The Enduring Vision

The Enduring Vision

A History of the American People

Concise Third Edition

Paul S. Boyer
University of Wisconsin, Madison

Clifford E. Clark, Jr.
Carleton College

Sandra McNair Hawley
San Jacinto College

Joseph F. Kett
University of Virginia

Neal Salisbury
Smith College

Harvard Sitkoff
University of New Hampshire

Nancy Woloch
Barnard College

Houghton Mifflin Company Boston New York

Sponsoring editor: Pat Coryell
Associate editor: Jeffrey Greene
Senior project editor: Rosemary Winfield
Production/design coordinator: Jennifer Meyer
Senior designer: Henry Rachlin
Manufacturing coordinator: Sally Culler
Marketing manager: Charles Cavaliere

Cover: design by Len Massiglia; cover image: Larimer Avenue Bridge by John Kane, 1932. The Carnegie Museum of Art, Pittsburgh, PA.

Printed in the U.S.A.

Library of Congress Catalog Card Number: 97-72448

ISBN: 0-395-85826-7

56789-VH-01 00

Preface

In this new concise edition of *The Enduring Vision* we have tried to maintain the strengths of the previous edition—a strong narrative that interweaves political, diplomatic, and economic history with social, cultural, and environmental analysis in a brief but thorough text that reflects both traditional concerns and the cutting edge of contemporary historical research. We have tried to use a readable style throughout, eliminating the social science jargon that both instructors and students (quite correctly) dislike.

This concise edition of *The Enduring Vision* interweaves traditional and more recent approaches to the study of history. In addition to political, diplomatic, and economic history, for example, the book examines and integrates social history, cultural history, the histories of the diverse peoples who make up our pluralistic society, and environmental history. We have maintained a balance that reflects the best of both traditional and the new emphases in historical scholarship, a blend that will serve the modern student well.

Like its predecessor, this is not a "lite" version of American history. We have retained all the major topics and issues from the original text to make this a book suitable for any introductory United States history course at the freshman or sophomore level, whether in four-year colleges and universities or two-year community and junior colleges. With nearly 40 percent fewer pages than the longer book, this concise edition affords the instructor the opportunity to assign more outside readings for greater depth.

Throughout this third edition the reader will encounter substantial changes, changes meant to deepen, broaden, and clarify our discussion of major issues. For example, Chapters 2 and 3 have been extensively reordered to bring together diverse aspects of early colonization and to strengthen the discussion of slavery and its transfer across the Atlantic. Other significant changes include greater discussion of the Taos pueblo and the Pueblo Revolt; British perspectives of the coming of the American Revolution; the rise of the Republican party; the Civil War in the Trans-Mississippi West; shifting attitudes toward the environment; fuller analysis of both Keynesianism and the roots of isolationist ideology; the Kennedy presidency; recent social and cultural trends such as mass marketing, mass entertainment, and the growing political clout of evangelical Christians; and the complexities and paradoxes of the first Clinton administration, the "Republican Revolution," the new worlds of the post–Cold War era and the postindustrial economy, and the 1996 presidential election. Chronologies and suggested readings have been brought up to date as well.

This concise edition features a generous array of maps. Reproduced in two colors, they vividly establish the physical and spatial setting of American history, enabling the student to grasp both the immensity of the United States and of the North American continent and the complexities of Native American and European settlement of that continent. We chose photographs not only for their freshness and visual impact but also for their complementarity with the text. Clear, easily understood charts and other graphics round out the illustrations. Each chapter has an extensive chronology at the end to help the student to set events in historical context, and an extensive annotated bibliography of the works for further reading or research.

A wide range of ancillaries to aid both instructor and student is available with *The Enduring Vision*, Concise Third Edition. They include the *Instructor's Resource Manual with Test Items*, the *Study Guide with Map Exercises*, and a computerized test bank for

Macintosh and IBM-compatible computers. The instructor may also opt to use some of the following additional supplements for the course and should contact a Houghton Mifflin sales representative for more information:

- *Getting the Most out of Your U.S. History Course: The History Student's Vade Mecum* by Neil R. Stout—a handy, concise student guide to getting the most out of the U.S. history survey course
- *Reading and Writing American History* by Peter Charles Hoffer and William W. Stueck, Volumes 1 and 2—a skills-based sourcebook for U.S. history students
- Map transparencies
- *Enduring Voices Document Sets* by James J. Lorence, Volumes 1 and 2
- *Surveying the Land: Skills and Exercises in U.S. Historical Geography* by Robert B. Grant, Volumes 1 and 2
- *Atlas of American History*
- *The Houghton Mifflin Guide to the Internet for History*

Writing and publishing a book of this complexity is never easy, and I would like to thank those individuals whose support and help has made this revised edition possible with minimum stress: my daughter, Lee Anne Hawley; my friends, especially James D. Heil; my colleagues, especially James A. Hall; and the editorial and production staff at Houghton Mifflin. We changed publishers in the midst of preparations for this third edition, and the hard work and intelligence of the Houghton Mifflin people made what could have been a logistical nightmare into a smooth transition. My special thanks to Pat Coryell, senior sponsoring editor; Jeff Greene, senior associate editor; and Rosemary Winfield, senior project editor.

Finally, reviewers at all stages of the revision process have made this a stronger and better book through their suggestions and their general enthusiasm. However, we must note that errors are ours alone.

Robert H. Tomlinson, Southwest Virginia Community College

Ronald C. McArthur, Atlantic Community College

James W. McKee, Jr., East Tennessee State University

George C. Rable, Anderson University

Karin A. Wulf, American University

Martin B. Cohen, George Mason University

Geoffrey Plank, University of Cincinnati

Michael J. Morgan, Rose State College

We are most grateful to them all.

We welcome all our readers' suggestions, queries, and criticisms. Please send them to Houghton Mifflin at this e-mail address: history@hmco.com.

S. M. H.

Contents

Colonial Society Comes of Age, 1660–1750

The Road to Revolution, 1744–1776

The Forge of Nationhood, 1776–1788

Launching the New Republic, 1789–1800

Jeffersonianism and the Era of Good Feelings

Life, Leisure, and Culture, 1840–1860

The Old South and Slavery, 1800–1860

Immigration, Expansion, and Sectional Conflict, 1840–1848

271

From Compromise to Secession, 1850–1861

293

Reforging the Union: Civil War, 1861–1865

315

21

Politics and Expansion in an Industrializing Age

The Progressive Era

The Turbulent Sixties

A Troubled Journey: From Port Huron to Watergate

Turning Inward: Society and Politics from Ford to Reagan

Maps

Charts, Graphs, and Tables

The Enduring Vision

CHAPTER 1

America Begins

The history of the Americas began thousands of years before Christopher Columbus's first voyage. Over that time, an indigenous American history unfolded, separate from that of the Old World of Africa, Asia, and Europe.

Some Native Americans eked out their existences in precarious environments, whereas others enjoyed prosperity; some lived in small bands, but others dwelled in large cities; some believed that the first humans came from the sky, and others thought that they originated underground. Wherever and however they lived, and whatever they believed, native peoples together made North America a human habitat and gave it a history.

(Right) Adena stone effigy pipe, c. 400–100 B.C.

The First Americans

The origins of the human species extend far back in time. More than 5 million years ago, direct human ancestors evolved in the temperate grasslands of Africa. Between 300,000 and 100,000 years ago, humans began peopling the Old World. Between 40,000 and 15,000 years ago, northern Asian hunting bands pursued large game animals across a broad land bridge then connecting Siberia and Alaska. In doing so, they became the first Americans.

Most Native Americans are descended from these earliest migrants, but a few trace their ancestry to later arrivals who crossed the land bridge about 9,000 years ago, and spread over much of northern and western Canada and southern and central Alaska. Some later migrated southward to become the Apaches and the Navajos of the Southwest. Eskimos and Aleuts began crossing the Bering Sea—which had submerged the land bridge—from Siberia about 5,000 years ago, and the Hawaiian Islands remained uninhabited until after A.D. 300.

The First Americans

The arrow shows the "ice corridor" through which most ancestors of Native Americans passed before dispersing throughout the Western Hemisphere.

SOURCE: Dean R. Snow, *The Archaeology of North America*. Copyright © 1989 by Chelsea House Publishers, a division of Main Line Book Co. Used by permission.

The Peopling of North America: The Paleo-Indians

About 10,000 B.C., the Ice Age neared its end. Melting glaciers opened an ice-free corridor from Alaska to the northern Plains, and bands of hunters moved along this route. Others probably traveled south along the Pacific coast in boats. As they emerged from the glacier-covered north, they discovered a hunter's paradise. Giant mammoths, mastodons, bison, caribou, and moose roamed the continent, innocent of the ways of human predators. In this bountiful world, the Paleo-Indians, as archaeologists call these hunters, fanned out and multiplied with astonishing speed. Within 1,000 years, descendants of the first Americans had spread throughout the Western Hemisphere.

Most Paleo-Indians lived in small bands of fifteen to fifty people. The men hunted; the women prepared the food and cared for the children. The band lived together for the summer but split into smaller groups of one or two families for fall and winter. Although they moved constantly, they remained within informal boundaries except when they traveled to favored quarries to obtain jasper or flint for making tools. Here they encountered other bands, with whom they traded and joined in religious ceremonies.

Even before leaving Alaska, the Paleo-Indians developed distinctly "American" ways. Their most characteristic innovation was the fluted point, which the Indians fitted to spears. Fluted points have been found throughout the Western Hemisphere, but none in Siberia. By 9000 B.C. many big-game species, including mammoths and mastodons, had vanished. Paleo-Indian hunters contributed to this extinction, as did a warming climate and ecological changes that altered or destroyed the large animals' food chains.

Archaic Societies

Climatic warming continued until about 4000 B.C. with dramatic effects for North America. Sea levels rose, flooding the shallow continental shelf, and glacial runoff filled the Great Lakes, the Mississippi River basin, and other waters. As the glaciers receded northward, so did the cold, icy arctic or subarctic environments that had previously extended into what are now the "lower forty-eight" states of the United States. Treeless plains and evergreen forests yielded to deciduous forests in the East, grassland prairies on the Plains, and desert in much of the West. An immense range of plants and animals covered the landscape.

Descendants of the Paleo-Indians prospered amid this abundance and diversity. These Archaic peoples, as archaeologists term native North Americans from 8000 B.C. to 1500 B.C., lived off wide varieties of smaller mammals, fish, and wild plants rather than big game. Greater efficiency in hunting and gathering permitted larger populations to inhabit smaller areas. In rich areas such as the East and Midwest, large populations lived in villages for virtually the entire year. For example, a year-round village that flourished near present-day Kampsville, Illinois, from 3900 to 2800 B.C. supported 100 to 150 people. Its residents procured fish and mussels from local lakes to supplement the deer, birds, nuts, and seeds available in the surrounding area.

Archaic peoples' cultures were diverse in other ways. Besides using many varieties of stone, they utilized bone, shell, copper, ivory, clay, leather, asphalt, and horn to make tools, weapons, utensils, and ornaments. Often Native Americans obtained these materials through trade with neighbors and through long-distance networks. Obsidian from the Yellowstone region, copper from the Great Lakes, and marine shells from ocean coasts appear at sites thousands of miles from their points of origin. Archaic peoples, like their Indian descendants, believed that such minerals contained supernatural power. A few large sites, among them Indian Knoll in western Kentucky, which dates to 2500–2000 B.C., served as major trade centers for such minerals.

Ideas as well as materials traveled along the trade networks. Techniques that developed in one place for making tools, procuring food, or using medicinal plants eventually spread over wide areas, far beyond the boundaries of community, language, and ethnicity. This diffusion created regional cultural patterns. Trade also served to spread religious beliefs, including ideas and practices relating to death. Archaic burials grew increasingly elaborate as Native Americans interred their dead with personal possessions and with objects fashioned from valued substances such as obsidian and copper. They often sprinkled the corpses with bright red hematite (an iron-bearing ore) so that they resembled a newborn. Ideas of death as a kind of rebirth were widespread in North America by the time Europeans arrived.

Archaic Americans developed neither ranks nor classes, nor did they centralize political power. However, the growing complexity of their diets and technologies led them to sharpen many distinctions between women's and men's roles. Men took responsibility for fishing and hunting; women harvested and prepared wild plants, including grinding and milling seeds. Men and women each made the tools needed for their tasks. In general, men's activities entailed travel, and women's work kept them close to the village, where they bore and raised children. At Indian Knoll and elsewhere, men were buried with tools related to hunting and fishing, and women with implements related to nut cracking and seed grinding. Objects used by shamans, or religious healers, were distributed equally between male and female graves, a practice implying that these key roles were not divided by gender.

The Indians' Continent

By 1500 B.C. in much of North America, Indians were developing new cultures that transcended those of the Archaic peoples. Some practiced specialized methods of food production and actively shaped their environment to their needs. In the Southwest, the Southeast, and the Eastern Woodlands, the advent of agriculture and of large centers of trade and population constituted a radical departure from Archaic patterns and hunting-gathering bands. Most Indians, however, still dwelled in small bands and retained their traditional reliance on hunting, fishing, and gathering.

Despite the differences emerging among native societies, ties among them remained strong. Expanded trade networks permitted goods and ideas to be carried over ever-widening areas. Ceramic pottery and the bow and arrow came into extensive use. Virtually everywhere, Indians continued to prefer seasonal food procurement and communities based on kinship, abandoning or resisting more centralized systems when they proved to be unworkable or oppressive.

The Northern and Western Perimeters

In western Alaska the post-Archaic period marked the beginning of a new arctic way of life. Eskimos and Aleuts had brought sophisticated tools and weapons from their Siberian homeland, including harpoons and spears for hunting sea mammals and caribou. By 1500 B.C., through their continued contacts with Siberia, the Eskimos were making and using the Americas' first bows and arrows, ceramic pottery, and pit houses, structures set partially below ground level. As they perfected ways of living in regions of vast tundras (treeless plains with a permanently frozen subsoil), Eskimos spread across upper Canada to the shores of Labrador, western Newfoundland, and Greenland.

Long before Columbus, the Eskimos made contact with Europeans and used certain of their material goods. From about A.D. 1 some iron tools reached Alaska by way of Russia and Siberia, but not enough to affect Eskimo culture substantially. Direct contacts with Europeans began in Greenland, Newfoundland, and Labrador, where Norse people from Scandinavia planted colonies in the late tenth century. At first the Norse traded metal goods for ivory near their Newfoundland settlement, but growing hostility ended peaceful commerce. By the eleventh century, the Norse had withdrawn from Vinland, as they called Newfoundland. The Norse colonies had no long-term impact on the indigenous peoples of North America. The colonies were short-lived, colonists were few, and, most important, the Norse did not carry the epidemic diseases that would be brought, with disastrous results for the Native Americans, by later colonists.

Along the Pacific coast, from Alaska to southern California, improvements in the production and storage of food enabled Indians to develop more settled ways of life. From the Alaskan panhandle to northern California, natives spent brief periods each year catching salmon and other fish. The Northwest Coast Indians dried and stored enough fish to last the year, and their seasonal movements gradually gave way to settled life in permanent villages of cedar-plank houses. In the Columbia Plateau, Indians built villages of pit houses and ate salmon through the summer. They left these communities in spring and fall for hunting and gathering.

By A.D. 1 many Northwest Coast villages numbered several hundred people. Trade and warfare strengthened the power of chiefs and other leaders, whose families had greater wealth and prestige than commoners. Leading families proclaimed their status in elaborate totem poles depicting supernatural beings linked to their ancestors and in potlatches, ceremonies in which the Indians gave away or destroyed much of their material wealth. The artistic and architectural achievements of Northwest Coast Indians awed Europeans. "What must astonish most [observers]," a French explorer wrote in 1791, "is to see painting everywhere, everywhere sculpture, among a nation of hunters."

At about the same time, Indians farther south, along the coast and in the interior valleys of what is now California, began to live in villages of one hundred or more people. Acorns dominated their diet. After the fall harvest, Indians ground the

Culture Areas of Native Americans and Locations of Selected Tribes, A.D. 1500 *"Culture area" is a convention enabling archaeologists and anthropologists to generalize about regional patterns among pre-Colombian Native American cultures.*

acorns into meal, leached them of bitter tannic acid, and then roasted, boiled, or baked the nuts before eating or storing them. Intense competition for acorns forced California bands to define territorial boundaries rigidly and to combine several villages under a single chief. Chiefs conducted trade, diplomacy, and religious ceremonies with neighboring groups and, when necessary, led their people in battle. Supplementing game, fish, and plants, acorns enabled California's Indians to prosper.

The end of the Archaic period produced little change in the forbidding aridity of the Great Basin, encompassing present-day Nevada, western Utah, southern Idaho, and eastern Oregon. The area continued to support small hunting and gathering bands. Change came only in the fourteenth or fifteenth century A.D., when Paiute, Ute, and Shoshone Indians absorbed or displaced earlier inhabitants across the Great Basin. The newcomers' more efficient seed processing enabled them to support increased populations, which in turn occupied ever-larger territories.

The Hawaiian Islands were part of the south and central Pacific lands of Oceania. By 1600 B.C. the Austronesian peoples of Australia and New Guinea had developed agriculture and were making pottery, tools, and giant outrigger canoes. They began settling formerly uninhabited South Pacific islands but did not reach Hawaii until the fourth century A.D.

These first Hawaiians lived in self-sufficient communities. They cultivated sweet potatoes, yams, and taro (which they made into a fermented paste) and exploited a variety of fish and shellfish. Each community distinguished sharply between commoners and chiefs. Hawaiian chiefs collected food and goods from subordinate communities and allies and occasionally waged war for territorial conquest and subjugation of other peoples.

When Europeans arrived in Hawaii in the late eighteenth century, the islands contained about 400,000 people in communities averaging 200 people each. Thereafter, European diseases devastated the native population, which plummeted to 40,000 by 1890.

The Southwest

Although peoples of the Pacific coast cultivated tobacco, they never farmed food-bearing plants. Abundant food resources left them little incentive to take the risks that agriculture entailed, especially in California, with its dry summers. In other areas of North America, however, agriculture became central to Indian life. In the arid Southwest, natives concentrated community energies on irrigation for agriculture, but in the humid Eastern Woodlands, plant cultivation came more easily. In both regions the advent of agriculture was a long, slow process that never entirely replaced other food-procuring activities.

New World farming began about 5000 B.C.—the same era in which agriculture was being introduced in Europe from southwestern Asia—when Indians in central Mexico planted seeds of certain wild crops that they had customarily harvested, including squash, corn, and beans. Plant domestication slowly spread, first reaching western New Mexico about 3500 B.C. Agriculture remained relatively unimportant for several thousand years, until a more drought-resistant strain of corn from Mexico enabled the inhabitants to move to dry lowlands. Populations then rose rapidly, and two influential new cultures arose, the Hohokam and the Anasazi.

Hohokam culture emerged in the third century B.C. when ancestors of Pima and Papago Indians began farming in the Gila River and Salt River valleys of southern Arizona. The Hohokam people built elaborate canal systems for irrigation that enabled them to harvest two crops each year, an amazing feat in such an arid environment. The construction and maintenance of the canals demanded large, coordinated work forces. The Hohokams therefore built permanent villages of several hundred residents, and many such communities were joined in confederations linked by canals. The central village in each confederation coordinated labor, trade, and religious and political life for all.

The Hohokam way of life drew on materials and ideas from outside the Southwest. From about the sixth century A.D., the larger Hohokam villages had ball courts and platform mounds such as those in Mexico, and ball games became major public events. Mexican art influenced Hohokam artists, who used clay, stone, turquoise, and shell. Seashells from California appeared in Hohokam pottery as backing for turquoise mosaics and as material for intricate etchings. Archaeologists have found Mexican items such as rubber balls, macaw feathers, and copper bells at Hohokam sites.

Among the last southwesterners to make farming the focus of their subsistence were a people known as the Anasazis, a Navajo term meaning "ancient ones." Their culture originated in the Four

Corners area where Arizona, New Mexico, Colorado, and Utah meet. Although they adopted village life and agriculture late, the Anasazis expanded rapidly in the sixth century A.D. and dominated a wide area. They traded with Indians in Mexico, California, and elsewhere but took few artistic or cultural ideas from them. Instead, their neighbors borrowed from the Anasazis.

The Anasazis had a distinctive architecture. They constructed their early dwellings, round pit houses, in the shape of *kivas*, the partly underground, circular structures where Anasazi men conducted religious ceremonies. Because the Anasazis believed that the first humans reached the earth from underground, their homes also featured small holes in the floor known as *sipapus*. As their population grew, the Anasazis built aboveground, rectangular apartment houses containing small *kivas*. Anasazi-style apartments and *kivas* are characteristic of the architecture of the modern-day Pueblo Indians, who are descendants of the Anasazis.

From the tenth through the mid-twelfth century, an unusually wet period, the Anasazis expanded over much of what today is New Mexico and Arizona. Village populations grew to 1,000 or more. In Chaco Canyon in northwestern New Mexico, a cluster of twelve villages forged a powerful confederation numbering 15,000 people. Perfectly straight roads radiated from the canyon to satellite pueblos up to sixty-five miles away. The builders carved out stairs or footholds in the sides of steep cliffs. The largest village, Pueblo Bonito, had 1,200 inhabitants and two Great Kivas, each fifty feet in diameter. People traveled from outlying areas to Chaco Canyon for religious ceremonies. Chaco Canyon was the center of the turquoise industry that manufactured beads for trade with Mexico, and its pueblos supplied the outlying people with food in times of drought. An elaborate system of controlling rainwater runoff through small dams, terraces, and other devices permitted this agricultural surplus.

Devastating droughts in the late twelfth and thirteenth centuries destroyed classic Anasazi culture. Suddenly, the amount of farmland was drastically reduced for a population that had grown rapidly during the preceding centuries. The Indians abandoned the great Anasazi centers and scattered. Some formed new pueblos along the upper Rio Grande, and others moved south and west to establish the Zuñi and Hopi pueblos. Descendants of the Anasazis still inhabit many of these pueblos. Other large agricultural communities, such as those of the Hohokams, also dispersed when droughts came. With farming peoples consequently clustered in the few areas with sufficient water, the drier southwestern lands attracted the foraging Apaches and Navajos, whose arrival at the end of the thirteenth century ended their long migration from northwestern Canada.

The Eastern Woodlands

Indians of the Eastern Woodlands, the vast forests from the Mississippi Valley to the Atlantic coast, also experimented with village life and political centralization, but without farming. After doing so, however, they developed an extraordinarily productive agriculture.

By 1200 B.C. about 5,000 people had concentrated in a single village at Poverty Point on the Mississippi River in Louisiana. Two large mounds flanked the village, and six concentric embankments—the largest over half a mile in diameter—surrounded it. During the spring and autumn equinoxes, a person standing on the larger mound could watch the sun rise directly over the village center. Solar observations formed the basis for these Indians' religious beliefs as well as for their calendar.

Poverty Point lay at the center of a large political and economic unit. It imported quartz, copper, obsidian, crystal, and other sacred materials from eastern North America and distributed them to nearby communities. These communities almost certainly supplied the labor for the earthworks. The Olmec peoples of Mexico clearly influenced the design and organization of Poverty Point. The settlement flourished for only three centuries and then declined, for reasons that are unclear. Nevertheless, it foreshadowed later Mississippi Valley developments.

A different mound-building culture, the Adena, emerged in the Ohio Valley in the fifth century B.C. Adena villages rarely exceeded 400 inhabitants, but

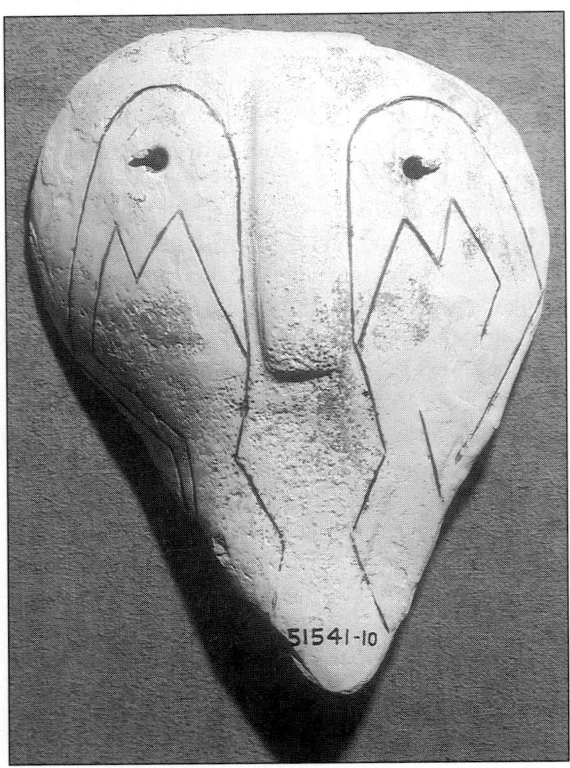

Mississippian Engraved Shell
Engraved conch shells, often with highly abstract designs, were among the goods traded by Mississippian peoples in the Southeast.

the Adena people spread over a wide area and built hundreds of mounds, most of them containing graves. The largest, Grave Creek Mound in West Virginia, was 240 feet in diameter and 70 feet high. In Adena culture, a person's social and political status apparently determined his or her treatment in death: some corpses were cremated (burned), others were placed in round clay basins, and still others were given elaborate tombs.

The Adena mounds constituted the heart of a religious movement whose adherents scattered over much of the Northeast. Although Adena burial practices—the inclusion of grave goods, the painting of red hematite on some corpses—were familiar in the Northeast, the burial rituals themselves and many of the manufactured objects were new. As the Adena culture flourished, trade networks distributed these objects far across the Northeast.

During the first century B.C., Adena culture evolved into a more developed and widespread culture known as Hopewell. Hopewell ceremonial centers, larger and more elaborate than those of the Adena, mushroomed along the Ohio and Illinois river valleys. Some centers contained two or three dozen mounds within enclosures of several square miles. The graves of elites contained elaborate burial goods: freshwater pearls, copper ornaments, mica, quartz, or other sacred substances. Hopewell artisans used raw materials from throughout America east of the Rockies. Through trade networks Hopewell influence spread to communities as distant as places in modern-day Wisconsin, Florida, and New York. The great Hopewell centers of the Ohio and Illinois Valleys were abandoned in the fifth century A.D. for reasons that remain unknown, but they exerted enormous influence.

Amazingly, the people who created the sophisticated Hopewell culture were primarily hunter-gatherers, not farmers. Although they did grow some crops, agriculture became a dietary mainstay for Woodlands people only between the seventh and twelfth centuries A.D.

The first full-time farmers in the East were the Mississippians, who lived on the flood plains of the Mississippi River and its major tributaries. Their culture incorporated elements from the Hopewell culture and new ideas from Mexico into their own traditions. The volume of Mississippian craft production and of long-distance trade dwarfed those of the Hopewell and Adena cultures. Mississippian towns, containing hundreds or even thousands of people, were built around open plazas like those of central Mexico. Religious temples and elite residences stood atop large mounds next to the plazas. Religious ceremonies focused on worship of the sun as the source of agricultural fertility. Chiefs claimed to be related to the sun, and when they died, wives and servants were killed to accompany them to the afterlife. Artisans produced sophisticated work in clay, stone, shell, copper, and wood, largely for religious and funeral rituals.

Many Mississippian centers were built not by local natives but by outsiders seeking to combine farming and riverborne trade. By the tenth century most Mississippian centers were part of larger confederacies based on trade and shared religious beliefs. Powerful "supercenters" and their chiefs dominated these confederacies. The most powerful confederacy revolved around the magnificent city of Cahokia, near modern St. Louis; its influence extended from the Appalachians to the edge of the Plains and from the Great Lakes to the Gulf of Mexico.

A city of about 20,000 people, Cahokia covered more than 6 square miles and contained more than 120 earthworks. At its center a four-terraced structure called Monk's Mound covered fifteen acres (more than the Great Pyramid of Egypt) and rose 100 feet at its highest point. Surrounding the city, a 125-square-mile metropolitan area encompassed ten large towns and more than fifty farming villages. In addition, Cahokia dominated a giant network of commercial and political alliances extending over much of the American heartland. Like other Mississippian societies, Cahokia, influenced by ideas and crops from Mexico, erected ever-more-complex political, economic, and religious institutions. Many scholars believe that by the twelfth century, Cahokia was the capital of a potential nation-state.

Cahokia reigned supreme for two and a half centuries, but by the thirteenth century, it and allied centers were beginning to suffer food shortages. Neighboring peoples, moreover, challenged them militarily, and the inhabitants fled. By the fifteenth century, Indians in the central Mississippi Valley were living in small villages linked by mutual interdependence, not coercion. Similar temple-mound centers in the Southeast also declined, and although new centers rose, European diseases destroyed them after 1500.

The demise of the Mississippian culture, like that of the Hopewell, ended a trend toward political centralization among Indians in eastern North America. Nonetheless, the Mississippians profoundly affected native culture in the East. They

Cahokia, c. A.D. 1200 *This depiction of Cahokia by a twentieth-century artist shows the Indian city's central area as defined by a defensive stockade. The four-terraced Monk's Mound and other public structures are within the stockade walls.*

spread not only new strains of corn and beans but also the techniques and tools to cultivate them. Only northern New England and the upper Great Lakes had growing seasons too short for corn to become a reliable crop.

By 1500 A.D. the North American continent presented a remarkable spectrum of cultures and societies. As they had for thousands of years, small, mobile hunting bands peopled the Arctic, Subarctic, Great Basin, and Plains. Stabler societies based on fishing or gathering predominated along the Pacific coast, while village-based agriculture dominated in the Southwest, the Eastern Woodlands, and parts of the Plains. Finally, Mississippian urban centers prevailed in parts of the Southeast.

Despite the vast differences among Native Americans, much bound them together. Trade facilitated the exchange of goods as well as of ideas, techniques, and beliefs. The bow and arrow, ceramic pottery, and burial rituals came to characterize Indians everywhere. Indians also shared a preference for independent, kin-based communities, an orientation probably reinforced by the failure of such highly centralized systems as Cahokia and the Anasazi centers.

New World Peoples on the Eve of European Contact

In 1492 the entire Western Hemisphere had about 75 million people, clustered thickly in Mexico and Central America, the Caribbean islands, and Peru. Between 7 and 10 million Native Americans lived north of Mexico. Sparse nomad populations inhabited the Great Basin, the high plains, and the northern forests. Denser concentrations, however, thrived along the Pacific coast, in the Southwest and Southeast, in the Mississippi Valley, and along the Atlantic coast. Speaking many diverse languages and dialects, these people constituted several hundred Indian nations and tribes. But for all Native Americans, the most important social groups were the family, clan, and village.

Family and Community

Kinship cemented Indian societies together. Ties to cousins, aunts, and uncles created complex patterns of social obligation. So did membership in a clan—a large kin group whose members reckoned their descent from a common ancestor embodying the admired qualities of some animal. Several different clans usually dwelled together in a single village. Clans in turn linked widely scattered groups within a larger social unit known as a tribe.

Kinship bonds were more important in Indian society than the bonds within nuclear families, that is, among married couples and their children. Indians did not necessarily expect spouses to be bound together forever; but kinship lasted for life. Divorce thus did not threaten the social order. Customs regulating marriage varied, but strict rules prevailed. In most cultures young people married in their teens, generally after a period of sexual experimentation. Although male leaders sometimes took several wives, nuclear families never stood alone. Instead, strong ties of residence and deference bound each couple to one or both sets of parents, producing what social scientists call extended families.

In addition, kinship was the basis for armed conflict. Indian societies typically considered homicide a matter to be resolved by the extended families of the victim and the perpetrator. If the perpetrator's family offered a gift that the victim's family considered appropriate, the question was settled. If not, the victim's kin might avenge the killing by armed retaliation. Chiefs or other leaders intervened to resolve disputes within the same village or tribe, but disputes between members of different groups could escalate into war. Densely populated societies that competed for scarce resources, as on the California coast, and centralized societies that attempted to dominate trade networks through coercion, such as the Hopewell culture, experienced frequent and intense warfare. However, warfare remained a low-level affair in most of North America. An exasperated New England officer, writing of his effort to obtain Indian allies in the early seventeenth century, described a battle between two Indian groups as "more for pastime than to conquer and subdue enemies." He concluded that "they might fight seven years and not kill seven men."

Among almost all agricultural Indians except those in the Southwest, women did the cultivating. Field work easily meshed with child care, as did such other tasks as preparing animal hides and gathering wild plants. Men did jobs that took them away from women and children: hunting, fishing, trading, negotiating, and fighting. With women producing much of the food supply, these communities gave women more power than European societies did. Among the Iroquois of what today is upstate New York, for example, women collectively owned the fields, distributed food, and played a major role in tribal councils. In New England women sometimes served as *sachems*, or chiefs.

In the Southwest wresting a living from the severe environment demanded concentrated effort, but the native peoples succeeded. The population was comparatively dense: 100,000 people may have lived in the pueblos and in river-valley settlements by the early sixteenth century. As in the rest of North America, extended families formed the foundation of village life.

Patterns of property ownership and gender roles in the Southwest differed considerably from those of Native Americans elsewhere. In addition, differences prevailed among local cultures. Unlike Indians elsewhere, men and women in the Southwest shared agricultural labor. River-valley peoples of the Southwest, moreover, owned land privately and passed it through the male line, and men dominated decision-making. In pueblo society, which in this respect resembled societies in the Northeast and Southeast, land was communally owned, and women played an influential role in community affairs. Clan membership passed through the mother's line. Yet pueblo communities depended on secret male societies to perform rituals that would secure the gods' blessings and bring life-giving rain. More than other Indians, pueblo society strictly subordinated the individual to the group and demanded rigorous cooperation.

Religion and Social Values

Indian myths, told by storytellers during religious ceremonies, explained the origin and destiny of the human race. In the beginning, said the Iroquois, a sky world of unchanging perfection existed. From it fell a beautiful pregnant woman, whom birds saved from plunging into the ocean. On the back of a tortoise that rose from the sea, birds created the earth's soil, in which the woman planted seeds. From these seeds sprang all nature; from her womb, human beings.

Native American religions revolved around the conviction that nature was alive, pulsating with spiritual power—*manitou* in the Algonquian language. A mysterious, awe-inspiring force that affected human life for both good and evil, such power united all nature in an unbroken web. *Manitou* encompassed "every thing which they cannot comprehend," wrote the English Puritan leader Roger Williams, one of the few Europeans who tried to understand the Indians' spiritual world. Belief in supernatural power led most Indians to seek constantly to conciliate all the spiritual forces in nature: living things, rocks, water, the sun and moon, even ghosts and witches. For example, Indians prayed to the spirits of animals that they hunted and generally killed just enough game to sustain themselves. To the Indians, humanity was only one link in the great chain of living nature. They would find very strange the Judeo-Christian view that God had given humanity dominion over nature.

Indians had many ways of gaining access to spiritual power. One was dreaming; most Native Americans took seriously the visions that came to them in sleep. They also sought access to the supernatural by using physical ordeals to alter their consciousness. Young men, for instance, commonly endured a traumatic rite of passage. Such rites often involved "questing"—going alone into a forest or up a mountain, fasting, and awaiting a mystical experience in which an animal spirit would reveal itself as a guide and offer a vision of the future. Girls went through comparable rituals at the onset of menstruation to initiate them into the spiritual world from which female reproductive power flowed. Entire communities often engaged in collective power-seeking rituals such as the Sun Dance (see Chapter 17).

Indians normally relied on shamans to understand the unseen. Shamans were healers who used medicinal plants and magical chants, but their role went further. They interpreted dreams, guided "questing" and other rituals, invoked war or peace spirits, and figured prominently in community councils. Chiefs had to maintain respectful relations with shamans, and by the sixteenth century, shamans formed organized priesthoods in the Southeast and Southwest.

Even as Indian societies grew larger and more complex, they maintained a strong sense of interdependence. Consequently, they demanded conformity and cooperation. From early childhood, Indians learned to be accommodating and reserved—careful not to reveal their feelings before they could sense others'. Indian parents generally punished by shaming. Fear of becoming an isolated social outcast forced individuals to maintain strict self-control. Communities made decisions by consensus, and leaders articulated slowly emerging agreements in passionate oratory. Both shamans and chiefs had to be dramatic speakers. In John Smith's words, they spoke in public "with vehemency and so great passions that they sweat till they drop and are so out of breath they can scarce speak."

Because Indians valued consensus so highly, their leaders' authority depended primarily on the respect that they invoked rather than on what they could demand by compulsion. Distributing gifts was central to establishing and maintaining leadership within a Native American community or to building alliances. As a seventeenth-century French-Canadian described this practice, it meant "I give thee, to the end thou shouldst give me." Thus for Indians, trade was not only an economic activity but also a means of ensuring goodwill with other peoples and of building their own prestige. Trade in flint and other toolmaking materials, salt, dyes, furs, food, seeds, and tobacco (which Indians treated as a ceremonial drug) spanned the continent. Native Americans eagerly assimilated the goods offered by European traders into their way of life. Metal tools were valued for their practical benefits, and dyed cloth and glass objects assumed symbolic, prestige-enhancing qualities.

Prestige, not material possessions, counted in Native American societies. If Indians did accumulate worldly goods, they did so to give them away in order to win prestige. Potlatch ceremonies of the Pacific Northwest were the most dramatic examples. An aspiring leader invited neighbors to a potlatch, at which he gave away or destroyed most of his possessions while chanting about his own greatness and taunting his rivals. Those who received were expected later to give away even more. Whoever gave away the most won the highest prestige and gained the most people obligated to him.

Scholars have used the word *reciprocity* to characterize Indian religious and social values. Reciprocity involved mutual give-and-take but did not aim to confer equality. Instead, societies based on reciprocity tried to maintain equilibrium and interdependence between individuals of unequal power and prestige. Indians also applied reciprocity to their religious concepts, viewing nature as a web of interdependent spiritual powers into which humans had to fit. And in social organizations, reciprocity required that communities be places of face-to-face, lifelong interaction. Trade and gift giving solidified such reciprocal bonds. Further, faith in social reciprocity underlay Indians' ideas of property rights. They believed that the people of one area might agree to share with others the right to use land for different but complementary purposes: hunting, gathering, farming, trapping, or traveling. The European notion that property ownership conferred perpetual and exclusive control of land was alien to Indians.

But Native American society was hardly a simple, noncompetitive world. All Indian cultures possessed a strong sense of order. Custom, the demands of social conformity, and the rigors of nature strictly regulated life. Everyday affairs mingled with the spiritual world at every turn. Nature and the supernatural could be frightening. Indians feared ghosts and believed that nonconformists could invoke evil spirits by witchcraft, the most dreaded crime in Indian cultures. Much of Indian religion involved placating evil spirits that caused sickness and death. Pueblo peoples, whose existence depended on rainfall, expressed their gratitude by frequent rituals. Even in the Southwest, where cooperation was stressed, life had an intensely competitive side. Individuals and communities eagerly strove to show physical prowess in such ritualized games as lacrosse, and some bet enthusiastically on the outcome. "They are so bewitched with these . . . games, that they will lose sometimes all they have," wrote an Englishman of the Massachusetts Indians in about 1630. Games served as both recreation and a means of acquiring prestige.

A breakdown of order in Indian communities could bring fearful consequences: accusations of witchcraft, demands for revenge against wrongdoers, war against enemies. Going to war or exacting personal revenge was a ritualized way of restoring order. A captured male could expect to meet death after prolonged torture. Indian men learned from childhood to inflict, and to bear, physical pain out of loyalty to kin and neighbors; they knew that they had to withstand torture without flinching and death without fear. Endurance was central to Indian life.

CONCLUSION

Well before the first Siberian hunters crossed the Bering land bridge, geographic isolation and ecological variety had been the New World's most striking characteristics. Native Americans' isolation made possible their social and cultural development untouched by alien influences and lethal epidemics. Meanwhile, great climatic and geographic variations among North American regions helped to ensure that native cultures—all of them shaped significantly by their natural environments—would be extremely diverse.

Native American history did not begin with Christopher Columbus's arrival. Despite what Europeans thought, they did not encounter an unchanging world of simple savages. Rather, for thousands of years native cultures and societies had transformed North America into a human habitat. Over millennia Indians learned the properties, uses, and values of plants, animals, soils, rocks, and minerals as well as the cycles of months, seasons, and years. Hunting camps, villages, cornfields, and trails transformed the landscape. Although occasionally wasteful—Plains Indians stampeding herds of bison over cliffs often killed far more animals than they could eat—Native Americans seem to have learned painful lessons from the collapse of the Anasazi and Cahokia cultures. Generally, the North American Indians practiced ecologically balanced ways of life. Indians saw themselves not as conquerors of nature but as participants in a natural and supernatural order that pervaded the universe. Religious practices expressed their gratitude and their constant concern that they not violate that order. As America's first people, Indians would often exert profound influence on European colonists, whether providing vitally needed knowledge of food crops or attempting to eliminate colonists or limit their expansion.

CHRONOLOGY

c. 5,000,000 B.C.	Earliest human ancestors appear in Africa.
c. 2,000,000 B.C.	Ice Age begins.
c. 300,000–100,000 B.C.	Humans spread throughout Eastern Hemisphere.
c. 40,000–15,000 B.C.	Ancestors of Native Americans cross Alaska-Siberia land bridge.
c. 10,000 B.C.	Ice Age ends.
c. 10,000–9000 B.C.	Paleo-Indians spread throughout Western Hemisphere.
c. 9000 B.C.	Extinction of big-game mammals.
c. 8000 B.C.	Archaic era begins.
c. 7000 B.C.	Athapaskan-speaking peoples arrive in North America.
c. 5000 B.C.	First domesticated plants grown in Western Hemisphere.
c. 3500 B.C.	First domesticated plants grown in North America.
c. 3000–2000 B.C.	Eskimo and Aleut peoples arrive in North America.
c. 1500 B.C.	Archaic era ends. Bow and arrow and ceramic pottery introduced in North America.
c. 1200 B.C.	Poverty Point flourishes in Louisiana.
c. 400–100 B.C.	Adena culture flourishes in Ohio Valley.
c. 250 B.C.	Hohokam culture begins in Southwest.
c. 100 B.C.	Anasazi culture begins in Southwest.
c. 100 B.C.–A.D. 600	Hopewell culture thrives in Midwest.
c. A.D. 300	First people arrive at Hawaiian Islands.
c. A.D. 700	Mississippian culture begins.
c. A.D. 900	Stockade and first mounds built at Cahokia.
c. A.D. 1000–1100	Norse settlement of Vinland flourishes on Newfoundland.
c. A.D. 1150	Anasazi peoples disperse to form pueblos.
c. A.D. 1200–1300	Cahokia declines.
c. A.D. 1400	League of the Iroquois formed.

FOR FURTHER READING

John Bierhorst, *The Mythology of North America* (1985). An excellent introduction to Native American mythology, organized regionally.

Brian Fagan, *Ancient North America: The Archaeology of a Continent* (1991). An informative, comprehensive introduction to the continent's history before Europeans' arrival.

Åke Hultkrantz, *The Religions of the American Indians* (1979). A stimulating discussion by the leading scholar on the subject.

Gwyn Jones, *The Norse Atlantic Saga*, rev. ed. (1986). A single volume combining recent scholarship on Norse, Eskimos, and Indians with translations of the most important sagas.

Alvin M. Josephy, Jr., *America in 1492: The World of the Indian Peoples Before the Arrival of Columbus* (1992). Outstanding essays on life in the Western Hemisphere on the eve of European contact.

William C. Sturtevant, gen. ed., *Handbook of North American Indians* (20 vols. projected, 1978–). A partially completed reference work providing basic information on the history and culture of virtually every known native society.

CHAPTER 2

Transatlantic Encounters and Colonial Beginnings, 1492–1630

The concepts of New World and Old World had not existed prior to Christopher Columbus's voyages from 1492 to 1504. To Europeans before Columbus, there was only one world—theirs, the world that stretched from Europe to Africa and Asia. Pre-Columbian Native Americans were equally sure that they inhabited the only world. In many ways the Columbian voyages triggered not just a meeting of two worlds previously unknown to each other but a collision between them.

Each group's fascination with the strangeness of the "other" world would all too quickly sour. The Indians, whom Europeans first saw as gullible, as potential servants or slaves, would become lazy and deceitful "savages" in whites' eyes. Native Americans would lose their wonder at European "magic"—guns and gunpowder, metal tools, and glass beads—and would realize that this magic, and the diseases that the Europeans brought, could be destructive.

(Right) ***Englishman Bartholomew Gosnold Trading with Indians at Martha's Vineyard, Massachusetts,*** *by Theodore de Bry, 1634*

In much of what is now Latin America, the arrival of the Europeans led to conquest. In the future United States and Canada, however, European mastery came more slowly; more than one hundred years would pass before self-sustaining colonies were established. Nevertheless, from the moment of Columbus's landing on October 12, 1492, the American continents became the stage for the encounter of the Old and New worlds.

Old World Peoples

The Eastern Hemisphere gave birth to the human race. Early humans evolved for several million years on Africa's warm savannas (grasslands) before spreading slowly across the rest of Africa, Asia, and Europe. These continents hosted a vast array of societies ranging from hunter-gatherers to powerful states with armed forces, bureaucracies, religious institutions, proud aristocracies, and toiling commoners. All would play a role in the collision of the Old and New worlds.

West Africa and Its Peoples

For almost 5,000 years the barren Sahara Desert across northern Africa cut most of the continent off from the rest of the Old World. West Africa was further isolated from the land to its north by the prevailing Atlantic winds, which carried old-fashioned sailing ships south but hampered their northward return. And the yellow fever rampant in the West African rain-forest coastline generally killed adult newcomers, who lacked immunity to the disease. But a broad, hospitable savanna covered much of the rest of Africa. In the first millennium B.C., the region's peoples radiated outward, eventually leaving their imprint on virtually all of sub-Saharan Africa. By the sixteenth century, sub-Saharan Africa, twice the landmass of the United States, had a population of perhaps 20 million.

Camel caravans crossing the Sahara ended West Africa's isolation and stimulated trade in gold and salt with Mediterranean North Africa. Powerful West African empires—Ghana, Mali, and Songhai—arose and flourished for a millennium, from 600 to 1600 A.D. Nominally Islamic, these wealthy empires were famed throughout North Africa. By 1492 the last of the great empires, Songhai, stood at the height of its power, its bureaucracy and army dominating much of the African interior. Songhai's major city, Timbuktu, boasted flourishing markets and a renowned university.

Compared to the savanna empires, coastal West Africa was relatively insignificant. During the first millennium A.D., small Islamic states arose in Senegambia, at Africa's westernmost bulge, and in Guinea's coastal forests. The best-known state was Benin, where artisans fashioned magnificent ironwork for centuries.

Then in the fifteenth century foreign demand for the gold that Africans panned from streams and dug from the earth triggered a population rise in Guinea. Savanna warriors and merchants poured into Guinea and Senegambia, seeking opportunity and occasionally founding or expanding Islamic states. By the mid-fifteenth century, the Portuguese, using new maritime technology, were sailing along West Africa's coast in search of gold and slaves.

West African leaders wielded sharply different amounts and kinds of political power. Grassland emperors claimed semigodlike status, which they only thinly disguised after adopting Islam. Rulers of smaller kingdoms depended on their ability to persuade, to conform to custom, and sometimes to redistribute wealth justly among their people.

In sub-Saharan Africa, kinship groups knitted societies together. Parents, aunts, uncles, distant cousins, and those who shared clan ties formed networks of mutual obligation. In centuries to come, the tradition of strong extended families would help enslaved Africans to endure the breakup of nuclear families by sale. In addition, polygyny (the custom whereby a man had several wives) and bridewealth (a prospective husband's payment to his bride's kin before marriage) were widespread in West Africa. Europeans often saw both practices as evidence of African barbarism. Wives generally maintained lifelong links with their own kin group, and children

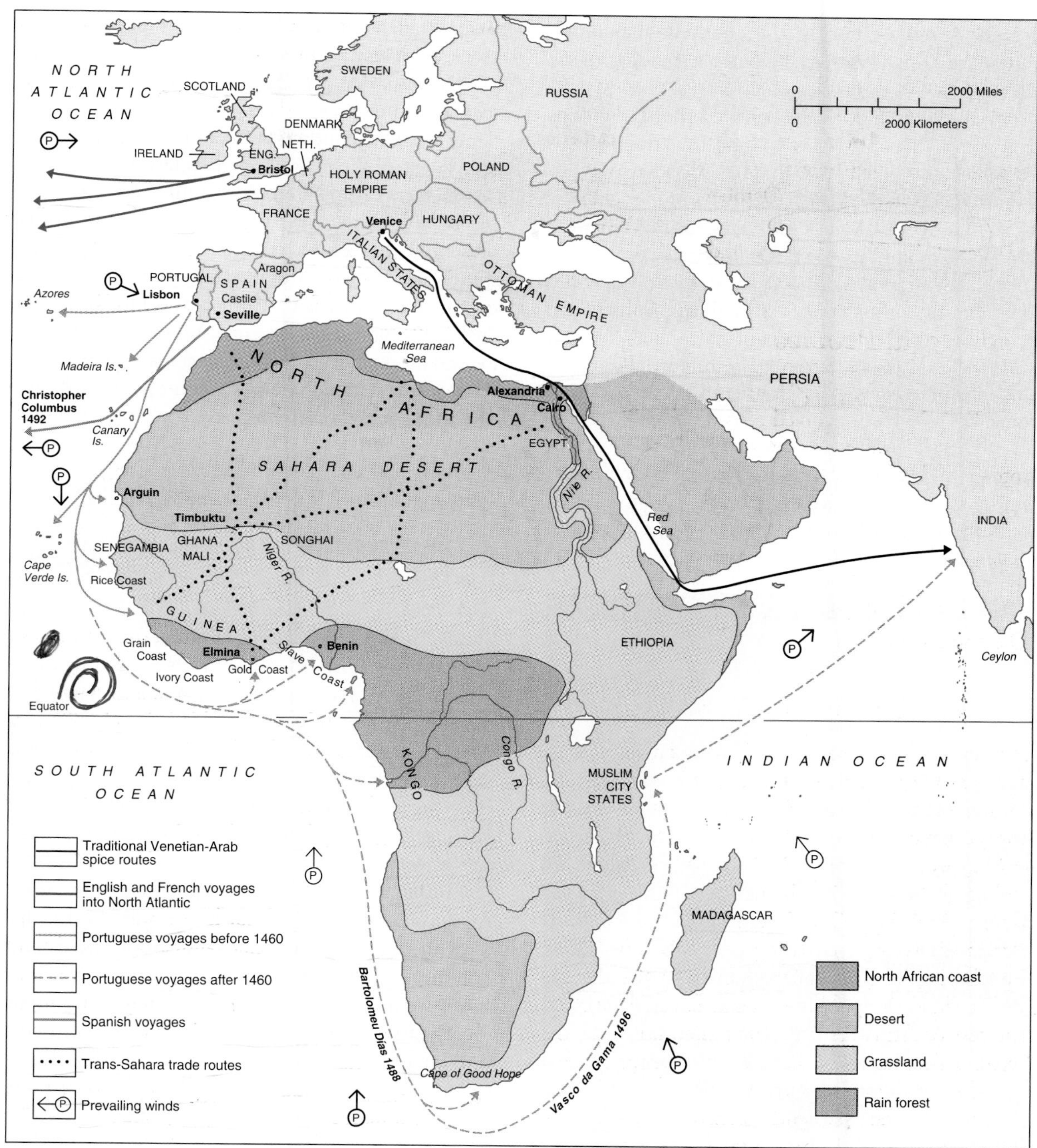

Europe, Africa, and the Near East in 1492

In 1492 Europeans had little knowledge of the outside world apart from the Mediterranean basin and Africa's west coast. Since the Azores, the Canary Islands, and the Cape Verde Islands had been discovered recently in the eastern Atlantic, many Europeans were not surprised when Columbus found new islands farther west in 1492.

traced descent through the mother's bloodline. These traditions buttressed women's standing in society.

Sub-Saharan Africans believed that kin groups enjoyed inalienable rights to land that their ancestors had cultivated and that they had a duty to honor ancestors and earth spirits by proper cultivation. Like North Americans, Africans did not treat land as a commodity to be bought and sold.

Cultivation was difficult in Africa and required the labor of both genders. As in all tropical regions, scorching sunlight and frequent downpours lowered soil fertility. Like Indians in eastern North America, many Africans practiced slash-and-burn agriculture

Mali Horseman, c. 13th–14th century

This terra-cotta figure originated in Mali, one of several powerful empires in West Africa before the arrival of Europeans.

to maintain soil fertility. In coastal rain forests, root crops, primarily yams, dominated. On the Senegambia savanna, rice was the staff of life. In the seventeenth and eighteenth centuries, both rice and its Senegambian cultivators would be transplanted (the latter, as slaves) to North America.

Religion permeated African life. West African, like Native American, religion recognized spiritual presences throughout nature. The power of earth spirits and of agricultural ancestors reinforced the esteem that Africans accorded to cultivators. An enslaved eighteenth-century West African who eventually managed to purchase his freedom from slavery, Olaudah Equiano, gave Europeans a glimpse of African religion:

> *The natives believe that there is one Creator of all things, and that he lives in the sun, [and] . . . that he governs events. . . . Some . . . believe in the transmigration of souls [reincarnation] to some degree. Those spirits, who are not transmigrated, such as their dear friends or relations, they believe always attend them, and guard them from the bad spirits of their foes.*

Magic and the placating of spiritual powers, moreover, were important in African life. In both African and Native American societies, shamans maintained contact with the spiritual world, and belief in witchcraft was widespread. Unlike Indian religion, however, African religion focused on ancestor worship.

Religious motifs saturated African art. West Africans used their ivory, cast-iron, and wood sculptures in ceremonies reenacting creation myths and honoring spirits. A strong moralistic streak ran through African folktales. Oral reciters transmitted these stories in dramatic public presentations with ritual masks, dance, and music of a complex rhythmic structure. West African art and music powerfully influenced twentieth-century art and jazz.

Much in traditional African culture clashed with the great monotheistic religions, Islam and Christianity. Among Africans, Islam appealed primarily to merchants trading with Muslim North Africa and to grassland rulers eager to consolidate their power. By the sixteenth century, Islam had only just begun to affect the daily lives of grassland cultivators and artisans. Christianity, which accompanied the Portuguese to Africa in the fifteenth and sixteenth centuries, had little impact on Africans until the nineteenth century.

European Culture and Society

When Columbus reached the New World in 1492, Europe was approaching the height of the Renaissance, the rebirth of classical Greek and Roman culture. Splendid architecture decorated European cities, and wealthy patrons commissioned artists to create works of idealized human beauty. Scholars strove to reconcile Christian faith and ancient philosophy, to explore the mysteries of nature, to map the world, and to explain the motions of the heavens.

But European society was quivering with tension. The era's artistic and intellectual creativity stemmed partly from intense social and spiritual stress as Europeans groped for stability by glorifying order, hierarchy, and beauty. A concern for power and rank, or "degree," dominated European life in the fifteenth and sixteenth centuries. Gender, wealth, inherited position, and political power affected every European's status, and few lived beyond the reach of some political authority's claim to tax and rule. But this order was shaky. Conflicts between ranks, between religions, and between rich and poor threatened the balance, making Europeans cling all the more eagerly to order and hierarchy.

Democracy had no place in this world. To Europeans of the era, democracy meant mob rule and the destruction of social distinctions. Hierarchy and its strict rules seemed safer. Kings dominated the European hierarchy, but they were concerned less with their people's welfare than with consolidating and enlarging their own power. To that end, they waged costly wars using mercenary armies and spreading disease and misery everywhere.

Europeans believed that kings, not queens, were meant to rule. In addition, they knew that a queen's marriage would ultimately transfer the crown to a foreign dynasty or to a new domestic one. Either situation would threaten stability and hierarchy. In England, where Queens Mary I and Elizabeth I reigned for half a century, people felt this fear most keenly.

Although Mary (ruled 1553–1558) blundered repeatedly as queen and saved the day only by dying early, Elizabeth (ruled 1558–1603) took England's interests to heart. Remaining the unmarried "virgin queen," she artfully managed Parliament, which represented upper-class landowners and merchants. By choosing prudent advisers and shrewdly manipulating royal favors, Elizabeth retained control of the kingdom's intricate political system for a half century.

Elizabeth's reign demonstrated the degree to which royal power depended on the upper classes' cooperation. The men who dominated Parliament saw officeholding as a form of property and as a legitimate way to improve their fortunes. No monarch could ride roughshod over such men, and in defending their own liberties, they preserved the principle of limited government against encroaching despotism. But England's upper classes had problems of their own as well. A tradition of free spending to maintain status and a stagnant economy pinched not only members of the aristocracy, or noblemen with titles, but also many of the gentry, the "respectable" untitled landowners who traditionally lived without doing manual labor and who played prominent political roles in local government and Parliament.

At the bottom of the social heap toiled the ordinary people. Europe remained rural in these times, and four-fifths of its population were peasants. Taxes, rents, and other dues to landlords and church officials were heavy. Poor harvests or war drove even well-to-do peasants to starvation.

Sharp population increases worsened conditions. The plague known as the Black Death had killed one-third of Europe's people in the late fourteenth century, but by 1660 dramatic growth was driving up the population to 100 million. Food supplies, however, did not rise as rapidly. Peasant families survived on pitifully low yields of wheat, barley, and oats. Plowing, sowing, and harvesting together, they also grazed livestock on jointly owned "commons" composed of pastureland and forest. But with new land at a premium, landlords, especially the English gentry, began to "enclose" the commons, thus making them private property. Peasants with no *written* title to their lands were particularly vulnerable. Those with strong titles, however, could either keep their land or profit by joining the landlord in enclosing.

Though numerous, European towns usually contained only a few thousand inhabitants. London, a great metropolis of 200,000 people by 1600, was an exception. Large or small, towns were dirty and disease-ridden, and townspeople lived close-packed with their neighbors.

People of the times saw towns as centers of opportunity for the ambitious. Immigration from the countryside therefore swelled urban populations. But peasants transplanted to towns remained at the bottom of the social order, unable to earn enough money to marry and to live independently. Manufacturing took place in household workshops, where artisan masters ruled their subordinates. Successful artisans and merchants formed guilds to control employment, prices, and the sale of goods. Dominated by the richest citizens, urban governments enforced social conformity by "sumptuary laws" that forbade dressing inappropriately for one's social rank.

The consequences of rapid population growth were acute in England, where the population doubled from 2.5 million in 1500 to 5 million by 1620. In parts of the countryside, the gentry grew rich selling wool, but because of technological stagnation, per capita output and household income among textile workers fell. In effect, more workers competed for fewer jobs as European markets for English cloth diminished and as food prices rose. Land enclosure aggravated unemployment and forced large numbers of people to wander the countryside in search of work. These "vagabonds" seemed to threaten law and order. Parliament passed "Poor Laws" ordering vagrants whipped and sent home, where hard-pressed taxpayers maintained them on relief.

Thus the hopes and ambitions that drew people to towns usually yielded to frustration. Some English people blamed the wealthy for raising prices, goading the poor to revolt, and giving too little to charity. Others, such as writer Thomas Nashe, spread the blame more widely:

> *From the rich to the poor . . . there is ambition, or swelling above their states [proper place in society]; the rich citizen swells against the pride of the prodigal courtier; the prodigal courtier swells against the wealth of the citizen. One company swells against another. . . . The ancients [elderly], they oppose themselves against the younger, and suppress them and keep them down all that they may. The young men, they call [the elderly] dotards, and swell and rage.*

Nashe and other conservative moralists stoutly upheld the value of social reciprocity. As in the New World and Africa, traditional society in Europe rested on long-term, reciprocal relationships. Because it sought smooth social relationships between individuals of unequal status, reciprocity required the upper classes to act with self-restraint and dignity and the lower classes to show deference to their "betters." It demanded strict economic regulation, too, to ensure that sellers charged a "just" price—one that covered costs and allowed the seller to profit but barred him from taking advantage of buyers' and borrowers' misfortunes, or of shortages, to make "excessive" profits.

Yet the ideals of traditional economic behavior had been withering for centuries. By the sixteenth century, nothing could stop the practices of charging interest on borrowed money and of increasing prices in response to demand. New forms of business organization such as the joint-stock company, the ancestor of the modern corporation, steadily spread. Demand for capital investment grew, and so did the supply of accumulated wealth. Gradually, a new economic outlook arose that justified the unimpeded acquisition of wealth and unregulated economic competition. Its adherents insisted that individuals owed one another only the money necessary to settle each market transaction. This "market economy" capitalism stood counter to traditional demands for the strict regulation of economic activity to ensure social reciprocity and to maintain "just prices."

Sixteenth- and seventeenth-century Europeans therefore were ambivalent about economic enterprise and social change. A restless desire for fresh opportunity kept life simmering with competitive tension. However, even those who prospered still sought the security and prestige of traditional social distinctions, and the poor longed for the age-old values that they hoped would restrain irresponsible greed. Intellectuals and clergy defended traditional standards, but ideal and reality grew steadily further apart.

Fundamental change in European society could also be seen in the rising importance of the nuclear family. In such a family, the power of the senior male challenged traditional kinship networks. The nuclear family represented a "little commonwealth" within which the father's rule mirrored God's rule over Creation and kings' lordship over their subjects. The ideal, according to a German writer, was that "wives should obey their husbands and not seek to dominate them; they must manage the home efficiently. Husbands . . . should treat their wives with consideration and occasionally close an eye to their faults." In practice, however, the father's domination often had to make room for the wife's management of family affairs and her assistance in running the farm or the workshop.

Europeans and Their God

Sixteenth-century Europeans believed in the biblical explanation of the origins of the world and its peoples. Christianity taught that Jesus Christ, God's Son, redeemed sinners through his crucifixion and resurrection. As real as God to European Christians was the devil, Satan, who lured people to damnation by tempting them to do evil. Jewish and Muslim European minorities shared Christians' worship of a single supreme being, based on the God of the Old Testament.

But many sixteenth-century Europeans also believed in witchcraft, magic, and astrology. They saw nature as a "chain of being" infused by God with life and tingling with spiritual forces. Deeply embedded in folklore, such supernaturalism also marked the "high culture" of educated Europeans. Indeed, the sixteenth-century European "mentality" had more in common with Indian and African mindsets than with modern views.

The medieval Christian church taught that Christ had founded the church to save sinners from hell. Every time a priest said Mass, Christ's sacrifice was repeated, and divine grace flowed to sinners through sacraments that priests alone could administer—especially baptism, confession, and the Eucharist (communion). In most of Europe the "church" was a huge network of clergymen set apart from laypeople by ordination into the priesthood and by the fact that they did not marry. The pope, the "vicar (representative) of Christ," topped this hierarchy. His authority reached throughout Europe, except in Russia, Greece, and the Balkan peninsula.

The papacy wielded awesome spiritual power. Fifteenth- and sixteenth-century popes claimed the authority to dispense extra blessings, or "indulgences," to repentant sinners in return for "good works," such as donating money to the church. Indulgences also promised time off from future punishment in purgatory. Given peoples' anxieties over sin, indulgences were enormously popular. A German seller of indulgences even advertised that

> *As soon as the coin in the cash box rings,*
> *The soul from purgatory's fire springs.*

But the sale of indulgences provoked charges of materialism and corruption. In 1517 Martin Luther, a German friar, attacked the practice. When the papacy tried to silence him, Luther broadened his criticism to include the Mass, priests, and the pope. His revolt sparked the Protestant Reformation, which changed Christianity forever.

To Luther, the selling of indulgences was evil not only because it bilked people but also because the church did harm by falsely assuring people that they could "earn" salvation by doing good works.

Luther believed instead that God alone chose whom to save and that believers should trust only God's love, not the word of priests and the pope. Luther's own spiritual struggle and experience of being "born again" constituted a classic conversion experience—the heart of Protestant religion as it would be preached and practiced for centuries in England and North America.

Luther's assault on church abuses won a fervent following among the German public, but Protestant reformers themselves could not agree on what God's word really meant. Thus Luther and French reformer John Calvin (1509–1564) interpreted salvation differently. Calvin, unlike Luther, insisted on the doctrine of predestination, in which an omnipotent God "predestined" most sinful humans to hell, saving only a few to exemplify his grace. Calvinists and Lutherans, as the followers of the two Reformation leaders came to be called, alike were horrified by radical Protestants such as the Anabaptists, who criticized the rich and powerful and restricted baptism to adults who had undergone a conversion. Viewing the Anabaptists as a threat to the social order, governments and mainstream churches persecuted them.

The Catholic church's remarkable resilience also dismayed Protestants. Indeed, the papacy vigorously attacked church corruption and combated Protestant viewpoints. The popes also sponsored a new religious order committed to the papacy, the Jesuits, whose members would distinguish themselves for centuries as teachers, missionaries, and royal advisers. This Catholic revival, known as the Counter-Reformation, created the modern Roman Catholic church.

Those in all religious camps who hoped that eventual Christian harmony would overcome religious quarrels were disillusioned. Religious warfare consumed much of western and central Europe from the mid-sixteenth to the mid-seventeenth century. Well-established international rivalries, such as those between Protestant England and Catholic Spain, assumed religious dimensions. In England the crown itself was entangled in religious controversy. Henry VIII (ruled 1509–1547) wanted a male heir to ensure political stability. But when his queen, Catherine of Aragon, failed to bear a son, Henry in 1527 requested a papal annulment of their marriage. When the pope denied his request, in 1533–1534 Henry had Parliament dissolve his marriage and proclaim him "supreme head" of the Church of England (Anglican church). He then seized and sold vast tracts of land owned by Catholic monasteries as a means of raising revenue.

The Rise of Puritanism in England

Religious strife troubled England for over a century after Henry's break with Rome. Henry's sale of monastic lands had created a vested interest against returning to the old order, but Henry never quite decided that he was Protestant. Under his son Edward VI (ruled 1547–1553), however, the English church veered sharply toward Protestantism. Then Henry's daughter Mary assumed the throne in 1553 and tried to restore Catholicism, in part by burning several hundred Protestants at the stake.

The reign of Mary's successor, Elizabeth I, who became queen in 1558, marked a crucial watershed. Most English people were now Protestant; *how* Protestant was the question. A militant Calvinist minority, the Puritans, demanded wholesale "purification" of the Church of England from "popish abuses." As Calvinists, they affirmed salvation by predestination, denied Christ's presence in the Eucharist, and believed that a learned sermon was the heart of true worship. They wished to free each congregation from outside interference and encouraged lay members to participate in parish affairs.

Puritans argued that leading an outwardly moral life was not enough to earn salvation. They believed that Christians also must forge a commitment to serve God through an act of spiritual rebirth, the conversion experience. At this moment of being "reborn," a soul confronted its own unworthiness and felt the power of God's grace. Through "sanctification," the convert was cemented to God as a "saint"—a member of the "elect," or the chosen. Only saints could join Puritan congregations.

In preparing for spiritual rebirth, Puritans struggled to master their own wills, to internalize an idealistic code of ethics, and to forge the inner strength to survive in a world of economic and moral chaos. By the time of his or her redemption, the Puritan had undergone a radical transformation that replaced doubt with certainty, producing a strong sense of purpose, a willingness to sacrifice, and an ironclad discipline.

Puritanism appealed mainly to the growing middle sectors of English society—the gentry, university-educated clergymen and intellectuals, merchants, shopkeepers, artisans, and well-to-do peasants. Self-discipline had become central to both the worldly and the spiritual dimensions of these people's lives, and from their ranks would come the settlers of New England (see Chapter 3). Puritanism attracted few of the titled nobility, who enjoyed their wealth and privilege, and few of the desperately poor, who were struggling for mere survival.

Queen Elizabeth distrusted Puritan militancy and favored the traditional, dignified worship of the Anglican church. Until the pope declared her a heretic in 1570 and urged Catholics to overthrow her, she even avoided breaking with the Catholic church. Thereafter she saw all English Catholics as potential traitors and became more openly Protestant. Although Puritan sentiment steadily gained ground, Elizabeth never embraced it. By courting influential Puritans and embracing militant anti-Catholicism, Elizabeth maintained most Puritans' loyalty. But after her death, religious tensions came to a boil.

The Stuart monarchs, James I (ruled 1603–1625) and Charles I (ruled 1625–1649), bitterly opposed Puritan efforts to eliminate the office of bishop; not only did bishops, appointed by the king, compose one-quarter of Parliament's upper house, but they also could, and did, silence clerical critics of the monarchs. "No bishop, no king," snapped James I, more prophetically than he realized.

Abandoning the earlier hope of transforming the Church of England into independent congregations of "saints," Puritan *Separatists* decided to leave the corrupt state church. Some Separatists went first to Calvinist Holland and from there to Plymouth Plantation in New England. *Nonseparatists* continued to strive to reform the Church of England from within. Some of their rank would later lead the colonization of Massachusetts Bay and Connecticut (see Chapter 3).

Under Charles I, Anglican authorities campaigned to eliminate Puritan influence within the church. Bishops insisted that services be conducted according to the Book of Common Prayer, which prescribed rituals similar to Catholic practice, and they dismissed Puritan ministers who refused to perform these "High Church" rites. Church courts harassed Puritans with fines and even excommunication.

Hard economic times compounded the Puritans' plight. Wages fell by 50 percent between 1550 and 1650, a growing population spawned massive unemplotment, and war on the European continent threw the weaving industry of England's heavily Puritan southeastern counties into a recession as Germany was prevented from importing large amounts of English cloth after 1618. Puritans believed that these problems were contributing to a spiritual and moral crisis in England. Indeed, one Puritan minister wrote that the dwindling economic opportunities were tempting everyone "to pluck his means, as it were, out of his neighbor's throat."

Seeking escape from religious, political, and economic misery, a group of Puritan merchants bought the charter of the failed Virginia Company of Plymouth in 1628 and obtained a royal charter for land north of the Plymouth colony between the Charles and Merrimack rivers in 1629.

Legacies of the Reformation

The Reformation left four major legacies. First, it created almost all the major Christian traditions that took root on American soil: Protestantism, modern Roman Catholicism, and the radical Protestantism that would later flower into dozens of denominations and groups seeking human perfection. Second, Protestants valued literacy. Luther's conversion sprang from his long study of the Bible, and Protestants demanded that believers carefully read

God's Word translated from Latin into contemporary spoken languages. Newly invented printing presses spread the new faith; wherever Protestantism flourished, so did general education and religious teaching. Third, Protestants denied that God endowed priests with special powers. Instead, Luther claimed, the church was a "priesthood of all believers." People were responsible for their own spiritual and moral condition. Finally, the Reformation and Counter-Reformation created a new crusading spirit in Europe that coincided with overseas expansion. From Christopher Columbus onward, this spirit justified Europeans' assumption of superiority over the non-Christian peoples of Africa and the Americas and the seizing of their land, resources, and labor.

The Reformation also created in many people a longing for the simplicity and purity of the ancient Christian church. Protestantism condemned the replacement of traditional reciprocity by marketplace values and questioned the pursuit of excessive wealth. In a world of troubling change, it forged individuals of strong moral determination and gave them the fortitude to survive and prosper. Protestantism's greatest appeal was to those who brooded over their chances for salvation and valued the steady performance of duty.

European Expansion

Europe's outward thrust began centuries before Columbus's first voyage in 1492. Norse adventurers had reached North America in the tenth century, but their colonies had collapsed. European attention had turned eastward after 1096 as a series of crusading armies tried to wrest Palestine from Muslim control. A brisk trade with the Middle East begun in these years had brought silks and spices to Europe. Marco Polo and other thirteenth-century merchants had even traveled overland to East Asia, to buy directly from the Chinese. Fourteenth- and fifteenth-century Italian merchants grew rich from the spice and silk trade and used their fortunes to finance the early Renaissance and overseas expansion by European monarchs.

Seaborne Expansion

In the mid-fifteenth century Europe experienced renewed prosperity and population growth. Competing for commercial advantage, the newly centralized European states projected their power overseas.

Improved maritime technology permitted this European expansion. In the early fifteenth century shipbuilders added the triangular Arab sail to their heavy cargo ships, creating a highly maneuverable ship, the caravel, to sail the stormy Atlantic. Further, the growing use of the compass and astrolabe permitted mariners to calculate their bearings on the open sea. Hand in hand with the technological advances of this "maritime revolution," Renaissance scholars corrected ancient geographical data and drew increasingly accurate maps. The new geography and sophisticated use of Arabic mathematics sharpened Europeans' knowledge of the world.

The Portuguese first felt the itch to explore new worlds. Their zeal for continuing the struggle against the Muslims, recently driven from Portugal, combined with an anxious search for new markets. Prince Henry "the Navigator" of Portugal (1394–1460) embodied both impulses. He encouraged Portuguese seamen to pilot their caravels farther down the African coast searching for weak spots in Muslim defenses and for trade opportunities. By the time of Henry's death, the Portuguese had built a profitable slaving station at Arguin; shortly after, they had penetrated south of the equator. In 1488 Bartolomeu Días reached Africa's southern tip, the Cape of Good Hope, opening the possibility of direct trade with India, and in 1498 Vasco da Gama led a Portuguese fleet around the cape and on to India. For more than a century the Portuguese remained an imperial presence in the Indian Ocean and the East Indies (modern Indonesia). But far more significantly, they brought Europeans face to face with black Africans.

The "New Slavery"
In this early depiction, African slaves work and look for gold in the New World, under the supervision of a watchful European master.

The "New Slavery" and Racism

Slavery was well established in fifteenth-century West Africa, as elsewhere. The grassland emperors as well as individual families depended on slave labor. But most slaves or their children were absorbed into African families over time. First Arabs, and then Europeans, however, turned African slavery into an intercontinental business. A fifteenth-century Italian reported that the Arabs

> *have many Berber horses, which they trade, and take to the Land of the Blacks, exchanging them with the rulers for slaves. . . . These slaves are brought to the market town of Hoden. . . . [Some] are taken . . . and sold to the Portuguese leaseholders of Arguin. . . . Every year the Portuguese carry away from [Arguin] a thousand slaves.*

The Portuguese kept most competitors from the lucrative African slave trade until about 1600. They exploited existing African commercial and social patterns, often trading slaves and local products to other Africans for gold. The local African kingdoms were too strong for the Portuguese to attack, and black rulers traded—or chose not to trade—according to their own self-interest.

The coming of the Portuguese slavers changed West African societies. Small kingdoms in Guinea and Senegambia expanded to "service" the trade, and some of their rulers became rich. Farther south, in modern Angola, the kings of Kongo used the slave trade to consolidate their power and adopted Christianity. Kongo flourished until attackers from the interior severely weakened it at the end of the sixteenth century. African kings and their communities used the slave trade to dispose of "undesirables," including troublesome slaves whom they already owned, lawbreakers, and persons accused of witchcraft. But most slaves were simply victims of raids or wars. Muslim and European slave trading greatly stimulated conflicts among communities in Africa.

Europeans had used slaves since ancient Greece and Rome, but ominous changes took place in European slavery once the Portuguese began making voyages to Africa. First, the new slave trade was a high-volume business that expanded at a steady rate as Europeans colonized the Western Hemisphere and established plantation societies there. Between 1500 and 1600, perhaps 250,000 African slaves would reach the New World, and 50,000 would perish en route. Between 1601 and 1621, 200,000 more would arrive. Before the Atlantic slave trade ended in the nineteenth century, nearly 12 million Africans would be shipped across the sea. Slavery on this scale had been unknown since the Roman Empire. Second, African slaves received exceptionally harsh treatment. In medieval Europe slaves had primarily performed domestic service, but by 1450 the Portuguese and Spanish had created large slave-labor plantations on their Atlantic and Mediterranean islands. Using African slaves who toiled until death, these plantations produced sugar for European markets. In short, the African slaves owned

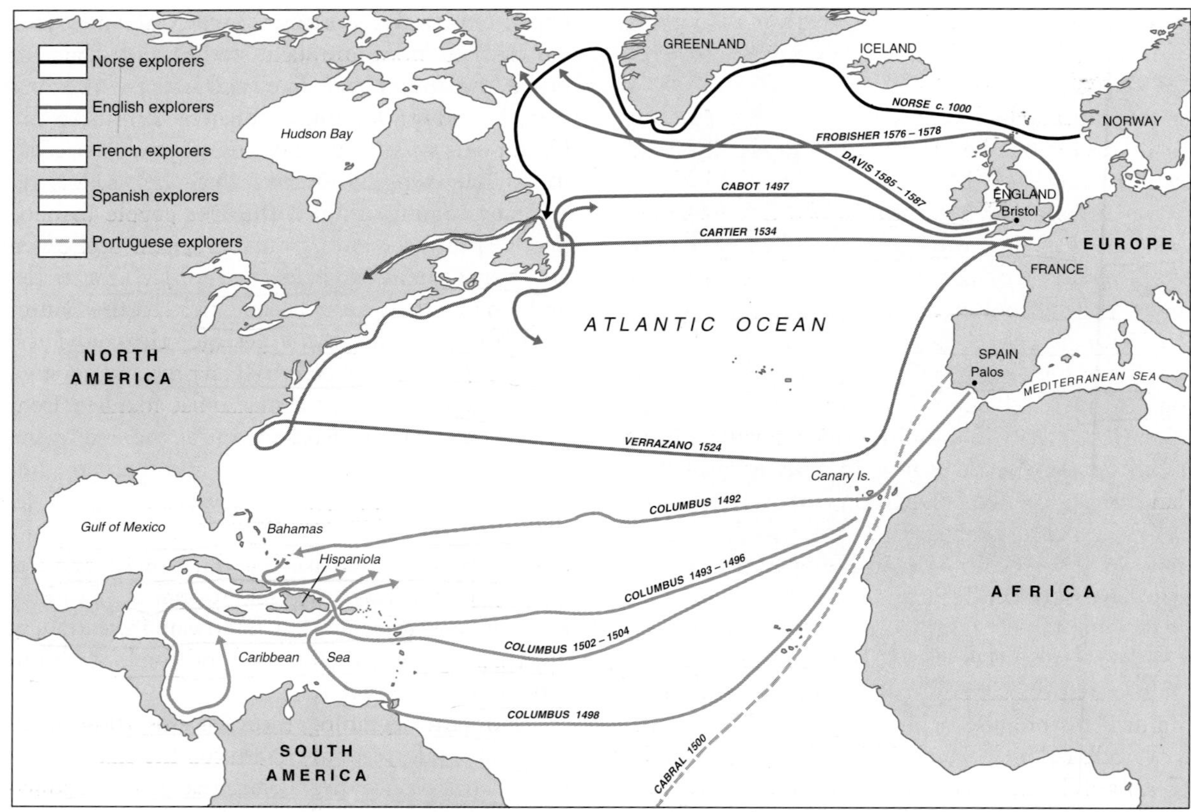

Major Transatlantic Explorations, 1000–1587 *Following Columbus's 1492 voyage, Spain's rivals soon began laying claim to parts of the New World based on the voyages of Cabot for England, Cabral for Portugal, and Verrazano for France. Later English and French exploration focused on finding a passsage to Asia around or through Canada.*

by Europeans performed exhausting, mindless labor. By 1600 the "new slavery" had become a brutal link in an expanding commerce that ultimately would encompass all major Western nations.

Finally, race became the explicit basis of the "new slavery." Africans' blackness and alien religion dehumanized them in European eyes. As racial prejudice hardened, Europeans found it easy to justify black slavery. European Christianity, moreover, made few attempts to soften slavery's rigors. Because the victims of the "new slavery" were physically distinctive and culturally alien, slavery became a lifelong, hereditary, and despised status.

Europeans Reach America

The fascinating, contradictory figure of Christopher Columbus (1451–1506) embodied Europeans' varied motives for expansion. The son of an Italian weaver, Columbus became obsessed by the idea that Europeans could reach Asia by sailing westward across the Atlantic. Combining an overestimation of Asia's eastward thrust with an underestimation of the earth's circumference, he concluded that the world was much smaller than it actually is and that the open-sea distance from Europe to Asia was roughly 3,000 miles, not the actual 12,000 miles.

Religious fervor led Columbus to dream of carrying Christianity around the globe, but he also hungered for wealth and glory.

Europeans had ventured far into the Atlantic before Columbus: besides the early Norse, fifteenth-century English fishers may have reached North America's coast. What distinguished Columbus was his persistence in hawking his "enterprise of the Indies" around Europe's royal courts. In 1492 the rulers of newly united Spain, Isabella of Castile and Ferdinand of Aragon, accepted Columbus's offer, hoping to break a threatened Portuguese monopoly on Asian trade. Picking up the westerly trade winds, Columbus's three small ships made landfall within a month off the North American coast at a small island that he named San Salvador.

Word of Columbus's discovery fired Europeans' imaginations. It also induced the Spanish and Portuguese to sign the Treaty of Tordesillas in 1494, dividing all future discoveries between themselves. Columbus made three further voyages, in the course of which he established Spanish colonies, but never fulfilled his promise of reaching Asia. Meanwhile, England's Henry VII (ruled 1485–1509) ignored the Treaty of Tordesillas and sent an Italian navigator known as John Cabot westward across the northern Atlantic in 1497. Cabot claimed Nova Scotia, Newfoundland, and the rich Grand Banks fisheries for England, but he vanished at sea on a second voyage. Like Columbus, Cabot believed that he had reached Asia.

The more Columbus and others explored, the more apparent it became that a vast landmass blocked the western route to Asia. In 1500 the Portuguese claimed Brazil, and other voyages outlined a continuous coastline from the Caribbean to Brazil. In 1507 a publisher brought out a collection of voyagers' tales, including one from the Italian Amerigo Vespucci. A shrewd marketer, the publisher devised a catchy name for the new continent: America.

Getting past America to Asia remained the early explorers' goal. In 1513 the Spaniard Vasco Núñez de Balboa crossed the narrow isthmus of Panama and chanced upon the Pacific Ocean. In 1519 the Portuguese mariner Ferdinand Magellan, sailing under the Castilian flag, began a voyage around the world through the stormy straits at South America's southern tip, now named the Straits of Magellan. He crossed the Pacific to the Philippines, only to die fighting with natives. One of his five ships and fifteen emaciated sailors returned to Spain in 1522, the first people to have sailed around the world. But Europeans desired an easier way to Asia's fabled wealth. The French dispatched Giovanni da Verrazano and Jacques Cartier to search for a "northwest passage" to Asia. Their voyages probed the North American coast from Newfoundland to the Carolinas but found neither gold nor a northwest passage.

The Conquerors

Columbus was America's first slave trader and the first Spanish *conquistador*, or conqueror. On Hispaniola he exported Indian slaves and created *encomiendas*, grants for both land and the labor of the Indians who lived on it.

From the beginning, *encomienderos*, those given the *encomiendas*, harshly exploited the native people. As disease, overwork, and malnutrition killed thousands of Indians, Portuguese slave traders supplied shiploads of Africans to replace them. Although shocked Spanish friars sent to convert the Native Americans reported the Indians' exploitation, and King Ferdinand attempted to forbid the practice, no one worried about African slaves' fate. Spanish settlers were soon fanning out across the Caribbean in pursuit of slaves and gold. In 1519 the young nobleman Hernán Cortés (1485–1547) led a small band of Spaniards to the Mexican coast. Destroying his boats and enlisting Indian allies, he marched inland to conquer Mexico.

Since reaching America, Spaniards had dreamed of a prize as rich as Mexico. The Aztec civilization, the product of 3,000 years of cultural evolution, was both powerful and wealthy. A centralized bureaucracy ruled from the capital, Tenochtitlán, whose 300,000 inhabitants made it one of the largest cities in the world. The Aztecs used fresh water carried by elaborately engineered aqueducts, and their artisans produced fine pottery as well as implements and statues of stone, copper, silver, and gold. "We were amazed . . . and some of our soldiers even asked whether the things that we saw were not a dream," recalled one *conquistador* of his first glimpse of Tenochtitlán's pyramids, lakes, and causeways. But the golden gifts that the Aztecs offered in vain hopes of buying off the invaders were no dream. Recalled an Indian, "Their bodies swelled with greed. . . . They hungered like pigs for that gold."

Cortés attacked and swiftly prevailed, owing partly to firearms and horses, which terrified the Aztecs, and partly to initial Aztec suppositions that the Spanish were the white, bearded gods foretold in legends. Cortés cunningly exploited the Aztec emperor Moctezuma's fears, the Indians' decimation by epidemics, and a revolt by the Aztecs' subject peoples. By 1521 Cortés had defeated the Aztecs and had begun to build Mexico City on the ruins of Tenochtitlán. Within twenty years, Central America lay at the Spaniards' feet. Thus was New Spain born.

During the rest of the sixteenth century, other *conquistadores* consolidated a great Hispanic empire stretching from New Spain (Mexico) to Chile. Spaniards stilled any doubts about the legitimacy of conquest by demanding that the Indians convert to Christianity—and by attacking them if they refused. From the beginning, however, the Spanish church and government had worried that the *conquistadores* were too powerful and abusive. The monarchy consequently sent hundreds of bureaucrats across the ocean to govern in the hierarchical European manner and to defend Indian rights. Further, an army of Spanish friars established missions among the Indians and tried to lessen their suffering, often clashing with civilian authorities. The result was a cumbersome system that seldom worked well.

The conquest came at enormous human cost. When Cortés landed in 1519, the Aztec empire contained 25 million people. By 1600 it had shrunk to between 1 and 2 million. Peru experienced similar devastation. Disease, not war or slavery, was the greatest killer. Native Americans lacked resistance to European and African infections, especially the

Indian View of Spanish Colonizers
This pictograph—a painting or drawing on rock—was sketched in the early colonial period in Cañón del Muerto, Arizona.

deadly, highly communicable smallpox. From the first years of contact with Europeans, terrible epidemics decimated Indian communities. In the West Indies the native population vanished within a half century, and disease opened the mainland for conquest as well. "The people began to die very fast, and many in a short space," an Englishman later remarked. From the early sixteenth century on, smallpox and other epidemics ravaged the defenseless Indians. Up to 90 percent of the native population was lost in some areas. In return, a virulent form of syphilis spread from the New World to the Old shortly after Columbus's first voyage.

The "Columbian exchange"—the biological encounter of the Old and New Worlds—went beyond deadly germs. Europeans brought horses, cattle, sheep, swine, chickens, wheat, coffee, sugar cane, and numerous fruits and vegetables with them, as well as an astonishing variety of weeds. African slaves carried rice and yams across the Atlantic. The list of New World gifts to the Old was equally impressive: it included corn, white and sweet potatoes, many varieties of beans, tomatoes, squash, pumpkins, peanuts, vanilla, chocolate, avocados, pineapples, chilis, tobacco, turkeys, canoes, kayaks, hammocks, snowshoes, and moccasins. European weeds and domesticated animals often, especially in North America, overwhelmed indigenous plant life and drove away native animals dependent on those plants. Settlers' crops, intensively cultivated on land never allowed to lie fallow, frequently exhausted American soils. Nonetheless, the worldwide exchange of food products enriched human diets and made possible enormous population growth. Today, nearly 60 percent of all food crops worldwide trace their roots to the Native American garden.

Another dimension of the meeting of the two worlds was the mixing of peoples. Within Spain's empire, a great human intermingling occurred. From 1500 to 1600 between 100,000 and 300,000 Spaniards immigrated to the New World, 90 percent of them male. A racially mixed population developed, particularly in towns. Spaniards fathered numerous children with African or Indian mothers, most of them slaves. Such racial mixing would

The Spanish and Portuguese Empires, 1610
By 1610 Spain dominated Latin America, including Portugal's possessions. Having devoted its energies to exploiting Mexico and the Caribbean, Spain had not yet expanded into what is now the United States, aside from establishing outposts in Florida and New Mexico.

occur, although far less commonly, in French and English colonies as well.

The New World supplied seemingly endless wealth for Spain. West Indian sugar plantations and Mexican sheep and cattle ranches enriched many. Much of Spain's wealth, however, was dug from the silver mines of Mexico and Peru. After 1540 enormous amounts of silver flowed across the Atlantic, far more than the small Spanish economy could absorb, setting off an inflation that eventually engulfed Europe. But, bent on dominating Europe, Spanish kings needed even more American silver to pay for their ships and armies. Several times they went bankrupt, and in the 1560s their efforts to squeeze more taxes from their subjects provoked revolt in Spain's Netherlands provinces (modern

Belgium, Holland, and Luxembourg). In the end, gaining access to American wealth cost the Spanish dearly.

The bloody history of Spain's American conquests and efforts to dominate Europe created the "Black Legend"—Protestant Europeans' vision of tyrannical, fanatically Catholic Spain intent on conquering everything in sight. Ironically, much of this grimly lurid picture came from the writings of a devout Spanish friar, Bartolomé de Las Casas (1474–1566), who had repented his own participation in the subjugation of Hispaniola and argued for a more humane Indian policy. By the end of the sixteenth century, Las Casas's hopes of justice for the Indians lay shattered. The Spanish church had grown increasingly bureaucratic and intolerant, fueling the Black Legend. As Spain's struggle to regain the Netherlands and to subdue France spilled near England, the Protestant English shuddered. They looked for opportunities across the Atlantic to strike back at Spain—and to enrich themselves.

Footholds in North America

Spain's New World wealth attracted other Europeans. Throughout the sixteenth century they sailed the North American coast, exploring, fishing, trading for furs, and smuggling. But except for a Spanish fort at St. Augustine, Florida, all sixteenth-century attempts at colonizing North America failed. Unrealistic dreams of easy wealth and pliant Indians brought French, English, and Spanish attempts to grief. Only the continued ravaging of the Indians by disease, declining Spanish power, and rising French, Dutch, and English power finally made colonization possible.

In 1607–1608 the English and French finally established permanent colonies. By 1614 the Dutch had followed. Within a generation North America's modern history took shape as each colony developed an economic orientation, pattern of Indian relations, and direction of geographic expansion.

New Spain's Northern Frontier

The Spanish built their New World empire on the wealth of the Aztec and other Indian states. But in the frontier lands north of Mexico, the absence of visible wealth and organized states discouraged conquest. Nonetheless, a succession of hopeful *conquistadores* marched across much of what would become the United States. Earliest came Juan Ponce de León, the conqueror of Puerto Rico, who trudged through Florida in search of gold and slaves twice, in 1512–1513 and in 1521, and then died in an Indian skirmish. The most astonishing early expedition began when 300 explorers left Florida in 1527 to explore the Gulf of Mexico. Indian attacks whittled their numbers until only a handful survived. Stranded in Texas, the survivors, led by Cabeza de Vaca, were passed from Indian tribe to tribe, often as slaves. They finally escaped and made their way to New Mexico and then south to Mexico in 1536.

Cabeza de Vaca inspired two would-be conquerors, Hernando de Soto and Francisco Vásquez de Coronado. In 1539–1543 de Soto and his party blundered from Tampa Bay to the Appalachians and back to southern Texas, scouring the land for gold and harrying the Indians. Although de Soto died without finding gold or conquering any Indians, his and other expeditions touched off epidemics that destroyed most of the remaining Mississippian societies. By the time Europeans returned to the southeastern interior late in the seventeenth century, only the Natchez people on the lower Mississippi River still inhabited their temple-mound center. Depopulated, the Cherokee and Creek Indians had adopted the less centralized village life of other eastern tribes.

As de Soto roamed the Southeast, the Southwest drew others with dreams of conquest, lured by rumors that the fabled Seven Golden Cities of Cíbola lay north of Mexico. In 1538 an expedition sighted the Zuñi pueblos and assumed them to be the golden cities. In 1540–1542 Francisco Vásquez de Coronado led a massive expedition bent on conquest. Coronado plundered several pueblos and roamed from the Grand Canyon to Kansas before returning to Mexico, thinking himself a failure. A third expedition under Juan Rodríguez Cabrillo sailed north along the California coast but found nothing worth seizing.

For decades after these failures, Spain's principal interest in the lands north of Mexico lay in establishing a few strategic bases in Florida to keep out intruders. In 1565 Spain planted the first successful European settlement on mainland North America, the fortress of St. Augustine. Then in the 1580s the Spanish returned to the southwestern pueblo country, preaching Christianity and scouting for wealth. In 1598 Juan de Oñate led 500 Spaniards into the upper Rio Grande valley, where he proclaimed the royal colony of New Mexico, distributed *encomiendas*, and demanded tribute from the Indians.

The new colony barely survived. In 1606 the Spanish replaced Oñate because of his excessive brutality. Finding no gold, many settlers left. In 1609 those who remained established Santa Fe; still others migrated to isolated ranches and fought off Navajo and Apache raiders. By 1630 Franciscan missionaries had established more than thirty missions stretching from the Rio Grande valley to Hopi villages in Arizona, 250 miles to the west. They had converted about 20,000 Indians to Christianity. Eventually, the missions' demands for labor and their attempts to uproot native religions would provoke an Indian backlash (see Chapter 3). Spanish New Mexico would not be secure for a century.

France: Initial Failures and Canadian Success

In 1534 Jacques Cartier of France, searching for the northwest passage, explored the St. Lawrence River, the center of French colonization after 1600. But a half century of failure preceded France's ultimate success.

France made its first attempt at colonizing North America in 1541, when ten ships sailed into the St. Lawrence Valley. Having alienated many of the Indians along the St. Lawrence in two previous expeditions, Cartier built a fortified settlement on Indian land and thus ended all possibility of peaceful Indian-French relations. Steady Indian attacks and scurvy (for which the Indians could have shown them a cure) drove the French off within two years.

This fiasco underlined one Spaniard's view that "this whole coast as far [south] as Florida is utterly unproductive." In 1562 French Huguenots (Calvinists) made the next French attempt at colonization, establishing a base in modern South Carolina. Two years later they founded a settlement in Florida, which the Spanish quickly destroyed. These failures as well as a civil war between French Catholics and Huguenots ended France's first attempts at colonization.

The Enterprising Dutch

Having secured independence from Spain by 1588, the Dutch Republic became one of the seventeenth century's great powers. The Dutch empire, based on sea power, would stretch from Brazil to West Africa to the East Indies, modern Indonesia. North American colonies were a small part of this vast empire, but the Dutch nonetheless played a key role in European colonization of the continent.

In 1609 Henry Hudson sailed up the broad, deep river that today bears his name, and in the next year Dutch ships sailed up the Hudson to trade with Indians. In 1614 the Dutch established Fort Nassau at the site of modern Albany, New York, and in 1625 planted another fort on an island at the mouth of the Hudson. Within two years Peter Minuit, director-general of the colony, bought the island from local Indians, named it Manhattan, and began a settlement christened New Amsterdam.

Furs, particularly beaver pelts, became the New Netherlanders' chief economic staple. The Mohawks as well as the other nations of the Iroquois Confederacy became the Dutch colonists' chief sup-

Carolina Indians Fishing, *by John White, 1585*
Using weirs (traplike enclosures), nets, and spears, these Carolina coastal Indians depended on fishing as an important source of their food. The artist, John White, accompanied Sir Walter Raleigh in setting up the Roanoke colony.

pliers of furs and soon found themselves embroiled in competition with the French-supported Hurons.

Elizabethan England and the Wider World

When Elizabeth I became queen in 1558, England, a minor power, stood on the sidelines as Spain and France grappled for European supremacy. England's claims to North America had receded, and religious division and domestic instability preoccupied the English.

This very instability, however, helped to propel Elizabethan expansion. Shipping the unemployed poor overseas would relieve England's economic woes, and these "surplus" people could provide markets for English cloth and produce raw materials. And the gentry of England's West Country—including the adventurers and seafarers Sir Francis Drake, Sir John Hawkins, Sir Humphrey Gilbert, and Sir Walter Raleigh—were lusting for action and ready to lead overseas ventures.

But Spain blocked the way. Good relations between Elizabethan England and imperial Spain had broken down as England worried about Spanish attempts to crush rebellion in the Netherlands and about Spain's intervention in France's religious wars. By 1570 Elizabeth was secretly aiding the French Huguenots and Dutch rebels as well as encouraging English "sea dogs" such as Sir Francis Drake and Sir John Hawkins, from whose voyages she took a share of the plunder.

Meanwhile, England's position in Ireland had deteriorated. By 1565 English troops were fighting to impose Elizabeth's rule throughout the island, where a Protestant English government was battling Irish Catholic rebels aided by Spain. In a war that ground on through the 1580s, English troops drove the Irish clans from their strongholds and established "plantations," or settlements, of Scottish and English Protestants. The English resorted to starvation and mass slaughter to break the Irish spirit. Elizabeth's generals justified these atrocities by calling the Irish savages. The Irish experience gave England strategies that it later used against North American Indians, whose customs, religion, and method of fighting seemed to absolve the English from guilt in waging exceptionally cruel warfare.

England had two objectives in the Western Hemisphere in the 1570s. The first was to find the northwest passage to Asia, preferably one lined with gold. The second, as Drake said, was to "singe the king of Spain's beard" by raiding Spanish fleets and cities. The search for a northwest passage proved fruitless, but the English did stage spectacularly successful and profitable privateering raids against the

Spanish. The most breathtaking enterprise of the era was Drake's voyage around the world in 1577–1580 in quest of sites for colonies.

In 1587 Sir Walter Raleigh, dreaming of founding an American colony where English, Indians, and even blacks liberated from Spanish slavery could live together productively, sponsored a colony on Roanoke Island, off the modern North Carolina coast. An earlier settlement (1585) had failed, in part because the colonists refused to grow their own food, expecting the Indians to feed them, and had worn out their welcome. One hundred ten colonists, many of them members of families, reached Roanoke in late summer 1587. Almost immediately the colony's leader, John White, returned to England for more supplies, leaving behind the settlers.

Spain's attempt to crush England with the Great Armada in 1588 prevented White from returning to Roanoke until 1590. When he did, he found only rusty armor, moldy books, and the word CROATOAN carved into a post. To this day, no one knows what happened to the "Lost Colony." The miserable failure at Roanoke would postpone the establishment of English colonies for seventeen more years.

Roanoke's fate illustrated several stubborn realities. First, even a large-scale, well-financed colony could fail, given settlers' unpreparedness for the American environment. Second, Europeans falsely assumed that the Indians would feed them and thus neglected to carry enough food supplies to carry them through the first winter. Third, colonizing attempts would have to be self-financing: a fiscally

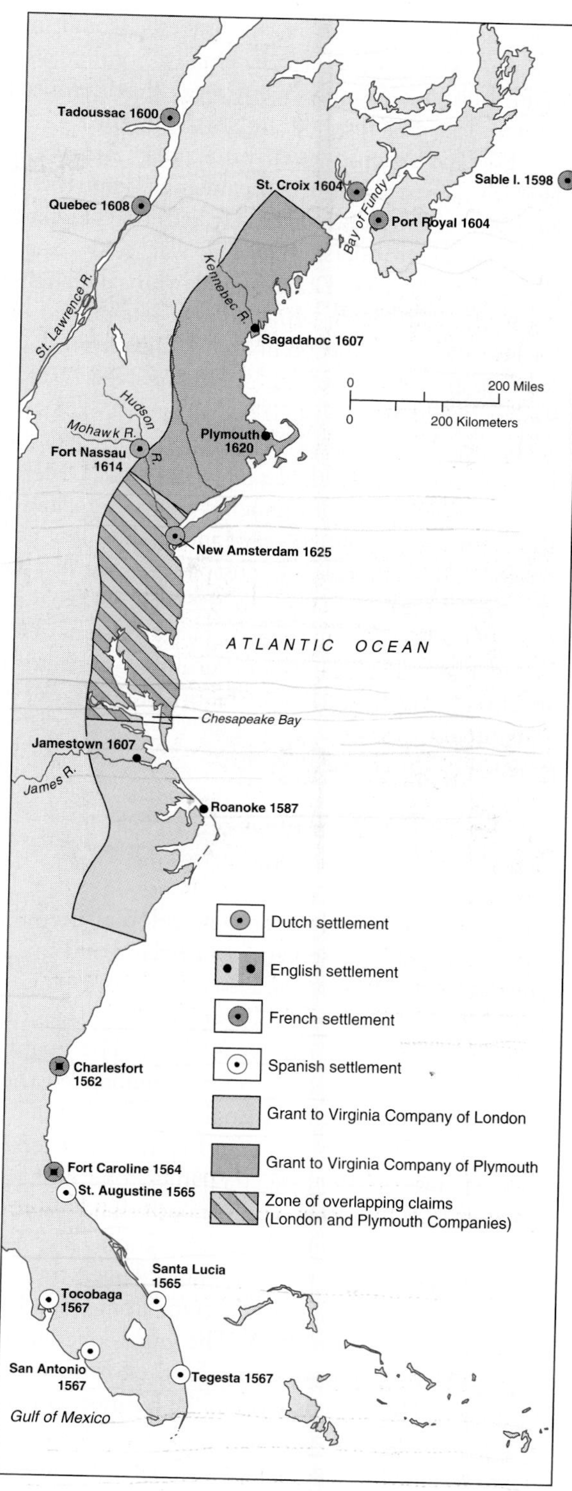

European Settlements in Eastern North America, 1565–1625

Except for St. Augustine, Florida, and Sante Fe, New Mexico, all European settlements founded before 1607 were abandoned by 1625. Despite the migration of 10,000 Europeans to North America's Atlantic coast by 1625, the total number of Spanish, English, French, and Dutch on the continent was then about 1,800, of whom two-thirds lived in Virginia. For French and Spanish settlement in the late colonial period, *see map on p. 80.*

strapped monarch such as Elizabeth would not throw good money after bad. Finally, conflict with Spain hung menacingly over every other European attempt to gain a foothold in North America.

England's victory over the Spanish Armada in 1588 preserved English independence, kept the island Protestant, and demonstrated that England could repel invaders. But the war with Spain churned on. In 1595 Drake and Hawkins died fighting in the Caribbean, while Raleigh squandered his fortune and his health on unsuccessful ventures.

To sustain public interest in the New World, Richard Hakluyt published collections of explorers' accounts, *The Principal Navigations, Voyages, and Discoveries of the English Nation* (1589, 1601). Meanwhile, a new means of financing colonies appeared, the joint-stock company. A kind of business corporation, the joint-stock company raised capital through the sale of stock to the public. Each investor faced only a limited risk, but large sums could be amassed. The English government henceforth would leave colonization to the private initiative of individuals or groups.

The Beginnings of English Colonization: Virginia

The hopes of would-be English colonial investors rose after 1600. Peace between England and Spain, concluded in 1604 by Elizabeth's successor, James I (ruled 1603–1625), opened the way for new colonization attempts in the New World. The Spanish not only agreed to peace but also renounced their claims to Virginia, leaving England a free hand.

On April 10, 1606, James I granted charters to two separate joint-stock companies, one based in London and the other in Plymouth. The Virginia Company of Plymouth received a grant extending from modern Maine to the Potomac River; the Virginia Company of London, a grant from Cape Fear north to the Hudson River. The grants overlapped, with the land in question to go to the first successful colonizer. The colonists would be business employees, not citizens of a separate political jurisdiction, and the stockholders of each company would regulate the colonists' behavior. Both companies dispatched colonists in 1607.

The Virginia Company of Plymouth sent 120 men to Sagadahoc at the mouth of the Kennebec River in Maine. The following year the colony disintegrated, the victim of Indian hostility (generally provoked) and hard Maine winters. The company subsequently became dormant. The Virginia Company of London dispatched 105 settlers to a site on the James River near Chesapeake Bay that they named Jamestown. But the first colonists, who included many gentry, hunted for gold and failed to plant crops. When relief ships arrived in January 1608, they found only 38 survivors.

Near anarchy reigned at Jamestown until September 1608, when desperate councilors, representatives of the Virginia Company of London, turned to a brash soldier of fortune, Captain John Smith. Only twenty-eight, Smith found that his experiences fighting the Spanish and the Turks had prepared him well to assume control in Virginia. By instituting harsh discipline, organizing the settlers, and requiring them to build houses and plant food, he ensured Jamestown's survival. During the winter of 1608–1609, Smith lost just 12 men out of 200.

Smith also became the colony's best diplomat. After local Indians captured him late in 1607, Smith displayed such impressive courage that Powhatan, the leader of the nearby Powhatan Confederacy, arranged an elaborate ceremony in which Pocahontas, his daughter, "saved" Smith's life during a mock execution. Smith maintained satisfactory relations with the Powhatan Confederacy partly through his personality and partly through calculated demonstrations of English military strength.

When serious injuries forced Smith to return to England in 1609, discipline again crumbled. Expecting the Indians to furnish corn, the settlers had not laid away enough food for winter. One colonist reported that Jamestown residents ate dogs, cats, rats, and snakes in order to survive. He gruesomely added that "many besides fed on the corpses of dead men." Of the 500 residents at Jamestown in September 1609, only 100 lived to May 1610. An influx of new recruits and the imposition of military rule, however, enabled Virginia to win the First Anglo-

Powhatan War (1610–1614) and, by 1611, to expand west to modern Richmond. The English population remained small—only 380 by 1616—and produced nothing of value for the stockholders.

Tobacco saved Virginia. John Rolfe, an Englishman who married Pocahontas, perfected a salable variety of tobacco for planting there, and by 1619 Virginia was exporting large, profitable amounts of the crop. Thereafter the Virginia Company poured supplies and settlers into the colony.

To attract labor and capital, the company awarded fifty-acre land grants ("headrights") to anyone paying his or her own passage or that of a laborer. By financing the passage of indentured servants, planters could accumulate large tracts of land. Thousands of single young men and a few hundred women became indentured servants, choosing the uncertainty of Virginia over poverty in England. In return for their passage, they worked a fixed term, usually four to seven years.

In 1619 the Virginia Company ended military rule and provided for an elected assembly, the House of Burgesses. Although the company could veto the assembly's actions, 1619 marked the beginning of representative government in North America. However, Virginia still faced three serious problems. First, local officials systematically defrauded shareholders, in the process sinking the company deeply into debt. Second, the colony's death rate soared. Malnutrition, typhus, dysentery, and salt poisoning (from drinking polluted river water) killed thousands of immigrants. Third, Indian relations worsened. After Powhatan's death in 1618, the new leader, Opechancanough, worried about the relentless expansion of the English colony. In 1622 the Indians killed 347 of the 1,200 settlers in a surprise attack. With their livestock destroyed, spring planting impossible, and disease spreading through crowded stockades, hundreds more colonists died in the ensuing months.

The Virginia Company sent more men, and Governor Francis Wyatt took the offensive. Using tactics developed during the Irish war, Wyatt destroyed the Indians' food supplies, conducted winter campaigns to drive them from their homes when they would suffer most, and fought (according to John Smith) as if he had "just cause to destroy them by all means possible." By 1625 the English had won the war, and the Indians had lost their best chance of forcing out the intruders.

But the struggle bankrupted the Virginia Company. After receiving complaints about its management, James revoked its charter and made Virginia a royal colony in 1624. Only 500 Old World settlers lived there, including a handful of Africans of uncertain status. The roots from which Virginia's Anglo-American and African-American peoples grew were fragile indeed.

The Origins of New England: Plymouth Plantation

Another rival entered the competition for the North American fur trade: the English who settled New England. In 1620 the Virginia Company of London granted a patent for a settlement to some English merchants headed by Thomas Weston. Weston dispatched eighteen families (102 people) in a small, leaky ship, the *Mayflower*. The colonists promised to send back lumber, furs, and fish for seven years, after which they would own the tract.

The expedition's leaders, and half its members, belonged to a small religious community from the northern English town of Scrooby. Separatist Puritans, they had earlier fled to the Netherlands to practice their religion freely. Fearing that their children were adopting Dutch ways, they decided to immigrate to America under Weston's sponsorship.

In November 1620 the *Mayflower* landed at Plymouth, outside the bounds of Virginia. Because they had no legal right to be there, the leaders forced the adult males in the group to sign the Mayflower Compact before they landed. By this document they constituted themselves a "civil body politic"—a civil government—under James I's sovereignty and established the colony of Plymouth Plantation.

Weakened by their journey and unprepared for winter, half the self-styled Pilgrims died within four months. Two Indians helped the others to survive: Squanto, a local Patuxet, and Samoset, an Abenaki from Maine who had traded with the English. To stop the Pilgrims from stealing their food, the Indians taught the newcomers how to grow corn. Squanto and Samoset also arranged an alliance between the Pilgrims and the local Wampanoag Indians, who were headed by Chief Massasoit. With firearms, the Pilgrims became the dominant partner, and the Wampanoags were forced to acknowledge English sovereignty.

Plymouth's relations with the Indians gradually worsened. Learning of the Virginia massacre of 1622, the Pilgrims militarized their colony and threatened their Indian "allies" with their monopoly of firepower. Although Massasoit remained loyal, this conduct offended many Wampanoags.

Meanwhile, systematically cheated by English patrons, the Pilgrims had sunk deeply into debt after seven years and faced fifteen years' additional labor to free themselves. Fishing was unprofitable, but the Pilgrims traded their surplus corn with nonagricultural Indians for furs, and in 1627 they agreed to divide the New England fur and wampum trade with the Dutch. By the time Plymouth fulfilled its financial obligations, the settlement had grown to several hundred people on Cape Cod and in the southeastern corner of modern Massachusetts.

The Pilgrims' importance was twofold. First, they helped to inspire the ideal of Americans as sturdy, self-reliant, God-fearing folk who endured hardship to govern themselves freely. Second, they foreshadowed the coercive methods that later generations of white Americans would use to gain mastery over the Indians. In both respects, the Pilgrims represented the vanguard of a massive Puritan migration in the 1630s.

CONCLUSION

The founding of North American colonies was part of Europe's halting modernization, which saw commercial capitalism, nation-states, and postmedieval Christianity emerge during the sixteenth century. In fact, expansion and colonization strengthened the forces of modernity by providing new fields for investment and profit as well as new foundations for national power.

The displacement of Indians and the enslavement of Africans tarnished the early history of European settlement in the New World. Despite devastation by disease, however, Native Americans yielded only slowly to foreign incursions. As for Africans, even the horrors of the Atlantic slave trade did not strip them of their heritage, which became the basis of a distinctive African-American culture.

During the first third of the seventeenth century, the general outlines of European claims in North America emerged, as did the basic elements of the various colonies' economic life. Establishing ranches in New Mexico and fortresses in Florida, Spain advanced as far north as seemed worthwhile. Virginia's victory over the Indians strengthened the English position in the Chesapeake, where tobacco became the principal crop. Here, as in the fragile Plymouth colony, English settlers depended mainly on farming. Dutch, Swedish, and French colonists traded in fish and furs, with New France positioned to penetrate deep into the continent. All these enterprises needed stable relations with Native Americans for success and security.

By the 1630s the tiny European outposts in North America had an air of permanence. Discontented Europeans began to dream of creating new societies across the Atlantic free of the Old World's inherited problems. Most of these dreamers seldom crossed the ocean, and those who did generally lost their illusions—and often their lives—to the rigors of a strange environment. The transplantation of Europeans into North America was hardly a story of inevitable triumph.

CHRONOLOGY

c. 600–1600	Rise of the great West African empires.
1271–1295	Marco Polo travels to East Asia.
c. 1400–1600	Renaissance era—first in Italy, then elsewhere in Europe.
1440	Portuguese slave trade in West Africa begins.
1488	Bartolomeu Días reaches the Cape of Good Hope.
1492	Christopher Columbus lands at San Salvador.
1497	John Cabot reaches Nova Scotia and Newfoundland.
1512–1521	Juan Ponce de León explores Florida.
1517	Protestant Reformation begins in Germany.
1519	Ferdinand Magellan embarks on round-the-world voyage. Hernán Cortés begins conquest of Aztec empire.
1534	Church of England breaks from Roman Catholic Church.
1534–1542	Jacques Cartier explores eastern Canada for France.
1539–1543	Hernando de Soto explores the southeastern United States.
1540–1542	Francisco Vásquez de Coronado explores the southwestern United States.
1558	Elizabeth I becomes queen of England.
1565	St. Augustine founded by Spanish.
1565–1580s	English attempt to subdue Ireland.
1577	Francis Drake circumnavigates the globe.
1578	Humphrey Gilbert secures a patent to establish an English colony in Newfoundland.
1584–1587	Roanoke colony explored and founded.
1588	English defeat the Spanish Armada.
1598	New Mexico colony founded.
1603	James I becomes king of England.
1607	English found colonies at Jamestown and Sagadahoc.
1608	Samuel de Champlain founds Quebec.
1609	Henry Hudson explores the Hudson River for the Dutch Republic.
1610–1614	First Anglo-Powhatan War.
1614	New Netherland colony founded.
1619	Large exports of tobacco from Virginia begin. House of Burgesses, first elected assembly, established in Virginia First Africans arrive in Virginia.
1620	Mayflower Compact signed; Plymouth Plantation founded.
1622–1632	Second Anglo-Powhatan War.
1624	James I revokes Virginia Company's charter.

FOR FURTHER READING

J. F. A. Aiayi and Michael Crowder, eds., *History of West Africa*, vol. I (1972). A comprehensive collection of essays covering the period prior to 1800.

Robert J. Berkhofer, Jr., *The White Man's Burden: Images of the American Indian from Columbus to the Present* (1978). A penetrating analysis of the shaping of European and American attitudes, ideologies, and policies toward Native Americans.

Carl Bridenbaugh, *Vexed and Troubled Englishmen, 1590–1642* (1968). A highly readable account of England at the start of the colonial era.

Alfred W. Crosby, Jr., *Ecological Imperialism: The Biological Expansion of Europe, 900–1900* (1986). An outstanding discussion of the environmental and medical history of European overseas expansion.

D. W. Menig, *The Shaping of America, vol. I: Atlantic America, 1492–1800* (1986). A geographer's engrossing study of Europeans' encounter with North America and the rise of colonial society.

J. H. Parry, *The Age of Reconnaissance* (1963). A comprehensive analysis of European exploration and the rise of European overseas empires from the fifteenth to the seventeenth century.

David B. Quinn, *North America from Earliest Discoveries to First Settlements: the Norse Voyages to 1612* (1977). A thorough, learned account of European exploration, based on a wide range of scholarship.

Kirkpatrick Sale, *The Conquest of Paradise: Christopher Columbus and the Columbian Legacy* (1990). A polemical but informed critique of Columbus and his role in opening the Americas to European exploitation.

Eric Wolf, *Europe and the People without History* (1982). An anthropologist's sweeping view of the causes and consequences of Europe's worldwide expansion.

CHAPTER 3

Expansion and Diversity: The Rise of Colonial America

The seventeenth century witnessed a flood of English migration across the Atlantic. In 1600 no English person had lived along the North American seacoast. By 1700, however, nearly 250,000 people of English birth or ancestry were dwelling in the New World, 200,000 of them in what became the United States. Large numbers of Dutch, French, Spanish, Irish, Scottish, and German settlers joined them. A second wave carried 300,000 West Africans to the New World. Whereas English immigrants to America hoped to realize economic opportunity or religious freedom, Africans and their descendants were owned by others. The majority of Africans taken to the Caribbean and North America went to West Indies sugar plantations; a minority, to the mainland plantation colonies; and a few, to New England. A third demographic upheaval, the depopulation and uprooting of Native Americans, made these two other migrations possible. Epidemic disease did much of the work of destroying the Indians, but warfare played an important role as well. About 1 million Indians had died as a result of contact with Europeans by 1700.

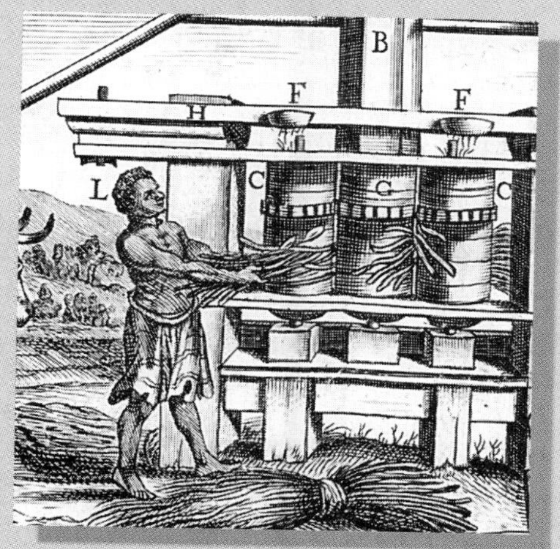

(Right) African slave making sugar (detail)

Invading Englishmen and their African slaves settled not in wilderness but on lands that Indian peoples had long inhabited. The wealth and vitality of the English colonies by 1700 resulted from this unequal encounter of peoples from three continents.

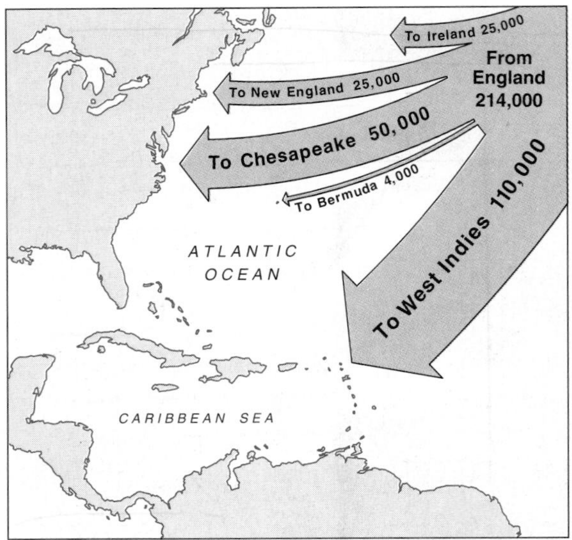

The Great English Migration, 1630–1660
During the great transatlantic English migration, the present-day United States received just one-third of English immigrants. The West Indies attracted twice as many colonists as went to the Chesapeake and over four times as many as settled in New England.

The New England Way

As England's religious and political environment grew worse in the 1620s, many Puritans became interested in colonizing New England. Large-scale Puritan migration would begin in 1630, as the intensely religious Puritans built a community based on religious ideals, the first utopian society in America.

A City upon a Hill

In 1628 several Puritan merchants obtained a charter to settle north of the Separatist colony at Plymouth. Organized as the Massachusetts Bay Company, they moved the seat of their colony's government to New England, paving the way for Massachusetts to be self-governing.

In 1630 the company dispatched a "great fleet," eleven ships and 700 passengers, to New England. As the ships crossed the Atlantic, Governor John Winthrop delivered a lay sermon, "A Model of Christian Charity," in which he explained how and why the new colony would differ from England itself.

Winthrop boldly announced that "we shall be as a city upon a hill, the eyes of all people are upon us." The settlers would build a godly community whose compelling example would shame England. The English government would then truly reform the church, and a revival of piety would create a nation of saints. Denouncing economic jealousy, Winthrop explained that God intended "in all times some must be rich and some poor." The rich would practice charity and mercy, and the poor show their faith in God's will by practicing patience and fortitude. In a godly state, the government would prevent the greedy among the rich from exploiting the poor and the lazy among the poor from burdening their fellow citizens.

Winthrop's sermon expressed both traditional European ideas of social reciprocity (see Chapter 2) and the Puritans' dismay at the economic forces battering—and changing—English society.

The old England of self-sufficient farm families living for generations in tight-knit communities had vanished. Instead, a handful of gentry families owned half of England's village land, while "yeoman" farmers, 20 percent of the remaining population, owned the other half.

For much of England's village population, life was brutal and desperate. Community ties frayed and family life deteriorated as people scattered to find work and as children were hired out as servants or apprentices. Lacking land, England's people competed fiercely for jobs and became individualistic, acquisitive, and materialistic. Winthrop blamed this competitive spirit for fostering apathy toward human suffering. Charity should moderate the drive for profit, he believed, so that goods would be ex-

John Winthrop (1588–1649)
During the passage to America, Winthrop urged his shipmates to build a society about which "men shall say of succeeding plantations: 'The Lord make it like that of New England.'"

changed, wages set, and interest calculated in a way that would allow a decent life for all. The rich would serve God with their money, giving generously in time of need, and the less fortunate would sacrifice their time to serve in church, government, or the military.

Winthrop and his fellow Puritans saw Massachusetts Bay not, like other colonies, as an extension of England and its harshly competitive ways, but as a reaction to it. Moral self-restraint would prevent merchants from squeezing out excessive profits; if necessary, the government could step in. Above all, the Puritans wanted to turn religious idealism into a renewed sense of community. "It is a great thing," wrote an early New Englander, "to be a foundation stone in such a spiritual building."

Development of a Puritan Orthodoxy

The great fleet of Puritans reached Boston Harbor in June 1630; by fall six towns had sprung up. During the unusually severe first winter, one-third of the Puritans died; however, spring brought 1,300 new settlers, and thousands more followed. The disciplined and highly motivated Puritans put Massachusetts Bay Colony on a firm footing in its first year. Though Nonseparatists, they created a system of self-governing congregations (congregationalism) unique to America. Unlike the Separatists of Plymouth and (later) Rhode Island, the Puritans of Massachusetts and Connecticut proclaimed themselves spiritual members of the Church of England, but at the same time they completely ignored the authority of Anglican bishops.

The chief architect of the Nonseparatists' congregationalism was the Reverend John Cotton. His plan placed the control of each congregation in the hands of the male saints, in contrast to the system in England, where a few wealthy members of the gentry controlled each congregation. In New England the male saints chose their minister, elected "elders" to handle finances, and otherwise controlled their church. The New England system thus was more democratic than Anglicanism.

Congregationalism fused elements of separating and nonseparating Puritanism. It followed the Separatist tradition by allowing only saints to take communion and to baptize their children, but adopted the Nonseparatist practice of requiring all adults (except for a few scandalously wicked individuals) to attend services and to pay for the support of the churches. New England thus had a state-sponsored, "established" church; the meetinghouse, used for both religious services and town business, symbolized the relationship of church to government.

This "New England Way" set high standards for identifying saints. Massachusetts Puritans insisted that candidates for church membership provide a soul-baring "relation," or account of their conversion, before the congregation. This public revelation of intimate spiritual matters could be embarrassing and painful for candidate and congregation, and it often intimidated those seeking church membership. The conversion relation ultimately became the New England Way's most vulnerable point and a major cause of its demise.

Literacy was essential to conversion. Children were drilled in catechism, young people read the Bible to feel the quickening of God's grace, and saints recorded their lapses and spiritual insights in diaries. In 1647 the Massachusetts Bay Colony passed the Old Deluder Act because "one chief project of that old deluder, Satan [is] to keep men from knowledge of the Scriptures." Every town of fifty or more households was to appoint one teacher from whom all children could receive instruction, and every town of one hundred households or more was to maintain a grammar school with a teacher capable of preparing students for university-level learning. This law, echoed by other Puritan colonies, was New England's first step toward public education, although attendance remained optional and boys were more likely to be taught reading and writing than girls. In any case, the family remained the chief guardian of education.

Clergymen bore responsibility for leading people to repentance and for stimulating piety. The minister was to stir his congregation's faith with direct, logical, and moving sermons understandable to average listeners. An educated clergy was essential, and so in 1636 Massachusetts founded Harvard College to produce learned ministers. In its first thirty-five years, the college turned out 201 graduates, 111 of them ministers. These alumni made New England the only American colony with a college-educated elite during the seventeenth century and ensured that the New England Way would not falter for lack of properly trained clergymen.

Dissenting Puritans

Some Puritans dissented from their leaders' vision of social order and religious conformity. The first to challenge the New England Way was Roger Williams, who arrived in America in 1631. Radiating the joy of serving God, he quickly became one of the most respected and popular figures in Massachusetts Bay. But when he questioned the legal basis of congregationalism, insisting that church and state be separate, the Massachusetts Bay government silenced him.

Although agreeing that the church must be free of state control, Puritans believed that a holy commonwealth required cooperation between church and state. Williams argued that civil government had to remain absolutely uninvolved with religious matters. He derived his ideas from the Anabaptist tradition (see Chapter 2), which held that saints had to limit their association with sinners to prevent contamination. Williams opposed compulsory church service and interference with private religious beliefs because he feared that the state would eventually corrupt the church and its saints.

Believing that the purpose of the colony was to protect true religion and to prevent heresy, political authorities declared Williams's opinions subversive and banished him in 1635. Williams went south to the edge of Narragansett Bay to a place that he later named Providence, which he purchased from the Indians. A steady stream of dissenters drifted to the group of settlements near Providence, forming Rhode Island in 1647. The only New England colony to practice religious toleration, Rhode Island grew to 800 settlers by 1650.

Anne Hutchinson, "a woman of haughty and fierce carriage, of a nimble wit and active spirit" according to her enemy John Winthrop, presented a second challenge to the New England Way. Ironically, Hutchinson's ideas derived from the much-respected minister John Cotton. Cotton insisted that true congregationalism required the saints to be free of religious or political control by anyone who had not undergone a conversion experience. His refusal to give authority or power over religion to anyone not "reborn" applied even to those who led blameless lives—at least until they had been reborn spiritually.

Hutchinson extended Cotton's ideas to a broad attack on clerical authority. She began to imply that her own minister was not a saint and then asserted that saints in the congregation could ignore his views if they believed that he lacked saving grace. Ultimately, she declared that only two ministers in the colony, John Cotton and her brother-in-law John Wheelright, had been reborn and thus were fit to exercise authority over the saints.

Hutchinson's ideas directly attacked the clergy's authority to interpret and teach Scripture; critics charged that her beliefs would delude individuals into imagining that they were accountable only to themselves. Her followers were labeled Antinomians, meaning those opposed to the rule of law. Anne Hutchinson bore the additional liability of being a woman challenging traditional male roles in church and state. Her gender made her seem an especially dangerous foe.

Massachusetts Bay split into pro- and anti-Hutchinson forces. Her opponents prevailed, bringing Hutchinson to trial for sedition before the Massachusetts Bay legislature (the General Court) and then for heresy before a panel of ministers. Hutchinson's knowledge of Scripture was so superior to that of her inquisitors that she might well have been acquitted had she not claimed to communicate directly with the Holy Spirit. Because Puritans believed that God had ceased to make known matters of faith by personal revelation since New Testament times, Hutchinson was condemned by her own words. Banished from the colony along with other Antinomians, Hutchinson settled in Rhode Island and then moved to New Netherland, where she was killed in that colony's war with Indians in 1643. Her banishment effectively ended the last challenge capable of splitting congregationalism and ensured the survival of the New England Way for two more generations.

New restrictions on women's independence and on equality within Puritan congregations followed antinomianism's defeat. Increasingly, women were prohibited from assuming the kind of public religious role claimed by Hutchinson and were even required to relate their conversion experiences in private to their ministers rather than publicly before their congregations.

Economics as well as ideas posed serious threats to Winthrop's "city upon a hill." While most Puritans shared Winthrop's view of community, self-discipline, and mutual obligation, a large minority had come to America for prosperity and social mobility. The most visibly ambitious colonists were merchants, whose activities fueled New England's economy but whose way of life challenged its ideals.

Merchants fit uneasily into a religious society that equated financial shrewdness with greed. They clashed repeatedly with government leaders, who were trying to regulate prices so that consumers would not suffer from the chronic shortage of manufactured goods that afflicted New England. In 1635 the General Court forbade the sale of any item at above 5 percent of its cost. Led by Robert Keayne, merchants protested that they needed to sell some goods at higher rates to offset losses incurred by shipwreck and inflation. In 1639 authorities heavily fined Keayne for selling nails at 25 percent above cost and forced him to apologize in front of his congregation.

Though he was a pious Puritan whose annual profits averaged just 5 percent, Keayne symbolized the danger that a headlong rush for prosperity would lead New Englanders to forget that they were their brothers' keepers. Controversies such as that involving Keayne were part of a struggle for the New England soul. At stake was the Puritans' ability to insulate their city upon a hill from a market economy that threatened to strangle the spirit of community within a harsh world of frantic competition.

Puritan Government and Community Life

To preserve the New England Way, the Puritans created political and religious institutions with far more popular participation than those in England. Its headquarters established in America, the Massachusetts Bay Company allowed all male saints to elect the governor and his council. By 1634 each town had gained the right to send two delegates to the General Court; ten years later court and council separated to create a bicameral (two-chamber) legislature. Although in England stringent property requirements allowed less than 30 percent of adult males to vote, 55 percent of Massachusetts's adult males could vote.

In England the basic unit of local government was the county court. Its magistrates, appointed by the king, not only decided legal cases but also performed administrative duties. By contrast, in New England the county court was primarily a court of law; the town meeting oversaw matters of local administration.

Towns were formed when a legislature granted land to several dozen heads of families. These individuals had almost unlimited freedom to lay out the settlement, design its church, distribute land among themselves, and make local laws. Generally, all adult male taxpayers, even nonsaints, participated in town meetings. In turn, the meetings ran the town and granted land rights to new settlers.

Most New England towns were uniform farm communities resembling traditional English villages; seaports, with their transient populations, were the chief exception. Each family generally received a one-acre house lot (just enough room for a vegetable garden) within a half mile of the meetinghouse. Each household also received strips of land or small fields farther away for crops and livestock. Individuals often owned several scattered parcels of land and had the right to graze a few extra animals on the town "commons."

Most towns attempted to maintain communities of tightly clustered settlers by distributing only as much land as was necessary for each family to support itself. The remaining land would be distributed to future generations as needed. Forcing residents to live close together was an attempt to foster social reciprocity. New England's generally compact system of settlement made people interact with each other and established an atmosphere of mutual watchfulness that promoted godly order. Town meetings open to all property-owning males and Sunday church services attended by everyone reinforced this strong sense of community.

Puritan Families

"The little commonwealth"—the nuclear family—was the foundation of Puritan society. "*Well-ordered families*," declared minister Cotton Mather in 1699, "naturally produce a *Good Order* in other *Societies*." A well-ordered family was one in which wife, children, and servants dutifully obeyed the husband and in which the "true wife" thought of herself "in subjection to her husband's authority."

New Englanders defined matrimony as a contract, not a sacrament. Puritans were thus married by justices of the peace rather than ministers. As a civil institution, marriage could be dissolved by the courts in cases of desertion, bigamy, adultery, or physical cruelty. However, New England courts saw divorce as a remedy only for extremely wronged spouses, such as the Plymouth woman who discovered that her husband also had wives in Boston, Barbados, and England. Massachusetts courts granted just twenty-seven divorces from 1639 to 1692.

Because Puritans believed that healthy families were crucial to the community's welfare, they intervened whenever they discovered serious problems in a household. Courts disciplined unruly youngsters, disobedient servants, disrespectful wives, and irresponsible husbands. Churches also censured, and even expelled, spouses who did not maintain domestic tranquillity.

New England wives enjoyed significant legal protections against spousal violence and nonsupport and had more freedom than their English counterparts to escape a failed marriage. But they suffered the legal disabilities borne by all women under English law. A wife had no property rights independent of her husband except by premarital agreement. Only if there were no other heirs or if a will so specified would a widow receive control of household property, although law entitled her to lifetime use of one-third of the estate.

New England's families enjoyed greater stability and lived longer lives than their English counterparts. The region's cold climate limited the impact of disease, especially in winter, when limited travel between towns slowed the spread of infection. Easy access to land contributed to a healthy diet, which strengthened resistance to disease and lowered death rates associated with childbirth. Life expectancy for Puritan men reached sixty-five, and women lived nearly that long. These life spans were ten years or more longer than those of England. More than 80 percent of all infants survived long enough to marry. Because so many of the 20,000 immigrants who arrived in New England between 1630 and 1642 came as members of families, an even sex ratio and a rapid natural increase of population followed.

Families were economically interdependent. Male heads of family managed the household's crops and livestock, conducted its business transactions, and represented it at town meetings. Wives bore and nurtured children; performed or oversaw work in the house, garden, and barn; and participated in community networks that assisted at childbirths and aided the poor and vulnerable. Sons depended on parents to provide them with acreage for a farm, and parents encouraged sons to stay at home and work in return for a bequest of land later on. Young males often tended their fathers' fields until their late twenties before receiving their own land. The average family, raising four sons to adulthood, could count on thirty to forty years of work if their sons delayed marriage until age twenty-six. Families with many sons and daughters enjoyed a labor surplus and sometimes hired out their children to work for others. Although inefficient, this system of family labor was all that New Englanders could afford.

There were other benefits. Prolonged dependence for sons ensured that the family line and property would continue in the hands of capable, experienced men. Although daughters performed vital labor, they would marry into another family. Young women with many childbearing years ahead of them were the most valuable potential wives, and first-generation women tended to marry by the age of twenty-one.

Saddled with the triple burdens of a short growing season, rocky soil salted with gravel, and an inefficient system of land distribution that forced farmers to cultivate widely scattered strips, the colonists nevertheless managed to feed their families and to keep ahead of their debts. Few grew wealthy from farming. For wealth, New Englanders turned lumbering, shipbuilding, fishing, and rum distilling into major industries that employed perhaps one-fifth of all adults full-time. As its economy diversified, New England prospered. Increasingly concerned more with profit than prophecy, the Puritans discovered, to their dismay, that fewer of their children were emerging as saints.

The Demise of the Puritan Errand

As New England struggled for stability and conformity, old England fell into chaos and civil war. Alienated by years of religious harassment, Puritans gained control of the revolt, beheaded Charles I in 1649, and governed without a king for more than a decade. In 1660 a provisional English government recalled the Stuarts and restored Charles II to the throne.

The Stuart Restoration doomed Puritanism in England as High Church Anglicans took their revenge; "God has spit in our face," lamented one Puritan. The Restoration also left American Puritans without a mission. Having conquered a wilderness and built their city upon a hill, they found that the eyes of the world were no longer fixed on them.

An internal crisis also gripped New England. First-generation Puritans had believed that they held a covenant, a holy contract, with God to establish a scripturally ordained church and to charge their descendants with its preservation. However, understandably reluctant to submit to a public review of their spirituality, relatively few second-generation Puritans were willing to join the elect by making the required conversion relation before the congregation. Through its passivity, the second generation expressed a preference for a more inclusive religious community, organized on traditional English practices. This generation also rejected the ritual of public conversion relation as an unnecessary source of division and bitterness that undermined Christian fellowship.

Because Puritan churches baptized only babies born to saints, first-generation Puritans faced the prospect that their own grandchildren would remain unbaptized unless the standards for church membership were lowered. They solved their dilemma in 1662 through a compromise known as the Half-Way Covenant, which permitted the children of all baptized members, including nonsaints, to be baptized. Church membership would pass down from generation to generation, but nonsaints would be "halfway" members, unable to take communion or to vote in church affairs. When forced to choose between a church system founded on a pure membership of the elect and one that embraced the entire community, New Englanders opted to sacrifice purity for community.

The Half-Way Covenant marked the end of the New England Way. The elect had been unable to raise a new generation of saints whose religious fervor equaled their own. Most adults chose to remain in "halfway" status for life, and the saints became a shrinking minority in the third and fourth generations. By the 1700s there were more female than male saints in most congregations. But because women could not vote in church affairs, religious authority stayed in male hands. Nevertheless, ministers publicly recognized women's role in upholding piety and the church itself.

Expansion and Native Americans

In contrast to the settlement of Virginia, the Puritan colonization of New England initially met little resistance from Native Americans, whose numbers had been drastically reduced by disease. Between 1616 and 1618 an epidemic killed 90 percent of New England's coastal Indians, and a second epidemic in 1643–1644 inflicted comparable casualties on Indians throughout the Northeast. The Massachusett Indians dwindled from 20,000 in 1600 to a few dozen in 1635 and sold most of their land. By 1675, New England's Native American population had shrunk from 125,000 in 1600 to about 10,000. During the 1640s Massachusetts Bay passed laws prohibiting Indians from practicing their own religion and encouraging missionaries to convert them to Christianity. Beginning in 1651 the Indians surrendered much of their independence and moved into "praying towns" such as Natick, a reservation established by the colony.

The expansion of English settlement farther inland, however, aroused Indian resistance. As settlers moved into the Connecticut River valley, beginning in 1633, friction developed with the Pequots, who controlled the trade in furs and wampum with New Netherland. After tensions escalated into violence, the English waged a ruthless campaign against the Pequots, using tactics similar to those devised to break Irish resistance (see Chapter 2). In a predawn attack, troops led by Captain John Mason surrounded and set fire to a Pequot village at Mystic, Connecticut, and then cut down all who tried to escape. Several hundred Pequots, mostly women and children, were killed. The Puritans found the grisly massacre a cause for celebration. Wrote Plymouth's governor William Bradford, "It was a fearful sight to see them [the Pequots] thus frying in the fire and the streams of blood quenching the same . . . but the victory seemed a sweet sacrifice, and they [the English] gave the praise to God, who had wrought so wonderfully for them." By late 1637 Pequot resistance was crushed, and English settlement of the new colonies of Connecticut and New Haven could proceed unimpeded.

Indians felt the English presence in many ways. The fur trade, initially beneficial to Native Americans of the interior, became a burden. Once Indians began hunting for trade instead of for their subsistence needs alone, they quickly depleted the supply of beavers and other fur-bearing animals. Because English traders advanced trade goods on credit before the hunting season began, many Indians fell into debt. Traders increasingly took Indian land as collateral and sold it to settlers.

English townspeople, eager to expand their agricultural output and provide for their sons, voted themselves much larger amounts of land after 1660.

For example, Dedham, Massachusetts, had distributed only 3,000 acres from 1636 to 1656; by 1668 it had allocated another 15,000 acres. Many farmers built their homes on their outlying tracts, crowding closer to the Indians' settlements and their hunting, fishing, and gathering areas.

Expansion put pressure on the natives and the land alike. By clearing trees for fields and for use as fuel and building material, the colonists were altering the entire ecosystem by the mid-1600s. Deer no longer grazed freely, and the wild plants on which the Indians depended for food and medicine could not grow. Deforestation not only dried the soil but also brought frequent flooding. Encroaching white settlers allowed their livestock to run wild, according to English custom. Pigs damaged Indian cornfields and shellfish-gathering sites. Cattle and horses devoured native grasses, which the settlers replaced with English varieties.

Powerless to reverse the alarming decline of population, land, and food supplies, many Indians became demoralized. Some turned to alcohol, which became increasingly available during the 1660s despite colonial attempts to suppress its sale to Native Americans. Interpreting the crisis as one of belief, other Indians converted to Christianity. By 1675 Puritan missionaries had established about thirty "praying towns." Supervised by missionaries, each praying town had its own Native American magistrate, and many congregations had Indian preachers. Although missionaries struggled to convert the Indians to "civilization"—English culture and ways of life—most Indians integrated the new faith with their native cultural identities, reinforcing the hostility of settlers who believed that all Indians were irrevocably "savage" and heathen.

Anglo-Indian conflict became acute in the 1670s because of pressure on the Indians to sell their land and to accept missionaries and the legal authority of white courts. Tension was especially high in the Plymouth colony, where Puritans had engulfed the Wampanoag tribe and forced a series of humiliating concessions from their leader Metacom, "King Philip," the son of the Pilgrims' onetime ally Massasoit.

In 1675 Plymouth hanged three Wampanoags for killing a Christian Indian; several other Wampanoags were shot while burglarizing a farmhouse. In response to the escalation of violence, Metacom organized two-thirds of the Native Americans, including many praying Indians, into a military alliance. "But little remains of my ancestors' domain. I am resolved not to see the day when I have no country," Metacom declared as he and his men touched off the conflict known as King Philip's War.

The war raged across New England. Metacom's forces, as well armed as the Puritans, devastated the countryside, wiping out twelve of New England's ninety towns and killing 600 colonists. The following year, 1676, saw the tide turn as Puritan militia destroyed their enemies' food supplies and sold hundreds of captives into slavery, including Metacom's wife and child. Perhaps 3,000 Indians died in battle or starved, including Metacom himself.

King Philip's War reduced southern New England's Indian population by almost 40 percent and eliminated open Indian resistance to white expansion. It also deepened whites' hostility toward all Native Americans, even the Christian Indians who had fought against King Philip. In 1677 ten praying towns were disbanded and all Indians were restricted to the remaining four. Missionary work ceased. "There is a cloud, a dark cloud upon the work of the Gospel among the poor Indians," mourned Puritan missionary John Eliot. In the face of poverty and discrimination, the remaining Indians struggled to maintain their communities and cultural identity. To compensate for the loss of traditional sources of sustenance, many became seamen or indentured servants, served in English wars against French Canada, or made and sold baskets and other wares.

Economics, Gender, and Satan in Salem

In the three decades after adoption of the Half-Way Covenant, the Puritan clergy unleashed a stream of jeremiads (angry lamentations, named after the Old Testament prophet Jeremiah) at their congregations, berating them for failing to preserve the idealism of the first generation. "New-England is originally a plantation of Religion, not a plantation of trade," one minister proclaimed, but in fact New Englanders were becoming more worldly, more individualistic, and far less patient with restrictions on their economic behavior. Indeed, by 1690 the Puritans, having built a society from the ground up, no longer felt an overriding need to place collective, community interests first. As New Englanders pursued economic gain more openly and as populations dispersed away from town centers, the fabric of community frayed. Friction easily arose between the townspeople still dwelling near the meetinghouse (who usually dominated politics) and the "outlivers," those living on outlying tracts of land, who were less influential because of their distance from town.

The rough equality of early New England, when most people had been small landowners with few luxuries, also began to vanish. By the late seventeenth century, the distribution of wealth was growing more uneven, especially in large, prosperous port cities. New England's rising involvement in international trade, moreover, encouraged competitiveness and impersonality. John Winthrop's vision of a religious community sustained by reciprocity and charity faded before the reality of a world increasingly materialistic and acquisitive—like the one that the early Puritans had fled.

Nowhere in New England did these trends have more disturbing effects than in Salem, Massachusetts, made up of the port of Salem Town and the farm community of Salem Village. Trade and rapid growth had made Salem Town the region's second-largest port. By 1690 prosperous merchants controlled much of the wealth and political power of Salem as a whole, and the community was vulnerable to conflict between its prosperous merchants and its struggling farmers.

Salem Village (now Danvers) lay six miles west of Salem Town's meetinghouse, and its citizens resented Salem Town's political dominance. Salem Village was divided between the supporters of two families, the Porters and the Putnams. Well connected with the merchant elite, the Porters enjoyed political prestige in Salem Town and lived in the village's eastern section, whose residents farmed richer soils and benefited more from Salem Town's prosperity. In contrast, most Putnams lived in Salem Village's less fertile western half, shared little in Salem Town's commercial expansion, and had lost their political influence. Rivalry between Porters and Putnams mirrored the tensions between Salem's urban and rural dwellers.

In late 1691 several Salem Village girls encouraged an African slave woman, Tituba, to tell fortunes and talk about sorcery. When the girls began behaving strangely, villagers assumed that they were victims of witchcraft. Pressed to identify their tormenters, they named two local white women and Tituba.

So far the incident was not unusual. Belief in witchcraft existed at all levels of American and European society. But by April 1692 the girls had denounced two prosperous farm wives long considered saints in the local church and had identified the village's former minister as a wizard (male witch). Fear of witchcraft soon overrode considerable doubts about the girls' credibility and led local judges to sweep aside normal procedural safeguards. Specifically, the judges ignored legal bans on "spectral evidence," testimony that a spirit resembling the accused had been seen tormenting a victim. Thereafter charges multiplied until the jails overflowed with accused witches.

The pattern of hysteria and accusations reflected Salem Village's internal divisions. Most charges came from the western side of the village—one-third from the Putnams alone—and were lodged against people who lived outside the western half and who were connected by economics or marriage to the Porters. Two-thirds of all accusers were girls aged eleven to twenty, and more than one-half had lost one or more parents in conflicts between Indians and settlers in Maine. They and other survivors had fled to Massachusetts, where most worked as servants in other families' households. They most frequently named as witches middle-aged wives and widows—women who had escaped the poverty and uncertainty that they themselves faced. At the same time, the "possessed" accusers

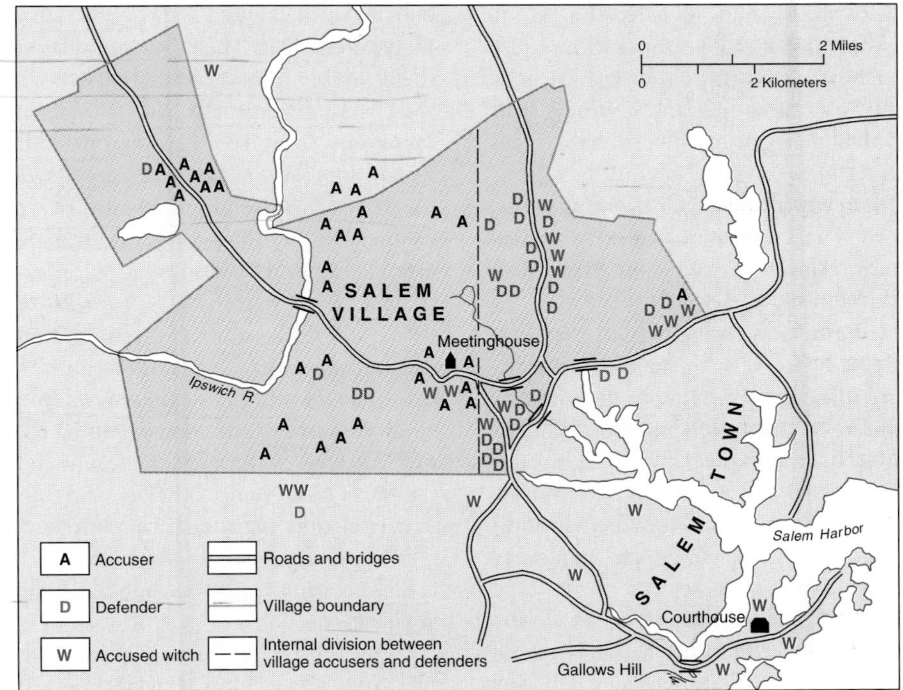

The Geography of Witchcraft: Salem Village, 1692

Geographic patterns of witchcraft testimony mirrored tensions within Salem Village. Accused witches and their defenders lived mostly in the village's eastern division or in Salem Town, whereas their accusers overwhelmingly resided in the village's western sector.

SOURCE: Adapted from *Salem Possessed: The Social Origins of Witchcraft* by Paul Boyer and Stephen Nissenbaum. Copyright © 1974 by the President and Fellows of Harvard College. Reprinted by permission of Harvard University Press.

gained momentary power and prominence by voicing the anxieties and hostilities of many others in their community and by virtually dictating the course of events in and around Salem for months.

Those found guilty of witchcraft tried to stave off death by implicating others. As the pandemonium spread, fear dissolved ties of friendship and family. A minister was condemned by his granddaughter, a mother by her seven-year-old daughter, and a husband and father by his wife and daughter. Fifty saved themselves by confessing, but twenty were condemned and executed.

By late 1692 doubts about the charges were surfacing. Clergymen objected to the emphasis on spectral evidence, crucial to most convictions. By accepting such evidence in court, minister Increase Mather warned, the Puritans had fallen victim to a deadly game of "blind man's buffet" set up by Satan and were "hotly and madly mauling one another in the dark." In October Governor William Phips forbade any further imprisonments for witchcraft. One hundred were still in jail, and 200 more stood accused. In early 1693 Phips ended the terror by pardoning all those who were convicted or suspected of practicing witchcraft.

The witchcraft hysteria reflected profound anxieties over social change. The underlying causes of this tension became clear as Salem Village's communally oriented farmers directed their wrath toward Salem Town's competitive and individualistic merchants. This clash of values revealed the extent to which John Winthrop's city upon a hill had lost its relevance to new generations forced into economic enterprise by New England's stingy soil, harsh climate, and meager natural resources. The tensions pervading New England society had been heightened by the crown's revoking the Massachusetts charter in 1684 and subsuming several colonies in the Dominion of New England in 1686 (see Chapter 4).

By 1700 New Englanders had begun a transition from Puritans to "Yankees." True to their Puritan roots, they retained strong religious convictions and an extraordinary capacity for perseverance. Increasingly grafted to these roots were ingenuity, sharpness, and an eye for opportunity, traits that would enable New Englanders to build a thriving international commerce and later an industrial revolution.

As New England moved away from its roots, the Chesapeake region to the south also underwent radical transformation. But the differences between the two areas of English settlement remained as great as ever.

Chesapeake Society

Virtually ignored by King James I (who took over the colony in 1624 from the bankrupt Virginia Company) and his successors, Virginia developed on its own. The English monarch's indifference worked to the colonial elite's advantage, leaving them room to experiment with local administration and to force reluctant royal governors to cooperate with their legislature. Tobacco and the environment shaped the colonists' destiny not only in Virginia but also in Maryland and in what became North Carolina.

State and Church in Virginia

James I planned to rule Virginia through appointed officials, but Virginians petitioned repeatedly for the restoration of their elected assembly, the first in the New World. James I's successor, Charles I, grudgingly relented in 1628, but only in order to induce the assembly to tax tobacco exports so as to transfer the cost of government from the crown to Virginia's taxpayers. After 1630, seeking more taxes, Virginia's royal governors called regular assemblies. During the 1650s the assembly split into two chambers, the elected House of Burgesses and the appointed Governor's Council. Later royal colonies also adopted this bicameral pattern.

Local government officials were appointed, rather than elected, during Virginia's first quarter-century. In 1634 Virginia adopted England's county-court system. Appointed by the royal governor, justices of the peace acted as judges, set local tax rates, paid county officials, and oversaw the construction and maintenance of roads, bridges, and public buildings. Thus south of New England, unelected county courts became the basic unit of local government.

In contrast to Puritan New England, Virginia had the Church of England as its established church. Anglican vestries governed each parish; elected vestrymen handled church finances, determined poor relief, and investigated complaints against the minister. Taxpayers were legally obliged to pay fixed rates to the Anglican church. Because of the large distances between settlements and churches as well as a chronic shortage of clergymen, few Virginians regularly attended services. In 1662 Virginia had just ten ministers to serve its forty-five parishes. Compared to New Englanders, Chesapeake dwellers felt religion's influence lightly.

Virginia's First Families

Three generations passed before Virginia evolved a social elite willing and able to provide disinterested public service. The gentry sent out by the Virginia Company were ill suited for a frontier society; by 1630 most had either died or returned to England. Then from 1630 to 1660 a generation of leaders emerged who had acquired great wealth through tobacco or through fraud. They dominated the Royal Council and used their power to increase their

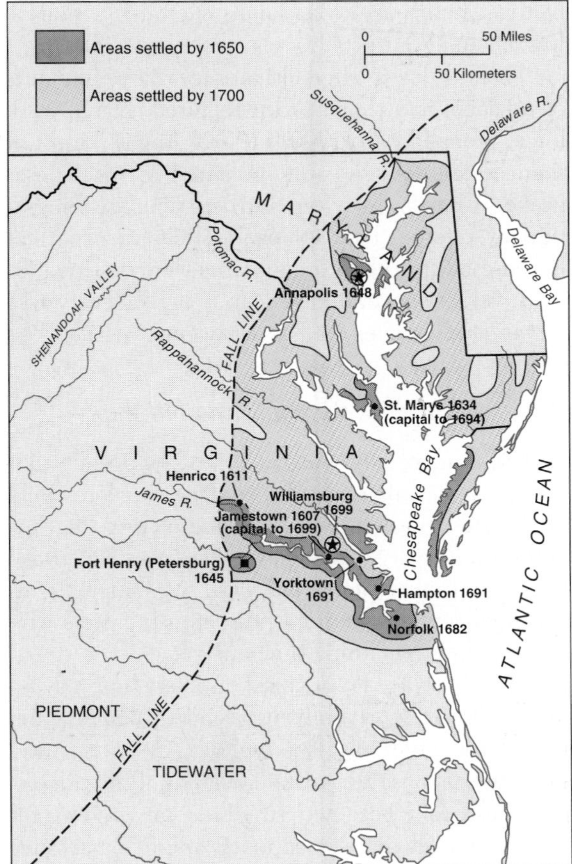

Colonizing the Chesapeake, 1607–1660
The Chesapeake frontier expanded slowly until after Indian defeat in the Second Powhatan War of 1644–1646. By 1700, when the European and African population had reached 110,000, newcomers had spread virtually throughout the tidewater.

wealth, but few had children to assume their place, and their influence died with them.

From 1660 to 1675 a third cycle of immigrants reached for power in Virginia. Generally the members of English merchant families who traded with Virginia, they brought wealth, education, and ambition with them. Becoming planters, they soon controlled the Royal Council; many profited from "public" service by obtaining huge land grants. They bequeathed both wealth and power to future generations, later known as the First Families of Virginia. Among them, Burwell, Byrd, Carter, Harrison, Lee, Ludwell, Randolph, and Taylor were prominent names. The First Families would dominate Virginia politics for two centuries, and four of the first five American presidents would be descended from them.

Maryland

Beginning in the 1630s, grants by the crown to reward English politicians replaced joint-stock companies as the primary mechanism of colonization. The first such grant, or proprietorship, went in 1632 to Lord Baltimore (Cecilius Calvert); he named the large tract east of Chesapeake Bay Maryland in honor of England's Queen Henrietta Maria. Lord Baltimore enjoyed broad power, lessened only by the stipulations that an elected assembly had to approve all laws and that the crown would control both war and trade.

With Charles I's consent, Baltimore intended to make Maryland a refuge for England's Catholics, who could neither worship in public nor hold political office and who had to pay tithes to the Anglican church. To make Maryland a haven, Baltimore tried to install the old English manor system. In theory, a manor lord would employ a Catholic priest as chaplain and allow others to hear Mass and to receive the sacraments on the manor. In practice, this arrangement never worked, for relatively few Catholics settled in Maryland, which was overwhelmingly Protestant from the beginning. Cheap land lured settlers who did not need to become tenants on the manors, and Baltimore's scheme fell apart. By 1675 all sixty of Maryland's nonproprietary manors had become plantations.

Religious tension gradually developed in Maryland society. The Protestant majority dominated the elected lower house of government, but many Catholics had become large landowners, held high public office, and dominated the appointive upper house. Until 1642 Catholics and Protestants shared the chapel at St. Mary's, the capital, but they began to argue over its use. As antagonisms intensified, Baltimore drafted, and the assembly passed, the Act for Religious Toleration (1649), America's first law affirming liberty of worship.

Unfortunately, the toleration act did not secure religious peace. In 1654 the Protestant majority barred Catholics from voting; ousted Governor William Stone, a Protestant; and repealed the toleration act. Stone raised an army, both Protestant and Catholic, to regain the government but met defeat at the Battle of the Severn River in 1655. The victors imprisoned Stone and hanged three Catholic leaders. Maryland remained in Protestant hands until 1658. Although Lord Baltimore was restored to control that year (ironically, at the command of English Puritans), Protestant resistance to Catholic political influence continued to cause problems in Maryland.

Tobacco Shapes a Way of Life

Chesapeake settlers were scattered across the landscape. A typical community included only 24 families in a twenty-five-square-mile area, a mere six people per square mile. (In contrast, New England often had 500 people squeezed onto one square mile.) Most Chesapeake inhabitants lived in a world of few friendships and considerable isolation; typical was Robert Boone, a Maryland farmer, who died at age seventy-nine "on the same Plantation where he was born in 1680, from which he never went 30 miles in his Life."

Isolated Chesapeake settlers shared a life governed by one overriding factor: the price of tobacco. After an initial boom, tobacco prices plunged 97 percent in 1629 before stabilizing at 10 percent of their original high. Tobacco was still profitable as long as it was grown on fertile soil near navigable water. As a result, 80 percent of Chesapeake homes were located along a riverbank, both for the fertile soil and for the cheap transportation thus afforded; ships literally could come to the plantation's front door. Wealthy planters shipped their tobacco and small farmers' crops from their own wharves and distributed imported goods. Neither towns nor a merchant class was needed, and urbanization was slow in the Chesapeake. Maryland's capital, St. Mary's, was a hamlet of thirty houses as late as 1678.

Wealth lay in the cultivation of large amounts of tobacco, and that in turn required a large work force. From 1630 to 1700, 110,000 English, most of them indentured servants, migrated to the Chesapeake. A headright system further stimulated migration by offering land for each person transported. Because most of these immigrants were destined for field work, men dominated; four out of every five servants were males aged about twenty.

Mortality, Gender, and Kinship

So few women immigrated to the Chesapeake that before 1650, only one-third of male servants could find brides and then only after completing their indentures. Female scarcity gave women an advantage in negotiating favorable marriages. Many female indentured servants married prosperous planters who paid off their remaining time of service.

Death ravaged Chesapeake society and left domestic life exceptionally fragile. In 1650 malaria joined the killer diseases typhoid, dysentery, and salt poisoning as the marshy lowlands of the tidewater Chesapeake became fertile breeding grounds for the mosquitoes that spread malaria. Life expectancy in the 1600s was twenty years lower in the Chesapeake than in New England. Servants died at appalling rates; 40 percent were dead within a decade of arrival and 70 percent before reaching age fifty.

Chesapeake widows often enjoyed substantial property rights. The region's men wrote wills giving their wives perpetual and complete control of their estates so that their own children could inherit them. A widow in such circumstances had a degree of economic independence but faced enormous pressure to remarry, particularly a man who could produce income by farming her fields.

The lopsided sex ratio and high death rates contributed to slow population growth in the Chesapeake. Although perhaps 110,000 English immigrated to the Chesapeake between 1630 and 1700, the white population was just 69,000 in 1700. Change come gradually as children acquired childhood immunities, life spans lengthened, and the sex

Virginia Indian, c. 1645
At the time that this contemporary sketch was made, Virginia's white settlers and Indians were embroiled in the Third Anglo-Powhatan War.

ratio evened out. By 1720 most Chesapeake residents were native born.

Tobacco's Troubles

Chesapeake society became increasingly unequal. A few planters used the headright system to build up large landholdings and to profit from their servants' labor. Wretchedly exploited, and poorly fed, clothed, and housed, servants faced a bleak future even when their indentures ended. Although some were able to claim fifty acres of land in Maryland, the majority who went to Virginia had no such prospects. Indeed, in Virginia after 1650 most riverfront land was held by speculators, and upward mobility became virtually impossible.

In 1660 Chesapeake tobacco prices plunged by 50 percent, setting off a depression that lasted fifty years. Despite losses, large planters earned some income from rents, interest on loans, and shopkeeping, while small landowners scrambled to sell corn and cattle in the West Indies. A typical family in this depression era lived in a small wooden shack, slept on rags, and ate mush or stew cooked in the single pot. Having fled poverty in England or the West Indies, people often found utter destitution in the Chesapeake. Ex-servants in particular became a frustrated and embittered underclass that seemed destined to remain landless and poor.

Bacon's Rebellion

By the 1670s these bleak conditions had locked most Virginia landowners into a losing battle against poverty and had left the colony's freedmen in despair. Both groups were capable of striking out in blind rage if an opportunity to stave off economic disaster presented itself. In 1676 this human powder keg exploded in violence.

Virginians had been free of serious conflict with the Indians since the end of the Third Anglo-Powhatan War in 1646. By 1653 tribes encircled by English settlements had begun agreeing to remain within boundaries set by the government—in effect, on reservations. White settlement continued to expand northward to the Potomac River, and by 1675 whites outnumbered Indians by a ten-to-one ratio.

In June 1675 a dispute between some Doeg Indians and a Virginia farmer escalated. A force of Virginia and Maryland militia pursuing the Doegs murdered fourteen friendly Susquehannocks and later executed five of their chiefs. The violence was now unstoppable. While Governor William Berkeley proposed defending the frontier by a costly system of forts, small farmers preferred the cheaper solution: a war of extermination against the Indians. Some 300 settlers elected Nathaniel Bacon, a distant relative of Berkeley and member of the Royal Council, to lead them against nearby Indians in April 1676. The expedition found only peaceful Indians but slaughtered them anyhow.

Returning to Jamestown, Virginia's capital, in June 1676, Bacon asked for authority to wage war "against all Indians in general." The legislature voted for a program designed to appeal to both hard-pressed taxpayers and landless ex-servants. All Indians who had left their villages without permission (even if fleeing Bacon) were declared enemies, and their lands were forfeited. Bacon's troops could seize any "enemy" property and enslave Indian prisoners.

But Governor Berkeley soon had second thoughts about the slaughter and recalled Bacon and his 1,300 men. Forbidden to attack Indians, Bacon's forces turned against the government and burned Jamestown. The rebels offered freedom to any servants or slaves owned by Berkeley's allies who would join them and then looted enemy plantations. What had begun as Indian warfare was now a social rebellion. Before the uprising could proceed further, however, Bacon died of dysentery in late 1676, and his followers dispersed.

Bacon's Rebellion revealed a society under deep internal stress. Begun as an effort to displace escalating tensions among whites onto the Indians, it became an excuse to plunder other whites. Economic opportunism as well as racism had spurred the small farmers and landless ex-servants to rise up. This rebellion was an outburst of pent-up frustrations by marginal taxpayers and ex-servants driven to desperation by the tobacco depression.

Slavery

The tensions and social instability underlying Bacon's Rebellion grew in large part from the plight of indentured servants trying to become free agents in an economy that offered them little. Even before the rebellion, however, potential for class conflict was diminishing as planters gradually substituted black slaves for white servants.

Racial slavery developed in three stages in the Chesapeake. Africans first appeared in 1619, but their early status was generally indistinguishable from the standing of white servants. By 1640 blacks and some Indians were being treated as slaves, and their children inherited their status. Thus their situation had become inferior to that of indentured white servants. In the final phase, after 1660, laws defined slavery as a lifelong, inheritable status based on color. By 1705 strict legal codes defined the place of slaves in society and set standards of racial etiquette.

Slavery was a system for blacks and Indians only. Whites never enslaved their white enemies; rather, they reserved the complete denial of human rights for nonwhites. The English embarked on slavery as a response to nonwhite peoples, whom they considered inferior to whites.

Not until the 1680s were there significant numbers of black slaves in the Chesapeake, but by 1700 nearly 20,000 slaves resided in the region. Economics as well as race underlay the replacement of indentured servitude by slavery. In England a population decline between 1650 and 1700 reduced the potential pool for overseas labor and drove up wages. In addition, with the end of the Royal African Company's monopoly on the shipping and sale of slaves in the 1690s, an expanded supply of slaves arrived in the Chesapeake.

The emergence of slavery served to relax the economic tensions that had triggered Bacon's Rebellion. After 1690 even poor whites who owned no slaves believed that they shared a common interest with upper-class planters in maintaining social control over an alien and dangerous race.

Slavery's establishment as the principal form of labor in the Chesapeake was part of a larger trend among England's plantation colonies, one that had begun in the Caribbean and would spread to the new mainland colony of Carolina.

Spread of Slavery: The Caribbean and Carolina

As Puritans settled New England, a second immigrant wave carried twice their number, some 40,000 English people, to the West Indian islands in the Caribbean. The English West Indies strongly influenced English North America. First, the islands were a major market for New England's surplus foodstuffs, dried fish, and lumber. Second, they

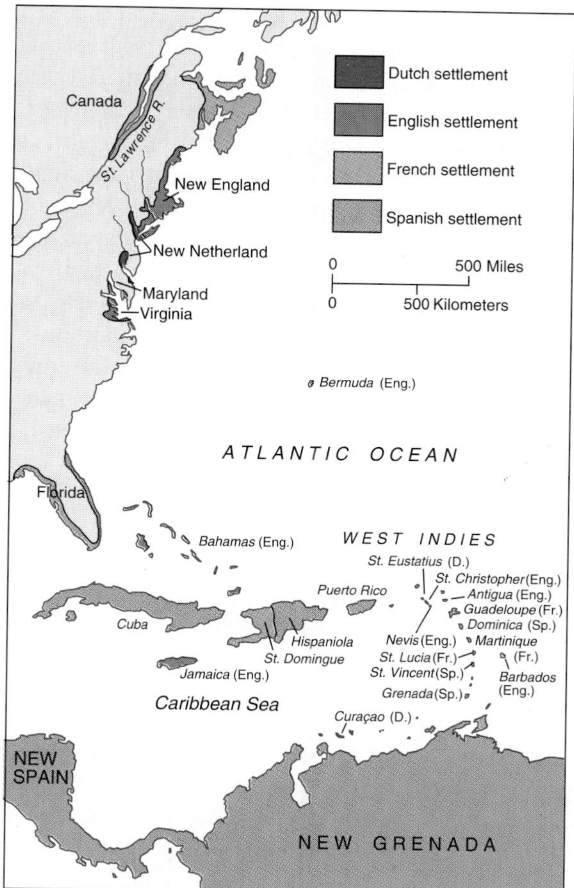

The Caribbean Colonies, 1660

Aside from Jamaica, England's sugar colonies were clustered in the eastern Caribbean's Leeward Islands. Lying within easy reach of seaborne attack, every English island but Barbados was the scene of major fighting.

adapted their economy to large-scale slave labor and devised a code of social conduct for nonwhites. In these latter ways, the West Indies pioneered techniques of racial control that were later adopted in the mainland colonies' plantation societies.

After 1660 large numbers of English islanders migrated to the Chesapeake and to Carolina, carrying with them the habits and prejudices of plantation slaveholding. By 1710 the population of Carolina, like that of the Caribbean colonies, was predominantly black and enslaved.

The Chaotic Caribbean

In the sixteenth century Spain claimed the entire Caribbean but concentrated on holding the four largest islands: Santo Domingo (Hispaniola), Puerto Rico, Cuba, and Jamaica. The English, French, and Dutch all scrambled to settle the uninhabited Caribbean islands. English freebooters became especially bold after Spain and Holland went to war in 1621. By 1640 England had established twenty communities from the Bahamas to the Nicaraguan coast. St. Kitts, Barbados, Montserrat, Nevis, and Antigua survived a Spanish counterattack, and Jamaica fell to England in 1655.

Born of war, England's West Indian colonies matured in turmoil. Between 1640 and 1713 they suffered the constant threat and frequent reality of both invasion and piracy. Seven slave revolts rocked the English islands before 1713 and left a bitter legacy of racial hatred.

Caribbean life went on amid constant violence inflicted on slaves by masters, on Catholics by Protestants, and on humans by nature. Bubonic plague killed one-third of the islanders from 1647 to 1649. Five thousand militiamen (every sixth Englishman in the Caribbean) died in the battle to capture Jamaica from Spain in the 1650s. Hurricanes regularly killed hundreds, and malaria and yellow fever felled thousands. In 1692 an earthquake killed 7,000 on Jamaica, one-sixth of the population. Few lived more than twenty years from their arrival in the islands.

Sugar and Slaves

Initially, the English West Indies developed along lines similar to Virginia, with tobacco the dominant crop. Because a single worker could tend only three acres of tobacco, tobacco farming demanded a large population. By 1640 more colonists lived on England's five West Indian islands than in all of Virginia.

Tobacco Label
The slave's central role in growing tobacco and serving his white master (here enjoying a smoke) is depicted.

Tobacco, requiring little equipment beyond a curing shed, was cheap to raise, and tobacco cultivation gave individuals with little money a chance at upward mobility. Through the 1630s the West Indies remained a society with a large percentage of independent landowners, an overwhelmingly white population, and no extreme inequality of wealth.

Sugar cane soon changed that, revolutionizing the islands' economy and society. Encouraged by Dutch merchants, wealthy English planters began to raise this enormously lucrative crop. Sugar sold at high prices, which escalated steadily over the next century, and could make a planter fabulously wealthy, but it required large amounts of capital and labor and elaborate machinery. With tobacco prices remaining low, most farmers could not afford to raise sugar. On Barbados a few sugar planters closed off all opportunity to small farmers by aggressively bidding up the price of land by more than 1,000 percent; by 1680 a mere 7 percent of landowners held over half the acreage. A typical sugar planter's estate was 200 acres, whereas most Barbadians scratched a meager living from 10 acres or less.

Because the profit from sugar vastly exceeded that from any other crop, West Indian planters turned every available acre into cane fields. Deforesting the islands (except Jamaica's mountains), they also virtually eliminated land for growing grain or raising livestock. Suddenly dependent on outside sources even for food, the Indies became a flourishing market for New England farmers, fishers, and loggers.

Moreover, the demand for labor soared because sugar required triple the labor force of tobacco. African slaves soon replaced indentured white servants in the fields. Most planters preferred black slaves to white servants because they could be driven harder and maintained more cheaply. Also, African slaves could better withstand the tropical diseases of the Caribbean, they had no rights under contract, and they toiled until they died. Although slaves initially cost two to four times more than indentured servants, they were an economical long-term investment. Some English immigrants to the Caribbean copied the example already set by the Spanish and enslaved both Indians and Africans.

By 1670 the sugar revolution had transformed the British West Indies into a predominantly black and slave society. In 1713 slaves outnumbered whites by four to one; the slave population had leaped from 40,000 in 1670 to 130,000 in 1713, with the white population remaining stable at 33,000. Meanwhile, driven from the Indies by high land prices, thousands of English settlers went north to the mainland. Settling in Carolina, they resumed tobacco cultivation.

West Indian Society

At the bottom of Caribbean society were the slaves, who lived under a ruthless system of racial control expressed in laws known as slave codes. The Barbados slave code of 1661 served as a model for both the Caribbean and the mainland colonies. The code required but never defined adequate shelter and diet for slaves, in effect allowing masters to let their slaves run almost naked, to house them in rickety shacks, and to work them to exhaustion. Slaves were stripped of all legal rights and protections: they could not be tried by juries and had no guarantee of a fair legal hearing.

In this way West Indian governments granted masters almost total control over their human property. As there were no limits on punishment, slaves suffered vicious beatings and whippings. A master who killed a slave could be punished only if a jury determined that the act was intentional—and then the punishment was limited to fines. Slave codes effectively legalized assault, battery, and manslaughter. The codes left slaves at the mercy of all whites, not just their owners; any white who caught a slave at large without a pass could give the slave a "moderate whipping," up to fifty lashes. Cruel and extreme punishments were prescribed to guarantee obedience. Judges could order ears sliced off, slaves torn limb from limb, and accused rebels burned alive.

Mortality among slaves was frightfully high. Sugar production required arduous labor, but it was so profitable that planters had little incentive to keep slaves healthy; they could easily replace those killed by overwork. Exhaustion and abuse killed most slaves within a decade of their arrival. Although planters imported 264,000 slaves between 1640 and 1699, the slave population stood at just 100,000 in 1700.

Despite these appalling conditions, slaves tried to maintain a semblance of normal existence. Many married and formed families. But the staggering rate of mortality cut most slave marriages short, and more than one-half of slave children died before reaching age five. Slaves preserved much of their African heritage in work songs, ceremonial dances and chants, and lamentations. Few slaves became Christian; most kept their faith in ancestral spirits, and some committed suicide in the belief that their ghosts would return home to Africa. The islands' black culture retained far more of an African imprint than the African-American life that would emerge on the mainland.

Among island whites, family cohesion was weak. Men outnumbered women four to one, and most white islanders lived wild bachelor lives. Organized religion withered in the absence of family and community support. A Caribbean joke maintained that on founding a settlement, the Spanish built a church, the Dutch built a fort, and the English built a barroom. "Old Kill-Devil," the local rum, was consumed in great quantities.

Wealthy island planters generally hired overseers to run their estates and retired in luxury to England. Poor whites left in droves for other colonies. The English Caribbean was a society of fortune seekers trying to get rich quickly before death overtook them and of slaves being worked to death.

The West Indies were the first English colonies to become plantation societies. They contained the most extreme examples of labor exploitation, racial subordination, and social inequality, but similar patterns would also characterize the Chesapeake Bay settlements and the coastal region known as Carolina.

Carolina: The First Restoration Colony

In 1663 Charles II bestowed the swampy coast between Virginia and Spanish Florida on several English supporters, making it the first of several Restoration colonies. The proprietors named their colony Carolina in honor of Charles (*Carolus* in Latin).

Settlers from New England and the West Indies had established outposts along the northern Carolina coast in the 1650s; the proprietors organized them into a separate district with a bicameral legislature. In 1669 one of the proprietors, Anthony Ashley Cooper, accelerated settlement by offering immigrants fifty-acre headright grants for every family member, indentured servant, or slave they brought in. The next year 200 Barbadian and English people began the settlement of southern Carolina near modern Charleston, "in the very chops of the Spanish." In the settlement they called Charles Town, they formed the colony's nucleus, with a bicameral legislature distinct from that of the northern district.

Cooper and his secretary, John Locke, devised an intricate plan for Carolina's settlement and government. Their Fundamental Constitutions of Carolina attempted to ensure the colony's stability by decreeing that political power and social rank should accurately reflect settlers' landed wealth. Thus they invented a three-tiered nobility that would hold two-fifths of all land, make laws through a council of nobles, and dispense justice through manorial courts. Ordinary Carolinians were expected to defer to the nobility and pay them rent, although they would enjoy religious toleration and the benefits of English common law. But new arrivals, hungry for land, saw no reason to accept the system and all but ignored it.

In the early years Carolina's population mainly consisted of small landowners. Southern Carolinians raised livestock, and colonists in northern Carolina exported tobacco, lumber, and pitch. In neither north nor south did the people realize enough profit to maintain slaves, and so self-sufficient white families predominated. But southern Carolinians eagerly sought a cash crop. In the early 1690s they found it—rice. Probably introduced to America by enslaved West Africans, rice cultivation enriched the few settlers with capital enough to acquire the dikes, dams, and slaves necessary to grow it. By earning annual profits of 25 percent, successful rice planters within a generation became the only colonial mainland elite whose wealth rivaled that of the Caribbean sugar planters.

Rice planters reaped their riches at the expense of African slaves. Knowledgeable about rice cultivation, slaves became tutors to their owners. The typical rice planter, with 130 acres in cultivation, needed sixty-five slaves. Demand drove the proportion of slaves in southern Carolina's population from 17 percent in 1680 to 67 percent in 1720, when the region officially became South Carolina. By 1776 the colony, with at least 100,000 slaves, would have more bondsmen than any other mainland colony in the eighteenth century. It would be Britain's only eighteenth-century mainland colony with a black majority.

Rice thrived in a narrow coastal strip extending from Cape Fear (now in North Carolina) to Georgia. Malaria, carried in from Africa but to which many Africans had partial immunity, ravaged this hot, humid lowland. In the worst months planters' families escaped to the relatively healthful climate of Charles Town, while overseers supervised the harvest.

As the black majority increased, whites relied on force and fear to control their slaves. In 1696 Carolina adopted the galling restrictions and gruesome punishments of the Barbados slave code. Bondage in the mainland colony grew as cruel and harsh as in the West Indies.

White Carolinians' attitudes toward Native Americans likewise hardened. The most vicious result was the trade in Indian slaves. White Carolinians armed allied Indians, encouraged them to raid and capture unarmed Indians to the south and west, and sold the captives to the West Indies during the 1670s and 1680s. A recent study estimates that the Carolina traders enslaved tens of thousands of Indians. Once shipped to the West Indies, most Native Americans died because they lacked immunities to European and tropical diseases.

Not surprisingly, Indian wars racked Carolina in the early eighteenth century. In 1711 some Tuscaroras, provoked by whites' encroachments and enslavement of Indians, destroyed the frontier settlement of New Bern. North Carolinians enlisted the aid of southern Carolina and its Indian allies. By 1713, after 1,000 Tuscaroras (about one-fifth of their population) had been killed or enslaved, the Native Americans surrendered.

Having helped to defeat the Tuscaroras, Carolina's Indian allies grew increasingly resentful of English traders' cheating, violence, and encroachment on their land. In 1715 the Yamasees attacked English trading houses and settlements. Only by arming some 400 slaves and enlisting the aid of the powerful Cherokees did the Carolinians crush the uprising. The surviving Yamasees fled to Florida or to the Creek nation.

In two generations Carolinians, with little help

from distant proprietors, had developed a thriving economy and had ended resistance from hostile Native Americans. Exasperated South Carolinians asked the British monarchy to take control, and in 1720 a temporary royal governor was appointed. Proprietary rule came to an end in 1729 when both North Carolina and South Carolina became royal colonies.

The Middle Colonies

Between the Chesapeake and New England, the third mainland colonial regions, the middle colonies, gradually emerged. In 1664 England seized New Netherland from the Dutch, and in 1681 Charles II authorized a colony where New Sweden had stood. Thus were laid the foundations for the Restoration colonies of New York, New Jersey, and Pennsylvania. By the end of the seventeenth century, the middle colonies composed North America's fastest-growing region.

Precursors: New Netherland and New Sweden

New Netherland became North America's first multiethnic society. Barely half the settlers were Dutch; most of the rest comprised Germans, French, Scandinavians, and Africans, both free and slave. In 1643 the population included Protestants, Catholics, Jews, and Muslims, speaking eighteen European and African languages. The trading company that had established the settlement struggled to control the settlers, whose get-rich-quick attitude sapped company profits as private individuals traded illegally in furs. Eventually, the company legalized the private trade.

Privatization rapidly increased the number of guns in the hands of New Netherland's Iroquois allies, giving them a distinct advantage over other tribes. As overhunting depleted local fur supplies and smallpox epidemics raged, the Iroquois encroached on Huron territory for pelts and captives (who were adopted into Iroquois families to replace the dead). After 1648 the Dutch-armed Iroquois destroyed the Hurons and attacked French settlements

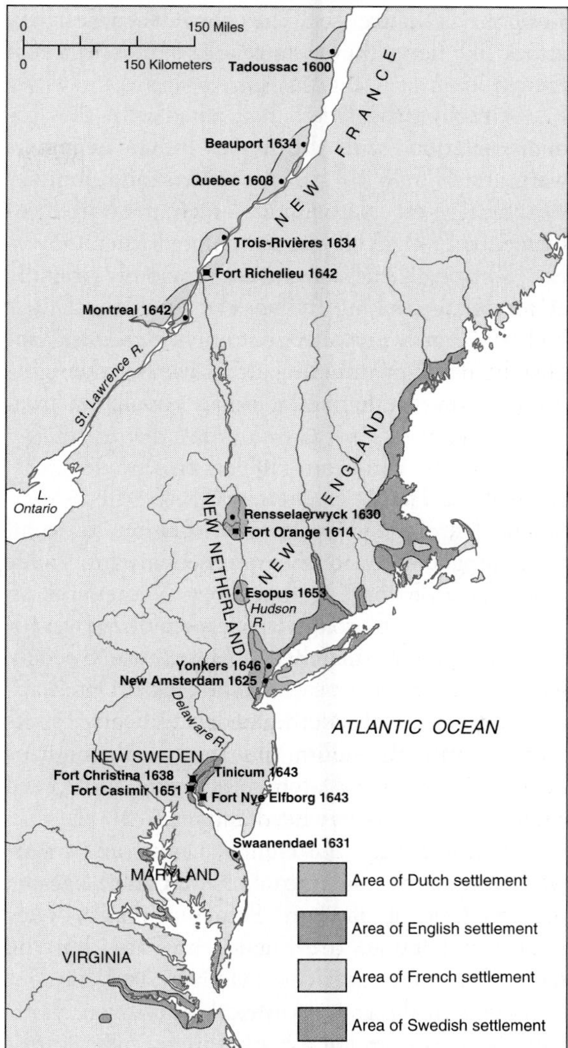

The Riverine Colonies of New France, New Netherland, and New Sweden, c. 1650
England's imperial rivals located their colonies along major river routes to the interior so that they could easily buy furs trapped by Indians farther inland. The French settled along the St. Lawrence, the Dutch along the Hudson, and the Swedes along the Delaware.

along the St. Lawrence. "They come like foxes, they attack like lions, they disappear like birds," wrote a French Jesuit.

Although the Dutch had allied with the Iroquois, relations with the nearer Indian neighbors were terrible. With greedy settlers and military weakness, New Netherland largely had itself to blame. In 1643 an all-out war erupted when Governor Willem Kiefft massacred previously friendly Algonquian-speaking Indians. By 1645 the Dutch had temporarily prevailed, but only by enlisting English help and by inflicting atrocities. But the fighting cut New Netherland's Indian population from 1,600 to 700.

Another European challenger, Sweden, distracted the Dutch in their war with the Algonquians. In 1638 Sweden had planted a small fur-trading colony in the lower Delaware Valley that was diverting furs from New Netherland. In 1655 the Dutch colony's stern soldier-governor Peter Stuyvesant marched against New Sweden, whose 400 residents peacefully accepted Dutch annexation. But New Netherland paid dearly for its victory. With the militia absent, the Algonquians destroyed scattered Dutch settlements and forced Stuyvesant to ransom white captives.

Although tiny, the French, Dutch, and Swedish colonies were significant. New France became the nucleus of modern French Canada. New Netherland fell to the English in 1664, but the Dutch presence in what became New York has lent a distinctive flavor to American life. Even short-lived New Sweden left a mark, the log cabin, introduced to the continent by Finnish settlers in the Swedish colony. Above all, the Dutch and Swedish colonies bequeathed a religious and ethnic diversity that would continue in England's "middle colonies."

English Conquests: New York and the Jerseys

Like the Carolinas, New York and the Jerseys originated with Restoration-era proprietors hoping to grow rich from rents collected from settlers within a hierarchical society. New York marginally achieved this dream, but the Jerseys did not.

In 1664, at war with the Dutch Republic, Charles II attacked the Dutch colony of New Netherland. Four hundred poorly armed Dutch civilians under Governor Peter Stuyvesant surrendered peacefully. Charles II made his brother James, duke of York, proprietor of the new English colony and renamed it New York. With James's ascension to the throne in 1685, he converted New York into a royal colony. By 1700 immigration had swelled the population to 20,000, of whom just 44 percent were descended from the original Dutch settlers.

New York's governors rewarded their influential political supporters with large land grants. By 1703 five families held 1.75 million acres, which they carved into manors and rented to tenants. By 1750 the enormous income they earned from rents had made the New York *patroons* a landed elite second in wealth only to the Carolina rice planters.

Ambitious plans collided with American realities in the Jerseys, also carved out of New Netherland. In 1664 the duke of York awarded a group of supporters the Jerseys, at the time inhabited by a few hundred Dutch and Swedes and several thousand Delaware Indians. Within a decade thousands of troublesome New England Puritans settled in the Jerseys, and the proprietors sold the region to Quakers, who split the territory into East and West Jersey.

East Jersey's new Scottish Quaker proprietors worked no more successfully with the local Puritans than had their predecessors, and in West Jersey the English Quakers squabbled constantly among themselves. The Jerseys' Quakers, Anglicans, Puritans, Scottish Presbyterians, and Dutch Calvinists quarreled with each other and got along even worse with the proprietors. The governments collapsed between 1698 and 1701, and in 1702 the disillusioned proprietors surrendered their political powers to the Crown, which made New Jersey a royal colony.

Quaker Pennsylvania

In 1681 Charles II paid off a huge debt by appointing a supporter's son, William Penn, as proprietor

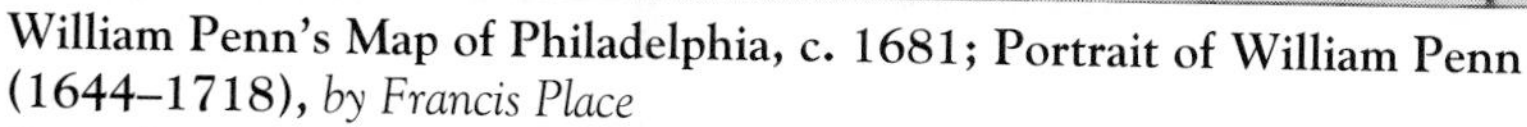
William Penn's Map of Philadelphia, c. 1681; Portrait of William Penn (1644–1718), *by Francis Place*

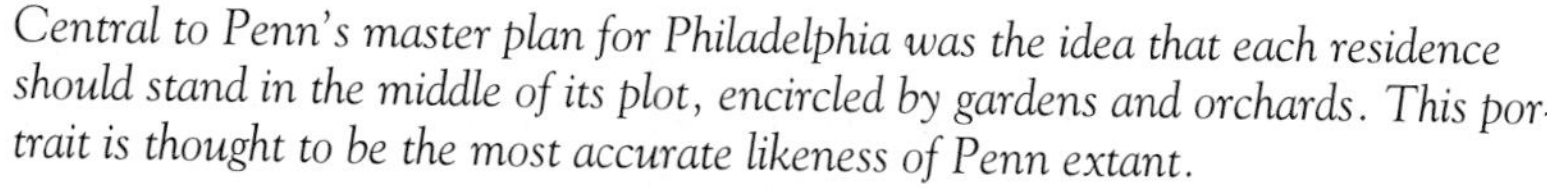
Central to Penn's master plan for Philadelphia was the idea that each residence should stand in the middle of its plot, encircled by gardens and orchards. This portrait is thought to be the most accurate likeness of Penn extant.

of the last unallocated tract of American territory at the king's disposal. Penn, a Quaker, thus founded the colony as a "holy experiment" based on the teachings of the English preacher George Fox. Penn also hoped for financial gain.

Quakers in late-seventeenth-century England stood well beyond the fringe of respectability. Challenging conventional foundations of social order, they appealed to those at the bottom of the economic ladder. But they also attracted some well-educated, well-to-do individuals disillusioned by the quarreling of rival religious faiths, including significant numbers of merchants. The members of this radical religious sect, which had been born in war-torn England during the 1640s and 1650s, called themselves the Society of Friends, but most others dubbed them Quakers.

At the heart of their founder George Fox's theology was the belief that the Holy Spirit, or "Inner Light," could inspire every soul. Mainstream Christians found this claim highly suspicious. Although trusting such direct inspiration, Quakers took pains to ensure that individual opinions would not be mistaken for God's will. Indeed, they felt confident that they understood the Inner Light only after having reached near-unanimous agreement through intensive discussion. In their religious services ("meetings"), Quakers sat silently until the Inner Light prompted one of them to speak. Quakers believed that the Inner Light could "speak in the female as well as the male," and they thus accorded women unprecedented equality.

Quaker behavior often seemed disrespectful to government and to the social elite and thus aroused hostility. For example, Quakers refused to tip their hats to their social betters, insisting that spiritual state, not wealth or status, deserved recognition. Their refusal to bear arms, moreover, appeared unpatriotic and cowardly.

Quakers in England faced intense pressure to conform to the established church, but they throve on persecution. Quakers absent from Anglican services were fined, and constables seized their farm tools, equipment, and livestock. Under Charles II, 15,000 Quakers were jailed. But Quakers maintained their reputation for industriousness even in prison. Jailed in 1669, Penn found his fellow Quaker inmates weaving, spinning, and absorbed in prayer during work breaks.

Care and planning made the Quaker migration

to Pennsylvania one of the most successful initial transplantations of Europeans in any North American colony. After sending an advance party, Penn arrived in 1682. He named his new capital Philadelphia, the "City of Brotherly Love." Within five years, 8,000 English Quakers had joined him. Quakers migrated in family groups, and the resulting high birthrate generated rapid population growth. (Pennsylvania's religious toleration attracted not only Quakers but also many other religious groups: Presbyterians, Baptists, Anglicans, and Catholics from England and Lutherans and radical sectarians from Germany.)

A victim of persecution, Penn hated intolerance and arbitrary governance. He offered Quakers the opportunity to make laws according to their ideals. His Frame of Government (constitution) featured a strong executive branch (a governor and governor's council) and a lower chamber (the assembly) with limited power. Friends, a majority in the colony, dominated the assembly, and Penn generally named Quakers to other positions. Hardly a democrat, Penn feared "the ambitions of the populace which shakes the Constitution" and intended to check the "rabble" as much as possible. To prevent wrangling and to achieve an orderly disposition of property, Penn personally oversaw land sales. He also designed a grid plan for Philadelphia, reserving park areas to keep it a "greene country towne." Penn sought peace with Native Americans by reassuring the Indians that the Quakers wished "to live together as Neighbours and Friends" and by buying land from them fairly.

Pennsylvania seemed an ideal colony—intelligently organized, well financed, tolerant, open to all industrious settlers, and at peace with the Indians. Rich lands and a lengthy growing season produced bumper crops. West Indian demand for grain generated widespread prosperity. By 1700 Philadelphia had become a major port. In 1704 counties along the lower Delaware River, where Swedes and Dutch had settled long before Penn, gained the right to elect their own legislature and became the colony of Delaware.

However, by this time Penn's "peaceable kingdom" had bogged down in human bickering. In 1684 Penn had returned to England, and during his fifteen-year absence the settlers had quarreled incessantly. An opposition party had attacked his efforts to monopolize foreign trade and to collect a small annual fee from each landowner. Struggles between pro- and anti-Penn forces had deadlocked the government. Penn's return from 1699 to 1701 had restored some order, but before leaving again, he made the legislature unicameral (one chamber) and allowed it to initiate measures.

Religious controversy meanwhile had erupted in the 1690s when prominent Quaker preacher George Keith urged the Quakers to adopt a formal religious creed. Doing so would have changed the democratically functioning Quakers into a conventional clergy-dominated church. In 1692 a majority of Quakers had rejected Keith's views, and he had joined the Church of England. But Keith's departure had begun a major decline in the Quaker share of Pennsylvania's population. In 1748 Penn's sons, who inherited the proprietorship, would become Anglican, and Anglicans thereafter would hold the highest political offices, although Friends would still dominate the colony's assembly.

Sadness darkened Penn's last years. His fortune spent in Pennsylvania, he served time in a debtor's prison and died in debt in 1718. He had long despaired at battling the legislature's politicians, bent as they were on economic and political advantage. As early as 1685 he had begged them, "For the love of God, me, and the poor country, be not so governmentish; so noisy and open in your disaffection."

Penn's anguish summed up the dilemmas of the English who had established the Restoration colonies. Little had gone as planned. Yet the Restoration colonies had succeeded. Before they were a quarter century old, the middle colonies had demonstrated that English America could benefit by encouraging pluralism. New York and New Jersey successfully integrated Dutch and Swedish populations; Pennsylvania, New Jersey, and Delaware refused to require residents to support any official church. But the virtual completion of English claim staking along the Atlantic coast had set England on a collision course with France and Spain, which also were vying for American territory.

Rivals for North America

Unlike England, with its compact seacoast colonial settlements in North America, France and Spain had cast enormous nets of widely separated trading posts and missions across the interior. The two Catholic nations had converted many Indians to Christianity and made them trading partners and allies. By 1720 scattered missionaries, fur traders, and merchants had spread French and Spanish influence across two-thirds of today's United States. The French government invested heavily in its American enterprise, but Spain, its empire decaying, made little effort to influence North American affairs. Local officials and settlers assumed the burden of extending imperial control for both powers.

France Claims a Continent

Under King Louis XIV (reigned 1661–1715), France sought to subordinate its American colony to French interests, following the doctrine of *mercantilism*. According to this doctrine, colonies should serve as sources of raw materials and as markets for manufactured goods so that the colonial power did not have to depend on rival nations for trade. The French wanted New France in order to increase fur trade, provide agricultural surplus to ship to France's West Indies colonies, and export timber for those colonies, and for the French Navy. To achieve this, the French government transformed New France into a royal colony, confronted and sought to stifle the Iroquois, and encouraged French immigration to Canada.

The Iroquois had long limited French colonial profits by intercepting convoys of fur pelts. In the 1660s Louis XIV had dispatched French troops to New France. The French Army had burned Mohawk villages. Sobered by the destruction, the Iroquois Confederacy had made a peace that had permitted New France's rapid expansion of fur exports. The French obtained furs in exchange for European goods, including guns.

In the 1660s France dispatched about 600 settlers a year to Canada, half of them indentured servants. But many immigrants gave up farming for the fur trade. By 1670 one-fifth had become *coureurs de bois*, independent traders free of government authority. Living and intermarrying with the Indians, the *coureurs* built a French empire resting on trade and goodwill among native peoples throughout central North America. Alarmed by the rapid expansion of England's colonies, France sought to contain them, and to prevent Spain from linking Florida with New Mexico, by dominating the North American heartland.

The Spanish Borderlands

English and French expansion, particularly René-Robert La Salle's building a fort in Spanish Texas in the 1680s, alarmed the Spanish. Yet the first permanent Spanish settlements in Texas did not appear until 1716. Instead, Spain concentrated on New Mexico. By 1680, 2,300 Europeans and 17,000 Pueblo Indians lived in New Mexico's Rio Grande valley.

However, many of the Indians chafed under Spanish control. Taos, a large pueblo in northern New Mexico, had long been a magnet for Native Americans resentful of Spanish rule, and in 1680 it would become the center of a major rebellion against the Spanish. Several factors triggered the uprising: prolonged drought, epidemics of European diseases, and Spanish attempts to suppress traditional religious ceremonies and symbols. The leader of the Taos revolt was Popé, a religious leader from a nearby pueblo who had fled to Taos to avoid persecution. In August 1680 Popé and others—many disillusioned Christian converts—led a massive uprising against the Spanish. The rebels slew more than 400 colonists and missionaries; hundreds more fled south into Mexico, leaving behind their horse herds and other livestock. Twelve years would pass before the Spanish recaptured Taos and the rebel Indians submitted to Spanish rule once again. The

Taos Pueblo, North House Block, 1880
The Taos pueblo of northern New Mexico became the site of a major anti-Spanish rebellion by Native Americans in 1680. As a result of this rebellion and the Spanish flight, Plains tribes gained access to horses for the first time.

Pueblo Revolt of 1680 would remain the largest Native American rebellion against Spain, although resentment continued to simmer. Perhaps the most important legacy of the Pueblo Revolt was the acquisition of the horse by Plains Indians quick to recognize the enormous advantages of mobility and speed; within a generation mounted warriors peopled the Great Plains from Canada to Texas, a formidable force arrayed first against Spanish and then against Anglo-American settlers.

In Florida the Spanish fared little better. Forced labor and missionization led to periodic Indian rebellions before 1680, and after that slave raiders from Carolina wreaked havoc among Indians under Spanish rule, as did disease. After 1715 Creek neutrality permitted the Spanish to enter the deerskin trade and even to stage counterraids into the British colony of Carolina. The Spanish also offered freedom to English-owned slaves who made their way to Florida. When a new round of warfare erupted in Europe at the end of the decade, Spain was ill prepared to defend its beleaguered North American colonies.

CONCLUSION

In less than a century, from 1630 to 1715, Europeans had laid claim to most of the area composing the United States from the Atlantic Ocean to the Rocky Mountains. Although France and Spain claimed vast domains, the population of England's colonies stood at 250,000, compared with 15,000 for France and 4,500 for Spain.

With the English colonies, several distinct regions emerged. Southern colonies, like those of the West Indies, focused on plantation production of cash crops, relying more and more on slave labor. New England's Puritans became far more worldly as a commercial economy boomed, and religious fervor slackened. The middle colonies, ethnically and religiously pluralistic, also embraced the market economy. During the first half of the eighteenth century, all three regions would be integrated into the first empire in history rooted in commercial capitalism.

CHRONOLOGY

1627 English establish Barbados.

1630 John Winthrop, "A Model of Christian Charity." Massachusetts Bay colony founded.

1630–1660 The great English migration to North America.

1633 First English settlements in Connecticut.

1634 Cecilius Calvert (Lord Baltimore) founds proprietary colony of Maryland.

1635 Roger Williams banished from Massachusetts Bay; founds Providence, Rhode Island, in 1636.

1636 Harvard College established.

1637 Anne Hutchinson tried by Massachusetts Bay Colony and banished to Rhode Island.
Pequot War.

1638 New Sweden established.

1640s Large-scale slave-labor system takes hold in the West Indies.

1642 English Civil War begins.

1644 Williams obtains permission to establish a legal government in Rhode Island.

1644–1646 Third Anglo-Powhatan War in Virginia.

1649 Maryland's Act for Religious Toleration.
King Charles I beheaded.

1651 First New England "praying town" established at Natick, Massachusetts.

1653 First Indian reservation established in Virginia.

1655 New Netherland annexes New Sweden.

1660 Charles II becomes king of England.

1661 Barbados government creates first comprehensive slave code.
Maryland defines slavery as a lifelong, inheritable racial status.

1662 Half-Way Covenant drafted.

1663 Carolina founded as English colony.
New France made a royal colony.

1664 English conquer the Dutch colony of New Netherland, which becomes the English colony of New York.
New Jersey established.

1670 Settlement of southern Carolina begins.
Virginia defines slavery as a lifelong, inheritable racial status.

1672 Louis Jolliet and Jacques Marquette explore the Mississippi River.

1675–1676 King Philip's War in New England.

1676 Bacon's Rebellion in Virginia.
Quakers organize the colony of West Jersey.

1680–1692 Pueblo revolt in New Mexico.

1681 William Penn founds the Pennsylvania colony.

1682 Quakers organize the colony of East Jersey. The Sieur de La Salle descends the Mississippi River to the Gulf of Mexico and claims the Mississippi basin for France.

1690s Collapse of the Royal African Company's monopoly on selling slaves to the English colonies; large shipments of Africans begin reaching the Chesapeake.

1692–1693 Salem witchcraft trials.

1698 French begin settlements near the mouth of the Mississippi River.

1711–1713 Tuscarora War in Carolina.

1715–1716 Yamasee War in Carolina.

FOR FURTHER READING

Paul Boyer and Stephen Nissenbaum, *Salem Possessed: The Social Origins of Witchcraft* (1974). A study of the witchcraft episode as the expression of social conflict in one New England community.

William Cronon, *Changes in the Land: Indians, Colonists, and the Ecology of New England* (1983). A pioneering study of the interactions of Native Americans and European settlers with the New England environment.

W. J. Eccles, *France in America*, rev. ed. (1991). An interpretive overview of French colonization in North America and the Caribbean by a distinguished scholar.

Jack P. Greene, *Pursuits of Happiness: The Social Development of Early Modern British Colonies and the Formation of American Culture* (1988). A brilliant synthesis of the colonial history of English America.

Winthrop D. Jordan, *The White Man's Burden: Historical Origins of Racism in the United States* (1974). A brief, yet definitive analysis of racism's origins.

Carol F. Karlsen, *The Devil in the Shape of a Woman: Witchcraft in Colonial New England* (1987). An examination of the relationship between witchcraft episodes and gender in New England society.

Edmund S. Morgan, *American Slavery, American Freedom: The Ordeal of Colonial Virginia* (1975). The most penetrating analysis yet written on the origins of southern slavery.

Alan Simpson, *Puritanism in Old and New England* (1955). A good brief introduction to Puritanism.

David J. Weber, *The Spanish Frontier in North America* (1992). A masterful synthesis of Spanish colonial history north of the Caribbean and Mexico.

CHAPTER 4

Colonial Society Comes of Age, 1660–1750

Restoration and Rebellion

A Maturing Colonial Economy and Society

Competing for a Continent

Enlightenment and Awakening

With the English Civil War's end in 1646, the flow of English settlers to America became a torrent. New colonies soon dotted the Atlantic seaboard from French-held Canada to Spanish-controlled Florida. Although English immigrants peopled most of these colonies, significant numbers of Germans, Irish, Scottish, Dutch, and French arrived and contributed to the emerging American culture. So, too, did the increasing African-American population, which slowly became English-speaking and Christian.

A generation of imperial crisis and war against the French from 1685 until 1713 forged among Anglo-America's whites a strong sense of shared allegiance to the English crown and of deeply felt Protestant heritage. During the peace that prevailed from 1713 to 1744, two vital but conflicting currents of European culture challenged British-American provincialism. The first was the Enlightenment, a movement among the educated public

(Right) Rhode Island colonists relaxing at teatime (detail)

characterized by a faith in reason and an appreciation of natural science. Joining and opposing this movement was a second current, a religious revival that pulsed across Protestant Europe in the 1730s and 1740s, a movement known as the Great Awakening in the American colonies.

The peace and prosperity of mid-eighteenth-century British North America would have astonished the seventeenth-century colonists who had clung to their uncertain footholds on the edge of the wilderness. But even though life had become reasonably stable and secure by the 1740s, especially for upper-class Anglo-Americans, the Great Awakening unleashed spiritual and social tremors that jolted colonial self-confidence.

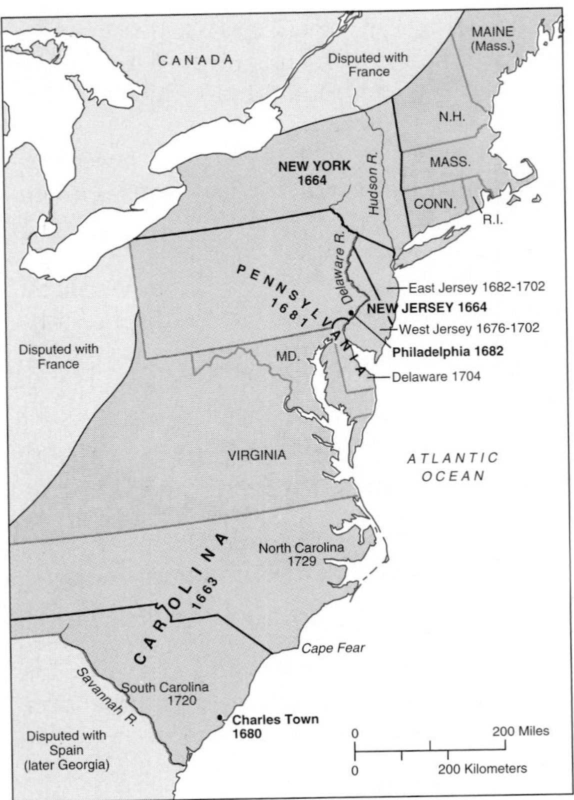

The Restoration Colonies
England's Restoration colonies were carved out of the claims or earlier colonial territory of rival European powers. Spain claimed the territory chartered as Carolina in 1663. Out of England's takeover of Dutch New Netherland in 1664 came the colonies of New York, East Jersey, West Jersey, Pennsylvania, and Delaware.

Restoration and Rebellion

Although English colonies dated to Virginia in 1607, there was no serious attempt to weld the diverse colonies into an empire until Charles II (ruled 1660–1685) ascended the throne. The "restoration" of the Stuart dynasty ended two decades of civil war and republican experiment. England began to expand its overseas trade and tried to subordinate to its own interests the commercial and political interests of the colonies.

Stuart Policies

To benefit England's commercial interests, Parliament began "tidying up" the North American colonies by passing a series of laws collectively known as the Navigation Acts beginning in 1651. The 1660 and 1663 acts, expanding on the 1651 act, forced colonial merchants to export valuable commodities such as sugar and tobacco only to England and banned the importation of goods in non-English ships. Meanwhile, a new wave of colony building gave England control of the North American coast from Maine to South Carolina.

Charles II intended the Navigation Acts and the new colonies to reward his supporters in England. The proprietors who oversaw the colonies' government expected to create prosperous settlements and a stable social hierarchy. But such plans collided with the colonists' determination to better themselves, and by 1689 English attempts to impose a uniform system of rule had provoked a series of colonial rebellions.

Royal Centralization

The sons of a king executed by Parliament, the last Stuart monarchs, Charles II and James II, disliked representative government. They tried to rule England as much as possible without Parliament and eyed American colonial assemblies suspiciously.

As Duke of York during his brother Charles's rule, James showed his disdain for colonial assemblies almost as soon as he became the proprietor of New York. Calling elected assemblies "of dangerous consequence," he forbade legislatures to meet from 1664 to 1682. Charles himself often appointed high-ranking army officers as colonial governors. Technically civilians, these officers commanded the militia and used it to crush civilian dissent. In his twenty-five-year reign, more than 90 percent of the governors whom Charles II appointed were army officers, a serious violation of the English tradition of holding the military accountable to civilian authority. When James became king, he continued the policy.

Ever resentful of outside meddling, New Englanders resisted such centralization of power. In 1661 the Massachusetts assembly declared its citizens exempt from all English laws and royal decrees except declarations of war. Ignoring the Navigation Acts, New Englanders welcomed Dutch traders. "The New England men . . . trade to any place that their interest lead them," lamented Virginia's governor William Berkeley.

Provoked, Charles targeted Massachusetts for punishment. In 1679 he carved a new royal territory, New Hampshire, from Massachusetts. In 1684 he declared Massachusetts a royal colony and revoked its charter, the very foundation of the Puritan city upon a hill. Puritan minister Increase Mather called on the colonists to resist, even to the point of martyrdom.

James II's accession to the throne intensified royal centralization in America. In 1686 the new king merged five separate colonies—Massachusetts, New Hampshire, Connecticut, Rhode Island, and Plymouth—into the Dominion of New England, later adding New York and the Jerseys. Under the new system, these colonies' legislatures ceased to exist. Sir Edmund Andros, a former army officer, became the Dominion's governor.

Andros's arbitrary actions ignited burning hatred. He limited towns to one annual meeting and jailed prominent citizens in order to crush protests. He forced a Boston Puritan congregation to share its meetinghouse with an Anglican minister. And Andros enforced the Navigation Acts. "You have no more privileges left you," Andros reportedly told a group of colonists, "than not to be sold for slaves."

Tensions also ran high in New York, where Catholics held high political and military posts under the Duke of York's rule. Anxious colonists feared that these Catholic officials would betray the colony to France. When Andros's local deputy allowed harbor forts to deteriorate, New Yorkers suspected the worst.

The Glorious Revolution in England and America

Puritans in England also worriedly monitored Stuart displays of pro-Catholic sympathies. The Duke of York himself became a Catholic in 1676, and Charles II converted on his deathbed. Both rulers violated English law by allowing Catholics to hold high office and to worship openly. James II had Anglican bishops who denounced these practices tried as state enemies.

The English tolerated James II's Catholicism only because his heirs, daughters Mary and Anne, remained Anglican. But in 1688 his second wife bore a son, who would be raised—and perhaps would rule—as a Catholic. Aghast at the idea, English political leaders asked Mary and her husband, William of Orange (the Dutch Republic's leader), to intervene. When William and Mary led a small army to England in November 1688, royal troops defected to them, and James II fled to France.

This bloodless coup, the "Glorious Revolution," created a "limited monarchy" as defined by England's Bill of Rights of 1689. The monarchs promised to summon Parliament annually, to sign its bills, and to respect civil liberties. Neither the English nor Anglo-Americans would ever forget this vindication of limited representative government. Anglo-Americans struck their own blows for political liberty as well when Massachusetts, New York, and Maryland rose up against their Stuart-appointed rulers.

News of the Glorious Revolution electrified Massachusetts Puritans, who arrested Andros and his councilors. (He tried to flee in women's clothing but was caught when a guard spotted this "lady" in army boots.) Acting in the name of William and Mary, the Massachusetts elite resumed its own government. In fact, the new monarchs would have preferred continuing the Dominion but prudently consented to its dismantling. They allowed Connecticut and Rhode Island to resume election of their own governors and permitted Massachusetts to absorb the Plymouth colony. But Massachusetts enjoyed only a partial victory. The colony's new royal charter of 1691 reserved to the crown the appointment of the governor. Moreover, property ownership, not church membership, became the criterion for voting. Worst of all, the Puritan colony had to tolerate Anglicans, who were proliferating in the port towns.

New York's counterpart of the anti-Stuart uprising was Leisler's Rebellion. In May 1689 the city militia, under Captain Jacob Leisler, had seized the harbor's main fort, begun to repair its defenses, and called elections for an assembly. Andros's deputy, his authority strangled, had sailed for England. In 1691 Leisler, still riding high, denied newly arrived English troops entry to key forts for fear that they were loyal to James II. But after a brief skirmish, Leisler was arrested and charged with treason for firing on royal troops. New Yorkers who considered themselves ill treated by Leisler packed the jury, and both he and his son-in-law were convicted and hanged.

Arbitrary government and fears of Catholic plots had also brought turmoil to Maryland by 1689, where the Protestant-dominated lower house and the Catholic upper chamber were feuding. When the Glorious Revolution had toppled James II, Lord Baltimore, away in England, had dispatched a courier to Maryland, commanding obedience to William and Mary. But the courier died en route. Maryland's Protestants widely suspected that their proprietor was a traitor who supported James II.

Protestant rebel John Coode organized the Protestant Association to secure Maryland for William and Mary. In July 1689 Coode and his co-conspirators seized the capital, removed Catholics from office, and requested that the crown take over the colony. Maryland became a royal province in 1691 and made the Church of England an established religion in 1692. Catholics, composing less than one-fourth of the population, lost the right to vote and to worship in public. In 1715 the fourth Lord Baltimore joined the Church of England and regained the proprietorship of Maryland. Maryland remained a proprietary colony until 1776.

The revolutionary events of 1688–1689 reestablished the colonies' legislative government and ensured Protestant religious freedom. William and Mary allowed colonial elites to reassert local control and encouraged Americans to identify their interests with England, laying the foundation for an empire based on voluntary allegiance, not raw force.

A Generation of War

The Glorious Revolution ushered in a quarter century of war that convulsed both England and the colonies. In 1689 England joined a European coalition against France's Louis XIV and plunged into the War of the League of Augsburg (which Anglo-Americans called King William's War).

In 1690, at the outbreak of King William's War, New Yorkers and Yankees launched an invasion of England's enemy, New France. The invasion deteriorated into cruel but inconclusive border raids by both sides. The Iroquois, allied to the English and Dutch, bore the brunt of the war. French forces, enlisting the aid of virtually every other tribe from Maine to the Great Lakes, played havoc with Iroquois land and peoples. By 1700 one-fourth of the Iroquois warriors had been killed or taken prisoner, or had fled to Canada. In twelve years the Iroquois population fell from 8,600 to 7,000. By comparison, English and Dutch casualties were fewer than 900, while the French probably lost no more than 400. In 1701 the Iroquois agreed to let Canada's governor settle their disputes with other Indians and to remain neutral in future wars. Thereafter, playing French and English off against each other, the Iroquois maintained control of their lands, rebuilt their population, and held the balance of power along the Great Lakes.

In 1702 a new European war pitted England against France and Spain. During what the colonists called Queen Anne's War, Anglo-Americans became painfully aware of their own military weakness. French and Indian raiders from Canada destroyed New England towns, while the Spanish invaded southern Carolina and nearly took Charles Town in 1706. Colonial vessels fell to French and Spanish warships. English forces, however, gained control of the Hudson Bay region, Newfoundland, and Acadia (henceforth called Nova Scotia). The peace signed in 1713 allowed Britain to keep these lands but left the French and Indians in control of their interior.

These wars had a profound political consequence. Anglo-Americans, newly aware of their military weakness, realized how much they needed the protection of the Royal Navy, and consequently they became more loyal than ever to the English crown. War thus reinforced the Anglo-American sense of British identity.

A Maturing Colonial Economy and Society

Britons visiting mid-eighteenth-century America found a sophisticated society and widespread prosperity. "The nobleness of the town surprized me more than the fertile appearance of the country," wrote an English naval officer of New York in 1756. "I had no idea of finding a place in America, consisting of near 2,000 houses, elegantly built of brick . . . and the streets paved and spacious, . . . but such is this city that very few in England can rival it in its show."

Such prosperity and social development were relatively new. By 1750 the colonies' brisk economic growth had been under way for fifty to seventy-five years, depending on the region. During that time colonial exports had grown steadily, allowing Anglo-Americans to enjoy a relatively high living standard despite parliamentary controls.

British Economic Policy Toward America

Between 1651 and 1733 Parliament enacted laws to govern commerce between Britain and its overseas colonies. Historians label the rules of trade set forth in these laws the navigation system, and they use the word *mercantilism* to describe the underlying legal assumptions. The navigation system and mercantilism deeply affected North America's relationship with Great Britain.

Mercantilism was not an elaborate economic theory. Instead, the word refers in general to European policies aimed at guaranteeing prosperity by making their own country as self-sufficient as possible—by eliminating its dependence on foreign suppliers, damaging its foreign competitors' commerce, and increasing the national stock of gold and silver by selling more goods abroad than it bought. Mercantilism was the direct opposite of a competitive free-market system, which would receive its first great theoretical description in Scottish economist Adam Smith's *The Wealth of Nations* (1776). Until then, mercantilism would dominate British policy.

In 1651 the English Parliament passed the first Navigation Act to undercut the Dutch Republic. It excluded the Dutch from English trade in order to force England to build its own merchant fleet. The Stuart restoration in 1660 brought more laws to protect English manufacturers from foreign competition. By 1750 a long series of Navigation Acts was affecting the colonial economy in four major ways.

First, the laws limited imperial trade to British-owned ships whose crews were three-quarters British (which was broadly defined to include all colonists, even blacks). At first the American colonists and some in the English business community objected because the Dutch offered better prices, credit, and merchandise. After 1700, however, the rising quality of the British merchant marine removed this cause for complaint.

This new shipping restriction helped Britain to become Europe's foremost shipping nation and laid the foundations for an American merchant marine. By the 1750s Americans owned one-third of all imperial vessels. The swift growth of this merchant marine diversified the colonial economy and made it more self-sufficient. The expansion of colonial shipping in turn demanded centralized docks, warehouses, and repair shops, and thus hastened urbanization. Philadelphia and New York both grew rapidly. Shipbuilding became a major industry, and by 1770 one-third of the British merchant marine was American built.

Second, the Navigation Acts barred the colonies' export of "enumerated goods" unless they first passed through England or Scotland. Among these were tobacco, rice, furs, indigo, and naval stores (masts, hemp, tar, and turpentine). (Before the mid-eighteenth century, at least, Parliament did not restrict grain, livestock, fish, lumber, or rum, which constituted 60 percent of colonial exports.) Furthermore, American tobacco exporters received a monopoly on the British tobacco market. Parliament also refunded taxes on tobacco and rice later shipped from Britain to other countries—amounting eventually to about 85 percent of American tobacco and rice.

Third, the navigation system encouraged economic diversification. Parliament paid modest bounties to Americans producing silk, iron, dyes, hemp, lumber, and other products that Britain would otherwise have had to import from foreign countries. Parliament also erected protective tariffs against foreign goods.

Fourth, the trade laws forbade Americans from competing with British manufacturers of clothing and steel—an apparently negative consequence for the colonies. In practice this regulation meant little because it referred to *large-scale* manufacturing and thus did not interfere with the tailors, hatters, and housewives who produced most American clothing in their households or in small shops. Americans would establish a profitable clothing industry only after 1820 and did not develop a successful steel industry until the 1840s. The colonists were free to produce iron, however, and by 1770, 250 colonial ironworks were employing 30,000 men. That year the colonies produced more iron than England and Wales; and only Sweden and Russia exceeded American output.

Before the mid-eighteenth century, the Navigation Acts did not overburden the colonists. The trade regulations, which fell primarily on rice and tobacco producers, lowered their income by only 3 percent. The cost of non-British merchandise rose, but not enough to encourage smuggling (except for tea from India and molasses from the French Caribbean). The great volume of colonial trade proceeded lawfully. In addition, Anglo-American commerce provided mutual advantages. Although Parliament intended the laws only to benefit Britain, British North America's economy grew at a per capita rate of 0.6 percent annually from 1650 to 1770 under the navigation system—twice as fast as Britain's.

A Burgeoning, Diversifying Population

European cities were too poor and crowded for marriage and families, Benjamin Franklin noted in 1751, but British America, with its open spaces and small cities, seemed destined to grow and flourish. Estimating the colonies' population at 1 million, Franklin predicted that it would double every 25 years. Not only were his estimates amazingly precise, but modern research has also confirmed his analysis of factors affecting population growth.

After 1700, when life expectancy and family size in the South rose to levels typical of those of the North, Anglo-America's growth far outpaced Britain's. Colonial women had an average of eight children and forty-two grandchildren, compared to five children and fifteen grandchildren for their British counterparts. In 1700 England's population outnumbered the colonies' by twenty to one; by 1775 the ratio would be only three to one.

In the eighteenth century continuing immigration contributed significantly to colonial population growth. In the forty years after Queen Anne's War, 350,000 newcomers had reached the colonies. The percentage of English-born immigrants among whites decreased sharply. Rising employment and higher wages in England made emigration less attractive than before, but economic hardship elsewhere in the British Isles and in northern Europe guaranteed an ethnically more diverse North America.

Ironically, enslaved Africans, some 140,000 in number, constituted the largest group of newcomers. Most were from Africa's west coast, and all had survived a sea crossing of sickening brutality. Ship captains closely calculated how many slaves they could jam into their vessels. Kept below deck in near-darkness, surrounded by filth and stench, numbed by depression, the Africans frequently fell victim to disease.

More than 100,000 newcomers in this era were from Ireland. Two-thirds of these were "Scots-Irish," the descendants of sixteenth-century Scottish Presbyterian settlers of northern Ireland. The Scots-Irish generally immigrated as complete families. In contrast, 90 percent of Irish Catholic immigrants consisted of unmarried males who, once in America, typically abandoned their faith to marry Protestant women.

Germany contributed some 65,000 settlers, the majority seeking escape from desperate poverty. One-third were "redemptioners" who had sold themselves or their children as indentured servants. Lutherans and Calvinists predominated, but a significant minority belonged to small, pacifist sects that desired above all to be left alone.

Immigrants shunned areas where land was scarce and expensive because most of them were poor. Philadelphia became the immigrants' primary port of entry. By 1775 the English accounted for only one-third of Pennsylvania's population.

Indentured servants had to work one to four years for a master who might exploit them cruelly.

Architect's Plan of a Slave Ship

This plan graphically depicts the crowded, unsanitary conditions under which slaves were transported across the Atlantic.

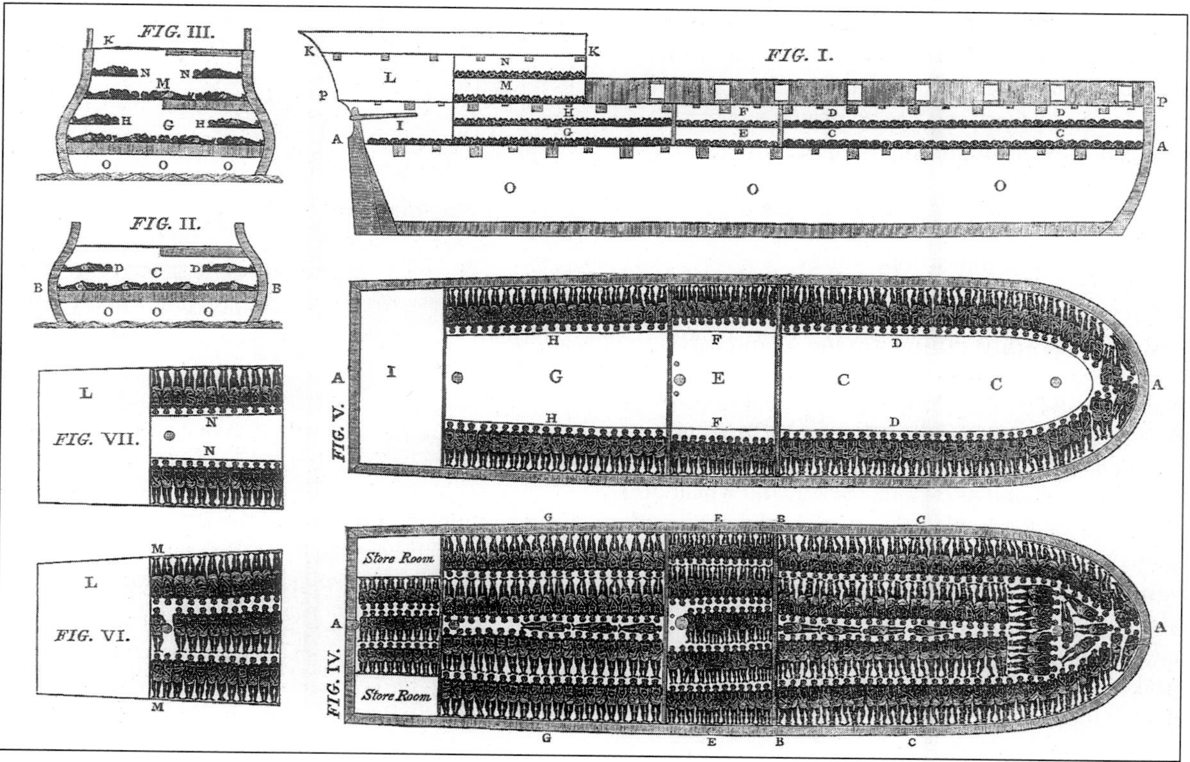

Servants could be sold or rented out, beaten, kept from marrying, and sexually harassed; attempted escape usually meant an extension of service. At the end of their term, most collected "freedom dues," which helped them to marry and to acquire land.

The piedmont, a broad, rolling upland stretching along the eastern slope of the Appalachians, drew many immigrants. Upper New York, Pennsylvania, and Maryland attracted large numbers of Germans and Scots-Irish. Charles Town became a popular gateway for immigrants who later moved westward to the Carolina piedmont to become small farmers. In 1713 few Anglo-Americans lived more than fifty miles from the Atlantic, but by 1750 one-third of the colonists resided in the piedmont.

English-descended colonists did not relish the arrival of so many foreigners. Benjamin Franklin wrote:

> *Why should the Palatine boors [Germans] be suffered to swarm into our settlements, and, by herding together, establish their language and manners, to the exclusion of ours? Why should Pennsylvania, founded by the English, become a colony of aliens, who will shortly be so numerous as to Germanize us instead of us Anglicizing them, and will never adopt our language or customs any more than they can acquire our complexion?*

Franklin also objected to slave trade because, he argued, it would increase America's black population at the expense of industrious whites.

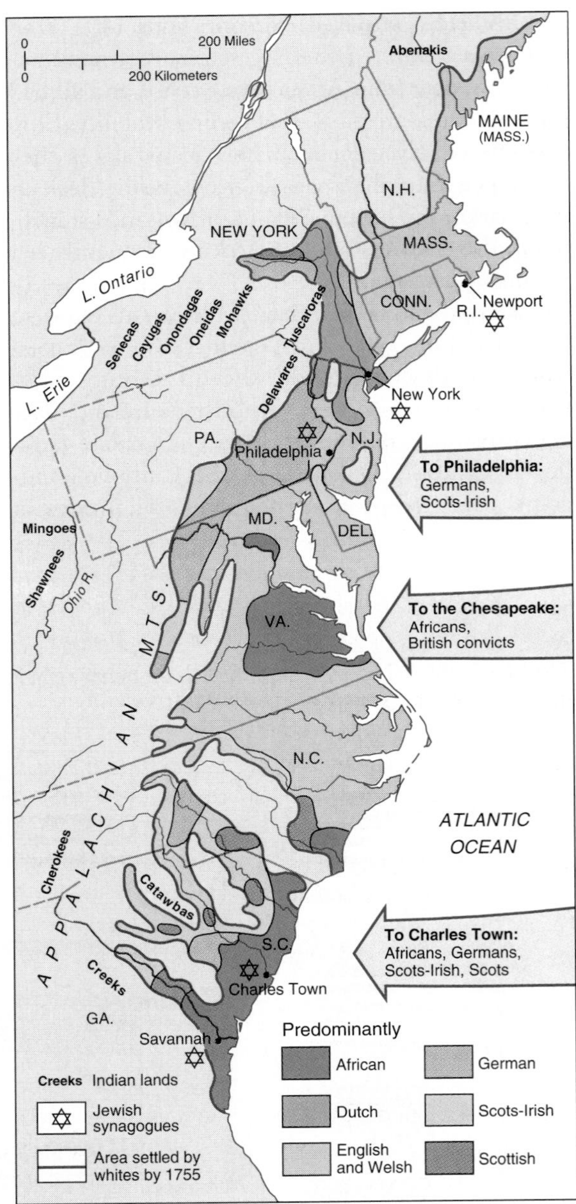

Immigration and Frontier Expansion, to 1755
A sharp rise in the importance of African slaves made much of the southern tidewater a predominantly African-American region. Immigrants from Germany, Ireland, and Scotland tended to settle in the piedmont. A significant Jewish population emerges in the seaports.

Eighteenth-Century Living Standards

A tenfold increase in exports drove colonial living standards up dramatically after 1700, especially in the Chesapeake. As tobacco exports tripled from 1713 to 1774, and as exports of corn and wheat also soared, prosperity replaced poverty in the region, although slaves and a small underclass of struggling white farmers remained poor. A landholding small-planter class arose, and a wealthy elite of large landowners and slavemasters flourished atop Chesapeake society after 1700. Perhaps 30 percent of white families owned slaves.

The mid-Atlantic, stretching from New York to Delaware, had the highest living standards. In 1770 per capital wealth here stood 40 percent above the colonial average. Prosperity rested on the region's rich soil, on a long-term climatic warming that lengthened the growing season, and on a brisk demand for livestock, wheat, and corn in the West Indies and southern Europe.

New Englanders prospered least. Their wealth, on average, was only half that of other colonists. Mediocre soil and a short growing season forced New Englanders to import grain. A long-term decline in the price of lumber also hurt the New England economy. By 1750 New England towns teemed with more young men than the land could support. Migration to the frontier eased this population pressure. The sea also provided a means of survival for many New Englanders. By 1700 the Yankee merchant marine and fishing industry were the largest in the colonies, providing employment for every seventh man. But prosperity carried a heavy price: the sea took one sailor in five to a watery grave.

By 1750 the American colonies enjoyed a standard of living roughly equal to that of England and far higher than those of Scotland and Ireland. Steady overseas demand for colonial products spawned a prosperity that enabled Americans to consume a huge volume of British products. In 1700 the colonies took just 5 percent of Britain's exports; by 1760 they absorbed almost 40 percent.

Rural Men and Women

Because the vast majority of colonial landowners had just enough acreage for a working farm, most could not provide land for their children when they married. Moreover, with longevity increasing, children often did not receive their inheritances until middle age or later; and, because families were large, a farmer's wealth was typically divided into small portions. Under these circumstances, a young man typically worked from about age sixteen to twenty-three as a field hand to save money just to buy farm equipment, and a young husband generally had to rent land until he reached his mid-thirties. Landownership came fastest to those farmers who took part-time work to increase their savings. Carpentry, fur trapping, and wintertime jobs such as draining meadows and fencing land supplemented farm incomes.

The payment of mortgages was slow. A farmer could expect to earn 6 percent cash income per year, which barely equaled mortgage interest. After making a down payment of one-third, a husband and wife generally paid the next third through their inheritances. The final third would be paid when the children reached their teens and helped to double the regular farm income. Most colonial parents found themselves free of debt only as they reached their late fifties.

Rural families depended somewhat on barter and much more on what wives and daughters manufactured: soap, preserved food, knitted goods, yarn,

Women's Work

Rural women were responsible for most household and garden tasks. This print, dating to 1780, shows young women tending onions in Wethersfield, Connecticut.

and the products of dairy, orchard, and garden. In this way women made significant contributions to the family's cash income and well-being. Legal constraints, however, bound colonial women. A woman's most independent decision was her choice of a husband. Once married, she lost control of her dowry. Nevertheless, widows controlled substantial property—an estimated 8 to 10 percent of all property in eighteenth-century Anglo-America—and some ran large estates or plantations.

Colonial Farmers and the Environment

As English settlement expanded, the environment east of the Appalachians changed rapidly. Eighteenth-century settlers cleared forest land in order to plant crops in its fertile soil. New England farmers also cleared from their land innumerable large rocks, debris from the last Ice Age. The felled trees provided timber to construct houses, barns, and fences and to burn as fuel for cooking and heating. Urban dwellers bought their firewood and construction timber from farmers and planters. Six years after Georgia's founding, a colonist noted that there was "no more firewood in Savannah; . . . it must be brought from the plantations [and is] already right expensive."

Removal of trees (deforestation) deprived large forest creatures such as bears, panthers, and wild turkeys of their habitat, while the planted land provided free lunch for rabbits, mice, and possums. Deforestation removed protection from winds and sun, producing warmer summers and harsher winters and, ironically, reinforcing the demand for firewood. By hastening the runoff of spring waters, deforestation led to heavier flooding and, where water could not escape, to more extensive swamps. Volatile temperatures and water levels rapidly reduced the number of fish in colonial streams and lakes. By 1766 naturalist John Bartram noted that fish "abounded formerly when the Indians lived much on them" but that "now there is not the 100th or perhaps the 1000th [portion] to be found."

Deforestation also dried and hardened the soil; colonial crops had even more drastic effects. Native Americans had rotated their crops to protect against soil depletion, but many colonial farmers lacked enough land to do so—and many more were unwilling to sacrifice short-term profits for long-term benefits. As early as 1637 a dismayed New England farmer found that his soil "after five or six years [of planting corn] grows barren beyond belief and puts on the face of winter in the time of summer." Tobacco yields in the Chesapeake region declined in fields planted only three or four consecutive years. As the Chesapeake tobacco growers abandoned tidewater fields and moved to the piedmont, they contributed to increased soil erosion. By 1750, in order to remain productive, many shifted from tobacco to wheat.

Well-to-do Europeans had already turned to conservation and "scientific farming." North American colonists ignored such techniques. Some could not afford to implement them, and virtually all believed that America's vast lands, including those still held by Indians, would sustain them and future generations indefinitely.

The Urban Paradox

Cities were colonial America's economic paradox. Although they shipped the livestock, grain, and lumber that enriched the countryside, at the same time they were caught in a downward spiral of declining opportunity.

After 1740 the 4 percent of colonists in cities found economic success elusive. Philadelphia, New York, and Boston faced escalating poverty. Debilitating ocean voyages left many immigrants too weak to work, and every ship from Europe carried widows and orphans. The cities' poor rolls, moreover, always bulged with the survivors of mariners lost at sea; unskilled, landless men; and women (often widows) and children from the countryside. And a high population density and poor sanitation left colonial cities vulnerable to the rapid spread of contagious diseases. As a result, half of all city children died before twenty-one, and urban adults averaged ten fewer years of life than rural residents.

Even the able-bodied found cities economically treacherous. Traditionally, artisans trained apprentices and employed them as journeymen until they could open their own shops. After 1750, however, more employers released their workers when business slowed. And from 1720 onward recessions hit frequently, creating longer spells of unemployment. As urban populations ballooned, wages shrank, while the cost of rent, food, and firewood shot up. Economic frustration bred violence. Between 1710 and 1750, for example, Boston experienced five major riots.

In the South most cities were little more than large towns, although Charles Town was North America's fourth-largest city. South Carolina's capital offered gracious living to wealthy planters during the months of heat and insect infestations on their plantations. But shanties on the city's outskirts sheltered a growing crowd of destitute whites. Like their counterparts in northern port cities, Charles Town's poor whites competed for work with urban slaves whose masters rented out their labor. Racial tensions simmered.

Middle-class urban women faced less manual drudgery than their rural counterparts. Nonetheless, they managed complex households, often including servants and other nonfamily members. Although they raised poulty and vegetables, sewed, and knitted, urban women generally purchased their cloth and most of their food. Household servants, usually young single women or widows, helped with cooking, cleaning, and laundering. Wives also worked in family businesses, usually located in the owner's home.

Widows and less affluent wives took in boarders and often spun and wove cloth for local merchants. Grim conditions in Boston forced many widows with children to look to the community for relief. Although their Puritan ancestors had seen providing care for poor dependents a matter of Christian charity, affluent Bostonians turned an increasingly wary eye toward the needy.

Slavery's Wages

From 1713 to 1754 five times as many slaves poured into mainland Anglo-America as in all the preceding years. The proportion of African-Americans in the colonies doubled, reaching 20 percent by midcentury. Fifteen percent of American slaves lived north of Maryland, mostly in New York and New Jersey.

Because West Indian and Brazilian slave buyers outbid North Americans, only 5 percent of transported Africans reached the mainland Anglo-American colonies. Mainland slaveowners, unable to buy enough male field hands, bought female workers and protected their investment by maintaining their slaves' health. These factors promoted family formation and increased life expectancy far beyond the levels in the Caribbean. By 1750 population growth among African-Americans equaled that of whites.

Masters could usually afford to keep slaves healthy, but they rarely made their human chattels comfortable. Slave upkeep generally cost 60 percent less than the maintenance of indentured servants. White servants ate 200 pounds of beef or pork a year; slaves, 50 pounds. A master would spend as much providing beer and hard cider for a servant as food and clothing for a slave. Adult slaves received eight quarts of corn and one pound of pork weekly and were expected to grow vegetables and to raise poultry.

Slaves worked for a longer portion of their lives than whites. Slave children worked part-time from the age of seven and full-time as early as eleven. African-American women performed hard work alongside men and tended tobacco and rice crops even when pregnant. Most slaves toiled until they died, although those in their sixties rarely did hard labor. The rigors of bondage, however, did not crush the slaves' spirits. Slaves proved resourceful at maximizing opportunities. Some even accumulated small amounts of property by staking out exclusive rights to their gardens and poultry. And in the Carolina and Georgia rice country, the task system gave slaves some control of their work. Under tasking, each slave spent a half day caring for a quarter acre, after which his or her duties ended. Ambitious slaves used the rest of the day to keep hogs or to grow vegetables for sale in Charles Town.

By midcentury slaves constituted 20 percent of New York City's population and formed a majority

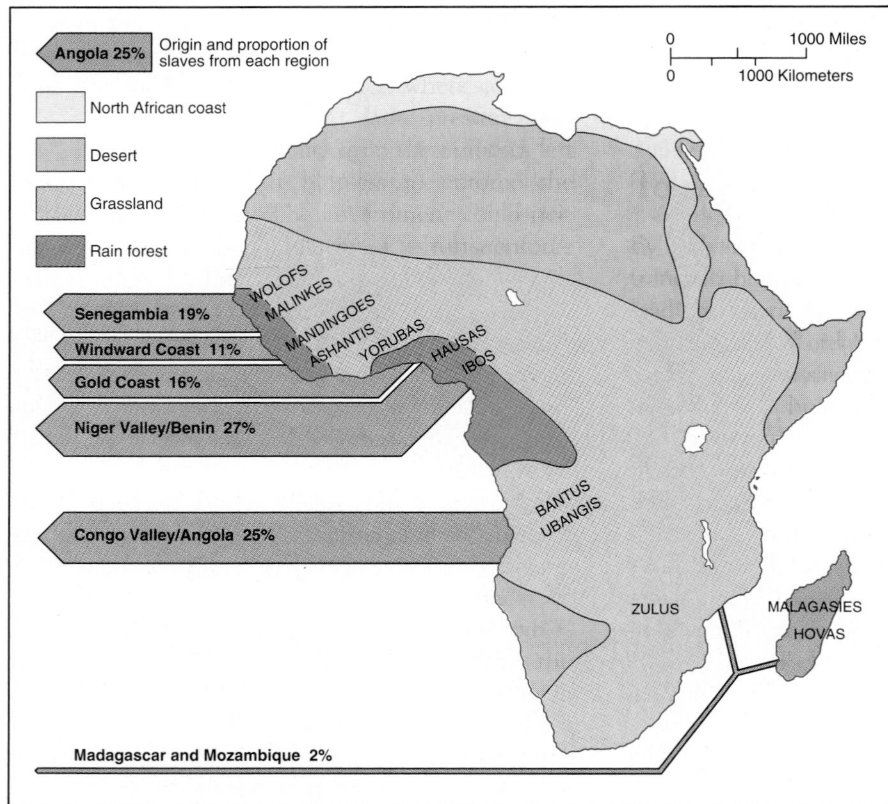

African Origins of North American Slaves, 1690–1807
Virtually all slaves brought to English North America came from West Africa, between Senegambia and Angola. Most were captured or bought inland and marched to the coast, where they were sold to African merchants who in turn sold them to European slave traders.

in Charles Town and Savannah. Skilled urban slaves hired themselves out and kept part of their wages. By 1770 one-tenth of Savannah's slaves were living in rented rooms away from their owners. Despite substantial personal freedom, they remained slaves. Although city life afforded them some freedom of association, it did not extend to them the opportunities of their owners.

The independence of South Carolina's slaves, and the fact that they constituted a majority in the colony, aroused planters' fears. To retain control, the white minority passed a number of laws restricting slaves' behavior. A 1735 law imposed a dress code limiting slaves to fabrics worth less than ten shillings a yard and prohibited their wearing their owners' cast-off clothes. Concern about the dangers of gatherings of large numbers of blacks uncontrolled by whites led in 1721 to a 9:00 P.M. curfew on blacks in Charles Town; the colony of South Carolina placed local slave patrols under the colonial militia. Slaves responded to such vigilance, and to harsher punishments, with increased incidents of arson, theft, flight, and violence.

Tensions erupted in 1739 when a slave uprising known as the Stono Rebellion jolted South Carolina. Stealing guns and ammunition from a store at the Stono River Bridge, one hundred slaves headed for Florida crying "Liberty!" Along the way they burned seven plantations and killed twenty whites. Within a day, however, mounted militiamen surrounded the runaways, cut them down, and spiked a rebel head on every milepost back to Charles Town. Whites expressed their fears in a new slave code stipulating constant surveillance for slaves. The code threatened masters with fines for not disciplining slaves and required legislative approval for manumission (the freeing of individual slaves). The Stono Rebellion thus accelerated South Carolina's emergence as a racist and fear-ridden society. The rebels' failure showed slaves that armed uprisings were suicidal. After the uprising slaves' resistance took the form of feigning stupidity, running away, committing arson or sabotage, or poisoning masters. Not until 1831 would significant slave violence of a comparable scale erupt on the mainland.

The Carolinas' phenomenal economic and political success cost innumerable lives and untold suffering for enslaved blacks and displaced Native Americans. Whites meanwhile lived in an atmosphere of anxiety. Grim reality had triumphed over hazy English dreams of a stable society.

The Rise of the Colonial Elites

For white colonial Americans, wealth defined status. "A man who has money here, no matter how he came by it, he is everything," wrote a Rhode Islander in 1748. Once wealthy, a man was expected to be responsible, dignified, and generous and to act as a community leader—to act like a gentleman. His wife was expected to be a skillful household manager and a refined, yet deferential hostess—a lady.

Before 1700 class structure in the colonies was relatively invisible; the rural elite spent its resources on land, servants, and slaves instead of conspicuous luxuries. A traveler visiting one of Virginia's richest planters noted that his host owned only "good beds but no curtains and instead of cane chairs . . . stools made of wood." After 1720, however, the display of wealth became more ostentatious. The greater gentry—the richest 2 percent of the population—built splendid estate homes such as New Jersey's Low House and Virginia's Shirley Mansion. The lesser gentry, or second-wealthiest 2 to 10 percent, lived in more modest fieldstone or wood-frame houses, and middle-class farmers typically inhabited one-story wooden buildings with four small rooms.

The gentry also exhibited their wealth after 1720 by living in the European "grand style." They wore costly English fashions, drove carriages, and bought expensive china, books, and furniture. They pursued a gracious life by studying foreign languages, learning formal dances, and cultivating polite manners. Horse racing replaced cockfighting as a preferred spectator sport. A few young colonial males received English educations.

Chesapeake planters, even the frugal, accumulated debt. Tobacco planters, perpetually short of cash, were in hock to British merchants who bought their crops and sold them expensive goods on credit. Planters had two options. They could strive for self-sufficiency, or they could diversify by growing wheat or cutting timber. Both self-sufficiency and economic diversification became more widespread as the eighteenth century progressed.

In eighteenth-century colonial cities wealth remained concentrated. New York's wealthiest 10 percent owned 45 percent of the property. Similar patterns characterized Philadelphia and Boston. Juxtaposed against the growth of a poor urban underclass, these statistics underscored the polarization of status and wealth in urban America on the eve of the Revolution. No American cities, however, experienced the vast gulf between wealth and poverty typical of European cities.

Elites and Colonial Politics

The colonial elite dominated politics as well as society. Governors appointed members of the greater gentry to serve on councils and as judges in the highest courts. The upper gentry, along with militia majors and colonels, also dominated among the representatives elected to the legislatures' lower houses (the assemblies). Members of the lesser gentry sat less often in the legislatures, but they commonly served as justices of the peace in the county courts.

Outside New England property restrictions barred 80 percent of white men from running for the assembly. In any case few ordinary citizens could have afforded the high costs of elective office. Assemblymen received meager living expenses, which did not cover the cost of staying at the capital,

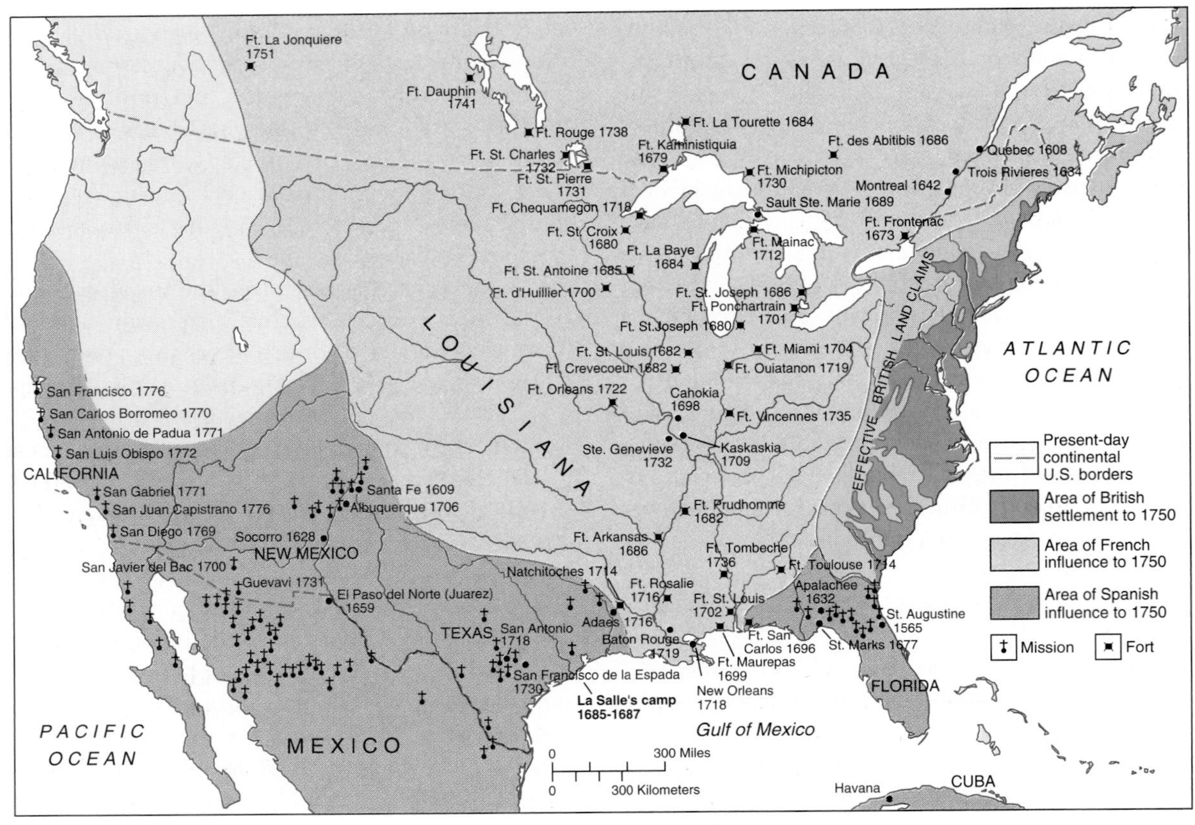

French and Spanish Occupation of North America, to 1776
French fur traders became entrenched along the Great Lakes and upper Mississippi River between 1666 and 1700, after which they built many settlements in territory claimed by Spain along the Gulf of Mexico. Spanish colonization was concentrated in Florida, central Texas, the Rio Grande Valley, and (after 1769) southern California.

much less make up for six to ten weeks of missed work. Even members of the gentry grumbled about legislative duty, many of them viewing it as "a sort of tax . . . to serve the public at their own Expense besides the neglect of their business." Consequently, political leadership fell to a small number of wealthy families with a tradition of public service.

The colonies generally set liberal qualifications for male voters, but all excluded women, blacks, and Indians from voting. In seven colonies voters had to own land (usually forty to fifty acres), and in the others they had to have enough property to furnish a house and to work a farm. Most of the 40 percent who could not meet these requirements were indentured servants, single sons living with parents, or young men just beginning family life. Most white males in Anglo-America could vote by age forty, whereas across the Atlantic, two-thirds of all Englishmen and 90 percent of Irishmen could never vote.

Rural voting participation was low, averaging 45 percent. Governors called elections randomly so that after years without an election one could be called on short notice. Voters in isolated areas often did not know of an upcoming election. Voting took place at the county seat, and many voters did not risk traveling long distances over poor roads to reach the voting place. In many colonies voters stated their preference publicly, often face to face with the candidates, a practice that discouraged dissenters. There were no political parties to stimulate popular interest or to mobilize voters. Candidates nominated themselves and ran on their reputations, not on issues.

In view of these factors, political indifference was widespread. For example, to avoid paying legislators' expenses, many Massachusetts towns refused to elect assemblymen. From 1731 to 1760 one-third of South Carolina's elected assemblymen neglected to take their seats. Apathy might have been even greater had not candidates plied voters with alcohol. George Washington dispensed almost two quarts of liquor for each voter when first elected to Virginia's assembly in 1758.

Only in the major seaports did political life flourish. Here greater population density, better communications, and the use of secret ballots (except in New York) accounted for a relatively high voter turnout. Furthermore, the cities' acute economic difficulties stimulated political participation among voters, ever hopeful that government might ease their problems.

The most important political development after 1700 was the rise of the assembly as the dominant force in colonial government. Except in Connecticut and Rhode Island, the crown or proprietors chose colonial governors, who in turn named a council, or upper legislative house. Only in the lower house, or assembly, could members of the gentry defend their interests. Until 1689 governors and councils drafted laws, and the assemblies generally followed passively. Thereafter assemblies assumed a more central role in politics as colonial leaders argued that their legislatures should exercise the same rights as Parliament. Indeed, they viewed their assemblies as miniature Houses of Commons and believed that colonial governors should be as restricted as monarchs. Parliament's victory in the Glorious Revolution convinced Americans that their governors had limited powers and should defer to the assemblies.

The lower houses refused to permit meddling in their procedures, took control over taxes and budgets, and kept a tight rein on executive salaries. Governors remained vulnerable to such financial pressure: they received no salary from Britain and relied on the assemblies for income. This "power of the purse" often forced governors to sign laws opposed by the crown.

Moreover, Britain's lack of interest in colonial politics allowed the assemblies to seize considerable power. The Board of Trade, established by Parliament in 1696 to monitor American affairs, had neither the staff, the energy, nor the vision to maintain royal authority by supporting embattled governors. This vacuum in royal power allowed the colonies to become self-governing in most respects except for regulating trade, printing money, and declaring war. This autonomy, reinforced by self-assertive assemblies, would haunt British authorities when they attempted to exercise more direct rule after 1763 (see Chapter 5).

From 1700 to 1750, then, class distinctions sharpened as many colonists flourished and some grew wealthy. The upper classes' hold on wealth ensured their domination of public life.

Competing for a Continent

Europeans transformed North America in the first half of the eighteenth century as they expanded their territorial claims, opened new areas for settlement, and engaged in more intensive trade and warfare with Native Americans. In turn, Native Americans welcomed some of these developments and resisted others.

France and Native Americans

With the end of the War of the Spanish Succession in 1713, France aggressively expanded and strengthened its North American empire, especially Louisiana. The French began to settle the mouth of the Mississippi and its environs, founding New Orleans in 1718. French traders moved onto the southern plains, exchanging goods, including guns, with Comanches and other Plains tribes that raided Spanish Texas.

Louisiana quickly acquired a foul reputation, and few French immigrated there willingly. To boost its population, the government sent paupers and criminals, recruited German refugees, and encouraged slave importation. By 1732 two-thirds of lower Louisiana's 5,800 people were slaves. Life was dismal for everyone. Corruption riddled local government, famine threatened constantly, and the missionary priests quarreled among themselves.

Louisiana's sluggish export economy forced settlers and slaves to find other means of support. Like the Indians, they hunted, fished, gathered wild plants, and cultivated gardens. And red, white, and black Louisianans traded with one another. Indians provided corn, tallow, and above all deerskins to merchants in return for blankets, kettles, axes, chickens, hogs, guns, and alcohol. Indians from west of the Mississippi brought horses and cattle, usually stolen from Spanish ranches in Texas. West African slaves, familiar with cattle from their homelands, managed many of Louisiana's herds; some became rustlers and illicit traders of beef.

French attention also turned to the Ohio Valley, which, thanks to Iroquois neutrality, had become a refuge for dislocated Native American tribes such as the Kickapoos, Shawnees, and Delawares. In order to counter growing English influence and to secure commercial and diplomatic ties with the Indians, the French expanded their trade. Several French posts, including Detroit, ballooned into sizable villages of Indian, French, and mixed-ancestry residents. Nonetheless, increased English trade in the area led most Indians to prefer an independent course.

Although the French were generally more successful than the English among the Indians, the French never won over the Chickasaws, who were supported by Carolina and whose frequent attacks made life miserable for the French and their Indian allies. Another southeastern tribe, the Creeks, played French, Spanish, and British off against one another, while the Fox Indians kept French traders from direct contact with Sioux tribes. In 1729–1730 the French brutally suppressed the Natchez Indians, the last of the Mississippian peoples, in order to open up land in Louisiana for tobacco and sugar cultivation.

By 1744 French traders had explored as far west as North Dakota and Colorado, buying beaver pelts and Indian slaves on the Great Plains. These traders and their competitors spread trade goods, including guns, to Native Americans throughout central Canada and the Plains. Meanwhile, Indians in the southern Plains and Great Basin had acquired horses from the thousands left behind by fleeing Spaniards after the Pueblo Revolt of 1680. Horses and guns enabled tribes such as the Lakota Sioux and Comanche to move onto the Plains and build a new, highly mobile way of life based on the pursuit of the buffalo. Widely scattered settlements along the Mississippi in modern-day Illinois and Missouri completed France's domain, an immense territory precariously dependent on often shaky relations with Native Americans.

Native Americans and British Expansion

The depopulation and dislocation of Native Americans made possible the colonies' rapid expansion. Epidemic diseases, environmental changes, war, and political pressure opened new land for Europeans. Pennsylvania coerced the Delawares into selling more than 50,000 acres between 1729 and 1734. In 1735 the colony's leaders produced a patently fraudulent treaty, dated to 1686, in which the Delawares promised to sell their land as far west as a man could walk in a day and a half. The colony hired three men to walk west as fast as they could. They covered nearly 60 miles, forcing the Delawares to cede 1,200 square miles of land in what became known as the Walking Purchase. The Delawares were forced to move, and the proprietors made a huge profit from land sales.

By helping remove the Delawares from Pennsylvania, the Iroquois tried to accommodate the English and consolidate their own power. Late in the seventeenth century the Iroquois had entered into a series of agreements, known as the Covenant Chain, to relocate Indians whose lands the colonists desired. These tribes were moved to areas of New York and Pennsylvania, on the periphery of the Iroquois' homeland, to serve as buffers against English expansion. By agreeing to the covenant, and by incorporating the Tuscaroras into their confederacy, the Iroquois created a center of Native American power distinct from, but cooperative with, the British.

Indians elsewhere along the westward-moving frontier faced pressure from settlers on one side and the Iroquois on the other. For example, having earlier abandoned some villages being encroached on by white settlers, the Catawbas of the Carolina piedmont, facing a dramatic decrease in wild game, moved westward and ran into the Iroquois. To counter the Iroquois, whose alliances with most of the northern colonies left them well armed, the Catawbas turned for aid to South Carolina. By ceding land and helping to defend that colony against other Indians, the Catawbas received guns, food, and clothing. Temporarily, their relationship with the English afforded the Catawbas security. But the growing gap in numbers between them and the settlers, and their competition with settlers for resources, made the Indians vulnerable and dependent.

British Settlement in the South: Georgia

In 1732 Parliament chartered a new colony, Georgia. It was to be a refuge for debtors, whose settlement would buffer South Carolina against attacks from Spanish Florida. Further, the new English colony would export expensive commodities such as wine and silk. To fulfill these plans, Parliament even spent money on the colony, the only North American colony except Nova Scotia in which the British government invested.

James Oglethorpe, who dominated the provincial board of trustees, shaped Georgia's early years. He established the port of entry, Savannah, in 1733. By 1740 nearly 3,000 colonists resided in Georgia. Almost half were non-English, immigrants from Germany, Switzerland, and Scotland, and most had their overseas passage paid by the government. A small number of Jews were among the early settlers. Thus Georgia began as the least English colony.

Idealism and concerns about security led Oglethorpe to ban slavery from Georgia. "If we allow slaves," he wrote to the trustees, "we act against the very principles by which we associated together, which was to relieve the distressed." Olglethorpe thought that slavery degraded blacks, made whites lazy, and presented a terrible risk. Aware of the Stono Rebellion, he worried that reliance on slave labor courted a slave revolt. Parliament thus made Georgia the only colony where slavery was forbidden. Oglethorpe also tried to bar the importation of rum. An abstainer from hard liquor, he feared the effects of encouraging local Indians to drink.

Oglethorpe's well-intentioned plans failed completely. Few debtors arrived because of Parliament's restrictions on their release from prison. Limitations that Oglethorpe had secured on settlers' rights to enlarge or sell their holdings discouraged immigrants, as did the ban on slavery. Georgia exported neither wine nor silk; only rice proved profitable. After a decade of struggle against economic reality, Oglethorpe yielded. In 1750 slavery became legal, and restrictions on landholdings vanished. As a result, Georgia boomed. Its 4,000 residents of 1750 mushroomed to 23,000 by 1770, almost half of them African-American.

Georgia's founding completed British settlement of the Atlantic seaboard. After 1750 westward expansion virtually halted—Anglo-Americans would not cross the Appalachians until the 1770s—but the population continued to grow at the rapid rates that Franklin had predicted.

Spain's Struggles

While trying to maintain an empire in the face of Native American, French, and British adversaries, Spain spread its language and culture over much of North America, especially the Southwest. To repopulate New Mexico with settlers after the Pueblo Revolt (see Chapter 3), Spain handed out huge land grants and constructed fortifications, primarily for defense against the Apaches. Settlers typically built houses on small lots around the church plaza, farmed separate fields nearby, grazed livestock, and shared community woodlands and pasture. Livestock-raising *ranchos* (ranches) monopolized vast amounts of land along the Rio Grande and blocked the establishment of further towns. On these *ranchos* mounted herders of cattle and sheep *(vaqueros)* created the way of life later adopted by the American cowboy, featuring lariat and roping skills, cattle drives, and roundups.

By 1750 New Mexico contained just 5,200 Spanish and 13,500 Pueblos. Intergrated into New Mexico society, most Pueblos practiced both Catholicism and their traditional religion. Along the frontier, Navajos and Apaches made peace with New Mexico to gain support against raids by Utes from the north and Comanches from the east.

To counter growing French influence among the Comanches and other Native Americans on the southern plains, Spain colonized Texas. In 1716 the Spanish established four missions. The most successful of the missions was San Antonio de Valero, where friars constructed a fortified building known as the Alamo. The Spanish presence in Texas remained light, however; by midcentury only 1,200 Spaniards and 1,300 mission Indians lived there under constant threat of Indian raids.

By 1750 the French and Spanish empires had reached their limits in North America. Spain controlled much of the Southeast and Southwest, and France claimed the Mississippi, Ohio, and Missouri River valleys. Both empires, spread thin, depended heavily on Indian goodwill. In contrast, British North America, compact and aggressively expansionist, was generally antagonistic toward Native Americans.

Enlightenment and Awakening

Eighteenth-century Anglo-America was probably the world's most literate society. Ninety percent of New England's adult white males and 40 percent of its women could write well enough to sign documents. In other colonies the literacy rate varied from 35 to 50 percent. In contrast, in England it stood at just over 30 percent. Nevertheless, ordinary Americans' reading encompassed only a few books: an almanac, a psalter, and the Bible. They inhabited a world of oral culture, in which ideas and information were passed through the spoken word—in conversations, debates, and sermons.

However, members of the gentry, well-off merchants, and educated ministers lived in a world of print culture. Though costly, books and writing paper opened eighteenth-century European civilization to men and women of these classes who could read. And a rich, exciting world it was. Great advances in natural science seemed to explain the laws of nature, human intelligence appeared poised to triumph over ignorance and prejudice, and life itself would surely become more pleasant. For those with time to read and think, an age of optimism and progress had dawned: the Enlightenment.

The Enlightenment in America

American intellectuals drew inspiration from Enlightenment ideals, which combined confidence in reason with skepticism toward beliefs not based on science or logic. Enlightenment thought drew on the work of the English physicist Sir Isaac Newton (1642–1727), who explained how gravitation ruled the universe. Newton's work demonstrated the harmony of natural laws and stimulated others to search for rational principles in medicine, law, psychology, and government.

No American more embodied the Enlightenment spirit than Benjamin Franklin (1706–1790). Born in Boston, Franklin migrated to Philadelphia at age seventeen, bringing considerable assets: skill as a printer, ambition, and insatiable curiosity. Within a few years he had gathered a small group of other young men with a zest for learning into a club called the Junto. Its members pledged to debate highbrow questions and to collect useful information for their "mutual improvement." In 1732 Franklin began publishing *Poor Richard's Almanack*, a collection of proverbs that made him famous. By age forty-two he had saved enough money to retire from printing and to devote himself to science and community service.

To Franklin, science and community service were intertwined; true science would make everyone's life more comfortable. For example, his experiments in flying a kite during a thunderstorm proved that lightning was electricity and led to the invention of the lightning rod. In 1743 Franklin organized the American Philosophical Society to encourage "all philosophical experiments that let light into the nature of things, tend to increase the power of man over matter, and multiply the conveniences and pleasures of life." By 1769 the society had blossomed into an intercolonial network of amateur scientists.

Although some plantation owners, among them Thomas Jefferson, championed the Enlightenment, it flourished in the seaboard cities, where the latest ideas from Europe circulated and gentlemen and artisans met in small societies to investigate nature. To these individuals, the Royal Society in London, the foremost learned society in the English-speaking world, represented the ideal. The Enlightenment thus initially strengthened ties between British and colonial elites. Its adherents envisioned progress as gradual and proceeding from the top down. They trusted reason far more than they trusted the common people, whose judgment seemed too easily deranged.

Just as Newton inspired the scientific bent of Enlightenment intellectuals, the English philosopher John Locke's *Essay Concerning Human Understanding* (1690) led many to embrace "reasonable" or "rational" religion. Locke contended that ideas are not inborn but are acquired by investigation of, and reflection on, experience. Enlightenment intellectuals believed that the study of the harmony and order of nature provided the best argument for God, a rational Creator. A handful insisted that where the Bible conflicted with reason, one should follow reason. Those—including Franklin and Jefferson—who took the argument furthest were called Deists. They concluded that God, having created a perfect universe, did not miraculously intervene in its workings but instead left it alone to operate according to natural law.

Most Americans influenced by the Enlightenment described themselves as Christians and attended church. But they feared Christianity's excesses, especially the influence of fanatics who persecuted others in religion's name and of "enthusiasts" who claimed miraculous visions and direct mandates from God. Before 1740 colonial intellectuals associated fanaticism and bigotry with the early Puritans and looked on their own time as an era of progressive reasonableness. But a series of religious revivals known as the Great Awakening would shatter their complacency.

The Great Awakening

Rationalists viewed the world as orderly and predictable. Many Americans, however, had neither worldly goods nor orderly and predictable lives. A diphtheria epidemic in 1737–1738 that killed every tenth child under sixteen from New Hampshire to Pennsylvania starkly reminded the colonists how fragile life was and turned their thoughts to religion.

A quickening of religious fervor in scattered places in the 1730s became passionate revivalism throughout Anglo-America in the 1740s. This "Great Awakening" cut across lines of class, status, and education as even elites realized the inadequacy of reason alone to move their hearts. Above all, the Great Awakening represented an unleashing of anxiety and longing among ordinary people living in a world of oral culture—anxiety about sin, longing for salvation. And it was the spoken word that brought the answers that they craved. But for all—colonial elites comfortable in the print world and commoners accustomed to the oral world—religion was primarily a matter of emotional commitment.

In contrast to rationalists, who stressed the human potential for betterment, the ministers of the Great Awakening emphasized the corruption of human nature, the fury of divine wrath, and the need for immediate repentance. Although well aware of contemporary philosophy and science,

Jonathan Edwards (1703–1758)
Edwards is best known for his sermon "Sinners in the Hands of an Angry God," which warned the wicked of the terrible punishments awaiting them in the afterlife.

Congregationalist minister Jonathan Edwards drove home this message with breathtaking clarity. In 1735 during a revival in Northampton, Massachusetts, Edwards preached his great sermon "Sinners in the Hands of an Angry God." "The God that holds you over the pit of Hell, much as one holds a spider or other loathsome insect over the fire, abhors you," Edwards intoned. "His wrath toward you burns like fire; He looks upon you as worthy of nothing else but to be cast into the fire."

Other colonial ministers—Presbyterian William Tennent and Dutch Reformed Theodore Frelinghuysen—had anticipated Edwards's fire-and-brimstone style. Pulling the diverse threads of revival together was the arrival in 1739 of the charismatic English cleric George Whitefield. A man of overpowering presence and a booming voice, Whitefield attracted some crowds exceeding 20,000. On a tour through the colonies Whitefield inspired thousands, mainly young adults, to seek salvation. Within four years of Whitefield's arrival, 20 percent of those under age forty-five had been "born again."

Whitefield's powerful allure awed even his critics. But divisions over the revivals developed in Whitefield's wake and were widened by the tactics of his most extreme followers. For example, after leaving Boston in October 1740, Whitefield invited Gilbert Tennent (William's son) to follow "in order to blow up the divine flame lately kindled there." Denouncing Boston's established clergy as "dead Drones" and lashing out at elites, Tennent built a following among the poor and downtrodden.

Exposing colonial society's divisions, Tennent and other radicals corroded support for revivals among established ministers and officials. Increasingly, lines hardened between the revivalists, the "New Lights," and the rationalist clergymen, or "Old Lights," who dominated the Anglican, Presbyterian, and Congregational churches. In 1740 Gilbert Tennent hinted that most Presbyterian ministers lacked saving grace and were bound for hell, and he urged parishioners to abandon them for the New Lights. By sowing doubts about ministers, Tennent undermined one of the foundations of the social order, for if people could not trust their ministers, whom *could* they trust? Old Light rationalists fired back. In 1742 Charles Chauncy, a Boston Congregationalist, condemned revivals as an epidemic of the "enthusiasm" that Enlightened intellectuals so hated. Chauncy especially blasted enthusiasts who mistook the ravings of their overheated imaginations for direct communications from God.

The Great Awakening thus split American Protestantism. In 1741 Old and New Light Presbyterians formed rival branches that reunited in 1758 when the revivalists emerged victorious. The Anglican church lost many members to New Light Presbyterians and Baptists. Congregationalists also splintered badly; by 1760 New Lights had seceded from one-third of all churches and formed separate parishes.

In Massachusetts and Connecticut, where the Congregational church was established by law, the secession of New Light parishes provoked bitter conflict. Old Lights denied new parishes legal status and tried to force New Lights into paying tithes to their former churches. Many New Lights were expelled from the legislature. In Windham County, Connecticut, an extra story was added to the jail to hold the New Lights arrested for failure to pay tithes.

The Great Awakening peaked in 1742 but made steady gains into the 1770s, and its long-term effects far exceeded its immediate impact. First, the revival started a decline in the influence of older sects such as the Quakers, Anglicans, and Congregationalists. In turn, the number of Presbyterians and Baptists increased after 1740, and that of Methodists rose steadily after 1770. These churches have since dominated American Protestantism. Second, the Great Awakening stimulated the founding of new colleges unscarred by religious wars. The College of New Jersey (Princeton, 1746), King's College (Columbia, 1754), the College of Rhode Island (Brown, 1764), Queen's College (Rutgers, 1766), and Dartmouth (1769) trace their roots to this era. Third, the revival drew many African Americans and Native Americans to Protestantism for the first time. Its oral and communal nature and emphasis on piety, rather than learning, blended aspects of both groups' traditional cultures. The Great Awakening marked the real emergence of black Protestantism as New Lights reached out to slaves, some of whom joined white churches and even preached at revival meetings. Meanwhile, a few New Light preachers became missionaries to Indians still residing in the colonies. Some Christian Indians, such as the Mohegan Samson Occom, became preachers themselves.

The Great Awakening, moreover, gave women added prominence in colonial religion. For several decades ministers had praised women—the majority of church members—as the embodiment of Christian piety. Now some New Light sects, mainly Baptist and Congregationalist, granted women the right to speak and vote in church meetings. Some women, like Anne Hutchinson a century earlier, presided over prayer meetings that included women, men, and sometimes even slaves. Unlike Anne Hutchinson, none was prosecuted. The Great Awakening also fostered religious tolerance by blurring theological differences among New Lights. Indeed, revivalism's emphasis on inner experience, rather than doctrinal fine points, helped to prepare Americans to accept the denominational pluralism that emerged after the Revolution.

Historians disagree about whether the Great Awakening had political effects. Although New Lights flayed the wealthy, they neither advocated a social revolution nor developed a political ideology. Yet by empowering ordinary people to criticize those in authority, the revivals laid the groundwork for political revolutionaries a generation later who would preach that royal government had grown corrupt and unworthy of obedience.

CONCLUSION

By the 1750s the mainland British colonies had matured. For fifty years their wealth and population had risen impressively. The mainland colonies were more populous than Scotland and almost one-third the size of England. White colonists' living standard equaled that of England. Literacy was widespread in the northern mainland colonies, and Anglo-America had more institutions of higher learning than England, Scotland, and Ireland combined. Britain and its colonies were a far more formidable presence in North America than their French and Spanish rivals. But after France's defeat, and Spain's weakening, in the Seven Years' War (1756–1763), latent tensions in colonial relations with Britain quickly became irreconcilable differences.

CHRONOLOGY

1651–1733 Parliament creates the navigation system to regulate British imperial commerce.

1660 Restoration of the Stuart dynasty to the English throne.

1685 Duke of York becomes King James II of England.

1686–1689 Dominion of New England.

1688 Glorious Revolution in England; James II deposed.

1689 William and Mary ascend to English throne.
Protestant Association seizes power in Maryland.
Leisler's Rebellion in New York.

1689–1697 King William's War (in Europe, War of the League of Augsburg).

1690 John Locke, *Essay Concerning Human Understanding*.

1698 French begin settlements near the mouth of the Mississippi River.

1701 Iroquois adopt neutrality policy toward European powers.

1702–1713 Queen Anne's War (in Europe, War of the Spanish Succession).

1716 San Antonio founded.

1718 New Orleans founded.

1732 Georgia colony chartered.
Benjamin Franklin begins publishing *Poor Richard's Almanack*.

1734 "Walking Purchase" of Delaware Indians in Pennsylvania.

1735 Jonathan Edwards leads revival in Northhampton, Massachusetts.

1739 Great Awakening begins.
Stono Rebellion in South Carolina.

1739–1744 Anglo-Spanish War.

1750 Slavery legalized in Georgia.

FOR FURTHER READING

Bernard Bailyn, *The Peopling of British North America: An Introduction* (1986). A brief interpretive overview of the causes and effects of European immigration to British North America.

Bernard Bailyn and Philip D. Morgan, eds., *Strangers Within the Realm: Cultural Margins of the First British Empire* (1991). Essays by leading historians examine the interplay of ethnicity and empire occurring in North America, the Caribbean, Scotland, and Ireland.

Richard L. Bushman, *From Puritan to Yankee: Character and the Social Order in Connecticut, 1690–1765* (1967). The best examination of social and cultural transformation in any eighteenth-century colony.

Rhys Isaac, *The Transformation of Virginia, 1740–1790* (1982). Pulitzer Prize–winning study of class relationships, race relations, and folkways during the Great Awakening and American Revolution.

John J. McCusker and Russell R. Menard, *The Economy of British America, 1607–1789*, rev. ed. (1991). A comprehensive discussion of the colonial economy in light of current scholarship.

James H. Merrell, *The Indians' New World: Catawbas and Their Neighbors from European Contact Through the Era of Removal* (1989). A pathbreaking examination, with broad implications for understanding the Native American past, of the interaction between South Carolina colonists and Catawba Indians.

Gary B. Nash, *The Urban Crucible: The Northern Seaports and the Origins of the American Revolution*, abridged ed. (1986). A study of social, economic, and political change in Boston, New York, and Philadelphia during the eighteenth century.

Timothy Silver, *A New Face on the Countryside: Indians, Colonists, and Slaves in South Atlantic Forests, 1500–1800* (1990). A highly readable discussion of the interactions of humans and their environment in one region.

Peter H. Wood, *Black Majority: Negroes in Colonial South Carolina from 1670 Through the Stono Rebellion* (1974). An engrossing study of slavery, racism, and African-American life in the lower South.

CHAPTER 5

The Road to Revolution, 1744–1776

By 1763 Britain had defeated France, its chief competitor for preeminence in North America, and stood at the height of eighteenth-century imperial power. British rule ran undisputed from the Atlantic seacoast to the Mississippi River and from northernmost Canada to the Florida straits. Ironically, this greatest of British triumphs would turn into one of the greatest of British defeats.

The imperial reorganization that war and conquest made necessary after 1763 radically altered Britain's relationship with its American colonies. Conflict arose between Britain and the colonies when Parliament, searching for ways to pay off the enormous debt accumulated during the war, attempted to tighten control over colonial affairs. The colonists, accustomed to legislating for themselves, widely resisted this effort to centralize decision making in London. American leaders interpreted Britain's clampdown as calculated antagonism, intended to deprive them of both prosperity and relative independence.

(Right) **Captain and Mrs. John Purves** *(detail), by Henry Benbridge, 1775*

Other groups, nonelites, had their own perspectives, shaped as much by social-economic tensions as by constitutional crisis. In port cities crowds of poor and working people clashed with British authority in sometimes violent demonstrations, in concert with or in defiance of elite radicals. In remote "backcountry" areas settlers used the language and ideas of urban radicals to resist domination by large landowners and seaboard elites. Throughout the colonies women brought their own perspective to the unfolding crisis.

Colonial resistance to British policies also reflected democratic stirrings in America and throughout the North Atlantic world. Among the products of this democratic urge were both the American Revolution, which erupted in 1776, and the French Revolution, which soon followed in 1789.

Despite apprehension among colonial politicians, they expressed their opposition peacefully from 1763 to 1775, through legislative resolutions and commercial boycotts. Even after fighting erupted, the colonists agonized for more than a year about whether to sever their political relationship with England—which even native-born Americans sometimes referred to affectionately as "home." Of all the world's colonial peoples, none became rebels more reluctantly than Anglo-Americans did in 1776.

Imperial Warfare

Imperial rivalries between England, on the one hand, and France and Spain, on the other, triggered two major wars that spilled into North America. The War of the Austrian Succession (1740–1748), known as King George's War to the colonists, saw England and its allies emerge victorious. Within a few years the conflict resumed as the Seven Years' War (1756–1763). England and France fought these wars not on the continent of Europe but on the high seas; in India, where they were competing for influence among local rulers; and in North America. Despite the European roots of these conflicts, few colonists doubted that their continued prosperity depended on British victories.

The wars produced mixed results. They strengthened the bonds between the British and the Anglo-Americans as they fought side by side. But the conclusion of each war planted the seeds first of misunderstanding, then of suspicion, and finally of hostility between the former compatriots.

King George's War

King George's War followed the pattern of earlier conflicts in the colonies. Battles generally involved fewer than 600 men, and skirmishes consisted of raids along the New French–British frontier. In attacks on New England frontier towns, the French and Indians killed or captured many civilians. Some captives, particularly women and children, chose to remain with their captors after the conflict ended.

King George's War produced a single major engagement. In 1745 almost 4,000 New Englanders assaulted the French bastion of Louisbourg in northern Nova Scotia, which guarded the entrance to the St. Lawrence River. The raw American recruits battered away at the fortress's 250 cannons and thirty-foot-high stone walls for almost seven weeks. Victory cost the Americans only 167 men and brought them control of the fortress and 1,500 prisoners.

But the triumph proved short-lived. In the treaty signed with the French in 1748, Britain traded Louisbourg back to France in exchange for a British outpost in India. The memory of how the stunning achievement at Louisbourg went for naught would embitter the colonists for a decade.

A Fragile Peace

Neither Britain nor France emerged from King George's War as the dominant power in North America, and each prepared for another war. Although French forts remained on British soil in New York and Nova Scotia, the Ohio Valley became the tinderbox for conflict.

For more than half a century Indians—Delawares, Shawnees, and others—had sought

refuge in the Ohio Valley. Initially welcomed as trade partners and bulwarks against English expansion, these Indians irritated the French by their independence, especially their willingness to trade with Anglo-Americans and to fight against France in King George's War. The French derided these Native Americans as "republicans" for their defiance of all outside authority, whether of the French or English or the Iroquois, some of whom had also moved to the area.

By the mid-eighteenth century these "republican" Indians were seeking to balance the French and British off against each other, while the two powers grew increasingly impatient with the Indians' neutrality. After King George's War Virginia pressured some Iroquois into ceding western lands occupied by the Delawares and agreeing to the construction of a fortified trading post at the junction of the Allegheny and Monongahela rivers—the site of modern Pittsburgh, headwaters of the Ohio River, and key to the Ohio Valley. The "republican" Indians consequently began to fear that the English represented the greater threat.

By 1752 Virginia, Pennsylvania, France, the Iroquois, and the "republican" Indians had all claimed the Ohio Valley. In 1753 France started building a chain of forts in order to regain control of the Virginia and Pennsylvania Indian trade. Virginia retaliated by sending a twenty-one-year-old surveyor, George Washington, to demand that the French abandon their forts. When the French refused, Washington recommended that Virginia occupy the point where the Monongahela and Allegheny rivers joined. In 1754 he led 300 colonial volunteers and 100 British regulars west, only to find the French already constructing Fort Duquesne at the juncture of the rivers. Washington withdrew sixty miles southeast to build a crude defensive post christened Fort Necessity, near which his men killed several French soldiers in an ambush that brought swift retaliation. On July 4, 1754, with one-fourth of his men dead, Washington surrendered Fort Necessity.

In mid-1754 seven northern colonies sent delegates to Albany, New York, to plan their mutual defense in the face of certain French retaliation. By showering the wavering Iroquois with wagonloads of presents, the colonists bought Iroquois neutrality. The delegates endorsed a plan for a colonial confederation, the Albany Plan of Union, drawn up by Pennsylvania's Benjamin Franklin and Massachusetts's Thomas Hutchinson. However, the Albany Plan collapsed because no colonial legislature would surrender control over its powers of taxation, not even to fellow Americans and in the face of grave danger. But the Albany Plan would provide a precedent for future American unity.

The Seven Years' War in America

Although France and Britain remained at peace in Europe until 1756, Washington's action at Fort Necessity had created a virtual state of war in North America. In response, nearly 8,000 colonists enlisted in 1755 to attack the French strongholds in New York and Nova Scotia. The British government sent General Edward Braddock and 1,000 regulars to take Fort Duquesne that same year.

Scornful of colonial soldiers, Braddock expected his disciplined regulars to make short work of the French. He only dimly perceived the strength and resourcefulness of the forces gathering against him. Washington's failure at Fort Necessity and Braddock's arrogance wiped out hope of any Indian support. On July 9, 1755, about 850 French and Indians ambushed Braddock's 2,200 Britons and Virginians near Fort Duquesne. After three hours of steady fire, the British regulars broke and retreated, leaving Washington's Virginians to cover the withdrawal. Nine hundred regular soldiers and colonists died, including Braddock.

After Braddock's defeat Indian raids convulsed Pennsylvania, Maryland, Virginia, and New Jersey. Two thousand New Englanders managed to seize two French forts that were threatening Nova Scotia. In the aftermath thousands of French-Canadians, or Acadians, were driven from Nova Scotia, and their villages were burned. French Louisiana became the new home for many of these people, who became known there as Cajuns.

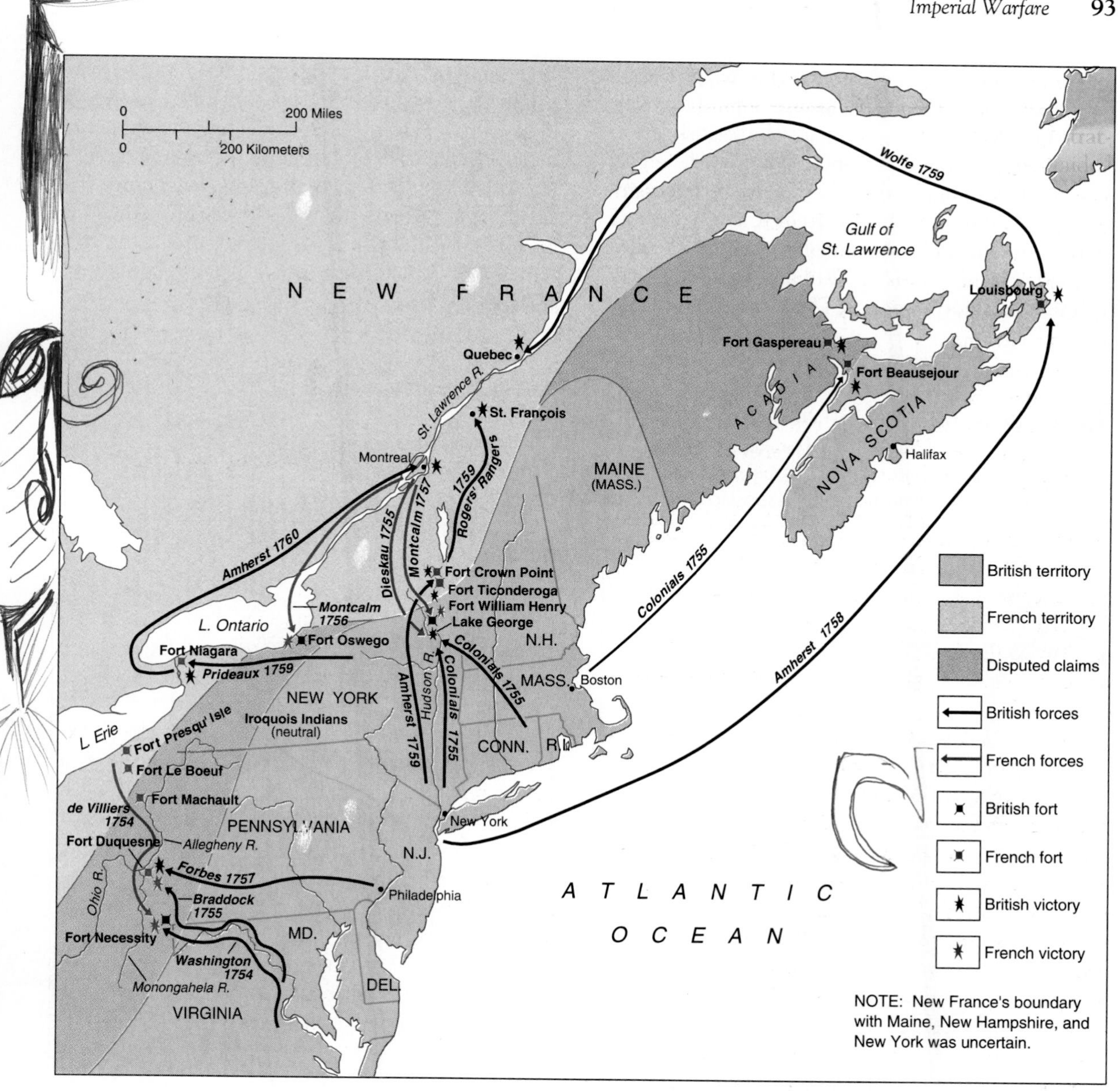

The Seven Years' War in America *After experiencing major defeats early in the war, Anglo-American forces turned the tide against the French by taking Fort Duquesne and Louisbourg in 1758. After Canada fell in 1760, the fighting shifted to Spain's Caribbean colonies.*

In 1756–1757 New France's daring commanding general Louis Joseph Montcalm maintained the offensive. Anglo-Americans outnumbered Canadians twenty to one, but Montcalm benefited from large numbers of French regulars, Indian support (including that of the neutral but usually British-leaning Iroquois), and full-scale mobilization of the Canadian population. The Anglo-American colonies supported the war grudgingly, providing few and usually poorly trained troops. However, 1758 proved a turning point for the British. First, Indian support for the French evaporated, largely because France appeared to hold a decisive margin. Their withdrawal enabled Britain to easily capture Fort Duquesne and win control of the Ohio Valley. Second, British minister William Pitt took over Britain's military affairs. The imaginative and single-minded Pitt reinvigorated the military campaign. Hard pressed in Europe by France and its allies (which after 1761 included Spain), Pitt believed that the mobilization of colonial forces would provide the key to crushing New France. He therefore kept fewer than 4,000 British regulars in North America, at the same time promising that Parliament would bear the cost of maintaining colonial troops.

European Powers in the New World Before 1754 and in 1763

The Treaty of Paris (1763) divided France's North American empire between Britain and Spain. Hoping to prevent unnecessary violence between whites and Indians, Britain forbade any new white settlements west of the Appalachians' crest in the Proclamation of 1763.

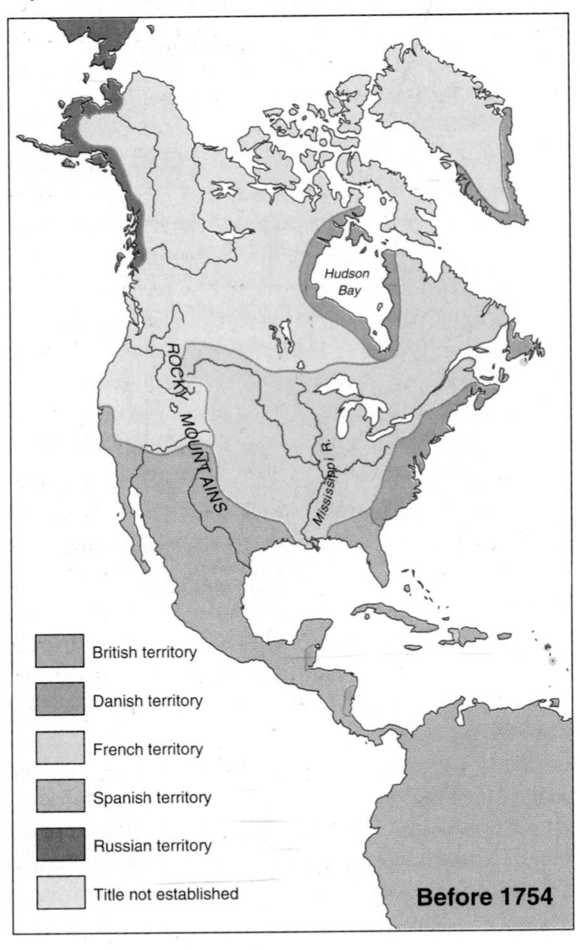

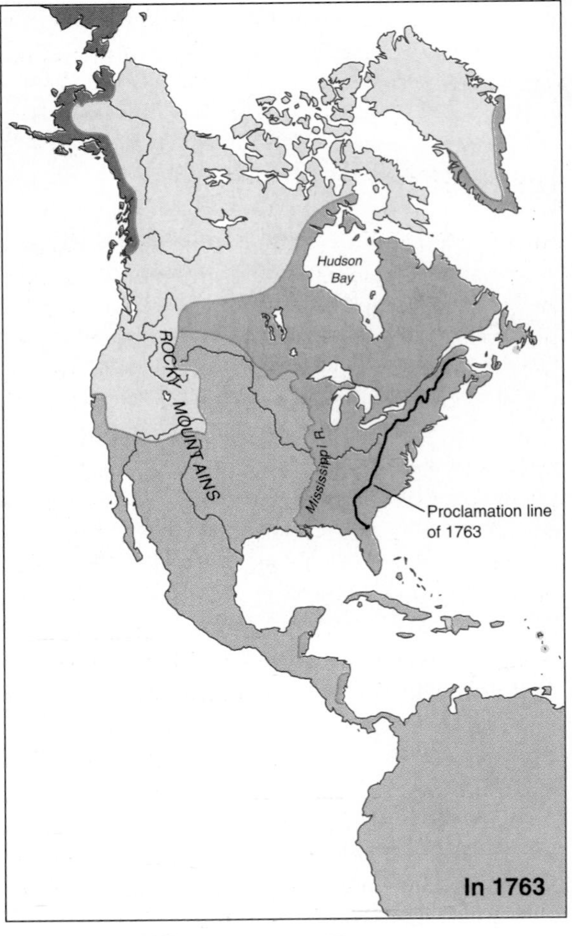

Pitt's offer to free Americans from the war's financial burden generated unprecedented support. In 1758 and again in 1759 the colonies organized 21,000 troops. As a result, Britain took the offensive and captured Louisbourg and Fort Duquesne in 1758 and Quebec in September 1759. In 1760, with Montreal's surrender, French resistance ended.

In the Treaty of Paris of 1763 France ceded all its territories on the North American mainland. Britain received all French lands east of the Mississippi; Spain acquired the port of New Orleans and all French lands west of the Mississippi. Spain traded Florida to Britain for Cuba. Spain's New World empire thus remained intact, while France's shrank to a handful of islands off Newfoundland and the West Indies. Supreme in eastern North America and victorious in a first global war, Britain appeared unchallengeable.

Imperial Reorganization

After the Seven Years' War Britain tried to finance its greatly expanded empire through new revenue measures on both sides of the Atlantic and to exercise more direct control over its colonies. Opponents of these measures rose in protest in Britain and in North America, decrying the economic costs of the new policy and painting it as a dangerous extension of tyrannical power. In America protest quickly escalated into conflict over the proper relationship between Parliament and the colonies.

This controversy coincided with the ascent of George III (ruled 1760–1820) to the throne. The twenty-two-year-old king was determined to play a strong role in government policy. Clashes of personality and policy led him to dismiss prime ministers abruptly, at the cost of disrupting the imperial reorganization under way in the 1760s. After the fall of Lord Bute in 1763 came the ministries of George Grenville (1763–1765), the Marquis of Rockingham (1766), and William Pitt (1766). A period of uncertain leadership ended in 1770 with the appointment of Frederick, Lord North, as prime minister.

Friction Among Allies

An extraordinary coalition of Britons, colonists, and Native Americans had defeated France, but when peace returned, so, too, did deep-seated tensions among these allies. In particular, Anglo-Americans chafed that they received little credit for their role in defeating New France. Writing about the capture of two French forts on Nova Scotia's border by 2,000 New Englanders and 300 British regular troops in 1755, Benjamin Franklin observed that "it could not be discovered by the Account . . . published in the *London Gazette*, that there was a single New England man concern'd in the Affair."

Pitt's strategy caused much of the misunderstanding. Recognizing that Americans could not perform as well as veteran regulars, Pitt had used Americans in vital support roles: forming the reserve for battle, handling supplies, and garrisoning frontier forts.

These American contributions had freed large numbers of British regulars to fight, but British officers complained that colonial troops not only fought poorly but also tended to return home, even in the midst of campaigns, when their terms were up or when their pay lagged. In turn, colonial soldiers complained that British officers treated their troops "little better than slaves."

Tensions flared as well between British officers and colonial civilians. Officers groused about colonial unwillingness to provide food or shelter; colonists resented the officers' arrogance. Pennsylvania Quakers, pacifist by conviction, refused to vote funds for the war effort, while New York and Massachusetts saw the quartering of British troops on their soil as an encroachment on their English liberties. In the meantime, British authorities viewed these actions as affronts to the king's prerogative and as threats to the defense of British territories. Moreover, Pitt's promise to reimburse the colonies for their military expenses enraged Britons. Wartime spending had brought substantial profits to colonial farmers, artisans, and merchants. And some merchants had continued their illicit trade with the French West Indies, thus violating the Navigation

Acts *and* trading with the enemy simultaneously. Britain's national debt had nearly doubled during the war, to more than £123 million. In contrast, the total colonial debt amounted to less than £1 million. Staggering under debt and taxes, the British thought it outrageous to repay the Americans for defending themselves.

Many colonists felt equally burdened. Wartime profits had gone to pay for British goods as thousands of people purchased what they had previously produced. Britain's manufacturing sector flourished—and then the wartime boom ended when peace returned. Now accustomed to new middle-class life-styles, colonists went into debt, and British creditors obliged by extending repayment terms from six months to a full year. Newly prosperous colonists found themselves mired in debt and even bankruptcy, and many began to suspect Britain of plotting to "enslave" the colonies in order to protect its own merchants and manufacturers.

Worse, Britain's victory over the French generated new Indian-white conflicts that drove the British debt even higher. No longer able to play the two imperial powers off against each other, Indians feared the consequences. They were right. To cut costs after the war, the British had stopped distributing food and ammunition to their Indian allies. Meanwhile, colonial squatters were moving onto Indian lands, raising both fears and tensions.

In early 1763 the Delaware Indian religious prophet Neolin called for Indians' repudiation of European culture, goods, and alliances. Other Native Americans in the Great Lakes and the Ohio Valley wished for the return of the French so that they could again play the European powers off against each other. Pontiac, an Ottawa Indian, and other leaders forged an anti-British coalition that sacked eight British forts along the Great Lakes and besieged British positions at Detroit and Pittsburgh. Short on food and ammunition, suffering a smallpox epidemic (deliberately spread by the British), and recognizing that the French would not return, the Indians surrendered in early fall.

But the British victory over the Indians was indecisive. Hoping to end the frontier fighting, the British government issued the Proclamation of 1763, which asserted royal control of land transactions, settlements, and trade of non-Indians west of the Appalachians and recognized existing Indian land titles everywhere west of the "proclamation line," which ran down the crest of the Appalachian Mountains. Although the policy calmed Indian fears, it angered the colonies by subordinating their western land claims to imperial authority and slowing colonial expansion.

Pontiac's rebellion also led the British government to station 10,000 regular troops in North America to occupy the western lands that France had ceded and to intimidate the Indians. The cost of administering British North America reached almost £440,000 yearly. Britons believed it perfectly reasonable for the colonists to help offset this expense. The colonists, however, struggling with their own postwar economic recession, saw it as none of their responsibility.

Despite offsetting the colonies' unfavorable balance of payments with Britain, these troops raised fears of a peacetime "standing army" that could threaten American liberty. With the French menace gone, increasing numbers of colonists viewed Indian lands to the west as the key to future prosperity. The British troops that enforced the Proclamation Act of 1763 thus became not protectors but threats to that future.

The Writs of Assistance

To halt American trade with the enemy in the French West Indies during the Seven Years' War, Britain had cracked down on colonial smuggling. In 1760 the royal governor of Massachusetts authorized the use of the writ of assistance to seize illegally imported goods. A general search warrant, the writ permitted customs officials to enter any ship or building where smuggled goods might be hidden. Because it required no evidence of probable cause for suspicion, the writ was considered unconstitutional by most English legal authorities. The writ also threatened the privacy of family residences, from which most merchants conducted business, by allowing customs agents to ransack a house in search of illegal goods without any evidence of lawbreaking.

The writ of assistance proved a powerful weapon against smuggling. Merchants in Boston, the colonies' smuggling capital, hired James Otis to challenge the device's constitutionality. The former prosecuting attorney for Boston's vice-admiralty court, Otis had resigned to protest the use of the writ. Before the Massachusetts supreme court in 1761, he argued that "an act against the Constitution is void"—even an act of Parliament. But the court, noting the use of an identical writ of assistance in England, ruled against the merchants.

Despite having lost his case, Otis had stated with clarity the colonial conception of Parliament's role under the British constitution. Most British politicians assumed that Parliament's laws themselves were part of the unwritten constitution and that Parliament could in effect alter the constitution at will. But like most colonists, Otis believed that Parliament had no authority to violate the traditional "rights of Englishmen" and that there were limits "beyond which if Parliaments go, their Acts bind not."

The Sugar Act

In 1764, three years after Otis's court challenge, Parliament passed the Sugar Act to offset part of Britain's North American military expenses. In ending the long-standing exemption of colonial trade from revenue-raising measures, the Sugar Act triggered new tension between Britain and the colonies. (The Navigation Acts, in contrast, had been intended not to raise revenue but to benefit the imperial economy indirectly by stimulating trade and protecting English manufactures from foreign competition.)

The Sugar Act amended the Molasses Act of 1733, which was a protective tariff against French molasses, not a revenue-producing device. The Molasses Act's 6-pence-per-gallon duty, however, was too high for American importers to pay, and they commonly bribed customs inspectors 1½ pence per gallon to look the other way when they unloaded smuggled molasses. In designing the Sugar Act, British officials, well aware of the widespread bribery, wrongly assumed that the colonists would willingly pay a lower, 3-pence-per-gallon tax.

Colonists found other features of the Sugar Act equally objectionable. The act brought a wide range of colonial commerce under imperial control. It stipulated that the colonists had to export valuable raw commodities *through* Britain instead of going directly to foreign ports, as they had been doing. Also, by slapping a heavy tax on the thriving American business of carrying duty-free Portuguese wine to the colonies, the law aimed to increase English merchants' sale of European wine. These restrictions set financial burdens on previously legal American commerce.

The Sugar Act also complicated the requirements for shipping colonial goods. A captain had to fill out a confusing series of documents certifying the legality of his trade. The absence of any document left his cargo liable to seizure. Moreover, the Sugar Act's broad definitions of oceanic commerce put much trade between colonies, which had never been regulated, under new and complex rules. The law's petty regulations made it virtually impossible for many colonial shippers to avoid committing technical violations of the act.

Finally, the Sugar Act discarded many traditional English protections for a fair trial. First, the law allowed customs officials to transfer smuggling cases from the colonial courts, in which juries decided the outcome, to vice-admiralty courts, in which a judge delivered the verdict. Because the act awarded vice-admiralty judges 5 percent of any confiscated cargo, it gave them a financial incentive to find defendants guilty. Second, until 1767 the law required all cases to be heard in the vice-admiralty court at Halifax, Nova Scotia, and reversed normal procedure by presuming the guilt of the accused and requiring the defendant to prove innocence.

The Sugar Act alarmed the colonists because it sacrificed their economic interests and legal rights to benefit British merchants. It was no idle threat. Rather than pay the 3-pence tax, however, Americans continued smuggling. In 1766 Britain lowered the duty to 1 pence, less than the usual bribe.

Colonial opponents hesitated to denounce the Sugar Act, which seemingly only amended the Molasses Act. Although nine provincial legislatures protested that the Sugar Act represented an abuse of Parliament's authority to regulate trade, opposition to the law remained fragmented and ineffective. A far more controversial measure would soon overshadow the Sugar Act.

The Stamp Act

Revenues raised by the Sugar Act did little to ease Britain's financial crisis. Britons groaned under the second-highest tax rates in Europe and looked resentfully at the lightly taxed colonists, who paid an average of 1 shilling per person compared to their 26 shillings per person. Most agreed with Prime Minister George Grenville that fairness demanded a larger colonial contribution.

In March 1765, to force colonists to pay their share of imperial expenses, Parliament passed the Stamp Act. The law obliged Americans to purchase and use specially marked or stamped paper for newspapers, customs documents, wills, contracts, and other public legal documents. Violators faced prosecution in vice-admiralty courts, without juries. Grenville projected yearly revenues of £60,000 to £100,000, which would defray up to 20 percent of North American military expenses. Unlike the Sugar Act, an *external* tax levied on imports, the Stamp Act was an *internal* tax levied directly on property, goods, and services in the colonies. External taxes regulated trade and fell primarily on merchants and ship captains, but internal taxes were designed to raise revenue and had far wider effects. The Stamp Act would tax anyone who made a will, bought or sold property, purchased newspapers, or borrowed money.

William Pitt and others objected to such an internal tax, arguing that the colonies taxed themselves through their elected assemblies. But to Grenville and his supporters, the tax seemed a small price for the benefits of empire, especially since Britons had paid a similar tax since 1695. Grenville

Stamp Act Protest
A Boston crowd burns bundles of the special watermarked paper intended for use as stamps.

agreed with Stamp Act opponents that Parliament could not tax British subjects unless they enjoyed representation in that body. He contended, however, that the colonists, like many other British adult males who did not vote for members of Parliament, were *virtually* represented. Theoretically, with virtual representation, every member of Parliament considered the welfare of *all* subjects, not just his constituents, in deciding issues. No Briton was represented by any particular member of the House of Commons; but all imperial subjects, including Americans, could depend on each member of Parliament to protect their well-being.

Grenville and his supporters also held that the colonial assemblies had no powers other than those Parliament allowed them. This view clashed directly with the stance of the many colonists who had argued for decades that their assemblies exercised legislative power equivalent to that of Britain's House of Commons.

The Colonial Perspective

The Stamp Act made many colonists believe that they had to confront parliamentary taxation head-on or surrender any claim to meaningful self-government. However much they admired Parliament, few Americans thought that it represented them. While virtual representation might apply to England and Scotland, they argued, it certainly did not extend across the Atlantic. In the American view, unless a lawmaker shared his constituents' interests, he would have no personal stake in opposing bills contrary to their welfare. Thus the colonists favored *actual*, rather than virtual, representation.

To the colonists, the Stamp Act demonstrated both Parliament's indifference to their interests and the shallowness of virtual representation. Colonial agents in London had lobbied against the law, and colonial assemblies had sent petitions warning against its passage, but to no avail. Parliament "must have thought us Americans all a parcel of Apes and very tame Apes too," concluded Christopher Gadsden of South Carolina, "or they would never have ventured on such a hateful, baneful experiment." The colonists did still concede, however, that Parliament possessed *limited* powers of legislation, and they accepted the parliamentary regulation of imperial trade.

Anglo-Americans considered the essential obligation of British allegiance to be loyalty to the Crown and their one unequivocal duty to be defending the empire in wartime. The colonists insisted that they enjoyed a substantial measure of self-government similar to that of the Protestants in Ireland, whose Parliament alone could tax its people but could not interfere with laws, such as the Navigation Acts, passed by the British Parliament. In a speech opposing the Sugar Act, James Otis had expressed Americans' basic argument: "that by [the British] Constitution, every man in the dominions is a free man; that no parts of His Majesty's dominions can be taxed without consent; that every part has a right to be represented in the supreme or some subordinate legislature." In essence, the colonists saw the empire as a loose federation (union) in which their legislatures possessed considerable autonomy.

Resisting the Stamp Act

In 1765 a political storm generated by the Stamp Act rumbled through all the colonies. The tempest caught up nearly every member of colonial society, but before it ended, elite leaders had assumed direction of the resistance movement.

In late May Patrick Henry, a twenty-nine-year-old Virginia lawyer with a gift for fiery oratory, expressed the rising spirit of resistance. He persuaded Virginia's House of Burgesses to adopt strong resolutions denying Parliament's power to tax the colonies. Garbled accounts of his resolutions and speeches—he probably never said, "Give me liberty or give me death"—electrified other colonists. By year's end, eight other colonial legislatures had rejected parliamentary taxation.

Meanwhile, active resistance took shape. In Boston by late summer, middle-class artisans and businessmen had created the Loyal Nine to fight the Stamp Act. They recognized that the stamp distributors, who alone could sell the specially watermarked paper, represented the law's weak link. If public pressure could force them to resign before the tax went into effect on November 1, the Stamp Act would not work. The Loyal Nine would propel Boston to the forefront of resistance.

Boston's preeminence in opposing Parliament was no accident. Bostonians lived primarily by trade and distilling, and in 1765 they were not living well, thanks to the Sugar Act. The heavy tax on molasses burdened rum producers, and the act's trade restrictions dried up the wine-import business and interfered with the direct export of New England products to profitable overseas markets. To add to the general distress, the city was still recovering from a disastrous fire in 1760 that had left every tenth family homeless.

This widespread economic distress produced an explosive situation. There was good reason to blame British policy for hard times. Furthermore, Bostonians seemed to enjoy mayhem for its own sake. The high point of each year was Guy Fawkes Day, November 5, when thousands commemorated the failure of a supposed Catholic plot in 1605 to blow up Parliament and to kill King James I. Crowds from the North End and the South End of Boston burned gigantic effigies of the pope as well as of local political leaders and generally poked fun at the "better sorts." High spirits usually overflowed into violent confrontations as crowds battled each other with fists, stones, and barrel staves. In 1764 after Guy Fawkes Day brawlers accidentally killed a small child, a truce united the rival mobs under a South End shoemaker named Ebenezer MacIntosh, the leader of 2,000 young toughs. The Loyal Nine enlisted MacIntosh's frustrated street fighters against Boston's stamp distributor, Andrew Oliver.

The morning of August 14, 1765, found a likeness of Oliver swinging from a tree. Oliver did not take the hint to resign, so at dusk MacIntosh and several hundred followers demolished a new building of his at the dock. The mob then surged toward Oliver's house and vandalized it. Oliver announced his resignation the following morning.

Groups similar to the Loyal Nine, calling themselves the Sons of Liberty, formed throughout the colonies. Several more houses were wrecked, and by November 1 the colonies had only two stamp distributors, who soon resigned. Within three months a movement without central leadership killed Grenville's tax.

The violence was spontaneous and directed against property, not persons. But some of the rampages and assaults raised warning flags, and leaders of the Sons of Liberty recognized that violence could alienate elite opponents of the tax. Thus they began to direct public demonstrations with firm discipline, maneuvering hundreds of protesters like a small army and forbidding their followers to carry weapons. Recognizing the value of martyrs, they resolved that the only lives lost over the issue of British taxation would come from their own ranks.

In October 1765 representatives from nine colonies met in New York City in the Stamp Act Congress. There the colonies agreed on, and boldly articulated, the principle that Parliament had no authority to levy taxes outside Britain or to deny any person a jury trial. The united front of the Stamp Act Congress was a far cry from the only other intercolonial meeting, the Albany Congress of 1754. But while emboldening and unifying the colonies, declarations of principle such as the Stamp Act Congress resolutions seemed futile to many colonists, in view of Parliament's earlier refusal to consider their objections to the stamp duties.

By late 1765 most stamp distributors had resigned or fled, and, without the watermarked paper required by law, most customs officials and court officers refused to perform their duties. In response, legislators compelled them to resume operations by threatening to withhold their pay. At the same time, merchants obtained sailing clearances by insisting that they would sue if their cargoes spoiled while delayed in port. By late December the colonial courts and harbors were again functioning.

In these ways the colonial upper class assumed control of the public outcry against the Stamp Act. Respectable gentlemen kept an explosive situation under control by taking over leadership of local Sons of Liberty, by coordinating protest through the Stamp Act Congress, and by having colonial legislatures resume normal business. But the Stamp Act remained in effect. To force its repeal, New York's merchants agreed on October 31, 1765, to boycott all British goods. Others followed. Because the colonies purchased 40 percent of England's manufactures, this nonimportation strategy triggered panic within England's business community. Its members descended on Parliament to warn that continuing the Stamp Act would result in bankruptcies, massive unemployment, and political unrest.

Meanwhile, the Marquis of Rockingham had succeeded George Grenville as prime minister. Rockingham hesitated to advocate repeal, but parliamentary support for repeal gradually grew—the result of practicality, not principle. In March 1766 Parliament revoked the Stamp Act. Simultaneously, however, Parliament passed the Declaratory Act, affirming parliamentary power to legislate for the colonies "in all cases whatsoever."

Because Americans interpreted the Declaratory Act as merely a face-saving measure on Parliament's part, they ignored it. In truth, however, the House of Commons intended that the colonists take the Declaratory Act literally to mean that they were not exempt from *any* parliamentary statute, including a tax law. The Stamp Act crisis thus ended in a fundamental disagreement between Britain and America over the colonists' political rights.

Although philosophical differences between Britain and America remained unresolved, most colonists put the events of 1765 behind them. Still loyal to "Old England," Anglo-Americans concluded that their resistance to the law had slapped Britain's leaders back to their senses. Yet the crisis led many to ponder British policies and actions more deeply than ever.

Ideology, Religion, and Resistance

The Stamp Act crisis had caused some Anglo-Americans to discern for the first time a sinister quality in the imperial relationship with Britain. To understand these perceptions, some educated colonists turned to philosophers, historians, and political writers. Many more looked to religion.

The colonists were familiar with John Locke and other Enlightenment political thinkers. Locke argued that in a state of nature, people enjoyed the "natural rights" of life, liberty, and property. To form governments to protect these rights, people entered into a "social contract." A government that encroached on natural rights broke its contract with the people. In such cases the people could resist their government. To many colonial leaders, Locke's concept of natural rights justified opposition to Parliament's arbitrary legislation.

The political writers read most widely in the colonies included a group known as oppositionists. According to John Trenchard and Thomas Gordon, among others, Parliament—the freely elected representatives of the people—formed the foundation of England's unique political liberties and protected them against the inherent corruption and tyranny of executive power. But since 1720, the oppositionists argued, prime ministers had exploited the treasury to provide pensions, contracts, and profitable offices to politicians and had bought elections by bribing voters. Most members of Parliament, they held, no longer represented the true interest of their constituents; instead, they had sold their souls for financial gain and joined a "conspiracy against liberty." Referring to themselves as the "country party," these oppositionists feared that a power-hungry "court party" of nonelected officials close to the king was using a corrupt Parliament to gain absolute power.

During the 1760s and 1770s English radicals, notably Joseph Priestly and James Burgh, drew from both Enlightenment and oppositionist authors to fashion a critique of English government and a new way of thinking about politics. At the heart of all political relationships, they argued, raged a struggle between the aggressive extension of artificial *power*, represented by corrupt governments, and the natural *liberty* of the people. To protect their liberty, free people had to avoid corruption in their own lives and resist the encroachment of tyranny. Above all, they had to remain alert for "conspiracies" against liberty.

Influenced by such ideas, a number of colonists detected a conspiracy behind British policy during the Stamp Act crisis. Joseph Warren of Massachusetts wrote that the act "induced some to imagine that [Prime Minister Grenville intended] by this to force the colonies into a rebellion, and from thence to take occasion to treat them with severity, and, by military power, to reduce them to servitude." Over the next decade a thundershower of pamphlets denounced British efforts to "enslave" the colonies through taxation and the imposition of officials, judges, and a standing army directed from London.

Many colonists also followed the lead of Massachusetts assemblyman Samuel Adams, who expressed hope that America would become a "Christian Sparta." By linking religion and ancient history, Adams combined two potent rhetorical appeals. Virtually every colonial American was steeped in Protestantism, and those whose education had gone beyond the basics had imbibed Greek and Latin learning as well as seventeenth-century English literature. These traditions, Americans believed, confirmed the legitimacy of their cause.

Thomas Jefferson of Virginia was typical of educated men of the day in revering the classical Greeks and Romans for their virtuous devotion to liberty. The pamphlets and speeches of gentlemen such as Jefferson, John Dickinson, and Patrick Henry resounded with quotations from the ancients that served as constant reminders of the righteous dignity of their cause. But appeals to ordinary Americans drew on deeper wellsprings of belief, notably the religious fervor that the Great Awakening had stirred.

Beginning with the Stamp Act crisis, New England's clergymen summoned their flocks to stand up for God and liberty. Exhorted one minister, "We are bound in conscience to stand fast in the liberty with which Christ has made us free." (Only Anglican ministers, whose church the king headed, tried to stay neutral or opposed the protest.) Clergymen who exalted the cause of liberty exerted an enormous influence on popular opinion. Far more Americans heard or read sermons than had access to newspapers or pamphlets. A popular theme was how God sent the people woes only to strengthen and sustain them until victory. Even Virginia gentlemen not known for their piety felt moved by such messages and ordered their families to comply with the days of "fasting and public humiliation" proclaimed by the clerical leaders. Moreover, protest leaders' calls to boycott British luxuries meshed neatly with ministers' traditional warnings against frivolity and wastefulness. Few Americans could ignore the unceasing public reminders that solidarity against British tyranny and "corruption" meant rejecting sin and obeying God.

The ebbing of the Stamp Act crisis removed the urgency from such extreme views. But the alarm raised by British actions was not easily quieted. After a gap of two years it would become clear that British and American views of the colonies' place in the empire remained far apart.

Era of Anglo-American Crisis

From 1767 to 1773 Parliament pursued a confrontational policy that eroded Americans' trust of Britain. The resulting climate of fear and alienation left most colonists convinced that the Stamp Act had been not an isolated mistake but part of a deliberate design to undermine colonial self-government. Growing numbers in Britain likewise questioned economically costly policies and actions that seemed to threaten Britons as well as colonists.

The Quartering Act

In August 1766 George III dismissed the Rockingham government and summoned William Pitt to form a cabinet. An opponent of taxing the colonies, Pitt had the potential to repair the Stamp Act's damage; the colonists respected him highly. However, Pitt's health collapsed in March 1767, and Charles Townshend, the chancellor of the exchequer (treasurer), became the effective leader.

Just as Townshend took office, a conflict arose with the New York legislature over the Quartering Act of 1765, which ordered colonial legislatures to pay for certain goods used by British soldiers stationed within their borders—candles, windowpanes, mattress straw, and a small liquor ration. The act applied only to troops in settled areas, not on the frontier. It did not force citizens to accept soldiers in private homes or require legislatures to erect barracks. The law aroused resentment, however, because it constituted an *indirect* tax. That is, although it did not empower royal officials to collect money directly from the colonists, it obligated assemblies to raise revenue by whatever means they considered appropriate. The act fell lightly on the colonies except New York, where more soldiers were stationed than in any other province. New York refused to grant the supplies.

New York's resistance unleashed a torrent of anti-American feeling in Parliament, still bitter after revoking the Stamp Act. Townshend responded by drafting the New York Suspending Act, which threatened to nullify all laws passed by the colony after October 1, 1767, if it refused to vote the supplies. By the time George III signed the measure, New York had already appropriated the funds. Nonetheless, the conflict over the Quartering Act revealed the depth of anticolonial sentiment in the House of Commons. It demonstrated that British leaders would not hesitate to defend Parliament's sovereignty through the most drastic of all steps: interfering with colonial self-government.

The Townshend Duties

This new wave of British resentment toward the colonies coincided with an outpouring of frustration over the government's failure to cut taxes from wartime levels. Discontent seethed among the landed gentry, whose members took advantage of their domination of the House of Commons to slash their own taxes in 1767. This move cost the government £500,000 and prompted Townshend to tax imports entering America and to propose laws to increase colonial customs revenues.

Townshend sought to tax the colonists by exploiting a loophole in their arguments against the Stamp Tax. Americans had emphasized their opposition to *internal* taxes but had said nothing about *external* taxes—Parliament's right to tax imports as they entered the colonies. Townshend interpreted this silence as evidence that the colonists accepted Britain's right to impose external taxes. But a now much wiser George Grenville predicted, "They will laugh at you for your distinctions about regulations of trade." Brushing aside such warnings, Parliament passed Townshend's Revenue Act of 1767 (popularly called the Townshend duties) in the summer. The new law taxed glass, paint, lead, paper, and tea imported into the colonies.

On the surface Townshend's case for external taxation was convincing, as the colonists had long accepted parliamentary regulation of trade and had in principle acknowledged taxation as a form of regulation. Americans had protested the Sugar Act not because it imposed taxes but because it set impractical regulations for conducting trade and violated traditional guarantees of a fair trial. But the Townshend duties differed significantly from what Americans considered a legitimate way of regulating trade through taxation. To the colonists, charging a duty was a lawful way for British authorities to control trade only if it excluded foreign goods by making them prohibitively expensive. The Revenue Act of 1767, however, set moderate rates that did not price goods out of the colonial market; clearly, its purpose was to collect money for the treasury. Thus from the colonial standpoint, Townshend's duties were taxes just like the Stamp Act duties.

Townshend had an ulterior motive for establishing an American source of revenue. Traditionally, colonial legislatures set colonial royal governors' salaries and often refused to pay them until the governors signed bills that they opposed. Townshend hoped that the Revenue Act would establish a fund to pay governors' and other royal officials' salaries, freeing them from the assemblies' control. In effect, he would strip the assemblies of their most potent weapon, the power of the purse, and tip the balance of power away from elected representatives and toward appointed royal officials.

The Revenue Act never yielded the income that Townshend had anticipated. Of all the items taxed, only tea produced any significant revenue—£20,000 of the £37,000 expected. And because the measure would serve its purpose only if the colonists could afford British tea, Townshend eliminated £60,000 in import fees paid on East Indian tea entering Britain before transshipment to America. On balance, the Revenue Act *worsened* the British treasury's deficit by £23,000. By 1767 Britain's financial difficulties were more an excuse for political demands to tax the colonies than a driving force. From Parliament's standpoint, the conflict with America was becoming a test of national will over the *principle* of taxation.

The Colonists' Reaction

Americans learned of the Revenue Act shortly before it went into operation, and they hesitated over their response. The strong-arm tactics that had sent stamp distributors into flight would not work against the Townshend duties, which the Royal Navy could easily collect offshore.

Resistance to the act remained weak until December 1767, when John Dickinson, a Delaware planter and Philadelphia lawyer, published *Letters from a Farmer in Pennsylvania*. These twelve essays, which appeared in nearly every colonial newspaper, emphasized that Parliament had no right to tax trade for the simple purpose of raising revenue. No tax designed to produce revenue could be considered constitutional unless a people's elected representatives voted for it. Dickinson's writings convinced Americans that their arguments against the Stamp Act also applied to the Revenue Act.

In early 1768 the Massachusetts assembly asked Samuel Adams to draft a "circular letter" to other legislatures. Possessing a flair for the push and shove of local politics, the Harvard-educated Adams had helped organize the Sons of Liberty in Boston. Adams's circular letter denounced taxation without representation and the threat to self-governance posed by Parliament's making governors and royal officials independent of the legislatures. Nevertheless, the document acknowledged Parliament as the "supreme legislative Power over the whole Empire" and advocated no illegal activities.

Samuel Adams (1722–1803)
A central player in the drive for American liberty, Adams wrote in 1774 that "I wish for a permanent union with the mother country, but only in terms of liberty and truth. No advantage that can accrue to America from such a union, can compensate for the loss of liberty."

Virginia's assembly warmly approved Adams's eloquent measure and sent out a more strongly worded letter of its own, urging all the colonies to oppose imperial policies that would "have an immediate tendency to enslave them." But most colonial legislatures reacted indifferently to these letters. In fact, resistance might have disintegrated had not the British government overreacted to the circular letters.

Indeed, parliamentary leaders saw even the mild Massachusetts letter as "little better than an incentive to Rebellion." Disorganized because of Townshend's sudden death in 1767, the king's Privy Council (advisers) directed Lord Hillsborough, the first appointee to the new post of secretary of state for the colonies, to express the government's displeasure. Hillsborough ordered the Massachusetts assembly to disown its letter, forbade all overseas assemblies to endorse it, and commanded royal governors to dissolve any legislature that violated his instructions.

The tactic backfired. Protesting Hillsborough's bullying, many legislatures previously indifferent to the Massachusetts letter adopted it enthusiastically. The Massachusetts House of Representatives voted 92–17 not to recall its letter. Royal governors responded by dismissing legislatures in Massachusetts and elsewhere, playing into the hands of Samuel

Adams and others who wished to ignite widespread opposition to the Townshend duties.

Increasingly outraged, the colonists still needed an effective means of pressuring Parliament for repeal. Nonimportation seemed especially promising because it offered an alternative to violence and would distress Britain's economy. Thus in August 1768 Boston's merchants adopted a nonimportation agreement, and the tactic spread southward. "Save your money, and you save your country!" trumpeted the Sons of Liberty, which reorganized after two years of inactivity. However, not all colonists supported nonimportation. Many merchants whose livelihood depended on imported goods waited until early 1769 to join the boycott. Far from complete, it probably kept out no more than 40 percent of British imports.

Wilkes and Liberty

British merchants and artisans, hit hard by the exclusion of 40 percent of imports, demanded repeal of the Townshend duties. Their protests became part of a larger movement in the 1760s against the policies of George III and a Parliament dominated by wealthy landowners. John Wilkes, a fiery London editor whose newspaper regularly and irreverently denounced the king, became both leader and focal point of the protest. A member of Parliament, Wilkes was tried for seditious libel and acquitted, to great popular acclaim. George III's government then shut down his newspaper and persuaded members of the House of Commons to deny Wilkes his seat. After publishing another slashing attack on the king, Wilkes fled to Paris.

In 1768 Wilkes returned to England, defying an arrest warrant, and again ran for Parliament. By then government policies, including the Townshend Acts, had unleashed a flood of protests against the "obnoxious" government ministers, a flood that swept along manufacturers and merchants as well as weavers and other workers. They all rallied around the cry "Wilkes and Liberty."

When the newly elected Wilkes was once again arrested 20,000 to 40,000 angry "Wilkesites" massed on St. George's Fields, outside the prison where he was being held. Soldiers and police responded to rock-throwing demonstrators by opening fire on them, killing eleven protesters. The "massacre of St. George's Fields" furnished martyrs to the protesters, and Wilkes received enormous outpourings of public support from the North American colonies as well as from Britain. Twice more elected from his prison cell, and twice more denied his seat, Wilkes maintained a regular correspondence with Boston's Sons of Liberty. Bostonians celebrated his release from prison in April 1770 with a massive celebration honoring this "illustrious martyr to liberty."

The Wilkes furor sharpened the political ideas of government opponents on both sides of the Atlantic. English voters sent petitions to Parliament proclaiming that its refusal to seat Wilkes was an affront to the electorate's will and calling "virtual representation" a sham. To guard against further arbitrary government actions, some formed the Society of the Supporters of the Bill of Rights "to defend and maintain the legal, constitutional liberty of the subject[s of the King]." Emboldened by the Wilkes and Liberty movement, William Pitt, Edmund Burke, and others forcefully denounced the government's colonial policies. The colonists themselves concluded that Parliament and the government represented a small but powerful minority whose authority they could legitimately question.

Women and Colonial Resistance

Nonimportation convinced the British—and the colonists—that all Americans were determined to sustain resistance, and it demonstrated that the American cause rested on foundations of impeccable morality and sensible moderation. It also provided a unique opportunity for women to join the protest.

Calling themselves Daughters of Liberty, upper-class female patriots assumed a highly visible role during the Townshend crisis. Convinced that colonial women could exert a persuasive moral influence on public opinion, American leaders encouraged them to protest the Revenue Act's tax on tea. Accordingly, in early 1770 more than 300 "mistresses of families" in Boston denounced the consumption of the beverage. In some ways nonconsumption was more effective than nonimportation, for the colonists' refusal to consume imports would chill merchants' economic incentive to import British goods.

Nonconsumption agreements therefore became popular and were extended to include other goods, mainly clothes. Again, women played a vital role because the boycott would fail unless the colonists replaced British imports with apparel of their own making. Responding to leaders' pleas for an expansion of domestic cloth production, women of all social ranks organized spinning bees. These attracted intense publicity as evidence of American determination to fight parliamentary taxation. The colonial cause, noted a New York woman, had enlisted "a fighting army of amazons . . . armed with spinning wheels." Spinning bees not only helped to undermine the masculine prejudice that women had no place in public life but also endowed spinning and weaving, previously considered routine tasks, with political virtue.

Colonial leaders were waging a battle to convince British public opinion that their society would stand firm in opposing unconstitutional taxes. Only if the Britons believed that Americans—male and female alike—were truly united would they accept repeal of the Townshend duties. Female participation in symbolic protests forced the British public to appreciate the depth of colonial commitment.

Customs Racketeering

Townshend also sought to increase revenues by extending British surveillance of colonial trade. In 1767 he induced Parliament to create the American Board of Customs Commissioners to strictly enforce the Navigation Acts. At the same time, Parliament increased the number of port officials, funded a colonial coast guard to catch smugglers, and provided money for secret informers. Townshend's hope was that the new system would end widespread bribery of customs officials by colonial shippers and merchants by bringing honesty, efficiency, and greater revenue to overseas customs operations. Instead the law quickly drew protests because of the ways it was enforced and because it reversed traditional legal process by assuming the accused to be guilty until proved otherwise.

The rapid expansion of the customs service in 1767 coincided with new provisions that awarded an informer one-third of the value of all goods and ships appropriated through a conviction of smuggling. The fact that fines could be tripled under certain circumstances provided an even greater incentive to seize illegal cargoes. Smuggling cases were heard in vice-admiralty courts, where the probability of conviction was extremely high. The prospect of accumulating a small fortune proved too tempting to most commissioners.

Revenue agents commonly perverted the law by filing charges for technical violations of the Sugar Act even when no evidence existed of intent to conduct illegal trade. They most often exploited the provision that declared any cargo illegal unless it had been loaded or unloaded with a customs officer's written authorization. Many vessels transporting lumber or tobacco found it impossible to comply because they typically picked up items piecemeal at a succession of small wharves far from a customhouse. Customs officials created other opportunities for seizures by bending the rules for a time and then suddenly enforcing the law.

Customs commissioners also fanned anger by invading sailors' traditional rights. Long-standing maritime custom allowed crews to supplement their incomes by making small sales between ports. Anything stored in a sailor's chest was considered private property, exempt from the Navigation Acts. But after 1767 revenue agents treated such belongings as cargo, thus establishing an excuse to seize the entire ship. Under this policy, crewmen saw arrogant inspectors break open their trunks and then lost trading stock worth several months' wages. Sailors waited for chances to get even. Not surprisingly, after 1767 inspectors increasingly fell victim to riots dominated by vengeful sailors.

In these ways the commissioners embarked on a program of "customs racketeering" that constituted legalized piracy. This program fed an upsurge in popular violence. Above all, customs commissioners' use of informers provoked retaliation. The *Pennsylvania Journal* in 1769 scorned these agents as "dogs of prey, thirsting after the fortunes of worthy and wealthy men." Informers aroused hatred in those whom they betrayed. Nearly all instances of tarring and feathering in these years represented private revenge against informers, not political reprisals.

Nowhere were customs agents and informers more detested than in Boston, where citizens retaliated in June 1768. When customs agents seized colonial merchant John Hancock's sloop *Liberty* on a technicality, a crowd tried to prevent the towing of Hancock's ship and then began assaulting customs officials. Swelling to several hundred, the mob drove all revenue inspectors from the city.

The wealthy Hancock, a leading opponent of British taxation, had became a chief target of the customs commissioners. Despite a lack of evidence that he was a smuggler, customs commissioners in 1768 used a perjured statement from a customs inspector to seize the *Liberty* for allegedly avoiding £700 in duties on wine worth £3,000. By then requesting the payment of triple charges, they made Hancock liable for a total fine of £9,000, thirteen times greater than the taxes supposedly evaded. During the prosecution that followed, British agents perjured themselves and the judge denied Hancock his right to a fair trial.

Hancock's case made Americans rethink their acceptance of the principle that Parliament had limited authority to pass laws for them. By 1770 it was clear that measures such as the Sugar Act and the act creating the American Board of Customs Commissioners endangered property rights and civil liberties as much as taxes. Realizing this fact, many Americans began to reject any legislation without representation. By 1774 a consensus had emerged that Parliament had no lawmaking authority over the colonies except the right to regulate imperial commerce.

By 1770 the British government, aware of its customs officers' excesses, had begun reforming the service. Smuggling charges against Hancock were dropped. Although the abuses ended, the damage had been done. Townshend's American Board of Customs Commissioners reinforced the colonists' growing suspicion of British motives and their alienation from England.

Repeal of the Townshend Duties

Meanwhile, in January 1770 Lord North had become prime minister. An able administrator, North favored eliminating most of the Townshend duties to end the commercial boycott, but he insisted on retaining the tax on tea to underscore British authority. In April 1770 Parliament again yielded to colonial pressure and repealed most of the Townshend duties.

This partial repeal presented a dilemma to American politicians. They considered it intolerable that taxes remained on tea, the most profitable item for the royal treasury. In July 1770 the general nonimportation movement collapsed, but the Sons of Liberty resisted external taxation by voluntary agreements not to drink British tea. Revenue from the tea tax consequently fell to only one-sixth the anticipated amount, far too low to pay royal governors' salaries.

Yet American leaders remained dissatisfied. The tea duty was a galling reminder that Parliament still claimed broad authority. The tea tax became a festering sore that slowly poisoned relations between Britain and the colonies. The Townshend crisis had begun the gradual dissolution of American loyalty to Britain.

The Boston Massacre

Nowhere was the fraying of loyalties more obvious than in Boston. In response to Bostonians' violence, 1,700 British troops landed in Boston in October 1768. In 1770 this military occupation provoked a fresh round of violence as armed sentries and resentful civilians traded insults. The mainly Protestant townspeople resented the authority of the soldiers, especially blacks and Irish Catholics, and bristled at job competition from enlisted men, most of whom could seek work after morning muster.

It was a situation tailor-made for Samuel Adams, a genius in shaping public opinion. By imposing nearly 2,000 redcoats on a crowded, economically distressed, and violence-prone city of 20,000 bullheaded Yankees, the British government had given Adams grist for his propaganda mill. In October 1768 he began publishing the *Journal of the Times*, a magazine claiming to offer factual accounts of abuses committed by the army and customs services. Adams's purpose was to kindle outrage, and thus resistance, toward British authority. The *Journal* seldom lacked stories of citizens assaulted, insulted, or simply annoyed, and Adams exaggerated every incident. With each issue, Boston's hatred of the redcoats grew.

Bostonians endured their first winter as a garrison town without undue trouble and saw half the British troops sail home in mid-1769. But relations between civilians and the remaining soldiers deteriorated. Resentment of British authority boiled over on February 22, 1770, when a customs informer fired bird shot at several children throwing rocks at his house and killed an eleven-year-old boy. Adams organized a burial procession to maximize the horror at a child's death, relying on grief to unite the community in opposition to British policies. "My Eyes never beheld such a funeral," wrote his cousin John Adams. "A vast Number of Boys walked before the Coffin, a vast Number of Women and Men after it. . . . This Shows there are many more Lives to spend if wanted in the Service of their country."

Although the army had played no part in the shooting, it became a target for Bostonians' rage. A week after the funeral, tension erupted at the guardpost protecting the customs office. When an officer tried to disperse a crowd led by Crispus Attucks, a seaman of African and Native American ancestry,

The Boston Massacre, 1770,
Engraving by Paul Revere
Shortly after this incident, one Bostonian observed that "unless there is some great alteration in the state of things, the era of the independence of the colonies is much nearer than I once thought it, or now wish it."

the mob responded with a barrage of flying objects. One soldier, knocked down by a block of ice, fired, and the others opened fire. Their volley killed five people, including Attucks.

Samuel Adams orchestrated a martyrs' funeral for the victims of this so-called Boston Massacre, named to recall the "St. George's Field Massacre" of Wilkes's supporters in London, and used the occasion to solidify American opposition to British authority. To defuse the explosive situation, the product of burning hatreds that sprang from an intolerable situation, royal authorities isolated the British troops on a fortified harbor island and promised a trial for the soldiers who had fired. Patriot leader John Adams defended the men to demonstrate American commitment to impartial justice. But the light punishments given these soldiers, who had shot unarmed civilians, forced the colonists to confront the stark possibility that Britain intended to coerce and suppress them through naked force.

The Committees of Correspondence

The colonies enjoyed a brief truce in their relations with Britain, but it ended in June 1772 when the customs schooner *Gaspee* ran aground near Providence, Rhode Island. A revenue cutter that engaged in customs racketeering by plundering cargoes for technical violations of the Sugar Act, the *Gaspee* also had an odious reputation among Rhode Islanders for its high-handed captain and crew of petty thieves. Stuck in the mud, the *Gaspee* presented an irresistible target for local inhabitants. That night more than 100 men took revenge by burning it to the waterline.

The British government dispatched a commission with instructions to send all suspects to England for trial. Although the investigators failed to identify any raiders, colonists took alarm at the government's willingness to dispense with another essential civil liberty, an accused citizen's right to be tried by a local jury.

Meanwhile, in fall 1772 Lord North prepared to implement Townshend's goal of paying royal governors from customs revenue, freeing them from the control of the colonial assemblies. With representative government deeply threatened, Samuel Adams persuaded Boston's town meeting to request that every Massachusetts community appoint people to exchange information and to coordinate measures to defend colonial rights. Within a year most Massachusetts communities had established "committees of correspondence," and the idea spread throughout New England.

The committees of correspondence, the colonists' first attempt to maintain close political cooperation over a wide area, allowed Samuel Adams to conduct a campaign of political education for all New England. He sent messages for each local committee to read at its town meeting, which debated the issues and adopted formal resolutions. The system made tens of thousands of citizens consider evidence that their rights were endangered and committed them to take a stand. Adams's most successful venture in whipping up public alarm came in June 1773 when he published letters from Massachusetts governor Thomas Hutchinson, obtained by Benjamin Franklin, advocating "an abridgement of what are called English liberties" and "a great restraint of natural liberty." The Hutchinson correspondence confirmed Americans' suspicions that a plot was afoot to destroy their basic freedoms.

Patrick Henry, Thomas Jefferson, and Richard Henry Lee had proposed in March 1773 that Virginia establish committees of correspondence, and within a year every province but Pennsylvania had such committees. By early 1774 a communications web linked colonial leaders.

In contrast to the brief, intense Stamp Act crisis, the dissatisfaction spawned by the Townshend duties persisted and gradually poisoned relations between Britain and America. In 1765 strong ties of loyalty and affection had disguised the depth of the division over taxation. By 1773, however, colonial allegiance was becoming conditional.

Frontier Tensions

On the Appalachian frontier tensions among natives, recent settlers, and colonial authorities underlined a continuing sense of emergency. Rapid population growth had spurred the migration of people and capital to the frontier, where colonists sought access to Indian lands. Land pressures and the lack of adequate revenue from the colonies left the British government helpless to enforce the Proclamation of 1763. The government could neither maintain garrisons at many of its forts, enforce laws and treaties, nor provide gifts to its native allies. Rising violence by colonists against Indians often went unpunished.

Under such pressures, Britain and the Iroquois, in the Treaty of Fort Stanwix (1768), turned land along the Ohio River that was occupied by the Shawnees, Delawares, and Cherokees over to the Virginia and Pennsylvania governments. The Shawnees assumed leadership of the "republican" Indians, who, with the Cherokees, were convinced that appeasement would not stop colonial expansion.

The treaty resolved Virginia's and Pennsylvania's overlapping land claims in Ohio at the Indians' expense. Other frontier disputes led to conflict among the colonists themselves. Settlers in western Massachusetts in the early 1760s, for example, found their titles challenged by New Yorkers. In 1766, threatened with eviction, the New Englanders staged an armed uprising. And in 1769 New Hampshire settlers calling themselves the Green Mountain Boys began guerrilla warfare against New York landlords. The independent government that they formed ultimately became that of Vermont.

Expansion also provoked conflict between frontier settlers and their own colonial governments. In North Carolina westerners, underrepresented in the assembly, found themselves exploited by dishonest officeholders appointed by eastern politicians. Twenty-five hundred armed westerners, known as Regulators, clashed with 1,300 North Carolina militia on May 16, 1771, at the battle of Alamance Creek. Although the Regulator uprising disintegrated, it crippled the colony's subsequent ability to resist British authority. A Regulator movement also arose in South Carolina, in this case to counter the government's unwillingness to prosecute bandits who terrorized the settlers. Fearful that the colony's slave population might revolt if the militia was dispatched, South Carolina's government yielded to the Regulators by establishing new courts and allowing jury trials in recently settled areas.

Toward Independence

By early 1773 British-colonial relations were again tranquil, but deceptively so. Wishful thinking was leading Americans to ignore the tax on tea. Indeed, they expected Lord North to have it repealed. But Parliament's passage of the Tea Act in May 1773 shattered this hope and set off a chain reaction of events from the Boston Tea Party in late 1773 to the colonies' declaration of their independence from England in July 1776.

The Tea Act

Smuggling and nonconsumption had taken a heavy toll on Britain's East India Company, the holder of the legal monopoly on importing tea into the British Empire. By 1773, as tons of tea rotted in warehouses, the East India Company was teetering on the brink of bankruptcy. But Lord North could not let the company fail because by maintaining British authority in India at its own expense, the East India Company had become a vital component in the British imperial structure.

If the company could control the colonial market, North reasoned, it could increase its profits and its survival would be guaranteed. Americans consumed vast amounts of tea but by 1773 were purchasing just one-quarter of it from the company. In May 1773, to save the beleaguered East India Company, Parliament passed the Tea Act, which eliminated all import duties on tea entering England and thus lowered the selling price to consumers. To reduce the price further, the Tea Act also permitted the company to sell tea directly to consumers rather than through wholesalers. These provisions reduced the cost of East India Company tea in the colonies to well below the price of smuggled tea. Parliament expected economic self-interest to overcome American scruples about buying taxed tea.

But the Tea Act alarmed many Americans,

who recognized that the revenues raised by the law would place royal governors' purses beyond the reach of the colonial assemblies. The law also threatened to seduce Americans into accepting parliamentary taxation in return for a frivolous luxury. The committees of correspondence decided to resist the importation of tea by pressuring the East India Company's agents to refuse acceptance or by preventing the landing of East India Company cargoes.

In Boston on November 28, 1773, the first ship came under jurisdiction of the customhouse, to which duties would have to be paid within twenty days or the cargo would be seized from the captain and the tea would be claimed by the company's agents and placed on sale. When Samuel Adams, John Hancock, and others asked customs officers to issue a special clearance for the ship's departure (to avoid the seizure and sale), Governor Hutchinson refused.

On the evening of December 16, 1773, Samuel Adams convened a meeting in Old South Church, at which he told 5,000 citizens about Hutchinson's insistence on landing the tea, warned them that the grace period would expire in a few hours, and proclaimed that "this meeting can do no more to save the country." About fifty young men disguised as Indians then loosed a few war whoops and headed for the wharf, followed by the crowd. Thousands lined the waterfront to watch them heave forty-five tons of tea overboard; for an hour the only sounds echoing through the crisp, moonlit night were the steady chop of hatchets breaking open wooden chests and the soft splash of tea on the water. Their work finished, the participants left quietly. They had assaulted no one and damaged nothing but the tea.

The Coercive Acts

Boston's "Tea Party" enraged the British. Only "New England fanatics" could imagine that cheap tea oppressed them, fumed Lord North. A Welsh member of Parliament declared that "the town of Boston ought to be knocked about by the ears, and destroy'd." The great orator Edmund Burke pled in vain for the one action that could end the crisis: "Leave America . . . to tax herself." But the British government swiftly asserted its authority through the passage of four Coercive Acts, which, along with the Quebec Act, became known to many colonists as the Intolerable Acts.

The first Coercive Act, the Boston Port Bill, was passed on April 1, 1774. It ordered the navy to close Boston harbor unless the town arranged to pay for the ruined tea by June 1. The impossibly short deadline was meant to ensure the harbor's closing, which would plunge Boston into economic distress. The second Coercive Act, the Massachusetts Government Act, revoked the Massachusetts charter and made the colony's government less democratic. The upper house would be appointed for life by the Crown, not elected annually by the assembly. The royal governor gained absolute control over the appointment of judges and sheriffs. Finally, the new charter limited town meetings to one a year. Although these changes brought Massachusetts government into line with other colonies, the colonists interpreted them as hostile toward representative government.

The final two Coercive Acts—the Administration of Justice Act and a new Quartering Act—rubbed salt into the wounds. The first of these permitted any person charged with murder while enforcing royal authority in Massachusetts to be tried in England or in another colony. The second went beyond the Quartering Act of 1765 by allowing the governor to requisition *empty* private buildings for quartering, or housing, troops. These measures, coupled with the appointment of General Thomas Gage, Britain's military commander in North America, as governor of Massachusetts, struck New Englanders as proof of a plan to place them under a military despotism.

Americans learned of the unrelated Quebec Act at the same time as the Coercive Acts. Intended to cement loyalty to Britain among conquered French-Canadian Catholics, the law established Roman Catholicism as Quebec's official religion. Protestant Anglo-Americans, who associated Catholicism with arbitrary government, took alarm. Furthermore, the Quebec Act gave Canada's governor sweeping powers but established no legislature. It also allowed property disputes to be decided by French law, which used no juries. The law extended Quebec's territorial claims south to the Ohio River and west to the Mississippi, a vast area populated by Indians and some French and claimed by several colonies.

The Intolerable Acts convinced New Englanders that the crown planned to corrode traditional English liberties throughout North America. Once the Coercive Acts destroyed these liberties in Massachusetts, many believed, the Quebec Act would serve as a blueprint for extinguishing representative government in other colonies. Parliament would replace all colonial governments with ones like Quebec's. Elected assemblies, freedom of religion for Protestants, and jury trials would vanish.

Intended only to punish Massachusetts, the Coercive Acts thus pushed most colonies to the brink of revolution. Repeal of these laws became the colonists' nonnegotiable demand. The Declaration of Independence would refer to these laws six times in listing colonial grievances justifying the break with Britain.

Virginia's response to the Coercive Acts was crucial, for it could provide more military manpower than any other colony in the event of war. After sentiment for active resistance solidified in the Virginia assembly, leading planters began a program of political education for the colony's apathetic citizens, emphasizing the need to support Massachusetts and persuading voters to commit themselves to resistance by signing petitions against the Coercive Acts. Within two years the gentry mobilized Virginia's free population against Parliament. It was clear that if war erupted, Britain would face united resistance not only in New England but also in Virginia.

The First Continental Congress

In response to the Intolerable Acts, the committees of correspondence of every colony but Georgia sent delegates to a Continental Congress in Philadelphia. The fifty-six delegates who assembled on September 5, 1774, included the colonies' most prominent politicians: Samuel and John Adams of Massachusetts; John Jay of New York; Joseph Galloway and John Dickinson of Pennsylvania; and Patrick Henry, Richard Henry Lee, and George Washington of Virginia. They were determined to find a way to defend American rights without war.

The Continental Congress endorsed the Suffolk Resolves, extreme statements of principle that proclaimed that the colonies owed no obedience to the Coercive Acts, advocated a provisional government until restoration of the Massachusetts charter, and vowed that defensive measures should follow any attack by royal troops. The Continental Congress also voted to boycott British goods after December 1, 1774, and to stop exporting goods to Britain and its West Indies possessions after September 1775. This agreement, called the Continental Association, would be enforced by locally elected committees of "observation" or "safety." But not all the delegates embraced such bold defiance. Jay, Dickinson, Galloway, and other moderates who dominated the middle-colony contingent feared that a confrontation with Britain would spawn internal colonial turmoil. They vainly opposed nonimportation and unsuccessfully sought support of a plan for an American legislature that would share with Parliament the authority to tax and to govern the colonies.

Finally, the delegates summarized their principles and demands in a petition to George III. They conceded to Parliament the power to regulate colonial commerce but argued that parliamentary efforts to impose taxes, enforce laws through admiralty courts, suspend assemblies, and revoke charters were unconstitutional. By addressing the king rather than Parliament, Congress was imploring George III to end the crisis by dismissing the ministers responsible for passing the Coercive Acts.

The Fighting Begins

Most Americans hoped that resistance would jolt Parliament into renouncing its claims of authority over the colonies. Only a minority of the colonial elite charged that Congress had made the "breach with the parent state a thousand times more irreparable than it was before," as one colonist observed. In England George III saw rebellion in Congress's actions. His instincts, like those of American loyalists—people loyal to England—were correct: a revolution was indeed brewing.

To solidify defiance, American resistance leaders used coercion against waverers and loyalists ("Tories"). Committees elected to enforce the Continental Association became vigilantes, compelling merchants to burn British imports, browbeating clergymen who preached pro-British sermons, and pressuring Americans to free themselves of dependence on British imports by adopting simpler diets and homespun clothing. In colony after colony, moreover, the committees assumed governmental functions by organizing volunteer military companies and extralegal legislatures. By spring 1775 colonial patriots had established provincial "congresses" that rivaled existing royal governments.

In April 1775 events in Massachusetts shattered the uneasy calm. Citizens had collected arms and organized militia units ("minutemen") to respond instantly in an emergency. The British government ordered Massachusetts governor Gage to quell the "rude rabble" and to arrest the patriot leaders. Aware that most of these had fled Boston, Gage, on April 19, 1775, sent 700 British soldiers to seize colonial military supplies stored at Concord. Two couriers, William Dawes and Paul Revere, alerted nearby towns of the British troop movements. At Lexington on the road to Concord, about 70 minutemen faced the British on the town green. After a confused skirmish in which eight minutemen died and a single redcoat was wounded, the British marched to Concord. They found few munitions but encountered a swarm of armed Yankees. When some minutemen mistakenly concluded that the town was being burned, they exchanged fire with British regulars and touched off a running battle that continued most of the sixteen miles back to Boston. By day's end the redcoats had lost 273 men.

These engagements awakened the countryside. Within a day some 20,000 New Englanders were besieging the British garrison in Boston. In the New England interior the Green Mountain Boys under Ethan Allen overran Fort Ticonderoga on Lake Champlain on May 10, partly with the intent of using its captured cannon in the siege of Boston. That same day the Continental Congress reconvened in Philadelphia. Most delegates still opposed independence and agreed to send a "loyal message" to George III. The resulting Olive Branch Petition presented three demands: a cease-fire in Boston, repeal of the Coercive Acts, and negotiations to establish guarantees of American rights. But the Olive Branch Petition reached London along with news of the battles of Breed's Hill and Bunker Hill just outside Boston. Although the British dislodged the Americans in the clashes, they suffered 2,200 casualties, compared to colonial losses of only 311. After Bunker Hill the British public wanted retaliation, not reconciliation. On August 23 the king proclaimed New England in a state of rebellion, and in December Parliament declared all the colonies rebellious.

The Failure of Reconciliation

Most Americans still clung to hopes of reconciliation. Even John Adams, who believed separation inevitable, said that he was "fond of reconciliation, if we could reasonably entertain Hopes of it on a constitutional basis." Yet the same Americans who pleaded for peace passed measures that the British could only see as rebellious. Delegates to the Continental Congress voted to establish an "American continental army" and appointed George Washington as commander.

The majority of Americans who resisted independence blamed evil ministers, rather than the king, for unconstitutional measures and expected saner heads to rise to power in Britain. On both counts they were wrong. Americans exaggerated the influence of Pitt, Burke, Wilkes (who finally took his seat in 1774), and their other friends in Britain. In March 1775 when Burke proposed that Parliament acknowledge the colonists' right to raise and dispose of taxes, a thumping majority of Parliament voted him down. Lord North's sole counterproposal was to allow the colonists to tax themselves on condition that they collect whatever sum Parliament ordered, in effect practicing involuntary self-taxation.

Americans' sentimental attachment to the king, the last emotional barrier to independence, crumbled in January 1776 with the publication of Thomas Paine's *Common Sense*. Paine had immigrated to the colonies from England in 1774 with a penchant for radical politics and a gift for plain and pungent prose. Paine told Americans what they had been unable to bring themselves to say: that at the root of the conspiracy against American liberty lay not corrupt politicians but the very institutions of monarchy and empire. Further, America did not need its British connection. "The commerce by which she [America] hath enriched herself are the necessaries of life, and will always have a market while eating is the custom in Europe," Paine argued. And, he pointed out, the events of the preceding six months had made independence a reality. Finally, Paine linked America's awakening nationalism with a sense of religious mission: "We have it in our power to begin the world over again. A situation, similar to the present, hath not happened since the days of Noah until now." America, Paine wrote, would be a new *kind* of nation, a model society free of oppressive English beliefs and institutions.

Common Sense, "a landflood that sweeps all before it," sold more than 100,000 copies in three months, one copy for every fourth or fifth adult male in the colonies. By spring 1776 Paine's pamphlet had dissolved lingering allegiance to George III and removed the last psychological barrier to independence.

Independence at Last

John Adams described the movement toward independence as a coach drawn by thirteen horses, which could not reach its destination any faster than the slowest were willing to run. New England was already in rebellion, and Rhode Island declared itself independent in May 1776. The middle colonies hesitated to support revolution because they feared, correctly, that the war would largely be fought over control of Philadelphia and New York. The South began to press for separation. In April North Carolina authorized its congressional delegates to vote for independence, and in June Virginia followed suit. On July 2 the Continental Congress formally adopted the Virginia resolution and created the United States of America.

The drafting of a statement to justify the colonies' separation from England fell to Virginia's Thomas Jefferson. Congress approved his manuscript on July 4, 1776. Even though parliamentary authority had been the focal point of dispute since 1765, the Declaration of Independence never mentioned Parliament by name because Congress was unwilling to imply that Parliament held any authority over America. Jefferson instead focused on George III, citing "repeated injuries and usurpations" against the colonies. He added that the king's "direct object [was] the establishment of an absolute tyranny over these states."

Like Paine, Jefferson elevated colonial grievances to a struggle of universal dimensions. In the tradition of Enlightenment thought, Jefferson argued that Britain had violated its contract with the colonists, giving them the right to replace it with a government of their own. His emphasis on the equality of all individuals and their natural entitlement to justice, liberty, and self-fulfillment expressed the Enlightenment's deep longing for government that rested on neither legal privilege nor the exploitation of the majority by the few—and deliberately ignored the existence of slavery.

Jefferson addressed the Declaration of Independence as much to Americans uncertain about the wisdom of independence as to world opinion. He wanted to convince his fellow citizens that social and political progress could no longer be accomplished within the British Empire. The declaration never claimed that perfect justice and equal opportunity existed in the now former American colonies, which had become the United States; instead, it challenged the Revolutionary generation and all who followed to bring this ideal closer to reality.

CONCLUSION

Throughout the long imperial crisis, Americans pursued the goal of reestablishing the empire as it had functioned before 1763, when colonial trade was protected and encouraged and when colonial assemblies exercised exclusive power over taxation and internal legislation. These reluctant revolutionaries now had to face Europe's greatest imperial power and win independence on the battlefield. They also had to decide to what degree they would implement the ideals evoked in Jefferson's declaration. Neither task would prove easy.

CHRONOLOGY

1733 Molasses Act.

1754–1760 French and Indian War (in Europe, the Seven Years' War, 1756–1763).

1760 George III becomes king of Great Britain.
Massachusetts controversy over writs of assistance.

1763 Indian uprising in Ohio Valley and Great Lakes.
Proclamation of 1763.

1764 Sugar Act.

1765 Stamp Act.
Quartering Act.
Loyal Nine formed in Boston to oppose the Stamp Act.
Sons of Liberty band together throughout the colonies.
Stamp Act Congress.
Colonists begin boycott of British goods.

1766 Stamp Act repealed.
Declaratory Act.

1767 New York Suspending Act.
Revenue Act (Townshend duties).
John Dickinson, *Letters from a Farmer in Pennsylvania*.
American Board of Customs Commissioners created.

1768 Massachusetts "circular letter."
Boston merchants adopt the colonies' first nonimportation agreement.
John Hancock's ship *Liberty* seized.
British troops arrive in Boston.
John Wilkes elected to Parliament; arrested.
St. George's Fields Massacre in London.

1770 Townshend duties, except tea tax, repealed.
Boston Massacre.

1771 Battle of Alamance Creek in North Carolina.

1772 *Gaspee* incident in Rhode Island.
Committees of correspondence begin in Massachusetts and rapidly spread.

1773 Tea Act.
Boston Tea Party.

1774 Coercive Acts.
Quebec Act.
First Continental Congress meets in Philadelphia and adopts Suffolk Resolves.
Continental Association.

1775 Battles of Lexington and Concord.
Second Continental Congress meets.
Olive Branch Petition.
Battles at Breed's Hill and Bunker Hill.

1776 Thomas Paine, *Common Sense*.
Declaration of Independence.

FOR FURTHER READING

Bernard Bailyn, *The Ideological Origins of the American Revolution* (1967). Pulitzer Prize–winning examination of the political heritage that shaped colonial resistance to British authority.

Edward Countryman, *The American Revolution* (1985). An outstanding introduction to the Revolution.

Robert A. Gross, *The Minutemen and Their World* (1976). An eloquent and evocative examination of Concord, Massachusetts, in the revolutionary era.

Pauline Maier, *From Resistance to Revolution: Colonial Radicals and the Development of American Opposition to Britain, 1765–1776* (1972). An insightful, definitive examination of how colonial leaders strove to force the repeal of unconstitutional laws with a minimum use of violence.

Robert Middlekauff, *The Glorious Cause: The American Revolution, 1763–1789* (1982). A learned and highly readable narrative of the events leading to independence.

Edmund S. Morgan and Helen M. Morgan, *The Stamp Act Crisis: Prologue to Revolution*, rev. ed. (1963). A classic analysis of colonial constitutional principles regarding limits on Parliament's taxing power.

Robert R. Palmer, *The Age of the Democratic Revolution: Vol. I, The Challenge* (1959). Bancroft Prize–winning examination of the American Revolution in comparison to events in England, Ireland, and France.

Gordon S. Wood, *The Radicalism of the American Revolution* (1992). A sweeping account of the Revolution's long-range impact on American society.

CHAPTER 6

The Forge of Nationhood, 1776–1788

America's First Civil War

Revolutionary Society

Forging New Governments

The Revolution would teach Americans a hard lesson: that *proclaiming* a new nation, as they had done so proudly in 1776, was much easier than *making* a new nation, which they struggled to do from 1776 to 1788.

Before 1775 the outlooks of inhabitants of the various colonies had been narrowly confined within the borders of their individual provinces. With little opportunity and less necessity to work together, each colonist had regarded his own colony as superior to all others. But eight years of war transformed the colonists from citizens of thirteen disparate provinces into American citizens. Only through the collective hardships of the War for Independence did the colonists learn to see each other not just as military allies but as fellow citizens.

Independence and peace in 1783, however, gave Americans a false security. Major problems remained unsolved. The national government's authority withered as states failed to provide financial support for its operations. During the 1780s

(Right) ***A Daughter of Liberty,*** *woodcut, 1779*

farsighted leaders saw two great challenges. Could they preserve the national spirit born during the war? If so, could they provide the central government with adequate authority, yet not interfere with the rights of individual states or endanger civil liberties? Not until 1789 would they begin to overcome these challenges.

America's First Civil War

The Revolution was simultaneously a collective struggle of the American people against Britain and a civil war among North Americans, the latter conducted without restraint, mutual respect, or compassion. Militarily, the war's outcome depended on the ability of the supporters of independence, called Whigs, to wear down the British army, and on the Whigs' success in suppressing their fellow North Americans' opposition to independence. The magnitude of these twin tasks often disheartened the Whigs, but it united them as well. The common disappointments and sacrifices endured from 1775 to 1783 forged among Americans the commitment to nationhood that ultimately prevented their new country from splintering into small republics.

Loyalists and Other British Sympathizers

When independence came in July 1776, many colonists remained unconvinced of its necessity. About 20 percent of all whites actively opposed the rebellion or supported it only when threatened with fines and imprisonment. These opponents of the Revolution called themselves loyalists, but Whigs labeled them Tories.

Loyalists, like Whigs, typically opposed parliamentary taxation of the colonies. Many loyalists thus found themselves fighting for a cause with which they did not entirely agree, and as a result many switched sides during the war. Maryland loyalist Reverend Jonathan Boucher expressed a widespread apprehension: "For my part, I equally dread a Victory by either side." But loyalists believed that separation was illegal and was not necessary to preserve the colonists' constitutional rights. Above all, they revered the crown and equated any failure to defend their king with a sacrifice of personal honor.

Loyalist strength in an area depended on how well prominent local Whigs had convinced voters that the king and Parliament were endangering representative government. From 1772 to 1776 elites in New England, Virginia, and South Carolina mobilized citizens by organizing public meetings and repeatedly explaining the issues. The majority opted for resistance; by 1776 loyalists constituted barely 5 percent of whites in these areas. In contrast, elites in New York and New Jersey remained reluctant to declare allegiance to either side, and their indecision resulted in divided communities. These two states provided half of the 21,000 Americans who would fight in loyalist units.

A second major factor in loyalist strength was the geographic distribution of recent British immigrants, who identified closely with their homeland. These newcomers included thousands of British veterans of the French and Indian War who had remained in the colonies, usually in New York. Further, the 125,000 British immigrants who arrived between 1763 and 1775 formed major centers of loyalist sympathy. In New York, Georgia, and the Carolina piedmont, where these newcomers clustered, loyalists probably constituted 25 to 40 percent of the white population in 1776.

Third, loyalism thrived on the presence of ethnic and religious minorities outside the main currents of colonial society. For example, a few German, Dutch, and French religious congregations that had resisted use of the English language felt indebted to Britain for their religious freedom and doubted that their rights would remain safe in an independent Anglo-American nation. However, German colonists in Virginia, Pennsylvania, and Maryland had embraced emergent American republicanism by 1776, and they would overwhelmingly support the Revolution.

Canada's French Catholics became the most significant white loyalist minority. The Quebec Act of 1774 had guaranteed their religious freedom and their continued use of French civil law. Remembering the bitter denunciations of this measure by their southern neighbors, French Catholics feared that Protestant Anglo-Americans would be far less tolerant. Canadian anxieties intensified in mid-1775 when the Continental Congress ordered Continental forces to "free" Canada from British tyranny and to block a British invasion from the north. In 1775 Continental armies attacked Quebec but were defeated. French Catholics emerged more loyal to the British crown than ever.

Black slaves and Native Americans also widely supported the British. In the earlier 1770s the British, not the Americans, had most often offered liberty to American slaves. In 1775 nearly 800 African-Americans had joined Lord Dunmore, Virginia's governor, who had promised them freedom if they supported the British cause. Hundreds of South Carolina slaves sought refuge on British ships in Charles Town's harbor. During the war itself at least 20,000 slaves would run away to sign on as laborers or soldiers in the Royal Army. Deeply alienated from white society, slaves realized that the Revolution would not benefit them. Finally, most Indians, recognizing the threat that expansion-minded colonists posed, likewise supported the British. Of the handful of tribes that sided with the colonists, the most prominent were two Iroquois tribes, the Oneidas and the Tuscaroras.

Whigs hated loyalists, and loyalists responded to Whigs with equal venom. Each side saw its cause as sacred and viewed opposition to it by a fellow American as a betrayal. Consequently, the worst atrocities of the war were inflicted by Americans on each other.

The Opposing Sides

Britain entered the war with what should have been two major advantages. First, Britain's 11 million people greatly outnumbered the 2.5 million colonists, one-third of whom were either slaves or loyalists. Second, Britain possessed the world's largest navy and one of its best armies. During the war the army's size more than doubled, from 48,000 to 111,000 men, and Britain hired 30,000 Hessian mercenaries and enlisted 21,000 loyalists to supplement its own fighting force.

Despite a smaller population, the new nation mobilized its people more effectively than Britain. By the war's end the rebels had enlisted or drafted half of all free males aged sixteen to forty-five—about 220,000 troops—compared to the 162,000 Britons, loyalists, and Hessians who served in the British army. Further, peacetime budget cuts after 1763 had weakened British seapower and thus Britain's ability to crush the rebellion. Midway through the war, half of Britain's ships languished in dry dock, awaiting repairs. Of 110,000 new sailors, the navy lost 42,000 to desertion and 20,000 to disease or wounds. In addition, American privateers cost Britain's merchant marine dearly. During the war U.S. Navy ships and privateers would capture more than 2,000 British merchant vessels and 16,000 crewmen.

Britain could ill afford such losses, for supplying its troops in North America was a Herculean task. Although at various times the British army controlled all the major American cities, British soldiers seldom ventured into the agricultural hinterland and thus could not easily round up supplies. Virtually all the food consumed by the army, one-third of a ton per soldier per year, was imported from Britain. Seriously overextended, the navy barely kept the army supplied and never effectively blockaded American ports.

Maintaining public support presented another serious problem for Britain. The war more than doubled the British national debt, adding to the problems of a people already paying record taxes. Burdened by record taxes, the politically influential landed gentry would not vote against their pocketbooks forever.

The new United States faced different but equally severe problems. First, one-fifth of its population was openly pro-British. Second, state militias lacked the training to fight pitched battles. Their hit-and-run guerrilla tactics could not bring victory, nor could avoiding major battles and allowing the British to occupy population centers. Moreover, the

U.S. dependence on guerrilla warfare would convince potential European allies that the Americans could not drive out the British and would doom American efforts to gain foreign loans and diplomatic recognition.

The Continental Army would thus have to fight in European fashion, relying on precision movements of mass formations of troops. Victory would depend on rapid maneuvers to crush an enemy's undefended flank or rear. Attackers would need exceptional skill in close-order drill to fall on an enemy before it could re-form and return fire. After advancing within musket range, opposing troops would stand upright and fire at each other until one line weakened. Discipline, training, and nerve would be essential if soldiers were to hold their line as comrades fell around them. The stronger side would attack at a quick walk, with bayonets drawn, and drive off its opponents.

In contrast to Britain, which had a well-trained army with a tradition of bravery under fire, the Continental Army had neither an inspirational heritage nor experienced officers in 1775. In the war's early years, it suffered heartbreaking defeats. However, to win, the Continentals did not have to destroy the British army but only to prolong the rebellion until Britain's taxpayers lost patience. Until then, American victory depended on the ability of one man to keep his army fighting despite defeat—George Washington.

George Washington

Few generals looked and acted the role as much as Washington. He spoke with authority and comported himself with dignity. At six feet two inches, he stood a half foot taller than an average contemporary. Powerfully built, athletic, and hardened by a rugged outdoor life, he could inspire troops to heroism.

Washington's military experience had begun at age twenty-two, when he had commanded a Virginia regiment raised to resist French claims in the Ohio Valley (see Chapter 5). Vastly outnumbered, he had lost his first battle. A year later at Braddock's defeat, Washington had assumed the point of greatest danger, had had two horses shot out from under him, and had his hat shot off and his coat ripped by bullets. But Washington's mistakes and lost battles had taught him lessons that easy victories might not have. He had discovered the dangers of overconfidence and the need for determination. He had also learned that Americans fought best when led by example and treated with respect.

In 1758, with Virginia's borders secured, Washington had resigned his commission and become a tobacco planter. He had sat in the House of Burgesses, where others respected him and sought his opinion. An early opponent of parliamentary taxation, he had also served in the Continental Congress. In the eyes of the many who valued his advice and his military experience, Washington was the logical choice to head the Continental Army.

War in Earnest

In March 1776 the British evacuated Boston and moved south to New York, which they wished to use as a base for conquering New England. Under two brothers, General William Howe and Admiral Richard, Lord Howe, 130 warships carried 32,000 troops to New York City in summer 1776. Defending the city were 18,000 poorly trained soldiers under Washington. On August 27, 15,000 British troops nearly annihilated 10,500 American troops on Long Island, just across a river from New York City. But Washington executed a masterly night evacuation, saving 9,500 troops and most of his artillery from capture.

In mid-September 1776 the Continental Army counted 16,000 men. Over the next three months the British killed or took prisoner one-quarter of these troops and drove the survivors across New Jersey. By early December, when Washington retreated from New Jersey into Pennsylvania, he commanded fewer than 7,000 men fit for duty. Thomas Paine called these demoralizing days "the times that try men's souls."

Washington took the offensive before military and national morale collapsed. On Christmas night 1776 he attacked a Hessian garrison at Trenton, New Jersey, and captured nearly 1,000 Germans

George Washington (1732–1799),
by John Trumbull, 1780
Washington's brilliant victories at Trenton and Princeton made patriot morale soar and forced the British to reconsider their military strategy.

with the loss of only 4 men. On January 3, 1777, Washington attacked Princeton, New Jersey, killing or capturing one-third of his 1,200 British opponents and losing only 40. The American victories at Trenton and Princeton had important consequences. First, they boosted civilian and military morale. Second, they undermined the Howes' plans to rally loyalists and skeptics to Britain's cause and forced the British evacuation of New Jersey in early 1777. Washington established winter quarters only twenty-five miles from New York City.

The rebel militia meanwhile drove thousands of New Jersey loyalists, who had been plundering Whig property, into British-held New York, where many joined the Royal Army. The New Jersey militia became a police force dedicated to rooting out political dissent. It disarmed known loyalists, jailed their leaders, and constantly watched suspected Tories. Ironically, the failure by British commanders to prevent widespread looting by their troops undermined New Jersey loyalists' support for the Crown. Facing constant danger of arrest, most loyalists who remained in New Jersey bowed to the inevitable and swore allegiance to the Continental Congress.

British invasions of New York in 1777, Georgia in 1778, and the Carolinas in 1779 produced similar results. As Whigs regained the upper hand, they pursued loyalists and coerced most into renouncing the Crown. But not all loyalists shifted sides; some became political refugees and fled the country. Indeed, the war drove one out of six loyalists into exile.

The Turning Point

Shortly after the battles of Trenton and Princeton, the marquis de Lafayette, a young French aristocrat, joined Washington's staff. Lafayette was twenty years old, idealistic, brave, infectiously optimistic—and closely connected to the French court. His arrival indicated that France might recognize American independence and declare war on Britain. However, the French first wanted proof that the Americans could win a major battle.

That victory came quickly. In summer 1777 the British planned a two-pronged attack to crush New York State and to isolate New England. Two British columns, one from Montreal and the other from Quebec, were to link up near Albany. Complicating an already intricate scheme, General William Howe launched another major campaign that summer aimed at the American capital, Philadelphia. Because of Howe's fateful decision, no British troops would be able to come to the aid of the Canadian columns.

The first British column, moving south from Montreal under Lieutenant Colonel Barry St. Leger, encountered a Continental force holding a chokepoint at Fort Stanwix. Unable to defeat the rebels after a three-week siege, the British retreated north. Meanwhile, the second British column, led by Gen-

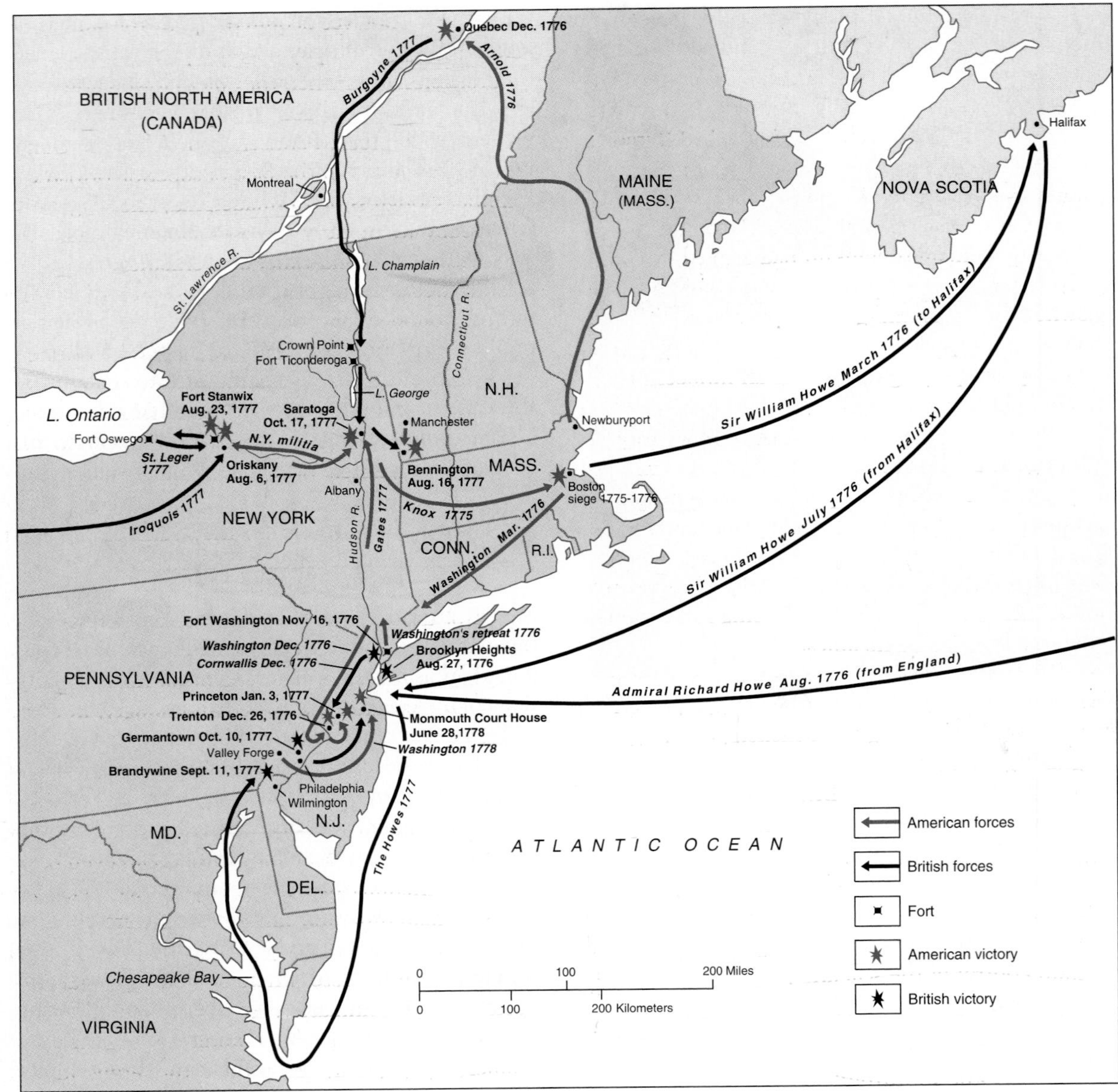

The War in the North, 1776–1779

Following the British evacuation of Boston, the war shifted to New York City, which the British held from 1776 to 1783. In 1777 Britain's success in taking the U.S. capital, Philadelphia, was offset by defeat in upstate New York. The hard-fought battle of Monmouth Court House, New Jersey, ended the northern campaigns in 1778.

eral John Burgoyne, became stranded in western New York, his supply lines overextended and his 8,300 troops depleted by combat and hunger. General Horatio Gates of the Continental Army gathered a force of 17,000 rebels and attacked Burgoyne near Saratoga. Burgoyne's troops, surrounded and outnumbered, surrendered on October 17, 1777.

Saratoga was as important diplomatically as militarily. Benjamin Franklin had arrived in France only a few weeks before news of Saratoga. Renowned for his learning and sophistication, Franklin shrewdly captured French imaginations by wearing a fur cap and playing the part of an innocent backwoods philosopher. Already pro-American, the French court received news of the victory at Saratoga as proof that the Americans could win the war and thus deserved diplomatic recognition. In February 1778 France formally recognized the United States. Four months later France went to war with Britain. Spain and Holland ultimately joined the war as French allies. Facing a coalition of enemies, Britain had no allies.

The colonies' allies made their presence felt. Between 1779 and 1781 Spanish troops prevented the British from taking the Mississippi Valley, and beginning in 1781 French troops contributed to rebel victories. Moreover, Britain sent thousands of soldiers to Ireland and the West Indies to guard against a French invasion, further stretching already depleted manpower reserves. The French and Spanish navies, which together approximately equaled the British fleet, won several large battles, denied Britain control of the sea, and punctured the Royal Navy's blockade.

The Continentals Mature

In late August 1777 British general Howe landed 18,000 troops near Philadelphia. With Washington at their head and Lafayette at his side, 16,000 Continentals paraded through the imperiled city. "They marched twelve deep," John Adams reported, "and yet took above two hours in passing by." Adams noted that the troops, although uniformed and well armed, had not yet acquired "quite the air of soldiers." They would pay a fearful price for their lack of professionalism when they met Howe's army.

The armies collided on September 11, 1777, at Brandywine Creek, Pennsylvania. After the Continentals crumbled in the face of superior British discipline, Congress fled Philadelphia, allowing Howe to occupy it. In early October Howe defeated the Americans a second time, at Germantown. In four bloody weeks 20 percent of the Continentals were killed, wounded, or captured.

In early December 1777 the 11,000 Continental survivors left Whitemarsh, Pennsylvania. Short on rations and chilled to the bone from marching into a wall of sleet, they took a week to reach their winter headquarters only eleven miles away. One-fourth of them had worn out at least one shoe. On days when the roads froze, they suffered horribly. Washington later recalled, "You might have tracked the army from White Marsh to Valley Forge by the blood of their feet." As the British rested comfortably in Philadelphia, eighteen miles away, the Continentals stumbled around the bleak hills of Valley Forge and huddled, exhausted and hungry, in crude huts.

The army slowly regained its strength but still lacked training. The Saratoga victory had resulted from the Americans' overwhelming numbers, not their superior skill. Meeting Howe on an even basis, the Continentals had lost badly—twice. The key skills of marching and maneuvering were nonexistent. Then in February 1778 the Continental Army's fortunes rose when a German soldier of fortune and drillmaster, Friedrich von Steuben, reached Valley Forge. An administrative genius and immensely popular, he turned the army into a formidable fighting force.

Just how formidable became clear in June 1778. The British, now under General Henry Clinton, evacuated Philadelphia and marched toward New York. The Continentals caught up on June 28 at Monmouth Court House, New Jersey. The battle blazed for six hours, with the Continentals throwing back Clinton's best units. The British finally broke off contact and slipped away under cover of darkness. Never again would they win easy victories against the Continental Army.

The Battle of Monmouth ended the contest for the North. Clinton occupied New York, which the Royal Navy made safe from attack. Washington kept his army on watch nearby, while Whig militia hunted down the last few Tory guerrillas.

Frontier Campaigns

West of the Appalachians and along New York and Pennsylvania's western borders, a different kind of war unfolded. The numbers engaged along the frontier were small, but the stakes were enormous. In 1776 few Anglo-Americans had any clear idea of the country's western boundaries. By 1783 when the

The War in the West, 1776–1779

George Rogers Clark's victory at Vincennes in 1779 gave the United States effective control of the Ohio Valley. Carolina militiamen drove attacking Cherokees far back into the Appalachians in 1776. In retaliation for raids on New York and Pennsylvania, John Sullivan inflicted widespread starvation on the Iroquois by burning their villages and winter food supplies in 1779.

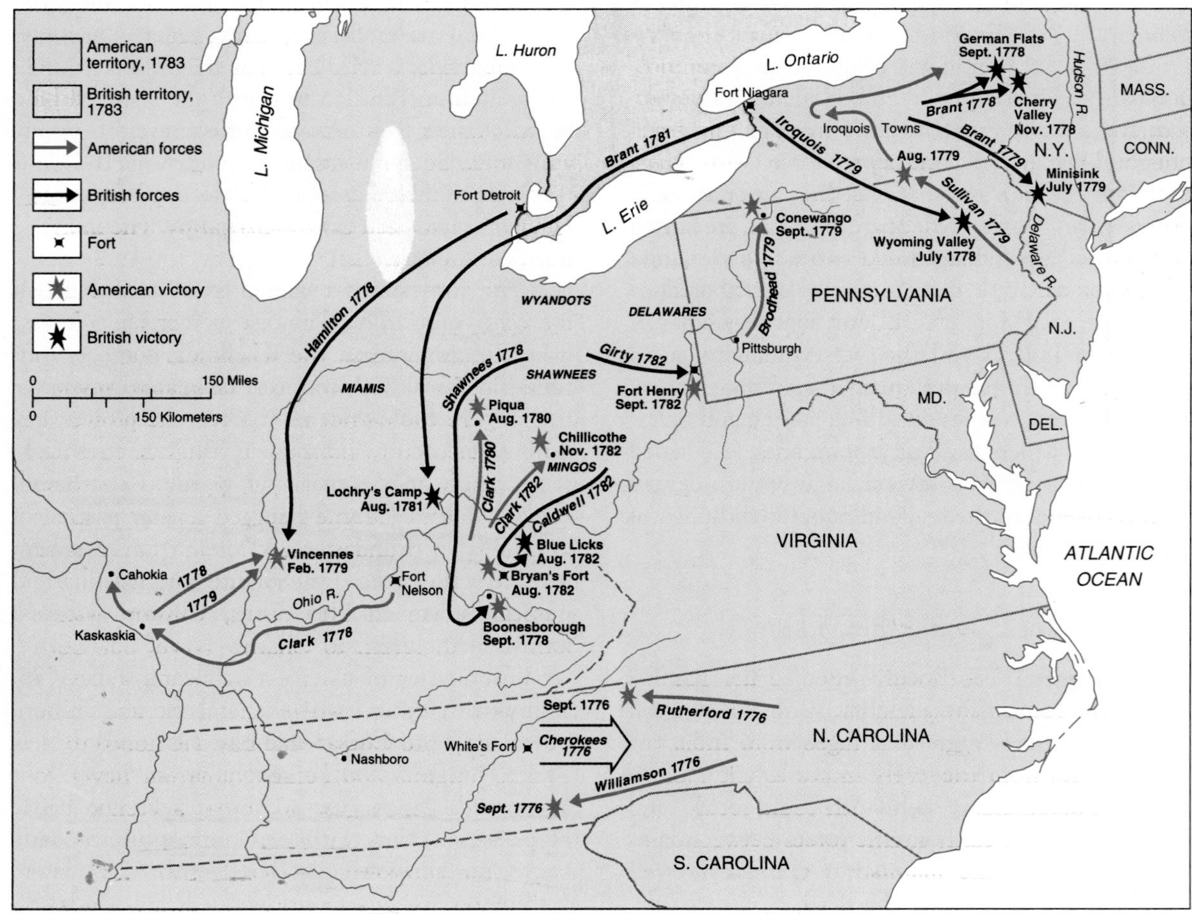

Peace of Paris concluded the war, the new nation would claim the Mississippi River as its western border. So although the frontier campaigns would not determine the war's outcome, they would significantly shape the future of the United States.

Frontier fighting first erupted in the South when Cherokees had begun attacking frontier settlements from Virginia to Georgia in 1776. Within a year retaliatory expeditions had burned most Cherokee towns and forced the Cherokees to cede most of their lands in South Carolina and large tracts in North Carolina and Tennessee. Elsewhere in the region the intense warfare lasted longer. Kentucky saw fierce fighting as rebels under Colonel George Rogers Clark established control of the Ohio River valley from Pittsburgh to the Mississippi after defeating both the British and Native Americans.

In the East pro-British Iroquois under the gifted Mohawk leader Joseph Brant devastated the New York and Pennsylvania frontiers in 1778. General John Sullivan led a Continental force, with Tuscarora and Oneida allies, against the Iroquois. Victorious at what is now Elmira, New York, in 1779, Sullivan and his forces burned two dozen Iroquois villages and destroyed a million bushels of corn. The Iroquois fled north to Canada, and hundreds starved to death. Sullivan had destroyed the heartland of the Iroquois; their population declined by one-third during the Revolutionary War. Although Brant's warriors laid waste to Pennsylvania and New York in one final spasm of fury in 1780, the Iroquois never recovered.

Victory in the South

After 1778 the British focus shifted to the South. France and Spain's entry had embroiled Britain in an international struggle that raged from India to Gibraltar and from the West Indies to the North American mainland. If the British could secure the South, they could easily shuffle forces between the West Indies and the mainland. And the South looked like an easy target: in 1778, 3,500 British troops had taken Savannah, Georgia, without difficulty, and Clinton expected a southern invasion to tap a huge reservoir of loyalist support. British strategy called for seizing key southern ports and, aided by loyal militiamen, moving back north, pacifying one region after another.

At first the plan unfolded smoothly. Sailing from New York with 4,000 men, Clinton captured Charles Town, South Carolina, in May 1780. He then returned to New York, leaving the mop-up operation to Lord Charles Cornwallis. Clinton's miscalculation of loyalist strength rapidly became apparent. Southern Tories used the British occupation to take revenge for their harsh treatment under rebel rule, and patriots struck back. The war engulfed the lower South and became intensely personal, with individuals choosing sides not for political reasons but for simple revenge.

Meanwhile, battles between British troops and Continental regulars led to a string of Continental defeats. America's worst loss of the entire war came at Camden, South Carolina, in August 1780. General Horatio Gates's combined force of professionals and militiamen faced Cornwallis's army. The militiamen fled after the first volley, and the badly outnumbered Continentals were overrun. Washington sent General Nathanael Greene to confront Cornwallis. Under Greene, the rebels lost three major battles in 1781 but won the campaign anyhow. Greene gave the patriot militiamen the protection that they needed to hunt down loyalists, stretched British supply lines until they snapped, and inflicted heavy casualties. Greene's dogged resistance forced Cornwallis to abandon the Carolina backcountry and to lead his battered troops into Virginia.

Still secure in New York, Clinton wanted Cornwallis to return to Charles Town, but Cornwallis had other plans. He established a base at Yorktown, Virginia, where the York and James rivers empty into Chesapeake Bay. He hoped to fan out into Virginia and Pennsylvania but never got the chance. On August 30, 1781, a French fleet dropped anchor off the Virginia coast and landed troops near Yorktown. Lafayette joined them, and Washington led his Continental Army south to

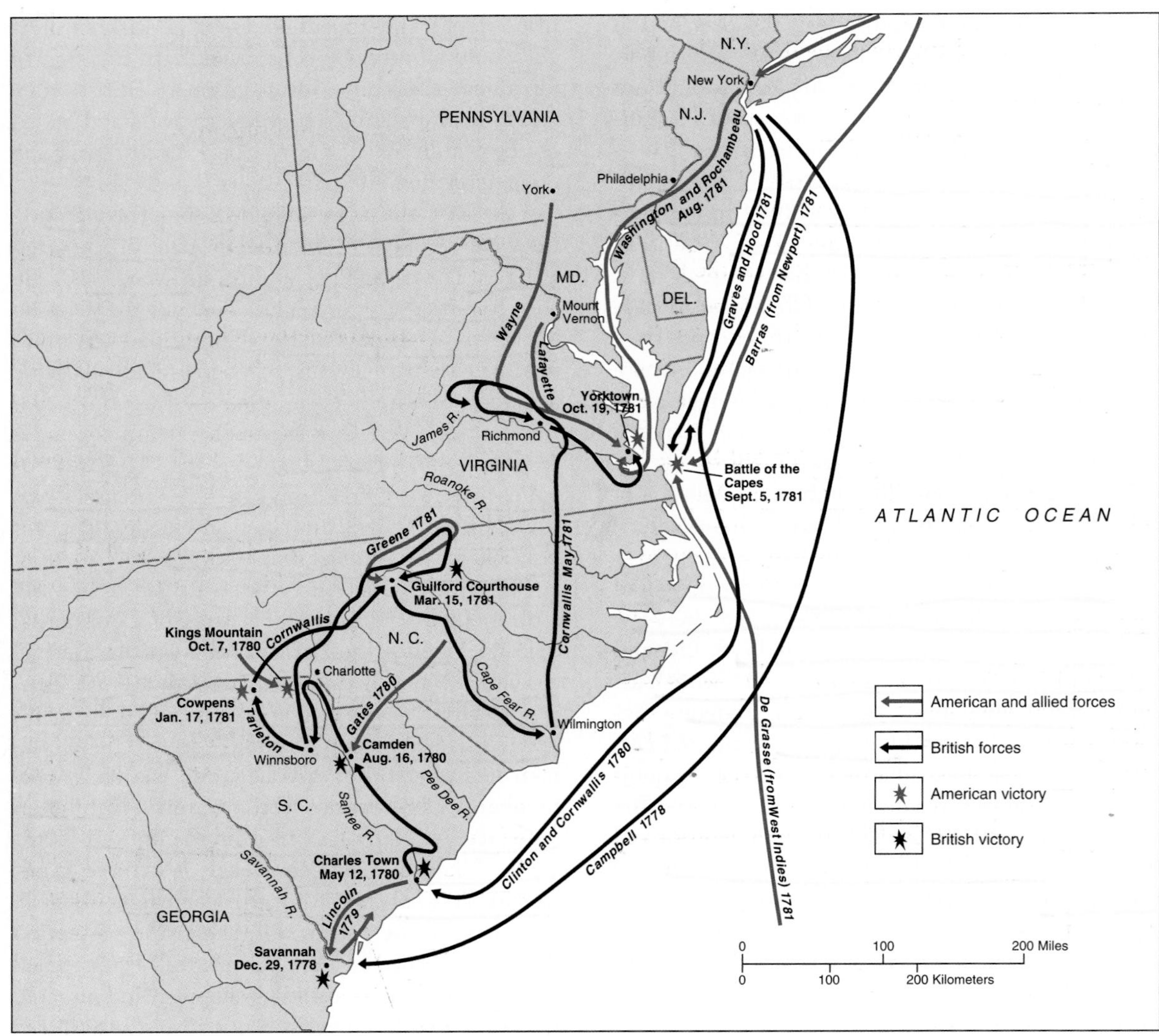

The War in the South, 1778–1781

By 1780 Britain held the South's major cities, Charles Town and Savannah, but could not establish control over the backcountry because of resistance from Nathanael Greene's Continentals. By invading Virginia, Lord Cornwallis placed himself within striking distance of Washington's U.S. and French forces, a decision that rapidly led to the British surrender at Yorktown in October 1781.

tighten the noose. Trapped and besieged at Yorktown, Cornwallis's 6,000 troops lasted three weeks against 8,800 Americans and 7,800 French. On October 19, 1781, they surrendered.

The Peace of Paris

"Oh God!" Lord North exclaimed on hearing of Yorktown. "It's all over." Indeed, Cornwallis's surrender had extinguished the overtaxed people's will to fight and forced the government to begin peace negotiations. Talks opened in Paris in June 1782, with John Adams, Benjamin Franklin, and John Jay as America's principal diplomats.

Military realities largely dictated the terms of the peace treaty. Britain recognized American independence and promised the evacuation of all royal troops from U.S. soil. Moreover, the British had little choice but to award the new nation the vast territory east of the Mississippi, for by 1783 20,000 Anglo-American settlers lived west of the Appalachians and George Rogers Clark's victories had given Americans control of the Northwest.

The settlement favored the United States but left some problems unresolved. In a separate treaty Britain transferred East and West Florida back to Spain, but the designated boundaries were ambiguous. Further, the Peace of Paris contained seeds of future British-American controversy: although the United States promised to urge state legislatures to compensate loyalists for property losses, several states would later refuse to comply. And notably missing from the treaty was any reference to the Native Americans, most of whom had supported the British. The treaty left them to deal with the new American republic on their own. Not surprisingly, many Indians did not acknowledge the new nation's claims to sovereignty over their territory.

Independence carried a heavy price. At least 5 percent of free white males aged sixteen to forty-five had died in the war. If the present-day United States were to suffer comparable casualties, 2.5 million would die. And the peace left two important issues unsettled: what kind of society the United States would become and what sort of government it would possess.

Revolutionary Society

Two forces shaped the Revolution's social effects: the principles articulated in the Declaration of Independence and the dislocations caused by the war. These factors combined to change relationships between members of different classes, races, and genders momentously.

Egalitarianism

Between 1700 and 1760 social relations between elites and common people had grown more formal, distant, and restrained. Members of the colonial gentry lived sumptuously to emphasize their position. By the late 1760s, however, many in the upper class were wearing homespun clothing in support of boycotts of British goods. When the First Families of Virginia organized militia companies in 1775, they dressed in plain hunting shirts so that even the poorest farmer would not find his humble appearance too embarrassing to enlist. By 1776 visible distinctions of wealth had noticeably lessened.

The war accelerated the erosion of class differences by forcing gentry-officers to respect ordinary men serving as privates. Indeed, the soldiers demanded to be treated with consideration, especially in light of the ringing statement of the Declaration of Independence that "all men are created equal." Soldiers followed commands, but not if they were addressed and treated as inferiors. The best officers realized this fact immediately. For example, General Israel Putnam of Connecticut, inspecting fortifications being dug near Boston in 1776, ordered a noncommissioned officer to throw a large stone onto the outer wall. "Sir, I am a corporal," the man protested. "Oh," Putnam responded, "I ask your pardon, sir," and he hurled the rock himself.

The war exposed most men of military age to such treatment. Soldiers who expected officers to recognize their worth as individuals carried their new self-esteem and insistence on respect back into civilian life. Personal pride gradually translated into political behavior and beliefs, and candidates took care not to scorn the common people. The war thus fundamentally democratized Americans' political assumptions. The gentry's sense of social rank also diminished as they met men who rose through ability and observed middle-class farmers and artisans handling duties previously thought above their station. This egalitarianism did not extend to propertyless males, women, and nonwhites, but it did undermine the tendency to believe that wealth or family background conferred a special claim to public office.

In short, Revolutionary-generation Americans insisted that virtue and sacrifice, not wealth, defined worth. They came to see the "natural aristocracy"—those who demonstrated fitness for government service by their personal accomplishments—as ideal candidates for political office. This natural aristocracy included self-made men such as Benjamin Franklin as well as those, like Thomas Jefferson and John Hancock, born into wealth.

A Revolution for African-Americans

The wartime condition of African-Americans contradicted the ideals of equality and justice for which Americans fought. About 500,000 black persons, composing one-fifth of the total population, inhabited the United States in 1776. All but 25,000 were slaves. Free blacks could not vote, lived under curfews, and lacked the guarantees of equal justice afforded to even the poorest white criminal. Grudging toleration was all that free blacks could expect, and few slaves ever became free.

The war nevertheless presented new opportunities to African-Americans. Some slaves took advantage of the confusion of war to run off and pose as freemen. A 1775 ban on black soldiers was collapsing by 1777. All states but Georgia and South Carolina eventually recruited blacks. Approximately 5,000 African-Americans, mainly from the North, served in the Continental Army. Most were slaves serving with their masters' consent, usually in racially integrated units.

Manpower demands, not a white commitment to equal justice, largely opened these opportunities. In fact, until the mid-eighteenth century most in the Western world saw slavery as part of the natural order. By the 1760s, however, some American opposition to slavery had blossomed. The Quakers led the way; by 1779 most Quaker slaveowners had freed their slaves. The Declaration of Independence's broad assertion of natural rights and human equality spurred a larger attack on slavery. By 1804 all the states from Pennsylvania north, except New Hampshire, had abolished slavery.

The antislavery movement reflected the Enlightenment's emphasis on gradual change. By priming public opinion to favor a weakening of the institution over time, leaders sought to bring about its demise. Most state abolition laws provided for gradual emancipation, typically declaring free all children born of a slave woman after a certain date, often July 4. (These individuals still had to work, without pay, for their mother's master for up to twenty-eight years.) Furthermore, Revolutionary leaders did not press for decisive action against slavery in the South, where the institution was embedded in the economy. They feared that widespread southern emancipation would either bankrupt or disrupt the Union. They argued that the United States, deeply in debt, could not finance immediate abolition in the South and that any attempt to do so without compensation would drive the region to secession.

Although slavery gnawed at Whig consciences even in the South, no state south of Pennsylvania abolished slavery. Most, however, passed laws making it easier to free slaves. Between 1775 and 1790 the number of free blacks in Virginia and Maryland rose from 4,000 to 21,000, or about 5 percent of all African-Americans residing there.

These "free persons of color" faced a future of destitution and second-class citizenship. Most had used up their cash savings to purchase their freedom and were past their physical prime. They found few whites willing to hire them or to pay equal wages. Most free blacks remained poor laborers or tenant farmers. But a few became landowners or skilled artisans. Benjamin Banneker of Maryland, a self-taught mathematician and astronomer, served on the commission that designed Washington, D.C., and published a series of almanacs.

Free blacks relied on one another for help, generally through religious channels. Because many white congregations spurned them, and because racially separate churches provided mutual support, self-pride, and a sense of accomplishment, free blacks began founding their own Baptist and Methodist congregations after the Revolution. In 1787 Philadelphia blacks established the Methodist congregation that by 1816 would become the African Methodist Episcopal church. Black churches, a great source of inner strength and community cohesion for most African-Americans ever since, had their roots in the revolutionary period.

Most states granted important civil rights to free blacks during and after the Revolution. For example, male free blacks who met property qualifications gained the right to vote everywhere by the 1780s. Most northern states repealed or stopped enforcing curfews and other restrictive laws; most also guaranteed free blacks equal treatment in court.

The Revolution neither ended slavery nor brought equality to free blacks, but it did begin a process by which slavery could be extinguished. In half the nation, public opinion no longer condoned human bondage, and southerners increasingly saw slavery as a necessary evil, implicitly admitting its immorality. The shift proved short-lived, as the trend toward egalitarianism faded in the 1790s.

Women in the New Republic

"To be adept in the art of Government is a prerogative to which your sex lay almost exclusive claim," wrote Abigail Adams to her husband, John, in 1776. One of the era's tartest political commentators and her husband's confidante and best friend, Adams had no public role. Indeed, most Americans in the 1780s believed that a woman's duty lay in maintaining her household and rearing her children.

Apart from some states' easing of women's difficulties in obtaining divorces, the Revolution had little effect on women's legal position. Women gained no new political rights, although New Jersey's constitution of 1776 did not exclude white female property holders from voting, which they did in significant numbers until barred (along with free blacks) in 1807. The assumption of women's natural dependence—on parents and then husbands—dominated discussions of the female role. Nevertheless, the Revolution's ideological currents emphasizing liberty and equality were significant for white American women.

Women greatly broadened their involvement in the cause, creating a wide range of support activities during the war. Female "camp followers," many of them soldiers' wives, cooked, laundered, and nursed the wounded for both sides. A few women disguised themselves as men and joined the fighting. Women who remained at home managed families, households, farms, and businesses on their own. Despite—and because of—enormous struggles, women gained confidence in their ability to think and act on matters traditionally reserved for men.

The revolutionary era witnessed a challenge to traditional attitudes toward women. American republicans increasingly recognized a woman's right to choose her husband rather than wait for an arranged marriage. Especially in the Northeast, daughters often, deliberately or otherwise, forced fathers' consent by becoming pregnant by prospective husbands. This secured young women economic support in a region depleted of suitors by the exodus of young, unmarried men.

Overall, white women had fewer children than their mothers and grandmothers had had. Before 1770, 40 percent of Quaker women had borne nine or more children; after then, only 14 percent would have that many children. Declining farm size and urbanization were incentives for smaller families, but just as clearly, women were finding some relief from the endless cycle of pregnancy and nursing that had consumed their forebears.

As women's roles expanded, so did republican ideas of male-female relations. A female author calling herself Matrimonial Republican denounced the word *obey* in the marriage service. "The obedience between man and wife," she wrote, "is, or ought to be, mutual." Lack of mutuality contributed to a rising number of divorce petitions submitted by women. A few women even dared challenge the prevailing sexual double standard that portrayed extramarital affairs by men as proof of virility and the same affairs by women as proof of bad character. In 1784 a woman writer calling herself Daphne appealed to her "sister Americans" to "stand by and support the dignity of our own sex" by publicly condemning the seducers, not their victims.

Gradually, the subordination of women became the subject of debate. In the essay "On the Equality of the Sexes," written in 1779, Massachusetts poet and essayist Judith Sargent Murray wrote that the genders had equal intellectual ability and deserved equal education. She hoped that "sensible and informed" women would improve their minds rather than rush into marriage and would instill republican ideals in their children. Like many of her contemporaries, Murray advocated "republican motherhood," which emphasized the importance of educating women in the values of liberty and independence in order to strengthen virtue in the new nation. Women were to infuse their sons as well as their daughters with these values. Even conservative John Adams reminded his daughter that she would be "responsible for a great share of the duty and opportunity of educating a rising family, from whom much will be expected."

After 1780 the urban elite founded numerous private schools, or academies, for girls, providing American women their first widespread opportunity for advanced education. Massachusetts also established an important precedent in 1789 by forbidding any town to exclude girls from its elementary schools. And although the great struggle for female political equality would not begin until the nineteenth century, Revolutionary-era assertions of women's intellectual and moral equality provoked scattered cries for women to be treated as men's political peers. However, republican egalitarianism faced a serious limitation: even an educated woman would be confined to being a virtuous wife and mother.

Native Americans and the Revolution

Revolutionary ideology held out at least abstract hope for African-Americans and women, but it made no provisions for the many Indians who sought to maintain political and cultural independence. Moreover, in an overwhelmingly agrarian society, the Revolution's promise of equal economic opportunity for all set the stage for territorial expansion beyond settled areas, thereby threatening Indian lands. Even where Indians retained land, the influx of settlers posed dangers in the form of deadly diseases, farming practices hostile to Indian subsistence, and alcohol. Indians were all the more vulnerable because during the wars between 1754 and 1783, their population east of the Mississippi had fallen by about one-half and many villages had been uprooted.

In the face of these uncertainties, Native Americans continued to incorporate aspects of European culture into their lives. From the early colonial period, they had adopted European-made goods of cloth, metal, and glass while retaining some of their traditional clothing, tools, and weapons. Indians also participated in the American economy by occasionally working for wages or selling food, craft items, and other products. Such interweaving of old and new characterized Indian communities throughout the newly independent states.

Thus Native Americans did not hold stubbornly to traditional ways, but they did insist on retaining control of their communities and ways of life. In 1745 some Iroquois had told an Anglo-American missionary, "We are Indians and do not wish to be transformed into white men. The English are our Brethren, but we never promised to become what they are." In the Revolution's aftermath, it remained unclear whether the new nation would accommodate Native Americans on these terms.

The Revolution and Social Change

The American Revolution left the distribution of wealth in the nation unchanged. Because fleeing Tories represented a cross-section of the population, and because wealthy Whigs snapped up confiscated Tory estates, the upper class owned about the same proportion of national wealth in 1783 as it had in 1776.

In short, the Revolution neither erased nor challenged social distinctions. Class distinctions, racial injustice, and the subordination of women persisted. Slavery remained intact in the South. Yet the Revolutionary era set in motion substantial changes. The gentry increasingly had to treat the common people with courtesy and to earn their respect. The Revolution dealt slavery a decisive blow in the North, enlarged the free-black population, and granted it important political rights. The Revolution also placed issues about relations between the genders on the agenda of national debate. Inevitably, these social changes shaped the new nation's political debates.

Forging New Governments

Before the Declaration of Independence, few Americans had thought about the colonies' forming governments of their own. The Continental Congress lacked the sovereign powers associated with governments, including the authority to impose taxes.

During the war rebels recognized the need to establish government institutions to sustain the war and to buttress the American claim to independence. But the task of forging a national government proved arduous. Moreover, the state governments formed in wartime reflected two often conflicting impulses: on the one hand, traditional Anglo-American ideas and practices; on the other, new, republican ideals. Americans would find that it was far easier to win a revolution than to transform revolutionary ideals into everyday institutions.

Tradition and Change

In establishing the Revolutionary state governments, the patriots relied heavily on the colonial experience. For example, most took the value of bicameral legislatures for granted. Colonial legislatures in the royal provinces had consisted of two houses: an appointed upper chamber (council) and an elected lower chamber (assembly). These two-part legislatures resembled Parliament's division into the House of Lords and the House of Commons and symbolized the assumption that a government should represent aristocrats and commoners separately. Despite the Revolution's democratic tendencies, few questioned the long-standing practice of setting property requirements for voters and elected officials. Property ownership, they argued, enabled voters and officeholders to think and act independently.

Americans generally agreed, too, that their elected representatives should exercise independent judgment rather than simply carry out the popular will. The idea of political parties as instruments for identifying and mobilizing public opinion was alien to the Revolutionary era, which equated parties with "factions"—selfish groups that advanced their interests at the expense of the public good. Candidates campaigned on the basis of their reputation and qualifications, not issues. In general, they did not present voters with a clear choice between policies calculated to benefit rival interest groups. Thus voters did not know how candidates stood on specific issues and found it hard to influence government actions.

As in the colonial era, legislatures were divided equally among all counties or towns in the 1780s, regardless of population distribution. A minority of voters normally elected a majority of assemblymen. Offices such as sheriff and county court justice remained appointive.

In sum, the colonial experience provided no precedent for democratization. Yet the imperial crisis of the 1760s and 1770s had pulled political elites in a democratic direction. The assemblies, the most democratic parts of colonial government, had led the fight against British policy. Colonists had embarked on the Revolution dreading executive officeholders and convinced that they could not trust even elected governors. Their recent experience seemed to confirm the "country party" view (see Chapter 5) that those in power tended to become corrupt or dictatorial. Thus revolutionary statesmen proclaimed the need to strengthen legislatures at the governors' expense.

But Revolutionary leaders described themselves as republicans, not democrats. These words had strongly charged meanings in the eighteenth century. At worst, democracy suggested mob rule; at best, it meant the concentration of power in an uneducated people. In contrast, republicanism presumed that government would be entrusted to capable leaders, elected for their talent and wisdom. For republicans, the ideal government would balance the interests of different classes to prevent any group's gaining absolute power. Most Whigs believed that a republic could not include a hereditary aristocracy or even a monarchy. Yet by rejecting these institutions, Whigs created a problem: how to maintain balance in government amid a pervasive distrust of executive power.

Reconstituting the States

The state governments organized during the Revolution reflected a struggle between democratic elements and elites. Eleven of the thirteen states set up bicameral legislatures. In most states the majority of officeholders continued to be appointed. The most radical constitution, Pennsylvania's, tried to establish election districts roughly equal in population so that a minority of voters could not elect a majority of legislators. Nine states reduced property requirements for voting, but none abolished them.

The persistence of these features should not obscure the pathbreaking nature of the state constitutions. First, their adoption required ratification by the people. Second, they could be changed only by popular vote. Above all, counter to the British view of a constitution as a body of customary practices, the state constitutions were *written* compacts that defined and limited rulers' powers. As a final check on government power, the Revolutionary constitutions contained bills of rights outlining fundamental freedoms beyond government control. Governments would no longer serve as the final judge of the constitutionality of their activities.

The state constitutions strictly limited executive power. In most states the governor became an elected official, and elections were held far more frequently than before—usually every year. In the majority of states legislatures, not governors, appointed judges and other officials. Stripped of the veto and most appointive powers, governors became figureheads.

Having weakened the executive branch and vested more power in the legislatures, the state constitutions also made the legislatures more responsive to the will of the people. Nowhere could the governor appoint the upper chamber. Eight states allowed voters to select *both* houses of the legislature. Pennsylvania and Georgia abolished the upper house and substituted a unicameral (one-chamber) legislature. The Whigs' assault on executive power reflected bitter memories of arbitrary royal governors and underscored the influence of country-party ideologues who had warned against executives' usurpation of authority.

During the 1780s, however, elites gradually reasserted their desires for centralized authority and the political prerogatives of wealth. The Massachusetts constitution of 1780, which established stiff property qualifications for voting and holding office, created state senate districts apportioned according to property values, and increased the governor's powers of veto and appointment, signaled a general trend. Georgia and Pennsylvania had reverted to bicameral legislatures by 1790. Other states raised property qualifications for the upper chamber to make room for men of "Wisdom, remarkable integrity, or that Weight which arises from property."

Troubled far less by differences among social classes and restrictions on the expression of popular will than by the prospect of tyranny, elites nevertheless feared that deep-seated and permanent social divisions could jeopardize republican liberty. Although more committed to liberty than equality, some republicans did use state government legislation to implement major social changes. In Virginia between 1776 and 1780, Thomas Jefferson drafted a series of bills to promote equality. He also attacked two legal bastions of the British aristocracy, primogeniture and entail. Primogeniture required that the eldest son inherit all property if there was no will; entail dictated that an heir and his descendants keep an estate intact—that is, neither sell nor divide it. Jefferson hoped that this legislation would

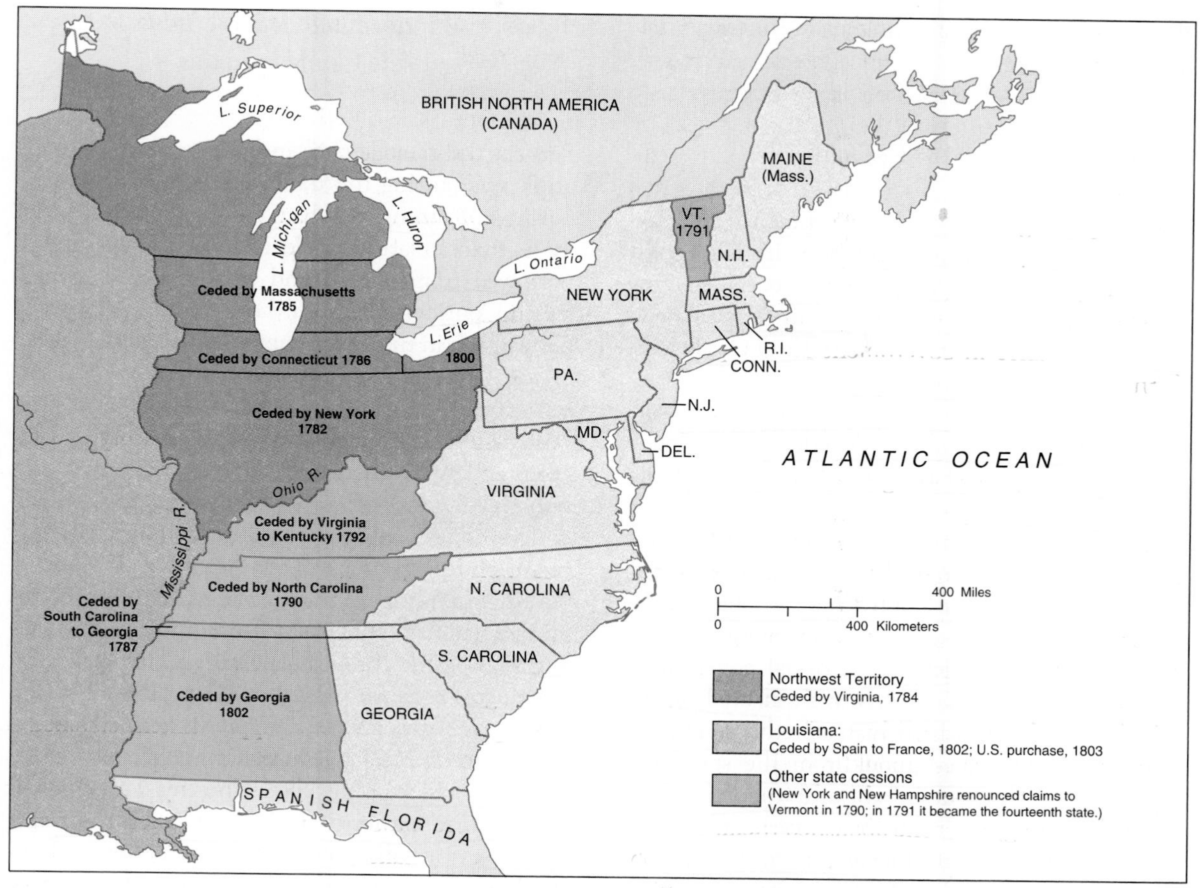

State Claims to Western Lands and State Cessions to the Federal Government, 1782–1802

Eastern states' surrender of land claims paved the way for new state governments in the West. Georgia was the last state to cede its western lands, in 1802.

ensure a continuous division of wealth and prevent wealthy families from amassing huge landholdings and becoming an aristocracy. By 1791 no state provided for primogeniture, and only two allowed entails.

These years also witnessed the end of most state-established churches. Religiously conservative New Hampshire, Connecticut, and Massachusetts resisted this reform until 1817, 1818, and 1833, respectively, but in every state where the Anglican church was established, such status was abolished by 1786. Jefferson's Statute for Religious Freedom (1786) resoundingly defended religious freedom. "Truth is great," he proclaimed, "and will prevail if left to itself."

In 1782 Thomas Paine wrote that the American Revolution was intended to ring in "a new era and give a new turn to human affairs." In this ambitious declaration, Paine expressed the heart of the republican ideal: that *all* political institutions would be judged by whether they served the public good, not the interests of a powerful few. More than anything else, this way of thinking made American politics revolutionary.

The Articles of Confederation

Americans' first national government reflected their fears of centralized authority. In 1776 John Dickinson drafted a proposal for a national government, and in 1777 Congress sent a weakened version of this document, the Articles of Confederation, to the states for ratification.

The Articles reserved to each state "its sovereignty, freedom and independence" and made Americans citizens of their states first and of the United States second. John Adams later explained that the Whigs never thought of "consolidating this vast Continent under one national Government" but created instead "a Confederacy of States, each of which must have a separate government."

Under the Articles, the national government consisted of a unicameral congress, elected by the state legislatures, in which each state had one vote. Congress could request funds from the states but could not tax without every state's approval, nor could it regulate interstate or overseas commerce. The Articles provided for no executive branch. Rather, congressional committees oversaw financial, diplomatic, and military affairs. Nor was there a judicial system by which the national government could compel allegiance to its laws.

All thirteen states had to approve the Articles. Maryland refused to sign them until states claiming lands north of the Ohio River turned them over to the national government. Maryland lawmakers wanted to keep Virginia and New York from dominating the new nation. As individual states gradually abandoned their northwestern claims, Maryland relented, and the Articles became law in March 1781.

The new government represented an important step in the process of defining the role of national sovereignty in relation to the sovereignty of individual states and in creating a formal government. Nonetheless, the Whigs' misgivings left the new government severely limited.

Finance and Trade Under the Confederation

Perhaps the greatest challenge facing the Confederation was putting the nation on a sound financial footing. Winning the war cost $160 million, far more than taxation could raise. The government borrowed from abroad and printed paper money, called Continentals. But from 1776 to 1791 lack of public faith in the government destroyed 98 percent of the Continentals' value—an inflationary disaster. Congress turned to Robert Morris, a wealthy Philadelphia merchant who became the nation's superintendent of finance in 1781. Morris proposed a national import duty of 5 percent to finance the congressional budget and to guarantee interest payments on the war debt, but the duty failed to pass.

In 1783, hoping to panic the country into creating a regular source of national revenue, Morris and New York congressman Alexander Hamilton engineered a dangerous gamble, later known as the Newburgh Conspiracy. They secretly persuaded some army officers, encamped at Newburgh, New York, to threaten a coup d'état unless the treasury obtained the taxation authority necessary to raise their pay, which was months late. George Washington forestalled the conspiracy by appealing to his officers' honor. Morris never intended a mutiny to take place, but his risk taking demonstrated the new nation's perilous financial straits and its political institutions' vulnerability.

When peace came in 1783, Morris found it impossible to fund the government adequately. After New York blocked another congressional tax measure sent to the states, state contributions to Congress fell steadily. By the late 1780s the states lagged 80 percent behind in providing the funds that Congress requested.

Nor could the Confederation pry trade concessions from Britain. Before independence, New England had depended heavily on exports to the West Indies. After independence, Britain had slapped strict limitations on U.S. commerce, allowing British shippers to increase their share of the Atlantic trade at American expense. This loss of

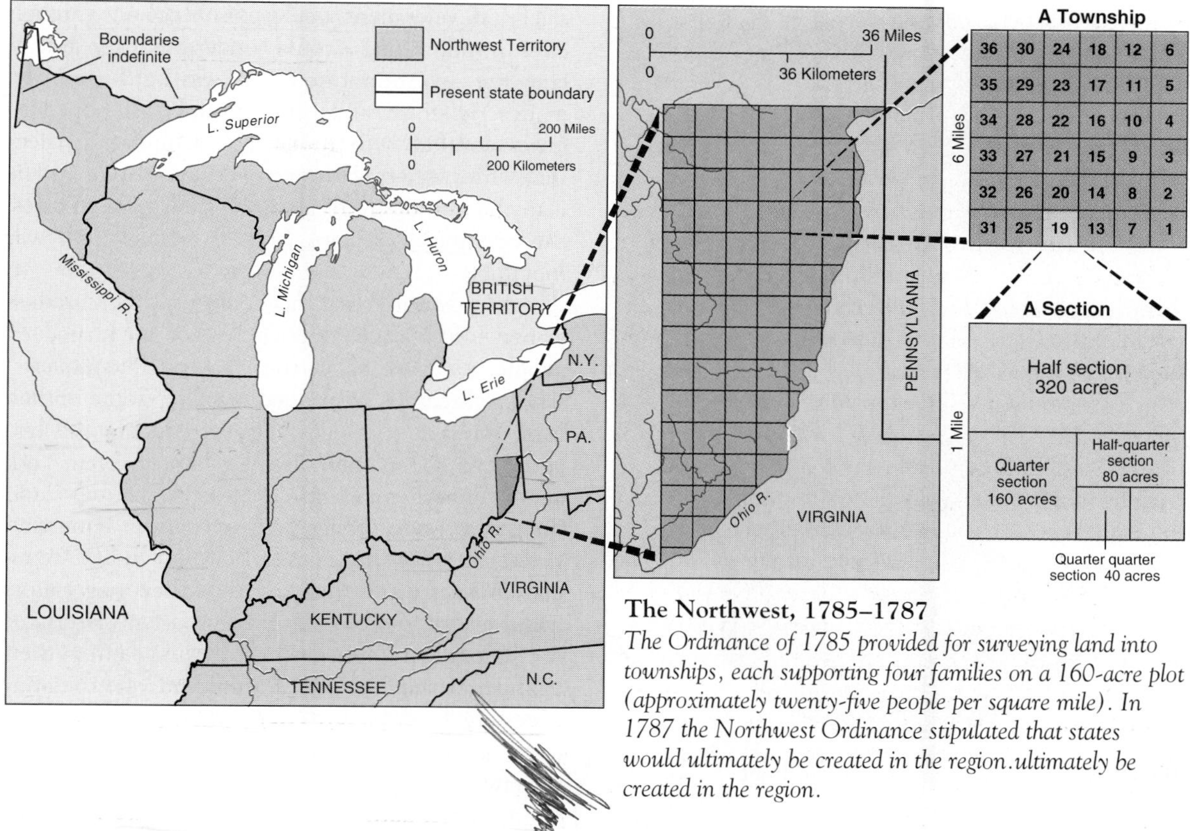

The Northwest, 1785–1787

The Ordinance of 1785 provided for surveying land into townships, each supporting four families on a 160-acre plot (approximately twenty-five people per square mile). In 1787 the Northwest Ordinance stipulated that states would ultimately be created in the region.ultimately be created in the region.

trade contributed to an economic depression that gripped the nation beginning in 1784.

The Confederation and the West

The postwar settlement and administration of western lands posed another formidable challenge to the new government. Settlers and speculators were determined to possess these lands, and Native Americans were equally determined to keep them out. At the same time, Britain and Spain sought to contain the new nation's territorial expansion.

After the states surrendered claims to more than 160 million acres north of the Ohio River, Congress, in the Ordinance of 1785, established uniform procedures for surveying the region. The law made the basic unit of settlement a township six miles square, subdivided into thirty-six sections of 640 acres each, with one section reserved as a source of income for public schools. A subsequent law, the Northwest Ordinance of 1787, defined the land north of the Ohio River as the Northwest Territory, provided for its later division into states, and forbade slavery in the territory. The Northwest Ordinance outlined three steps for admitting states to the Union. First, Congress would appoint a territorial governor and judges. Second, as soon as 5,000 adult males lived in a territory, the people would write a temporary constitution and elect a legislature. Third, when the population reached 60,000, the settlers would write a state constitution, which Congress would approve before granting statehood.

The Ordinance of 1785 and the Northwest Ordinance became the Confederation's major contributions to American life. They set the principles for surveying the frontier, allowed territorial self-

Phillis Wheatley, African-American Poet
Though a slave, Wheatley was the best-known poet in America at the time of the Revolution. Some of her poems linked the liberty sought by the colonists with a plea for the liberty of slaves. Despite her fame, Wheatley died in poverty in 1784.

government at an early stage of settlement, and provided reasonable standards for statehood. They became models for organizing territories west of the Mississippi River and established precedents for banning slavery from certain territories. However, because Indians, determined to bar white settlement, controlled virtually the entire Northwest, Congress's ordinances had no immediate effect.

The Northwest Territory offered enough rich land to guarantee future citizens landownership, thus satisfying the republican belief that opening the West would prevent the rise, east of the Appalachians, of a large class of tenant farmers and poor laborers lacking the property needed to vote. Such a development would poison politics through class conflict and would undermine republican equality. In the anticipated westward push by whites, Jefferson and other republicans hoped to avoid conflict with Indians by assimilating them into white society. However, because Native Americans had no desire to abandon their own cultures, the opening of western lands to whites made war inevitable.

At postwar treaty negotiations U.S. commissioners told Native Americans, "You are a subdued people. . . . We claim the country by conquest." Under threat of continued warfare, some Indian leaders initially yielded. Through treaties the Iroquois lost about one-half their land in New York and Pennsylvania, while the Delawares and Shawnees were obliged to recognize American sovereignty over their lands. But most Indians repudiated the treaties, denying that their negotiators had the authority to give up their nations' lands.

The Indians' resistance also stemmed from their confidence that the British would provide the arms necessary to defy the Americans. Britain had refused to abandon seven forts along the nation's northwestern frontier, ostensibly because Tories remained uncompensated for property losses. In April 1784 the British colonial office secretly ordered Canada's governor to hold onto the forts, hoping to reestablish Britain's claim to the Northwest Territory.

The Mohawk Joseph Brant led Indian resistance to white settlement. Courageous, skilled in diplomacy, and well educated, he organized the northwestern Indians into a military alliance in 1786 to keep out white settlers. But Brant and his followers, who had relocated beyond American reach in Canada, could not win support from other Iroquois such as the Senecas of Jenuchshadago, who remained in New York and feared a military invasion.

The Confederation faced similar problems in the Southeast, where Spain and its Indian allies worked to block American encroachment on their land. The Spanish found an ally in the shrewd Creek diplomat Alexander McGillivray, who was determined to regain surrendered Creek territory. McGillivray negotiated a secret treaty with Spain that promised the Creeks weapons to protect themselves "from the Bears and other fierce Animals." In 1786 he launched an attack on occupants of disputed lands. He offered a cease-fire after winning his objective.

The Spanish also attempted to prevent American infiltration by denying western settlers permission to ship crops down the Mississippi River to New Orleans. After the Spanish closed New Orleans to Anglo-American commerce in 1784, John Jay went to Spain to negotiate trading privileges at New Orleans. Although he failed to win concessions, he returned with a treaty that opened Spanish markets to eastern merchants at the price of relinquishing American export rights through New Orleans. In 1786 Congress rejected this Jay-Gardoqui Treaty, but westerners and southerners, whose interests seemed to have been sacrificed to benefit northern commerce, felt betrayed.

Shays's Rebellion

Had not violence erupted in Massachusetts, the Confederation might have lasted indefinitely. Massachusetts had suffered two major blows: in the depression that had set in in 1784, it had lost its best market, the British West Indies, and early in 1786 the state legislature had imposed high taxes to pay off its Revolutionary debt rapidly. British creditors and Massachusetts bankers and tax collectors demanded payment in specie (gold and silver coin). Thousands of small farmers, accustomed to paying local creditors with goods and services, often over a period of years, found the idea of paying all debts in hard currency not only alien but also impossible. Farmers in western Massachusetts were hard hit. As they had more than a decade earlier, farmers held rallies to discuss "the Supressing of tyrannical government." This time, however, tyranny stemmed from the state house in Boston, not Parliament in London. Late in 1786 Daniel Shays, a Revolutionary War officer and hard-pressed farmer, led 2,000 angry men in an attempt to shut down the courts and to prevent foreclosures and tax auctions. Although routed by the state militia, Shays's followers won control of the Massachusetts legislature in 1787, cut taxes, and secured a pardon for Shays.

Although Shays's Rebellion caused little bloodshed and never raised a serious threat of anarchy, critics of the Confederation painted it and similar, less radical movements elsewhere as a taste of the disorder to come under the weak national government. By threatening to seize weapons from a federal arsenal at Springfield, Massachusetts, the Shaysites had unintentionally reminded nationalists how vulnerable to "mobocracy" the United States had become. Meanwhile, rumors that Spain had offered westerners export rights at New Orleans if they would secede from the Union sowed fears that the United States was on the verge of coming apart.

The mid-Atlantic and southern states, emerging from the depression that still gripped New England, generally did not share this alarm about the Confederation's fragility. However, a growing minority was dissatisfied. Urban artisans wanted a strong government that could impose high tariffs to protect their products. Merchants and shippers desired a government powerful enough to secure trading privileges for them, and land speculators and westerners wanted a strong government that would pursue aggressive anti-Indian policies.

Shortly before Shays's Rebellion, delegates from five states, meeting at Annapolis, Maryland, had called for a convention to propose amendments to the Articles of Confederation. Accepting their suggestions, Congress asked the states to send delegates to meet in Philadelphia.

The Philadelphia Convention

In May 1787 fifty-five delegates, from every state but Rhode Island, began gathering at the Pennsylvania State House (later called Independence Hall) in Philadelphia. Among them were men of established reputation—George Washington, Benjamin Franklin, Robert Morris—as well as talented newcomers such as Alexander Hamilton and James Madison. Most were wealthy, were in their thirties

James Madison (1751–1836)
Although one of the Philadelphia Convention's youngest delegates, Madison of Virginia was among its most politically astute. He played a central role in the Constitution's adoption.

or forties, and had legal training. Nineteen owned slaves. Most important, they shared a "continental" or "nationalist" perspective. Thirty-nine had served in Congress and knew firsthand the weaknesses of the Articles. They were convinced that without a strong national government, the country would fall victim to foreign aggression or simply disintegrate.

Two basic issues confronted the convention. First, should the delegates merely tinker with the Articles, or should they draw up a new frame of government? Second, how could any government balance the conflicting interests of large and small states? Thirty-six-year-old James Madison of Virginia proposed answers to both questions.

Madison's Virginia Plan, introduced by fellow Virginian Edmund Randolph in late May, boldly called for a national government, not a confederation of states. It gave Congress virtually unrestricted rights of legislation and taxation, power to veto state laws, and authority to use military force against states. As delegate Charles Pinckney of South Carolina immediately saw, the Virginia Plan was designed "to abolish the State Govern[men]ts altogether." The Virginia Plan specified a bicameral legislation and made representation in both houses of Congress proportional to each state's population. The voters would elect the lower house, which would then choose delegates to the upper house from nominations submitted by the state legislatures. The houses would jointly name the country's president and judges. But opposition to Madison's plan surfaced immediately, particularly his call for proportional representation, which favored Virginia, the largest state.

On June 15 William Paterson of New Jersey offered a counterproposal that, like Madison's plan, strengthened the national government at the states' expense. The New Jersey Plan featured a unicameral legislature in which each state had one vote, just as under the Articles. It went even further than the Virginia Plan by defining congressional laws and treaties as the "supreme law of the land."

The New Jersey Plan exposed the convention's greatest problem: the question of representation. The Virginia Plan gave the four largest states—Virginia, Massachusetts, New York, and Pennsylvania—a majority in both houses. The New Jersey Plan allowed the seven smallest states, with only 25 percent of the U.S. population, to control Congress. By early July the convention was stalemated. To end the impasse, the delegates appointed a "grand committee" dedicated to compromise. This panel adopted a proposal by the Connecticut delegation: an equal vote for each state in the upper house and proportional representation in the lower house. The convention accepted the compromise on July 17 and in two months overcame the remaining hurdles.

As finally approved on September 17, 1787, the Constitution of the United States was an extraordinary document. In addition to reconciling the interests of large and small states, it balanced the delegates' desire for a strong national government against their fear of tyranny. It increased national authority in several ways. It vested in Congress the authority to levy and collect taxes, to regulate interstate commerce, and to conduct diplomacy. Under the Constitution, all acts and treaties of the United States would become "the supreme law of the land." State officials would have to uphold the Constitution, even against acts of their own states. The national government could use military force against any state.

In effect, the Constitution abandoned the principle on which the Articles of Confederation had rested: that the United States was a federation of independent republics known as states. However, the Constitution's framers restrained the new national government in two key ways. First, they established three distinct branches within the new government—the legislative, the executive, and the judicial. Second, they designed a system of checks and balances to prevent one branch from dominating the others. States' equal representation in the Senate offset proportional representation by population in the House, and each chamber could block hasty measures demanded by the other. Further, the president could veto acts of Congress, but to prevent capricious use of the presidential veto, a two-thirds majority in each house could override a veto. The president would conduct diplomacy, but only the Senate could ratify treaties. The president appointed his cabinet, but only with Senate approval. Congress could, by joint vote, remove the president and his appointees from office, but only for "high crimes," not for political disagreements.

To further guarantee the independence of each branch, the Constitution provided that the members of one branch would not choose those of another, except judges, whose independence was protected by lifetime appointments. For example, an electoral college, composed of members chosen by the various state legislatures, would select the president. State legislatures would also elect senators, whereas popular vote would determine delegates to the House of Representatives.

In addition to checks and balances, the Constitution embodied a novel form of federalism—a system of shared power and dual lawmaking by the state and national governments—to limit central authority. Not only did the state legislatures have a key role in electing the president and senators, but the Constitution could be amended by the votes of three-fourths of the state legislatures. This system differed greatly from Madison's original plan to establish a national government entirely independent of and superior to the states. Federalism assumed that the national government would limit its activities to foreign affairs, national defense, regulation of commerce, and coining of money. Most other political matters were left to the states. The states could otherwise act autonomously on purely internal matters, including slavery.

The Philadelphia convention faced a dilemma: were slaves property or persons? In general, southern states regarded slaves as property; however, since slaves constituted substantial portions of the southern population, southern delegates wanted to count them as persons in determining representation in the lower house. Many northern delegates from the states that were abolishing slavery hesitated to give southern states a political edge by counting as persons slaves who had neither civil nor political rights. At the same time, northern delegates, themselves property owners, balked at questioning southern notions of property rights. Thus they agreed to allow three-fifths of all slaves to be counted for congressional representation and forbade any state's people to prevent the return of runaway slaves to another state. The Constitution did limit slavery by not repudiating the Northwest Ordinance's restrictions on slavery and by permitting Congress to ban the importation of slaves after 1808.

Although leaving much authority to the states, the Constitution established a national government clearly superior to the states in several spheres and utterly abandoned the notion of a confederation of virtually independent states. Having thus strengthened national authority, the convention faced the issue of ratification. Two factors argued against submitting the Constitution to the state legislatures for ratification. First, the state legislatures would probably reject the Constitution, which shrank their power relative to the national government. Second, most of the framers believed that the government had to rest on the consent of the American people themselves. The Constitution's opening words—"We the People of the United States"—embodied this view. In the end the Philadelphia Convention provided for the Constitution's ratification by special state conventions composed of delegates elected by the people. Approval by nine such conventions would enable the new government to operate.

Under the Constitution, the framers expected the nation's "natural aristocracy" to continue exercising political leadership; but did they also intend to rein in the democratic currents that the Revolution had set in motion? In one respect they did—by curtailing the power of popularly elected state legislatures. However, the Constitution made no attempt to control faction and disorder by suppressing liberty—a "remedy," wrote Madison, that would have been "worse than the disease." The House of Representatives did provide one crucial democratic element in the new government. Equally important, the Constitution recognized the American people as the ultimate source of political legitimacy. By making the Constitution flexible and amendable and by dividing political power among competing branches of government, the framers made it possible for the national government to be slowly democratized.

The Constitution's Ratification

At first the Constitution had little national support. Many Americans hesitated to accept the idea of a radically restructured government. To quiet fears of centralized national authority, the Constitution's supporters shrewdly dubbed themselves Federalists, a term implying that the Constitution successfully balanced the relationship between state and national governments.

The Constitution's opponents became known as Antifederalists, a negative-sounding name that conveyed little of their fears that the Constitution *did not* balance the power of the state and national governments. In fact, many Antifederalists doubted that such a balance was even possible. By augmenting national authority, they believed, the Constitution would ultimately doom the states.

Antifederalist arguments reflected the deep-seated Anglo-American suspicion of any concentration of power, a suspicion that had driven events from the Stamp Act Congress through the War of Independence and the early years of the new republic. Unquestionably, the Constitution gave the national government unprecedented authority in an age when most writers on politics agreed that the sole means of preventing despotism was restraining the power of government officials. Distant from the people, especially in an era when news traveled slowly, the national government would be far less responsive to the popular will than state governments would be. "The vast Continent of America cannot be long subjected to a Democracy if consolidated into one Government. You might as well attempt to rule Hell by Prayer," wrote a New England Antifederalist. Furthermore, no one could be sure that the untried scheme of checks and balances would work. And the Constitution contained no guarantees that the new government would protect the liberties of individuals or the states. The absence of a bill of rights prompted Madison's nationalist ally and fellow Virginian George Mason, the author of the first state bill of rights in 1776, to oppose the Constitution.

The Antifederalists confronted several major disadvantages. For one thing, the Federalists included most of the country's wealthiest and most honored men, including Washington and Franklin. In addition, the majority of newspapers were Federalist and did not hesitate to bias their reporting. Finally, the Antifederalists, largely drawn from state and local leaders, lacked their opponents' contacts and experience at the national level. Ultimately, however, Federalist superiority in funds and political organizing proved decisive. The Antifederalists failed to create a sense of urgency among their supporters, assuming that most would automatically rally to them. However, only one-quarter of the voters turned out to elect delegates to the state ratifying conventions, and most had been mobilized by Federalists.

Federalist delegates prevailed in eight state

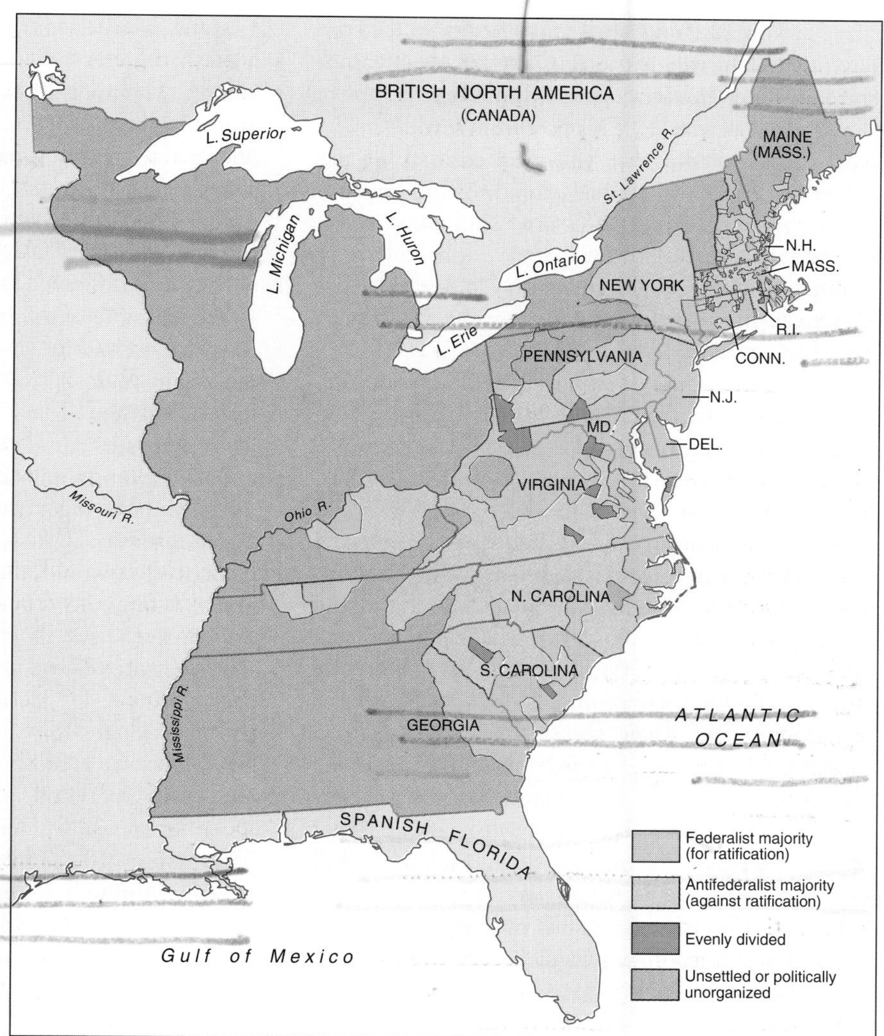

Federalist and Antifederalist Strongholds, 1787–1790

Federalists drew their primary backing from densely populated areas along major transportation routes, where trade, mobility, and frequent contact with people in other states encouraged a nationalistic identity. Antifederalist support came from interior regions where geographic isolation bred a localistic perspective. However, some frontier regions, among them Georgia and western Virginia, voted for a strong central government that would push back the Indians or the Spanish.

conventions between December 1787 and May 1788, in all cases but one by margins of two-thirds or more. Such lopsided voting in favor of the Constitution reflected Federalist aggressiveness more than popular support. In a Pennsylvania Antifederalist's words, the Federalists rammed through approval in some states "before it can be digested or deliberately considered." Only Rhode Island and North Carolina rejected the Constitution.

But unless the large states of Virginia and New York ratified, the new government would be unworkable. Antifederalism ran high in both, especially among small farmers, who believed that the Constitution favored city dwellers and monied interests. Prominent Antifederalists included New York's governor George Clinton and Virginia's Richard Henry Lee, George Mason, Patrick Henry, and future president James Monroe.

On June 21, 1788, the Constitution became the law of the land when the ninth state, New Hampshire, ratified. Debate continued in Virginia, where the Federalists won wide support from settlers in the western part of the state who wanted a strong national government capable of ending Indian raids along the Ohio River. Western Virginians' votes, combined with Madison's logic and tidewater planters' support, ruled the day. On June 25 the Virginia delegates ratified by a narrow 53 percent majority.

The struggle was even hotter in New York. Antifederalists controlled the state convention and probably would have voted down the Constitution had not news arrived of New Hampshire's and Virginia's ratification. Federalists, led by Alexander Hamilton and John Jay, hinted strongly that if the convention rejected the Constitution, New York City would secede and join the Union alone, leaving upstate New York a landlocked enclave. Alarmed, a number of Antifederalists switched sides and New York ratified on July 26 by a 30–27 vote.

Despite the defeat, the Antifederalists left an important legacy. At Antifederalist insistence, the Virginia, New York, and Massachusetts conventions ratified the Constitution with requests that the new charter be amended to include a bill of rights protecting Americans' basic freedoms. Widespread support for a bill of rights made it a major item on the new government's agenda, even as states were choosing members of Congress and presidential electors were unanimously designating George Washington president of the United States.

Antifederalists in New York also stimulated one of the greatest works of political analysis ever written: *The Federalist*, a series of eighty-five newspaper articles by Alexander Hamilton, James Madison, and John Jay. Although *The Federalist* papers did little to influence the New York vote, they provided a glimpse of the framers' intentions in designing the Constitution and thus powerfully shaped the American philosophy of government. The Constitution, insisted *The Federalist*'s authors, had two main purposes: to defend minority rights against majority tyranny and to prevent a stubborn minority from blocking measures necessary for the national interest. There was no reason to fear that the Constitution would allow a single economic or regional interest to dominate. In the most profound essay in the series, *Federalist* No. 10, Madison argued that the nation's size and diversity would neutralize the attempts of factions to steer unwise laws through Congress.

Madison's analysis was far too optimistic, however. The Constitution did indeed afford enormous scope for special interests to influence government. The great challenge for Madison's generation would be maintaining a government that provided equal benefits to all but special privileges to none.

CONCLUSION

By May 1790 North Carolina and Rhode Island had entered the Union, marking the final triumph of the nationalism born of the War for Independence. The eight-year conflict had swept up one-half of all men of military age and made casualties of one-fifth of them. Never before had such a large part of the population sacrificed in a common cause of this magnitude.

The experience of sacrificing and fighting together made many of the former colonists self-consciously American. Many shared the view of General Nathanael Greene of Rhode Island, who condemned the "prejudices" of those with "local attachments." "I feel the cause and not the place," he said; "I would as soon go to Virginia [to fight] as stay here [New England]." The distractions of peace almost allowed this sentiment to evaporate, but the Constitution offered clear proof that large numbers of Americans viewed themselves as a common people rather than as the citizens of allied states.

CHRONOLOGY

1775 Virginia governor Lord Dunmore promises freedom to any slave assisting in the restoration of royal authority.
Mercy Otis Warren, *The Group*.

1776 British troops evacuate Boston.
British defeat American forces under George Washington in fighting around New York City.
American victory in Battle of Trenton.

1777 American victory in Battle of Princeton.
British surrender at Saratoga.
Battle of Brandywine Creek; British occupy Philadelphia.
American defeat at Battle of Germantown.
Congress approves Articles of Confederation.

1778 France formally recognizes the United States.
France declares war on Britain.
Philadelphia evacuated by British; Battle of Monmouth Court House (New Jersey).
British occupy Savannah.
Joseph Brant leads Iroquois attacks in western Pennsylvania and New York.

1779 Spain declares war on Britain.
George Rogers Clark's recapture of Vincennes.
John Sullivan leads U.S. raids on Iroquois.
Judith Murray, "On the Equality of the Sexes" (published in 1790).

1780 British seize Charles Town.
Dutch Republic declares war on Britain.

1781 Articles of Confederation become law.
Battle of Yorktown; British general Charles Cornwallis surrenders.

1782 Paris peace negotiations begin.

1783 Peace of Paris.
Newburgh Conspiracy.

1784 Spain closes New Orleans to American trade.
Economic depression begins.

1785 Ordinance of 1785.

1786 Congress rejects Jay-Gardoqui Treaty.
Joseph Brant organizes Indian resistance to U.S. expansion.
Virginia adopts Thomas Jefferson's Statute for Religious Freedom.

1786–1787 Shays's Rebellion in Massachusetts.

1787 Northwest Ordinance.
Philadelphia Convention; federal Constitution signed.

1788 Alexander Hamilton, James Madison, and John Jay, *The Federalist*.
Federal Constitution becomes law.

FOR FURTHER READING

Edward Countryman, *The American Revolution* (1985). An excellent introduction to developments from the Revolution through ratification of the Constitution.

Jack P. Greene, ed., *The American Revolution: Its Character and Limits* (1987). Leading scholars' analysis of how Americans dealt with the problem of applying their political ideals to an imperfect society without endangering the nation's survival.

Robert Middlekauff, *The Glorious Cause: The American Revolution, 1763–1789* (1982). A comprehensive account of military and political developments through the Philadelphia Convention.

Mary Beth Norton, *Liberty's Daughters: The Revolutionary Experience of American Women, 1750–1800* (1980). A wide-ranging study of changes in the lives and roles of women during the revolutionary era.

Benjamin Quarles, *The Negro in the American Revolution* (1961). An authoritative study of blacks' role in the Revolution and its consequences for them.

Charles Royster, *A Revolutionary People at War: The Continental Army and American Character* (1980). An illuminating analysis of how revolutionary Americans created and fought in an army.

Gordon Wood, *The Creation of the American Republic, 1776–1787* (1969). Comprehensive treatment of the evolution of American political thought from the first state governments to the Philadelphia Convention.

CHAPTER 7

Launching the New Republic, 1789–1800

The Fragile New Nation

Constitutional Government Takes Shape

National Economic Policy and Its Consequences

The United States in a Hostile World

Battling for the Nation's Soul

Deferring Equality

The problems facing George Washington in 1789 underlined the fragility of the United States. North Carolina and Rhode Island still remained outside the Union, westerners were flirting with Spanish agents, and the splintering of the nation into several smaller countries seemed a real threat. In addition, Indians and frontier whites were fighting ceaselessly, foreign restrictions were strangling American exports, the treasury was bankrupt, and government credit was a shambles. Finally, France, Spain, and Britain all menaced American prosperity and independence.

By the end of his second administration in 1797, Washington had helped to overcome some of the most serious obstacles, but at the price of unleashing fiercely emotional party divisions. By 1798 a sense of crisis again gripped the nation. The party in power resorted to political oppression. Afraid of despotism and an unfair election, the opposition party desperately maintained that state legislatures could veto federal laws.

(Right) ***Liberty and Washington,*** *anonymous artist, early nineteenth century*

In the election of 1800, each side damned the other in irresponsible rhetoric. Only after the election, with Thomas Jefferson in office, was it clear that the United States had avoided dissolution and preserved civil liberties.

The Fragile New Nation

The postwar years brought problems, not prosperity, to many Americans. Restrictions on export markets endangered the livelihoods of farmers, sailors, and merchants. Foreign efforts to prevent American settlement of the frontier frustrated land speculators as well as pioneers. The Confederation's default on the national debt had injured thousands of Revolutionary creditors by delaying their compensation, and there was no guarantee that the new government would honor their claims. These conditions had convinced Americans of the need for a new constitution, but because of the scope of the problems, the new system could still fail.

Conflicting regional interests would prevent the new government from providing equal nationwide benefits for two decades. And other fissures were deepening within American society: among blacks, Indians, and whites; between emerging capitalists and wage earners; and above all, among citizens with different interpretations of republicanism. These regional and ideological conflicts would not only split the new Congress into hostile parties but also bring into focus a rising demand for a *democratic* republic.

The West and the South

Most U.S. territory from the Appalachians to the Mississippi River belonged to Native Americans. Divided into more than eighty tribes numbering perhaps 150,000 people in 1789, Indians struggled to preserve their way of life. During the Revolutionary War patriot forces had dealt the Iroquois and Cherokees punishing blows, but most Indians, though bloodied, had continued to hold their land. In 1786 Ohio River tribes formed a defensive confederacy (see Chapter 6). Powerful southeastern nations refused to acknowledge American rule. Great Britain backed Indian resistance in the Northwest, as did Spain in the Southeast.

Confronting the inland Indians were about 200,000 frontier settlers, many of them isolated and vulnerable. By 1786 Indian war parties had spread death, destruction, and panic from Pennsylvania to Georgia. Fifteen hundred of Kentucky's 74,000 settlers were captured or killed in Indian raids from 1784 to 1790, a casualty rate twice that of the Revolutionary War. Frontier people retaliated ruthlessly. "The people of Kentucky," wrote an army officer, "will carry on private expeditions against the Indians and kill them whenever they meet them, and I do not believe there is a jury in all Kentucky will punish a man for it."

Massive military force—enough to raze Indian villages, destroy food supplies, and threaten starvation—represented the key to whites' conquering the Indians. Frontier militias, poorly equipped and trained, lacked sufficient force. In 1786 a lack of supplies forced 1,200 Kentuckians under George Rogers Clark to abandon a campaign against Great Lakes Indians. Defeat of the Indians clearly called for federal forces. But in 1789 the U.S. Army's total strength stood at 672 soldiers, less than one-half the number of warriors in the northwestern Indian confederation. Despairing frontier settlers concluded that the United States had forfeited their loyalty. Clark spoke for many Kentuckians in 1786 when he declared that "no property or person is safe under a government so weak as that of the United States."

Nevertheless, militia raids gradually forced Miamis, Shawnees, and Delawares to evacuate southern Indiana and Ohio. In spring 1788 fifty New Englanders sailed down the Ohio in a bullet-proof barge christened the *Mayflower* to found the town of Marietta. Later that year Pennsylvanians and New Jerseyites established Cincinnati. The contest for the Ohio Valley was nearing its decisive stage.

Westerners felt a special bitterness toward the British, whose continued occupation of seven northwestern forts seemed the mainspring of the endless border fighting. British complaints about American failure to compensate the loyalists were a fig leaf for slowing U.S. expansion until Britain could establish an Indian buffer state south of the Great Lakes and annex the region to Canada.

Spain, unable to prevent American settlers' occupation of land it claimed in the Southeast, sought their allegiance by offering citizenship—and bribes. Most westerners who accepted the gold doled out by Spanish officials meant only to pocket badly needed cash in return for vague promises of goodwill. Nevertheless, many talked openly of secession. "I am decidedly of the opinion," wrote Kentucky's attorney general in 1787, "that this western country will in a few years Revolt from the Union and endeavor to erect an Independent Government."

Meanwhile, southerners watched with concern as Anglo-American fortunes in the West deteriorated. Many southern citizens had acquired a stake in trans-Appalachian affairs when Virginia and North Carolina had awarded revolutionary soldiers with western land. Whether they intended to move west or to sell their rights, the veterans wanted the western territories to prosper. Many planters (including George Washington) hoped to make a quick fortune in land speculation. They had borrowed heavily to buy frontier land, but uncertainty about the West's future endangered their investments. By 1789 a potent combination of small farmers and landed gentry in the South were enraged at foreign barriers to expansion. They eagerly supported politicians, including Thomas Jefferson and James Madison, who urged strong measures against the British and Spanish.

Regional Economies

The failure of tobacco and rice to regain their prewar export levels intensified the frustrations of southern planter-speculators. In 1770 the South had produced two-thirds of the mainland colonies' exports; by 1790 this portion had shrunk to less than half. Southerners' attempts to diversify their crops had had little effect. Their failure to recover their export base, along with the persistence of barriers to western expansion, raised doubts about the South's future.

In the mid-Atlantic region New York and Pennsylvania benefited from a steady demand for foodstuffs and quickly recovered from the Revolution's ravages. As famine stalked Europe, American farmers in the Delaware and Hudson valleys prospered from climbing export prices.

New England enjoyed less fortune. A short growing season and poor soil kept farm yields low. Farmers barely produced enough grain for local consumption. New Englanders also faced both high taxes to repay Revolutionary debts and tightened credit that spawned countless lawsuits against debtors. And economic depression only aggravated the region's chronic overpopulation. Moreover, British restrictions on West Indian trade (see Chapter 6) hit New England hard. Some resourceful captains carried cargoes to the French West Indies or even to China, and others smuggled foodstuffs to the British West Indies under the nose of the British navy. But with British policy as it was, the number of seamen in the Massachusetts cod and whale fisheries had fallen 42 percent between the 1770s and 1791. Because New Englanders could not force Britain to grant trade concessions, they preferred peaceful accommodation rather than the direct confrontation with Britain that southerners supported.

Entrepreneurs, Artisans, and Wage Earners

After 1783, however, ambitious, aggressive businessmen reduced northern dependence on farming by investing their profits in factories, ships, government bonds, and banks. Convinced that American strength required a balancing of agriculture with banking, manufacturing, and commerce, they sought to limit U.S. dependence on British manufactures. They also insisted that the nation needed a healthy merchant marine to augment its naval forces in wartime.

These entrepreneurs' innovative business ventures pointed toward the future. In the 1780s the country's first private banks appeared in Philadelphia, Boston, and New York. In 1787 Philadelphia merchants created the Pennsylvania Society for the

Encouragement of Manufactures and the Useful Arts. Among the English artisans whom the society encouraged to bring their knowledge of industrial technology across the Atlantic was Samuel Slater, who helped to establish an early cotton-spinning mill in Rhode Island in 1793 (see Chapter 9). In 1791 New York and Philadelphia investors founded the Society for the Encouragement of Useful Manufactures, and New York merchants and insurance underwriters organized America's first association for trading government bonds, which evolved into the New York Stock Exchange.

Yet in 1789 northeastern cities lacked large factories. Half the work force consisted of "mechanics," or master artisans and journeymen, who produced handmade goods. Journeymen changed jobs frequently; master artisan Samuel Ashton's Philadelphia cabinet shop, for example, kept journeymen an average of just six months. Master artisans and other employers drew on the increasing ranks of low-paid day workers—orphans, widows, drifters, and free blacks.

Mechanics tended to follow their fathers' occupations. They lived in close-knit neighborhoods and drank, marched, and "mobbed" together. Facing stiff competition from British manufacturers using labor-saving machinery and cheap unskilled labor, they supported a national tariff to raise the price of imported goods and wanted a strong, assertive national government. Although a few artisans employed new technologies, most were reluctant to abandon their traditional ways or could not raise the capital to modernize. With opportunities shrinking, many formed societies to set wages and hours.

In 1789 virtually all politically conscious Americans—entrepreneurs and merchants, urban mechanics and frontier settlers, nationalists and Antifederalists, northerners and southerners—expressed their hopes for the nation's future in terms of republican ideals. These lofty goals of selfless service to the general good had helped leaders to rally public resistance to British encroachment since the 1760s. Republican ideology had shaped the state constitutions and the new Constitution and Antifederalist doctrines as well. By the 1790s most Americans thought that they knew what republican virtue meant, and most condemned rival views as the road to corruption.

Constitutional Government Takes Shape

The men entrusted with the federal experiment began assembling in the new national capital, New York, in March 1789. The new leaders had to reach decisions on critical questions that the Constitution's framers had left unresolved. For example, the Constitution neither gave the president formal responsibility for preparing a legislative agenda nor specified whether cabinet officers were accountable to Congress or to the president. The Constitution did not say how the federal courts should be organized, and there was no bill of rights. Under these circumstances, the First Congress could have weakened presidential authority, limited access to federal courts, or even called a convention to rewrite the Constitution. In 1789 the nation's future remained unsettled in these and many other regards.

Defining the Presidency

No office in the new government aroused more suspicion than the presidency. Many feared that the president's powers could make him a king. But George Washington's reputation for honesty checked public apprehension, and Washington himself tried to calm fears of unlimited executive power.

The Constitution mentioned the executive departments of the federal government only in passing, required Senate approval of presidential nominees to head these bureaus, and made all executive personnel liable to being impeached or to being charged with wrongdoing in office. Otherwise, Congress was free to establish the organization and accountability of what became known as the cabinet. The first cabinet consisted of four departments, headed by the secretaries of state, treasury, and war and by the attorney general. A proposal to forbid the president's dismissal of cabinet officers without Senate approval was defeated. This outcome reinforced presidential authority to make and carry out policy; it also separated executive and legislative powers beyond what the Constitution required and made the president a more equal partner of Congress.

President Washington suggested few laws to Congress, seldom criticized opponents of government policy, and generally limited his public statements to matters of foreign relations and military affairs. He deferred to congressional decisions on domestic policy whenever possible and vetoed only two measures in his eight-year tenure. To reassure the public that he was above favoritism and conflicts of interest, Washington balanced his cabinet with southerners and northeasterners. When Secretary of State Thomas Jefferson opposed policies of Secretary of the Treasury Alexander Hamilton, Washington implored Jefferson not to resign, even though the president supported Hamilton.

"He is polite with dignity, affable without familiarity, distant without haughtiness, grave without austerity, modest, wise, and good." So Abigail Adams, the wife of Vice President John Adams, described Washington. The nation's first president genuinely sought to understand the hopes of the two groups that dominated American society—southern planters and northeastern merchants and entrepreneurs. Like most republican leaders, he believed that the proper role for ordinary citizens was not to set policy through elections but to choose well-educated men to make laws in the people's best interest, independently of direct popular influence.

Only reluctantly did Washington accept reelection in 1792. He dreaded dying while in office and setting the precedent for a lifetime presidency. He realized that "the preservation of the sacred fire of liberty and the destiny of the republican model of government are . . . *deeply*, perhaps *finally*, staked on the experiment entrusted to the hands of the American people." Should he contribute to that experiment's failure, Washington feared, his name would live only as an "awful monument."

National Justice and the Bill of Rights

The Constitution authorized Congress to establish federal courts below the level of the Supreme Court but provided no plan for their structure. The absence of a comprehensive bill of rights, moreover, had led several delegates at Philadelphia to refuse to sign the Constitution and had been a major Antifederalist point of attack. The task of dealing with these gaps fell to Congress.

In 1789 many citizens feared that the new federal courts would ride roughshod over local customs. Every state had a blend of judicial procedures suited to its needs, and any attempt to force the states to abandon their legal heritage would have produced counterdemands for narrowly restricting federal justice. In the face of such sentiments, Congress might have drastically curtailed the scope and power of the federal judiciary or limited the federal judiciary system to the Supreme Court. Congress might also have forbidden federal judges to accept cases from the states on a range of subjects (as permitted by Article III, Section 2). Such actions by Congress would have tipped the balance of power to the states.

However, when it created the federal court system through the Judiciary Act of 1789, Congress did not seek to hobble the national judiciary. The act quieted popular apprehensions by establishing in each state a federal district court that operated according to local procedures. As the Constitution stipulated, the Supreme Court exercised final jurisdiction. Congress's compromise respected state traditions while offering wide access to federal justice.

Behind the movement for a bill of rights lay Americans' long-standing fear that a strong central government would lead to tyranny. Many Antifederalists believed that the best safeguard against tyranny would be to strengthen the powers of the state governments at the expense of the federal government, but many others wanted simply to guarantee basic personal liberties. From the House of Representatives, James Madison battled to preserve a powerful national government. He played the leading role in drafting the ten amendments that became known as the Bill of Rights when ratified in December 1791.

Madison insisted that the first eight amendments guarantee personal liberties, not strip the national government of authority. The First Amendment safeguarded the most fundamental freedoms of expression—religion, speech, press, and political activity. The Second Amendment ensured that each state could form its own militia. Like the Third Amendment, it sought to protect citizens from what Americans saw as the most sinister embodiment of tyranny: standing armies. The Fourth through the Eighth Amendments limited the police powers of the states by guaranteeing fair treatment in legal and judicial proceedings. The Ninth and Tenth Amendments reserved to the people or to the states powers not allocated to the federal government, but Madison headed off proposals to limit federal power more explicitly.

With the Bill of Rights in place, the federal judiciary established its authority. In the case of *Chisholm* v. *Georgia* (1793), the Supreme Court ruled that a nonresident could sue a state in federal court. In 1796 the Court declared its right to determine the constitutionality of federal statutes in *Hylton* v. *United States* and to strike down state laws in *Ware* v. *Hylton*. But in 1794 Congress decided that the *Chisholm* case had encroached too far on states' authority and overturned the decision through a constitutional amendment. Ratified in 1798, the Eleventh Amendment revised Article III, Section 2, so that private citizens could not undermine states' financial autonomy by using federal courts to sue another state's government in civil cases and claim money from that state's treasury.

By endorsing the Eleventh Amendment, Congress expressed its recognition that federal power could threaten vital local interests. The same awareness had ruptured the nationalist coalition that had written the Constitution, secured its ratification, and dominated the First Congress. James Madison's shift from nationalist to critic of excessive federal power in 1790–1791 dramatically illustrated the split. Up to this time, of the nationalists, only Alexander Hamilton had thought much about how federal power should be used. His bold program alienated many nationalists by demonstrating that federal policies could be shaped to reward special interests.

National Economic Policy and Its Consequences

Aware that war would jeopardize national survival, Washington concentrated on diplomacy and military affairs. His reluctance to become involved with legislation enabled Secretary of the Treasury Alexander Hamilton to set domestic priorities. Hamilton emerged as the country's most imaginative and dynamic statesman by formulating a sweeping program for national economic development. However, his agenda proved deeply divisive.

Alexander Hamilton and His Objectives

Born in the West Indies in 1755, Hamilton had arrived in New York in 1772 to enroll at King's College (now Columbia University), where he had passionately defended American rights. Having entered the Continental Army in 1775, Hamilton had distinguished himself in battle, and during four years on Washington's staff had developed a close relationship with the commander in chief. For Hamilton, Washington filled the emotional void created by his own father's desertion. For the childless Washington, Hamilton became almost a son. Hamilton thus enjoyed extraordinary influence over Washington.

Hamilton's financial policies had two goals: to strengthen the nation against foreign enemies and to lessen the threat of disunion. The possibility of war with Britain, Spain, or both presented the most immediate danger. To finance a war, the Republic would have to borrow, but because Congress under the Articles had failed to redeem or pay interest on the Revolutionary debt, the nation had little credit. Thus the country's economy seemed unequal to fighting a major European power. War with Britain would mean a blockade, strangling commerce and halting the importation of necessary manufactured goods. The French navy, so helpful during the Revolution, had declined greatly since 1783, while Britain's Royal Navy had vastly improved. In addition, political instability in France made the Revolutionary ally an uncertain friend. Without self-sufficiency in vital industrial products and a strong merchant marine ready for combat, America stood little chance of surviving another war with Britain.

Hamilton also feared that the Union might disintegrate because he believed that Americans tended to think first of local loyalties and interests. His own service in the Continental Army had imbued him with burning nationalistic faith and had weakened his identification with his adopted state, New York, or any other American locale. To him, the Constitution represented a close victory of national over state authority. Now he worried that the states might reassert power over the new government. If they succeeded, he doubted whether the nation could prevent ruinous trade discrimination between states, deter foreign aggression, and avoid civil war.

His view of human nature as well as his wartime experiences shaped Hamilton's political beliefs. He shared the conviction of many nationalists that the vast majority of the Republic's population, like the rest of humanity, would never display the degree of self-sacrifice and virtue that he had shown. Hamilton concluded that the federal government's survival depended on building support among politically influential citizens through a direct appeal to their financial interests. Private ambitions would then serve the national welfare.

Charming and brilliant, vain and handsome, a notorious womanizer, thirsty for fame and power, Hamilton exemplified the worldly citizens whose fortunes he hoped to link to the Republic's future. To his opponents, however, Hamilton embodied the dark forces luring the Republic to doom—a man who, Jefferson wrote, believed in "the necessity of either force or corruption to govern men."

Alexander Hamilton (1755–1804), *by John Trumbull*
As President George Washington's secretary of the treasury, the boldly self-confident Hamilton designed national economic programs that aimed to expand the power and influence of wealthy Americans within society.

Report on the Public Credit

In 1789 Congress directed the Treasury Department to evaluate the Revolutionary debt. Hamilton seized the opportunity to devise policies to strengthen the nation's credit, enable it to defer paying its debt, and entice the upper class to place its prestige and capital at the nation's service. In January 1790 Congress received his Report on the Public Credit. It listed \$54 million in U.S. debt: \$42 million owed to Americans and the rest to foreigners. Hamilton estimated that on top of the national debt, the

states had debts of $25 million that the United States had promised to reimburse.

Hamilton recommended that the federal government "fund" the national debt by raising $54 million in new securities to honor the Revolutionary debt. Purchasers of these securities could choose from several combinations of federal "stock" and western lands. Those who wished could retain their original bonds and earn 4 percent interest. All these options would reduce interest payments on the debt. Creditors would approve this reduction because their investments would become more valuable and secure. The report proposed that the federal government use the same means to pay off state debts remaining from the Revolution.

A deeper motive lay behind Hamilton's argument that the failure of some states to honor their obligations would undermine American credit overseas. Hamilton saw the federal assumption of state debts as a chance for the national government to win the gratitude and loyalty of state creditors. Because state legislatures, awash in debt, were anxious to avoid piling more taxes on voters, they would accept any relief, regardless of the reason.

Hamilton exhorted the government to use the money earned by selling federal lands in the West to pay off the $12 million owed to Europeans as soon as possible, but he suggested that the remaining $42 million owed to Americans be made a permanent debt. If the government paid only the interest on its bonds, investors would hold them for long terms. The sole burden on taxpayers would be the small annual interest. Thus the United States could uphold its credit at minimal expense without ever having to pay off the debt itself.

Above all, Hamilton believed, a permanent debt would tie the economic fortunes of the nation's creditors to the government. In an age of notoriously risky investments, the federal government would protect the savings of wealthy bond holders through conservative policies but still pay an interest rate competitive with that of the Bank of England. The guarantee of future interest payments would link the interests of the moneyed class to those of the nation.

Hamilton's proposals provoked controversy. Many members of Congress objected that those least deserving reward would gain the most. The original owners of more than 60 percent of the debt certificates issued by the Continental Congress had long since sold at a loss, often out of dire necessity. Wealthy speculators, anticipating Hamilton's intentions, had snapped up large holdings at the expense of the unsuspecting original owners and would reap huge gains.

To Hamilton's surprise, Madison became a chief opponent of reimbursing current holders at face value. Sensing disapproval of the plan in Virginia, Madison tried but failed to obtain compensation for original owners who had sold their certificates. Hamilton's policy generated widespread resentment by rewarding rich profiteers while ignoring wartime sacrifice by ordinary citizens.

Opposition to assuming the state debts also ran high, especially in the South. But Hamilton saved his proposal by exploiting Virginians' desire to relocate the national capital in their region. They hoped that moving the capital would keep Virginia the nation's largest, most influential state. Essentially, Hamilton traded the votes necessary to locate the capital along the Potomac for enough votes to win his battle for assumption.

Enactment of the Report on the Public Credit reversed the nation's fiscal standing. By 1792 the United States' soaring fiscal reputation allowed some U.S. bonds to sell at 10 percent above face value.

Reports on the Bank and Manufactures

In December 1790 Hamilton presented Congress with his Report on a National Bank. Having restored full faith in greatly undervalued certificates, Hamilton had in effect expanded the capital available for investment. Now he intended to direct that money toward projects to diversify the national economy through a federally chartered bank.

The proposed bank would raise $10 million through a public stock offering. Fully four-fifths of the control of the bank would fall to private hands. Private investors could purchase shares by paying for three-quarters of their value in government bonds. In this way the bank would capture a substantial portion of the recently funded debt and make it available for loans; it would also receive steady interest payments from the Treasury. Shareholders would profit handsomely.

Hamilton argued that the Bank of the United States would cost taxpayers nothing and greatly benefit the nation. It would provide a safe place for federal deposits, make inexpensive loans to the government when taxes fell short, and relieve the scarcity of hard cash by issuing paper notes. Further, the bank would regulate the business of state banks and, above all, provide much-needed credit for economic expansion.

Hamilton also called for American economic self-sufficiency. An admirer of the way that factory expansion had stimulated British wealth, he wanted to encourage industrialization in the United States. His Report on Manufactures of December 1791 advocated protective tariffs on imports to foster domestic manufacturing, which would in turn attract immigrants and create national wealth. He also called for assisting the merchant marine against British trade restrictions by reducing duties on goods brought into the country on U.S. ships and by offering subsidies for fishermen and whalers.

Hamilton's Challenge to Limited Government

To many, Hamilton's plan to establish a permanent national debt violated the principle of equality among citizens by favoring the interests of public creditors. Some detractors also denounced the national bank as a dangerous scheme that gave a small elite special power to influence the government.

The bank controversy drew Thomas Jefferson into the ranks of Hamilton's opponents. Like Madison, Jefferson believed that the Bank of England had undermined the integrity of the government in Britain. Shareholders of the Bank of the United States could just as easily become tools of unscrupulous politicians. Members of Congress who owned bank stock would likely vote in support of the bank even at the cost of the national good. To Jefferson, the bank represented "a machine for the corruption of the legislature [Congress]."

Constitutional issues presented the bank's opponents with their strongest argument. The Constitution did not authorize Congress to issue charters of incorporation; in fact, the constitutional convention had rejected such a proposal. Unless Congress adhered to a "strict interpretation" of the Constitution, critics argued, the central government might oppress the states and trample individual liberties. Strict limits on government powers seemed the surest way to prevent the United States from degenerating into a corrupt despotism, as Britain had.

Congress approved the bank by only a thin margin. Dubious about its constitutionality, Washington asked Jefferson and Hamilton for advice. Jefferson distrusted banking and did not want to extend government power beyond the letter of the Constitution. But Hamilton urged Washington to sign the bill. Because Article I, Section 8, of the Constitution specified that Congress could enact all measures "necessary and proper," Hamilton contended that the only unconstitutional activities were those *forbidden* to the national government. Washington accepted Hamilton's argument, and in February 1791 the Bank of the United States obtained a twenty-year charter. Washington's acceptance of a "loose interpretation" of the Constitution marked the first victory for advocates of an active, assertive national government.

Madison and Jefferson also strongly opposed Hamilton's proposal to use protective tariffs to encourage industry. Such protection, they thought, constituted an unfair subsidy promoting uncompetitive industries that would founder without government support. They argued, moreover, that tariffs doubly injured most citizens, first by imposing heavy import taxes passed on to the consumer and then by reducing the incentive for American manufacturers to produce low-cost goods. The only beneficiaries would be individuals shielded from overseas competition and the institutions, such as the bank, that lent them money. Fearful that American cities would spawn a dangerous class of politically volatile poor, Jefferson and Madison viewed industrialization as a potential menace.

Congress ultimately refused to approve a high protective tariff. Hamilton nevertheless succeeded in setting higher duties on goods brought in by non-American than by American ships, and consequently the tonnage of such goods imported on American ships tripled from 1789 to 1793.

Hamilton's Legacy

Hamilton built a political base by appealing to people's economic self-interest. His "rescue" of the national credit provided enormous gains for speculators, merchants, and other urban "moneyed men" who by 1790 possessed most of the Revolutionary debt. As holders of bank stock, these same groups had reason to use their prestige on behalf of national authority. Moreover, federal assumption of state debts liberated taxpayers from crushing burdens in New England, New Jersey, and South Carolina, while Hamilton's promotion of industry, commerce, and shipping won favor with the Northeast's budding entrepreneurs and hard-pressed artisans.

Supporters of Hamilton's policies called themselves Federalists in order to associate themselves with the Constitution. But they actually favored a centralized ("consolidated") national government, not a truly federal system that left substantial power to the states. They dominated public opinion in the states that were most benefited by assumption and enjoyed considerable support in Pennsylvania and New York.

However, Hamilton's economic program sowed dissension in areas where it provided little advantage. Resentment ran high among those who felt that the government was rewarding special interests. Southerners especially detested Hamilton's program. Southern states had generally paid off their Revolutionary debts, and few southerners still held Revolutionary certificates. Moreover, the Bank of the United States had few southern stockholders and allocated little capital for southern loans.

Hamilton's plan for commercial expansion and industrial development appeared similarly irrelevant to the West, where agriculture promised exceptional profit once the right of export through New Orleans was guaranteed. Even in New York and Pennsylvania, Hamilton's policies generated some dissatisfaction. Resentment of a supposedly national program that benefited eastern "moneyed men" and Yankees who refused to pay their debts gradually united westerners, southerners, and many people in the mid-Atlantic into a political coalition. Challenging the Federalists for control of the government, these opponents called for a return to true republicanism.

The Whiskey Rebellion

Hamilton's program helped to ignite a civil insurrection called the Whiskey Rebellion. Severely testing federal authority, this uprising posed the young Republic's first serious crisis.

To augment national revenue, Hamilton had proposed an excise tax on domestically produced whiskey. He maintained that such a tax would not only distribute the expense of financing the national debt evenly but also improve the country's morals by lowering liquor consumption. Although Congress passed Hamilton's program in March 1791, many doubted that Americans, who drank an average of six gallons of hard liquor per adult per year, would submit tamely to sobriety.

Western Pennsylvanians found the new tax especially burdensome. Unable to ship their crops to world markets through New Orleans, most local farmers habitually were distilling their rye or corn into alcohol, which could be carried across the Appalachians at a fraction of the price charged for bulky grain. Hamilton's excise tax, equal to 25 percent of whiskey's retail value, would wipe out frontier farmers' profit.

Because the law specified, in addition, that federal courts would try all cases of alleged tax evasion, any western Pennsylvanian indicted for noncompliance would have to travel 300 or so miles to Philadelphia. Not only would the accused face a jury of unsympathetic easterners, but he would also have to shoulder the cost of a long journey and lost earnings as well as fines and penalties if convicted. Moreover, because Treasury Department officials rarely enforced the law outside western Pennsylvania, the efforts of an especially diligent excise inspector who lived near Pittsburgh to collect the tax enraged local residents.

Initially, most western Pennsylvanians preferred peaceful protest. But a minority turned violent, assaulting federal revenue officers and sometimes their own neighbors, until, in a scene reminiscent of colonial protests against Britain, large-scale resistance erupted in July 1794. One hundred men attacked a U.S. marshal serving delinquent taxpayers with summonses to appear in court in Philadelphia. A crowd of 500 burned the chief revenue officer's house following a shootout with federal soldiers. Roving bands torched buildings, assaulted tax collectors, and raised a flag symbolizing an independent country that they hoped to create from six western counties.

The frontier turmoil played into the Washington administration's hands. Echoing British denunciation of colonial protests, Hamilton blasted the rebellion as simple lawlessness. Washington concluded that a federal failure to respond strongly would encourage outbreaks in other frontier areas where lax enforcement had allowed distillers to escape paying taxes. The president accordingly summoned 12,900 militiamen to march west under his command, but opposition evaporated once the troops reached the Appalachians. Of 150 suspects later seized, 20 were sent in irons to Philadelphia.

The Whiskey Rebellion was a milestone in determining the limits of public opposition to federal policies. In the early 1790s many Americans assumed that it was still legitimate to protest unpopular laws by using the methods that they had employed against British policies. By firmly suppressing the first major challenge to national authority, President Washington served notice that citizens could change the law only through constitutional procedures—by making their dissatisfaction known to their elected representatives and, if necessary, by electing new representatives.

The United States in a Hostile World

By 1793 disagreements over foreign affairs had become the primary source of friction in American public life. The division created by controversy over Hamilton's economic program hardened into ideologically oriented factions that disagreed vehemently over whether American foreign policy should become pro-French or pro-British.

The United States faced a particularly hostile international environment in the 1790s. European powers restricted American trade, supported Indian trouble along the frontier, strengthened and expanded their North American empires, and maintained garrisons on U.S. soil. Because the new nation's economic well-being depended on exports, foreign policy issues loomed large in national politics. Disputes over foreign relations roiled public life from 1793 to 1815.

Foreign Powers and Native Americans in the West

At the same time, Spain attempted to counter potential rivals for North American territory—Russia and Britain on the Pacific coast and the United States and Britain in the Mississippi Valley. In the 1740s traders from Siberia had begun trading with Alaskan natives for sea-otter pelts, spreading deadly diseases in the process. Britain continued its search for a "northwest passage" to link the Canadian interior to the Pacific. To counter these twin threats, Spain flung colonists and missionaries northward along the California coast from San Diego to Sonoma (north of San Francisco). In "New California," the missions fared better than the handful of settlers. However, epidemic and venereal diseases carried by the Spanish raged among the native coastal tribes; between 1769 and 1830 the Indian population plummeted from about 72,000 to about 18,000. Priests sought to "civilize" the survivors by placing them in missions, imposing rigid discipline, and putting them to work in vineyards and other enterprises. Meanwhile, Spain strengthened its position in the southwest by making peace with the Comanches, the Navajos, and most of the Apache nations that threatened its settlements.

Revitalized by these western successes, Spain joined Britain and Native Americans as a formidable barrier to U.S. aims in the Mississippi Valley. In the 1790s the Spanish bribed many well-known political figures in Tennessee and Kentucky, including James Wilkinson, one of Washington's former generals, whose intrigues continued into the next century. Thomas Scott, a congressman from western Pennsylvania, meanwhile schemed with the British. The admission of Vermont, Kentucky, and Tennessee as states between 1791 and 1796 was meant in part to strengthen their sometimes shaky loyalty to the Union.

President Washington tried to keep tight control of foreign policy. Recognizing that the complex western problems would not easily yield, he pursued patient diplomacy to "preserve the country in peace if I can, and to be prepared for war if I cannot." The prospect of peace improved in 1789 when Spain unexpectedly opened New Orleans to American commerce. Secessionist sentiment subsided.

Washington then moved to weaken Spanish influence in the West by neutralizing Spain's most important ally, the Creek Indians. The Creeks numbered more than 20,000, including perhaps 5,000 warriors, and were fiercely hostile toward Georgian settlers, whom they called "the greedy people who want our lands." Under terms of the 1790 Treaty of New York, American settlers could occupy the Georgia piedmont but not other Creek territory. Washington insisted that Georgia restore to the Chickasaws and Choctaws, Creek allies, a vast area along the Mississippi River that Georgia had already begun selling off to land speculators.

Hoping to conclude a similar agreement with Britain's Indian allies, the United States sent an

Stimafachki of the Koasati Creeks,
by John Trumbull, 1790
This portrait was sketched during the U.S.-Creek conference that resulted in the Treaty of New York.

envoy to the Great Lakes tribes. The Miamis responded by burning a captured American to death. Two military campaigns, in 1790 and 1791, failed to force peace and cost the United States 1,100 men.

The Washington administration tried to pacify the Indians through a benevolent policy. Alarmed by the chaos on the frontier, where trespassers invaded Indian lands and the native peoples rejected U.S. claims to sovereignty, the government formally recognized Indian title as secure and inalienable except by the "free consent" of the Indians themselves. To reinforce this policy, Congress passed laws to prohibit trespassing on Indian lands, to punish crimes committed there by non-Indians, to outlaw alcohol, and to regulate trade. The administration also encouraged Indians to become "civilized." By adopting private property and a strictly agricultural livelihood, officials believed, Indians would find a place in American society—and make land available for non-Indians.

Indians, however, were unwilling to give up their traditional ways entirely and to assimilate into an alien culture. And most whites did not want to integrate Native Americans into their society. Consequently, the United States continued to pressure Indians to sell their lands and to move farther west. Washington's frontier policy became a wreck. Not only had two military expeditions suffered defeat in the Northwest, but in 1792 the Spanish had persuaded the Creeks to renounce their treaty with the federal government and to resume hostilities. Ultimately, the damage to U.S. prestige from these setbacks convinced many Americans that only an alliance with France could counterbalance the combined strength of Britain, Spain, and the Indians.

France and Factional Politics

One of the most momentous events in history, the French Revolution, began in 1789. Americans watched sympathetically as the French abolished nobles' privileges, wrote a constitution, and repelled invading armies. In 1793, after becoming a republic, France proclaimed a war of all peoples against all kings and assumed that the United States would eagerly enlist.

Enthusiasm for a pro-French foreign policy burned brightest in the South and along the frontier. France's war against Britain and Spain, begun in 1793, raised hopes among southern land speculators and western settlers that a French victory would leave those nations too exhausted to continue meddling in the West. The United States could then insist on free navigation of the Mississippi, evacuation of British garrisons, and termination of both nations' support of Indian resistance.

In addition, a slave uprising in France's Caribbean colony of Saint Domingue (later renamed Haiti), in which Britain became involved, aroused passionate anti-British sentiment in the South. White southerners grew alarmed for slavery's future and their own lives as terrified French planters fled to the United States from Saint Domingue with vivid accounts of how British invaders in 1793 had supported the rebellious slaves. The blacks had inflicted heavy casualties on the French. Southern whites concluded that Britain had intentionally provoked a bloodbath, and they worried that a British-inspired race war would engulf the South as well.

After 1790 economics led to sharp differences between northern and southern reactions to the French Revolution. Growing antagonism toward France among northern merchants reflected their basic conservatism and their awareness that their prosperity depended on good relations with Britain. Virtually all the nation's merchant marine operated from northern ports, and the largest share of U.S. foreign trade was with Britain. Fearful that an alliance with France would provoke British retaliation against this valuable commerce, northerners argued that the United States could win valuable concessions by demonstrating friendly intentions toward Britain.

Southerners had no such reasons to favor Britain. They perceived American reliance on British commerce as a menace to national self-determination and wished to divert most U.S. trade to France. Southern spokesmen such as Jefferson and Madison demanded discriminatory duties on British cargoes. These recommendations threatened ties with Britain, which sold more manufactured goods to the United States than to any other country. Federalist opponents of a discriminatory tariff warned that the English would not stand by while a weak French ally pushed them into depression. If Congress adopted trade retaliation, Hamilton predicted, "an open war between the United States and Great Britain" would result.

After declaring war with Spain and Britain in 1793, France sought to enlist the United States in the war and to strengthen the treaty of alliance between the two nations. France dispatched Edmond Genet as minister to the United States with orders to recruit American mercenaries to conquer Spanish territories and to attack British shipping. Much to France's disgust, President Washington issued a proclamation of neutrality on April 22, 1793.

Meanwhile, Citizen Genet (as he was known in French Revolutionary style) had arrived on April 8. He found numerous southern volunteers for his American Foreign Legion despite official U.S. neutrality. Making generals of George Rogers Clark of Kentucky and Elisha Clarke, Genet ordered them to seize New Orleans and St. Augustine. Clark openly defied the neutrality proclamation by advertising for recruits, and Clarke drilled 300 soldiers along the Florida border. However, the French failed to provide adequate funds for either campaign, and in 1794 both expeditions disintegrated.

However, Genet did not need funds to outfit privateers, whose crews were paid from captured plunder. By summer 1793 nearly 1,000 Americans were at sea in a dozen ships flying the French flag. These privateers seized over eighty British ships and towed them to American ports, where French consuls sold the ships and cargoes at auction.

The British Crisis

Although Washington swiftly closed the nation's harbors to Genet's buccaneers, the episode provoked an Anglo-American crisis. Britain decided that only a massive show of force would deter American aggression. Thus on November 6, 1793, Britain's Privy Council issued orders confiscating foreign ships trading with the French islands in the Caribbean. The orders were kept secret until most American ships carrying winter provisions to the Caribbean left port so that their captains would not know that they were sailing into a war zone. The Royal Navy seized more than twenty-five American ships, a high price for Genet's mischief making.

Meanwhile, the U.S. merchant marine suffered another galling indignity—the drafting of its crewmen into the Royal Navy. Thousands of British sailors had fled to American ships looking for an easier life than the tough, poorly paying British system. In late 1793 British naval officers began inspecting American crews for British subjects, whom they then impressed (forcibly enlisted) as the king's sailors. Overzealous commanders sometimes exceeded orders by taking U.S. citizens—and in any case Britain did not recognize its former subjects' right to adopt American citizenship. Impressment struck a raw nerve in most Americans.

Next the British challenged the United States for control of the West. In February 1794 at an Indian council, Canada's governor denied U.S. claims north of the Ohio River and urged his listeners to destroy every white settlement in the Northwest. Britain soon erected Fort Miami near Toledo, Ohio. That same year Spain encroached further on U.S. territory by building Fort San Fernando at what is now Memphis, Tennessee.

Hoping to halt the drift toward war, Washington launched a desperate diplomatic initiative, sending Chief Justice John Jay to Great Britain and Thomas Pinckney to Spain. The president also authorized General Anthony Wayne to negotiate a treaty with the Indians of the Ohio Valley.

The Indians scoffed at Washington's peace offer until "Mad Anthony" Wayne led 3,000 regulars and militiamen deep into their homeland, ravaging every village in reach. On August 20, 1794, Wayne's troops routed 2,000 Indians at the Battle of Fallen Timbers, two miles from Britain's Fort Miami. Wayne's army staged a provocative victory march past the British garrison and then built Fort Defiance to challenge British authority in the Northwest. Indian morale plummeted. In August 1795 Wayne compelled twelve northeastern tribes to sign the Treaty of Greenville, which opened most of Ohio to white settlement and temporarily ended Indian hostilities.

Wayne's success allowed John Jay a major diplomatic victory in London: a British promise to withdraw troops from American soil. Jay also gained American access to West Indian markets, but only by bargaining away U.S. rights to load cargoes of sugar, molasses, and coffee from the Caribbean. On other points the British remained unyielding. Few Americans could interpret Jay's Treaty as preserving peace with honor.

Jay's Treaty left Britain free not only to violate American neutrality but also to restrict U.S. trade with French ports during wartime. Moreover, Jay did not succeed in ending impressment. He also failed to gain compensation for slaves taken by the British during the Revolution, an outcome especially galling to southerners. In 1795 the Federalist-dominated Senate ratified the treaty by just one vote.

Jay's Treaty probably represented the most that a weak, politically divided United States could extract from Britain. A major achievement for the Washington administration, it defused an explosive crisis with Britain, ended British occupation of U.S. territory, and provided for arbitration to settle both American and British claims for compensation. Jay's Treaty also stimulated American trade as British governors in the West Indies used the treaty's ratification as an excuse to open their harbors to U.S. ships. Other British officials permitted Americans to develop a thriving commerce with India. Within a few years of 1795, American exports to the British Empire had shot up 300 percent.

On the heels of Jay's Treaty came an unqualified diplomatic triumph engineered by Thomas Pinckney. Ratified in 1796, the Treaty of San Lorenzo (also called Pinckney's Treaty) with Spain gave westerners unrestricted, duty-free access to world markets via the Mississippi River. Spain also promised to recognize the thirty-first parallel as the United States' southern boundary, to dismantle all fortifications on American soil, and to discourage Indian attacks against western settlers.

By 1796 the Washington administration had defended the nation's territorial integrity, restored peace to the frontier, opened the Mississippi for western exports, reopened British markets to U.S. shipping, and kept the nation out of a European war. However, as the outcry over Jay's Treaty showed, foreign policy had left Americans far more divided in 1796 than in 1789.

Battling for the Nation's Soul

Besides distrusting centralized executive authority, colonial and Revolutionary Americans feared organized political parties, which they assumed were formed by corrupt conspirators operating against the liberties of the people. Despite these views, politically conscious Americans had split into two hostile political parties, Federalists and Republicans, by the end of Washington's second term.

The struggle transcended the economic and social differences evident in earlier disputes about Hamiltonian finance and the possibility of war with Britain. After 1796 the battle was fought over the very future of representative government. The election of 1800 would determine whether the political elite could accommodate demands from ordinary citizens for more influence in determining policy. No issue was more important or more hotly argued than that of officeholders' accountability to their constituents.

Ideological Confrontation

The French Revolution led many Americans to reassess their political values. The Revolution's radical turn in 1793–1794, which sent thousands to the guillotine, polarized public opinion, generally along regional lines.

Northern Federalists damned revolutionary France as an abomination—"an open Hell," thundered Massachusetts Federalist Fisher Ames, "still ringing with agonies and blasphemies, still smoking with sufferings and crimes." Conservative and religiously oriented, New Englanders detested the French government's disregard for civil rights and its adoration of reason over the worship of God. Middle Atlantic businessmen, perhaps less religious but no less conservative, condemned French leaders as evil radicals who incited the poor against the rich. But a minority of well-off northern merchants and professionals, loyal to deeply held republican principles, supported the Revolution.

Federalists trembled at the thought of "mob rule" in the nation's future. They took alarm when artisans in New York and Philadelphia bandied the French revolutionary slogan "Liberty, Equality, Fraternity" and exalted pro-French political leaders such as Jefferson. Citizen Genet's recruitment of hundreds of Americans to fight for France reinforced their fears.

By the mid-1790s Federalist leaders had concluded that it was dangerous to involve the public deeply in politics. The people were undependable, too easy a prey for rabble-rousers like Genet. As Senator George Cabot of Massachusetts said, "The many do not think at all." But properly led, they believed, the people presented a powerful (albeit passive) bulwark against anarchy. Federalists in fact trusted ordinary property owners to judge a candidate's personal fitness for high office, but only that personal fitness. They consequently argued that citizens need not be presented with policy choices during elections. Thus Federalists favored a representative government in which elected officials would rule in the people's name, independently of direct popular influence.

Preserving order, Federalists maintained, required forging a close relationship between the government and the upper class. Doing so would reassure citizens that their future was in competent hands and would set high standards that few radicals could meet. As early as 1789 Vice President John Adams had tried (unsuccessfully) to give the president and other officials titles such as "His High Mightiness." In the 1790s government officials dramatized their social distance from average citizens. Congress and the cabinet dressed in high fashion and flaunted their wealth at endless balls and formal dinners. While insisting that they ruled *of* and *for* the people, Federalists took pains to symbolize that their government was not *by* the people.

The Federalists aimed to limit public office to wise and virtuous men who would protect liberty. This objective was consistent with eighteenth-century fears that corruption and unchecked passion would undermine society. In republican theory a "virtuous" government need not be directly responsible to public opinion. If (as many assumed) democracy meant mob rule, then political virtue and direct democracy were incompatible. Conservative colonial political traditions, republican ideology, and social reciprocity (see Chapter 2) shaped Federalists' suspicion of the ordinary people.

Federalist measures alienated many Americans, including Jefferson and Madison, who had a vastly different understanding of republican ideology. Antifederalist sentiment ran high in the South, where republican ideology stressed the corruption inherent in a powerful government dominated by a few highly visible men. Southern Republicans insisted that only the distribution of power among virtuous, independent citizens would protect liberty. Further, many southern planters had absorbed the Enlightenment's faith that the free flow of ideas would ensure progress. Exhilarated by events in France, many white southerners saw the French as fellow republicans, carrying on a revolution that would replace hereditary privilege with liberty, equality, and brotherhood. With their own labor force consisting of enslaved blacks, not free wage workers, southern elites did not fear popular participation in politics. Unlike northern Federalists, then, southern planters faced the future with optimism and viewed attempts to inhibit widespread political participation as unworthy of educated gentlemen.

Self-interest also drove Jefferson, Madison, and likeminded Americans to rouse ordinary citizens' concerns about civic affairs. In the early 1790s widespread political apathy favored the Federalists, making it unlikely that they would be criticized for passing unwise laws. However, if the public held Federalists accountable, they would think twice before enacting measures opposed by the majority; or if they persisted in advocating such policies, they would be removed from office.

In October 1791 organized efforts to turn public opinion against the Federalists began with the publication of the *National Gazette*. Then in 1793–1794 popular dissatisfaction with government policies led to the formation of several dozen Democratic (or Republican) societies. Their membership ranged from planters and merchants to artisans and sailors. Conspicuously absent were clergymen, the poor, and nonwhites. Sharply critical of Federalists, the societies spread dissatisfaction with the Washington administration's policies.

Federalists interpreted the societies' emotional appeals to ordinary people as demagoguery and denounced their followers as "democrats, mobocrats, & all other kinds of rats." They feared that the societies would become revolutionary organizations. Washington privately warned that "if [the clubs] were not counteracted . . . they would shake the government to its foundation." By criticizing them, Washington abandoned his nonpartisanship and aligned himself with the Federalists, a move that would cost him dearly.

The Republican Party

Neither Jefferson nor Madison belonged to a Democratic society. However, the clubs' criticism of the administration galvanized into political activity many who would later support Jefferson and Madison's Republican party.

In the early 1790s Americans believed that organizing a political faction or party was corrupt and subversive. Republican ideology assumed that parties would fill Congress with politicians of little ability and less integrity, pursuing selfish goals at national expense. Good citizens would shun such partisan scheming. However, these ideals wavered as controversy mounted over Hamilton's program and the Washington administration's foreign policy. Washington tried to set an example of impartial leadership by seeking advice from both camps, but Jefferson resigned from the cabinet in 1793, and thereafter not even the president could halt the widening political split. Each side saw itself as the guardian of republican virtue and attacked the other as an illegitimate faction.

In 1794 party development reached a decisive stage. Shortly after Washington aligned himself with Federalist policies, supporters of Jefferson who had begun to call themselves Republicans won a slight majority in the House of Representatives. The election signaled their transformation from a faction to a broad-based party, the Republican party, capable of coordinating national political campaigns.

Federalists and Republicans alike used the press to mold public opinion. American journalism came of age in the 1790s as the number of newspapers multiplied from 92 to 242. By 1800 newspapers had perhaps 140,000 paid subscribers (about one-fifth of the eligible voters), and their secondhand readership probably exceeded 300,000. Newspapers of both camps, libelous and irresponsible, cheapened public discussion through constant fear mongering and character assassination. Republicans stood accused of plotting a reign of terror and scheming to turn the nation over to France. Federalists faced charges of favoring hereditary aristocracy and planning to establish an American dynasty by marrying off John Adams's daughter to George III. But despite the mutual distrust thus created, newspaper warfare stimulated citizens to become politically active.

Underlying the inflammatory rhetoric was the Republican charge that the Federalists were bent on enriching the wealthy at taxpayers' expense. Although most Republican leaders were themselves well born, Republicans asserted that the Federalists planned to create a privileged order of men and to re-create the atmosphere of a European court through highly publicized formal dinners and balls. Although wrong in claiming that opponents wanted to introduce aristocracy and monarchy, the Republicans correctly identified the Federalists' fundamental assumption: that citizens' worth could be measured in terms of their money.

Accusations that he secretly supported a plot to establish a monarchy enraged Washington. "By God," Jefferson reported him swearing, "he [the president] would rather be in his grave than in his present situation. . . . He had rather be on his farm than to be made *emperor of the world*." Alarmed by the furor over Jay's Treaty, Washington dreaded the nation's polarization into hostile factions. And Republican abuse stung him. Lonely and surrounded by mediocre men after Hamilton returned to private life, Washington decided in spring 1796 to retire after two terms and called on Hamilton to give a sharp political twist to a farewell address.

In the farewell message Washington vigorously condemned political parties. Partisan alignments, he insisted, endangered the republic's survival, especially if they became entangled in foreign policy disputes. Aside from fulfilling existing treaty obligations and maintaining foreign commerce, the United States had to avoid "political connection" with Europe and its wars. If the United States gathered its strength under "an efficient government," it could defy any foreign challenge; but if it was drawn into Europe's quarrels and corruption, the republican experiment would be doomed. Washington and Hamilton thus turned the central argument of republicanism against their Republican critics. They also evoked a vision of a United States virtuously isolated from foreign intrigue and power politics, an ideal that would remain a potent inspiration until the twentieth century.

Washington left the presidency in 1797 amid a barrage of criticism. The nation's political division into Republicans and Federalists meanwhile hardened. Each party consolidated its hold over particular states and groups of voters, leaving the electorate almost equally divided.

The Election of 1796

As the election of 1796 approached, the Republicans cultivated a large, loyal body of voters, the first time since the Revolution that the political elite effectively mobilized ordinary Americans. The Republican constituency included the Democratic societies, workingmen's clubs, and immigrant-aid associations.

Immigrants became a prime target for Republican recruiters. During the 1790s the United States absorbed 20,000 French refugees from Saint Domingue and 60,000 Irish. Although few immigrants could vote, the Irish exerted critical influence in Pennsylvania and New York, where public opinion was so closely divided that a few hundred voters could tip the balance. In short, Irish immigrants could provide Republicans a winning margin in both states, and the Republicans' pro-French, anti-British rhetoric ensured enthusiastic Irish support.

In 1796 the presidential candidates were Vice President John Adams, whom the Federalists supported, and the Republicans' Jefferson. Republican strength in the South offset Federalist strength in New England, leaving Pennsylvania and New York as crucial "swing" states where the Irish vote might tip the scales. In the end Jefferson carried Pennsylvania but not New York and lost the presidency by three electoral votes. The Federalists kept control of Congress. But by a political fluke, Jefferson became vice president under the constitutional provision (quickly changed by the Twelfth Amendment) that the candidate receiving the highest number of electoral votes would become president and the candidate amassing the next-highest number would become vice president.

President Adams exemplified the paradoxes of the intellectual. His brilliance, insight, and idealism have seldom been equaled among American presidents. He was more comfortable, however, with ideas than with people, more theoretical than practical, and rather inflexible. He inspired trust and admiration but could not command loyalty or stir the electorate. As Benjamin Franklin observed, Adams was "always an honest man, often a wise one, but sometimes, and in some things, absolutely out of his senses." He was utterly unsuited to unify the country.

The French Crisis

To Adams's initial good fortune, French provocations produced a sharp anti-Republican backlash. France interpreted Jay's Treaty as an American attempt to assist the British in their war against France. Learning of Jefferson's defeat, the French ordered the seizure of American ships; within a year they had plundered more than 300 U.S. vessels. The French also ordered that every American captured on a British naval ship, even those involuntarily impressed, be hanged.

Seeking to avoid war, Adams dispatched a peace commission to France. The French foreign minister, Charles de Talleyrand, refused to meet with the Americans, instead promising through three unnamed agents ("X, Y, and Z") that talks could begin after he received $250,000 and France obtained a $12 million loan. This barefaced demand for a bribe became known as the XYZ Affair. Outraged Americans adopted the battle cry "Millions for defense, not one cent for tribute."

The XYZ Affair discredited Republican foreign policy views. The party's leaders compounded the damage by refusing to condemn French aggression and opposing Adam's call for defensive measures. While Republicans tried to excuse French behavior, the Federalists rode a wave of patriotism to an enormous victory in the 1798 congressional elections.

Congress responded to the XYZ Affair by arming fifty-four ships to protect U.S. commerce. The new warships joined what became known as the Quasi-War—an undeclared Franco-American naval conflict in the Caribbean from 1798 to 1800, during which U.S. forces seized ninety-three French privateers at the loss of just one ship. The British navy meanwhile extended the protection of its convoys to the U. S. merchant marine. By early 1799 the French no longer posed a serious threat at sea.

Despite Adam's misgivings, the Federalists Congress tripled the regular army to 10,000 men in 1798, with an automatic expansion of land forces to 50,000 in case of war. But the risk of a land war with France was minimal. What Federalist actually wanted was a strong military force ready in case of a civil war, for the crisis had produced near-hysterical fears that French and Irish malcontents were hatching treasonous conspiracies.

The Alien and Sedition Acts

The Federalists insisted that the possibility of war with France demanded stringent legislation to protect national security. In 1798 the Federalist Congress accordingly passed four measures known collectively as the Alien and Sedition Acts. Although President Adams neither requested nor wanted the laws, he deferred to Congress and signed them.

The least controversial of the four laws, the Alien Enemies Act, was designed to prevent wartime espionage or sabotage. It outlined procedures for determining whether a hostile country's citizens, when staying in America, posed a threat to the United States; if so, they would be deported or jailed. It also established principles to respect the rights of enemy citizens. This law would not be used until the War of 1812.

The second of the laws, the Alien Friends Act, enforceable in peacetime until June 25, 1800, authorized the president to expel foreign residents whose activities he considered dangerous. It required no proof of guilt. Republicans maintained that the law's real purpose was to deport immigrants critical of Federalist policies. Republicans also denounced the third law, the Naturalization Act. This measure increased the residency requirement for U.S. citizenship from five to fourteen years (the last five continuously in one state) to reduce Irish voting.

Finally came the Sedition Act, the only one of these measures enforceable against U.S. citizens. Although its alleged purpose was to distinguish between free speech and attempts to encourage the violation of federal laws or to seed a revolution, the act defined criminal activity so broadly that it blurred distinctions between sedition and legitimate political discussion. Thus it forbade an individual or a group "to oppose any measure or measures of the United States"—wording that could be interpreted to ban any criticism of the party in power. Another clause made it illegal to speak, write, or print any statement that would bring the president "into contempt or disrepute." A newspaper editor could therefore face imprisonment for criticizing Adams or his cabinet. Juries heard sedition cases and could decide whether a defendant had intended to stir up rebellion or merely to express political dissent. However one regarded it, the Sedition Act interfered with free speech. The Federalists wrote the law to expire in 1801 so that it could not be used against them if they lost the next election.

The real target of all this Federalist repression was the opposition press. Four of the five largest Republican newspapers were charged with sedition just as the election of 1800 was getting under way. The attorney general used the Alien Friends Act to drive the Irish journalist John Daly Burk underground. After failing to deport Scottish editor Thomas Callender, an all-Federalist jury sent him to prison for criticizing the president. Federalist leaders intended that a small number of highly visible prosecutions would intimidate journalists and candidates into silence during the election. The attorney general charged seventeen persons with sedition and won ten convictions. Among the victims was Republican congressman Matthew Lyon of Vermont, who spent four months in prison for publishing an article blasting Adams.

Vocal criticism of Federalist repression erupted only in Virginia and Kentucky. In summer 1798 militia commanders in these states mustered their regiments to hear speeches demanding that the federal government respect the Bill of Rights. Entire units signed petitions denouncing the Alien and Sedition Acts. Young men stepped forward to sign the documents on drumheads, a pen in one hand and a gun in the other. Older officers who had fought in the Continental Army looked on approvingly. It was not hard to imagine rifles replacing quill pens as the men who had led one revolution took up arms again.

Ten years earlier opponents of the Constitution had warned that giving the national government extensive powers would endanger freedom. By 1798 these predictions had come true. Shocked Republicans realized that with the Federalists in control of all three branches of government, neither the Bill of Rights nor the system of checks and balances protected individual liberties. In this context the doctrine of states' rights was advanced as a way to prevent the national government from violating freedoms.

James Madison and Thomas Jefferson anonymously wrote two manifestos on states' rights that the assemblies of Virginia and Kentucky endorsed in 1798. Madison's Virginia Resolutions and Jefferson's Kentucky Resolutions proclaimed that state legislatures retained both their right to judge the constitutionality of federal actions and an authority called interposition, which enabled them to protect the liberties of their citizens. A set of Kentucky Resolutions adopted in November 1799 added that states could "nullify" objectionable federal laws. The authors intended interposition and nullification to protect residents from being tried for breaking an unconstitutional law. Although most states disapproved the resolutions, their passage demonstrated the potential for rebellion in the late 1790s.

The Election of 1800

In 1800 the Republicans rallied around Thomas Jefferson for president and New York politician Aaron Burr for vice president. The Federalists became mired in wrangling between Adams and the "High Federalists" who looked to Hamilton for guidance. That the nation survived the election of 1800 without a civil war or the disregard of voters' wishes owed much to the good sense of moderates in both parties. Jefferson and Madison discouraged radicalism that might provoke intervention by the national army. Even more credit belonged to Adams for rejecting High Federalist demands that he ensure victory by sparking an insurrection or asking Congress to declare war on France.

"Nothing but an open war can save us," declared one High Federalist. But when the president discovered the French willing to seek peace in 1799, he proposed a special diplomatic mission. "Surprise, indignation, grief & disgust followed each other in quick succession," reported a Federalist senator. Adams obtained Senate approval for his envoys only by threatening to resign and so make Jefferson president. Outraged High Federalists tried, unsuccessfully, to dump Adams. Hamilton denounced him as a fool, but this ill-considered tactic backfired when most New Englanders rallied around the president.

Adams's negotiations with France did not achieve a settlement until 1801, but the expectation of normal relations prevented Federalists from exploiting charges of Republican sympathy for the enemy. With the immediate threat of war removed, voters grew resentful that in just two years taxes had soared 33 percent to support an army that had done virtually nothing. As the danger of war receded, voters gave Federalists less credit for standing up to France and more blame for ballooning the national debt by $10 million.

Two years after triumphing in the 1798 elections, Federalists found their support badly eroded. High Federalists spitefully withheld the backing that Adams needed to win the presidency. Republicans successfully mobilized voters in Philadelphia and New York who were ready to forsake the Federalists. Voter turnouts more than doubled those of 1788, rising from 15 percent to 40 percent, and in hotly contested New York and Pennsylvania more than one-half the eligible voters participated.

Adams lost the presidency by just eight electoral votes, but Jefferson's election was not assured. Because all seventy-three Republican electors voted for both their party's nominees, the electoral college deadlocked in a Jefferson-Burr tie. The election went to the House of Representatives, where, after thirty-five ballots, Jefferson won the presidency by history's narrowest margin.

Deferring Equality

The election of 1800 did not make the United States more democratic, but it did prevent antidemocratic prejudices from blocking future political liberalization. The Republican victory also repudiated the Federalist campaign to create a base of support through special-interest legislation. After 1800 government policies would be judged by Jefferson's standard of "equal rights for all, special privileges for none."

But not all Americans won equal rights. Women and African-Americans took almost no part in politics, and few people felt that they should. In the case of the Indians, U.S. diplomatic gains came largely at their expense; and national issues rarely were concerned with African-Americans. Meanwhile, white Americans lost much of their Revolutionary idealism and began to assume that racial minorities would always be second-class citizens at best.

Indians in the New Republic

By 1795 most eastern Indian tribes had suffered severe reductions in population and territory, owing to battle, famine, and disease. From 1775 to 1795 the Cherokees declined from 16,000 to 10,000 and the Iroquois from 9,000 to 4,000. Between 1775 and 1800 Indians forfeited more land than the area inhabited by whites in 1775. Settlers crowded Indians onto reservations (often illegally), liquor dealers and criminals trespassed on Indian lands, and government agents and missionaries pressured Indians to abandon their lands and cultures.

Demoralized and unable to strike back, Indians often consumed enormous amounts of whiskey and became violent. The Iroquois were typical. "The Indians of the Six Nations," wrote a federal official in 1796, "have become given to indolence, drunkenness, and thefts, and have taken to killing each other." A social and moral crisis gripped tribes threatened by whites' expansion.

Beginning in 1799 a Seneca prophet, Handsome Lake, led his people in a creative effort to resolve the crisis. He tried to end alcoholism among Indians by appealing to their religious traditions. He welcomed Quaker missionaries and federal aid earmarked for teaching Euro-American agricultural methods to Iroquois men in search of new livelihoods after the collapse of the fur trade and the loss of most of their lands. Many Iroquois men welcomed the change. Iroquois women, however, resisted because they stood to forfeit their collective ownership of farmland, their control of the food supply, and their place in tribal councils. Women who rejected Handsome Lake's advice to exchange farming for housewifery were accused of witchcraft, and some were killed.

Redefining the Color Line

The Republic's first years marked the high tide of African-Americans' Revolutionary-era success in

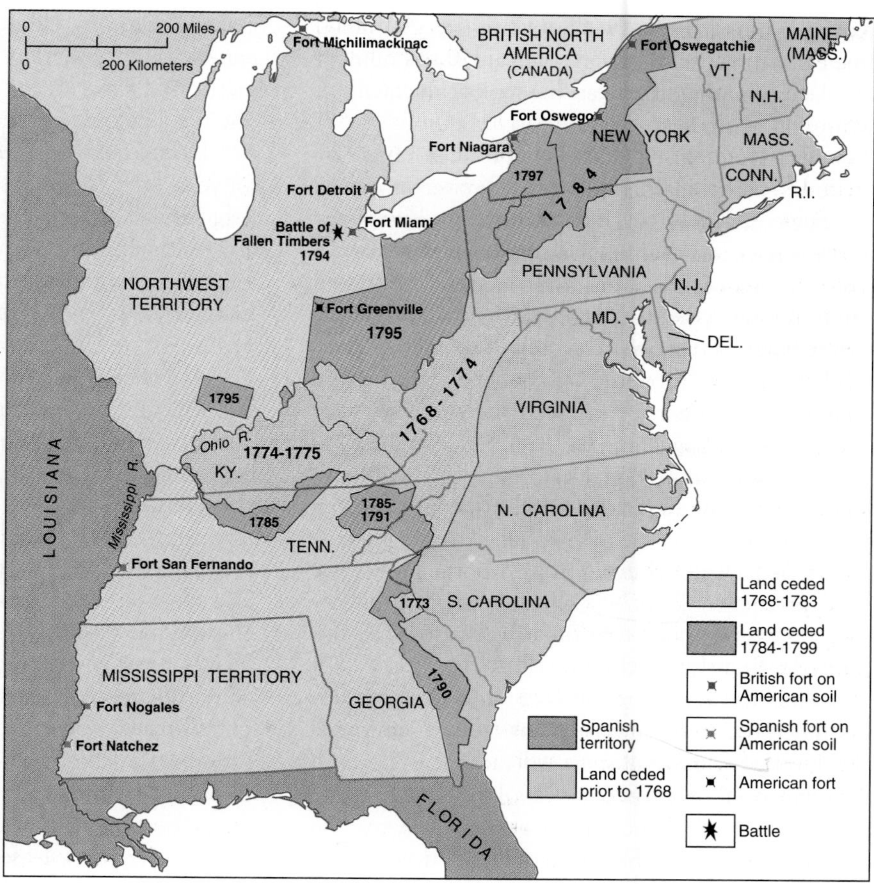

Indian Land Cessions, 1768–1799

Between 1768 and 1775 western Indians sold off vast territories, mostly hunting grounds in mountainous regions. The upheavals of the Revolutionary War, followed by conflicts with U.S. military forces from 1784 to 1799, led to large cessions of inhabited Indian lands.

bettering their lot. Although racism persisted, Jefferson's eloquent words "all men are created equal" awakened many white consciences. In 1790, 8 percent of African-Americans enjoyed freedom. By 1800, 11 percent were free. State reforms meanwhile attempted to improve slaves' conditions. In 1791 the North Carolina legislature declared that the "distinction of criminality between the murder of a white person and one who is equally an human creature, but merely of a different complexion, is disgraceful to humanity" and authorized the execution of whites who murdered slaves. By 1794 most states had outlawed the Atlantic slave trade.

Hesitant measures to ensure free blacks' legal equality appeared in the 1780s and early 1790s. Most states dropped restrictions on their freedom of movement, protected their property, and allowed them to enroll in the militia. All but three states either permitted free blacks to vote or made no specific attempts to exclude them. But before the 1790s ended, the trend toward lessening the social and legal distances between the races ended. Abolitionist sentiment ebbed, slavery became more entrenched, and whites demonstrated reluctance to accept free blacks as fellow citizens.

Federal law led the way in restricting the rights of African Americans. In 1790 congressional procedures for naturalizing aliens limited eligibility to foreign whites. The federal militia law of 1792 allowed states to exclude free blacks. The navy and marine corps forbade nonwhite enlistments in 1798. By 1807 Delaware, Maryland, Kentucky, and New Jersey had stripped free blacks of the vote. Although free blacks enjoyed rights in some areas, the number of places treating them as the political equals of whites dropped sharply in the early 1800s.

An especially revealing symptom of changing attitudes occurred in 1793 when Congress passed the Fugitive Slave Law. The law required judges to award possession of a runaway slave on a formal request by a master or his representative. Accused runaways were denied jury trials and sometimes were refused permission to present evidence. Slaves' legal status as property disqualified them from claiming these constitutional privileges, but the Fugitive Slave Law denied even *free* blacks the legal protections guaranteed to them under the Bill of Rights. The law marked a striking departure from the atmosphere of the 1780s, when state governments had given whites and free blacks the same legal privileges. By 1793 white Americans clearly found it easy to forget that the Constitution had not limited citizenship to their race.

The bloody slave revolt on Saint Domingue undermined the trend toward abolition and reinforced the kind of fears that spawned racism. Reports of the slaughter of French slaveholders made white Americans more reluctant to criticize slavery and helped to transform the image of blacks from that of victims of injustice to one of potential menaces. In August 1800 a planned insurrection of more than 1,000 slaves in Richmond, Virginia, kindled smoldering white fears. The militia put down the conspiracy and executed 35 slaves, including the leader, Gabriel Prosser. "I have ventured my life in endeavoring to obtain the liberty of my countrymen, and I am a willing sacrifice to their cause," said one rebel before his execution.

Isolated uprisings occurred in the United States for years after "Gabriel's Rebellion," and rumors persisted that a massive revolt was brewing. Antislavery sentiment diminished rapidly. The antislavery movement would not recover from the damage inflicted by the Saint Domingue revolt until the early 1830s.

Another development would strengthen slavery. In the 1790s demand in the British textile industry stimulated the cultivation of cotton in coastal South Carolina and Georgia. Here the soil and climate were ideal for growing long-staple cotton, whose fibers could be separated easily from its seed. In the South's upland and interior regions, however, only short-staple cotton thrived. Its seed clung tenaciously to the fibers and defied cleaning. It was as if southerners had discovered gold but could not mine it. In 1793 a Connecticut Yankee, Eli Whitney, rescued the South by inventing a cotton gin that efficiently cleaned short-staple cotton. Improved by others, Whitney's machine removed a major obstacle to cotton cultivation, gave plantation slavery a new lease on life, and undermined the doubts of those who considered slavery economically outmoded. Thus by the time Thomas Jefferson became president in 1801, free blacks had suffered a subtle erosion of their political gains, and slaves stood no closer to freedom.

CONCLUSION

The United States had survived its perilous birth. George Washington had steered the country through its initial uncertain years even as political strife led to the formation of political parties and threatened the unity of the fragile nation. In 1800 a peaceful transition of power occurred when the Federalists allowed Thomas Jefferson to become president. By 1801 the dangers of civil war and national disintegration had abated. Yet ideological hatreds remained strong and the West's allegiance to the Union shaky. Racial tensions were growing, not diminishing. It remained to be seen whether Jefferson's liberal version of republicanism could serve as a better philosophy of government than the Federalists' conservative republicanism.

CHRONOLOGY

1789 First Congress convenes in New York.
George Washington sworn in as first president.
Judiciary Act of 1789.
French Revolution begins.

1790 Alexander Hamilton submits his Report on the Public Credit and Report on a National Bank to Congress.
Treaty of New York.

1791 Bank of the United States is granted a twenty-year charter.
Bill of Rights ratified.
Slave uprising begins in French colony of Saint Domingue.
Hamilton submits his Report on Manufactures to Congress.

1792 Washington reelected president.

1793 Fugitive Slave Law.
Chisholm v. *Georgia.*
Large-scale exodus of French planters from Saint Domingue to the United States.
France declares war on Britain and Spain.
Washington's Neutrality Proclamation.
Citizen Genet arrives in United States.
Democratic societies established.

1794 Whiskey Rebellion.
General Anthony Wayne's forces rout Indians in the Battle of Fallen Timbers.

1795 Treaty of Greenville.
Jay's Treaty with Britain ratified.

1796 *Hylton* v. *United States*.
Ware v. *Hylton*.
Treaty of San Lorenzo (Pinckney's Treaty) ratified.
Washington's Farewell Address.
John Adams elected president.

1798 XYZ Affair.
Alien and Sedition Acts.
Eleventh Amendment to the Constitution ratified.

1798–1799 Virginia and Kentucky Resolutions.

1798–1800 United States fights Quasi-War with France.

1800 Gabriel's Rebellion in Virginia.
Thomas Jefferson elected president.

FOR FURTHER READING

Joyce Appleby, *Capitalism and a New Social Order: The Republican Vision of the 1790s* (1984). A brief, penetrating analysis of Jeffersonian ideology.

Stanley Elkins and Eric McKitrick, *The Age of Federalism: The Early American Republic, 1788–1800* (1993). A magisterial account of politics and diplomacy through the decisive election of 1800.

Richard Hofstadter, *The Idea of a Party System: The Rise of Legitimate Opposition in the United States, 1780–1840* (1969). A classic account of how and why America's founders, originally fearing political parties, came to embrace them.

Drew R. McCoy, *The Elusive Republic: Political Economy in Jeffersonian America* (1980). An insightful portrayal of the influence of economic considerations on early national political thought.

James M. Smith, *Freedom's Fetters: The Alien and Sedition Laws and American Civil Liberties*, rev. ed. (1966). The most comprehensive study of the country's first great crisis in civil rights.

Laurel Thatcher Ulrich, *A Midwife's Tale: The Life of Martha Ballard, Based on Her Diary, 1785–1812* (1990). A Pulitzer Prize–winning study of a woman's life in rural America.

Anthony F.C. Wallace, *The Death and Rebirth of the Seneca* (1969). An anthropologist's masterful account of the Senecas' devastation during the Revolution and their remarkable cultural recovery afterward.

CHAPTER 8

Jeffersonianism and the Era of Good Feelings

Jefferson's election, a turning point in the history of the young Republic, marked the peaceful transfer of power from one political party to another, a process never before attempted. Given the absence of precedent—the very newness of it all—relatively minor questions such as the replacement of Federalist officeholders spawned major philosophical debates. Perhaps the most important task facing Jefferson was to create and to gain support for ground rules to guide the operations of republican government.

This objective accomplished, the United States experienced extraordinary events in the two decades after Jefferson's election. In swift succession it doubled its land area; stopped all trade with Europe in an attempt to avoid war; went to war anyhow, nearly lost, and proclaimed a moral victory; almost disintegrated in a conflict over slavery and statehood; and staked its claim to preeminence in the New World. An age that began with ferocious political controversy culminated in the "Era of Good Feelings."

(Right) ***Dolley Madison,*** *by Gilbert Stuart, 1804*

The Age of Jefferson

The Gathering Storm

The War of 1812

The Awakening of American Nationalism

The Age of Jefferson

Unemotional himself, Thomas Jefferson aroused deep emotions in others. To admirers, he was an aristocrat who trusted the people and defended popular liberty; to detractors, he was an infidel and a radical. Jefferson had so many facets that misunderstanding him was easy. Trained in law, he had spent much of his life in public service—as governor of Virginia, Washington's secretary of state, Adams's vice president. He designed his own neoclassical mansion, Monticello; studied the violin and numerous languages (including several Native American tongues); and served twenty years as president of the American Philosophical Society, America's oldest and most important scientific organization. Although he saw himself as a humanitarian, he owned more than 200 slaves.

History taught Jefferson that republics fell from within; governments that undermined popular liberty, not hostile neighbors, were the real threat to freedom. Taxes, standing armies, and corrupt officials made governments masters, rather than servants, of the people. In Europe the collapse of the French Revolution and the rise of Napoleonic dictatorship had both dismayed Jefferson and convinced him that he had read history correctly.

To prevent the United States from sinking into tyranny, Jefferson advocated that state governments retain great authority because they were immediately responsive to popular will. Popular liberty required popular virtue, he believed, virtue being the disposition to place public good above private interest and to exercise vigilance in keeping government under control. To Jefferson, the most vigilant and virtuous people were educated farmers, accustomed to acting and thinking with sturdy independence. Least vigilant were the inhabitants of cities, which he saw as breeding grounds for mobs and as menaces to liberty. When Americans "get piled upon one another in large cities, as in Europe," he warned, "they will become corrupt as in Europe."

Although opponents labeled him a dreamy philosopher incapable of governing, Jefferson was in fact intensely practical. He studied science not for its abstract theories but because scientific advances would augment human happiness. Jefferson's practical cast of mind revealed itself in his inventions—including an improved plow and a gadget for duplicating letters—and in his presidential agenda.

Jefferson's "Revolution"

Jefferson described his election as a revolution, but the revolution he sought was to restore the liberty and tranquillity that (he thought) the United States had enjoyed in its earliest years and to reverse what he saw as a drift into despotism. The $10 million growth in the national debt under the Federalists alarmed Jefferson and his secretary of the treasury, Albert Gallatin. They rejected Alexander Hamilton's argument that debt strengthened the government by giving creditors a stake in its health. Just paying interest on the debt would require taxes, which would suck money from industrious farmers, the backbone of the Republic. The money would then fall into the hands of creditors, parasites who lived off interest payments. Increased tax revenues might also tempt the government to create a standing army, always a threat to liberty.

Jefferson and Gallatin asked Congress to repeal most internal taxes, and they slashed expenditures by closing some embassies and reducing the army. The navy was a different matter because of the Barbary pirates. For centuries rulers in North Africa (the "Barbary Coast") had tried to solve their own budget problems by engaging in piracy and demanding ransom for captured seamen. Jefferson refused to meet their demands for tribute: he calculated that war would be cheaper than giving in to such bribery. In 1801 he dispatched a naval squadron to the Barbary Coast. After the navy had bombarded several ports and the marines had landed at Tripoli, in 1805 the United States concluded a peace treaty with the Barbary rulers. The military solution had cost less than half the annual bribe!

To Jefferson and Gallatin, federal economy outweighed the importance of military preparedness; Gallatin calculated that by holding the line on expenditures, the government could pay off the

The World of Thomas Jefferson at Monticello

Jefferson spent much of his adult life building and remodeling Monticello, his "simple and elegant" Virginia mansion, and he died there on July 4, 1826, fifty years to the day after the signing of the Declaration of Independence. Preferring the useful to the showy, he omitted the grand staircase evident in other mansions, designed the house to appear smaller than it actually was, and filled it with labor-saving gadgets.

national debt in sixteen years. A lull in the European war between France and England that had threatened American shipping in the 1790s convinced Jefferson that minimal military preparedness was a sound policy. "We can now proceed without risks in demolishing useless structures of expense . . . and fortifying the principles of free government," he wrote.

Jefferson and the Judiciary

In his first inaugural address Jefferson reminded Americans that their agreements were more basic than their disagreements. "We have called by different name brothers of the same principle," he proclaimed. "We are all republicans; we are all federalists." Political conflict might not evaporate, but he hoped to win over moderate Federalists. After all, Jefferson and John Adams had once been friends, although bitterness over the composition and control of the federal judiciary would prevent their reconciliation during Jefferson's administration.

In theory, both Jefferson and the Federalists believed that talent and virtue, not political affiliation, were the primary qualifications for judgeships. In practice, Federalists had found neither talent nor virtue among Republicans, and in 1800 not a single Republican sat on the federal bench. For Republicans, the crowning blow was the Federalist-sponsored Judiciary Act, passed in February 1801. Ostensibly nonpartisan, the act created sixteen new federal judgeships to relieve Supreme Court justices of circuit-riding responsibilities but reduced the number of justices from six to five. This latter provision threatened to strip Jefferson of his first opportunity to appoint a justice—and threatened also to perpetuate Federalist domination of the judiciary.

The act confirmed Jefferson's fears that the Federalists would use the judiciary as a stronghold from which "all the works of Republicanism are to be beaten down and erased." Outgoing president John Adams strengthened Jefferson's suspicions by appointing Federalists to the new positions. These last-minute "midnight appointments" included candidates who had lost in the 1800 elections, a former loyalist Revolutionary War captain, and several relatives of John Marshall, a staunch Federalist and the new chief justice.

Although Jefferson rejected the radical view that judges should be elected rather than appointed, the Federalists seemed bent on turning the judiciary into an arm of their party. Ironically, an unfinished "midnight appointment" prompted Jefferson to seek repeal of the Judiciary Act of 1801. On the last day in office, Adams appointed William Marbury justice of the peace in the District of Columbia but failed to deliver Marbury's commission. When Jefferson's secretary of state, James Madison, refused to release the commission, Marbury petitioned the Supreme Court for a writ of mandamus* ordering Madison to make the delivery. Chief Justice Marshall then called on Madison to show cause why he should not be compelled to deliver the commission. Already wary, Jefferson saw Marshall's maneuvers as early signs of Federalist politics with the judiciary, so in 1802 the president pushed for, and won, congressional repeal of the Judiciary Act. Federalists despaired. The Constitution, one moaned, "is dead. It is dead."

The Federalist judiciary, however, was alive and well. Chief Justice John Marshall was a Virginian but the son of a farmer, not an aristocrat. His service in the Revolution had instilled in him a burning attachment to the Union rather than to any state. In 1803 Marshall's long-awaited decision in *Marbury* v. *Madison* came down. It would be immensely important in the evolution of the Constitution, for in this decision Marshall declared an act of Congress unconstitutional for the first time in American history. He denied Marbury's petition for a writ of mandamus to force Madison to deliver the commission on the grounds that when Congress had granted the Court authority to issue such a writ in 1789, it had exceeded its constitutional authority. By overturning an act of Congress, the justices set an important precedent and solidified the role of the Court as a third, coequal branch of the federal government.

President Jefferson, like most Republicans, believed that the Court possessed the right of judicial review (the right to declare acts of Congress unconstitutional), but he did not believe that the Supreme Court alone had the power of judicial review. Instead, he believed that all branches of the government had the right to decide the constitutionality of measures before them. Thus it was not Marshall's assertion of the Court's power of judicial review that troubled Jefferson—it was what he interpreted as Marshall's gratuitous lecture to Madison on his moral duty that upset the president, who perceived it as another example of Federalist partisanship in respect to the judiciary.

Even before the Court handed down *Marbury*, Republicans had taken the offensive against the Federalist judiciary by moving to impeach two Federalist judges. One of them, John Pickering of the New Hampshire District Court, was an insane alcoholic given to bizarre behavior in court. The other, Samuel Chase of the Supreme Court, was a notoriously partisan Federalist, the devil incarnate to Republicans. All of them knew that Chase's name formed the correct ending to a popular verse.

Cursed of thy father, scum of all that's base,
Thy sight is odious, and thy name is ______.

Although the details clearly differed, the two cases raised the same issue. Under the Constitution, impeachment was the only way to remove federal judges, but it could be considered only in cases of "Treason, Bribery and other high Crimes and Misdemeanors." Was impeachment an appropriate way to get rid of mad or partisan judges? On March 12, 1804, the Senate convicted Pickering, despite some senators' misgivings. Although the House voted to indict Chase that same day, John Randolph, a Jefferson supporter, botched the prosecution so badly that he failed to obtain the two-thirds majority necessary to convict. Even had Randolph done a more competent job, the prosecution might have failed anyhow because moderate Republicans were begin-

*Mandamus: an order from a higher court commanding that a specified action be taken.

ning to doubt that impeachment was a solution to the issue of judicial partisanship.

Chase's acquittal ended Jefferson's skirmishes with the judiciary. Unlike his radical followers, Jefferson objected neither to judicial review nor to an appointed judiciary; he merely challenged Federalist use of judicial power for political goals. Yet there was always a gray area between law and politics. To Federalists, there was no conflict between protecting the Constitution and advancing their party's cause. Nor did Federalists use their domination of the courts to undo Jefferson's "revolution" of 1800; the Marshall court, for example, upheld the constitutionality of the repeal of the Judiciary Act of 1801. In turn, Jefferson never proposed impeaching Marshall. And in the Pickering and Chase cases, Jefferson had merely tried to make the judiciary more responsive to popular will by challenging judges who had behaved outrageously. No other federal judge would be impeached for more than fifty years.

The Louisiana Purchase

Jefferson's goal of avoiding foreign entanglements would remain beyond reach as long as European powers held large territories in North America. In the Treaty of San Ildefonso (1800), a weakened Spain had returned the vast Louisiana Territory to France, which, under Napoleon Bonaparte, was emerging as Europe's strongest military power. Jefferson was appalled.

The president had long imagined that the inevitable expansion of a free and virtuous American people would create an "empire of liberty." Spain was no obstacle, but Napoleonic France posed a real danger; Bonaparte's capacity for mischief was boundless, and American fears were great. If Bonaparte gave England a free hand in the Mediterranean in exchange for a license for French expansion in North America, the United States could be sandwiched between British Canada and French Louisiana. And if Britain refused to cooperate with France, the British might seize Louisiana, trapping the Americans between two large British territories.

Bonaparte's real goal was different but no less dangerous to American interests. Sure of his destiny as a conqueror, he dreamed of re-creating a French New World empire bordering the Caribbean and the Gulf of Mexico. The island of Santo Domingo (modern Haiti and the Dominican Republic) would be the fulcrum of the empire and Louisiana its breadbasket. Before this dream could become reality, however, the French would have to subdue Santo Domingo, where a bloody slave rebellion had led to the creation of a government under the black statesman Toussaint L'Ouverture. Napoleon accordingly dispatched an army to reassert French control and to reestablish slavery, but yellow fever and fierce resistance by the former slaves doomed the French forces.

As a slaveholder, Jefferson tacitly approved Napoleon's attempted reconquest of Santo Domingo; as a nationalist, he continued to fear the French presence in Louisiana. This fear turned to alarm when the Spanish colonial administrator in New Orleans prohibited the deposit of American produce in that city for transshipment to foreign lands. Because American farmers west of the Appalachians depended on access to the sea via New Orleans, the Spanish order was a major provocation. Most Americans assumed (wrongly) that the order had come from Napoleon, who had not yet taken formal possession of Louisiana. A concerned Jefferson wrote that "the day that France takes possession of N. Orleans . . . we must marry ourselves to the British fleet and nation."

The combination of France's failure to subdue Santo Domingo and the termination of the American right of deposit at New Orleans stimulated two crucial decisions, one by Jefferson and the other by Napoleon, that led to the American purchase of Louisiana. First, Jefferson nominated James Monroe and Robert R. Livingston to negotiate with France for the purchase of New Orleans and as much of the Floridas as possible. (Because West Florida had repeatedly changed hands among France, Britain, and

Spain, no one was sure who owned it.) Meanwhile, Napoleon had concluded that his Caribbean empire was not worth the cost. In addition, he planned to resume war in Europe and needed cash—so he decided to sell *all* of Louisiana. The American commissioners and the French government settled on a price of $15 million. Thus the United States bought this immense, uncharted territory. No one knew its exact size, but the Louisiana Purchase virtually doubled the area of the United States.

Unsure of his constitutional authority to acquire Louisiana, Jefferson drafted an amendment that would have given him that power. But few Republicans shared his reservations, and Jefferson soon began to worry that the long process of ratifying an amendment might give Napoleon time to change his mind. In addition, aware that most Federalists opposed the Louisiana Purchase because it would decrease the relative importance of their eastern-seaboard strongholds, the Republican Jefferson saw

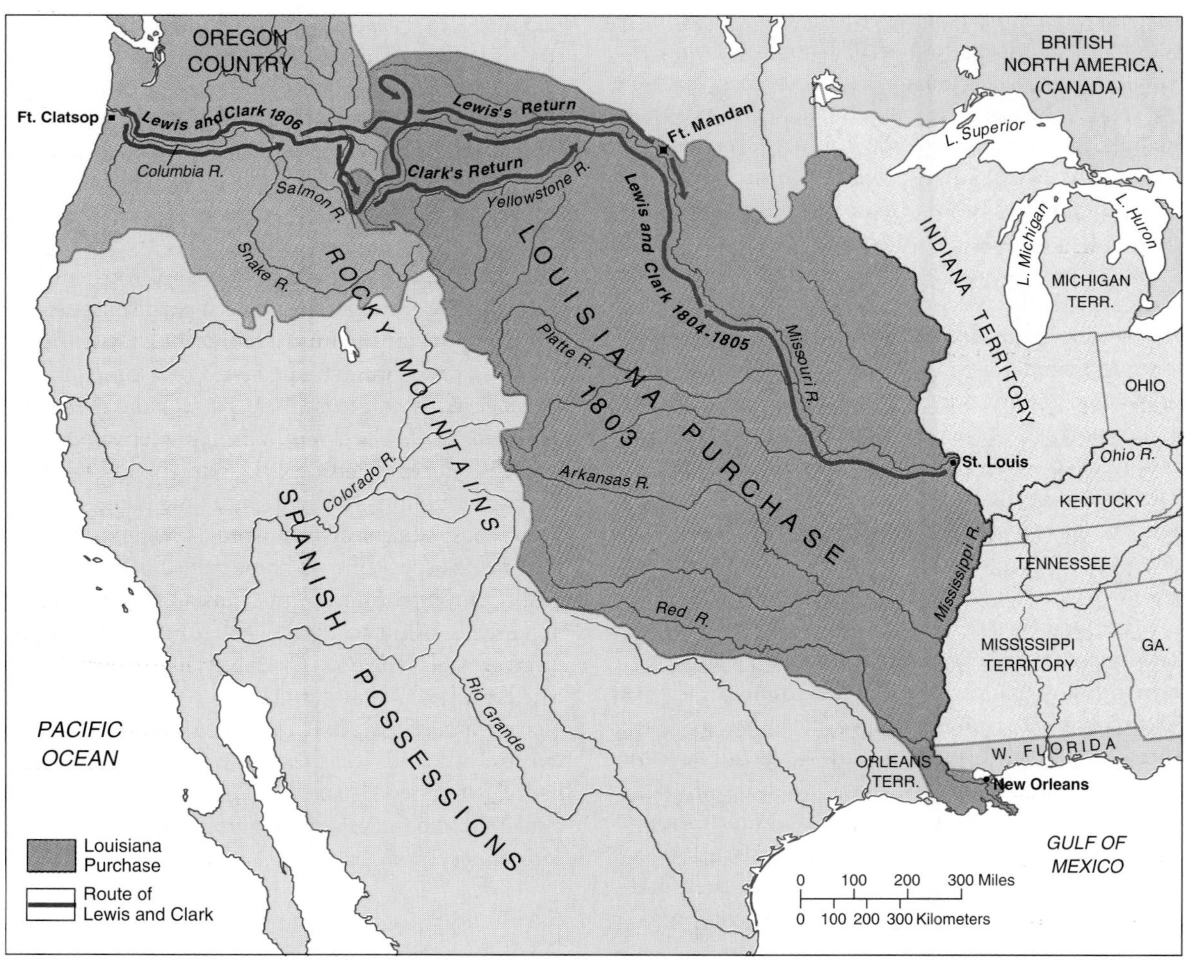

The Louisiana Purchase and the Exploration of the West *The explorations of Lewis and Clark demonstrated the vast extent of the area purchased from France.*

no reason to hand the Federalists an issue by dallying over ratification. The president quietly dropped the amendment, and the Senate quickly ratified the purchase.

The Lewis and Clark Expedition

Louisiana dazzled Jefferson's imagination. Americans knew virtually nothing about the immense territory, not even its western boundary. A case could be made for the Pacific Ocean, but Jefferson was content to claim that Louisiana extended at least to the mountains west of the Mississippi, mountains that few Americans had seen. Thus the Louisiana Purchase was both a bargain and a surprise package.

Even before the purchase, Jefferson had planned an exploratory expedition. He had chosen Lieutenant Meriwether Lewis, his personal secretary, as commander and had sent him to Philadelphia for a crash course in zoology, astronomy, and botany. Lewis was to trace the Missouri River to its source, cross the western highlands, and follow the best water route to the Pacific. Although Jefferson stressed commercial possibilities in requesting congressional funding for the expedition, he probably cared more about advancing scientific knowledge. His instructions to Lewis focused on obtaining accurate measurements of latitude and longitude, gathering information about Native American languages and customs, and studying climate, volcanoes, and plant and animal life.

Leaving St. Louis in May 1804, Lewis; his second-in-command, William Clark; and about fifty others followed the Missouri and then the Snake and Columbia rivers. In the Dakota Country they hired a French-Canadian fur trader, Toussaint Charbonneau, as guide and interpreter. Charbonneau proved less than ideal, but his shortcomings were offset by his wife, Sacajawea, a sixteen-year-old Shoshone stolen by a rival tribe and then married to Charbonneau. During the expedition the presence of Sacajawea's newborn son helped to persuade skeptical tribes of Lewis and Clark's peaceful intent; she also showed the whites how to forage for wild plants, often their only food, by raiding rodent dens. After reaching the Pacific in November 1805, the expedition returned to St. Louis. The explorers had collected vast amounts of scientific information, including the disturbing fact that more than 300 miles of mountains separated the Missouri from the Columbia. Nonetheless, the Lewis and Clark expedition stimulated interest in the West.

The Election of 1804

Candidates	*Parties*	*Electoral Vote*
THOMAS JEFFERSON	Democratic-Republican	162
Charles C. Pinckney	Federalist	14

The Election of 1804

The main threat to Jefferson's reelection in 1804 was not the Federalists, who were dispirited and lacked a popular national issue, but Aaron Burr, his own vice president, who had tried to take advantage of a tie in the electoral college to gain the presidency in 1800. The Twelfth Amendment had clarified the electoral process but had not eliminated Burr's conniving; he had spent much of his vice presidency intriguing with the Federalists. The Republicans dispensed with the threat by unceremoniously dumping him from the ticket in 1804 in favor of George Clinton. In the election the Federalist nominees, Charles C. Pinckney and Rufus King, carried only two states. Jefferson's overwhelming victory brought his first term to a fitting close; between 1801 and 1804 the United States had doubled its territory, started to pay off its debt, and remained at peace. President Jefferson basked in the sun of success.

The Gathering Storm

But the sky was not cloudless for long. For one thing, the lull in the European wars had ended; between 1803 and 1814 the renewed Napoleonic Wars turned the United States into a pawn in a foreign chess game and made Jefferson's second term far less successful than his first. For another, the collapse of the Federalists proved a mixed blessing. As long as the Federalists and Republicans had competed equally, the Republican leadership could demand party unity. But as the Federalists weakened, unity became less important and Republicans fell victim to internal squabbles.

Jefferson's Coalition Fragments

The election of 1804 temporarily eliminated the Federalists as a force in national politics. Intraparty factionalism, however, provided trouble enough for the Republicans. Aaron Burr, dropped from the 1804 ticket, began to intrigue with a faction of extreme, or High, Federalists who were scheming to form a "Northern Confederacy" that would include Nova Scotia, New England, New York, and even Pennsylvania. To advance their plot, the Federalists helped Burr to gain the Federalist nomination for governor of New York. Alexander Hamilton, who had thwarted Burr's grab for the presidency in 1800 by supporting Jefferson, now foiled Burr a second time by allowing publication of his "despicable opinion" of Burr. After his defeat in the New York election, Burr challenged Hamilton to a duel and mortally wounded him at Weehawken, New Jersey, on July 11, 1804.

Indicted in two states for murdering Hamilton, Burr next hatched a scheme so audacious that not even his opponents could believe that he was capable of such treachery. Burr allied himself with General James Wilkinson, the military governor of the Louisiana Territory, who had been taking Spanish money since the 1780s. Their plot had several dimensions: they would create an independent confederacy of western states, conquer Mexico, and invade West Florida. The scheming duo presented the plot imaginatively. To westerners, they said that it had the covert support of the Jefferson administration; to the British, that it was a way to attack Spanish lands; and to the Spanish, that it would open the way to dividing up the United States.

In fall 1806 Burr and some sixty followers made their way down the Ohio and Mississippi rivers to join Wilkinson at Natchez. Wilkinson was not there. Recognizing that Jefferson was ready to move against Burr and that the British were not interested in supporting the plot, Wilkinson had double-crossed Burr, reporting the conspiracy in a letter to Jefferson. Wilkinson then took refuge in New Orleans and proclaimed himself the most loyal of the president's followers.

In October 1806 Jefferson denounced the conspiracy. Former vice president Burr panicked, tried to flee, but was captured and returned to Richmond to stand trial for treason. Chief Justice John Marshall presided and advised the jury that the prosecution had to prove actual treasonable acts—an impossible task because the conspiracy had never reached fruition. Jefferson was furious, but Marshall followed the clear wording of the Constitution, which deliberately made treason difficult to prove. The jury returned a "not proved" verdict, which Marshall entered as "not guilty." Still under indictment for the murder of Hamilton, Burr fled to Europe, where he tried but failed to involve Napoleon in a grand scheme that would be the prelude to a proposed Anglo-French invasion of the United States. Burr returned to the United States in 1812 and practiced law in New York; perhaps the most puzzling man in American history, he died in 1836.

Jefferson and the Quids

Jefferson also faced a challenge from a group of fellow Republicans known as the Quids.* Their leader was John Randolph of Virginia, a man of abounding eccentricities and acerbic wit. Randolph still subscribed to the "country ideology" of the 1770s, which celebrated the wisdom of the farmer against rulers and warned against governments' tendency to

*Quid: a name taken from the Latin *tertium quid,* or "third thing"; roughly, a dissenter.

encroach on liberty. Originally, Jefferson had shared these beliefs, but he had recognized them as an ideology of opposition, not of power; once in office, he therefore compromised. In contrast, Randolph remained frozen in the 1770s, denouncing every change as decline and proclaiming that he would throw all politicians to the dogs if he had less respect for dogs.

Not surprisingly, Randolph turned on Jefferson. First, he blasted the president for backing a compromise in the Yazoo land scandal. In 1795 the Georgia legislature had sold the huge Yazoo tract (35 million acres composing most of present-day Alabama and Mississippi) for a fraction of its value to land companies that had bribed virtually the entire legislature. The next legislature canceled the sale, but many investors had already bought land, some of them in good faith. The scandal was a moral challenge to Jefferson because of the good-faith purchases and a political dilemma as well, for some buyers were northerners whom Jefferson hoped to woo to the Republican Party. In 1803 a federal commission compromised with an award of 5 million acres to the Yazoo investors. To Randolph, the compromise was itself a scandal—further evidence of the decay of republican virtue.

Randolph also clashed with Jefferson over the president's request for a congressional appropriation to purchase the Floridas from Spain. Randolph raged not so much at the land purchase as at Jefferson's "deception" in requesting money for extraordinary diplomatic expenses without officially informing Congress of the real object of the expenditures. In fact, however, Jefferson had privately informed members of Congress, including Randolph, of his plans, but to Randolph it still seemed another betrayal of virtue.

The Suppression of American Trade

Burr's acquittal and Randolph's taunts shattered the aura of invincibility that had surrounded Jefferson. Now foreign affairs posed even sharper challenges. As Britain and France resumed their war, the United States prospered at Britain's expense by carrying sugar and coffee from French and Spanish Caribbean colonies to Europe. This trade not only provided Napoleon with supplies but also drove down the price of sugar and coffee from British colonies by adding to the glut of these commodities on the world market. The British concluded that their economic problems stemmed from American prosperity.

This prosperity rested on the reexport trade, which created conflicts with Britain. According to the British Rule of 1756, any trade closed during peacetime could not be opened during war. For example, France usually restricted the sugar trade to French ships during peacetime and thus could not open it to American ships during war. The U.S. response to the Rule of 1756 was the "broken voyage," by which U.S. ships would carry French sugar or coffee to American ports, unload it, pass it through customs, and then reexport it as *American* produce. Britain tolerated this dodge for nearly a decade but in 1805 initiated a policy of total war toward France, including the strangulation of French trade. In the *Essex* case (1805), a British court declared broken voyages illegal.

Next came a series of British trade decrees ("Orders in Council"), through which Britain intended to blockade part of continental Europe and thus staunch the flow of any products that might aid the French war effort. French counterdecrees, proclaiming the British Isles blockaded, followed. In effect, if Americans obeyed the British regulations, they would violate the French rules, and vice versa. In total war, however, there was no room for neutrality, so both Britain and France seized U.S. ships. The British captures were far more humiliating and infuriating, for although most French seizures took place in European ports, many British takeovers occurred within sight of the U.S. coastline.

Impressment

To these provocations the British added impressment. At issue was Britain's seizing purported Royal

Navy deserters from American merchant ships and subsequently forcing them back into service. British sailors had good reason to be discontented with their navy. Discipline on the Royal Navy's "floating hells" was often brutal, and the pay low; sailors on American ships earned up to five times more than those on British ships. Consequently, at a time when war raised the demand for sailors, the Royal Navy suffered a high rate of desertion to American ships. In 1807, for example, 149 of the 419 sailors on the USS *Constitution* were British subjects.

Impressed sailors led harrowing lives that included frequent escapes and recaptures. One seaman endured impressment eleven times. Another, facing his third recapture, drowned himself rather than spend another day in the Royal Navy. Impressment was, moreover, galling to American pride, for even though many deserters had become American citizens, the British impressed them anyway. The British also impressed U.S.-born seamen, including those who could prove their American birth; between 1803 and 1812, 6,000 Americans were impressed.

The *Chesapeake* incident heightened British-American tensions. In June 1807 a British warship, HMS *Leopard,* attacked an American frigate, the USS *Chesapeake,* just off Virginia. The British boarded the vessel and seized four supposed deserters. One, an actual deserter, was later hanged; the other three, former Britons, had "deserted" only from impressment and were now American citizens. Never before had the British claimed the right to seize deserters off government ships. Public outrage mounted; Jefferson claimed that he had not seen so belligerent a spirit in America since 1775. Yet while making some preparations for a possible war, Jefferson sought peace, first by engaging in fruitless negotiations with Britain to gain redress for the *Chesapeake* and then by steering the Embargo Act through Congress in December 1807.

The Embargo Act

By far the most controversial legislation of Jefferson's presidency, the Embargo Act prohibited vessels from leaving American harbors for foreign ports. Technically, it prohibited only exports, but it stopped imports as well, for few foreign ships would enter American ports if they had to leave empty. An amazed British newspaper called the embargo "little short of an absolute secession from the rest of the civilized world."

Jefferson defended the embargo as "peaceable coercion," a way of forcing France and, especially, Britain to respect American neutrality. But it did not work. Although British trade with the United States plummeted, the British opened new markets in South America. France's Napoleon, for his part, treated the act as a joke, seizing American ships and then informing the United States that he was only helping to enforce the embargo. Furthermore, the discovery of a major loophole that allowed American ships blown off course to put in at European ports led to an epidemic of U.S. captains reporting that adverse winds had forced them across the Atlantic.

The United States itself felt the harshest effects. Thirty thousand seamen lost their jobs, hundreds of merchants went bankrupt, and debtors swelled the jail population. Unable to export produce or to sell it at a decent price in the cities, farmers suffered as well. Land speculators discovered that cash-starved farmers could not buy land. "I live and that is all," wrote one New York speculator. "I am doing no business, cannot sell anybody property, nor collect any money." New England suffered most; in Massachusetts, which accounted for a third of foreign trade, the embargo was a calamity.

Yet there were benefits. Unable to export goods, merchants used their capital to begin manufacturing. In 1808 the United States had only fifteen cotton textile mills; by the end of 1809 eighty-seven more had been built. But merchants already ruined or seamen driven to soup kitchens took little comfort. Nor could New Englanders forget that the source of their misery was one of the "Virginia lordlings," "Mad Tom" Jefferson, who knew little about New England and loathed cities, the foundation of the region's prosperity. A Massachusetts poet wrote:

Our ships all in motion once whitened the ocean,
They sailed and returned with a cargo;
Now doomed to decay they have fallen a prey
To Jefferson, worms, and embargo.

The Election of 1808

With Jefferson's blessing, the Republicans nominated James Madison and George Clinton for the presidency and vice presidency in 1808. The Federalists renominated Charles C. Pinckney and Rufus King, the same ticket that had failed in 1804. In 1808 the Federalists staged a modest comeback, but Madison handily won the presidency, and the Republicans continued to control Congress.

The Federalists' revival, modest as it was, rested on two factors. First, the Embargo Act gave them the national issue that they had long lacked. Second, younger Federalists had abandoned their elders' "gentlemanly" disdain for campaigning and deliberately imitated vote-winning techniques such as barbecues and mass meetings that had worked for the Republicans.

The Election of 1808

Candidates	*Parties*	*Electoral Vote*
JAMES MADISON	Democratic-Republican	122
Charles C. Pinckney	Federalist	47
George Clinton	Democratic-Republican	6

The Failure of Peaceable Coercion

To some contemporaries, "Little Jemmy" Madison, five feet four inches tall, seemed a weak, shadowy figure compared to Jefferson. In fact, Madison's intelligence and capacity for systematic thought equaled Jefferson's. Like Jefferson, Madison believed that American liberty rested on the virtue of the people and that virtue was critically tied to the growth and prosperity of agriculture. Madison also recognized that agricultural prosperity depended on trade—farmers needed markets. The British West Indies, dependent on the United States for much lumber and grain, struck Madison as both a natural trading partner and a tempting target. Britain alone could not fully supply the West Indies. By embargoing its own trade with the Indies, Madison reasoned, the United States could force Britain to its knees before Americans would suffer severe losses.

The American embargo, however, was coercing no one. Increased trade between Canada and the West Indies made a shambles of Madison's plan to pressure Britain. On March 1, 1809, Congress replaced the Embargo Act with the weaker, face-saving Non-Intercourse Act, which opened U.S. trade to all nations except Britain and France and authorized the president to restore trade with either of those nations if it stopped violating neutral rights. But neither nation complied. Meanwhile, American shippers kept up their profitable trade with the British and French, despite the restrictions. In May 1810 Congress substituted a new measure, Macon's Bill No. 2, for the Non-Intercourse Act. This legislation reopened trade with both belligerents, France and Britain, and then offered a clumsy bribe to each: if either nation repealed its restrictions on neutral shipping, the United States would halt all trade with the other. Napoleon seized the opportunity to confound both English-speaking nations by promising to repeal his edicts against American trade, hoping to provoke hostility between Britain and the United States. But the French continued to seize American ships. Peaceable coercion had become a fiasco.

The Push into War

Madison now faced not only a hostile Britain and France but also militant Republicans demanding more aggressive policies. Primarily southerners and westerners, the militants were infuriated by insults to the American flag. In addition, economic recession between 1808 and 1810 had convinced the firebrands that British policies were wrecking their regions' economies. The election of 1810 brought several young militants, christened "war hawks," to Congress. Led by Henry Clay of Kentucky, who preferred war to the "putrescent pool of ignominious peace," the war hawks included John C. Calhoun of South Carolina, Richard M. Johnson of Kentucky, and William R. King of North Carolina—all future vice presidents. Clay was elected Speaker of the House.

Tecumseh and the Prophet

More emotional and pugnaciously nationalistic than Jefferson or Madison, the war hawks called for expelling Britain from Canada and Spain from the Floridas. Their demands merged with westerners' fears that the British in Canada were recruiting Indians to halt the march of United States settlement. These fears, groundless but plausible, intensified when the Shawnee Indian chief Tecumseh and his half-brother, the Prophet, tried to unite several Ohio and Indiana tribes against westward-moving settlers. Demoralized by the continuing loss of the Indians' land and by alcoholism's ravages on Native American society, Tecumseh and the Prophet (a recovered alcoholic) tried to unite their people and to revive traditional values. Both believed that the Indians had to purge themselves of liquor and other corruptions of white civilization.

The Shawnee leaders were on a collision course with the governor of the Indiana Territory, William Henry Harrison. In the Treaty of Fort Wayne (1809), Harrison had purchased much of central and western Indiana from the Miami and the Delaware tribes for a paltry $10,000. After Tecumseh's Shawnees refused to sign the treaty, Harrison saw the charismatic leader as an enemy and even as a British cat's-paw. Accordingly, in September 1811 Harrison led an army against a Shawnee encampment at the junction of the Wabash and Tippecanoe Rivers. Two months later when the Prophet prematurely attacked Harrison (Tecumseh was away recruiting Creek Indians), Harrison won a decisive victory. Ironically, the Battle of Tippecanoe, which made Harrison a national hero, accomplished what it had been designed to prevent: it prompted Tecumseh to join with the British.

Congress Votes for War

By spring 1812 President Madison had concluded that war was inevitable, and he sent a war message

Tenskwatawa (1768?–1834?), the Prophet

In periods of crisis Native American cultures often gave rise to prophets—religious revivalists of sorts—such as Tecumseh's brother Tenskwatawa. Known to non-Indians as the Prophet, Tenskwatawa tried to revive traditional Indian values and customs such as the common ownership of land and the wearing of animal skins and furs. His religious program blended with Tecumseh's political program to unite the western tribes.

to Congress on June 1. Ironically, an economic slump prompted Britain to repeal its Orders in Council on June 23, but by then Congress had declared war. With the partial settlement of the maritime issues, the British hoped that Madison would revoke the declaration. However, they miscalculated the belligerence of American political leaders, especially Republicans.

The war hawks constituted a Senate minority, so the key to the declaration of war was the support of Republicans from populous states such as Pennsylvania, Virginia, and Maryland. Most opposition to war came from Federalist strongholds in Massachusetts, Connecticut, and New York. Southern Federalists joined their northern counterparts in opposition to the war, while northern Republicans supported it. In short, the vote for war followed party, rather than sectional, lines. Much like the president, most Republicans had not wanted war but had been led to demand it by an accumulation of grievances.

Madison, in his war message, listed impressment, the presence of British ships in U.S. waters, and British violation of neutral rights as wrongs that justified war. None of these complaints fully explains why America declared war in 1812. Neither do continuing Indian problems (blamed on the British) along the frontier. A more important underlying cause for the war was the economic recession that affected the South and West after 1808. Finally, the fact that Madison, rather than Jefferson, was president was vitally important. Jefferson had believed that Britain was motivated primarily by its desire to defeat Napoleon; time was on America's side, Jefferson thought, for once the war in Europe ended, the provocations would stop. Madison held that Britain's real motive was to strangle American trade and thus to eliminate the United States as a trading rival. European war or not, Madison saw Britain as a menace to America. In his war message he stated flatly that Britain was meddling with U.S. trade not because of the European war but because it "frustrated the monopoly which she [Britain] covets for her own commerce and navigation."

The War of 1812

Although Americans unfurled the slogan "Free Trade and Sailors' Rights" in summer 1812, they marched, rather than sailed, to war; Canada, not the Royal Navy, was the principal target. Madison considered Canada a key prop of the British Empire and a main component of the British plan to strangle American trade. Moreover, an attack on Canada was also more practical. Republican emphasis on economy had shrunk both the national debt—from \$83 million to \$27.5 million—and the navy, which was down to six frigates, three sloops, and a number of smaller vessels, including gunboats. These latter craft were essentially floating gun platforms designed for harbor defense; they often sank while under sail or were blown to sea while anchored in port.

Not only could Americans march to Canada, but it also seemed an easy target. Indeed, the United States was much more populous than its northern neighbor and had vastly larger armies and militias. Further, the British army was occupied with Napoleon, and 60 percent of Canadians were Americans by birth, lured north by cheap land. To Jefferson, the conquest of Canada seemed "a mere matter of marching."

It was not that easy. First, the British had an invaluable ally in the Native Americans, whose practice of taking and displaying scalps frightened many Americans. Second, most U.S. generals were aged and incompetent, and Andrew Jackson, one of the few able generals, was long denied a commission for political reasons. Third, the Americans' state militias overflowed with Sunday soldiers who "hollered for water half the time, and whiskey the other." The militiamen and their compatriots supported the war lukewarmly at best, and Madison could raise only 10,000 one-year volunteers out of the 50,000 authorized by Congress. For most people, Canada was remote and national political issues were almost as remote. Local attachments remained stronger than national ones in 1812.

The war's military campaigns developed in two

broad phases. From summer 1812 to spring 1814, the Americans took the offensive, launching a series of poorly coordinated and unsuccessful attacks on Canada. From spring 1814 to early 1815, the British retaliated and achieved several spectacular victories while losing key battles.

On to Canada

Despite some sympathy for the idea of an attack on Montreal, the American offensive opened in the West, largely for political reasons. In July 1812 the sixty-year-old general William Hull led an American army from Detroit into Canada, but Tecumseh cut his supply lines. Unnerved, Hull retreated to Detroit. The British commander played on Hull's fears by warning that he might not be able to control the Indians, and Hull promptly surrendered 2,000 men to 1,300 British and Native American troops.

In two other thrusts in 1812, the United States fared no better. A mixed force of regulars and New York militia was ordered into Canada north of Niagara Falls, but the militia refused to leave the state and watched as the British crushed the American regulars at the Battle of Queenston (October 13, 1812). The Indian presence was again decisive; the American commander, Winfield Scott, negotiated the U.S. surrender as Mohawks were attacking his men. In November General Henry Dearborn, en route to Montreal, had marched twenty miles north of Plattsburgh, New York, when the militia refused to advance. Dearborn retreated to Plattsburgh.

Renewed U.S. offensives and subsequent reverses in 1813 convinced the Americans that they could not retake Detroit while the British controlled Lake Erie. During winter 1812–1813 U.S. captain Oliver Hazard Perry constructed a little fleet out of green wood and outfitted it with captured cannon and supplies dragged across the snow from Pittsburgh to his headquarters at Presqu'ile (Erie). On September 10, 1813, the homemade American fleet destroyed a British squadron at Put-in-Bay on the western end of Lake Erie; "we have met the enemy, and they are ours," Perry triumphantly reported. The British then pulled out of Detroit, but American forces under General William Henry Harrison overtook and defeated a combined British-Indian force at the Battle of the Thames on October 5. Tecumseh, a legend among whites, died in the battle.

The Naval War

The American navy, although small, boasted three of the largest, fastest frigates afloat—the *Constitution*, the *United States*, and the *President*. In 1812 the *Constitution* destroyed two British warships, HMS *Guerrière* in the mid-Atlantic and HMS *Java* off Brazil, but these victories had no military significance. By 1814 superior British naval strength had clamped a blockade along the American coast and trapped the frigates in harbor. Nor did Perry's and Harrison's victories in the West hasten the conquest of Canada. Efforts to invade Canada in the Niagara area and to gain control of Lake Ontario also failed.

The British Offensive

Britain's military fortunes crested in spring 1814. Defeated in Europe, Napoleon abdicated in April, and Britain began moving regulars from Europe to North America. They quickly discovered that battle-toughened Americans defending their homes would not fold as easily as the earlier militiamen had.

Britain's main offensive thrust was meant to split the New England states, which were skeptical of the war, from the rest of the country. General Sir George Prevost headed a force of 10,000 British veterans, the largest and best-equipped British force ever sent to North America. They advanced readily down Lake Champlain until reaching the entrenched American forces at Plattsburgh; after his fleet met defeat on September 11, Prevost abandoned the campaign.

Ironically, Britain's most spectacular success began as a diversion from Prevost's offensive. A

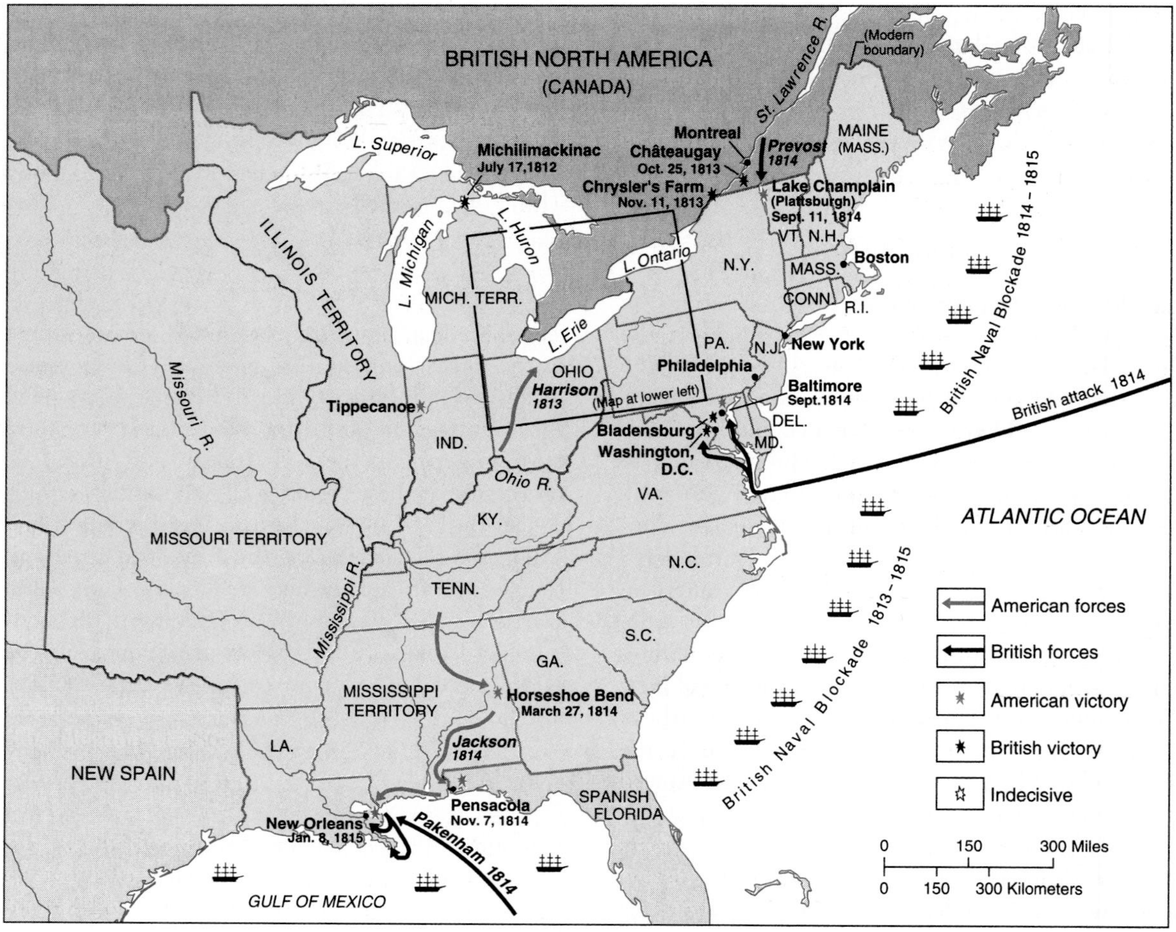

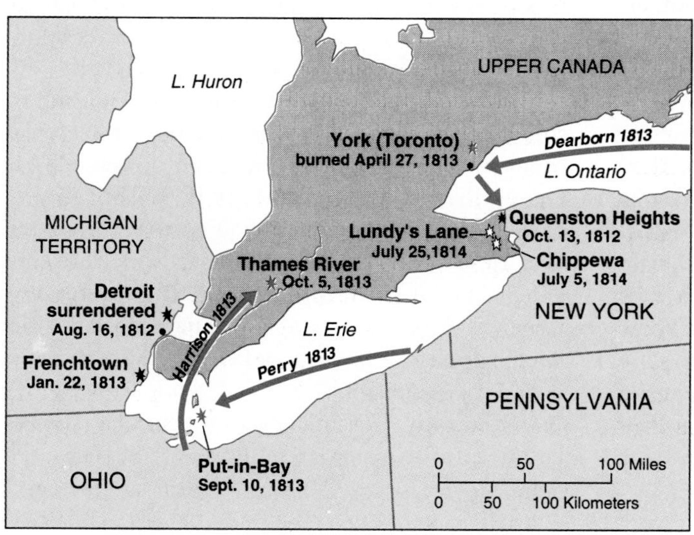

Major Battles of the War of 1812

Most of the war's major engagements occurred on or near the United States' northern frontier; but the Royal Navy blockaded the entire Atlantic coast, and the British army penetrated as far south as Washington and New Orleans.

British army that had come up from Bermuda entered Chesapeake Bay and on August 24, 1814, met a larger American force (mainly militiamen) at Bladensburg, Maryland. The Battle of Bladensburg deteriorated into the "Bladensburg Races" as the American troops fled, virtually without firing a shot. The British then descended on Washington, D.C. Madison, who had witnessed the Bladensburg fiasco, fled into the Virginia hills. His wife, Dolley, loaded her silver, a bed, and a portrait of Washington onto her carriage before joining her husband. British troops ate the supper prepared for the Madisons and then burned the presidential mansion and other public buildings in the capital. Beyond embarrassing and angering Americans, the Washington raid accomplished little, for after a failed attack on Baltimore, the British broke off the operation.

The Treaty of Ghent

English and American commissioners met at Ghent, Belgium, in August 1814 to negotiate a peace. Although the British appeared to be in a commanding position, they were not.

Napoleon's abdication had made Britain's primary goal a lasting European peace, and thus the British had little to gain by prolonging a minor war in America. At first they demanded territorial concessions from the United States, but they yielded on the issue after the Battle of Plattsburgh. The treaty, signed on Christmas Eve, 1814, restored the *status quo ante bellum:** the United States neither gained nor lost territory. The fixing of the Canadian-American border was referred to a joint commission for future settlement. Impressment was left hanging, but the end of the European war made neutral rights a dead issue.

Ironically, America's most dramatic victory came on January 8, 1815, two weeks after the treaty had been signed but before word of it had reached America. A British force had descended on New Orleans. U.S. troops commanded by General Andrew ("Old Hickory") Jackson, legendary as a fierce Indian fighter, shredded the line of advancing redcoats, inflicting more than 2,000 casualties while suffering only 13 of their own.

The Hartford Convention

Although it meant nothing in terms of the war, the Battle of New Orleans proved devastating for the Federalist Party. The Federalists' comeback had continued into the election of 1812, when their candidate, DeWitt Clinton, an antiwar Republican, had carried all of New England except Vermont, along with New York and New Jersey. American military setbacks had intensified Federalist disdain for Madison. He seemed to epitomize a decade of Republican misrule at New England's expense. The Louisiana Purchase, constitutionally dubious, had reduced the importance of New England, the Embargo Act had nearly destroyed the region's commerce, and "Mr. Madison's War" had brought fresh misery in the form of the British blockade. A few New England Federalists began to talk of secession from the Union.

In late 1814 a special Federalist convention met in Hartford, Connecticut. Although some supported secession, moderates took control and passed a series of resolutions expressing New England's grievances. Convinced that New England was becoming a permanent minority in a nation dominated by southern Republicans who failed to understand the region's commercial interests, the convention leaders proposed a series of constitutional amendments: to abolish the three-fifths clause, which allowed southerners to count slaves as a basis for representation; to require a two-thirds vote of Congress to declare war and to admit new states into the Union; to limit the president to a single term; to prohibit the election of two successive presidents from the same state; and to bar embargoes lasting more than sixty days. These proposals were as bold as their timing was disastrous. News of the peace and of Jackson's victory at New Orleans dashed Federalist hopes of gaining popular support, while the states' rights emphasis of the convention smelled of treason to many delegates. The restoration of peace stripped the Federalists of their primary grievance. In the presidential election of 1816,

---

**Status quo ante bellum:* Latin for "the state of affairs before the war."

The Election of 1812

Candidates	Parties	Electoral Vote
JAMES MADISON	Democratic-Republican	128
DeWitt Clinton	Federalist	89

The Election of 1816

Candidates	Parties	Electoral Vote
JAMES MONROE	Democratic-Republican	183
Rufus King	Federalist	34

The Election of 1820

Candidates	Parties	Electoral Vote
JAMES MONROE	Democratic-Republican	231
John Quincy Adams	Independent Republican	1

James Monroe, Madison's hand-picked successor and another Virginia Republican, swept the nation over negligible Federalist opposition. Four years later he would receive every electoral vote but one. The Federalists were finished as a force in national politics.

The Awakening of American Nationalism

The United States emerged from the War of 1812 bruised but intact. In its first major war since independence, the American republic had demonstrated that it could fight on even terms against a major power and that republics could conduct wars without becoming despotisms. The war also produced several major symbols of American nationalism: the presidential mansion, whitewashed to hide smoke damage, became the White House; Britain's failed attack on Fort McHenry in Baltimore Harbor inspired Francis Scott Key's "Star-Spangled Banner"; and the Battle of New Orleans made Andrew Jackson a national hero and reinforced legends about the prowess of American frontier people and their "long rifles." Much of the legend spun around the Battle of New Orleans was untrue, but Americans loved it nonetheless, especially because it confirmed their conviction that amateur soldiers and militiamen could outfight a professional army.

Madison's Nationalism and the Era of Good Feelings

The War of 1812 had three major political consequences. First, it eliminated the Federalists as a national political force. Second, it went far toward convincing the Republicans that the nation was strong and resilient, capable of fighting a war while maintaining liberty. Third, with political rivals removed, the Republicans began to embrace some Federalist ideas. Both President Madison and Henry Clay became advocates of federal support for internal improvements, tariff protection for new industries, and the creation of a new national bank; Clay christened these ideas the American System and proclaimed that they would make the nation economically self-sufficient. In 1816 Congress chartered the Second Bank of the United States and enacted a moderate tariff, but federally supported internal improvements were more difficult. Madison vetoed an internal improvements bill in 1817, believing that a constitutional amendment was necessary to authorize such improvements.

As Republicans adopted positions they once had disdained, an "Era of Good Feelings" dawned. Coined by a Boston newspaper editor, the term describes both of James Monroe's presidential administrations. Compared to Jefferson and Madison, Monroe was neither brilliant, polished, nor wealthy, but he wanted to heal America's political divisions, and he tried to avoid political controversies. Yet the good feelings were paper-thin, and Madison's veto of the internal improvements bill showed that disagreements lingered about the role of the federal government under the Constitution. The embargo, the War of 1812, and the continuation of slavery had aroused sectional animosities that no phrase could paper over. Not surprisingly, the postwar consensus unraveled rapidly.

John Marshall and the Supreme Court

In 1819 Jefferson's old antagonist John Marshall, still chief justice, issued two opinions that stunned Republicans. The first case, *Dartmouth College* v. *Woodward*, focused on New Hampshire's attempt to transform a private corporation, Dartmouth College, into a state university. Marshall concluded that Dartmouth's original charter was a contract and thus was protected under the constitutional prohibition against state interference in contracts. Marshall's ruling had enormous implications. In effect, Marshall said that once a state had chartered a college or business, that state surrendered its power to alter the charter and, in large measure, its authority to regulate the beneficiary. Buttressed by Marshall's decision, businesses and colleges increasingly sought the legal privileges of a charter or an act of incorporation.

A few weeks later the chief justice handed down an even more momentous decision in *McCulloch* v. *Maryland*. At issue was whether the state of Maryland had the power to tax a national corporation, specifically the Baltimore branch of the Second Bank of the United States. Marshall focused on two issues. First, did Congress have power to charter a national bank? The Constitution, Marshall conceded, did not explicitly grant this power, but the broad sweep of enumerated powers implied the power to charter a bank. This was a clear enunciation of a broad, or "loose," construction (interpretation) of the Constitution. The second issue revolved around whether a state could tax an agency of the federal government that was located within its borders. Marshall argued that any power of the national government, enumerated or implied, was supreme within its sphere. States could not interfere with the exercise of federal power; thus Maryland's attempt to tax the bank was plainly unconstitutional.

Marshall's decision in *McCulloch* dismayed many Republicans. For one thing, it placed the unpopular bank beyond the regulatory power of any state government. Far more important, the *McCulloch* decision attacked state sovereignty. The Constitution, Marshall said, was the creation not of state governments but of the people of *all* the states and thus overrode state laws. Like Jefferson, most Republicans considered the Union a compact among states and saw state governments as the guarantors of popular liberty. In Republican eyes, the *Dartmouth* and *McCulloch* cases stripped state governments of the power to impose the will of their people on corporations and thus threatened liberty.

The Missouri Compromise

The fragility of the Era of Good Feelings again became apparent in a two-year-long controversy over the territory of Missouri. In February 1819 the House of Representatives considered a bill to admit Missouri as a slave state. A New York Republican, James Tallmadge Jr., offered an amendment that prohibited the further introduction of slaves into Missouri and provided for the emancipation, at age twenty-five, of all slave offspring born after Missouri joined the Union. Following rancorous debate, the House accepted the amendment and the Senate rejected it. Both chambers voted along sectional lines.

Sectional differences had long troubled American politics, but the issues had been primarily economic. The Missouri question now thrust slavery into the center of this long-standing sectional conflict. "This momentous question," Jefferson worried, "like a fire bell in the night, awakened and filled me with terror."

The matter of slavery surfaced at this time for a number of reasons. In 1819 the Union had eleven slave and eleven free states; the admission of Missouri as a slave state would upset this balance, to the South's advantage. Noting that every president since John Adams had been a Virginian, Federalists painted the admission of Missouri as part of a conspiracy to perpetuate the rule of Virginia slaveholders. Republicans, pointing to the sudden emergence in the House of Representatives of a vocal antislavery block, began to see all efforts to restrict slavery as a Federalist plot to regain power by dividing northern and southern Republicans. In sum, by 1819 the slavery issue had become intertwined with the prevailing distrust between the parties and between the sections.

Virtually every issue that would wrack the Union in the next forty years was present in the Missouri controversy: southern charges that the North was conspiring to destroy the Union and to end slavery; northern accusations that southerners were conspiring to extend slavery. For a while leaders doubted that the Union would survive the crisis; the words *disunion* and *civil war* were freely uttered, Henry Clay wrote.

A series of congressional agreements known collectively as the Missouri Compromise resolved the crisis. To balance the number of slave states and free states, Congress in 1820 admitted Maine as a free state and Missouri as a slave state; to forestall a further crisis, it also prohibited slavery in the remainder of the Louisiana Purchase north of 36°30', Missouri's southern border. An attempt by Missourians to bar free blacks from entering the territory nearly undid the compromise, but in 1821 a second Missouri Compromise opened the way for Missouri's admission by prohibiting Missouri from discriminat-

The Missouri Compromise, 1820–1821

The Missouri Compromise temporarily quelled controversy over slavery by admitting Maine as a free state and Missouri as a slave state and by prohibiting slavery in the remainder of the Louisiana Purchase north of 36°30'.

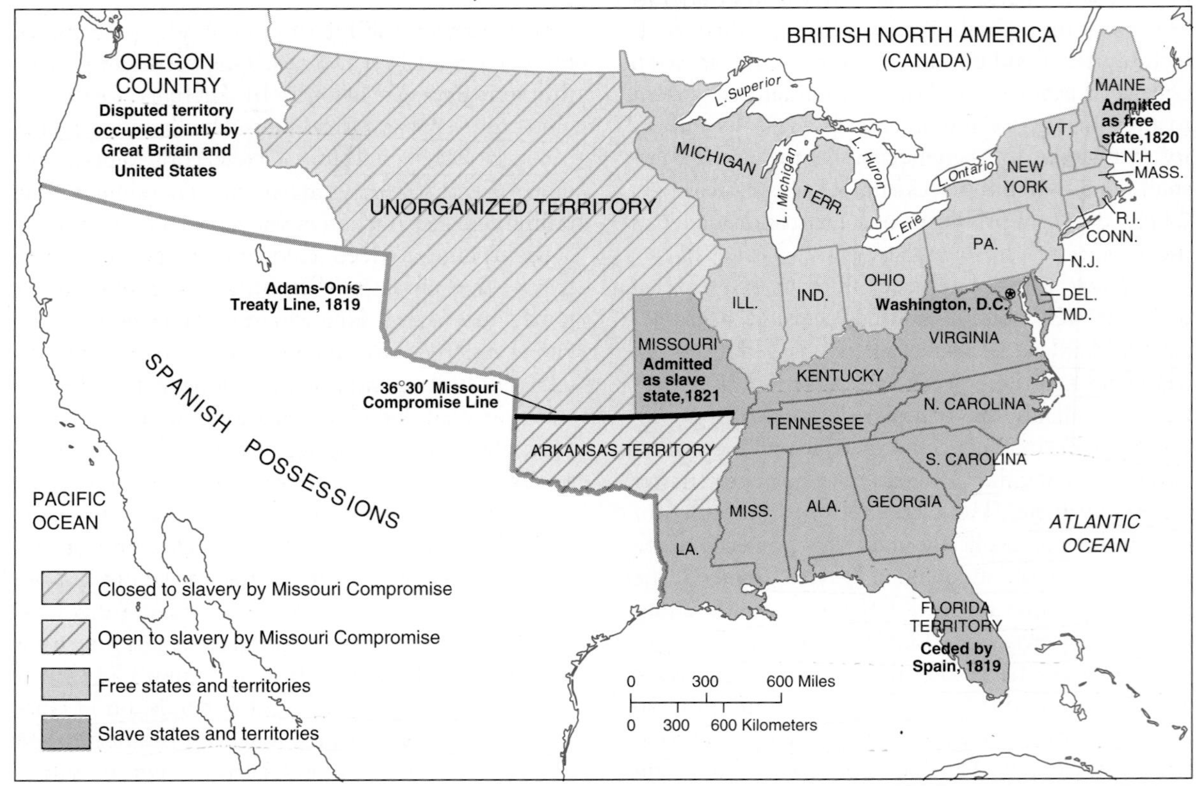

ing against citizens of other states, without stating whether free blacks were citizens.

The Missouri Compromise was widely viewed as a southern victory. The South had gained admission of Missouri, whose acceptance of slavery was controversial, while the North had merely gained Maine, whose rejection of slavery sparked no controversy. But at the same time, the South had allowed slavery to be banned from a vast territory north of 36°30', an area that would not long remain a wilderness. The Missouri Compromise also reinforced the principle that Congress could prohibit slavery in some territories. Southerners had implicitly agreed that slaves were not like other forms of property that could be moved from place to place at will.

Foreign Policy Under Monroe

"Good feelings" also characterized American foreign policy from 1816 to 1824. The end of the War of 1812 and of the Napoleonic Wars had removed most Federalist-Republican disagreements over foreign policy. Moreover, President Monroe had as his secretary of state an extraordinary diplomat, John Quincy Adams, a tough negotiator and an ardent nationalist. The only Federalist in the Senate to support the Louisiana Purchase, and the son of the last Federalist president, Adams had backed the embargo, joined the Republican Party, and helped to negotiate the Treaty of Ghent.

Adams moved quickly to strengthen the peace with Great Britain. During his term the Rush-Bagot Treaty of 1817 demilitarized the Great Lakes and the British-American Convention of 1818 fixed the Canadian-American boundary and restored U.S. fishing rights off Newfoundland. With its northern border secure, the United States could turn its attention southward and westward.

Adams was equally successful with the Spanish, who still owned East Florida and claimed West Florida. It had never been clear whether the Louisiana Purchase included West Florida. Acting as if it did, the United States in 1812 had simply added a slice of West Florida to the state of Louisiana and another piece to the Mississippi Territory. Using the pretext that it was a base for Seminole Indian raids and a refuge for fugitive slaves, Andrew Jackson, now a military commander in the South, invaded West Florida in 1818, hanged two British subjects, and captured Spanish forts. Although Jackson had acted without explicit orders, Adams supported the raid, guessing correctly that it would panic the Spanish into further concessions. In 1819 Spain agreed to the Adams-Onís (or Transcontinental) Treaty, ceding East Florida to the United States, renouncing all claims to West Florida, and agreeing to a border that ran north along the Sabine River (separating Spanish Texas from Louisiana), then west along the Red and Arkansas Rivers to the Rockies, and then along the forty-second parallel to the Pacific. Finally, the United States had a legitimate claim to the Pacific coast.

The Monroe Doctrine

John Quincy Adams had long believed that God and nature had ordained that the United States would eventually span the entire continent of North America. While negotiating the purchase of Florida, he made it clear to Spain that the United States might well seize what it could not purchase—including Texas and Mexico. Besides, Spain had other pressing concerns, primarily anticolonial revolutions that had erupted in South America. The failing imperial power sought aid in crushing the revolts from the Holy Alliance, which had been formed in Europe in 1815 to quash revolutions in the name of Christian principles. However, Britain had not joined the alliance. Its foreign minister, George Canning, now proposed a joint U.S.-British statement opposing European interference in South America and pledging that neither nation would annex any part of Spain's New World empire.

Adams shared Canning's opposition to European intervention in the New World, but rejected his insistence on a joint Anglo-American pledge never to annex any of Spain's former territories. The American secretary of state wanted to keep open the possibility of annexing Texas or Cuba.

This was the background of the Monroe Doctrine, as President Monroe's message to Congress on December 2, 1823, became known. Largely written by Adams, the message announced three key principles: that U.S. policy was to avoid European wars unless American interests were involved, that the "American continents" were not "subjects for future colonization by any European power," and that the United States would construe any European attempt at colonization as an "unfriendly act."

Europeans widely derided the Monroe Doctrine as a unilateral pronouncement by a United States that could not enforce it. Fear of Britain's Royal Navy, not the Monroe Doctrine, prevented European intervention in South America. Nonetheless, the doctrine had two major implications. First, in pledging not to interfere in European wars, the United States in effect declined to support any future revolutionary movements in Europe. Second, by keeping open options to annex territory in the Americas itself, the United States was claiming for itself a preeminent position in the New World.

CONCLUSION

Although James Monroe and John Quincy Adams engineered formidable diplomatic achievements, the chief task of the Republic's early leaders was to fashion political institutions and customs to govern the young nation and to do so within a framework of contending political parties not anticipated in the Constitution. Fears that a victorious party, to assure its continued dominance, might amend or twist the Constitution were very real; Jefferson's early actions against the judiciary provoked a strong reaction by Federalists because they suspected a plot to destroy them.

But Jefferson did not have to destroy the Federalists; they destroyed themselves in the furor over the embargo and the War of 1812. The postwar surge of national pride swept the Federalists aside, and the Republican embrace of Federalist policies such as the tariff and internal improvements blurred divisions once sharp. The Republican presidencies of Jefferson, Madison, and Monroe settled critical debates over foreign policy and opened the way for internal expansion and economic development.

Monroe's reelection in 1820 marked the high point of the Republican ascendancy and the Era of Good Feelings. The signs of future divisions subsequently grew. The controversy over Missouri in particular shattered sectional harmony, while other, subtler changes were shaping new issues and divisions that would surface by 1830.

CHRONOLOGY

1800–1801 John Adams's midnight appointments.

1802 The Judiciary Act of 1801.
Yazoo land compromise.
American right of deposit at New Orleans revoked.

1803 *Marbury* v. *Madison*.
Conclusion of the Louisiana Purchase.

1804 Judge John Pickering convicted by the Senate.
Impeachment of Justice Samuel Chase.
Aaron Burr kills Alexander Hamilton in a duel.
Jefferson elected to a second term.

1804–1806 Lewis and Clark expedition.

1805 Start of the Burr conspiracy.
Chase acquitted by the Senate.
Essex case.

1806 British government issues the first Order in Council.

1807 Burr acquitted of treason.
Chesapeake affair.
Embargo Act passed.

1808 James Madison elected president.

1809 Non-Intercourse Act passed; Embargo Act repealed.

1810 Macon's Bill No. 2.

1811 Battle of Tippecanoe.

1812 Orders in Council revoked.
United States declares war on Britain.
Madison reelected to a second term.
General William Hull surrenders at Detroit.
Battle of Queenston.

1813 Battle of Lake Erie (Put-in-Bay).

1814 Battle of Bladensburg.
British burn Washington, D.C.
Battle of Plattsburgh.
Hartford Convention.
Treaty of Ghent signed.

1815 Battle of New Orleans.

1816 James Monroe elected president.
Second Bank of the United States chartered.

1817 Rush-Bagot Treaty.

1818 British-American Convention of 1818.
Andrew Jackson invades East Florida.

1819 Adams-Onís (Transcontinental) Treaty.
Dartmouth College v. *Woodward*.
McCulloch v. *Maryland*.

1820 Monroe reelected to a second term.

1820–1821 Missouri Compromise.

1823 Monroe Doctrine.

FOR FURTHER READING

Henry Adams, *History of the United States During the Administrations of Jefferson and Madison*, 9 vols. (1889–1891). A classic study by the great-grandson of John Adams.

Drew R. McCoy, *The Last of the Fathers: James Madison and the Republican Legacy* (1989). The best recent book on Madison.

Forrest McDonald, *The Presidency of Thomas Jefferson* (1976). A lively overview.

Dumas Malone, *Jefferson and His Time*, vols. 4 and 5 (1970, 1974). An extremely comprehensive biography.

Merrill Peterson, *Thomas Jefferson and the New Nation: A Biography* (1970). The best one-volume biography of Jefferson.

Marshall Smelser, *The Democratic Republic, 1801–1815* (1968). A thorough general work.

J. C. A. Stagg, *Mr. Madison's War: Politics, Diplomacy, and Warfare in the Early Republic* (1983). An important reinterpretation of the causes of the War of 1812.

G. Edward White, *The Marshall Court and Cultural Change, 1815–1835* (1991). A seminal reinterpretation of the Supreme Court under John Marshall.

CHAPTER

9

The Transformation of American Society, 1815–1840

The years 1815 to 1840 saw rapid, often disorienting changes that affected both those who followed the frontier westward and those who stayed in the East. A revolution in transportation stimulated interregional trade and migration and encouraged an unprecedented development of towns and cities. The new urban dwellers provided a market not only for agricultural produce but also for the manufactures of the industries springing up in New England and major northeastern cities.

Viewed superficially, these changes might seem to have had little effect on the way Americans lived. Whether in 1815 or in 1840, most Americans dwelled outside the cities, practiced agriculture for a living, and traveled on foot or by horse. Yet this impression of continuity misleads us, for by 1840 many farmers had moved west. In addition, the nature of farming had changed as farmers increasingly raised crops for sale in distant markets rather than for their own use. By 1840, moreover, alternatives to farming as a liveli-

(Right) Rocky Mountain trappers, or "mountain men," were hunters, explorers, and adventurers who lived "a wild Robin Hood kind of life" with "little fear of God and none at all of the Devil."

hood abounded. And the rise of such alternatives impinged on some of the most basic social relationships: between parents and children and between wives and husbands.

Westward Expansion and the Growth of the Market Economy

The spark igniting these changes was the spread of Americans across the Appalachian Mountains. In 1790 most Americans lived east of the mountains, within a few hundred miles of the Atlantic; by 1840 one-third dwelled between the Appalachians and the Mississippi River. Unforeseen social and economic forces buffeted the settlers of this new West.

The Sweep West

This westward movement occurred in several thrusts. Americans leapfrogged the Appalachians after 1791 to bring four new states into the Union by 1803: Vermont, Kentucky, Tennessee, and Ohio. From 1816 to 1821 momentum carried settlers farther west, even across the Mississippi River, and six more states entered: Indiana, Mississippi, Illinois, Alabama, Maine, and Missouri. Ohio's population soared from 45,000 in 1800 to more than 1.5 million by 1840 and Michigan's from 5,000 in 1810 to 212,000 in 1840.

Exploration carried some Americans even farther west. Zebulon Pike explored the Spanish Southwest in 1806, sighting the Colorado peak later named after him. By 1811, in the wake of Lewis and Clark, the New York merchant John Jacob Astor had founded a fur-trading post at the mouth of the Columbia River in the Oregon Country. At first whites relied on the Native Americans for furs, but in the 1820s such "mountain men" as Kit Carson and Jedediah Smith penetrated deep beyond the Rockies.

Smith typified these men and their exploits. Originally from western New York, he had moved west as far as Illinois by 1822. That year he signed on with an expedition bound for the upper Missouri River. In the course of this and later explorations, Smith nearly fell victim to a grizzly bear in South Dakota's Black Hills, crossed the Mojave Desert into California and explored the San Joaquin Valley, and hiked back across the Sierras and the Great Basin to the Great Salt Lake, a forbidding trip. His thirst for adventure led to his early death at the hands of Comanche Indians in 1831.

The mountain men, though celebrated, were not themselves typical westward migrants. For most pioneers, the West meant the area between the Appalachians and the Mississippi River, and their goal was stability, not adventure. Pioneers' letters home stressed the bounty and peacefulness of the West rather than its dangers. According to a Missourian in 1816, "There neither is, nor, in the nature of things, can there ever be, any thing like poverty [in this area]. All is ease, tranquility, and comfort."

Western Society and Customs

Pioneers usually migrated in family groups. To reach markets with their produce, most settled along navigable rivers, particularly the great Ohio-Mississippi system. Not until the coming of canals and then railroads did westerners venture far from rivers. Settlers often clustered with people from the same eastern region; when New Englanders found southerners well entrenched in Indiana, they pushed on to Michigan.

These new westerners craved sociability. Even before towns sprang up, farm families joined their neighbors for sports and festivities. Men met for games that tested strength and agility: wrestling, lifting weights, pole jumping (for distance, not height), and hammer throwing. The games could be brutal. In gander pulling, riders competed to pull the head off a gander whose neck had been stripped of feathers and greased. Women usually combined work and play in quilting and sewing bees, carpet tackings, and even goose and chicken pluckings. At "hoedowns" and "frolics," the settlers danced to a fiddler's tune.

Merrymaking at a Wayside Inn,
by Pavel Svinin

Country inns served as social centers for rural neighborhoods as well as stopping places for travelers. Although this painting evokes rustic charm, guests at inns complained of the stale odor of rum, pie crusts that tasted like leather, cheese that defied digestion, and a lack of privacy that made them look forward to another day on the road.

Western farm households usually practiced a clear gender division of labor. Men performed the heavy work such as cutting down trees and plowing fields. Women cooked, spun and wove, sewed, milked, and tended their large families. They also often helped with the butchering—slitting the hog's throat while it was still alive, bleeding it, scooping out the innards, washing the heart and liver, and hanging the organs to dry. Daintiness had been left behind, east of the mountains.

Compared to the East, the West was rough: cowpaths substituted for sidewalks and hand-hewn cabins for comfortable homes. The relative lack of refinement made westerners targets for eastern taunts. Jibed at as half-savage yokels, westerners responded that they at least were honest democrats, not soft would-be aristocrats. Pretension got short shrift. A sojourner at a tavern who hung a blanket to cover his bed from public gaze might find it ripped down, a woman who sought privacy in a crowded room might be dismissed as "uppity," and a politician who came to a rally in a buggy, rather than on horseback, might lose votes.

The Federal Government and the West

The federal government's growing strength spurred westward expansion. Under the Articles of Confederation, several states had ceded western lands to the national government, creating a bountiful public domain. The Land Ordinance of 1785 had provided for the survey and sale of these lands, and the Northwest Ordinance of 1787 had established a mechanism for transforming them into states. The Louisiana Purchase had brought the entire Mississippi River under American control, and the Adams-Onís Treaty had wiped out the remnants of Spanish control east of the Mississippi. Six million acres of public land had been promised to volunteers during the War of 1812. The National Road, a highway begun in 1811, stretched farther westward, reaching Wheeling, Virginia, in 1818 and Vandalia,

Illinois, by 1838. People crowded along it. One traveler wrote, "We are seldom out of sight, as we travel on this grand track toward the Ohio, of family groups before and behind us."

The same governmental strength that aided whites brought misery to the Indians. Virtually all the foreign policy successes of the Republicans worked to the Native Americans' disadvantage. The Louisiana Purchase and Adams-Onís Treaty had stripped them of Spanish protection, and the War of 1812 had deprived them of British protection. Lewis and Clark bluntly told the Indians that they should "shut their ears up to the counsels of bad birds" and listen only to the Great White Father in Washington.

The Removal of the Indians

Westward-moving white settlers found in their path sizable numbers of Native Americans, especially in the South, home to the "Five Civilized Tribes"—the Cherokees, Creeks, Choctaws, Chickasaws, and Seminoles. Years of commercial dealings and intermarriage with Europeans had created in these tribes influential minorities of mixed-bloods who had embraced Christianity and agriculture. The Cherokees had adopted Anglo-American culture to a greater extent than any other tribe. Among them were farmers, millers, and even slave owners; they also had a written form of their language, written laws, and their own bilingual newspaper, the *Cherokee Phoenix*.

While welcoming such signs of "civilization" among the Indians, whites did not hesitate to push the tribes out of their way. Although some mixed-bloods sold tribal lands and moved west, others resisted because their prosperity depended on trade with close-by whites. And full-blooded members of the Five Civilized Tribes, contemptuous of whites and mixed-bloods alike, wanted to retain their ancestral lands. When the Creek chief William McIntosh, a mixed-blood, sold most Creek lands in Georgia and Alabama, other Creeks executed him.

Whites' demands for Native American lands reached the boiling point in the 1820s. Andrew Jackson of Tennessee embodied the new militancy of those who rejected piecemeal and tribe-by-tribe treaties. Jackson believed that the balance between Indians and whites had shifted drastically in recent decades and that the Indians were far weaker than commonly believed. There was no justification for "the farce of treating with the Indian tribes," Jackson proclaimed; the Indians were not independent nations but subject to the laws of their state of residence.

When Jackson became president in 1829, he instituted a coercive removal policy that reflected his disdain for the Indians and his conviction that

Andrew Jackson as the Indians' Great Father
This political cartoon of c.1830 depicts the Native Americans as children or dolls, subject to a fatherly Jackson's dictates.

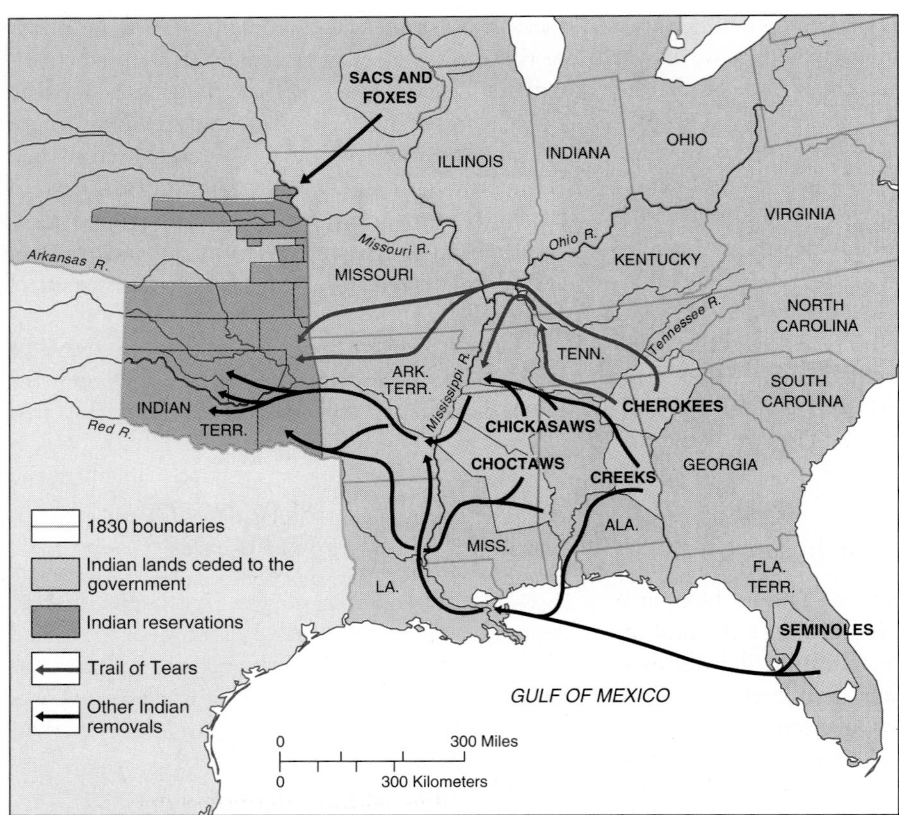

The Removal of the Native Americans to the West, 1820–1840
The so-called Trail of Tears, followed by the Cherokees, was one of several routes along which various tribes migrated on their forced removal to reservations west of the Mississippi.

"real" Indians, who retained their original ways, were being exploited by whites and mixed-bloods. In 1830 Jackson secured from a divided Congress the Indian Removal Act, granting the president authority to remove the Indians by force if necessary. By then, southern states had intensified pressure on the remaining tribes: a Georgia law had extended state jurisdiction over Cherokee country, begun the confiscation of tribal land, and made it illegal for Indians to testify against whites. The Creeks of Georgia and Alabama had started moving west in the late 1820s. In 1836 the Georgia militia attacked those still in the state, and when starving Creeks raided white settlements for food, federal troops finished the job begun by the militia. In 1836, 15,000 Creeks, most of the Creek nation, were removed—many in chains—and resettled west of the Mississippi River.

The other southern "civilized" tribes suffered a similar fate. Chickasaws and Choctaws were removed by the early 1830s. French visitor Alexis de Tocqueville witnessed the arrival of the Choctaws along the Mississippi. "I saw them embark to cross the great river, and the sight will never fade from my memory. Neither sob nor complaint rose from that silent assembly. Their afflictions were of long standing, and they felt them to be irremediable." Of the Seminoles, more than half were removed from Florida in 1842 after seven years of bitter warfare.

The Cherokees, however, pursued peaceful resistance by seeking an injunction from the Supreme Court against Georgia's attempts to extend its laws over them and to confiscate their lands. In *Worcester v. Georgia* (1832), Chief Justice John Marshall ruled that the Cherokees, who had their own constitution and government, were a "domestic dependent nation" and hence were entitled to federal protection of their lands against Georgia's claims. Marshall concluded that Georgia laws were not valid in Cherokee territory.

President Andrew Jackson reportedly sneered, "John Marshall has made his decision; now let him enforce it," and ignored the ruling. Then in 1835 the U.S. government negotiated the fraudulent Treaty of New Echota with a handful of unauthorized individuals. It ceded most remaining Cherokee lands to the United States for $5.6 million and the Indians' transportation west. The principal signers were killed by other Cherokees in 1839, but by then the tribe's fate was sealed. Sixteen thousand Cherokees straggled west to the Indian Territory between 1835 and 1838 along the so-called Trail of Tears. A total of perhaps 4,000 died along the trail itself and within a year of the initial roundup and hard journey.

Indians in the Northwest Territory fared no better after they signed land-cession treaties. Two uprisings marked their westward removal. The first was quickly crushed, but the second, led by a Sac and Fox chief, Black Hawk, raged along the frontier in Illinois until federal troops and state militiamen virtually annihilated the Indians in 1832. After Black Hawk's defeat, the other northwestern tribes agreed to removal. Between 1832 and 1837 the United States consequently acquired nearly 190 million acres of Indian land in the Northwest for $70 million.

The Agricultural Boom

In clearing the Indians from their territory, the federal government was responding to whites' pressures for land. Depleted soil and overcrowding had long driven farmers west, but after the War of 1812 soaring agricultural commodity prices and rising demand for western foodstuffs sharpened the land hunger. England and France, exhausted by war, were importing substantial amounts of American wheat and corn; New England needed food for its burgeoning industrial population. With produce prices skyrocketing, western farmers took advantage of the Ohio-Mississippi river system to ship their grain to foreign markets through New Orleans. In short, federal Indian policy, although devastating to Native Americans, made farming possible in the West, and high prices and high demand made it attractive.

Cotton, and Eli Whitney's cotton gin, provided the impetus for settlement of the Old Southwest, especially Alabama and Mississippi. Indeed, the explosive westward thrust of southern farmers and planters after the War of 1812 resembled a gold rush. By 1817 land prices had shot up from $30 to $50 an acre. By 1820 Alabama and Mississippi produced half the nation's cotton. With a seemingly unlimited British market for raw cotton, production tripled between 1816 and 1831. Between 1831 and 1836 the value of cotton exports rose 300 percent, and cotton accounted for two-thirds of U.S. exports.

The Market Economy and Federal Land Policy

American farmers, accustomed to growing enough food for their families (subsistence farming) and some grain or cotton for sale (commercial farming for the "market economy"), pursued national and foreign markets with zeal after the War of 1812. But the new commercial farmers encountered serious problems, including wildly fluctuating markets. They also routinely had to borrow money to cover the often long interval between harvest and sale. Thus commercial agriculture forced farmers to accept short-term debt in hope of reaping long-term profits. This debt was frequently worse than expected, particularly because many western farmers had also borrowed money to buy their land.

Federal efforts in this period to put the public domain into the hands of small farmers floundered. In the face of partisan and sectional pressures, the federal government passed various land laws in quick succession, each intended to undo the damage caused by its predecessors.

The Ordinance of 1785 had aimed to ensure the orderly settlement of the public domain by creating townships of thirty-six square miles, divided into 640-acre sections. Because ordinary farmers could not afford such large purchases, the assumption was that they would pool their money to buy sections. It was also assumed that a population of compatible settlers living on adjoining lots would be easier to govern than one of isolated settlers on scattered homesteads.

However, the Federalist administrations of the 1790s undermined this orderly process by encouraging the sale of huge tracts of land to wealthy speculators, who held the land until prices rose and then sold it to farmers. When the Republicans came to power in 1801, they tried to reverse this trend by dropping the minimum land sale to 320 acres; by 1832 the minimum acreage had fallen to 40 acres.

But land speculators remained one step ahead of federal policy, selling more affordable, easier-to-clear 40-acre lots (which farmers preferred) long before 1832. Soaring agricultural prices and easier credit after the War of 1812 also favored speculators; between 1812 and 1817 the value of bank notes in circulation increased from $45 million to $100 million. Many new banks were funded primarily to lend money to their directors for personal investment in land speculation. By 1819 sales of public lands were 1,000 percent greater than average sales from 1800 to 1814.

The Speculator and the Squatter

Nonetheless, most of the public domain found its way into the hands of small farmers. The desire to recoup investments led speculators to sell quickly, as did the proliferation of squatters.

Squatters had long helped themselves to western land. Proud and independent, they hated land speculators and pressured Congress to allow "preemption" rights—that is, the right to purchase at the minimum price the land that they already lived on and had improved. After passing a series of limited preemption laws, Congress acknowledged a general right of preemption in 1841.

But these laws were of little use to farmers who had to purchase land from speculators. For them, interest rates ranged as high as 40 percent. Many western farmers, drowning in debt, had to skimp on food and plant cash crops in the hope of paying off creditors. Having moved west to fulfill dreams of self-sufficiency, they found themselves caught in the cash-crop economy, which quickly exhausted their land and forced them to move farther westward in search of new land. Abraham Lincoln's parents, who migrated from the East through several farms in Kentucky and then to Indiana, typified this "moving frontier."

The Panic of 1819

In 1819 the land boom collapsed like a house of cards, the victim of a financial panic. State banks' loose practices played a major role in causing the panic. These state banks issued their own bank notes, little more than a promise to pay the bearer a certain amount of specie (gold and silver coin) on demand. Such notes were plentiful and had helped fuel the land boom after 1815. Farmers also borrowed to buy more land and plant more crops, certain that sales to Europe would enable them to repay loans. But even as American farmers were becoming more dependent on agricultural exports to repay their debts, bumper crops in Europe combined with an economic slump in England to trim foreign demand for U.S. crops.

The result was a cascade of economic catastrophes. In summer 1819 the Bank of the United States, holder of large amounts of state bank paper, began to insist that the state banks redeem this paper in specie. To pay these debts, state banks demanded that farmers and land speculators repay their loans—in specie. Credit contracted sharply throughout the nation, particularly in the West.

Land speculators suffered as credit dried up and land prices tumbled. Land prices plummeted from $69 an acre to $2 an acre as the credit squeeze drove down commodity prices. Hard-pressed farmers could not pay their debts, speculators could not collect their money, and land values collapsed.

The panic had three major consequences for Americans. First, they came to despise banks, especially the Bank of the United States. Second, they recognized how vulnerable American factories were to foreign competition and began to favor higher tariffs. Third, farmers recognized how deeply they depended on distant markets and began to look for better and cheaper ways to transport their products to these markets.

The Transportation Revolution: Steamboats, Canals, and Railroads

The transportation systems available in 1820 had serious weaknesses. The great rivers west of the Appalachians ran primarily north to south and hence could not by themselves connect western farmers to eastern markets. Roads were expensive to maintain, and horse-drawn wagons were slow and limited in range. Consequently, after 1820 attention and investment shifted to the development of waterways.

In 1807 Robert R. Livingston and Robert Fulton introduced the steamboat *Clermont* on the Hudson River. They soon gained a monopoly from the New York legislature to run a New York–New Jersey ferry service. Spectacular profits lured competitors, who secured a license from Congress and then filed suit to break the Livingston-Fulton monopoly. In 1824 Chief Justice John Marshall handed down his decision in what was known as the *Gibbons* v. *Ogden* case. Marshall ruled that Article I, Section 8, of the Constitution, which empowered Congress to regulate interstate commerce, applied to navigation as well. In this case, he wrote, the power of Congress to regulate interstate commerce had to prevail over the power of New York; thus the Livingston-Fulton monopoly was void. Marshall's decision not only opened the way for rapid expansion of steamboat traffic but also forcefully reasserted the supremacy of national power over that of the states. In the aftermath of this decision, other state-granted monopolies collapsed and steamboat traffic increased rapidly. The number of steamboats operating on western rivers jumped from 17 in 1817 to 727 by 1855.

Steamboats assumed a vital role along the Mississippi-Ohio river system. They were far more useful than rafts, which journeyed only one way, or keelboats, which took up to four months to travel upstream from New Orleans to Louisville; in 1817 a steamboat made the identical trip in just twenty-five days. The development of long, shallow hulls permitted navigation of the Mississippi-Ohio system even when hot, dry summers lowered the river level. Steamboats became more ornate as well as more practical. To compete for passengers, they offered luxurious cabins and lounges, called saloons. The saloon of one steamboat, the *Eclipse*, was the length of a football field and featured skylights, chandeliers, and velvet-covered mahogany furniture.

While steamboats proved their value, canals replaced roads and turnpikes as the focus of popular enthusiasm and financial speculation. Although the cost of canal construction was mind-boggling—Jefferson dismissed the idea of canals as "little short of madness"—canals offered the possibility of connecting the Mississippi-Ohio system with the Great Lakes and even the East Coast.

The first major canal project was the Erie Canal, completed in 1825. Ten times longer than any existing canal in North America, it stretched 363 miles from Buffalo to Albany, linking Lake Erie to the Hudson River, New York City, and the Atlantic Ocean. Other canals followed in rapid succession. One of the most spectacular was the Main Line (or Pennsylvania) Canal, which crossed the Alleghenies to connect Philadelphia with Pittsburgh. Canal boats used on the Main Line were built in collapsible sections; taken apart on reaching the mountains, they were carried over the crest on cable cars.

The canal boom slashed shipping costs. Before the Erie Canal, transporting wheat from Buffalo to New York City cost three times its market value; corn, six times its market value; and oats, twelve times. The Erie dramatically cut freight charges, which in the period 1817–1830 dropped from nineteen cents to two cents a ton per mile between the two cities. Similar reductions prevailed nationwide.

Railroads soon were competing with canals and gradually overtook them. In 1825 the first railroad for general transportation began operation in England. The new technology quickly reached the United States, and by 1840 there were 3,000 miles of railroad track, equal to the total canal mileage. Faster, cheaper to build, and able to reach more places, railroads enjoyed obvious advantages over canals, but Americans realized their potential only slowly.

Early railroads connected eastern cities rather than crossing the mountains and carried more passengers than freight. Not until 1849 did freight revenue exceed passenger revenue, and not until 1850 did railroads link the East Coast to Lake Erie. There were two main reasons for this slow pace of development. First, unlike canals, most railroads were built by private companies that tended to skimp on costs, as a result producing lines requiring constant repair. In contrast, canals needed little maintenance. Second, shipping bulky commodities such as iron, coal, and grain was cheaper by canal than by rail.

The Growth of Cities

The transportation revolution accelerated the growth of towns and cities. Indeed, the forty years before the Civil War, 1820 to 1860, saw the most rapid urbanization in U.S. history. In that time the percentage of people living in places of 2,500 or more inhabitants rose from 6.1 percent to nearly 20 percent. The Erie Canal transformed Rochester, New York, from a village of several hundred in 1817 to a town of 9,000 by 1830. By 1860 New York City's population had rocketed from 124,000 to 800,000, and the number of towns with more than 2,500 inhabitants climbed from 56 to 350 between 1820 and 1850.

Urban growth was particularly fast in the West. The War of 1812 stimulated manufacturing and transformed villages into towns, as did the agricultural boom and the introduction of steamboats after 1815. Virtually all the major western cities were river ports. Of these, Pittsburgh, Cincinnati, Louisville, and New Orleans were the largest and most prominent. Pittsburgh was a manufacturing center, but the others were basically commercial hubs flooded by people eager to make money.

What the transportation revolution gave, it could also take away. The completion of the Erie Canal gradually shifted the center of western economic activity away from the river cities and toward the Great Lakes; Buffalo, Cleveland, Detroit, Chicago, and Milwaukee were the ultimate beneficiaries of the canal. In 1830 nearly 75 percent of western city dwellers lived in the river ports of New Orleans, Louisville, Cincinnati, and Pittsburgh, but by 1840 the proportion had dropped to 20 percent. The advent of modern manufacturing would multiply the effect of the transportation revolution on the growth of cities.

The Rise of Manufacturing

Although we associate the word *manufacturing* with factories and machines, it literally means "making by hand." In the colonial era most products were in fact handmade, either in the home or in the workshops of skilled artisans. The years 1815–1860 mark the transition from colonial to modern manufacturing, although factories remained small. Indeed, as late as 1860 the average manufacturing establishment contained only eight workers.

Americans continued to think of themselves as a nation of farmers in this era, but industrialization was taking hold. By 1850, 20 percent of the labor force worked in manufacturing and produced 30 percent of the national output.

Industrialization occurred gradually, in distinct stages. In early manufacturing the production of goods was divided so that each worker made parts rather than entire products. As manufacturing advanced, workers were gathered into factories with rooms devoted to specialized operations performed by hand or simple machines. Finally, power-driven machinery replaced hand manufacturing. Because industrialization grew gradually and unevenly, people did not always realize that traditional manufacturing by skilled artisans was becoming obsolete and that machines would soon tumble artisans from their pedestals.

Causes of Industrialization

Multiple domestic and foreign factors stimulated industrialization. The Era of Good Feelings saw general agreement that the United States needed tariffs; once protected from foreign competition, American cloth production rose by an average of 15 percent *every year* from 1815 to 1833. At the same time, the transportation revolution enlarged markets and demand. Americans began to prefer factory-made products to homemade ones. Especially in the West, farmers concentrated on their farming and bought shoes and cloth.

Immigration was also vital. Five million people emigrated from Europe to the United States between 1790 and 1860, most of them to pursue economic opportunity. The majority was German or Irish, but the smaller number of British immigrants was most important to industrialization. That process in Britain was a generation ahead of the United States, and British immigrants understood the workings of machines. For example, immigrant Samuel Slater had learned the "mystery" of textile production as an apprentice in England. Although British law forbade emigration by skilled "mechanics" such as Slater, he disguised himself and brought his knowledge of machines and factories to eager Americans.

Americans also freely experimented with various machines and developed their own technologies. In the 1790s wagon maker Oliver Evans built an automated flour mill that a single person could supervise: grain was poured in one side, and flour poured out on the other. With labor scarce in the early Republic, manufacturers sought to cut costs by replacing expensive workers with machines. Eli Whitney borrowed the European idea of interchangeable parts and employed unskilled (and thus cheap) workers to make 10,000 muskets for the U.S. Army. The use of interchangeable parts become so common in the United States that Europeans and Americans alike called it the American system of manufacturing.

Mill Girls

New England's humming textile mills were a magnet for untold numbers of independence-seeking young women in antebellum America.

New England Industrializes

New England became America's first industrial region. The trade wars leading up to the War of 1812 had devastated the Northeast's traditional economy and stimulated capital investment in manufacturing. New England's many swift-flowing rivers were ideal sources of waterpower for mills. The westward migration of New England's young men, unable to wrest a living from rocky soil, left a surplus of young women, who supplied cheap industrial labor.

Cotton textiles led the way. Samuel Slater arrived in Pawtucket, Rhode Island, in 1790 and helped to design and build a mill that used Richard Arkwright's spinning frame to spin cotton yarn. His work force quickly grew from nine to one hundred, and his mills multiplied. Slater's mills performed only two operations: carding the cotton (separating cotton bolls into fine strands) and spinning the fiber into yarn. In what was still essentially "cottage" manufacturing, Slater contracted out the weaving to women working in their homes.

The establishment of the Boston Manufacturing Company in 1813 opened a new chapter in U.S. manufacturing. Backed by ample capital, the Boston Company built textile mills in the Massachusetts towns of Lowell and Waltham; by 1836 the company employed more than 6,000 workers.

Unlike Slater's mills, the Waltham and Lowell factories turned out finished products, thus elbowing aside Slater's cottage industry. Slater had tried to preserve tradition by hiring entire families to work at his mills—the men to raise crops, the women and children to toil in the mills. In contrast, 80 percent of the workers in the Lowell and Waltham mills were unmarried women fifteen to thirty years old. Hired managers and company regulations, rather than families, provided discipline. The workers ("operatives") boarded in factory-owned houses or licensed homes, observed a curfew, attended church, and accepted the "moral police of the corporations."

The corporations enforced high moral standards, at least in part to attract New England farm girls to the mills, where working conditions were less than attractive. To prevent threads from snapping, the factories had to be kept humid; windows were nailed shut, and water was sprayed in the air. Flying dust and deafening noise were constant companions. In the 1830s conditions worsened as competition and recession led mill owners to reduce wages and speed up work schedules. The system's impersonality intensified the harshness of the work environment. Owners rarely visited factories; their agents, all men, gave orders to the workers, mainly women. In 1834 and again in 1836 women at the Lowell mills quit work to protest low wages.

Manufacturing in New York City and Philadelphia

In the 1830s and 1840s New York, Philadelphia, and other cities witnessed a different kind of industrialization. It involved few machines or women workers and encompassed a wide range of products, including shoes, saddles, tools, ropes, hats, and gloves.

Despite these differences, factories in New York City and Philadelphia exposed workers to the same forces encountered by their New England counterparts. The transportation revolution had expanded markets and turned urban artisans and merchants into aggressive merchandiser who scoured the country for orders. By 1835 New York's ready-made clothing industry was supplying cheap shirts and dungarees to western farmers and southern slaves; by the 1840s it was providing expensive suits for the well-to-do. Fierce competition spurred wage cuts and work speedups in the urban factories. Whereas New England's entrepreneurs had introduced machines, New York City's manufacturers lacked both cheap waterpower and readily available machines. To increase production, New York and Philadelphia factory owners alike hired large numbers of unskilled workers and paid them low wages. A worker would perform one simple hand operation such as stitching cloth or soling shoes. Unlike their colonial counterparts, these workers neither made whole shoes nor saw a customer. Such subdivision of tasks (performed without machines) and specialization of labor characterized much early industrialization. In Massachusetts's boot and shoe industry, workers gradually were gathered into large factories to perform specialized operations in different rooms. But in New York City and Philadelphia, high population density made grouping workers unnecessary; instead, middlemen subcontracted out tasks to widows, immigrants, and others who would fashion parts of shoes or saddles or dresses anywhere that light would enter.

The skilled artisans of New York City and Philadelphia tried to protect their interests by forming trade unions and "workingmen's" political parties. Initially, they sought to restore privileges and working conditions that artisans had once enjoyed, but gradually they joined forces with unskilled workers. When coal heavers in Philadelphia struck for a ten-hour day in 1835, carpenters, cigar makers, leather workers, and other artisans joined in what became the first general strike in the United States. The emergence of organized worker protests underscored the mixed blessings of economic development. Where some people prospered, others found their economic position deteriorating. By 1830 many Americans were questioning whether their nation was truly a land of equality.

Equality and Inequality

Visitors to the United States sensed changes sweeping the country but could neither describe them nor agree on their direction. One of the most astute of these observers, the French nobleman Alexis de Tocqueville, whose *Democracy in America* (1835, 1840) is a classic, cited the "general equality of condition among the people" as the fundamental shaping force of American society. But Tocqueville also was keenly aware of inequalities in that society, inequalities less visible but no less real than those in France. The United States might not have a permanent servant class, but it surely had its rich and its poor.

Even today historians disagree about the meaning and extent of inequality in antebellum (pre–Civil War) America. Nonetheless, we have a more detailed and complete understanding of that society than did its contemporaries, such as Tocqueville. The following discussion applies mainly to northern society; we examine the South's distinctive social structure in Chapter 12.

Growing Inequality: The Rich and the Poor

The gap between rich and poor continued to widen in the first half of the nineteenth century. Although striking inequalities separated rich and poor farmers, the inequalities were far greater in the cities, where a small fraction of the people owned a huge share of the wealth. In Boston the richest 4 percent of the people owned almost 70 percent of the wealth by 1848, whereas 81 percent of the population owned only 4 percent of the wealth. New York and other major cities mirrored these statistics.

Although commentators celebrated the self-made man and his rise "from rags to riches," few actually fit this pattern. Less than 5 percent of the wealthy had started life poor; almost 90 percent of well-off people had been born rich. Clearly, the old-fashioned way to wealth was to inherit it, to marry more of it, and to invest it wisely. Occasional rags-to-riches stories like that of John Jacob Astor and his fur-trading empire sustained the myth, but it was mainly a myth.

The rich built their splendid residences close to one another. In New York half the city's wealthy families lived on only eight streets, and they belonged to the same clubs. Tocqueville noted these facts and also observed that the rich feigned respect for equality, at least in public. They rode in ordinary carriages, brushed elbows with the less privileged, and avoided the conspicuous display of wealth that marked their private lives.

At the opposite end of the social ladder were the poor. By today's standards most antebellum Americans were poor; they lived at the edge of destitution, depended on their children's labor to meet expenses, had little money for medical care or recreation, and suffered frequent unemployment. In 1850 an estimated three out of eight males over twenty owned little more than their clothing.

Antebellum Americans distinguished between poverty, a common condition, and *pauperism*, which meant both poverty and dependency—the inability to care for oneself. The elderly, the ill, and the widowed often fell into the category of pauperism, although they were not seen as a permanent class. Pauperism caused by illness, old age, or circumstance would not pass from generation to generation.

Moralists' assumption that the United States would be free of a permanent class of paupers was comforting but misleading. Immigrants, especially the Irish who fled famine in their homeland only to settle in wretched slums in New York City, found it difficult to escape poverty. Moreover, as some Americans convinced themselves that success lay within everyone's grasp, they also tended to believe that the poor were responsible for their own poverty. Ironically, even as many Americans blamed the poor for being poor, discrimination mired some groups in enduring poverty. Among the chief victims were northern free blacks.

Dancing for Eels, Catharine Market, 1820
Expressive dancing was part of African-American street festivals in the eighteenth-century cities. Fearing that such street dancing perpetuated white stereotypes of blacks, antislavery whites and black leaders tried to suppress it after 1800, but black dancing survived in dance cellars in New York City's Five Points slum. As this sketch indicates, African-Americans sometimes danced in public for applause, "a bunch of eels" or other fish, and perhaps money. The African-American at the left is "patting juba," which meant keeping time by hand clapping or by beating hands against legs. "Juba" also became the nickname of William Henry Lane. After seeing Lane perform in 1842 in a Five Points cellar, the novelist Charles Dickens lableled him "the greatest dancer known."

Free Blacks in the North

Prejudice against African-Americans was deeply ingrained in white society throughout the nation. Although slavery had largely disappeared in the North by 1820, discriminatory laws remained. The voting rights of African-Americans were severely restricted; for example, New York eliminated property requirements for whites but kept them for blacks. There were attempts to bar free blacks from migrating. And segregation prevailed in northern schools, jails, and hospitals. Most damaging of all to free blacks was the social pressure that forced them into unskilled, low-paying jobs throughout the northern cities. Recalling his youth as a free black in Rhode Island, William J. Brown wrote, "To drive carriages, carry a market basket after the boss, and brush his boots, or saw wood and run errands was as high as a colored man could rise." Although a few free blacks accumulated moderate wealth, free blacks in general were only half as likely as other city dwellers to own real estate.

The "Middling Classes"

Most antebellum Americans were neither fabulously rich nor grindingly poor but part of the "middling classes." Even though the wealthy owned an increasing proportion of wealth, per capita income grew at 1.5 percent annually between 1840 and 1860, and the standard of living generally rose after 1800.

Americans applied the term *middling classes* to farmers and artisans, who held the ideal of self-employment and were considered steady and dependable. Often, however, farmers and artisans led lives considerably less stable than this ideal. Asa G. Sheldon of Massachusetts described himself as a farmer, offered advice on growing corn and cranberries, and gave speeches glorifying farming. But Sheldon actually practiced it very little; he instead derived his living from transporting grain, harvesting timber, and clearing land for railroads. The Irish immigrants whom he hired did the shoveling and hauling, and Sheldon the "farmer" prospered—but his prosperity owed little to farming.

The increasingly commercial and industrial American economy allowed, and sometimes forced, people to adapt. Not all succeeded. Allan Melville, the father of novelist Herman Melville, was one who failed. An enterprising import merchant with boundless faith in the inevitable triumph of honesty and prudence, Melville did well until the late 1820s, when his business sagged. By 1830 he was "destitute of resources and without a shilling—without immediate assistance I know not what will become of me." Despite loans of $3,500, Melville's downward spiral continued, and he died two years later, broken in spirit.

Artisans shared the perils of life in the middling classes. During the colonial period many had attained the ideal of self-employment, owning their tools, taking orders, making their products, and training their children and apprentices in the craft. By 1850 this self-sufficient artisan class had split into two distinct groups. The few artisans who had access to capital became entrepreneurs who hired journeymen to do the actual work. Without capital, most remained journeymen, working for the artisans-turned-entrepreneurs with little prospect of self-employment.

Like the poor, the middling class was transient. When debt-burdened farmers hoping to get out of debt exhausted land quickly by their intense cultivation of cash crops, they simply moved on. Artisans, increasingly displaced by machines, found that skilled jobs were seasonal, and so they, too, moved from place to place to survive.

The multiplying risks and opportunities that confronted Americans both widened the gap between social classes and increased the psychological burdens on individuals. Commercial and industrial growth placed intense pressure on basic social relationships—for example, between lawyer and client, minister and congregation, and even parents and children.

The Revolution in Social Relationships

Following the War of 1812 the growth of interregional trade, commercial agriculture, and manufacturing disrupted traditional social relationships and forged new ones. Two broad changes took place. First, Americans began to question traditional forms of authority and to embrace individualism; wealth, education, and social position no longer received automatic deference. Second, Americans created new foundations for authority. For example, women developed the idea that they possessed a "separate sphere" of authority in the home, and individuals formed voluntary associations to influence the direction of society.

The Attack on the Professions

An intense criticism of lawyers, physicians, and ministers exemplified the assault on and erosion of traditional authority. Between 1800 and 1840 the wave of religious revivals known as the Second Great Awakening (see Chapter 10) sparked fierce attacks on the professions. Revivalists blasted the clergy for creating complex theologies, drinking expensive wines, and fleecing the people. One revivalist accused physicians of inventing fancy Latin and Greek names for diseases to disguise their inability to cure them.

These attacks on the learned professions peaked between 1820 and 1850. Samuel Thomson led a successful movement to eliminate all barriers to entry into the medical profession, including educational requirements. By 1845 every state had repealed laws requiring licenses or education to practice medicine. In religion ministers found little job security as finicky congregations dismissed clergymen whose theology displeased them. In turn, ministers became more ambitious and more inclined to leave poor, small churches for large, wealthy ones.

The increasing commercialization of the economy led to both more professionals and more attacks on them. In 1765 America had one medical school; by 1860 there were sixty-five. The newly minted doctors and lawyers had neither deep roots in the towns where they practiced nor convincing claims to social superiority. "Men dropped down into their places as from clouds," one critic wrote. "Nobody knew who or what they were, except as they claimed." A horse doctor would hang up a sign as "Physician and Surgeon" and "fire at random a box of his pills into your bowels, with a vague chance of killing some disease unknown to him, but with a better prospect of killing the patient."

This questioning of authority was particularly sharp on the frontier. Easterners sneered that every man in the West claimed to be a "judge," "general," "colonel," or "squire." In a society in which *every* person was new, titles were easily adopted and just as readily challenged. Would-be gentlemen substituted an exaggerated sense of personal honor for legal or customary claims of authority. Obsessed with their fragile status, these "gentlemen" could react testily to the slightest insult, and consequently duels were common on the frontier.

The Challenges to Family Authority

Meanwhile, children quietly questioned parental authority. The era's economic change forced many young people to choose between staying at home to help their parents and venturing out on their own. Writing to her parents just before beginning work at a Lowell textile mill, eighteen-year-old Sally Rice explained:

> *I must of course have something of my own before many more years have passed over my head, and where is that something coming from if I go home and earn nothing. You may think me unkind, but how can you blame me if I want to stay here. I have but one life to live and I want to enjoy myself as I can while I live.*

This desire for independence fueled westward migration as well. Restless single men led the way. Two young men from Virginia put it succinctly: "All the promise of life now seemed to us to be at the other end of the rainbow—somewhere else—anywhere else but on the farm. . . . All our youthful plans had as their chief object the getting away from the farm."

As young antebellum Americans tried to escape close parental supervision, courtship and marriage patterns also changed. No longer dependent on parents for land, young people wanted to choose their own mates. Romantic love, rather than parental preference, increasingly determined marital decisions. Colonial Puritans had advised young people to choose marriage partners whom they *could* love; but by the early 1800s young men and women viewed romantic love as the indispensable basis for successful marriage.

One clear sign of lessening parental control over courtship and marriage was the number of women marrying out of their birth order. Traditionally, fathers had wanted their daughters to marry in the order of their birth to avoid suspicion that there was something wrong with any of them. Another mark of the times was the growing popularity of long engagements; young women were reluctant to tie the knot, fearing that marriage would snuff out their independence. Equally striking was the increasing number of young women who chose not to marry. Catharine Beecher, for example, the daughter of minister Lyman Beecher, broke off her engagement to a young man during the 1820s, later renewed the engagement, and after her fiancé's death remained single.

Thus young people lived more and more in a world of their own. Moralists reacted with alarm and flooded the country with books of advice to youth, all of which stressed the same message: that the newly independent young people should develop rectitude, self-control, and "character." The self-made adult began with the self-made youth.

Wives, Husbands

Another class of advice books counseled wives and husbands about their rights and duties. These books were a sign that relations between spouses were also changing. Young men and women accustomed to making their own decisions would understandably approach marriage as a compact among equals. Although inequalities within marriage remained—especially the legal tradition that married women could not own property—the trend was toward a form of equality.

One source of this change was the rise of the doctrine of separate spheres. The traditional view of women as subordinate in all ways yielded to a separate-but-equal doctrine that portrayed men as superior in making money and governing the world and women as superior in exerting moral influence on family members. Most important was the shift of responsibility for child rearing from fathers to mothers. Advice books instructed mothers to discipline children by withdrawing love rather than using corporal punishment. A whipped child might obey but would remain sullen and bitter. The gentler methods advocated in manuals promised to penetrate the child's heart, to make the child want to do the right thing.

The idea of a separate women's sphere blended with the image of family and home as secluded refuges from a disorderly society. Popular culture painted an alluring portrait of the pleasures of home in such sentimental songs as "Home, Sweet Home" and poems such as "A Visit from St. Nicholas." Even the physical appearance of houses changed; one prominent architect published plans for peaceful single-family homes to offset the hurly-burly of daily life. "There should be something to love," he wrote. "There must be nooks about it, where one would love to linger; windows, where one can enjoy the quiet landscape at his leisure; cozy rooms, where all fireside joys are invited to dwell."

But reality diverged far from this ideal. Ownership of a quiet single-family home lay beyond the reach of most Americans, even much of the middle class. Farm homes, far from tranquil, were beehives of activity, and city dwellers often had to sacrifice privacy by taking in boarders to supplement family income.

Nevertheless, these intertwined ideas—separate spheres for men and women and the home as a sanctuary from the harsh world—were virtually the only ones projected in antebellum magazines. Although ideals, they intersected with the real world at points. The decline of cottage industry and the growing number of men (merchants, lawyers, brokers) who worked outside the home gave women more time to lavish on children. Married women found these ideals sources of power: the doctrine of separate spheres subtly implied that women should control not only the discipline but also the number of children.

In 1800 the United States had one of the highest birthrates ever recorded. Statistically, the average woman bore 7.04 children. Children were valuable for the labor they provided and for the relief from the burdens of survival that they could bring to aging parents. The more children, the better, most couples assumed. However, the growth of the market economy raised questions about children's economic value. Unlike a farmer, a merchant or lawyer could not send his children to work at the age of seven or eight. The birthrate gradually dropped, especially in towns and cities, so that statistically, by 1900 the average woman would bear 3.98 children. Birthrates remained higher among African-Americans and immigrants and in the rural West, where land was plentiful.

Abstinence, *coitus interruptus* (the withdrawal of the penis before ejaculation), and abortion were common birth-control methods. Remedies for "female irregularity"—unwanted pregnancy—were widely advertised. The rubber condom and vaginal diaphragm were familiar to many Americans by 1865. Whatever the method, husbands and wives jointly decided to limit family size. Economic and ideological considerations blended together. Husbands could note that the economic value of children was declining; wives, that having fewer children would give them more time to nurture each one and thereby to carry out their womanly duties.

Most supporters of the ideal of separate spheres did not advocate full legal equality for women. Indeed, the idea of separate spheres was an explicit *alternative* to legal equality. But the concept enhanced women's power within marriage by giving them influence in such vital issues as child rearing and the frequency of pregnancies.

Horizontal Allegiances and the Rise of Voluntary Associations

As some forms of authority weakened, Americans devised new ways by which individuals could extend their influence over others. The antebellum era witnessed the widespread substitution of *horizontal* allegiances for *vertical* allegiances. In vertical allegiances, authority flows from the top down, and people in a subordinate position identify their interests with those of superiors rather than others in the same subordinate roles. The traditional patriarchal family is an example of vertical allegiance, as is the traditional apprentice system. When social relationships assumed a horizontal form, new patterns emerged. Vertical relationships remained but became less important. New relationships linked those who were in a similar position: for example, in the large textile mills, operatives realized they had more in common with one another than with their supervisors. Wives tended to form associations that bound them with other married women, and young men developed associations with other young men.

Voluntary (and horizontal) associations proliferated in the 1820s and 1830s. Tocqueville described Americans as "a nation of joiners." At the most basic level these organizations promoted sociability by providing contact with people who shared similar interests, experiences, or characteristics. Women and free blacks formed their own voluntary associations. Beyond that, voluntary associations allowed members to assert their influence at a time when traditional forms of authority were weakening. To promote the concept of a separate sphere for women, women joined maternal associations to exchange ideas about child rearing; temperance associations to work for abstinence from alcoholic beverages; and moral-reform societies to combat prostitution.

Temperance and moral-reform societies served dual purposes. In addition to trying to suppress well-known vices, they enhanced women's power over men. Temperance advocates assumed that intemperance was a male vice, and moral reformers attributed prostitution to men who, unable to control their passions, exploited vulnerable girls. These organizations represented collective action by middle-class women to increase their influence in society.

CONCLUSION

Tocqueville described the United States of the 1830s as remarkable not for "the marvellous grandeur of some undertakings" but for the "innumerable multitude of small ones." Indeed, despite grand projects such as the Erie Canal, the era's distinguishing feature was the number of small to medium-sized enterprises that Americans embarked on: commercial farms of modest proportions, railroads of a few hundred miles, manufacturing companies employing five to ten workers. Even so, antebellum Americans thought that the world of their ancestors was breaking apart. As traditional assumptions eroded, however, new ones replaced them. Ties to village leaders and parents weakened, but people of the same age or same ideas formed new bonds. A widening circle of Americans insisted on the right to shape their own economic destinies, but individualism did not mean isolation from others, as the proliferation of voluntary associations testified.

Beyond changing the private lives of Americans, the social transformations of 1815 to 1840 also created a host of new political issues, as we shall see in Chapter 10.

CHRONOLOGY

1790 Samuel Slater opens his first Rhode Island mill.

1793 Eli Whitney invents the cotton gin.

1807 Robert R. Livingston and Robert Fulton introduce the steamboat *Clermont* on the Hudson River.

1811 Construction of the National Road begins at Cumberland, Maryland.

1819 Economic panic, ushering in four-year depression.

1820–1850 Growth of female moral-reform societies.

1820s Expansion of New England textile mills.

1824 *Gibbons* v. *Ogden*.

1825 Completion of the Erie Canal.

1828 Baltimore and Ohio Railroad chartered.

1830 Indian Removal Act passed by Congress.

1831 Alexis de Tocqueville begins visit to the United States to study American penitentiaries.

1832 *Worcester* v. *Georgia*.

1834 First strike at the Lowell mills.

1835–1838 Trail of Tears.

1837 Economic panic begins a depression that lasts until 1843.

1840 System of production by interchangeable parts perfected.

FOR FURTHER READING

William L. Anderson, ed., *Cherokee Removal Before and After* (1991). An anthology containing the latest research on Cherokee relocation.

Rowland Berthoff, *An Unsettled People: Social Order and Disorder in American History* (1971). A stimulating interpretation of American social history.

Ray A. Billington, *Westward Expansion: A History of the American Frontier* (1949). The standard study of westward movement and settlement.

Carl Degler, *At Odds: Women and the Family in America from the Revolution to the Present* (1980). A fine overview of the economic and social experiences of American women.

Gary Nash, *Forging Freedom: The Formation of Philadelphia's Black Community, 1720–1840* (1988). An imaginative reconstruction of the emergence of a semi-autonomous African-American community.

Harry N. Scheiber, *The Ohio Canal Era: A Case Study of Government and the Economy, 1820–1861* (1969). An analysis that speaks volumes about economic growth in the early republic.

George R. Taylor, *The Transportation Revolution, 1815–1860* (1951). The standard general study of the development of canals, steamboats, highways, and railroads.

Sean Wilentz, *Chants Democratic: New York City and the Rise of the American Working Class, 1788–1850* (1983). A stimulating synthesis of economic, social, and political history.

CHAPTER 10

Politics, Religion, and Reform in Antebellum America

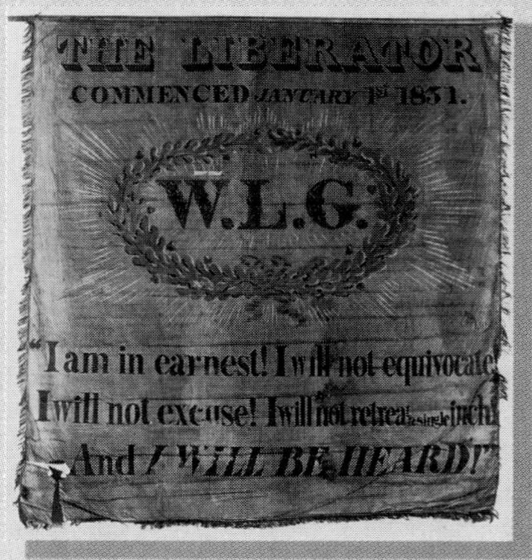

The 1820s were a period of transition. As the Revolutionary generation passed from the scene—both Thomas Jefferson and John Adams died on July 4, 1826—new generations of Americans grappled with new problems born of westward migration, growing economic individualism, and increasing sectional conflict over slavery. Massive social and economic change shattered old assumptions and created a vigorous new brand of politics.

This transformation led to the birth of a second American party system, with Democrats and Whigs replacing Republicans and Federalists. The changes went far beyond names. The new parties organized grassroots support, molded government in response to the people's will, and welcomed conflict as a way to sustain interest in political issues.

Reform movements paralleled, and sometimes replaced, politics as idealistic men and women worked for temperance, abolition, education reform, and equality for women. Strongly held religious beliefs, often the product of evangelism and nontraditional sects, impelled reformers into

(Right) The Liberator *banner*

these and other crusades, and they soon discovered that their success rested on their ability to influence politics.

Both the political and the reform agendas of the 1820s and 1830s diverged from those of the nation's founders. They had feared popular participation in politics, left an ambiguous legacy on slavery, and displayed little interest in women's rights. Yet even as Americans shifted their political and social priorities, they continued to venerate the founders. Histories of the United States, biographies of Revolutionary patriots, and torchlight parades that bore portraits of Washington and Jefferson alongside depictions of Andrew Jackson reassured the men and women of the young nation that they were remaining loyal to their heritage.

The Transformation of American Politics, 1824–1832

In 1824 Andrew Jackson and John Quincy Adams were both members of Jefferson's Republican party; by 1834 Jackson was a Democrat and Adams a Whig. Tensions spawned by industrialization, the rise of the Cotton South, and westward expansion split Jefferson's old party. Generally, supporters of states' rights joined the Democrats, and advocates of national support for economic development became Whigs.

Democrat or Whig, leaders had to adapt to the rising notion that politics should be an expression of the will of the common people rather than an activity that gentlemen conducted on the people's behalf. Americans still looked up to their political leaders, but those leaders could no longer look down on the people.

Democratic Ferment

Democratizing forces in politics took several forms. One of the most common was the abolition of the requirement that voters own property; no western states had such a requirement, and eastern states gradually liberalized their laws. Moreover, written ballots replaced the custom of voting aloud, which had enabled elites to influence others at the polls. And appointive offices became elective. The selection of members of the electoral college shifted gradually from state legislatures to the voters, and by 1832 only South Carolina followed the old custom.

The fierce tug of war between Republicans and Federalists in the 1790s and early 1800s had taught both parties to court voters and listen to their will. At grand party-run barbecues from Maine to Maryland, potential voters washed down free clams and oysters with free beer and whiskey. Republicans sought to expand suffrage in the North, and Federalists did likewise in the South, each in hopes of transforming itself into a majority party in that section.

The pace of political democratization was uneven, however. The parties were still run from the top down as late as 1820, with candidates nominated by caucus, that is, a meeting of party members in the legislature. Moreover, few party leaders embraced the principle of universal white manhood suffrage. Finally, the democratization of politics did not necessarily draw more voters to the polls. Waning competition between Federalists and Republicans after 1816 deprived voters of clear choices and made national politics boring. Yet no one disputed that to oppose the people or democracy would be a formula for political suicide. The people, one Federalist moaned, "have become too saucy and are really beginning to fancy themselves equal to their betters."

The Election of 1824

Sectional politics shattered the harmony of the Era of Good Feelings. In 1824 five candidates, all Republicans, battled for the presidency. John Quincy Adams emerged as the New England favorite. John C. Calhoun and William Crawford fought to represent the South. Henry Clay of Kentucky assumed that his leadership in promoting the American System would endear him to the East as well as to his native West. Tennessean Andrew Jackson stunned

The Election of 1824

Candidates	*Parties*	*Electoral Vote*	*Popular Vote*	*Percentage of Popular Vote*
JOHN QUINCY ADAMS	Democratic-Republican	84	108,740	30.5
Andrew Jackson	Democratic-Republican	99	153,544	43.1
William H. Crawford	Democratic-Republican	41	46,618	13.1
Henry Clay	Democratic-Republican	37	47,136	13.2

the four by emerging as a favorite of frontier people, southerners, and some northerners as well.

Most Republicans in Congress refused to support Crawford, the caucus's choice, and a paralyzing stroke soon removed him from the race. Impressed by Jackson's support, Calhoun withdrew to run unopposed for the vice presidency. Jackson won the popular and electoral vote but failed to win the majority electoral vote required by the Constitution. When the election went to the House of Representatives, Clay threw his support, and thus the presidency, to Adams; Adams then promptly appointed Clay secretary of state. Jackson's supporters raged that a "corrupt bargain" had cheated their candidate, "Old Hickory," of the presidency. Although no evidence of any outright deal was uncovered, the widespread belief in a corrupt bargain hung like a cloud over Adam's presidency.

John Quincy Adams as President

Failing to understand the changing political climate, Adams made several other miscalculations that would cloak his presidency in controversy. For example, he proposed federal support for internal improvements, although Old Republicans had continued to attack them as unconstitutional. Adams then infuriated southerners by proposing to send American delegates to a conference of newly independent Latin American nations. Southerners opposed U.S. participation because it would imply recognition of Haiti, the black republic created by slave revolutionaries. Both the sharp debate over Missouri and the discovery of Denmark Vesey's conspiracy to ignite a slave rebellion in South Carolina had shaken southern slaveholders. Instead of building new bases of support, Adams clung to the increasingly obsolete view of the president as custodian of the public good, aloof from partisan politics. He alienated his supporters by appointing his opponents to high office and wrote loftily, "I have no wish to fortify myself by the support of any party whatever." Idealistic though his view was, it guaranteed him a single-term presidency.

The Rise of Andrew Jackson and Martin Van Buren

As Adams's popularity fell, Andrew Jackson's rose. His victory over the British at the Battle of New Orleans made him a national hero, and southerners admired him as a Tennessee slaveholder, a renowned Indian fighter, and an advocate of Indian removal. Too, southerners praised Jackson's demand that they be allowed a free hand in pushing the Indians westward as a noble application of Jeffersonian ideals of states' rights—and a way to satisfy their land hunger. As the only candidate in 1824 not linked to the Monroe administration, Jackson was also in a position to capitalize on discontent after the Panic of 1819, which, in Calhoun's words, left people with "a general mass of disaffection to the Government" and "looking out anywhere for a leader."

By 1826 towns and villages across the country buzzed with political activity. Because supporters of Jackson, Adams, and Clay all still called themselves

Republicans, few realized that a new political system was being born. The man most alert to the new currents was Martin Van Buren, who would be Jackson's vice president and then president.

Van Buren exemplified a new breed of politician. A tavernkeeper's son, he had worked his way up through New York politics and created a powerful statewide machine, the Albany Regency, composed of men like himself from the middling and lower ranks. A genial man who befriended even his political rivals, Van Buren loved the game of politics and possessed an uncanny ability to sense which way the political winds were shifting.

The election of 1824 had convinced Van Buren of the need for two-party competition. Without the discipline imposed by party competition, the Republicans had splintered into sectional factions. The country would be better served, he thought, by reducing the shades of opinion in the country to just two so that parties could clash and a clear winner emerge. Jackson was the logical leader, and presidential nominee, of one new party, becoming known as the Democratic party; its opponents, calling themselves National Republicans, nominated Adams. The second American party system was taking shape.

The Election of 1828

The 1828 campaign was a vicious, mudslinging affair. The National Republicans attacked Jackson as a murderer, a drunken gambler, and an adulterer. He had in fact killed several men in duels and had several more executed militarily; and in 1791 he had married Rachel Robards, erroneously believing that her divorce from her first husband had become final. Jackson supporters retaliated that Adams was rich and in debt, had tried to gain favor with the Russian tsar by providing him with a beautiful American prostitute, and—perhaps worst of all to westerners—wore silk underwear.

The Adams supporters' charges that Jackson was an illiterate backwoodsman backfired and endeared "Old Hickory" to ordinary people. Jackson's

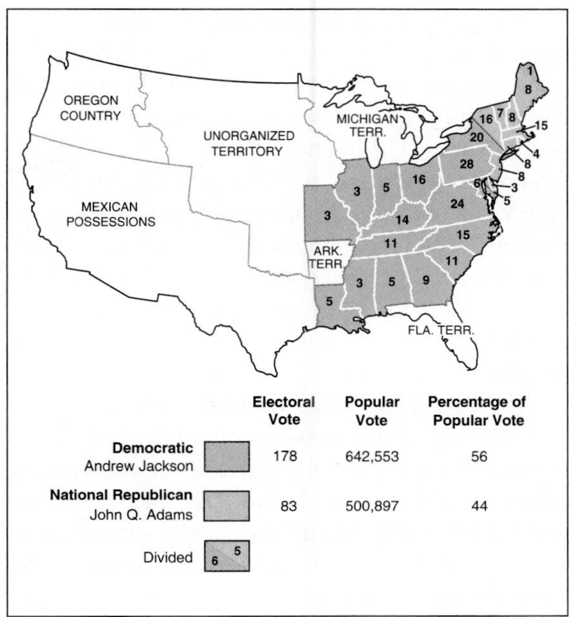

The Election of 1828

mudslingers, moreover, had the better aim. They proclaimed that Jackson was the common man incarnate—his mind unclouded by learning, his morals simple and true, his will fierce and resolute. Adams, in contrast, was an aristocrat, a scholar whose learning obscured the truth, a man who could write but not fight.

The election swept Jackson into office with twice Adams's electoral votes. The popular vote, much closer, reflected the strong sectional bases of the new parties. Adams doubled Jackson's vote in New England, while Jackson doubled Adams's vote in the South and nearly tripled it in the Southwest.

Jackson in Office

For all the furor, the campaign had revealed little about Jackson's position on major issues. On such key questions as federal aid for internal improvements and the tariff, Jackson had sent out conflicting signals. He would, as president, use the office to express the will of the majority.

Jackson's first policy on assuming office was to support "rotation in office," the removal of officeholders of the rival party. Jackson neither invented this policy, popularly known as the spoils system, nor abused it, but he moved to new ground in defending it. Rotation in office was fundamentally democratic, he argued. Officeholders' duties were so plain and simple that any intelligent man could perform them. By moving people into and out of office at will, Jackson hoped to prevent the emergence of an elite bureaucracy unresponsive to the will of the people.

Jackson's interpretation of the spoils system ruffled feathers, but the issues of internal improvements and tariffs ignited real controversy. Like most southerners, Jackson believed that federal support for internal improvements was simply a lavish giveaway. He thought that such funding violated the Constitution, which stated that Congress could appropriate money only for national purposes, not for the benefit of particular sections or interests. Accordingly, in 1830 Jackson vetoed a bill to provide federal support for a road in Kentucky between Maysville and Lexington.

The Maysville Road Bill veto and the almost simultaneous Indian Removal Act enhanced Jackson's popularity in the South. The tariff issue, however, would test southern loyalty. In 1828 while Adams was still president, Congress passed a high protective tariff favorable to western agriculture and New England manufacturing. Southerners fumed at the tariff, which raised the price of the manufactured goods that they had to buy and also created the threat of retaliatory tariffs against southern cotton exports. To the surprise of Jackson and his followers, he, rather than Adams, bore the brunt of southern ire.

Nullification

The 1828 tariff, the "Tariff of Abominations," laid the foundation for a split between Jackson and his vice president, John C. Calhoun. Although he had entered Congress as a "war hawk" and had championed nationalism early in his career, Calhoun had gradually become a states' rights sectionalist. He had supported the tariff of 1816 but would fiercely oppose that of 1828.

Calhoun also burned with ambition to be president. Jackson had stated that he would serve only one term and as vice president Calhoun assumed that he would succeed Jackson. To do so, he needed to maintain the support of the South, which was increasingly taking an anti-tariff stance. Calhoun's own state, South Carolina, had suffered economic decline throughout the 1820s; its citizens blamed protective tariffs for driving up the price of manufactured goods and for threatening cotton prices by lowering American demand for British cotton cloth, which was spun and woven from southern cotton. Whereas New Englanders, among them Senator Daniel Webster of Massachusetts, supported the tariff and protectionism, southerners responded with militant hostility.

Calhoun also accepted the Virginia and Kentucky Resolutions of 1798–1799, which defined the Union as a compact among the states, an association conferring limited powers on the central government. He insisted that the only constitutional tariff was one that raised money for the common national defense, not one that favored a particular section at the expense of others. Calhoun expressed these views anonymously in the widely circulated *South Carolina Exposition and Protest* (1828), which argued not only that the 1828 tariff was unconstitutional but also that states had the right to nullify that tariff within their borders.

More was at stake than the price of manufactured goods. Southerners feared that a government capable of passing tariffs favoring one section over another might also pass laws meddling with slavery. Although this idea seemed far-fetched—Jackson himself was a slaveholder—South Carolina's whites were edgy about the safety of slavery. African-Americans composed a majority of their state's population, the slave Nat Turner's bloody rebellion in Virginia in 1831 raised fears of a similar threat to South Carolina, and William Lloyd Garrison's new newspaper, *The Liberator*, advocated immediate aboli-

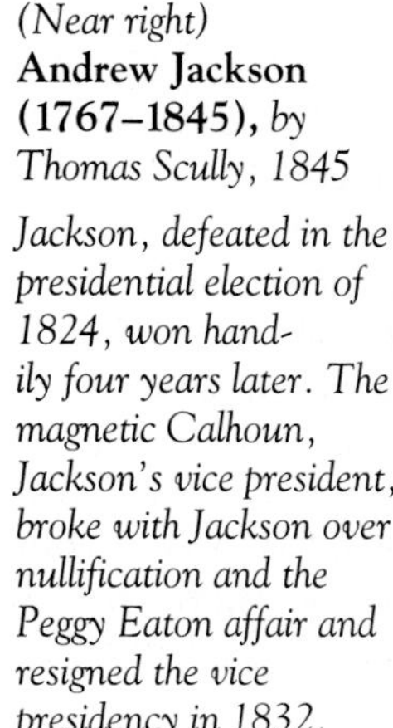

(Near right) **Andrew Jackson (1767–1845),** *by Thomas Scully, 1845*

Jackson, defeated in the presidential election of 1824, won handily four years later. The magnetic Calhoun, Jackson's vice president, broke with Jackson over nullification and the Peggy Eaton affair and resigned the vice presidency in 1832.

(Above) **John C. Calhoun (1782–1850),** *by Charles Bird King, c. 1825*

tion. To many South Carolinians, these were ominous signs warning that a line had to be drawn against tariffs and possible future interference with slavery.

Jackson Versus Calhoun

Like Calhoun, Jackson was strong-willed and proud. Unlike Calhoun, he already was president and the leader of a national party that included supporters of the tariff. To mollify both pro-tariff and anti-tariff forces, he devised two policies.

First, he distributed surplus federal revenue, largely derived from the tariff duties, to the states, hoping to remove the taint of sectional injustice from the tariff. Second, he tried to ease tariffs down from the sky-high 1828 rates, and Congress passed slight reductions in 1832. But these measures did little to satisfy Calhoun and the South Carolinians.

By the time the somewhat lower tariff was passed, other issues had ruptured relations between the president and vice president. Jackson learned that in 1818, then–Secretary of War Calhoun had urged that Jackson be punished for his unauthorized raid into Spanish Florida. Combined with the snubbing by Calhoun's wife, Floride, of Peggy Eaton, the scandal-tainted spouse of Jackson's ally and secretary of war, John H. Eaton, this revelation convinced Jackson that he had to "destroy [Calhoun] regardless of what injury it might do me or my administration." A Jefferson Day dinner in April 1830 featured a symbolic confrontation between Jackson and Calhoun. Jackson proposed the toast "Our Union: It must be preserved." Calhoun responded, "The Union next to Liberty the most dear. May we always remember that it can only be preserved by distributing equally the benefits and burdens of the Union."

The stage was set for the president and the vice president to clash over nullification. In November 1832 a South Carolina convention, citing Calhoun's states' rights doctrine, nullified the tariffs of

1828 and 1832 and forbade the collection of customs duties within the state. Jackson reacted quickly. He despised nullification as an "abominable doctrine" that would reduce the government to anarchy and denounced the South Carolinians as "unprincipled men who would rather rule in hell than be subordinate in heaven." He sent arms to Unionists in South Carolina and issued a proclamation that lambasted nullification as unconstitutional; the Constitution, he emphasized, had established "a single nation," not a league of states.

In March 1833 the crisis eased as President Jackson signed "the olive branch and the sword," in one historian's words. The Compromise Tariff of 1833, the olive branch or peace offering, provided for a gradual but significant lowering of tariff duties from 1833 to 1842. The Force Bill, the sword, authorized the president to use arms to collect customs duties in South Carolina. Although South Carolina did not abandon the principle of nullification—in fact, it petulantly nullified the Force Bill—it accepted the Compromise Tariff and rescinded its nullification of the tariffs of 1828 and 1832.

This so-called Compromise of 1833 grew out of a mixture of partisanship and statesmanship. Its chief architect was Henry Clay of Kentucky, who had long favored high tariffs. Clay not only feared the outbreak of civil war but also wanted to keep control of the tariff issue away from the Jacksonians, even if that meant a lower tariff. The nullifiers, recognizing that no other states had supported them, preferred giving Clay, not Jackson, credit for defusing the crisis; they therefore supported the Compromise Tariff and rescinded the nullification proclamation. Americans everywhere hailed Henry Clay as the Great Compromiser.

The Bank Veto

One reason that Jackson signed Clay's Compromise Tariff into law was that he had no strong convictions about an alternative. In fact, he was relatively open-minded on the subject of tariffs. The same could not be said of his attitude toward banks. Owing to disastrous financial speculations early in his career, Jackson was deeply suspicious of all banks, all paper money, and all monopolies. On each count the Bank of the United States was guilty.

The Bank of the United States had received a twenty-year charter from Congress in 1816. As a creditor of state banks, the Bank of the United States in effect restrained their printing and lending of money by its ability to demand the redemption of state notes in specie (gold or silver coin).

Many other aspects of the Bank of the United States made it controversial. For example, it was widely blamed for the Panic of 1819. Second, it was a privileged institution at a time when privilege was coming under fierce attack. Third, as the official depository for federal revenue, the bank had far greater lending capacity than state banks and thus dominated them. Fourth, although chartered by the federal government, the bank was controlled by its stockholders, who were private citizens—"moneyed capitalists" in Jackson's view. Finally, its location in Philadelphia, rather than Washington, symbolized the bank's independence of supervision by the national government. The bank's president, the aristocratic Nicholas Biddle, saw himself as a public servant duty-bound to keep the bank above politics.

After Jackson questioned "both the constitutionality and the expediency" of the Bank of the United States in his first annual message to Congress, Biddle sought an early rechartering of the bank. He was urged on by Henry Clay, who hoped to ride the probank bandwagon into the White House in 1832. Congress passed, and Jackson promptly vetoed, the recharter bill. The president denounced the bank as a private and privileged monopoly that drained the West of specie, was immune to taxation by states, put inordinate power in the hands of a few men, and made "the rich richer and the potent more powerful."

The Election of 1832

By 1832 Jackson had made clear his views on major issues. He was simultaneously a strong defender of

The Election of 1832

Candidates	Parties	Electoral Vote	Popular Vote	Percentage of Popular Vote
ANDREW JACKSON	Democratic	219	687,502	55.0
Henry Clay	National Republican	49	530,189	42.4
William Wirt	Anti-Masonic	7	33,108	2.6
John Floyd	National Republican	11		

states' rights *and* a staunch Unionist. Although he cherished the Union, Jackson believed the states far too diverse to accept strong direction from the federal government. The safest course was to allow the states considerable freedom so that they would remain contentedly within the Union and would reject such a dangerous doctrine as nullification.

Throwing aside earlier promises to retire, Jackson ran for the presidency again in 1832, with Martin Van Buren as his running mate. Henry Clay ran on the National Republican ticket, stressing his American System of protective tariffs, national banking, and federal support for internal improvements. Jackson's overwhelming personal popularity swamped Clay, 219 to 49 electoral votes. Secure in office for another four years, Jackson was ready to finish dismantling the Bank of the United States.

The Bank Controversy and the Second Party System

Coming late in Jackson's first term, the veto of the recharter of the Bank of the United States had little impact on the election of 1832. However, between 1833 and 1840 banking became an issue that ignited popular passion as Jackson's veto of the bank recharter unleashed a tiger that threatened to devour all banks.

Banking created such controversy in part because the United States had no paper currency of its own. Instead, private bankers (widely viewed as sinister figures) issued paper notes, which they promised to redeem in specie. Yet there was a more basic issue: what sort of society would the United States become? Abundant paper money would foster a speculative economy that would enrich some Americans but leave many poor. Would the United States embrace swift economic development at the price of allowing some people to get rich quickly while others languished? Or would the nation undergo more modest growth in traditional molds, anchored by "honest" manual work and frugality?

Before the answer to these questions was clear, the banking issue dramatically transformed politics. It contributed both to the growth of opposition to the Democrats and to the steady expansion of popular interest in politics.

The War on the Bank of the United States

Jackson could have allowed the Bank of the United States, "the monster," as he termed it, to die a natural death when its charter expired, but he and his followers believed that if the bank escaped with a breath of life, "it will soon recover its wonted strength, its whole power to injure us, and all hope of its destruction must forever be renounced." When Biddle began calling in bank loans and contracting credit to forestall further moves by Jackson, Jacksonians saw their darkest fears confirmed. The bank, Jackson said, "is trying to kill me, but I will kill it." So the president began removing federal deposits from the Bank of the United States and putting them in state banks.

In turn, this policy raised new problems. State banks that were depositories for federal funds could use these moneys as the basis for issuing more notes and extending more loans. Jackson hoped to head off the danger of a credit-fueled speculative economy by limiting the number of state banks used for federal revenue. But he discovered that doing so was impossible; indeed, by the end of 1833 there were twenty-three "pet banks," chosen in part for their loyalty to the Democratic party. Jackson could not stem the rapid economic expansion fueled by paper money and by foreign specie flowing in to purchase cotton. In 1836 the president thus reluctantly signed the Deposit Act, increasing the number of deposit banks and lessening federal control over them.

The Democratic party split between advocates of soft money (paper) and proponents of hard money (specie). The two Democratic camps agreed that the Bank of the United States was evil, but for different reasons. Soft-money Democrats, especially strong in the West, resented the bank's restriction of credit and wanted more paper money. Hard-money Democrats, typically wage-earning urban workers, disliked the speculative economy based on paper money and easy credit, and they deeply feared inflation.

The Rise of Whig Opposition

During Jackson's second term the National Republicans changed their name to the Whig Party and broadened their base of support in both the North and the South. As Jackson's policies became clearer and sharper, the opposition attracted people alienated by his positions.

For example, Jackson's crushing of nullification led some southerners to the Whigs in order to oppose Jackson. Jackson's war against the Bank of the United States and his opposition to federal aid for internal improvements alienated other southerners and drove them to the Whigs as well. Most of the South remained Democratic, but the Whigs made substantial inroads nonetheless. Northern reformers also joined the Whigs, who were far more willing than the Democrats to effect social change by government intervention. And supporters of Henry Clay's American System joined advocates of public education and temperance in seeking a more activist, interventionist national government.

One remarkable source of Whig strength was Anti-Masonry, a protest movement against the secrecy of Masonic lodges, which had long provided prominent men with fraternal fellowship and exotic rituals. In 1826 William Morgan, a stonemason from Genesee County, New York, was kidnapped after threatening to expose Masonic secrets. Efforts to solve the mystery of Morgan's disappearance foundered because local officials, themselves Masons, obstructed the investigation. Rumors spread that Masonry was a conspiracy of the rich to suppress liberty, a secret order of men who loathed Christianity, and an exclusive retreat for drunkards.

Anti-Masons, who began as a movement of moral protest, organized the Anti-Masonic party, which became a potent political force in part of New England. In many ways Anti-Masons' hatred of vice paralleled that of the Whig reformers, and so their entry into the Whig party was natural. Anti-Masonry brought into the Whig party a broad-based constituency that protested "aristocracy" with the same zeal as Jacksonian Democrats, and the presence of Anti-Masons in the party countered the charge that the Whigs were tools of the rich.

By 1836 the Whigs had become a national party with widespread appeal. Whigs everywhere assailed Andrew Jackson as an imperious dictator, "King Andrew I"; and the name "Whigs" evoked memories of the American patriots who had opposed George III in 1776.

The Election of 1836

As the election of 1836 approached, the Whigs lacked a national leader. Henry Clay came close, but he carried political scars and a reputation for spending his days at the gaming table and his nights in brothels. In the end the Whigs ran four sectional candidates, hoping to draw enough votes to prevent the Democratic candidate, Martin Van Buren, from gaining a majority of electoral votes. Although the strategy failed—Van Buren captured 170 electoral

The Election of 1836

Candidates	Parties	Electoral Vote	Popular Vote	Percentage of Popular Vote
MARTIN VAN BUREN	Democratic	170	765,483	50.9
William H. Harrison	Whig	73	739,795	49.1
Hugh L. White	Whig	26		
Daniel Webster	Whig	14		
W. P. Mangum	Whig	11		

votes to the Whigs' 124—the Whigs made substantial gains in the South, a clear sign of trouble ahead for the Democrats.

The Panic of 1837

Hailed as "the greatest man of his age," Jackson left office in 1837 in a sunburst of glory. Yet he bequeathed to his successor a severe depression, the legacy of the bank war and the "pet banks."

In the speculative boom of 1835 and 1836, born of Jackson's policy of placing federal funds in state banks, the total number of banks doubled, the value of bank notes in circulation nearly tripled, and both commodity and land prices soared skyward. But the overheated economy began to cool rapidly in May 1837 as prices tumbled and as bank after bank suspended specie payments. After a short rally, 1839 saw a second crash as banks across the nation again suspended specie payments.

The prolonged depression had multiple roots. Domestically, Jackson's Specie Circular of July 1836, declaring that only specie, not paper money, could be used to purchase public lands, dried up credit. International causes played a large role as well, especially Britain's decision in 1836 to halt the flow of specie from its shores to the United States.

The Search for Solutions

Van Buren, known as "the sly fox" and "the little magician" for his political craftiness, would need those skills to confront the depression, which was battering ordinary citizens and the Democratic party alike. The president called for the creation of an independent treasury that would hold government revenues and keep them from the grasp of corporations. When Van Buren finally signed the Independent Treasury Bill into law on July 4, 1840, his supporters hailed it as a second Declaration of Independence.

The Independent Treasury reflected the basic Jacksonian suspicion of an alliance between the federal government and banking. However, the Independent Treasury Act failed to address banking on the state level, where newly chartered state banks—more than 900 in number by 1840—lent money to farmers and businessmen, fueling the speculative economy feared by Jacksonians.

Whigs and Democrats differed sharply in their approach to the multiplication of state banks. Whigs, convinced that Jackson's Specie Circular, not banks themselves, had brought on the depression, supported policies allowing any group to start a bank as long as its members met state requirements. Democrats, who tended to blame banks and paper money for the depression, adopted the hard-money position favored by Jackson and his advisers. After 1837 the Democrats were in effect an antibank, hard-money party.

The Election of 1840

Despite the depression, the Democrats renominated Van Buren. Avoiding the mistake of 1836, the Whigs nominated a single candidate, Ohio's William Henry Harrison, and ran John Tyler of Virginia for vice president. The Whigs chose Harri-

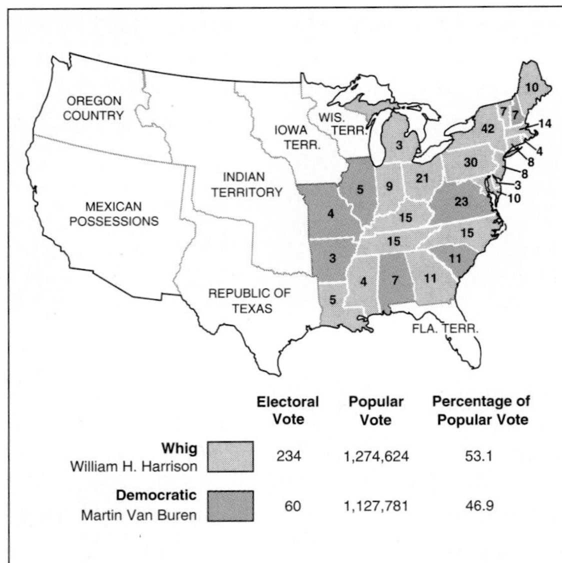

The Election of 1840

son, sixty-seven years old, largely because he had few enemies.

Early in the campaign the Democrats made a fatal mistake, ridiculing Harrison as "Old Granny" who desired only to spend his declining years in a log cabin sipping cider. In so doing, they handed the Whigs the most famous campaign symbol in American history. The Whigs saluted Harrison as a rugged frontiersman, the hero of the Battle of Tippecanoe, and a defender of all those people who lived in log cabins. Disdaining a platform, the Whigs ran a "hurrah" campaign using log cabins for headquarters, singing log cabin songs, and ladling out log cabin cider. Instead of a platform, they trumpeted, "Tippecanoe and Tyler, too!" and attacked Van Buren as an aristocrat who lived in "regal splendor."

Harrison was elected in a clear victory. The depression would have made it difficult for any Democrat to win, and Van Buren lacked the halo of military glory that gleamed around Jackson and Harrison. However, many of Van Buren's problems stemmed from his style of campaign. While the Whigs ran a rousing race aimed directly at the "common man," Van Buren quietly wrote letters of encouragement to key supporters. Ironically, the Whigs beat the master politician at his own game.

The Second Party System Matures

The strong contrasts between the two parties and the sharp choices they presented jolted the American electorate. Nearly 2.4 million people voted in 1840, up an astonishing 60 percent from 1836. Most of that change was in the number of people who chose to vote; prior to 1840 the proportion of white males who voted had ranged from 55 to 58 percent; in 1840 it rose to 80 percent.

Both the depression and the frenzied log cabin campaign had brought voters to the polls in 1840, but voter turnouts stayed high even after prosperity returned. The second party system reached a high plateau in 1840 and remained there over a decade. The gradual hardening of the line between the two parties piqued popular interest in politics.

By 1840 reform issues were drawing as many to the polls as tariffs and banking. Religion, rather than politics, however, was the source of many of these reforms.

The Rise of Popular Religion

In *Democracy in America,* Alexis de Tocqueville called religion "the foremost of the political institutions" in the United States. "In France I had almost always seen the spirit of religion and the spirit of freedom pursuing courses dramatically opposed to each other; but in America I found that they were intimately united, and that they reigned in common over the same country."

Tocqueville was referring to the way religious impulses reinforced democracy and liberty. Just as Americans demanded that politics be accessible to average people, they insisted ministers preach doctrines that appealed to ordinary men and women. Successful ministers used plain language to move the heart, not theological complexity to dazzle the intellect. Increasingly, Americans put individuals in charge of their own religious destiny, thrusting aside

Calvinist predestination in favor of the belief that anyone could attain heaven. A series of religious revivals known as the Second Great Awakening contributed to the growing harmony between religion and politics and to the growing conviction that heaven itself was democratic.

The Second Great Awakening

The Second Great Awakening first flared in Connecticut in the 1790s, and during the following half century it set ablaze one section of the nation after another. As the revivals moved westward, they underwent striking changes, typified by the rise of camp meetings. Here the members of several denominations gathered together in sprawling open-air camps to hear revivalists proclaim that the Second Coming of Jesus was near and that the time for repentance was now. The most famous camp meeting took place at Cane Ridge, Kentucky, in August 1801. A huge crowd gathered on a hillside to listen to thunderous sermons, sing hymns, and experience divine grace.

The Cane Ridge revival was part of the Great Kentucky Revival of 1800–1801. These frontier revivals featured "exercises" in which men and women rolled around like logs, jerked their heads furiously, and grunted like animals. Critics blasted the frontier frenzy for encouraging fleshly lust and complained that "more souls were begot than saved" at the camp meetings. But although these early frontier revivals challenged traditional religious customs—indeed, the most successful preachers were farmers and artisans who had experienced powerful conversions and scorned those whose religion came from books—the revivalists promoted law, order, and morality.

Methodists, the most successful frontier denomination, became the largest American Protestant denomination, soaring from 70,000 members in 1800 to more than 1 million in 1844. The Methodists emphasized that religion was a matter of the heart rather than the head and relied on itinerant circuit riders, young, unmarried men who traveled ceaselessly and preached in houses, open fields, or wherever else listeners would gather. After the Methodist circuit riders left, their converts held weekly "classes" to provide mutual encouragement and to chastise members for drunkenness, fighting, gossiping, fornication, and even shrewd business practices.

Eastern Revivals

By the 1820s the Second Great Awakening had begun to shift back to the East. The hottest revival fires blazed in an area of western New York known as the Burned-Over District. No longer a frontier, western New York teemed with descendants of Puritans who hungered for religious experience and with people drawn by the hope of wealth after the completion of the Erie Canal. It was a fertile field of high expectations and bitter discontent. The man who harnessed these anxieties to religion was Charles Grandison Finney, a lawyer-turned-Presbyterian minister. His greatest "harvest" came in the thriving canal city of Rochester in 1830–1831.

Finney's innovations at the Rochester revival justified his reputation as the "father of modern revivalism." First, he pioneered in generating cooperation among Protestants, and all denominations participated in his revivals. In addition, he introduced such novelties as the "anxious seat," a bench where those ready for conversion could be made objects of special prayer, and the "protracted meeting," which ran nightly for a week or more. Finally, although a Presbyterian, Finney rejected the Calvinist doctrine of total depravity, humankind's irresistible inclination to sin. Instead, he proclaimed, sin was a voluntary act, and those who willed themselves to sin could just as readily will themselves not to sin. In theory, men and women could live perfect lives, free of sin. Those converted by Finney or other evangelists believed that they were cleansed of past guilt and were beginning a new life. "I have been born again," a young convert wrote. "I am three days old when I write this letter."

Originally controversial, Finney's ideas came to dominate "evangelical" Protestantism, which focused on the need for an emotional religious conversion. He succeeded because he told people what they wanted to hear: that their destinies were in their own hands. A society that celebrated the "self-made" individual embraced Finney's assertion that even in religion people could make of themselves what they chose. Finney multiplied his success by emphasizing the role of women, who outnumbered male converts nearly two to one. Finney encouraged women to give public testimonials of their conversion, and he often converted men by first winning over their wives and daughters.

Critics of Revivals: The Unitarians

Although some praised revivals for saving souls, others doubted their lasting effects. The Unitarians were a small but influential group of critics. Although their basic doctrine—that Jesus Christ was less than fully divine—had gained acceptance among religious liberals in the eighteenth century, Unitarianism became a formal denomination only in the early nineteenth century. Hundreds of New England Congregational churches were torn apart by the withdrawal of socially prominent families who had embraced Unitarianism and by legal battles over which group, Congregationalists or Unitarians, could occupy church property. Unitarians won few converts outside New England, but their tendency to attract the wealthy and educated gave them influence beyond their numbers.

Unitarians criticized revivals as uncouth emotional exhibitions and argued that "character building" was more effective than sudden emotional conversion. Yet they and the revivalists agreed in rejecting the Calvinist emphasis on human wickedness. Christianity had only one purpose, a Unitarian leader proclaimed: "the perfection of human nature, the elevation of men into nobler beings."

The Rise of Mormonism

Far more controversial than the Unitarians were the Mormons and their church, the Church of Jesus Christ of Latter-day Saints, another new denomination of the 1820s. Joseph Smith, its founder, grew up in the heart of the Burned-Over District. Conflict among the various religious denominations that thrived in the region left Smith confused: "Some were contending for the Methodist faith, some for the Presbyterian, and some for the Baptists," he later wrote. He wondered who was right and who wrong or whether they were "all wrong together."

Smith resolved this conflict, which was not uncommon in the Burned-Over District, in a unique way. He claimed that an angel had led him to a buried book of revelation and to special stones for use in translating it. The Book of Mormon, which Smith translated, tells the story of an ancient Hebrew prophet, Lehi, whose descendants migrated to America and created a prosperous civilization. Jesus had appeared and performed miracles in the New World, but Lehi's descendants had departed from the Lord's ways and quarreled among themselves. God had cursed some of these defectors with dark skin; these were the American Indians, who had long since forgotten their history.

Smith quickly gathered followers. Mormonism's appeal lay partly in its placing America at the center of Christian history and partly in its resolving the conflicting claims within Protestantism by additional revelations beyond those in the Bible. The Mormons moved steadily west, both to escape persecution and to draw closer to the Indians, whom they wished to convert. Smith's claim of a new revelation guaranteed a hostile reception for the Mormons wherever they went because it undermined the authority of the Bible, which, along with the Constitution, contained the ideals on which the American republic rested.

In 1843 Smith added fuel to the fire by proclaiming yet another revelation, this one sanctioning polygyny, the practice of taking multiple wives. Smith's claims that he was a prophet, the "Second Mohammed," also intensified the controversy that boiled around Mormonism. He proclaimed that Mormonism would be to Christianity what Christianity had been to Judaism: a grand, all-encompassing, and higher form of religion. Smith called himself "Prophet of the Kingdom of God." But in 1844 the state of Illinois charged him with treason and jailed him in the town of Carthage. There, in June 1844, a mob murdered Smith and his brother.

Although deprived of a founder, Mormonism grew rapidly in the next three decades; by 1870 it boasted 200,000 believers. Brigham Young, who assumed leadership after Smith's murder, led the Mormons westward into Utah, at the time still under Mexican control. There he established the independent republic of Deseret, and the Mormons prospered. Young's firm control kept the rank and file in line, while polygyny guaranteed that Mormons would remain a people apart from the mainstream of American society. Above all, the Mormons were industrious and deeply committed to the welfare of their people. They transformed the Great Salt Lake Valley into a rich oasis and continued to dominate Utah after it became part of the United States.

Although it pushed against main currents of American society, Mormonism offered the downcast and the outcast an alternative to dominant religious and social practices. In this respect it mirrored the efforts of several religious communal societies, among them the Shakers, whose members likewise set themselves apart from society.

The Shakers

The founder of the Shakers (who derived their name from a convulsive religious dance that was part of their ceremony) was Mother Ann Lee, the illiterate daughter of an English blacksmith. Lee and her followers had established a series of tightly knit agricultural-artisan communities in America after her arrival in 1774. Shaker artisanship, particularly in furniture, had quickly gained renown for its simple lines, beauty, and strength. Shaker advances in the development of new farm tools and seed varieties would be a boon to the growing market economy. However, the Shakers were fundamentally other worldly and hostile to materialism. Lee had insisted that her followers abstain from sexual intercourse, believed that the end of the world was imminent, and derived many of her doctrines from trances and visions. She had also taught that at the Second Coming, Jesus would take the form of a woman.

Shaker missionaries took advantage of revivalism's appeal. At Cane Ridge and other revivals, Shaker proselytizers attracted converts whom the revivals had loosened from their traditional religious moorings. By the 1830s the Shakers numbered about 6,000.

Although the Shakers and the Mormons lived apart from traditional society, most evangelical Protestants taught that religion and the pursuit of wealth were compatible. Revivalists taught that getting ahead in the world was acceptable as long as people were honest, temperate, and bound by their consciences. By encouraging involvement in society, evangelism provided a powerful stimulus to the multiple social reform movements of the 1820s and 1830s.

The Age of Reform

Despite rising popular interest in politics between 1824 and 1840, large numbers of people were excluded from political participation. Women and free blacks could not vote, and political parties shunned controversial issues, including slavery and women's rights.

During the 1820s and 1830s unprecedented numbers of men and women joined organizations aimed at improving society. The abolition of slavery, women's rights, temperance, better treatment of criminals and the insane, public education, and even the establishment of perfect, utopian communities were on the various reformers' agenda. Although they occasionally cooperated with political parties, especially the Whigs, reformers gave their loyalty to their causes, not to parties.

Religious revivalism intensified the righteousness of reformers, who believed that they were on God's side of any issue. Abolitionists and temperance reformers tended to come from evangelical backgrounds, but others, school reformers and women's rights advocates particularly, were often hostile or indifferent to revivals. Yet even reformers opposed to revivalism borrowed evangelical preachers' language and psychology by painting drunkenness, ignorance, and inequality as sins calling for immediate repentance and change. Reformers had a dark side. So sure were many reformers of the worthiness of their cause that they became self-righteous, paying more attention, for example, to drunkenness than to conditions that bred drinking.

Reform movements lacked a national scope. New England and those parts of the Midwest settled by New Englanders were hotbeds of reform, while southerners actively suppressed abolition, displayed only mild interest in temperance and educational reform, ignored women's rights, and saw utopian communities as proof of the mental instability of northern reformers.

The War on Liquor

Agitation for temperance (either total abstinence from alcoholic beverages or moderation in their use) intensified during the second quarter of the nineteenth century. Alcohol abuse was a growing problem: per capita consumption of rum, whiskey, gin, and brandy had risen steadily until it exceeded seven gallons per year by 1830, nearly triple today's rate. The average adult male downed a half pint of liquor a day, and reformers saw alcohol excess as a male indulgence whose bitter consequences (for example, spending money on liquor instead of food) fell on women and children. Not surprisingly, millions of women marched behind the temperance banner.

The movement took off in 1825 when the popular evangelist Lyman Beecher, in six widely acclaimed lectures, thundered against all use of alcohol. Evangelical Protestants established the American Temperance Society the following year, and by 1834 it enjoyed some 5,000 state and local affiliates. The American Temperance Society demanded total abstinence and flooded the country with tracts denouncing the "amazing evil" of strong drink.

The laboring class became a chief target for temperance reformers. Passing a jug around the workplace every few hours had been a time-honored way to relieve on-the-job fatigue, but large factories demanded a more disciplined, sober work force. Manufacturers quickly supported the evangelical temperance reformers. Uninterested in temperance at first, workers flocked to reform after the Panic of 1837, forming the Washington Temperance Societies beginning in 1840. Many workers who joined the Washingtonians were reformed drunkards who had concluded that hard times required temperance and frugality. Because so many of the forces dislocating workers in the late 1830s were beyond their control, they looked to something that they could control: drinking. Take care of temperance, a Washingtonian told his audience, and the Lord would take care of the economy.

As temperance won new supporters, the crusaders shifted their emphasis from the individual drinker to the entire community and demanded that towns and even states ban all traffic in liquor. By the late 1830s prohibition was scoring victories, especially in New England. The steady rise of alcohol consumption halted in the early 1830s and then began to fall; by the 1840s the rate of consumption was less than half that in the 1820s.

Public-School Reform

Like temperance crusaders, school reformers worked to encourage orderliness and thrift in the common people. Rural "district" schools were a main target. Here students ranging in age from three to twenty crowded into a single room and learned to read and count, but little more.

District schools enjoyed considerable support from rural parents. However, reformers insisted that schools had to equip children for the emerging competitive and industrial economy. In 1837 Horace Mann of Massachusetts, the most articulate and influential of the reformers, became the first secretary of his state's newly created board of education. He presided over sweeping reforms to transform schools from loose organizations into highly structured institutions that occupied most of a child's time and energy. Mann's goals included shifting financial support of schools from parents to the state, compelling attendance, extending the school term, introducing standardized textbooks, and grading schools (that is, classifying students by age and attainment).

School reformers sought to spread uniform cultural values as well as to combat ignorance. Requiring students to arrive at a set time would teach punctuality, and matching children against their peers would stimulate the competitiveness needed in an industrializing society. Children would read the same books and absorb the same moral lessons. The McGuffey readers, which sold 50 million copies between 1836 and 1870, preached industry, honesty, sobriety, and patriotism.

Mann's reforms took root primarily in the North, despite challenges from farmers satisfied with the district school, from Catholics objecting to anti-Catholic and anti-Irish barbs in the textbooks, and from the working poor, who widely saw compulsory education as a menace to families dependent on children's wages. He and other school reformers prevailed in part because their opponents could not cooperate with each other and in part because the reformers attracted influential allies, including urban workers, manufacturers, and women. Many people doubted that a woman could control a one-room school with students of widely variant ages, but managing a classroom of eight-year-olds was different. Reformers predicted that school reform would make teaching a suitable profession for women, and they were right. By 1900, 70 percent of the nation's teachers were women.

School reform also appealed to native-born Americans alarmed by the swelling tide of immigration. The public school became a vehicle for forging a common American culture out of an increasingly diverse society. However, few reformers stressed the integration of black and white children. When black children got any schooling, it was usually in segregated schools; black children in integrated schools encountered such virulent prejudice that African-American leaders in northern cities often preferred segregated schools.

Abolitionism

Antislavery sentiment had flourished among whites during the Revolutionary era but faded in the early nineteenth century. The American Colonization Society, founded in 1817, was the main antislavery organization of this period. It proposed gradual emancipation, compensation for slave owners when slaves became free, and the shipment to Africa of freed blacks. Although these proposals attracted some support from slave owners in the Upper South, they were unrealizable. The growing cotton economy had made slavery more attractive than ever to most southerners, and few owners would have freed their slaves, even if compensated. The U.S. slave population, fed by natural increase, soared in the early nineteenth century, from 1.2 million in 1810 to more than 2 million by 1830, but only 1,400 blacks migrated to Africa, and most were already free.

Radical antislavery views flourished primarily among African-Americans themselves. Opposing colonization in Africa—for most American blacks were native born—they formed scores of abolition societies. One free black, David Walker of Boston, even called for a rebellion to crush slavery.

In 1821 Benjamin Lundy, a white Quaker, began a newspaper, the *Genius of Universal Emancipation*, that trumpeted repeal of the Constitution's three-fifths clause, the outlawing of the internal slave trade, and the abolition of slavery in U.S. territories. Seven years later Lundy hired a young New Englander, William Lloyd Garrison, as an editorial assistant. The prematurely bald, bespectacled Garrison looked like a genial schoolmaster, but he would become a potent force in the antislavery movement.

In 1831 Garrison launched a newspaper, *The Liberator*, to spread his radical antislavery message. "I am in earnest," he wrote. "I will not equivocate—I will not excuse—I will not retreat a single inch—AND I WILL BE HEARD." His battle cry was "immediate emancipation"; his demand, civil and legal equality for African-Americans. However, even Garrison did not believe that all slaves could be freed overnight. People first had to realize that slavery was sinful and its continued existence intolerable.

Black abolitionists supported Garrison; in its early years three-fourths of *The Liberator*'s subscribers were African-American. Other blacks were emerging as powerful writers and speakers. Frederick Douglass, an escaped slave, could rivet an audience with an opening line: "I appear before the immense

Lucretia Mott (1793–1880)

Dorothea Dix (1808–1887)

Mott, a Quaker minister, worked for the antislavery cause as well as for women's rights. Dix, after devoting herself to reforming prison conditions and the treatment of the insane, served her country in the Civil War as superintendent of women nurses.

with pursuits beyond the family and thus blunted demands for full equality.

Penitentiaries and Asylums

Beginning in the 1820s, reformers tried to combat poverty, crime, and insanity by establishing regimented institutions, themselves the products of bold new assumptions about the causes of deviancy. As poverty and crime had increased and become more visible in the early nineteenth century, alarmed investigators had concluded that indigence and deviant behavior resulted not from defects in human nature, as colonial Americans had thought, but from drunken fathers and broken homes. The failure of parental discipline, not the will of God or the wickedness of human nature, lay at the root of evil. In light of the growing belief that the moral qualities of the individual could be changed, reformers turned their energies to finding the right combination of moral influences and structured environments to improve human nature.

Reformers created, for example, highly ordered and disciplined penitentiaries as substitutes for failed parental discipline. Sincere reformation, rather than simple incarceration, became the goal. Solitary confinement would purge offenders' violent habits, reformers believed; at new prisons in Auburn and Ossining, New York, prisoners could neither speak nor look at one another during the day and spent their nights in small, windowless cells. Critics of the "Auburn system" preferred the "Pennsylvania system," in which each prisoner was isolated in a single cell and received no news or visits from the outside.

Antebellum America also witnessed a transformation in the treatment of the poor. The infirm poor crowded into almshouses, while the able-bodied poor entered workhouses. Idealistic reformers argued that taking the poor from demoralizing surroundings and putting them into such highly regimented institutions could change them into virtuous, productive citizens. But the results were often dismal. In 1833 a legislative committee found that

FOR FURTHER READING

Lee Benson, *The Concept of Jacksonian Democracy: New York as a Test Case* (1961). A major revisionist interpretation of the period.

William W. Freehling, *Prelude to Civil War* (1966). A major study of the nullification crisis.

Richard P. McCormick, *The Second American Party System: Party Formation in the Jacksonian Era* (1966). An influential work stressing the role of political leaders in shaping the second party system.

Edward Pessen, *Jacksonian America: Society, Personality, and Politics*, rev. ed. (1979). A comprehensive interpretation of the period, emphasizing the lack of real democracy in American society and politics.

Robert V. Remini, *Henry Clay: Statesman for the Union* (1991). An important new biography of the leading Whig statesman of the period.

Arthur M. Schlesinger Jr., *The Age of Jackson* (1945). A classic study, now dated in some of its interpretations but still highly readable.

Fred Somkin, *Unquiet Eagle: Memory and Desire in the Idea of American Freedom, 1815–1860* (1967). A penetrating study of American political values.

Ronald G. Walters, *American Reformers, 1815–1860* (1978). A balanced study that addresses the negative as well as the positive aspects of nineteenth-century reform.

Chilton Williamson, *American Suffrage: From Property to Democracy, 1760–1860* (1960). The standard study of changing requirements for voting.

CHAPTER 11

Life, Leisure, and Culture, 1840–1860

Americans, wrote Alexis de Tocqueville, "care but little for what has been, but they are haunted by visions of what will be." Belief in irreversible progress captivated Americans in the 1840s and 1850s. Each year advances in technology confirmed Thomas Jefferson's prediction that Europe "will have to lean on our shoulders and hobble by our side." Improvements in agriculture, industry, and transportation led to calls for the development of a distinctive American literary and artistic style, and writers and artists responded. For the most part Americans equated material, cultural, and moral progress; inventor Samuel F. B. Morse expected that his telegraph would end war.

But progress had a dark side. It neither prevented nor softened the economic depressions of the late 1830s and 1840s. Cholera epidemics demonstrated that diseases as well as people could travel swiftly by railroad and steamboat. Some leading writers questioned the easy assumption that material progress meant moral progress. And for the first time anxieties arose about the despoliation of the American landscape.

(Right) Family relaxing in their parlor, c. 1852

Technology and Economic Growth

As evidence of progressiveness, Americans increasingly pointed to the march of "technology," the use of scientific principles to transform the practical conveniences of life. "We have invented more useful machines within twenty years," a Bostonian reported, "than have been invented in all Europe."

To optimistic Americans, technology was both democratic and progressive. Machines would advance civilization because they could perform the work of ten people without needing food or clothing, Daniel Webster contended. A Lowell mill girl wrote, "It is emphatically the age of improvement. The arts and sciences have been more fully developed and the great mass of society are feeling its improvement."

Woman at Singer Sewing Machine

Asked to repair a sewing machine that did not do continuous stitching, Isaac M. Singer invented one that did. Patented in 1851, the Singer machine quickly dominated the market. Although most early sewing machines were used in factories, some had made their way into households by 1860.

The technology that transformed life in antebellum America included the steam engine, the cotton gin, the reaper, the use of interchangeable parts in manufacturing, the sewing machine, and the telegraph. Some of these originated in Europe, but Americans had a flair for investing in others' inventions and perfecting their own. Sadly, these advances did not benefit everyone. The cotton gin, for example, riveted slavery firmly in place by intensifying southern dependence on cotton. By rendering traditional skills obsolete, technology also undercut the position of artisans. Nonetheless, the improved transportation and increased productivity that technology made possible raised the living standards of a sizable body of free Americans between 1840 and 1860.

Agricultural Advancement

Although few settlers ventured onto the treeless, semiarid Great Plains before the Civil War, settlement edged west after 1830 from the woodlands of Ohio and Kentucky into parts of Indiana, Michigan, and Illinois where flat grasslands (prairies) alternated with forests. The prairies' matted soil was difficult to break for planting, but in 1837 John Deere invented a steel-tipped plow that halved the labor required to clear prairie for planting. Timber for housing and fencing was available near the prairies, and settlement occurred rapidly.

Wheat quickly became the Midwest's major cash crop. Technology eased the task of harvesting wheat. The traditional hand sickle consumed enormous amounts of time and labor and collecting and binding the cut wheat, even more. Experiments with horse-drawn machines to replace sickles had failed until Cyrus McCormick of Virginia developed the mechanical reaper. In 1834 McCormick patented his machine; in 1847 he opened a factory in

Chicago, and by 1860 he had sold 80,000 reapers. During the Civil War McCormick made immense profits by selling 250,000 reapers. The mechanical reaper, which harvested grain seven times faster than traditional methods with half the labor force, guaranteed that wheat would dominate the midwestern prairies.

Although Americans generally remained wasteful farmers—abundant cheap land made it more "practical" to move west than to try to improve played-out soil—a movement for more efficient cultivation developed before the Civil War, primarily in the East. Because eastern soils could not compete with fertile western lands, eastern farmers had little choice. For example, some farmers in Orange County, New York, fed their cattle only clover and bluegrass; combining better feed with an emphasis on cleanliness in processing dairy products, they could then charge twice as much as others for the superior butter they marketed. Virginia wheat growers fertilized their soil with plaster left over from construction of the James River Canal and raised their average yield 250 percent between 1800 and 1860. In the 1840s cotton planters began importing guano, the droppings of sea birds on islands off Peru, for use as a fertilizer. By applying fertilizers, eastern cotton growers could close the gap created by the superior fertility of soils in the Southwest.

Technology and Industrial Progress

The early growth of U.S. manufacturing relied primarily on imported technology. That dependence lessened during the 1830s as American industries became more innovative.

Eli Whitney had pioneered in the application of interchangeable parts in the United States in 1798, but the manufacture of guns and other products using interchangeable parts still required a great deal of handwork before the components could be fitted together. By the 1840s, however, American factories had eliminated the need for hand-fitting by improving the quality of machine tools. In 1853 the superintendent of the Springfield, Massachusetts, armory staged a spectacular demonstration of interchangeable parts for a British commission investigating American technology. Rifles that had been produced in ten consecutive years were stripped and their parts easily reassembled at random.

The American system of manufacturing offered multiple advantages. Damaged machines no longer had to be discarded but could be repaired simply by installing new parts. Improved machine tools allowed entrepreneurs to mass-produce new inventions rapidly, and the speed of production attracted investors. By the 1850s Connecticut firms, among them Smith and Wesson, were mass-producing the revolving pistol, which Samuel Colt had invented in 1836. Sophisticated machine tools made it possible to increase production "by confining a worker to one particular limb of a pistol until he had made two thousand." Elias Howe's sewing machine, invented in 1846, entered mass production only two years later.

Americans were eager to use technology to conquer time and space. An impatient people inhabiting a huge area, they seized enthusiastically on Samuel F.B. Morse's invention of the telegraph in 1844. A British engineer noted how quickly Americans adapted the invention: "A system of communication that annihilates distances was felt to be of vital importance, both politically and commercially, in a country so vast, and having a population so widely scattered." The speed with which Americans formed telegraph companies and strung lines stunned that same engineer. By 1852 more than 15,000 miles of lines connected cities as far-flung as Quebec, New Orleans, and St. Louis. And in 1857 a transatlantic cable linked New York and London for four months before snapping. (A new cable had to wait until 1867, after the Civil War.)

The Railroad Boom

The desire to conquer time and space also drove antebellum Americans to make an extraordinary investment in railroads. Even more than the telegraph, the railroad embodied progress through advances in technology.

In 1790 even European royalty could travel no faster than fourteen miles an hour and that only with frequent changes of horses. By 1850 an ordinary American could travel three times as fast on a train. The swift, comfortable transportation that American railroads provided for the common person dramatized technology's democratic promise. U.S. railroads offered only one class of travel, in contrast to the several classes on European railroads. With the introduction of adjustable upholstered seats that could serve as couches at night, every American in effect traveled first class—except for African-Americans, who often were forced to sit separately.

Americans loved railroads "as a lover loves his mistress," one Frenchman wrote, but there was little to love about the earliest railroads. Sparks from locomotives showered the passengers riding in open cars, which were common. Travelers sometimes had to get out and pull trains to stations. Lacking lights, trains rarely ran at night. Before the introduction of standard time zones in 1883 (see Chapter 18), scheduling was a nightmare; at noon in Boston it was twelve minutes before noon in New York City. Delays were frequent, for trains on single-track lines had to wait on sidings for other trains to pass. Because a train's location was a mystery once it had left the station, these waits could seem endless.

Between 1840 and 1860 the size of the rail network and the power and convenience of trains underwent stunning transformations. Railroad track went from 3,000 to 30,000 miles, flat-roofed coaches replaced open cars, kerosene lamps made night travel possible, and increasingly powerful engines let trains climb even the steepest hills. Fifty thousand miles of telegraph wire enabled dispatchers to communicate with trains en route and thus to reduce delays.

Problems nonetheless lingered. Sleeping accommodations remained crude, and schedules erratic. Because individual railroads used different gauge track, frequent changes of train were necessary: there were eight changes between Charleston and Philadelphia in the 1850s. Yet nothing slowed the advance of railroads or cured America's mania for them. By 1860 the United States had more track than all the rest of the world.

Railroads spearheaded the second phase of the transportation revolution. Canals remained in use, but railroads, both faster and less vulnerable to winter freezes, gradually overtook them, first in passengers and then in freight. By 1860 the value of goods transported by railroads greatly exceeded that carried by canals.

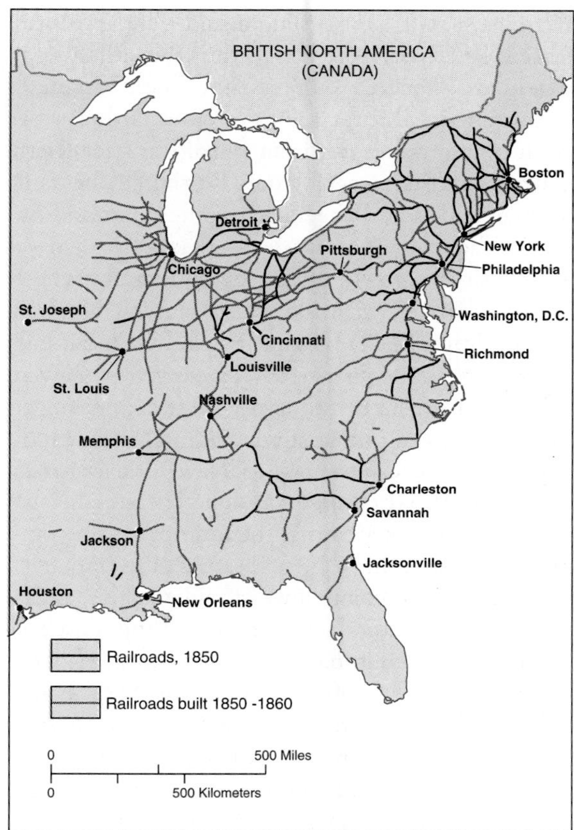

Railroad Growth, 1850–1860

Rail ties between the East and the Midwest greatly increased during the railroad "boom" of the 1850s.

During the 1850s the nation's rail net grew by 22,000 miles, and most of the expansion took place east of the Mississippi River. Cities such as Chicago, Chattanooga, and Atlanta boomed because of the railroads. Most important, the railroads crossed the Appalachian Mountains to link the East and the Midwest. The New York Central and the Erie railroads joined New York City to Buffalo; the Pennsylvania Railroad connected Philadelphia and

Pittsburgh; and the Baltimore and Ohio Railroad linked the Chesapeake Bay to the Ohio-Mississippi system at Wheeling, Virginia (now West Virginia). Trunk lines tied these routes to cities farther west. By 1860 rail routes ran from Buffalo to Cleveland, Toledo, and Chicago; from Pittsburgh to Fort Wayne; and from Wheeling to Cincinnati and St. Louis.

Chicago's growth illustrates the impact of these rail links. In 1849 it was a village of a few hundred people with virtually no rail service. By 1860 it had become a metropolis of 100,000, served by eleven railroads. Farmers in the upper Midwest no longer had to send their grain, livestock, and dairy products down the Mississippi to New Orleans; they could now ship their products directly east. Chicago supplanted New Orleans as the interior's main commercial hub.

The east-west rail lines stimulated the settlement and agricultural development of the Midwest. By 1860 Illinois, Indiana, and Wisconsin had replaced Ohio, Pennsylvania, and New York as the leading wheat-growing states. Enabling farmers to speed their produce to the East, railroads increased the value of farmland and promoted additional settlement. In turn, this population growth stimulated industrial development in cities such as Chicago and Minneapolis, for the new settlers needed lumber for fences and houses and mills to grind wheat into flour. Railroads also spurred the growth of small towns along their midwestern routes. Some lines, such as the Illinois Central, made profits from real-estate speculation. After purchasing land for stations along its route, the Illinois Central laid out towns around the stations and even stipulated street names. By the Civil War, few viewed the Midwest as a frontier or its inhabitants as pioneers.

As the nation's first big business, railroads transformed the conduct of business, particularly in finance. State money had helped to finance many lines, but by the 1840s it began to dry up. Federal aid would not be widely available until the Civil War. Although local and county governments tried to fill the void, the dramatic expansion of the rail net in the 1850s required new sources of financing. Private investors had long purchased railroad stock, but the large trunk lines of the 1850s needed far more capital than small investors could generate. Thus the railroads turned to the capital market in New York City. The railroad boom helped to make Wall Street the nation's greatest capital market, as the securities of all the leading railroads were traded on the floor of the New York Stock Exchange. New York also became the center of modern investment firms. These companies evaluated securities issued by railroads in Toledo or Chattanooga and then found purchasers in New York, Paris, London, and Amsterdam. Controlling the flow of funds to the railroads, investment bankers soon influenced their internal affairs. A Wall Street analyst noted in 1851 that railroad men seeking financing "must remember that money is power, and that the [financier] can dictate to a great extent his own terms."

Rising Prosperity

Technology also improved life by lowering prices. Clocks that cost $50 to make by hand in 1800 could be produced for 50¢ by 1850. Widespread use of steam power led to a 25 percent rise in the average worker's real income (purchasing power) between 1840 and 1860; unlike water wheels, steam engines could run in all seasons, and so workers did not have to face long winter layoffs. Although cotton textile workers saw little gain in hourly wages, their average annual wages rose from $160 to $201 between 1830 and 1869.

The growth of towns and cities also contributed to the upward trend in average annual wages. In contrast to rural farming areas, with their heavily seasonal labor, urban settings offered year-round opportunities for jobs. Towns and cities also provided women and children—who seldom were paid for farm labor—new opportunities for paid work. Children's wages played an important role in family finances for working-class families. An average New York or Philadelphia working-class family spent $500 to $600 per year on food, rent, clothing, and fuel. However, an average male head of household earned $300 a year. Clearly, the survival of many families depended on the wages of children and wives.

The average urban worker was marginally better off than the average rural worker, primarily because of seasonal fluctuations in agricultural work. Most antebellum Americans continued to see farming as the ideal occupation, but comparatively few could raise the $500 or so in cash necessary to purchase, clear, and stock a farm and then wait three to five years for any reward. The economic advantages of urban life explain in part why so many Americans moved to urban areas in the first half of the nineteenth century. So does the unprecedented range of comforts and conveniences that the city offered.

The Quality of Life

Subtle but critical changes in the quality of daily life accompanied the large-scale transformations in transportation, production, and income in the two decades before the Civil War. These changes occurred within the home and affected routine activities such as eating, drinking, and washing. Americans became far more comfortable as machine-made furniture, stoves, and fresh food entered the home.

But change occurred unevenly. Technology made it possible for the middle class to enjoy luxuries formerly reserved for the rich, yet it widened the gulf between middle class and poor. As middle-class homes became increasingly lavish, the urban poor crowded into cramped tenements. And some critical elements—medicine, for example—lagged far behind in the technological explosion. Nevertheless, Americans embraced the benefits of progress and ignored its limitations. Few accepted the possibility that progress could neglect such an important aspect of everyday life as health. Lacking medical advances, Americans embraced popular health movements that stressed diet and regimen over doctors.

Housing

During the early 1800s the unattached and distinctive wood-frame houses dotting colonial urban skylines yielded to quickly constructed, uniform-looking brick row houses. Where some praised the row houses as democratic, others condemned "their extreme uniformity—when you have seen one, you have seen all." The typical row house was narrow and long, fifteen to twenty feet across and thirty to forty feet from front to back. Most had open spaces in the rear for gardens, pigs, privies (outhouses), and cisterns (water-storage vessels). Middle-class row houses, with cast-iron balconies, elegant doors, and curved staircases emphasizing the owner's individuality and taste, were larger and more elaborate than those of the working class.

As land values soared (as much as 750 percent in Manhattan between 1785 and 1815), renting, rather than owning, homes became common. By 1815 more than half of the homes in large cities were rented. Skyrocketing land values also led to the subdivision of row houses for occupancy by several families. The worst of these, known as tenements, were the usual habitats of Irish immigrants and free blacks.

In rural areas the quality of housing depended as much on the date of settlement as on social class. In recently settled areas the standard dwelling was a one-room log cabin with split-log floors that allowed in drafts, roofs that let in snow, crude chimneys made of sticks and clay, and windows covered by oiled paper or cloth. As rural communities matured, log cabins gave way to frame houses of two or more rooms with glass windows and better insulation.

Home Furniture

Furniture also revealed the widening gap between the prosperous and the poor. Families in the middle and upper classes increasingly decorated their parlors with a style of furniture known as rococo. Such furniture was ornate and featured elaborately carved wooden frames supporting heavily upholstered backs and seats topped with medallions; vines, leaves, and flowers covered both wooden and upholstered surfaces. The fashion of the day required the crowding of seven matched pieces into the parlor. Contemporary style also dictated the hanging of mirrors with intricate gilded moldings depicting birds, flowers, and young women.

Such highly ornamental furniture marked its

possessors as people of substantial wealth. The rise of mass-produced furniture brought rococo style within the reach of the middle class, which could not afford to import furniture from France, as the wealthy did. Most Americans, however, were unable to afford either imported or domestic rococo and had to be content with simpler furniture. Technological advances in furniture making tended to level taste between the middle and upper classes while marking those classes off from everyone else.

Heating, Cooking, and Diet

The transportation and industrial revolutions also affected heating, cooking, and diet. Iron foundries took advantage of distant markets by specializing in the production of cast-iron stoves, which had displaced open hearths in urban areas by the late 1840s. Country dwellers continued to prefer open wood-fired hearths, partly because clearing farm land left abundant wood. City people, however, increasingly opted for coal-fired stoves. The discovery of high-grade hard coal in eastern Pennsylvania guaranteed a steady supply of the fuel.

Coal burned longer and hotter than wood and reduced the time and expense of acquiring fuel. The drawbacks of using coal, among them its sooty residue and the ever-present danger of carbon monoxide poisoning, paled beside its benefits, which included ease of cooking. With coal, open flames no longer threatened clothing and person, meals could be left unattended, and several dishes could be cooked at once on the stove. In this way stoves contributed to a growing variety in the American diet.

Meanwhile, better transportation brought a greater variety of foodstuffs to urban markets, particularly fresh vegetables. For most people, diet was still subject to seasonal fluctuation; only the rich could afford fruit out of season. Preserving any kind of food was a problem, for few homes had iceboxes—the forerunners of refrigerators—before 1860. Housewives could bury meat in the snow to keep it from spoiling, but salt remained the most widely used preservative. Americans ate far more pork than beef because salt affected the taste of pork less.

Water and Sanitation

Rural homes rarely had running water. Instead, water was brought in from wells, springs, or cisterns; once used, it was carried outside and dumped. But antebellum cities had begun constructing public waterworks to deal with threats to well water posed by leakage from outdoor privies. By 1823 Philadelphia had completed a system that brought water from the Schuylkill and Delaware rivers to street hydrants. Charles Dickens marveled that the city "is most bountifully provided with fresh water, which is showered and jerked about, and turned on, and poured off everywhere." By 1860 sixty-eight public water systems were operating in the United States.

Although public waterworks were engineering marvels, their impact was uneven. Most smaller cities had no waterworks before the Civil War, and even in New York less than a tenth of the city's population were customers of the water system. Few urban houses had running water, and so families carried water from street hydrants into their homes. Because hot running water was rare, the water had to be heated on the stove before one could take a bath. Not surprisingly, people rarely bathed.

Infrequent baths meant pungent body odors, but they mingled with a multitude of strong scents. Even fashionable residential streets contained stables backed by mounds of manure. Street cleaning was left to private contractors, who often discharged their duties casually, and so urban Americans relied on hogs, which they let roam freely to scavenge, for cleaning public thoroughfares. Outdoor privies added to the stench. Flush toilets were rare outside cities, and within cities sewer systems lagged behind water systems. Boston had only 5,000 flush toilets in 1860 for a population of 178,000, a far higher ratio of toilets to people than most cities. Americans normally answered calls of nature by trips to outdoor privies and suppressed their odors with shovelsful of dirt.

Stoves and other conveniences did little to liberate women from housework; they merely elevated the standards of housekeeping. Technology would let women fulfill their duty to make every house "a glorious temple." However, middle-class Americans boasted how comfortable their lives were becoming and pointed to the steady improvement in wages, diet, and water supplies as tangible marks of betterment.

Disease and Health

Despite the slowly rising living standard, Americans remained vulnerable to disease. Epidemic disease swept through antebellum American cities and felled thousands. Yellow fever and cholera killed one-fifth of New Orlean's population in 1832–1833, and cholera alone killed 10 percent of St. Louis's population in 1849.

Ironically, the transportation revolution increased the danger of epidemic diseases. The cholera epidemic of 1832, the first truly national epidemic, followed shipping routes: one branch of the epidemic ran from New York City up the Hudson River, across the Erie Canal to Ohio, and down the Ohio River to the Mississippi and New Orleans; the other branch followed shipping up and down the East Coast from New York.

The inability of physicians to explain epidemic diseases led to general distrust of the medical profession and to the making of public health a low-priority issue (see Chapter 9). No one understood that bacteria caused cholera and yellow fever. Instead, doctors debated the "contagion" theory versus the "miasm" theory of disease. Contagionists, who believed that touch spread disease, called for quarantines of affected areas. Supporters of the miasm theory argued that poisonous gases (miasms) emitted by rotten vegetation or dead animals carried disease through the air. They concluded that swamps had to be drained and streets cleaned. It quickly became apparent that neither theory worked.

Although epidemic disease baffled antebellum physicians, the discovery of anesthesia opened the way for remarkable advances in surgery. Laughing gas (nitrous oxide) had long provided partygoers who inhaled it enjoyable sensations of giddiness and painlessness, but it was difficult to handle. Crawford Long, a Georgia physician who had attended laughing gas frolics in his youth, employed sulfuric ether (an easily transportable liquid with the same properties as nitrous oxide) during surgery. Long did not follow up his discovery, but four years later William T.G. Morton, a dentist, successfully employed sulfuric ether during an operation at Massachusetts General Hospital. Within a few years ether was widely used.

The discovery of anesthesia improved the public image of surgeons, who had long been viewed as brutes hacking away at agonized patients. It also permitted longer and thus more careful operations. However, the failure of most surgeons to recognize the importance of clean hands and sterilized instruments partially offset the value of anesthesia. As early as 1843, Oliver Wendell Holmes Sr., a poet and physician, published a paper on how unclean hands spread puerperal fever among women giving birth, but disinfection was accepted only gradually. Operations remained as dangerous as the conditions they tried to heal. The mortality rate for amputations hovered around 40 percent, and during the Civil War 87 percent of soldiers who suffered abdominal wounds died from them.

Popular Health Movements

Doubtful of medicine and skeptical of the benefits of public health, antebellum Americans turned to various therapies that promised a longer, healthier life. Hydropathy, the "water cure," offered "an abundance of water of dewy softness and crystal transparency, to cleanse, renovate, and rejuvenate the disease-worn and dilapidated system." Well-to-do women flocked to hydropathic sanitoriums both to relieve pain and to enjoy relaxation and exercise in a congenial gathering place.

Sylvester Graham, a temperance reformer turned health advocate, popularized dietary changes as the way to better health. He urged Americans to eat less; to substitute vegetables, fruits, and whole-grain bread (called Graham bread) for meat; to abstain from spices, coffee, tea, and alcohol; and to avoid sexual "excess" (by which he meant most sex).

Reformers became enthusiastic proponents of Graham's ideas. Abolitionists and others agreed with Graham that Americans' unnatural cravings, whether for red meat or sex, stimulated violence and aggressive impulses. But Graham's doctrines also attracted a broad audience beyond the reform movements. His books sold well, and his public lectures were thronged. His commonsense ideas appealed to Americans wary of orthodox medicine, and he used familiar religious terms to describe disease, which was hell, and health, which amounted to a kind of heaven on earth. Graham provided simple assurances to an audience as ignorant as he was of disease's true causes.

Phrenology

The belief that each person was master of his or her own destiny underlay not only evangelical religion and health movements but also the most popular of the antebellum scientific fads: phrenology. Created by a Viennese physician, Franz J. Gall, phrenology rested on the idea that the human mind comprised thirty-seven distinct faculties, or "organs," each localized in a different part of the brain. Phrenologists thought that the degree of each organ's development determined skull shape, so that they could accurately analyze an individual's character by examining the bumps and depressions of the skull.

In the United States two brothers, Orson and Lorenzo Fowler, became the chief promoters of phrenology in the 1840s. Orson Fowler was a missionary of sorts for phrenology, opening a publishing house (Fowlers and Wells) that marketed phrenology books everywhere. The Fowlers met criticisms that phrenology was godless by pointing out a huge organ called "Veneration" to prove that people were naturally religious, and they answered charges that phrenology was pessimistic by claiming that exercise could improve every desirable mental organ. Lorenzo Fowler reported that several of his own skull bumps had grown.

Phrenology appealed to Americans as a "practical" science. In a mobile, individualistic society, it promised a quick assessment of others. Merchants sometimes used phrenological charts to hire clerks, and some young women even induced their fiancés to undergo a phrenological analysis before marriage.

Phrenologists had close ties to popular health movements. Fowlers and Wells published the *Water-Cure Journal* and Sylvester Graham's *Lectures on the Science of Human Life*. Orson Fowler filled his popular phrenological books with tips on the evils of coffee, tea, meat, spices, and sex that could have been plucked from Graham's writings. Phrenology shared with the health movement the belief that anyone could understand and obey the "laws" of life.

Unlike hydropathy, phrenology required no money; unlike Grahamism, it required no abstinence. Easily understood and practiced, and filled with the promise of universal betterment, phrenology was ideal for antebellum America. Just as Americans had invented machines to better their lives, they could invent "sciences" that promised human betterment.

Democratic Pastimes

Between 1830 and 1860 technology transformed recreation into a commodity that could be purchased in the form of cheap newspapers and novels and equally cheap tickets to plays, museums, and lectures. Imaginative entrepreneurs seized technology to make and sell entertainment. Fortunes awaited men who could sense what people wanted and who could use available technology to satisfy them. James Gordon Bennett, one of the founders of the penny press, and P. T. Barnum, the greatest showman of the century, made the public want what they had to sell.

Bennett and Barnum saw themselves as purveyors of democratic entertainment: they sold their wares cheaply to anyone. Barnum's American Museum in New York City catered to varied social classes that paid to see paintings, dwarfs, mammoth bones, and other attractions. By marketing his museum as a family entertainment, Barnum helped to break down barriers between pastimes of husband and wife. Racy news stories in Bennett's *New York Herald* provided a vast audience with common information and topics of conversation.

Technology also changed the way Americans amused themselves. People had long found ways to enjoy themselves, and even the gloomiest Puritans had indulged in games and sports. After 1830, however, individuals increasingly became spectators rather than creators of amusements, relying on entrepreneurs who supplied entertainment.

Newspapers

In 1830 the typical American newspaper was four pages long, with the front and back pages filled almost completely with advertisements. The interior pages contained editorials, reprints of political speeches, notices of political events, and information about shipping. Even the most prominent papers had a daily circulation of only 1,000 to 2,000; subsidies from political parties or factions supported them. "Journalists," a contemporary wrote, "were usually little more than secretaries dependent upon cliques of politicians, merchants, brokers, and office seekers for their prosperity and bread."

Because they could be profitable without being popular, most early newspapers had limited appeal. Priced at six cents an issue, the average paper was too expensive for a worker who earned less than a dollar a day. Moreover, with few eye-catching news stories or illustrations, papers seemed little more than bulletin boards.

In the 1830s technology began to transform newspapers. Cheaper paper and steam-driven presses drastically lowered production costs, and enterprising journalists, among them James Gordon Bennett, saw the implications: slash prices, boost circulation, and reap vast profits. In 1833 New York's eleven daily newspapers had a combined daily circulation of only 26,500. Two years later the combined circulation of the three largest "penny" newspapers had soared to 44,000. From 1830 to 1840 national newspaper circulation rose from 78,000 to 300,000, and the number of weekly newspapers more than doubled.

The penny press also revolutionized the marketing and format of newspapers. Newsboys hawked the penny papers on busy street corners, and reporters filled the papers with gripping news stories designed to attract readers. As sociologist Michael Schudson observes, "The penny press invented the modern concept of 'news.' " The penny papers also used the telegraph to speed both news and human-interest stories to readers.

Some penny papers were little more than scandal sheets, but others, such as Bennett's *New York Herald* and Horace Greeley's *New York Tribune*, pioneered modern financial and political reporting. The *Herald* featured a daily "money article" that analyzed and interpreted financial events. "The spirit, pith, and philosophy of commercial affairs is what men of business want," Bennett wrote. The relentless snooping by the *Tribune's* Washington reporters outraged politicians. In 1841 *Tribune* correspondents were temporarily barred from the House of Representatives for reporting that an Ohio representative ate his lunch in the House chamber, picked his teeth with a jackknife, and wiped his greasy hands on his pants and coat.

The Popular Novel

Novels became affordable and enormously popular between 1830 and 1860. In the 1830s technology and transportation began to lower the price of novels, and in the 1840s cheap paperbacks selling for as little as seven cents flooded the national market. Serial versions appeared in newspapers devoted mainly to printing novels.

Sentimental novels dominated the fiction market in the 1840s and 1850s. The tribulations of orphans and deaths of children filled the pages of these tearjerkers. In Susan Warner's *The Wide, Wide World,* the heroine bursts into tears on an average of every other page for two volumes. Another popular writer, Lydia Sigourney, wrote a poem on a canary accidentally starved to death.

Women constituted the main audience for sentimental novels; these works were written by women, about women, and mainly for women. Writing, the most lucrative occupation open to women prior to the Civil War, attracted those desperately in need of cash. Susan Warner, for example, raised in luxury, had been thrown into poverty by her family's ruin in the Panic of 1839. Mrs. E. D. E. N. Southworth turned to writing after a broken marriage left her supporting two children on a teacher's salary of $250 a year.

A major theme in the novels of Warner, Southworth, and their female contemporaries was that women could conquer any obstacle. These novels challenged stereotypes of men as trusty providers and of women as delicate dependents. Instead, men were portrayed as liars, drunken lechers, and vicious misers and women as resourceful and strong-willed. A typical plot featured a female orphan or a spoiled rich girl thrown on hard times or a dutiful daughter plagued by a drunken father. Each learned to master her life. The moral was clear: women could overcome trials and make the world a better place.

The Theater

During the 1850s popular novelists such as Charles Dickens and Harriet Beecher Stowe were as well known through dramatizations of their work as through sales of their books. Antebellum theaters were large and crowded; cheap seats drew a democratic throng of lawyers and merchants and their wives, artisans and clerks, sailors and noisy boys, and a sizable body of prostitutes. The presence of prostitutes in the audience was only one of many factors that made theaters vaguely disreputable. Theater audiences were notoriously rowdy: they stamped their feet, hooted at villains, and threw potatoes and garbage at the stage when they disliked the characters or the acting.

Actors developed huge followings. In 1849 a long-running feud between leading American actor Edwin Forrest and popular British actor William Macready ended with a riot in New York City that left twenty people dead. The riot demonstrated theater's broad popularity. Forrest's supporters included Irish workers who loathed the British and who appealed to "working men" to rally against the "aristocrat" Macready. Macready, projecting a polished, intellectual image, attracted the better-educated classes. Had not all classes patronized the theater, the riot probably never would have occurred.

The plays themselves were as diverse as the audiences. Melodramas, whose plots resembled those of sentimental novels, were popular; vice was punished, virtue was rewarded, and the heroine married the hero. Yet the single most popular dramatist was William Shakespeare. In 1835 Philadelphia audiences witnessed sixty-five performances of his plays. Shakespeare himself might not have recognized some of these performances, adapted as they were for popular audiences. Theatrical managers highlighted swordfights and assassinations, cut long speeches, and changed tragic endings to happy ones. Producers arranged for short performances or demonstrations between acts. In the middle of *Macbeth,* the audience might see an impersonation of Tecumseh or of Aaron Burr, jugglers and acrobats, a drummer beating twelve drums at once, or a three-year-old who weighed one hundred pounds.

Minstrel Shows

The minstrel shows that Americans flocked to see in the 1840s and 1850s forged enduring stereotypes that buttressed white Americans' sense of superiority by diminishing blacks. The shows arose in northern cities in the 1840s as blackfaced white men took the stage to present an evening of songs, dances, and humorous sketches.

Although the performances featured elements of African-American culture, especially dance steps,

Dan Bryant, the Minstrel

Bryant was one of many antebellum popularizers of black minstrelsy. One of the earliest known minstrelsy performances occurred in Boston in 1799 when a white man, Gottlieb Graupner, reportedly made up as a black, sang and accompanied himself on the banjo.

most of the songs were from white culture. Stephen Foster's "Camptown Races" and "Massa's in the Cold, Cold Ground," first performed in minstrel shows, reflected whites' notions of how blacks sang, not authentic black music. The images of blacks projected by minstrelsy catered to the prejudices of the working-class whites who dominated the audiences. Minstrel troupes depicted blacks as stupid, clumsy, and obsessively musical and emphasized their Africanness. At a time of intensifying political conflict over race, minstrel shows planted images and expectations about blacks' behavior through stock characters such as Uncle Ned, the tattered, humble, and docile slave; and Zip Coon, the arrogant urban free black who paraded around in a high hat and long-tailed coat and lived off his girlfriends' money.

P. T. Barnum

No one understood better than P.T. Barnum how to turn the public's craving for entertainment into a profitable business. He was simultaneously a hustler who cheated his customers before they could cheat him and an idealist who founded a newspaper to attack wrongdoing and who thought of himself as a public benefactor.

After moving to New York City in 1834, Barnum began his career as an entrepreneur of entertainment. His first venture exhibited an African-American woman, Joyce Heth, whom Barnum billed as the 169-year-old former slave nurse of George Washington. In Barnum's mind, the truth or falsehood of the claim was irrelevant. What mattered was that people would pay. It was the beginning of a lifelong game between Barnum and the public.

In 1841 Barnum purchased a run-down museum in New York City, rechristened it the American Museum, and opened a new chapter in the history of popular entertainment. Avoiding the educational slant of other museums, Barnum concentrated on curiosities and faked exhibits; he wanted to interest people, not to educate them. The American Museum included ventriloquists, magicians, albinos, a five-year-old midget named Tom Thumb, and the "Feejee Mermaid," a shrunken oddity "taken alive in the Feejee Islands." By 1850 Barnum's entertainment emporium was the best-known museum in the nation.

A genius at publicity, Barnum recognized that newspapers could invent as well as report news. Thus he frequently wrote letters (under various names) to newspapers hinting that the scientific world was agog over some astonishing curiosity that the public could soon view at the American Museum. Barnum's success rested on more than people's curiosity, however. A temperance advocate, he provided lectures on the evils of alcohol and gave the place a reputation as a center for safe family amusement. In addition, Barnum tapped the public's insatiable appetite for natural wonders. At a time when each year brought new technological marvels, Americans would believe in anything, even the Feejee Mermaid.

The Quest for Nationality in Literature and Art

Sentimental novels, melodramas, minstrel shows, and the American Museum belonged to the world of popular culture. They did not represent the serious culture in which many Americans sought to reflect the American spirit. During the 1830s Ralph Waldo Emerson emerged as the most influential spokesman for those who sought a national literature and art.

"The American Scholar," an address by Emerson in 1837, constituted an intellectual Declaration of Independence. His message had an electrifying effect. Americans had too long deferred to European precedents, he proclaimed. The democratic spirit of the age had made Americans more self-reliant, and the time had come for them to break free of European standards and to trust themselves. In addition, Emerson's address adopted romanticism, the major intellectual movement of the first half of the nineteenth century, which celebrated the nation and the individual. Rejecting the idea of universal standards, romantics first in Europe and then in the United States insisted that great literature had to reflect both the national character and the author's emotions.

The transcendentalism of Emerson and his colleagues formed a uniquely American romanticism. Transcendentalists argued that knowledge went beyond, or transcended, the intellect. Like sight, it was an instantaneous, direct perception of truth. Intuition and emotion could provide knowledge as accurately as intellect could. Emerson concluded that learned people had no special advantage in the pursuit of truth. Rather, truth itself was democratic—all could see the truth if only they would trust the promptings of their hearts. Transcendentalist doctrine led to the exhilarating belief that a young, democratic society such as the United States could produce as noble a literature and art as the established societies of Europe simply by drawing on the inexhaustible resources of the common people.

Literary Geography

"The American Scholar" coincided with the American Renaissance, a flowering of art and literature that had been gaining momentum since the 1820s.

New England's rocky soil had proved fertile ground for literature. Its poets ranged from the urbane Henry Wadsworth Longfellow to the self-taught Quaker John Greenleaf Whittier. Boston was home to George Bancroft, Francis Parkman, William Hickling Prescott, and John Lothrop Motley, the four most distinguished historians of the age. Twenty miles from Boston lay Concord, where Emerson, Nathaniel Hawthorne, the eccentric Henry David Thoreau, and the brilliant philosopher Margaret Fuller lived. Close by was Fruitlands, a utopian community where Louisa May Alcott had spent part of her childhood. West of that lay Amherst, where the shy, reclusive, and brilliant poet Emily Dickinson lived her entire fifty-six years on the same street.

New York, home to Washington Irving, James Fenimore Cooper, Walt Whitman, and Herman Melville, supported a flourishing literary culture. Southerners, including William Gilmore Simms, acquired national reputations. Virginia-born Edgar Allan Poe did most of his writing in New York and Philadelphia.

Many reputations that burned brightly in nineteenth-century America have dimmed, but the genius of seven writers continues to gleam: Cooper, Emerson, Thoreau, Whitman, Hawthorne, Melville, and Poe. Cooper and Emerson were the only writers who basked in public esteem in their day;

neither Hawthorne nor Poe gained the audience that each believed he deserved, and the antebellum public largely ignored Thoreau and Whitman. Melville's light works were popular, but his serious fiction received little acclaim. Creativity, not popularity, linked these seven writers. Each challenged existing literary conventions and created new ones.

James Fenimore Cooper and the Stirrings of Literary Independence

Until well after 1800 British literature dominated American literary taste. Sir Walter Scott's historical novel *Waverly* (1814) had catapulted the British author to enduring fame and influence in America and created a demand for historical novels. Born in 1789, James Fenimore Cooper, called the American Scott because he wrote historical novels, introduced American characters and American themes to literature. In his frontiersman Natty Bumppo, "Leatherstocking," Cooper created an American archetype. Natty first appears in *The Pioneers* (1823) as an old man, a former hunter, who blames the farmers for wantonly destroying upstate New York's game and turning the silent and majestic forests into deserts of tree stumps. As a spokesman for nature against the march of civilization, Natty became a highly popular figure, and his life unfolded in several other enormously popular novels, such as *The Last of the Mohicans* (1826), *The Pathfinder* (1840), and *The Deerslayer* (1841). The prolific Cooper averaged a novel a year for thirty-four years and said that he found it harder to read his novels than to write them.

The success of James Fenimore Cooper and other early-nineteenth-century writers was the first step in the development of an American literature. Americans still read British novels, but more and more they enjoyed American authors. In 1800 American authors had accounted for a negligible proportion of the output of American publishers, but by 1830, 40 percent of the books published in the United States were written by Americans and by 1850, 75 percent.

Emerson, Thoreau, and Whitman

Ralph Waldo Emerson's advocacy of a national literature extended beyond "The American Scholar." In his own writing he tried to capture the brisk language of the common people, and he also encouraged younger writers, among them Thoreau and Whitman. Whitman, extravagantly patriotic, contrasted sharply with Emerson and Thoreau, who criticized the materialism and aggressiveness of their compatriots. But all three shared a common trait: their uniquely American work emphasized the spontaneous and vivid expression of personal feeling rather than learned analysis.

Born in 1803, Emerson had served briefly as a Unitarian minister before fashioning a career as a public lecturer. Pungency and vividness characterized his lectures, which Emerson published as essays. The true scholar, he stressed, must be independent: "Let him not quit his belief that a popgun is a popgun, though the ancient and honorable of the earth affirm it to be the crack of doom." A transcendentalist who believed that knowledge reflected the voice of God within every person and that truth was inborn and universal, Emerson relied not on a systematic analysis of the world around him but on vivid and arresting—although unconnected—assertions. Listening to Emerson, someone said, was like trying to see the sun in a fog; one could see light but never the sun.

In addition to dazzling his audiences, Emerson had a magnetic attraction for young intellectuals ill at ease in conventional society. Henry David Thoreau, born in 1817, typified the younger Emersonians. Unlike Emerson, whose adventurousness was largely intellectual, Thoreau was both a thinker and a doer. At one point he went to jail rather than pay poll taxes that would support the Mexican War, a conflict that he saw as part of a southern conspiracy to extend slavery. The experience of jail led Thoreau to write *Civil Disobedience* (1849), in which he defended disobedience of unjust laws.

In spring 1845 Thoreau moved a few miles from Concord into the woods near Walden Pond. He constructed a simple cabin on land owned by Emer-

Louisa May Alcott, c. 1858
Raised in bleak, if genteel, poverty, Louisa May Alcott first gained recognition for her sketches of her experiences as a nurse in a military hospital during the Civil War. The publication of Little Women, *her largely autobiographical novel of New England family life, brought her fame and enough money to support herself and her sisters.*

son and spent the next two years providing for his wants away from civilization. Thoreau's stated purpose for his retreat to Walden was to write a book about a canoe trip that he and his brother had taken, but he soon discovered a larger purpose and undertook a much more important book. *Walden* (1854), although it abounded with descriptions of nature and wildlife, carried a larger, transcendentalist message. Thoreau proclaimed that his woodland retreat had taught him that only a few weeks' work was needed to satisfy material needs; most of the year could be used to examine life's purpose. The problem with Americans, he wrote, was that they turned themselves into "mere machines" to acquire wealth without asking why. Thoreau prodded Americans with the uncomfortable truth that material progress and moral progress were not as intimately related as they liked to think.

Emerson sympathized with personalities as dissimilar but distinctively American as Thoreau and Walt Whitman—the former was eccentric, reclusive, and critical, the latter was self-taught, exuberant, outgoing, and in love with everything American except slavery. A journalist and fervent Democrat, Whitman had an intimate, affectionate knowledge of ordinary Americans. His reading of Emerson nurtured his belief that the United States would be the cradle of a new citizen in whom natural virtue would flourish. The threads of Whitman's early career came together in his major work, *Leaves of Grass,* a book of poems first published in 1855.

Leaves of Grass shattered existing poetic conventions. Whitman composed in free verse, and his blunt, often lusty words assailed "delicacy." He wrote of "the scent of these armpits finer than prayer" and "winds whose soft-tickling genitals rub against me." Whitman became the subject as well as the writer of his poems, especially in "Song of Myself." He saw himself—crude, plain, self-taught, passionately democratic—as the personification of the American people.

To some contemporary critics, *Leaves of Grass* seemed the work of an escaped lunatic. One derided it as a "heterogeneous mass of bombast, egotism, vulgarity, and nonsense." Emerson and a few others, however, reacted enthusiastically. Emerson had long awaited the appearance of "the poet of America" and knew immediately that in Whitman that poet had arrived.

Hawthorne, Melville, and Poe

Emerson's call on American writers to create a democratic literature by comprehending "the near, the low, the common" had a negligible impact on the major fiction writers during the 1840s and 1850s: Nathaniel Hawthorne, Herman Melville, and Edgar Allan Poe. Hawthorne, for example, set *The Scarlet Letter* (1850) in New England's Puritan past, *The House of the Seven Gables* (1851) in a mansion haunted by memories of the past, and *The Mar-*

ble Faun (1859) in Rome. Poe set several of his short stories in Europe; and Melville's novels *Typee* (1846), *Omoo* (1847), and *Mardi* (1849) took place in the exotic South Seas, and his masterpiece, *Moby-Dick* (1851), aboard a whaler.

In part, these three writers felt that American life lacked the materials for great fiction. Hawthorne bemoaned the difficulty of writing about a country "where there is no shadow, no antiquity, no mystery, no picturesque and gloomy wrong." Psychology, not society, fascinated these writers. Each probed the depths of the human mind rather than the intricacies of social relationships. Their preoccupation with analyzing the characters' mental states grew out of their underlying pessimism about the human condition. All three viewed individuals as bundles of conflicting forces that might never be reconciled.

Pessimism led them to create characters obsessed by pride, guilt, a desire for revenge, or a quest for perfection and then to set their stories along the byways of society, where the authors could freely explore the complexities of human motivation without the jarring intrusions of everyday life. For example, in *The Scarlet Letter* Hawthorne returned to the Puritan era in order to examine the psychological and moral consequences of the adultery committed by Hester Prynne and the minister Arthur Dimmesdale, although he devoted little attention to depicting the Puritan village in which the action takes place. Melville, in *Moby-Dick*, created the frightening Captain Ahab, whose relentless pursuit of a white whale fails to fill the chasm in his soul and brings death to all his crew except the narrator. Poe, too, channeled his pessimism into creative work of the first rank. In his short story "The Fall of the House of Usher" (1839), he interwove the symbol of a crumbling mansion with the mental agony of a crumbling family.

Although these three authors ignored Emerson's call to write about the everyday experiences of their fellow Americans, they fashioned a distinctively American fiction. Their works, preoccupied with analysis of moral dilemmas and psychological states, fulfilled Tocqueville's prediction that writers in democratic nations, while rejecting traditional sources of fiction, would explore the abstract and universal questions of human nature.

American Landscape Painting

American painters between 1820 and 1860 also sought to develop nationality in their work. Lacking a mythic past of gods and goddesses, they subordinated historical and figure painting to landscape painting. The American landscape, though barren of the "poetry of decay" that Europe's ruined castles and crumbling temples provided, was fresh and relatively unencumbered by the human imprint. These conditions posed a challenge to the painters of the Hudson River school, which flourished from the 1820s to the 1870s. Its best-known representatives—Thomas Cole, Asher Durand, and Frederic Church—painted scenes of the unspoiled region around the Hudson River.

The works of Washington Irving and the opening of the Erie Canal had piqued interest in the Hudson during the 1820s. Then, after 1830 Emerson and Thoreau lauded primitive nature; "in wildness is the preservation of the world," Thoreau wrote. By this time, much of the original American forest already had fallen to pioneer axes, and one writer urgently concluded that "it behooves our artists to rescue from [civilization's] grasp the little that is left before it is too late."

The Hudson River painters did more than preserve a passing wilderness; they also emphasized emotional effect. Cole's rich colors; billowing clouds; massive, gnarled trees; towering peaks; and deep chasms so heightened the dramatic impact of his paintings that poet William Cullen Bryant compared them to "acts of religion." In powerful, evocative canvases, American artists aimed to capture the natural grandeur of their land.

Like Cole, George Catlin tried to preserve a vanishing America through his art. His goal was to paint as many Native Americans as possible in their pure and "savage" state. By 1837 he had created 437 oil paintings and thousands of sketches of faces and customs from nearly fifty tribes. Catlin's romantic view of the Indians as noble savages was a double-edged sword. His admirers delighted in his dignified portrayals of Indians but shared his foreboding that the march of progress had already doomed these noble creatures to oblivion.

Landscape architects tried to create small enclaves of nature to provide spiritual refreshment to harried city dwellers. "Rural" cemetaries with pastoral names such as Harmony Grove, placed near major cities, became tourist attractions, designed as much for the living as for the dead. On a grander scale Frederick Law Olmsted and Calvert Vaux designed New York City's Central Park to look like undisturbed countryside. Drainage pipes carried water to man-made lakes, and trees screened out the surrounding buildings. Central Park became an idealized version of nature, meant to remind visitors of landscapes that they had seen in pictures. Thus nature was made to mirror art.

The Diffusion of Knowledge

Just as Emerson contended that the democratizing spirit of his age would encourage Americans to discover their cultural identity, many of his contemporaries argued that the educated had a duty to "diffuse," or spread, enlightenment among the common people. Some believed that inexpensive books and magazines would bring fine literature to the masses, but others thought that only organized efforts could instruct and uplift American minds.

Advocates of systematic popular instruction turned to both public schools and lyceums, local organizations that sponsored public lectures on topics as diverse as astronomy, biology, physiology, geology, memory, Iceland, the true mission of women, and the domestic life of the Turks. Audiences usually included professional men, merchants, farmers, artisans, and middle-class women. The lecturers mirrored their audiences' diversity. After 1840 the spread of railroads contributed to the rise of a group of nationally known lecturers, including Ralph Waldo Emerson. Tickets cost as little as 12¢ but the crowds were so large that some lecturers could command the then astounding fee of $250 per talk.

Not only railroads but also the growth of public education and the advent of low-priced newspapers and books helped to bring audiences and lecturers together. Originating in New England, lyceums expanded across the northern states and made inroads into the South. Their spread revealed a popular hunger for knowledge and refinement. By 1840, 3,500 towns had lyceums, yet in that year's presidential election, the Whigs' log cabin campaign blasted Democratic candidate Martin Van Buren for displays of refinement. Americans were clearly of two minds on the subject of learning. Nowhere was this ambivalence sharper than in the West. Westerners prided themselves on their rough ways, but eastern missionaries swarmed across the West to build not only lyceum halls but also academies and colleges. In 1800 there was only one college in what is now the Midwest; by 1850 there were nearly seventy, more than in any other region. Audiences flocked to listen to emissaries of eastern refinement.

The movement to popularize knowledge and art bridged the cultural gap between classes but never closed it. The popularization of culture carried a hidden price, as lyceum lecturers usually softened their ideas to avoid controversy. Even Emerson, whose early pronouncements on religion were controversial, pulled his punches on the lyceum circuit; his vagueness of style made it possible to quote him on both sides of most issues.

CONCLUSION

Hailed as progressive and democratic, advances in technology transformed the lives of millions of Americans between 1840 and 1860. Mechanical reapers increased the food supply, steam power drove up productivity and income, and coal-burning stoves brought warmer homes and a better diet to millions of people. Even leisure felt the impact of technology, which brought down the cost of printing, stimulated the rise of the penny press and the dime novel, expanded the size of the reading public, and encouraged efforts to popularize knowledge.

The bright possibilities, rather than the dark potential, of technology impressed most antebellum Americans, but technology neither erased class and ethnic differences nor quieted a growing conflict between North and South. As the penny press and the telegraph spread, Americans discovered that speedier communication could not bridge their differences over slavery.

CHRONOLOGY

1820 Washington Irving, *The Sketch Book*.

1823 Philadelphia completes the first urban water-supply system.

1826 Josiah Holbrook introduces the idea for lyceums. James Fenimore Cooper, *The Last of the Mohicans*.

1832 A cholera epidemic strikes the United States.

1833 The *New York Sun*, the first penny newspaper, is established.

1834 Cyrus McCormick patents the mechanical reaper.

1835 James Gordon Bennett establishes the *New York Herald*.

1837 Ralph Waldo Emerson, "The American Scholar."

1839 Edgar Allan Poe, "The Fall of the House of Usher."

1841 P. T. Barnum opens the American Museum.

1844 Samuel F. B. Morse patents the telegraph. The American Art Union is established.

1846 W. T. G. Morton successfully uses anesthesia.

1849 Second major cholera epidemic.

1850 Nathaniel Hawthorne, *The Scarlet Letter*.

1851 Hawthorne, *The House of the Seven Gables*. Herman Melville, *Moby-Dick*.

1853 Ten small railroads are consolidated into the New York Central Railroad.

1854 Henry David Thoreau, *Walden*.

1855 Walt Whitman, *Leaves of Grass*.

1857 Baltimore–St. Louis rail service completed.

FOR FURTHER READING

Carl Bode, *The Anatomy of American Popular Culture, 1840–1861* (1959). A useful general survey.

Mary Kupiec Cayton, *Emerson's Emergence: Self and Society in the Transformation of New England* (1989). A sensitive interpretaion of the major figure in the American Renaissance.

William Cronon, *Chicago and the Great West* (1991). Analysis emphasizing environmental factors in the emergence of Chicago as the dominant city in the mid-nineteenth-century West.

Ann Douglas, *The Feminization of American Culture* (1977). An analysis of the role of the middle-class women and liberal ministers in the cultural sphere during the nineteenth century.

Siegfried Giedion, *Mechanization Takes Command* (1948). An interpretive overview of the impact of technology on Europe and America.

Barbara Novak, *Nature and Culture: American Landscape Painting, 1825–1875* (1982). An insightful study of the relationships between landscape painting and contemporary religious and philosophical currents.

Gwendolyn Wright, *Building the Dream: A Social History of Housing in America* (1981). An exploration of the ideologies and policies that have shaped American housing since Puritan times.

CHAPTER 12

The Old South and Slavery, 1800–1860

During winter 1831–1832 an intense debate over the future of slavery raged across Virginia. In part, the debate was a continuation of discussions begun during the Revolution; in part, it sprang from the anxieties created by an August 1831 slave insurrection led by Nat Turner. Virginians advanced various plans for the slaves' emancipation, and opponents of slavery, many of them nonslaveholders from western Virginia, briefly held the initiative. Slavery was denounced as "a mildew which has blighted in its course every region it has touched from the creation of the world."

The ultimate victory of proslavery forces in the Virginia legislature marked a point of no return in U.S. history. From this time on southern society increasingly diverged from the rest of the nation; the word *South* referred to a distinct political and economic region. The key to defining the South was the institution of slavery. Although slavery had been spread throughout all thirteen colonies, by the early 1830s it had been banned in every

(Right) **Charlotte Helen and Her Faithful Nurse, Lydia,** *1857*

northern state and outlawed in the entire British Empire. Opposition to slavery continued to intensify in the United States, Europe, and South America—but not in the South. As Senator James Buchanan of Pennsylvania observed in 1842, "All Christendom is leagued against the South upon the question of domestic slavery."

However, even within the South there existed profound divisions between the slaveholders, who were in the minority, and the nonslaveholders, who made up the majority of the population. Their common race, not slavery, bound them together. Similarly, major differences separated the Upper South (Virginia, North Carolina, Tennessee, and Arkansas) from the Lower South (South Carolina, Georgia, Florida, Alabama, Mississippi, Louisiana, and Texas). Nonetheless, the ties created by slavery powerfully bound the two Souths together.

African-Americans could do little to escape bondage directly. But they defied its most devastating effects indirectly by creating strong families (often extended to include nonblood members) and by undermining the system through sabotage and through the vitality of a distinctive black culture.

Slavery shaped and scarred all social relationships in the Old South: between blacks and whites, among whites, and even among blacks. Without slavery, there would never have been an Old South.

King Cotton

In 1790 the South was essentially stagnant. Tobacco, its primary cash crop, had lost its economic

Growth of Cotton Production and the Slave Population, 1790–1860

Cotton and slavery rose together in the Old South.

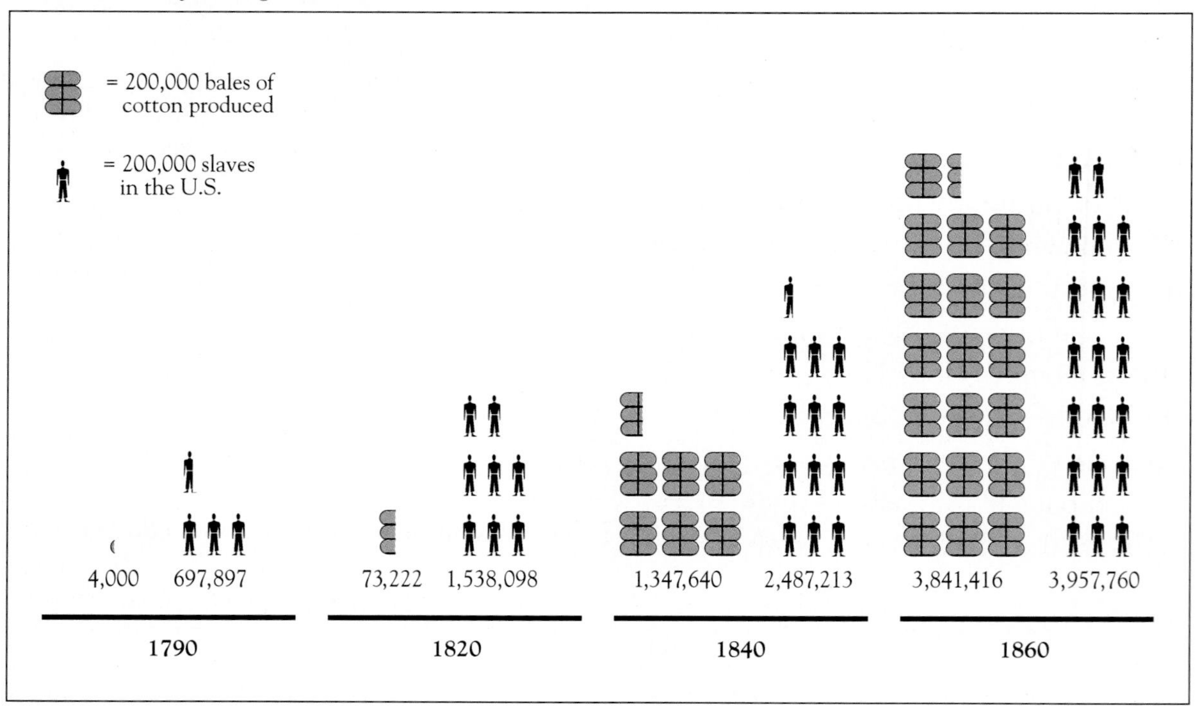

vitality even as it had depleted the once-rich southern soils, and neither rice nor cotton could replace tobacco's economic importance. Three out of four southerners still lived along the Atlantic seaboard, specifically in the Chesapeake and the Carolinas. One of three resided in Virginia alone.

The contrast between that South and the dynamic South of 1850 was stunning. By 1850 southerners had moved south and west—now only one of seven southerners lived in Virginia—and cotton reigned as king, shaping this new South. The growth of the British textile industry had created a huge demand for cotton, while Indian removal had made way for southern expansion into the "Cotton Kingdom," a broad swath of land that stretched from South Carolina, Georgia, and northern Florida in the east through Alabama, Mississippi, central and western Tennessee, and Louisiana, and from there on to Arkansas and Texas.

The Lure of Cotton

To the British traveler Basil Hall, southerners talked incessantly of cotton. "Every flow of wind from the shore wafted off the smell of that useful plant; at every dock or wharf we encountered it in huge piles or pyramids of bales, and our decks were soon choked with it. All day, . . . the captain, pilot, crew, and passengers were talking of nothing else." A warm climate, wet springs and summers, and relatively dry autumns made the Lower (or Deep) South ideal for cultivating cotton. A cotton farmer needed neither slaves nor cotton gins nor the capital required for sugar cultivation. Indeed, perhaps 50 percent of farmers in the "cotton belt" owned no slaves, and to process their harvest, they could turn to the widely available commercial gins. In short, cotton profited everyone; it promised to make poor men prosperous and rich men kings.

Yet large-scale cotton cultivation and slavery grew together as the southern slave population nearly doubled between 1810 and 1830. Three-fourths of all southern slaves worked in the cotton economy in 1830. Owning slaves enabled a planter to harvest vast fields of cotton speedily, a crucial advantage because a sudden rainstorm at harvest time could pelt cotton to the ground and soil it.

Cotton offered an added advantage: it was compatible with corn production. Corn could be planted either earlier or later than cotton and harvested before or after. Because the cost of owning a slave remained the same regardless of whether he or she was working, corn production allowed slaveholders to shift slave labor between corn and cotton. By 1860 the acreage devoted to corn in the Old South actually *exceeded* that devoted to cotton. Economically, corn and cotton gave the South the best of two worlds. Intense demand in Britain and New England kept cotton prices high and money flowing into the South. Because of southern self-sufficiency in growing corn and raising hogs that thrived on the corn, money did not drain away to pay for food. In 1860 the twelve wealthiest counties in the United States were all in the South.

Ties Between the Lower and Upper South

Two giant cash crops, sugar and cotton, dominated agriculture in the Lower South. The Upper South, a region of tobacco, vegetable, hemp, and wheat growers, depended far less on the great cash crops. Neverthless, a common dependence on slavery unified the Upper and the Lower South and made the Upper South identify more with the Lower South than with the nation's free states.

A range of social, political, and psychological factors promoted this unity. First, many settlers in the Lower South had come from the Upper South. Second, all white southerners benefited from the Constitution's three-fifths clause, which let them count slaves as a basis for congressional representation. Third, abolitionist attacks on slavery stung all southerners and bound them together. Fourth, economic ties linked the two Souths. The profitability of cotton and sugar increased the value of slaves throughout the South. The sale of slaves from the declining plantation states of the Upper South to

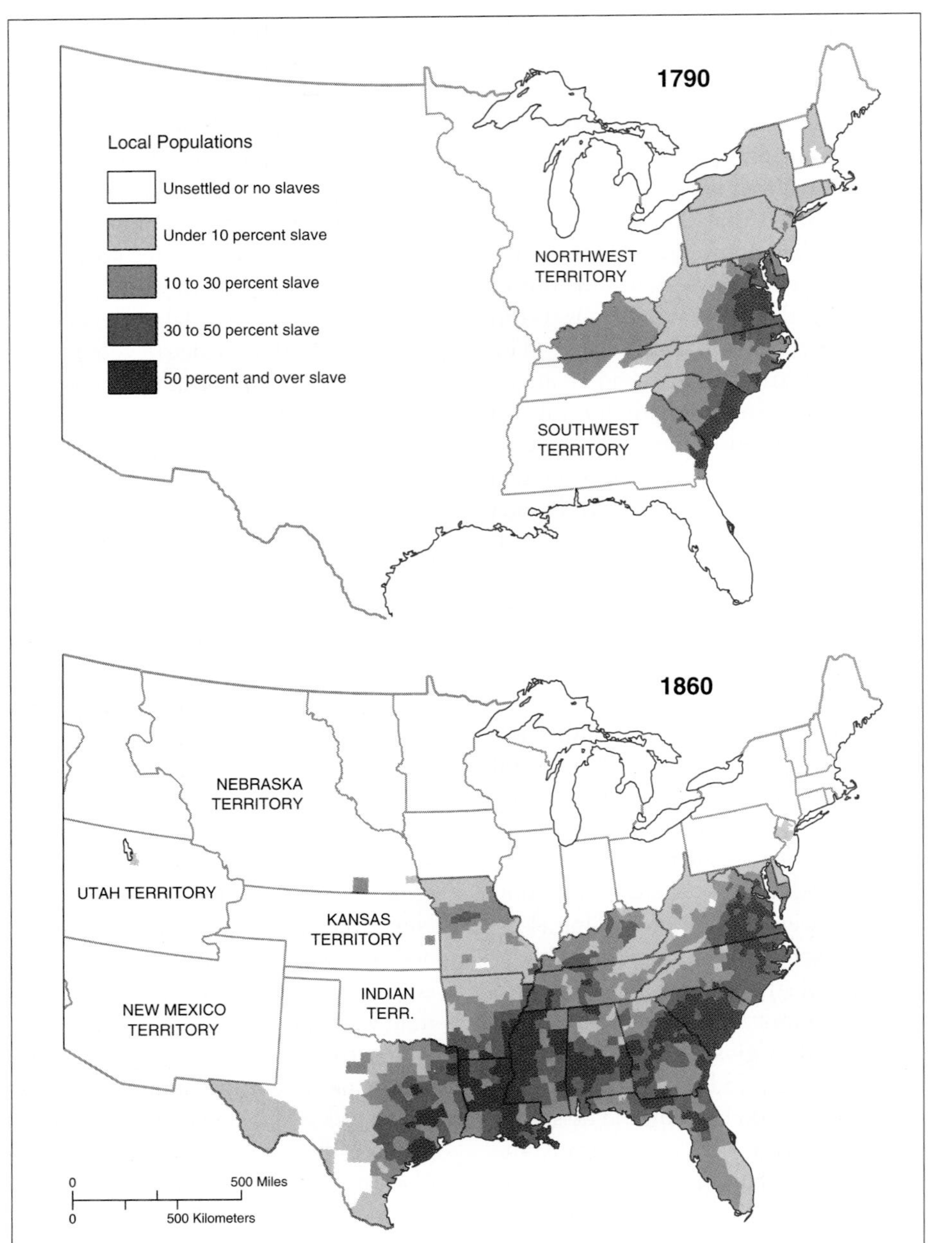

Distribution of Slaves, 1790 and 1860

In 1790 the majority of slaves resided along the southeastern seaboard. By 1860, however, slavery had spread throughout the South, and slaves were most heavily concentrated in the Deep South states.

SOURCE: Reprinted with permission of the McGraw-Hill Companies, from *Ordeal by Fire: The Civil War and Reconstruction*, Second Edition, by James M. McPherson. Copyright © 1992 by the McGraw-Hill Companies.

the booming Lower South was a huge business. Eliminate the slave trade, one Virginian argued, and "Virginia will be a desert."

The North and South Diverge: Economic Patterns

However, the changes responsible for the dynamic growth of the South widened the distance between it and the North. The South remained predominantly rural as the North became more and more urban.

Lack of industry kept the South rural; by 1850 it had one-third of the U.S. population but accounted for only a tenth of the nation's manufacturing. In 1850 the industrial output of the entire South was less than a third that of Massachusetts alone. Between 1840 and 1860 the southern share of capital invested in U.S. manufacturing actually *declined*, from 20 percent to 16 percent.

Some southerners advocated and created factories in the South, but they were a minority. By 1860 cotton-textile mills were scattered throughout the South, and Richmond boasted the nation's fourth-largest producer of iron products, the Tredegar Iron Works. Despite these successes, industrial output in the South trailed far behind that of the New England and Middle Atlantic states. Southern factories were small; they produced mainly for nearby markets, and they were closely tied to agriculture. While northern factories manufactured cloth and shoes, southern factories turned grain into flour, corn into meal, and trees into lumber.

Slavery posed a major obstacle to southern industrialization, but not because slaves were unfit for factories; the Tredegar Iron Works was among many factories that employed slaves. However, the prospect of industrial slavery troubled slaveholders. Away from the strict discipline and supervision possible on a plantation, slaves sometimes behaved as if they were free, shifting jobs, working overtime, and even negotiating better working conditions. A Virginia planter summed up whites' lamentations about urban, industrial slaves: they "got the habit of roaming about and *taking care of themselves*."

But the chief brake on southern industrialization was money, not labor. To raise the capital needed to build factories, planters would have had to sell their slaves. They seldom did. Cash crops such as cotton and sugar were proved, but the benefits of industrialization were remote and doubtful. Successful industrialization also would disrupt social relations, a southerner contended, by introducing "filthy, overcrowded, licentious factories" and attracting abolitionists. As long as southerners believed that the cash-crop economy remained profitable, they had little reason to plunge into the uncertainties of industrialization.

The North and South Diverge: Education in a Cotton Economy

In education, as in industry, the South lagged behind the North. Where northerners recognized the benefits of an educated work force for their growing manufacturing economy, agriculturally oriented southerners rejected compulsory education and were reluctant to tax property to support schools. They abhorred the thought of educating slaves, and southern lawmakers made it a crime to teach slaves to read. For most whites, the only available schools were private. White illiteracy thus remained high in the South as it declined in the North.

Southern education trailed northern education for a number of reasons. As the southern states' revenues rose and fell with the fluctuating price of cotton, so did enthusiasm for public education. Low population density also impeded the expansion of southern education. Having a public school within walking distance of each child was virtually impossible. But the primary reason for the South's failure to develop effective public schools was widespread indifference. Agricultural, self-sufficient, and independent, the middling and poor whites of the South remained unconvinced of the need for public education. They had little dependency on the printed word, few complex commercial transactions, and infrequent dealings with urban people. Planters did not need an orderly and disciplined white work force; they already had a black one that they were determined to keep illiterate lest it acquire ideas about freedom.

Cotton and Southern Progress

Because the South diverged so sharply from the North, outsiders often dismissed it as backward. A northern journalist wrote of white southerners in the 1850s, "They work little, and that little, badly; they earn little, they sell little; they buy little, and have little—very little—of the common comforts and consolations of civilized life."

But the South did not lack progressive features. By 1860 white per capita income in the South exceeded the national average. And although southerners lagged behind northerners in general technology, they did advance in the area that concerned them most: scientific agriculture.

Thus the Old South was not economically backward—it was merely different. Cotton was a wonderful crop, and southerners could hardly be blamed for making it their ruler. As a southern senator wrote in 1858, "You dare not make war upon cotton; no power on earth dares to make war upon it. Cotton is king."

Social Relations in the White South

Antislavery northerners often charged that slavery warped the South's entire social structure. By creating a permanent black underclass of bond servants, they alleged, slavery robbed lower-class whites of the incentive to work, reduced them to shiftless misery, and rendered the South a premodern throwback in an otherwise progressive era. Southerners retorted that the real center of white inequality was the North, where merchants and financiers paraded in fine silks and never soiled their hands with manual labor.

In reality, the white South mixed aristocratic and democratic, premodern and modern features. Although the South featured considerable class inequality, property ownership was widespread. Rich planters dominated social life and the legislature, but they did not necessarily get their way, and often their political agenda paralleled that of other whites. Like white northerners, white southerners were restless, acquisitive, eager to make money, and skillful at managing complex commercial enterprises. Yet practices such as slaveholding and dueling thrived in the South when they were dying out elsewhere.

The Social Groups of the White South

There was wide diversity within and between the South's slaveholding and nonslaveholding classes. Although some planters owned hundreds of slaves and lived lavishly, most lived more modestly. In 1860, one-fourth of all white families in the South owned slaves; nearly half of those owned fewer than five slaves, and three-fourths had fewer than ten slaves. Only 12 percent owned twenty or more slaves, and only 1 percent a hundred or more. Nonslaveholders were equally diverse. Most owned farms and drew on the labor of family members, but other whites squatted on land in the pine barrens or piney woods and scratched out a living by raising livestock, hunting, fishing, and planting a few acres of corn, oats, or sweet potatoes.

Planters, small slaveholders, family farmers, and pine-barrens folk composed the South's four main white groups. Many southerners—lawyers, physicians, merchants, and artisans—did not fall into any of these four, but they tended to identify their interests with one or another of the agricultural groups. Urban merchants and lawyers depended on the planters and shared their views on most issues, whereas rural artisans and merchants dealt with, and were thus attuned to, the family farmers, or yeomen.

Planters and Plantation Mistresses

The plantation, with its porticoed mansion and fields teeming with slaves, stands at the center of the popular image of the Old South. This romanticized view, reinforced by novels and movies such as *Gone with the Wind,* is not entirely false, for the South did contain plantations that travelers found "superb beyond description." Abundant slaves and the division of labor they afforded, and plentiful land, allowed large plantations to generate incomes of $20,000 or more a year, an immense sum in those years.

In the eighteenth century during the initial flush of settlement in the piedmont and trans-Appalachian South, even well-off planters generally had lived in humble log cabins. After 1810, however, elite planters competed with one another to build stately mansions. Yet most planters counted their wealth not in grand mansions and elegant furnishings but in the value of their slaves. A field hand was worth as much as $1,700 in the 1850s, and few planters sold their slaves to buy furniture and silver plate.

But in their constant worry about profit, planters enjoyed neither repose nor security. High fixed costs—housing and feeding slaves, maintaining cotton gins, hiring overseers—led them to search for more and better land, higher efficiency, and greater self-sufficiency. Because cotton prices tended to fluctuate seasonally, planters often assigned their cotton to commercial agents in cities, who held the cotton until the price was right. The agents extended credit so that the planters could pay their bills before the cotton was sold. Indebtedness became part of the plantation economy and intensified the planters' quest for profitability. Psychological strains compounded economic worries. Frequent moves disrupted circles of friends and relatives, particularly as migration to the Southwest (Alabama and Mississippi) carried families into less settled, more desolate areas. Until 1850 this area was still the frontier.

Migration to the Southwest often deeply unsettled plantation women. They suddenly found themselves in frontier conditions with neither friends, neighbors, nor relatives nearby and surrounded by slaves. "I am sad tonight, sickness preys upon my frame," wrote a bride who moved to Mississippi in 1833. "I am alone and more than 150 miles from any near relatives in the wild woods of an Indian nation." Frequent absences by husbands, whether

Ye Southern Planter, 1838
Although they aspired to be leisured gentlemen and live in mansions, most planters resided in modest dwellings and actively managed their estates.

they were looking for new land, supervising outlying plantations, or conducting business in the city, intensified wives' loneliness.

Planters and their wives found various ways of coping with their isolation. Employing overseers to run the plantation, some lived in cities; in 1850 one-half the planters in the Mississippi Delta lived in New Orleans or Natchez. Most planters acted as their own overseers, however, and dealt with the problems of harsh living conditions by opening their homes to visitors. The responsibility for such hospitality fell heavily on wives, who might have to entertain as many as fifteen people for breakfast and attend to the needs of visitors who stayed for days. Plantation wives also bore the burdens of raising their children, supervising house slaves, making clothes and carpets, looking after smokehouses and dairies, planting gardens, and, often, keeping the plantation accounts. Plantation wives were anything but the delicate idlers of legend.

Among the heaviest sorrows of some plantation mistresses was the presence of mulatto children, constant reminders of their husbands' infidelities. Charlestonian Mary Boykin Chesnut, a famous diarist, observed tartly, "Any lady is ready to tell you who is the father of all the mulatto children in everybody's household but her own. These, she seems to think, drop from clouds." Southern men insisted on sexual purity for white women but allowed themselves a looser standard. The father of abolitionist sisters Sarah and Angelina Grimké fathered three mulatto children after his wife's death. The gentlemanly code usually tolerated such transgressions.

Yet isolation, drudgery, and humiliation did not turn planters' wives against the system. Indeed, when the Civil War came, they supported the Confederacy as enthusiastically as any group. However much they might have hated living as white islands in a sea of slaves, they recognized that their wealth and position depended on slavery.

The Small Slaveholders

In 1860, 88 percent of all slaveholders owned fewer than twenty slaves, and most possessed fewer than ten. One out of every five slaveholders worked outside of agriculture, as a lawyer, physician, merchant, or artisan.

Small slaveholders experienced conflicting loyalties and ambitions. In upland regions they absorbed the outlook of the more numerous yeomen (nonslaveowning small farmers); they owned only a few slaves and rarely aspired to become large planters. In contrast, in the plantation-dominated low country and delta regions, small slaveholders often aspired to planter status. There someone with ten slaves could realistically look forward to owning thirty. And ambitious, acquisitive individuals equated success with owning more slaves. The logic of slavery remained the same: the only way to justify the investment in slaves was to set them to work on profitable crops. Such crops demanded more and better land, and both the planters and the small slaveholders of the deltas were restless and footloose.

The social structure of the deltas was fluid. In the early antebellum period large planters had been reluctant to risk transporting their hundreds of valuable slaves in a still turbulent region. It was small slaveholders who led the initial westward push into the cotton belt in the 1810s and 1820s. Gradually, large planters, too, moved westward, buying up the land that the small slave owners had developed and turning the region from Vicksburg to Natchez into large plantations. Small slave owners took the profits from selling their land, bought more slaves, and moved on. They gradually transformed the region from Vicksburg to Tuscaloosa, Alabama, into a belt of medium-sized farms with a dozen or so slaves on each.

The Yeomen

Nonslaveholding family farmers, or yeomen, composed the largest single group of southern whites. Most owned land, and many hired slaves to help at harvest. In areas of poor soil, such as eastern Tennessee, yeomen were typically subsistence farmers, but most yeomen grew some cash crops. Their landholdings were comparatively small, ranging from 50 to 200 acres. Yeomen generally inhabited uplands far from the rich coastal plains and deltas, such as the piedmont of the East or the hilly upcountry of the Southwest. Young, landless yeomen lived with and worked for relatives.

Above all, the yeomen valued self-sufficiency. Unlike planters, who were driven to acquire more land and to plant more cash crops, the yeomen devoted much of their acreage to subsistence crops such as corn, sweet potatoes, and oats. The planter's ideal was profit with modest self-sufficiency; the yeoman's goal, self-sufficiency with modest profit.

Yeomen living in planter-dominated regions were often dismissed as "poor white trash," but in the upland regions that they dominated, the yeomen were highly respected. Upland slaveholders tended to own only a few slaves; like the yeomen, they were essentially family farmers. With or without the aid of slaves, yeomen fathers and sons cleared the land and cultivated the fields. Wives and daughters planted and tended vegetable gardens, helped at harvest, occasionally cared for livestock, cooked, and made the family's clothes.

Unlike southern planters, yeomen marketed their cash crops locally, trading cotton, wheat, and tobacco for goods and services from nearby artisans and merchants. In some areas yeomen sold their surplus corn to drovers and herdsmen who specialized in raising hogs. Along the French Broad River in eastern Tennessee, for example, 20,000 to 30,000 hogs a year were fattened for market. At peak season a traveler would see 1,000 hogs a mile. The hogs were penned at night in huge stock stands—veritable hog hotels—and fed with corn supplied by the local yeomen.

The People of the Pine Barrens

Independent whites of the wooded "pine barrens" were one of the most controversial groups in the Old South. About 10 percent of southern whites, they usually squatted on the land; put up crude cabins; cleared some acreage, where they planted corn between tree stumps; and grazed hogs and cattle in the woods. They neither raised cash crops nor engaged in the daily routine of orderly work that characterized family farmers. With their ramshackle houses and handful of stump-strewn acres, they appeared lazy and shiftless.

Abolitionists cited the pine-barrens people as proof that slavery degraded whites, but southerners responded that, while the pine-barrens folk were poor, they could at least feed themselves, unlike the paupers of northern cities. In general, the people of the pine barrens were both self-sufficient and fiercely independent. Pine-barrens men were reluctant to hire themselves out as laborers to do "slave" tasks, and the women refused to become servants.

Neither victimized nor oppressed, these people generally lived in the pine barrens by choice. The grandson of a farmer who had migrated from Emanuel County, Georgia, to the Mississippi pine barrens explained his grandfather's decision: "The turpentine smell, the moan of the winds through the pine trees, and nobody within fifty miles of him, [were] too captivating . . . to be resisted, and he rested there."

Conflict and Consensus in the White South

Planters tangled with yeomen on several issues. With extensive economic dealings and need for credit, planters inclined toward the Whig party, which generally supported economic development. The independent yeomen, cherishing their self-sufficiency, tended to be Democrats.

Yet few conflicts arose between these groups. An underlying political unity reigned in the South. Geography was in part responsible: planters, small slaveowners, yeomen, and pine-barrens folk tended to cluster in different regions, each independent of the others. In addition, with landownership widespread and factories sparse, few whites worked for other whites, and so friction among whites was minimized.

The white South's political structure was sufficiently democratic to prevent any one group from gaining exclusive control over politics. Planters dominated state legislatures, but they owed their election to the popular vote. And the democratic currents that had swept northern politics between 1815 and 1860 had affected the South as well; newer southern states entered the Union with democratic constitutions that included universal white manhood suffrage—the right of all adult white males to vote.

Although yeomen often voted for planters, the nonslaveholders did not give their elected representatives a blank check to govern as they pleased. During the 1830s and 1840s Whig planters who favored banks faced intense and often successful opposition from Democratic yeomen. These yeomen blamed banks for the Panic of 1837 and pressured southern legislatures to restrict bank operations. The nonslaveholders got their way often enough to nurture their belief that they, not the slaveholders, controlled politics.

Conflict over Slavery

Nevertheless, considerable *potential* existed for conflict between slaveholders and nonslaveholders. The southern white carpenter who complained in 1849 that "unjust, oppressive, and degrading" competition from slave labor depressed his wages surely had a point. Between 1830 and 1860 the slaveholding class shrank in size in relation to the total white population, but its share of total wealth increased. As a Louisiana editor wrote in 1858, "The present tendency of supply and demand is to concentrate all the slaves in the hands of the few, and thus excite the envy rather than cultivate the sympathy of the people."

Yet although pockets of opposition dotted the South, slavery did not create profound or lasting divisions between slaveholders and nonslaveholders. For example, antagonism to slavery flourished in parts of Virginia up to 1860, but proposals for emancipating the slaves dropped from the state's political agenda after 1832. Kentucky had a history of antislavery activity dating back to the 1790s, but after calls for emancipation suffered a crushing defeat in an 1849 referendum, slavery ceased to be a political issue there.

The rise and fall of pro-emancipation sentiment in the South raises a key question: as most white southerners were non-slaveholders, why did they not attack slavery more consistently? To look ahead, why were so many southerners willing to fight ferociously and to die bravely during the Civil War in defense of an institution in which they apparently had no real stake? There are several reasons. First, some nonslaveholders hoped to become slaveholders. Second, most southerners accepted the racist assumptions on which slavery rested; they dreaded the likelihood that emancipation would encourage "impudent" blacks to entertain ideas of social equality with whites. Slavery appealed to whites as a legal, time-honored, and foolproof way to enforce the social subordination of blacks. Third, no one knew where the slaves, if freed, would go or what they would do. Colonizing freed blacks in Africa was unrealistic, southerners concluded, but they also believed that without colonization, emancipation would lead to a race war. In 1860 Georgia's governor sent a blunt message to his constituents, many of them nonslaveholders: "So soon as the slaves were at liberty thousands of them would leave the cotton and rice fields . . . and make their way to the healthier climate of the mountain region [where] we should have them plundering and stealing, robbing and killing."

The Proslavery Argument

Between 1830 and 1860 southerners constructed a defense of slavery as a positive good rather than a necessary evil. St. Paul's injunction that servants obey their masters became a biblical justification for some. Others looked to the classical past to argue that slavery was both an ancient and classical institution; the slave society of Athens, they said, had produced Aristotle and Plato, and Roman slaveholders had laid the foundations of Western civilization. A third proslavery argument, advanced particularly by George Fitzhugh of Virginia, contrasted the plight of the northern "wage slaves," callously discarded when they became too ill or too old to work, with the lot of southern slaves, cared for by masters who attended to their health, their clothing, and their discipline.

At the same time, southerners increasingly suppressed any open discussion of slavery within the South. In the 1830s they seized abolitionist literature from southern mails and burned it. Although Kentucky abolitionist Cassius Marcellus Clay protected his press with two cannons, in 1845 a mob dismantled it anyway. By 1860 any southerner found with a copy of Hinton R. Helper's antislavery *The Impending Crises* might well fear for his life.

The rise of the proslavery argument coincided with a shift in the position of southern churches on slavery. During the 1790s and early 1800s some Protestant ministers had assailed slavery as immoral, but by the 1830s most clergymen had convinced themselves that slavery was both compatible with Christianity and necessary for the proper exercise of Christian religion. Slavery, they proclaimed, provided the opportunity to display Christian responsibility toward one's inferiors, and it helped African-Americans to develop Christian virtues such as humility and self-control. Southerners increasingly attacked antislavery evangelicals in the North for disrupting the "superior" social arrangement of the South. In 1837 southerners and conservative northerners had combined forces to drive antislavery New School Presbyterians out of that denomination's main body, in 1844 the Methodist Episcopal Church split into northern and southern wings, and in 1845 Baptists formed a separate Southern Convention. In effect, southern evangelicals seceded from national church organizations long before the South seceded from the Union.

Honor and Violence in the Old South

Almost everything about the Old South struck northern visitors as extreme. Although inequality flourished in both the North and the South, no group was as deprived as southern slaves. Not only did northerners find the gap between the races in the South extreme, but also individual southerners seemed to run to extremes. One minute they were hospitable and gracious; the next, savagely violent. "The Americans of the South," Tocqueville wrote, "are brave, comparatively ignorant, hospitable, generous, easy to irritate, violent in their resentments, without industry or the spirit of enterprise."

Violence in the White South

Throughout the colonial and antebellum periods, violence deeply colored the daily lives of white southerners. In the 1760s a minister described backcountry Virginians "biting one anothers Lips and Noses off, and gowging one another—that is, thrusting out anothers Eyes, and kicking one another on the Cods [genitals], to the great damage of many a Poor Woman." Gouging out eyes became a specialty of sorts among poor southern whites. On one occasion a South Carolina judge entered his court to find a plaintiff, a juror, and two witnesses all missing one eye. Stories of eye gougings and ear bitings became part of Old South folklore. Mike Fink, a legendary southern fighter and hunter, boasted that he was so mean in infancy that he refused his mother's milk and howled for whiskey. Yet beneath the folklore lay the reality of violence that gave the Old South a murder rate as much as ten times higher than that of the North.

The Code of Honor and Dueling

At the root of most violence in the white South lay intensified feelings of personal pride that reflected the inescapable presence of slaves. White southerners saw slaves degraded, insulted, and powerless to resist. In turn, whites reacted violently to even trivial insults to demonstrate that they had nothing in common with slaves.

Among gentlemen this exaggerated pride took the form of a code of honor, with honor defined as an extraordinary sensitivity to one's reputation. Northern moralists celebrated a rival idea, character, the quality that enabled an individual to behave in steady fashion regardless of how others acted toward him or her. In the honor culture of the Old South, however, even the slightest insult, as long as it was perceived as intentional, could become the basis for a duel.

Formalized by French and British officers during the Revolutionary War, dueling gained a secure niche in the Old South as a means by which gentlemen dealt with affronts to their honor. Seemingly trivial incidents—a harmless brushing against the side of someone at a public event, a hostile glance—could trigger a duel. Yet dueling did not necessarily lead to violence. Gentlemen viewed dueling as a refined alternative to the random violence of lower-class life. Instead of leaping at his antagonist's throat, a gentleman remained cool, settled on a weapon with his opponent, and agreed to a meeting place. In the interval, friends of the parties negotiated to clear up the "misunderstanding" that had provoked the challenge. Most confrontations ended peaceably rather than on the field of honor at dawn.

Although dueling was as much a way of settling disputes peacefully as of ending them violently, the ritual could easily end in death or maiming. Dueling bypassed the court system, which would have guaranteed a peaceful result; in disputes involving honor, recourse to the law struck many southerners as cowardly and shameless.

Dueling rested on the assumption that gentlemen could recognize each other and know when to respond to a challenge. Nothing in the code of honor compelled a person to duel with someone who was not a gentleman, for such a person's opinion hardly mattered. An insolent porter who insulted a gentleman might get a whipping but did not merit a duel. Yet it was often difficult to determine who was a gentleman. Indeed, the Old South teemed with would-be gentlemen. A clerk in a country store in Arkansas in 1850 found it remarkable that ordinary farmers who hung around the store talked of their honor, and that the proprietor, a German Jew, carried a dueling pistol.

The Southern Evangelicals and White Values

With its emphasis on the personal redress of grievances and its inclination toward violence, the ideal of honor conflicted with the values preached by the southern evangelical churches, notably the Baptists, Methodists, and Presbyterians. These denominations stressed humility and self-restraint, virtues that sharply contrasted with the culture of display that buttressed the extravagance and violence of the Old South.

Before 1830 most southern gentlemen looked down on the evangelicals as uncouth fanatics. But the evangelicals shed their backwoods image by founding colleges such as Randolph Macon and Wake Forest and by exhorting women (two-thirds of the average congregation) to make every home "a sanctuary, a resting place, a shadow from the heats, turmoils, and conflicts of life, and an effectual barrier against ambition, envy, jealousy, and selfishness." During the 1830s evangelical values and practices penetrated even the Episcopal church, long preferred by the gentry.

Southern evangelicals rarely attacked honor as such, but they condemned dueling, brawling, intemperance, and gambling. By the 1860s the South counted many gentlemen like the Bible-quoting Presbyterian general Thomas J. "Stonewall" Jackson, fierce in a righteous war but a sworn opponent of strong drink, gambling, and dueling.

Life Under Slavery

Slavery, the institution at the root of the code of honor and other distinctive features of the Old South, has long inspired controversy among historians. Some have seen slavery as a benevolent institution in which African-Americans lived contentedly under kindly masters; others, as a brutal system that drove slaves into constant rebellion. Neither view is accurate, but both contain a germ of truth. There were kind masters, and some slaves developed genuine affection for their owners. Yet slavery inherently oppressed its African-American victims by forcibly appropriating their life and labor. Even kind masters exploited blacks in order to earn profits. And kindness was a double-edged sword; the benevolent master expected grateful affection from his slaves and interpreted that affection as loyalty to slavery itself. When northern troops descended on the plantations during the Civil War, masters were genuinely surprised and dismayed to find many of their most trusted slaves deserting to Union lines.

The kindness or cruelty of masters was important, but three other factors primarily determined slaves' experience: the kind of agriculture in which they worked, whether they resided in rural or urban areas, and what century they lived in. The experiences of slaves working on cotton plantations in the 1830s differed drastically from those of slaves in 1700, for reasons unrelated to the kindness or brutality of masters.

The Maturing of the Plantation System

Slavery changed significantly between 1700 and 1830. In 1700 the typical slave was a man in his twenties, recently arrived from Africa or the Caribbean, who worked on an isolated small farm. Drawn from different regions of Africa, few slaves spoke the same language. Because slave ships carried twice as many men as women, and because slaves were widely scattered, blacks had difficulties finding partners and creating a semblance of family life. Severe malnutrition sharply limited the number of children slave women bore. Without continuing importations, the number of slaves in North America would have declined between 1710 and 1730.

In contrast, by 1830 the typical North American slave was as likely to be female as male, had been born in America, spoke English, and worked beside numerous other slaves on a plantation. The rise of plantation agriculture in the eighteenth century was at the heart of the change. Plantation slaves found mates more easily than slaves on scattered farms. The ratio between slave men and women fell into balance, and marriage between slaves on the same or nearby plantations increased. The native-born slave population soared after 1750. The importation of African slaves declined, and in 1808 Congress banned it.

Work and Discipline of Plantation Slaves

In 1850 the typical slave worked on a large farm or plantation with at least ten other slaves. Almost three-quarters of all slaves belonged to masters with ten or more slaves, and just over one-half lived in units of twenty or more slaves. Thus understanding the life of a typical slave requires examining plantation routines.

An hour before sunrise, a horn or a bell awakened the slaves. After a sparse breakfast, they marched to the fields. A traveler in Mississippi described such a procession: "First came, led by an old driver carrying a whip, forty of the largest and strongest women I ever saw together; they were all in a simple uniform dress of bluish check stuff, the skirts reaching little below the knee; their legs and feet were bare; they carried themselves loftily, each having a hoe over the shoulder, and walking with a free, powerful swing." The plow hands followed, "thirty strong, mostly men, but few of them women. . . . A lean and vigilant white overseer, on a brisk pony, brought up the rear."

Slave men and women worked side by side in the fields. Those female slaves who did not labor in the fields remained busy. A former slave, John Curry, described how his mother milked cows, cared for children whose mothers worked in the fields, cooked for field hands, washed and ironed for her master's household, and looked after her own seven children. Plantations never lacked tasks for slaves of either gender. As former slave Solomon Northup noted, "Ploughing, planting, picking cotton, gathering the corn, and pulling and burning stalks, occupies the whole of the four seasons of the year. Drawing and cutting wood, pressing cotton, fattening and killing hogs, are but incidental labors." In any season the slave's day stretched from dawn to dusk. When darkness made field work impossible, slaves toted cotton bales to the ginhouse, gathered wood for supper fires, and fed the mules. Weary from their labors, they slept in log cabins on wooden planks.

Although virtually all antebellum Americans worked long hours, no others experienced the combination of long hours and harsh discipline that slave field hands endured. Northern factory workers did not live in fear of drivers walking among them with a whip. Repulsive brutality pervaded American

African-American Women and Men on a Trek Home, South Carolina *Much like northern factories, large plantations made it possible to impose discipline and order on their work force. Here African-American women loaded down with cotton join their men on the march home after a day in the fields.*

slavery. For example, pregnant slave women were sometimes forced to lie in depressions in the ground and endure whipping on their backs, a practice that supposedly protected the fetus while abusing the mother. Masters often delegated discipline and punishment to white overseers and black drivers. The barbaric discipline meted out by others twinged the consciences of many masters, but most justified it as their Christian duty to ensure the slaves' proper "submissiveness." Frederick Douglass recalled that his worst master had been converted at a Methodist camp meeting. "If religion had any effect on his character at all," Douglass related, "it made him more cruel and hateful in all his ways."

Despite the system's brutality, some slaves advanced—not to freedom but to semiskilled or skilled indoor work. Some became blacksmiths, carpenters, or gin operators, and others served as cooks, butlers, and dining-room attendants. These house slaves became legendary for their disdain of field hands and poor whites. Slave artisans and house slaves generally enjoyed higher status than the field hands. But legend often distorted reality, for house slaves were as subject to discipline as field hands.

Slave Families

Masters thought of slaves as naturally promiscuous and flattered themselves into thinking that they alone held slave marriages together. Masters had powerful incentives to encourage slave marriages: bringing new slaves into the world and discouraging slaves from running away. James Henry Hammond, governor of South Carolina and a large slaveholder, noted in his diary how he "flogged Joe Goodwyn and ordered him to go back to his wife. Ditto Gabriel and Molly and ordered them to come together."

This picture of benevolent masters holding together promiscuous slaves is misleading. Slavery itself posed the keenest challenge to slave families. The law provided neither recognition of nor protection for the slave family. Masters reluctant to break slave marriages by sale could neither bequeath their reluctance to heirs nor avoid economic hardship that might force them to sell slaves. The reality, one historian has calculated, was that on average a slave would see eleven family members sold during his or her lifetime.

Inevitably, the buying and selling of slaves disrupted attempts to create a stable family life. Poignant testimony to the effects of sale on slave families appeared in advertisements for runaway slaves. An 1851 North Carolina advertisement said that a particular fugitive was probably "lurking in the neighborhood of E. D. Walker's, at Moore's Creek, who owns most of his relatives, or Nathan Bonham's who owns his mother; or perhaps, near Fletcher Bell's, at Long Creek, who owns his father." Small wonder that a slave preacher pronounced a couple married "until death or *distance* do you part."

Other factors disrupted slave marriages. The marriage of a slave woman did not protect her against the sexual demands of her master or, indeed, of any white. Slave children of white masters sometimes became targets for the wrath of white mistresses. Sarah Wilson, the daughter of a slave and her white master, remembers that as a child she was "picked on" by her mistress until the master ordered his wife to let Sarah alone because she "got big, big blood in her." Field work kept slave mothers from their children, who were cared for by the elderly or by the mothers of other children.

Despite these enormous obstacles, relationships within slave families were often intimate and, where possible, long lasting. Lacking legal protection, slaves developed their own standards of family morality. A southern white woman observed that slaves "did not consider it wrong for a girl to have a child before she married, but afterwards were extremely severe upon anything like infidelity on her part." Given the opportunity, slaves solemnized their marriages before members of the clergy. White clergymen who accompanied Union armies into Mississippi and Louisiana during the Civil War conducted thousands of marriage rites for slaves who had long viewed themselves as married and desired a formal ceremony and registration.

Broad kinship patterns—close ties between children and grandparents, aunts, and uncles as well as parents—had marked West African cultures, and they were reinforced by the separation of children and parents that routinely occurred under slavery. Frederick Douglass never knew his father and saw his mother rarely, but he vividly remembered his grandmother. In addition, slaves often created "fictive" kin networks, naming friends as their uncles, aunts, brothers, or sisters. In this way they helped to protect themselves against the disruption of family ties and established a broader community of obligation. When plantation slaves greeted each other as "brother," they were not making a statement about actual kinship but about obligations to each other.

The Longevity, Health, and Diet of Slaves

Of the 10 million to 12 million Africans imported to the New World between the fifteenth and nineteenth centuries, North America received only 550,000 of them (about 5 percent), whereas Brazil received 3.5 million (nearly 33 percent). Yet by 1825, 36 percent of all slaves in the Western Hemisphere lived in the United States, and only 31 percent in Brazil. The reason for this difference is that slaves in the United States reproduced faster and lived longer than those in Brazil and elsewhere in the Western Hemisphere.

Several factors account for U.S. slaves' longer lives and higher rates of reproduction. First, with the gender ratio among slaves equalizing more rapidly in North America, slaves there married earlier and had more children. Second, because raising corn and livestock was compatible with growing cotton, the Old South produced plentiful food. Slaves generally received a peck of cornmeal and three to four pounds of fatty pork a week, which they often supplemented with vegetables grown on small plots and with catfish and game.

Slaves enjoyed greater immunity from malaria and yellow fever than whites but suffered more from cholera, dysentery, and diarrhea. Lacking privies, slaves usually relieved themselves behind bushes, and consequently urine and feces contaminated the sources of their drinking water. Slave remedies for stomach ailments, though commonly ridiculed by whites, often worked. For example, slaves ate white clay to cure dysentery and diarrhea. We now know that white clay contains kaolin, a remedy for these disorders.

Nonetheless, slaves experienced a higher mortality rate than whites. The very young suffered most; infant mortality among slaves was double that among whites, and one in three African-American children died before age ten. Plantations in the disease-ridden lowlands had the worst overall mortality rates, but overworked field hands often miscarried or bore weakened infants even in healthier areas.

Slaves off Plantations

Greater freedom from supervision and greater opportunities awaited slaves who worked off plantations in towns and cities. Most southern whites succumbed to the lure of cotton and established small farms; the resulting shortage of white labor created a steady demand for slaves outside the plantation economy. Driving wagons, working as stevedores on the docks, manning river barges, and toiling in mining and lumbering gave slaves an opportunity to work somewhere other than the cotton fields. Other African-Americans served as engineers for sawmills or artisans for ironworks. African-American women and children constituted the main labor force for the South's fledgling textile industry.

The draining of potential white laborers from southern cities also provided opportunity for slaves to become skilled artisans. In the eighteenth century Charleston, Savannah, and other cities had a large class of highly skilled slave blacksmiths and carpenters, and the tradition endured into the nineteenth century. Slave or free, blacks found it easier to pursue skilled occupations in southern cities than in northern ones, where immigrant laborers competed with blacks for work.

Despite slavery's stranglehold, urban African-Americans in the South enjoyed opportunities denied their counterparts in the North. Generally, slaves who worked in factories, mining, or lumbering were hired out by their masters rather than owned by their employers. If working conditions for hired-out slaves deteriorated badly, masters would refuse to provide employers with more slaves. Consequently, working conditions for slaves off the plantation generally stayed at a tolerable level. Watching workers load cotton onto a steamboat, Frederick Law Olmsted was amazed to see slaves sent to the top of the bank to roll the bales down to Irishmen who stowed them on the ship. Asking the reason for this arrangement, Olmsted was told, "The niggers are worth too much to be risked here; if the Paddies [Irish] are knocked overboard, or get their backs broke, nobody loses anything."

Life on the Margin: Free Blacks in the Old South

Free blacks were likelier than southern blacks in general to live in cities. In 1860 one-third of the free blacks in the Upper South and more than half in the Lower South were urban.

Urban specialization allowed free blacks the chance to become carpenters, coopers (barrel makers), barbers, and small traders. Most of the meat, fish, and produce in an antebellum southern market was prepared for sale by free blacks. Urban free blacks formed their own fraternal orders and churches; in New Orleans free blacks also had their own opera and literary journals. In Natchez a free black barber, William Tiler Johnson, invested profits from his shop in real estate, acquired stores that he rented out, and bought a plantation and slaves.

Despite such successes, free blacks were vulnerable in southern society. They continued to increase in absolute numbers (a little more than 250,000 free people of color lived in the South in 1860), but the rate of growth of the free black population slowed radically after 1810. Fewer masters freed their slaves after that time, and following the Nat Turner rebellion in 1831, states legally restricted the liberties of free blacks. Every southern state forbade free blacks to enter, and in 1859 Arkansas ordered all free blacks to leave.

Although a free-black culture flourished in certain cities, that culture did not reflect the conditions under which the majority of blacks lived. Most free blacks dwelled in rural areas, where whites lumped them together with slaves, and a much higher percentage of blacks were free in the Upper South than in the Lower South.

Many free blacks were mulattos, the product of white masters and black women, and looked down on "darky" field hands and laborers. But as discrimination against free people of color intensified during the late antebellum period, many free blacks realized that whatever future they had was as blacks, not whites. Feelings of racial solidarity increased during the 1850s, and after the Civil War, the leaders of the ex-slaves were usually blacks who had been free before the war.

Slave Resistance

Fear of slave insurrection haunted the Old South. In lowland and delta plantation areas slaves often outnumbered whites. In the cities free blacks could have provided leadership for rebellions. Rumors of slave conspiracies flew within the southern white community, and all whites knew of the massive black revolt that had destroyed French rule in Santo Domingo.

Yet only three organized rebellions occurred in the Old South during the nineteenth century. Taken together, they say more about the futility than the possibility of slave rebellion. In 1800 the Virginia slave Gabriel Prosser's planned rebellion was betrayed by other slaves, and Prosser and his followers were executed. That same year Denmark Vesey, a South Carolina slave, used $1,500 won in a lottery to buy his freedom. Purchasing a carpentry shop in Charleston, Vesey preached at the city's African Methodist Episcopal church and built a sizable African-American following. In 1822 he and his loyalists devised a plan to attack Charleston and seize the city's arms and ammunition; betrayed by other slaves, they were captured and executed.

The Nat Turner rebellion, which occurred in 1831 in Southampton County, Virginia, was the only slave insurrection to lead to white deaths. Gloomy and introspective by nature, the slave Nat Turner taught himself to read and write in childhood. He became an electrifying preacher and gained a reputation for prophecy, including visions of white and black angels warring in the sky. For all his gifts, Turner's life as a field hand was onerous, and the sale of his wife reminded him that whites measured him only by his cash value.

In 1831 Turner's anger over slavery's injustice boiled over. In August he and a handful of slaves set out, armed with axes and clubs. Gathering recruits as they moved from plantation to plantation, Turner and his followers killed all whites whom they encountered, men, women, and children alike. Before the rebellion was suppressed, fifty-five whites and more than a hundred blacks had died.

Turner's rebellion stunned the South. Coupled with the slave uprising of the 1790s on Santo Domingo, it convinced white southerners that a slave insurrection constituted an ever-present threat. Yet the Nat Turner rebellion, like the Prosser and Vesey conspiracies, never had a chance of success. During the Turner rebellion several slaves alerted their masters to the threat, less from loyalty than from a correct assessment of Turner's chances. Despite constant fears of slave rebellion, the Old South experienced far fewer threats than the Caribbean or South America.

Several factors explain this apparent tranquillity. First, although slaves formed a majority in South Carolina and a few other areas, they did not constitute a *large* majority in any state. Second, unlike Caribbean slave owners, most southern masters lived on their plantations; they possessed armed force and were willing to use it. Third, family ties among U.S. slaves made them reluctant to risk death and thereby to orphan their children. Finally, slaves who ran away or plotted rebellion had no allies. Southern Indians routinely captured runaway slaves and claimed rewards for them; some Indians even owned slaves.

Unable to rebel, many slaves tried to escape to freedom in the North. Some light mulattos who passed as whites succeeded. More often, slaves borrowed, stole, or forged passes from plantations or obtained papers describing them as free. Frederick Douglass borrowed a sailor's papers to make his escape from Baltimore to New York City. Some former slaves, including Harriet Tubman and Josiah Henson, returned to the South to assist others to escape. Despite legends of an "Underground Railroad" of abolitionists helping slaves to freedom, fugitive slaves owed little to abolitionists. The "safe houses" of white sympathizers in border states were better known to slave catchers than to runaways. Probably fewer than a thousand slaves actually escaped to the North.

Despite poor prospects for permanent escape, slaves could disappear for prolonged periods into the free-black communities of southern cities. Slaves enjoyed a fair degree of practical freedom to drive wagons to market and to come and go when they were off plantations. Slaves sent to a city might overstay their leave and pass themselves off as free. This kind of practical freedom did not change slavery's underlying oppressiveness, but it did give slaves a sense of having certain rights, and it helped to channel slave resistance into activities that were furtive and relatively harmless rather than open and violent. Theft, for example, was so common that planters kept tools, smokehouses, and closets under lock and key. Overworked field hands might leave tools out to rust, feign illness, or simply refuse to work. Slaves could not be fired for such malingering or negligence. And Frederick Law Olmsted even found masters afraid to punish a slave "lest [he or she] should abscond, or take a sulky fit and not work, or poison some of the family, or set fire to the dwelling." Indeed, not all furtive resistance was harmless. Arson and poisoning, both common forms of vengeance in African culture, flourished in the Old South. So did fear. Masters afflicted by dysentery never knew for sure that they had not been poisoned.

Arson, poisoning, theft, work stoppage, and negligence acted as alternatives to violent rebellion, but their goal was not freedom. Their object was merely to make slavery bearable. Most slaves would have preferred freedom but settled for less. "White folks do as they please," an ex-slave said, "and the darkies do as they can."

The Emergence of African-American Culture

Enslaved blacks combined elements of African and American culture to create a distinctive culture of their own.

The Language and Religion of Slaves

Before slaves could develop a common culture, they needed a common language. During the colonial period African-born slaves, speaking a variety of languages, had developed a "pidgin"—that is, a language that has no native speakers but in which people with different native languages can communicate. Many African-born slaves spoke English pidgin poorly, but their American-born descendants used it as their primary language.

Like all pidgins, English pidgin was a simplified language. Slaves usually dropped the verb *to be* (which had no equivalent in African tongues) and ignored or confused genders. Instead of saying "Mary is in the cabin," they typically said, "Mary, he in cabin." They substituted *no* for *not,* as in "He no wicked." Some African words, among them *banjo,* moved from pidgin to standard English, and others, such as *goober* (peanut), entered southern white slang. Although many whites ridiculed pidgin, and black house servants struggled to speak standard English, pidgin proved indispensable for communication among slaves.

Religion played an equally important role in forging an African-American culture. Africa contained rich and diverse religious customs and beliefs. Despite the presence of a few Muslims and Christians in the early slave population, most of the slaves brought from Africa followed one of many native African religions. Most of these religions drew little distinction between the spiritual and natural worlds—storms, illnesses, and earthquakes were all assumed to stem from supernatural forces. God, spirits that inhabited woods and waters, and ancestor spirits all constituted these supernatural forces. The religions of West Africa, the region where most American slaves originated, attached special significance to water, which suggested life and hope.

However, African religions did not unify American slaves. African religions differed greatly, and the majority of slaves in the colonial period were young men who had not absorbed this religious heritage. Remnants of African religion remained, however, in part because before the 1790s whites made few attempts to convert slaves to Christianity. When whites' conversion efforts increased, dimly remembered African beliefs such as the reverence for water may have aided Christian missionaries in influencing slaves to accept Christianity and to undergo baptism. Evangelical Christianity, like African religions, drew few distinctions between the sacred and the worldly. Just as Africans believed that droughts and plagues resulted from supernatural forces, revivalists knew in their hearts that every drunkard who fell off his horse and every Sabbath breaker struck by lightning had experienced a deliberate, direct punishment from God.

By the 1790s African-Americans formed about a quarter of the membership of the Methodist and Baptist denominations. The fact that converted slaves played significant roles in the South's three slave rebellions reinforced whites' fears that a Christian slave would be a rebellious slave. These slave uprisings, especially the Nat Turner rebellion, spurred Protestant missionaries to intensify their efforts among slaves. They pointed to the self-taught Turner as proof that slaves could learn about Christianity and claimed that only organized efforts at conversion would ensure that the slaves were taught correct versions of Christianity. After Methodists, Baptists, and Presbyterians split into northern and southern wings, missionaries argued that it was safe to convert slaves, for the southern churches had rid themselves of antislavery elements. Between 1845 and 1860 the number of African-American Baptists doubled.

Christian blacks' experience in the Old South illustrates the contradictions of life under slavery. Urban blacks often had their own churches, but rural blacks and slaves worshipped in the same churches as whites. Although African-Americans sat in segregated sections, they heard the same service as whites. Churches became the most interracial institutions in the Old South, and biracial churches sometimes disciplined whites for abusing black Christian members. But Christianity was not a route to black liberation. Ministers went out of their way to remind slaves that spiritual equality was not the same as civil equality. The conversion of slaves succeeded only to the extent that it did not challenge the basic inequality of southern society.

However, slaves listening to the same sermons as whites often came to different conclusions. For example, slaves drew parallels between their captivity and that of the Jews, the Chosen People. Like the Jews, slaves concluded, they were "de people of de Lord." If they kept the faith, they would reach the Promised Land.

"The Promised Land" could refer to Israel, to heaven, or to freedom. Whites agreed that Israel and heaven were the only permissible meanings, but some African-Americans thought of freedom as well. Many plantations had black preachers, slaves trained by white ministers to spread Christianity among blacks. In the presence of masters or ministers, African-American preachers repeated the familiar biblical command "Obey your master." Often, however, slaves met for services apart from whites, and then the message changed.

Some slaves privately interpreted Christianity as a religion of liberation, but most recognized that their prospects for freedom were slight. Generally, Christianity neither turned blacks into revolutionaries nor made them model slaves. It did provide slaves with a view of slavery different from their masters' outlook. Masters argued that slavery was a benign and divinely ordained institution, but Christianity told slaves that the institution was an afflic-

The Banjo Lesson,
by Henry O. Tanner, c. 1893
Tanner, a black artist, captured African-Americans' rich musical traditions and close family bonds in this evocative painting. Africans brought the banza, or banjo, to the Americas.

tion, a terrible and unjust system that God had allowed in order to test their faith. For having endured slavery, he would reward slaves. For having created it, he would punish masters.

African-American Music and Dance

African-American culture expressed blacks' feelings. Long after white rituals had grown sober and sedate, the congregation in African-American religious services shouted, "Amen" and let their body movements reflect their feelings. Slaves also expressed their emotions in music and dance. Southern law forbade them to own "drums, horns, or other loud instruments, which may call together or give sign or notice to one another of their wicked designs and intentions." Instead, slaves made rhythmical clapping, called "patting juba," an indispensable accompaniment to dancing. Slaves also played an African instrument, the banjo, and beat tin buckets as substitutes for drums. Slave music was tied to bodily movement; slaves expressed themselves in a dance African in origin, emphasizing shuffling steps and bodily contortions rather than quick footwork and erect backs as in whites' dances.

Whether at work or prayer, slaves liked to sing. Work songs usually consisted of a leader's chant and a choral response. Masters encouraged such songs, believing that singing induced slaves to work harder and that the innocent content of work songs proved that slaves were happy. However, Frederick Douglass, recalling his own past, observed that "slaves sing most when they are most unhappy. The songs of the slave represent the sorrows of his heart; and he is relieved by them, only as an aching heart is relieved by its tears."

African-Americans also sang religious songs, later known as spirituals, which reflected the powerful emphasis that slave religion placed on deliverance from earthly travails. Whites took a dim view of spirituals and tried to make slaves sing "good psalms and hymns" instead of "the extravagant and nonsensical chants, and catches, and hallelujah songs of their own composing." But enslaved blacks clung to their spirituals, drawing hope from them that "we will soon be free, when the Lord will call us home," as one spiritual promised.

CONCLUSION

The emergence of an African-American culture was one of many features that made the Old South distinctive. With its huge black population, plantation slavery, lack of industries, and scattered white population, the South seemed a world apart to antebellum northerners, who were convinced that slavery had cut the South off from progress and turned it into "sterile land, and bankrupt estates." Southerners, for their part, believed that their agricultural base was far more stable than northern industry. Southerners portrayed slavery as a time-honored and benevolent response to the natural inequality of the black race and believed that their slaves were content. In reality, however, few slaves accepted slavery. African-Americans resisted slavery covertly, by sabotage or poison, rather than openly, by escape or rebellion. The Christianity that whites used to justify slavery taught slaves the injustice of human bondage.

CHRONOLOGY

1790s Methodists and Baptists start to make major strides in converting slaves to Christianity.

1793 Eli Whitney invents the cotton gin.

1800 Gabriel Prosser leads a slave rebellion in Virginia.

1808 Congress prohibits external slave trade.

1816–1819 Boom in cotton prices stimulates settlement of the Southwest.

1822 Denmark Vesey's conspiracy is uncovered in South Carolina.

1831 William Lloyd Garrison starts *The Liberator*. Nat Turner leads a slave rebellion in Virginia.

1832 Virginia legislature narrowly defeats a proposal for gradual emancipation.

1837 Economic panic begins, lowering cotton prices.

1844–1845 Methodist and Baptist churches split over slavery into northern and southern wings.

1849 Sugar production in Louisiana reaches its peak.

1849–1860 Period of high cotton prices.

FOR FURTHER READING

John B. Boles, *Black Southerners, 1619–1869* (1983). An excellent synthesis of scholarship on slavery.

Wilbur J. Cash, *The Mind of the South* (1941). A brilliant interpretation of southern history.

Bruce Collins, *White Society in the Antebellum South* (1985). A very good, brief synthesis of southern white society and culture.

William J. Cooper, *Liberty and Slavery: Southern Politics to 1860* (1983). A valuable synthesis and interpretation of recent scholarship on the antebellum South in national politics.

Robert W. Fogel, *Without Consent or Contract: The Rise and Fall of American Slavery* (1989). A comprehensive reexamination of the slaves' productivity and welfare.

Robert W. Fogel and Stanley L. Engerman, *Time on the Cross: The Economics of American Negro Slavery* (1974). A controversial book that uses mathematical models to analyze the profitability of slavery. (Fogel won the Nobel Prize in Economics in 1993.)

Lacy K. Ford, *Origins of Southern Radicalism: The South Carolina Upcountry, 1800–1860* (1988). An important recent study that underscores the commitment of poorer whites in the hill regions to their personal independence and to widespread property ownership.

Eugene D. Genovese, *Roll, Jordan, Roll: The World the Slaves Made* (1974). The most influential work on slavery in the Old South written during the last twenty-five years; a penetrating analysis of the paternalistic relationship between masters and slaves.

Peter Kolchin, *Unfree Labor: American Slavery and Russian Serfdom* (1987). A comparative study that sets American slavery within the context of unfree labor in the early nineteenth century.

James Oakes, *The Ruling Race: A History of American Slaveholders* (1982). An important attack on the ideas of Eugene D. Genovese.

James Oakes, *Slavery and Freedom: An Interpretation of the Old South* (1990). A study stressing slavery's development in the context of liberal capitalism.

U. B. Phillips, *American Negro Slavery* (1918) and *Life and Labor in the Old South* (1929). Works marred by racial prejudice but containing a wealth of information about slavery and the plantation system.

Kenneth M. Stampp, *The Peculiar Institution: Slavery in the Antebellum South* (1956). A standard account of the African-American experience under slavery.

CHAPTER 13

Immigration, Expansion, and Sectional Conflict, 1840–1848

Newcomers and Natives

The West and Beyond

The Politics of Expansion

"Americans regard this continent as their birthright," thundered Sam Houston, the first president of the Republic of Texas, in 1847. Indeed, antebellum Americans widely believed that God had ordained the spread of their civilization, progressive and unique, from ocean to ocean. Indians and Mexicans must make way "for our mighty march," Houston concluded.

This was not idle talk. In less than 1,000 fevered days during President James K. Polk's administration (1845–1849), the United States doubled its land area through annexation, negotiation, and war. Meanwhile, immigrants poured in. The push and pull of expansion and immigration were closely intertwined, and most immigrants gravitated to the expansionist Democratic party.

The benefits of expansion emerged as an article of faith among most antebellum Americans. Opening new lands to settlement, the thinking went, would create more yeoman farmers, and the Jeffersonian ideal of the United States as a nation of

(Right) California Forty-Niner, c. 1850

self-sufficient farmers would be recaptured. Westward expansion would reduce sectional strife as well. Such optimism was unfounded. By 1850 expansion would heat sectional antagonisms to the boiling point, split the Democratic party, and set the nation on the path to the Civil War.

Newcomers and Natives

Between 1815 and 1860, 5 million European immigrants reached the United States. Of these, 4.2 million arrived between 1840 and 1860, and 3 million crowded in just from 1845 to 1854, the largest immigration relative to population in U.S. history. The Irish and the Germans dominated this wave of newcomers; by 1860 three-fourths of foreign-born Americans were Irish or German.

Expectations and Realities

Although a desire for religious freedom drew some immigrants to U.S. shores, hopes of economic betterment lured the majority. Travelers' accounts and relatives' letters assured Europeans that America was an ideal world, a utopia. Yet typically, emigrants faced hard times. Because ships sailed irregularly, many were forced to spend their small savings in waterfront slums while awaiting departure. Squalid cargo ships carried most of the emigrants, who endured wretched conditions in quarters as crowded as those of slave ships.

But for many, the greatest shock came after landing. In the depression years of the 1840s, immigrants quickly discovered that farming in America was a perilous prospect, radically different from what they had known in Europe. Unlike the compact farming communities of Europe, American agricultural areas featured scattered farms, and Americans' individualism led them to speculate in land and to move frequently.

Clear patterns emerged amid the shocks and dislocations of immigration. For example, most Irish immigrants lacked the capital to purchase land and consequently crowded into urban areas of New England, New York, New Jersey, and Pennsylvania, where they could find jobs. German immigrants often arrived at southern ports, but slavery, climate, and lack of economic opportunity gradually drove them north to settle in Illinois, Ohio, Wisconsin, and Missouri.

Cities, rather than farms, attracted most antebellum immigrants; by 1860 German and Irish newcomers constituted half or more of the population of St. Louis, New York, Chicago, Cincinnati, Milwaukee, Detroit, and San Francisco. These fast-growing cities needed people with strong backs willing to work for low wages. Irish construction gangs built the houses, streets, and aqueducts that were changing the face of urban America and dug the canals and railroads that linked these cities. In addition to jobs, cities provided immigrants with the community life lacking in farming areas.

The Germans

In 1860 there was no German nation-state, only a collection of principalities and kingdoms. Immigrants from this area thought of themselves as Bavarians, Westphalians, or Saxons, not Germans. They included Catholics, Protestants, Jews, and freethinkers who denounced all religions.

German immigrants spanned a wide spectrum of class and occupation. Most were farmers, but professionals, artisans, and tradespeople made up a sizable minority. For example, Levi Strauss, a Jewish tailor from Bavaria, reached the United States in 1847. When gold was discovered in California the next year, Strauss gathered rolls of cloth and sailed for San Francisco. There he fashioned tough work overalls from canvas. Demand soared, and Strauss opened a factory to produce his cheap overalls, later known as blue jeans or Levi's.

A common language transcended the differences among German immigrants and bound them together. They clustered in the same neighborhoods, formed their own militia and fire companies, and established German-language parochial schools and newspapers. The diversity of the German-speaking population further fostered solidarity. Because Germans supplied their own lawyers, doctors, teachers, and merchants from their midst, they had no need to go outside their neighborhoods. Native-born Americans simultaneously admired German industriousness and resented German self-sufficiency, which they interpreted as clannishness. In a vicious cycle, the Germans responded by becoming even more clannish. In effect, they isolated themselves from gaining the political influence that Irish immigrants acquired.

The Irish

There were three waves of Irish immigration. Between 1815 and the mid-1820s, most Irish immigrants were Protestants, small landowners and tradespeople drawn by enthusiastic veterans of the War of 1812 who reported that America was a paradise where "all a man needed was a gun and sufficient ammunition to be able to live like a prince." From the mid-1820s to the mid-1840s, Irish immigration became both more Catholic and poorer, primarily comprising tenant farmers evicted by Protestant landlords as "superfluous." Rich or poor, Protestant or Catholic, nearly a million Irish crossed the Atlantic to the United States between 1815 and 1845.

Then, between 1845 and the early 1850s the character of Irish immigration changed dramatically. In Ireland blight destroyed harvest after harvest of potatoes, virtually the only food of the peasantry, and triggered one of the most gruesome famines in history. The Great Famine killed a million people. Those who survived, a landlord wrote, were "famished and ghastly skeletons." To escape suffering and death, 1.8 million Irish migrated to the United States in the decade after 1845.

Overwhelmingly poor and Catholic, these newest Irish immigrants entered the work force at the bottom. Paddy with his pickax and Bridget the maid were simultaneously stereotypes and realities. While Irish men dug streets and canals and railroads, Irish women worked as maids and textile workers. Poverty drove women to work at early ages, and the outdoor, all-season labor performed by their husbands turned many of them into working widows. Because the Irish usually married late, almost half the Irish immigrants were single adult women, many of whom never married. Most of these Irish-Americans lived a harsh existence. One immigrant described the life of the average Irish-born laborer as "despicable, humiliating, [and] slavish"; there was "no love for him—no protection of life—[he] can be shot down, run through, kicked, cuffed, spat upon—and no redress." Nevertheless, a few Irish struggled up the social ladder, becoming foremen in factories or small storeowners.

It sometimes seemed that no matter what the Irish did, they clashed with other Americans. The poorer Irish who dug canals, took in laundry, or worked as domestics competed with equally poor free blacks. The result was Irish animosity toward blacks and Irish hatred of abolitionists. At the same time, the Irish who secured skilled or semiskilled jobs clashed with native-born white workers.

Anti-Catholicism, Nativism, and Labor Protest

In the 1840s swelling Catholic immigration led to a Protestant counterattack in the form of nativist (anti-immigrant) societies. Many nativist societies began as secret or semisecret fraternal orders but developed political offshoots; for example, the Order of the Star-Spangled Banner evolved into the "Know-Nothing" party, a major political force in the 1850s. During the 1840s, however, nativist societies played their most influential part in flare-ups over local issues. In 1844 after a nativist political party won a handful of offices in Philadelphia, fiery Protestant orators denounced "popery," and Protestant mobs put Catholic neighborhoods to the torch. By the time militia quelled these "Bible Riots," sixteen people lay dead and thirty buildings had been reduced to charred ruins.

An explosive mixture of fears and discontents fueled nativism. Protestants generally saw their doctrines such as the responsibility of each individual to interpret scripture as far more democratic than Catholicism, which made doctrine the province of the pope and the hierarchy. Native-born artisans and journeymen, already hard pressed by the subdivision of tasks and the aftermath of the Panic of 1837, feared that desperately poor Catholic immigrants represented threats to their jobs. Nativism fed on such fears and anxieties.

Demands for land reform joined nativism as a proposed solution to workers' economic woes. Americans had long believed that abundant land guaranteed security against a permanent class of "wage slaves." In 1844 George Henry Evans, an English-born radical, organized the National Reform Association and exhorted workers to "Vote Yourself a Farm." Such neo-Jeffersonian ideas gained Evans support among artisans and middle-class intellectuals. Land reformers argued that workers in an industrial economy abandoned all possibility of economic independence; their only hope lay in claiming land and becoming farmers. However, in an age when a horse cost the average worker three months' pay, and most factory workers dreaded "the horrors of wilderness life," the idea of solving industrial problems by turning "wage slaves" into self-sufficient farmers seemed a pipe dream.

Labor unions appealed to workers left cold by the promises of the land reformers. For example, desperately poor Irish immigrants, refugees from an agricultural society, believed that they could gain more through unions and strikes than through farming. Even women workers organized unions in these years; the leader of a seamstresses' union proclaimed, "Too long have we been bound down by tyrant employers."

Probably the most important development for workers in the 1840s was a state court decision. In *Commonwealth* v. *Hunt* (1842), the Massachusetts Supreme Court ruled that labor unions were not illegal monopolies that restrained trade. However, because less than 1 percent of the work force at that time belonged to unions, their impact was sharply limited. Thus Massachusetts employers easily brushed aside the *Commonwealth* decision, firing union agitators and replacing them with cheap immigrant labor. "Hundreds of honest laborers," a labor paper reported in 1848, "have been dismissed from employment in the manufactories of New England because they have been suspected of knowing their rights and daring to assert them." This repression effectively blunted agitation for a ten-hour workday in an era when the twelve- or fourteen-hour day was typical.

Ethnic and religious tensions also split the antebellum working class during the 1830s and 1840s. Friction between native-born and immigrant workers inevitably became intertwined with the political divisions of the second party system.

Labor Protest and Immigrant Politics

Few immigrants had voted before reaching America, and even fewer had fled political persecution. Political upheavals had erupted in Austria and some German states in the turbulent year 1848, but among the 1 million German immigrants to the United States, only 10,000 were political refugees, or "Forty-Eighters." Once settled in the United States, however, many immigrants became politically active. They discovered that urban political organizations could help them to find housing and jobs—in return for votes. Both the Irish and the Germans identified overwhelmingly with the Democratic party. By 1820 the Irish controlled Tammany Hall, the New York City Democratic organization; Germans became staunch Democrats in Milwaukee, St. Louis, and other cities.

Immigrants' fears about jobs partly explained their widespread Democratic support. Former president Andrew Jackson had given the Democratic party an antiprivilege, anti-aristocratic coloration, making the Democrats seem more sympathetic than the Whigs to the common people. In addition, antislavery was linked to the Whig party, and the Irish loathed abolitionism because they feared that freed slaves would become their economic competitors. Moreover, the Whigs' moral and religious values seemed to threaten those of the Irish and Germans. Hearty-drinking Irish and German immigrants shunned temperance-crusading Whigs, many of whom were also rabid anti-Catholics. Even public-school reform, championed by the Whigs, was perceived as a menace to the Catholicism of Irish children and as a threat to the integrity of German language and culture.

The Bible Riots illustrate both the interplay of

Defenders of the True Faith
This cartoon portrays the mob that attacked a Roman Catholic convent in Charlestown, Massachusetts, in 1834, as composed of bigoted ruffians who flatter themselves that their deed will live as a heroic act in the national memory.

nativism, religion, and politics and the way in which local issues shaped the immigrants' political loyalties. Both Democrats and Whigs became adept at attracting voters initially drawn to politics by local issues such as liquor regulations and school laws. Nativists usually voted for Whig candidates rather than those of overtly nativist parties, while immigrants followed the Democratic party from local battles into national politics. There the Democrats taught immigrants to revere George Washington, Thomas Jefferson, and Andrew Jackson; to view "moneyed capitalists" as parasites who would tremble when the people spoke; and to think of themselves as Americans. During the 1830s the Democrats had persuaded immigrants that such national issues as the Bank of the United States and the tariff were vital to them. Similarly, in the 1840s the Democrats would try to convince immigrants that national territorial expansion would advance their interests.

The West and Beyond

As late as 1840 the American West meant the area between the Appalachian Mountains and the Mississippi River or just beyond. West of that lay the inhospitable Great Plains. A semiarid treeless plateau, the Plains sustained huge buffalo herds and the nomadic Indians who lived off the buffalo. Because the Great Plains presented would-be farmers with formidable obstacles, public interest shifted toward the Far West, the fertile region beyond the Rockies.

The Far West

By the Transcontinental (or Adams-Onís) Treaty of 1819, the United States had relinquished to Spain its claims to Texas west of the Sabine River and in return had received Spanish claims to the Oregon Country north of California. Two years later the

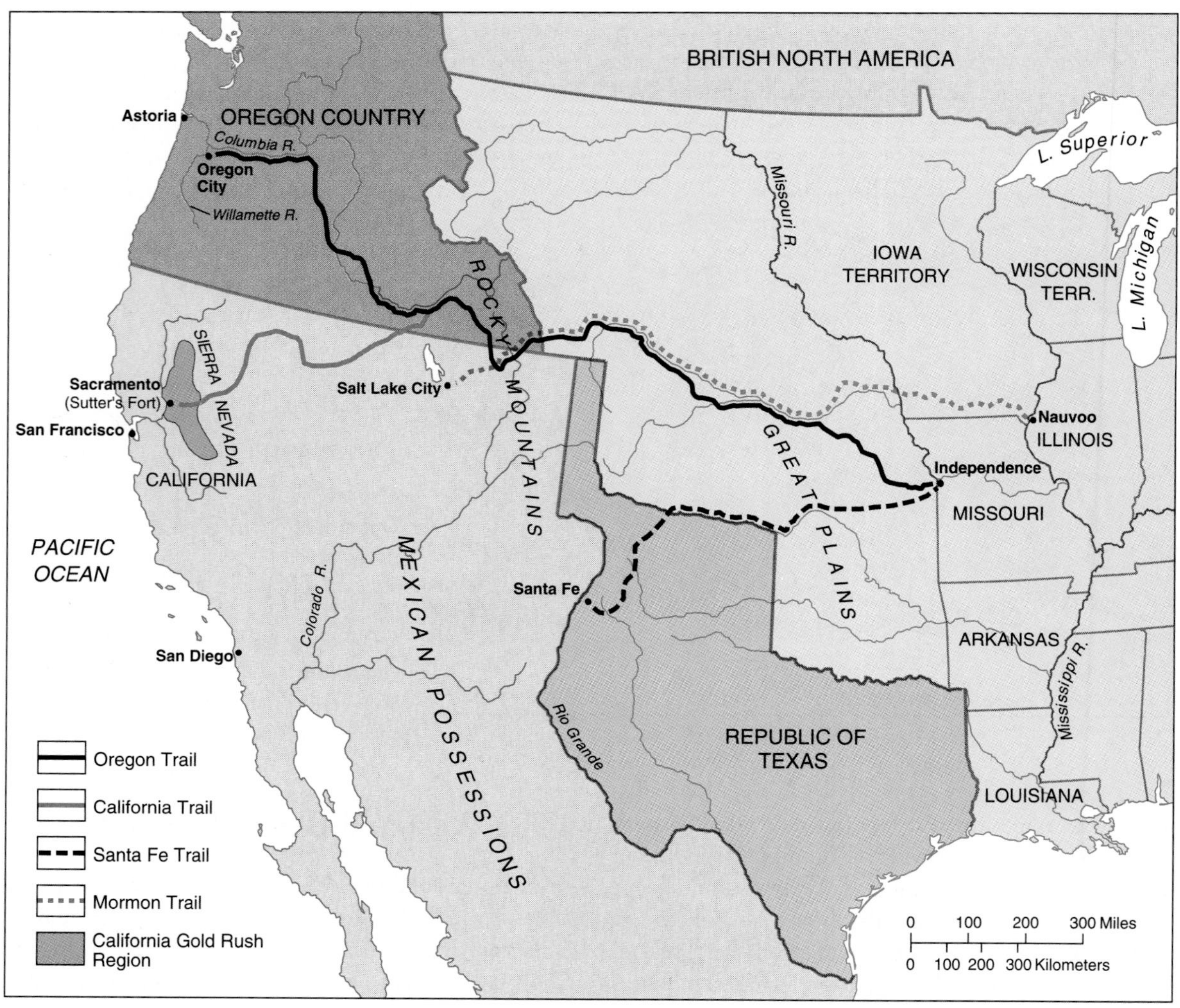

Trails to the West, 1840 *By 1840 several trails carried pioneers from Missouri and Illinois to the West.*

Mexican Revolution had brought Mexico independence from Spain and possession of all North American territory claimed by Spain—Texas, California, and the southwest quadrant of the continent. In 1824 and 1825 Russia yielded its claims to Oregon south of Alaska, and in 1827 the United States and Great Britain revived an earlier agreement for the joint occupation of the Oregon Territory.

Despite these agreements and treaties, the vast Far West remained a remote and shadowy frontier during the 1820s. The American line of settlement reached only to Missouri, a 2,000-mile trek (allowing for mountains) from the West Coast.

Far Western Trade

After sailing around South America and up the Pacific coast, early merchants had established American and British outposts on the West Coast. Between the late 1790s and the 1820s, for example, Boston merchants had built a thriving trade, exchanging goods from the eastern United States for western sea-otter fur, cattle, hides, and tallow (rendered from cattle fat and used for making candles and soap). The British Hudson's Bay Company developed a similar trade in Oregon and northern California. The California trade generated little friction with Mexico. Californians were as eager to buy as the traders were to sell. Traders who settled in California, such as the Swiss-born John Sutter, learned to speak Spanish and became assimilated into Mexican culture.

Also during the 1820s, trading links developed between St. Louis and Santa Fe. Each spring, midwesterners loaded wagon trains with tools, clothing, and household sundries and rumbled westward to Santa Fe, where they traded their goods for mules and silver. Mexico welcomed the trade. By the 1830s more than half the goods trucked west along the Santa Fe Trail trickled into the mineral-rich Mexican provinces of Chihuahua and Sonora and were exchanged for Mexican silver pesos, which became the principal medium of exchange in Missouri.

Some Americans ventured north from Santa Fe to trap beaver in what is today western Colorado and eastern Utah. Americans from St. Louis soon found themselves competing with both the Santa Fe traders and the agents of the Hudson's Bay Company for lucrative beaver pelts. In 1825 William Ashley of St. Louis initiated an annual rendezvous along the Green River in Mexican territory, where midwestern traders could exchange beaver pelts for supplies and thereby save themselves the long trip back to St. Louis. Gradually, the St. Louis traders wrested the beaver trade from their Santa Fe competitors.

For the most part, American traders and trappers operating on the northern Mexican frontier in the 1820s and 1830s provided a service to Mexico's provinces. The Mexican people of New Mexico and California depended on American trade for manufactured goods, and the Mexican government in both provinces needed revenues from customs duties. The New Mexican government often had to wait until the caravan of American traders arrived from St. Louis before it could pay its officials and soldiers.

Yet despite the mutually beneficial relations between Mexicans and Americans, the potential for conflict was always present. Spanish-speaking, Roman Catholic, and accustomed to a hierarchical society, the Mexicans formed a striking contrast to the Protestant, individualistic Americans. Furthermore, American traders returned to the United States with glowing reports about the fertility and climate of Mexico's northern provinces. Consequently, by the 1820s American settlers were moving into eastern Texas. At the same time, the ties binding Mexico's government to its northern provinces were fraying.

Mexican Government in the Far West

Spain, and later Mexico, recognized that the key to controlling their frontier provinces lay in promoting settlement there by Spanish-speaking people—Spaniards, Mexicans, and Indians who had embraced Catholicism and agriculture. Thus by the early nineteenth century, Spanish missions, which had long been the chief instrument of Spanish expansion, stretched up the California coast as far as San Francisco and into the interior of New Mexico and Texas.

The Spanish missions combined political, economic, and religious goals. Paid by the government, the Franciscan priests who staffed the missions tried to convert Native Americans and to settle them on mission lands. By 1823 more than 20,000 Indians lived on the lands of the twenty-one California missions, most of them protected by a fort, or presidio, like that at San Francisco.

In the late 1820s the mission system began to decline, the victim of Mexican independence and the new government's decision to secularize the missions by distributing their lands to ambitious government officials and private ranchers. Some of the mission Indians became forced laborers, but most returned to their nomadic ways and joined with Indians who had resisted the missions. During the 1820s and 1830s these "barbaric Indians"—notably the Comanches, Apaches, Navajos, and Utes—terrorized the Mexican frontier, carrying off women and children as well as livestock. Mexican policy was partly responsible for the upsurge in terrorism. With the secularization of the missions, Hispanic ranchers had made some Native Americans virtual slaves on ranches bloated by the addition of mission lands. Frontier dwellers, moreover, sometimes raided Native American tribes for domestic servants. "To get Indian girls to work for you," a descendant of Hispanic settlers recalled, "all you had to do was organize a company against the Navajos or Utes or Apaches and kill all the men you could and bring captive the children." Thus the "barbaric Indians" had many scores to settle.

Overofficered and corrupt, the Mexican army had little taste for frontier fighting and less for protecting frontier settlers. Consequently, few people ventured into the undeveloped, lawless territories, and most of the Mexican empire remained underpopulated. In 1836 New Mexico contained 30,000 settlers of Hispanic culture; California, about 3,200; and Texas, 4,000. Separated by vast distances from an uncaring government in Mexico City, and dependent on American traders for the necessities of civilization, the frontier Mexicans constituted a frail barrier against the advance of Anglo-American settlement.

American Settlements in Texas

Unlike the provinces of New Mexico and California, the Mexican state known as Coahuila-Texas had neither mountains nor deserts to protect its boundaries. By 1823, 3,000 Americans had drifted into eastern Texas, some in search of cotton lands, others in flight from creditors after the Panic of 1819. In 1824 the Mexican government began to encourage American colonization of Texas as a way to bring in manufactured goods and to gain protection against the Indians. The government bestowed generous land grants on agents known as *empresarios* to recruit peaceful American settlers for Texas. Stephen F. Austin, the most successful of the *empresarios,* had brought in 300 families by 1825. By 1830, 7,000 Americans lived in Texas, more than double the Mexican population there.

This large number of Americans proved a mixed blessing. Unlike the assimilated traders of California, the American settlers in Texas were generally farmers living in their own communities, far from the Mexican settlements to the west. Although naturalized Mexican citizens and nominal Catholics, the American settlers distrusted the Mexicans and complained constantly about the creaking, erratic Mexican judicial system. Mexico had not bargained for the size and speed of American immigration. The first news of the Americans, wrote a Mexican general in 1828, "comes from discovering them on land already under cultivation."

As early as 1826 an American *empresario,* Haden Edwards, led a revolt against Mexican rule, but Mexican forces, aided by Austin, crushed the uprising. However, Mexican policies in the early 1830s quickly eroded the American settlers' allegiance to the Mexican government. In 1830 the government closed Texas to further immigration from the United States and forbade the introduction of more slaves to Texas, a troubling matter because many American settlers were slaveholders. But Mexico could not enforce its decrees, and between 1830 and 1834 the number of Americans in Texas doubled. Austin secured repeal of the prohibition against American migration in 1834; within a year an estimated 1,000 Americans a month were entering Texas. In 1836 Texas counted some 30,000 white Americans, 5,000 black slaves, and 4,000 Mexicans.

At the same time, the Mexican government grew more and more erratic. "The political character of this country," Austin wrote, "seems to partake of its geological features—all is volcanic." From the beginning, the government had featured a precarious balance between liberals who favored decentralized government and conservatives who wanted a highly centralized state with power in the hands of the military and church officials in Mexico City. When Antonio López de Santa Anna became president of Mexico in 1834, he restricted the power of the individual states, including Coahuila-Texas. His actions ignited a series of rebellions in the Mexican states, the most important of which became the Texas Revolution.

The Texas Revolution

At first the insurgent Anglo-Texans sought the restoration of the liberal Constitution of 1824 and greater autonomy for Texas, not independence. But Santa Anna's brutal treatment of the rebels alarmed the initially moderate Austin and others. When Santa Anna invaded Texas in fall 1835, Austin cast his lot with the radicals who wanted outright independence.

Santa Anna's armies met with initial success. In February 1836, 4,000 of his men laid siege to San Antonio, where 200 rebels had retreated into an abandoned mission, the Alamo. On March 6—four days after Texas had declared its independence, although they did not know about it—the defenders of the Alamo were overwhelmed by Mexican troops. Under Santa Anna's orders, the Mexican army killed all the Alamo's defenders, including the wounded. A few weeks later Mexican troops massacred 350 Texas prisoners at Goliad.

Meanwhile, the Texans had formed an army with Sam Houston at its head. A giant man of extensive political and military experience, Houston retreated east to pick up recruits, many of them Americans who crossed the Sabine River border to fight Santa Anna. On April 21, 1836, Houston's army turned and surprised the complacent Mexican forces under Santa Anna, which had encamped on a prairie just to the east of what is now the city of Houston. Shouting, "Remember the Alamo!" and "Remember Goliad!" Houston's army of 1,200 tore through the Mexican lines, killing nearly half of Santa Anna's men in fifteen minutes and capturing the general himself. This engagement, the Battle of San Jacinto, gave Texas its independence from Mexico, although the Mexican government never ratified the treaty that Santa Anna signed. However, Texas became an independent republic, not the American state that most had envisioned.

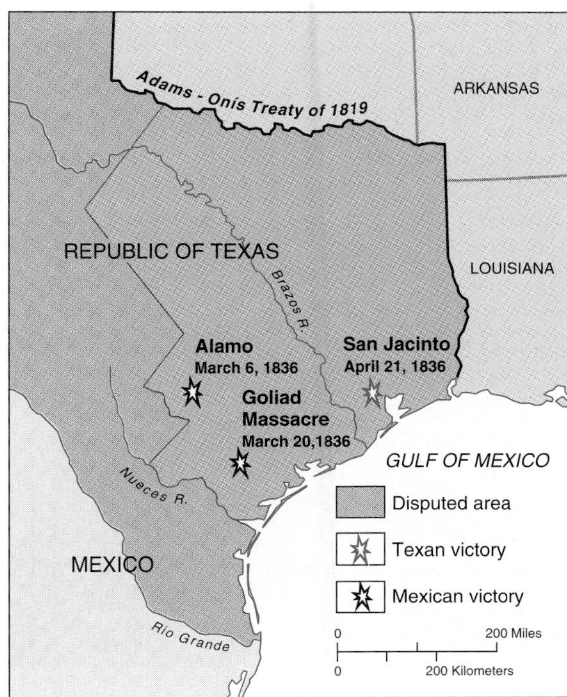

Major Battles in the Texas Revolution, 1835–1836
Sam Houston's victory at San Jacinto was the decisive action of the war and avenged the massacres at the Alamo and Goliad.

American Settlements in California, New Mexico, and Oregon

Before 1840 California and New Mexico, both less accessible than Texas, exerted only a mild attraction for American settlers. That year a mere 100 Americans lived in New Mexico and perhaps 400 in California. According to a contemporary, these Americans "are scattered throughout the whole Mexican population, and most of them have Spanish wives. . . . They live in every respect like the Spanish."

Yet the beginnings of change were evident. During the 1840s Americans streamed into the Sacramento Valley, lured by favorable reports of the region and welcomed by the Hispanic population as a way to encourage economic development. To these land-hungry settlers, geographically and culturally separated from the Mexican population, no sacrifice was too great if it led to California.

To the north, Oregon's abundant farmland

Sam Houston (1793–1863)
This photo shows Houston as a prosperous, successful elder statesman. But in his youth, Houston had a reputation for wildness. In 1829 he resigned Tennessee's governorship and lived dissolutely for three years among the Cherokee Indians.

beckoned settlers from the Mississippi Valley. By 1840 some 500 Americans had settled there, in what was described as a "pioneer's paradise" where "the pigs are running around under the great acorn trees, round and fat and already cooked, with knives and forks sticking in them so that you can cut off a slice whenever you are hungry." To some, Oregon was more attractive than California, especially because the joint British-American occupation seemed to herald eventual U.S. annexation.

The Overland Trail

Whether bound for California or Oregon, Americans faced a four-month ordeal crossing terrain little known in reality but vividly depicted in fiction as an Indian killing ground. Cautious pioneers stocked up on enough guns to equip an army in jump-off towns such as Independence and St. Joseph, Missouri. In fact, they were more likely to shoot one another than to be shot by the usually cooperative Indians and much more likely to be scalped by Independence or St. Joseph merchants selling their goods at inflated prices.

Along the Overland Trail the emigrants faced hardships and hazards: ornery mules that kicked, bit, and balked; oxen that collapsed from thirst; and overloaded wagons that broke down. Trails were difficult to follow and too often marked by the debris of broken wagons and the bleached bones of oxen. Guidebooks were more like guessbooks. The Donner party, which left Illinois in 1846, lost so much time following one such guidebook that it became snowbound in the High Sierra during a bitter winter. To survive, members of the party guaranteed themselves a place in future textbooks by turning to cannibalism.

Emigrants met the challenges of the overland trail by close cooperation with one another, traveling in huge wagon trains rather than alone. Men yoked and unyoked the oxen, drove the wagons and stock, and hunted. Women packed, cooked, and assisted in childbirths. Men also stood guard against Indian raids, although these were rare.

Between 1840 and 1848, an estimated 11,500 pioneers followed an overland trail to Oregon, and some 2,700 reached California. Such small numbers made a difference, for the British did not settle Oregon at all and the Mexican population of California was small and scattered. By 1845 California was clinging to Mexico by the thinnest of threads. The territory's Hispanic population, the *californios*, felt little allegiance to Mexico, which they contemptuously called "the other shore." Some of them wanted independence from Mexico, while others contemplated British or French rule. By the mid-1840s these *californios*, with their tenuous allegiances, faced a growing number of American settlers with definite political sympathies.

The Politics of Expansion

Westward expansion raised the question of whether the United States should annex Texas. In the 1840s the Texas issue sparked political passions and became entangled with other unsettling issues about the West. Between 1846 and 1848 a war with Mexico and a dramatic confrontation with Britain settled these questions on terms favorable to the United States.

At the start of the 1840s western issues received little attention in a nation concerned with issues relating to economic recovery—tariffs, banking, and internal improvements. Only after politicians failed to address the economic problems coherently did opportunistic leaders thrust expansion-related issues to the top of the political agenda.

The Whig Ascendancy

The election of 1840 brought the Whig candidate William Henry Harrison to the presidency and installed Whig majorities in both houses of Congress. The Whigs proposed to replace Van Buren's Independent Treasury (see Chapter 10) with some sort of national fiscal agency such as the Bank of the United States. The Whig party also favored a revised tariff that would increase government revenues but remain low enough to permit the importation of foreign goods. According to the Whig plan, the states would then receive tariff-generated revenues for internal improvements.

The Whig program might well have breezed into law. But Harrison died after only a month in office, and his successor, John Tyler, a Virginia aristocrat put on the ticket for his southern appeal, proved a disaster for the Whigs. A former Democrat, Tyler continued to favored the Democratic philosophy of states' rights. As president, he used the veto to shred his new party's program. In August 1841 a Whig measure to create a new national bank fell to Tyler's veto, as did a subsequent modification.

Tyler also played havoc with Whig tariff policy by vetoing one bill to lower tariffs to 20 percent in accord with the Compromise Tariff and rejecting another to distribute revenue from a higher tariff to the states. Whig leaders were understandably furious; some Whigs talked of impeaching Tyler. In August 1842 the president, needing money to run the government, signed a new bill that maintained some tariffs above 20 percent but abandoned distribution to the states.

Tyler's erratic course confounded and disrupted his party. By maintaining some tariffs above 20 percent, the tariff of 1842 satisfied northern manufacturers, but by abandoning distribution, it infuriated southerners and westerners. The issue cut across party lines. In the congressional elections of 1842, the Whigs paid a heavy price for failing to enact their program; they lost control of the House to the Democrats. Now the nation had one party controlling the Senate, another controlling the House, and a president who appeared to belong to neither.

Tyler and Texas Annexation

Although disowned by his party, Tyler ardently desired a second term as president. Domestic issues offered him little hope of building a popular following, but foreign policy was another matter. In 1842 Tyler's secretary of state, Daniel Webster, concluded the Webster-Ashburton Treaty with Great Britain, settling a long-festering dispute over the Maine-Canadian border. Tyler reasoned that if he could follow the treaty, which was highly popular in the North, with the annexation of Texas, he could build a national following.

The issue of slavery clouded every discussion of Texas. Antislavery northerners saw proposals to annex Texas as part of a southern conspiracy to extend American territory into Mexico, Cuba, and Central America. Thus an unlimited number of new slave states could be created, but British Canada would eliminate the possibility of free states expanding to the north. And some southerners talked openly of carving Texas into four or five slave states.

Nevertheless, in summer 1843 Tyler launched a campaign for Texas annexation. He justified his crusade by reporting that he had learned of an attempt to make Texas a British, rather than an

American, ally. John C. Calhoun, who became secretary of state in 1844, embroidered these reports with his own theories of British plans to use abolition as a way to destroy rice, sugar, and cotton production in the United States.

In spring 1844 Tyler and Calhoun submitted to the Senate a treaty annexing Texas. Accompanying the treaty was a letter from Calhoun to the British minister in Washington defending slavery as beneficial to African-Americans, the only way to protect them from "vice and pauperism." Abolitionists now had evidence that the annexation of Texas was linked to a conspiracy to extend slavery. Consequently, both Whig and Democratic leaders came out in opposition to the annexation of Texas, and the treaty went down to crushing defeat in the Senate. But however ostensibly decisive, the Senate vote simply dumped the annexation question into the upcoming presidential election.

The Election of 1844

Tyler's ineptitude turned the presidential campaign into a free-for-all. Unable to gather support as an independent, he dropped out of the race. Henry Clay had a secure grip on the Whig nomination, but Martin Van Buren's apparently clear path to the head of the Democratic ticket vanished as the issue of annexation split his party. A deadlocked Democratic party finally turned to James K. Polk of Tennessee, the first "dark-horse" nominee in American history.

Little known outside the South, the slaveholding Polk enjoyed broad southern support as the "bosom friend of [Andrew] Jackson, and a pure whole-hogged Democrat, the known enemy of banks and distribution." Polk supported the immediate "reannexation" of Texas—like Jackson, he believed that Texas had been part of the Louisiana Purchase until ceded to Spain in the Transcontinental (Adams-Onís) Treaty of 1819. Indeed, Polk followed Old Hickory's lead so often that he became known as Young Hickory.

Jeering "Who is James K. Polk?" the Whigs derided the nomination. However, Polk, a wily campaigner, convinced many northerners that annexation of Texas would benefit them. In an imaginative scenario, Polk and his supporters argued that if Britain succeeded in abolitionizing Texas, slavery would not be able to move westward, racial tensions in existing slave states would intensify, and the chances of a race war would increase. However farfetched, this argument played effectively on northern racial phobias and helped Polk to detach annexation from Calhoun's narrow, prosouthern defense.

In contrast to the Democrats, whose position was clear, Clay and the Whigs wobbled. After several shifts Clay finally came out against annexation, but not until September. His wavering alienated his southern supporters and prompted some of his northern supporters to bolt the Whigs for the antislavery Liberty party, formed in 1840. The Whigs also infuriated Catholic immigrant voters by nominating Theodore Frelinghuysen for the vice presidency. A supporter of temperance and an assortment of other causes, Frelinghuysen confirmed fears that the Whigs were the orthodox Protestant

The Election of 1844

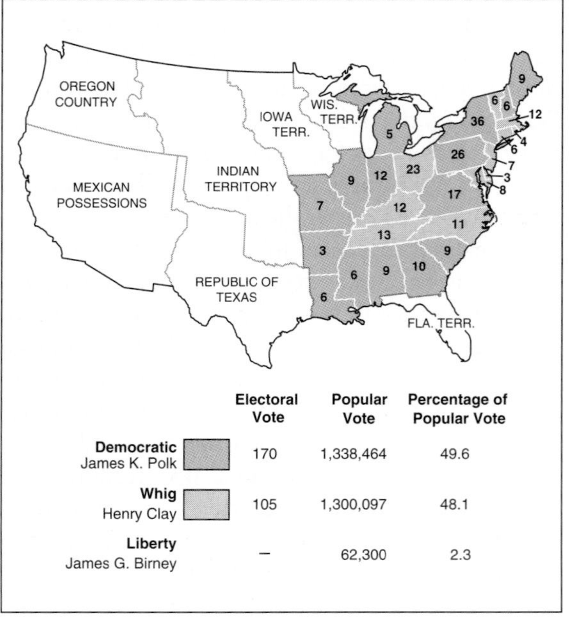

	Electoral Vote	Popular Vote	Percentage of Popular Vote
Democratic James K. Polk	170	1,338,464	49.6
Whig Henry Clay	105	1,300,097	48.1
Liberty James G. Birney	–	62,300	2.3

party. Catholic immigrants turned out in large numbers to vote for the Democrats.

On the eve of the election in New York City, so many Irish marched to the courthouse to be qualified for voting that the windows had to be opened to allow people to enter and leave. "Ireland has reconquered the country which England lost," moaned an embittered Whig. Polk won the electoral vote 170–105, but his margin in the popular vote was only 38,000 out of 2.6 million votes cast. A shift of 6,000 votes in New York, where the immigrant vote and Whig defections to the Liberty party had hurt Clay, would have given Clay the state and the presidency.

Manifest Destiny

The election of 1844 demonstrated the strength of national support for the annexation of Texas. The surging popular sentiment for expansion reflected a growing conviction that America's natural destiny was to expand into Texas and all the way to the Pacific Ocean.

Expansionists emphasized extending the "area of freedom" and talked of "repelling the contaminating proximity of monarchies upon the soil that we have consecrated to the rights of man." For young Americans such as Walt Whitman, such restless expansionism knew few limits. "The more we reflect upon annexation as involving a part of Mexico, the more do doubts and obstacles resolve themselves away," Whitman wrote. "Then there is California, on the way to which lovely tract lies Santa Fe; how long a time will elapse before they shine as two new stars in our mighty firmament?" Americans needed only a phrase to capture this ebullient spirit. In 1845 John L. O'Sullivan, a New York Democratic journalist, supplied that phrase when he wrote of "our manifest destiny to overspread and to possess the whole of the continent which Providence has given us for the development of the great experiment of liberty and federated self-government entrusted to us."

Advocates of Manifest Destiny used lofty language and invoked God and nature to justify expansion. Because most champions of Manifest Destiny were Democrats who favored annexing Texas, northern Whigs dismissed Manifest Destiny as a smoke screen to conceal an evil intent to extend slavery. In fact, many expansionists supported neither slavery nor annexation. Most had their eyes not on Texas but on Oregon and California. Blaming the post-1837 depression on the failure of Americans to find markets for their agricultural surplus, they saw California and Oregon as solutions. A Missouri Democrat observed that "the ports of Asia are as convenient to Oregon as the ports of Europe are to the eastern slope of our confederacy, with an infinitely better ocean for navigation." An Alabama Democrat praised California's "safe and capacious harbors," which "invite to their bosoms the rich commerce of the East."

More than trade was at stake. To many, expansion presented an opportunity to preserve the agricultural character of the American people and thus to safeguard democracy. Fundamentally Jeffersonian, expansionists equated industrialization and urbanization with social stratification and class strife. To avoid the "bloated wealth" and "terrible misery" that afflicted Britain, the United States *had to* expand.

Democrats saw expansion as a logical complement to their support of low tariffs and their opposition to centralized banking. High tariffs and banks tended to "favor and foster the factory system," but expansion would provide farmers with land and with access to foreign markets. Americans would continue to be farmers, and the foundations of the Republic would remain secure.

This message, trumpeted by the penny press, made sense to the working poor, many of them Irish immigrants. Expansion would open economic opportunity for the common people and thwart British plans to free American slaves, whom the poor viewed as potential competition for already scarce jobs.

Expansionism drew on the ideas of Thomas Jefferson, John Quincy Adams, and other leaders of the early Republic who had proclaimed the American people's right to displace any people, uncivilized or European, from their westward path. Early expansionists had feared that overexpansion might create an ungovernable empire, but their successors had no such qualms. Although they pointed with alarm to the negative effects of industrialization, the expansionists also relied on the technology of industrialization. The railroad and the telegraph, they said, had annihilated the problem of distance and made expansion safe.

Polk and Oregon

The growing spirit of Manifest Destiny intensified the Oregon issue. To soften northern criticism of the pending annexation of Texas, the Democrats had included in their 1844 platform the assertion that American title "to the whole of the Territory of Oregon is clear and unquestionable." Taken literally, this statement, which Polk repeated in his inaugural address, pressed an American claim to the entire Oregon Territory between California and 54°40', a claim never before advanced.

Polk's objectives in Oregon were far subtler than his language. He knew that it would take a war with Britain for the United States to claim the entire Oregon Territory, and he wanted to avoid war. He hoped the belligerent language would persuade the British to accept what they had previously rejected, a division of Oregon at the forty-ninth parallel. This settlement would give the United States the superb deep-water harbor of Puget Sound and the southern tip of Vancouver Island.

Polk's position succeeded in rousing furious interest in the nation's acquiring the entire territory. Mass meetings adopted such resolutions as "The Whole or None!" Each year brought new American settlers into Oregon. John Quincy Adams, though no supporter of the annexation of Texas or the 54°40' boundary for Oregon, believed that American settlements gave the United States a stronger claim than discovery and exploration had given the British. The United States, not Britain, he contended, was destined "to make the wilderness blossom as the rose, to establish laws, to increase, multiply, and subdue the earth," all "at the first behest of God Almighty."

In April 1846 Polk forced the issue by notifying Britain that the United States was terminating the joint British-American occupation of Oregon. In effect, this message was that the British could either go to war over the American claims to 54°40′ or negotiate. They chose to negotiate. Although raging against "that ill-regulated, overbearing, and aggressive spirit of American democracy," Britain faced too many other problems to wage war over "a few miles of pine swamp." The ensuing treaty divided Oregon at the forty-ninth parallel, although Britain retained all of Vancouver Island and navigation rights on the Columbia River. On June 15, 1846, the Senate ratified the treaty, stipulating that Britain's navigation rights on the Columbia were temporary.

The Origins of the Mexican War

While Polk challenged Britain over Oregon, the United States and Mexico moved toward war. The conflict had both immediate and remote causes. One long-standing grievance lay in the failure of the Mexican government to pay $2 million in debts

Oregon Boundary Dispute

Although demanding that Britain cede the entire Oregon Territory south of 54°40′, the United States settled for a compromise at the forty-ninth parallel.

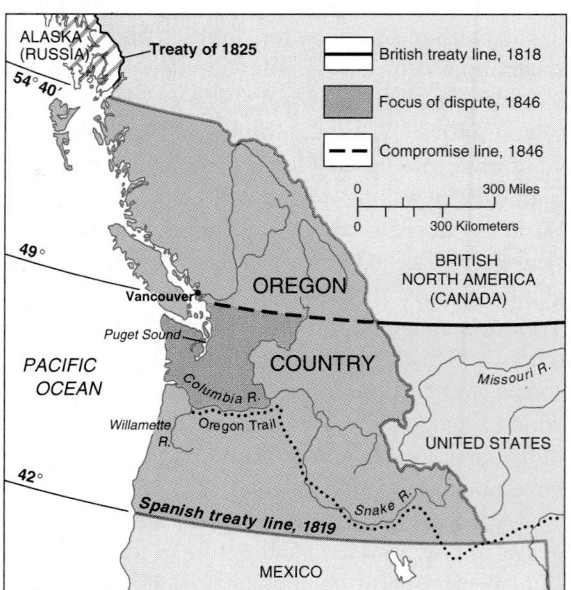

Patriotism and the Mexican War
U.S. soldiers commonly wore tall hats known as shako caps during the Mexican War. The caps were adorned with decorative plates showing the eagle spreading its wings, the symbol of Manifest Destiny. Inexpensive and mass-produced lithographs such as the one on the left, depicting the Battle of Sacramento, aroused patriotic support for the war.

owed to U.S. citizens. Bitter memories of the Alamo and of the Goliad massacre, moreover, reinforced American loathing of Mexico. Above all, the issue of Texas poisoned relations. Mexico still hoped to regain Texas or to keep it independent of the United States. Should Texas join the United States, Mexico feared, Americans might seize other provinces and even Mexico itself and treat Mexicans as they treated slaves.

Polk's election increased the strength of the pro-annexationists, as his campaign had persuaded many northerners that Texas's annexation would bring national benefits. In February 1845 both houses of Congress responded to popular sentiment by passing a resolution annexing Texas. However, Texans balked, in part because some feared that union with the United States would provoke a Mexican invasion and war on Texas soil.

Polk moved rapidly. To sweeten the pot for Texans, he supported their claim that the Rio Grande constituted Texas's southern border, despite Mexico's contention that the Nueces River, 100 miles farther north, bounded Texas. Because the Rio Grande meandered west and north nearly 2,000 miles, it encompassed a huge territory, including part of modern New Mexico. The Texas that Polk proposed to annex thus was far larger than the Texas that had gained independence from Mexico. On July 4, 1845, reassured by Polk's support, Texas voted to accept annexation. To counter Mexican belligerency, Polk ordered American troops under General Zachary Taylor to the edge of the disputed territory. Taylor deployed his army at Corpus Christi, south of the Nueces River, in territory still claimed by Mexico.

California and its fine harbors influenced Polk's actions, for he had entered the White House with the firm intention of extending American control over that province, too. If Mexico went to war with the United States over Texas, Polk's supporters claimed, "the road to California will be open to us." Reports from American agents convinced Polk that the way lay open for California to join the United States as Texas would—by revolution and then annexation.

Continued turmoil in Mexican politics further complicated this complex situation. In early 1845 a new Mexican government agreed to negotiate with the United States, and Polk decided to give negotiations a chance. In November 1845 he dispatched John Slidell to Mexico City with instructions to gain Mexican recognition of the annexation of Texas with the Rio Grande border. In exchange, the U.S. government would assume the debt owed by Mexico to American citizens. Polk also authorized Slidell to offer up to $25 million for California and New Mexico. However, by the time Slidell reached Mexico City, the government there had become too weak to make concessions to the United States, and its head, General José Herrara, refused to receive Slidell. Polk then ordered Taylor to move southward to the Rio Grande, hoping to provoke a Mexican attack and to unite the American people behind war.

The Mexican government, however, dawdled over taking the bait. Polk was about to send a war message to Congress when word finally arrived that Mexican forces had crossed the Rio Grande and attacked the U.S. army. *"American blood has been shed on American soil!"* Polk's followers jubilantly proclaimed. On May 11, 1846, Polk informed Congress that war "exists by the act of Mexico herself" and called for $10 million to fight the war.

Polk's disingenuous assertion that the United States was already at war provoked furious opposition in Congress. For one thing, the Mexican attack on Taylor's troops had taken place on land never before claimed by the United States. Equally grievous, in announcing that war already existed, Polk seemed to undercut congressional power to declare war. He was using a mere border incident as a pretext to plunge the nation into a general war to acquire more slave territory. Whig papers warned readers that Polk was "precipitating you into a fathomless abyss of crime and calamity." But Polk had backed the Whigs into a corner. They could not afford to appear unpatriotic—they remembered vividly what opposition to the War of 1812 had cost the Federalists—so they swallowed their outrage and supported war.

Polk's single-minded pursuit of his goals had prevailed. A humorless, austere man who banned dancing and liquor at White House receptions, Polk inspired little personal warmth. But he had clear objectives and pursued them unflinchingly. He triumphed over all opposition, in part because of his opponents' fragmentation, in part because of expansion's popular appeal, and in part because of his foreign antagonists' weakness. Reluctant to fight over Oregon, Britain had negotiated. Too weak to negotiate, Mexico chose to fight over territory that it had already lost (Texas) and where its hold was feeble (California and New Mexico).

The Mexican War

Most European observers expected Mexico to win the war. Its army was four times the size of the American forces, and it was fighting on home ground. The United States, having botched its one previous attempt to invade a neighbor, Canada in 1812, now had to sustain offensive operations in an area remote from American settlements. American expansionists, however, hardly expected the Mexicans to fight at all. Racism and arrogance convinced many Americans that the Mexican people, degraded by their mixed Spanish and Indian population, were "as sure to melt away at the approach of [American] energy and enterprise as snow before a southern sun," as one newspaper publisher insisted.

In fact, the Mexicans fought bravely and stubbornly, although unsuccessfully. In May 1846 Taylor, "Old Rough and Ready," routed the Mexican army in Texas and pursued it across the Rio Grande, eventually to capture the major city of Monterrey in September. War enthusiasm surged in the United States, and recruiting posters blared, "Here's to old Zach! Glorious Times! Roast Beef, Ice Cream, and Three Months' Advance!" After taking Monterrey, Taylor, starved for supplies, halted and granted Mexico an eight-week armistice. Eager to undercut Taylor's popularity—the Whigs were already touting him as a presidential candidate—Polk stripped him of half his forces and reassigned them to General Winfield Scott. He was to mount an amphibious attack on Vera Cruz and proceed on to Mexico City, following the path of Cortés and his *conquistadores*. Events outstripped Polk's scheme, however, when Taylor defeated a far larger Mexican army at the Battle of Buena Vista, on February 22–23, 1847.

Farther north, American forces took advantage of the shakiness of Mexican rule to strip away New

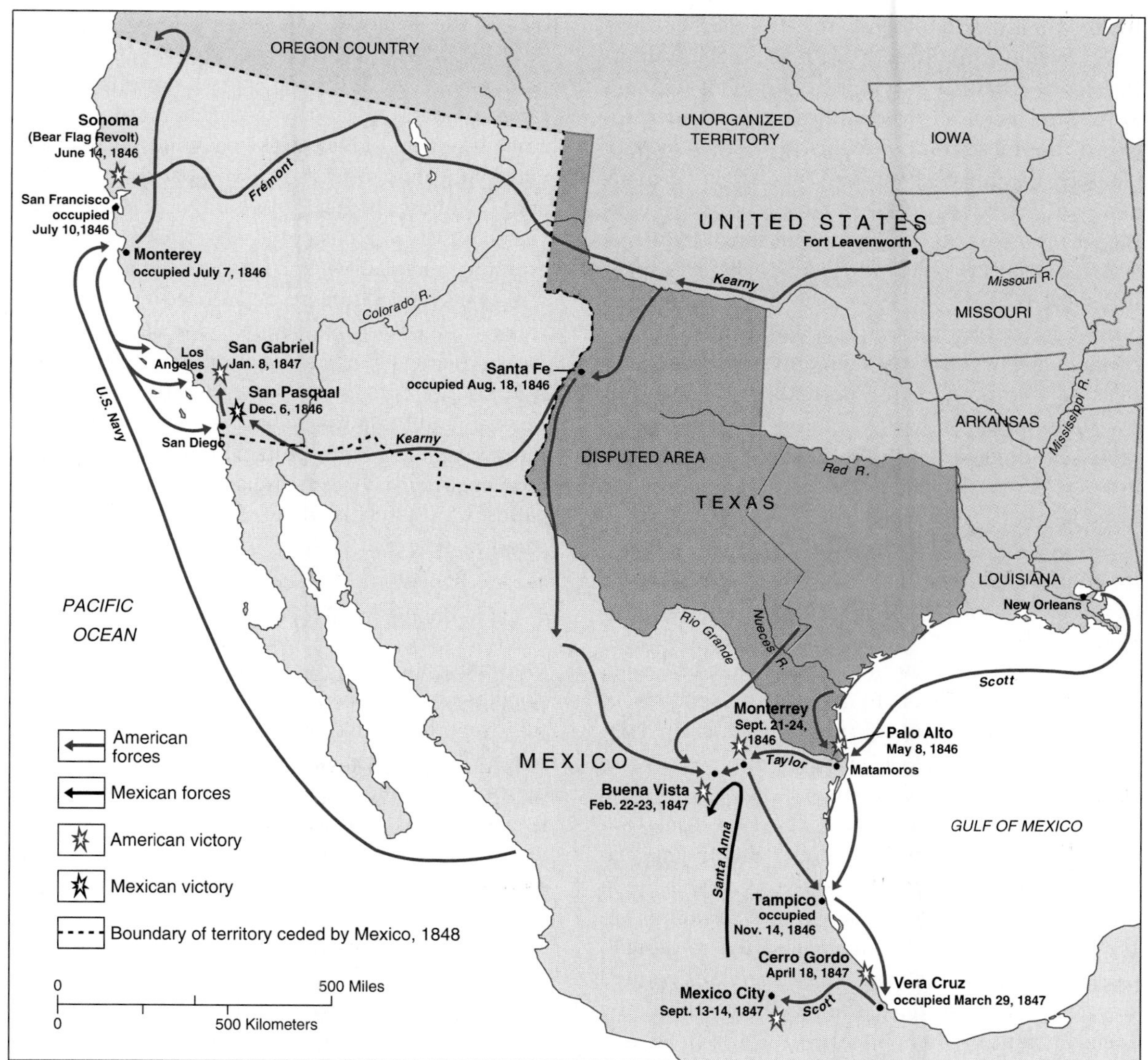

Major Battles of the Mexican War *The Mexican War's decisive campaign began with General Winfield Scott's capture of Vera Cruz and ended with his conquest of Mexico City.*

Mexico and California. In spring 1846 Colonel Stephen Kearny led an army from Fort Leavenworth, Kansas, toward Santa Fe. Having overcome immense natural obstacles to reach New Mexico, Kearny took the territory by a combination of bluff, bluster, and, perhaps, bribery. The Mexican governor, who had said that "it is better to be thought brave than to be so," fled at Kearny's approach. Once he had suppressed a brief rebellion by Mexicans and Indians, Kearny controlled New Mexico securely enough that he could dispatch part of his army south into Mexico to support Taylor at Buena Vista.

California also fell easily into American hands.

In 1845 Polk had ordered the Pacific Squadron under Commodore John D. Sloat to occupy California's ports in event of war. The president had also dispatched a courier overland with secret orders for one of the most colorful actors in the conquest of California, John C. Frémont. A Georgia-born adventurer, Frémont had taken advantage of his marriage to the daughter of a powerful senator to have accounts of his explorations in the Northwest published as official government documents, then basked in glory as "the Great Pathfinder." Polk's courier caught up with Frémont in Oregon. Instructed to proceed to California and "watch over the interests of the United States," Frémont interpreted his orders liberally. In June 1846 he rounded up some American insurgents, captured the town of Sonoma, and proclaimed the independent "Bear Flag Republic." The combined efforts of Frémont, Sloat, and Kearny (who had continued on to California after his successful New Mexico campaign) established U.S. control over California.

The war's final and most important campaign brought Winfield Scott to glory in the conquest of Mexico City itself. In March 1847 Scott carried out a successful amphibious landing near Vera Cruz, pounded the city into submission, and moved inland to attack Mexico City. The U.S. army encountered a Mexican force under Santa Anna at the seemingly impregnable Cerro Gordo pass, but a young captain, Robert E. Lee, helped to find a trail that outflanked the Mexicans and led to a small peak overlooking the pass. The Americans planted howitzers there, stormed the pass, and routed the Mexican army. On September 13, 1847, Mexico City fell to Scott, and he joined Zachary Taylor in the pantheon of new American heroes.

Although the Mexican army had outnumbered the U.S. forces in virtually every battle, it could not match the superior artillery or the superior logistics and organization of the "barbarians of the North." American soldiers died like flies from yellow fever, and they carried into battle the agonies of venereal disease, which they picked up (and left) in every Mexican town they captured, but they benefited enormously from the unprecedented quality of their weapons, supplies, and organization.

By the Treaty of Guadalupe-Hidalgo (February 2, 1848), Mexico ceded Texas with the Rio Grande boundary, New Mexico, and California to the United States; from the Mexican cession would come the states of New Mexico, California, Nevada, and Utah, most of Arizona, and parts of Colorado and Wyoming. In turn, the United States assumed the claims of U.S. citizens against the Mexican government and paid Mexico $15 million. Although some rabid expansionists denounced the treaty because it failed to include all of Mexico, Polk, like most Americans, was satisfied. Empty territory was fine, but few Americans wanted to annex the mixed Spanish and Indian population of Mexico itself and incorporate into the United States "ignorant and indolent half-civilized Indians," in one writer's words. On March 10, 1848, the Senate ratified the treaty by a vote of 38–10.

The Mexican War in the Popular Mind

Occurring amid the rise of the penny press and the popular novel, the Mexican War became the most fully reported war that the United States had yet fought and the first conflict in which war correspondents were employed. The extensive coverage given to battlefield victories fueled soaring nationalism and helped to submerge political divisions. "We are now all Whigs and all Democrats," an Indiana newspaper exulted.

Romance as well as patriotism gripped the popular mind. Writers portrayed the war as evidence that the noble streak in the American character could prevail over the grasping materialism of U.S. society. A generation raised on the historical novels of Sir Walter Scott believed that the age of chivalry had returned. Popular novels such as *The Texas Ranger; or, the Maid of Matamoros* mingled patriotism and romance in tales of how American soldiers routed Mexican men, only to fall in love with Mexican women.

Zachary Taylor became the main beneficiary of public infatuation with the war. "Old Rough and Ready" seemed to combine, in equal parts, military genius, a democratic bearing, and a conspicuously ordinary manner. In contrast to the more punctilious Winfield Scott ("Old Fuss and Feathers"), Taylor went into battle wearing a straw hat and plain brown coat. To a people searching for heroes, even his short, stocky stature seemed vaguely Napoleonic. The war made Taylor a hero, and the conflicts spinning out of that war would now boost his political career.

Intensifying Sectional Divisions

Despite wartime patriotic enthusiasm, sectional conflict sharpened between 1846 and 1848. Questions related to territorial expansion intensified this conflict, but so, too, did President Polk's uncompromising and literal-minded Jacksonianism.

Polk had restored the Independent Treasury, to the Whigs' dismay, and had eroded Democratic unity by pursuing Jacksonian policies on tariffs and internal improvements. Despite Polk's campaign promise to combine a revenue tariff with mild protection, his administration's Tariff of 1846 slashed duties to the minimum necessary for revenue. Having alienated his northern supporters, Polk then disappointed western Democrats, thirsting for federal aid to internal improvements, by vetoing the Rivers and Harbors Bill of 1846.

Important as these issues were, territorial expansion generated the Polk administration's major battles. To Polk, it mattered little whether new territories were slave or free. Expansion would meet its purposes by dispersing the population, weakening dangerous tendencies toward centralized government, and ensuring the agricultural and democratic character of the United States. Focusing attention on slavery in the territories struck him as "not only unwise but wicked." To Polk, the Missouri Compromise, prohibiting slavery north of 36°30', embodied a simple, permanent solution to the question of territorial slavery.

But many northerners were coming to see slavery in the territories as a profoundly disruptive issue that neither could nor should be solved simply by extending the 36°30' line. Abolitionist Whigs, who opposed any expansion of slavery on moral grounds, posed a lesser threat to Polk than northern Democrats who feared that extending slavery into New Mexico and California would deter free laborers from settling those territories. Those Democrats argued that competition with slavery degraded free labor, that the westward extension of slavery would create a barrier to the westward migration of free labor, and that such a barrier would intensify social problems already evident in the East: excessive concentration of population, labor protest, class strife, and social stratification.

The Wilmot Proviso

A young Democratic congressman from Pennsylvania, David Wilmot, galvanized these disaffected northern Democrats. In August 1846 he introduced an amendment to an appropriations bill. This amendment, which became known as the Wilmot Proviso, stipulated that slavery be prohibited in any territory acquired by the negotiations. Wilmot represented the Democrats who had supported annexing Texas on the assumption that it would be the last slave state. Like other northern Democrats, he believed that Polk had made an implicit bargain: Texas for slaveholders, California and New Mexico for free labor. But Polk and southern Democrats opposed any barrier to the expansion of slavery south of the Missouri Compromise line; they believed that the westward expansion of slavery would reduce the concentration of slaves in older southern regions and thus lessen the chances of a slave revolt.

The proviso raised unsettling constitutional questions. Calhoun and other southerners contended that because slaves were property, the Constitution protected slaveholders' right to carry their slaves wherever they chose. This position led to the conclusion that the Missouri Compromise was unconstitutional. On the other side, many northerners cited the Northwest Ordinance of 1787, the Missouri Compromise, and the Constitution itself, which gave Congress the power to "make all needful rules and regulations respecting the territory or other property belonging to the United States," as justification for congressional legislation over slavery in the territories.

The Election of 1848

The Whigs watched in dismay as prosperity returned under Polk's program of an independent treasury and low tariffs. Never before had Henry Clay's American System of national banking and high tariffs seemed so irrelevant. But the Wilmot Proviso gave the Whigs a political windfall; originating in the Democratic party, it allowed the Whigs to portray themselves as the South's only dependable friends.

These considerations inclined the majority of Whigs toward Zachary Taylor. As a Louisiana slaveholder, he had obvious appeal to the South. As a political newcomer, he had no loyalty to a discredited American System. And as a war hero, he had broad national appeal. Nominating Taylor as presidential candidate in 1848, the Whigs presented him as an ideal man "without regard to creeds or principles" and ran him without any platform.

The Democrats faced a greater challenge because David Wilmot was one of their own. They could not ignore the issue of slavery in the territories, but if they embraced the positions of either Wilmot or Calhoun, the party would split along sectional lines. When Polk declined to run for reelection, the Democrats nominated Lewis Cass of Michigan, who solved their dilemma by announcing the doctrine of "squatter sovereignty," or popular sovereignty as it was later called. Cass argued that Congress should let the question of slavery in the territories be decided by the people who settled there. Squatter sovereignty appealed to many because of its arresting simplicity and vagueness; it loftily ignored such questions as whether Congress actually possessed power to prohibit territorial slavery and (if squatter sovereignty were to become law) what timetables for territorial action should be followed. In fact, few Democrats wanted definitive answers. As long as the doctrine remained vague, northern and southern Democrats alike could interpret it to their respective benefit.

In the campaign both parties tried to avoid the issue of slavery in the territories, but neither succeeded. A pro-Wilmot faction of the Democratic party linked up with the abolitionist Liberty party and antislavery "Conscience" Whigs to form the Free-Soil party. Declaring their dedication to "Free Trade, Free Labor, Free Speech, and Free Men," the Free-Soilers nominated Martin Van Buren on a platform opposing any extension of slavery.

Zachary Taylor benefited from the opposition's alienation of key northern states over the tariff issue, from Democratic disunity over the Wilmot Proviso, and from his war-hero stature. He captured a majority of electoral votes in both North and South. Although it failed to carry any state, the Free-Soil party ran well enough in the North to demonstrate the grassroots popularity of opposition to the extension of slavery. By showing that opposition to the spread of slavery had far more appeal than outright abolitionism, the Free-Soilers sent both Whigs and Democrats a message that they would be unable to ignore in future elections.

The California Gold Rush

When Wilmot had introduced his proviso, the issue of slavery in the West was more abstract than immediate, for Mexico had not yet ceded any territory. The picture quickly changed when an American carpenter discovered gold while building a sawmill in the foothills of California's Sierra Nevada only

The Election of 1848

Candidates	*Parties*	*Electoral Vote*	*Popular Vote*	*Percentage of Popular Vote*
ZACHARY TAYLOR	Whig	163	1,360,967	47.4
Lewis Cass	Democratic	127	1,222,342	42.5
Martin Van Buren	Free-Soil		291,263	10.1

San Francisco Saloon, *by Frank Marryat*

Mexicans, Chinese, Yankees, and southerners drink together in an ornate San Francisco saloon in the booming gold-rush days.

nine days before the Treaty of Guadalupe-Hidalgo was signed. A frantic gold rush erupted. A San Francisco paper complained that "the whole country from San Francisco to Los Angeles, and from the shore to the base of the Sierra Nevada, resounds with the sordid cry to gold, GOLD, GOLD! while the field is left half-planted, the house half-built, and everything neglected but the manufacture of shovels and pickaxes." By December 1848 pamphlets with such titles as *The Emigrant's Guide to the Gold Mines* had hit the streets of New York City, and the gold rush was on. Overland emigrants to California rose from 400 in 1848 to 44,000 in 1850.

The gold rush made the issue of slavery in the West an immediate, practical concern. The newcomers to California included Mexicans, free blacks, and slaves brought by southern planters. White prospectors loathed the idea of competing with these groups and wanted to drive them from the gold fields. Violence mounted, and demands grew for a strong civilian government to replace the ineffective military government left over from the war. The gold rush guaranteed that the question of slavery in the Mexican cession would be the first item on the agenda for Polk's successor and the nation.

CONCLUSION

By calling their destiny manifest, Americans of the 1840s implied that they had no choice but to annex Texas, to seize California and New Mexico, and to take the lion's share of Oregon. The idea of inevitable expansion had deep roots in American experiences and values. Fed by immigration, the population had grown dramatically, increasing nearly 500 percent between 1800 and 1850. Overwhelming numbers of U.S. settlers did as much to seal the fate of Texas as did Sam Houston's victory in the Battle of San Jacinto. Expansion also rested on ideas that seemed self-evident to antebellum Americans: that a nation of farmers would never experience sustained misery, that most Americans would rather work on farms than in factories, and that expansion would provide more land for farming, reduce the dangerous concentration of people in cities, and restore opportunity for all.

But expansion did little to heal deepening divisions between immigrants and native-born Americans or between northerners and southerners. Instead, it split the Democratic party, widened the gap between northern and southern Whigs, and spurred the emergence of the Free-Soil party. As the 1840s ended, Americans, victorious over Mexico and enriched by the discovery of gold in California, would begin to discover the high price of expansion.

CHRONOLOGY

1818 The United States and Britain agree on joint occupation of Oregon for a ten-year period.

1819 Transcontinental (Adams-Onís) Treaty.

1821 Mexico gains independence from Spain.

1822 Stephen F. Austin founds the first American community in Texas.

1824–1825 Russia abandons its claims to Oregon south of 50°40'.

1826 Haden Edwards leads an abortive rebellion against Mexican rule in Texas.

1827 The United States and Britain renew their agreement on joint occupation of Oregon for an indefinite period.

1830 Mexico closes Texas to further American immigration.

1834 Antonio López de Santa Anna comes to power in Mexico.
Austin secures repeal of the ban on American immigration into Texas.

1835 Santa Anna invades Texas.

1836 Texas declares its independence from Mexico.
Fall of the Alamo.
Goliad massacre.
Battle of San Jacinto.

1840 William Henry Harrison elected president.

1841 Harrison dies; John Tyler becomes president.
Tyler vetoes Whig National Banking Bill.

1842 Webster-Ashburton Treaty.

1843 Tyler launches campaign for Texas annexation.

1844 Philadelphia Bible Riots.
Senate rejects treaty annexing Texas.
James K. Polk elected president.

1845 Texas accepts annexation by the United States.
Mexico rejects Slidell mission.

1846 Congress ends the joint occupation of Oregon.
Zachary Taylor defeats the Mexicans in two battles north of the Rio Grande.
The United States declares war on Mexico.
John C. Frémont proclaims the Bear Flag Republic in California.
Congress votes to accept a settlement of the Oregon boundary issue with Britain.
Colonel Stephen Kearny occupies Santa Fe.
Wilmot Proviso introduced.
Taylor takes Monterrey.

1847 Taylor defeats Santa Anna at the Battle of Buena Vista.
Vera Cruz falls to Winfield Scott.
Mexico City falls to Scott.
Lewis Cass's principle of "squatter sovereignty."

1848 Gold discovered in California.
Treaty of Guadalupe-Hidalgo signed.
Taylor elected president.

FOR FURTHER READING

Ray A. Billington, *The Far Western Frontier, 1830–1860* (1956). A comprehensive narrative of the settlement of the Far West.

William R. Brock, *Parties and Political Conscience: American Dilemmas, 1840–1850* (1979). An excellent interpretive study of the politics of the 1840s.

William H. Goetzmann, *When the Eagle Screamed: The Romantic Horizon in American Diplomacy, 1800–1860* (1966). A lively overview of antebellum expansionism.

Maldwyn A. Jones, *American Immigration* (1960). An excellent brief introduction to immigration.

Patricia Nelson Limerick, *Legacy of Conquest* (1987). A provocative interpretation of western history.

Charles G. Sellers, *James K. Polk: Continentalist, 1843–1846* (1966). An outstanding political biography.

Henry Nash Smith, *Virgin Land: The American West as Symbol and Myth* (1950). A classic study of westward expansion in the American mind.

CHAPTER 14

From Compromise to Secession, 1850–1861

The Compromise of 1850

The Collapse of the Second Party System

The Crisis of the Union

From December 1859 to February 1860 Congress deadlocked over the selection of the Speaker of the House of Representatives. Tempers flared as northerners and southerners collided ideologically. A South Carolinian observed that "the only persons who do not have a revolver and a knife are those who have two revolvers." The election of an inoffensive New Jersey congressman to the speakership broke the deadlock, but the tension in Congress reflected the divisions between North and South that would lead to civil war.

Confrontations with the North over slavery in the territories fed a deepening desperation in the South and spawned thoughts of secession—withdrawal from the Union. During the 1850s a growing number of northerners embraced the doctrine of free soil, the belief that Congress had to prohibit slavery in all the territories. Prominent free-soilers such as William Seward of New York and Abraham Lincoln of Illinois, who sought to limit but not to abolish slavery, made the

(Right) ***John Brown*** *by John Steuart Curry, 1939*

conflict over slavery a national issue. Seward spoke of an "irrepressible conflict" between slavery and freedom, and Lincoln said, "I believe this government cannot endure permanently half *slave* and half *free*."

To free-soil advocates, the ideal society was composed of free people working to achieve economic self-sufficiency as landowning farmers, self-employed artisans, and small shopkeepers. Southerners also valued economic independence, but they insisted that without slaves to do menial jobs, whites could never attain self-sufficiency. By 1850 most southerners had persuaded themselves that slavery treated blacks humanely while enabling whites to live comfortably.

These differing images of the good society made conflict over slavery in the territories virtually unavoidable. Free-soil attacks on territorial slavery infuriated southerners, who believed they should be able to take slaves—their property—anywhere they wanted. They interpreted free-soilers' hostility as a thinly disguised attempt to erode slavery's foundations. When abolitionist John Brown recklessly attempted to launch a slave insurrection in 1859, many southerners concluded that secession offered their only protection. "Not only our property," a southern editor proclaimed, "but our honor, our lives and our all are involved."

The Compromise of 1850

Ralph Waldo Emerson's grim prediction that a U.S. victory in the Mexican War would be like swallowing arsenic proved disturbingly accurate. When the war ended in 1848, the United States contained an equal number (fifteen each) of free and slave states, but the vast territory gained by the war threatened to upset this balance. Any solution to the question of slavery in the Mexican cession—a free-soil policy, extension of the Missouri Compromise line, or popular sovereignty—ensured controversy. The prospect of free soil angered southerners, while extension of the Missouri Compromise line antagonized free-soil northerners as well as southern extremists who proclaimed that Congress could not bar slavery's expansion. Popular sovereignty offered the greatest hope for compromise by taking the question of slavery out of national politics and handing it to each territory, but this notion pleased neither free-soil nor proslavery extremists.

As the rhetoric escalated, events plunged the nation into crisis. Utah and then California, both acquired from Mexico, sought admission to the Union as free states. Texas, admitted to the Union as a slave state in 1845, aggravated matters by claiming the eastern half of New Mexico, thus potentially opening the door to slavery's extension into other newly acquired territory.

By 1850 other issues had become intertwined with territorial questions. Northerners had grown increasingly unhappy with slavery in the District of Columbia, within the shadow of the Capitol; southerners complained about lax enforcement of the Fugitive Slave Act of 1793. Any broad compromise would have to take both matters into account.

Zachary Taylor at the Helm

President Zachary Taylor believed that the South must not kindle the issue of slavery in the territories because neither New Mexico nor California was suited for slavery. In 1849 he asserted that "the people of the North need have no apprehension of the further extension of slavery."

Taylor's position differed significantly with the thinking behind the still controversial Wilmot Proviso, which proposed that Congress bar slavery in the territories ceded by Mexico. Taylor's plan, in contrast, left the decision to the states. He prompted California to apply for admission as a free state, bypassing the territorial stage, and hinted that he expected New Mexico (where the Mexican government had abolished slavery) to do the same. This strategy appeared to offer a quick, practical solution to the problem of extending slavery. The North would gain two new free states, and the South would gain acceptance of the right of the individual state to bar or to permit slavery.

But southerners rejected Taylor's plan. Not

only would it yield the Wilmot Proviso's goal—the banning of slavery from the lands acquired from Mexico—but it rested on the shaky assumption that slavery could never take root in California or New Mexico. Southerners also protested the addition of two new free states. "If we are to be reduced to a mere handful . . . wo, wo, I say to this Union," John C. Calhoun warned. Disillusioned with Taylor, a slaveholder from whom they had expected better, nine southern states agreed to send delegates to a convention to meet in Nashville in June 1850.

Henry Clay Proposes a Compromise

Had Taylor held a stronger position in the Whig party, he might have blunted mounting southern opposition. But many leading Whigs had never accepted this political novice, and in early 1850 Kentucky senator Henry Clay challenged Taylor's leadership by forging a compromise bill to resolve the whole range of contentious issues. Clay proposed (1) the admission of California as a free state; (2) the division of the remainder of the Mexican cession into two territories, New Mexico and Utah, without federal restrictions on slavery; (3) the settlement of the Texas–New Mexico boundary dispute on terms favorable to New Mexico; (4) as a pot-sweetener for Texas, an agreement that the federal government would assume the state's large public debt; (5) continuation of slavery in the District of Columbia but abolition of the slave trade; and (6) a more effective fugitive slave law.

Clay rolled all these proposals into a single "omnibus" bill. The debates over the compromise bill during late winter and early spring 1850 marked the last major appearance on the public stage of Clay, Calhoun, and Webster, the trio who had stood at the center of American political life since the War of 1812. Clay, the conciliator as ever, warned the South against the evils of secession and assured the North that nature would check the spread of slavery. Gaunt and gloomy, the dying Calhoun listened as another senator read Calhoun's address for him, a repetition of his warnings that only if the North treated the South as an equal could the Union survive. Webster spoke vividly in favor of compromise, "not as a Massachusetts man, nor as a Northern man, but as an American," and chided the North for trying to "reenact the will of God" by excluding slavery from the Mexican cession. Strident voices countered these attempts at conciliation. The antislavery Whig William Seward of New York enraged southerners by talking of a "higher law than the Constitution"—namely, the will of God against the extension of slavery. Clay's compromise faltered as Clay broke with President Taylor, who attacked him as a glory hunter.

Henry Clay (1777–1852)
Eloquent but at the same time earthy, Clay was first elected to the Senate during Jefferson's administration. Subsequently, Clay himself made five unsuccessful bids for the presidency. A European visitor was struck by his penchant for chewing tobacco, drinking whiskey, putting his legs on the table, and spitting "like a regular Kentucky hog-driver."

Even as the Union faced its worst crisis since 1789, events in summer 1850 eased the way toward

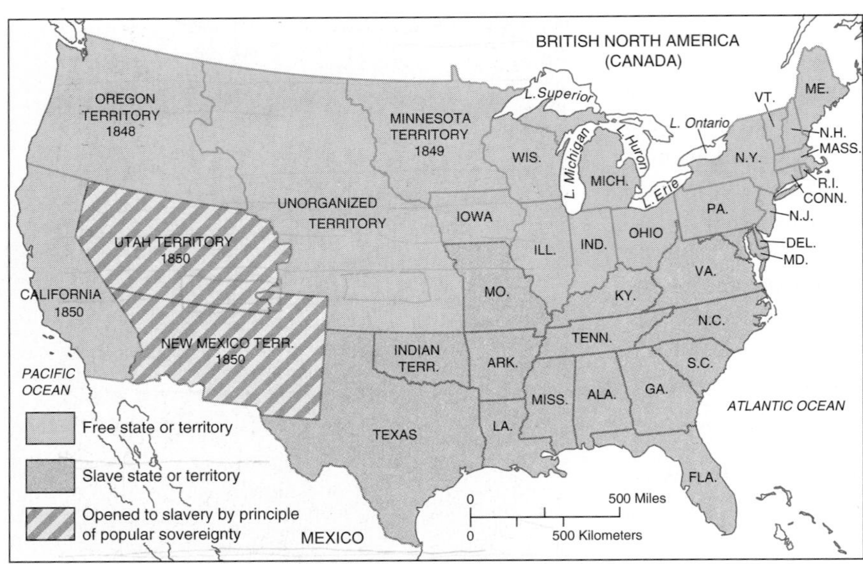

The Compromise of 1850

The Compromise of 1850 admitted California as a free state. Utah and New Mexico were left open to slavery or freedom according to the principle of popular sovereignty.

resolution. When the Nashville convention met in June, only nine of the fifteen slave states, primarily in the Lower South, sent delegates. Despite the reckless pronouncements of the "fire-eaters" (extreme advocates of "southern rights"), moderates dominated. Then Zachary Taylor celebrated too extravagantly on July 4 and died five days later of a stomach ailment. His successor, Millard Fillmore of New York, supported Clay's compromise. Finally, Senator Stephen A. Douglas of Illinois took over stewardship of the bill from the exhausted Clay and ingeniously secured its passage by chopping the omnibus bill into a series of individual measures. By summer's end Congress had passed each component of Clay's plan and the Compromise of 1850 had become reality.

Assessing the Compromise

Although President Fillmore hailed the compromise as a final settlement of sectional issues, it failed to bridge the underlying differences between North and South. Few members of Congress had supported each separate proposal: southerners had voted against the admission of California and northerners against the Fugitive Slave Act. Only shifting alliances between moderates and northerners or southerners on specific issues had achieved passage of the compromise.

Each section could claim victories from the compromise. Northern victories were clear: admission of California and abolition of the slave trade in the District of Columbia. However, southern victories, such as the stricter fugitive slave law, were clouded by the legislators' failure to resolve the issue of congressional authority over slavery in territories outside the Mexican cession.

Southerners therefore reacted ambivalently to the Compromise of 1850. In state elections during fall 1850 and 1851, procompromise candidates generally thrashed the law's opponents. At the same time, Unionists in Georgia wrote the celebrated Georgia platform, which threatened secession if Congress prohibited slavery in the Mexican cession or repealed the Fugitive Slave Act. And the South's one clear victory, the passage of a new, more stringent fugitive slave law, quickly proved a mixed blessing.

Enforcement of the Fugitive Slave Act

Northern moderates accepted the Fugitive Slave Act of 1850 as the price of saving the Union, but the law outraged antislavery northerners. It denied alleged fugitives the right of trial by jury, forbade them to testify at their own trial, permitted their return to slavery merely on the testimony of a claimant, and enabled court-appointed commissioners to collect ten dollars if they ruled for the slaveholder but only five if they ruled for the fugitive. As one commentator noted, the law threatened to turn the North into "one vast hunting ground." It targeted *all* runaways, putting at risk even fugitives who had lived as free blacks for thirty years or more. Above all, the law brought home to northerners the uncomfortable truth of their own complicity in slavery's continuation. By legalizing the activities of slave catchers on northern soil, the law reminded northerners that slavery was a national problem, not merely a southern institution. Antislavery northerners assailed the law in such terms as the "vilest monument of infamy of the nineteenth century."

Efforts to catch and return runaways inflamed emotions in both North and South. In 1854 a Boston mob aroused by antislavery speeches killed a courthouse guard in an abortive effort to rescue fugitive slave Anthony Burns. Determined to enforce the law, President Franklin Pierce sent federal troops to escort Burns to the harbor, where a ship carried him back to slavery. As five platoons of troops marched Burns to the ship, 50,000 people lined the streets. One Bostonian hung from his window a black coffin bearing the words "THE FUNERAL OF LIBERTY." The Burns incident shattered the complacency of conservative supporters of the Compromise of 1850. "We went to bed one night old fashioned conservative Compromise Union Whigs," textile manufacturer Amos A. Lawrence wrote, "and waked up stark mad Abolitionists." A Boston committee later purchased Burns's freedom, but other fugitives had worse fates. Margaret Garner, about to be captured and sent back to Kentucky as a slave, tried to kill her children rather than witness their return to slavery.

Harriet Beecher Stowe (1811–1896)
Stowe did extensive research before writing Uncle Tom's Cabin. *By making the demonic Simon Legree a northerner and by portraying southerners as well meaning, she effectively indicted slavery as an institution.*

Northerners devised ways to interfere with the enforcement of the Fugitive Slave Act. "Vigilance" committees spirited endangered blacks to Canada, lawyers dragged out hearings to raise slave catchers' expenses, and "personal liberty laws" hindered state officials' enforcement of the law. These obstructionist tactics convinced southerners that opposition to slavery boiled just beneath the surface of northern opinion. The southern "victory" represented by the passage of the Fugitive Slave Act seemed increasingly illusory.

Uncle Tom's Cabin

Harriet Beecher Stowe's novel *Uncle Tom's Cabin* (1852) drummed up wide northern support for fugitive slaves. Stowe, the daughter of famed evangeli-

The Election of 1852

Candidates	Parties	Electoral Vote	Popular Vote	Percentage of Popular Vote
FRANKLIN PIERCE	Democratic	254	1,601,117	50.9
Winfield Scott	Whig	42	1,385,453	44.1
John P. Hale	Free-Soil		155,825	5.0

cal Lyman Beecher, greeted the Fugitive Slave Act with horror. In one of the novel's most memorable scenes, she depicted the slave Eliza, clutching her infant son, bounding across ice floes on the Ohio River to freedom. Slavery itself was Stowe's main target. Much of her novel's power derives from its view that good intentions mean little in the face of so evil an institution. The good intentions of a kindly slave owner die with him, and Uncle Tom is sold to the vicious Yankee Simon Legree, who whips Tom to death. Stowe also played effectively to the emotions of her audience by demonstrating how slavery ripped slave families apart.

Three hundred thousand copies of *Uncle Tom's Cabin* were sold in 1852, and 1.2 million by summer 1853. Stage dramatizations reached perhaps fifty times as many people as the novel did. As a play, *Uncle Tom's Cabin* enthralled working-class audiences normally indifferent or hostile to abolitionism. Yet the impact of *Uncle Tom's Cabin* cannot be precisely measured. Although it hardly lived up to the prediction of one abolitionist leader that it would convert 2 million people to abolitionism, it did push many waverers toward an aggressive antislavery stance. As historian David Potter concluded, the northern attitude toward slavery "was never quite the same after *Uncle Tom's Cabin*."

The Election of 1852

The Fugitive Slave Act fragmented the Whig party. Northern Whigs took the lead in defying the law, and southern Whigs had a difficult time explaining away the power of vocal free-soil Whigs.

In 1852 the Whigs' nomination of Mexican War hero General Winfield Scott as their presidential candidate widened the sectional split in the party. Although a Virginian, Scott owed his nomination to the northern free-soil Whigs. His single, feeble statement endorsing the Compromise of 1850 undercut southern Whigs trying to portray the Democrats as the party of disunion and themselves as the party of both slavery and the Union.

The Democrats had their own problems. Substantial numbers of free-soilers who had left the party in 1848 gravitated to the Whig party in 1852. The Democrats nominated Franklin Pierce of New Hampshire, a dark-horse candidate whose chief attraction was that no faction of the party violently opposed him. The "ultra men of the South," a friend of his noted, "say they can cheerfully go for him, and none, none say they cannot." Northern and southern Democrats alike rallied behind the Compromise of 1850 and behind the ideal of popular sovereignty, and Pierce won a smashing victory. In the most one-sided election since 1820, he carried twenty-seven of the thirty-one states and collected 254 of 296 electoral votes. Following the Whigs' devastating defeats throughout the South in both presidential and local elections, one stalwart lamented "the decisive breaking-up of our party."

The Collapse of the Second Party System

Franklin Pierce was the last presidential candidate of the nineteenth century to carry the popular and electoral vote in both North and South. Not until Franklin D. Roosevelt swept into office in 1932

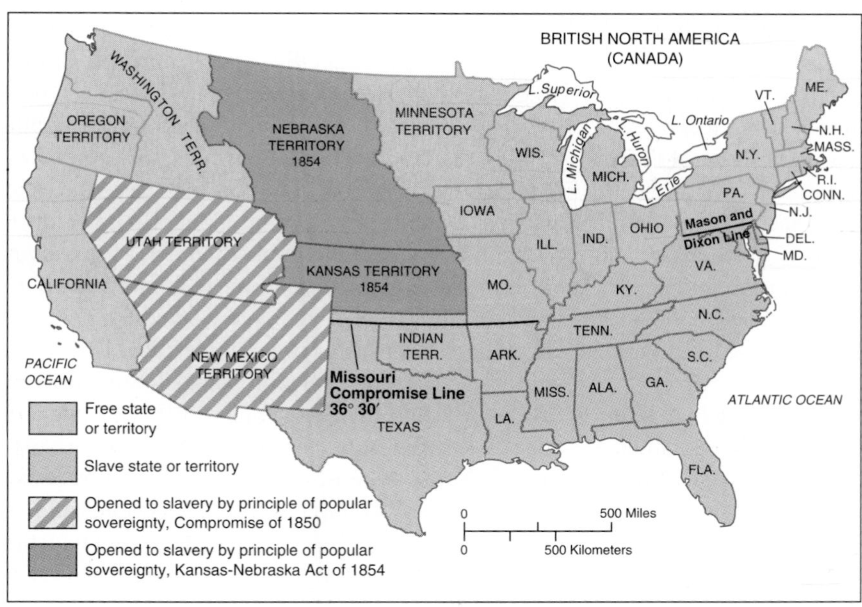

The Kansas-Nebraska Act, 1854

Kansas and Nebraska lay within the Louisiana Purchase, north of 36°30′, and hence were closed to slavery until Stephen A. Douglas introduced his bills in 1854.

would another president do so. Pierce also became the last president to hold office under the second party system—Whigs against Democrats. Within four years of Pierce's election, the Whig party would disintegrate, to be replaced by two newcomers, the American (Know-Nothing) party and the Republican party.

Unlike the Whigs, the Republican party was a purely sectional, northern party, drawing its support from both former Whigs and discontented Democrats. The Democrats survived as a national party, but with a base so shrunken in the North that the newborn Republican party captured two-thirds of the free states in the election of 1856.

For decades the second party system had kept the conflict over slavery in check by providing Americans other issues to argue about—banking, internal improvements, tariffs, and temperance. By the 1850s the debate over slavery extension overshadowed such issues and exposed raw divisions in each party. Whigs, with their larger, more aggressive free-soil wing, were much more vulnerable to disruption than the Democrats. Thus when Stephen A. Douglas put forth a proposal in 1854 to organize the vast Nebraska territory with no restrictions on slavery, he ignited a fire-storm that consumed the Whig party.

The Kansas-Nebraska Act

Signed in late May 1854, the Kansas-Nebraska Act shattered the already weakened second party system and triggered renewed sectional strife. The bill's roots lay in the seemingly uncontroversial desire of farmers to organize the large territory west of Iowa and Missouri. Railroad enthusiasts who dreamed of a rail line linking the Midwest to the Pacific also wanted the territory organized.

In January 1854 Democratic senator Stephen A. Douglas of Illinois proposed a bill to organize Nebraska as a territory. Douglas believed that a railroad to the Pacific would bring national benefits, including a continuous line of settlement, and thought that a railroad-based western expansion would unite the splintering Democratic factions.

Two sources of potential conflict loomed. First, some southerners advocated a southern-based Pacific route rather than a midwestern one. Second, Nebraska lay north of the Missouri Compromise line in the Louisiana Purchase, a region closed to slavery. Under Douglas's bill, the South would lose the Pacific rail route *and* face the possibility of more free territory in the Union. To placate southerners and win their votes, Douglas made two concessions. First, he proclaimed the Missouri Compromise now void, superseded by the Compromise of 1850 and its doctrine of popular sovereignty. Second, Douglas agreed to divide the territory into northern and southern parts, Nebraska and Kansas. Implicit in this, at least to southerners, was the idea that Nebraska would be free soil but Kansas would be open to slavery.

These modifications to Douglas's original bill set off a storm of protest. Despite Douglas's belief that national expansion was the critical issue, most attention focused on the extension of slavery. Antislavery northerners assailed the bill as "an atrocious plot" to violate the Missouri Compromise and to turn Kansas into a "dreary region of despotism, inhabited by masters and slaves." Their anger provoked an equal response among southerners and added the issue of regional pride to the already volatile mix of expansion and slavery.

Despite the uproar, Douglas guided the bill easily through the Senate. Matters were far more tumultuous in the House, where the bill passed by a narrow margin. Ominously, not a single northern Whig in the House voted for the bill, and northern Democrats split evenly.

The Surge of Free Soil

Amid the clamor over his bill, Douglas ruefully observed that he could now travel to Chicago by the light of his own burning effigies. Neither a fool nor a political novice, he was the victim of a political bombshell, free soil, that exploded under his feet.

Support for free soil united many who agreed on little else. Many free-soilers were racists who opposed allowing any African-Americans, slave or free, into the West. Others repudiated slavery on moral grounds and rejected blatantly racist legislation. However, as one abolitionist noted, the free-soil convictions of many westerners rested on a "perfect, if not supreme" hatred of African-Americans.

Although split over the morality of slavery, most free-soilers agreed that slavery impeded whites' progress. Most accepted Abraham Lincoln's portrayal of the North as a society of upwardly mobile farmers, artisans, and small-business operators. Any enterprising individual could escape wage labor and attain self-employment. "The man who labored for another last year," Lincoln insisted, "this year labors for himself, and next year he will hire others to labor for him." Because a slave worked for nothing, free-soilers claimed, no free laborer could compete with a slave. In any territory that allowed slavery, free labor would therefore vanish. Wherever slavery appeared, a free-soiler argued, "labor loses its dignity; industry sickens; education finds no schools; religion finds no churches, and the whole land of slavery is impoverished." Free-soilers also rejected the idea that slavery had natural limits. "Slavery is as certain to invade New Mexico and Utah, as the sun is to rise," insisted a free-soiler. If slavery secured a toehold in Kansas, free-soilers warned, Minnesota would fall to slavery as well.

The Kansas-Nebraska Act, in free-soilers' opinion, was "a part of a continuous movement of slaveholders to advance slavery over the entire North." Free-soilers saw southern planters, southern politicians, and their northern dupes, such as Stephen A. Douglas, entangled in a gigantic conspiracy to extend slavery. To free-soilers, a *pattern* of events—the Fugitive Slave Act, the repeal of the Missouri Compromise, and the division of Nebraska—demonstrated that a diabolical "Slave Power" was spreading its tentacles like an octopus.

The Ebbing of Manifest Destiny

The uproar over the Kansas-Nebraska Act embarrassed the Pierce administration. It also doomed Manifest Destiny, the one issue that had held the Democrats together in the 1840s.

Franklin Pierce had come to office championing Manifest Destiny, but increasing sectional rivalries sidetracked his efforts. In 1853 his emissary James Gadsden negotiated the purchase of a strip of land south of the Gila River (now southern Arizona

and part of southern New Mexico), an acquisition favored by advocates of a southern railroad route to the Pacific. Fierce opposition to the Gadsden Purchase revealed mounting free-soilers' suspicions of expansion, and the Senate approved the treaty only after slashing 9,000 square miles from the purchase. The sectional rivalries beginning to engulf the Nebraska bill clearly threatened any proposal to gain new territory.

Cuba provided even more vivid proof of the change in public attitudes toward expansion. In 1854 a former Mississippi governor, John A. Quitman, planned a filibuster (an unofficial military expedition) to seize Cuba from Spain. Pierce wanted to acquire Cuba and may first have encouraged Quitman's plans, but the president backed down in the face of northern opposition. Northerners saw the filibuster as another manifestation of the Slave Power's conspiracy to grab more territory for the South's "peculiar institution."

Events, however, slipped out of Pierce's control. In October 1854 the American ambassadors to Great Britain, France, and Spain, two of them southerners, met in Belgium and issued the unofficial Ostend Manifesto, calling on the United States to acquire Cuba by any means, including force. Beset by the storm over the Kansas-Nebraska Act and northern fury over Quitman's proposed filibuster, Pierce repudiated the manifesto.

Despite the Pierce administration's disavowal of the Ostend Manifesto, the idea of expansion into the Caribbean continued to attract southerners, including the Tennessee-born adventurer William Walker. Between 1853 and 1860, the year a firing squad in Honduras executed him, Walker led a succession of filibustering expeditions into Mexico and Nicaragua. Taking advantage of civil chaos in Nicaragua, he made himself the chief political force there, reinstituted slavery, and talked of making Nicaragua a U.S. colony. Southern expansionists, moreover, kept the acquisition of Mexico and Cuba at the top of their agenda and received some support from northern Democrats. As late as 1859 James Buchanan, Pierce's successor, asked Congress to appropriate funds to purchase Cuba.

Although some southerners were against expansion—among them the Louisiana sugar planters who opposed acquiring Cuba because Cuban sugar would compete with their product—southern expansionists stirred up enough commotion to worry antislavery northerners that the South aspired to establish a Caribbean slave empire. Like a card in a poker game, the threat of expansion southward was all the more menacing for not being played. As long as the debate on the extension of slavery focused on territories in the continental United States, slavery's prospects for expansion were limited. However, adding Caribbean territory to the equation changed all calculations.

The Whigs Disintegrate

While straining Democratic unity, the Kansas-Nebraska Act wrecked the Whig party. Although Democrats lost ground in the 1854 congressional elections, the Whigs failed to benefit. No matter how furious the free-soil Democrats were at Douglas for introducing the act, they could not forget that southern Whigs had supported him. Northern Whigs split into two camps: antislavery "Conscience" Whigs, led by Senator William Seward of New York, and conservatives, led by former president Millard Fillmore. The conservatives believed that the Whig party had to adhere to the Compromise of 1850 to maintain itself as a national party.

This deep division within the Whig party repelled anti-slavery Democrats and prompted anti-slavery Whigs to look for an alternative party. By 1856 the new Republican party would become home for these anti-slavery refugees; however, in 1854 and 1855 the American, or Know-Nothing, party emerged as the principal alternative to the faltering established parties.

The Rise and Fall of the Know-Nothings

The Know-Nothings evolved out of a nativist organization, the Order of the Star-Spangled Banner. (The party's popular name derived from its members' standard response to inquiries about its activities: "I know nothing.") One of many nativist societies that had mushroomed in response to the immigration boom of the 1840s, the Order of the Star-Spangled Banner had pressured existing parties to nominate and appoint only native-born Protestants. It had also urged lengthening the naturalization period before immigrants could vote.

Winfield Scott's compaign for the presidency in 1852 had alienated many nativists, who had previously voted Whig. Trying to revitalize his badly split party, Scott had courted the traditionally Democratic Catholic vote. Most Catholics had voted for Franklin Pierce, but many nativists bailed out of the Whig party. The Kansas-Nebraska Act cemented nativist allegiance to the Know-Nothings, opposed both to the extension of slavery and to Catholicism. An obsessive fear of conspiracies unified the Know-Nothings. They simultaneously denounced a papal conspiracy against the American republic and a Slave Power conspiracy reaching its tentacles throughout the United States.

The Know-Nothings enjoyed a meteoric rise and an equally rapid fall. For example, in 1854 they captured the governorship, almost the entire state legislature, and all the congressional seats of Massachusetts. Such Know-Nothing successes wrecked Whig hopes of capitalizing on hostility to the Kansas-Nebraska Act.

By 1856 the Know-Nothings had become a falling star soon to plummet below the horizon. They proved as vulnerable to sectional conflicts over slavery as the Whigs. In 1855 southern Know-Nothings, mainly proslavery former Whigs, combined with northern conservatives to make acceptance of the Kansas-Nebraska Act part of the Know-Nothing platform, blurring the attraction of Know-Nothingism to northern voters more antislavery than anti-Catholic. One such former Whig, Illinois congressman Abraham Lincoln, asked pointedly, "How can anyone who abhors the oppression of negroes be in favor of degrading classes of white people?" Most Know-Nothings eventually concluded that, as one observer put it, "neither the Pope nor the foreigners ever can govern the country or endanger its liberties, but the slavebreeders and slavetraders *do* govern it, and threaten to put an end to all government but theirs." Chief beneficiary of the Know-Nothing dilemma was the emerging Republican party, which had no southern wing to blunt its antislavery message.

The Origins of the Republican Party

Born in the chaotic aftermath of the Kansas-Nebraska Act, the Republican party would become the main opposition to the Democratic party by 1856 and would win each presidential election from 1860 until 1884. In 1855, however, few might have predicted such a bright future. Although united in opposition to the Kansas-Nebraska Act, the fledgling party was host to conservatives who wanted to restore the Missouri Compromise, radicals who had been part of the Liberty party abolitionists, and a sizable middle of free-soilers.

Building organizations at the state level was essential, for state issues often shaped voters' allegiances. The Know-Nothings, for example, linked support for temperance, strong at the state level, with anti-Catholicism and antislavery. Frequently antislavery voters were also protemperance and anti-Catholic, believing that addiction to alcohol and submission to the pope were both forms of enslavement to be eradicated. Competing with the Know-Nothings for these intensely moralistic voters at the state level, Republicans faced a dilemma: if they attacked the Know-Nothings for stressing anti-Catholicism over antislavery, they might well alienate the voters, but if they compromised with the Know-Nothings, they might well lose their own identity as a party.

Alternately attacking and conciliating, the Republicans succeeded in some state elections in 1855 but lost ground as popular ire against the Kansas-Nebraska Act cooled. By the start of 1856 they were organized in only half the northern states and lacked any national organization. The Republicans desperately needed something to make voters more concerned about the Slave Power than about rum or Catholicism. Salvation for the nascent party came in the form of violence in Kansas, which quickly became known as Bleeding Kansas. This violence united the party around its free-soil center, intensified antislavery feelings, and boosted Republican fortunes.

Bleeding Kansas

In the wake of the Kansas-Nebraska Act, Boston abolitionists had organized a company to send antislavery settlers into Kansas, but most of the territory's early settlers came from Missouri or other parts of the Midwest. Few of these opposed slavery on moral grounds. Some supported slavery; others wanted to keep all African-Americans out of Kansas. "I kem to Kansas to live in a free state," exclaimed one clergyman, "and I don't want niggers a-trampin' over my grave."

Despite most settlers' racist leanings and hatred of abolitionists, Kansas became a battleground between proslavery and antislavery forces. In March 1855 thousands of proslavery Missouri "border ruffians" crossed into Kansas to vote illegally in the first elections for the territorial legislature. Drawing revolvers, they quickly silenced judges who challenged their right to vote in Kansas. Ironically, proslavery forces probably would have won an honest election. But the proslavery legislature established in 1855 in Lecompton, Kansas, operated under a cloud of fraud. "There is not a proslavery man of my acquaintance in Kansas," wrote the antislavery wife of a farmer, "who does not acknowledge that the Bogus Legislature was the result of a gigantic and well-planned fraud, that the elections were carried by an invading mob from Missouri." The Lecompton legislature shredded what little good reputation it had by passing a series of outrageous laws, punishing the harboring of fugitive slaves by ten years' imprisonment, and making the circulation of abolitionist literature a capital offense.

The legislature's actions set off a chain reaction. In summer 1855 free-staters, including many aroused to oppose the Lecompton legislature, organized a rival government at Topeka. In May 1856 the Lecompton government dispatched a posse to Lawrence, where some free-staters were organizing a militia. The Lecompton posse, bearing banners emblazoned "SOUTHERN RIGHTS" and "LET YANKEES TREMBLE AND ABOLITIONISTS FALL," tore through Lawrence, burning buildings and destroying two printing presses. There were no deaths, but Republicans immediately dubbed the incident "THE SACK OF LAWRENCE."

The next move belonged to John Brown, a Connecticut-born abolitionist with an overpowering sense of divinely ordained mission. The "sack" of Lawrence convinced Brown that God now beckoned him "to break the jaws of the wicked." In late May Brown led seven men, including his four sons and his son-in-law, toward Pottawatomie Creek near Lawrence. They shot to death one man associated with the Lecompton government and hacked four others to pieces with broadswords. Brown's "Pottawatomie Massacre" terrified southerners and transformed "Bleeding Kansas" into a battleground between North and South. Supporters of slavery armed themselves for, as one South Carolinian wrote, "no Proslavery man knows when he is safe in this Ter[ritory]."

Popular sovereignty had failed in Kansas. Instead of resolving the issue of the extension of slavery, popular sovereignty had institutionalized the division over slavery by creating two rival governments. The Pierce administration compounded its problems, and Kansas's, by denouncing the antislavery Topeka government and recognizing the proslavery Lecompton government, thus forcing northern Democrats into the awkward appearance of supporting the "Bogus Legislature" at Lecompton. Nor did popular sovereignty keep the slavery issue out of politics. On the day before the proslavery attack on Lawrence, Republican senator Charles Sumner of Massachusetts delivered a wrathful speech, "The Crime Against Kansas," in which he verbally lashed the Senate for its complicity in slavery. Sumner singled out Senator Andrew Butler of South Carolina for making "the harlot, slavery" his mistress. The speech stunned the Senate. Two days later a relative of Butler, Democratic representative Preston Brooks of South Carolina, strode into the

The Election of 1856

Candidates	*Parties*	*Electoral Vote*	*Popular Vote*	*Percentage of Popular Vote*
JAMES BUCHANAN	Democratic	174	1,832,955	45.3
John C. Frémont	Republican	114	1,339,932	33.1
Millard Fillmore	American	8	871,731	21.6

Senate chamber and beat Sumner with a cane. The hollow cane broke after five or six blows, but Sumner, who required stitches, took three years to recuperate. Brooks immediately became a hero in the South.

Now "Bleeding Kansas" and "Bleeding Sumner" united the North. The "sack" of Lawrence, President Pierce's recognition of the proslavery Lecompton government, and Brooks's actions seemed to clinch the Republican argument that an aggressive slaveocracy was in power and holding white northerners in contempt. By denouncing the Slave Power rather than slavery, the Republicans sidestepped the divisive question of slavery's morality. Instead, they focused on portraying planters as arrogant aristocrats, the natural enemies of the laboring people of the North.

The Election of 1856

The presidential race of 1856 revealed the scope of the political realignment of the preceding few years. The Republicans, in their first presidential contest, nominated John C. Frémont, the "pathfinder" of California "Bear State" fame. Northern Know-Nothings also endorsed Frémont, while southern Know-Nothings nominated Millard Fillmore, the last Whig president. The Democrats dumped the battered Pierce for James Buchanan of Pennsylvania, who had had the luck to be out of the country (as minister to Great Britain) during the Kansas-Nebraska furor. A signer of the Ostend Manifesto, Buchanan was popular in the South.

The campaign became two separate races: Frémont versus Buchanan in the free states and Fillmore versus Buchanan in the slave states. Buchanan in effect was the only national candidate. Although Frémont attracted wide support in the North and Fillmore equal support in the South, Buchanan carried enough votes in both North and South to win the presidency.

The election of 1856 made three facts clear. First, the American party was finished as a major national force. Having worked for the Republican Frémont, most northern Know-Nothings joined that party. Fillmore's dismal showing in the South convinced southern Know-Nothings to abandon their party and seek a new political affiliation. Second, although in existence for barely a year, lacking any base in the South, and running a political novice, the Republican party did very well. A purely sectional party had nearly captured the presidency. Third, as long as the Democrats could unite behind a single national candidate, they would be hard to defeat. To achieve unity, however, the Democrats would have to find more James Buchanans—"doughface" moderates acceptable to southerners and northerners alike.

The Crisis of the Union

No one ever accused James Buchanan of impulsiveness or fanaticism. Although a moderate who wished to avoid controversy, Buchanan would preside over one of the most controversy-ridden administrations in American history. A Supreme Court decision concerning Dred Scott, a Missouri slave who had resided in free territory for several years; the creation of the proslavery Lecompton constitution in Kansas; a raid by John Brown on Harpers Ferry, Virginia; and secession itself would wrack Buchanan's administration. The forces driving the nation apart were spinning out of control by 1856, and Buchanan could not stop them. By his inauguration, southerners saw creeping abolitionism in the guise of free soil and northerners detected an ever more insatiable Slave Power. Once these potent images took hold in the minds of the American people, politicians could do little to erase them.

The Dred Scott *Case*

Pledged to congressional "noninterference" with slavery in the territories, Buchanan looked to the courts for resolution of the vexatious issue of slavery's extension. A case that appeared to promise a solution had been winding its way through the courts for years; on March 6, 1857, two days after Buchanan's inauguration, the Supreme Court handed down its decision in *Dred Scott* v. *Sandford*.

During the 1830s his master had taken Dred Scott, a slave, from the slave state of Missouri into Illinois and the Wisconsin Territory, both closed to slavery. After his master's death, Scott sued for his freedom on the grounds of his residence in free territory. Scott's case reached the Supreme Court in 1856.

The Court faced two key questions. Did Scott's residence in free territory during the 1830s make him free? Did Scott, again enslaved in Missouri, have the right to sue in the federal courts? The Supreme Court could have neatly sidestepped controversy by ruling that Scott had no right to sue, but it chose not to.

Instead, Chief Justice Roger B. Taney, a seventy-nine-year-old Marylander, handed down a sweeping decision that touched off another firestorm. First, Taney wrote, Scott, a slave, could not sue for his freedom. Further, no black, whether a slave or a free descendant of slaves, could become a U.S. citizen. Continuing his incendiary opinion, Taney ruled that even had Scott been entitled to sue, his residence in free territory did not make him free because the Missouri Compromise, whose provisions prohibited slavery in the Wisconsin Territory, was itself unconstitutional. The compromise, declared Taney, violated the Fifth Amendment's protection of property (including slaves).

The *Dred Scott* decision, instead of settling the issue of expansion of slavery, touched off another blast of controversy. The antislavery press flayed it as "willful perversion" filled with "gross historical falsehoods." Republicans saw the decision as further evidence that the fiendish Slave Power gripped the nation. The Slave Power, a northern paper bellowed, "has marched over and annihilated the boundaries of the states. We are now one great homogeneous slaveholding community."

Like Stephen A. Douglas after the Kansas-Nebraska Act, James Buchanan now appeared as another northern dupe of an evil slaveocracy. Republicans restrained themselves from open defiance of the decision only by insisting that it did not bind the nation; Taney's comments on the constitutionality of the Missouri Compromise, they contended, were opinions unnecessary to settling the case and therefore technically not binding.

The savage reaction to the decision provided more proof that no "judicious" or nonpartisan solution to slavery was possible. Any doubter needed only to read the fast-breaking news from Kansas.

The Lecompton Constitution

While the Supreme Court wrestled with the abstract issues raised by the expansion of slavery, President Buchanan sought a concrete solution to the problem of Kansas, where the free-state government at Topeka and the officially recognized proslavery government at Lecompton regarded each other with profound distrust. Buchanan's plan for Kansas looked simple: an elected territorial convention would draw up a constitution that would either prohibit or permit slavery; Buchanan would submit the constitution to Congress; Congress would then admit Kansas as a state.

Unfortunately, the plan exploded in Buchanan's face. Popular sovereignty, the essence of the plan, demanded fair play, a commodity scarce in

Stephen A. Douglas
Douglas's politics was founded on his unflinching conviction that most Americans favored national expansion and would support popular sovereignty as the fastest and least controversial way to achieve it. Douglas's self-assurance blinded him to rising northern sentiment for free soil.

Abraham Lincoln
Clean-shaven at the time of his famous debates with Douglas, Lincoln would soon grow a beard to give himself a more distinguished appearance.

Kansas. The territory's history of fraudulent elections left both sides reluctant to commit their fortunes to the polls. In June 1857 an election for a constitutional convention took place, but free-staters, by now a majority in Kansas, boycotted the election on grounds that the proslavery forces would rig it. A constitutional convention dominated by proslavery delegates then met and drew up the Lecompton constitution, which protected the rights of slaveholders already residing in Kansas and provided for a referendum to decide whether to allow more slaves into the territory.

Buchanan faced a dilemma. A supporter of popular sovereignty, he had favored letting Kansas voters decide the slavery issue. But now he confronted a constitution drawn up by a convention chosen by less than 10 percent of the eligible voters, a referendum that would not allow voters to remove slaves already in Kansas, and the prospect that the proslavery side would conduct the referendum no more honestly than it had other elections. However, there were compelling reasons to accept the Lecompton constitution. The South, which had provided Buchanan's winning margin in the 1856 election, supported it. To Buchanan, the wrangling over slavery in Kansas was a case of extremists' turning minor issues into major ones, especially because only about 200 slaves resided in Kansas and because prospects for slavery in the remaining territories were slight. The admission of Kansas to the Union as free or slave seemed the quickest way to end the commotion, and so in December 1857 Buchanan endorsed the Lecompton constitution.

Stephen A. Douglas and other northern Democrats broke with Buchanan. To them, the Lecompton constitution, in allowing voters to decide only whether more slaves could enter Kansas, violated the spirit of popular sovereignty. "I care not whether [slavery] is voted down or voted up," Douglas proclaimed, but refusal to allow any vote on slavery amounted to "a system of trickery and jugglery to defeat the fair expression of the will of the people."

Meanwhile, the turbulent swirl of events continued in Kansas. The newly elected territorial legislature called for a referendum on the Lecompton constitution and thus for a referendum on slavery itself. Two elections followed. In December 1857 the referendum called by the constitutional convention took place. Free-staters boycotted it, and the Lecompton constitution passed overwhelmingly. Two weeks later the election called by the territorial legislature took place. This time proslavery forces boycotted, and the constitution went down to crushing defeat. Buchanan tried to ignore this second election, but when he attempted to bring Kansas into the Union under the Lecompton constitution, Congress blocked him and forced yet another referendum. In this third election Kansans could accept or reject the entire constitution, with the proviso that rejection would delay statehood. Despite the proviso, Kansans overwhelmingly voted down the Lecompton constitution.

Buchanan simultaneously had failed to tranquilize Kansas and alienated northerners in his own party, who now more than ever believed that the southern Slave Power pulled all the important strings in the Democratic party. Douglas emerged as the hero of the hour for northern Democrats but saw his cherished formula of popular sovereignty become a prescription for strife rather than harmony.

The Lincoln-Douglas Debates

Despite the acclaim that he received for his stand against the Lecompton constitution, Douglas faced a stiff challenge in the 1858 Illinois senatorial election. Of his Republican opponent, Abraham Lincoln, Douglas remarked: "I shall have my hands full. He is the strong man of his party—full of wit, facts, and dates—and the best stump speaker with his droll ways and dry jokes, in the West." Indeed, the campaign pitted the Republican party's rising star against the Senate's leading Democrat. Thanks to the railroad and the telegraph, it received unprecedented national attention.

Physically and ideologically, the two candidates presented a striking contrast. Tall and gangling, Lincoln possessed energy, ambition, and a passion for self-education that had carried him from the

Kentucky log cabin where he was born into law and politics in his adopted Illinois. First elected as a Whig, he joined the Republican party in 1856. The New England–born Douglas stood a foot shorter than Lincoln, but to the small farmers of southern origin who populated the Illinois flatlands, he was the "little giant," the personification of the Democratic party in the West.

Despite Douglas's position against the Lecompton constitution, Lincoln saw him as author of the Kansas-Nebraska bill and a man who cared not whether slavery was voted up or down as long as the vote was honest. Opening his campaign with his famous "House Divided" speech ("this government cannot endure permanently half *slave* and half *free*"), Lincoln stressed the gulf between his free-soil position and Douglas's popular sovereignty. Douglas dismissed the house-divided doctrine as an invitation to secession. What mattered to him was not slavery but the continued expansion of white settlement. Both men wanted to keep slavery out of the path of white settlement, but Douglas believed that popular sovereignty was the surest way to do so without disrupting the Union.

The high point of the campaign came in a series of seven debates held from August to October 1858. Douglas used the debates to portray Lincoln as a virtual abolitionist and advocate of racial equality. Lincoln replied that Congress had no constitutional authority to abolish slavery in the South. He also asserted that "I am not, nor ever have been in favor of bringing about the social and political equality of the white and black man."

In the debate at Freeport, Illinois, Lincoln tried to make Douglas squirm by asking how popular sovereignty could be reconciled with the *Dred Scott* decision. Douglas responded that, although the Supreme Court had ruled that Congress could not exclude slavery from the territories, the voters in a territory could do so by refusing to enact laws that gave legal protection to slave property. This "Freeport doctrine" salvaged popular sovereignty but did nothing for Douglas's reputation among southerners, who preferred the guarantees of *Dred Scott* to the uncertainties of popular sovereignty. Trying to move beyond debates on free soil and popular sovereignty, Lincoln shifted in the closing debates to attacks on slavery as "a moral, social, and political evil."

Neither man scored a clear victory in the debates, and the senatorial election, which Douglas won, settled no major issues. Nonetheless, the candidates' contest was crucial. It solidified the sectional split in the Democratic party and made Lincoln famous in the North—and infamous in the South.

John Brown's Raid

Although Lincoln explicitly rejected abolitionism, he called free soil a step toward the "ultimate extinction" of slavery. Many southerners ignored the differences between free soil and abolitionism, seeing them as inseparable components of an unholy alliance against slavery. To many in the South, the entire North seemed locked in the grip of demented leaders bent on civil war.

Nothing reinforced this image more than John Brown's raid on the federal arsenal at Harpers Ferry, Virginia. Brown, the religious zealot responsible for the Pottawatomie massacre, seized the arsenal on October 16, 1859, hoping to ignite a slave rebellion throughout the South. Federal troops overpowered the raiders, and Brown, apprehended and convicted of treason, was hanged on December 2, 1859.

Had Brown been a lone fanatic, southerners might have dismissed the raid, but captured correspondence revealed that he enjoyed ties to prominent abolitionists. They had provided both moral and financial support for Brown's plan to "purge this land with blood." When the North responded to Brown's execution with memorial services and tolling bells, southerners saw proof positive of widespread northern support for abolition and even for race war. Although Republicans, including Lincoln and Senator William Seward of New York, denounced Brown's raid, southerners suspected that they regretted the conspiracy's failure more than the attempt itself.

Brown's abortive raid also rekindled southern fears of a slave insurrection. Rumors flew around the South, and vigilantes turned out to battle conspiracies that existed only in their own minds. Volunteers, for example, mobilized to defend northeastern Texas against thousands of abolitionists supposedly on their way to pillage Dallas and its environs. The hysteria generated by such rumors played into the hands of the extremists known as fire-eaters, who encouraged the witch hunts in order to gain political support.

Although fears of a slave insurrection proved groundless, they strengthened southern anxieties about abolitionism. More and more southerners concluded that the Republican party itself directed abolitionism and deserved blame for John Brown's plot as well. After all, had not influential Republicans assailed slavery, unconstitutionally tried to ban it, and spoken of an "irrepressible conflict" between slavery and freedom? The Tennessee legislature reflected southern views when it passed resolutions declaring that the Harpers Ferry raid was "the natural fruit of this treasonable 'irrepressible conflict' doctrine put forth by the great head of the Black Republican party and echoed by his subordinates."

The South Contemplates Secession

Convinced that the menace to southern rights lay not just with eccentrics such as abolitionist editor William Lloyd Garrison but also with the Republican party that had swept two-thirds of the northern states in the election of 1856, some southerners saw secession from the United States as their only recourse. "The South must dissever itself," a South Carolinian insisted, "from the rotten Northern element." Most southerners, however, reached this conclusion gradually and reluctantly. In 1850, insulated from the main tide of immigration, southerners thought themselves the most American of Americans. The events of the 1850s led growing numbers of southerners to conclude that the North had deserted the principles of the Union and had virtually declared war on the South by using such headline-grabbing phrases as "irrepressible conflict" and "a higher law." To southerners, the North, not slavery, was the problem. For some, venturing into the North became entering "enemy territory" and "a totally different country."

As sectional ties frayed, John Brown's raid electrified southern opinion. A Richmond editor observed that thousands of southerners "who, a month ago, scoffed at the idea of a dissolution of the Union as a madman's dream . . . now hold the opinion that its days are numbered, its glory perished."

Secession made no sense as a tactic to win concrete goals, but logic had yielded to emotion in much of the South. Fury at what southerners considered the irresponsible, unconstitutional course taken by Republicans in attacking slavery drove the talk of secession, and so did the belief that the North treated the South as inferior, even as a slave. "Talk of Negro slavery," wrote one angry southerner, "is not half so humiliating and disgraceful as the slavery of the South to the North." White southerners, certain that slavery made it possible for them to enjoy unprecedented freedom and equality, took great pride in their homeland. They bitterly resented Republican portrayals of the South as a region of arrogant planters and degraded common whites.

As long as the pliant James Buchanan occupied the White House, southerners only talked of secession. However, once Buchanan declined to seek reelection, they anxiously awaited the next presidential election.

The Election of 1860

Republicans had done well in the elections of 1856 as a single-issue, free-soil party, but they had to broaden their base in order to win in 1860. Republican leaders needed an economic program to complement their advocacy of free soil. A severe economic slump following the Panic of 1857 provided them an opening. The depression shattered a decade of prosperity and thrust economic concerns to the fore. In response, the Republicans developed an economic program based on support for a protective tariff, federal aid for internal improvements, and grants to settlers of free 160-acre homesteads carved from public lands.

To broaden their appeal, the Republicans chose Abraham Lincoln as their presidential candidate

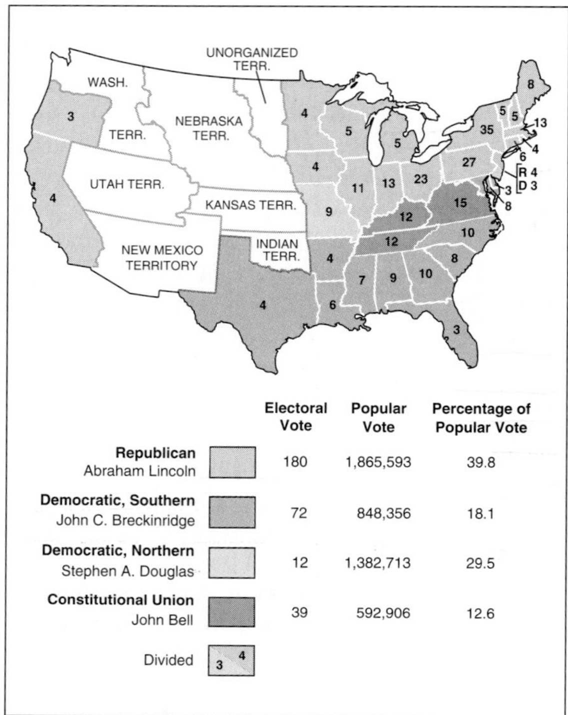

The Election of 1860

over the better-known William H. Seward. Lincoln offered a stronger possibility of carrying key states such as Pennsylvania and his home state of Illinois and projected a more moderate image than Seward, whose penchant for phrases like "irrepressible conflict" and "higher law" made him appear radical. In contrast, Lincoln repeatedly had said that Congress had no constitutional right to interfere with slavery in the South and had rejected the "higher law" doctrine.

The Democrats, still clinging to national party status, had to bridge their own sectional divisions. The *Dred Scott* decision and the conflict over the Lecompton constitution had weakened northern Democrats and strengthened southern Democrats. While Douglas still desperately defended popular sovereignty, southern Democrats stretched *Dred Scott* to conclude that Congress now had to protect slavery in the territories.

The Democratic party's internal turmoil boiled over at its Charleston convention in spring 1860. Failing to win a platform guaranteeing the federal protection of slavery in the territories, delegates from the Lower South stormed out. The convention adjourned to Baltimore, where a new fight erupted over whether to seat the pro-Douglas delegates hastily chosen to replace the absent delegates from the Lower South. When the convention voted to seat these new delegates, representatives from Virginia and the Upper South walked out. What remained of the original Democratic convention nominated Douglas, but the seceders marched off to yet another hall in Baltimore and nominated Buchanan's vice president, John C. Breckinridge of Kentucky, on a platform calling for the congressional protection of slavery in the territories. The spectacle of two different Democratic candidates for the presidency signaled the complete disruption of the party.

The South still contained a sizable number of moderates, often former Whigs. In 1860 these southern moderates joined former northern Whigs in the new Constitutional Union party. They nominated John Bell of Tennessee, a slaveholder who had opposed the Kansas-Nebraska Act and the Lecompton constitution. Calling for the Union's preservation, the new party took no stand on slavery's extension.

The four candidates presented a relatively clear choice. At one end of the spectrum, Lincoln conceded that the South had the constitutional right to preserve slavery, but he demanded that Congress prohibit its extension. At the other end, Breckinridge insisted that Congress had to protect slavery anywhere it existed. In the middle were Bell and Douglas, the latter still trying to salvage popular sovereignty. In the end Lincoln won 180 electoral votes; his three opponents, only 123. However, Lincoln's popular votes, 39 percent of the total, came almost completely from the North. Douglas, the only candidate to run in both sections, ran second in the popular vote but carried only Missouri. Bell won most of the Upper South, and Breckinridge took Maryland and the Lower South.

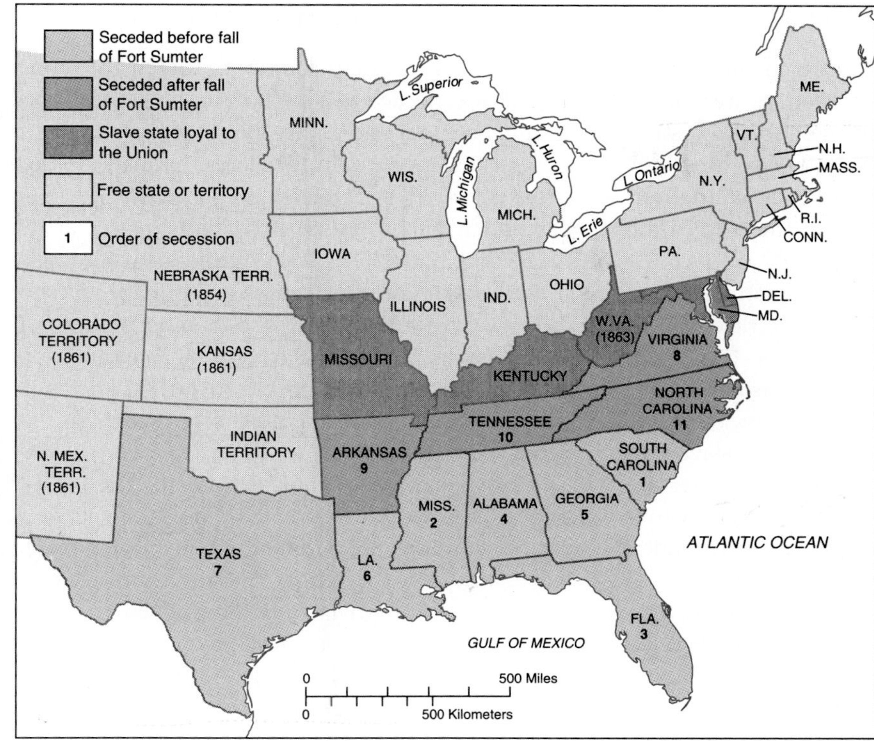

Secession

Four key states—Virginia, Arkansas, Tennessee, and North Carolina—did not secede until after the fall of Fort Sumter. The border slave states of Maryland, Delaware, Kentucky, and Missouri stayed in the Union.

The Movement for Secession

Southerners faced a dilemma. The president-elect was so unpopular in the South that his name had not even appeared on the ballot in many southern states. Lincoln's victory struck many southerners as a calculated insult. The North, a South Carolina planter said, "has got so far toward being abolitionized as to elect a man avowedly hostile to our institutions." Few southerners believed that Lincoln would fulfill his promise to protect slavery in the South, and most feared that he would act as a tool for more John Browns.

Some southerners had threatened secession at the prospect of Lincoln's election, and now the moment of decision had arrived. On December 20, 1860, a South Carolina convention voted unanimously for secession; in short order Alabama, Mississippi, Florida, Georgia, Louisiana, and Texas followed. On February 4, 1861, delegates from these seven states met in Montgomery, Alabama, and established the Confederate States of America. But uncertainty colored the secession movement. Many southerners, even in the Deep South, had resisted the fire-eaters' call to leave the Union. Jefferson Davis, inaugurated in February 1861 as president of the Confederacy, was a reluctant secessionist who had remained in the Senate two weeks after his own state of Mississippi had seceded.

At first the Upper South rejected secession completely. More economically dependent on the North, it had proportionately fewer slaves and more nonslaveholders, whose loyalty in case of secession was dubious. Finally, if secession precipitated a war, the Upper South was the likely battleground. Consequently, the secession movement that South Carolina had begun so boldly in December 1860 seemed to be falling apart by March 1861.

The Search for Compromise

The lack of southern unity confirmed the view of most Republicans that the secessionists were more bluster than substance. Seward described secession as the work of "a relatively few hotheads," and Lincoln believed that the loyal majority of southerners would soon wrest control from the fire-eating minority.

This perception stiffened Republican resolve to resist compromise. Moderate John J. Crittenden of Kentucky suggested compensation for owners of runaway slaves, repeal of northern personal-liberty laws, a constitutional amendment to prohibit the federal government from interfering with slavery in southern states, and another amendment to restore the Missouri Compromise line. But in the face of adamant Republican opposition, the Crittenden plan collapsed.

Lincoln's faith in a "loyal majority" of southerners exaggerated both their numbers and their dedication to the Union. Many southern opponents of the fire-eating secessionists sat on the fence, waiting for major concessions from the North; their allegiance to the Union thus was conditional. But compromise would have meant the abandonment of free soil, a basic principle on which the Republican party had been founded, and Lincoln, who misread southern opinion, resisted.

Beyond the issue of compromise, the precipitous secession of the Lower South had changed the question that Lincoln faced. The issue no longer revolved around slavery's extension but around secession. The Lower South had left the Union in the face of losing a fair election. For Lincoln to cave in to such pressure would violate majority rule, the sacred principle on which the nation had been founded.

The Coming of War

By the time Lincoln took office in March 1861, only a spark was needed to set off a war. Lincoln pledged in his inaugural address to "hold, occupy, and possess" federal property in the states that had seceded, a statement that committed him to the defense of Fort Pickens in Florida and Fort Sumter in the harbor of Charleston, South Carolina. Accordingly, the president informed South Carolina's governor of his intention to supply Fort Sumter with provisions but neither reinforcements nor ammunition. Shortly before dawn on April 12, 1861, Confederate shore batteries bombarded the fort, which surrendered the next day.

Proclaiming an insurrection in the Lower South, Lincoln called for 75,000 militia to suppress the rebellion. The outbreak of hostilities ended fence-sitting in the Upper South. "I am a Union man," one southerner wrote, "but when they [the Lincoln administration] send men south it will change my notions. I can do nothing against my own people." In quick succession Virginia, North Carolina, Arkansas, and Tennessee joined the Confederacy. Acknowledging that "I am one of those dull creatures that cannot see the good of secession," Robert E. Lee resigned from the U.S. Army rather than lead troops against his native Virginia.

The North, too, was ready for a fight, less to abolish slavery than to punish secession. Stephen Douglas, exhausted by his efforts to find a peaceable solution to the issue of slavery extension, assaulted "the new system of resistance by the sword and bayonet to the results of the ballot-box" and affirmed, "I deprecate war, but if it must come I am with my country, under all circumstances, and in every contingency."

CONCLUSION

During the 1850s disagreements over the extension of slavery drove the North and the South far apart. When popular sovereignty failed, support for free soil grew in the North, while at the same time southerners decided that the *Dred Scott* decision mandated the congressional protection of slavery in the territories and elsewhere.

The decade had begun with the Compromise of 1850, which papered over, rather than solved, divisive issues. Decades of industrial expansion had left northerners convinced of the value of free labor, and decades of agricultural prosperity had left southerners equally convinced of the economic and moral value of slavery.

Nonetheless, secession festered ten years before erupting. Southerners would not take the drastic step of seceding until they believed that the North aimed not merely to bar the expansion of slavery but also to corrode the moral and political foundations of southern society. The Kansas-Nebraska furor, the emergence of the purely sectional Republican party, northern opposition to the *Dred Scott* decision, and John Brown's raid on Harpers Ferry finally persuaded southerners that the North intended to reduce them to subjection and "slavery." Secession seemed a natural recourse.

These conflicts were deeply embedded in the nation's political heritage, with the North and the South holding vastly different views of what that heritage was. For northerners, liberty meant an individual's freedom to pursue self-interest without competition from slaves. For white southerners, liberty meant freedom to use their legal property, including slaves, as they saw fit. Each side proclaimed that *it* subscribed to the rule of law, which it accused the other of deserting. Ultimately, war broke out between siblings who, although they claimed the same inheritance, had become virtual strangers.

CHRONOLOGY

1846 Wilmot Proviso.

1848 Treaty of Guadalupe-Hidalgo ends Mexican War.
Free-Soil party formed.
Zachary Taylor elected president.

1849 California seeks admission to the Union as a free state.

1850 Nashville convention assembles to discuss the South's grievances.
Compromise of 1850.

1852 Harriet Beecher Stowe, *Uncle Tom's Cabin*.
Franklin Pierce elected president.

1854 Ostend Manifesto.
Kansas-Nebraska Act.

1854–1855 Know-Nothing and Republican parties emerge.

1855 Proslavery forces steal the election for a territorial legislature in Kansas.
Proslavery Kansans establish a government in Lecompton.
Free-soil government established in Topeka, Kansas.

1856 The "sack" of Lawrence, Kansas.
John Brown's Pottawatomie massacre.
James Buchanan elected president.

1857 *Dred Scott* decision.
President Buchanan endorses the Lecompton constitution in Kansas.
Panic of 1857.

1858 Congress refuses to admit Kansas to the Union under the Lecompton constitution.
Lincoln and Douglas debate.

1859 John Brown's raid on Harpers Ferry.

1860 Abraham Lincoln elected president.
South Carolina secedes from the Union.

1861 The remaining Lower South states secede.
Confederate States of America established.
Crittenden compromise plan collapses.
Lincoln takes office.
Firing on Fort Sumter; Civil War begins.
Upper South secedes.

FOR FURTHER READING

Tyler Anbinder, *Nativism and Slavery: The Northern Know Nothings and the Politics of the 1850s* (1992). A study of the Know-Nothings' striking success in the North in the mid-1850s.

Eric Foner, *Free Soil, Free Labor, Free Men: The Ideology of the Republican Party Before the Civil War* (1970). An outstanding analysis of the thought, values, and components of the Republican party.

William W. Freehling, *The Road to Disunion: Secessionists at Bay, 1776–1854* (1990). A major study that traces the roots of secession.

William E. Gienapp, *The Origins of the Republican Party, 1852–1856* (1988). A major recent study of the party's formative period.

Michael F. Holt, *The Political Crisis of the 1850s* (1978). A lively reinterpretation of the politics of the 1850s.

Allan Nevins, *The Ordeal of the Union* (vols. 1–2, 1947). A very detailed, highly regarded account of the coming of the Civil War.

David Potter, *The Impending Crisis, 1848–1861* (1976). The best one-volume overview of the events leading to the Civil War.

CHAPTER 15

Reforging the Union: Civil War, 1861–1865

With Fort Sumter's fall in April 1861, northerners and southerners rushed to arms. "They sing and whoop, they laugh; they holler to de people on de ground and sing out 'Good-by,'" remarked a slave watching rebel troops depart. "All going down to die." Longing for the excitement of battle, the first troops enlisted with hopes of adventure and glory. Neither the volunteers nor the politicians expected a long or bloody war.

These expectations of military glory and quick fame proved the first of many miscalculations. Actual battlefield experiences scarcely conformed to the early volunteers' rosy visions. War brought not glory but fetid army camps and the stench of death. "We don't mind the sight of dead men no more than if they were dead hogs," a Union soldier claimed.

One out of every five soldiers who fought in the Civil War died in it. The 620,000 American soldiers killed between 1861 and 1865 nearly equaled the number of U.S. soldiers killed in all other American wars combined. As it became clear

(Right) Armless or legless veterans were a common sight in American cities, towns, and rural districts well into our present century.

that a few battles would not decide the war, leaders on both sides contemplated, and often adopted, previously unthinkable strategies. The Confederacy, despite its states' rights basis, had to draft men into its army and virtually extort supplies from civilians. By the end of the war, the Confederacy was even prepared to arm slaves in a desperate effort to save a society founded on slavery. The North, which began the war with the objective of overcoming secession, explicitly disclaiming any intention of interfering with slavery, found that in order to win, it had to destroy slavery.

Mobilizing for War

Neither North nor South was prepared for war. In April 1861 most of the Union's small army, a scant 16,000 men, was scattered across the West. One-third of its officers had resigned to join the Confederacy. The nation had not had a strong president since James K. Polk in the 1840s, and many viewed the new president, Abraham Lincoln, as a yokel. It seemed doubtful that such a government could marshal its people for war. The Confederacy was even less prepared: it had no tax structure, no navy, only two tiny gunpowder factories, and poorly equipped, unconnected railroad lines.

During the first two years of war, both sides would have to overcome these deficiencies, raise and supply large armies, and finance the war. In each region mobilization would expand the powers of the central government to a degree that few had anticipated.

Recruitment and Conscription

The Civil War armies were the largest organizations ever created in America; by the end of the war, more than 2 million men had served in the Union army and 800,000 in the Confederate army. In the first flush of enthusiasm for war, volunteers rushed to the colors. "War and volunteers are the only topics of conversation or thought," an Oberlin College student wrote to his brother in April 1861. "I cannot study. I cannot sleep. I cannot work."

At first the raising of armies was a local, rather than a national or state, effort. Regiments usually consisted of volunteers from the same locale. Southern cavalrymen provided their own horses, and uniforms were left to local option. In both armies the troops themselves elected officers up to the rank of colonel. This informal, democratic way of raising and organizing soldiers reflected the nation's political traditions but could not withstand the stresses of the Civil War. As early as July 1861 the Union began examinations for officers. With casualties mounting, moreover, military demand exceeded the supply of volunteers. The Confederacy felt the pinch first and in April 1862 enacted the first conscription law in American history, requiring all able-bodied white men aged eighteen to thirty-five to serve in the military. (By war's end the limits would be seventeen and fifty.) The Confederacy's Conscription Act aroused little enthusiasm. A later amendment exempting owners or overseers of twenty or more slaves evoked complaints about "a rich man's war but a poor man's fight."

Despite opposition, the Confederate draft became increasingly difficult to evade, and this fact stimulated volunteering. Only one soldier in five was a draftee, but four out of every five eligible white southerners served in the Confederate army. An 1864 law requiring all soldiers to serve for the duration of the war ensured that a high proportion of Confederate soldiers would be battle-hardened veterans.

Once the army was raised, the Confederacy had to supply it. At first the South imported arms and ammunition from Europe or relied on weapons taken from federal arsenals and captured on the battlefield. Gradually, the Confederacy assigned contracts to privately owned factories such as the Tredegar Iron Works in Richmond, provided loans to establish new plants, and created government-owned industries such as the giant Augusta Powder Works in Georgia. The South lost few, if any, battles for want of munitions.

Supplying troops with clothing and food proved more difficult. When the South invaded Maryland in 1862, thousands of Confederate soldiers remained behind because they could not march barefoot on Maryland's gravel-surfaced roads. Late in the war, Robert E. Lee's Army of Northern Virginia ran out of food but never out of ammunition. Supply problems had several sources: railroads that fell into disrepair or were captured, an economy that grew more cotton and tobacco than food, and Union capture of the livestock and grain-raising districts of central Tennessee and Virginia. Close to desperation, the Confederate Congress in 1863 passed the Impressment Act, authorizing army officers to take food from reluctant farmers at prescribed rates. One provision, bitterly resented, empowered agents to impress slaves into labor for the army. Slave owners were willing to give up their relatives to military service, a Georgia congressman noted, "but let one of their negroes be taken and what a howl you will hear."

The industrial North more easily supplied its troops with arms, clothes, and food, but keeping a full army was another matter. When the initial tide of enthusiasm for enlistment ebbed, Congress turned to conscription with the Enrollment Act of March 1863. Every able-bodied white male citizen aged twenty to forty-five faced the draft.

The Enrollment Act provided some exemptions and offered two ways of escaping the draft: substitution, or paying another man to serve; and commutation, or paying a $300 fee to the government. As enrollment districts competed for volunteers by offering cash bounties, "bounty jumpers" repeatedly enrolled and then deserted after collecting their payment. Democrats denounced conscription as a violation of individual liberties and states' rights, and ordinary citizens resented the substitution and commutation privileges and leveled their own "poor man's fight" charges. Nevertheless, as in the Confederacy, the law stimulated volunteering: only 8 percent of all Union soldiers were draftees or substitutes.

Financing the War

The recruitment and supply of huge armies lay far beyond the capacity of American public finance at the start of the war. During the 1840s and 1850s federal spending had averaged only 2 percent of the gross national product.* With such meager expenditures, the federal government met its revenue needs from tariff duties and income from the sale of public lands. During the war, however, as annual federal expenditures rose to 15 percent of the gross national product, the need for new sources of revenue became urgent. When neither additional taxes nor war bond sales produced enough revenue, the Union and the Confederacy began to print paper money. Early in 1862 President Lincoln signed into law the Legal Tender Act, authorizing the issue of $150 million in paper "greenbacks." Although the North's financial officials distrusted paper money, they resorted to it because, as the Union's treasury secretary bluntly put it, "*The Treasury is nearly empty*." Unlike gold and silver, which had established market values, the value of paper money depended on the public's confidence in the government that issued it. To bolster that confidence, Union officials made the greenbacks legal tender (that is, acceptable in payment of most public and private debts).

In contrast, the Confederacy never made paper money legal tender, and so suspicions arose that the southern government had little faith in its own money. The fact that the Confederacy raised little of its wartime revenue from taxes compounded the problem. Northern invasions and poor internal transportation made collecting taxes difficult, and ultimately the South raised less than 5 percent of its wartime revenue from taxes (compared to 21 percent in the North).

Confidence in the Confederacy's paper money quickly evaporated, and the value of paper money in relation to gold plunged. The Confederate response—printing more paper money—merely accelerated inflation. Prices in the North rose 80 percent during the war, but those in the South soared more than 9,000 percent.

---

*Gross national product (GNP): the sum, measured in dollars, of all goods and services produced in a given year. By contrast, in the 1980s the federal budget averaged about 25 percent of GNP.

By raising taxes, floating bonds, and printing paper money, both North and South broke with the hard-money, minimal-government traditions of American public finance. In the North, Republicans took advantage of the departure of southern Democrats to push through Congress a measure that they and their Whig predecessors had long advocated: a national banking system. Passed in February 1863, the National Bank Act allowed banks to obtain federal charters and to issue national bank notes (backed by the federal government). The North's ability to revolutionize its system of public finances reflected both its greater experience with complex financial transactions and its stronger political cohesion.

Political Leadership in Wartime

The Civil War pitted rival political systems as well as armies and economies against each other. The South entered the war with several apparent political advantages. Lincoln's call for militiamen to suppress the rebellion had transformed southern waverers into secessionists. "Never was a people more united or more determined," wrote a New Orleans resident. "There is but one mind, one heart, one action." Since the founding of the United States, the South had produced a disproportionate share of the nation's strong presidents: Washington, Jefferson, Madison, Monroe, Jackson, and Polk. Jefferson Davis, the president of the Confederacy, possessed experience, honesty, courage, and what one commentator called "a jaw sawed in *steel*."

In contrast, the Union's list of political liabilities appeared lengthy. Loyal but contentious northern Democrats wanted no conscription, no National Bank, and no abolition of slavery. Even within the Republican party, Lincoln, with little national experience, had trouble commanding respect. A small but vocal group of Republicans known as the Radicals—including Secretary of the Treasury Salmon P. Chase, Senator Charles Sumner of Massachusetts, and Representative Thaddeus Stevens of Pennsylvania—vigorously criticized Lincoln. First they focused on his failure to make the slaves' emancipation a war goal, and later they would lash him for being too eager to readmit the conquered rebel states into the Union.

Abraham Lincoln
When Lincoln became president in March 1861, he faced more severe problems than any predecessor. Washington photographer Matthew Brady captured this image of the solemn president-elect on February 23, 1861, a few weeks after the formation of the Confederacy and shortly before Lincoln's inauguration.

Lincoln's style of leadership both encouraged and disarmed opposition within the Republican party. Keeping his counsel to himself until ready to act, he met criticism with homespun anecdotes that threw his opponents off guard. Caught between Radicals and conservatives, Lincoln used his cautious reserve to maintain open communications with both wings of the party and to fragment his opposition. He also co-opted some members of the opposition, including Chase, by bringing them into his cabinet.

In contrast, Jefferson Davis had a knack for making enemies. A West Pointer, he would rather have led the army than the government, and he used his sharp tongue to win arguments rather than friends. Davis's cabinet suffered frequent resignations; for example, the Confederacy had five secretaries of war in four years. Relations between Davis and his vice president, Alexander Stephens of Georgia, were disastrous. Stephens left Richmond, the Confederate capital, in 1862 and spent most of the war in Georgia sniping at Davis as "weak and vacillating, timid, petulant, peevish, obstinate."

The clash between Davis and Stephens involved not just personalities but also the ideological divisions that lay at the heart of the Confederacy. The Confederate Constitution explicitly guaranteed the sovereignty of the Confederate states and prohibited the government from enacting protective tariffs or supporting internal improvements. For Stephens and other influential Confederate leaders, the Confederacy existed to protect slavery and to enshrine states' rights. For Davis, the overriding objective of the Confederacy was to secure the independence of the South from the North, if necessary at the expense of states' rights.

This difference between Davis and Stephens somewhat resembled the discord between Lincoln and the northern Democrats. Lincoln believed that winning the war demanded increasing the central government's power; like Stephens, northern Democrats resisted centralization. But Lincoln could control his opponents more effectively than Davis controlled his. By temperament Lincoln was more suited to reconciliation than Davis was, and the different nature of party politics in the two sections favored him as well.

In the South the Democrats and the remaining Whigs agreed to suspend party politics for the war's duration. Although intended to encourage unity, this decision led to discord. As southern politics disintegrated along personal and factional lines, Davis found himself without organized political support. In contrast, in the Union northern Democrats' opposition to Lincoln tended to unify the Republicans. After Democrats won control of five states in the election of 1862, Republicans swallowed a bitter lesson: no matter how much they disdained Lincoln, they had to rally behind him or risk being driven from office. Ultimately, the Union developed more political cohesion than the Confederacy not because it had fewer divisions but because it managed those divisions more effectively.

Securing the Union's Borders

Even before large-scale fighting began, Lincoln moved to safeguard Washington, which was bordered by two slave states (Virginia and Maryland) and filled with Confederate sympathizers. A week after Fort Sumter's fall, a Baltimore mob attacked a Massachusetts regiment bound for Washington, but enough troops slipped through to protect the capital. Lincoln then dispatched federal troops to Maryland and suspended the writ of habeas corpus;* federal troops could now arrest Marylanders without formally charging them with specific offenses. Both Maryland and Delaware, another border slave state, voted down secession. Next Lincoln authorized the arming of Union sympathizers in Kentucky, a slave state with a Unionist legislature, a secessionist governor, and a thin chance of staying neutral. Lincoln also stationed troops just across the Ohio River from Kentucky, in Illinois, and when a Confederate army invaded Kentucky early in 1862, those troops drove it out. Officially, at least, Kentucky became the third slave state to declare for the Union. Four years of murderous fighting ravaged the fourth, Missouri, as Union and Confederate armies and bands of guerrillas clashed. Despite savage fighting and the divided loyalties of its people, Missouri never left the Union.

By holding the border slave states in the

*Habeas corpus: a court order requiring that the detainer of a prisoner bring the person in custody to court and show cause for his or her detention.

Union, Lincoln kept open his lines to the free states and gained access to the river systems in Kentucky and Missouri that led into the heart of the Confederacy. Lincoln's firmness, particularly in the case of Maryland, scotched charges that he was weak-willed.

In Battle, 1861–1862

The Civil War was the first war in which both sides relied extensively on railroads, the telegraph, mass-produced weapons, joint army-navy tactics, iron-plated warships, rifled guns and artillery, and trench warfare. Thus there is some justification for its description as the first modern war.

Armies, Weapons, and Strategies

Compared to the Confederacy's 9 million people, who included 3 million slaves, the Union had 22 million people in 1861. The North also enjoyed 3.5 times as many white men of military age, 90 percent of all U.S. industrial capacity, and two-thirds of its railroad track. But the North faced a daunting challenge: to force the South back into the Union. The South, in contrast, fought only for independence. To subdue the Confederacy, the North would have to sustain offensive operations over an area comparable in size to the part of Russia that Napoleon had invaded in 1812 with disastrous results.

Measured against this challenge, the North's advantages in population and technology shrank. The North had more men but needed them to defend long supply lines and to occupy captured areas. Consequently, it could commit a smaller proportion of its overall force to combat. The South, relying on slaves for labor, could assign a higher proportion of its white male population to combat. And although the Union had superior railroads, it had to move its troops and supplies huge distances, whereas the Confederacy could shift its troops relatively short distances within its defense area without railroads. The South's poor roads hampered the supply-heavy northern forces as well. Finally, southerners had an edge in morale, for Confederate troops usually fought on home ground.

The Civil War witnessed experiments with a variety of new weapons, including the submarine, the repeating rifle, and the multibarreled Gatling gun, the predecessor of the machine gun. Whereas smoothbore muskets had an effective range of 80 yards, the Springfield or Enfield rifles widely in use by 1863 were accurate at 400 yards. The rifle's development posed a challenge to long-accepted military tactics, which stressed the mass infantry charge. Armed with muskets, defenders could fire only a round or two before being overwhelmed. Armed with rifles, however, defenders could fire several rounds before closing with the enemy.

As the fighting wore on, both sides recognized the value of trenches, which offered defenders protection against withering rifle fire. In addition, the rifle forced generals to depend less on cavalry. Traditionally, cavalry had been among the most prestigious components of an army, in part because cavalry charges were often devastatingly effective and in part because the cavalry helped to maintain class distinctions within the army. More accurate rifles reduced the cavalry's effectiveness, for the bullet that missed a rider could hit his horse. Thus the cavalry increasingly was relegated to reconnaissance and raids.

Much like previous wars, the Civil War was fought basically in a succession of battles during which exposed infantry traded volleys, charged, and countercharged. The side that withdrew first from the battlefield was considered the loser, even though it frequently sustained lighter casualties than the "victor." The defeated army usually moved back a few miles to lick its wounds; the winners stayed in place to lick theirs. Although politicians raged at generals for not pursuing a beaten foe, they seldom understood the difficulties that a mangled victor faced in gathering horses, mules, supply trains, and exhausted soldiers for an attack. Not surprisingly, generals on both sides concluded that the best defense was a good offense.

What passed for long-range Union strategy in 1861 was the Anaconda plan, which called for the

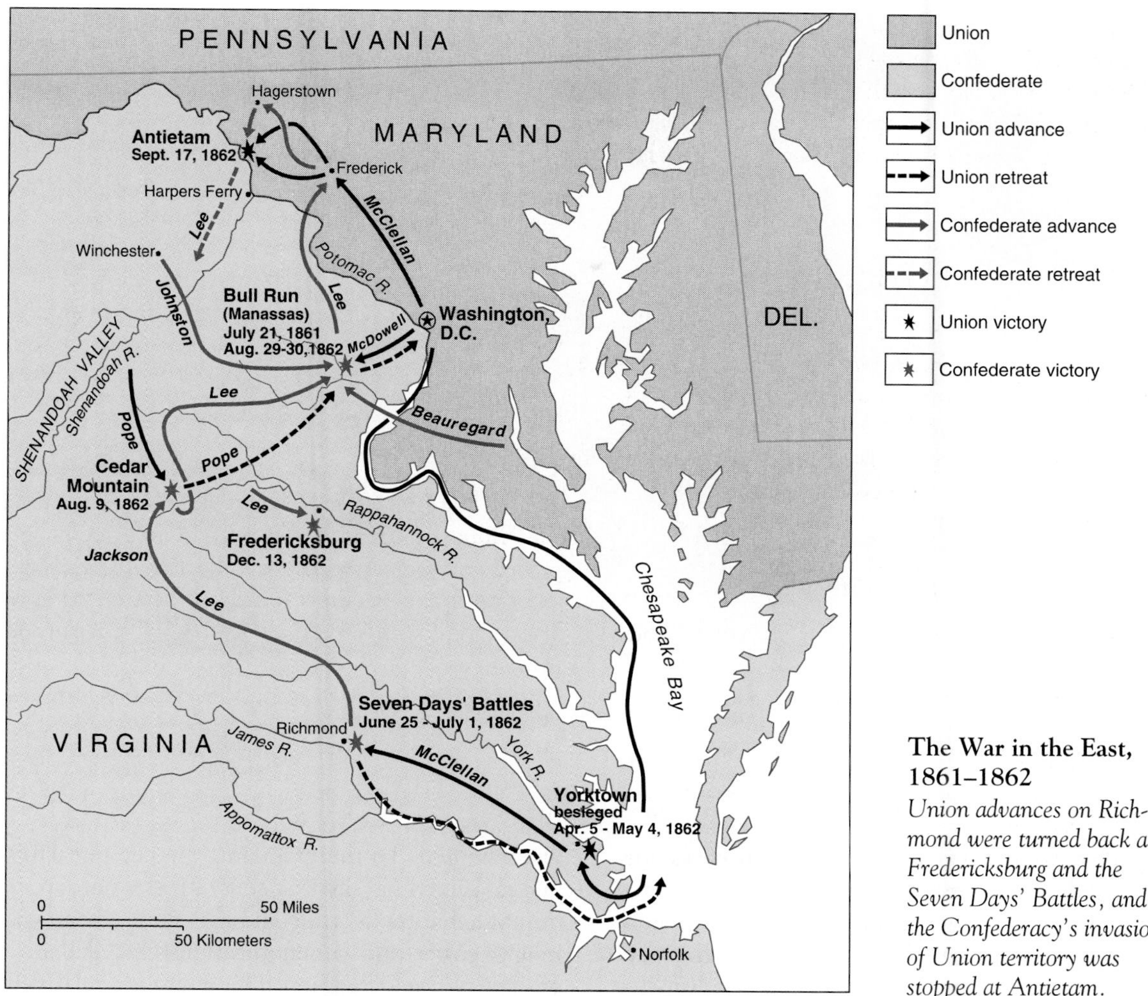

The War in the East, 1861–1862
Union advances on Richmond were turned back at Fredericksburg and the Seven Days' Battles, and the Confederacy's invasion of Union territory was stopped at Antietam.

Union to blockade the southern coast and to thrust, like a huge snake, down the Mississippi River. In theory, sealing off and severing the Confederacy would make the South recognize the futility of secession and end the war as bloodlessly as possible. However, the lack of adequate ships and men to seize the Mississippi in 1861 prevented the implementation of this ambitious plan.

Early in the war the need to secure the border slave states, especially Kentucky and Missouri, dictated Union strategy in the West, sending northern armies plunging southward from Kentucky into Tennessee. The Appalachian Mountains tended to separate this western theater from the eastern theater. East of the mountains, the Confederates' decision to locate their capital in Richmond, Virginia, shaped Union strategy. "Forward to Richmond!" became the Union's first war cry.

Stalemate in the East

Before Union troops could reach Richmond, one hundred miles southwest of Washington, they

Dead Soldiers at Antietam

These dead rebel gunners lie next to the wreckage of their battery at Antietam. The building, a Dunker church, was the site of furious fighting.

would have to dislodge a Confederate army brazenly encamped at Manassas Junction, Virginia, only twenty-five miles from the Union capital. Lincoln ordered General Irvin McDowell to attack the rebel force. In the resulting First Battle of Bull Run (or First Manassas*), amateur armies clashed in bloody chaos under a blistering sun in July 1861 as well-dressed, picnicking Washington dignitaries watched the carnage. The Confederates routed the larger Union army.

After Bull Run, Lincoln appointed General George B. McClellan to replace McDowell as commander of the Union's Army of the Potomac. McClellan, a master of administration and training, transformed a ragtag mob into a disciplined fighting force. His soldiers adored him, but Lincoln became disenchanted. To the president, the key to victory lay in launching simultaneous attacks on several fronts so that the North could exploit its advantages in manpower and communications. McClellan, a proslavery Democrat, hoped for a series of relatively bloodless victories that would result in the readmission of southern states into the Union with slavery still intact.

In spring 1862 McClellan got an opportunity to demonstrate the value of his strategy. After Bull Run, the Confederates had pulled back behind the Rappahannock River to block a Union march toward Richmond. McClellan decided to go around the southerners by transporting his troops down the Chesapeake Bay to the tip of the peninsula formed by the York and James rivers and then to attack Richmond from the rear.

At first McClellan's Peninsula Campaign unfolded smoothly. But after luring the Confederacy to the brink of defeat, he hesitated, refusing to

*Because the North often named battles after local landmarks, usually bodies of water, and the South after the nearest town, some Civil War battles are known by two names.

launch the final attack without the reinforcements he expected. Confederate forces under General Thomas "Stonewall" Jackson had turned back the reinforcements. As McClellan delayed, General Robert E. Lee assumed command of the Confederacy's Army of Northern Virginia. An opponent of secession, a man so courteous that he seemed almost too gentle, Lee nevertheless was McClellan's opposite, bold and willing to accept casualties.

Lee immediately took the offensive, attacking the much larger Union forces in the Seven Days' Battles (June–July 1862). Raging through forests east of Richmond, the battles cost the Confederacy nearly twice as many men as the Union, but McClellan, not Lee, blinked. Unnerved by mounting casualties, he sent a series of panicky reports to Washington. Lincoln, who cared little for McClellan's peninsula strategy, ordered him to call off the campaign and return to Washington.

With McClellan out of the picture, Lee and his lieutenant, Stonewall Jackson, pushed north, routing a Union army at the Second Battle of Bull Run (Second Manassas) in August 1862. Lee followed up this victory with a typically bold stroke: he took his army across the Potomac and northward into Maryland, hoping that the fall harvest could provide him with desperately needed supplies. McClellan met Lee at the Battle of Antietam (Sharpsburg) on September 17, 1862. North and South together suffered 24,000 casualties in this bloodiest day of the entire war. Tactically, the battle was a draw, but strategically it constituted a major Union victory because it forced Lee to withdraw south of the Potomac. Most important, Antietam provided Lincoln the occasion to issue the Emancipation Proclamation, freeing all slaves under rebel control.

Lincoln complained that McClellan had "the slows" and faulted him for not pursuing Lee after Antietam. McClellan's replacement, General Ambrose Burnside, thought himself unfit for high command. He was right. In December 1862 he led 122,000 federal troops against 78,500 Confederates at the Battle of Fredericksburg (Virginia). Burnside captured the town but then sacrificed his army in futile charges up the heights west of the town. The carnage shook even Lee. "It is well that war is so terrible—we should grow fond of it," he told an aide during the battle. Richmond remained, in the words of a southern song, "a hard road to travel." The war in the East had become a stalemate.

The War in the West

The Union fared better in the West. Unlike the geographically limited eastern theater, the war in the West shifted over a vast terrain that provided access to rivers leading directly into the South. The West also spawned new leadership in the person of an obscure Union general, Ulysses S. Grant. A West Point graduate with a reputation for heavy drinking, and a failed farmer and businessman, Grant soon proved one of the Union's best leaders.

In 1861–1862 Grant had stabilized control of Missouri and Kentucky and then moved south to attack Corinth, Mississippi, a major rail junction. In early April 1862 Confederate forces staged a surprise attack on Grant's army, encamped at Shiloh Church in southern Tennessee. Driven back on the first day, Union forces counterattacked on the second day and drove the Confederate army from the field. Of 77,000 men who fought at Shiloh, 23,000 were killed or wounded. Perhaps the most important casualty was General Albert Sydney Johnston, whose death deprived the Confederacy of its best commander west of the Appalachians. Defeated at Shiloh, the Confederates evacuated Corinth.

For the Corinth-Shiloh Campaign, the Confederacy had stripped New Orleans of its defenses, leaving its largest city guarded by only 3,000 militia. A combined land-sea force under Union general Benjamin Butler and Admiral David G. Farragut took advantage of the weakened defenses and captured New Orleans in late April. Farragut continued up the Mississippi as far as Natchez. When a Union flotilla moved down the river in June and took Memphis, the North controlled the great river except for a 200-mile stretch between Port Hudson, Louisiana, and Vicksburg, Mississippi.

In 1862 Union and Confederate forces also clashed in the Transmississippi West, a vast region that stretched from the Midwest to the Pacific Coast. On the banks of the Rio Grande, Union vol-

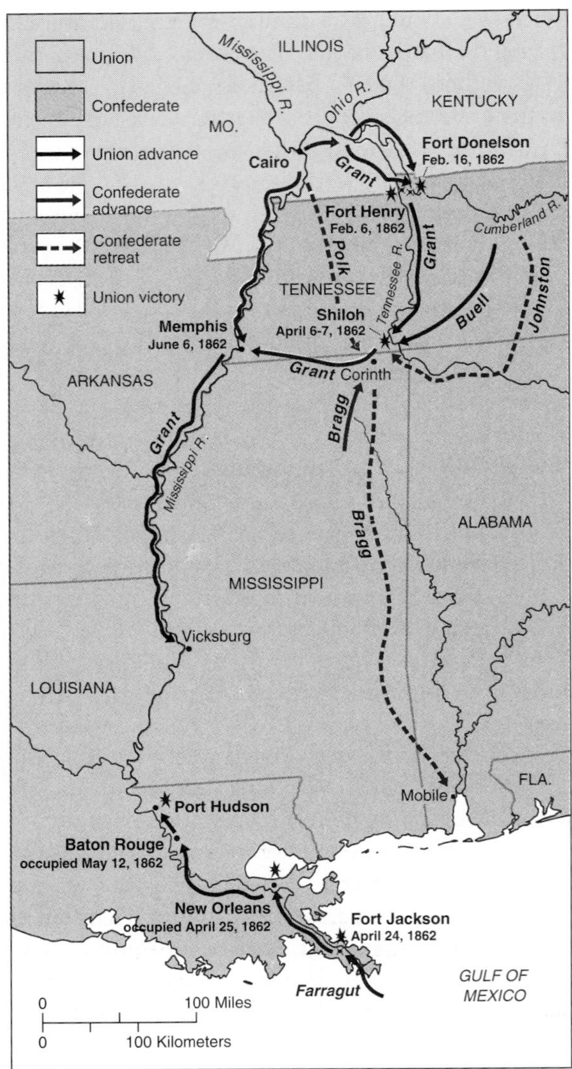

The War in the West, 1861–1862
By the end of 1862 the North held New Orleans and the entire Mississippi River except for the stretch between Vicksburg and Port Hudson.

unteers and Mexican-American companies drove a Confederate army from Texas out of New Mexico. A thousand miles to the east, opposing armies battled for control of the crucial Missouri River. In Pea Ridge, Arkansas, in March 1862, northern troops scattered a Confederate force of 16,000.

These Union victories changed the Trans-Mississippi war. As the rebel threat faded, western volunteers who had mobilized to crush Confederates turned to fighting Indians. Conflict between Union forces and Native Americans erupted in Minnesota, Arizona, Nevada, Colorado, and New Mexico. After 1865 federal troops moved west to complete the rout of the Indians that had begun during the Civil War.

Ironclads and Cruisers: The Naval War

By plunging the navy into the Confederacy like a dagger, the Union exploited one of its clearest advantages. The North began the war with more than forty active warships—the South had none—and by 1865 northern industrial advantages had given the United States the largest navy in the world. Steamships could penetrate the South's river systems from any direction. Yet the Union navy faced an extraordinary challenge in its efforts to blockade the South's 3,500 miles of coastline. Sleek Confederate blockade runners darted in and out of southern harbors with little chance of capture early in the war. Their chances of success gradually diminished, however, as the North tightened the blockade and began to capture key southern ports. In 1861 almost 90 percent of blockade runners made it through; by 1865 the rate had sunk to 50 percent.

Despite meager resources, the South made impressive efforts to offset the North's naval advantages. Early in the war the Confederates raised a scuttled Union frigate, the *Merrimac;* sheathed its sides in iron; rechristened it the *Virginia;* and deployed it to attack wooden Union ships at Hampton Roads, Virginia. The *Virginia*'s success ended on March 9, 1862, when it tangled with the hastily built Union ironclad *Monitor* in the first battle ever fought between ironclads. The battle ended in a draw, but the South eventually lost the naval war because it could not build enough ships to overcome the northern lead. Even successful commerce raiders, such as the British-built *Alabama* and the *Florida,* although they wreaked havoc on the Union's merchant marine, did comparatively little to tip the balance in the South's favor because the North did not depend on imports for war materials.

The Diplomatic War

While armies and navies clashed in 1861–1862, conflict developed on a third front, diplomacy. At the war's start southerners had confidently opened a campaign to gain swift diplomatic recognition for the Confederacy. They were sure of the support of Britain and France's upper classes and even more certain that Britain, dependent on the South for four-fifths of its cotton, would have to break the Union blockade.

In 1861 Confederate diplomats James Mason and John Slidell sailed for Europe to lobby for recognition of an independent South, but their ship, the *Trent,* fell into Union hands. When the pair ended up as prisoners in Boston, British tempers exploded. Considering one war at a time quite enough, President Lincoln ordered Mason and Slidell released. But settling the *Trent* affair did not eliminate friction between the United States and Britain. Union diplomats protested the construction of Confederate commerce raiders such as the *Alabama* and the *Florida* in British shipyards and threatened war if two British-built ironclads were turned over to the Confederacy. Britain gave in and purchased the vessels for its own navy.

The South fell far short of its diplomatic objectives. Neither Britain nor France ever recognized the Confederacy as a nation. Southerners had badly overestimated the leverage of "cotton diplomacy" and the power of King Cotton, exaggerating the impact of their threats to withhold raw cotton supplies. Britain had an enormous cotton surplus on hand when the war began and developed other sources of cotton during the war, especially in India and Egypt. Although the South's share of England's cotton imports plummeted from 77 percent to 10 percent during the war, Britain's textile industry never faltered.

Lincoln's issuance of the Emancipation Proclamation, freeing the slaves, effectively preempted any British or French move toward recognition of the Confederacy. By transforming the war into a struggle about slavery, Lincoln won wide support among liberals and the working class in Britain. The proclamation, wrote Henry Adams (diplomat Charles Francis Adams's son) from London, "has done more for us here than all of our former victories and all our diplomacy."

Emancipation Transforms the War

"I hear old John Brown knocking on the lid of his coffin and shouting 'Let me out! Let me out!'" abolitionist Henry Stanton wrote to his wife after the fall of Fort Sumter. "The Doom of Slavery is at hand." In 1861 this prediction seemed wildly premature. In the inaugural address Lincoln had stated bluntly, "I have no purpose, directly or indirectly, to interfere with the institution of slavery in the states where it exists." Yet within two years both necessity and ideology made emancipation a primary northern goal.

The rise of emancipation as a war goal reflected the changing character of the conflict itself. As the fighting raged on, demands for the prosecution of a "total war" intensified in the North, and many people who were unconcerned about the morality of slavery accepted abolition as a military necessity.

From Confiscation to Emancipation

The Union's policy on emancipation developed in several stages. As soon as northern troops invaded the South, questions arose about captured rebel property, including slaves. Generally, slaves who fled behind Union lines were considered "contraband"—enemy property liable to seizure—and were put to work for the Union army. In August 1861 Congress passed the first Confiscation Act, which authorized the seizure of all property, including slaves, used in military aid of the rebellion. This law did not free slaves, nor did it apply to those who had not worked for the Confederate army.

Several factors determined the Union's cautious approach. For one thing, Lincoln maintained that the South could not legally secede and thus argued that the Constitution's protection of property still applied. Second, Lincoln did not want to alienate slaveholders in the border states and proslavery Democrats. In December 1861 he assured Congress that the war would not become a "remorseless revolutionary struggle." At the same time, however, the Radical Republicans pressured Lincoln to make the Civil War a second American Revolution, one that would abolish slavery. Thaddeus Stevens urged that the Union "free every slave—slay every traitor—burn every Rebel mansion, if these things be necessary to preserve this temple of freedom." Radicals agreed with African-American abolitionist Frederick Douglass that "to fight against slaveholders without fighting against slavery, is but a half-hearted business."

Emancipation also took on military significance with each Union setback, as northerners began to recognize that slavery permitted the South to commit a higher percentage of its white men to battle. In July 1862 Congress therefore passed the second Confiscation Act, which authorized the seizure of property belonging to all rebels, stipulated that slaves who entered Union lines "shall be forever free," and authorized the use of blacks as soldiers.

Nevertheless, Lincoln continued to stall. "My paramount object in this struggle *is* to save the Union, and is *not* either to save or destroy slavery," Lincoln averred. "If I could save the Union without freeing *any* slave, I would do it, and if I could save it by freeing *all* the slaves, I would do it; and if I could save it by freeing some and leaving others alone, I would also do that." But Lincoln, who had always loathed slavery, gradually came around to the view that the war had to lead to abolition. Reluctant to push the issue while Union armies reeled in defeat, he drafted a proclamation of emancipation and waited for the right moment to announce it. After the Union victory at Antietam, Lincoln issued the Preliminary Emancipation Proclamation (September 1862), which declared all slaves under rebel control free as of January 1, 1863. The final Emancipation Proclamation, issued on January 1, 1863, declared "forever free" all slaves in areas in rebellion.

The proclamation had limited practical impact. It applied only to areas in which it could not be enforced, those still in rebellion, and did not touch slavery in the border states. But the Emancipation Proclamation was a brilliant political stroke. By making it a military measure, Lincoln pacified northern conservatives, and by issuing the proclamation himself, he stole the initiative from the Radical Republicans. Through the proclamation, moreover, Lincoln mobilized support for the Union among European liberals, pushed the border states toward emancipation (both Missouri and Maryland abolished slavery before the war's end), and increased slaves' incentives to escape as Union troops neared. Fulfilling the worst of Confederate fears, the proclamation also enabled African-Americans to join the Union army.

The Emancipation Proclamation did not end slavery everywhere or free "*all* the slaves," but it changed the war. From 1863 on the war for the Union was also a war against slavery.

Crossing Union Lines

The attacks and counterattacks of the opposing armies turned many slaves into pawns of the war, free when Union troops overran their area, slaves again if the Confederates regained control. One North Carolina slave celebrated his liberation twelve different times. By 1865 about 500,000 former slaves were in Union hands.

Although in the first year of the war masters could retrieve slaves from Union armies, after 1862 slaves who crossed Union lines were considered free. The continual influx of freed slaves created a huge refugee problem for army commanders. Many freed slaves served in army camps as cooks, teamsters, and laborers. Some worked for pay on abandoned plantations or were leased out to planters who swore allegiance to the Union. Whether in camps or on plantations, freedmen questioned the value of liberation. Deductions for clothing and food ate up most of their earnings, and labor contracts bound them for long periods of time. Moreover, the freedmen encountered fierce prejudice among Yankee soldiers, who widely feared that emancipation would propel blacks northward after the war. The best solution to the widespread "question of what to do with the darkies," wrote one northern soldier, "would be to shoot them."

But this was not the whole story. Contrabands who aided the Union as spies and scouts helped to break down bigotry. "The sooner we get rid of our foolish prejudice the better for us," a Massachusetts soldier wrote home. In March 1865 Congress established the Freedmen's Bureau to provide relief, education, and work for the former slaves. The same law also provided that forty acres of abandoned or confiscated land could be leased to each freedman or southern Unionist, with an option to buy after three years. This was the first and only time that Congress provided for the redistribution of confiscated Confederate property.

African-American Soldiers in the Union Army

During the first year of the war the Union had rejected African-American soldiers. Only after the Emancipation Proclamation did the large-scale enlistment of blacks begin. Prominent blacks, including Frederick Douglass, worked as recruiting agents in northern cities. Douglass clearly saw the link between military service and citizenship. "Once let the black man get upon his person the brass letters, U.S.; let him get an eagle on his button, and a musket on his shoulder and bullets in his pocket, and there is no power on earth which can deny that he has earned the right to citizenship." By the war's end 186,000 African-Americans had served in the

African-American Artillerymen

African-American troops were organized after the Emancipation Proclamation. The soldiers in the photograph belonged to the Second U.S. Colored Light Artillery, which took part in the Battle of Nashville in 1864.

Union army, one-tenth of all Union soldiers. One-half came from the Confederate states.

White Union soldiers commonly objected to the new recruits on racial grounds. Others, including Colonel Thomas Wentworth Higginson, a liberal minister and former John Brown supporter who led a black regiment, welcomed the black soldiers. "There is a fierce energy about them [in battle] beyond anything of which I have ever read, except it be the French Zouaves [troops in North Africa]," he observed. Even Union soldiers who held African-Americans in contempt came to approve of "anything that will kill a rebel." Black recruitment offered opportunities for whites to secure commissions, for blacks served in separate regiments under white officers. For most of the war, black soldiers earned far less pay than whites. "We have come out Like men and Expected to be Treated as men but we have bin Treated more Like Dogs then men," an African-American soldier complained. Not until June 1864 did Congress belatedly equalize the pay of black and white soldiers.

African-American soldiers also suffered a far higher mortality rate than whites. Seldom committed to combat, they were far more likely to die of disease in bacteria-ridden garrisons. The Confederacy refused to treat captured black Union soldiers as prisoners of war; instead they were sent back to the states from which they had come to be reenslaved or executed. In an especially gruesome incident, when Confederate troops captured Fort Pillow, Tennessee, in 1864, they massacred 262 blacks.

Although fraught with inequities and hardships, military service symbolized citizenship for African-Americans. A black private explained, "If we hadn't become sojers, all might have gone back as it was before. But now things can never go back because we have showed our energy and our courage . . . and our natural manhood." And the Union's use of African-American soldiers, especially former slaves, struck a military as well as psychological blow at the Confederacy. "They will make good soldiers," General Grant wrote in 1863, "and taking them from the enemy weakens him in the same proportion they strengthen us."

Slavery in Wartime

Anxious white southerners on the home front felt as if they were perched on a volcano. To maintain control over their 3 million slaves, they tightened slave patrols, spread scare stories among slaves, and sometimes even moved entire plantations to relative safety in Texas. "The whites would tell the colored people not to go to the Yankees, for they would harness them to carts . . . in place of horses," remembered one African-American fugitive.

Some slaves remained faithful to their owners, hiding treasured belongings from marauding Union soldiers. Others were torn between loyalty and desire for freedom; one body servant, for example, accompanied his master to war, rescued him when he was wounded, and then escaped on his master's horse. Given the chance to flee to Union lines, most slaves did. Freedom was irresistible. But the majority of southern slaves stayed on their plantations under the nominal control of their masters. Despite the fears of southern whites, no general slave uprising occurred, and the Confederate war effort continued to utilize slave labor. Thousands of slaves worked in war plants, toiled as teamsters and cooks in army camps, and served as nurses in field hospitals. However, wartime conditions reduced overall slave productivity. The women and boys who remained on plantations complained of hard-to-control slaves who refused to work, worked inefficiently, or even destroyed property.

Whether slaves fled to freedom or merely stopped working, they effectively undermined the plantation system. Slavery disintegrated even as the Confederacy fought to preserve it. By 1864 a desperate Confederate Congress considered impressing slaves into the army in exchange for their freedom at the war's end. Although Robert E. Lee himself favored making slaves into soldiers, others were adamantly opposed. "If slaves will make good soldiers," a Georgia general argued, "our whole theory of slavery is wrong." In March 1865 the Confederate Congress passed a bill to arm 300,000 slave soldiers.

Although the plan to arm the slaves never took effect, the debate over it damaged southern morale

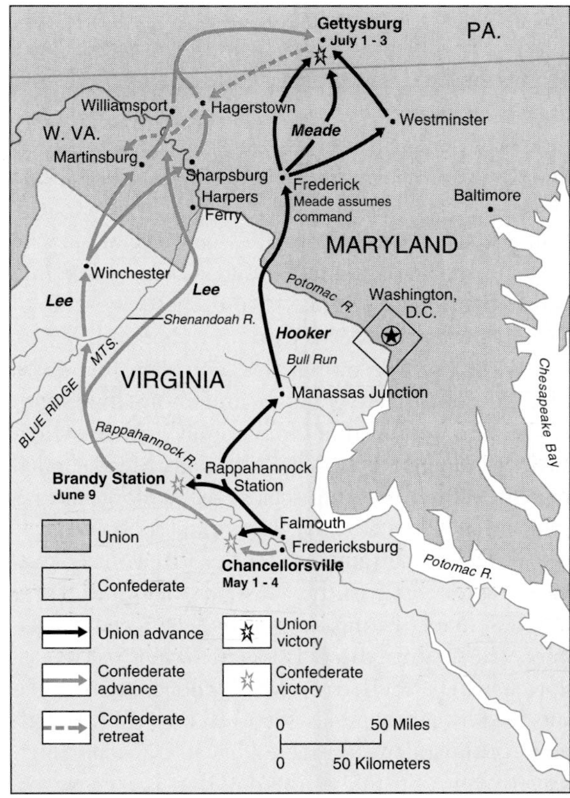

The War in the East, 1863

Victorious at Chancellorsville in May 1863, Lee again invaded Union territory but was decisively stopped at Gettysburg.

Robert E. Lee (1807–1870)

Lee had a distinguished military career before assuming command of the Army of Northern Virginia in 1862. He had served in the Mexican War under Winfield Scott and as lieutenant colonel of the cavalry performed frontier duty in Texas beginning in 1855. In 1859 he had led the troops that put down John Brown's raid on Harpers Ferry.

by revealing deep internal divisions over war goals. Even before these conflicts had become obvious, the South's military position had deteriorated.

The Turning Point of 1863

In summer and fall 1863 Union fortunes improved dramatically in every theater of the war. However, the spring had gone badly as General Joseph "Fighting Joe" Hooker, a windbag fond of issuing pompous proclamations to his troops, suffered a crushing defeat at Chancellorsville, Virginia, in May 1863. Although Chancellorsville cost the South dearly—Stonewall Jackson was accidentally killed by his own troops—it humiliated the North, whose forces had outnumbered the Confederate troops two to one. "What will the country say?" Lincoln moaned. Reports from the West brought no better news: Grant was still unable to take Vicksburg, and the rebels clung to a vital 200-mile stretch of the Mississippi.

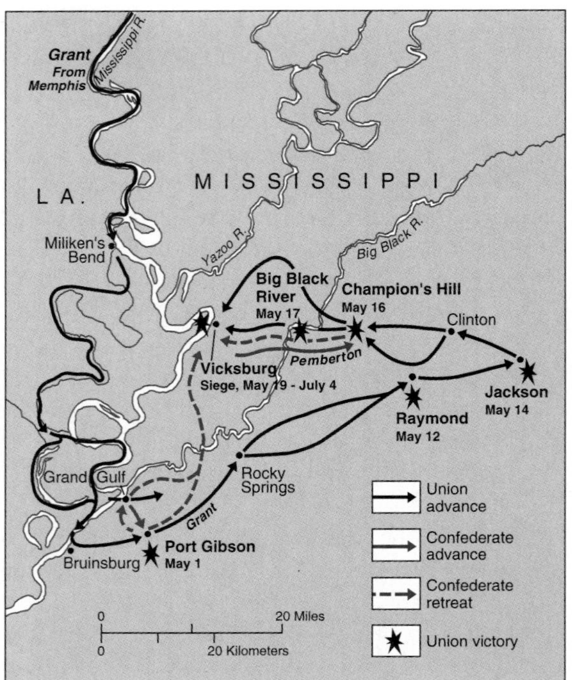

The War in the West, 1863: Vicksburg
Grant first moved his army west of Vicksburg to a point on the Mississippi south of the town. Then he marched northeast, taking Jackson, and finally west to Vicksburg.

Union fortunes rose when Lee determined to invade the North. The decision provoked dissension within the Confederate government, but Lee needed supplies that war-racked Virginia could no longer provide. He also hoped that Lincoln would move troops from Vicksburg back into the eastern theater, and he believed that a major Confederate victory on northern soil could tip the balance to propeace northern Democrats and gain European recognition for the Confederacy. Lee led his 75,000 men into Maryland and then pressed forward into southern Pennsylvania. Lincoln, rejecting Hooker's plan to attack a virtually unprotected Richmond, replaced him with General George G. Meade.

Early in July 1863 Lee's offensive ground to a halt at a Pennsylvania road junction, Gettysburg. Confederates foraging for shoes in the town stumbled into Union cavalry, and both sides called for reinforcements. Thus began the war's greatest battle. The Union fielded 90,000 troops against Lee's 75,000, and the struggle raged for the first three days of July. On the afternoon of the third day, Lee ordered a direct frontal assault on the Union lines, and 15,000 men under General George E. Pickett charged across the open field, flags bright in the brilliant sunshine. Union rifles poured volley after volley into the onrushing Confederates, whose line wavered and then broke. More than one-half of Pickett's force lay dead, dying, or captured. When Lee withdrew to Virginia the next day, July 4, he had lost seventeen generals and more than one-third of his army. Total Union and Confederate casualties numbered 50,000. Although Meade failed to pursue the retreating rebels, the Union men rejoiced that they had parried Lee's stab northward.

Almost simultaneously, the North won a strategically vital battle in the West, at Vicksburg. After arduous maneuvering, Grant had besieged Vicksburg, the key to the Mississippi. After six weeks, during which southern soldiers and civilians alike survived by eating mules and even rats, the Confederate commander surrendered his 30,000-man garrison to Grant on July 4, the day that Lee began his withdrawal from Pennsylvania. Port Hudson, the last Confederate stronghold on the Mississippi, soon surrendered. "The Father of Waters flows unvexed to the sea," Lincoln proclaimed.

A second crucial Union victory in the West soon followed as armies stormed back and forth across Tennessee. By November 1863 the Union forces had finally captured and held Chattanooga, and the way lay open for a Union strike into Georgia.

Coming on the heels of reverses that had driven northern morale to its lowest point of the war, Union successes in the second half of 1863 stiffened the North's will to continue fighting and plunged some Confederate leaders into despair. After the fall of Vicksburg, chief of ordnance Josiah Gorgas lamented, "Yesterday we rode the pinnacle of success—today absolute ruin seems our portion. The Confederacy totters to its destruction."

Totter it might, but the South was far from falling. Lee and his Army of Northern Virginia still defended Virginia and Richmond. Although the loss of Vicksburg had cut the Confederacy in half, southern states west of the Mississippi could still provide soldiers. And the heart of the Confederacy—the Carolinas, Georgia, Florida, Mississippi, and Virginia—remained in southern hands. Few contemporaries thought that the fate of the Confederacy had been sealed.

War and Society, North and South

The Civil War, engulfing two economies and societies, extended far beyond the battlefields. By 1863 the contrasts between North and South were stark: superior resources enabled the Union to meet wartime demands that the imperiled Confederacy could not. But both sides confronted similar problems: labor shortages, inflation, and disunity and dissent. The war disrupted and dislocated families in the Union and Confederacy alike but especially in the South. Women on both sides took on new roles at home, in the workplace, and in relief efforts.

The War's Economic Impact: The North

The war had a wildly uneven effect on the Union's economy. Deprived of southern markets, the shoe industry in Massachusetts declined; deprived of raw cotton, the textile industry went into a tailspin. But northern industries directly related to the war effort, such as the manufacture of arms and uniforms, benefited from huge government contracts. Railroads flourished. Now an overwhelming majority in Congress, and with no need to balance southern interests against those of the North, the Republican party carried through a vigorous probusiness legislative agenda. Congress hiked the tariff in 1862 and again in 1864 to protect domestic industries. In 1862 it passed the Pacific Railroad Act to build a transcontinental railroad. The government chartered the Union Pacific and Central Pacific corporations and gave each large land grants and generous loans, a total of 60 million acres of land and $20 million. The issuance of greenbacks and the creation of a national banking system brought a measure of uniformity to the nation's financial system.

The Republicans designed these measures to help all social classes and partially succeeded. The Homestead Act (passed in May 1862), embodying the party's ideal of "free soil, free labor, free men," granted 160 acres of public land to settlers after five years of residence on the land. By 1865, 20,000 homesteaders had occupied new land in the West under this act. To bring higher education within the reach of the common people, the Morrill Land Grant Act of July 1862 gave states proceeds from public land to establish universities emphasizing "such branches of learning as are related to agriculture and mechanic arts [engineering]."

Despite the idealistic goals underlying such laws, the war benefited the wealthy more than the average citizen. Corrupt contractors grew rich by selling the government substandard merchandise such as the notorious "shoddy," clothing made from compressed rags, which quickly disintegrated. Speculators made millions in the gold market, profiting more from Union defeats than from Union victories. Dealers with access to scarce commodities reaped astonishing profits. Manpower shortages in agricultural areas stimulated demand for Cyrus McCormick's mechanical reaper. McCormick redoubled his profits by investing in pig iron and watching as wartime demand drove the price of iron from twenty-three to forty dollars a ton.

Ordinary workers suffered. Protective tariffs, wartime excise taxes, and inflation bloated the price of finished goods, while wages lagged 20 percent or more behind cost increases. As boys and women poured into government offices and factories to replace men serving in the army, they drew lower pay, and the threat that employers could hire more youths and females undercut the bargaining power of men remaining in the labor force.

The War's Economic Impact: The South

The war shattered the South's economy. In fact, if both regions are considered together, the war retarded *American* economic growth. For example, the U.S. commodity output, which had increased 51 percent and 62 percent in the 1840s and 1850s, respectively, rose only 22 percent during the 1860s. Even this modest gain depended wholly on the North, for during that same decade commodity output in the South *declined* 39 percent.

Multiple factors offset the South's substantial wartime industrial growth. For example, the war destroyed the South's railroads. Cotton production plunged from 4 million bales in 1861 to 300,000 in 1865. Southern food production also declined because of Union occupation and a shortage of manpower. Food scarcities occurred late in the war. "The people are subsisting on the ungathered crops and nine families out of ten are left without meat," lamented one Mississippian.

Part of the blame for the South's food shortage rested with the planters. Despite government pleas to grow more food, many planters continued to raise cotton. To feed its hungry armies, the Confederacy impressed food from civilians. Farms and plantations run by the wives of active soldiers provided the easiest targets for food-impressment agents, and the women sent desperate pleas to their husbands to return home. By late 1864, half the Confederacy's soldiers were absent from their units.

In one respect the persistence of cotton growing aided the South as cotton became the basis for the Confederacy's flourishing trade with the enemy. In July 1861 the U.S. Congress virtually legalized this trade by allowing northern commerce with southerners loyal to the Union. In practice, it proved impossible to tell loyalists from rebels, and northern traders happily swapped bacon, salt, blankets, and other necessities with whomever would sell them southern cotton. By 1864 traffic through the lines was providing the South with enough food daily to feed Lee's Army of Northern Virginia. To one disenchanted northern congressman, it seemed that the Union's policy was "to feed an army and fight it at the same time."

Trading with the enemy alleviated the South's food shortages but intensified its morale problems. The prospect of traffic with the Yankees gave planters an incentive to keep growing cotton, and it fattened merchants and middlemen. "Oh! the extortioners," complained a War Office clerk in Richmond. "Our patriotism is mainly in the army and among the ladies of the South. The avarice and cupidity of men at home could only be exceeded by ravenous wolves."

Dealing with Dissent

Both wartime governments faced mounting dissent and disloyalty. Within the Confederacy, dissent assumed two basic forms. First, a vocal group of states' rights supporters persistently attacked Jefferson Davis's government as a despotism. Second, loyalty to the Union flourished among the nonslaveholding small farmers who lived in the Appalachian region. To these people, the Confederate rebellion was a slave owners' conspiracy. An Alabama farmer complained of the planters, "All they want is to get you pupt up and to fight for their infurnal negroes and after you do there fighting you may kiss there hine parts for o they care." On the whole, the South responded mildly to such popular disaffection. In 1862 the Confederate Congress gave President Davis the power to suspend the writ of habeas corpus, but he used it sparingly.

Lincoln faced similar challenges in the North, where the Democratic minority opposed both emancipation and the wartime growth of centralized power. One faction, the "Peace Democrats" (called Copperheads by their opponents, to suggest a resemblance to a species of easily concealed poisonous snakes), demanded a truce and a peace conference. They charged that the administration's war policy would "exterminate the South," make reconciliation impossible, and spark "terrible social change and revolution" nationwide.

Strongest in the border states, the Midwest, and northeastern cities, the Democrats mobilized farmers of southern background and the urban working class, especially recent immigrants, who feared losing their jobs to free blacks. In 1863 this volatile mix of political, ethnic, racial, and class antagonisms exploded into antidraft protests in several cities. By far the most violent eruption occurred in July 1863 in New York City, where mobs of Irish working-class men and women roamed the streets for four days until federal troops suppressed them. The Irish loathed the idea of being drafted to fight a war on behalf of slaves who, once freed, might compete with them for jobs. They also bitterly resented the provision of the draft law that allowed the rich to purchase substitutes. The mobs' targets reflected their grievances: the rioters lynched at least a dozen blacks, injured hundreds more, and burned draft offices and the homes of wealthy Republicans.

President Lincoln's speedy dispatch of federal troops to quash these riots typified his forceful response to dissent. Lincoln imposed martial law with far less hesitancy than Davis; he suspended the writ of habeas corpus nationwide in 1863 and authorized the arrest of rebels, draft resisters, and anyone engaged in "any disloyal practice." The contrasting responses of Davis and Lincoln to dissent underscored the differences between the two regions' wartime political systems. Lincoln and the Republicans used dissent to rally patriotic fever against the Democrats, but Davis lacked the institutionalization of dissent provided by party conflict and thus had to tread lightly lest he be branded a despot.

Yet Lincoln did not unleash a reign of terror against dissent. In general, the North preserved freedom of the press, speech, and assembly. In 1864 the Union became the first warring nation in history to hold a contested national election. Moreover, most of the 15,000 civilians arrested in the North were quickly released. A few cases aroused concern. In 1864 a military commission sentenced an Indiana man to be hanged for an alleged plot to free Confederate prisoners. Two years later in *Ex parte* Milligan (1866), the Supreme Court overturned the conviction, ruling that military courts could not try civilians when civil courts were open. The arrest of outspoken dissident politicians raised protests as well. Clement L. Vallandigham, an Ohio Peace Democrat, challenged the administration, denounced the suspension of habeas corpus, and proposed an armistice. In 1863 a military commission sentenced him to jail for the duration of the war; when Ohio Democrats nominated him for governor, Lincoln changed the sentence to banishment. Escorted to enemy lines in Tennessee, Vallandigham was left in the hands of bewildered Confederates and escaped to Canada. The Supreme Court refused to review his case.

The Medical War

The Union and the Confederacy alike witnessed remarkable wartime patriotism that propelled civilians, especially women, to work tirelessly to alleviate soldiers' suffering. The United States Sanitary Commission, organized to assist the Union's medical bureau, depended on women volunteers. Described by one woman as a "great artery that bears the people's love to the army," the commission raised funds, bought and distributed supplies, and ran special kitchens to supplement army rations. One widow, Mary Ann "Mother" Bickerdyke, served sick and wounded Union soldiers as both nurse and surrogate mother.

Women also reached out to aid the battlefront through the nursing corps. Some 3,200 women served the Union and the Confederacy as nurses. Dorothea Dix, famed for her campaigns on behalf of the insane, became head of the Union's nursing corps. Clara Barton, an obscure clerk in the Patent Office, found ingenious ways of channeling medicine to the sick and wounded. Catching wind of Union movements before the Battle of Antietam, she showed up at the battlefield on the eve of the clash with a wagonload of supplies. When army surgeons ran out of bandages and started to dress wounds with corn husks, she raced forward with lint and bandages. In 1881 she would found the American Red Cross. The Confederacy also had extraordinary nurses, among them Belle Boyd, who served as both nurse and spy and once dashed through a field, waving her bonnet, to give Stonewall Jackson information. Nurses witnessed horrible sights. One reported, "About the amputating table lay large piles of human flesh—legs, arms, feet, and hands."

Pioneered by British reformer Florence Nightingale in the 1850s, nursing was a new vocation for women. In the eyes of critics, it marked a brazen departure from women's proper sphere. Male doctors were unsure about how to react to female nurses and sanitary workers. Some saw a potential for mischief in women's presence in male hospital wards. But other physicians viewed nursing and sanitary work as useful. The miasm theory of disease (see Chapter 11) won wide respect among physicians and stimulated valuable sanitary measures. In partial consequence, the ratio of disease to battle deaths was much lower in the Civil War than in the Mexican War. Nonetheless, for every soldier killed during the Civil War, two died of disease. The germ theory of disease was unknown, and arm and leg wounds often led to gangrene or tetanus. Typhoid, malaria, diarrhea, and dysentery were rampant in army camps.

Prison camps posed a special problem. The two sides had far more prisoners than they could handle, and prisoners on both sides suffered gravely. The worst conditions plagued the southern camps. Squalor and insufficient rations turned the Confederate prison camp at Andersonville, Georgia, into a virtual death camp; 3,000 prisoners a month (out of a total of 32,000) were dying there by August 1864. After the war an outraged northern public demanded, and got, the execution of Andersonville's commandant. Although the commandant was partly to blame, the deterioration of the southern economy was primarily responsible for such wretched conditions. Union prison camps were only marginally better.

The War and Women's Rights

Nurses and Sanitary Commission workers were not the only women to serve society in wartime. In North and South alike, women took over jobs vacated by men. In rural areas, where manpower shortages were most acute, women often plowed, planted, and harvested.

Northern women's rights advocates hoped that the war would yield equality for women as well as for slaves. A grateful North, they contended, should reward women for their wartime service and recognize the link between black rights and women's rights. In 1863 feminists Elizabeth Cady Stanton and Susan B. Anthony organized the National Woman's Loyal League. Its members principally gathered signatures on petitions calling for a constitutional amendment to abolish slavery, but Stanton and Anthony used the organization to promote woman suffrage as well. Despite high expectations, the war did not bring women significantly closer to economic or political equality. Nor did it much change the prevailing definition of women's sphere. Men continued to dominate the medical profession, and for the rest of the century the census classified nurses as domestic help.

This failure to win the vote for women by capitalizing on the rising sentiment for abolition keenly disappointed women's rights advocates. The North had compelling reasons to abolish slavery, but northern politicians saw little practical value in woman suffrage. The *New York Herald,* which supported the Loyal League's attack on slavery, dismissed its call for woman suffrage as "nonsense and tomfoolery." Stanton wrote bitterly, "So long as woman labors to second man's endeavors and exalt his sex above her own, her virtues pass unquestioned; but when she dares to demand rights and privileges for herself, her motives, manners, dress, personal appearance, and character are subjects for ridicule and detraction."

The Union Victorious, 1864–1865

Successes at Gettysburg and Vicksburg in 1863 notwithstanding, the Union stood no closer to taking Richmond at the start of 1864 than in 1861, and most of the Lower South remained under Confederate control. The North's persistent inability to destroy the main Confederate armies eroded the Union's will to attack. War weariness strengthened

The Election of 1864

Candidates	*Parties*	*Electoral Vote*	*Popular Vote*	*Percentage of Popular Vote*
ABRAHAM LINCOLN	Republican	212	2,206,938	55.0
George B. McClellan	Democratic	21	1,803,787	45.0

the Democrats and jeopardized Lincoln's reelection in 1864.

The year 1864 was crucial for the North. A Union army under General William Tecumseh Sherman captured Atlanta in September, boosting northern morale and helping to reelect Lincoln. Sherman then marched unimpeded across Georgia and into South Carolina and devastated the states. In Virginia Grant backed Lee into trenches around Petersburg and Richmond and forced the evacuation of both cities—and ultimately the Confederacy's collapse.

The Eastern Theater in 1864

Early in 1864 Lincoln made Grant the commander of all Union armies and promoted him to lieutenant general. At first glance, the stony-faced, cigar-puffing Grant seemed an unlikely candidate for so exalted a rank, held previously only by George Washington. But Grant's successes in the West had made him the Union's most popular general. He moved his headquarters to the Army of the Potomac in the East and mapped a strategy for final victory.

Grant shared Lincoln's belief that the Union had to coordinate its attacks on all fronts to exploit its numerical advantage. He planned a sustained offensive against Lee in the East while ordering Sherman to attack the rebel army in Georgia. Sherman's mission was "to break it [the Confederate army] up, and to get into the interior of the enemy's country . . . inflicting all the damage you can."

In early May 1864 Grant led 118,000 men against Lee's 64,000 in a forested area near Fredericksburg, Virginia, called the Wilderness. The Union army fought the Army of Northern Virginia in a series of bloody engagements in May and June. These battles ranked among the war's fiercest; at Cold Harbor, Grant lost 7,000 men in one hour. Instead of recoiling from such an immense "butcher's bill," Grant pressed on, forcing Lee to pull back to trenches guarding Petersburg and Richmond.

Once entrenched, Lee could not threaten the Union rear with rapid moves as he had done for three years. Lee sent General Jubal A. Early on raids down the Shenandoah Valley, which served the Confederacy as a granary and as an indirect way to menace Washington. Grant countered by ordering General Philip Sheridan to march down the valley from the north and lay it waste. By September 1864 Sheridan controlled the devastated valley.

Sherman in Georgia

While Grant and Lee grappled in the Wilderness, Sherman led 98,000 men into Georgia. Opposing him with 53,000 men (later reinforced to 65,000), General Joseph Johnston slowly retreated toward Atlanta, conserving his strength for a defense of the city. Dismayed by this defensive strategy, President Davis replaced Johnston with the adventurous John B. Hood. He gave Davis what he wanted, a series of attacks on Sherman, but Sherman pressed relentlessly forward against Hood's increasingly depleted army. Unable to defend Atlanta, Hood evacuated the city, which Sherman took on September 2, 1864.

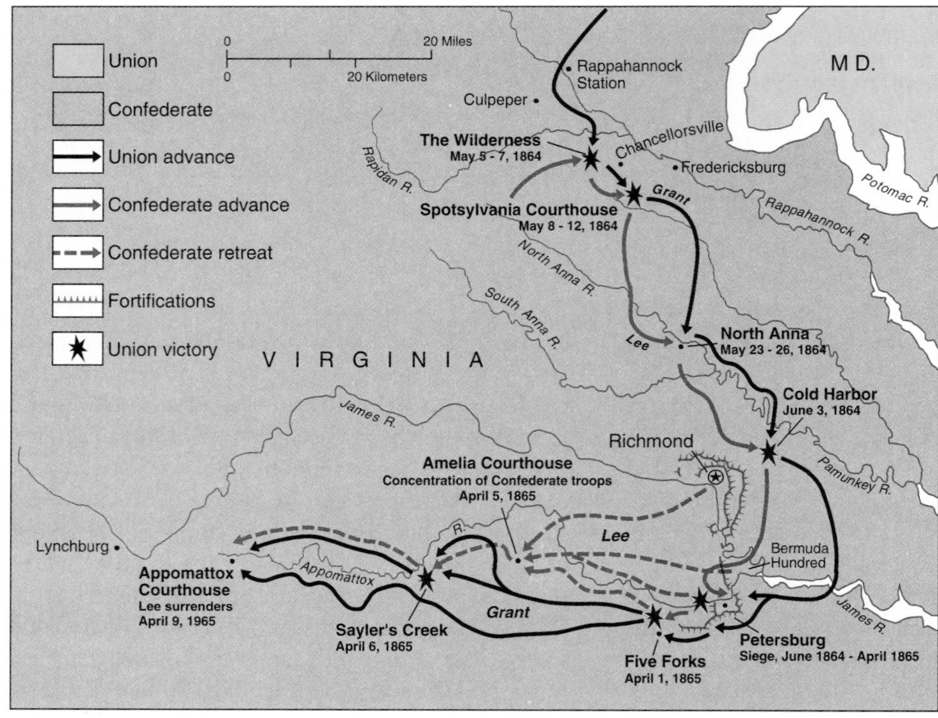

The Final Virginia Campaign, 1864–1865

The Election of 1864

Atlanta's fall came at a timely moment for Lincoln, in the thick of a tough campaign for reelection. Radical Republicans opposed his renomination, largely because of his desire to restore occupied parts of the Confederacy to the Union, and rallied around Secretary of the Treasury Salmon P. Chase. The Democrats, meanwhile, had never forgiven Lincoln for making emancipation a war goal, and now the Copperheads demanded an immediate armistice followed by negotiations.

Lincoln, however, benefited from his own resourcefulness and his foes' problems. Chase's challenge failed, and by the time of the Republican convention, Lincoln's managers controlled the nomination. To isolate the Peace Democrats, the Republicans formed a temporary organization, the National Union party, and chose a southern Unionist, Democratic senator Andrew Johnson of Tennessee, for the vice presidency. The Democrats nominated George B. McClellan, former commander of the Army of the Potomac, who advocated military victory and tried to distance himself from the Democratic platform, which called for peace without victory.

Lincoln doubted that he would be reelected, but the fall of Atlanta provided an enormous boost. With 55 percent of the popular vote and 212 out of 233 electoral votes, he swept to victory.

Sherman's March Through Georgia

Meanwhile, Sherman gave the South a lesson in total war. Refusing to chase Hood back into Tennessee, he decided to abandon his own supply lines, to march his army across Georgia to Savannah, and to live off the countryside. He would break the South's will to fight, terrify its people, and "make war so terrible . . . that generations would pass before they could appeal to it again."

Sherman began by burning much of Atlanta and forcing the evacuation of its civilian population. This harsh measure freed him of the need to feed and garrison the city. Then he led the bulk of his army, 62,000 men, out of Atlanta toward Savannah. Four columns of infantry, augmented by cavalry squads and followed by thousands of jubilant slaves, moved on a front sixty miles wide and at a pace of ten miles a day, destroying everything that could aid the Confederacy—arsenals, railroads, munitions plants, cotton gins, crops, and livestock. This ruin far exceeded Sherman's orders. Although told not to destroy civilian property, foragers ransacked and demolished homes. Indeed, havoc seemed a vital part of Sherman's strategy. By the time he occupied Savannah, he estimated that his army had destroyed $100 million worth of property. After taking Savannah in December 1864, Sherman's army wheeled north toward South Carolina and advanced unimpeded to Columbia, where fires set by looters, slaves, soldiers of both sides, and liberated Union prisoners razed the city. Sherman headed for North Carolina. By spring 1865 his army had left behind 400 miles of ruin. Other Union armies controlled the entire Confederacy, except Texas and Florida, and destroyed its wealth. "War is cruelty and you cannot refine it," Sherman wrote. "Those who brought war into our country deserve all the curses and maledictions a people can pour out."

Toward Appomattox

While Sherman headed north, Grant renewed his assault on the entrenched Army of Northern Virginia. His main objective was Petersburg, a railroad hub south of Richmond. The fall of Atlanta and the devastation wrought by Sherman's army took a heavy toll on Confederate morale. Desertions reached epidemic proportions. Late in March 1865 Grant, reinforced by Sheridan, swung his army around the western flank of the Petersburg defenders. Lee could not stop him. On April 2 a courier brought the grim news to Jefferson Davis, attending church in Richmond: "General Lee telegraphs that he can hold his position no longer."

Davis left his pew, gathered his government, and fled. On the morning of April 3 Union troops entered Richmond, pulled down the Confederate flag, and raised the Stars and Stripes over the capital. Explosions set by retreating Confederates left the city "a sea of flames." Union troops liberated the jail, which held slaves awaiting sale, and its rejoicing inmates poured into the streets. On April 4 Lincoln toured the city and, for a few minutes, sat at Davis's desk with a dreamy expression on his face.

Lee led a last-ditch effort to escape westward to Lynchburg and its rail connections. But Grant and Sheridan choked off the route, and on April 9 Lee bowed to the inevitable. He asked for terms of surrender and met Grant in a private home in the village of Appomattox Courthouse, east of Lynchburg. As stunned troops gathered outside, Lee appeared in full dress uniform, complete with sword. Grant entered in his customary disarray, smoking a cigar. The final surrender came four days later as Lee's troops laid down their arms between federal ranks. "On our part," wrote a Union officer, "not a sound of trumpet . . . nor roll of drum; not a cheer . . . but an awed stillness rather." Grant paroled Lee's 26,000 men and sent them home with the horses and mules "to work their little farms." Within a month the remnants of Confederate resistance collapsed.

Grant headed back to Washington. On April 14 he turned down a theater date with the Lincolns; his wife found Mrs. Lincoln overbearing. That night at Ford's Theater an unemployed pro-Confederate actor, John Wilkes Booth, entered Lincoln's box and shot him in the head. Assassination attempts on the secretary of state and vice president failed, and Booth escaped. Within two weeks Union troops hunted him down and shot him to death (or he shot himself). Four accused accomplices were hanged, and four more were imprisoned. On April 15 Lincoln died and Andrew Johnson became president. Six days later Lincoln's funeral train left Washington on its mournful journey to Springfield, Illinois. Crowds of thousands gathered at stations to weep as the black-draped train passed.

CONCLUSION

The Civil War took a larger human toll than any other war in American history. More than 600,000 persons died during the tragic four years of war. Most families in the nation suffered losses. Vivid reminders remained well into the twentieth century. For many years armless and legless veterans gathered at regimental reunions, and thousands of communities built monuments to the dead.

The war's costs were high, but only the southern economy was destroyed. By war's end the North had most of the nation's wealth and industrial capacity. Spurring economic modernization, the war provided opportunities for industrial development and capital investment. No longer the largest slave-owning power in the world, the United States would become a major industrial nation.

The war had political ramifications as well. States never regained their antebellum range of powers. The national banking system gradually supplanted state banks, and greenbacks provided a national currency. The war also promoted large-scale organization in both the business world and public life.

Finally, the Civil War fulfilled abolitionists' prophecies as well as Union goals, producing the very sort of radical upheaval within southern society that Lincoln had tried to avoid. Beaten Confederates wondered whether blacks and Yankees would permanently take over the South. "Hello, massa," an African-American Union soldier called out when he spotted his former owner among Confederate prisoners whom he was guarding. "Bottom rail top dis time." The nation now shifted its attention to the reconstruction of the conquered South and the fate of 3.5 million newly freed slaves.

CHRONOLOGY

1861 President Abraham Lincoln calls for volunteers to suppress the rebellion (April).
Virginia, Arkansas, Tennessee, and North Carolina join the Confederacy (April–May).
Lincoln imposes a naval blockade on the South (April).
First Battle of Bull Run (July).
First Confiscation Act (August).

1862 Legal Tender Act (February).
George B. McClellan's Peninsula Campaign (March–July).
Battle of Shiloh (April).
Confederate Congress passes the Conscription Act (April).
David G. Farragut captures New Orleans (April).
Homestead Act (May).
Seven Days' Battles (June–July).
Pacific Railroad Act (July).
Morrill Land Grant Act (July).
Second Confiscation Act (July).
Second Battle of Bull Run (August).
Battle of Antietam (September).
Preliminary Emancipation Proclamation (September).
Battle of Fredericksburg (December).

1863 Emancipation Proclamation issued (January).
Lincoln suspends writ of habeas corpus nationwide (January).
National Bank Act (February).
Congress passes the Enrollment Act (March).
Battle of Chancellorsville (May).
Battle of Gettysburg (July).
Surrender of Vicksburg (July).
New York City draft riots (July).
Battle of Chickamauga (September).

1864 Ulysses S. Grant given command of all Union armies (March).
Wilderness campaign (May–June).
Surrender of Atlanta (September).
Lincoln reelected (November).
William T. Sherman's march to the sea (November–December).

1865 Sherman moves through South Carolina (January–March).
Grant takes Richmond (April).
Robert E. Lee surrenders at Appomattox (April).
Lincoln dies (April).
Joseph Johnston surrenders to Sherman (April).

FOR FURTHER READING

Iver Bernstein, *The New York Draft Riots: The Significance for American Society and Politics in the Age of the Civil War* (1990). An exploration of the social, economic, and political facets of the riots, and their ramifications.

Albert Castel, *Decision in the West: The Atlanta Campaign of 1864* (1992). A critical examination of William T. Sherman's legendary brilliance of command.

Catherine Clinton and Nina Silber, eds., *Divided Houses: Gender and the Civil War* (1992). Essays focusing on changes in women's roles and activities.

David H. Donald, *Lincoln* (1995). An impressive new biography of one of America's greatest presidents.

Alvin M. Josephy Jr., *The Civil War in the American West* (1993). A penetrating look at a relatively unexamined arena of the war.

Leon Litwack, *Been in the Storm So Long: The Aftermath of Slavery* (1979). A prize-winning examination of slaves' responses to the process of emancipation, continuing into the Reconstruction era.

James M. McPherson, *Battle Cry of Freedom: The Civil War Era* (1988). An award-winning study of the war years, skillfully integrating political, military, and social history.

Philip Shaw Paludan, *The Presidency of Abraham Lincoln* (1994). An assessment of Lincoln as statesman, party leader, commander in chief, and emancipator.

Charles Royster, *The Destructive War: William Tecumseh Sherman, Stonewall Jackson, and the Americans* (1991). An insightful exploration of the meaning of violence and nationality in the Civil War era.

Emory M. Thomas, *The Confederate Nation, 1861–1865* (1979). An engaging narrative history, emphasizing the rise and fall of southern nationalism.

CHAPTER 16

The Crises of Reconstruction, 1865–1877

When the Civil War ended, parts of the South resembled a wasteland. The landscape "looked for many miles like a broad black streak of ruin and desolation," wrote a Union general. Homes, crops, and railroads had been destroyed; farming and business had come to a standstill. Refugees, demobilized soldiers, and former slaves flooded the roads. The prevailing mood was as grim as the landscape. "The South lies prostrate—their foot is on us—there is no help," a Virginia woman lamented. That 200,000 Union troops occupied the former Confederacy contributed to the sense of despair.

After most wars victors care little for the mood of the vanquished, but the Civil War was different. The Union had sought not merely victory but the return of national unity. The federal government faced unprecedented questions. How could the Union be restored and the South reintegrated? Who would control the process—Congress or the president? Should Confederate leaders be tried for treason? Most important, what would happen to the 3.5 million former slaves?

(Right) Richmond in ruins, 1865

The freedmen's future was *the* crucial postwar issue, for emancipation had set in motion the most profound upheaval in the nation's history. Slavery had been both a labor system and a means of racial control; it had determined the South's social, economic, and political structure. The end of the Civil War, in short, posed two huge challenges that had to be addressed simultaneously: readmitting the Confederate states to the Union and defining the status of free blacks in society.

From 1865 to 1877 the drama of Reconstruction—the restoration of the former Confederate states to the Union—unfolded in several theaters. In Washington conflict between president and Congress led to stringent measures. In the South Republicans temporarily took power, and far-reaching social and economic changes transformed the former Confederacy. Freed slaves wrestled with new identities and new problems. Meanwhile, the North hurtled headlong into an era of industrial expansion, labor unrest, and financial crises. By the mid-1870s, however, northern Republicans had abandoned Reconstruction and southern Democrats had regained control of their states. Reconstruction collapsed in 1877, and the nature and causes of its failure have engaged historians ever since.

Reconstruction Politics

The end of the Civil War offered multiple possibilities for chaos and vengeance. The federal government could have imprisoned Confederate leaders; former rebel troops could have become guerrillas; freed slaves could have waged a racial war against their former masters. None of this happened. Instead, intense *political* conflict dominated the immediate postwar period. The political upheaval, sometimes attended by violence, produced new constitutional amendments, an impeachment crisis, and some of the most ambitious domestic legislation ever enacted by Congress, the Reconstruction Acts of 1867–1868. It culminated in something that few expected, the enfranchisement of African-American men.

In 1865 only a handful of Radical Republicans advocated African-American suffrage. Any plan to restore the Union, Representative Thaddeus Stevens of Pennsylvania proclaimed, would have to "revolutionize Southern institutions, habits, and manners . . . or all our blood and treasure have been spent in vain." In the complex political battles of Reconstruction, the Radicals won broad support for their program, including African-American male enfranchisement. Just as the Civil War had led to emancipation, so Reconstruction led to African-American suffrage.

Lincoln's Plan

Conflict over Reconstruction began even before the war ended. In December 1863 President Lincoln issued the Proclamation of Amnesty and Reconstruction, which allowed southern states to form new governments if at least 10 percent of those who had voted in the 1860 elections swore an oath of allegiance to the Union and accepted emancipation. This plan excluded most Confederate officials and military officers, who would have had to apply for presidential pardons, as well as African-Americans, who had not voted in 1860. Lincoln hoped both to undermine the Confederacy and to build a southern Republican party.

Radical Republicans in Congress wanted a slower readmission process that would exclude even more ex-Confederates from political life. The Wade-Davis bill, passed by Congress in July 1864, provided that a military government would rule each former Confederate state and that at least one-half of the eligible voters would have to swear allegiance before they could choose a convention to repeal secession and abolish slavery. In addition, to qualify as a voter or a delegate, a southerner would have to take the "ironclad" oath, swearing that he had never voluntarily supported the Confederacy. The Wade-Davis bill would have delayed readmission of southern states almost indefinitely.

Lincoln pocket-vetoed* the Wade-Davis bill, and an impasse followed. Arkansas, Louisiana, Tennessee, and parts of Virginia moved toward readmission under variants of Lincoln's plan, but Congress refused to seat their delegates. Lincoln hinted that he might be moving toward a more rigorous policy than his original one, a program that would include African-American suffrage. But his death foreclosed the possibility that he and Congress might draw closer to agreement, and Radicals now looked with hope to the new president, Andrew Johnson.

Presidential Reconstruction Under Johnson

At first glance, Andrew Johnson seemed a likely ally for the Radicals. The only southern senator to remain in Congress when his state seceded, Johnson had taken a strong anti-Confederate stance and had served as military governor of Tennessee for two years. Self-educated, an ardent Jacksonian, a foe of the planter class, a supporter of emancipation—Johnson carried impeccable credentials. However, as a lifelong Democrat he had his own political agenda, sharply different from that of the Radicals.

In May 1865, with Congress out of session, Johnson shocked Republicans by announcing his own program to bring the southern states still without Reconstruction governments—Alabama, Florida, Georgia, Mississippi, North Carolina, South Carolina, and Texas—back into the Union. Virtually all southerners who took an oath of allegiance would receive pardon and amnesty, and all their property except slaves would be restored to them. Confederate civil and military officers would still be disqualified, as would well-to-do former Confederates (anyone owning taxable property worth $20,000 or more). By purging the plantation aristocracy, Johnson claimed, he would aid "humble men, the peasantry and yeomen of the South, who have been decoyed . . . into rebellion." Oath takers could elect delegates to state conventions, which would call regular elections, proclaim secession illegal, repudiate debts incurred under the Confederacy, and ratify the Thirteenth Amendment, which abolished slavery.

This presidential Reconstruction took effect in summer 1865, with unforeseen results. Johnson handed out pardons liberally (some 13,000) and dropped his plans for the punishment of treason. By the end of 1865 all seven states had created new civil governments that in effect restored the *status quo ante bellum*. Confederate officers and large planters resumed state offices, and former Confederate congressmen and generals won election to Congress. Because many of these new representatives were former Whigs who had not supported secession, southerners believed that they genuinely had elected "Union" men. Some states refused to repudiate their Confederate debts or to ratify the Thirteenth Amendment.

Most infuriating to the Radicals, every state passed a "black code" intended to ensure a landless, dependent black labor force—to "secure the services of the negroes, teach them their place," in the words of one Alabamian. These codes, which replaced earlier slave codes, guaranteed the freedmen some basic rights—marriage, ownership of property, the right to testify in court against other blacks—but also harshly restricted freedmen's behavior. Some states established segregation, and most prohibited racial intermarriage, jury service by blacks, and court testimony by blacks against whites. Most harmful, black codes included economic restrictions to prevent blacks from leaving the plantation, usually by establishing a system of labor contracts and then stipulating that anyone who had not signed a labor contract was a vagrant and thus subject to arrest.

These codes left freedmen no longer slaves but not really liberated. Although many of their provisions never actually took effect—for example, the Union army and the Freedmen's Bureau suspended the enforcement of the racially discriminatory laws—

*Pocket-vetoed: failed to sign the bill within ten days of Congress's adjournment.

King Andrew

This Thomas Nast cartoon, published just before the 1866 congressional elections, conveyed Republican antipathy to Andrew Johnson. The president is depicted as an autocratic tyrant. Radical Republican Thaddeus Stevens, upper right, has his head on the block and is about to lose it. The Republic sits in chains.

the black codes reflected white southern attitudes and showed what "home rule" would have been like without federal intervention.

When former abolitionists and Radical Republicans decried the black codes, Johnson defended them and his restoration program. Former Confederates should not become "a degraded and debased people," he said. To many northerners, both the black codes and the election of former Confederates to high office reeked of southern defiance. "What can be hatched from such an egg but another rebellion?" asked a Boston newspaper. When the Thirty-ninth Congress convened in December 1865, it refused to seat the southern delegates and prepared to dismantle the black codes and to lock ex-Confederates out of power.

Congress Versus Johnson

Southern blacks' status became the major issue in Congress. With Congress split into four blocs—Democrats, and radical, moderate, and conservative Republicans—a politically adroit president could have protected his program. Ineptly, Johnson alienated the moderates and pushed them into the Radicals' arms by vetoing some key moderate measures.

In late 1865 Congress voted to extend the life of the Freedmen's Bureau for three more years. Staffed mainly by army officers, the bureau provided relief, rations, and medical care; built schools for former slaves; put them to work on abandoned or confiscated lands; and tried to protect their rights as laborers. To strengthen the bureau, Congress had voted to allow it to run special military courts that would settle labor disputes and invalidate labor contracts forced on African-Americans under the black codes. In February 1866 Johnson vetoed the bill; the Constitution, he declared, neither sanctioned military trials of civilians in peacetime nor supported a system to care for "indigent persons." Then in March 1866 Congress passed the Civil Rights Act of 1866, which made African-Americans U.S. citizens with the same civil rights as other citizens and authorized federal intervention to ensure African-Americans' rights in court. Johnson vetoed this measure also, arguing that it would "operate in favor of the colored and against the white race." In April Congress overrode his veto, and in July it enacted the Supplementary Freedmen's Bureau Act over another presidential veto.

These vetoes puzzled many Republicans, for the new laws did not undercut the basic structure of presidential Reconstruction. Although the vetoes gained support for Johnson among northern Democrats, they cost him dearly among moderate Republicans, who began to ally with the Radicals. Was Johnson a political incompetent, or was he merely trying, unsuccessfully, to forge a centrist coalition? Whatever the case, he drove moderate and Radical Republicans together toward their next step: the passage of a constitutional amendment to protect the new Civil Rights Act.

The Fourteenth Amendment

In April 1866 Congress adopted the Fourteenth Amendment, its most ambitious attempt to deal with the problems of Reconstruction and the freed slaves. In the first clause, the amendment proclaimed that all persons born or naturalized in the United States were citizens and that no state could abridge their rights without due process of law or deny them equal protection under the law. Second, the amendment guaranteed that if a state denied suffrage to any male citizen, its representation in Congress would be proportionally reduced. Third, the amendment disqualified from state and national offices *all* prewar officeholders who had supported the Confederacy. Finally, it repudiated the Confederate debt and maintained the validity of the federal debt. In effect, the Fourteenth Amendment nullified the *Dred Scott* decision, threatened southern states that deprived African-American men of the right to vote, and invalidated most of the pardons that President Johnson had ladled out. Beyond demonstrating widespread receptivity to the Radicals' demands, including African-American male suffrage, the Fourteenth Amendment represented the first national effort to limit the states' control of civil and political rights.

Passage of the amendment created a fire-storm. Abolitionists said that it did not go far enough to protect African-American voting rights, southerners blasted it as vengeful, and President Johnson denounced it. The president's unwillingness to compromise solidified the new alliance between moderate and Radical Republicans and transformed the congressional elections of 1866 into a referendum on the Fourteenth Amendment.

Over the summer Johnson set off on a whistle-stop train tour campaigning against the amendment. Humorless and defensive, the president made fresh enemies, however, and doomed his hope of creating a new political party, the National Union party, opposed to the amendment. Meanwhile, the moderate and Radical Republicans defended the amendment, condemned President Johnson, and branded the Democratic party "a common sewer . . . into which is emptied every element of treason, North and South."

Republicans carried the congressional elections of 1866 in a landslide, winning nearly two-thirds of the House and three-fourths of the Senate. They had secured a mandate for the Fourteenth Amendment and their own Reconstruction program.

Congressional Reconstruction

The congressional debate over reconstructing the South began in December 1866 and lasted three months. Radical leaders, anxious to stifle a resurgence of Confederate power, called for African-American suffrage, federal support for public schools, confiscation of Confederate estates, and extended military occupation of the South. Moderate Republicans accepted part of this plan. The lawmakers debated every ramification of various legislative proposals, and in February 1867, after complex political maneuvers, Congress passed the Reconstruction Act of 1867. Johnson vetoed it, and on March 2 Congress passed the law over his veto. Three more Reconstruction acts, passed in 1867 and 1868 over presidential vetoes, refined and enforced the first act.

The Reconstruction Act of 1867 invalidated the state governments formed under the Lincoln and Johnson plans; only Tennessee, which had already ratified the Fourteenth Amendment and had been readmitted to the Union, escaped further Reconstruction. The new law divided the other ten former Confederate states into five military districts. It provided that voters—all black men, plus whites not disqualified by the Fourteenth Amendment—

The Reconstruction of the South

The Reconstruction Act of 1867 divided the former Confederate states, except Tennessee, into five military districts and set forth the steps by which new state governments could be created.

could elect delegates who would write a new state constitution granting African-American suffrage. After congressional approval of the state constitution, and after the state legislature's ratification of the Fourteenth Amendment, Congress would readmit the state into the Union. The enfranchisement of African-Americans and disfranchisement of so many ex-Confederates made the Reconstruction Act of 1867 far more radical than Johnson's program. Even then, however, it provided only temporary military rule, made no provisions to prosecute Confederate leaders for treason, and neither confiscated nor redistributed property.

Radical Republican leader Thaddeus Stevens had proposed confiscation of large Confederate estates to "humble the proud traitors" and to provide land for the former slaves. He hoped to create a new class of self-sufficient African-American yeomen farmers. Because political independence rested on economic independence, he contended, land grants would be far more valuable to African-Americans than the vote. But moderate Republicans and others backed away from Stevens's proposal. Tampering with property rights in the South might well jeopardize them in the North, they argued, and could endanger the entire Reconstruction program. Thus Congress rejected the most radical parts of the Radical Republican program.

Congressional Reconstruction took effect in spring 1867, but Johnson impeded its implementation by replacing pro-Radical military officers with conservative ones since Reconstruction could not be enforced without military power. Furious and more suspicious than ever of the president, congressional moderates and Radicals again joined forces to block Johnson from further hampering Reconstruction.

The Impeachment Crisis

In March 1867, responding to Johnson's obstructionist tactics, Republicans in Congress passed two laws to restrict presidential power. The Tenure of Office Act prohibited the president from removing civil officers without Senate consent. Its purpose was to protect Secretary of War Edwin Stanton, a Radical ally needed to enforce the Reconstruction acts. The other law banned the president from issuing military orders except through the commanding general, Ulysses S. Grant, who could not be removed without the Senate's consent. Not satisfied with clipping the president's wings, Radicals also began to look for grounds for impeachment and conviction to remove all possible obstacles to Reconstruction. Intense investigations by the House Judiciary Committee and private detectives turned up no impeachable offenses, but Johnson himself soon provided the charges that his opponents needed.

In August 1867 Johnson suspended Stanton and in February 1868 tried to remove him. The president's defiance of the Tenure of Office Act drove moderate Republicans back into alliance with the Radicals. The House approved eleven charges of impeachment, nine of them based on violation of the Tenure of Office Act and the other two accusing Johnson of being "unmindful of the high duties of the office," of seeking to disgrace Congress, and of not enforcing the Reconstruction acts.

Johnson's trial by the Senate, which began in March 1868, riveted public attention for eleven weeks. Seven congressmen, including leading Radicals, served as prosecutors, or "managers." Johnson's lawyers maintained that he was merely seeking a court test of a law that he believed unconstitutional, the Tenure of Office Act, by violating it. They also contended that the law did not protect Stanton because Lincoln, not Johnson, had appointed him. And they asserted that Johnson was guilty of no crime indictable in a regular court.

The congressional "managers" countered that impeachment was a political process, not a criminal trial, and that Johnson's "abuse of discretionary power" constituted an impeachable offense. Some Senate Republicans wavered, fearful that the removal of a president would destroy the balance of power within the federal government. They also were reluctant to see Benjamin Wade, a Radical Republican who was president pro tempore of the Senate, become president, as the Constitution then provided.

Intense pressure weighed on the wavering Republican senators. Ultimately, seven Republicans risked political suicide by voting with the Democrats against removal, and the Senate failed by one vote to convict Johnson. In so doing, the legislators set two critical precedents: in the future, no president would be impeached on political grounds, nor would he be impeached because two-thirds of Congress disagreed with him. In the short term, nonetheless, the anti-Johnson forces achieved their goals, for Andrew Johnson had no future as president. Republicans in Congress could now pursue their last major Reconstruction objective: guaranteeing African-American male suffrage.

The Fifteenth Amendment

African-American suffrage was the linchpin of congressional Reconstruction. Only with the support of African-American voters could Republicans secure control of the southern states. The Reconstruction Act of 1867 had forced southern states to enfranchise black men in order to reenter the Union, but most northern states still refused to grant suffrage to African-Americans. The Fifteenth Amendment, drawn up by Republicans and approved by Congress in 1869, aimed both to protect black suffrage in the South and to extend it to the northern and border states, on the assumption that newly enfranchised African-Americans would gratefully vote Republican. The amendment prohibited the denial of suf-

The Reconstruction Amendments

Amendment and Date of Congressional Passage	*Provisions*	*Ratification*
Thirteenth (January 1865)	Prohibited slavery in the United States.	December 1865
Fourteenth (June 1866)	Defined citizenship to include all persons born or naturalized in the United States. Provided proportional loss of congressional representation for any state that denied suffrage to any of its male citizens. Disqualified prewar officeholders who supported the Confederacy from state or national office. Repudiated the Confederate debt.	July 1868, after Congress made ratification a prerequisite for readmission of ex-Confederate states to the Union.
Fifteenth (February 1869)	Prohibited the denial of suffrage because of race, color, or previous condition of servitude.	March 1870; ratification required of Virginia, Texas, Mississippi, and Georgia for readmission to the Union.

frage by the states to anyone on account of race, color, or previous condition of servitude.

Democrats opposed the amendment on the grounds that it violated states' rights, but they did not control enough states to prevent its ratification. However, to some southerners, the amendment's omissions made it acceptable; as a Richmond newspaper pointed out, it had "loopholes through which a coach and four horses can be driven." Indeed, the new amendment did not guarantee African-American officeholding, nor did it prohibit restrictions on suffrage such as property requirements and literacy tests, both of which might be used to deny African-Americans the vote.

The debate over black suffrage drew new participants into the fray. Women's rights advocates had tried to promote both black suffrage and woman suffrage, but Radical Republicans rejected any linkage between the two, preferring to concentrate on black suffrage. Supporters of women's rights were themselves divided. Frederick Douglass argued that black suffrage had to receive priority. "If the elective franchise is not extended to the Negro, he is dead," explained Douglass. "Woman has a thousand ways by which she can attach herself to the ruling power of the land that we have not." Women's rights leaders Elizabeth Cady Stanton and Susan B. Anthony disagreed. If the Fifteenth Amendment did not include women, they emphasized, it would establish an "aristocracy of sex" and increase the disabilities under which women already labored. The argument fractured the old abolition–women's rights coalition and would lead to the development of an independent women's rights movement.

By the time the Fifteenth Amendment was ratified in 1870, Congress could look back on five years of momentous achievement. Three constitutional amendments had broadened the scope of democracy by abolishing slavery, affirming the rights of citizens, and prohibiting the denial of suffrage on the basis of race. Congress had readmitted the former Confederate states into the Union. At the same time, momentum had slowed at the federal level. In 1869 the center of action shifted to the South, where tumultuous change was under way.

Reconstruction Governments

During the years of presidential Reconstruction, 1865–1867, the southern states faced formidable tasks: creating new governments, reviving war-torn economies, and dealing with the impact of emancipation. Racial tensions flared as freedmen organized political meetings to protest ill treatment and demand equal rights, and deadly race riots erupted in major southern cities. In May 1866 white crowds attacked African-American veterans in Memphis and rampaged through African-American neighborhoods, killing forty-six people. Two months later in New Orleans, whites assaulted black delegates on their way to a political meeting and left forty people dead.

Congressional Reconstruction, supervised by federal troops, began in spring 1867 with the dismantling of existing governments and the formation of new state governments dominated by Republicans. By 1868 most former Confederate states had rejoined the Union, and within two years the process was complete.

But Republican rule did not long endure in the South. Opposition from southern Democrats, the landowning elite, vigilantes, and most white voters proved insurmountable. Nevertheless, these Reconstruction governments were unique because African-American men, including former slaves, participated in them. Slavery had ended in other societies, too, but only in the United States had freedmen gained democratic political rights.

A New Electorate

The Reconstruction laws of 1867–1868 transformed the southern electorate by temporarily disfranchising 15 percent of potential white voters and by enfranchising more than 700,000 freed slaves. Black voters outnumbered whites by 100,000 overall and held voting majorities in five states.

This new electorate provided a base for the Republican party, which had never existed in the South. To scornful Democrats, the Republicans comprised three types of scoundrels: northern "carpetbaggers" who had come south for wealth and power; southern scalawags, poor and ignorant, looking to profit from Republican rule; and hordes of uneducated freedmen, easily manipulated. In fact, the hastily assembled Republican party, crossing racial and class lines, constituted a loose coalition of diverse factions with often contradictory goals.

To northerners who moved south after the war, the former Confederacy was an undeveloped region, ripe with possibilities. The carpetbaggers included many former Union soldiers who hoped to buy land, open factories, build railroads, or simply enjoy the warmer climate. Wielding disproportionate political power—they held almost one in three state offices—carpetbaggers recruited African-American support through a patriotic society called the Union League, which urged African-Americans to vote and escorted them to the polls.

A handful of scalawags (white southerners who supported the Republicans) were old Whigs, but most were small farmers from the mountain regions of North Carolina, Georgia, Alabama, and Arkansas. Former Unionists who had owned no slaves and who felt no loyalty to the old plantation elite, they wanted to improve their economic position and cared little one way or the other about black suffrage. Scalawags held the most political offices during Reconstruction but proved the least stable element of the Republican coalition. Many drifted back into the Democratic fold.

Freedmen, the backbone of southern Republicanism, provided eight out of ten Republican votes. They sought land, education, civil rights, and political equality and remained loyal Republicans. "We know our friends," an elderly freedman said. Although Reconstruction governments depended on African-American votes, freedmen held at most one in five political offices and constituted a legislative majority only in South Carolina, whose population was more than 60 percent black. No African-Americans won the office of governor, and only two served in the U.S. Senate. A mere 6 percent of southern members of the House were African-American, and almost 50 percent came from South Carolina.

A significant status gap divided high-level African-American officials from African-American voters. Most freedmen cared mainly about their economic future, especially about acquiring land, whereas African-American officeholders concerned themselves far more with attaining equal rights. Still, both groups shared high expectations and prized enfranchisement. "We are not prepared for this suffrage," admitted a former slave. "But we can learn. Give a man tools and let him commence to use them and in time he will learn a trade. So it is with voting. . . . In time we shall learn to do our duty."

Republican Rule

Large numbers of African-Americans participated in government for the first time in the state constitutional conventions of 1867–1868. The South Carolina convention had an African-American majority, and in Louisiana one-half the delegates were freedmen. In general, these conventions instituted democratic changes such as universal manhood suffrage and public-school systems but failed to provide either integrated schools or land reform. Wherever proposed, plans for the confiscation and redistribution of land failed.

Once civil power shifted to the new state governments, Republican administrations began ambitious public-works programs. They built roads and bridges, promoted railroad development, and funded institutions to care for orphans, the insane, and the disabled. Republican regimes also expanded state government and formed state militia in which African-Americans often were heavily represented. Finally, they created public-school systems, almost nonexistent in the antebellum South.

These reforms cost millions, and state debts and taxes skyrocketed. During the 1860s taxes rose 400 percent. Although northern tax rates still exceeded southern tax rates, southerners, particularly landowners, resented the new levies. In their view, Reconstruction strained the pocketbooks of the propertied in order to finance the vast expenditures of Republican legislatures, the "no property herd."

Opponents of Reconstruction viewed Republican rule as wasteful and corrupt, the "most stupendous system of organized robbery in history." Indeed, corruption did permeate some state governments, as in Louisiana and South Carolina. The main profiteers were government officials who accepted bribes and railroad promoters who doled them out. But neither group was exclusively Republican. In fact, corruption increasingly characterized government *nationally* in these years and was both more flagrant and more lucrative in the North. But such a comparison did little to quiet the critics of Republican rule.

Counterattacks

For ex-Confederates, African-American enfranchisement and the "horror of Negro domination" created nightmares. As soon as congressional Reconstruction began, it fell under attack. Democratic newspapers assailed delegates to the North Carolina constitutional convention as an "Ethiopian minstrelsy . . . baboons, monkeys, mules . . . and other jackasses." They demeaned Louisiana's constitution as "the work of ignorant Negroes cooperating with a gang of white adventurers."

But Democrats delayed any political mobilization until the readmission of the southern states was completed. Then they swung into action, often calling themselves Conservatives to attract former Whigs. At first, they pursued African-American votes, but when that initiative failed, they switched tactics. In every southern state the Democrats contested elections, backed dissident Republican factions, elected some Democratic legislators, and lured scalawags away from the Republican Party.

Vigilante efforts to reduce black votes bolstered Democratic campaigns to win white ones. Antagonism toward free blacks, long present in southern

The Ku Klux Klan
The menacing symbol and hooded disguise characterized the Ku Klux Klan's campaign of intimidation during Reconstruction. Hooded Klansmen, like this Tennessee nightrider, wore colored robes with astrological symbols such as the moon and stars. The Klan strove to end Republican rule, restore white supremacy, and obliterate, in a southern editor's words, "the preposterous and wicked dogma of negro equality."

life, grew increasingly violent. As early as 1865 Freedmen's Bureau agents itemized a variety of outrages against blacks, including shooting, murder, rape, arson, and "severe and inhuman beating." White vigilante groups sprang up in all parts of the former Confederacy, but one organization became dominant. In spring 1866 six young Confederate war veterans in Tennessee formed a social club, the Ku Klux Klan, distinguished by elaborate rituals, hooded costumes, and secret passwords. New Klan dens spread rapidly. By the election of 1868, when African-American suffrage had become a reality, the Klan had become a terrorist movement directed against potential African-American voters.

The Klan sought to suppress black voting, to reestablish white supremacy, and to topple the Reconstruction governments. It targeted Union League officers, Freedmen's Bureau officials, white Republicans, black militia units, economically successful blacks, and African-American voters. Some Democrats denounced Klan members as "cutthroats and riff-raff," but some prominent Confederate leaders, including General Nathan Bedford Forrest, were active Klansmen. Vigilantism united southern whites of different social classes and drew on the energy of many Confederate veterans.

Republican legislatures tried to outlaw vigilantism, but when state militia could not enforce the laws, state officials turned to the federal government for help. In response, between May 1870 and February 1871 Congress passed three Enforcement Acts, each progressively more stringent. The First Enforcement Act protected African-American voters. The Second Enforcement Act provided for federal supervision of southern elections, and the Third Enforcement Act (also known as the Ku Klux Klan Act) authorized the use of federal troops and the suspension of habeas corpus. Although thousands were arrested under the Enforcement Acts, most terrorists escaped conviction.

By 1872 the federal government had effectively suppressed the Klan, but vigilantism had served its purpose. A large military presence in the South could have protected black rights, but instead troop levels fell steadily. Congress allowed the Freedmen's Bureau to die in 1869, and the Enforcement Acts became dead letters. White southerners, a Georgia politician explained in 1871, could not discard "a feeling of bitterness, a feeling that the Negro is a sort of instinctual enemy of ours." The battle over Reconstruction was in essence a battle over the implications of emancipation, and it had begun as soon as the war had ended.

The Freedmen's School

Supported by the Freedmen's Bureau, northern freedmen's aid societies, and African-American denominations, freedmen's schools reached about 12 percent of school-age African-American children in the South by 1870. Here, a northern teacher poses with her students at a school in rural North Carolina.

The Impact of Emancipation

"The master he says we are all free," a South Carolina slave declared in 1865. "But it don't mean we is white. And it don't mean we is equal." Yet despite the daunting handicaps they faced—illiteracy, lack of property, lack of skills—most former slaves found the exhilaration of freedom overwhelming. Emancipation had given them the right to their own labor and a sense of autonomy, and during Reconstruction they asserted their independence by casting off white control and shedding the vestiges of slavery.

Confronting Freedom

For the ex-slaves, mobility was often liberty's first fruit. Some left the slave quarters; others fled the plantation completely. "I have never in my life met with such ingratitude," a South Carolina mistress exclaimed when a former slave ran off.

Emancipation stirred waves of migration within the former Confederacy. Some slaves headed to the Deep South, where desperate planters would pay higher wages for labor, but more moved to towns and cities. Urban African-American populations doubled and tripled after emancipation. The desire to find lost family members drove some migrations. "They had a passion, not so much for wandering as for getting together," explained a Freedmen's Bureau official. Parents sought children who had been sold; husbands and wives who had been separated reunited; and families reclaimed children who were being raised in masters' homes. The Freedmen's Bureau helped former slaves to get information about missing relatives and to travel to find them, and bureau agents also tried to resolve entanglements over the multiple alliances of spouses who had been separated under slavery.

Not all efforts at reunion succeeded. Some fugitive slaves had died during the war or were untraceable. Other ex-slaves had formed new partnerships and could not revive old ones. But the success stories were poignant. "I's hunted an' hunted till I track you up here," one freedman told the wife whom he found twenty years after their separation by sale.

Once reunited, freed blacks quickly legalized unions formed under slavery, sometimes in mass ceremonies of up to seventy couples. Legal marriage had a tangible impact on family life. In 1870 eight out of ten African-American families in the cotton-producing South were two-parent families, about the same proportion as white families. Men asserted themselves as household heads, and their wives and children often withdrew from the work force. Thus severe labor shortages followed immediately after the war because women had made up half of all field workers. However, by Reconstruction's end, many African-American women had rejoined the work force out of economic necessity, either in the fields or as cooks, laundresses, and domestic servants.

African-American Institutions

The freed blacks' desire for independence also led to the growth of African-American churches. The African Methodist Episcopal Church, founded by Philadelphia blacks in the 1790s, gained thousands of new southern members. Negro Baptist churches, their roots often in plantation "praise meetings" organized by slaves, sprouted everywhere.

The influence of African-American churches extended far beyond religion. They provided relief, raised funds for schools, and supported Republican policies. African-American ministers assumed leading political roles. Even after southern Democrats excluded most freedmen from political life at Reconstruction's end, ministers remained the main pillars of authority within African-American communities.

Schools, too, played a crucial role for freedmen as the ex-slaves sought literacy for themselves and above all for their children. At emancipation, African-Americans organized their own schools, which the Freedmen's Bureau soon supervised. Northern philanthropic organizations paid the wages of instructors, half of whom were women. In 1869 the bureau reported more than 4,000 African-American schools in the former Confederacy. Within three more years each southern state had a public-school system, at least in principle, generally with separate schools for blacks and whites. The Freedmen's Bureau and others also helped to establish Howard, Atlanta, and Fisk Universities in 1866–1867 and Hampton Institute in 1868. Nonetheless, African-American education remained limited. Few rural blacks could reach the schools, and those who tried were sometimes the targets of vigilante attacks. Thus by the end of Reconstruction, more than 80 percent of the African-American population remained illiterate, although literacy was rising among children.

Not only school segregation but also other forms of racial separation were taken for granted. Whether by law or by custom, segregation continued on streetcars and trains as well as in churches, theaters, and restaurants. In 1875 Congress passed the Civil Rights Act, banning segregation except in schools, but in the 1883 *Civil Rights Cases*, the Supreme Court threw the law out. The Fourteenth Amendment did not prohibit discrimination by individuals, the Court ruled, only that perpetrated by the state.

White southerners adamantly rejected the prospect of racial integration, which they insisted would lead to racial amalgamation. "If we have social equality, we shall have intermarriage," contended one white southerner, "and if we have intermarriage, we shall degenerate." Urban blacks occasionally protested segregation, but most freed blacks were less interested in "social equality" than in African-American liberty and community. Moreover, the new black elite—teachers, ministers, and politicians—served African-American constituencies and thus had a vested interest in separate black institutions. Too, rural blacks had little desire to mix with whites; rather, they sought freedom from white control. Above all, they wanted to secure personal independence by acquiring land.

Land, Labor, and Sharecropping

"The sole ambition of the freedman," a New Englander wrote from South Carolina in 1865, "appears to be to become the owner of a little piece of land, there to erect a humble home, and to dwell in peace and security, at his own free will and pleasure." Indeed, to free blacks everywhere, "forty acres and a mule" promised emancipation from plantation labor, white domination, and cotton, the "slave crop." Landownership signified economic independence. "We want to be placed on land until we are able to buy it and make it our own," an African-American minister told General Sherman in Georgia during the war.

But the freedmen's visions of landownership failed to materialize, for large-scale land reform never occurred. Proposals to confiscate or to redistribute Confederate property failed. A few slaves did obtain land, either through the pooling of resources or through the Southern Homestead Act. In 1866 Congress passed this law, setting aside 44 million acres of land in five southern states for freedmen; but the land was poor, and few slaves had resources to survive until their first harvest. About 4,000 blacks claimed homesteads, though few could establish farms. By the end of Reconstruction, only a fraction of former slaves owned working farms. Without large-scale land reform, barriers to African-American landownership remained overwhelming.

Three obstacles impeded African-American landownership. Freedmen lacked capital to buy land or tools. Furthermore, white southerners generally opposed selling land to blacks. Most important, planters sought to preserve a cheap labor force and forged laws to ensure that black labor would remain available on the plantations.

The black codes written during presidential Reconstruction were designed to preserve a captive labor force. Under labor contracts in effect in 1865–1866, freedmen received wages, housing, food, and clothing in exchange for field work. But cash was scarce, and wages often became a small share of the crop, typically one-eighth or less, to be divided among the entire work force. Freedmen's Bureau agents encouraged African-Americans to sign the contracts, seeing wage labor as a step toward economic independence. "You must begin at the bottom of the ladder and climb up," bureau head O. O. Howard told the freedmen.

Problems arose immediately. Freedmen disliked the new wage system, especially the use of gang labor, which resembled the work pattern under slavery. Moreover, postwar planters had to compete for labor even as many scorned African-American workers as lazy or inefficient. One landowner estimated that workers accomplished only "two-fifths of what they did under the old system." As productivity fell, so did land values. Plummeting cotton prices and poor harvests in 1866 and 1867 combined with these other factors to create an impasse: landowners lacked labor, and freedmen lacked land.

Southerners began experimenting with new labor schemes, including the division of plantations into small tenancies. Sharecropping was the most widespread arrangement. Under this system, landowners subdivided large plantations into farms of thirty to fifty acres and rented them to freedmen under annual leases for a share of the crop, usually one-half. Freedmen liked this decentralized system, which let them use the labor of family members and represented a step toward independence. A half share of the crop far exceeded the fraction that they had received under the black codes. Planters benefited, too, for the leases gave them leverage over their tenants and tenants shared the risk of poor harvests with them. Most important, planters retained control of their land. The most productive land thus remained in the hands of a small group of owners, and in effect sharecropping helped to preserve the planter elite.

Although the wage system continued on sugar and rice plantations, by 1870 the plantation tradition had yielded to sharecropping in the cotton South. A severe depression in 1873 drove many blacks and independent white farmers into sharecropping. By 1880 sharecroppers, white and black, farmed 80 percent of the land in cotton-producing states. In fact, white sharecroppers outnumbered black,

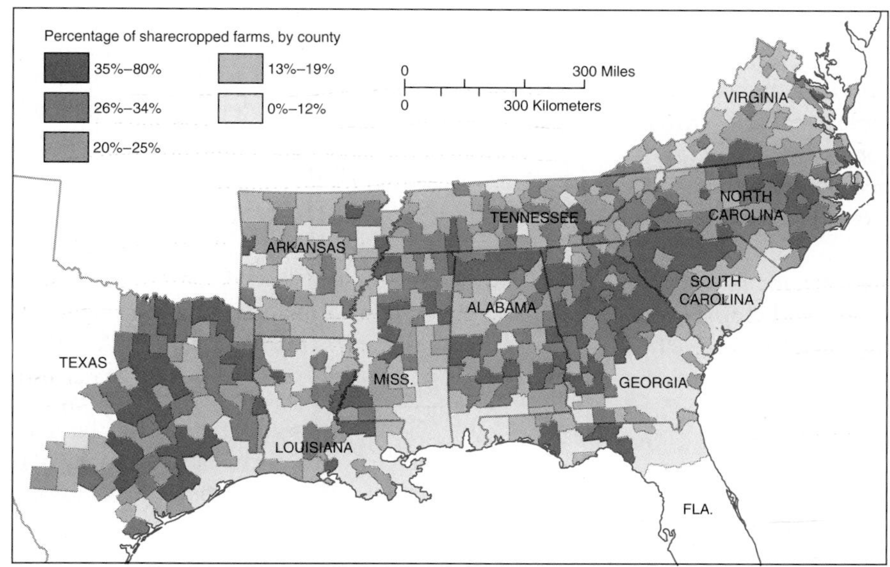

Southern Sharecropping, 1880

The depressed economy of the late 1870s caused poverty and debt, increased tenancy among white farmers, and forced many renters, black and white, into sharecropping. By 1880 the sharecropping system pervaded most southern counties, with highest concentrations in the cotton belt from South Carolina to eastern Texas.

SOURCE: U.S. Census Office, Tenth Census, 1880, *Report of the Production of Agriculture* (Washington, D.C.: Government Printing Office, 1883), Table 5.

although a higher proportion of southern blacks, almost 75 percent, were involved in the system. Changes in marketing and finance, meanwhile, made the sharecroppers' lot increasingly precarious.

Toward a Crop-Lien Economy

Before the Civil War planters had depended on factors, or middlemen, who sold them supplies, extended credit, and marketed their crops through urban merchants. Because the high value of slave property had backed these long-distance credit arrangements, this system collapsed with the end of slavery. The postwar South, with its hundreds of thousands of tenant farmers and sharecroppers, needed a local credit system.

Into this gap stepped rural merchants, who advanced supplies to tenants and sharecroppers on credit and sold their crops to wholesalers. Because renters had no property to serve as collateral, merchants secured their loans with a lien, or claim, on each farmer's next crop. Exorbitant interest rates, 50 percent or more, quickly forced many tenants and sharecroppers into a cycle of indebtedness. The sharecropper might well owe part of his crop to the landowner and another part (the rest of his crop, or more) to the merchant. Illiterate tenants who could not keep track of their financial arrangements were at the mercy of sometimes unscrupulous merchants. "A man that didn't know how to count would always lose," an Arkansas freedman explained. Once a tenant's real or alleged debts exceeded the value of his crop, he was tied to the land, to cotton, and to sharecropping.

By the end of Reconstruction, sharecropping and crop liens had bound the South to easily marketable cash crops such as cotton and prevented crop diversification. Soil depletion, land erosion, and outmoded equipment stranded capital-short planters in a cycle of poverty. Postwar changes in southern agriculture left the region with bleak economic prospects.

Trapped in perpetual debt, tenant farmers became the chief victims of the new agricultural order. Cotton remained the only survival route open to poor farmers, regardless of race, but low income from cotton locked them into sharecropping and crop liens. African-American tenants, for whom neither landownership nor economic independence ever materialized, saw their political rights dwindle as rapidly as their hopes for economic freedom. When Reconstruction ended, neither state governments nor the national government offered them protection, for northern politicians were preoccupied with their own problems.

New Concerns in the North

The nomination of Ulysses S. Grant for president in 1868 launched a chaotic era in national politics. His eight years in office featured political scandals, a party revolt, a massive depression, and a steady retreat from Reconstruction. By the mid-1870s northern voters cared more about economics, unemployment, labor unrest, and currency problems than the "southern question." Eager to end sectional conflict, Republicans turned their backs on the freedmen.

Grantism

Republicans had good reason to nominate General Grant. A war hero, he was endorsed by veterans, admired throughout the North, and unscathed by the bitter feuds of Reconstruction politics. To oppose Grant, the Democrats nominated Horatio Seymour, arch-critic of the Lincoln administration and an opponent of Reconstruction and greenbacks. Grant ran on his personal popularity more than on issues. Although he carried all but eight states, the popular vote was close; newly enfranchised freedmen provided Grant's margin in the South. When he was inaugurated, Grant pledged to execute all the laws, whether he agreed with them or not, to support sound money, and to follow a humane policy toward the Indians.

Grant's presidential leadership proved as weak as his war leadership had been strong. He had little political skill; his cabinet appointments were at best mediocre, and a string of scandals plagued his administration. In 1869 financier Jay Gould and his partner Jim Fisk attempted to corner the gold market with the help of Grant's brother-in-law. When gold prices tumbled, investors were ruined, and Grant's reputation was tarnished. Near the end of Grant's first term, his vice president, Schuyler Colfax, got caught up in the Crédit Mobilier scandal, an elaborate scheme to skim off the profits of the Union Pacific Railroad. Then in 1875 Grant's personal secretary, Orville Babcock, was found guilty of accepting bribes from the "whiskey ring," distillers who preferred bribery to payment of federal taxes. And in 1876 voters learned that Grant's secretary of war, William E. Belknap, had taken bribes to sell lucrative Indian trading posts in Oklahoma.

The Election of 1868

Candidates	*Parties*	*Electoral Vote*	*Popular Vote*	*Percentage of Popular Vote*
ULYSSES S. GRANT	Republican	214	3,013,421	52.7
Horatio Seymour	Democratic	80	2,706,829	47.3

The Election of 1872

Candidates	Parties	Electoral Vote	Popular Vote	Percentage of Popular Vote
ULYSSES S. GRANT	Republican	286	3,596,745	55.6
Horace Greeley*	Democratic		2,843,446	43.9

*On Greeley's death shortly after the election, the electors supporting him divided their votes among minor candidates.

Although Grant was not personally involved in the scandals, he did little to restrain such activities, and "Grantism" came to stand for fraud, bribery, and corruption in office. Such evils, however, spread far beyond Washington. The New York City press in 1872 revealed that Democrat boss William M. Tweed led a ring that had looted the city treasury and collected some $200 million in kickbacks and bribes. When Mark Twain and coauthor Charles Dudley Warner published their scathing satire *The Gilded Age* (1873), readers recognized the novel's speculators, self-promoters, and maniacal opportunists as familiar types in public life.

Grant did enjoy some foreign policy successes. His administration engineered the settlement of the *Alabama* claims with England: an international tribunal ordered Britain to pay $15.5 million to the United States in compensation for damage inflicted by Confederate-owned but British-built raiders. But the administration went astray when it tried to add nonadjacent territory to the Union. In 1867 the Johnson administration had purchased Alaska from Russia at the bargain price of $7.2 million. The purchase had rekindled expansionists' hope, and in 1870 Grant decided to annex the Caribbean island nation of Santo Domingo (the modern Dominican Republic). The president believed that annexation would promote Caribbean trade and provide a haven for persecuted southern blacks. Despite speculators' hopes for windfall profits, the Senate rejected the annexation treaty and further diminished Grant's reputation.

As the election of 1872 approached, dissident Republicans feared that "Grantism" would ruin the party. Former Radicals and other Republicans left out of Grant's "Great Barbecue" formed their own party, the Liberal Republicans.

The Liberals' Revolt

The Liberal Republican revolt split the Republican party and undermined Reconstruction. Liberals demanded civil service reform to bring the "best men" into government. In the South they demanded an end to "bayonet rule" and argued that African-Americans, now enfranchised, could fend for themselves. Corruption in government posed a greater threat than Confederate resurgence, the Liberals claimed, and they demanded that the "best men" in the South, ex-Confederates barred from holding office, be returned to government.

New York Tribune editor Horace Greeley, inconsistently supporting both a stringent Reconstruction policy and leniency toward the ex-Confederates, received the Liberal Republican nomination, and the Democrats endorsed Greeley as well. Republican reformers found themselves allied with the party that they had recently castigated as a "sewer" of treasonable sentiments.

Despite Greeley's arduous campaigning (he literally worked himself to death on the campaign trail and died a few weeks after the election), Grant carried 56 percent of the popular vote and won the electoral vote handily. But his victory had come at a high price: to nullify the Liberals' issues, "regular" Republicans passed an amnesty act allowing all but a few hundred ex-Confederates to resume office. And during Grant's second term Republicans' desire to discard the "southern question" grew as a depression gripped the nation.

The Panic of 1873

The postwar years brought accelerated industrialization, rapid economic expansion, and frantic speculation as investors rushed to take advantage of seemingly unlimited opportunities. Railroads led the speculative boom. The transcontinental line reached completion in 1869 (see Chapter 17), and by 1873 almost 400 railroads crisscrossed the Northeast. But in addition to transforming the northern economy, the railroad boom led entrepreneurs to overspeculate, with drastic results.

In 1869 Philadelphia banker Jay Cooke took over a new transcontinental line, the Northern Pacific. For four years Northern Pacific securities sold briskly, but in 1873 construction costs outran bond sales. In September Cooke, his bank vaults stuffed with unsalable bonds, defaulted on his obligations. His bank, the largest in the nation, shut down. Then the stock market collapsed and smaller banks and other firms followed; and the Panic of 1873 plunged the nation into a devastating five-year depression. Thousands of businesses went bankrupt. By 1878 unemployment had risen to more than 3 million. Labor protests mounted, and industrial violence spread (see Chapter 18). The depression of the 1870s demonstrated ruthlessly that conflicts born of industrialization had replaced sectional divisions.

The depression also fed a dispute over currency that had begun in 1865. During the Civil War Americans had used greenbacks, a paper currency not backed by a specific weight in gold. "Sound-money" supporters demanded the withdrawal of greenbacks from circulation as a means of stabilizing the currency. Their opponents, "easy-money" advocates such as farmers and manufacturers dependent on easy credit, wanted to expand the currency by issuing additional greenbacks. The deepening depression created even more demand for easy money, and the issue split both major parties.

Controversy over the type of currency was compounded by the question of how to repay the federal debt. In wartime the Union government had borrowed astronomical sums through the sale of war bonds. Bond holders wanted repayment in "coin," gold or silver, even though many of them had paid for the bonds in greenbacks. The Public Credit Act of 1869 promised payment in coin.

Senator John Sherman, the author of the Public Credit Act, put together a series of compromises to satisfy both "sound-money" and "easy-money" advocates. Sherman's measures, exchanging Civil War bonds for new ones payable over a longer period of time and defining "coin" as gold only, preserved the public credit, the currency, and Republican unity. His Specie Resumption Act of 1875 promised to put the nation back on the gold standard by 1879.

But Sherman's measures, however ingenious, did not placate the Democrats, who gained control of the House in 1875. Many Democrats, and a few Republicans, were "free-silver" advocates who wanted the silver dollar restored in order to expand the currency and end the depression. The Bland-Allison Act of 1878 partially restored silver coinage by requiring the government to buy and coin several million dollars' worth of silver each month. In 1876 other expansionists formed the Greenback party to keep the paper money in circulation for the sake of debtors, but they enjoyed little success. As the depression receded, the clamor for "easy money" subsided, only to return in the 1890s (see Chapter 21). Although never settled, the controversial "money question" diverted attention away from Reconstruction and thus contributed to its demise.

Reconstruction and the Constitution

During the 1870s the Supreme Court also played a role in weakening northern support for Reconstruction as new constitutional questions surfaced.

Would the Court support laws to protect freedmen's rights? The decision in *Ex Parte Milligan* (1866) had suggested not. In *Milligan,* the Court had ruled that a military commission could not try civilians in areas where civilian courts were functioning, thus dooming the special military courts that had been established to enforce the Supplementary Freedmen's Bureau Act. Would the Court sabotage the congressional Reconstruction plan? In 1869 in *Texas* v. *White,* the Court had let Reconstruction stand, ruling that Congress had the power to ensure each state a republican form of government and to recognize the legitimate government in any state.

However, during the 1870s the Supreme Court backed away from Reconstruction. The process began with the *Slaughterhouse* decision of 1873. In this case the Court ruled that the Fourteenth Amendment protected the rights of *national* citizenship, such as the right to interstate travel, but that it did not protect the civil rights that individuals derived from *state* citizenship. The federal government, in short, did not have to safeguard such rights against violation by the states. The *Slaughterhouse* decision effectively gutted the Fourteenth Amendment, which was intended to secure freedmen's rights against state encroachment.

The Supreme Court retreated even further from Reconstruction in two cases involving the Enforcement Act of 1870. In *U.S.* v. *Reese* (1876), the Court threw out the indictment of Kentucky officials who had barred African-Americans from voting. The Fifteenth Amendment, the Court said, did not "confer the right of suffrage upon anyone"; it merely prohibited the hindrance of voting on the basis of race, color, or previous condition of servitude. Crucial sections of the Enforcement Act, the Court ruled, were invalid. Another decision that same year, *U.S.* v. *Cruikshank,* again weakened the Fourteenth Amendment. In the *Cruikshank* case, the Court ruled that the amendment barred *states,* but not *individuals,* from encroaching on individual rights. The decision threw out the indictments against white Louisianians charged with murdering more than thirty black militiamen who had surrendered after a battle with armed whites.

Continuing this retreat from Reconstruction, the Supreme Court in 1883 invalidated both the Civil Rights Act of 1875 and the Ku Klux Klan Act of 1871; later it would uphold segregation laws (see Chapter 21). Taken cumulatively, these decisions dismantled Republican Reconstruction and confirmed rising northern sentiment that Reconstruction's egalitarian goals were unenforceable.

Republicans in Retreat

The Republicans gradually disengaged from Reconstruction, beginning with the election of Grant as president in 1868. Grant, like most Americans, hesitated to approve the use of federal authority in state or local affairs.

In the 1870s Republican idealism waned. Instead, commercial and industrial interests dominated both the Liberal and "regular" wings of the party, and few had any taste left for further sectional strife. When Democratic victories in the House of Representatives in 1874 showed that Reconstruction had become a political liability, the Republicans prepared to abandon it.

By 1875, moreover, the Radical Republicans had virtually disappeared. The Radical leaders Chase, Stevens, and Sumner had died, and others had grown tired of "waving the bloody shirt," or defaming Democratic opponents by reviving wartime animosity. Party leaders reported that voters were "sick of carpet-bag government" and tired of the "southern question" and the "Negro question." It seemed pointless to prop up southern Republican regimes that even President Grant found corrupt. Finally, Republicans generally agreed with southern Democrats that African-Americans were inferior. To insist on black equality, many party members believed, would be a thankless, divisive, and politically suicidal course that would quash any hope of reunion between North and South. The Republican retreat set the stage for Reconstruction's end in 1877.

Reconstruction Abandoned

"We are in a very hot political contest just now," a Mississippi planter wrote his daughter in 1875, "with a good prospect of turning out the carpetbag thieves by whom we have been robbed for the past six to ten years." Indeed, an angry white majority

southern votes were fraudulent: Republicans had discarded legitimate Democratic ballots, and Democrats had illegally prevented freedmen from voting. In January 1877 Congress created a special electoral commission to resolve the conflict. The commission originally consisted of seven Republicans, seven Democrats, and one independent, but when the independent resigned, a Republican replaced him. The commission gave the Republican Hayes the election by an 8–7 vote.

Congress now had to certify the new electoral vote. But the Democrats controlled the House, and some planned to forestall approval of the electoral vote. For many southern Democrats, regaining control of their states was far more important than electing a Republican president—*if* the new Republican administration would leave the South alone. Republican leaders, for their part, were willing to bargain, for Hayes wanted not just victory but also southern approval. Informal negotiations followed, with both parties exchanging promises. Ohio Republicans and southern Democrats agreed that if Hayes won the election, he would remove federal troops from all southern states. Other negotiations led to the understanding that southerners would receive federal patronage, federal aid to railroads, and federal support for internal improvements. In turn, southerners promised to accept Hayes as president and to treat the freedmen fairly.

Congress thus ratified Hayes's election. Once in office, Hayes fulfilled many of the agreements made by his colleagues. Republican rule toppled in Louisiana, South Carolina, and Florida. But some of the bargains struck in the so-called Compromise of 1877 fell apart, particularly Democratic promises to treat the freedmen fairly and Hayes's pledges to ensure the freed slaves' rights. "When you turned us loose, you turned us loose to the sky, to the storm, to the whirlwind, and worst of all . . . to the wrath of our infuriated masters," Frederick Douglass had charged at the 1876 Republican convention. "The question now is, do you mean to make good to us the promises in your Constitution?" By 1877 the answer was clear: "No."

CONCLUSION

The end of Reconstruction benefited both major political parties. The "southern question" no longer burdened the Republicans. The Democrats, who had regained power in the ex-Confederate states, would remain entrenched there for almost a century. The postwar South was tied to sharecropping and economic backwardness as surely as it once had been tied to slavery; but "home rule" was firmly in place.

Reconstruction's end also signaled the triumph of nationalism and reconciliation. Battlefields became national parks. Jefferson Davis, who had served two years in prison but had never gone to trial, urged young men to "lay aside all rancor, all bitter sectional feeling." Americans increasingly dismissed Reconstruction as a fiasco, a tragic interlude of "radical rule" and "black reconstruction" fashioned by carpetbaggers, scalawags, and Radical Republicans.

Historians, too, still consider Reconstruction a failure, although for different reasons from those of Americans who lived through the era. Today scholars view Reconstruction as an unsuccessful democratic experiment that did not go far enough. They cite two main failings. First, Congress did not promote land reform and thus left African-Americans propertyless, without the economic power to defend their rights. More important, the federal government did not back congressional Reconstruction militarily. Reconstruction's failure lay with the federal government's inability to fulfill its own goals and to create a biracial democracy in the South. Consequently, the nation's adjustment to emancipation would continue into the twentieth century.

The Reconstruction era left significant legacies, including the Fourteenth and Fifteenth Amendments, monuments to Congress's democratic zeal in the 1860s. Above all, Reconstruction gave freedmen the opportunity to reconstitute their families, to form schools and churches, and to participate in government for the first time in U.S. history. However, in the 1880s the United States would consign Reconstruction to history and the freed slaves to their fate as Americans focused on their economic futures—on railroads, factories, and mills and on the exploitation of bountiful natural resources.

CHRONOLOGY

1863 President Abraham Lincoln issues Proclamation of Amnesty and Reconstruction.

1864 Wade-Davis bill passed by Congress and pocket-vetoed by Lincoln.

1865 Freedmen's Bureau established.
Civil War ends.
Lincoln assassinated; Andrew Johnson becomes president.
Johnson issues Proclamation of Amnesty and Reconstruction.
Ex-Confederate states hold constitutional conventions (May–December).
Thirteenth Amendment added to the Constitution.
Presidential Reconstruction completed.

1866 Congress enacts the Civil Rights Act of 1866 and the Supplementary Freedmen's Bureau Act over Johnson's vetoes.
Ku Klux Klan founded in Tennessee.
Congress proposes the Fourteenth Amendment.
Race riots in southern cities.
Thirty-ninth Congress begins debates over Reconstruction policy.

1867 Reconstruction Act of 1867.
William Seward negotiates the purchase of Alaska.
Constitutional conventions meet in the ex-Confederate states.
Howard University founded.

1868 President Johnson is impeached, tried, and acquitted.
Fourteenth Amendment added to the Constitution.
Ulysses S. Grant elected president.

1869 Transcontinental railroad completed.

1870 Fifteenth Amendment added to the Constitution.
Enforcement Act of 1870.

1871 Second Enforcement Act.
Ku Klux Klan Act.

1872 Liberal Republican Party formed.
Alabama claims settled.
Grant reelected president.

1873 Panic of 1873 begins (September–October), setting off a five-year depression.

1875 Civil Rights Act of 1875.
Specie Resumption Act.

1876 Disputed presidential election: Rutherford B. Hayes versus Samuel J. Tilden.

1877 Electoral commission decides election in favor of Hayes.
The last Republican-controlled governments overthrown in Florida, Louisiana, and South Carolina.

1879 "Exodus" movement spreads through several southern states.

FOR FURTHER READING

Eric Foner, *Reconstruction: America's Unfinished Revolution, 1863–1877* (1988). A thorough exploration of Reconstruction that draws on recent scholarship and stresses the centrality of the African-American experience.

John Hope Franklin, *Reconstruction After the Civil War* (1961). An overview that dismantles the traditional view of Reconstruction as a disastrous experiment in radical rule.

William Gillette, *Retreat from Reconstruction, 1869–1879* (1979). A survey of the era's national politics, indicting Republican policy makers for vacillation and lack of commitment to racial equality.

Leon Litwack, *Been in the Storm So Long: The Aftermath of Slavery* (1979). A comprehensive study of the African-American response to emancipation in 1865–1866.

Roger L. Ransom and Richard Sutch, *One Kind of Freedom: The Economic Consequences of Emancipation* (1977). Economic assessment of the impact of free black labor on the South and explanation of the rise of sharecropping and the crop-lien system.

Kenneth M. Stampp, *The Era of Reconstruction, 1865–1877* (1965). A classic revisionist interpretation of Reconstruction, focusing on the establishment and fall of Republican governments.

Joel Williamson, *The Negro in South Carolina During Reconstruction, 1861–1877* (1965). A pioneer study of African-American life and institutions after emancipation.

CHAPTER 17

The Trans-Mississippi West

Native Americans and the Frontier

Settling the West

Exploiting the West

The West of Life and Legend

In the second half of the nineteenth century, Americans launched one of the greatest migrations in modern history: the exploration and development of half a continent. Optimistic, thirsting for fresh starts, they flooded westward seeking land and fortune.

Even before the Civil War, Americans had seen the trans-Mississippi West as a land of adventure, opportunity, and inexhaustible natural resources. Three hundred thousand Americans had poured into California during the gold rush in 1849 and 1850. Thousands of other midcentury pioneers had moved onto the fertile prairies of Iowa, Minnesota, Kansas, and Nebraska.

When the Civil War ended, the vision of the western frontier as a land of economic promise and limitless natural resources lured another generation west. Pushing aside the Native Americans, settlers swarmed onto the rolling prairies of the Great Plains. They quickly filled the

(Right) Chief Joseph (1840?–1904) of the Nez Percés

rich, rain-soaked farmlands of Wisconsin, Minnesota, Iowa, and eastern sections of Kansas, Nebraska, and the Dakotas. A few continued westward onto the semiarid High Plains, hoping to make their fortunes in ranching and mining, and a handful forged beyond them, through the Rocky Mountains and into the near-desert Great Basin of Nevada.

Viewing the West as a seedbed of economic opportunity, the migrants exploited its natural resources ruthlessly, in the process damaging the environment and destroying the Native Americans' traditional ways—and occasionally even themselves. Convinced of their cultural superiority, they saw nothing unjust in taking land from the resident Native Americans or Mexicans. Under the banner of progress, these new westerners stripped the landscape of trees, slaughtered millions of buffalo, skinned the mountainsides in search of minerals, and tore up the prairie sod to build farms.

However, Indian resistance and the rugged Plains landscape slowed development and drove thousands away. This was stark, weather-beaten country, seared by hot winds in summer and lashed by blizzards in winter, and some could not take it. Still, in the post–Civil War era enough western development had occurred that the region required federal government support: military intervention, land subsidies, and financial aid to railroad builders. Investments by eastern bankers and foreign capitalists were also crucial to western growth. Yet the new westerners clung to their ideal of the self-reliant, independent individual who could overcome all obstacles. That ideal, often sorely tested, has survived as the bedrock of western Americans' outlook even today.

Native Americans and the Frontier

The trans-Mississippi West was hardly empty before the newcomers arrived. About 360,000 Indians lived there, their cultures already shaped by European contact. Many pueblo dwellers, among them the Hopis and Zuñis of the Southwest, had reached accommodation with the Spanish-speaking *rancheros* (ranchers). Maintaining their traditional ways based on agriculture and sheepherding, the Indians traded mutton and produce for metal hoes, glass beads, knives, and guns. The fierce Apaches and Navajos, who raided pueblo dwellers and *rancheros* alike, also traded with Europeans for manufactured goods.

On the Great Plains, the acquisition of Spanish horses and British firearms had transformed the native peoples from walking nomads into the mounted warriors whom nineteenth-century pioneers encountered. Commercial and other contacts with the non-Indian world remained important to the Plains Indians as new settlers moved in. But beyond these generally positive exchanges, European contact disrupted Native American cultures. Diseases such as measles and diphtheria, contracted from traders and settlers, ravaged tribes everywhere.

However, it was the physical disruption of Indian life on the Great Plains, home to nearly half the Native Americans of the West, that caught the public eye and weighed on the public conscience. The Americans who descended on the Plains after 1850 had little understanding of, and less respect for, traditional "savage" ways. Consequently, the Plains Indians, defeated by the American military, forced onto reservations, and demoralized by disease, alcohol, and impoverishment, plunged along a downward spiral. By 1890 relocation to generally inadequate lands had become the fate of almost every Indian nation of the Great Plains. But from the wreckage of the Native Americans' traditional ways of life arose signs of a strong cultural response to conquest and forced modernization.

The Plains Indians

The Indians of the Great Plains inhabited two major subregions. Several large Siouan-speaking tribes, including the Sioux, Crows, and Assiniboins, dominated the northern Plains from the Dakotas

Buffalo Head Trophies
To encourage buffalo hunting as a sport, railroads crossing the Great Plains had animal heads mounted by their own taxidermists for display at ticket stations.

and Montana southward to Nebraska. Mandans, Flatheads, Blackfeet, Cheyennes, and Arapahos also roamed the northern Plains. A few were allies, but most were bitter enemies constantly at war. The central and southern Plains were home to the agricultural "Five Civilized Tribes" driven there from the Southeast in the 1830s, to the partially settled Osages and Pawnees, and to the nomadic Comanches, Kiowas, southern Arapahos, and Kiowa Apaches.

Diversity characterized the Plains Indians and sometimes even flourished within divisions of the same tribe. The Dakota Sioux of Minnesota led a semisedentary life of agriculture, maple-sugar harvesting, and deer and bison hunting. In contrast, the Lakota Sioux ranged the High Plains to the west, following the buffalo. Nonetheless, life for all Plains Indians revolved around extended family ties and tribal cooperation. Within the Sioux nation, for example, families and clans joined forces to hunt and farm and reached decisions by consensus. Extended families formed small winter villages or larger summer encampments. Leaders relied on persuasion rather than authority; they governed by example, giving food and supplies to the needy and initiating projects in the hope that others would follow.

Religious and harvest celebrations provided the cement for life in Sioux villages and camps. Sioux religion was complex and very different from the Judeo-Christian tradition. Life consisted of a series of circles: family, band, tribe, and Sioux Nation. The Lakota Sioux also believed in plant and animal spirits, some more powerful than humans, whose help could be invoked in the Sun Dance. In this ceremony, young men would "sacrifice" themselves by suffering self-torture—stabbing their chests with skewers hung with buffalo skulls, hanging suspended from poles, or cutting pieces of their own flesh to place at the foot of the Sun Dance pole.

Many Plains tribes followed the buffalo migration. The huge herds, at their peak containing an estimated 32 million bison, served as an "ambulatory supermarket," for Indians used every part of the animal. They ate its meat, made clothing and shelter from its hides, fashioned its bones into tools, and burned dried buffalo dung ("chips") as fuel. They even used buffalo skulls for religious purposes, as in the Sun Dance.

High demand for buffalo hides to make industrial belting and buffalo robes for use on carriages and sleighs led to the destruction of the herds upon which the Plains Indians depended. Ruthless entrepreneurs used the expanding railroad networks to kill the animals and transport their pelts.

Railroads hired hunters, usually whites, to slay bison with which to feed construction gangs. William F. "Buffalo Bill" Cody killed 4,300 buffalo in only eight months during 1867–1868 to provide food for Union Pacific crews. Eastern sport hunters and sightseers chartered trains to shoot animals for profit or adventure. Army commanders, seeing the destruction of the buffalo as a way to undermine the resistance of buffalo-dependent tribes, encouraged the slaughter. The resultant carnage was almost unbelievable. Between 1872 and 1875, non-Indian hunters killed 9 million buffalo, taking the skins but leaving the carcasses to rot. One railroad conductor recalled that a traveler "could have journeyed more than one hundred miles along the railroad right of way, without stepping off the carcass of a slaughtered bison." By the 1880s the relentless killing had reduced the herds to a few thousand animals, destroyed a way of life dependent on the buffalo, and cleared the path for farmers to settle former Indian hunting grounds.

The Transformation of Indian Life

Non-Indians not only exterminated the buffalo but also seized control of much of the land. Between 1837 and 1867, for example, the Ojibwa and Dakota Sioux in the Minnesota territory ceded 24 million acres to the federal government. Treaties established two large reservations within the Minnesota Territory and promised annual government support. However, federal authorities failed to give the Dakota Sioux their yearly payments on time and neglected to provide promised agricultural aid. Driven by hunger and anger at unfulfilled promises, the Sioux returned to their former hunting grounds in August 1862 and killed an estimated 700 white settlers. Reinforced by the U.S. Army, the settlers crushed the uprising in two weeks, hanged 38 Indian leaders, and jailed more than 200, and exiled the rest to poor-quality reservations in the Dakotas and northeastern Nebraska. By 1866 the number of Sioux in Minnesota had plummeted from 7,000 to 374.

In the 1860s the federal government abandoned its previous policy of treating much of the West as a vast Indian reservation and created a system of smaller, separate tribal reservations on which the Native Americans were to be concentrated, by force if necessary. There, federal officials hoped, the Indians would abandon nomadism for a settled agricultural life. Some Indians, including southwestern Pueblos and the Crows of Montana, accepted this fate. Others, among them the Navajos of Arizona and New Mexico and the Dakota Sioux, initially opposed the new policy, but to no avail. However, the remaining Plains Indians, 100,000 strong, resisted. From the 1860s through the 1880s, these tribes—the western Sioux, Cheyennes, Arapahos, Kiowas, Comanches, Nez Percés, Bannocks, and Apaches—faced the U.S. Army in a final battle for the West.

In this protracted, bitter conflict, both sides committed atrocities. Two examples illustrate the tragic pattern. In 1864 Cheyennes and Arapahos in southern Colorado, weary of fighting gold miners encroaching on their already-reduced lands, sued for peace and encamped by Sand Creek. Colorado militia attacked the camp, clubbing and slaughtering about 200 Indian men, women, and children even after the Indians had raised a white flag of surrender. "Kill and scalp all, big and little," shouted Colonel John M. Chivington, the militia leader; "nits make lice." Two years later the Teton Sioux fought a ferocious war against U.S. cavalry to defend land along Wyoming's Powder River. Trying to stop construction of the Bozeman Trail, a road from Wyoming to the gold fields of Montana that intersected the native people's buffalo-hunting grounds, the Tetons lured eighty soldiers out of their stockade and killed and mutilated them.

These massacres by both whites and Indians rekindled public debate over federal Indian policy. As western settlers pressed Congress to establish a strict reservation policy under army control instead of the present federal agents and local militia, critics urged a cessation of violence on both sides. In response, Congress in 1867 halted construction on the Bozeman Trail, sent a peace commission to end the fighting, and set aside two large districts where, it was hoped, the nomadic tribes would settle and become Christians. Behind the government's persuasion lay the threat of force. Native Americans who refused to "locate in [the] permanent abodes provided for them," warned the commissioner of Indian affairs, "would be subject wholly to the control and supervision of military authorities, [and] . . . treated as friendly or hostile as circumstances might justify."

At first the plan appeared to work. Representatives of 68,000 southern Plains Indians signed a treaty at Medicine Lodge Creek, Kansas, promising to live on reservations in present-day Oklahoma. The next year, scattered bands of Sioux, 54,000 in number, agreed to move to the Great Sioux Reserve in the western part of modern South Dakota in return for provisions. But Indian dissatisfaction with the treaties ran deep, and many refused to move to, or to remain on, the reservations. A Sioux chief explained, "We do not want to live like the white man. . . . The Great Spirit gave us hunting grounds, gave us the buffalo, the elk, the deer, and the antelope. Our fathers have taught us to hunt and live on the Plains, and we are contented."

In August 1868 war parties of defiant Cheyennes, Arapahos, and Sioux raided frontier settlements in Kansas and Colorado, burning homes and killing whites. In retaliation, army troops attacked Indians, even peaceful ones. That autumn a raiding party under the command of Lieutenant Colonel George Armstrong Custer attacked a sleeping Cheyenne village, killing more than 100 warriors, shooting more than 800 horses, and taking 53 women and children prisoner. Other Cheyennes and Arapahos were pursued, captured, and returned to reservations.

Spurred on by evangelical Christian reformers, Congress in 1869 established the Board of Indian Commissioners to mold reservation life along "desirable" lines. The board wanted to use the major Protestant denominations to break the Indians' nomadic tradition and to force them to remain on the reservations, where they would become Christian farmers. However, the new, inexperienced, church-appointed Indian agents encountered obstacles in trying to implement these policies. Lawrie Tatum, a pacifist Quaker, failed to persuade Comanches and Kiowas to cease raiding Texas settlements and to stay on their Oklahoma reservations. Kiowa chiefs Satanta and Big Tree insisted that they could be at peace with the federal government while remaining at war with Texas. Scheming by whites who fraudulently purchased reservation lands and squabbling among the Protestant denominations further undermined the new policy. By the 1880s, the federal government, frustrated with the churches, was ignoring their nominations for Indian agents and made its own appointments.

Caught in an ambiguous and faltering U.S. policy that vacillated between removal and assimilation, and infuriated by continuing non-Indian settlement of the Plains, Native Americans struck back. In 1874 a Kiowa, Comanche, and Cheyenne raid on the Adobe Walls trading post in the Texas panhandle ignited the Red River War. Regular army troops retaliated, destroying Indian supplies, slaughtering one hundred Cheyenne fugitives near the Sappa River in Kansas, and sending more than seventy "ringleaders" to military prison in Florida. Thus, Native American independence on the southern Plains ended. In the Southwest, in modern Arizona and New Mexico, Apaches under Geronimo fought a guerrilla war but were subdued by 1886.

Custer's Last Stand

Of all the acts of Indian resistance against the reservation policy, none aroused more passion or caused more bloodshed than the conflict between the western Sioux and the U.S. Army in the Dakotas, Montana, and Wyoming. Its roots went back to the Treaty of Fort Laramie (1868), which ended the Powder River War and set aside the Great Sioux

Reserve "in perpetuity." But not all the Sioux had fought in the war or signed the treaty. For example, the highly respected Sitting Bull had kept his Hunkpapa Sioux out of the fighting. And western Sioux who had not signed the treaty, including the Oglala and Brulé Sioux, had no intention of moving to the reservation.

Skillfully playing off local officials against the federal government, the Oglala and Brulé bands in 1873 won permission to stay near the Indian agencies along the upper reaches of the White River in Nebraska, near their traditional hunting grounds. They enjoyed the best of both worlds, receiving government provisions but hunting on their customary range. To protect these hunting grounds, they raided white settlements, intimidated federal agents, and harassed miners, surveyors, and others who ventured onto their lands.

The Indian agents' inability to prevent the Sioux from entering and leaving the reservations at will, coupled with growing pressure from would-be colonists and developers, prompted the army to take action. In 1874 General William Tecumseh Sherman sent a force under George Armstrong Custer (now a colonel) into the Black Hills of South Dakota. Lean and mustachioed, with shoulder-length red-blond hair, Custer had been a celebrity since the Civil War. Now decked out in a fringed buckskin uniform and a crimson scarf, the ambitious Custer saw himself in the heroic mold of western adventurers Davy Crockett and Kit Carson.

Ostensibly, Colonel Custer was to find a location for a new fort and keep an eye on renegade Indians, but his real objective was to confirm rumors about gold deposits. While Custer's troops mapped the lush meadows and chose a site for the fort, two "practical miners" panned the streams. In a report telegraphed to the *New York World,* Custer described the region as excellent farm country and casually mentioned finding "gold among the roots of the grass." The resulting gold rush gave the army a new justification for proceeding against the Indians. Custer had in fact become part of an army plan to force concessions from the Sioux. In November 1875 after an attempt to purchase the Black Hills, President Ulysses S. Grant and his generals decided to remove all roadblocks to the entry of miners. As of January 31, 1876, Indians outside the reservations would be taken in by force.

When the Indians refused to return to the reservations, the army mobilized, with Custer in the thick of things. In June 1876 he led 600 troops of the Seventh Cavalry to the Little Bighorn River area of modern Montana, a hub of Indian resistance. On the morning of June 25, Custer, after dividing his forces and underestimating the number of Indians, recklessly led his 209 men against the Indian encampment of 1,500 to 5,000 warriors. Custer and the outnumbered cavalry were surrounded and wiped out.

"Custer's Last Stand" shocked Americans. Most agreed that the federal government must crush the Native American resistance. "It is inconsistent with our civilization and with common sense," trumpeted the *New York Herald,* "to allow the Indian to roam over a country as fine as that around the Black Hills, preventing its development in order that he may shoot game and scalp his neighbors. . . . This region must be taken from the Indian."

The Indians' unexpected coup at Little Bighorn made the army more cautious than before. In Montana troops harassed Sioux bands for the next five years to drive them back onto the reservations. The army attacked Indian camps in the dead of winter and destroyed all supplies. In 1881 lack of provisions forced Sitting Bull, a leader at Little Bighorn, to give up; for a time after his surrender, he suffered the ignominy of appearing as an attraction in Buffalo Bill's Wild West Show.

Similar tactics were used against Chief Joseph and the Nez Percés in Oregon and against the Northern Cheyennes, who had been transported to Oklahoma after the Battle of Little Bighorn. In September 1878 the Northern Cheyennes' chief, Dull Knife, led 150 survivors north to join the Sioux. The army chased them down and imprisoned them at Fort Robinson, Nebraska. Denied the opportunity to stay on a reservation near their traditional lands, the Cheyennes refused to leave the fort, and the army then withheld all food, water, and fuel. In January 1879 a desperate Dull Knife and his followers shot the guards and broke for freedom.

Soldiers gunned down half the Indians in the snow, including women, children, and Dull Knife himself. Although sporadic Indian resistance continued until the end of the century, such brutal tactics sapped the Indians' ability to resist.

"Saving" the Indians

Bloody massacres were not the nation's only answer to the "Indian problem." In 1879 army officer Richard H. Pratt founded the Carlisle Indian School in Pennsylvania to give Indians the skills and cultural attitudes necessary to succeed in American society. Pratt claimed to want to "kill the Indian and save the man." Uprooted from family and tribe, young Indians who attended Carlisle encountered teachers with no respect for traditional Indian culture. Reeducation represented as determined an assault on the Native American world as the slaughter of the buffalo, the seizure of hunting land, and military repression. And because reeducation appealed to humanitarians' sincere concern for the Indians, it was more insidious.

The federal government's flagrant abuse of Indian treaties and atrocities such as the Fort Robinson massacre outraged humanitarians, mainly well-educated easterners. A lecture tour by Chief Standing Bear, whose peaceful Ponca tribe had been driven from land guaranteed by treaty, further aroused the reformers' indignation. Standing Bear's eloquence particularly affected Helen Hunt Jackson. In *A Century of Dishonor* (1881), Jackson, an easterner transplanted to Colorado, rallied public opinion against the government's record of broken treaties. "It makes little difference," she wrote, ". . . where one opens the record of the history of the Indians; every page and every year has its dark stain."

Well-intentioned humanitarians concluded that the best way to protect Indian interests lay in breaking up reservations, ending all recognition of the tribes, and propelling Native Americans into mainstream society. They would solve the "Indian problem" by eliminating Indians as a culturally distinct entity. They consequently threw their support to the passage in 1887 of the Dawes Severalty Act.

The Dawes Act aimed at reforming the "weaknesses" of Indian life—the absence of private property and the nomadic tradition—by forcing Indians to be farmers and landowners. The law emphasized severalty, the treatment of Indians as individuals instead of as members of tribes, and called for the breakup of reservations. Each head of an Indian family who accepted the law would receive 160 acres of land for farming or 320 acres for grazing. The government would carve this acreage from reservation lands and would sell off the remaining lands (often the richest). To prevent unscrupulous people from gaining control of parcels granted to individuals, the government would hold the property of each tribal member in trust for twenty-five years. The Dawes Act also made Indians U.S. citizens,

Major Indian–White Clashes in the West

Although never recognized as such in the popular press, the battles between Native Americans and the U.S. Army on the Great Plains amounted to a major undeclared war.

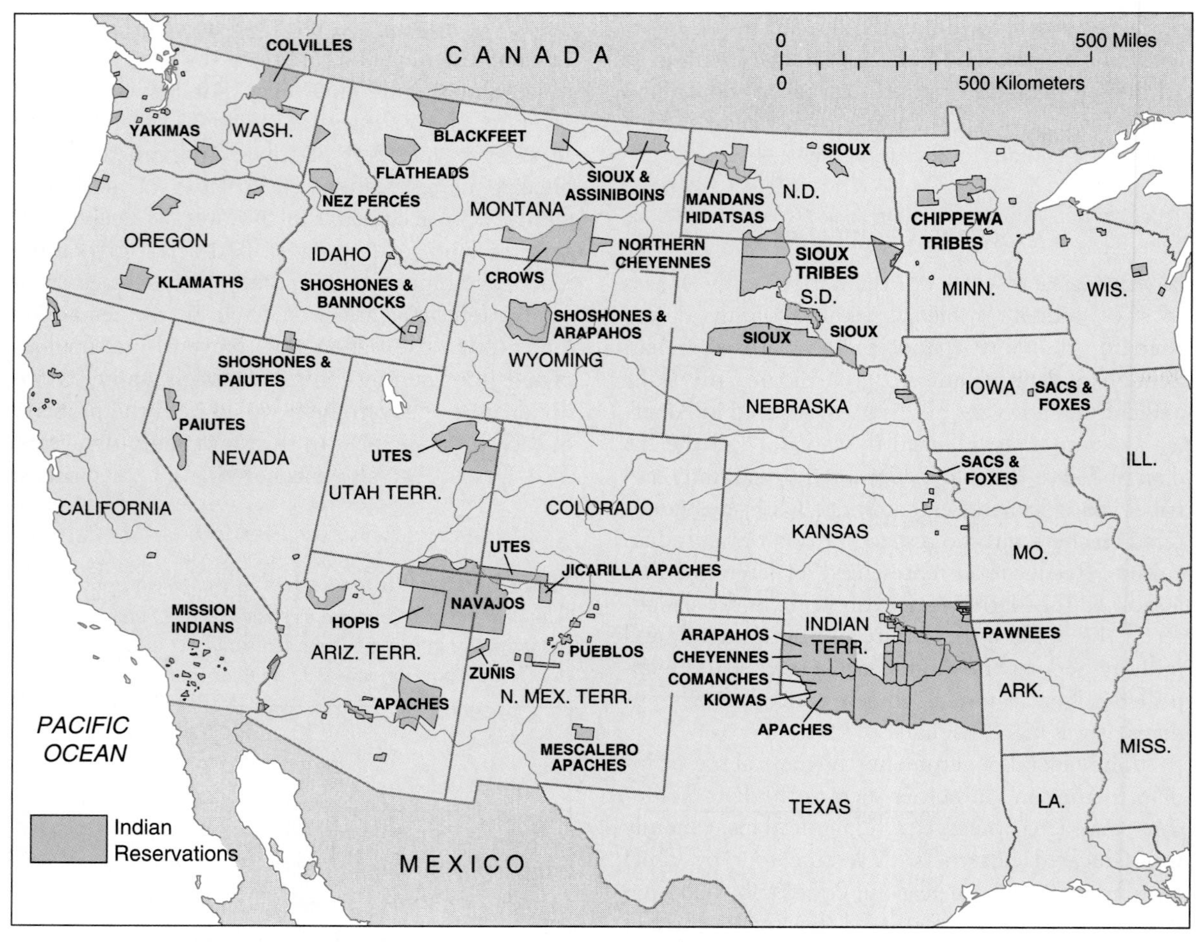

Western Indian Reservations, 1890

Native American reservations were almost invariably located on poor-quality lands. Consequently, when the Dawes Severalty Act broke up the reservations into 160-acre farming tracts, many of the semiarid divisions would not support cultivation.

with all the rights and responsibilities thereof, including the protection of federal laws and the requirement to pay taxes.

Western speculators who coveted reservation lands and military authorities who wanted to break up reservations lobbied heavily for the Dawes Act. But the bill's strongest support came from such "friends of the Indian" as Helen Hunt Jackson, who wanted to relieve the native peoples' suffering but also believed in the innate superiority of white American culture. Convinced that citizenship would best protect the Indians, the reformers tried to "civilize" the Native Americans by weaning them from their traditional culture.

Few land allotments were made until the 1890s, but then the breakup of the reservations accelerated. Ultimately, the Dawes Act proved a boon not to Indians but to speculators, who obtained the best land. By 1934 total Indian acreage had declined by 65 percent, and much of what remained in Indian hands was too dry and gravelly for farming.

Some Native Americans who received land under the Dawes Act became large-scale farmers or ranchers, but countless others languished. Hunting restrictions prevented many from supplementing their land yields, and government support steadily increased Indian dependence on federal aid. Alcoholism, a continuing problem worsened by the easy availability of whiskey as a trade item and by boredom, became more prevalent as Native Americans struggled with the constraints of reservation life.

The Ghost Dance and the End of Indian Resistance on the Great Plains

In the late 1880s the Sioux grew desperate. The federal government had reduced their meat rations, and disease had killed one-third of their cattle. They turned to Wovoka, a prophet popular among the Great Basin Indians of Nevada, who promised to restore the Sioux to their original dominance if they performed the Ghost Dance. In this ritual the dancers, wearing sacred Ghost Shirts decorated to ward off evil, moved in a circle, accelerating until they reached a trance in which they believed they saw visions of the future. Some dancers claimed special powers to kill non-Indian settlers, and many believed that Ghost Shirts would protect them from harm.

In fall 1890 the spread of the Ghost Dance movement among the Sioux in the Dakota Territory alarmed military authorities. The local reservation agent, Major James McLaughlin, decided to arrest Chief Sitting Bull, whose cabin had become a rallying point for Ghost Dancers. On a freezing December morning, McLaughlin dispatched forty-two Indian policemen to take Sitting Bull into custody. As two policemen pulled the chief from his cabin, his bodyguard shot one of them, and the policeman in turn shot Sitting Bull. Then, in the midst of bloody hand-to-hand fighting, Sitting Bull's horse began to perform tricks from its days in the Wild

Wounded Knee
Piled up like cordwood, the frozen bodies of the Sioux slaughtered at Wounded Knee were a grim reminder that the U.S. Army would brook no opposition to its control of Indian reservation life.

West show. The macabre scene terrified observers, who concluded that the dead chief's spirit had entered his horse.

Sitting Bull's violent death preceded by only two weeks one of the bloodiest episodes in the history of Plains Indian–white relations. On December 29, 1890, the Seventh Calvary began rounding up 350 starving Sioux at Wounded Knee, South Dakota. When several Indians refused to surrender, the soldiers retaliated with rapid-fire Hotchkiss cannons, and within a short time as many as 300 Indians, including infants, lay dead.

As the frozen corpses at Wounded Knee were being dumped into mass graves, a generation of Indian-white conflict on the Great Plains shuddered to a close. Some Indians succeeded in adapting to non-Indian ways, but many were devastated at being forced to abandon their religious beliefs and a way of life rooted in hunting, cooperative living, and nomadism. Driven onto reservations, the Plains Indians became almost completely dependent as their cultural traditions, modes of survival, and social organization were crushed. By 1900 the Plains Indian population had shrunk from nearly 250,000 to just over 100,000. Nevertheless, after 1900 the population gradually rose. Against overwhelming odds, the pride, group memory, and cultural identity of the Plains Indians survived all efforts to trample them.

Unlike the nomadic western Sioux, the more settled Navajos of the Southwest adjusted to the reservation system and preserved traditional ways while incorporating elements of the new order. By 1900 the Navajos had tripled their reservation land, dramatically increased their numbers and their herds, and carved out for themselves a distinct place in Arizona and New Mexico.

By the end of the century, the U.S. government had forced extraordinary changes on Indians. In the name of civilization and progress, civic leaders mixed sincere (if misguided) benevolence, coercion wrapped in an aura of legality, and outbursts of naked violence. Some white Americans felt contempt and hatred toward the Indians, but others sought to uplift, educate, and Christianize them. Government officials and ordinary citizens were equally blind to any inherent value in Native American life and traditions, and both played their part in shattering a proud people and an ancient culture. The Indians' fate would weigh on the American conscience for generations.

Settling the West

The Native Americans' defeat opened the way for the settlement of a vast territory stretching from the prairie Plains to the Sierra Nevada and the Cascade Mountains. As railroad expansion lessened the time and hazards of the journey west, migration accelerated. In the next three decades, new settlers started up 2.5 million farms in the Dakotas, Kansas, and Nebraska. More land was parceled out into farms than in the previous 250 years of American history, and agricultural production doubled.

The First Transcontinental Railroad and the Movement West

On May 10, 1869, pealing church bells and booming cannons announced the completion of the first railroad spanning North America. At Promontory Point, Utah, beaming officials drove in a golden spike to link the Union Pacific and the Central Pacific tracks. With the new route's completion, the transcontinental journey shrank from several months to a single week.

The Pacific Railroad Act of 1862 had paved the way for railroad construction. Immigrant labor had done most of the backbreaking work of building the railroad. Chinese workers had blasted through solid rock in the Sierra Nevada, while Irish immigrants had dug their way across Nebraska and Wyoming. Americans of many other backgrounds, including blacks and Mexican-Americans, had joined in.

The building and financing of the railroads had enormous consequences for the United States. The railroads acquired millions of acres of public land and became the largest landholders in the West under the Pacific Railroad Act. By 1893 many states had deeded to the railroad companies huge tracts of land, including one-quarter of Minnesota and Washington and one-fifth of the public lands in Wisconsin, North Dakota, and Montana. As landowners, the railroads shaped settlement of much of the West while reaping huge profits.

Between 1870 and 1900 railroads brought nearly 2.2 million immigrant settlers to the West. Entire villages of Germans and Eastern Europeans relocated. By 1905 the Santa Fe Railroad alone had brought 60,000 German-speaking Mennonites from Ukraine to Kansas. To ensure quick payment of money owed for land purchased by immigants, railroads encouraged new immigrants to grow cash crops—wheat on the Plains, corn in Kansas and Iowa, cotton in Texas. These crops brought high revenues but left farmers dangerously vulnerable to fluctuating market prices.

Transcontinental Railroads and Federal Land Grants, 1850–1900

Despite the laissez-faire ideology that argued against government interference in business, Congress heavily subsidized American railroads and gave them millions of acres of land. As illustrated in the box, belts of land were reserved on either side of a railroad's right of way. Until the railroad claimed the exact one-mile-square sections it chose to possess, all such sections within the belt remained closed to settlement.

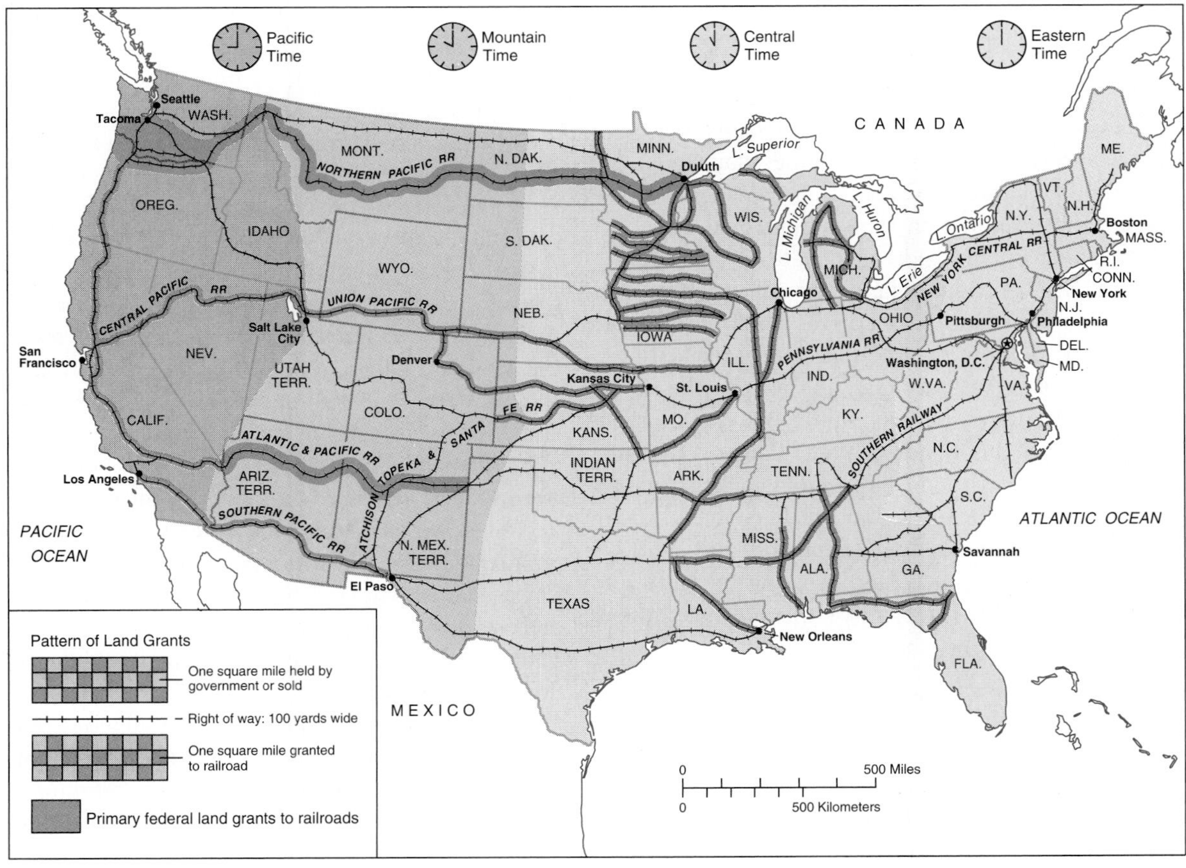

Homesteaders on the Great Plains

Liberalized land laws also drew settlers west. The Homestead Act of 1862 offered 160 acres of free land to any individual who paid a $10 registration fee, lived on the land for five years, and cultivated and improved it. Because reaching the Great Plains was expensive, most settlers migrated from nearby states. In 1860 Kansas contained 31,000 settlers from Illinois but only 4,200 from New England. Many homesteaders had previously worked at other jobs; on the Dakota frontier, only one-third of the native-stock settlers had farmed before migrating.

The Homestead Act attracted immigrants from the British Isles and other areas of Europe where good-quality land was prohibitively expensive. Urged on by land promoters, waves of English, Irish, Germans, Swedes, Danes, Norwegians, and Czechs formed their own communities on the Great Plains. Town names such as New Ulm, New Sweden, and New Prague testified to residents' origins. Within a generation, Minnesota's Red River valley boasted the largest Norwegian population outside Norway.

Although nearly 400,000 families claimed land under the Homestead Act between 1869 and 1900, the law did not function as its authors had intended. Speculators, railroads, and state governments acquired huge portions of land, and only one acre in every nine went to the pioneers for whom it was intended. In addition, the 160-acre limit specified by the Homestead Act was ample for farming the rich lands of Minnesota but not sufficient on the arid lands west of the hundredth meridian. Congress passed legislation to address this problem, but speculators, lumber companies, and ranchers abused the laws to amass large holdings. Even though families did not receive as much land as Congress had intended, federal laws kept alive the dream of the West as a place for new beginnings.

New Farms, New Markets

Railroad expansion and liberal land laws coincided with advances in farm mechanization and the development of improved strains of wheat and corn. Thanks to efficient steel plows, specially designed wheat planters, and improved threshers and windmills, the Great Plains farmer of the late nineteenth century harvested ten times more wheat than his counterpart of 1840. Barbed wire, patented in 1874, allowed farmers to keep roving livestock off their land and touched off violent conflict between farmers and ranchers. Generally, the farmers won, and the "open range" began to vanish.

The leap in wheat productivity was fueled by the spiraling growth of eastern urban populations, which increased 400 percent between 1870 and 1910. New milling techniques encouraged consumption by allowing the wheat's husk and bran to be culled out, producing a silky, better-tasting all-white flour. Minnesota's Washburn Mills (later called General Mills) used the new technology to market bread and cake flour nationally and around the world.

As farming entered a period of seemingly unparalleled prosperity, enthusiastic promoters claimed that anyone could make an easy living in the West. But few people fully understood the sacrifices and perils of agriculture. Land remained expensive, and the cost of horses, machinery, and seed could easily mount to more than $1,200, far more than the average industrial worker earned. Reliant on cash crops to pay off mortgages, farmers depended on the railroads and were at the mercy of the international grain market's shifting currents.

Western grain growers lost their independence and became players in a world market economy. High demand could bring prosperity, but when overproduction pushed prices down, the heavily indebted farmer faced ruin. The emergence of a global grain trade also drove European peasants onto the Great Plains, where they, too, competed for land and markets. These stark realities forced many Plains farmers to abandon their illusions of independence and easy wealth.

On the western Plains, low rainfall, less than twenty inches a year, increased homesteaders' problems. Farmers compensated by "dry farming"—plowing deeply to stimulate the soil's capillary action and harrowing lightly to raise a moisture-protective covering of dirt. They also diverted creeks for irrigation. But a drought that began in the 1870s, together with terrible grasshopper infestations and a national depression between 1873 and 1878, drove many to despair.

Building a Society and Achieving Statehood

No matter where homesteaders hailed from, they faced difficult adjustments to frontier life. Dawn-to-dusk work in strange places combined with fierce storms and other natural disasters to drive many off the Plains. Others persisted, establishing ties to the land and building communities.

The early years were grueling. Pioneers averaged sixty-eight hours a week of backbreaking work to build a house, plow and plant, and drill a well. Their visions of a new Eden on the Plains quickly dimmed. Blacks who migrated from the South to the Plains after the Civil War found that prejudice and racism compounded their difficulties.

Frontier life posed daunting obstacles for middle-class women settlers swept up in the romantic conventions of the day. The landscape enchanted many at first, and their letters home described the undulating plains as arrestingly beautiful. But soon "horrible tribes of mosquitoes," violent and extreme weather, isolation and loneliness, and the crude sod huts they called home made many miserable. In a typical reaction, a young bride burst into tears upon first seeing her new sod home, and she told her husband that her father had better housing for his hogs.

Many people failed to adapt to their new environment, and the transiency rate on the frontier was high. Seventy-nine percent of the families in one typical Wisconsin county in 1880 had moved by 1895. The rigors of frontier life forced some out, and the hope of finding better land lured others westward. But those who "stuck it out" came to identify closely with the land. Wood-frame homes eventually replaced "soddies," and farm settlements blossomed into towns. Churches and Sunday schools became centers of social activity as well as worship. Farmers gathered for barn raisings and group threshings; families pooled their energies in quilting and husking bees. Cooperation was both a practical necessity and a form of insurance in a rugged environment where everyone was vulnerable to disaster. As settlements mushroomed into towns, their residents eagerly established libraries, lyceums, and Masonic lodges and other social clubs, in part to dispel the image of small towns as cultural backwaters. Larger communities built fashionable hotels and imported entertainers for their new "opera houses." Basically conservative, the new pioneers patterned their churches, schools, courts, and government after the ones they had left behind.

To achieve statehood, the residents of a territory had to petition Congress to pass an enabling act establishing the proposed state's boundaries and authorizing an election to select delegates for a state constitutional convention. Once a state constitution had been drawn up and ratified by popular vote, the territory applied to Congress for admission as a state. Under these procedures, Kansas entered the Union in 1861, followed by Nevada in 1864, Nebraska in 1867, and Colorado in 1876. Not until 1889 did North Dakota, South Dakota, Montana, and Washington become states. Wyoming and Idaho entered the Union the following year. Utah, its admission long delayed because of the Mormon practice of polygyny, finally outlawed plural marriages and entered in 1896. With Oklahoma's entry in 1907 and Arizona's and New Mexico's in 1912, the process of creating permanent political institutions in the trans-Mississippi West was complete.

Although conservative, several of the new state governments supported woman suffrage. Pioneer women battled for the vote, and between 1870 and 1910 seven western states held referenda on the issue. Success came first in the Wyoming Territory, where the legislature enfranchised women in 1869. By attracting the "gentler sex," who were outnumbered six to one, Wyoming lawmakers hoped to improve the territory's reputation as a haven of rowdy mining camps. Utah also supported woman suffrage, and Nebraska and Colorado permitted women to vote in school elections. Still, by 1910 only four states—Idaho, Wyoming, Utah, and Colorado—had granted women full voting rights.

The Grange

Plains farming remained risky. Between 1873 and 1877 terrible grasshopper infestations consumed half the midwestern wheat crop. After 1870 production rose and prices fell. Wheat tumbled from $2.95 a bushel in 1866 to $1.06 in 1880. Farmers who had borrowed to finance their homesteads and machinery went bankrupt or barely survived. In 1874 an elderly Minnesotan wrote, "We can see nothing but starvation in the future if relief does not come."

When relief did not come, farmers established their own cooperative ventures. In 1867, under the leadership of Oliver H. Kelley, a Department of Agriculture clerk, midwestern farmers formed the Grange, or "Patrons of Husbandry." The Grange offered education, emotional support, and fellowship; membership had climbed to more than 1.5 million by the early 1870s. The Grange maintained a library of information on planting and livestock and organized covered-dish dinners and songfests. Farmers isolated on remote farms could find "an opportunity for social, intellectual, and moral improvement."

At the heart of the Grange was farmers' concern over their economic plight. An 1874 circular defined its purpose: to help farmers to "buy less and produce more, in order to make our farms more self-sustaining." Grangers shared the old republican, Jeffersonian-Jacksonian belief that the bounty of the soil formed the basis of all honorable wealth and that the producers formed the true backbone of society. The Grangers wanted to restore self-sufficiency to family farms. The Grange negotiated discounts from farm-machinery dealers and established "cash-only" cooperative stores and grain elevators to eliminate the "middlemen"—bankers, grain brokers, and merchants who grew rich at the farmers' expense. And the Grangers attacked the railroads, which hurt farmers by giving discounts to large shippers, bribing state legislators for land grants, and charging higher rates for short runs than for long hauls. Although supposedly nonpolitical, midwestern Grangers lobbied state legislatures for laws setting maximum rates for freight shipments.

The railroads appealed these "Granger laws" to the Supreme Court. But in *Munn* v. *Illinois* (1877), the Court not only ruled against the railroads but also upheld an Illinois law fixing a maximum rate for grain storage. The case of *Wabash* v. *Illinois* (1886), however, later prohibited states from regulating *interstate* railroad rates. Then in 1887 Congress passed the Interstate Commerce Act, establishing a new agency, the Interstate Commerce Commission, to investigate and oversee railroad operations. The commission did little to curb the railroads, but it did establish the principle of federal regulation of interstate transportation.

Was the Grange correct in blaming greedy railroads and middlemen for farm problems? The answer is not simple. From 1873 to 1878, the entire economy was trapped in a depression that stung railroads and farmers alike. Although farm commodity prices fell between 1865 and 1900, so did prices on manufactured goods. Railroads could justify their stiff freight rates in part by the thin pattern of western settlement and the seasonality of grain shipments. Nonetheless, farmers and Grangers had reason to complain. Farmers had no control over the prices they received for their crops and were at the mercy of local merchants and farm-equipment dealers who held monopolies. Railroads sometimes transported wheat to only one mill or refused to stop at small towns. These policies struck farmers as arbitrary and left them feeling powerless.

Despite gains, the Grange movement soon faltered. By 1878 intense railroad lobbying had won repeal of most state regulations. The cash-only cooperatives failed because few farmers had cash, and the Grange ideal of financial independence proved unrealistic. Under the conditions prevailing on the Plains after the Civil War, it was impossible to farm without borrowing money. Although the Grange movement had peaked by 1880, it laid the groundwork for an even more powerful wave of agrarian protest in the 1880s and 1890s (see Chapter 21).

The Southwestern Frontier

Until 1848 when the Treaty of Guadalupe-Hidalgo ceded an immense territory to the United States, Mexicans had controlled the Southwest. There they had built their own churches, maintained ranches, and traded with the Indians. Although the peace treaty pledged the United States to protect the liberty and property of Mexicans who remained on U.S. soil, over the next three decades aggressive American ranchers and settlers forced the Spanish-speaking population off much of the land. Mexicans who stayed behind adapted to Anglo society with varying degrees of success.

In Texas, where the revolution against Mexico and later the Mexican War had left a legacy of bitterness and misunderstanding, Anglos frequently harassed Mexican-Americans and confiscated their lands. Border raids by Mexican bandits worsened the situation. Tensions peaked in 1859 when Juan Cortina, a Mexican rancher, led an attack on Brownsville, Texas, and freed all the prisoners in jail. Cortina slipped back and forth across the U.S.-Mexican border for years until the Mexican government, fearing an American invasion, imprisoned him in 1875.

Similar violence erupted in California in the 1850s and 1860s after a cycle of flood and drought ruined many large ranches owned by the *californios*, Spanish-speaking descendants of the original Spanish and Mexican settlers. The collapse of the ranch economy forced many *californios* to retreat into barrios—socially segregated urban neighborhoods. A rapid increase in Anglo migration left the Mexican-American minorities stranded within the cities, where they survived as low-paid day workers and kept a tenacious hold on their cultural traditions.

The adaptation of Spanish-speaking Americans to Anglo society unfolded more smoothly in Arizona and New Mexico, where the original Spanish settlement was sparse and where a small class of wealthy Mexican landowners dominated a poor, illiterate peasantry. As early as the 1820s, wealthy Mexicans in Arizona had sent their children to the United States for education and had formed trading and business partnerships with Americans. Perhaps the most successful was Estevan Ochoa, who began a freighting business in 1859 with an American partner and expanded it into a lucrative merchandising, mining, and sheep-raising operation. The achievements of Ochoa (who rose to become Tucson's mayor) and other Mexican businessmen helped to moderate Anglo antagonism toward the Mexican-American population.

But in the 1880s violence erupted between Mexican-American and Anglo ranchers in Arizona and New Mexico. Organized as *Las Gorras Blancas* (The White Caps) in 1888, Mexican-American ranchers attacked Anglo settlers who had fenced acreage in northern New Mexico that had previously been public grazing land. In the cities Mexican-American businessmen commonly restricted their professional dealings to their own people, and the Spanish-speaking population as a whole became more impoverished. Even in Tucson, where the Mexican-American elite enjoyed considerable prosperity, 80 percent of Mexican-Americans in the work force were laborers by 1880, employed as butchers, barbers, cowboys, and railroad workers.

As increasing numbers of Mexican-American males lost title to their land and became seasonal migrant workers, Mexican-American women held their communities together. These women ran their households and created community solidarity by emphasizing traditional values, kinship, and the Catholic Church. By raising children, even those of other women, by gardening, and by trading food, soap, and other produce, they maintained stable communities in the face of drought or persecution by Anglos.

During the 1890s, a time of rising racism on the national level, violence and discrimination against the Southwest's Spanish-speaking citizens escalated. Riots occurred in the Texas communities of Beeville and Laredo in 1894 and 1899. Expressions of anti-Catholicism and verbal attacks on Mexican-Americans as violent and lazy increased among Anglos. Spanish-speaking citizens' battle for fair treatment and cultural respect would continue into the twentieth century.

Exploiting the West

From gold mines to cattle ranches to huge farms, the West appeared ripe with get-rich-quick opportunities between 1850 and 1890. Banner headlines across the country publicized bonanza after bonanza,

Adobe House, Santa Barbara, c. 1890
Although Spanish-speaking families in Santa Barbara were excluded from certain sections of town, they posed as proudly in front of their homes as did local Anglos.

building up the myth of the frontier as a place of boundless opportunity. In reality, the bonanzas set in motion a boom-and-bust economy in which a few became fabulously rich, many lost their shirts, and most barely survived.

The Mining Frontier

Beginning with the California gold rush of 1849, mining booms consumed the west. The original California strike was followed by a gold strike in British Columbia in 1857. Then in 1858 prospector Henry Comstock stumbled on the rich Comstock Lode of gold and silver along Nevada's Carson River; and a few months later gold and silver seekers found still more precious ore along Clear Creek, Colorado, near present-day Denver. By 1900 gold strikes dotted the map from Idaho, Montana, Wyoming, and South Dakota all the way north to the Alaskan Klondike. California yielded more than $1 billion in gold; the Comstock Lode alone produced more than $300 million in gold and silver.

Early discoveries often consisted of "placer" gold, panned from riverbeds and streams. These finds reinforced the myth of the mining country as "a poor man's paradise." In 1860 almost one of every four Californians claimed mining as his occupation. Although a few prospectors mined huge fortunes, the majority remained poor. Most of the West's mining wealth fell into the hands of bankers and companies that could afford the huge amounts of capital necessary to tap the rich veins of gold and silver ore deep within the earth. Large mining companies, backed by eastern and British capital, soon took over the major discoveries. Henry Comstock sold one claim for $11,000 and another for two mules.

The great discoveries such as the Comstock Lode and the Clear Creek strike might not have brought wealth to many prospectors but did create boom towns. Virginia City, Nevada, was typical. A shantytown in 1859, it had blossomed by 1873 into a metropolis of 20,000 residents. Males outnumbered females three to one. Among its buildings stood mansions, a six-story hotel, an opera house, 131 saloons, 4 banks, and uncounted brothels.

Word of new discoveries lured miners, ever anxious to get rich, to mining towns such as Virginia City. The chaotic rush to stake new claims led to widespread cheating and theft. When Virginia City's small, corrupt police force failed to maintain order, vigilantes took over the town, hanged two notorious outlaws, and forced others off the lode. Miners typically earned about $2,000 a year (teachers made $450 to $650), but meals and a room could cost between $480 and $720 annually in a boom town. Furthermore, mining was difficult and dangerous—more than 300 workers died in the Virginia City mines in less than twenty years. And when miners had exhausted the ore-bearing veins, they left for new territories. By 1900 Virginia City's population had shrunk to below 4,000.

Virginia City's boom-and-bust story was replayed again and again across the West between 1870 and 1900. Mark Twain captured the thrill of mining "stampedes" in his book *Roughing It* (1872). "Every few days," he wrote,

> *news would come of the discovery of a brand-new mining region; immediately the papers would teem with accounts of its richness, and away the surplus population would scamper to take possession. By the time I was fairly inoculated with the disease, 'Esmeralda' had just had a run and 'Humboldt' was beginning to shriek for attention. 'Humboldt! Humboldt!' was the new cry, and straightway*

Chinese Immigrant Labor

These young Chinese workers at the Deadwood mines in the Dakota Territory served as a colorfully dressed hose squad.

> *Humboldt, the newest of the new, the richest of the rich, the most marvelous of the marvelous discoveries in silver-land, was occupying two columns of the public prints to 'Esmeralda's' one.*

Most miners earned only enough to go elsewhere and try again, pursuing the elusive dream of riches across the West. The myth of the frontier exaggerated the opportunities of the mining West, but it contained just enough reality to sustain people's hopes.

Cowboys and the Cattle Frontier

Just as romanticized accounts of gold strikes fueled the feverish expansion of the mining frontier, romantic tales of hardy cowboys driving longhorns north from Texas helped to spark the transformation of the cattle industry in these same decades. Businessmen and railroad entrepreneurs promoted cattle herding as the new route to fame and fortune. The cowboy, once scorned as a ne'er-do-well and drifter, was glorified as a man of rough-hewn integrity and self-reliant strength who lived a life of adventurous simplicity on the Chisholm, Shawnee, and other fabled cattle trails of the Southwest.

In 1868 Joseph G. McCoy, a young cattle dealer from Illinois, combined organizational and promotional skills to make the cattle industry a new bonanza. McCoy had reaped substantial profits trading livestock during the Civil War. He was well aware that attempts in the 1850s to drive longhorn cattle from south Texas grasslands northward to markets in Arkansas, Illinois, and Missouri had failed because of frequent Indian attacks and outbreaks of "Texas fever" that had killed thousands of cattle. But with the Plains Indians' relocation onto reservations and the railroads' extension into Kansas, McCoy saw a renewed potential in cattle shipping.

Having formed a partnership in 1867 with a company that shipped cattle to New Orleans and New York, McCoy went to Kansas to construct a new stockyard in Abilene. He overcame opposition by purchasing supplies from neighboring ranchers at high prices and reimbursing them for any stock that died of Texas fever. By guaranteeing to ship his steers by rail to hungry eastern markets, McCoy gained a five-dollar kickback on each cattle car. To make the overland drive from Texas easier, he helped to survey and shorten the Chisholm Trail. Finally, in a clever feat of showmanship, he organized the first Wild West show, sending four Texas cowboys to St. Louis and Chicago, where their roping and riding exhibitions attracted both exuberant crowds and eager buyers for the cattle he shipped. At the end of McCoy's first year in Abilene, 35,000 steers were trailed north and sold; the following year, the number more than doubled to 75,000.

The great cattle drives of the 1860s and 1870s became a bonanza for herd owners. Steers purchased in Texas for $9 a head sold for $28 in Abilene. A herd of 2,000 head could generate a tidy $30,000 profit. But cattlemen lived at the mercy of high interest rates and unstable markets. During the Panic of 1873, hundreds of cattle drovers fell into bankruptcy. At the same time, railroad promoters kept investors interested by shamelessly exaggerating the potential for profit.

Persuaded by these claims, miners, farmers, and others anxious to get rich quickly turned to ranching. Foreign investors sank huge sums into the cattle business. The English alone put $45 million into ranch companies in the 1870s and 1880s; by 1883 British companies owned or controlled nearly 20 million acres of western grazing land. American businesses dived in; during the 1880s twenty domestically owned companies, worth from $20,000 to $3 million, operated in Wyoming alone.

Little money found its way into the pockets of the cowboys themselves. Cowpunchers who drove herds 800 miles through dirt and dust from Texas to Kansas earned $30 a month, about the same as common laborers. Long hours, low pay, and hazardous work discouraged many older ranch hands from applying. Most cowboys were young men in their teens and twenties who worked for a year or two for quick money and then pursued different livelihoods.

One-fifth of trail riders were black or Mexican. Barred from many other trades, African-American cowboys enjoyed the freedom of life on the trail and distinguished themselves as shrewd and resourceful cowpunchers. One of the best-known African-American cowboys was Nat Love, the son of Tennessee slaves. By his own account, he was "wild, reckless, free" and "afraid of nothing." On July 4, 1876, with the Black Hills gold rush in full swing, Love delivered 3,000 head of cattle and then rode into Deadwood to celebrate. That same day, he won roping and shooting contests and a new title, Deadwood Dick.

At odds with the lonely, dirty, and often boring cowboy life were the exploits of the mythic frontier cowboy, glamorized by the eastern press as early as the 1870s. The image of the West as a lawless land where cowboys-turned-vigilantes battled brutish bandits fired easterners' imaginations. In 1877 Edward L. Wheeler wrote his first dime novel, *Deadwood Dick, The Prince of the Road: or, the Black Rider of the Black Hills*. Over the next eight years, Wheeler churned out thirty-three Deadwood Dick novels about the adventures of his muscular young hero, who turned his blazing six-shooters on ruthless ruffians and dishonest desperadoes. The fictional character had much in common with the real-life Deadwood Dick except that Wheeler, to appeal to his white readership, made Dick a white man. The vigilante justice and lynch law that reigned in these novels presented the western frontier as a throwback to a semilegendary earlier age in which honor had triumphed when the righteous took matters into their own hands.

The reality was much less picturesque. In Abilene, for example, a brief period of violence and turmoil ended when the town established a police force. City ordinances forbade the carrying of firearms and regulated saloons, gambling, and prostitution. James B. ("Wild Bill") Hickok served as town marshal in 1871, but his tenure was less eventful than legend has it. Dime novelists described him as "a veritable terror to bad men on the border," but Marshal Hickok killed just two men, one of them by mistake. "Cow towns" like Abilene, Wichita, and Dodge City did not have unusually high homicide rates.

More typical of western conflicts were the "range wars" that pitted ranchers, who thought that the open range existed for them, against farmers anxious to fence and plow it. Gaining the upper hand in state legislatures, farm interests tried to cripple the cattlemen with quarantine laws and inspection regulations. Ranchers retaliated against the spread of barbed-wire fence, first by cutting settlers' fences and then by buying and enclosing thousands of acres of their own. Small-scale shooting incidents broke out between farmers and cattle drivers and between rival cattlemen and sheep ranchers.

Peaking during 1880–1885, the bonanza produced more than 4.5 million head of cattle for eastern markets. However, as early as 1882 prices sagged and some ranchers fell into debt. In 1885 President Grover Cleveland, trying to improve federal observance of Indian treaties, ordered cattlemen to remove their stock from the Cheyenne-Arapaho reservation, and 200,000 more cattle crowded onto already overgrazed ranges. In 1885 and 1886 a devil's brew of winter blizzards, searing droughts, and Texas fever destroyed 90 percent of the cattle in some areas of open range and pushed thousands of ranchers into bankruptcy. Survivors had to irrigate and fence their land and raise their cattle on smaller ranches. The open range and the great cattle drives were finished.

Bonanza Farms on the Plains

The heady enthusiasm that permeated mining and ranching in the 1870s and 1880s also percolated into agriculture. A wheat boom in the Dakota Territory attracted large capital investments that produced the nation's first "agribusiness."

The boom began during the Panic of 1873, when bank failures caused Northern Pacific Railroad bond values to plummet and the railroad exchanged land for the depreciated bonds. Speculators purchased more than 300,000 acres in the fertile Red River valley of North Dakota for between fifty cents and a dollar an acre. Singly or in groups, they established enormous factorylike farms run by hired managers, and they invested heavily in labor and equipment. The Cass-Cheney-Dalrymple farm near Fargo, North Dakota, for example, covered twenty-four square miles and hired fifty men to plow and an additional one hundred workers to harvest.

The publicity generated by the success of such large investors created an unprecedented wheat boom in the Red River valley. Banking syndicates and small farmers rushed to buy land, North Dakota's population tripled, and wheat production skyrocketed. But the profits soon evaporated, and by 1890 some Red River valley farmers were destitute. Overproduction, high investment costs, erratic rainfall, excessive reliance on one crop, and depressed international grain prices had all contributed to the boom's collapse. Large-scale farmers who had dreamed of getting rich felt lucky simply to survive. By 1889 Oliver Dalrymple, the "king" of the wheat growers, lamented that "it seems as if the time has come when there is no money in wheat raising."

The Oklahoma Land Rush

Meanwhile, would-be homesteaders greedily eyed the huge Indian Territory (modern Oklahoma). Considering much of the land worthless, the federal government in the 1830s had reserved it for the Five Civilized Tribes. But to punish the tribes for supporting the Confederacy during the Civil War, the government had settled thousands of Indians from *other* tribes in the territory. In the 1880s land-hungry non-Indians argued that the Civilized Tribes' betrayal of the Union justified further confiscation of their land.

In 1889 Congress transferred 2 million acres of unassigned Oklahoma land to the federal public domain. At noon on April 22, 1889, thousands of men, women, and children in buggies and wagons stampeded onto the new lands to stake out homesteads. (Others, the so-called Sooners, had infiltrated the lands illegally and were already plowing fields.) Before nightfall, tent communities had risen at Oklahoma City and Guthrie, near the Santa Fe Railroad. Within two months, 6,000 claims had been filed. As the Dawes Severalty Act freed up additional land, new torrents of homesteaders poured into the territory.

The land rush demonstrated the continuing power of the frontier myth, which tied "free" land to the ideals of self-determination and individual opportunity. Most early Oklahoma homesteaders succeeded as farmers because ample rainfall and fertile soil yielded substantial crops. But within two generations, a combination of exploitive farming, poor land management, and drought would turn Oklahoma into the desolate center of the Dust Bowl.

The West of Life and Legend

In 1893, four years after the Oklahoma land rush, the young historian Frederick Jackson Turner delivered a lecture entitled "The Significance of the Frontier in American History." Turner declared that "the frontier has gone, and with its going has closed the first period of American history." Although inaccurate, Turner's linking of economic opportunity to the development of the West caught the popular imagination and created a new school of historians. Today, however, scholars recognize that Turner's ethnocentric omission of Native Americans' claims to the land represented a mythic West that had taken root in the American imagination. Originally the product of nineteenth-century novels, songs, and paintings, the legend would be perpetuated by twentieth-century mass media. Its evolution is fascinating, and its influence, far-reaching.

The American Adam and the Dime-Novel Hero

James Fenimore Cooper and other nineteenth-century writers presented the frontiersman as an American Adam—simple, virtuous, innocent, and untainted by a corrupt social order. Similarly, an early biographer of Kit Carson portrayed the mountain man as an antidote to refined society, a person of "genuine simplicity . . . truthfulness . . . [and] bravery." And in Mark Twain's *The Adventures of*

Huckleberry Finn (1885), Huck heads west "because Aunt Sally she's going to adopt me and sivilize [*sic*] me, and I can't stand it." Themes of adventure, romance, contemplation, and escape from society and its pressures pervaded these works.

An alternative West emerged in the dime novels that blanketed the nation in the 1860s and 1870s. This West featured a frontiersman deeply immersed in society and its concerns. In a fictionalized biography of "Buffalo Bill" Cody, Edward Judson (who used the pen name Ned Buntline) made Cody a powerful force for justice and social order as he drives off treacherous Indians and rounds up horse thieves and cattle rustlers. So wildly popular was this new fictional frontiersman that the real Cody started his own Wild West show in 1883. Cody also presented mock "battles" between army scouts and Indians, morality dramas of good versus evil. The Wild West show thus reinforced the dime-novel image of the West as an arena of moral encounter where virtue always triumphed.

Revitalizing the Frontier Legend

Three notable members of the eastern establishment, historian and essayist Theodore Roosevelt, painter and sculptor Frederic Remington, and novelist Owen Wister, used both mythical Wests—the refuge from society and the stage for moral conflict—in their work. In the 1880s all three spent much time in the West, and the experience intensely affected them. Feeling constrained by their genteel urban world, they went west for the physical challenges and moral simplicities of the dime novels. Each found what he sought.

The frontier that Roosevelt glorified in *The Winning of the West* (1889–1896) and other works, and that Remington portrayed in his art, was a stark physical and moral environment that tested true character. Viewing the West through the lens of Charles Darwin's evolutionary theory, which characterized life as a struggle that only the fittest and the best survived, Roosevelt and Remington exalted the disappearing frontier as the last outpost of an honest and true social order. This version of the frontier myth reached full flower in Owen Wister's popular novel *The Virginian* (1902). In Wister's tale, the physical and social environment of the Great Plains produced individuals like his unnamed cowboy hero "the Virginian," an honest, strong, compassionate man, quick to help the weak and to fight the wicked. The Virginian is one of nature's aristocrats—ill educated and unsophisticated but upright, steady, and deeply moral. For Wister, and for Roosevelt and Remington, too, the cowboy was the Christian knight on the Great Plains, indifferent to material gain as he upheld virtue, pursued justice, and attacked evil.

Western myth was far removed from western realities. The mythical West ignored the hard physical labor of the cattle range and glossed over the ugly underside of frontier expansion—the brutalities of Indian warfare, the racist discrimination against blacks and Mexican-Americans, the perils of commercial agriculture and cattle ranching, and the boom-and-bust mentality rooted in the selfish exploitation of natural resources. Further, the myth obscured the complex links between the settlement of the frontier and the emergence of the United States as a major industrial nation. Indeed, eastern and foreign capital bankrolled mining, ranching, and farming; technology underlay agricultural productivity; and without railroads, western expansion would have been unthinkable.

Beginning a Conservation Movement

Despite a one-sided, idealistic vision, Wister's celebration of the western experience reinforced a growing recognition that overeager entrepreneurs might well ruin the western landscape. Two important results of the western legend were surging public support for national parks and the beginning of an organized conservation movement.

The natural beauty of the landscape awed the explorers and mappers of the High Plains and Rocky Mountains. Major John Wesley Powell, who charted the Colorado River in 1869, wrote eloquently about the region's towering rock formations and thundering cataracts. Powell's *Report on the*

Lands of the Arid Regions of the United States (1878) not only recognized the awesome beauty of the Colorado River basin but also argued that settlers needed to adjust their expectations about the use of water in the dry western terrain.

At the same time that Powell was exploring the Grand Canyon, General Henry D. Washburn led a party to the Yellowstone River area of Wyoming and Montana. The explorers were stunned. "Amid the canyon and falls, the boiling springs and sulphur mountains, and, above all, the mud volcano and the geysers of the Yellowstone, your memory becomes filled and clogged with objects new in experience, wonderful in extent, and possessing unlimited grandeur and beauty," one member of the party later wrote. The Washburn explorers abandoned their plan to claim this area for the Northern Pacific Railroad and instead petitioned Congress to protect it from settlement, occupancy, and sale. In 1872 Congress created Yellowstone National Park to "provide for the preservation . . . of all time, mineral deposits, natural curiosities, or wonders within said park . . . in their natural condition."

These steps to conserve the West's natural resources reflected the beginnings of a changed awareness of the environment. George Perkins Marsh, a Vermont architect and politician, used his influential study *Man and Nature* (1864) to attack the view that nature existed to be conquered. He warned Americans to stop their destructive use of the land. "Man," he wrote, "is everywhere a disturbing agent. Wherever he plants his foot, the harmonies of nature are turned to discords."

Marsh's plea for conservation found its most eloquent support in the work of John Muir, a Scottish immigrant who had grown up in Wisconsin. Muir fell in love with the redwood forests of the Yosemite Valley, and for forty years he tramped the rugged mountains of the West. A romantic at heart, he struggled to experience the wilderness at its most elemental level. Once, caught high in the Rockies during a summer storm, he climbed the tallest pine around and swayed back and forth in the raging wind. Muir became the late nineteenth century's most articulate publicist for wilderness protection. His campaign to preserve the wilderness contributed to the establishment of Yosemite National Park in 1890 and the creation two years later of the Sierra Club, committed to encouraging the enjoyment and protection of the wilderness in the mountain region of the Pacific coast.

The wilderness-protection movement reaffirmed the image of the West as a unique region whose magnificent landscape produced tough individuals of superior ability. Overlooking the senseless violence and ruthless exploitation of the land, writers, historians, and politicians kept alive the legend of the western frontier as a seedbed of American virtue.

CONCLUSION

The divergence between the mythic and the real West offers clues to the power and the importance of the myth. Ill at ease with changes produced by industrialization, urbanization, and immigration, countless Americans embraced the West as an uncomplicated Eden where flourished the social simplicity and moral clarity that for easterners were lost forever. Molded by writers, politicians, and artists, the myth captivated Americans. The more tenaciously they clung to the myth, the harder it became for them to understand, and adjust to, the transformations around them.

Of all those who tried to come to terms with the meaning of the West, Frederick Jackson Turner, who insisted that the frontier was the key to understanding American history, remains one of the most fascinating. "The expansion westward with its new opportunities, its continuous touch with the simplicity of primitive society," he argued, "furnish[es] the forces dominating [the] American character." The frontier experience, he continued, produced a practical, inventive, self-reliant people who valued individualism and freedom. As a description of social reality, Turner's analysis left much to be desired. But in his articulation and distillation of ideas about the West, Turner demonstrated the powerful hold of the frontier myth on the national imagination and became one of its most persuasive advocates.

The settlement of the West occupies two separate dimensions. First, it was a formidable episode in the social, economic, and political history of the United States. Second, it was a process that lived in the popular imagination long after the frontier had vanished, influencing Americans' ideas about society, government, and themselves.

CHRONOLOGY

1849 California gold rush.

1858 Henry Comstock strikes gold in Nevada.
Gold discovered at Clear Creek, Colorado.

1862 Homestead Act.
Sioux War breaks out in Minnesota.

1864 Massacre of Cheyennes at Sand Creek, Colorado.
George Perkins Marsh, *Man and Nature*.

1867 Joseph McCoy organizes cattle drives to Abilene, Kansas.
The Grange (Patrons of Husbandry) founded.
New Indian policy of smaller reservations adopted.
Medicine Lodge Treaty.

1868 Fort Laramie Treaty.

1869 Board of Indian Commissioners established to reform Indian reservation life.

1872 Mark Twain, *Roughing It*.
Yellowstone National Park established.

1873 Panic allows speculators to purchase thousands of acres in the Red River valley of North Dakota cheaply.
Biggest strike on Nevada's Comstock Lode.

1874 Invention of barbed wire.
Gold discovered in the Black Hills of South Dakota.
Red River War pits the Kiowas, Comanches, and Cheyennes against the U.S. Army.
Grasshopper infestations ruin crops in Iowa and Kansas.

1876 Colorado admitted to the Union, gives women the right to vote in school elections.
Massacre of Colonel George Armstrong Custer and his troops at Little Bighorn.

1877 *Munn* v. *Illinois*.

1878 John Wesley Powell, *Report on the Lands of the Arid Regions of the United States*.

1879 Massacre of northern Cheyennes at Fort Robinson, Nebraska.

1881 Helen Hunt Jackson, *A Century of Dishonor*.

1883 William ("Buffalo Bill") Cody organizes Wild West show.

1886 Severe drought on the Plains destroys cattle and grain.
Wabash v. *Illinois*.

1887 Dawes Severalty Act.

1888 *Las Gorras Blancas* (The White Caps) raid ranchers in northern New Mexico.

1889 Oklahoma Territory opened for settlement.

1889–1896 Theodore Roosevelt, *The Winning of the West*.

1890 Ghost Dance movement spreads to the Black Hills.
Massacre of Teton Sioux at Wounded Knee, South Dakota.
Yosemite National Park established.

1892 John Muir organizes the Sierra Club.

1893 Frederick Jackson Turner, "The Significance of the Frontier in American History."

1902 Owen Wister, *The Virginian*.

FOR FURTHER READING

William Cronon, George Miles, and Jay Gitlin, eds., *Under the Open Sky: Rethinking America's Western Past* (1992). Perceptive essays on western race relations, Native Americans, and regional identity.

Peter Iverson, *The Navajos* (1990). A brief, insightful history of the culture and everyday life of the Navajos.

Patricia Nelson Limerick, *The Legacy of Conquest: The Unbroken Past of the American West* (1987). A critical assessment of the movement westward that critiques Turner's frontier thesis.

Clyde A. Milner II, Carol A. O'Connor, and Martha A. Sandweiss, eds., *The Oxford History of the American West* (1994). A comprehensive reference work with chapters on many facets of the western experience.

Ruth B. Moynihan, Susan Armitage, and Christiane Fischer Dichamp, eds., *So Much to Be Done: Women Settlers on the Mining and Ranching Frontier* (1990). Firsthand accounts by women who struggled to adapt to living in the West.

Richard White, *"It's Your Misfortune and None of My Own": A New History of the American West* (1991). A revisionist work depicting the nineteenth-century West as a meeting place and arena of conflict for many cultures.

CHAPTER 18

The Rise of Industrial America

The industrial transformation of the late nineteenth century both exhilarated and unsettled Americans. In thirty years (1870–1900), the United States became the world's leading industrial power, doubling its iron and textile production, quadrupling the number of workers in manufacturing, and increasing overall manufacturing output more than 600 percent. But while new technologies and new inventions made life vastly more comfortable and convenient, they also led to the victimization of laborers and the deterioration of the environment.

Much of the rest of this book will examine the profound consequences of industrialization. First, we will examine how the transformation occurred and how it affected the people whose labor made it possible.

(Right) Late nineteenth-century coal miners such as these often faced extremely dangerous working conditions.

The Character of Industrial Change

Five features dominated the birth of modern industrial America: the exploitation of immense coal deposits for cheap energy; rapid technological innovation and the spread of the factory system; pressures to compete tooth and nail; an unprecedented, relentless drop in price levels; and an inadequate money supply that drove interest rates up and restricted credit.

These five factors were interwoven. The great coal deposits of Pennsylvania, West Virginia, and Kentucky provided cheap energy to fuel railroads, factories, and urban growth. New technologies that exploited these energy sources stimulated productivity and served as a catalyst for explosive industrial expansion. Technology also allowed manufacturers to cut costs and to hire cheap unskilled or semiskilled labor. This cost cutting drove firms to undersell each other, pushing weak firms out of business and prompting stronger, more efficient, and more ruthless ones to consolidate. Until the mid-1890s, cost reduction, technology, and competition forced prices down. Farmers suffered from low commodity prices, and workers felt the sting of low wages, but both groups benefited as store-bought goods cheapened. Meanwhile, high interest rates and tight credit hurt farmers and small entrepreneurs. And the depressions of the 1870s and 1890s hit all Americans hard. Above all, business leaders' unflagging drive to maximize efficiency produced colossal fortunes for a handful even as it forced millions to live near the subsistence level.

The skyrocketing demand for consumer goods stimulated the production of "capital goods," machinery to boost farm and factory output. Railroads and corporations that manufactured capital goods, refined petroleum, and made steel propelled the economy forward.

A stunning expansion in the scale of industry reflected the magnitude of economic change. Until the 1870s Americans defined a company employing one hundred workers as a large business. By 1900, however, mammoth corporations dominated industry. Singer Sewing Machines employed more than 90,000 employees and sold 1.25 million sewing machines yearly. Similar marvels of production and size characterized railroads, meatpacking, steel, sugar, and oil. But nowhere was the aggressive competition that characterized the emergence of industrial America more intense than among the railroads, the symbol of industrial progress.

Singer Sewing Machines
The Singer Company's success was built not only on its innovative use of interchangeable parts but also on advertising campaigns that stressed how easy its machines were to use.

Railroad Innovations

By 1900, 193,000 miles of railroad track crisscrossed the United States—more than in all of Europe, including Russia. Connecting every state in the

Union, the railroads opened an immense internal market and epitomized the new technological order. Railroad companies pioneered crucial aspects of large-scale corporate enterprise: issuing stock to meet capital needs, separating ownership from management, creating national distribution and marketing systems, diversifying production facilities, and forming new management structures.

Early railroad entrepreneurs faced huge financial problems. Buying land, laying track, building engines and cars, and erecting stations were horrendously expensive. The Pennsylvania Railroad, formed by the merger of seventy-three smaller lines in the 1850s, required $35 million in capitalization. Enormous subsidies from federal, state, and local governments helped to provide capital, but the large railroad companies also borrowed heavily by selling stocks and bonds. By 1900 the combined debt of all U.S. railroads stood at $5.1 billion, five times the federal debt.

Although stockholders owned the railroads, company officials directed day-to-day operations. Concerns about indebtedness and safety drove these managers to systematize operations nationally. Railroads relied on the telegraph to coordinate the complex flow of cars. By the end of the Civil War, the telegraph was the backbone of a network knitting together the entire nation. Using hierarchical structures and elaborate accounting systems that allowed tight control of expenditures, railroads could accurately predict profits on a daily basis. Such management innovations became models for other businesses seeking national markets.

Creativity, Cooperation, and Competition

The larger-than-life men who expanded the railroad industry in the 1870s and 1880s often seemed villainous; they were "robber barons" to their contemporaries. Jay Gould, the president of the Union Pacific, drew scorn as a "perfect eel" and "one of the most sinister figures that have ever flitted batlike across the vision of the American people." Recent historians have been kinder, viewing the great industrialists as a diverse group, some of them iron-fisted pirates but others sophisticated businessmen of breathtaking originality and inventiveness.

The expansion and consolidation of railroading reflected both ingenuity and dishonesty. Although railroads had become the nation's major transportation system by the end of the Civil War, the industry was in chaos. Hundreds of small companies differed on everything from track width to engine size. By 1893 the small companies had been consolidated into major trunk lines.

Consolidation also meant standardization. In 1886 all railroads shifted to the new standard 4' 8½"–gauge track; they also adopted standard couplings, signals, and cooperative billing procedures that let one road ship cargo on several other lines. Perhaps the most symbolic example of standardization, and of the changes being wrought by industrialization, was the adoption of standard time zones in 1883. Many Americans felt far more comfortable with "God's time," based on the rising and setting of the sun, but the railroads certainly operated more efficiently on standard time.

The establishment of integrated transportation and communications networks cut both ways. Companies gained access to national markets, and consumers to goods produced in faraway factories. However, rancorous competition often saddled companies with massive debts and led to "watering" of stock, the issuing of stock certificates that far exceeded the company's assets. By 1885 one-third of the nation's railroad stock had been watered.

Entangled in heavy indebtedness, overextended systems, and crooked business practices, railroads fought each other recklessly for traffic. They cut rates for large shippers, offered special arrangements for handling bulk goods, dispensed free passes to influential politicians, and granted rebates and kickbacks to favored clients. The competition became so ferocious that railroads tried to curb it by establishing pools, agreements to divide traffic proportionately and to charge uniform rates. None of these tactics shored up the railroads' precarious finances, and some overbuilt lines careened into bankruptcy.

Caught in the middle of the railroads' tug of

war, farmers and small businessmen turned to state governments for help. In the 1870s Granger-led protests drove many midwestern state legislatures to outlaw rate descrimination. In the 1880s, however, the Supreme Court began negating such laws, thus breaking down local autonomy and supporting the capitalist integration of the economy at the national level. In 1887 Congress passed the Interstate Commerce Act, which established the Interstate Commerce Commission (ICC) to oversee railroad practices and banned pooling, rebates, and other monopolistic activity. However, the Supreme Court ruled in favor of railroads over regulators until the Hepburn Act of 1906 strengthened the ICC by empowering it to set rates (see Chapter 22).

Vicious competition in the rail industry lessened only when the national depression that began in 1893 forced several roads into the hands of investment bankers. Supported by major investment houses in Boston, New York, and Philadelphia, J. Pierpont Morgan took over the weakened systems, reorganized them, refinanced their debts, and built intersystem alliances by purchasing blocks of stock in competing lines. By 1906, thanks to the bankers' centralized management, seven giant networks controlled two-thirds of the nation's track.

Railroad development thus reflected an enormous paradox. The massive trunk systems represented the largest business enterprise in the world, with the most advanced methods of accounting and organization. Their insatiable appetite for rails and engines stimulated the demand for steel and other products, and the transportation network they built opened up exciting possibilities for a truly national economy. But despite such power and innovations, the railroads remained unstable. Cutthroat expansion inflated operating costs, reduced revenues, and made them vulnerable to economic downturns. In the depression of 1893, only intervention by investment bankers saved the industry from collapse.

Applying the Lessons of the Railroads to Steel

The career of Andrew Carnegie illustrates the link between railroad expansion and the growth of heavy industry. Carnegie's salesmanship and managerial genius played a major role in his successful adaptation of railroad organization and finance to the steel industry.

Carnegie embodied the rags-to-riches dream. Born in Scotland, he immigrated to the United States in 1848 at age twelve. In his first job, bobbin boy in a textile mill, he earned $1.20 a week for sixty hours of work. In 1849 the ambitious youth became a Western Union messenger boy, and soon he was Pittsburgh's fastest telegrapher, "reading" the sound of the keys by ear. Decoding messages for the city's business leaders, Carnegie gained an insider's view of their operations.

In 1852 Tom Scott, superintendent of the Pennsylvania Railroad's western division, hired the seventeen-year-old Carnegie as his secretary and personal telegrapher. Carnegie quickly mastered the complex details of the most innovative business of the time. Seven years later Scott became vice president of the Pennsylvania, and Carnegie took Scott's former job as head of the Pennsylvania's western division. In his six years as division chief, the daringly innovative Carnegie doubled the road's mileage and quadrupled its traffic. By 1868 his investments alone brought him nearly $60,000 a year, a substantial fortune.

Carnegie decided in the early 1870s to build his own steel mill, in part because of his connections with the railroad industry, the nation's largest purchaser of steel. His J. Edgar Thompson Mill incorporated the new Bessemer production technology, blasting air through molten iron to burn off carbon and other impurities. Carnegie also used the cost-analysis techniques pioneered by the railroads to cut production costs. His management philosophy was deceptively simple: "Watch the costs, and the profits will take care of themselves." He learned how to produce steel twenty dollars per ton more cheaply than his competitors and how to parlay his railroad connections into huge orders.

Vertical integration—that is, controlling all aspects of manufacturing, from extracting raw materials to selling the finished product—enabled

Carnegie to achieve even greater efficiency. From iron-ore fields to a huge sales force, Carnegie Steel controlled every phase of the industry. The shrewd selection of associates also aided Carnegie, particularly his partnership with Henry Clay Frick, who became chairman of Carnegie Steel in 1889. Under Frick's aggressive leadership, Carnegie Steel's profits rose each year, reaching $40 million in 1900. Carnegie Steel demonstrated how sophisticated technology and innovative management (combined with brutally low wages) could slash prices. By 1900 Carnegie was producing steel rails at $11.50 per ton, down from $65 per ton in the 1870s.

Frick's management of daily operations left Carnegie free to pursue philanthropy. Carnegie, who had decided that fortunes corrupted their possessors, established foundations and donated more than $300 million for libraries, universities, and international-peace causes. (He also knew that such actions would buttress his popularity.)

By 1900 Carnegie Steel, employing 20,000 people, had become the world's largest industrial corporation. But internal squabbling produced disgruntled subordinates, and a confrontation between Carnegie and Frick forced the latter out of the company. At the same time, rival firms, including Federal Steel, formed in 1898 by J. Pierpont Morgan, threatened Carnegie Steel's sales to the wire, nail, and pipe industries.

When Carnegie cunningly responded by announcing plans to produce seamless pipes by new and highly efficient techniques, his two largest competitors sought compromise and consolidation. Morgan asked Charles Schwab, the president of Carnegie Steel, to find out how much Carnegie wanted for his share of the company. Schwab tracked Carnegie to a golf course, and Carnegie informed Schwab that he would require nearly $500 million. "Tell Carnegie I accept his price," Morgan responded, and United States Steel was born. Morgan combined the Carnegie companies with his own Federal Steel to create the first business capitalized at more than $1 billion. U.S. Steel, with its 200 member companies employing 168,000 people, marked a new scale in industrial enterprise.

Carnegie portrayed himself as a self-made man who rose through discipline, hard work, thrift, patience, and quick action in the face of opportunity. The reality was more complex. Carnegie had an uncanny ability to see the larger picture and to hire talented associates; he combined this gift with ingenuity in transferring techniques like cost accounting from railroads to steel, and he callously kept wages as low as possible. To a public little interested in details, Carnegie's success reaffirmed the possibilities of the American economic system and promised that anyone could rise from rags to riches.

Consolidating the Industrial Order

Between 1870 and 1900 rapacious competition also swept the oil, salt, sugar, tobacco, and meatpacking industries. Entrepreneurs raced to reduce costs and dominate rivals. For example, Chicago meatpackers Philip Armour and Gustavus Swift introduced multiple efficiencies into the packing industry and

Industrial Consolidation: Iron and Steel Firms, 1870 and 1900

	1870	*1900*
No. of firms	808	669
No. of employees	78,000	272,000
Output (tons)	3,200,000	29,500,000
Capital invested	$121,000,000	$590,000,000

SOURCE: Figure from *The Economic Transformation of America: 1600 to Present,* Second Edition by Robert L. Heilbroner and Aaron Singer. Copyright © 1984 by Harcourt Brace & Company. Reproduced by permission of the publisher.

reaped fortunes by using refrigerated railcars to supply meat to eastern cities.

The evolution of the oil industry typified this process. After Edwin L. Drake drilled the first successful petroleum well in 1859 near Titusville in northwestern Pennsylvania, entry into the oil business came relatively easily. By the 1870s rickety drilling rigs, collection tanks, and ramshackle refineries littered the landscape near Pittsburgh and Cleveland, the sites of the first discoveries.

A young Cleveland merchant, John D. Rockefeller, gradually dominated in this new race for wealth. His methods reflected those of Carnegie: cost cutting and efficiency. After founding the Standard Oil Company in 1870, Rockefeller scrutinized the smallest detail of daily operations, insisting that one refinery manager find 750 missing barrel stoppers or that another reduce from 40 to 39 the number of drops of solder used to seal a kerosene can. He recognized that in a mass-production enterprise, small changes could save thousands of dollars. Rockefeller also stressed the importance of providing a reliable product and adopted the latest techniques to ensure the quality of his fuels and lubricants. In addition, he advertised heavily and made the red five-gallon can of Standard Oil kerosene instantly recognizable.

Like Carnegie, Rockefeller possessed an extraordinary ability to understand the workings of an entire industry. Seeing that the firm that controlled the shipment of oil could dominate the industry, Rockefeller purchased his own tanker cars. He wangled a 10 percent rebate from the railroads and a kickback on his competitors' shipments. When new technology made pipelines the most efficient method of transporting oil, Rockefeller established his own massive interregional pipeline network. And Rockefeller used aggression and deception to

Mergers in Mining and Manufacturing, 1895–1910

A wave of business mergers occurred after the Supreme Court's 1897 and 1898 rulings that any firms concluding price-fixing or market-allocating agreements violated the Sherman Anti-Trust Act. But the merger mania died down when business leaders quickly discovered that companies could remain profitable only through vertical integration.

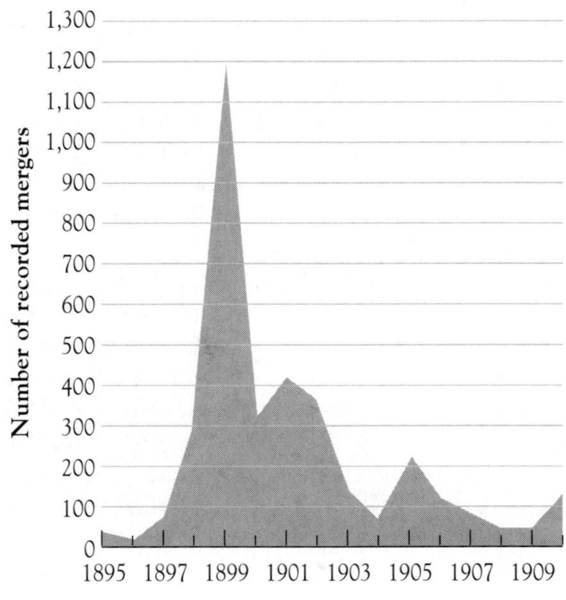

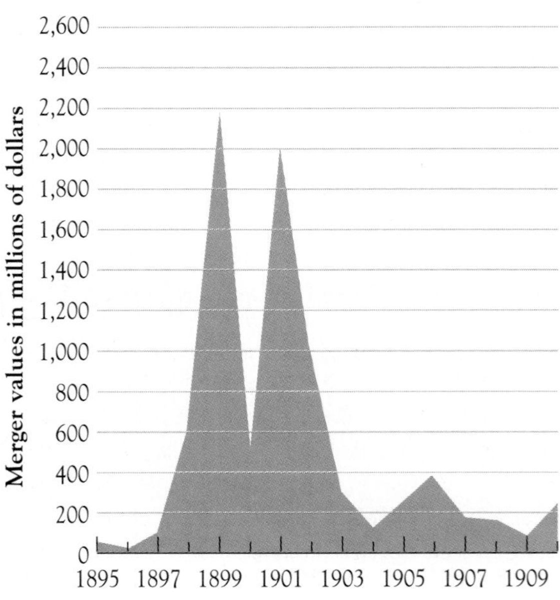

force out competitors. He priced his products below cost to strangle rivals and drove merchants who would not sell his products out of business. "The Standard Oil Company brooks no competition," a congressional investigating committee reported; "its settled policy and firm determination is to crush out all who may be rash enough to enter the field against it." By 1879 Rockefeller controlled 90 percent of the nation's oil-refining capacity.

Convinced that competition wasted resources, Rockefeller established the Standard Oil Trust in 1882. Rockefeller and his associates persuaded stockholders of forty companies to exchange their stock for certificates of trust and then established a board of trustees to run all the companies. Within three years, the Standard Oil Trust had consolidated crude-oil buying throughout its member firms and cut the number of refineries by half. In this way Rockefeller went beyond Carnegie by integrating the petroleum industry both *vertically*, by controlling every function from production to local retailing, and *horizontally*, by merging competing companies into a single giant system. Consequently, Standard Oil grew into an industrial titan and spread to Asia, Africa, and South America. By 1890 Rockefeller's personal fortune had mushroomed to more than $800 million.

Success bred imitation, and trusts bloomed in the copper, sugar, whiskey, and lead industries. But rapacious tactics, monopolistic control, and sky-high earnings provoked a public outcry and led to investigations of the trusts' unscrupulous practices. In 1890 Congress, under the leadership of Ohio senator John Sherman, passed the Sherman Anti-Trust Act, outlawing trusts and any other contracts or combinations in restraint of trade and establishing both fines and jail time as penalties. However, the act never defined clearly either *trust* or *restraint of trade*, and the government prosecuted only a handful of cases before 1904. When Standard Oil was challenged in 1892, it simply reorganized as a holding company;* the nine trustees became the board of directors for Standard Oil (New Jersey), and profits soared.

Supreme Court decisions hamstrung antitrust efforts. In 1895, for example, the federal government brought suit against the sugar trust in *United States* v. *E. C. Knight Company*, arguing that the trust, which controlled more than 90 percent of all U.S. sugar refining, operated in restraint of trade. The Court, however, chose to define manufacturing as a local concern, not part of interstate commerce, and threw out the suit. Thus protected, corporate mergers and consolidations surged ahead. By 1900 mammoth firms controlled nearly 40 percent of all capital investment in manufacturing.

The Triumph of Technology

New technologies and machines offered another way in which to build profits, lower costs, and improve efficiency. They also created markets hungry for new products. After 1870 business corporations stepped up their research efforts and introduced a remarkable variety of new consumer goods.

The major inventions that stimulated industrial output and underlay mass production remained hidden from public view. Few Americans had heard of the Bessemer process for making steel or of the refrigerated railroad cars that allowed Swift to slaughter beef in Chicago and sell it fresh in New York City. But the public saw the *fruits* of technology—the sewing machine, the telephone, the light bulb, and other inventions that eased the drudgery of everyday life and reshaped social interactions. Mass-produced sewing machines replaced hand-sewn with factory-stitched clothing, relieved women of the tedium of hand-making the family apparel, and expanded personal wardrobes. Telephones not only transformed communications but also undermined the social conventions for polite behavior that had governed face-to-face or written exchanges. The light bulb made possible longer and more regular working hours. These wonders inspired optimism that technology would lead to the betterment of society.

Thomas A. Edison (1847–1931) epitomized

*Holding company: a corporation that owns a controlling share of the stock of one or more other firms the inventive impulse. Largely self-educated, Edison was a born salesman and self-promoter. Although he modestly stated that "genius is one percent inspiration and ninety-nine percent perspiration," he reveled in his own image as an inventing "wizard." Like Carnegie, Edison envisioned a large, interconnected industrial system resting on a foundation of technological innovation.

In his early work, Edison concentrated on the telegraph; his first major invention was a stock-quotation printer. In 1876 his profits enabled him to establish an "invention factory" in Menlo Park, New Jersey, where he predicted "a minor invention every ten days, and a big one every six months."

When the advent of the telephone undercut the telegraph market, Edison turned his attention to the electric light. He realized that practical electrical lighting had to be part of a complete system—generators, voltage regulators, electric meters, insulated wiring—as well as cheap. In 1877, buoyed by the success of his invention of the phonograph, Edison set out to develop a new filament for incandescent light bulbs. He perfected a process for generating electricity and discovered a carbon filament that would glow dependably in a vacuum. In 1882, backed by J. Pierpont Morgan, the Edison Illuminating Company opened a power plant in New York City's financial district, furnishing lighting for eighty-five buildings.

Others rushed into the electrical field. Most important, Edison competitor George Westinghouse developed an efficient system to deliver cheap high-voltage power through the use of alternating current. In the process, he stole many of Edison's ideas, and Edison angrily sued. Embittered by legal battles—defense of his patents cost him more than $2 million—Edison relinquished control of his enterprises in the late 1880s. In 1892 his company merged with a competitor to form the General Electric Company. Four years later, GE and Westinghouse agreed to exchange patents under a joint board. Such patent pooling agreements became another way in which to dominate markets.

Edison meanwhile continued to pump out invention after invention, including the mimeograph machine, the microphone, the motion-picture camera and film, and the storage battery. Over his long life, he patented 1,093 inventions and amassed an estate worth more than $6 million. Perhaps his greatest contribution was his Menlo Park laboratory, a model for industrial research, which demonstrated that the systematic use of science in support of industrial technology paid large dividends.

Mass Production, Mass Marketing

The technological and managerial innovations of Edison, Carnegie, and Rockefeller proved adaptable throughout U.S. industry, spurring marvels of production. When production outstripped demand, industries developed advertising and marketing techniques to whet the consumers' appetites and to differentiate the products.

The growth of the flour industry illustrates the spread of mass production and the emergence of new marketing concepts. In the 1870s adoption of advanced technology allowed companies to produce vast amounts of flour, more than they could sell. To solve this problem, companies developed product differentiation. Mills thought up new product lines such as cake flours and breakfast cereals and used hard-hitting advertising to sell them. Henry P. Crowell, for example, heavily promoted his new milled oat product under the easily remembered Quaker Oats brand name. Brand names, trademarks, guarantees, slogans, endorsements, and other gimmicks built product demand and consumer loyalty. Americans bought Ivory Soap because of the impressive pledge that it was "99 and 44/100s percent pure." The American Tobacco Company used trading cards, circulars, boxtop premiums, prizes, and scientific endorsements to convert Americans to cigarette smoking and to its own products.

In the 1880s George Eastman invented a paper-based photographic film as an alternative to the bulky, fragile glass plates then in use. When professional photographers resisted the innovation, Eastman realized that "in order to make a large business we would have to reach the general public and create a new class of patrons." Mass-producing a cheap camera, the Kodak, and devising a catchy slogan ("You press the button, we do the rest"), Eastman introduced a system in which customers returned both the one-hundred-exposure film *and* the camera to his Rochester factory. For ten dollars, the company developed and printed the film, reloaded the camera, and returned everything to the customer. Eastman had revolutionized an industry and democratized a visual medium previously confined to a few.

Other companies with names well known today contributed to the production and marketing revolution—H. J. Heinz, Campbell Soup, Pabst Beer, and Borden Milk, to name a few. Benefiting from savings made possible by new machinery, organizational efficiencies, high volume, and national distribution, such firms won a large share of the market with advertising that stressed their products' high quality and low cost.

Pittsburgh in the 1890s
For many Americans, the price of progress was often pollution. Lacking the technology to filter carbon and gases from smoke, factory owners had no choice but to fill the skies with soot.

Industrialization: Costs and Benefits

By 1900 an industrial economy dominated by a few mammoth firms had replaced the chaos of early competition among thousands of small companies. The industrial transformation begun by the railroads had spread throughout U.S. business. For those that fell behind in an unforgiving economic environment, the cost was measured in ruined fortunes, bankrupt companies, and shattered dreams. John D. Rockefeller summed up the prevailing atmosphere when he said that in the Standard Oil Trust he wanted "only the big ones, only those who have already proved they can do a big business. As for the others, unfortunately they will have to die."

The cost was high, too, for millions of workers. The new industrial order rested on the backs on laborers who received subsistence wages and could be fired at a moment's notice. Environmental devastation was part of the cost as well. Polluted rivers, smoky skies, and a landscape littered with reeking garbage and toxic by-products bore mute witness to the relentless drive for efficiency and profit.

But industrialization also brought social benefits: labor-saving products, lower prices for goods, and advances in transportation and communication. Benefits and liabilities seemed inextricably interconnected. The sewing machine, for example, created thousands of new jobs, made a wide variety of clothing available, and eased the lives of millions of housewives. However, it also encouraged greedy entrepreneurs to operate sweatshops in crowded tenements and unsafe lofts where immigrants toiled long hours for pitifully low wages.

Whatever the balance sheet of social gains and costs, one thing was clear: the United States had muscled its way onto the world stage as an industrial titan. In 1870 the United States turned out less than a quarter of the world's manufactured goods;

by 1900 it produced nearly a third. The ambition of countless inventors, financiers, managerial innovators, and marketing wizards had laid the groundwork for a new social and economic order.

The New South

The South entered the industrial era far more slowly than the North. Many factors hindered its progress: the Civil War's physical devastation, the relatively small number of towns and cities, lack of capital, illiteracy, northern control of financial markets and capital, and a low rate of technological innovation. The myth of the Lost Cause—the nostalgic portrayal of the antebellum South as traditional and unchanging—also impeded the region's economic growth.

Obstacles to Southern Economic Development

Much of the South's difficulty in industrializing stemmed from its lack of capital. The Civil War shattered the South's credit system and destroyed its assets. The fighting left cities burned, fields trampled, livestock slaughtered, and farms and plantations ruined. Banks failed in large numbers; by 1865 the South, with 25 percent of the nation's population, had only 2 percent of its banks.

Federal policies adopted during the war restricted the expansion of the southern banking system. Obtaining a national bank charter required $50,000 in capital, far beyond most southerners' postwar means. Federal laws also prohibited national banks' extension of mortgages on real estate, so even those with the necessary capital faced obstacles. Southern banks in effect were confined to cities and could lend only relatively small amounts.

Rural merchants, shopkeepers, and large landowners became bankers by default with the establishment of the crop-lien system (see Chapter 16). In exchange for the provision of seed and tools, they insisted that farmers specialize in cotton and tobacco, crops that initially brought high returns. Prosperity did not follow, however. Instead, the shift from planting corn to raising cotton and tobacco made small southern farmers vulnerable to the fluctuations of commercial agriculture and reduced their self-sufficiency.

The South also remained the victim of federal policies designed to aid northern industry. High protective tariffs raised the price of imported machine technology, the retirement of federal greenbacks and the demonetization of silver (see Chapter 16) further limited capital, and discriminatory railroad freight rates hiked shipping prices.

The South's chronic shortage of funds affected the economy indirectly as well by limiting resources available for education. Reconstruction had seen a modest expansion of public schooling for both whites and blacks, but many southern states refused to tax property for school support until 1889. Low school attendance limited the number of educated people available for technical positions in business and industry.

The myth of the Lost Cause further retarded economic progress. After the war, southern states often contributed the modest funds they had to veterans' pensions. This practice not only built a white patronage system for Confederate veterans and reinforced the myth of the Lost Cause, but also left little for economic and educational development.

The New South Creed and Southern Industrialization

In the 1870s, fearful that the South would become an economic backwater, some southern newspaper editors, planters, merchants, and industrialists championed "the New South creed" to encourage southern industrialization. Natural resources and cheap labor, they argued, made the South a natural site for industrial development. During the 1880s, the movement to industrialize the South gained momentum. Southern states offered tax exemptions for new businesses, set up industrial and agricultural expositions, and leased convicts from state prisons to serve as cheap labor. States sold forest and mineral rights on 6 million acres of land to speculators.

Between 1869 and 1899 lumber production increased 500 percent as the forests of Alabama and Louisiana were denuded. Southern iron and coal industries also expanded. Founded in 1871 in the heart of a region blessed with coal, limestone, and iron-ore deposits, Birmingham, Alabama, became a bustling city of noisy railroad yards and roaring blast furnaces. By 1900 it was the nation's largest pig-iron shipper.

Recruiting black workers, southern iron and steel mills contributed to the migration of African-Americans cityward. By 1900, 20 percent of the southern black population was urban. However, southern industry reflected the patterns of racism permeating other aspects of southern life. The burgeoning textile mills of the piedmont were lily-white; in the iron and steel industry, blacks composed 60 percent of the work force but had no chance of advancement. In a rare reversal of usual patterns, black workers in iron and steel on average earned more than white textile workers.

Textile Workers
Textile mills hired both adults and children. Here a man and two boys stand before the machines that they operated for sixty hours a week. Child laborers in the mills often went home so tired that they fell asleep before supper and could not be wakened until morning.

The Southern Mill Economy

The textile mills that mushroomed in the South in the 1880s took southern industrialization down a different path than that of the North and Midwest. The southern textile industry did not cluster in existing cities but sprang up in the countryside and often became a catalyst for the rise of new towns. Rural ways and values suffused the South's new industrial workplace.

The cotton-mill economy grew largely in the piedmont, a beautiful country of rolling hills and rushing rivers stretching from central Virginia to northern Georgia and Alabama. After the war most of the region's farmers had fallen into the crop-lien and sharecropping systems. But postwar railroad construction opened the piedmont to outside markets and sparked intense town building and textile-mill expansion. Between 1880 and 1900 track mileage in North Carolina grew more than 250 percent. Some 120 new mills were built in that state alone.

Merchants and newspaper editors hailed the prospect that cotton mills would lift the South out of poverty, and at first sharecroppers and tenant farmers looked hopefully to the mills, which seemed to offer a way out of misery. But appearances deceived. The cotton-mill promoters were the same men who had profited from the commercialization of southern agriculture and the rise of sharecropping and crop liens. They made low-skilled, low-paid workers the backbone of their operations.

Mill superintendents drew their workers from

impoverished nearby farms and commonly hired entire families, usually poor whites. Although superintendents promised that textile work would free these families from poverty, they shamelessly exploited them. By the 1880s, when mills earned 30 to 75 percent profit for their investors, mill workers twelve to eighteen years of age received seven to eleven cents an hour, half of comparable wages in New England.

The mill dominated the piedmont textile community. The mill operator built and owned workers' housing and the company store, supported the village church, financed the local elementary school, and pried into the mill hands' morals and behavior. Mill owners usually kept workers dependent and immobile by paying them only once a month, often in scrip—a certificate redeemable exclusively at the company store. Most families had to buy on credit during the month, overspent, and fell behind in their payments. As charges were deducted from the next month's paycheck, workers fell into a cycle of indebtedness indistinguishable from that of sharecroppers.

To help make ends meet, mill workers kept their own gardens and raised chickens and an occasional cow or pig. Southern mill hands thus brought communal farm values into the mills and mill villages. Although they had to adapt to machine-paced work and earned barely enough to live on, the working poor in the mill districts eased the shift from rural to village-industrial life by clinging to a cooperative country ethic.

Southern textile mills, like their northern counterparts, exploited the cheap rural labor around them, settling transplanted farm people in paternalistic, company-run villages. The industry shot up 1,400 percent, and by 1920 the South was the nation's leading textile-mill center.

The Southern Industrial Lag

Still, in the South industrialization was slower, slighter, and more dependent on outside forces than in the North, and the southern economy remained essentially colonial, subject to control by northern industries and financial syndicates. Except for the American Tobacco Company, southern industry was dominated by northern companies and bankers. For example, U.S. Steel controlled the foundries in Birmingham, and it forced southerners to pay higher prices for steel than northerners, even though southern production cost less. Inevitably, environmental damage—polluted streams, blasted forests, grimy coal towns, and soot-blackened cities—accompanied industrialization.

Unfavorable federal banking regulations, scarce capital, staggering debt, and discriminatory business practices by northern-controlled enterprises hampered the South's economic development. Dragged down by a poorly educated and poorly trained population, both white and black, southern industry languished. Limited by outside forces, economic progress in the South occurred in its own distinctly regional way.

Industrial Work and the Work Force

Nationally, industrialization proceeded unevenly: during the late nineteenth century most Americans still worked in small factories and locally run businesses. But as the century closed, more and more large factories appeared, with armies of skilled and semiskilled workers. Between 1860 and 1900 the number of industrial workers jumped from 885,000 to 3.2 million, and the trend toward large-scale production became unmistakable.

From Workshop to Factory

The changes that led to the factory economy involved a fundamental restructuring of work habits and a new emphasis on workplace discipline. The boot and shoe industry illustrates the impact of these changes. As late as the 1840s, shoemakers were the aristocrats of labor, working in small, independent shops where they set their own hours. A distinctive working-class culture evolved around them. Foreign-born English, German, and Irish shoe workers set up ethnic trade organizations; took time off for religious observances, funerals, and holidays; drank sociably on the job; and helped each other weather accidents or illness. Living in tenements within tight-knit ethnic neighborhoods, they developed strong ethnic and community pride.

As early as the 1850s, however, changes in the ready-made shoe industry began to erode the role and status of skilled labor. Management moved its growing production staffs into large buildings and broke the manufacturing process into a series of repetitive tasks. Skilled artisans now worked in teams, with each member responsible for a specific task. Workers lost the freedom to drink on the job or to take time off for special occasions. The working-class culture that had reinforced group solidarity appeared wasteful and inefficient to owners and foremen. Then in the 1880s, as shoe factories became larger and more mechanized, traditional skills vanished. Sophisticated machines allowed companies to replace skilled workers with low-paid, unskilled women and children. By 1890 unskilled women made up more than 35 percent of the work force in an industry that skilled men had once dominated.

Skilled artisans in other trades also found their responsibilities changing. With the exception of crafts such as carpentry and bricklaying, artisans no longer participated in the production process *as a whole*. Rather, skilled workers performed numbingly repetitious, monotonous tasks. Factory work had become specialized, machine-paced, and deadeningly routine.

The Hardships of Industrial Labor

The expansion of the factory system created an unprecedented demand for unskilled labor. By the 1880s nearly one-third of the workers in the railroad and steel industries were common laborers. In the construction trades, the machine and tool industries, and garment manufacturing, industrialists used the contract system to hire unskilled laborers. Subcontractors hired, managed, and fired these common workers, who were taken on when needed and laid off in slack periods. The steel industry employed them to shovel ore, coal, and limestone around the yards and to move ingots inside the mills. Foremen drove the gangs hard.

Unskilled workers drifted from city to city and from industry to industry. They earned about one-third the wages of skilled artisans. In the late 1870s, bricklayers earned $3.00 a day, but unskilled laborers a mere $1.30. Only southern mill workers, averaging $.84 a day, earned less.

Skilled and unskilled workers alike put in twelve-hour shifts, often under hazardous, unhealthful conditions. An alarming incidence of industrial accidents stemmed from workers' inexperience with the complicated, heavy machinery and employers' unconcern for plant safety. One steelworker recalled that, on his first day at the mill, "I looked up and a big train carrying a big vessel with fire was making towards me. I stood numb, afraid to move, until a man came to me and led me out of the mill." The accident rate in steel mills was extremely high.

Children as young as eight worked in coal mines and cotton mills. Their attempts to play while on the job made them vulnerable to accidents. In cotton mills, when supervision was lax, child workers would grab the belts that powered the machines and see who could ride them farthest up toward the drive shaft in the ceiling before letting go and falling to the floor. In coal mines, children who worked as slate pickers sat in a cloud of black dust beneath the breakers that crushed coal, removing slate and other impurities. Black lung disease occurred commonly and often led to emphysema and tuberculosis. Cotton-mill workers, both children and adults, contracted brown lung, another crippling pulmonary disease, from breathing cotton dust.

For adult workers, the railroads presented the greatest peril. In 1889, the first year that reliable statistics were compiled, almost 2,000 railwaymen were killed on the job and more than 20,000 were injured. Disabled workers and widows received minimal aid from employers. Until the 1890s the courts considered employer negligence one of the normal risks borne by the employee. Employers fought the adoption of safety and health standards on the grounds that the costs would be excessive. Workers joined fraternal organizations and ethnic clubs for sickness and accident benefits, but usually the amounts set aside were too low to give them much relief. When a worker was killed or maimed, the family depended on relatives or neighbors for help.

Immigrant Labor

Outside the South, factory owners turned to unskilled immigrants for the muscle needed in factories, mills, railroads, and heavy construction. In Philadelphia native-born Americans and recent German immigrants dominated the highly skilled metal-working trades, and Irish immigrants remained in unskilled occupations until the 1890s, when the "new immigrants" from southern and eastern Europe replaced them (see Chapter 19). On the West Coast, Chinese immigrants performed the dirtiest, most physically demanding jobs in mining, canning, and railroad construction.

Immigrants who lived frugally in a boardinghouse and worked an eighty-four-hour week could save fifteen dollars a month, far more than they could have earned in the old country. Intent on improving their economic standing, many immigrants readily accepted the exhausting work schedule and volunteered for overtime work. One worker summed up the typical routine: "A good job, save money, work all time, go home, sleep, no spend."

Rural peasants from southern and eastern Europe who immigrated after 1890 found abandoning their traditional work patterns and adjusting to factory schedules difficult. Changing daylight patterns shaped farm work, but the relentless speed of the machines dictated factory operations. When immigrant workers resisted the tempo of factory work, or drank on the job or took unexcused absences, employers enforced discipline. Some sponsored temperance societies and Sunday schools to teach punctuality and sobriety. Others published rule books outlining specific codes of behavior. When persuasion proved ineffective, employers cut wages and put workers on the piecework system, paying them only for items produced.

Workers sometimes fought attempts to tighten discipline by demanding a say in production quotas. Seeking to re-create a village atmosphere, immigrant workers also often persuaded their employers to hire friends and relatives. Factory workers who came from farms where the entire family had toiled together sought to work with as many family members as possible.

In the face of immigrant labor's desire for a sociable, humane work environment, the proliferation of machines in factories kindled employer-employee tensions. When the factory owners' desire to increase output coincided with the immigrants' desire to maximize income, long hours at the machines were welcomed. But when employers cut wages or unreasonably accelerated the work schedule, unrest boiled to the surface.

Women and Work in Industrializing America

Marital status as well as social class shaped women's work experiences. Married women of all classes accepted the doctrine of separate spheres for men and women (see Chapter 20). Believing women uniquely capable of nuturing children, married women tended to remain home rearing children and looking after the household; men labored in factories and offices. Well-to-do women hired maids and cooks to ease their burdens; working-class married women, in contrast, often had to earn money at home to make ends meet.

Working at home for wages—sewing, buttonmaking, taking in boarders, or doing laundry—predated industrialization. However, economic expansion and the growth of cities enabled unscrupulous entrepreneurs to exploit the home work force. Cigar manufacturers would buy or lease a tenement and require "their" families to live there. Working-class married women and their children often labored long hours in their crowded apartments to finish needlework for the garment industry.

Unlike these married women with little choice but to accept home work, working-class single women often saw outside work as an opportunity. In 1870 only 13 percent of all women worked outside the home, but between 1870 and 1900 the number of women working outside the home nearly tripled, and by the turn of the century women made up 17 percent of the country's labor force. Many women workers abandoned domestic employment for better-paying, less demeaning jobs in the textile, food-processing, and garment industries.

Changes in agriculture prompted countless young farm women to seek employment in the industrial sector, and young immigrant women, too, worked in factories to increase their families' meager income. Factory owners welcomed young foreign-born women as a ready source of inexpensive unskilled labor; but because many of them would soon marry and leave the work force, employers treated them as temporary help. Young women in the clothing industry earned as little as five dollars for seventy hours of work but widely relished the independence of working. Although most of their income went to their parents, they delighted in having a little spending money.

When the typewriter and the telephone came into general use in the 1890s, office work became more specialized, and women with high-school educations moved into clerical and secretarial positions earlier filled by men. The clean, safe working conditions and relatively good pay attracted them; a first-rate typist could earn seven dollars a week. Even though women were excluded from managerial positions, office jobs carried higher prestige and offered steadier work than employment in factories or shops.

Nonetheless, women's work outside the home was seen as temporary. Society defined women's real achievement in terms of marriage and the family. A woman experienced vicarious satisfaction when her husband received a promotion or her son earned a raise. Few people imagined that women could attain national or even local prominence in the emerging corporate order.

Hard Work and the Gospel of Success

Influential opinion molders in these years preached that any man could achieve success in the new industrial era. In *Ragged Dick* (1867) and scores of later tales, minister-turned-novelist Horatio Alger recounted the adventures of poor but honest lads who rise through ambition, initiative, and self-discipline. Life is a struggle in Alger's America, but success comes from seizing the unexpected opportunities that fortune thrusts in one's path. In his widely read stories, shoeshine boys stop runaway horses or save children from drowning and are rewarded for their bravery by rich benefactors who give them a start in business. Andrew Carnegie served as proof that the United States remained the land of opportunity and "rags to riches."

Recent studies reveal that Carnegie was a rare exception. Ninety-five percent of industrial leaders had middle- and upper-class backgrounds. However, small companies provided opportunities for skilled immigrants and native-born working-class Americans to rise to the top. In Paterson, New Jersey, the most successful owners of small to medium-sized industrial companies between 1850 and 1880 had begun as workers, broadened their skills through apprenticeships, and then opened their own factories. Few reaped immense fortunes, but many attained substantial incomes.

Unskilled workers found far fewer opportunities for advancement. Many did move into semiskilled and even skilled positions that allowed them to increase their earnings and even to own a home. However, most immigrants, especially the Irish and Italians, progressed far more slowly than the sons of middle- and upper-class Americans who enjoyed educational advantages and family financial backing. Upward mobility for unskilled workers generally meant mobility *within* the working class. Immigrants who got ahead went from rags to respectability, not rags to riches.

Between 1860 and 1900 real wages rose 31 percent for unskilled workers and 74 percent for skilled workers. But high incidences of injury and unemployment kept unskilled immigrant workers in a precarious position. Even in a prosperous year such as 1890, one in every five workers was unemployed for at least a month. During the depressions of the 1870s and 1890s, wage cuts, extended layoffs, and unemployment pushed those at the base of the industrial work force to the brink of starvation.

The question of economic mobility in the late nineteenth century is complex. At the top, the rich amassed enormous fortunes; in 1890 a mere 10 percent of American families owned 73 percent of the national wealth. At the bottom, recent immigrants struggled to survive, with only 45 percent of U.S. industrial laborers taking in earnings above the $500 poverty line. Nevertheless, between these extremes, skilled immigrant workers and shopkeepers swelled the middle class. The standard of living rose for millions of Americans, although the gap between rich and poor remained an abyss.

Labor Unions and Industrial Conflict

Toiling long hours for low wages, often under dangerous conditions, some workers turned to labor unions. Unions, however, faced formidable obstacles. For one thing, employers could hire poor immigrants to work for lower wages than unionized help or to serve as strikebreakers. For another, ethnic and racial divisions hampered labor organization as immigrant workers, who tended to socialize and marry within their own tight groups, resisted appeals to unionize. In addition, not only did relatively prosperous skilled workers feel little in common with low-paid laborers, but also workers (skilled and unskilled alike) in radically different work environments saw little reason for cooperation.

Two groups, the National Labor Union and the Knights of Labor, attempted to build mass labor movements but failed. The most successful late-nineteenth-century labor movement, the American Federation of Labor (AFL), was an amalgamation of powerful craft unions that represented only a fraction of the labor force. With unions so weak, labor unrest often led to unplanned wildcat walkouts that sometimes exploded into violence.

Organizing the Workers

The Civil War marked a watershed in the rise of organized labor. Small craft unions, with goals of fighting wage reductions and providing sickness benefits, had existed since the eighteenth century, but after the war labor leaders sought to increase union clout. To many, the answer lay in the formation of a single association that would transcend craft lines and draw a mass membership.

William H. Sylvis, elected president of the Iron Moulders' International Union in 1863, dreamed of creating such a superunion. Condemning "the monied aristocracy—proud, imperious and dishonest, . . . blasting and withering everything it [comes] in contact with," Sylvis quickly built his union from "a mere pygmy" to a membership of 8,500. In 1866 he called a convention that formed the National Labor Union (NLU). The new organization embraced an eight-hour workday, currency and banking reform, an end to convict labor, a federal department of labor, and restrictions on immigration, particularly of Chinese. Under Sylvis's leadership the NLU also endorsed the cause of working women and elected the head of a union of female laundry workers as one of its national officers. The NLU urged African-American workers to organize as well, although in racially separate unions.

After an iron founders' strike failed in winter 1866–1867, Sylvis concluded that national political reform held the key to labor's future. In 1868 a number of reformers, including woman-suffrage advocates Susan B. Anthony and Elizabeth Cady Stanton, attended the NLU convention. However, Sylvis's sudden death in 1869 shattered the NLU, which disintegrated by 1873.

The dream of a national labor movement lived on in a new organization, the Noble and Holy Order of the Knights of Labor. Founded in 1869 by Philadelphia tailors as a secret society modeled on the Masonic order (see Chapter 10), the Knights

Ethnic and Racial Hatred

Conservative business owners used racist advertising, such as this trade card stigmatizing Chinese laundry workers, to promote their own products and to associate their company with patriotism.

welcomed all wage earners; they excluded only bankers, physicians, lawyers, stockbrokers, professional gamblers, and liquor dealers. The Knights advocated equal pay for women, an end to child and convict labor, a graduated income tax, and cooperative employer-employee ownership of factories, mines, and other businesses.

At first the Knights grew slowly, in part because the Catholic church forbade Catholics to join. In the 1880s membership skyrocketed after the church lifted its prohibition and an Irish Catholic, Terence V. Powderly, became the Knights' head. The eloquent Powderly orchestrated successes in a series of labor clashes and brought in thousands of new members.

The Knights of Labor reflected its idealistic origins and Powderly's collaborative vision. Powderly condemned strikes as "a relic of barbarism" and organized producer and consumer cooperatives. He also advocated temperance and offered membership to both African-Americans and women. By 1886 women made up 10 percent of the Knights' membership.

Powderly and the Knights supported immigration restriction and a total ban on Chinese immigration. Union members feared that immigrants would steal jobs by working too cheaply. Westerners, especially Californians, saw the Chinese as a major threat. In 1877 a San Francisco demonstration for the eight-hour day turned into a riot that destroyed twenty-five Chinese laundries and terrorized the local Chinese population. Congress passed the Chinese Exclusion Act in 1882, placing a ten-year moratorium on Chinese immigration, but sporadic anti-Chinese violence continued.

Although inspired by Powderly's vision of a harmonious and cooperative future, most rank-and-file members cared more about immediate issues such as wage cuts, production speedups, and deteriorating working conditions. Most, moreover, rejected Powderly's antistrike position. In 1883–1884 spontaneous local strikes led by Knights gained reluctant support from the national leadership. However, in 1885 when Jay Gould tried to drive the Knights out of his Wabash Railroad by firing active union members, Powderly recognized that the union's survival was at stake. He therefore authorized a strike against the Wabash and ordered Knights working for other lines to refuse to handle Wabash cars. With his railroad crippled, Gould halted his campaign against the Knights.

Membership soared; by 1886, 6,000 locals served more than 700,000 workers. That fall the Knights entered politics, mounting campaigns in nearly two hundred towns and cities, electing several mayors and judges, and helping a dozen congressmen to gain office. In state legislatures they secured passage of laws banning convict labor, and at the national level they lobbied successfully for legislation outlawing the importation of foreign contract labor. Conservatives warned darkly that the Knights could cripple the economy and take over the country.

In fact, the Knights' strength soon waned. Leaders lost control of the membership because of the union's explosive growth, and a series of failed (and unauthorized) strikes left members disillusioned. The national reaction to the Haymarket riot also contributed to the union's decline. By the late 1880s, the Knights of Labor was a shadow of its former self. But it had given major impetus to the labor movement and awakened a sense of group solidarity in hundreds of thousands of workers.

Even as the Knights became weaker, another labor organization, pursuing more immediate and practical goals, was growing strong. The skilled craft unions had long felt threatened by the Knights' broad base and emphasis on sweeping reform goals. In May 1886 the craft unions left the Knights to form the American Federation of Labor (AFL), which replaced the Knights' grand visions with practical tactics aimed at "bread-and-butter issues." "We have no ultimate ends," one skilled craft official commented; "we are going on from day to day. We fight only for immediate objectives."

Samuel Gompers, an English immigrant cigar maker who headed the AFL from its formation until his death in 1924, believed in "trade unionism, pure and simple." Having lost faith in utopian social reforms and catch-all labor organizations, he believed that "the poor, the hungry, have not the strength to engage in a conflict even when life is at stake." To stand up to corporations, Gompers argued, labor had to harness the bargaining power of skilled workers, who were not easily replaced, and concentrate on practical goals of raising wages and reducing hours.

A master tactician, Gompers believed that large-scale industrial organization required comparable labor organization. At the same time, he knew that the individual skilled craft unions were committed to controlling their own affairs. To meet the challenge of persuading workers to join forces without violating their sense of craft autonomy, Gompers organized the AFL as a *federation* of trade unions, each retaining control of its own members but linked by an executive council to coordinate strategy. Focusing the federation's efforts on short-term improvements in wages and hours, Gompers sidestepped divisive political issues. The AFL advocated an eight-hour workday, employers' liability, and mine-safety laws. By 1904 the AFL had grown to more than 1.6 million members.

As a whole, although late-nineteenth-century labor organizations held up ideals toward which workers might strive, these organizations remained weak. They enlisted less than 5 percent of the work force. Split between skilled artisans and common laborers, separated along ethnic and religious lines, and divided over tactics, the unions enjoyed only occasional success against the growing power of corporate enterprise. More often, they watched from the sidelines as unorganized workers launched sudden strikes that sometimes turned violent.

Strikes and Labor Violence

From 1881 to 1905, 7 million workers participated in some 37,000 strikes, some of which involved property damage and looting. Shaken middle-class Americans, unaware of the hardships endured by workers, feared that they were on the verge of a class war.

The Wall Street crash of 1873 triggered a major depression. Businesses collapsed, tramps roamed New York and Chicago streets, and labor unrest mounted. In 1877 a wildcat railroad strike turned deadly. Ignited by a wage reduction on the Baltimore and Ohio Railroad in July, the strike exploded up and down the rail lines and spread quickly from coast to coast. Rioters in Pittsburgh torched Union Depot and the Pennsylvania Railroad roundhouse. By the time newly inaugurated president Rutherford

B. Hayes called out the troops and quelled the strike, nearly one hundred people had died and two-thirds of U.S. railroads stood idle.

The strike stunned middle-class America. Hysterical voices proclaimed that "if the club of the policeman, knocking out the brains of the rioter, will answer, then well and good, [but if not] then bullets and bayonets . . . constitute the one remedy." Employers exploited the public hysteria to crack down on labor. Many required workers to sign "yellow dog" contracts, in which they promised not to strike or join a union. Some hired Pinkerton agents to serve as a private police force and, as in the 1877 rail strike, relied on the U.S. Army (or state militias) to suppress unrest.

The 1880s saw more strikes and violence. On May 1, 1886, 340,000 workers walked off their jobs to support the eight-hour workday. On May 3 Chicago police shot and killed four strikers at the McCormick Harvester plant. At a protest rally the next evening in the city's Haymarket Square, someone threw a bomb from a nearby building, killing or fatally wounding seven policemen. In turn, the police fired wildly into the crowd and slew four demonstrators. Business leaders and middle-class citizens lashed out at labor activists, particularly the Haymarket meeting sponsors, most of whom were associated with German anarchism. Eight were arrested. No evidence connected them directly to the bomb throwing, but all were convicted, and four were executed; a fifth committed suicide in prison. Illinois governor John Altgeld pardoned the three survivors in 1893. As Americans became convinced that a deadly foreign conspiracy gripped the nation, animosity toward labor unions intensified.

Confrontations between business and labor continued into the 1890s. Federal troops were called out to crush strikes by Idaho silver miners and Carnegie steelworkers. The most systematic use of troops to smash unions came in 1894 in a strike against the Pullman Palace Car Company. George Pullman, a self-taught pioneer in the manufacture of elegant railroad sleeping and dining cars, had constructed a factory and a town called Pullman south of Chicago. The carefully planned community provided Pullman workers with brick houses, parks, playgrounds, a bank, a library, and even a sewage-treatment plant. However, Pullman policed workers' activities, banned saloons, and insisted that his properties turn a profit.

When the depression of 1893 hit, Pullman responded to declining orders by slashing wages. But he did not lower rents. Thousands of workers joined the newly formed American Railway Union and went on strike. They were led by a fiery young organizer, Eugene V. Debs, who vowed "to strip the mask of hypocrisy from the pretended philanthropist and show him to the world as an oppressor of labor." Union members working for other railroads refused to switch Pullman cars, paralyzing rail traffic in and out of Chicago and over the western half of the United States.

In response to the crisis, the General Managers' Association, composed of top railroad executives, decided to break the union. After importing strikebreakers, the organization asked U.S. attorney general Richard Olney, who sat on the board of directors of three major railroads, for a federal injunction against the strikers for allegedly refusing to move rail cars carrying U.S. mail. In fact, however, union members had volunteered to switch mail cars onto trains that did not carry Pullman cars; it was the railroads' managers who had delayed the mail by refusing to dispatch trains without the full complement of cars. Olney, supported by President Grover Cleveland, cited the Sherman Anti-Trust Act and secured an injunction against leaders of the American Railway Union for restraint of commerce. When the union refused to order its members back to work, Debs was arrested and federal troops poured in. During the ensuing rioting, 700 freight cars were burned, thirteen people died, and fifty-three were wounded. The strike was crushed.

By exploiting the popular identification of strikers with anarchism and violence, corporate leaders hobbled organized labor's ability to bargain. When the Supreme Court upheld Debs's prison sentence and legalized the use of injunctions against labor unions (*In re Debs*, 1895), business gained a powerful new weapon against labor. Aggressive employer associations and conservative federal, state, and local officials hamstrung efforts to build a strong working-class movement. Blocked by officials and frustrated by court decisions, American unions could not expand their base of support. Not until the 1930s would the labor movement regain the vitality sapped by post–Civil War turmoil and shed its negative public image.

Social Thinkers Probe for Alternatives

The widespread industrial turmoil was particularly unsettling when juxtaposed with growing evidence of working-class destitution. A general public debate considered the social meaning of the new industrial order. At stake was a critical issue: should government become the mechanism for helping the poor and regulating big business?

Defenders of capitalism embraced a philosophy of laissez-faire ("hands-off"), insisting that government should never attempt to control business. They cited the argument of Scottish economist Adam Smith (1723–1790) that self-interest acted as an "invisible hand" in the marketplace, automatically balancing the supply of and demand for goods and services. In "The Gospel of Wealth," an influential essay published in 1889, Andrew Carnegie applied British scientist Charles Darwin's evolutionary theories to human society. "The law of competition," Carnegie wrote, "may be sometimes hard for the individual, [but] it is best for the race, because it insures the survival of the fittest in every department." Ignoring the contemporary scramble among businesses to eliminate competition and to form trusts, Carnegie praised unregulated competition as a source of positive long-term social benefits.

Yale professor William Graham Sumner shared Carnegie's Social Darwinism, as this conservative, laissez-faire outlook came to be known. Unchangeable laws controlled the social order, he contended; "a drunkard in the gutter is just where he ought to be. . . . The law of survival of the fittest was not made by man, and it cannot be abrogated by man. We can only, by interfering with it, produce the survival of the unfittest." Social theorists, sentimental humanitarians, and "labor fakers" intent on uplifting the poor and needy actually harmed the "forgotten man"—the hardworking individual whose taxes were expected to fund their do-good schemes. The state, declared Sumner, owed its citizens only law, order, and basic political rights.

Social Darwinism did not go unchallenged. In *Dynamic Sociology* (1883), geologist Lester Frank Ward argued that human will *could* circumvent the supposed "laws" of nature. Just as scientists had bred superior livestock, government experts could regulate big business, protect society's weaker members, and prevent the reckless exploitation of natural resources.

Henry George, a newspaper editor and economic theorist, proposed to solve the nation's uneven distribution of wealth through the "single tax." In *Progress and Poverty* (1879), he proposed that government tax the "unearned increment" that speculators reaped from rising land prices. These funds could then ameliorate the misery caused by industrialization. Americans could enjoy the benefits of socialism—a state-controlled economic system that distributed resources according to need—without abandoning capitalism.

Another newspaper editor, Edward Bellamy, turned to fiction to evoke visions of a harmonious industrialized society. In *Looking Backward* (1888), Bellamy's protagonist, Julian West, falls asleep in 1888 and awakens in 2000 to find a nation without poverty or strife, thanks to a centralized, state-run economy. Centralization and a new religion of solidarity have created a society in which everyone works for the common welfare. Bellamy's utopian novel resonated among middle-class Americans. Fearful of corporate power and working-class violence, they formed nearly 500 Nationalist clubs to implement Bellamy's scheme.

Ward, George, and Bellamy did not deny the industrial order's benefits; rather, envisioning a harmonious society whose members all worked together, they sought to humanize it. Marxist socialists advanced a different view. In *Das Kapital*

(1867) and other works, German radical Karl Marx argued that the labor required to produce a commodity was the only true measure of that commodity's value. Profit made by a capitalist employer was "surplus value" appropriated from exploited workers. Competition among capitalists would increase, Marx predicted; wages would decline to starvation levels, and finally the impoverished working class would seize control of the state *and* the means of production and distribution. Class struggle would lead to a classless utopia in which the state would "wither away" and exploitation would end. But Marxism had little appeal in late-nineteenth-century America beyond a handful of mainly German-born immigrants. More alarming were the anarchists, mainly immigrants, who rejected Marxist discipline and preached the destruction of capitalism, the violent overthrow of the state, and the immediate introduction of a stateless utopia.

CONCLUSION

In the Republic's early years, Thomas Jefferson had warned of industrialization's threat to American virtue and democracy, even as Alexander Hamilton had promoted industrialization as essential to national prosperity and greatness. By 1900 Americans realized that both men had been right. Industrialization *had* catapulted the United States to world power, lowered the cost of goods, generated thousands of jobs, and made available a wide range of consumer products. But as Jefferson had foreseen, the cost was high. Savage competition, exploited workers, shady business practices, polluted landscapes, and the erosion of traditional skills had accompanied the rise of giant corporations. Labor violence, urban slums, and grinding poverty underlined the high cost.

Americans were uncertain about the new industrial order. Enjoying the higher standard of living that industrialization made possible, but fearing capitalist power and social chaos, they tried to keep the material benefits while alleviating the social harm. The Interstate Commerce Act, the Sherman Anti-Trust Act, and the vogue of Nationalist clubs testify to middle-class qualms. In the Progressive Era of the early twentieth century (see Chapter 22), Americans would redouble their efforts to create political and social solutions to the changes wrought by economic transformation.

CHRONOLOGY

1837 Magnetic telegraph invented.

1859 First oil well drilled, in Titusville, Pennsylvania.

1866 National Labor Union founded.

1869 First transcontinental railroad completed.
Knights of Labor organized.

1870 Standard Oil Company established.

1873 Panic of 1873 triggers a depression lasting until 1879.

1876 Alexander Graham Bell invents and patents the telephone.
Thomas A. Edison opens research laboratory at Menlo Park, New Jersey.

1877 Edison invents the phonograph.
Railway workers stage the first nationwide strike.

1879 Henry George, *Progress and Poverty*.
Edison perfects the incandescent lamp.

1882 Standard Oil Trust established.
Edison opens the first electric power station on Pearl Street in New York City.
Chinese Exclusion Act.

1883 Railroads divide the country into time zones. Lester Frank Ward, *Dynamic Sociology*.

1886 American Federation of Labor (AFL) formed. Police and demonstrators clash at Haymarket Square in Chicago.

1887 Interstate Commerce Act establishes the Interstate Commerce Commission.

1888 Edward Bellamy, *Looking Backward*.

1889 Andrew Carnegie, "The Gospel of Wealth."

1890 Sherman Anti-Trust Act.

1892 Standard Oil of New Jersey and General Electric formed.
Steelworkers strike at Homestead, Pennsylvania.
Silver miners strike in Idaho.

1893 Panic of 1893 triggers a depression lasting until 1897.

1894 Pullman Palace Car workers strike, supported by the American Railway Union.

1901 J. Pierpont Morgan organizes United States Steel.

FOR FURTHER READING

Edward L. Ayers, *The Promise of the New South: Life After Reconstruction* (1992). A comprehensive overview of economic and social change within the post–Civil War South.

Albro Martin, *Railroads Triumphant: The Growth, Rejection, and Rebirth of a Vital American Force* (1992). An excellent analysis of the railroad's impact on industrial and urban development in the late nineteenth century.

J. Carroll Moody and Alice Kessler-Harris, eds., *Perspectives on American Labor History: The Problems of Synthesis* (1989). Essays on the role of gender and class within the American labor movement.

William Serrin, *Homestead: The Glory and Tragedy of an American Steel Town* (1992). A balanced account of a steel-making community.

Kim Voss, *The Making of American Exceptionalism: The Knights of Labor and Class Formation in the Nineteenth Century* (1993). An important comparative analysis of American labor's attempts to mobilize workers in the face of business opposition.

CHAPTER 19

The Transformation of Urban America

Explosive growth transformed U.S. cities in the late nineteenth century. Between 1870 and 1900 New Orleans's population doubled, Buffalo's tripled, and Chicago's increased more than fivefold. By 1900 Philadelphia, New York City, and Chicago had each passed the 1-million-person mark and 40 percent of all Americans lived in cities.

This spectacular urban growth, fueled by the influx of 11 million immigrants, created a dynamic environment for job development. Lured by the prospect of finding work, newcomers to America provided cheap labor for countless small businesses and industries. In turn, these developments made possible an unparalleled concentration of resources and markets that dramatically stimulated national economic expansion. Like the frontier, the city symbolized opportunity for all comers.

But the city's unprecedented size and diversity threatened traditional American

(Right) Immigrant children, 1890 (detail); photograph by Jacob Riis

expectations of community life and stability. A medley of immigrant groups contended with each other and with native-born Americans for jobs, power, and influence. Rapid growth strained city services, generating terrible housing and sanitation problems.

Native-born American city dwellers found the noise, stench, and congestion disturbing. They worried about the newcomers' squalid tenements, fondness for drink, and strange social customs. Reformers who set out to "clean up" the cities aimed not only to improve the physical environment but also to destroy the distinctive customs of the immigrant cultures. The immigrants, resenting attacks on their way of life, fought to protect their traditions. The late nineteenth century thus witnessed an intense struggle among diverse urban constituencies to control the city politically and to benefit from its economic and cultural potential.

Urban Expansion

Between 1840 and 1900 a critical need for factory sites, housing, and offices transformed the physical appearance of U.S. cities. Residential neighborhoods, parks, downtown business districts, and commercial and manufacturing areas blossomed. New transportation systems moved commuters on streetcars, trains, electric trolleys, and subway cars. Suburbs developed along railroad lines in the countryside, where land was cheap and the environment pleasant.

The New Urban World

The rapid growth of cities after the Civil War created a national urban network—a web of regional metropolises, specialized manufacturing cities, and smaller communities of varying size and function. Major cities such as New York, Boston, and San Francisco became regional centers providing manufacturing plants, banks, and financial services for the surrounding towns and countryside. In the 1850s Chicago emerged as the upper Midwest's center for shipping and marketing lumber, meat, and grain. Thirty years later its factories employed 75,000 people, the largest industrial work force west of the Appalachians. Smaller cities specialized in particular products or processes: Holyoke, Massachusetts, in paper; Minneapolis, Minnesota, in milling and lumber; and Corning, New York, in glass.

Brisk expansion changed urban life forever. Small towns followed the seasonal rhythms of farming, but cities pulsed with people rushing to meet schedules and to beat deadlines. Although small-town residents knew their neighbors, city dwellers lived in a world of strangers. Time itself changed in the city as urbanites worked and played late into the night.

A Revolution in Transportation

Until the early nineteenth century, most cities were compact, densely settled communities of perhaps three square miles. Within these "walking" cities, rich and poor lived in close proximity. The advent of new transportation systems turned these cities inside out. The rich moved to the city's edge, and the poor relocated inward, crowding into abandoned mansions subdivided into apartments.

The first urban transportation networks operating at regular schedules over fixed routes appeared in New York in the 1820s; within two decades horse-drawn streetcars running along rails embedded in the streets had replaced the early, rough-riding stagecoaches. By the 1880s, 415 streetcar companies were carrying 188 million passengers a year over more than 6,000 miles of track, providing easy transportation between city dwellers' work and their homes. The horsecars, however, presented problems. Observers recoiled as they watched drivers whip horses straining to pull the crowded cars or as they saw fallen animals destroyed where they lay. In New York alone, an estimated 15,000 horses died from overwork each year in the 1880s. In addition, horse droppings fouled city streets. In 1900 health officials in Rochester, New York, estimated that the city's 15,000 horses produced enough manure every year to fill a hole one acre in area and 175 feet deep and to breed 16 billion flies.

Steam railroads were an obvious replacement. As early as 1849, fifty-nine commuter trains made the daily trip into Boston from as far away as fifteen miles. But because steam engines were not efficient for short runs, city officials began exploring more flexible alternatives, such as cable cars and electric streetcars.

Chicago pioneered the most extensive cable-car system, which operated over eighty-six miles of track by 1887. More sanitary, better on hills, and quieter than horsecars, cable cars nonetheless had drawbacks, too, particularly high construction costs. Eventually, cable cars proved profitable only in hilly cities.

By the 1890s electric streetcars or trolleys had replaced horsecars and cable cars in most cities. In effect, trolley companies subsidized long-distance commuting by charging a fixed price per ride rather than by distance. Thus families could move farther and farther from city centers without increasing their transportation costs. Urban sprawl ensued. Many streetcar companies lost money in their operations because of low population densities along their lines but earned towering profits by buying and selling suburban land.

Radiating outward from the city center like the spokes of a wheel, streetcar lines revitalized cities by requiring crosstown commuters to pass through the downtown. The arrangement improved commercial opportunities in the central business district, and entrepreneurs hastened to capitalize on this potential. In 1874 John Wanamaker of Philadelphia turned an old downtown railroad freight depot into an elaborate department store. Merchants in other cities duplicated his success. The inexpensive convenience of traveling by trolley made shopping downtown a new form of recreation.

A Mobile Population

The expansion of streetcar systems and the completion of regional railroad networks dramatically increased residential instability as more and more people succumbed to the fever to move. People fled congested neighborhoods for outlying residential areas—now conveniently accessible by streetcar—to gain open space and fresh air. Fashionable homes sprouted on the city's periphery. The availability of larger houses at lower prices also lured people to the suburbs.

Movement *between* cities paralleled the frantic residential shifts *within* cities. Families commonly moved from city to city to boost their income or to improve their living conditions. Most cities, although growing in overall numbers, lost more than half their current inhabitants every decade. Historical demographers calculate that most U.S. cities experienced an astonishing turnover of three to four times their total population every ten years.

Contemporaries deplored the speed and scale of residential change. They viewed the migration of the middle and upper classes as a selfish attempt to escape responsibility for improving inner-city neighborhoods. Well-to-do city dwellers might be concerned about the poor, but they put the happiness, health, and safety of their own families first, moving to neighborhoods with better housing and an improved quality of life.

Thus mobility and change represented the norm in nineteenth-century urban society. New transportation systems permitted residential movement, and rich and poor alike freely changed residences and jobs in search of new paths to happiness and success. The city beckoned to the restless and the ambitious.

Migrants and Immigrants

As the new industries concentrated in urban settings demanded thousands of new workers, the promise of good wages and plentiful jobs attracted many rural and small-town dwellers to the cities. So great was the migration from rural areas, especially in New England, that some farm communities vanished from the map.

Young women led the exodus. The growing commercialization and specialization of agriculture had turned much farm labor into male work. Mail-order sales of factory-made goods meanwhile reduced the need for women's work on subsistence tasks. So young farm women flocked to the cities, where they competed with immigrant, African-American, and city-born women for jobs.

From 1860 to 1890, the prospect of a better life also attracted nearly 10 million northern European immigrants to American cities, where they joined the more than 4 million who had settled there in the 1840s and 1850s. Their numbers included 3 million Germans; 2 million English, Scottish, and Welsh; and 1.5 million Irish. Moreover, by 1900 more than 800,000 French-Canadians had migrated southward to work in the New England mills, and nearly 1 million Scandinavians farmed the rich lands of Wisconsin and Minnesota. Then, in the three decades after 1890, more than 18 million "new immigrants" joined these "old immigrants." Predominantly peasants, they came from southern and eastern Europe.

The overwhelming majority of both old and new immigrants settled in cities in the northeastern and north-central states. Dreams fired by exuberant letters from earlier immigrants—and by the extravagant claims of steamship lines seeking passengers—brought throngs of new arrivals in search of work and fresh beginnings. The numbers were staggering. In 1890 New York City contained twice as many Irish as Dublin, as many Germans as Hamburg, half as many Italians as Naples, and two and a half times the Jewish population of Warsaw. Four out of five people in New York City were immigrants or the children of immigrants.

Overpopulation, crop failure, famine, and industrial depression had driven some of these immigrants from their homelands. However, many people, especially single young men, immigrated in the belief that the United States held a better future than their homeland. An eighteen-year-old Norwegian explained his decision: "My father is a

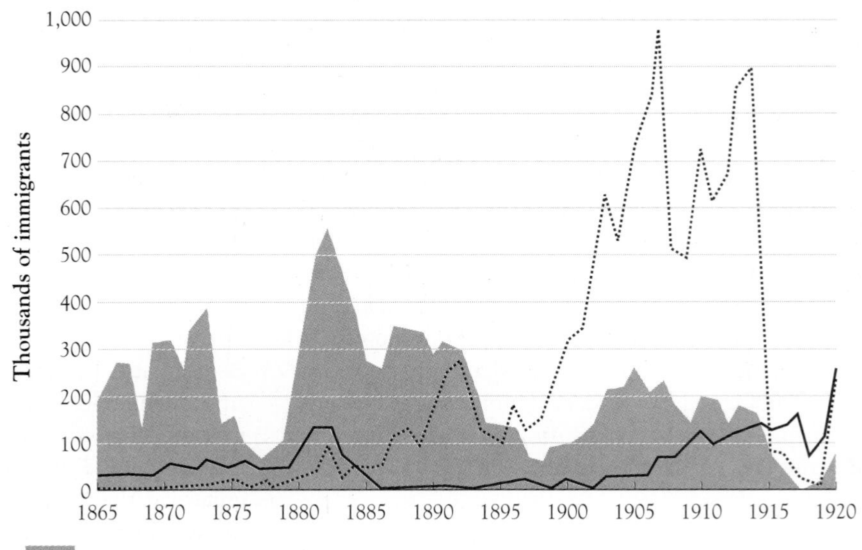

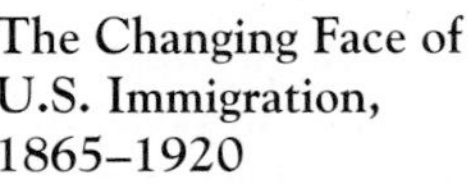

The Changing Face of U.S. Immigration, 1865–1920

Between 1865 and 1895, the majority of newcomers to America hailed from northern and western Europe. But the early twentieth century witnessed a surge of immigration from southern and eastern Europe.

Jakob Mithelstadt and Family, 1905

The Mithelstadts were Russian Germans who arrived in New York City on the S.S. Pretoria. *The poorest immigrants traveled in steerage, below-deck cargo areas that lacked portholes and originally housed the cables to the ship's rudder.*

schoolteacher and has, besides me, two younger sons, so that it often strains his resources to keep us in school here. . . . I have come to feel that the most sensible thing I can do is to emigrate to America."

The transatlantic journey, cramped and often stormy, featured poor food, little privacy, and rudimentary sanitary facilities. Immigrants arrived tired, fearful, and in some cases very sick. Then customs officials examined them for physical handicaps and contagious diseases. After 1891 those with a "loathsome" infection such as leprosy or a sexually transmitted disease were deported. Immigrants who passed the physical examination then had their names recorded. If a customs official had difficulty pronouncing a foreign name, he Anglicized it. One German Jew became flustered when asked for his name and mumbled "Schoyn vergessen [I forget]." The inspector, who did not know Yiddish, wrote, "Sean Ferguson."

In 1892 the federal government established a facility for admitting immigrants on Ellis Island, replacing a nearby facility run by the state of New York on Castle Garden. Here America's newest residents exchanged foreign currency for U.S. dollars, purchased railroad tickets, and arranged lodgings. Those who arrived with enough cash, including many Germans and Scandinavians, commonly traveled west to Chicago, Milwaukee, and the prairies beyond. But most of the Irish and Italians, largely from poor peasant backgrounds, stayed in eastern cities such as Boston, New York, and Philadelphia, where they filled the lowest-paying jobs. The Irish and Italians who did go west typically made the trip in stages, moving from job to job along the railroad and canal systems.

Adjusting to Urban Society

Immigrants tended to cluster together to ease the transition to life in a new society. In 1890 a reporter observed that if a map of New York City's streets were colored in by nationality, it "would show more stripes than on the skin of a zebra, and more colors than any rainbow."

Most newcomers preferred to live near others not merely of their own nationality but from their own region or village. New York's Lower East Side held not a single "Little Italy" but dozens of them, inhabited by Neapolitans and Calabrians at Mulberry Bend, Genoese on Baxter Street, northern Italians west of Broadway, and Tyrolese Italians on Sixty-ninth Street near the Hudson River.

Within these neighborhoods, immigrants endured incredibly crowded conditions. In New York City, where real-estate costs soared highest, landlords built virtually windowless five-story buildings on lots only twenty-five feet wide. In 1879 New York reformers secured passage of a law that forced landlords to construct buildings with central ten foot by four foot air shafts. Dubbed "dumbbell" tenements because of their shape, the buildings squeezed stairs, halls, and common bathrooms into the narrow central sections. By the 1890s a single New York block typically contained ten dumbbell tenements with between 2,000 and 4,000 immigrant residents. The worst conditions flourished in Manhattan, but in 1902 investigators in Buffalo, New York, found sixty Polish immigrants living in a single small row house.

Nonetheless, many immigrant families enjoyed richly textured lives. Within their tight ethnic neighborhoods, immigrants could speak their native language, purchase traditional foods, attend Old World church services, and celebrate their festivals. Ironically, reformers' attempts to change immigrants' behavior often heightened the newcomers' sense of ethnic identity.

Rates of assimilation varied. Not surprisingly, those whose work drew them into the currents of city life often shed their old ways and embraced the new U.S. culture; for them, dreams of upward mobility became reality. Older immigrant women, whose world revolved around their tenement flats and immediate neighborhood, tended to cling to their customs. As immigrant children learned the English language and American ways in public schools, many rejected their parents' Old World accents, dress, and customs. For the second and third generation of immigrant families, the appeal of the ethnic neighborhoods faded.

Some immigrant groups adjusted more easily than others. Those with skilled trades and familiarity with Anglo-American customs had relatively few problems. Ethnic groups that formed a substantial percentage of a city's population also had a major advantage. The Irish of Boston, New York City, and Chicago, as well as the Germans of Milwaukee, dominated local government and church organizations and eased the path for their fellow immigrants.

The larger the immigrant group was, the more effectively organized were its churches, newspapers, schools, banks, and benevolent associations. The New York Hebrew Free Loan Society (founded in 1892), one of numerous self-help organizations set up in this era, provided interest-free loans of up to $200 to Jewish immigrants who wanted to establish their own businesses. But the power of the larger immigrant groups sometimes made the adjustment to American society more difficult for members of the smaller groups. The English and Germans who dominated the building trades, for example, limited the numbers of Italians hired. In 1900 only 18 percent of New York's skilled brick masons were Italians, but 55 percent of its barbers and 97 percent of its poorly paid bootblacks were recent newcomers from Italy.

The smaller immigrant groups sometimes had trouble adjusting to American society, moreover, because many of their members did not intend to stay in the United States. Young Italian males often immigrated to America to earn enough money to return home, where they hoped to buy land or to establish a business. They made little effort to learn English or to understand American customs. Of the Italians who migrated to New York before 1914, nearly 50 percent went back to Italy.

By 1900, whatever the degree of adaptation to the English language and U.S. culture, all immigrant groups faced increasing hostility from native-born Americans, who not only disliked the newcomers' social customs but also feared their growing influence.

Slums and Ghettos

Every major city had run-down, overcrowded slum neighborhoods, created when landlords subdivided old buildings and packed in too many residents. The poorer the renters were, the worse the slums were. Slums became ghettos when laws, prejudice, and community pressure prevented inhabitants from moving out. During the 1890s, Italians in New York City, African-Americans in Philadelphia and Chicago, Mexicans in Los Angeles, and Chinese in San Francisco increasingly became locked into ghettos. Italian immigrants in particular were pushed into substandard housing. Because so many young males intended to return to Italy, they took the cheapest available housing and endured filth and congestion in the belief that their stay was temporary.

To an urban reformer such as Jacob Riis, the Italians themselves appeared to be the problem. Riis despised their custom of congregating in the streets to purchase food, chat with friends, or pass the time. In *How the Other Half Lives* (1890), he singled out a district called the Bend as the worst of New York City's slums and emphasized its Italian character. "Half of the people in 'the Bend' are christened Pasquale," he wrote. "When the police do not know the name of an escaped murderer, they guess at Pasquale and send the name out on an alarm; in nine cases out of ten it fits." Riis acknowledged the destructive effects of substandard housing, inadequate health care, and unsanitary conditions, as well as the social disruption of immigration, but still blamed the Italian residents for the crime, squalor, disease, and appallingly high infant death rate that plagued them. This tendency to fault the slum dwellers for their own plight, and to hold particular immigrant groups responsible for their living conditions, characterized even well-intentioned reformers and helped to shape, and to distort, middle-class perceptions of the immigrant city.

Epidemics of typhoid fever, smallpox, and diphtheria periodically ravaged the slums, and the slower killer tuberculosis claimed thousands of victims. Whooping cough, measles, and scarlet fever took a fearful toll among youth, and infant mortality was high. In 1900 one immigrant ward in Chicago saw 20 percent of all infants die in their first year.

Furthermore, tenements often bordered industrial districts, and so residents had to put up with the noise, pollution, and foul odors of tanneries, foundries, factories, and packing houses. Reliance on coal for steam engines and heating released vast quantities of soot and coal dust to drift over the slums. As smoke tinged the atmosphere a hazy gray, buildings took on a dingy, grimy patina.

The position of blacks was even worse than that of poor white immigrants. Driven from the skilled trades, confined to low-paying menial jobs, trapped in segregated districts, and excluded from other areas by restrictive real-estate covenants, African-Americans had no way out of the ghetto. By the turn of the century, growing competition between immigrants and black migrants moving up from the South left African-Americans segregated in the poorest sections of northern cities, such as Chicago's "Black Belt" on the South Side and Cleveland's Central Avenue District. Intimidation as well as segregation plagued urban blacks. In the 1880s a black newspaper asserted that white police officers, especially the Irish, "delight in arresting every little colored boy they see on the street, who may be doing something not at all offensive, and allow the white boys to do what they please."

Rivalry over housing and jobs sometimes sparked racial violence. Usually, the victim of an attack was a lone individual; however, sometimes interracial clashes escalated into full-scale riots, as in New York City during summer 1900. The mêlée began when a young black man knifed and killed a plainclothes policeman whom he believed was mishandling his wife. As news of the murder spread, lower Manhattan erupted in rage. "Men and women poured by the hundreds from the neighboring tenements," a local reporter wrote. "Negroes were set upon wherever they could be found and brutally beaten."

Fashionable Avenues and Suburbs

The same cities that harbored slums, suffering, and violence also boasted neighborhoods of dazzling opulence. The wealthy built monumental residences on exclusive thoroughfares just outside the downtown, among them Fifth Avenue in New York, Commonwealth Avenue in Boston, and Euclid Avenue in Cleveland. In Chicago, after a devastating fire in 1871, the elite moved south to Prairie Avenue around Eighteenth Street. Then in the 1880s, with the extension of the street-railway system, well-to-do Chicagoans moved to Lake Shore Drive, the so-called Gold Coast on the near North Side. The gradual northward migration of Chicago's well-heeled citizens paralleled the expansion of immigrant neighborhoods on the South Side, where once-fashionable mansions, converted to cramped apartments, quickly filled with newcomers.

Middle-class city dwellers followed the wealthy, moving to new suburbs. In the 1890s Chicago developer Samuel Eberly Gross created entire low-cost subdivisions north and west of the city and advertised homes for as little as ten dollars a month. Lawyers, doctors, small businessmen, and other professionals moved farther out along the main thoroughfares served by the street railway and purchased homes with large lots.

A pattern of informal residential segregation by income took shape in the cities and suburbs. Built for families of a particular income level, certain city neighborhoods and suburbs developed remarkably similar internal standards for lot size and house design. Commuters who rode the new street railways out from the city center could identify the changing neighborhoods along the way as readily as a geologist might distinguish different strata on a washed-out riverbank. And with the physical change in American cities came a new awareness of class and cultural disparities.

The Urban Challenge

Although middle- and upper-class Americans were abandoning their downtown residences in the 1880s and 1890s, the business and professional activities of merchants, journalists, manufacturers, lawyers, and others remained centered in the heart of the city. Growing evidence of social unrest and the occasional strikes and riots that swept through the cities deeply disturbed these old-stock citizens. Critics linked the disorder to the immigrant masses, who, they said, lacked self-discipline and behaved immorally. The corruption-riddled political machines that dominated city government became a chief target of the critics.

Convinced that urgent steps had to be taken to stem a rising tide of riot, robbery, and rotten government, concerned citizens waged a continual battle to eradicate urban crime, to reform "boss" politics, and to assimilate immigrants into mainstream society. A powerful blend of altruism and self-interest motivated them.

Policing the City

In the novel *Ragged Dick* (1867), Horatio Alger detailed the scams and violence awaiting unwary newcomers to the city, perpetrated by dishonest shopkeepers, pickpockets, muggers, con artists, and Irish street gangs. Alger and other writers who associated crime with the growth of cities did not exaggerate. As Philadelphia's population tripled between 1850 and 1900, for example, so did its homicides. Concerned citizens worried publicly about easily available cheap handguns.

In the 1830s and 1840s cities had established police forces to maintain law and order. Unlike their European counterparts, these regulatory agencies were civilian enterprises, separate from the military and controlled by local officials. Following New York's example, set in 1853, U.S. cities had outfitted their police officers with badges and uniforms and authorized them to carry clubs and revolvers. These police forces often had ill-defined responsibilities, ranging from maintaining order and preventing crime to cleaning streets, running lodging houses for the homeless, and supervising the sanitation of vegetable markets. The police made little headway in suppressing the rowdy street life, drinking, gambling, and prostitution that flourished in the immigrant working-class districts.

Middle-class civic leaders particularly deplored the neighborhood saloons, which provided a free lunch with a five-cent beer, meeting rooms, news of job openings, and, sometimes, gambling tables and prostitutes' services in back rooms. State legislatures, dominated by rural, native-born citizens who disapproved of the immigrants' drinking and gambling, regularly passed laws banning these practices, curtailing Sunday business operations, and regulating saloons.

Caught between moralistic state legislators and immigrant communities resentful of outside meddling, police tried to steer a middle course, tacitly allowing saloons to remain open on Sunday, for example, as long as their patrons behaved properly in public. Then in 1894 an investigation by a New York State legislator uncovered evidence that the New York City police not only were failing to suppress illegal activities but also were actually licensing them. In return for payoffs, the police permitted gamblers, prostitutes, and saloonkeepers to operate more or less at will in poor neighborhoods where little organized opposition existed, provided that they remained discreet. Instead of fighting vice, the shocked legislator concluded, the police were conniving in it.

The complex relationship between the police and those whom they were supposed to be policing manifested itself in other ways. By the 1870s most police departments in major cities had squads of detectives who worked out of inner-city saloons. Often not easily distinguishable from the crooks and con men with whom they rubbed shoulders, these police detectives sometimes even functioned as go-betweens for thieves and robbery victims, returning stolen property in exchange for a reward. In some cities professional criminals reached an understanding with detectives and returned property stolen from citizens of high prestige and standing.

In late-nineteenth-century cities, reformers tried to make law enforcement more professional by appointing independent, nonpartisan boards of commissioners to hire and fire police officers. Pressured by such reformers as young Theodore Roosevelt, who headed New York's Board of Police Commissioners from 1895 to 1897, civic leaders gradually removed police departments from political patronage and adopted regular hiring procedures. But urban reformers had less success in legislating the stricter morality that rural legislators desired. Given the large immigrant populations within the cities, many police officers, especially those drawn from the immigrant ranks, remained sympathetic to the social customs of the ethnic groups among which they circulated. By the turn of the century many urban police departments, unable to enforce the strict morality demanded by rural state legislators, had shifted their attention from trying to control the "dangerous classes" to deterring criminal behavior.

Governing the City

The competition for authority over the police reflected a deeper power struggle within urban politics. The demands placed on public utilities, rapid-transit systems, and fire and police departments forced cities to raise taxes, issue bonds, and create new municipal departments and positions. Large sums could be made by dominating any segment of this process, and state and local politicians fought for control of the city and the right to run these lucrative services. To complicate matters, city governments and state legislatures alike claimed jurisdiction over the urban environment. Ostensibly to curb governmental abuse, state legislatures altered city charters, bestowed special contracts and monopolies on railroad and utility magnates, and tried to minimize taxes by reducing the expenses of city government and limiting city services.

By midcentury, outside interference in local affairs had encouraged the rise of a new kind of professional politician, the "boss," who presided over the city's "machine," an unofficial political organization designed to keep a particular party or faction in office. The boss wielded enormous influence in city government. Often a former saloonkeeper or labor leader, the boss knew his constituents well. Cincinnati's George B. Cox was a typical boss, though more honest than many. The son of British immigrants, Cox worked his way up from newsboy and lookout for gamblers to saloon owner. Elected to Cincinnati's city council in 1879, Cox became head of the city's Republican machine, which swung elections to the GOP, controlled key public offices, and acted as a broker among competing corporate and political interests.

For better or worse, the political machine was America's unique contribution to the challenge of municipal government in an era of pell-mell urban growth. Typified by Tammany Hall, the Democratic organization that dominated New York politics from the 1830s to the 1930s, machines emerged in a host of cities during the late nineteenth century. Organized in a pyramidal hierarchy, the machine rested on precinct captains who operated at the neighborhood level and reported to ward bosses, frequently saloonkeepers. The ward bosses ladled out patronage, contracts, and political appointments. At the apex of the pyramid sat the city boss, controlling party activities throughout the city.

The machine ruled supreme within its orbit. The politicians who ran it controlled the jobs of thousands of policemen, firemen, sanitation workers, and other city employees; they exerted enormous influence over courts, schools, hospitals, and other municipal agencies. Democratic in some cities, Republican in others, the machine hammered out compromises and resolved conflicts among competing urban interest groups.

The machine rewarded its friends and punished its enemies through its control of taxes, licenses, and inspections. It gave tax breaks to favored contractors and slipped them information about upcoming street and sewer projects. The ward captain doubled as a kind of welfare agent, helping the needy and protecting the troubled. Apparent generosity enhanced the bosses' image, at little cost: $10 to pay a tenement dweller's rent or $3 to pay a fine meant a lot to the poor but was small change to bosses who raked in millions from public contracts and land deals. The machine may have helped some of the urban poor, but by entangling social services with political corruption, it often prevented the political process from responding to the needs of the city's neediest inhabitants.

An effective precinct captain could work his way up from local to state or even national power. In Kansas City, Missouri, "Big Jim" Pendergast, an Irish hotelkeeper and saloonkeeper in an industrial ward, clawed his way to power in the 1890s by providing welfare services for his African-American, Italian, and Irish constituents. By controlling his ward's delegates to the city's Democratic conventions, he rose to city alderman. When opponents threatened to root out gambling interests associated with his saloon, Pendergast used his influence with the governor to engineer the appointment of a sympathetic police chief. By the turn of the century, Pendergast held nearly absolute sway in Kansas City politics and wielded considerable clout at the state level.

Cox, Pendergast, and other bosses transformed urban politics into a form of entrepreneurship. As ambitious and ruthless as any Rockefeller or Carnegie, they pioneered new forms of political and social organization. In some cases they also amassed vast fortunes. At times greedy and unscrupulous, they nevertheless responded to immigrant and working-class concerns in a society increasingly dominated by the middle and upper classes.

Under boss William Marcy Tweed, the Tammany Hall machine sank to new depths of corruption. Between 1869 and 1871, the machine dispensed 60,000 patronage positions and pumped up the city's debt by $70 million through graft and inflated contracts. The details of the Tweed ring's massive fraud were widely reported in newspapers and satirized in *Harper's Weekly* by cartoonist Thomas Nast. In one cartoon, Nast portrayed Tweed and his cronies as vultures picking at the city's bones. The caption read, "Let us prey." Tweed bellowed in fury. "I don't care a straw for your newspaper articles—my constituents don't know how to read," he told *Harper's*; "but they can't help seeing

"Let Us Prey," 1871

Cartoonist Thomas Nast hated William Marcy Tweed's ostentatious style. Pictured here as the chief vulture standing over the body of New York City, Boss Tweed wears an enormous diamond, a symbol of his insatiable greed.

them damned pictures." Convicted of fraud and extortion, Tweed was sentenced to jail in 1873, served two years, escaped to Spain, was caught, and died in jail in 1878.

Not all bosses were as crooked as Tweed. Boss Cox of Cincinnati, who maintained that he had never received an illegal payoff, gained the backing of local reformers by supporting voter-registration laws and placing police and fire departments under independent bipartisan boards. He also supported the construction of a new city waterworks and the improvement of parks and other recreation facilities. Although Cox's opponents doubted that his administration was as free of corruption as he claimed, they did not overthrow his machine until 1897.

Despite the stereotype of city bosses as crude and vulgar, not all bosses fit that mold. San Francisco boss Abraham Ruef graduated from the University of California at age eighteen with highest honors. Ed Flynn, the boss of the Bronx, New York, was a brilliant lawyer. Whatever their backgrounds, bosses represented a new political style that stressed grass-roots ties to the neighborhood and ward. They made sure that their constituents' concerns were heard and displayed flexible, pragmatic, and opportunistic approaches to meeting the challenges of urban life.

Nevertheless, by the turn of the century bosses faced well-organized assaults on their power, led by an urban elite seeking to restore "good government." In this atmosphere, the bosses increasingly forged alliances with civic organizations and reform leagues that paved the way for new sewer and transportation systems, expanded parklands, and improved public services—a record of considerable accomplishment given the magnitude of the problems created by urban growth.

Battling Poverty

In contrast to the bosses' piecemeal attempts to aid the urban poor, middle-class reformers sought comprehensive solutions. Jacob Riis and other reformers believed that imigrants' lack of self-discipline and self-control led to their miseries. Thus reformers often focused on the moral improvement of the poor while ignoring the crippling effect of low wages and dangerous working conditions. Humanitarian campaigns to help the destitute often turned into crusades to Americanize the immigrants and eliminate their "offensive" and "self-destructive" behaviors.

Poverty-relief workers first targeted the young, considered the most malleable. Early Protestant social reformers started charitable societies to help transient youths and street waifs. In 1843 Robert M. Hartley, a former employee of the New York Temperance Society, founded the New York Association for Improving the Condition of the Poor. Convinced that slum children learned bad habits from their parents, Hartley organized a system of "home visitation" that sent volunteers into inner-city tenements to urge poor families to change their ways. The association also demanded pure-milk laws, public baths, and better housing.

The Young Men's Christian Association (YMCA), founded in England in 1841 and exported to America in 1851, focused on the dislocation and strain experienced by rural Americans who migrated to the cities in the post–Civil War years. The YMCA and later the YWCA (Young Women's Christian Association) provided decent housing and wholesome recreational facilities under close supervision and expelled members for drinking or other forbidden behavior.

Indeed, the departure of young people, especially farmers' daughters, from older rural areas had reached startling proportions. In one Vermont town, 73 percent of those aged five to fourteen in the 1880 census had left by 1900. The glamour and glitter of urban life dazzled the youthful rural migrants, who were drawn cityward mainly in search of economic opportunities. Far from home, with few friends and nowhere to stay, they easily fell victim to con artists. The YMCA and YWCA supplied these innocents safe temporary lodgings and reassuring reminders of home.

By 1900 more than 1,500 YMCAs acted as havens for nearly 250,000 men. But the YMCA and YWCA reached only a small portion of the young adult population. Their moralistic stance repelled some, and others preferred not to ask for help. Narrowly focused, the "Y" strategy could do little to relieve urban problems.

New Approaches to Social Work

The inability of relief organizations to cope with the explosive growth of the urban poor in the 1870s and 1880s convinced many middle-class Americans that urban poverty had reached dangerous proportions. In 1885 the Reverend Josiah Strong expressed this fear in his book *Our Country: Its Possible Future and Present Crisis*. Accusing cities of "multiplying and focalizing the elements of anarchy and destruction," Strong blamed immigration and Catholicism and pleaded for a cooperative Protestant effort to battle the dual plagues of intemperance and destitution.

Even before Strong mounted the battlements, social reformers had begun developing more coercive strategies to fight poverty. One of the earliest and most effective agencies to use tough-minded tactics was the Salvation Army. A church established along paramilitary lines in England in 1865 by Methodist minister "General" William Booth, the Salvation Army sent its uniformed volunteers to the United States in 1880 to provide food, shelter, and temporary employment for families. Known for its rousing music and attention-getting street meetings, the group ran soup kitchens and day nurseries and dispatched "slum brigades" to carry the message of morality to the immigrant poor. Funded by donations, the Salvation Army tried to aid—and to control—an urban population whose fondness for saloons, dance halls, and streetside entertainment threatened middle-class conceptions of a stable society. The organization's strategy was simple: attract the poor with marching bands and lively preaching; follow up with offers of food, assistance, and work; and then teach them the solid, middle-class virtues of temperance, hard work, and self-discipline.

New York's Charity Organization Society (COS), founded in 1882 by Josephine Shaw Lowell, implemented a similar approach, attempting to make the poor more honest and efficient. The society sent "friendly visitors" into the tenements to counsel families on how to improve their lives. Convinced that moral deficiencies lay at the root of poverty, and that the "promiscuous charity" of overlapping welfare agencies undermined the desire to work, the COS tried to foster self-sufficiency in its charges.

Critics justly accused the COS and similar groups of seeking more to control than to help the poor. More often than not, the friendly visitors wore cultural blinders, misunderstanding the real source of the difficulties faced by the poor and expecting to effect change by imposing middle-class standards.

One journalist dismissed the typical friendly visitor as "235 pounds of Sunshine." Unable to see slum problems from the vantage point of the poor, the organizations ultimately failed to convert the poor to their own codes of morality and decorum.

The Moral-Purity Campaign

Unable to eradicate urban poverty and crime, reformers pushed for tougher measures against sin and immorality. In 1872 Anthony Comstock, a pious young dry-goods clerk, founded the New York Society for the Suppression of Vice and demanded that municipal authorities close down gambling and lottery operations and censor obscene publications. His purity crusade gained widespread support from civic leaders frustrated by the lack of progress in flushing away urban vice.

Nothing symbolized the contested terrain between middle- and lower-class culture than prostitution, socially degenerate to some and a source of recreation to others. The "oldest profession" simultaneously exploited women and offered them good earnings and unbounded personal freedom. Brothels—houses of prostitution—expanded rapidly from the time of the Civil War until the 1880s, when saloons and cabarets, often controlled by politcal machines, replaced them. Reformers assumed, incorrectly, that immigrant women made up the majority of urban prostitutes.

In 1892 Charles Parkhurst, a Presbyterian minister and New York reformer, founded the City Vigilance League to clean up prostitiution, gambling dens, and saloons. Parkhurst blamed the "slimy, oozy soil of Tammany Hall" and the New York City police for the city's rampant evil. In September 1894 a nonpartisan Committee of Seventy elected a new mayor who pressured city officials to enforce the laws against prostitution, gambling, and Sunday liquor sales.

The purity campaign, however, lasted scarcely three years. Irish and German neighborhoods rallied in defense of their cherished saloons. Individuals who had championed Parkhurst scoffed at his self-righteous and bombastic rhetoric and deserted his movement; the reform coalition fell apart. Tammany Hall regained its power in 1897 and installed a new police chief willing to regulate, rather than to root out, vice. New York's population was too large and its ethnic constituencies were too diverse for the middle and upper classes to curb all the illegal activities flourishing within the sprawling metropolis.

The Social Gospel

Meanwhile, in the 1870s and 1880s a handful of Protestant ministers explored radical alternatives for aiding impoverished city dwellers. Appalled by slum conditions, they argued that the rich and wellborn deserved part of the blame for poverty and thus had a responsibility to do something about it.

William S. Rainsford, the minister of New York City's St. George's Episcopal Church, pioneered the so-called institutional church movement, whereby large downtown churches in once elite districts now overrun by immigrants provided their new neighbors with social services as well as a place to worship. Supported by his wealthy church warden, J. Pierpont Morgan, Rainsford organized a boys' club, built recreational facilities on the Lower East Side, and established an industrial training program.

When his unorthodox approach provoked conservative wrath, Rainsford, unfazed, redoubled his criticism of complacent churchgoers' lack of concern. He argued that excessive drinking in immigrant wards did not stem from peoples' lack of willpower but was a by-product of the larger problem of the slums, where millions were trapped in desperate circumstances. Closing saloons on Sundays would accomplish far less than prosecuting the slum landlords and sweatshop owners who victimized the poor. In the end Rainsford's efforts fell short because of the magnitude of slum problems, but his sympathetic approach reflected an important dimension of a crusade by a group of late-nineteenth-century ministers to awaken American Protestants to the realities of the immigrant city.

Supporting that drive were the leaders of the Social Gospel movement, launched in the 1870s

Greeting Neighbors at Hull House
Settlement-house workers were eager to work with immigrant families in order to ensure that the children received proper health care and nutrition. In addition to establishing a nursery, Hull House in Chicago provided classes for parents and helped find them jobs.

by Congregational minister Washington Gladden of Columbus, Ohio. Dismayed by the way that many middle-class churchgoers ignored the hardships of slum dwellers, Gladden insisted that true Christianity commits men and women to fight social injustice. If Gladden set the tone for the Social Gospel, Walter Rauschenbusch, a minister in New York City's notorious Hell's Kitchen neighborhood, articulated its philosophy. Strongly influenced by Henry George's and Edward Bellamy's criticism of laissez-faire ideology (see Chapter 18), Rauschenbusch sought to apply Jesus's teachings to society. A truly Christian society, he said, would unite all churches, reorganize the industrial system, and work for international peace.

The Social Gospel's fierce attacks on complacent Christian support of the status quo attracted only a handful of Protestants. Their earnest voices, however, blended with a growing chorus of critics bemoaning the nation's urban woes.

The Settlement-House Movement

By the 1880s many concerned citizens had become convinced that reform pressure applied from the top down, however well intentioned, was ineffective and wrongheaded. The passage of laws did not ensure obedience. A younger generation of charity workers, led by Jane Addams, developed a new weapon against destitution: the settlement house. Like the Social Gospelers, these reformers recognized that the hardships of slum life were often beyond individuals' control. Stressing the environmental causes of crime and poverty, settlement-house relief workers themselves moved into poor neighborhoods, where, in Addams's words, they could see firsthand "the struggle for existence, which is so much harsher among people near the edge of pauperism."

The Illinois-born Addams had graduated from Rockford College in 1882 and toured Europe a year later with her friend Ellen Gates Starr. Impressed by Toynbee Hall, a charity workers' residence deep in a London slum, the two women returned to Chicago and in 1889 purchased and repaired the dilapidated Charles J. Hull mansion, which they later opened as an experiment in the settlement-house approach. By living in Hull House and working in daily contact with poor immigrants, they hoped to provide a model creative outlet for college-trained women like themselves.

Drawing on the middle-class ideal of true womanhood as supportive and self-sacrificing, Addams turned Hull House into a social center for recent immigrants. She invited newly arrived Italian immigrants to plays; held classes in English, civics, cooking, and dressmaking; and encouraged them to preserve their traditional crafts. She also established a kindergarten, a laundry, an employment bureau, and a day nursery for working mothers. In the hope of upgrading filthy, overcrowded slum housing, Addams and her coworkers published systematic studies of city housing conditions and pressured politicians to enforce sanitary regulations.

By 1895 at least fifty settlement houses had opened around the nation. Their leaders trained a generation of young college students who later would serve as state and local government officials and would play an influential part in the regulatory movements of the Progressive Era (see Chapter 22). Through their sympathetic attitudes toward the immigrants and their systematic publication of data about slum conditions, settlement-house workers gave Americans new hope that the city's problems could be overcome.

Yet settlement houses enjoyed little success in their attempts to bridge the gap between rich and poor and to promote class cooperation and social harmony. Although immigrants appreciated the settlement houses' resources and activity, they widely felt that the reformers cared little for increasing immigrant political power. "They're like the rest," complained one immigrant, "a bunch of people planning for us and deciding what is good for us without consulting us or taking us into their confidence."

Reshaping the Urban Environment

While reformers battled slum conditions and municipal corruption, landscape architects and city planners who shared their goal of an orderly urban society sought to reshape the urban masses by transforming their physical surroundings. Entire sections of America's metropolises were rebuilt in an attempt to clean up pollution and to restore beauty, dignity, and order to the urban environment.

To raise the level of urban and cultural awareness, these self-proclaimed saviors of America's cities established monumental public libraries, endowed art museums, constructed theaters and symphony halls, and expanded park and recreational facilities. At the same time, real-estate and business interests remodeled the city in their own way, erecting great towers of commerce and finance.

The motivations behind commercial construction were simple—profit and growth—but sponsors of the new urban landscape had more complex social objectives. They wanted both to make the city a more appealing place and to instill a sense of order that would tame and restrain the urban masses.

Parks and Public Spaces

Architects Andrew Jackson Downing and Frederick Law Olmsted were prominent in envisioning a new urban landscape. The ideal metropolis, they argued, should clearly differentiate shopping and housing areas from the industrial district. The city should have a compact commercial nucleus, but spacious parks and roadways should open up the landscape. Most important, public buildings and boulevards should be built on a grand scale, to inspire and awe ordinary citizens.

In 1858 Olmsted, one of the earliest and most successful promoters of this vision, had teamed up with English architect Calvert Vaux to develop the original plan for Central Park in New York City. After their success in New York, they designed major parks for Brooklyn, Chicago, Philadelphia, and Boston.

Boston's Back Bay

Olmsted and others who called for revitalizing the urban environment through planning and design took Boston's fashionable Back Bay district as their model. This area was a 450-acre tidal flat until 1857, when the state of Massachusetts began a massive engineering project to fill it in and to raise it twenty feet. For more than forty years, gravel trains ran around the clock from Needham, nine miles away, to the Back Bay. The state deeded some of the lots thus created to contractors as payment for the filling work, reserved others for educational and philanthropic organizations, and sold the rest as building lots. Each deed specified the height of the building, the distance it should be set back from the street, and the materials that could be used.

Engineers laid out Commonwealth Avenue, the Back Bay's main thoroughfare, along the lines of a French boulevard, with a formal central section graced by trees, stone benches, and statues. Elegant side streets branched off the avenue, with back alleys for deliveries. The uniform height of the district's five-story row houses established a line of vision that imparted formality and consistency.

Various cultural institutions reinforced the Back Bay's image as a center of civilization and refinement. In addition to the monumental Boston Public Library, the Back Bay eventually contained two colleges, two museums, five schools, and twelve churches. In the eyes of many social reformers and civic leaders, the Back Bay represented the classic example of the charming, cosmopolitan environment that city planning could create.

Rebuilding Chicago

In contrast to Boston, postwar Chicago was a planner's nightmare. Chicago was America's shock city, the extreme example of the kind of problems spawned by unregulated growth. Between 1850 and 1870, the city's population rose like a tidal wave, from 30,000 to 300,000, inundating neighborhoods and swamping city services. Although crisis, rather than planning, often dictated changes in the city, the sheer magnitude of the changes forced Chicagoans to accept innovations that others elsewhere later copied.

For example, expansion in the 1840s had left residents with swampy, unpaved streets just above the water table. To remedy this soggy situation, the city council decided in 1855 that the streets' level had to be raised, and so owners jacked up their buildings to meet the new grade level. In 1857 a British traveler noted in amazement that "the Briggs House, a gigantic hotel, five stories high, solid masonry, weighing 22,000 tons, was raised four and a half feet, and new foundations built below. The people were in it all the time, coming and going, eating and sleeping."

Chicago faced a new crisis in October 1871 when a fire razed nearly four square miles of the central city, devouring 61,000 buildings, gutting the commercial district, and leaving nearly 100,000 people homeless. The urgent need for downtown reconstruction gave Chicago architects, engineers, and civic leaders an unprecedented opportunity. In the next two decades, they cooperatively pioneered innovative methods for tall office building construction and created a new American building, the skyscraper.

The skyscraper depended on three technological innovations: fireproofing, the internal metal frame, and the elevator. Not until the 1880s did Chicago architects combine them into a distinctive commercial style. In view of the city's recent fire, officials insisted that all new structures be built of noncombustible materials. Stone was the obvious choice, but its great weight severely limited the size of buildings that could be erected on Chicago's marshy soil. Louis Sullivan and other architects developed a far lighter alternative—a central metal skeleton, fireproofed with fired-clay tile, to support the exterior walls. By placing the metal frame on an expanded foundation and installing motorized elevators, Chicago architects increased the city's building heights from four to twenty-two stories. Once Chicago skyscrapers demonstrated the technical feasibility and commercial advantages of constructing tall, metal-supported buildings on small, expensive urban lots, other American cities began to raise their skylines.

The dramatic rebuilding of the urban environment in Boston and Chicago encouraged business leaders and reformers in smaller cities. By the turn of the century, municipal art societies, park and outdoor-art associations, and civic-improvement leagues had sprung up around the country. Cities launched programs to replace muddy streets and unsightly billboards in downtown business districts with broad boulevards, sparkling fountains, and gleaming marble public buildings.

Known as the "city-beautiful movement," this crusade favored the interests of the rich and wellborn, who took less interest in upgrading the slums than in making public buildings impressive and even monumental. They believed that attractive, imposing civic architecture would produce better citizens and reduce immorality and social disorder. In the early twentieth century, the city-beautiful impulse would evolve into a comprehensive city-planning movement (see Chapter 22) inspired by soaring visions of a transformed urban environment.

Toward a Metropolitan America

As city-beautiful advocates drafted plans for the urban future, harried city-hall bureaucrats, municipal administrators, and civic engineers wrestled with inadequate water supplies, antiquated sewer systems, and basic municipal services that lagged behind the pace of urban growth. To provide more efficient administration, new citywide agencies gradually took over matters once handled at the neighborhood and ward level. But while administration became centralized, urban power remained widely dispersed. Conflicts among different segments of the urban population—real-estate developers, businessmen, immigrants—ultimately encouraged compromise arrangements necessary for the smooth functioning of the entire city.

Around midcentury, city dwellers began to recognize that the deplorable quality of water and sewer systems threatened urban life. Even by the 1870s, most urbanites still relied on private wells, outhouses, and cesspools; sewer systems were primitive and few. An engineer pungently described such systems as "reservoirs of liquid filth, ever oozing through the defective joints, and polluting the very earth upon which the city stands." Pouring sewage directly into Lake Michigan, Chicago contributed to the frequent cholera, typhoid, and diphtheria epidemics that ravaged the city.

Early attempts to construct interconnected sewer systems fell victim to local politics. In Washington, D.C., contractors who had been hired for their political contacts produced lateral sewers that could not run uphill into the main trunk lines. In St. Louis and Cincinnati, politically motivated contracts resulted in inadequate systems that taxpayers had to replace within a decade, at enormous expense.

Gradually and painfully, cities developed the centralized administrative structures that their size required. In 1889 Chicago officials persuaded the Illinois legislature to create a 185-square-mile sanitary district encompassing the city and its suburbs. By 1899 the city built the enormous Ship and Sanitary Canal, which reversed the flow of the Chicago River to carry the city's processed sewage downstate. By 1900 the establishment of water and sewer systems had cut mortality rates from typhoid fever nationwide by 65 percent.

The movement to centralize control over water and sewer facilities represented a broader process of physical and political consolidation in urban America. As cities grew, they added unincorporated surrounding land and absorbed adjacent municipalities, a development that allowed city governments to coordinate transportation, water, and sewer networks as well as to increase tax revenues. The largest such consolidation occurred in 1898 when Brooklyn, Queens, Staten Island, and the Bronx joined Manhattan to create the modern New York City. In the process, New York added nearly 2 million people to its population and ballooned from 44 to nearly 300 square miles.

Practically every U.S. city pushed out its boundaries in these years. Merchants saw annexation as a way to dilute the political power of immigrants who "stood in the way of progress," reformers hailed annexation as a step toward more professional city services, and real-estate promoters welcomed it as a means of securing municipal sewer and water systems that would increase the value of their holdings. Most middle-class suburbanites, eager for access to efficient city services, went along with the process. Not until the mid-twentieth century would suburban communities, valuing local autonomy and wary of urban tax rates and social problems, successfully fight off annexation.

CONCLUSION

The movement toward a metropolitan America culminated a long struggle to control the changing urban world after the Civil War. The expanding cities' size and diversity sometimes seemed overwhelming, while the battles for power and wealth raging in urban America proved at once exciting and disturbing.

The urban population grappled with the stresses of a social environment unfamiliar to many and undergoing tremendous flux. Middle- and upper-class urban residents were disturbed by the industrial city's massive physical problems—housing, sanitation, policing, schooling—and even more by the city's corrosive effect on traditional values and expectations. Migrants from America's farms and homogeneous small towns found themselves in an impersonal, fast-paced commercial world where antagonistic economic interests and ethnic and racial groups struggled for influence and power. Immigrants uprooted from centuries-old rhythms of peasant life or from the urban ghettos of eastern Europe had to adapt to the unremitting demands of industrial labor, to the mortal hazards and casual indignities of tenement life, and to the head-spinning diversity of the city. Remarkably impervious to the assaults of middle-class political opponents, to the pieties of would-be uplifters, or to the efforts of moral reformers to legislate behavior, immigrants rallied around the political boss. Of all the city's actors in these years, the boss learned best how to wield the levers of power in the new urban world.

Thus the post–Civil War city was a place of constant contention among wildly different groups. But from this boisterous conflict emerged the recognition that all city dwellers shared a basic interest in clean water, adequate sewers, garbage collection, and fire protection. Out of this realization blossomed a conception of what some have called the service city—a city that could efficiently meet the collective needs of its diverse inhabitants. By 1900 city bureaucracies had established responsibility for sanitation, transportation, street lighting, public health, parks, and police. Metropolitan America had taken shape.

Despite dark warnings of chaos and social upheaval, a remarkable degree of order and stability prevailed in the United States as the nineteenth century closed. Cities had evolved governmental forms sufficient to assure an adequate quality of life for all and to intervene when necessary to protect the welfare of the urban populace. This enlarged conception of government only slowly penetrated the arena of national politics, but the lessons so painfully learned in late-nineteenth-century cities would profoundly shape the progressive movement that lay ahead.

CHRONOLOGY

1843 Robert M. Hartley founds the New York Association for Improving the Condition of the Poor.

1851 The American branch of the Young Men's Christian Association (YMCA) opens.

1853 Charles Loring Brace founds the New York Children's Aid Society.

1855 New York opens its Castle Garden immigrant center.

1857 Filling in of Boston's Back Bay begins.

1858 Frederick Law Olmsted and Calvert Vaux design Central Park.

1869 Boss William Marcy Tweed gains control of New York City's Tammany Hall political machine.

1871 The Great Chicago Fire.

1872 Anthony Comstock founds the New York Society for the Suppression of Vice and leads a "purity" campaign.

1874 John Wanamaker opens his Philadelphia department store.

1879 The New York "dumbbell" tenement law is passed.

1880 William Booth's followers establish an American branch of the Salvation Army.

1882 Josephine Shaw Lowell founds the New York Charity Organization Society (COS).

1888 First electric-trolley line, in Richmond, Virginia.

1889 Jane Addams and Ellen Gates Starr open Hull House.

1890 Jacob Riis, *How the Other Half Lives*.

1892 Immigrant-admitting station is opened on Ellis Island in the New York City harbor.
Reverend Charles Parkhurst organizes the City Vigilance League.
"Big Jim" Pendergast gains control of the Kansas City, Missouri, political machine.

1894 The Chicago Ship and Sanitary Canal is built.
Clarence Lexow's investigation of New York City reveals widespread police corruption.

1898 New York City consolidates five boroughs into Greater New York.

1900 Theodore Dreiser, *Sister Carrie*.

1907 Walter Rauschenbusch, *Christianity and the Social Crisis*.

1910 Jane Addams, *Twenty Years at Hull House*.

FOR FURTHER READING

Paul Boyer, *Urban Masses and Moral Order in America, 1820–1920* (1978). A richly detailed analysis of reformers' attempts to control city life.

Ruth H. Crocker, *Social Work and Social Order: The Settlement Movement in Two Industrial Cities, 1889–1930* (1992). An important, balanced assessment of the settlement-house movement.

William Cronon, *Nature's Metropolis: Chicago and the Great West* (1991). An innovative study of the link between urban growth and regional economic prosperity in the Midwest.

Kenneth T. Jackson, *Crabgrass Frontier: The Suburbanization of the United States* (1985). A stimulating comparative study of city expansion and suburban development in Europe and America.

Peter McCaffery, *When Bosses Ruled Philadelphia: The Emergence of the Republican Machine, 1867–1933* (1993). A revisionist look at political bosses that downplays their welfare role.

Martin V. Melosi, ed., *Pollution and Reform in American Cities, 1870–1930* (1980). A pioneering examination of the environmental impact of U.S. industrial and urban growth.

Walter Nugent, *Crossings: The Great Transatlantic Migrations, 1870–1914* (1992). A thoughtful overview of the reasons for the major migrations to the Americas.

Kathy Peiss, *Cheap Amusements:: Working Women and Leisure in Turn-of-the-Century New York* (1986). A forceful, provocative analysis of immigrant women's lives.

David Ward, *Poverty, Ethnicity, and the American City, 1840–1925* (1989). A penetrating analysis of the relationship among immigration, ethnicity, and the changing structure of industrial capitalism.

CHAPTER 20

Daily Life, Popular Culture, and the Arts, 1860–1900

Americans faced difficult adjustments as they shifted from a producer economy that valued hard work and thrift to a consumer economy stressing material possessions and leisure-time activities. A torrent of new products, including hot-air furnaces, indoor plumbing fixtures, sewing machines, and cast-iron kitchen ranges, poured out of U.S. factories, promising previously unimagined comforts and conveniences. But these advances were not equally available, and their great variety actually intensified class consciousness. The middle and upper classes, which included professionals and white-collar workers, increasingly defined their status in terms of material possessions, comfortable houses, education, genteel cultural standards, and leisure pursuits. In contrast, the larger proportion of farmers and working-class urbanites, paid low wages and frequently out of work, plucked only small benefits from the economic cornucopia.

Although many people improved their economic position and social standing in these years, the gulf between the

(Right) Ornate, imposing pianos and organs were a fixture of the middle-class Victorian parlor.

classes widened. The very rich lived in a world apart, the middle class embraced its own work code and life-style, and a vigorous working-class culture emerged in the heavily immigrant cities. Despite middle-class efforts to remake working-class ways, the mass lower-class culture ultimately proved most influential in shaping modern America.

Everyday Life in Flux

In the closing decades of the nineteenth century, industrialization not only introduced an unprecedented range of products but also created new jobs and destroyed old ones, in the process rearranging occupational structure and altering income distribution. These changes, together with the expansion of white-collar occupations, elevated expectations for family life and fostered a growing class awareness.

Rising Standards of Living

After 1850 mechanization increased output, decreased prices, and encouraged the development of new products that revolutionized life for many Americans. The widespread use of sewing machines, for example, transformed the way people dressed. Before the Civil War, handmade shirts required 30,000 stitches, so most people wore hand-me-downs in simple designs. By the 1880s machine-sewn shirts took only two hours to complete and came in standard sizes and elaborate designs. Personal wardrobes for the middle and elite classes expanded dramatically. Clothes closets were now common household features, and dress became an important badge of social class. Immigrants and rural migrants rushed to buy cheap factory-made clothes and to shed their "greenhorn" or "hayseed" look.

Innovations in food technology changed eating habits. In 1878 physician John Harvey Kellogg marketed Granola, a wheat-oat-corn mixture advertised as healthier than the standard breakfast of sausage, eggs, and potatoes. In the next three decades, Kellogg would also introduce wheat flakes, shredded wheat, and corn flakes. Competitors rushed in. Charles W. Post developed Grape Nuts Flakes and Postum, a breakfast drink made from bran, wheat, and molasses that was supposed to replace overstimulating, unhealthful coffee. By the turn of the century, health-conscious middle- and upper-class Americans who could afford the new cereals and hot drinks had shifted to them.

Not all inventions lived up to their promoters' claims. Lydia Pinkham's vegetable extract "for all those painful Complaints and Weaknesses so common to our best female population" contained nearly 23 percent alcohol. Other tonics featured significant amounts of opium, and countless patent medicines that promised to cure everything from backache to deafness were totally ineffective. But a public that believed that material and physical improvements lay within everyone's reach eagerly snapped them up.

Nonetheless, industrialization was significantly improving the level of comfort and convenience for many American families. In 1870 most urban women, lacking a means of refrigeration, shopped daily, baked their own bread, and canned their own fruits and vegetables. They spent hours preparing food, doing laundry by hand, firing up smoky stoves and furnaces, and carrying "slop jars" to outdoor sewers or malodorous waste-collection tanks. By 1900, however, indoor plumbing, better stoves and furnaces, commercially prepared foods, and mechanical washing machines had eased domestic burdens. Urban middle- and upper-class families took for granted such innovations as central heating, electric lights, and telephone service. Ninety percent of urban families ate store-bought bread; two-thirds used commercial laundries. Iceboxes kept food fresh, and stores featured canned vegetables, pickles, and soups.

Bringing New Commodities to Rural and Small-Town America

As new products changed the lives of city dwellers,

mail-order houses and chain stores reoriented the standards of rural and small-town America. The changes began with Aaron Montgomery Ward. In the 1860s as a traveling salesman, Ward saw that rural Americans depended on local merchants selling limited goods at high prices. In 1872 he joined forces with the Grangers, who pledged to reduce farmers' costs by eliminating the middlemen, and he circulated a list of products for sale at a 40 percent discount. By 1884 Ward's catalog offered nearly 10,000 items to rural customers. Ward encountered competition from Richard Warren Sears, who in 1886 established a mail-order company (now Sears, Roebuck) that shipped farmers everything from tools to baby carriages. Sears built customer loyalty by guaranteeing low prices and publishing testimonials from satisfied patrons. The firm carried many products at different prices to suit all pocketbooks. Pump organs, for example, ranged from "Our AA Grade Home Favorite" at $64.95 to "Our Happy Home Organ, Grade B" at $22.00. Distributed to millions of rural families, the encyclopedic Sears and Ward's catalogs (available in German and Swedish as well as English) opened the door to a new world of consumer goods and educated their readers in middle-class taste.

Chain stores offered another way to bring low-priced mass-produced goods to consumers. In 1879 F. W. Woolworth, a farm boy from upstate New York, opened a "Five and Ten Cent Store" in Utica that sold merchandise such as crochet needles, safety pins, and harmonicas from a "five-cent counter." His stores multiplied rapidly. Together with the Great Atlantic and Pacific Tea Company, which consolidated several food stores into the "A&P" operation in 1859, Woolworth's pioneered national "chains" that stressed low prices and consumer savings.

By the 1890s a barrage of advertising was presenting daily choices about what to buy. More conscious than ever of this sparkling array of material options, Americans had entered an era in which the goods and the services purchased dictated social position and status. Material possessions made possible new realms of comfort and convenience, but they also reinforced a pervasive sense of widening class differences.

A Shifting Class Structure

Patterns of consumption, culture, and everyday life are a reflection of a society's class structure, and in late-nineteenth-century America this structure underwent important modifications. Fundamental changes in the nature of work, in addition to shifts in residential location, massive immigration, and new patterns of consumption, redefined and sharpened the concept of social class. Life-style and self-identification joined income and occupation as determinants of social rank.

The working class felt these changes first and most keenly. In antebellum America the skilled artisans who had dominated the working class had shared a bond of common outlook and class identity with laborers. That bond began to dissolve in the mid-1870s as new production methods changed the work process and destroyed the jobs of skilled artisans. Unskilled immigrants who desperately needed work took the dangerous, low-paying jobs created in the steel mills and elsewhere. By the end of the century, skilled artisans looked down on these newcomers and identified themselves with the middle class.

As the working class fragmented, the middle class expanded. Demand for trained personnel increased in all sectors: growing municipal bureaucracies, school systems, businesses and corporations, and department stores, among others. These middle-class personnel worked in clean offices physically separated from the sooty factories and dirty mills that employed manual workers. Middle-class clerical and professional workers received fixed salaries considerably higher than the earnings of skilled artisans. Few skilled artisans took home more than $500 yearly, but clerks and bookkeepers were paid from $500 to $1,000, and other middle-class workers earned more than $1,000 a year.

Freed from worries about making ends meet, middle-class employees adopted long-term strategies for improving their income and maximizing their purchasing power. They devoted more resources to

Telephone Operators, 1885
The anonymity of the new technology of the telephone sometimes led to flirtations between male callers and the young women who manually transferred calls. Mark Twain's narrator in A Connecticut Yankee in King Arthur's Court *(1889) is so infatuated with telephone operators that he names his first child Hello Central.*

educating their children, buying expensive items on credit, and improving household comforts. A shorter workweek gave middle-class employees more time to spend with their families and greater opportunities for socializing and recreation than before.

The very wealthy flaunted their riches, honing public awareness of growing class divisions. The Carnegies, Morgans, and Rockefellers used their immense fortunes to build elaborate houses and country estates. Palatial houses offered the ultimate proof of success on the capitalist battlefield. Railroad financier Jay Gould built a Gothic castle of a home, with a 380-foot-long greenhouse filled with costly exotic plants. At resorts such as Newport, Rhode Island, the wealthy built stately mansions ("cottages"), kept stables of racehorses, and cruised on magnificent yachts.

Workplace restructuring, the expansion of the middle class, and the rise of enormous fortunes severely skewed income distribution. In 1896 a knowledgeable observer estimated that 5.5 million American families were working class, earning less than $500; 5.5 million were middle class, earning $500 to $5,000; and the remaining 1.5 million, composing 12 percent of the population, earned more than $5,000. This privileged 12 percent owned 86 percent of the nation's wealth. The middle class, 44 percent of the population, possessed 12.5 percent of the wealth, and the working class, the bottom 44 percent of the population, struggled to survive with a mere 1.5 percent of the wealth.

The Changing Family

This skewed distribution of resources had an important impact on family life. Income not only determined access to household technology and consumer goods but also affected family size, life expectancy, infant mortality, and relationships between parents and children.

Between 1860 and 1900 most Americans lived in nuclear families made up of parents and children. Boarders or servants might reside with them, but grandparents and other relatives typically did not. Families continued to become smaller as women bore fewer children. For white women, the number of live births fell from an average of 5.42 children in 1850 to 3.56 in 1900. At the same time, life expectancy rose from 38.4 years to 46.3 years for males and from 40.5 years to 48.3 years for females. The size of the typical nuclear family stabilized at five or six members.

Such statistics obscure important differences stemming from social class, race, and ethnicity. In 1900 a high infant mortality rate among black males dropped their average life expectancy at birth to 22.5 years, less than half that of white males. Farm and immigrant families continued to be large, typically with from six to eight children. Buffalo, New York, an industrial city with many immigrants, provides a striking confirmation of class differences. In 1900 the statistically average laborer's family had 5.7 children; a skilled worker's, 5.2; and a business owner's or manager's family, 3.5.

These statistics show how significantly middle- and upper-class families differed from working-class families. The correlation between income and family size indicates that the middle and upper classes practiced birth control, using either abstinence, contraception, or abortion. Women with small families had more free time, could give more attention to educating and training children, and enjoyed greater opportunities for leisure and recreation than those with many children.

Working-Class Family Life

Working-class families that lived just above or even below the poverty level relied on the labor of children and on a network of relatives who could pitch in when necessary. The poorer the family was, the more it depended on the work of all its members.

In the postwar South, African-American families, with few possessions and little money, relied heavily on extended families—cousins, aunts, uncles, and other relatives—to help with child care, housing, and expenses. The members of this extended kinship network, which could include as many as 200 people, practiced a remarkable degree of cooperation. They reached decisions jointly, shared economic resources, provided emotional support, and strengthened mutual ties through visits, reunions, and membership in the same church.

Poor white families in the South and Midwest, although often better off than their black counterparts, also depended heavily on the efforts of all family members. The men and older boys worked in the fields, and farm wives and younger children ran the house and dairy, kept up the kitchen garden, sewed and mended clothes, knitted hats and gloves, churned butter, made soap, and trimmed the oil lamps that illuminated the home. When necessary, rural women and their daughters took over the duties normally performed by men. They built homes, plowed the fields, cared for the livestock, and pitched in at harvest time. Many farm families owed their survival to the hard work and resourcefulness of everyone involved.

The same was true for urban working-class families; the contributions of *all* family members often spelled the difference between survival and modest prosperity. The average urban family of five or six members in the 1890s needed $600 to $800 annually to live comfortably, more than the father's earnings alone could provide. To supplement their income, urban working-class families rented rooms to boarders, and the women commonly took in laundry. Urban working-class women who could not afford store-bought clothes sewed the family's wardrobe. If a husband became sick or lost his job, a wife might take a job in a garment factory alongside her elder daughters, who usually worked until they married. Immigrant children commonly went to work at the age of ten and turned over their earnings to their parents. Such responsibilities forced children to grow up quickly but also instilled a strong sense of family loyalty.

This cooperative family ethic was the key to improving working-class families' financial position. Pooling wages allowed families to set aside part of their income for monthly mortgage payments. Such thrift, and the availability of small, affordable houses, helped many families to purchase their own homes. Homeownership served as a kind of insurance; if the principal breadwinner fell sick or became unemployed, families could take in boarders or use the house as collateral on a loan.

"Stem families" enabled working- and middle-class families to support elderly parents. In this arrangement, while most children mature, marry, and move away, one child remains in the parents' household even after marriage. This child cares for aged parents, often takes over the family farm or business, and inherits the house when the parents die. Working-class Americans particularly benefited from the stem family system.

The cooperative family ethic enabled working-class Americans to survive and even to get ahead in the rapidly changing economy of the late nineteenth century. But it also accentuated the differences between poor families and their middle- and upper-class counterparts, which managed comfortably on the salary of the main breadwinner alone.

Middle-Class Society and Culture

Spared the struggle for survival that confronted most Americans, the middle and upper classes faced a different challenge: explaining and rationalizing the material benefits of the emerging consumer society. To justify the achievements of society's wealthiest members, ministers, advice-book writers, and other commentators appealed to Victorian morality, a set of social ideas influential among the privileged classes of England and the United States during the reign (1837–1901) of Britain's Queen Victoria.

Proponents of Victorian morality argued that the success of the middle and upper classes rested on their superior talent, intelligence, morality, and self-control. Women were identified as the driving force for moral improvement. While men engaged in the world's work, women provided the gentle, elevating influence that would lead society in its upward march.

A network of institutions, from elegant department stores and hotels to elite colleges and universities, testified to the privileged position of the upper and middle classes.

Manners and Morals

The Victorian world view rested on several fundamental assumptions. Cautiously optimistic about human nature, the Victorian moral code held that only strenuous effort would bring progress. At its best, this code energized reform movements against suffering and injustice, including slavery; at its worst, this intense moralism could lead to an obsessive preoccupation with the details of personal behavior. Because more members of the elite and middle class believed that they had achieved their status through sobriety, industriousness, and self-restraint, they stressed these virtues. "Victorian morality" thus became synonymous with an intense emphasis on self-discipline and self-control. Often violated in practice, this code was widely preached as the standard for society.

To this emphasis on sobriety and self-control, the champions of Victorian morality added the importance of "culture" (knowledge of the social graces, literature, the fine arts, and classical music) as an agency of social uplift. Prominent clergymen, among them Henry Ward Beecher of Brooklyn, urged cultural refinement. To further the cause, the elite founded, and the middle class supported, a series of cultural institutions including the Metropolitan Museum of Art in New York (1870) and the Museum of Fine Arts in Boston (1870).

At its pettiest, the middle-class focus on conduct degenerated into a preoccupation with manners and social rituals. Behavior as well as income defined social standing. Good manners, including a knowledge of proper etiquette in all social occasions, especially dining and entertaining, became a badge of status. Meals evolved into rituals that differentiated the social classes. They presented occasions for displaying the elaborate silver and china that middle- and upper-class families exclusively possessed, and they provided telltale clues to a family's level of refinement and sophistication.

The Victorian code, with its emphasis on

morals, manners, and behavior, heightened the sense of class differences and created visible distinctions among social groups. Prominent Victorians might claim their sincere interest in helping others to improve themselves, but more often than not their self-righteous, intensely moralistic outlook simply widened the gap already opened by income disparities.

The Cult of Domesticity

Victorian views on morality and culture, coupled with rising pressures on consumers to make decisions about a mountain of domestic products, had a subtle but important impact on middle-class expectations about woman's role within the home. From the 1840s onward, the home had been idealized as "the woman's sphere," a protected retreat where she could express her special maternal gifts, including a sensitivity toward children and an aptitude for religion. "The home is the wife's province," asserted one writer; "it is her natural field of labor."

Victorian advocates of the cult of domesticity added a new obligation for women: to foster an artistic environment that would nurture the family's cultural improvement. Houses became statements of cultural aspirations, and elaborately ornamented architectural styles gained popularity. Like intricate sculptures, these houses featured detailed wood ornamentation, windows of varying dimensions, and ornate chimneys. Women turned the front parlor into a treasure house whose furnishings and curios reflected family social standing and refinement. Souvenir spoons and other knickknacks demonstrated the household's cosmopolitanism. Excluded from the world of business and commerce, women directed their energy to transforming their homes into "a place of repose, a refuge from the excitement and distractions of outside . . . , provided with every attainable means of rest and recreation."

Not all middle-class women pursued this domestic ideal. For some, the drudgery of housework and of running the family overwhelmed any concern for artistic accomplishment. For others, the artistic ideal itself was not to their taste. In the 1880s and 1890s women increasingly sought other outlets for their creative energies. Some, such as temperance crusader Frances Willard, would use the cult of domesticity as a rationale for political causes.

Department Stores and Hotels

Although Victorian thought justified the privileges of the well-to-do, many people found it difficult to shake the thriftiness of their early years and accept the new preoccupation with accumulation and display. In the 1880s merchandisers encouraged Americans to loosen their purse strings and enjoy prosperity by emphasizing the high quality and low cost of their goods.

Key to changing attitudes about consumption was the department store. In the final quarter of the nineteenth century, entrepreneurs such as Roland Macy, John Wanamaker, and Marshall Field made the department store an urban institution and transformed the shopping experience for their middle- and upper-class patrons.

In a radical departure from the rural general store, the department store sold every conceivable household item and article of clothing, purchased in large volume at low cost. The department store sold goods at fixed prices, allowed unconditional exchanges, and provided free delivery. Merchants such as Macy and Wanamaker overcame middle- and upper-class reluctance to spend by advertising products at "rock-bottom" prices and by waging price wars to validate their claims. End-of-season clearance sales at drastically marked-down prices prevented stock from piling up and attracted the thrifty.

Major downtown establishments tried to make shopping an adventure. The stores became more and more ornate, with stained-glass skylights, marble staircases, brilliant chandeliers, and plush carpets. When opened in 1876, John Wanamaker's Grand Depot in Philadelphia boasted a gaslit "tent" where women could examine silk gowns under ballroom conditions. Marshall Field's Chicago emporium contained a stained-glass dome, blue English carpets, and rare walnut paneling.

Rike's Department Store, Dayton, Ohio, 1893
Department stores set new standards for customer comfort and service in this era.

Department stores lavished care and attention on shoppers, especially women. Richly decorated lounges, elegant restaurants serving modestly priced lunches, and glittering holiday decorations enticed visitors to linger and to buy on impulse. Sales clerks greeted customers at the door, answered questions, and made women feel at home. The large urban department store became a social club and home away from home for affluent women.

The stately metropolitan hotels that proliferated in the late nineteenth century provided further examples of high fashion and elite taste. New York's Waldorf Astoria, Chicago's Palmer House, and San Francisco's Palace became public shrines, epitomizing efficient organization and upper-class taste. Built in 1892 in the German Renaissance style, the Waldorf Astoria was a self-contained community with offices, restaurants, ballrooms, courtyards, and 500 guest rooms. Household reformers of the 1890s held up the highly organized restaurants and laundry systems of the big hotels as models for efficient cooperative-apartment complexes.

Whether one marveled at their efficiency or gazed in wonder at their gilt mirrors and plush carpets, the grand hotels set the pattern for luxury, convenience, and service. In a society that shunned aristocratic pretensions, hotels and department stores made luxury acceptable by clothing it in the guise of efficiency and good taste. They provided a setting where newly affluent members of society could indulge and pamper themselves, if only for a few minutes or a day.

The Transformation of Higher Education

At a time when relatively few Americans possessed even a high-school education, colleges and universities represented another stronghold of the business and professional elite and of the moderately well-to-do middle class. Wealthy capitalists gained stature and a measure of immortality by endowing colleges and universities. In 1885 Leland Stanford and his wife, Jane Lathrop Stanford, launched Stanford University with a bequest of $24 million; in 1891 John D. Rockefeller donated $34 million to the University of Chicago. Industrialists and businessmen dominated the boards of trustees of many educational institutions, and colleges were viewed as a training ground for future business and professional leaders.

The athletic field as well as the classroom prepared affluent young men for business and the professions. Football, adapted from English rugby in 1869, became an elite sport played by college teams. Some college presidents dismissed football as a dangerous waste of time and money, but alumni and coaches credited the new sport with building character. Because Social Darwinism emphasized struggle, football seemed an ideal arena for improving the strength, courage, and self-discipline of youth. Some defenders of the sport insisted that football could substitute for the frontier experience in an increasingly urban society. By 1900 football had become a popular fall sport, stimulating alumni giving and building goodwill for those elite institutions that otherwise remained far outside the experience of the average American.

More than 150 new colleges and universities appeared between 1880 and 1900, and enrollments more than doubled, rising from 1.7 percent of college-age youth in 1870 to 4 percent in 1900. A small but growing number of these newcomers to higher education were women. Wealthy capitalists financed some institutions, but public funds supported the state universities of the Midwest, and religious denominations continued to support many colleges.

Debates about what should be taught and how it should be taught swept through higher education, especially in science and medicine. Antebellum medical education had occupied less than a year of medical students' time, and most received their degrees without ever having visited a hospital or seen a patient. The grim mortality rates of the Civil War, in which twice as many soldiers died from infections as from wounds, graphically illustrated the low state of medical education. In the 1880s and 1890s medical professors, many of whom had studied in France and Germany, began restructuring American medical education, insisting that students be trained in biology, chemistry, and physics. By 1900 the practice of medicine in America rested on a firm professional foundation. Similar reforms took place in architecture, engineering, and law.

These changes were part of a larger transformation in higher education that produced a new institution, the research university. Unlike antebellum colleges, which taught little beyond classical languages, theology, logic, and mathematics, the new research universities offered courses in a wide variety of subjects, established professional schools, and encouraged faculty members to pursue basic research. For Andrew D. White, the first president of Cornell University (1869), the goal was to create a school "where any person can find instruction in any study." Cornell, the University of Wisconsin, Johns Hopkins, Harvard, and others laid the groundwork for the central role that U.S. universities would play in the intellectual, cultural, and scientific life of the twentieth century. However, higher education remained the privilege of a few as the nineteenth century ended; the age when college attendance would become the norm lay many years ahead.

Working-Class Leisure in the Immigrant City

In colonial America the subject of leisure time had generally arisen only when ministers condemned "idleness" as the first step toward sin. In the rural culture of the early nineteenth century, the unremitting routines of farm labor had left little time for relaxation. Family picnics, horse races, county fairs, revivals, and holidays such as the Fourth of July and Christmas had provided permissible diversion, but even in relaxation earlier generations had guarded against "laziness."

As urban populations and factories multiplied after the Civil War, new patterns of leisure and amusement emerged, especially among the urban working class. After long hours in factories and mills or behind department-store counters, working-class Americans craved relaxation and diversion. They thronged the streets, patronized saloons and dance halls, cheered at boxing matches and baseball games, and organized boisterous group picnics and holiday celebrations. Amusement parks, vaudeville theaters, sporting clubs, and racetracks provided further entertainment for workers, and mass leisure became a big business.

As factory work became more routinized and more impersonal, working-class Americans, especially immigrants, cherished their few opportunities for interaction and recreation. Ironically, the same ethnic divisions that fragmented the labor movement in this era provided the foundation for a strong working-class culture beyond the factory gates.

Streets, Saloons, and Boxing Matches

Hours of tedious, highly disciplined, and physically exhausting labor left workers tired but thirsty for excitement and escape from their cramped living quarters. In 1889 a banner carried by a carpenters' union summed up their needs: "EIGHT HOURS FOR WORK, EIGHT HOURS FOR REST, AND EIGHT HOURS FOR WHAT WE WILL."

City streets provided some recreation. Relaxing after a day's work, shop girls and laborers clustered on busy corners, watching shouting pushcart peddlers and listening to organ grinders play familiar melodies. For a penny or a nickel, they could buy a bagel, a baked potato, or a soda. In the summer when the heat and humidity within the tenements reached unbearable levels, the streets became the center of neighborhood life.

The streets beckoned to all, but some leisure institutions drew a male clientele. For example, in cities, such as Baltimore, Milwaukee, and Cincinnati, with a strong German immigrant flavor, gymnastic clubs (*Turnvereine*) and singing societies (*Gesangvereine*) provided men with both companionship and the opportunity to perpetuate Old World traditions.

Saloons offered male companionship, conviviality, and five-cent beer, often with a free lunch thrown in. By 1900 New York City had an estimated 10,000 saloons. As gathering places in ethnic neighborhoods, saloons reinforced group identity and became centers for immigrant politics. Saloonkeepers often doubled as local ward bosses who performed small services for their patrons. With rich mahogany bars, shiny brass rails, and elegant mirrors, saloons provided a taste of luxury for their factory-worker clientele.

What explains the saloons' popularity, and what was their impact? The saloon provided an antidote to the socially isolating routines of factory labor. The saloon scene thus clashed with the increasingly private and family-centered social life of the middle class. But saloons often served as bases for prostitution and criminal activity. Moreover, drinking too much at the saloon frequently led to family violence, and "treating"—buying drinks for friends—cut deeply into already meager paychecks.

For working-class males, bare-knuckles prizefighting also became a popular amusement. Drawing heroes from society's poorer ranks, the boxing rings became an arena where lower-class men could assert their individuality and physical prowess. African-Americans, Irish, and Germans formed their own "sporting clubs" and used athletics to bolster their self-confidence and to reaffirm their racial or ethnic identity.

Amateur boxing gained unexpected elite support in the 1880s and 1890s as an antidote to what some people considered a dangerous tendency toward decadence among privileged males. Theodore Roosevelt, a New York patrician and rising Republican, did much to make the sport respectable. The introduction of the Marquis of Queensbury code—a set of rules devised in England that required the use of gloves, outlawed wrestling holds, standardized the three-minute round, and changed the time required for a knockout from thirty seconds to ten—increased boxing's acceptability to the upper crust. Meanwhile, the sport, like other popular leisure-time diversions, was becoming professionalized.

The Rise of Professional Sports

As an English game called rounders, baseball had

existed since the seventeenth century. If Americans did not create baseball, they nevertheless took this informal children's game and turned it into a major professional sport. In 1845 the New York Knickerbockers, the first organized baseball team, was established. In the 1860s rules were codified and the sport assumed its present form, featuring overhand pitching, fielders' gloves, nine-inning games, and bases spaced ninety feet apart. That same decade, promoters organized professional clubs and began to compete for players. In 1869 the Cincinnati Red Stockings, the first team to put its players under contract for the whole season, toured the country and ended the season with fifty-seven wins and no losses.

Team owners organized the National League in 1876 and took control of the game from the players by forbidding them to play for other teams and limiting each city to a single team. Crowds of 10,000 to 12,000 fans flooded into ballparks each game, creating enormous profits for the owners. By the 1890s baseball was big business. Clubs scheduled doubleheaders, ran promotions such as ladies' day, and made money by selling beer, peanuts, and hot dogs. The working class particularly took baseball to heart. The most profitable teams came from industrial cities with large working-class populations.

Newspapers thrived on baseball. Joseph Pulitzer introduced the first separate sports page when he bought the *New York World* in 1883, and baseball dominated the paper's sports reporting. Baseball, declared writer Mark Twain, had become "the very symbol . . . and visible expression of the drive and push and rush and struggle of the raging, tearing, booming nineteenth century."

Although no other organized sport attracted as large a following as baseball, horse racing and boxing also drew large crowds of spectators and received wide press coverage. But whereas races such as Louisville's Kentucky Derby became social events for the rich, professional boxing aroused passionate devotion in the working class.

The hero of nineteenth-century professional sports was heavyweight fighter John L. Sullivan. Of Irish-immigrant stock, Sullivan began boxing in 1877 at age nineteen. With his massive physique, handlebar mustache, and arrogant swagger, Sullivan was enormously popular. Barnstorming across the country, he vanquished a succession of local strong men, invariably wearing his trademark green tights with an American flag wrapped around his middle.

Vaudeville, Amusement Parks, and Dance Halls

In contrast to the male preserve of saloons and prizefights, the world of vaudeville shows, amusement parks, and neighborhood dance halls welcomed all comers regardless of gender and proved particularly congenial to working-class women.

Vaudeville, with roots in antebellum minstrel shows, offered a succession of acts designed for mass appeal. The vaudeville show typically opened with an animal act or a dance number, followed by a musical interlude. Then came comic skits ridiculing the trials of urban life, satirizing police and municipal ineptitude, poking fun at the babel of accents in the immigrant city, and mining a rich vein of ethnic humor and stereotypes. After more musical numbers and acts by ventriloquists and magicians, the program ended with a "flash" finale featuring flying-trapeze artists or the like. By the 1880s vaudeville was drawing larger crowds than any other form of theater. It provided an evening of inexpensive, lighthearted entertainment and let immigrants laugh at their own experiences, as translated into slapstick and caricature.

While vaudeville offered psychological release from the stresses of working-class life, amusement parks provided physical escape. The fun houses, thrill rides, and games of New York's Coney Island, the prototype of urban amusement parks, sprawled along the Brooklyn waterfront. By 1900 as many as 500,000 people would throng the beach, the boardwalk, and the amusement parks on a summer Saturday. Young couples rode through the dark Tunnel of Love, sped down the dizzying roller coaster, and watched bellydancers in the sideshows, momentarily surrendering to the spirit of exuberant play and forgetting the restrictions and demands of the industrial world.

By the end of the nineteenth century, New York City had well over 300,000 female wage earners, most of them young, unmarried women. The amusement parks with their exhilarating rides and glittering dance pavilions, and the dance halls in the immigrant districts of most cities, exerted a powerful lure. There these women could meet friends, spend time with young men beyond parents' watchful eyes, show off their new dresses, and try out the latest dance steps in a magical release from the drudgery of daily life.

Ragtime

Nothing more vividly illustrates the differences between the cultures of the middle class and the working class than the contrasting styles of popular music that each favored. While the middle class preferred hymns or songs with a moral message, the working class embraced ragtime, the product of African-American musicians in the saloons of the South.

Ragtime developed out of the rich tradition of songs through which black Americans had eased the burdens of their lives. Like spirituals, ragtime used syncopated rhythms and complex harmonies, but it blended them with marching-band musical structures to create a distinctive style. A favorite of "honky-tonk" piano players, ragtime was introduced to the broader public in the 1890s and became a national sensation. Its best-known composer, Scott Joplin, introduced his music at Chicago's Columbian Exposition in 1893. "Maple Leaf Rag," published in 1899, earned Joplin a national reputation.

Inventive, playful, and infectiously rhythmic, ragtime had an appealing originality. But part of its popularity also came from its origin in saloons and its association with blacks, whom white Victorians stereotyped as sexual and uninhibited. The "wild" and complex rhythms of ragtime supposedly reflected a freer and more "natural" expression of love and affection. When genteel critics sneered, the new dance music became all the more attractive to the urban working class.

Ragtime's popularity proved a mixed blessing for African-Americans. It testified to the achievements of brilliant composers such as Joplin, helped to break down barriers in the music industry, and contributed to a spreading rebellion against Victorian repressiveness. At the same time, it confirmed white stereotypes of blacks as primitive and sensuous, a bias that underlay the racism of the period and helped to justify segregation and discrimination.

Cultures in Conflict

Class conflict and cultural unrest embroiled the United States in the late nineteenth century, even within the middle class. As 1900 dawned, ethical questions about Victorian morality and new cultural stirrings intensified. At the center of the cultural turbulence stood women, increasingly dissatisfied with the restrictive code of feminine propriety. The growth of women's clubs and women's colleges, and even the bicycle fad of the 1890s, all contributed to the emergence of the "new woman."

At the same time, a widening chasm divided the well-to-do from the mass of immigrant laborers. Perhaps in no period of American history have class conflicts been as open and raw. Nervously eying the noisy culture of city streets, saloons, boxing clubs, dance halls, and amusement parks, middle-class leaders perceived a massive, if unconscious, challenge to their own cultural and social standing. Some middle-class reformers promoted public schools as a means to impose middle-class values on the urban masses, and others battled urban "vice" and "immorality." The genteel mores of the middle class proved particularly vulnerable, so that by 1900 the Victorian social and moral ethos was crumbling.

The Genteel Tradition and Its Critics

In the 1870s and 1880s a group of upper-class writers and editors, led by Charles Eliot Norton of

Harvard and E. L. Godkin of *The Nation*, codified standards for writing and design and tried to create a coherent national artistic culture. Joining forces with allies in Boston and New York, these elites lobbied to "improve" American taste in interior furnishings, textiles, ceramics, wallpaper, and books.

The drive to improve the arts was prompted in part by the flood of cheap reproductions and sensationalistic novels that poured off the nation's presses after the Civil War. Despondent about what they termed a "chromo civilization" enamored of trashy books and garish color art prints, Norton, Godkin, and others lectured the middle class about the value of high culture and the insights to be gained from the arts. They also censored their own publications to remove all sexual allusions, vulgar slang, disrespectful treatment of Christianity, and unhappy endings.

Godkin and editors of other "quality" periodicals created an important forum for serious writers in *The Nation* and *The Atlantic Monthly*. Novelist Henry James, who published virtually all of his work in the *Atlantic*, reflected the views of this elite literary establishment. He wrote, "It is art that *makes* life, . . . and I know of no substitute whatever for [its] force and beauty." This art-for-art's-sake movement also influenced architects, jewelers, and interior decorators.

Although these genteel magazines provided an important forum for new authors, their editors' strident elitism and imperialistic desire to control national literary standards bred opposition. Samuel Langhorne Clemens, better known as Mark Twain, spoke for many young writers when he declared as early as 1869 that he was through with "literature and all that bosh." Attacking aristocratic literary conventions, Twain and others who shared his concerns worked to broaden literature's appeal to the general public.

These efforts by a younger generation of writers to chart new directions for American literature rested on sweeping changes within the publishing industry. New magazines such as *Ladies' Home Journal*, *Cosmopolitan*, and *McClure's* competed with the elite publications. The new magazines slashed their prices and tripled their circulation. Supported by advertising rather than subscriptions, they provided an outlet for younger authors who wanted to write about real people in everyday life.

Some of these writers were labeled regionalists because they captured the distinctive dialects and details of their featured locale, whether New England or the South. Others, among them William Dean Howells, focused on a truthful, if optimistic, depiction of the commonplace. Another group, called naturalists, stressed economic and psychological determinants and often examined the dark underside of life. In *Maggie: A Girl of the Streets* (1893), a bleak story of an innocent girl's exploitation and suicide in an urban slum, Stephen Crane wrote what is generally considered the first naturalist American novel. Labels aside, all these writers shared a skepticism toward literary conventions and an intense desire to understand the society around them.

The careers of Mark Twain and Theodore Dreiser highlight the changes in the publishing industry and the evolution of new forms of writing. Both were products of the Midwest, outsiders to the East Coast literary establishment—Twain from Missouri and Dreiser from Indiana. As young men, both worked as newspaper reporters and traveled widely. Both learned from direct experience about the greed, speculation, and fraud of the era.

Twain and Dreiser called on their own experiences to write about the human impact of the wrenching social changes that surrounded them: the flow of people to the expanding cities and the relentless scramble for power, wealth, and fame. In the *Adventures of Huckleberry Finn* (1884), Twain uses the river journey of two runaways, the rebellious Huck and the slave Jim, to explore the nature of contemporary American society by contrasting the idyllic life on the raft to the tawdry, fraudulent world of the small riverfront towns. Dreiser's *Sister Carrie* (1900) traces the journey of Carrie Meeber, an innocent and attractive girl, from her Wisconsin farm home to Chicago. Seduced by a traveling salesman, Carrie moves in with Hurstwood, the married proprietor of a fancy saloon. Driven by her desire for

Samuel Langhorne Clemens (Mark Twain) (1835–1910)

Before winning fame as a writer, the adventurous Twain worked as a printer; a river pilot on the Mississippi; a mining prospector in Carson City, Nevada; and a newspaper reporter.

expensive department-store clothes and lavish entertainment, Carrie follows Hurstwood to New York, abandons him when his money runs out, and pursues her own career in the theater.

Twain and Dreiser broke sharply with the genteel tradition's emphasis on manners and decorum. *Century* magazine readers complained that *Huckleberry Finn* was "destitute of a single redeeming quality." The publisher of *Sister Carrie* found the novel so repugnant that he printed only 1,000 copies to fulfill his contract—and then stored them in a warehouse.

Similarly, growing numbers of scholars and critics challenged the elite's self-serving beliefs, including assumptions that moral worth and economic standing were closely linked and that the status quo represented a social order decreed by God and nature alike. Economist Thorstein Veblen's *The Theory of the Leisure Class* (1899) caustically critiqued the life-style of the new capitalist elite. The product of a poor Norwegian farm community in Minnesota, Veblen looked at the captains of industry and their families with a jaundiced eye. He mercilessly documented their "conspicuous consumption" and lamented the widening economic gap between "those who worked without profit" and "those who profited without working."

Within the new discipline of sociology, Annie MacLean exposed the exploitation of department-store clerks, Walter Wyckoff uncovered the hand-to-mouth existence of unskilled laborers, and W. E. B. Du Bois documented the hardships of African-Americans in Philadelphia. The publication of these writings, coupled with the economic depression and seething labor agitation of the 1890s, made it increasingly difficult for turn-of-the-century middle-class Americans to accept the smug, self-satisfied belief in progress and genteel culture that had been a hallmark of the Victorian outlook.

Modernism in Architecture and Painting

The challenge to the genteel tradition also found support among architects and painters. Architects followed the lead of Louis Sullivan, who argued that a building's form should follow its function. In their view, banks, for example, should look like financial institutions, not Greek temples. Rejecting elite pretensions, architects looked to the future—to modernism, a quest for new modes of expression—for inspiration.

Frank Lloyd Wright's "prairie-school" houses, first built in the Chicago suburb of Oak Park in the 1890s, represented a typical modernist break with the past. Wright scorned the bulky Victorian house, with its large attics and basements; his designs, featuring broad, sheltering roofs and low silhouettes harmonious with the flat prairie landscape, used open, interconnecting rooms to create a sense of spaciousness.

Modernism's rejection of Victorian gentility influenced late-nineteenth-century painting as well. Winslow Homer's watercolors pictured nature as brutally tough and unsentimental; in his grim, elemental seascapes, lone men struggle against massive waves that threaten to overwhelm them. Thomas Eakins's canvases of swimmers, boxers, and rowers (such as his well-known *The Champion Single Sculls*, 1871) captured moments of vigorous physical exertion. Obsessed with making his paintings realistic, Eakins studied anatomy at a medical school, did photographic studies and dissection on cadavers in preparation for painting, and used nude models in his drawing classes.

The architects' and painters' revolt symptomized a larger shift in middle-class thought driven by the emergence of a complex social environment. As one minister observed in 1898, the transition from muscle to mechanical power had "separated, as by an impassable gulf, the simple, homespun, individualistic world of the . . . past, from the complex, closely associated life of the present." The increasingly evident gap between the quiet parlors and flickering kerosene lamps of small towns and life in the big, glittering cities of glass and iron made nineteenth-century Americans acutely aware of differences in wealth and upbringing.

Distrusting idealistic Victorian assumptions about social progress, the middle class nevertheless disagreed over how to replace them. Not until the progressive period would social reformers combine new expertise in social research with an enlarged conception of the federal government's regulatory power to break sharply with their Victorian predecessors' social outlook.

From Victorian Lady to New Woman

The role of middle-class women in the revolt against Victorian refinement was complex and ambiguous. Some women's dissatisfaction with the cult of domesticity did not necessarily lead to their open rebellion. Though chafing against the constraints of the genteel code and the assumption that they should limit their activities to the home, many women remained committed to playing a supportive role within the family. In fact, early advocates of a "widened sphere" for women often fused the traditional Victorian ideal of womanhood with a firm commitment to political action.

The career of temperance leader Frances Willard illustrates how the cult of domesticity could evolve into a broader view of women's social and political responsibilities. Willard believed that by nature women were compassionate, nurturing, and sensitive to others; she was equally convinced that drinking encouraged men to squander their earnings and profoundly threatened family life. In 1874 Willard resigned her positions as dean of women and professor of English at Northwestern University to devote her energies completely to the temperance cause. Five years later, she became president of the newly formed Woman's Christian Temperance Union (WCTU).

Willard transformed the cult of domesticity's emphasis on women's unique moral virtues into a rationale for political action. The domestication of politics, she asserted, would protect the family and improve public morality. Choosing as her badge a white ribbon, symbolizing the purity of the home, in 1880 Frances Willard launched a crusade to win women's right to vote so that they could outlaw liquor. Willard also expanded the WCTU's activities to include welfare work, prison reform, labor arbitration, and public health. By 1890 the WCTU, with a membership of 150,000, had become the nation's first mass organization of women. Its members gained experience as lobbyists, organizers, and lecturers, undercutting the assumption of "separate spheres."

An expanding network of women's clubs offered another means by which middle- and upper-class women could hone their skills in civic affairs, public speaking, and intellectual analysis. Club women became involved in social-welfare projects, public-library expansion, and tenement reform. By 1892 the General Federation of Women's Clubs boasted 495 affiliates and 100,000 members.

College education also expanded women's roles. Coeducational colleges and universities in the Midwest enrolled increasing numbers of women, and private universities admitted women to affiliated but separate institutions such as Barnard (1889) and Radcliffe (1894). Between 1880 and 1900 the percentage of colleges admitting women jumped from 30 percent to 71 percent; by the turn of the century, women constituted more than one-third of the total college-student population.

Although the earliest women's colleges had been founded to reinforce prevailing concepts of femininity, participation in college organizations, athletics, and dramatics enabled female students to learn traditionally "masculine" strategies for gaining power. The generation of women educated at female institutions in the late nineteenth century developed the self-confidence to break with the Victorian ideal of passive womanhood and to compete on an equal basis with men by displaying strength, aggressiveness, and intelligence, popularly considered male attributes.

A bicycling vogue that swept urban America at the end of the century further loosened Victorian constraints on women. Fearful of waning vitality, middle- and upper-class Americans sought new means of improving their vigor, ranging from health products such as cod-liver oil and sarsaparilla to enthusiastic participation in basketball. Bicycling, which could be enjoyed individually or in groups, quickly became the most popular sport with those who wished to combine exercise with recreation. The advent in the 1880s of smaller wheels, ball-bearing axles, and air-filled tires helped to make bicycling a national craze, so that by the 1890s more than a million Americans owned bicycles.

Bicycling especially appealed to young women uncomfortable with restrictive Victorian ideas, which included the views that proper young ladies must never sweat, the female body must be fully covered at all times, and physical exertion should take place in private. Pedaling along without corsets or padded clothing, the woman bicyclist implicitly broke with genteel conventions.

Changing attitudes about femininity also found expression in shifting ideas about marriage. Charlotte Perkins Gilman, a suffrage advocate and speaker for women's rights, asserted that women would make an effective contribution to society only when they won economic independence from men through work outside the home. The climbing divorce rate between 1880 and 1900 testified to women's changing relationship to men; in 1880 one in twenty-one marriages ended in divorce, but by 1900 the rate had shot up to one in twelve. Women who sued for divorce increasingly cited their husbands' failure to act responsibly and to respect their autonomy. Accepting such arguments, courts fre-

Bicycling Lithograph, 1887

The first high-wheeler bicycles were difficult and dangerous to ride. One bump might pitch the rider forward over the handlebars. Therefore, the sport at first was restricted to males. Females who wished to accompany their male friends, as shown in this lithograph, could ride the more cumbersome "fairy tricycle."

quently awarded wives alimony, a monetary settlement payable by ex-husbands to support their former spouses.

Contemporary assessments of these changes differed widely. Riding a bicycle, demanding the vote, and "wearin' clothes that no lady shud wear," wrote humorist Peter Finley Dunne, "Molly Donahue have up an' become a new woman!" A more sympathetic male observer, illustrator Charles Dana Gibson, captured the popular image of this new woman with his folio of "Gibson girls," who exuded independence and freedom. Playing tennis or riding her bicycle, Gibson's tanned, vigorous young woman enjoyed the healthy outdoor life and active participation in the community.

Women writers generally welcomed the new female commitment to self-sufficiency and independence. Mary Wilkins Freeman's short stories, for example, compare women's expanding role to the frontier ideal of freedom. Her characters fight for their beliefs without concern for society's reaction. Feminist Kate Chopin pushed the debate to the extreme by having the married heroine of her 1899 novel *The Awakening* violate social conventions by falling in love with another man and then taking her life when his ideas about women prove as narrow and traditional as those of her husband.

Nonetheless, attitudes changed slowly. The enlarged concept of women's role in society had its greatest influence on middle-class women who enjoyed the privilege of higher education, possessed some leisure time, and could hope for success in journalism, education, social work, and nursing. For shop girls who worked sixty hours a week to make ends meet, such opportunities remained a distant goal. Although many women sought more independence and control over their own lives, most still viewed the home as their primary responsibility.

Public Education as an Arena of Class Conflict

Controversy over the scope and function of public education engaged Americans of all socioeconomic levels and highlighted class and cultural divisions in late-nineteenth-century society. Viewing public schools as an instrument for indoctrinating and controlling the lower ranks, middle-class educators and civic leaders campaigned to expand and centralize public schooling. These would-be reformers' efforts aroused opposition from ethnic and religious groups whose outlook and interests differed sharply from theirs.

Thanks to the crusade for universal public education started by Horace Mann, most states had public-school systems by the Civil War. More than half the nation's children received some formal education, but most attended only a few years, and few went to high school. In the 1870s middle-class activists, concerned that many Americans lacked sufficient knowledge to participate wisely in public affairs or to function effectively in the labor force, worked to raise the overall educational level and to increase the number of years spent in school.

One such reformer was William Torrey Harris, a Victorian moralist who viewed public schools as a "great instrument to lift all classes of people into . . . civilized life." Harris urged teachers to instill in students a sense of order, decorum, self-discipline, and civic loyalty. Believing that modern industrial society depended on citizens' conforming to the timetables of factory and train, he envisioned schools as models of punctuality and scheduling: "The pupil must have his lesson ready at the appointed time, must rise at the tap of the bell, move to the line, return; in short, go through all the evolutions with equal precision."

To achieve these goals, reform-minded educators such as Harris wrested control of schools from neighborhood leaders and ward politicians by stressing punctuality and order, compulsory-attendance laws, and a tenure system to insulate teachers from political favoritism and parental pressure. By 1900 thirty-one states required all children from eight to fourteen years of age to attend school. But the steamroller methods by Harris and others to systematize public education prompted protests. New York pediatrician Joseph Mayer Rice, after interviewing 1,200 teachers, lashed out at the schools' singsong memorization and prisonlike discipline. In city after city he discovered teachers who drilled students mercilessly and were more concerned about their posture than their learning.

But Rice overlooked real advances; for example, the national illiteracy rate dropped from 17 percent in 1880 to 13 percent by 1900, despite the influx of immigrants. He was on target, however, in assailing many teachers' rigid emphasis on silence, docility, and unquestioning obedience to rules. When a Chicago school inspector found a thirteen-year-old boy huddled in the basement of a stockyard building and ordered him back to school, the weeping boy blurted:

> *They hits ye if yer don't learn, and they hits ye if ye whisper, and they hits ye if ye have string in yer pocket, and they hits ye if yer seat squeaks, and they hits ye if ye don't stand up in time, and they hits ye if yer late, and they hits ye if ye ferget the page.*

By the 1880s several different groups were opposing the centralized urban public-school bureaucracies. Working-class families that depended on their children's meager wages for survival, for example, resisted attempts to force their sons and daughters to attend school past the elementary grades. Although some immigrant families sacrificed to give their children an education, many withdrew their offspring from school as soon as they had learned the rudiments of reading and writing and sent them to work. Catholic immigrants, moreover, objected to the public schools' overwhelmingly Protestant orientation. The Catholic church thus established separate parochial systems, and it rejected federal aid to public schools as a ploy to "gradually extinguish Catholicity in this country, and to form one homogeneous American people after the New England Evangelical type." At the other end of the social scale from working-class immigrants, upper-class parents, especially in the Northeast, commonly did not wish to send their children to the immigrant-thronged public schools. Many therefore enrolled their children in private seminaries and academies. Shielding their privileged students from the temptations of urban life while preparing them to go on to college, these institutions reinforced the elite belief that higher education should be the preserve of the well-to-do.

The proliferation of private and parochial schools, along with controversies over compulsory education, public funding, and classroom decorum, reveals the extent to which public education had become entangled in ethnic and class differences. Unlike Germany and Japan, which standardized and centralized their national educational systems in the nineteenth century, the United States created a diverse system of locally run public and private institutions that allowed each segment of society some influence over its schools. Amid the disputes, school enrollments expanded dramatically. In 1870 fewer than 72,000 students attended the nation's 1,026 high schools. By 1900 the number of high schools had jumped to more than 5,000 and the number of students to more than 500,000.

CONCLUSION

By the 1890s class conflict was evident in virtually every area of American life, from mealtime manners to entertainment. Middle- and upper-class Americans battled "indecent" lower-class pursuits such as gambling, prizefighting, and bawdy boardwalk sideshows. While the elite favored large, impeccably groomed urban parks, models of propriety and gentility, working people fought for neighborhood parks where they could play ball, drink beer, and escape the stifling heat of tenement apartments.

Not all members of the elite agreed. In *Democratic Vistas* (1881), Walt Whitman decried the attempts of "certain portions of the people" to force their cultural standards and moral values on others, who were made to feel "degraded, humiliated, [and] of no account." Charlotte Perkins Gilman criticized middle-class society for its obsession with manners and empty social rituals.

By the end of the century, a series of compromises between the elite and the working-class and immigrants was emerging. Eroded by dissension within and opposition without, Victorian morality waned, and new standards blended elements of earlier opposing ideas. For example, new rules regulated behavior in both boxing and baseball. The elite view of sports as a vehicle for instilling self-discipline faded, and sports became valued as entertainment and spectacle, big business, and an important part of the new consumerism.

Similarly, vaudeville houses evolved into movie theaters, ragtime music became jazz, and amusement parks like Coney Island became multimillion-dollar theme parks such as Disneyland. In short, the raffish, raucous, and frequently denounced working-class culture of the immigrant city served as the seedbed of modern mass culture. And everywhere commerical interests came to dominate popular culture, encouraging an increasingly prosperous nation to enjoy—and pay for—goods, leisure, sports, and entertainments.

CHRONOLOGY

1865 Vassar College founded.

1869 Cornell University founded.
First intercollegiate football game.
The Great Atlantic & Pacific Tea Company (A&P) organizes a chain of food stores.

1871 Thomas Eakins, *The Champion Single Sculls*.

1875 Smith College founded.
Frances Willard joins the Woman's Christian Temperance Union.

1876 National League of baseball players organized.

1879 F. W. Woolworth opens his "Five and Ten Cent Store" in Utica, New York.

1884 Mark Twain, *Adventures of Huckleberry Finn*.
Bryn Mawr College founded.

1885 Stanford University founded.

1886 Richard Warren Sears starts Sears, Roebuck.

1889 Columbia University adds Barnard College as a coordinate institution for women.

1891 University of Chicago founded.

1892 Joseph Mayer Rice writes his exposé of public education in *Forum* magazine.
General Federation of Women's Clubs organized.

1893 Stephen Crane, *Maggie: A Girl of the Streets*.

1895 Coney Island amusement park opens in Brooklyn.

1899 Scott Joplin, "Maple Leaf Rag."
Kate Chopin, *The Awakening*.

1900 Theodore Dreiser, *Sister Carrie*.

FOR FURTHER READING

Jessica Foy and Thomas J. Schlereth, eds., *American Home Life, 1880–1930* (1992). A probing look at the impact of technology and changing social practices on family life at the turn of the century.

Elliot Gorn and Warren Goldstein, *A Brief History of American Sports* (1993). A skillful analysis of the impact of urbanization, industrialization, and commercialization on American sports.

William Leach, *Land of Desire: Merchants, Power, and the Rise of a New American Culture* (1993). A balanced examination of the innovative advertising and merchandising strategies that underlay the shift to a consumer culture in the 1890s.

Sheila M. Rothman, *Woman's Proper Place: A History of Changing Ideals and Practices, 1870 to the Present* (1978). A perceptive study of shifting attitudes toward women's proper role in society.

Oliver Zunz, *Making America Corporate, 1870–1920* (1990). A pioneering exploration of corporate capitalism's impact on the creation of a consumer culture.

CHAPTER

21

Politics and Expansion in an Industrializing Age

Late-nineteenth-century politics was a boisterous affair. Elections attracted enormous interest, and voters participated in record numbers. Songs, parades, banners, and buttons transformed presidential campaigns into countrywide festivals.

Beneath the hoopla, serious national issues were at stake: tariff rates, veterans' pensions, railroad development, and monetary policy. Political feelings also ran high over local issues. Religious, ethnic, and cultural differences among voters shaped big-city and state politics.

But while industrialization and urbanization were transforming the nation, politicians seemed unable or unwilling to deal with the social consequences. The federal government's lack of engagement arose in part because a tradition of localism was deeply entrenched in American public life and in part because the business leaders who dominated national politics generally opposed government intervention in the economy. These same capitalists welcomed government economic

(Right) Trains such as this played a major role in the United States' industrial transformation.

policies such as tariffs and railroad subsidies, but otherwise their motto was "Hands off."

The government thus sidestepped social problems that in retrospect seem of central importance, even though officials spent an amazing amount of time passing out government jobs through a spoils system so notorious that a demand for civil-service reform swept the nation. As corporations restructured the economy and manipulated the political system to their advantage, major groups became either political outcasts or political victims. Natural catastrophes and economic grievances ignited a grass-roots movement among aggrieved farmers in the 1880s, while an avowedly racist society disfranchised, exploited, segregated, and even terrorized southern blacks.

In the 1890s agrarian discontent led to the rise of the Populist party, which proposed far-reaching government programs to remedy economic and social problems. After the devastating Depression of 1893, voters in 1896 would choose for the first time in years between candidates with radically different political and economic philosophies.

As the century ended, a potent combination of sensationalist journalism, humanitarianism, nationalistic fervor, and capitalistic pressures fueled a drive for expansion. In a short war in 1898, the United States defeated Spain and acquired Caribbean and Pacific lands, setting the stage for expansion in Latin America and confrontation in Asia.

Party Politics in an Era of Social and Economic Upheaval

Geography, ethnic loyalties, sectional conflict, and state and local alignments shaped politics in the 1870s and 1880s. Two issues dominated national politics: the nature and size of the money supply and the staffing of the government bureaucracy.

Patterns of Party Strength

Although American voters elected only one Democratic president, Grover Cleveland (on two separate occasions), between 1857 and 1912, presidential elections were often extremely close. In 1876 and again in 1888, the defeated Democrat received more popular votes than the victorious Republican. The two parties, moreover, often shared control of Congress in these years.

The Democrats' strength rested on three bases: the South; southern parts of border states such as Ohio, Indiana, and Illinois; and large northern cities. The bedrock of Republican strength was rural and small-town New England, Pennsylvania, and the upper Midwest; Republicans also received a substantial urban vote from businessmen and white-collar workers. But these broad geographic concentrations of party strength masked a far more complex reality. Family traditions, ethnic ties, religious affiliations, and other issues often determined how an individual voted. Nor did economic standing absolutely determine party affiliation.

With the two parties so evenly matched, "swing states" where elections could go either way—Connecticut, New York, New Jersey, Indiana, and Illinois—held the balance of power. By no coincidence, most presidential and vice-presidential candidates came from those states.

Voter participation ran high, although women were excluded from casting ballots and African-Americans increasingly were disfranchised. Participation among northern voters reached 80 percent or more and could rise to 95 percent in hard-fought state or local elections. Because only men could vote in most states, political parties functioned as male social organizations. Woman suffrage aroused resistance in part because it threatened the political subculture that offered men so many material and emotional rewards.

The Stakes of Politics

Late-nineteenth-century electoral campaigns centered on three issues that large numbers of voters considered important: the tariff, the nation's currency supply, and veterans' benefits. Import duties had a direct impact on entire regions, and government policies affecting the money supply and

Immigrant Entrepreneurs

This 1888 photograph of the staff of William C. Raue's house- and sign-painting business in Watertown, Wisconsin (a center of German immigrant culture), captures the expansive spirit of the 1880s—an exuberance reflected in the era's politics.

veterans' pensions similarly concerned millions of Americans directly.

Elections frequently involved emotional side issues as Republicans "waved the bloody shirt," reminding voters of the Civil War, and as southerners made crude racist appeals to white voters. However, presidential candidates rarely confronted the problems created by industrialization. Except for the Interstate Commerce Act of 1887 and the Sherman Anti-Trust Act of 1890, Washington seemed caught in a time warp as society plunged into the modern era.

Why was there such neglect? Most important, the capitalist elite used its massive political clout to resist public regulation or oversight. Additionally, a series of lackluster men occupied a much diminished presidential office. Party discipline in Congress had broken down, and members displayed little concern for large national issues. Jealously guarding their political turf, they were better at winning elections than at governing. The doctrine of laissez-faire, which emphasized that the federal government should promote economic development but not regulate the industries that it subsidized, was widely preached.

When people wanted help from government, they turned to state or local authorities. On the Great Plains, angry farmers demanded that their state legislatures regulate railroad rates, while in the cities, immigrants depended variously on machine bosses and reformers, who contended among themselves for political power.

Moreover, state and local governments fought furiously with each other for control. States often held iron sway over cities; when Chicago wanted to issue permits to street popcorn vendors, the Illinois legislature had to pass a special act. To complicate matters, rural legislators had disproportionate influence. In Connecticut, villages of a few hundred people had the same voting strength as such cities as Hartford and Bridgeport.

Also on the local level, grass-roots rivalries pitted ethnic and social groups against one another. In New York City, immigrant Catholics and native-born Protestants locked horns over tax support to parochial schools. In 1889 native-born Republican legislators in Wisconsin passed a law requiring all children to attend English-language schools, a direct attack on parochial schools that held classes in German, Swedish, or Norwegian. And electoral skirmishes often centered on cultural differences, notably the perennial Protestant attempt to force prohibition on Irish whiskey drinkers, German beer drinkers, and Italian wine drinkers.

Thus Gilded Age politics formed an intricate mosaic of individuals, groups, and political parties pursuing varied interests in city halls, statehouses, and Washington, D.C. But despite all the furious activity, the political system lagged behind in addressing the social problems of an increasingly urban and industrial nation.

The Hayes White House: Virtue Restored

In this era of locally based politics and a diminished presidency, the state leaders who controlled both major parties almost invariably chose appealing but pliable men as presidential candidates.

Rutherford B. Hayes (1877–1881) embodied this narrow view of the office. Hayes had won admiration as an honest Ohio governor, and his major presidential achievement was restoration of respect for the office after the Grant scandals. The benevolent, bearded Hayes brought dignity and decorum to the White House. His wife, Lucy, a highly intelligent, college-educated woman of great moral earnestness, actively supported the Woman's Christian Temperance Union (WCTU), and Hayes banished alcohol from the White House. After one presidential dinner, the secretary of state grumbled, "It was a brilliant affair. The water flowed like champagne."

Regulating the Money Supply

Meanwhile, a political issue surfaced in the 1870s that would agitate American politics for decades: how to create a money supply adequate for a diverse and growing economy. The chaotic antebellum system, featuring the circulation of currency from 1,600 state banks, had to be reformed. Many believed that the only trustworthy money was gold, silver, or certificates exchangeable for these scarce metals. All antebellum *federal* currency, about $228 million, consisted of gold or silver coins or U.S. Treasury notes redeemable in gold or silver.

There were other issues. Bankers, business leaders, and politicians believed that economic stability required a strictly limited currency supply, which would drive interest rates up and prices down. Debtors and manufacturers, however, wanted to expand the money supply, a policy that would help them to pay off their debts and would force up falling farm prices.

After the Civil War, these complex issues swirled around a specific question: should the wartime greenbacks still in circulation be retained or eliminated? The hard times associated with the Panic of 1873 (see Chapter 16) made this dispute even more bitter.

The money question entered electoral politics in the mid-1870s with the formation of the Greenback party, which called for an expanded money supply to benefit workers and farmers. In the 1878 midterm elections, Greenback candidates received more than 1 million votes and won fourteen seats in Congress.

As prosperity returned, the Greenback party declined, but the money issue did not disappear. An even longer-lasting controversy surged over the coinage of silver. In the Coinage Act of 1873, Congress instructed the U.S. mint to cease making silver coins, thus "demonetizing" silver. When discoveries in Nevada sharply increased the silver supply, the same coalition that had supported the Greenback party turned to silver with equal ardor, demanding that the government resume purchasing and coining silver.

In 1878 the passage of the Bland-Allison Act gave silver forces a partial victory. It required the treasury to purchase and mint $2 million to $4 million a month in silver. However, the conservative-controlled treasury sabotaged the law by purchasing the minimum amount and refusing to circulate the silver coins it minted.

Frustrated silver advocates tried a new approach in the Sherman Silver Purchase Act of 1890. This measure instructed the treasury to buy 4.5 million ounces of silver a month, almost exactly the amount produced by the nation's silver mines, and to issue treasury notes, redeemable in gold or silver, equivalent to the cost of the purchases. The money supply increased slightly, but as world silver prices plummeted from 1893 forward, the government paid less each month for its purchases and thus issued fewer treasury notes. The tangled controversy went on.

The Spoils System

Since Andrew Jackson's time, successful politicians had rewarded supporters and contributors with positions ranging from cabinet posts to post-office and customs-service jobs. Defenders called the system rotation in office and claimed that it was a democratic way of filling government positions. Critics, however, dubbed it the spoils system after the old expression "To the victor belong the spoils." Too often, the new officeholders were ill prepared or just incompetent, and even the well qualified often had to continue making campaign contributions to their patrons to keep their jobs.

In the 1870s the battle over patronage split the Republican party between rival factions, the Stalwarts and the Half-Breeds. The two differed primarily over who would control the party machinery and patronage. The vain Senator Roscoe Conkling of New York, who had gained control of his state's patronage in President Grant's day, led the Stalwarts, and Senator James G. Blaine of Maine led the Half-Breeds.

For years, a small but influential group of reformers had campaigned for a merit-based civil service. Well bred, well educated, and well heeled, these reformers little understood the immigrants for whom the public payroll could be a ticket out of poverty. They called for a civil service of "gentlemen . . . who need nothing and want nothing from government except the satisfaction of using their talents." In fact, as the government's functions grew more complex, a professional civil service became necessary.

In 1881 advocates of professionalism founded the National Civil Service Reform League; among its chief members were Senator Carl Schurz of Missouri, editor E. L. Godkin, and social-welfare advocate Josephine Shaw Lowell. Civil-service reformers displayed an almost religious fervor: "I have spent my life in fighting the spoils system," gasped one on his deathbed.

Cautiously embracing the civil-service cause, President Hayes in 1877 launched an investigation of the corrupt New York City customs office and demanded the resignations of two officials with strong ties to Conkling. When they refused Hayes's order, the president suspended them.

Civil-Service Reform

In 1880 a deadlocked Republican presidential convention turned to dark-horse candidate James A. Garfield of Ohio. Because Garfield had ties to the Half-Breeds, a Stalwart vice-presidential candidate was nominated, Chester A. Arthur—one of the two Conkling loyalists fired by Hayes. Garfield was healthy, so the choice of the unqualified Arthur on the ticket seemed safe.

Running against both Democratic and Greenback candidates, Garfield won the 1880 election by a razor-thin margin of under 40,000 votes. Conkling, to protest Garfield's appointment of several of

The Election of 1880

Candidates	*Parties*	*Electoral Vote*	*Popular Vote*	*Percentage of Popular Vote*
JAMES A. GARFIELD	Republican	214	4,453,295	48.5
Winfield S. Hancock	Democratic	155	4,414,082	48.1
James B. Weaver	Greenback-Labor		308,578	3.4

his foes to government posts, resigned from the Senate, confident that the New York legislature would reelect him and thus strengthen his political power. To his surprise, the legislature elected another senator and ended Conkling's political career.

Civil-service reformers sought more than the defeat of one spoilsman; they wanted a civil-service law. A tragic event helped them to realize their wish. On July 2, 1881, Charles J. Guiteau, a drifter, shot President Garfield in the delusion that the Stalwarts would reward him, Guiteau, with a job. Garfield eventually died, and Chester A. Arthur, the very symbol of the corrupt patronage system, became president. Guiteau was tried and hanged for assassinating the president.

Painting Garfield as a martyr to the spoils system, civil-service reformers in 1883 pushed through Congress the Pendleton Civil Service Act, drafted by the Civil Service Reform League. It established a civil-service commission to set up standards of merit for federal jobs and to prepare competitive examinations. Initially, the Pendleton Act covered only 12 percent of federal employees, but it was gradually expanded. The creation of a professional civil service marked an important step in the process by which the federal government gradually caught up with the transformation of America.

By becoming a mediocre president, Chester A. Arthur pleasantly surprised those who expected him to be an unmitigated disaster. He supported civil-service reform, but his easygoing nature made him a caretaker president at most. In 1882 frustrated voters gave Democrats an overwhelming majority in the House of Representatives, and in 1884 they put a Democrat, Grover Cleveland, in the White House for the first time since 1856.

Politics of Privilege, Politics of Exclusion

Grover Cleveland challenged powerful interests by calling for cuts in the tariff and veterans' pensions. After Cleveland served a single term (1885–1889), one of the most corrupt elections in American history put Republican Benjamin Harrison (1889–1893) in the White House—and restored big business and the veterans' lobby to the driver's seat. Simultaneously, debt-ridden farmers mounted a spirited protest movement. And in the South, the white majority used the machinery of politics to strip black citizens of their basic rights.

The Election of 1884: Cleveland Victorious

James G. Blaine, the Republican nominee in 1884, typified younger Republicans eager to build a truly national party that would promote economic development. But he carried a load of political baggage, including a series of damning letters that appeared to offer political favors in exchange for railroad stock and carried the unforgettable tag line "Burn this letter."

Sensing Blaine's vulnerability, the Democrats nominated Grover Cleveland of New York, who had enjoyed a meteoric career—first as Buffalo's mayor and then as New York's governor—as a reformer and opponent of bosses and spoilsmen. Cleveland's bulldog demeanor mirrored his determined independence.

Confronted with the sharp contrast between the soiled Blaine and the seemingly spotless Cleveland, Republican reformers bolted to Cleveland. However, early in the campaign Republicans made the shocking charge that as a young man Cleveland had fathered an illegitimate child. Cleveland immediately admitted the damaging accusation, but Republicans exploited the issue, chanting, "Ma, Ma, where's my pa?" Defiant Democrats responded, "He's gone to the White House, ha, ha, ha!"

Shortly before the election, a prominent New York Protestant clergyman denounced the Democrats as the party of "Rum, Romanism, and Rebellion." Immigrants and southerners who had contemplated sitting out the election rallied to Cleveland, and he carried New York, the key to electoral victory.

The Election of 1884

Candidates	Parties	Electoral Vote	Popular Vote	Percentage of Popular Vote
GROVER CLEVELAND	Democratic	219	4,879,507	48.5
James G. Blaine	Republican	182	4,850,293	48.2
Benjamin F. Butler	Greenback-Labor		175,370	1.8
John P. St. John	Prohibition		150,369	1.5

Tariffs and Pensions

The corpulent Cleveland settled comfortably into the shadowy role expected of Gilded Age presidents. From youth, he had embraced Jacksonian laissez-faire, the belief that progress and prosperity depended on government's not meddling in the economy. However, by the 1880s laissez-faire had become the rallying cry of an entrenched business elite staunchly opposed to public regulation of corporate America.

Enmeshed in the political views of his youth, Cleveland displayed little understanding of the United States' industrial transformation and warned people not to expect the government to bail them out of their troubles. But one issue did catch his attention: the tariff. A tangle of conflicting economic and political interests had wrapped themselves around this issue, particularly the question of which imports should be taxed and how high the duties should be. For example, producers of coal and other commodities wanted protective tariffs, as did many manufacturers. But other manufacturers sought low tariffs on commodities they needed, while farmers attacked *all* tariffs for inflating the price of farm equipment and endangering markets for U.S. farm products.

Business-oriented Republicans generally favored tariffs; Democrats, with their agrarian base, tended to oppose them. For his part, Cleveland supported tariff reform largely because the high protective tariffs of the era were creating huge federal-budget surpluses. To spend the surpluses, legislators devised expensive federally funded projects ("pork-barrel" projects) to benefit their home districts. The president believed that the system promoted corruption.

In 1887 Cleveland devoted his annual message to Congress to the tariff. He argued that lower tariffs not only would cut the federal surplus but also would reduce prices and slow the development of trusts. Although politicians paid little attention, corporate leaders equated talk of lower tariffs with a direct assault on business prosperity.

Cleveland stirred up another hornet's nest by opposing the routine payment of veterans' disability pensions. Fraudulent claims proliferated in this era; one veteran collected a disability pension for poor eyesight caused, he said, by wartime diarrhea. Cleveland personally investigated these claims and rejected many. He also vetoed a bill that would have pensioned all disabled veterans, whether or not the disabilities were war related, and their dependents. The pension roll should be an honor roll, he stressed, not a refuge for frauds.

1888: Big Business and the GAR Strike Back

By 1888 some influential groups had concluded that Cleveland had to go. Republican kingmakers nominated Benjamin Harrison, a corporation lawyer and former senator of such personal coldness that some ridiculed him as the human iceberg. Harrison's managers capitalized on the fact that he was

The Election of 1888

Candidates	*Parties*	*Electoral Vote*	*Popular Vote*	*Percentage of Popular Vote*
BENJAMIN HARRISON	Republican	233	5,477,129	47.9
Grover Cleveland	Democratic	168	5,537,857	48.6
Clinton B. Fisk	Prohibition		249,506	2.2
Anson J. Streeter	Union Labor		146,935	1.3

the grandson of William Henry Harrison, dubbing him Young Tippecanoe. Instead of sending the candidate around the country, they brought delegations to his Indiana home, where he read flowery speeches appealing to their interests and vanity.

The Republicans focused on the tariff. They portrayed Cleveland as an advocate of "free trade"—the elimination of all tariffs—and warned that only a high tariff could ensure business prosperity, decent wages, and a healthy home market for the farmer. Worried business leaders provided $4 million in campaign contributions, which purchased advertising and votes.

In the end, Cleveland received almost 100,000 more votes than Harrison but lost New York, Indiana, and the electoral vote. When Harrison piously observed that Providence had helped the Republican cause, his campaign chairman, Matthew Quay, snorted: "Providence hadn't a damn thing to do with it. . . . A number of men . . . approach[ed] the gates of the penitentiary to make him president."

Once in office, Harrison rewarded his supporters. He appointed a former Grand Army of the Republic commander to the position of commissioner of pensions. "God help the surplus!" exulted the new commissioner, who then swelled the roll of pensioners from 676,000 to nearly 1 million. Sociologist Theda Skocpol has called this massive pension system, coupled with medical care through a network of veterans' hospitals, America's first large public-welfare program. So freely was money appropriated for pensions and pork-barrel projects that the Republican-dominated Congress of 1890 became known as the Billion-Dollar Congress. In 1890 the triumphant Republicans also passed the McKinley Tariff, which pushed rates to an all-time high.

Rarely has the federal government been so subservient to entrenched economic interests, so saturated in the native-born Protestant outlook, and so out of touch with the plight of the disadvantaged as during the 1880s. But discontent was intensifying. In 1890 voters ousted the Republicans and put Democrats in control of the House of Representatives. This outcome reflected not only a stinging rebuke of the Billion-Dollar Congress and the business-ruled Harrison administration but also immigrant resentment at native-born Protestant attempts to "uplift" newcomers by force of law. Above all, the 1890 election awakened the nation to a tide of political activism engulfing the agrarian South and West.

Western Farmers Organize

Millions of farmers felt abandoned by the political process in the late nineteenth century. Agricultural productivity had grown, but many farmers, especially in the South and Midwest, faced a demoralizing cycle of falling prices, scarce money, and debt. In the Cotton South, the crop-lien system had entrapped many small planters in endless debt, forcing them into tenancy or sharecropping. On the Great Plains, wheat farmers faced equally perplexing problems. Plunging into debt to buy land at high interest rates, many owed the bank, the farm-implement

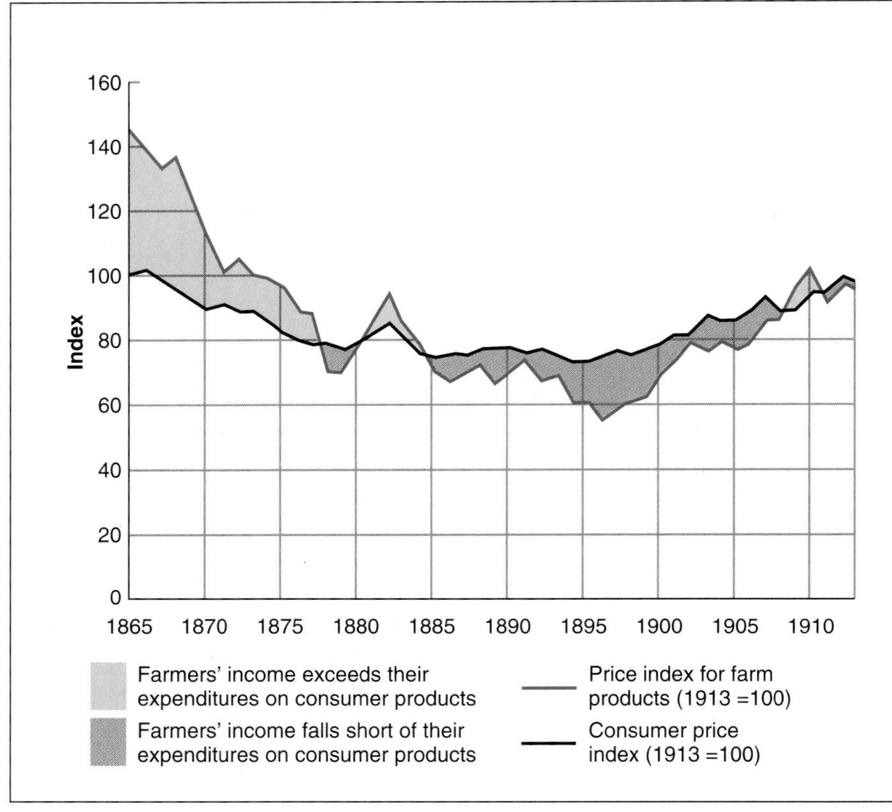

Consumer Prices and Farm-Product Prices, 1865–1913

As cycles of drought and debt battered Great Plains wheat growers, a Kansas farmer wrote, "At the age of 52, after a long life of toil, economy, and self-denial, I find myself and family virtually paupers."

dealer, the grain-elevator operator, and the railroad. The Greenback and Grange movements had collapsed.

Out of the despair emerged the alliance movement. This outburst of agrarian protest began in the 1870s when Texas farmers gathered to discuss their problems, and it spread eastward. Like Grangers, alliance members initially advocated farmers' cooperatives to purchase equipment and supplies and to market their cotton. And, as had the Grange cooperatives, these generally failed for lack of capital.

In 1887 a farsighted Texan, Charles W. Macune, assumed leadership of the alliance movement. By 1889 Macune had merged several regional groups into the National Farmers' Alliance and Industrial Union, or the Southern Alliance. A parallel organization of black farmers emerged, the National Colored Farmers' Alliance. By 1890 the Southern Alliance boasted 3 million members and its black counterpart another 1.2 million. Alliance members generally comprised the poorest farmers, growers dependent on a single crop, and geographically isolated farmers. Gathering for picnics and rallies, hard-hit farm families realized the political potential of their collective undertaking. As a member wrote in 1889, "Reform never begins with the leaders, it comes from the people." Southern Alliance leaders Tom Watson of Georgia and Leonidas Polk of North Carolina even urged black and white farmers to act together on their common problems. For a while, this message of racial cooperation in the name of reform carried promise.

At the same time, alliance fever was also burning across the Great Plains, where alliances had sprung up in Kansas, Nebraska, Iowa, and Minnesota in the drought-plagued years 1880 and 1881.

In 1886–1887 the alliance spirit was rekindled on the plains when killing winter blizzards gave way to severe drought. For the next decade, only two wheat crops were worth harvesting. Searing winds shriveled the half-ripe grain, and chinch bugs gnawed away the rest. Making matters worse, world grain prices fell.

Innumerable midwestern families packed up and returned East. "In God we trusted, in Kansas we busted," some scrawled on their wagons. Western Kansas lost 50 percent of its population between 1888 and 1892. But others hung on, and the organization that is usually called the Northwestern Alliance, including all the Great Plains states, grew rapidly, although it never approached the Southern Alliance in total size.

One of the best-known midwestern alliance leaders was the fiery Wichita lawyer Mary E. Lease. When she advised Kansans to "raise less corn and more hell," a conservative newspaper sneered, "[Kansas] has started to raise hell, as Mrs. Lease advised, and [the state] seems to have an overproduction. But that doesn't matter. Kansas never did believe in diversified crops." Many other women, veterans of the Granger and prohibition movements, rallied to the new movement, founding the National Women's Alliance (NWA) in 1891. Declared the NWA: "Put 1,000 women lecturers in the field and revolution is here."

From this scalding rhetoric and feverish activity came a political agenda. In 1889 the Southern and Northwestern alliances arranged a loose merger and supported candidates who agreed with them. Among their goals were tariff reduction, a graduated income tax, public ownership of railroads, federal funding for irrigation research, a prohibition on landownership by aliens, and "the free and unlimited coinage of silver."

The 1890 elections illuminated the depth of agrarian discontent. Alliance-backed candidates won four governorships and controlled eleven legislatures. Three alliance-backed senators and fifty congressmen went to Washington in 1890 as angry winds from the hinterland buffeted the political system.

Northwestern Alliance leaders favored a third party, and by 1892 many Southern Alliance officials had reluctantly come around to their position. In February 1892 the top alliance leaders organized the People's Party of the United States—a name quickly shortened to the Populist party. At their convention that August, 1,300 cheering delegates nominated for the presidency Iowan James B. Weaver, a Union general in the Civil War and a former Greenback candidate.

The Populist platform contained the goals announced by the alliance leaders in 1889 and added a call for the direct popular election of senators and other electoral reforms. Minnesota Populist Ignatius Donnelly's ringing preamble pronounced the nation "on the verge of moral, political, and material ruin" and proclaimed, "We seek to restore the government of the Republic to the hands of 'the plain people' with which class it originated."

As the Populists geared up for the 1892 campaign, other citizens with far more profound grievances found themselves even more marginalized.

African-Americans After Reconstruction

The end of Reconstruction in 1877 and the restoration of power to southern white elites spelled bad news for the nation's African-Americans, most of whom still lived in the South. Southern white opinion sought an end to "Negro rule" and tried to suppress the black vote. Initially, whites relied on intimidation, terror, and fraud to limit black voting rights, but in 1890 Mississippi amended its state constitution to exclude most African-American voters, and other southern states followed suit.

The Fifteenth Amendment (1870) had guaranteed all male citizens' right to vote, so indirect means such as literacy tests, poll taxes, and property requirements were used to disfranchise African-Americans. To ensure that these measures excluded only blacks, whites employed such devices as the grandfather clause, which exempted from these electoral requirements anyone whose ancestor had voted in 1860. African-American disfranchisement proceeded erratically, but by the early twentieth century it was effectively complete.

Disfranchisement was the keystone of an arch of white supremacy that stretched across the South. In a movement culminating early in the twentieth century, state after state also passed laws strictly segregating many realms of life by race (see Chapter 22). African-American caterers, barbers, contractors, bricklayers, carpenters, and other artisans lost their white customers. And blacks sent to prison—sometimes for minor offenses—got caught up in the convict-lease system, which allowed cotton planters and others to "lease" prison gangs and to put them to work under degraded conditions.

The lynch rope was the ultimate enforcer of white supremacy. Through the 1880s and 1890s, an average of one hundred African-Americans were lynched annually in the United States, mainly in the South. Rumors and unsubstantiated accusations of blacks' rape of white women frequently unleashed this mob violence. ("Attempted rape" could mean a wide range of behavior unacceptable to whites.) The lynch mob exerted social control, terrorizing blacks and demonstrating whites' absolute power. By no coincidence, lynching reached its highest point in 1892 as many poor African-Americans joined the agrarian protest and rallied to the Populist party banner.

The relationship between southern agrarian protest and white racism was complex. Some Populists, among them Georgia's Tom Watson, tried to build a genuinely interracial movement and denounced both lynching and the convict-lease system. When an African-American Populist leader pursued by a lynch mob took refuge in Watson's house during the 1892 campaign, he summoned 2,000 armed white Populists to defend the man. But most white Populists, encouraged by such rabble-rousers as "Pitchfork Ben" Tillman of South Carolina, held fast to racism; Watson complained that most poor whites "would joyously hug the chains of . . . wretchedness rather than do any experimenting on [the race] question."

The white ruling elite, eager to drive a wedge in the farm-protest movement, worked to inflame lower-class white racism. Addressing an alliance meeting in 1889, an Atlanta editor warned against division among white southerners; the South's only hope, he said, was "the clear and unmistakable domination of the white race." On balance, the rise of southern agrarian protest deepened racial hatred and worsened blacks' situation.

While southern African-Americans suffered racist oppression, the federal government did nothing. In 1877 President Hayes noted that black rights were being destroyed; however, like most northern politicians, he paid lip service to egalitarian principles and failed to apply them to African-Americans.

The Supreme Court similarly abandoned African-Americans to their fates. The Court ripped gaping holes into the Fourteenth Amendment and the Civil Rights Act of 1875 (see Chapter 16). In the *Civil Rights Cases* (1883), the Court threw out the Civil Rights Act of 1875 on the grounds that the Fourteenth Amendment prevented governments, but not individuals, from infringing on civil rights. In *Plessy* v. *Ferguson* (1896), the Court upheld a Louisiana law requiring segregated railroad cars. Racial segregation was legal, the justices ruled, provided that equal facilities were made available to each race.

With the Supreme Court's blessing, the South also segregated its public schools, ignoring the caveat that separate facilities must be equal. White children studied in nicer buildings, used newer equipment, and were taught by better-paid teachers than black children. Not until 1954 would the Court abandon the "separate but equal" doctrine. Rounding out a dismal record, the justices in 1898 upheld the poll tax and literacy tests by which Mississippi and other states had disfranchised African-Americans.

Few northerners protested the indignities that underlay the South's white-supremacist society. Until the North condemned lynching, declared aged abolitionist Frederick Douglass in 1892, "it will remain equally involved with the South in this common crime." The restoration of sectional harmony came at a high price: northern acquiescence in the utter debasement of a people whose freedom

The Election of 1892

Candidates	*Parties*	*Electoral Vote*	*Popular Vote*	*Percentage of Popular Vote*
GROVER CLEVELAND	Democratic	277	5,555,426	46.1
Benjamin Harrison	Republican	145	5,182,690	43.0
James B. Weaver	People's	22	1,029,846	8.5
John Bidwell	Prohibition		264,133	2.2

had cost the lives of thousands of northern men.

African-Americans responded in various ways to their plight. The best-known black southerner of the period, Booker T. Washington, counseled patience, accommodation, and the acquisition of skills. Black churches provided emotional support, as did black fraternal lodges. And a handful of African-Americans established banks and successful businesses such as insurance companies and barber shops.

Meanwhile, voices of black protest never wholly died out. Frederick Douglass urged African-Americans to press on for full equality; he proclaimed, "[Those] who would be free, themselves must strike the first blow." But for some African-Americans, the solution was to leave the South. In 1879 several thousand moved to Kansas (see Chapter 16), and 10,000 migrated to Chicago between 1870 and 1890. Blacks who went north, however, discovered that they had not left racism behind, for public opinion sanctioned many forms of de facto discrimination in the North. Northern African-American laborers encountered widespread prejudice. Although the Knights of Labor had welcomed blacks and counted 60,000 black members in its heyday, the AFL looked the other way as its member craft unions excluded African-Americans.

The rise of the "solid South," firmly established on racist foundations, had profound implications for American politics. For one thing, it made a mockery of the two-party system; for nearly a century, the only important election in most southern states was the Democratic primary. Furthermore, the large bloc of southern Democrats in Congress accumulated seniority and power, exerting a potent influence on public policy. Finally, the solid South wielded enormous clout in the Democratic party; no national candidate unacceptable to the South stood a chance.

Above all, the rigid caste system of the post-Reconstruction South molded the consciousness of those caught up in it, black and white alike. Describing her girlhood in the turn-of-the-century South, white novelist Lillian Smith wrote:

> *From the day I was born, I began to learn my lessons. . . . I learned it is possible to be a Christian and a white southerner simultaneously; to be a gentlewoman and an arrogant callous creature at the same moment; to pray at night and ride a Jim Crow car the next morning; . . . to glow when the word* democracy *was used, and to practice slavery from morning to night.*

The 1890s: Politics in a Depression Decade

The 1890s was one of the most unsettled decades in American history. Grover Cleveland, reelected president in 1892, faced a business panic, an erosion of the government's fiscal stability, and a depression. Bloody labor strikes and, as we have seen, the emergence of the Populist party added to the presidential predicament. The crises of the 1890s had paradoxical results. They dramatically spotlighted the paralysis of the federal government dominated by a capitalist elite and shaped by laissez-faire ideology in the face of industrialization and urbanization. Yet at the same time, these crises lead to profound changes in American politics and ideology.

1892: Populists Challenge the Status Quo

The year 1892 provided evidence of growing discontent. The Populist platform, adopted in July, angrily catalogued agrarian demands. The deaths of thirteen men in a gun battle between strikers and strikebreakers at the Homestead steel mill and the use of federal troops against silver-mine strikers in the Idaho panhandle seemed to justify the Populists' warning of a nation verging on class warfare.

Both major parties reacted cautiously in the 1892 campaign for the White House. The election was a replay of 1888, Harrison versus Cleveland, but this time Cleveland won by more than 360,000 votes, a decisive margin in an age of close elections. The Populists' strength proved spotty. Their presidential candidate, James B. Weaver, got more than 1 million votes, 8.5 percent of the total, and the Populists elected five senators, ten congressmen, and three governors. But the party made no dent in New England or the urban East and little in the Midwest.

In the South, racism, Democratic loyalty, distaste for the former Union general Weaver, and widespread intimidation and voter fraud kept the Populist tally under 25 percent. The party's failure killed the prospects for interracial agrarian reform. After 1892 southern politicians seeking to appeal to poor whites stayed within the Democratic fold and laced their populism with virulent racism.

The Panic of 1893: Capitalism in Crisis

No sooner did Cleveland take office than he confronted the worst crisis to face any president since the Civil War: an economic collapse that began in the railroad industry but quickly spread. Railroads had led in the awesome industrial growth of the 1880s, unleashing both investment and speculation. In the early 1890s railroad growth slowed, affecting other industries, especially iron and steel. The bubble burst in 1893.

The first hint of trouble came in the February failure of the Philadelphia and Reading Railroad. The bankruptcy occurred at a moment of weakened confidence in the government's ability to redeem paper money for gold on demand. Economic problems in London in 1890 had forced British investors to unload millions of dollars of American stocks; $68 million in U.S. gold reserves flowed across the Atlantic to Britain. But at the same time, the largesse of the Billion-Dollar Congress had substantially reduced the federal surplus, while the Sherman Silver Purchase Act was straining the gold reserve. Finally, the election of the Democrat Cleveland further eroded confidence in the dollar; although the president endorsed the gold standard, his party harbored many advocates of inflationary policies. From January 1892 to March 1893 (the month Cleveland was inaugurated), the gold reserve fell from $192 million to $100 million. Those who believed that the gold standard offered the only sure evidence of financial stability were alarmed.

With the collapse of the Philadelphia and Reading, fear fed on itself as panicky investors converted their stock holdings to gold. Stock prices plunged, the gold reserve plummeted, and by the end of the year 74 railroads, 600 banks, and 15,000 businesses had failed. Four years of hard times would follow the Panic of 1893.

The Depression of 1893–1897

The crisis worsened in 1894. By June nearly 200 railroads had failed, and by 1897 one-third of the nation's railroad mileage was in bankruptcy. The railroad boom had been the key to the prosperity of the 1880s, and the railroad collapse of the 1890s brought on a full-scale depression.

In human terms, the depression took a heavy toll. Industrial unemployment ranged from 20 to 25 percent. One-fifth of factory workers had no money to buy food or to heat their homes, and jobless men tramped the streets looking for work. Unusually harsh winters in 1893 and 1894 aggravated the misery. People were starving to death in New York City as a wealthy New Yorker named Bradley Martin threw a costume ball that cost hundreds of thousands of dollars. Popular outrage at this flaunting of wealth in a prostrate city drove Martin and his family abroad.

In rural America, already hard hit by declining agricultural prices, the depression turned trouble into ruin. Farm prices dropped by more than 20 percent: corn plummeted from $.50 to $.21 a bushel and wheat from $.84 to $.51.

Protest swelled among desperate Americans. The populist movement grew stronger. In Massillon, Ohio, self-taught monetary "expert" Jacob Coxey concluded that the answer to unemployment was a $500 million public-works program funded with paper money not backed by gold. Coxey organized a march on Washington in March 1894 to lobby for his scheme. Thousands joined him en route, and several hundred reached Washington in late April. Police arrested Coxey and other leaders for trespassing on Capitol grounds, and his "army" broke up. Though radical in the 1890s, Coxey's proposals anticipated programs that the government would adopt during the depression of the 1930s.

As disquiet intensified, fear and anger clutched middle-class Americans. A church magazine demanded that troops put a "pitiless stop" to all violent outbreaks of unrest. To some, a bloody upheaval seemed imminent.

Conservatives Hunker Down

In the face of the mass turmoil, Cleveland retreated into a laissez-faire fortress. Boom-and-bust economic cycles were inevitable, he insisted, and government could only ride out the storm. Moreover, not understanding the depression's complex causes, Cleveland focused on a single peripheral issue, the gold standard. In August 1893 he persuaded a special session of Congress to repeal the Sherman Silver Purchase Act, which he blamed for the dwindling gold reserve.

But the gold drain continued and the depression deepened. In early 1895, with the gold reserve down to $41 million, Cleveland turned to Wall Street. Bankers J. P. Morgan and August Belmont agreed to lend the government $62 million in exchange for discounted U.S. bonds. The government then purchased 3.5 million ounces of gold, stemming the drain on the reserve, and Morgan and Belmont resold their bonds for a substantial profit. Cleveland had saved the gold standard, but at a high price. His deal with Morgan and Belmont, and the handsome profits they made, seemed to show more concern for moneyed men than for the average American and confirmed agrarian radicals' suspicions of an unholy alliance between Washington and Wall Street.

As always, politics in the early 1890s reflected the maneuvering of competing interest groups. As the tariff battle made clear, corporate interests held the whip hand. Although Cleveland favored tariff reform, lobbyists swayed the Democrat-controlled Congress of 1892–1893 to reject such reforms. The Wilson-Gorman Tariff of 1894 made so many concessions to special interests that a disgusted president allowed it to become law without his signature.

One feature of the Wilson-Gorman Tariff suggested an enlarging vision of government's role in an age of towering fortunes: an income tax of 2 percent on all income over $4,000 (roughly $40,000 in present-day purchasing power). But in 1895 the Supreme Court declared the tax unconstitutional on the grounds that the Constitution forbade the direct federal taxation of individuals. Thus whether one looked at the executive, the legislature, or the judiciary, Washington's subordination to the corporate elite seemed nearly complete.

Cleveland's policies also split the Democratic party. The rift decisively affected the elections of 1894 and 1896 and led to a major political realignment as the century ended.

Laissez-faire ideology suffered a grievous setback in the 1890s as depression-worn Americans adopted a broader conception of government's proper role in dealing with the social consequences of industrialization. As progressivism, this new perspective would unleash powerful political energies. The depression was thus memorable not only for the suffering it caused but also for the lessons it taught.

The Watershed Election of 1896

Republican gains in the 1894 midterm elections revealed popular revulsion against Cleveland and the Democrats, whom Americans widely blamed for the hard times. In the 1896 presidential election, the monetary question became the overriding symbolic issue. Conservatives clung to the gold standard, but advocates of "free silver" triumphed at the Democratic convention when a young silver advocate, William Jennings Bryan, secured the nomination. However, his opponent, William McKinley, won the election, and his triumph laid the groundwork for a major political realignment.

1894: Protest Grows Louder

The midterm election of 1894 spelled Democratic disaster. The blizzard of protest votes, said one, left the party "buried under the drift a thousand feet deep." Republicans, aided by votes from immigrants battered by the depression, gained control of Congress and several key states. Populist candidates won nearly 1.5 million votes, 40 percent over their 1892 total. Most Populist gains came in the South. The party's leaders looked forward to 1896.

The Silver Issue

As serious economic divisions split Americans in the mid-1890s, a Supreme Court justice described the conflict as "a war of the poor against the rich: a war constantly growing in intensity and bitterness." It was a war of words, fought largely over a symbolic issue: free silver.

By clinging to the gold standard, Cleveland forced his opponents into an exaggerated obsession with silver. The genuine issues dividing rich and poor, creditor and debtor, and farmer and city dweller disappeared in murky debates over the two semimythic metals. Conservatives warned of nightmarish dangers in abandoning the gold standard, and agrarian radicals extolled silver as a universal cure-all. Both sides had a point. Gold advocates recognized the potential disaster of uncontrolled inflation if paper money rested only on the government's ability to run printing presses. Silver advocates knew from personal experience how tight-money, high-interest policies depressed prices and devastated farmers.

Silver Advocates Capture the Democratic Party

At the 1896 Democratic convention in Chicago, outnumbered Cleveland supporters protested in vain as western and southern delegates adopted a platform demanding the free and unlimited coinage of silver—in effect, repudiating the Cleveland administration. An ardent advocate of the sil-

The Election of 1896

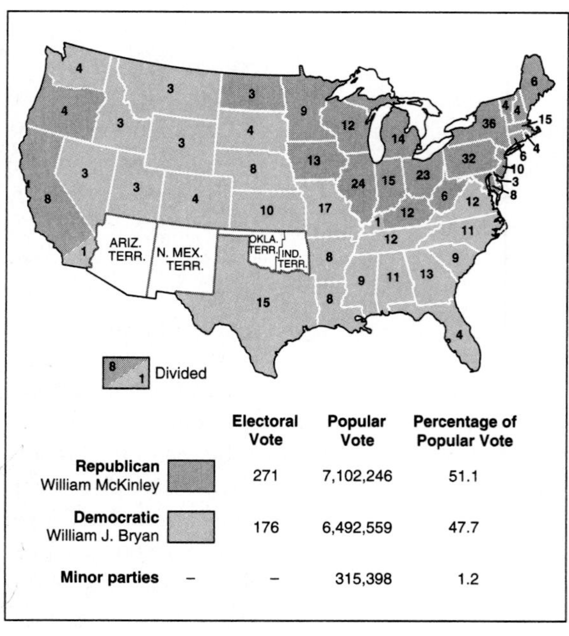

	Electoral Vote	Popular Vote	Percentage of Popular Vote
Republican William McKinley	271	7,102,246	51.1
Democratic William J. Bryan	176	6,492,559	47.7
Minor parties –	–	315,398	1.2

ver cause captured the party's nomination: William Jennings Bryan of Nebraska. Only thirty-six, the young lawyer had already served two terms in Congress.

Bryan brought mighty oratorical talents to politics. In Chicago during the debate over the platform, his booming voice carried his rousing words to the highest galleries of the convention hall. Praising farmers as the nation's bedrock, Bryan roared to the cheering delegates, "You shall not press down upon the brow of labor this crown of thorns, you shall not crucify mankind upon a cross of gold."

The silverites' capture of the Democratic party left the Populists with a dilemma. Free silver was only one reform among many that they advocated. If they jumped aboard the Bryan bandwagon, they would abandon their own program. But a separate Populist ticket would siphon votes from Bryan and guarantee a Republican victory. Reluctantly, the Populists endorsed Bryan. Meanwhile, the Republicans nominated former Ohio governor William McKinley on a platform endorsing the high protective tariff and the gold standard.

1896: Conservatism Triumphant

Bryan did his best to sustain the momentum of the Chicago convention, crisscrossing the country by train to deliver his free-silver campaign speech. One skeptic jeered that Bryan was well nicknamed the "Boy Wonder of the River Platte": his mouth was just as wide and his mind just as shallow.

Mark Hanna, a Cleveland industrialist, managed the Republican McKinley's campaign. Recognizing that the dignified, somewhat aloof McKinley could not match Bryan's popular touch—one wit noted that McKinley always seemed to be "determinedly looking for his pedestal"—Hanna built the campaign around posters and pamphlets that warned of the dangers of free silver, caricatured Bryan as a radical, and portrayed McKinley and the gold standard as twin pillars of prosperity.

Drawing on a war chest possibly as large as $7 million, Hanna spent lavishly. J. P. Morgan and John D. Rockefeller together contributed $500,000 to the McKinley campaign, more than Bryan's total campaign contributions. McKinley himself stayed

"Dubious"
A Republican poster called voters' attention to poverty-stricken nations that had a silver coinage, implying that the United States would sink to the same level if it adopted Bryan's panacea.

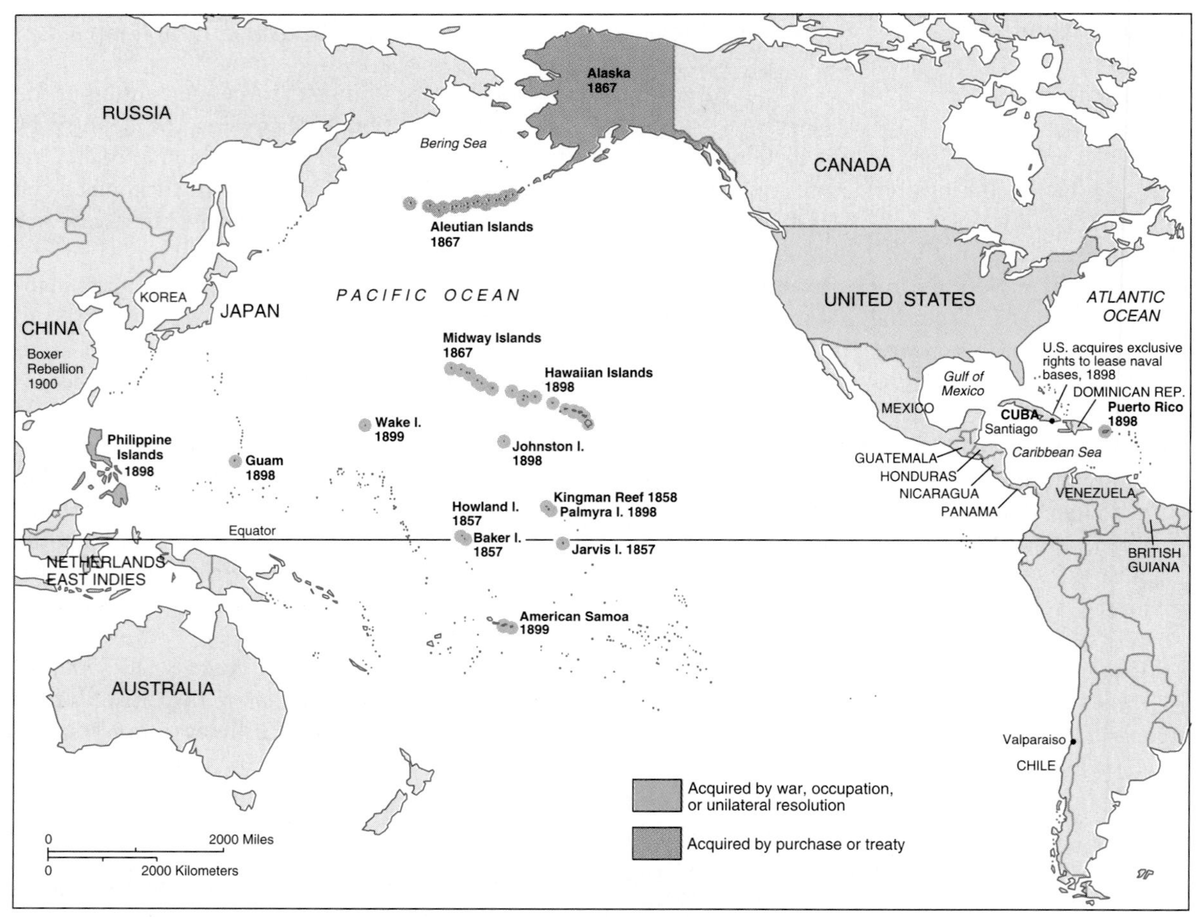

U.S. Territorial Expansion in the Late Nineteenth Century

The major period of U.S. territorial expansion abroad came in a short burst of activity in the late 1890s, when newspapers and some politicians beat the drums for empire.

home in Canton, Ohio, emerging occasionally to read speeches to a stream of visiting delegations.

On election day 1896, McKinley swamped Bryan by more than 600,000 votes; the Democrats carried only the South, the Great Plains, and the Rocky Mountains. In nominating Bryan, the Democrats had selected a candidate with little appeal for factory workers, the urban middle class, or immigrants. Furthermore, despite a telling critique of laissez-faire capitalism, the populist vision of returning to a premodern world of independent farmers and entrepreneurs seemed increasingly anachronistic in the face of the new corporate order's steady expansion.

The McKinley administration translated its conservative platform into law. The Dingley Tariff (1897) pushed rates to all-time highs, and the Currency Act of 1900 committed the United States to the gold standard. Because of returning prosperity, rising farm prices, and the discovery of gold in Alaska, these measures roused little opposition, and McKinley easily defeated Bryan again in 1900.

The Election of 1900

Candidates	*Parties*	*Electoral Vote*	*Popular Vote*	*Percentage of Popular Vote*
WILLIAM McKINLEY	Republican	292	7,218,491	51.7
William Jennings Bryan	Democratic; Populist	155	6,356,734	45.5
John C. Wooley	Prohibition		208,914	1.5

The elections of 1894 and 1896 produced a Republican majority that, except for Woodrow Wilson's presidency (1913–1921), would dominate national politics until the election of Franklin D. Roosevelt in 1932. Populism collapsed, but a new reform movement, progressivism, was picking up momentum and adopting many of its ideas.

Expansionist Stirrings and War with Spain

Beyond dominating domestic politics, the corporate elite influenced U.S. foreign policy in the late nineteenth century, contributing to surging expansionist pressures. Business leaders, politicians, statesmen, editorialists, and Fourth of July orators insisted that national greatness required America to join Europe in the imperialist theater. Fanned by sensationalistic newspaper coverage of Cuba's struggle for independence from Spain, public enthusiasm for international assertiveness sparked a war between the United States and Spain in 1898.

Roots of Expansionist Sentiment

Since the time of the first English settlements along the Atlantic seaboard, newcomers to America had been expansionist. The Louisiana Purchase testified to that fervor, as did the Manifest Destiny of the 1840s, which had led to war with Mexico and propelled America to the Pacific. Civil war and industrialization had temporarily damped expansionism, but it revived strongly after 1880 as the conviction grew that the United States had a global destiny.

European and Japanese imperialism intensified this expansionist sentiment. Great Britain, France, Belgium, Germany, Italy, and Japan were all collecting colonies from North Africa to remote Pacific islands, and many Americans concluded that true national greatness demanded an empire. Corporate leaders concluded that continued prosperity as well as national pride demanded overseas markets. In 1890 the secretary of state noted that national productivity was outrunning "the demands of the home market" and insisted that American business look abroad.

Other voices joined in the expansionist chorus. Proponents of a strong navy contributed to the expansionist mood. In *The Influence of Sea Power upon History* (1890), Alfred Thayer Mahan equated sea power with national greatness and urged a rapid U.S. naval buildup. To do so required the acquisition of territory overseas for bases. Some religious leaders talked of America's divine mission to spread Christianity, an argument with racist tinges. One minister averred that "God is training the Anglo-Saxon race for its mission"—a mission of bringing Christianity and civilization to the world's "weaker races." Theodore Roosevelt, Henry Cabot Lodge, and diplomat John Hay led a group of Republican expansionists who tirelessly preached imperial greatness and military might. "I should welcome almost any war," Roosevelt declared, "for I think this country needs one." A series of diplomatic skirmishes in the mid-1890s revealed the newly assertive American mood and paved the way for the war that Roosevelt desired.

In the mid-1880s, quarrels between the United States and Great Britain had flared over fishing rights in the North Atlantic and North Pacific, reawakening latent anti-British feelings and the old dream of acquiring Canada. A poem published in the *Detroit News* provided a new nickname for expansionists—jingoists:

We do not want to fight,
But, by jingo, if we do,
We'll scoop in all the fishing grounds
And the whole dominion too!

In 1898 a compromise settled the fishing-rights dispute, but by then attention had shifted to Latin America. In 1891 tensions had flared between the United States and Chile after a mob in Valparaiso killed two American sailors and injured seventeen others on shore leave. War fever subsided after Chile apologized and paid an indemnity of $75,000.

In 1895 another conflict erupted between the United States and Great Britain, this time over the boundary of British Guiana. Secretary of State Richard Olney sent the British a stern memorandum reminding them of the Monroe Doctrine, and the British condescendingly responded that this revered idea had no standing under law. Many Americans seriously contemplated war with Great Britain until the British agreed to accept the findings of a special arbitration commission.

Pacific Expansion

Even the far-off Pacific felt the stirrings of American expansionism. In the Samoan Islands, the U.S. Navy sought the port of Pago Pago as a refueling station. In March 1889 the United States narrowly avoided a naval clash with Germany over the islands when a timely hurricane intervened. Ultimately, America established a three-way protectorate over the islands with Germany and Great Britain.

The Hawaiian Islands with their great potential economic and strategic significance also beckoned U.S. imperialists. American missionaries and merchants had been active in the islands since the end of the eighteenth century. American-owned sugar plantations dominated the Hawaiian economy. Under an 1887 treaty, the United States built a naval base at Pearl Harbor, near Honolulu. Then in 1891, angered by American economic domination, islanders welcomed Liliuokalani to the Hawaiian throne. Strong-willed and hostile toward Americans, she became queen amid a crisis set off by a U.S. decision in 1890 to tax Hawaiian sugar. Hawaiian sugar prices plunged 40 percent as a result. Facing ruin, the planters deposed the queen in January 1893, proclaimed the independent Republic of Hawaii, and requested U.S. annexation.

Cleveland was skeptical about annexation and grew more so when an emissary whom he sent to Hawaii cast doubt on whether the Hawaiians desired annexation. Such scruples infuriated expansionists. "In ordering Old Glory pulled down at Honolulu, President Cleveland turned back the hand on the dial of civilization," a New York newspaper fulminated. "Queen Lil" made matters difficult for her American supporters by declaring that if restored to power, she would behead the coup leaders.

When McKinley succeeded Cleveland, the annexation of Hawaii moved rapidly forward, and in 1898 Congress proclaimed Hawaii an American territory. Sixty-one years later, it joined the Union as the fiftieth state.

Crisis over Cuba

In 1898 American attention shifted to Cuba, where a rebellion against Spanish rule had erupted in 1895. American businessmen had $50 million invested in the island and annually imported $100 million in sugar and other products from Cuba. Revolutionary turmoil would jeopardize these interests. Neither the Cleveland nor the McKinley administration supported the rebellion.

But the rebels won widespread popular backing from Americans, support that increased with revelations of the cruelty inflicted on the Cuban people by the Spanish commander, Valeriano Weyler. Under Weyler's "reconcentration" policy, the civilian population was herded into camps in order to isolate the rebels. Brutality, malnutrition, and disease turned the concentration camps into death camps; perhaps 200,000 Cubans died there.

Fueling American anger were sensational stories published by two New York newspapers, William Randolph Hearst's *Journal* and Joseph Pulitzer's *World,* which were embroiled in a circulation war. The Cuban tragedy was ready-made for Hearst's and Pulitzer's lurid reporting. Daily headlines blared the latest developments, and feature stories detailed "Butcher" Weyler's atrocities.

In 1897 a liberal Spanish government made significant concessions, and a peaceful solution to the Cuban crisis seemed near. But Hearst and Pulitzer continued to inflame public opinion. On February 8, 1898, Hearst's *Journal* published a private letter from a Spanish diplomat describing McKinley as "weak" and "a bidder for the admiration of the crowd." Many Americans would have agreed, but they resented hearing it from a Spanish diplomat.

Irritation turned to outrage on February 15, 1898, when an explosion rocked the battleship *Maine* in Havana harbor, killing 226 American crewmen. Newspaper headlines blazed with accusations of Spanish perfidy. In fact, a 1976 investigation confirmed what experts had thought even in 1898: that an internal explosion in the ammunition storage area had destroyed the battleship. In 1898, however, neither Washington nor the yellow press wanted to see the tragedy as accidental.

President McKinley still hung back from war, but he was not prepared to risk his popularity by resisting an aroused public. Despite further Spanish concessions, on April 11 McKinley sent a war message to Congress, and legislators passed a joint resolution recognizing Cuba's independence and authorizing force to expel the Spanish. An amendment introduced by Senator Henry M. Teller of Colorado declared that the United States had no desire for "sovereignty, jurisdiction, or control" in Cuba.

The Spanish-American War

The conflict with Spain lasted three months. Action began on May 1, 1898, when a U.S. fleet under Admiral George Dewey steamed into Manila Bay in the Philippines and destroyed or captured all ten Spanish ships anchored there, at the cost of 1 American and 381 Spanish lives. In mid-August U.S. troops occupied the capital, Manila.

In Cuba the war's only significant land engagement took place on July 1 when American troops seized two strongly defended Spanish garrisons on El Caney Hill and San Juan Hill overlooking the Spanish military stronghold of Santiago de Cuba. Leading the volunteer "Rough Riders" at San Juan Hill was Theodore Roosevelt, getting his taste of war—and abundant publicity—at last. Two days later, the Spanish fleet, which had been blockaded by the Americans at Santiago de Cuba, made a gallant but doomed break for the open sea. American ships sank the seven ancient vessels, killing 474 Spaniards and ending four hundred years of Spanish empire in America.

John Hay thought that it had all been "a splendid little war," but careful examination showed how terribly ill prepared the American forces had been. They went into battle in the tropical midsummer wearing heavy wool uniforms, received abysmal medical care, and died in droves from yellow fever and malaria. The United States lost more than 5,000 men in Cuba, only 379 of them in combat.

Negotiations in Paris followed a July 17 armistice. On December 10, 1898, the United States and Spain signed the Treaty of Paris. Spain recognized Cuba's independence and, after much pressure and a payment of \$20 million, ceded the Philippines, Puerto Rico, and Guam to the United States. Americans possessed an island empire stretching from the Caribbean to the Pacific.

Deepening Imperialist Ventures: The Philippines, China, and Panama

The Spanish-American War opened a period of intensified world involvement for the United States. In the Philippines, America fought a brutal four-year war to suppress a Filipino struggle for independence. In China, Washington sought an "open

U.S. Soldiers Question Filipino Women
The United States' military repression of the Filipino independence movement brought much suffering to the civilian population. As many as 200,000 people died of disease, malnutrition, and other wartime hazards.

door" for U.S. trade, and in Latin America President Theodore Roosevelt used dubious methods to clear the way for an American-controlled canal across the Isthmus of Panama.

The Platt Amendment

American troops remained in Cuba after the withdrawal of the Spanish, despite the Teller Amendment. Although the soldiers, commanded by General Leonard Wood, accomplished much in public health, education, and sanitation, they did little for Cuban independence.

The troops withdrew after four years, under terms that severely compromised Cuban sovereignty. An amendment to the 1901 army appropriations bill offered by Senator Orville Platt of Connecticut authorized the U.S. withdrawal only after Cuba accepted severe restrictions on treaty making and borrowing. The United States reserved the right to intervene in Cuba when it saw fit and to maintain a naval base there. The Cuban government accepted the Platt Amendment, which remained in force until 1934. The United States reoccupied Cuba in 1906–1909 and again in 1912 and established a large naval base at Guantanamo Bay. By 1920 U.S. investments in Cuba had soared from $50 million to $500 million.

Guerrilla War in the Philippines

When the Spanish-American War began, few Americans knew what or where the Philippine Islands were. President McKinley confessed that "I could not have told where those darn islands were within 2,000 miles." In fact, those 7,000 islands lay in the South China Sea, and American business saw them as a steppingstone to the rich China market. McKinley, as always reflecting public opinion, soon convinced himself that the United States had to help "our little brown brothers" in the islands, who, he believed, were unfit to govern themselves and could not be left to predatory German or Japanese imperialists. America's mission, according to the president, was "to educate the Filipinos, and to uplift and civilize and Christianize them, and by God's grace do the very best we could by them." (McKinley ignored the fact that after four hundred years of Spanish rule, most Filipinos were already Roman Catholics.) McKinley instructed the American peace negotiators in Paris to acquire the islands.

Ruling the Philippines proved difficult. Filipinos longed for independence, and in 1896 young Emilio Aguinaldo had organized a movement to drive out the Spanish. In summer 1898, with arms supplied by Admiral Dewey, Aguinaldo's forces captured most of Luzon, the Philippines' main island. In June, Aguinaldo proclaimed Filipino independence and drafted a democratic constitution. After the U.S. Senate ratified the Treaty of Paris in February 1899, fighting broke out between the

American army and Aguinaldo's forces, who felt betrayed.

It took the United States four years to crush the Filipino independence movement, which waged a guerrilla war against the U.S. forces. More than 125,000 Americans troops ultimately served in the Philippine jungles. American casualties—4,000 troops died—were ten times greater than in the entire Spanish-American War. As many as 20,000 Filipino independence fighters perished, and untold tens of thousands of civilians died when the Americans implemented the same sort of reconcentration policy that they had denounced in Cuba. In 1902 a Senate committee investigating the war heard sobering testimony from U.S. soldiers about the execution of prisoners, the torture of suspects, and the burning of Filipino villages. The humanitarian mood of 1898, when Americans had rushed to save Cuba from the Spanish, seemed remote indeed.

In 1902 Congress passed the Philippine Government Act, providing that a presidentially appointed governor would rule the islands and that a Filipino assembly would be elected. The law also promised eventual self-government. But the Philippines would not become independent until July 4, 1946, nearly half a century after Dewey's guns had boomed across Manila Bay.

Critics of Empire

Influential critics lashed out against American imperialism. William Jennings Bryan, editor E. L. Godkin, settlement-house founder Jane Addams, and novelist Mark Twain led the outcry, and steel king Andrew Carnegie contributed thousands of dollars. In November 1899 these critics of empire formed the Anti-Imperialist League.

The United States' takeover of foreign territories and subjugation of other peoples, the anti-imperialists believed, violated the sacred principles of human equality and self-government on which the nation had been founded. The United States has "puked up our ancient national heritage" and "turned pirate," fumed Harvard philosopher William James. Another anti-imperialist leader wrote, "Dewey took Manila with the loss of one man—and all of our institutions." Twain suggested a new design for the American flag, with black replacing the white stripes and with a skull and crossbones superseding the field of stars. Other anti-imperialists feared that prolonged contact with "our little brown brothers" might "mongrelize" the "American race."

In February 1899 the Senate ratified the expansionist peace treaty with Spain by a single vote, but Bryan's crushing defeat in 1900 seemed to validate McKinley's expansionist policies. Nevertheless, the anti-imperialists for the most part had upheld an older and finer vision of America than that evoked by the jingoistic rhetoric and military posturing that surrounded them.

The Open Door Notes: Competing for the China Market

As the Philippine war dragged on, Americans shifted their focus to China. The depression of 1893–1897 had heightened interest in foreign markets, and China was especially inviting. Opportunities for trade and investment seemed limitless in a land of 400 million potential customers. The tottering Manchu Dynasty, near collapse, could neither keep out nor limit foreign trade.

China's weakness had drawn other imperialists—including Russia, Germany, and Great Britain—who had won major concessions of land and trading rights. In September 1899, fearful of American businesses being shut out of China, Secretary of State John Hay sent notes to the imperialist powers in China requesting that they open the ports within their spheres of influence to all comers and not grant special privileges to traders of their own nations. Although the six imperialist nations returned noncommittal answers, Hay blithely announced that they had accepted the principle of an "Open Door" to American business.

The Open Door notes illuminate how commercial considerations influenced U.S. foreign policy. They reflected a quest for what has been called informal empire in contrast to the formal acquisition of overseas territories. In this kind of economic expansionism, the government played a subordinate and supporting role to private enterprise in a kind of laissez-faire imperialism.

In 1899, even as the Open Door notes were circulating, Chinese anger at foreign exploitation exploded. Urged on by an aged Manchu Dynasty empress, a fanatical secret society, the Harmonious Righteous Fists ("Boxers" to Westerners) rampaged across China, killing thousands of foreigners and Chinese Christians. In June 1900 the Boxers occupied Beijing (Peking), China's capital, and besieged the district housing the foreign legations. In August 1900 an international army, including 2,500 U.S. troops, marched on Beijing, drove back the Boxers, rescued the occupants of the besieged legations, and sacked the city.

The failed uprising nearly toppled the Manchu Dynasty, an outcome that would have opened the way for the total partitioning of China among the imperialists. To prevent this development, Hay issued a second series of Open Door notes, reaffirming the principle of open trade in China for all nations and announcing U.S. support for China's territorial and administrative integrity. In the 1930s, when Japanese expansionism would threaten China, this Open Door policy would mold America's response.

The Panama Canal: Hardball Diplomacy

The final episode in this expansionist cycle was the construction of the Panama Canal. Dreams of a canal across the ribbon of land linking North and South America dated back to the early Spanish conquest. Yellow fever and mismanagement brought a French company's late-nineteenth-century attempt to build a canal to disaster and left a half-completed waterway. To recoup some of the $400 million loss, the company offered to sell its assets, including a concession from Colombia, which then controlled the isthmus, for $109 million.

Americans considered alternative routes, including a canal across Nicaragua, but in 1901 the French lowered the asking price to $40 million. President Theodore Roosevelt pressed the offer, but in 1902 the Colombian government refused to ratify the Hay-Herrán agreement, which would have turned the French concession over to the United States. Furious, Roosevelt privately denounced the Colombians as "greedy little anthropoids."

Roosevelt found a willing collaborator in Philippe Bunau-Varilla, an official of the French company. To prevent the loss of $40 million to his firm, Bunau-Varilla organized a "revolution" in Panama, then still a Colombian province. Working from a room at the Waldorf Astoria Hotel in New York City, Bunau-Varilla wrote a declaration of independence and constitution. On November 3, 1903, the "revolution" erupted on schedule, with a U.S. warship anchored offshore as a warning to Colombia not to intervene. In short order, Bunau-Varilla proclaimed himself ambassador to Washington, gained American recognition of the newly hatched nation, and signed a treaty granting the United States a ten-mile-wide strip of land across Panama "in perpetuity" in return for $10 million and an annual payment of $250,000. Roosevelt later summarized the episode: "I took the Canal Zone, and let Congress debate, and while the debate goes on, the canal does also."

Before completing the canal, the United States first had to conquer yellow fever. After Dr. Walter Reed recognized the mosquito as its carrier, the U.S. Army carried out a prodigious drainage project that eradicated the disease-bearing pest. Construction began in 1906, and in August 1914 the first ship passed through the canal. The Atlantic and Pacific coasts were linked by a short sea route just in time for World War I.

A technical wonder, the canal also symbolized an arrogant American imperialism. For decades, the rancor generated by Roosevelt's high-handed actions, combined with other cases of U.S. interventionism, shadowed U.S.–Latin American relations.

CONCLUSION

The opening of the Panama Canal concluded thirty years of expansionism that trumpeted the United States' debut on the world stage and underscored the global reach of U.S. capitalism. Left unanswered at the time was the question of how a government designed for a small agrarian nation could meet the needs of an industrialized land of immigrant cities. Clearly, limited laissez-faire government was not the solution.

In the 1890s agrarian discontent underscored major problems and gave rise to the Populist party, which challenged laissez-faire assumptions and demanded that the government play an assertive role in solving social and economic problems. Although the party faded, its ideas became the basis for the progressive movement, to which we now turn.

CHRONOLOGY

1873 Panic of 1873.
Coinage Act demonetizes silver.

1877 Rutherford B. Hayes becomes president.

1878 Bland-Allison Act requires U.S. Treasury to purchase silver.

1880 James Garfield elected president.

1881 Assassination of Garfield; Chester A. Arthur becomes president.

1883 Pendleton Civil Service Act.

1884 Grover Cleveland elected president.

1887 Cleveland urges tariff reform and vetoes veterans' pension bill.

1888 Benjamin Harrison elected president.

1889 United States, Great Britain, and Germany establish protectorate over Samoan Islands.

1890 Sherman Silver Purchase Act.
Sherman Anti-Trust Act.
McKinley Tariff pushes tariffs to all-time high.

1891 Crisis between United States and Chile over attack on U.S. sailors.

1892 Cleveland elected to second term as president.

1893 Panic of 1893; depression of 1893–1897 begins.
Drain of treasury's gold reserve.
Repeal of Sherman Silver Purchase Act.
Overthrow of Queen Liliuokalani of Hawaii.

1894 "Coxey's Army" marches on Washington.
Pullman strike.
Wilson-Gorman Tariff.

1895 Supreme Court declares federal income tax unconstitutional.
Banker's loans end drain on gold reserve.
United States intervenes in Venezuela–Great Britain boundary dispute.

1896 Free-silver forces capture Democratic party and nominate William Jennings Bryan.
William McKinley elected president.

1898 Spanish-American War.

1898–1902 United States suppresses guerrilla uprising in Philippines.

1899 First United States Open Door notes on China.
United States helps put down Boxer uprising.

1900 Currency Act officially places United States on gold standard.
Second Open Door notes on China.
McKinley reelected.

1901 Platt Amendment retains U.S. role in Cuba.
Assassination of McKinley; Theodore Roosevelt becomes president.

1902 Philippine Government Act.

1903 Hay-Herrán agreement rejected by Colombia.
"Revolution" in Panama organized by Philippe Bunau-Varilla.
Hay-Bunau-Varilla Treaty.

1914 Completion of Panama Canal.

FOR FURTHER READING

Edward L. Ayers, *The Promise of the New South: Life After Reconstruction* (1992). A richly textured work that explores the complexity of the topic and pays close attention to nonelite men and women.

Robert L. Beisner, *From the Old Diplomacy to the New, 1865–1900*, 2d ed. (1986). A valuable study tracing the roots of expansionism.

W. Fitzhugh Brundage, *Lynching in the New South: Georgia and Virginia, 1880–1930* (1993). A careful analysis of lynching in two southern states over a fifty-year period.

William F. Holmes, ed., *American Populism* (1994). A well-selected set of nineteen scholarly essays interpreting the agrarian reform movement and surveying its varied aspects.

Morton Keller, *Affairs of State: Public Life in Late-Nineteenth-Century America* (1977). An excellent account of politics and government.

Robert C. McMath, *American Populism: A Social History, 1877–1898* (1993). A well-written study summing up recent scholarship on populism, especially its social and cultural dimensions.

John Offner, *An Unwanted War* (1992). A good recent history of the diplomacy leading up to the Spanish-American War.

CHAPTER 22

The Progressive Era

Industrialization brought benefits as well as problems to the United States. For the millions of immigrants working in unsafe factories and residing in unhealthful slums, life was a cycle of poverty, exhausting labor, and early death. But at the same time, corporations grew powerful, the new middle class of white-collar workers consolidated its position, and women demanded full participation in the political process. From this volatile milieu pulsed a current of reform that became the progressive movement, the response to the changes that transformed the United States between the Civil War and the twentieth century as Americans grappled with the new world of corporations, factories, cities, and immigrants.

The progressives were the first group of American reformers to view the government as an ally in the cause of reform. Neither glorifying the individual nor withdrawing from society as earlier reformers had done, they saw organizations and social engagement as essential to reform.

(Right) Boy working in a Lowell, Massachusetts, mill, c. 1920

Progressivism emerged first at the state and local levels, generated by groups as different as women's clubs and political radicals. At the national level, these reform impulses coalesced into a single movement that turned Washington into a hotbed of activism. By 1917, when reform gave way to war, progressivism had fundamentally altered U.S. government and society. This chapter will examine first the social changes that spawned progressivism and then the movement itself.

Japanese Immigrant Railroad Workers
America's phenomenal post–Civil War industrial growth would have been impossible without the millions of immigrants who labored long hours for low wages.

A Changing American Society and Economy

Urban growth and corporate consolidation brought dramatic changes to the United States in the early twentieth century. Farm-born Americans streaming into cities met a swirling tide of immigrants. During this era of booming prosperity, new forms of business organization transformed American capitalism. Some benefited, but millions of industrial workers faced long hours, low wages, dangerous working conditions, and pressures for ever greater output. They organized to improve their lot through the labor union and the ballot box.

Immigrant Masses and a New Urban Middle Class

Through all the turbulence of the early twentieth century, people continued to flock to the cities. By 1920 the urban population had passed the 50 percent mark, sixty-eight American cities had more than 100,000 residents, and New York City alone had grown by 2.2 million since 1900. Millions of the new urbanites had come from small-town and rural America. However, immigration still provided the greatest source of urban growth; more than 17 million people entered the United States between 1900 and 1917, and most of them became city dwellers.

As in the 1890s, the immigrant stream flowed primarily from southern and eastern Europe, but 200,000 Japanese, 40,000 Chinese, and thousands of Mexicans joined them. Although most came of economic necessity, revolution propelled many Mexicans northward, and religious persecution triggered the immigration of millions of eastern European Jews. By 1913 New York City's Lower East Side had a Jewish population of 1.4 million.

City life remained harsh. Urban governments' ability to provide decent schools and parks, safe water, sewers, garbage collection, and fire protection lagged behind the pace of growth. Death rates in the immigrant wards reached twice the national average, reflecting shockingly bad conditions.

Meanwhile, the urban middle class expanded rapidly. From 1900 to 1920, the white-collar work force jumped from 5.1 million to 10.5 million, twice the growth rate for the work force as a whole. This new middle class included such diverse groups as skilled engineers, technicians, bureaucrats, businessmen, lawyers, physicians, and teachers. Ambitious, well educated, and valuing self-discipline and social

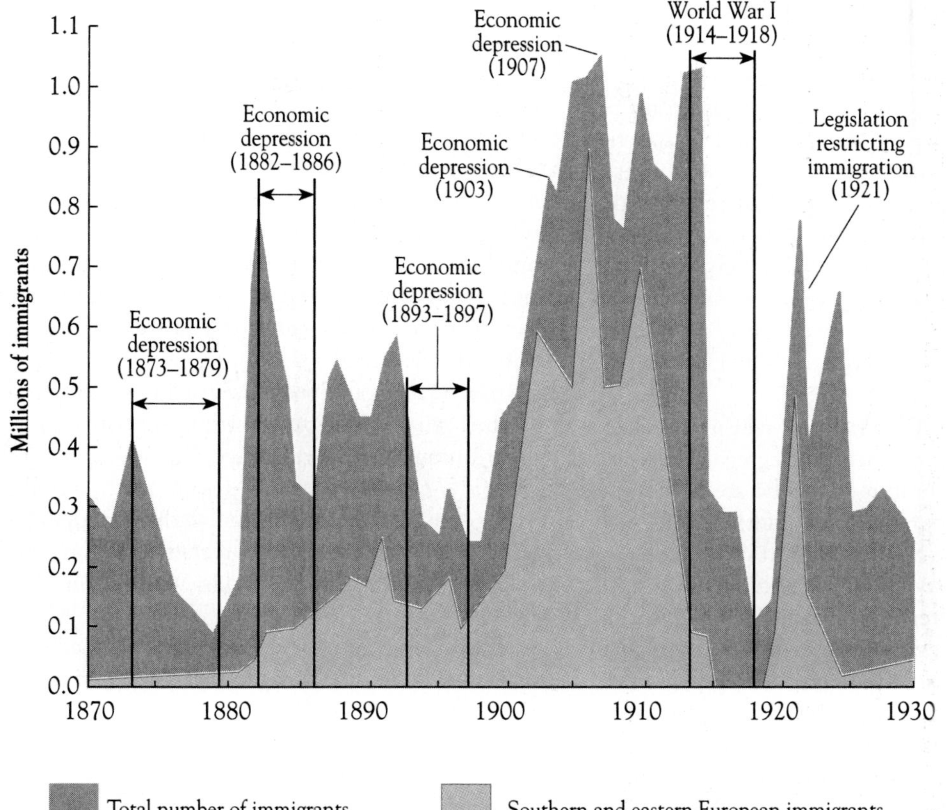

Immigration to the United States, 1870–1930

With the end of the depression of the 1890s, immigrants from southern and eastern Europe poured into America's cities, spurring an immigration-restriction movement, urban moral-control campaigns, and efforts to improve the physical and social conditions of immigrant life.

SOURCES: *Statistical History of the United States from Colonial Times to the Present* (Stamford, Conn.: Fairfield Publishers, 1965); and report presented by Senator William P. Dillingham, Senate document 742, 61st Congress, 3rd session, December 5, 1910: Abstracts of Reports to the Immigration Commission.

stability, they were eager to make their influence felt.

The city posed both opportunity and frustration for middle-class women. Some became public-school teachers, secretaries, librarians, and telephone operators, pushing the number of women in white-collar jobs from 949,000 in 1900 to 3.4 million in 1920. More and more women earned college degrees, and women made up 40 percent of the college population in 1910. But married urban middle-class women, hedged in by the demands of home and children and the ideology of domesticity, typically faced isolation and limited opportunity. The divorce rate crept up from one in twelve marriages in 1900 to one in nine by 1920. Many middle-class women who were mired in domestic routines joined white-collar and college-educated women in a resurgent women's movement.

African-Americans in a Racist Age

In 1900 more than two-thirds of the nation's 10 million blacks lived in the South as sharecroppers and tenant farmers. By 1910 the cotton boll weevil and ruinous floods had driven 20 percent of these southern blacks into cities. Urban African-American men took jobs in factories, mines, docks, and railroads or became carpenters or bricklayers, while African-American women became domestic servants, seamstresses, and laundry or tobacco workers. By 1910, 54 percent of America's black women worked.

"Jim Crow"—legally enforced racism—peaked in the early twentieth century. Segregation separated black from white in most public areas, including streetcars, trains, schools, parks, and even cemeteries. Until the Supreme Court outlawed it in 1917, a number of southern cities had legally imposed residential segregation. In some courts, black and white witnesses even took the oath on separate Bibles. Trapped on a treadmill of poverty, poor education, and discrimination, and prevented from voting, southern blacks faced formidable obstacles.

Meanwhile, the trek northward continued. Fleeing poverty and racism and drawn by job opportunities, two hundred thousand African-Americans migrated north between 1890 and 1910. World War I drew still more, and by 1920, 1.4 million African-Americans lived in the North. Northern blacks encountered conditions similar to those in the South. Racism had deepened after 1890 as depression and immigration heightened social tensions. Segregation, although not legally imposed, existed everywhere, supported by social pressure and occasional violence. Blacks lived in run-down "colored districts," attended dilapidated schools, and took the low-paying jobs. Although African-Americans voted, their allegiance to the Republican party gave them little influence. Even the newest mass medium, the movies, reinforced racism. D. W. Griffith's 1915 classic film *The Birth of a Nation* glorified the Ku Klux Klan and vilified and ridiculed African-Americans.

Smoldering racism occasionally ignited. In an antiblack riot in Atlanta in 1906, four African-Americans were murdered, many blacks' homes were burned, and the president of a black theological seminary was severely beaten by a white police officer. Lynchings had peaked in the late nineteenth century, but from 1900 to 1920 an average of about seventy-five lynchings occurred yearly. The victims were usually African-American men accused of murder, rape, or some other crime. Lynchings could involve incredible sadism, with large crowds attending to watch the victim's mutilation before he was killed.

In the face of adversity, African-Americans developed self-reliance and a strong support network. Their unique culture remained vigorous. Black religious life, centered in the African Methodist Episcopal church, provided a bulwark of support for many. Black colleges and universities, among them Fisk in Nashville and Howard in Washington, D.C., survived against heavy odds. The urban African-American community included black-owned insurance companies and banks and boasted a small elite of entrepreneurs, teachers, ministers, and lawyers. Blacks also rose socially through sports, among them Texan Jack Johnson, who won the heavyweight boxing championship in 1908.

New black musical idioms emerged. In addition to ragtime, the blues, rooted in the mournful chants of sharecroppers, gained recognition with the songs of W. C. Handy, including the classic "St. Louis Blues" (1914). Jazz gained popularity as well. Originating in New Orleans with the band of Buddy Bolden in the 1890s, jazz moved north to Chicago and other cities during World War I, eventually winning recognition as the United States' greatest musical achievement.

Corporate Boardrooms, Factory Floors

The process of consolidation that had produced Carnegie Steel and Standard Oil accelerated in the early twentieth century, with an average of 260 companies annually absorbed in mergers. Following the Carnegie Steel pattern, J. P. Morgan in 1902 consolidated six competing companies into the International Harvester Company, which controlled 85 percent of the farm-implement business. In 1908 William C. Durant founded the General Motors Company, which, backed financially by the Du Pont Corporation, bought up automobile manufacturers ranging from the inexpensive Chevrolet to the luxury Cadillac.

Many workers benefited from the prevailing good times. Industrial workers' average real (adjusted for inflation) wages had risen from $532 in the late nineteenth century to $687 by 1915. But even with the dollar's buying power much higher than today—a loaf of bread cost a mere seven cents—such pay barely supported a family and left no cushion for emergencies.

To make ends meet, entire immigrant families went to work. Two-thirds of immigrant girls had entered the labor force in the early 1900s, working in factories, as domestics, and in laundries and bakeries. Although the figures are imprecise, by 1910 the nonfarm labor force included at least 1.6 million children aged ten to fifteen. One investigator found a girl of five working at night in a South Carolina textile mill.

For all laborers, the hours were long and the hazards great. In 1900 the average worker toiled nine and one-half hours a day; some southern textile mill workers put in twelve- and thirteen-hour days. Few employers accepted responsibility for work-related accidents or injuries, and vacations and retirement benefits were rare. Generally, American capitalism extracted the maximum of labor from its work force and gave a bare minimum in return. Efficiency experts such as Frederick W. Taylor dreamed of making human workers as rational and predictable as machines.

Workers Organize; Socialism Advances

As workers continued to organize, the American Federation of Labor (AFL) grew from half a million members in 1897 to 4 million by 1920—but this was only 20 percent of the nonfarm labor force. With thousands of immigrants competing for jobs, union activities could be risky; bosses could easily fire an "agitator" and hire a newcomer. Judicial hostility also plagued the labor movement. In the 1908 *Danbury Hatters* case, a unanimous Supreme Court ruled that boycotts in support of strikes violated the Sherman Anti-Trust Act.

The AFL's strength continued to rest in the skilled trades, not in factory and mill work. Yet few unions tried to reach the unskilled laborers at the lowest end of the scale. In 1900 immigrants in New

Children in the Labor Force, 1880–1930

	Children Gainfully Employed, Nonagricultural Work		
Year	*Total number of children aged 10–15 (in millions)*	*Total number of children employed (in millions)*	*Percentage of children employed*
1880	6.6	1.1	16.8
1890	8.3	1.5	18.1
1900	9.6	1.7	18.2
1910	10.8	1.6	15.0
1920	12.5	1.4	11.3
1930	14.3	0.7	4.7

SOURCE: From *The Statistical History of the United States* by Ben J. Wattenberg. Introduction and User's Guide copyright © 1976 by Ben J. Wattenberg. Reprinted by permission of Basic Books, a division of HarperCollins Publishers, Inc.

York organized the International Ladies' Garment Workers Union (ILGWU), which conducted successful strikes in 1909 and 1911.

The Industrial Workers of the World (IWW), or Wobblies, founded in Chicago in 1905 and led by William D. "Big Bill" Haywood, also targeted the most exploited workers. Never large, and torn by dissent, the IWW peaked at around 30,000 members, mainly western miners, lumbermen, fruit pickers, and itinerant laborers. Its greatest success came in 1912 when it won a rancorous textile strike in Lawrence, Massachusetts. The victory owed much to Elizabeth Gurley Flynn, a fervent Irish-American orator, and Margaret Sanger, the leader of the birth-control movement, who publicized the cause by sending strikers' children to New York sympathizers for temporary care.

The IWW preached revolution. In 1908 it proclaimed, "The struggle must go on until the workers of the world . . . take possession of the earth and the machinery of production, and abolish the wage system." The Wobblies had a reputation, much exaggerated, for violence and sabotage, and they faced unremitting harassment through arrests and prosecution by government officials. By 1920 the IWW's strength was broken.

Others appalled by capitalism's human toll turned to socialism. Socialists advocated an end to capitalism and demanded public ownership of factories, utilities, railroads, and communications systems. But American workers generally rejected the revolutionary ideology of German social theorist Karl Marx in favor of democratic socialism achieved at the ballot box. In 1900 democratic socialists formed the Socialist Party of America (SPA). Eugene V. Debs, the Indiana labor leader converted to socialism during his imprisonment after the Pullman strike, became the SPA's most popular spokesman and its candidate for president five times between 1900 and 1920. The pinnacle of socialist strength came in 1912 when the SPA counted 118,000 members, Debs received over 900,000 votes for president, and the Socialists elected a congressman along with hundreds of municipal officials.

The upsurge in Socialist votes was only one sign of rising discontent with politics-as-usual. As the problems created by industrialism became obvious, the demand that government do something grew insistent.

The Progressive Movement Takes Shape

As the twentieth century began, intellectuals increasingly challenged the ideological foundations of a business-oriented social order, and writers publicized industrialization's human toll. Reformers sought to make government more democratic, to eradicate unhealthful and dangerous conditions in cities and factories, and to curb corporate power. Overwhelmed by the diversity of these reform efforts and awed at the political energies they unleashed, Americans grouped them under a single label: the progressive movement.

Progressivism: An Overview

Progressivism was a political response to industrialization and its social results: immigration, urban growth, the concentration of corporate power, and the widening of class divisions. Unlike populism, born of agrarian unrest, progressivism found its strength in the cities. And the progressives were *reformers*, not radicals or revolutionaries. They wanted to remedy the evils spawned by unregulated capitalism, not to destroy the system.

Progressivism never became a cohesive movement with a unified program; it remained a diverse array of reform activities that sometimes overlapped and sometimes sharply diverged. Many reformers insisted that the preservation of democracy required stricter regulation of business; others, emphasizing humanitarian themes, called for legislation to protect workers and the urban poor. Still others concentrated on reforming the structure of government, especially at the municipal level. And some, seeing immigration, urban immorality, and social disorder as the central problems, advocated social-control strategies such as immigration restriction and the abolition of prostitution and saloons.

The progressives themselves were a diverse lot, aligned in coalitions that shifted from issue to issue. At the center of the movement stood the native-born Protestant middle class. However, the urban-immigrant political machines provided critical support on issues affecting factory workers and slum conditions, and even corporate leaders at times helped to devise business-regulation measures, especially when pressures for such regulation became irresistible.

Public-citizen groups such as the American League for Civic Improvement provided the first impetus for reform. In an era of organizations, the roots of progressivism not surprisingly came from this organizational impulse. All the major progressive reforms, from woman suffrage and the abolition of child labor to prohibition, drew strength from such organizations.

Closely related to this organizational impulse was the progressive emphasis on a "scientific" approach to social problems. Scientific and technological expertise had shaped the industrial revolution, and progressives believed that such expertise would solve the social problems that industrialism had left in its wake. Progressives marshaled social research, expert opinion, and statistical data to support their causes.

Some historians, stressing the technological and managerial aspects of progressivism, portray the movement as an example of an organizing stage through which all modernizing societies pass. This is a useful interpretation, but one must remember that "progressivism" did not unfold automatically, independently of human will. Earnest and energetic leaders, journalists, ministers, and organizers all made a difference. Human drive and emotion propelled the movement forward. Progressivism, then, is not an impersonal historical abstraction but a useful term for the activities and concerns of thousands of individual Americans in the early twentieth century.

Intellectuals Lay the Groundwork

Building on the work of Lester Ward, Edward Bellamy, and the Social Gospel leaders, brilliant turn-of-the-century thinkers helped to reorient American social thought and laid the ideological foundation for progressivism.

William Graham Sumner and other Social Darwinists had argued that "survival of the fittest" justified unrestrained economic competition. Ward had begun the intellectual attack against these ideas, and the assault intensified in the opening years of the new century. Scholars in many disciplines produced work skeptical of the established order and implicitly supporting far-reaching changes.

Thorstein Veblen, a Norwegian-American, was prominent among the reshapers of economic thought. In *The Theory of the Leisure Class* (1899), he assailed the values and life-styles of the Gilded Age elite and their "conspicuous consumption." In later writings he argued that engineers, molded by the stern discipline of the machine, were better fitted to lead society than was the business class. Veblen epitomized the admiration of efficiency, science, and technical expertise that lay at the heart of the progressive impulse.

Historians also contributed to the new currents of thought that fed into progressivism. In "The Significance of the Frontier in American History" (see Chapter 17), Frederick Jackson Turner argued that the social and political experience of generations of western pioneers constituted the central dynamic of American history. Equally influential in this historical revisionism were Mary Ritter Beard and her husband, Charles A. Beard. In such books as *Woman's Work in Municipalities* (1915) and *A Short History of the American Labor Movement* (1920), Mary Beard spotlighted groups ignored by traditional historians. In *An Economic Interpretation of the Constitution* (1913), Charles A. Beard gave ammunition to the progressive critics of big business by arguing that the Constitution makers of 1787 had served the interests of the moneyed class of their day.

Harvard philosopher William James also contributed to this intellectual reconstruction in his seminal work *Pragmatism* (1907), which argued that truth emerges neither from universal laws nor abstract theories but from experience. Truth is what *works*. James's emphasis on the fluidity of knowledge and the importance of practical action contributed to the progressive model of skepticism toward established ideologies. Reformer Jane Addams, James believed, exemplified his pragmatic philosophy. While others theorize about reality, he wrote to her, "you *inhabit* reality." In *Democracy and Social Ethics* (1902), Addams rejected individualistic morality and called for a new social ideology rooted in awareness of modern society's complex interdependence.

More than anyone else, Herbert Croly embodied the progressive faith in the power of ideas to transform society. In his masterpiece, *The Promise of American Life* (1909), Croly called for an activist federal government that would serve *all* citizens, not just the capitalist class. To build public support for such a transformed conception of government, Croly argued, socially engaged intellectuals must play a key role. In 1914 he founded *The New Republic* magazine as a forum for progressive ideas.

New Ideas About Education and the Law

With public-school enrollment leaping from 7 million children in 1870 to more than 23 million by 1920, progressive intellectuals realized that schools could be a powerful engine of social change. Chief among educational reformers was the philosopher John Dewey, who insisted that the intelligent application of the scientific method to social problems could build a just and harmonious society. Viewing intelligence above all as an instrument of social action, he called his philosophy Instrumentalism.

Public schools could lead to significant reform if they embraced the new ethic of social interdependence, Dewey maintained. Banishing bolted-down chairs and desks from the model school that he started at the University of Chicago in 1896, he encouraged children to move around the room, to ask questions, and to interact with each other as well as with the teacher. In *Democracy and Education* (1916), Dewey argued that schools must embody the values of democracy and cooperation through their methods and curriculum. In the ideal school, children would work together in a harmonious process of intellectual inquiry and social growth.

This mood of civic idealism spread across colleges and universities as well. No longer could the university be a "home of useless and harmless recluses," one university president emphasized; it must dedicate itself to the public good. Princeton's president Woodrow Wilson summed up the new spirit in his 1902 inaugural address, "Princeton for the Nation's Service."

Even the natural sciences felt the pull of social activism. A Massachusetts Institute of Technology chemist, Ellen Richards, applied chemistry to the issues of nutrition, food adulteration, and public hygiene. Statisticians used their skills to study labor conditions, epidemic diseases, and urban housing density.

New ideas influenced the legal profession as well. Instead of citing ancient precedent, according to Oliver Wendell Holmes, Jr., in his influential *The Common Law* (1881), jurists must recognize that law evolves as society changes. "The life of the law has not been logic; it has been experience," he argued. Appointed to the Supreme Court in 1902 as the Progressive Era began, Holmes wrote eloquent dissents from the conservative majority, establishing the framework for a more flexible view.

Novelists and Journalists Spread the Word

As intellectuals chipped away at laissez-faire ideology and laid the foundations for a new social ethic, novelists and journalists helped to transform progressivism into a national movement by revealing to middle-class readers the seamy details of corporate wrongdoing and the harsh realities of slum and factory life. Advances in high-speed printing and photographic reproduction assured their message a mass audience and intensified its emotional impact. Henry Demarest Lloyd's *Wealth and Commonwealth* (1894), a biting exposé of the Standard Oil Company, was a pathbreaking early work. Novelists followed with compelling indictments of corporate greed and heedless urban growth. In *The Octopus* (1901), Frank Norris portrayed the struggle between wheat growers and railroad owners. David Graham Phillips's *Susan Lenox: Her Fall and Rise* (1917) explored links among slum life, political corruption, and prostitution. Theodore Dreiser's *The Financier* (1912) portrayed a hard-driving business tycoon devoid of social consciousness.

Mass-circulation magazines such as *McClure's*, *Cosmopolitan*, and *Everybody's* published expansive articles exposing political corruption and corporate wrongdoing. President Theodore Roosevelt, thinking some of these articles too one-sided, christened their authors "muckrakers" after a character in John Bunyan's *Pilgrim's Progress* who spends all his time raking up filth. The name became a badge of honor. The muckrakers' stark prose emphasized facts rather than abstractions. For example, in a 1903 series on working women, Maria Van Vorst offered a gripping account of a shoe factory where women's fingernails literally rotted off because the female employees had to immerse their hands in caustic dyes.

The muckrakers touched a nerve. *McClure's* circulation soared to 750,000 and *Cosmopolitan*'s to more than a million during their heyday in 1901–1903. Many magazine exposés appeared in book form, including Lincoln Steffens's *The Shame of the Cities* (1904), Ida Tarbell's damning *History of the Standard Oil Company* (1904), and David Graham Phillips's *Treason of the Senate* (1906).

Artists and photographers supplied a visual counterpoint. George Luks, John Sloan, and others of the "Ashcan School" painted realistic canvases of New York's teeming immigrant life. Lewis Hine photographed factory laborers, especially children with their stunted bodies, pale skin, and sad eyes.

Reforming the Political Process

The progressive movement had begun in the 1890s in well-to-do city neighborhoods as the urban elite and middle classes crusaded against "evil" political bosses. A succession of anti-Tammany reform waves set off by Protestant clergy had swept New York City. In Detroit, the reform administration of Mayor Hazen Pingree (1890–1897) had brought honesty to city hall, lowered transit fares, and made the tax structure more equitable. The shrewd Pingree once slapped a health quarantine on a brothel where a local business leader was paying a visit and refused to let the man leave until he promised to drop his opposition to Pingree's reforms.

The municipal-reform impulse strengthened after 1900. In 1907 San Francisco newspaper editor Fremont Older crusaded against the city's notoriously corrupt boss, Mayor Abe Reuf. Attorney Hiram Johnson, who took over the prosecution of the Reuf machine when the original prosecutor was gunned down in court, obtained a conviction of Mayor Reuf and his cronies. Sternly self-righteous, Johnson embodied the reform fervor of the day—one observer called him "a volcano in perpetual eruption"—and he rode the Reuf case to the California governorship and the U.S. Senate. In Toledo, Ohio, a colorful eccentric named Samuel M. "Golden Rule" Jones led the reform crusade. A self-made businessman converted to the Social Gospel, Jones introduced profit sharing in his factory; as mayor, he established playgrounds, free kindergartens, lodging houses for tramps, and an open-air church for all faiths.

As the urban reform movement matured, it systematically attacked the roots of urban misgovernment, including the uncontrolled private monopolies that provided such basic services as water, gas, electricity, and public transportation. Reformers passed laws regulating the rates that utilities could charge, taxing them more equitably, and curbing their political influence. Reformers also advocated, and sometimes achieved, the public ownership of utilities.

Reflecting the progressive enthusiasm for expertise and efficiency, some reformers advocated *structural* changes in city government. They wanted to replace mayors and aldermen elected on a ward-by-ward basis with professional managers and administrators chosen in citywide elections. Supposedly above politics, these experts were expected to run the city like an efficient business.

Virtually all elements of the urban population participated in reform. The native-born middle class provided the initial impetus for urban beautification and political reform. Business leaders often supported city-manager systems and citywide elections—structural changes that diminished the power of the ward bosses and increased that of the corporate elite. On matters of practical concern such as municipal services, immigrants and even political bosses supported the new urban-reform movement.

Municipal reform soon expanded to electoral reform at the state level. By 1910 all states had instituted secret ballots, making it much harder than before to rig elections. Another widely adopted Progressive Era reform was the direct primary, in which party members, rather than leaders, selected nominees for public office. And some western states inaugurated electoral reforms known as initiative, referendum, and recall. By an initiative, voters can instruct the legislature to consider a specific bill. In a referendum, they can actually enact a law or express their views on a measure. By a recall petition, voters can remove an official from office by gathering enough signatures. The culmination of this flurry of electoral reforms came in 1913 with the ratification of the Seventeenth Amendment to the Constitution, which shifted the election of U.S. senators from state legislatures to the voters at large.

These electoral changes produced mixed results. They were meant to democratize voting, but party leaders and organized interest groups learned to manipulate the new electoral machinery. Ironically, the new procedures appear primarily to have weakened party loyalties and reduced voter interest. Overall voter-participation rates declined steeply in the early twentieth century, but political activity by organized groups increased.

Protecting Workers and Beautifying the City

If issues of municipal government, utility regulation, and electoral reform represented the brain of progressivism, the impetus to improve conditions in factories, mills, and slums represented its heart. By 1907 thirty states had abolished child labor. A 1903 Oregon law limited women in industry to a ten-hour workday. Other reforms concentrated on industrial safety, welfare programs, and disability benefits for workers injured on the job.

Political bosses in cities with heavy immigrant populations supported such legislation. State senator Robert F. Wagner, a leader of New York City's Tammany Hall machine, headed the New York State Factory Investigating Committee. Thanks to this committee's efforts, New York enacted fifty-six worker-protection laws, tightening factory-safety standards, permitting pregnancy leaves, and requiring chairs with backs for garment workers. By 1914 twenty-five states had passed laws making employers liable for job-related injuries or deaths.

City reformers worked for practical goals such as better garbage collection and street cleaning, milk inspection, public-health programs, and housing codes. Urban-beautification advocates campaigned for new parks, boulevards, and streetlights and against billboards, smoky factories, and unsightly overhead wires. Daniel Burnham, the developer of innovative city plans for San Francisco and Cleveland, recognized that such blueprints had to be bold and comprehensive in order to capture the public imagination. His proposed plan for Chicago incorporated a completely new layout that would make the city both efficient and aesthetically harmonious. In Burnham's vision, Chicago's focal point would be a new civic center containing a majestic city hall and a vast plaza. Many features of his plan eventually became reality as Chicago spent more than $300 million on urban-development projects between 1910 and 1920. Other urban beautifiers of the Progressive Era shared Burnham's belief that broad boulevards, imposing squares, and monumental civic buildings would restore public pride in metropolitan America.

Old-Time Movies
Early moviegoers were greeted by humorous lantern slides attempting to instill good behavior.

Corporate Regulation

Progressives also believed that big business had to be brought to heel. Few wanted to destroy the giant corporations, but many became convinced that these enterprises that had benefited so enormously from the government's economic policies should be subject to government supervision. One state after another enacted legislation regulating railroads, mines, mills, telephone companies, and other businesses. Public-health officials, factory investigators, and other regulators monitored corporate America as never before.

Under Governor Robert La Follette (1901–1906), Wisconsin exemplified this process. A former Republican member of Congress, "Fighting Bob" was elected governor as an independent in 1900. Soon he was transforming state government just as reform mayors had transformed municipal government. Challenging the business interests long dominant in Wisconsin politics, the La Follette administration adopted the direct-primary system, set up a commission to regulate railroads operating within the state, increased corporate taxes, and passed a law limiting campaign spending.

Regulating national corporations at the municipal and state levels posed obvious problems. Once progressivism reached into national politics, however, the regulatory impulse, rooted in grass-roots activism, moved to the center of the reform agenda.

Progressivism and Social Control: The Movement's Coercive Dimension

Progressives believed that they could restore order to urban-industrial society through research, legislation, and enlightened social tinkering. This outlook underlay progressivism's confidence but also gave it a repressive and strongly moralistic edge; whereas some progressives focused on such issues as child labor and corporate regulation, others became obsessed with personal behavior and sought to impose morality by law. Although these reformers addressed serious social problems, their moralistic rhetoric and proposed remedies often betrayed an impulse to force the urban poor to conform to their own middle-class code.

Moral Control in the Cities

Quaint as early movies seem today, some of them, especially those featuring sexuality, struck many middle-class Americans as dangerously immoral. The shabbiness of the immigrant-district five-cent movie halls, called nickelodeons, intensified such feelings. But a New York garment worker who lived with her Italian immigrant parents recalled, "The one place I was allowed to go by myself was the movies. My parents wouldn't let me go anywhere else, even when I was twenty-four." This freedom from moral oversight was precisely what worried progressives. Warning of "nickel madness," they demanded film censorship. Several states did establish censorship boards, and Chicago empowered its police chief to ban movies that he considered immoral.

Prostitution, a major social problem in urbanizing America, became a target for the moral reformers. Young women could earn five times as much money as a prostitute than as a factory worker and put in far fewer hours. In true progressive fashion, the reformers began to investigate. The American Social Hygiene Association (1914), financed by John D. Rockefeller, sponsored medical research on sexually transmitted diseases, underwrote "vice investigations" in various cities, and drafted model municipal statutes against prostitution. Soon a "white slave" hysteria gripped the country. Sensationalizing books, articles, and films warned that innocent farm girls were being kidnapped and forced into a life of sin in the city. The Mann Act (1910) made it a federal crime to transport a woman across a state line "for immoral purposes." Amid much fanfare, the red-light districts of New Orleans, Chicago, and other cities were shut down or forced to operate more discreetly.

The progressive moral-control movement reached its zenith with the prohibition crusade. Temperance had long loomed large on the American reform agenda, but during the Progressive Era reformers' energies shifted to the legal abolition of alcoholic beverages.

The Anti-Saloon League (ASL), founded in 1895, was a typical progressive organization, with full-time professionals staffing a national office and Protestant ministers serving on a network of state committees. ASL presses produced tons of propaganda documenting the role of alcohol and the saloon in health problems, family disorder, political corruption, and workplace inefficiency and championing nationwide prohibition as a legislative cureall. A legitimate social issue, prohibition took on heavy symbolic overtones for middle-class reformers as a lurid symptom of urban America's rampant immorality. Supported by the Woman's Christian Temperance Union and influential church agencies, the ASL crusade led to the passage (1918) and ratification (1919) of the Eighteenth Amendment, outlawing the manufacture, sale, and transport of alcoholic beverages (see Chapter 23).

Like prostitution, alcohol abuse was a serious problem. Alcoholism contributed to public-health problems as well as to poverty, domestic abuse, and other social pathologies. But like the antiprostitution crusade, the prohibition campaign was also an episode in the culture wars between native-born citizens and immigrants. The ASL simultaneously raised legitimate issues and embodied Protestant America's desire to tame the immigrant city.

The Progressive Era also marks Americans' first attempts to deal with drug abuse, which was widespread. Medicines frequently contained opium or its derivatives, heroin and morphine, and physicians freely prescribed these opiates. Cocaine was widely used—it was part of Coca-Cola's secret formula until about 1900.

Progressivism's regulatory impulse quickly zeroed in on such dangerous drugs. The Pure Food and Drug Act and the Harrison Narcotics Act strictly regulated addictive substances such as the opiates and cocaine. In the battle against drugs, as in environmental concerns, the progressives at the dawn of the twentieth century anticipated some of the central issues that the Amercan nation confronts as another century prepares to dawn.

Immigration Restriction and Eugenics

The obvious answer to the threats posed by the immigrant city, some reformers concluded, lay in excluding immigrants. Many progressives supported immigration restriction. Those who did documented their case with a flourish of scientific expertise. In 1911 a congressional commission produced a statistical study "proving" the new immigrants' innate degeneracy. In 1914 the progressive sociologist Edward A. Ross described recent immigrants as "hirsute, low-browed, big-faced persons of obviously low mentality." In 1896, 1913, and 1915, Congress passed literacy-test bills aimed at slowing immigration, but they fell victim to veto by a succession of presidents. In 1917, however, such a bill became law over President Wilson's veto. This, too, was part of progressivism's ambiguous legacy.

The most sinister perversion of "science" in the Progressive Era was the eugenics movement. Eugenics is the control of reproduction to alter the characteristics of a plant or animal species. Some American eugenicists believed that controlled breeding could also improve society. In 1904 the Carnegie Foundation funded a research center to study heredity and genetic manipulation. Its director, zoologist Charles B. Davenport, was a racist, an anti-Semite, and an advocate of immigration restriction. Inspired by Davenport and other eugenicists, some states legalized the forced sterilization of criminals, sex offenders, and the mentally deficient. A 1927 Supreme Court case upheld such laws.

This ugly underside of early-twentieth-century thought was plainly revealed in Madison Grant's *The Passing of the Great Race* (1916). In many ways Grant, a patrician supporter of numerous civic causes, represented the best in progressivism. In *The Passing,* however, he stirred together a rancid brew of pseudoscientific data and spewed out a vicious diatribe against Jews, blacks, and southern and eastern Europeans. Grant called for absolute racial segregation, immigration restriction, and the forced sterilization of "unfit" groups, including "worthless race types." He chillingly previewed the ideas that Adolf Hitler would one day bring to fruition.

Racism and Progressivism

As Grant's work suggests, racism rose to a high pitch during the Progressive Era. Taken as a whole, the progressive movement did little as African-Americans were lynched, disfranchised, and discriminated against. For many progressives, African-Americans represented a source of social menace to be studied, controlled, and kept out of public life.

In the South, progressives often led the movement for African-American disfranchisement and segregation. Numerous southern politicians backed a variety of progressive reforms while simultaneously pursuing viciously antiblack policies. In Washington, D.C., racism pervaded the administration of Woodrow Wilson (1913–1921). The southern-born Wilson displayed a patronizing attitude toward blacks and acquiesced as southerners in his cabinet and in Congress imposed rigid segregation on all levels of the government.

But some progressives spoke up eloquently for immigrants and African-Americans. Settlement-house worker Mary White Ovington helped to found the National Association for the Advancement of Colored People and wrote *Half a Man* (1911), a study of the effects of racial prejudice on New York City's blacks. Progressive social thought nevertheless included some disturbing ingredients—an assurance of moral and intellectual superiority, an exaggerated confidence in the social application of science, a readiness to use state power to coerce individual behavior—that all too readily could turn repressive and destructive.

African-Americans and Women Organize

The early twentieth century was a time of intense organizational activity and intellectual ferment for African-Americans and women, especially those of the urban middle class. Both groups had ample cause for dissatisfaction, and among both, movements flowered to address those grievances.

Controversy Among African-Americans

The nation's foremost African-American leader from the 1890s until his death in 1915 was Booker T. Washington. Born into slavery in Virginia in 1856, the son of a slave woman and her white master, Washington enrolled at a freedman's school in Hampton, Virginia, in 1872. In 1881 he organized a state vocational school in Tuskegee, Alabama, that became Tuskegee University.

Washington attained prominence in 1895 when he gave an address in Atlanta insisting that the first task of African-Americans must be that of acquiring vocational skills. Once blacks proved their economic value, he predicted, racism would ebb; meanwhile, they must accept their lot. Although Washington's "Atlanta Compromise" publicly urged accommodation to a racist society, he secretly contributed to organizations fighting racial discrimination.

Much admired by white America, Washington traveled and lectured widely. His autobiography, *Up from Slavery* (1901), recounted his rise from poverty through honesty, hard work, and the help of kindly patrons—familiar themes to a generation of white readers reared on Horatio Alger. But African-Americans were divided over Washington's program. Although many southern blacks revered Washington, some northern blacks challenged his dominance. With racism escalating and blacks' status declining, Washington's philosophy of accommodation and his optimistic predictions seemed unrealistic to critics, one of whom wrote in 1902 that Washington's acceptance of African-American disfranchisement struck "a fatal blow . . . to the Negro's political rights and liberty."

Washington's most powerful challenge came from W. E. B. Du Bois (1868–1963). A cultivated scholar, Du Bois set forth his differences with Washington in *The Souls of Black Folk* (1903). Rejecting Washington's call for patience and the cultivation of manual skills, Du Bois demanded full access for blacks to the same educational advantages and intellectual opportunities open to whites. African-Americans would have to struggle ceaselessly against all forms of racial discrimination, he argued. In his assertiveness and militance, Du Bois set the direction of black activism in the new century.

The Founding of the NAACP

In the 1890s the Afro-American Council served as a forum for blacks who favored vigorous resistance to racism, but when Booker T. Washington gained control of the organization, his opponents turned elsewhere. In 1905, under Du Bois's leadership, these challengers met at Niagara Falls, and for the next few years participants in the "Niagara Movement" convened annually.

A small group of white reformers also rejected Washington's cautiousness, including newspaper publisher Oswald Garrison Villard, the grandson of abolitionist William Lloyd Garrison. In 1909 Villard and his allies joined with Du Bois and other blacks from the Niagara Movement to form the National Association for the Advancement of Colored People (NAACP). Rejecting Washington's accommodationist policy, the NAACP called for full political equality for African-Americans and an end to racial discrimination. Attracting the urban black middle class, the NAACP by 1914 had 6,000 members.

Revival of the Woman-Suffrage Movement

As late as 1910, women could vote in only four sparsely populated western states: Wyoming, Utah, Colorado, and Idaho. Six states voted down referenda on woman suffrage after 1896, but onrushing social and ideological currents infused the suffrage movement with new vitality after 1900. Middle-class women found it absurd that they could not vote, particularly because recently arrived (and often uneducated) immigrant men could. A vigorous suffrage movement in Great Britain therefore reverberated on this side of the Atlantic. Women's leadership in the larger progressive movement, moreover, powerfully boosted the cause.

The renewal of the women's movement began at the grass roots. In big cities such as New York and Chicago, suffragists used street meetings and parades to gain publicity. A new generation of leaders, drawing on the rhetoric of progressive reform, translated this energy into a revitalized national movement. Under Carrie Chapman Catt, who succeeded Susan B. Anthony as president of the National American Woman Suffrage Association (NAWSA) in 1900, the movement adopted the so-called Winning Plan: grass-roots organization with centralized coordination.

Following a strategy devised in NAWSA's executive office, women nationwide lobbied legislators, distributed literature, conducted referenda, and organized marches and rallies. State after state fell

Woman Suffrage Before the Nineteenth Amendment
Beginning with Wyoming in 1869, woman suffrage made steady gains in western states before 1920. In the East key breakthroughs came in New York (1917) and Michigan (1918). The South remained an anti-woman-suffrage bastion throughout the period.

into the suffrage column. A key victory came in 1917 when New York State voters approved a woman-suffrage referendum. Although a few black and immigrant women participated at the local level, NAWSA's membership remained largely white, native born, and middle class.

Not all suffragists accepted Catt's strategy. Alice Paul, who admired the militancy of British suffragists while a student in Great Britain, became a leading dissenter. Ambitious for leadership and impatient with NAWSA's state-by-state approach, Paul in 1913 founded the Congressional Union, later renamed the Woman's party, to bring direct pressure on the federal government to enact a woman-suffrage amendment. Insisting that the party in power—the Democrats under President Woodrow Wilson—must be held accountable for the continued denial of votes to women, Paul and her followers picketed the White House around the clock in the wartime year 1917. Several demonstrators were arrested, jailed, and, when they went on a hunger strike, force-fed.

Thanks in part to women's active participation in the war effort (see Chapter 23), the tide turned. The Nineteenth Amendment, granting women the vote, passed Congress in 1919 and was ratified by August 1920. That November, seventy-two years after the first American women's rights convention (at Seneca Falls, New York, in 1848), women all across America at last went to the polls.

Breaking out of the "Woman's Sphere"

The suffrage movement did not exhaust American women's talents or organizational energies. Organizations such as the General Federation of Women's Clubs and the National Association of Colored Women grew briskly in the early twentieth century.

A Revived Women's Movement
As the drive for woman suffrage gained momentum, these activists in Washington State put up posters for the cause.

Women's club members, settlement-house leaders, and individual female activists joined in various campaigns: to bring playgrounds and day nurseries to the slums, to abolish child labor, to improve conditions for women workers, and to ban unsafe foods and quack remedies.

Entrenched cultural assumptions about "woman's sphere" crumbled as women became active on many fronts. Katherine Bement Davis served as the innovative superintendent of a woman's reformatory before becoming New York City's commissioner of corrections. Anarchist Emma Goldman crisscrossed the country delivering riveting lectures on politics, feminism, and modern drama while coediting a radical monthly, *Mother Earth*. And in 1914 Margaret Sanger began a campaign for birth control, a term that she coined. A nurse and radical feminist, Sanger had witnessed the tragedy of unwanted pregnancies among slum women. In 1916 she opened the nation's first birth-control clinic, in Brooklyn, New York.

Leading feminist intellectual Charlotte Perkins Gilman, in her book *Women and Economics* (1898), traced the history of sexual discrimination, explored the cultural process of gender stereotyping, and linked the legal, political, and social subordination of women to their economic dependence on men. Gilman argued that confining women to the domestic sphere was outdated. She advocated women's economic independence through equality in the workplace and state-run day-care centers.

Alice Hamilton and Florence Kelley typify women's central role in progressivism. Hamilton, a professor of bacteriology at Northwestern University, worked closely with Jane Addams at Hull House. In 1910, combining scientific expertise with social-welfare advocacy, Hamilton conducted a pathbreaking study of lead poisoning in industry. Appointed an investigator for the U.S. Bureau of Labor in 1911, she became an expert on, and tireless campaigner against, work-related health hazards.

In 1893 the investigations by Florence Kelley of conditions in factories and tenement workhouses helped to secure passage of an Illinois law prohibiting child labor and limiting working hours for women. In 1899 she became general secretary of the National Consumers' League, which lobbied for improved factory conditions. Kelley angrily asked, "Why are seals, bears, reindeer, fish, wild game in the national parks, buffalo, [and] migratory birds all found suitable for federal protection, but not children?" Her efforts did much to awaken Americans to the evils of child labor.

National Progressivism—Phase I: Roosevelt and Taft

By 1905 localized reform movements had coalesced into a national effort. Symbolically, in 1906 Robert La Follette became a U.S. senator. He arrived in Washington as progressivism found its first national leader, Theodore Roosevelt.

Bombastic, self-righteous, and jingoistic—but also brilliant, politically masterful, and endlessly interesting—Roosevelt, "TR," became president in 1901. He made the White House a volcano of political activism. Skillfully orchestrating public opinion, the popular young president pursued his goals: labor mediation, consumer protection, conservation, business virtue, and activism abroad. TR's hand-picked successor, William Howard Taft, lacked his master's political genius, however, and sniping among former allies marred his term.

Roosevelt's Path to the White House

On September 6, 1901, in Buffalo, an anarchist shot then-president William McKinley. At first McKinley's survival seemed certain, so Vice President Theodore Roosevelt proceeded with a hiking trip into the Adirondack Mountains. Then an urgent message about McKinley's worsening condition propelled Roosevelt out of the mountains on a breakneck journey by horse and wagon and by train to Buffalo. On September 14 the forty-two-year-old Roosevelt took the presidential oath.

Reflecting the view of many politicians, Republican kingmaker Mark Hanna exclaimed, "My God, that damned cowboy in the White House!" Although Roosevelt was in fact the son of an aristocratic New York family, his emphasis on vigor and physical fitness reflected his love of the West. After a sickly childhood, Roosevelt used a body-building program and active summers in Wyoming to develop a strong physique. Later, two years on a Dakota ranch helped him to struggle past grief over his young wife's death in 1884 and nurtured the physical and mental toughness that he would later extol as "the strenuous life."

Plunging into politics when most of his social class considered it unbefitting gentlemen, Roosevelt held various posts in New York State before leading the Rough Riders in Cuba. He was elected New York's governor in 1898. Republican bosses, unsettled by this human dynamo, shunted him off to the limbo of the vice presidency in 1900. Angry at the maneuver, Roosevelt sputtered, "I would a great deal rather be anything, say a history professor, than Vice President."

Unexpectedly thrust into the White House, TR energized the presidency. "While President I have been President emphatically," he boasted; "I believe in a strong executive." Roosevelt enjoyed public life and loved the limelight. As a relative wryly observed, he wanted to be the bride at every wedding and the corpse at every funeral. Americans were fascinated by their rambunctious young president, with his toothy grin, machine-gun speech, and passion for the outdoors. After Teddy Roosevelt, the presidency was never quite the same. He enlarged the office in ways that permanently affected the balance of power within American government.

Labor Disputes and Corporate Regulation

The new president's political skills were quickly tested. In May 1902 the United Mine Workers Union (UMW) called a strike to gain higher wages, shorter hours, and recognition as a union. The mine owners refused to talk to UMW leaders. After five months, with coal reserves dwindling, TR sum-

The Election of 1904

Candidates	*Parties*	*Electoral Vote*	*Popular Vote*	*Percentage of Popular Vote*
THEODORE ROOSEVELT	Republican	336	7,628,461	57.4
Alton B. Parker	Democratic	140	5,084,223	37.6
Eugene V. Debs	Socialist		402,283	3.0
Silas C. Swallow	Prohibition		258,536	1.9

moned the deadlocked parties to the White House. Threatening to take over the mines, he won reluctant acceptance of an arbitration commission to settle the dispute. In 1903 the commission granted miners a 10 percent wage hike and reduced their workday to nine hours.

TR approached such labor disputes very differently from his predecessors, who had called out federal troops to break strikes. Though not consistently prolabor, he defended labor's right to organize, and when a well-known mine owner sanctimoniously claimed that miners' welfare could safely be left to "the Christian men to whom God in his infinite wisdom has given control of the property interests of the country," Roosevelt bristled at such "arrogant stupidity."

With his privileged social background, TR neither feared nor much respected the capitalists who had clawed their way to the top in Gilded Age America. Conservative at heart, he had no desire to abolish big corporations, but he embraced the progressive philosophy that corporate behavior must be carefully regulated. A strict moralist, he believed that corporations, like individuals, must meet a high standard of virtue.

As a political realist, Roosevelt recognized that many politicians did not share his views. Tensions involving sometimes conflicting characteristics—his moralism, his aristocratic conservatism, his cautious embrace of progressive ideas, and his understanding of the realities of capitalist America—would characterize his presidency.

J. P. Morgan's formation in 1901 of the United States Steel Company, the nation's first billion-dollar corporation, deepened public uneasiness over business consolidation. Dashing to the head of the parade, TR used his first State of the Union message to advocate "trustbusting," the breakup of business monopolies. In February 1902 Roosevelt's attorney general filed suit against the Northern Securities Company, a mammoth holding company formed to control railroading in the Northwest. To Roosevelt, the company clearly violated the Sherman Anti-Trust Act. He called for a "square deal" for all Americans and denounced special treatment for powerful capitalists. "We don't wish to destroy corporations," he insisted, "but we do wish to make them serve the public good." In 1904, by a 5–4 vote, the Supreme Court ordered the Northern Securities Company dissolved.

The Roosevelt administration sued forty-three other companies for violating the antitrust law. In two key cases in 1911, the Court ordered the breakup of the Standard Oil Company, the granddaddy of all trusts, and the reorganization of the American Tobacco Company to make it less monopolistic.

As the 1904 presidential election approached, Roosevelt made peace with the Republicans' big-business wing. When the convention that unanimously nominated Roosevelt adopted a conservative, probusiness platform, $2 million in corporate campaign contributions poured in. The conservative-dominated Democrats meanwhile rejected William Jennings Bryan, nominated New York judge Alton B. Parker, and wrote a platform firmly embracing the gold standard.

Easily defeating Parker, Roosevelt turned to one of his major goals: railroad regulation. He saw regulation, rather than trustbusting, as the most promising long-term role for government and viewed antitrust suits as a means of compelling corporations to accept regulation. His work for passage of the Hepburn Act (1906) reflected this shift in outlook. The Hepburn Act tightened railroad regulation by empowering the Interstate Commerce Commission to set maximum railroad rates and to examine railroads' financial records. It also required standardized bookkeeping to make such inspection easy, and it curtailed the distribution of free passes. Although the measure did not entirely satisfy some reformers, it significantly increased government's ability to regulate the railroads.

Consumer Protection and Racial Issues

No progressive reform aroused a more gut-level response than the fight against unsafe and falsely labeled food, drugs, and medicine. Upton Sinclair's stomach-turning *The Jungle* (1906) described the foul conditions under which sausages and cold cuts were produced. In a vivid passage, Sinclair wrote:

Theodore Roosevelt (1858–1919) and John Muir (1838–1914) at Yosemite
The conservation-minded politician and naturalist-conservationist pose on the rim of Yosemite Valley.

> *It was too dark in these [packing-house] storage places to see well, but a man could run his hand over these piles of meat and sweep off handfuls of dried dung of rats. These rats were nuisances, and the packers would put poisoned bread out for them, they would die, and then rats, bread, and meat would go into the hoppers together.*

A socialist, Sinclair had intended his book to publicize the exploitation of immigrant workers, but most readers focused on the unsanitary packing-house conditions he described. "I aimed at the nation's heart, but hit it in the stomach," he lamented.

Other muckrakers exposed useless, sometimes dangerous, patent medicines. Many popular nostrums, including children's medicines, contained cocaine, opium, and alcohol. "Colden's Liquid Beef Tonic," for example, "recommended for treatment of the alcohol habit," itself contained 26.5 percent alcohol. Peddlers of these potions claimed that they could cure cancer, grow hair, and restore sexual potency.

Ever sensitive to the public mood, Roosevelt strongly endorsed the Pure Food and Drug Act and the Meat Inspection Act, both passed in 1906. The former outlawed the sale of adulterated food and drugs and required the accurate labeling of ingredients; the latter imposed strict sanitary requirements for meatpackers, set up a quality-rating system, and created a program of federal meat inspection.

On racial matters, Roosevelt's record was marginally better than that of many other politicians in this racist age. On the positive side, he appointed an African-American as the head of the Charleston customhouse and closed a Mississippi post office rather than yield to racist demands that he dismiss the black postmistress. In a gesture of symbolic import, he met with Booker T. Washington at the White House. The worst blot on his record came in 1906 when he summarily discharged an entire regiment of black army troops charged with rioting in Brownsville, Texas.

The Conservation Movement

By 1900 decades of urban-industrial growth and western expansion had taken a heavy toll on the land. In the West, controversy over land use spilled into the political arena as mining and timber interests, farmers, ranchers, sheep growers, city officials, and preservationists advanced competing claims.

Western business interests and boosters preached the maximum exploitation of the region's resources, but the Sierra Club and other wilderness-protection groups sought to preserve large wild areas for their pristine beauty. After Congress in 1891 authorized the president to designate public lands as forest reserves, Presidents Harrison and Cleveland set aside 35 million acres.

A wilderness vogue swept the United States in the early twentieth century. From congested cities and clanging factories, Americans looked to the wilderness, with its unspoiled lakes, virgin forests, and inspiring vistas, for tranquillity and spiritual solace. Popular writers evoked the tang of the campfire and the lure of the primitive, and the Boy Scouts (1910) and Girl Scouts (1912) gave city children a taste of the outdoors.

The zest for wilderness colored the politics of the era. Resource-management issues pitted state and local authorities against the federal government. Local politicians, echoing their region's business groups, charged that mushy-headed preservationists were setting aside so much wilderness land that western economic development was suffering.

Between the wilderness enthusiasts and the proponents of unrestrained development stood a growing cadre of government professionals who saw the public domain as a resource to be managed scientifically. This characteristically progressive view found its ablest advocate in Gifford Pinchot. Named head of the new U.S. Forest Service in 1895, Pinchot campaigned for conservation—the planned, regulated use of forests for various public and commercial purposes.

Wilderness advocates saw Pinchot's Forest Service as a safeguard against mindless exploitation but worried that commercial development would ruin unspoiled nature and erase its intangible benefits. A Sierra Club member wrote, "It is true that trees are for human use. But there are aesthetic uses as well as commercial ones—uses for the spiritual wealth of us all, as well as for the material wealth of some." But the professional conservationists dismissed such wilderness advocates as sentimental amateurs.

By temperament, President Roosevelt was a preservationist, a champion of wilderness and

The Election of 1908

Candidates	*Parties*	*Electoral Vote*	*Popular Vote*	*Percentage of Popular Vote*
WILLIAM H. TAFT	Republican	321	7,675,320	51.6
William Jennings Bryan	Democratic	162	6,412,294	43.1
Eugene V. Debs	Socialist		420,793	2.8
Eugene W. Chafin	Prohibition		253,840	1.7

wildlife preservation. "When I hear of the destruction of a species," he wrote, "I feel just as if all the works of some greater writer had perished." However, Roosevelt the politician understood the conservationists' call for the planned development of natural resources. In this spirit he supported the National Reclamation Act of 1902, which earmarked the proceeds of public-land sales for water management in the Southwest and established the Reclamation Service to plan specific irrigation projects. Roosevelt also backed Pinchot's program of multiuse land management and set aside more than 200 million acres of public land as national forests, mineral reserves, and potential water-power sites. But because of opposition in the West, Congress in 1907 rescinded the president's power to create national forests in six timber-rich states. Roosevelt signed the bill—only, however, after designating twenty-one new national forests totaling 16 million acres in those six states.

Preservationists won important victories in this era. Initiatives by private citizens saved a large grove of California's giant redwoods and a lovely stretch of the Maine coastline. By 1916 thirteen national parks had been created, but without central management. That year, Congress established the National Park Service to oversee what one writer termed the nation's "crown jewels."

Environmental health hazards aroused concern as well. With factories pumping pollutants into the air and dumping poisons into rivers, urban reformers fought for restrictive legislation. Roosevelt was sympathetic, especially when a power plant spewing black smoke near the White House drove him to threaten legal action.

The Progressive Era saw environmental issues draw intense national concern for the first time. Roosevelt played a crucial part in the process; along with millions of acres of national forest, he created fifty-three wildlife reserves and five new national parks. Equally important, Roosevelt kept environmental concerns in the public mind. Declaring conservation the United States' "most vital internal question," he gave priority to an issue that would reverberate through the rest of the century.

Taft in the White House

Roosevelt had pledged not to run in 1908, and to the disappointment of millions, he kept his promise. The Republicans' most conservative wing regained control. Although they nominated Roosevelt's choice, William Howard Taft, for president, they selected a conservative vice-presidential candidate and drafted an extremely conservative platform.

On the Democratic side, the defeat of the conservative Alton B. Parker had opened the door for a last hurrah by William Jennings Bryan. Nominating him, the Democrats adopted a platform calling for a lower tariff, denouncing trusts, and embracing labor. Unlike its predecessors, Bryan's 1908 campaign aroused neither horror nor passionate support, and Taft coasted to victory.

Taft differed markedly from Roosevelt. Whereas TR kept in fighting trim, Taft was grossly overweight. TR sparred in a boxing ring that he had set up in the White House; Taft played golf. TR loved dramatic public donnybrooks against the forces of evil and greed, but Taft had little use for political conflict. Above all, TR loved being president, while Taft's happiest days would come later, as chief justice of the Supreme Court.

Pledged to carry on TR's program, Taft supported the Mann-Elkins Act (1910), which strengthened the Interstate Commerce Commission and extended its authority to include telephone and telegraph companies. The Taft White House filed more antitrust suits than the Roosevelt administration had, but its lack of fanfare left most people considering TR the quintessential "trustbuster."

A Divided Republican Party

During the Roosevelt administration, a small group of reform-minded Republican legislators, nicknamed the Insurgents, had challenged their party's congressional leadership. Counting senators La Follette of Wisconsin and Albert Beveridge of Indiana and congressman George Norris of Nebraska among their members, the Insurgents turned against President Taft in 1909 after a tariff struggle.

Taft had originally believed that the tariff should be lowered, but in 1909 he signed the high Payne-Aldrich Tariff, praising it as "the best tariff bill that the Republican party ever passed." The battle lines between conservative and progressive Republicans were drawn.

A major Insurgent target was Speaker of the House Joseph G. Cannon of Illinois, whose benevolent nickname, Uncle Joe, belied his reactionary ideas and ruthless politics. With near-absolute power, Cannon prevented most reform bills from reaching a vote. In March 1910 Republican Insurgents joined with Democrats to curtail Cannon's power sharply. This Insurgent victory represented a slap at Taft, who supported Cannon.

Relations between Taft and Roosevelt eroded in 1909–1910 as TR's Washington allies sent him stormy letters about Taft's lack of reform zeal. The so-called Ballinger-Pinchot affair brought matters to a head. Richard A. Ballinger, Taft's secretary of the interior, was a conservative western lawyer who believed in the private development of natural resources. Ballinger approved the sale of several million acres of public land in Alaska to some Seattle businessmen, who promptly sold it to a banking consortium that included J. P. Morgan, the very symbol of the money power. A low-level Interior official protested and was dismissed, and when Gifford Pinchot of the Forestry Service criticized Ballinger in congressional testimony, he, too, was fired. TR's supporters seethed.

When Roosevelt returned to the United States from an African safari in June 1910, Pinchot, not Taft, met the boat. TR came out with guns blazing in the midterm 1910 elections, supporting the Insurgents and defining a program called the New Nationalism that would make the federal government a powerful reform instrument. He appealed for expanded federal regulation of business, censured judges who struck down progressive laws, and endorsed the idea of reversing judicial rulings by popular vote.

Democrats captured the House of Representatives in 1910, and a coalition of Democrats and Insurgents controlled the Senate. As fervor for reform rose, Roosevelt sounded more and more like a presidential candidate. Meanwhile, a new challenger for national leadership of the progressive movement was emerging from the ranks of the Democrats. He was Woodrow Wilson.

The Election of 1912

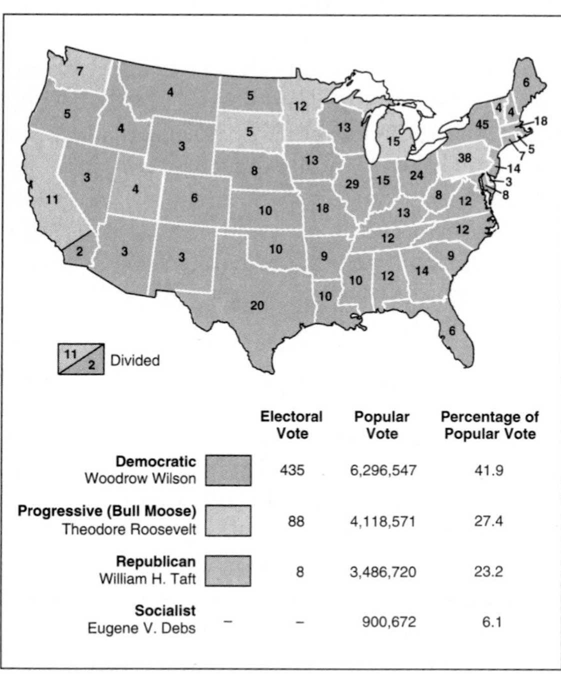

	Electoral Vote	Popular Vote	Percentage of Popular Vote
Democratic Woodrow Wilson	435	6,296,547	41.9
Progressive (Bull Moose) Theodore Roosevelt	88	4,118,571	27.4
Republican William H. Taft	8	3,486,720	23.2
Socialist Eugene V. Debs	–	900,672	6.1

National Progressivism—Phase II: Woodrow Wilson

Defeating two other reform candidates in the presidential election of 1912, Woodrow Wilson played a pivotal role as Congress enacted an imposing array of reform measures.

The Four-Way Election of 1912

In February 1912 Roosevelt announced that he would seek the Republican nomination. With Taft showing no intention of withdrawing, the stage was set for a Republican battle royal. Roosevelt won virtually all the state primaries and conventions in which he challenged Taft, but Taft controlled the party machinery. When the Republican convention that June disqualified many of Roosevelt's hard-won delegates, TR's outraged supporters stalked out. They reassembled in August to form a third party, the Progressive party.

Declaring himself "stripped to the buff and ready for the fight," Roosevelt proclaimed that he felt "as fit as a bull moose," thus giving his party the nickname the Bull Moose party. The euphoric delegates nominated TR by acclamation and endorsed virtually every reform cause of the day.

Meanwhile, the new political spirit had infused the Democratic party and produced reform administrations at state and local levels. In New Jersey, voters elected a political novice, Woodrow Wilson, as governor in 1910. A "Wilson for President" movement had gained momentum in 1911–1912, and by the time the Democrats convened in late June 1912, the Wilson boom proved irresistible.

The Republican Taft essentially gave up. Eugene V. Debs ran on the Socialist platform, demanding an end to capitalism, and Roosevelt and Wilson vied for the moderate reform vote. TR preached his New Nationalism: governmental regulation of big business in the public interest. Wilson called for a "New Freedom," evoking an earlier era of small entrepreneurs and free competition. Government should encourage competition, he proclaimed, not regulate business enterprise. "The history of liberty is the history of the limitation of government power, not the increase of it," he insisted. The divided Republicans proved no match for the united Democrats. Although Roosevelt won 4 million popular votes and eighty-eight electoral votes, Wilson prevailed with 6.3 million votes, and the Democrats took both houses of Congress.

The 1912 election solidly identified the triumphant Democrats with reform, launching a tradition on which Franklin D. Roosevelt would build in the 1930s. The breakaway Bull Moose movement simultaneously demonstrated the support for reform among grass-roots Republicans and left the Republican party in the grip of its most conservative elements.

Woodrow Wilson: The Scholar as President

The son, grandson, and nephew of Presbyterian ministers, Wilson grew up in southern towns during and after the Civil War in a churchly atmosphere that shaped his oratory and moral outlook. He graduated from Princeton, earned a Ph.D. in political science from Johns Hopkins University, taught at Princeton, and become president there in 1902. Admired for his educational ideas, Wilson gradually lost support at Princeton because of his unwillingness to compromise and left the academic world for the political arena in 1910. Two years later, he was president of the United States.

Wilson displayed the same strengths and weaknesses at the national level that he had at Princeton. An eloquent orator, he could galvanize listeners with his idealism, but he could as easily alienate them with a righteousness that allowed no compromise. However, when he chose, Wilson could be a master of statesmanship and compromise. During Wilson's eight years as president, all these facets of his complex personality would come into play.

Tariff and Banking Reform

The first item on Wilson's agenda was tariff reform. When a low-tariff bill bogged down in the Senate, Wilson demonstrated his talent for dramatic leadership by shining the spotlight on tariff lobbyists and on individual senators' interests in maintaining a high tariff. In the aftermath of this publicity, the Senate passed a bill slashing tariff rates even more than the House had earlier. The Underwood-Simmons Tariff reduced rates an average of 15 percent and imposed an income tax, recently authorized by the Sixteenth Amendment (1913).

In June 1913, with the tariff battle raging, Wilson called for banking and currency reform. A consensus existed about the need for a strong central bank; the question was whether it should be privately or publicly controlled. Wilson finally sided with the progressives, insisting on public control. He played a critical part in the complex bargaining process that led to the Federal Reserve Act of 1913, his greatest legislative achievement.

The act created a network of twelve regional Federal Reserve banks under mixed public and private control. Each regional bank could issue currency to private banks in its district. Overall control of the system rested in the hands of the heads of the regional banks and the Washington-based Federal Reserve Board. All national banks were required to join the new system. Although its power was diffuse at first, the Federal Reserve grew after the 1930s into a strong institution capable of directing the nation's monetary policy. The Federal Reserve Board provides safeguards against economic panic and shapes monetary policy to promote growth and dampen inflationary pressure. Its most important tool is the authority to raise or lower the interest rate on funds advanced to member banks, thus tightening or easing credit and controlling the rate of business expansion.

Corporate Regulation

Wilson and his congressional allies turned next to that quintessential progressive cause, business regulation. President Wilson, more sympathetic than candidate Wilson to regulation, shepherded two important regulatory measures through Congress.

The Federal Trade Commission Act (1914) reflected an administrative approach by creating a "watchdog" agency, the Federal Trade Commission (FTC), with power to investigate suspected violations, to require regular reports from corporations, and to issue "cease and desist" orders against unfair methods. The Clayton Antitrust Act (1914) amplified the Sherman Anti-Trust Act by spelling out a series of illegal practices, such as selling at a loss to monopolize a market. With the added clout of the Clayton Act, the Wilson administration filed antitrust suits against close to a hundred corporations.

Labor Legislation and Farm Aid

Sympathetic to labor, Wilson supported the American Federation of Labor, defended workers' right to organize, and endorsed a Clayton Act clause that exempted strikes, boycotts, and peaceful picketing from "restraint of trade." In 1916 he helped to push three important worker-protection laws through Congress: the Keating-Owen Act, barring from interstate commerce products manufactured by child labor (later declared unconstitutional); the Adamson Act, establishing an eight-hour workday for interstate railway workers; and the Workmen's Compensation Act, providing accident and injury protection to federal workers.

Wilson also championed the Federal Farm Loan Act and the Federal Warehouse Act (1916), which allowed farmers to secure long-term, low-interest loans using land or crops as security. The Federal Highway Act (1916) matched federal funds with state appropriations for highway construction, benefiting the new automobile industry as well as farmers plagued by bad roads.

Progressivism and the Constitution

The conservative, probusiness federal courts' tilt moderated as the Progressive Era ran its course. In 1908 the Supreme Court revealed the changing judicial climate when in *Muller* v. *Oregon* it upheld an Oregon law setting maximum working hours for women laundry workers at ten hours. To defend the constitutionality of the Oregon law, Boston attorney Louis Brandeis had offered economic, medical, and sociological evidence of the harmful effects of long hours on women workers. The Court's acceptance of the "Brandeis brief" marked a breakthrough in making the nation's legal system responsive to new social realities.

The Election of 1916

Candidates	*Parties*	*Electoral Vote*	*Popular Vote*	*Percentage of Popular Vote*
WOODROW WILSON	Democratic	277	9,127,695	49.4
Charles E. Hughes	Republican	254	8,533,507	46.2
A. L. Benson	Socialist		585,113	3.2
J. Frank Hanly	Prohibition		220,506	1.2

Progressivism also produced four constitutional amendments. The Sixteenth (ratified in 1913) granted Congress the authority to tax income. Quickly exercising its new authority, Congress in 1913 imposed a graduated federal income tax with a maximum rate of 7 percent on incomes in excess of $500,000. The Seventeenth Amendment (1913) completed a crusade begun by the Populists by mandating the direct popular election of U.S. senators. The Eighteenth (1919) established prohibition, and the Nineteenth (1920) granted women the vote. This array of amendments demonstrated how profoundly progressivism had resculpted the political landscape.

1916: Wilson Edges out Hughes

In 1916 Wilson easily won renomination for the presidency. The Republicans nominated Charles Evans Hughes, Supreme Court justice and former New York governor. With the Republicans more or less reunited, the election was extremely close. Wilson won the popular vote by more than 500,000, but the electoral-college outcome remained in doubt for weeks as the California tally seesawed back and forth. Ultimately, Wilson carried the state by under 4,000 votes, and with it, the election. War and its aftermath, not reform, would dominate Wilson's second term.

CONCLUSION

After the flurry of worker-protection legislation in fall 1916, the progressive movement lost momentum as the nation's attention turned to war. Yet progressivism left a remarkable legacy in specific laws and in a changed view of government. By 1916 most Americans agreed that it was proper and necessary for the government to play a central social and economic role. Progressivism had expanded the meaning of democracy and challenged the cynical view that government was nothing more than a tool of the economic elite. Progressives enlarged the government because they realized that in an era of gargantuan industries, sprawling cities, and concentrated corporate power, the government's role had to grow in order to serve the public interest, give people a decent life, and protect vulnerable members of society.

Progressive ideals often faltered in practice, however. Corporations proved remarkably adroit at manipulating the new regulatory state, and bureaucratic routine frequently gutted programs rooted in moral indignation and a vision of social justice. Unquestionably, too, progressivism had its repressive, illiberal, and coercive elements; on questions of racial justice, it chalked up a miserable record.

Nonetheless, the Progressive Era shines as a time when American politics began to confront the social upheavals wrought by industrialization. Americans learned to think of their government as an arena of possibility where they could address public issues and social problems. Twenty years later, another great reform movement, the New Deal, would draw heavily on progressivism's legacy.

CHRONOLOGY

1895 Anti-Saloon League founded.
Booker T. Washington's "Atlanta Compromise" address.

1898 Charlotte Perkins Gilman, *Women and Economics*.

1899 Thorstein Veblen, *The Theory of the Leisure Class*.

1900 International Ladies' Garment Workers' Union (ILGWU) founded.
Socialist Party of America organized.
Theodore Dreiser, *Sister Carrie*.
Carrie Chapman Catt becomes president of the National American Woman Suffrage Association (NAWSA).

1901 Assassination of McKinley; Theodore Roosevelt becomes president.

1902 Roosevelt mediates coal strike.
Jane Addams, *Democracy and Social Ethics*.

1903 W. E. B. Du Bois, *The Souls of Black Folk*.

1904 Roosevelt elected president.
Northern Securities case.
Lincoln Steffens, *The Shame of the Cities*.
Ida Tarbell, *History of the Standard Oil Company*.

1905 Industrial Workers of the World (IWW) organized.
Niagara Movement established.

1906 Hepburn Act.
Upton Sinclair, *The Jungle*.
Pure Food and Drug Act.
Meat Inspection Act.

1907 Walter Rauschenbusch, *Christianity and the Social Crisis*.
William James, *Pragmatism*.

1908 *Muller* v. *Oregon*.
William Howard Taft elected president.

1909 Payne-Aldrich Tariff.
Ballinger-Pinchot controversy.
National Association for the Advancement of Colored People (NAACP) founded.
Herbert Croly, *The Promise of American Life*.

1910 Mann Act.

1911 Supreme Court orders dissolution of Standard Oil Company.

1912 Progressive (Bull Moose) party founded.
Woodrow Wilson elected president.

1913 Underwood-Simmons Tariff.
Federal Reserve Act.
Sixteenth Amendment added to the Constitution.
Seventeenth Amendment added to the Constitution.
Thirty thousand march for woman suffrage in New York City.

1914 Federal Trade Commission Act.
Clayton Antitrust Act.

1915 D. W. Griffith, *The Birth of a Nation*.

1916 Federal Farm Loan Act.
Keating-Owen Act.
Workmen's Compensation Act.
Wilson reelected.
John Dewey, *Democracy and Education*.
Margaret Sanger opens nation's first birth-control clinic in Brooklyn, New York.
National Park Service created.

1919 Eighteenth Amendment added to the Constitution.

1920 Nineteenth Amendment added to the Constitution.

FOR FURTHER READING

Alan Dawley, *Struggle for Justice: Social Responsibility and the Liberal State* (1991). A thoughtful study placing the progressive movement in a larger historical and ideological context.

Noralee Frankel and Nancy S. Dye, eds., *Gender, Class, Race, and Reform in the Progressive Era* (1991). Selected essays exploring progressivism from various social perspectives.

Arthur S. Link and Richard L. McCormick, *Progressivism* (1993). Lucid, sensible unraveling of progressivism's diverse strands and comprehensive discussion of current interpretations.

William A. Link, *The Paradox of Southern Progressivism, 1880–1930* (1992). A regional study tracing the emergence of a reform-minded new administrative order in the urban South.

Robert B. Westbrook, *John Dewey and American Democracy* (1991). The definitive intellectual biography of an influential philosopher and social thinker.

CHAPTER 23

World War I

Defining America's World Role

War in Europe

Mobilizing at Home, Fighting in France

Promoting the War and Suppressing Dissent

Economic and Social Trends in Wartime America

Joyous Armistice, Bitter Aftermath

Somber, trembling with emotion, President Woodrow Wilson asked Congress for a declaration of war against Germany on the evening of April 2, 1917. Applause and shouts greeted his statement that the world must be made "safe for democracy," and many members of Congress waved silk American flags. When the speech ended, Senator Henry Cabot Lodge of Massachusetts, a fierce Wilson opponent, rushed forward to shake his hand. "Mr. President," said Lodge, "you have expressed in the loftiest manner the sentiments of the American people." But Wilson remained solemn. "Think what it was they were applauding," he mused to an aide; "my message today was a message of death for our young men. How strange it seems to applaud that."

Wilson delivered his message of death reluctantly, after months of trying to keep the United States out of the European war that had erupted in 1914. Elected in a gale of reformist enthusiasm, Wilson was caught up in—and ultimately consumed

(Right) Note the contrast between this idealized sketch by Harry Everett Townsend and the photograph on page 511.

by—the struggle engulfing Europe. He now brought to a series of foreign crises the same self-assured moralism that he had long applied to domestic issues.

Even before the United States slipped into the European war, an assertive foreign policy had shaped American relations with the rest of the world as presidents Roosevelt and Taft both pursued an activist course in Asia and Latin America. Roosevelt's balance-of-power chess game, Taft's concentration on business opportunities, and Wilson's moralism illustrate the diverse, sometimes contradictory motives that underlay America's expanding global influence.

Defining America's World Role

The United States' growing determination to assert its might, to protect and extend American business interests, and to impose its own standards of good government throughout the world led to continued American involvement in Asia and Latin America as the twentieth century unfolded.

The Roosevelt Corollary in Latin America and the Balance of Power in Asia

Theodore Roosevelt, president from 1901 to 1909, believed that the United States must strengthen its world role, protect U.S. interests in Latin America, and preserve the balance of power in Asia. In 1904 when several European nations threatened to invade the Dominican Republic, a small Caribbean island nation that had defaulted on its debts, Roosevelt concluded that American interests were in jeopardy. He feared that the Europeans would turn debt collecting into permanent occupation. If any big power were to intervene in the region, he felt, it should be the United States. In December 1904 Roosevelt declared that "chronic wrongdoing" by any Latin American nation would justify intervention by the United States, acting as an international policeman.

This pronouncement became known as the Roosevelt Corollary to the Monroe Doctrine. (The original "doctrine," issued in 1823, had warned European powers against meddling in Latin America.) The Roosevelt Corollary announced that in some circumstances the United States had the *right* to intrude. Suiting actions to words, the United States ran the Dominican Republic's customs service for two years and took over the management of the country's foreign debt.

On the other side of the world, meanwhile, the imperial rivalries that swirled over China continued unabated, catapulting Roosevelt into the role of peacemaker. In 1900 Russia tried to take advantage of the chaos unleashed by the Boxer uprising (see Chapter 21) by sending troops to occupy Manchuria, China's northeastern province. In February 1904 the Japanese, who had their own plans for Manchuria, launched a surprise attack on Russian forces at Port Arthur, Manchuria. In the Russo-Japanese War that followed, Japan dominated Russia.

Russian expansionism dismayed Roosevelt, but so did the possibility of a total Japanese victory—and disruption of the balance of power that TR considered essential to Asian peace and to the maintenance of America's role in the Philippines. In June 1905 he therefore invited Japan and Russia to a peace conference in Portsmouth, New Hampshire, and in early September the two exhausted foes signed a peace treaty. Russia recognized Japan's rule in Korea and made other territorial concessions. From then on, curbing Japanese expansionism became the United States' chief goal in Asia.

American relations with Japan deteriorated in 1906 when the San Francisco school board ordered Asian children to attend segregated schools. Roosevelt persuaded the board to reverse its decision, however, and in 1907 his administration tried to head off future problems by negotiating a "gentleman's agreement" by which Japan pledged to stop Japanese emigration to the United States. But racist attitudes along the Pacific coast continued to poison U.S.-Japan relations, particularly after 1913 when the California legislature prohibited Japanese aliens from owning land. A 1922 Supreme Court decision (*Ozawa* v. *U.S.*) preventing Japanese from becoming naturalized citizens intensified U.S.-Japanese friction.

As Californians worried about the "yellow peril," Japanese journalists watching America's growing military strength wrote of a "white peril." In 1907 Roosevelt ordered a flotilla of sixteen gleaming white battleships to steam on a "training operation" to Japan and then around the world. The 1908 visit of the "Great White Fleet" to Japan underscored the United States' growing naval might—and led to huge increases in Japan's naval building program.

Woodrow Wilson, Schoolteacher

This 1914 political cartoon captures the patronizing self-righteousness of Wilson's approach to Latin America that planted the seeds of long-term resentments.

Dollar Diplomacy in China and Nicaragua

The foreign policy of William Howard Taft, Roosevelt's successor, focused mainly on advancing American commercial interests; critics called it dollar diplomacy. After a futile attempt to involve American bankers in Manchurian railroad building demonstrated the shortcomings of the Open Door policy, Woodrow Wilson, after he took presidential office in 1913, shelved dollar diplomacy.

Closer to home, in Nicaragua, dollar diplomacy seemed more successful. In 1911 a U.S.-supported revolution in Nicaragua brought to power Adolfo Díaz, an officer of an American-owned Nicaraguan mining property. U.S. bankers loaned the Díaz government $15 million in exchange for control of the Nicaraguan national bank, the customs service, and the national railroad. A revolt against Díaz in 1912 triggered action under the Roosevelt Corollary: Taft sent in 2,500 marines to protect the American investment. Except for a brief interval, U.S. Marines remained in Managua, Nicaragua's capital, until 1933.

Wilson and Latin America

In 1913 the Democrat Wilson repudiated his Republican predecessors' expansionism and pledged that the United States would "never again seek one additional foot of territory by conquest." Nevertheless, Wilson, too, became deeply entangled in Latin America. In 1915 after bloody upheavals in Haiti and the Dominican Republic, Wilson ordered in the marines. A Haitian constitution favorable to American commercial interests was ratified in 1918 by a vote of 69,377 to 355—in a marine-supervised election—and marines brutally suppressed Haitian resistance to American rule. They remained in the Dominican Republic until 1924 and in Haiti until 1934.

From 1913 to 1914, Wilson's major foreign-policy preoccupation was Mexico, a nation divided between a tiny elite of wealthy landowners and a mass of poor peasants. In a particularly turbulent era for Mexico, Wilson tried to promote good government in Mexico City, to protect the large U.S. capital investments in the country, and ultimately to safeguard U.S. citizens traveling in Mexico or living along its border.

In 1911 rebels led by democratic reformer Francisco Madero had overthrown the autocratic Mexican president, Porfirio Díaz. Forty thousand Americans had settled in Mexico under Díaz, and $2 billion in U.S. investments had flowed into the country. Early in 1913, Mexican troops loyal to General Victoriano Huerta ousted and murdered Madero.

Wilson reversed the long-standing American policy of recognizing governments that held power regardless of how they had come to power. "I will not recognize a government of butchers," he declared, refusing to deal with Huerta. Wilson authorized arms sales to Venustiano Carranza, a Huerta foe, and blockaded Vera Cruz to prevent weapons from reaching Huerta. "I am going to teach the South American republics to elect good men," Wilson asserted. In April 1914 American troops occupied Vera Cruz and began fighting Mexican forces. Sixty-five Americans and 500 Mexicans were killed or wounded. Bowing to U.S. might, Huerta abdicated, Carranza took power, and American troops withdrew.

But the turmoil continued. In January 1916 a bandit chieftain in northern Mexico, Pancho Villa, murdered sixteen American mining engineers and then crossed the border; burned Columbus, New Mexico; and killed nineteen of its inhabitants. Sharing the public's outrage, Wilson sent into Mexico a punitive expedition that eventually totaled 12,000 U.S. troops. When Villa brazenly staged another raid across the Rio Grande into Texas, Wilson ordered 150,000 National Guardsmen into duty along the border.

Early in 1917, with the United States teetering on the brink of the European war, Wilson withdrew the army from Mexico. When Carranza was formally elected president later that year, Wilson extended U.S. recognition. Mexico adopted a new constitution that sharply curtailed the freewheeling operations of American capitalists by centralizing control of oil and mineral resources and imposed strict regulations on foreign investors.

Although comparatively minor, these episodes in Latin America and Asia revealed American foreign-policy goals in this era. The United States searched for a world order on *U.S.* terms—an international system founded on the uniquely American blend of liberalism, democracy, open trade, and capitalism. Washington planners envisioned a harmonious, stable global order of democratic societies that would welcome both American political values and American corporate expansion.

These episodes also foreshadowed the future. The maneuvering between the United States and Japan reflected a growing clash of interests, compounded by racism, that would lead to the exclusion of Japanese immigrants in 1924 and culminate in war with Japan in 1941. The revolutionary and nationalistic energies stirring in Latin America would explosively transform its politics half a century later. But of more immediate concern, the vision of a world order based on U.S. ideals would soon find expression in Woodrow Wilson's response to the crisis in Europe.

War in Europe

When war came to Europe in August 1914, most Americans wanted to remain aloof. For nearly three years, the United States did stay neutral, but then public opinion began to shift. Emotional ties to Britain and France, economic considerations, the vision of a world remade in America's image, and German violations of neutral rights, as defined by President Wilson, combined by April 1917 to draw the United States into the maelstrom.

The Coming of War

With minor exceptions, until the early twentieth century Europe had remained at peace after the conclusion of the Napoleonic Wars in 1815. Problems lurked beneath this serene surface, however. In 1914 a complex network of alliances bound European nations together, even as forces of nationalism threatened to tear some of them apart.

The slow-motion collapse in the 1870s of the ancient Ottoman Empire, centered in Turkey, had created such newly independent Balkan nations as Romania, Bulgaria, and Serbia (later a part of Yugoslavia) and presented opportunities for great-power meddling. Nationalism reached a fever pitch in Serbia, which dreamed of absorbing other South Slavic peoples. Russia, the largest Slavic nation, supported the Serbian dream. Meanwhile, the Austro-Hungarian Empire, itself menaced, saw opportunities for expansion as the Ottoman Empire receded. In 1908 Austria-Hungary annexed Bosnia-Herzogovina, a Slavic land wedged between Austria-Hungary and Serbia. The Russians were alarmed, and the Serbs furious.

Moreover, Germany, under the leadership of Kaiser Wilhelm II, was in an expansionist mood. Many Germans believed that their nation, united only since 1871, was lagging in the quest for national greatness and empire. Expansion, modernization, and military power became the order of the day in Berlin, the German Empire's capital.

Ordinary Europeans experienced a vague restlessness as the twentieth century opened. Life seemed soft, boring, and stale. Like Theodore Roosevelt on the eve of the Spanish-American War, some Europeans openly speculated that a war would strengthen national character and add excitement to a languid age.

In mid-1914, this volatile mixture exploded. In June a terrorist with close links to Serbia gunned down the heir to the Austrian throne and his wife as they rode through the Bosnian capital, Sarajevo. Austria delivered a harsh ultimatum to Serbia and five days later, after an "unacceptable" Serbian response, declared war on its Balkan neighbor. The intricate machinery of the alliance system rumbled into action. Linked to Serbia by a secret treaty, Russia mobilized for war. Germany declared war on Russia and on Russia's ally, France. Great Britain, linked by treaty to France, declared war on Germany. Thus a lone assassin plunged Europe into a war that altered history.

The American People's Initial Responses

President Wilson immediately proclaimed U.S. neutrality and exhorted the nation to be neutral "in thought as well as in action." Most Americans, grateful that the Atlantic Ocean lay between them and the battlefields, supported Wilson's position. As a popular song said, "I Didn't Raise My Boy to Be a Soldier."

Although most Americans shared Wilson's desire to stay out of the war, remaining neutral in thought proved difficult. Not only economic ties but also a common language, ancestry, and culture linked many Americans to Britain by strong emotional bonds. Still, not all Americans shared these ties. Because millions were of German origin, many sided with Germany. Irish-Americans, raised for generations on "twisting the [British] lion's tail," had little sympathy for Britain.

The Perils of Neutrality

By 1917 the American commitment to neutrality had been transformed into strong popular support for war. What caused this turnabout?

First, Wilson's vision of a world order built on American political and economic values conflicted with his commitment to neutrality. The international system that he favored, based on liberalism, democracy, and capitalistic enterprise, could never exist in a world dominated by imperial Germany. Wilson also believed that only U.S. leadership could ensure the achievement of this vision, and unless America helped to fight the war, America could not shape the peace.

This global vision influenced Wilson's approach to the first and perhaps most important problem confronting the United States: the question of neutral rights on the high seas. Within days of the war's outbreak, Britain had intercepted American merchant ships bound for Germany. In November 1914 Britain provoked more Wilsonian protests by declaring the North Sea a war zone and

Woman's Peace Party Parade
With fans to symbolize their point, these marchers urged President Wilson to continue the search for peace despite German provocations on the high seas.

planting it with explosive mines, and in March 1915 Britain blockaded all German ports. U.S. denunciations had no effect, for Britain had resolved to exploit its naval advantage no matter how it alienated American public opinion.

Ultimately, however, German violations of American ideas of neutrality drew the United States into the war. Determined to take advantage of a new and deadly weapon, the submarine, Germany in February 1915 designated the waters around the British Isles a war zone and warned off all ships, including those of Americans. Wilson again protested, warning that Germany would be held to "strict accountability" for the loss of American ships or lives.

Developments in May 1915 underscored the problems of neutrality. Germany placed announcements in U.S. newspapers advising against travel on British or French vessels. Six days later, on May 7, a U-boat sank the British liner *Lusitania,* with a loss of 1,198 lives, including 128 Americans. In increasingly strong notes to the German government, Wilson demanded specific pledges that Germany would stop its unrestricted submarine warfare. Nonetheless, he also insisted that America could use persuasion, rather than force, to press the belligerents to recognize neutral rights.

The *Lusitania* disaster exposed deep divisions in U.S. public opinion. Many Americans concluded that war was inevitable. Theodore Roosevelt, strongly pro-British, condemned Wilson for "abject cowardice and weakness." The National Security League, a lobby of bankers and industrialists, led a "preparedness" movement, stirring up patriotism and promoting an arms buildup and military training. By the fall of 1915, Wilson himself called for a military buildup. Many others, however, including pacifists, German-Americans, and those who had taken Wilson's speeches seriously, deplored the drift toward war. Leading feminists and social-justice reformers warned that the war spirit was eroding humanitarian values central to reform. As early as August 1914, 1,500 black-clad women marched down New York's Fifth Avenue protesting the war. In 1915 Jane Addams, Carrie Chapman Catt, and other feminists formed the Woman's Peace party, and later that year they and others sailed to Sweden on a ship chartered by industrialist Henry Ford in an attempt to mediate the war and bring peace before Christmas.

Wilson's firm but restrained policy seemed to work. In August 1915 when a U-boat violated orders and sank the *Arabic,* a British liner, with the loss of two American lives, Germany pledged that such an incident would not happen again. But in March 1916 it did, as a German sub sank a French vessel, *Sussex,* and injured several Americans. Wilson threatened to break diplomatic relations, a first step toward war, and Berlin pledged not to attack merchant vessels without warning. The crisis over neutral rights eased temporarily.

Corporate boardrooms as well as the high seas proved an arena for quarrels over neutral rights. Early in the war, American bankers trying to lend money to the belligerents were told that such loans were "inconsistent with the true spirit of neutrality." The policy did not last. In August 1915 Wilson's cabinet began to warn that only substantial loans to Great Britain could prevent "a serious financial situation" in the United States. Wilson finally permitted the Morgan bank to lend $500 million to the British and French governments. By April 1917 U.S. banks had lent $2.3 billion to the Allies (Great Britain, France, Russia, and Italy) and only $27 million to the Central Powers (Germany and Austria-Hungary). Trade with the Allies had consequently soared as commerce with the Central Powers plummeted, and the Allies' economic dependence on America increased. Although the United States remained neutral, Wilson had taken full advantage of the Allies' credit needs to strengthen the nation's commercial and financial position in the world economy.

Stalemate in the Trenches

While Americans focused on neutral rights, the land war in Europe degenerated into a costly stalemate. After Germany's initial offensive drive stalled, the two sides dug in, forming a line of trenches that snaked across France from the English Channel to the Swiss border. For more than three years, this line remained essentially unchanged. A German offensive in 1916 near the French town of Verdun alone cost hundreds of thousands of casualties but did little to break the stalemate. The war in the trenches was nightmarish, a ghastly inferno of mud, lice, rats, artillery bursts, poison gas, and sudden, random death.

Determined to win the propaganda war, Britain bombarded the United States with posters and articles portraying alleged German atrocities, such as the impaling of babies on bayonets. German propaganda proved relatively ineffective.

The United States Enters the War

As the war dragged on, German military leaders pushed for greater and greater use of the submarine. Although such stepped-up German aggression would almost certainly pull the United States into the war, American entry would have no significance, they said—"zero, zero, zero," according to one German naval officer. The generals prevailed. On January 9, 1917, the German government decided to return to the policy of unlimited U-boat attacks.

Events now rushed forward. Three days after Germany's formal announcement of the resumption of unrestricted submarine warfare, Wilson broke diplomatic relations. Five American ships fell victim to German torpedoes in February and March. And on February 24, the United States' discovery of the so-called Zimmermann telegram enormously widened the rift between the two nations. Attempting to create problems on the American side of the Atlantic, German foreign secretary Alfred Zimmermann had cabled the German ambassador in Mexico to propose a military alliance of Germany, Mexico, and Japan, with Mexico promised the return of its "lost" territories of Texas, Arizona, and New Mexico. Publication of the telegram raised a furor in the United States.

Finally, on April 2 Wilson went before Congress to call for a declaration of war. By wide margins, both the Senate and the House voted for war. Three key factors—German attacks on American shipping, U.S. investment in the Allied cause, and American cultural links to the Allies, especially England—had converged to draw the United States into war.

Mobilizing at Home, Fighting in France

World War I would leave the United States with relatively few scars. At war for only nineteen months, the nation took comparatively light casualties—112,000 of the 7.5 million dead—and the American homeland remained untouched. Still, the war constituted a major turning point. It changed the lives of almost all Americans, transformed the nation's government and economy, and thrust the United States into the arena of global politics.

Raising an Army

A woefully unprepared American military faced war in April 1917. The regular army of 120,000 enlisted men had virtually no combat experience. An aging officer corps was dozing away the years until retirement. There was enough ammunition for only two days of fighting, and the War Department was a snakepit of jealous bureaucrats.

Raising an army and imposing order on the War Department posed a daunting challenge. Wilson's secretary of war, Newton D. Baker, performed brilliantly on the first task, skillfully implementing the Selective Service Act passed in May 1917. Baker cleverly made the first draft registration day a "festival and patriotic occasion." Thanks to a carefully orchestrated public-relations campaign and local civilian draft boards' deft handling of the draft, 24 million men registered by November 1918, of whom nearly 3 million were drafted. In addition, following a precedent-breaking decision by the secretary of the navy, 11,000 women served in the navy during the war and several hundred in the marines. Although not assigned to combat, they performed crucial support functions as nurses, clerical workers, and telephone operators.

Army chief of staff General Peyton C. Marsh worked the same wonders in organizing and galvanizing the War Department that Baker had with the draft. In the military training camps, young men from all over the United States got their first taste of a soldier's discipline and often their first experience of the world beyond their hometown.

Organizing the Economy for War

The coming of the war in 1917 brought not only military mobilization but also unprecedented government oversight of the economy. The populist and progressive goal of more public control over corporations began to be achieved.

The War Industries Board (WIB) was established in 1917 to coordinate military purchasing, to fight waste, and to ensure that the military received the weapons, equipment, and supplies it needed. Especially under the wealthy Wall Street speculator Bernard Baruch, whom Wilson appointed to run the WIB in March 1918, the agency exercised enormous control over the industrial sector. In addition to allocating raw materials, the board established production priorities and introduced all kinds of efficiencies. To save steel, rubber, and other scarce commodities, competing companies coordinated their production processes. The standardization of bicycle manufacturing, for example, saved 2,000 tons of steel. The Fuel Administration, headed by Williams College president Harry Garfield, controlled coal output, regulated fuel prices and consumption, and in March 1918 introduced daylight savings time as a wartime conservation measure. Benjamin Franklin originally had proposed the idea of adjusting clocks to take advantage of long summer daylight hours, but it took the war emergency to bring the measure about.

Baruch's counterpart on the agricultural front was Herbert Hoover, the head of the Food Administration. A mining engineer who had amassed a fortune in Asia, Hoover oversaw the production and distribution of foodstuffs—especially wheat, meat, and sugar—to assure adequate supplies for the army and the food-short Allies. A master of persuasion, Hoover organized a public-relations campaign to convince Americans that they should conserve food. Bombarded with such slogans as "Serve Beans by All Means" and "Don't Let Your Horse Be More Patriotic Than You Are—Eat a Dish of Oatmeal,"

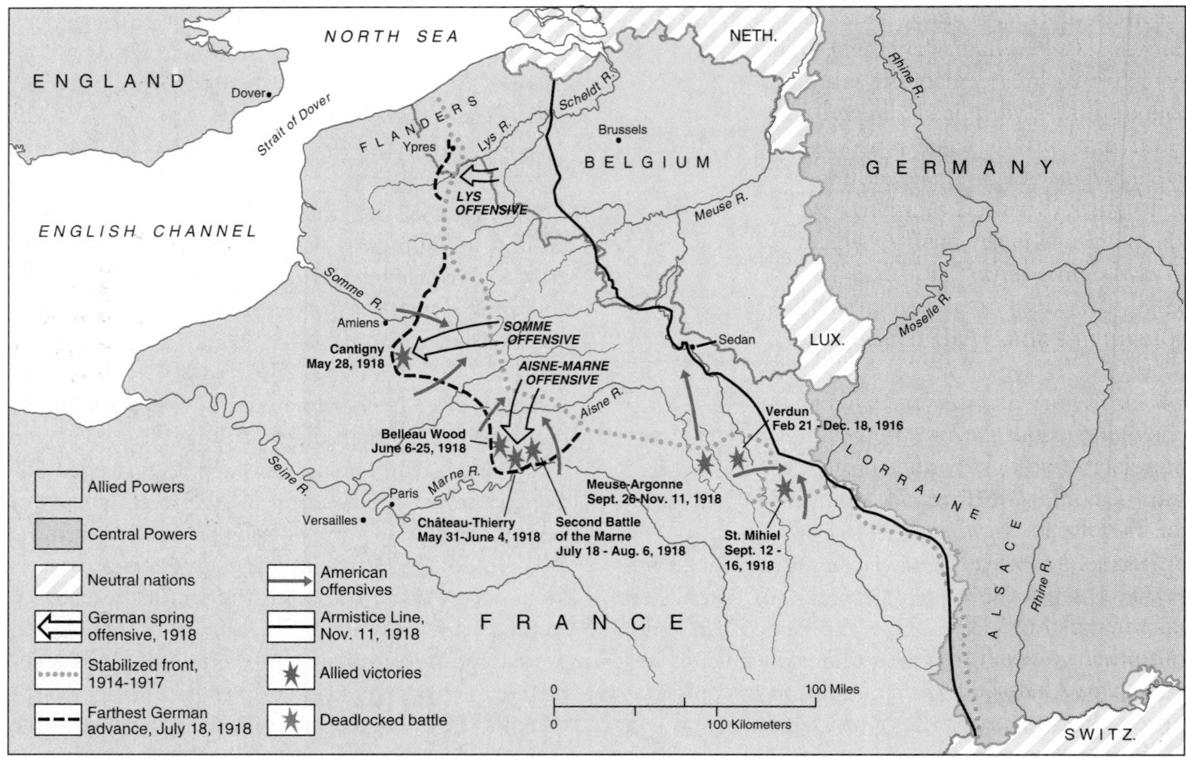

The United States on the Western Front, 1918

American troops first saw action in the campaign to throw back Germany's spring 1918 offensive in the Somme and Aisne-Marne sectors. The next heavy American engagement came that autumn as part of the Allies' Meuse-Argonne offensive that ended the war.

Americans observed "meatless days" and "wheatless days."

The War Industries Board and the Food Administration represented only the tip of the regulatory iceberg. Nearly 5,000 government agencies supervised home-front activities during the war. When a massive railroad tie-up during the snowy winter of 1917–1918 impeded the flow of supplies to Europe, the government took over and transformed the 3,000 competing companies into an efficient national transportation system.

The war accelerated the corporate consolidation and economic integration already under way as businesses worked together to make production and distribution more rational and more efficient. It was also highly profitable. Despite congressional imposition of an excess-profits tax, wartime corporate profits mushroomed. In place of trustbusting, moreover, the government actively encouraged industrial cooperation. In 1917 major corporate mergers soared to nearly two hundred, more than twice the annual average for the immediate prewar years.

This colossal regulatory apparatus fell apart when the war ended, but its influence lingered. The old laissez-faire suspicion of government, already eroded, suffered further blows in 1917–1918. In the 1930s when the nation faced a different kind of crisis, the government activism of World War I would be remembered. Indeed, the wartime agencies of 1917–1918 became models for many New Deal agencies (see Chapter 25.)

With the AEF in France

About 2 million American soldiers went to France in 1917–1918 as members of the American Expeditionary Force (AEF) under General John J. Pershing. A West Point graduate and commander of the 1916 expedition against Pancho Villa, Pershing was an iron-willed officer with a ramrod bearing, steely eyes, and trim mustache. For most men of the AEF, the war at first seemed a great adventure. After traveling to France on crowded freighters or even captured German liners, they piled aboard freight cars marked "HOMMES 40, CHEVAUX 8" (40 men, 8 horses) on their way to the front. Once there, they marched, trained, became acquainted with the French—and waited.

Aerial dogfights between German and Allied reconnaissance planes offered spectacular sideshows. The most famous World War I ace, Germany's Manfred von Richthofen, the "Red Baron," shot down eighty Allied aircraft before his luck ran out in April 1918. Although Secretary of War Baker was "thoroughly fascinated" by the recently invented airplane's possibilities and pressed Congress to appropriate large sums for aircraft construction, only thirty-seven planes were built.

The war would be won or lost on land and sea, however, and when the United States entered, Allied prospects looked bleak. German submarines took a horrendous toll on Allied shipping: 600,000 tons in March 1917, 900,000 tons in April. A failed French offensive in the spring led to an army mutiny, and an almost equally disastrous British-French offensive in November cost 400,000 casualties to gain four miles.

To make matters worse, Russia left the war in 1917. The all-out effort dictated by the massive war had undermined Russia's already toppling tsarist government, and in March 1917 the imperial government had collapsed. A provisional liberal government attempted to continue the war. Marxist revolutionaries under Vladimir Ilyich Lenin, however, capitalized on the provisional government's instability. On November 6, 1917, Lenin and Leon Trotsky led an armed coup that overthrew the provisional government and began a civil war for the entire Russian empire. In March 1918 Lenin's Bolshevik government signed a separate armistice with Germany, which freed thousands of German troops for transfer to the Western Front in France.

Life at the Front

A battle-weary infantry corporal during the Argonne Forest campaign. Wrote Florence Bullard, working as a volunteer behind the lines, "I have had to write many sad letters to . . . mothers. I wonder if it will ever end."

In these desperate circumstances, French and British commanders wanted to incorporate AEF troops into Allied units already at the front. But Pershing insisted that the AEF be "distinct and separate," in part because he scorned the defensive mentality of the Allied commanders and in part because separate combat would strengthen the United States' voice at the peace table.

American forces saw their first real combat in March 1918 when a German offensive threatened France's English Channel ports. The Allies created a unified command under French general Ferdinand Foch, and American troops were thrown into the fighting around Amiens and Armentières that stemmed the German advance. In May 1918 Germany launched the second phase of its spring offensive. By the end of the month, the Germans had broken through the Allied lines and had secured a nearly open road to Paris, only fifty miles away. At this critical moment, Americans spearheaded the forces that finally stopped the German advance at the town of Château-Thierry and nearby Belleau Wood. And 85,000 American troops helped to staunch the final German offensive of the war, a thrust at the ancient cathedral city of Rheims. This Allied victory marked the crucial turning point of the war. Germany's desperate attempt to take the offensive had failed. Now it was the Allies' turn.

Turning the Tide

On July 18, 1918, the Allies launched their counteroffensive. Of the 1 million American soldiers on French soil, 270,000 participated in a successful drive to push the Germans back.

In September Pershing took his first independent command and assembled nearly 500,000 American and 100,000 French troops to implement his strategy of hard-hitting offense. An American wrote in his diary, "It was zero hour and in one instant the entire front as far as the eye could reach in either direction was a sheet of flame, while the heavy artillery made the earth quake."

The war's last great battle began on September 26 as 1.2 million Americans joined the struggle to drive the Germans from the Meuse River and the dense Argonne Forest north of Verdun. Poison gas hung in the air, and bloated rats scurried through the mud, feasting on human remains, as the offensive pressed forward over land devastated by four years of trench warfare. Theodore Roosevelt's "great adventure" seemed remote indeed in the Meuse-Argonne campaign. Death came in many forms and without ceremony. Bodies, packs, rifles, photos, and letters from home sank into the all-consuming mud as more than 26,000 Americans died in the battle and thousands more perished in an influenza epidemic that would take 20 million lives worldwide. Religious principles and ethical scruples seemed irrelevant. "Love of thy neighbor is forgotten," lamented one young man. The war's brutality would shape the literature of the 1920s as writers such as Ernest Hemingway forced readers to confront the reality of mass slaughter. By early November the Allied counteroffensive had succeeded, but at terrible cost.

African-Americans in the AEF

More than 260,000 African-Americans volunteered or were drafted in World War I, and 50,000 went to France. Racism pervaded the military as it did American society itself.

One racist senator from Mississippi, warning that the sight of "arrogant, strutting" African-American soldiers would trigger race riots in the United States, had urged that African-Americans not be drafted. Tensions reached the breaking point in Houston in August 1917 when some black members of the Twenty-fourth Infantry, endlessly goaded by local whites, seized weapons from the armory and killed seventeen whites. After a hasty trial with no opportunity for an appeal, thirteen African-American soldiers were hanged, and forty-one went to jail for life.

In France, blacks worked mainly as messboys (mealtime aides), laborers, and stevedores (ship-cargo handlers). Four black infantry regiments served with distinction under French command. One entire regiment, the 369th, was honored with the French Croix de Guerre, and several hundred individual black soldiers received French decorations for bravery. Most French people, military and civilian alike, at least superficially treated whites and blacks the same. For African-American members of the AEF, this eye-opening experience would remain with them when they returned home.

Promoting the War and Suppressing Dissent

Patriotic fervor pervaded American society in 1917–1918, in part the result of an elaborate government campaign to whip up enthusiasm for the war. In its wake came stifling intellectual conformity and intolerance for dissent. Government authorities and private vigilante groups hounded and arrested socialists, pacifists, and other dissidents and in the process trampled the basic constitutional rights of thousands.

Advertising the War

For President Wilson, the war at home was no less important than the war abroad. "It is not an army we must shape and train for war, it is a nation," he declared. Wilson knew that millions of Americans opposed the war. They represented diverse viewpoints but collectively they posed a formidable obstacle to the president's dream of rallying the nation behind his crusade for a new world order.

Trying initially to overcome domestic opposition by voluntary means, the Wilson administration called upon the new professions of advertising and public relations. Treasury Secretary William Gibbs McAdoo set the patriotic tone, raising enormous sums to defray the expense of the war. Including loans to the Allies, World War I cost the United States $35.5 billion. Almost two-thirds of this amount ($21 billion) came from government bond sales, called Liberty Loan drives, organized by McAdoo.

McAdoo surrounded the Liberty Loan campaigns with great ballyhoo. Posters exhorted citizens to "FIGHT OR BUY BONDS." Parades, rallies, and appearances by movie stars all aided the cause. An undercurrent of coercion also contributed to heavy sales; McAdoo declared that "only a friend of Germany" would refuse to buy bonds.

Stiff taxes supplied the other one-third of the war's funding. Taking advantage of the new power to tax incomes granted by the Sixteenth Amendment (ratified in 1913), Congress imposed wartime income taxes that rose to 63 percent at the top level.

George Creel, a progressive reformer and journalist, headed Washington's most effective wartime propaganda agency, the Committee on Public Information (CPI). Established in April 1917, ostensibly to combat rumors by providing authoritative information, the Creel committee became a propaganda agency that communicated the government's official version of reality and discredited those who questioned it. Posters, news releases, advertisements, and movies all trumpeted the government's sanitized version of events. The CPI poured foreign-language publications into the cities to ensure the loyalty of recent immigrants. Creel also organized the "four minute men": a network of 75,000 speakers throughout the nation who gave patriotic talks to audiences of all kinds. Creel calculated that this small army of propagandists delivered 7.5 million speeches to listeners totaling 314 million.

Intellectuals, Cultural Leaders, and Reformers Present Arms

The nation's teachers, writers, religious leaders, and magazine editors overwhelmingly supported the war. These custodians of culture viewed the conflict as a struggle to defend threatened values and standards. Historians contrasted Germany's malignant power and glorification of brute force with the Allies' loftier, more civilized ideals. Alan Seeger, a young Harvard graduate who volunteered to fight for France in 1916, wrote highly popular poems romanticizing the war. An artillery barrage became "the magnificent orchestra of war." The "sense of being the instrument of Destiny," wrote Seeger, represented the "supreme experience" of combat. He was killed in action in 1916.

Progressives hoped that the wartime climate of heightened government activism and sacrifice for the common good would encourage further reforms. Some of George Creel's most effective coworkers on the Committee for Public Information were former muckrakers. Herbert Croly, Walter Lippmann, and other progressive intellectuals associated with the *New Republic* zealously supported the war.

The liberal philosopher and educational reformer John Dewey joined the prowar chorus. In *New Republic* articles in 1917–1918, Dewey condemned the war's opponents. Socially engaged intellectuals, he wrote, must accept reality as they found it and shape it toward positive social goals, not stand aside in self-righteous indignation. The war presented exciting "social possibilities" for the advance of society at home and abroad. Domestically, the wartime growth of government power could be channeled to reform purposes once peace returned. Internationally, America's entry would transform a crude imperialistic clash into a worldwide democratic crusade, Dewey argued.

Wartime Intolerance and Hysteria

Responding to this drumfire of propaganda, some Americans became almost hysterical in their hatred of all things German, their hostility to aliens and dissenters, and their strident patriotism. Isolated actions by German saboteurs, including the blowing-up of a New Jersey munitions dump, fanned the antiforeign flames. In Collinsville, Illinois, a mob of 500 lynched a young German-born man in April 1918. When a jury exonerated the mob leaders, a jury member shouted, "Nobody can say we aren't loyal now."

German books vanished from libraries, towns with German names changed them, and "liberty sandwich" and "liberty cabbage" replaced "hamburgers" and "sauerkraut" on restaurant menus. Popular evangelist Billy Sunday proclaimed, "If you turn hell upside down you will find 'Made in Germany' stamped on the bottom." Leopold Stokowski, the conductor of the Philadelphia Orchestra, dropped German opera and songs from the repertoire but asked President Wilson's permission to retain Bach, Beethoven, Mozart, and Brahms.

The zealots of ideological conformity fell with special ferocity on war critics and radicals. A mob hauled a Cincinnati pacifist minister to a woods and whipped him. Theodore Roosevelt, never the voice of moderation, branded antiwar senator Robert La Follette "an unhung traitor." In Bisbee, Arizona, a vigilante mob forced 1,200 miners who belonged to the IWW onto a freight train and shipped them into the New Mexico desert without food, water, or shelter.

Opponents of the War

Despite the overheated conformist climate, a few Americans refused to support the war. Some were German-Americans with ties to the land of their forebears, and some others belonged to historically pacifist churches. Sixty-five thousand men registered as conscientious objectors, and 21,000 of them were drafted. The army assigned most of these to "noncombatant" duty on military bases.

Jane Addams, a founder of the Woman's Peace party in 1915, remained a pacifist throughout the war. She did, however, lecture for the Food Administration's Speakers Bureau because she saw increased food production as a means of aiding the war's innocent victims.

Socialist party leaders, including Eugene V. Debs, opposed the war on political grounds. They viewed it as a capitalist contest for world markets, with the soldiers on both sides mere cannon fodder. The U.S. declaration of war, they insisted, mainly reflected Wall Street's desire to protect its loans to England and France.

The war's most incisive critic was Randolph Bourne, a young journalist. Although Bourne much admired John Dewey, he rejected his hero's prowar position. Like moths near a flame, Bourne said, intellectuals were mesmerized by the lure of being near the center of action and power. He dismissed as a self-serving delusion the belief that liberal reformers could direct the war to their own purposes. War took on its own terrible momentum, he wrote, and could no more be controlled by intellectuals than a rogue elephant crashing through the bush. Ultimately, Dewey, Lippmann, and other prowar intellectuals agreed with Bourne. By 1919 Dewey had conceded that the war, far from promoting liberalism, had unleashed the most reactionary and intolerant forces in the nation.

Suppressing Dissent by Law

Wartime intolerance also found expression in federal laws and in the actions of top government officials. The Espionage Act of June 1917 prescribed heavy fines and long prison sentences for a variety of loosely defined antiwar activities. The Sedition Amendment to the Espionage Act (May 1918) imposed heavy penalties on anyone convicted of using "disloyal, profane, scurrilous, or abusive language" about the government, the Constitution, the flag, or the military.

Wilson's reactionary attorney general, Thomas W. Gregory, freely employed these measures to stamp out dissent. Opponents of the war should expect no mercy "from an outraged people and an avenging government," he said. Under this sweeping legislation and equally sweeping state laws, hundreds of pacifists, socialists, and war opponents found themselves imprisoned. Kate Richards O'Hare, a midwestern socialist organizer, spent more than a year in prison for allegedly telling an audience that "the women of the United States are nothing more than brood sows, to raise children to get into the army and be made into fertilizer." Eugene V. Debs was sentenced to ten years in a federal penitentiary for a speech discussing the economic causes of the war.

The Espionage Act also authorized the postmaster general to bar suspect materials from the mail—a provision enthusiastically enforced by Wilson's postmaster general, Albert S. Burleson, a radical-hating superpatriot. In January 1919 Congressman-elect Victor Berger received a twenty-year prison sentence (later set aside by the Supreme Court) and was denied his seat in the House for publishing antiwar articles in his socialist newspaper, the *Milwaukee Leader*.

A few citizens protested. Muckraking novelist Upton Sinclair wrote to President Wilson to deplore that a man of Burleson's "pitiful and childish ignorance" should wield such power. Wilson did little to restrain either his postmaster general or his attorney general. Nor did the Supreme Court. In three 1919 decisions, the Court upheld Espionage Act convictions of people who had spoken out against the war. It also upheld Debs's conviction. Although the war was over, a vindictive Wilson refused to commute Debs's sentence. (President Warren Harding would at last release the ill and aging Debs in December 1921, but the government would not restore his rights as a U.S. citizen.)

Thus wartime idealism and high resolve deteriorated into fearful suspicion, narrow ideological conformity, and the persecution of those who failed to meet the zealots' notion of "100 percent Americanism." The effects of this ugly wartime climate would linger long after the armistice.

Economic and Social Trends in Wartime America

All wars usher in unanticipated economic and social changes, and World War I was no exception. The war affected the lives of millions of industrial workers (including large numbers of African-Americans and women) and farmers. The wartime mood also gave a significant boost to the moral-reform movement.

Boom Times in Industry and Agriculture

For all its horrendous human toll, World War I brought glowing prosperity to the American economy. Factory production climbed about 35 percent from 1914 to 1918, and the civilian work force grew by 1.3 million from 1916 to 1918. Wages rose, but prices soared. The real wages of unskilled workers climbed by nearly 20 percent from 1914 to 1918.

A no-strike rule prevailed in American industry during the war. Samuel Gompers of the American Federation of Labor ordered workers to stay on the job for the duration. Union membership increased from 2.7 million in 1916 to more than 5 million by 1920. The National War Labor Board guaranteed workers' rights to organize and bargain collectively. It also pressured war plants to introduce the eight-hour workday, which by the war's end had become the standard in U.S. industry.

American agriculture prospered during the war years. With European farm production disrupted, U.S. agricultural prices more than doubled from 1913 to 1918. Cotton jumped from $.12 to $.29 per pound by 1918 and corn from $.70 to $1.52 a bushel. At the same time, farmers' real income rose significantly. But in the long run, this agricultural boom proved a mixed blessing. Farmers borrowed heavily to expand their production, and when the artificially high wartime prices collapsed, they found themselves in a credit squeeze. During an ensuing, long agricultural depression in the 1920s and 1930s, farmers would look back to the war years as their last time of real prosperity.

Social disruption as well as prosperity came of the boom. The job seekers streaming into urban industrial centers strained housing, schools, and municipal services. Changes in social behavior occurred, taking many forms. The consumption of cigarettes shot up by 350 percent, to 48 billion a year. Automobile production quadrupled, reaching 1.8 million in 1917. With more cars on the road, American life began to change.

African-Americans Migrate Northward

The war sharply accelerated blacks' migration to northern cities. An estimated half-million African-Americans left the South during the war. Chicago's African-American population swelled from 44,000 in 1910 to 110,000 in 1920 and Cleveland's from 8,000 to 34,000.

Economic opportunity drew them north. When the war sharply reduced immigration from Europe, American industry recruited black workers to take up the slack. The economic inducements found a ready response. To the black sharecropper mired in poverty and confronting blatant racism, the prospect of a salary of three dollars a day, in a region where racism seemed less intense, appeared a heaven-sent opportunity. One black, newly settled near Chicago, wrote his southern relatives, "Nothing here but money, and it is not hard to get." By 1920, 1.5 million African-Americans were working in northern factories or other urban-based jobs.

Once the initial elation faded, African-American migrants often found they had traded one set of problems for another. White workers resented the competition, and white homeowners reacted in fear and hostility as crowded black neighborhoods spilled over into surrounding areas. Bloody violence broke out on July 2, 1917, in East St. Louis, Illinois, home to 10,000 blacks recently arrived from the South. In a well-coordinated action, a white mob torched black homes and then shot the residents as they fled. At least thirty-nine African-Americans were killed. A few weeks later, the newly founded National Association for the Advancement of Colored People (NAACP) organized a silent march down New York's Fifth Avenue to protest racial violence. Despite this and other demonstrations, racial enmity in northern cities did not end with the signing of the armistice.

Women and the War

From one perspective, World War I seems a supremely male experience. Male politicians and statesmen made the decisions that led to war. Male generals issued the orders that sent untold thousands of other men to their death in battle. Yet any event as vast as war touches all of society. The war affected women differently than men, but it affected them profoundly.

Women activists hoped that the war would lead to equality and greater opportunity for women. One author offered a feminist variation of Woodrow Wilson's theme: women should energetically support the war, she said, in order to win a role in shaping the peace.

For a bright, brief moment, the war promised dramatic gains for women. Thousands of women served in the military and in volunteer agencies, and about 1 million women worked in industry in 1917–1918. The woman-suffrage movement sped toward victory in 1917–1918 on a tide of wartime idealism. "The services of women during the supreme crisis have been of the most signal usefulness and distinction," wrote President Wilson; "it is high time that part of our debt should be acknowledged." By overwhelming margins, Congress passed a woman-suffrage amendment to the Constitution in 1919. This Nineteenth Amendment was ratified in 1920.

But hopes that the war would permanently improve women's status proved unfounded. Relatively few women actually *entered* the work force for the first time in 1917–1918; most simply moved from poorly paying jobs to better-paying positions. And even those in better-paying jobs generally earned less than the men whom they replaced. As soon as the war ended, moreover, women lost their jobs to make room for the returning troops. The New York labor federation stated, "The same patriotism which induced women to enter industry during the war should induce them to vacate their positions after the war."

Despite the short-lived spurt in employment during the war, the percentage of working women declined slightly from 1910 to 1920. As industrial researcher Mary Van Kleeck wrote, when "the immediate dangers" ended, traditional male attitudes "came to life once more." The dark underside of the war spirit—prejudice, intolerance, conformism—demonstrated remarkable tenacity in peace; positive effects such as the beginning of gender equality in the workplace were more fleeting.

The War and Progressivism

Exploring the war's impact on progressive reform, historians find a mixed picture. Without question, in the long run the war stifled reform energies and ushered in a decade of repression. During the war, socialists and dissenters endured hostility and persecution. And while the war brought increased corporate regulation, a long-sought progressive goal, wartime regulatory agencies were often dominated by the same business interests they supposedly supervised.

Yet the war also clearly benefited some reform causes. The woman-suffrage campaign prospered, as did the movement to better the lot of the industrial worker. The War Labor Board pushed for greater unionization and for an eight-hour workday, which became standard by the war's end. Social-justice progressives pressed for reforms that would promote social stability and industrial efficiency, both war-related goals. Under pressure from the War Labor Board and the War Department, several states banned child labor, set wage and hour rules, and enacted various protections and benefits for factory laborers. This flurry of social-justice reform activity quieted with the return of peace, but the laws remained on the books as precedents for future reform efforts.

The war also strengthened the coercive, moral-reform component of the progressive movement, including the drive for prohibition. Nineteen states had gone dry by 1917, and the war decisively boosted the cause. Prohibitionists pointed out that most of the nation's biggest breweries bore such German names as Pabst, Schlitz, and Anheuser-Busch. Beer, they hinted, was part of a German plot to undermine the United States' moral fiber and fighting qualities. Furthermore, the use of grain to manufacture whiskey and gin seemed unpatriotic. The Eighteenth Amendment, which banned the manufacture, transportation, and sale of alcoholic beverages, passed in December 1917. It drew wide support as a war measure.

The war also strengthened the antiprostitution movement and encouraged strict sexual morality. The War Department closed all brothels near military bases, and Congress appropriated $4 million to combat prostitution and sexually transmitted disease on the home front. Among the red-light districts closed on military orders was New Orleans's famed Storyville. Many jazz musicians who had been performing in Storyville's brothels and clubs moved up the Mississippi, carrying their music to Memphis, St. Louis, and Chicago. Thus, ironically, the moral reformism of World War I contributed to the diffusion of jazz northward.

Joyous Armistice, Bitter Aftermath

In November 1918 the war that had battered Europe for more than four years ground to a halt. Woodrow Wilson took the lead at the peace conference, but he failed in his cherished objective of securing American membership in the League of Nations. At home, racism and intolerance worsened. In the election of 1920, Americans repudiated Wilsonianism and sent conservative Republican Warren G. Harding to the White House.

Wilson's Fourteen Points

President Wilson planned to put a "Made in America" stamp on the peace. American involvement, he believed, could transform a sordid power conflict into something higher and finer—a struggle for a new, more democratic world order.

As the nation had mobilized in 1917, Wilson had striven to translate his vision into specific war aims. The need had grown urgent after Lenin's bolsheviks seized power in Russia late in 1917 and published many of the self-serving secret treaties signed by the European powers before 1914.

In his Fourteen Points speech to Congress in January 1918, Wilson summed up U.S. war aims. Eight points dealt with territorial settlement in postwar Europe, underscoring Wilson's belief in self-determination and autonomy for peoples formerly ruled by the Austro-Hungarian or the Ottoman empires. A ninth point insisted that colonial disputes be resolved in the interests of the colonial peoples as well as of the European powers. The remaining five points revealed Wilson's larger vision: a world of free navigation, lowered trade barriers, reduced armaments, openly negotiated treaties, and "a general association of nations" to ensure peace and resolve conflicts by negotiation. The Fourteen Points helped to solidify U.S. support for the war, especially among liberals. Such generous and high-minded goals proved that the nation had gone to war for noble objectives. Whether Wilson could achieve his goals remained to be seen.

Armistice

With the failure of Germany's spring 1918 offensive, and with Allied advances in the Meuse-Argonne and elsewhere, German military leaders acknowledged the inevitable. In early October they proposed to Wilson an armistice based on the Fourteen Points. The British and French hesitated, but in early November they agreed to peace on the basis of the Fourteen Points. Meanwhile, political turmoil in Berlin led to the abdication of Kaiser Wilhelm II and the proclamation of a German republic.

As dawn broke over the Forest of Compiègne on November 11, 1918, Marshal Foch and his German counterparts, seated in Foch's private railroad car, signed the armistice. Word spread swiftly: hostilities would cease at 11:00 A.M. As the booming guns fell silent, French, British, American, and German men cautiously approached each other. Rockets burst over the front that night in celebration. Back home, cheering throngs filled the streets. "Everything for which America has fought has been accomplished," Wilson's armistice message stated hopefully .

The Versailles Peace Conference

The challenge of forging a peace treaty remained. Wilson opted personally to lead the U.S. delegation to the peace conference. This decision was probably a mistake, for Wilson's oratorical skills outstripped his talent for negotiation and compromise. The president compounded his mistake by selecting only one Republican peace commissioner, an elderly diplomat. In the November 1918 congressional elections, Republicans gained control of both houses of Congress, an ominous sign for Wilson.

Wilson received a hero's welcome in Europe. Shouts of "Voodrow Veelson" rang out in Paris as Wilson and the French president headed a parade up the Champs-Elysées, the city's elegant ceremonial boulevard. When Wilson reached Britain, children spread flowers in his path, and in Italy an exuberant official compared his visit to the Second Coming of Jesus Christ.

The exhilaration evaporated when the peace conference began on January 18, 1919, at the palace of Versailles near Paris. A Council of Four, comprising the Allied heads of state, dominated the proceedings: Wilson; Italy's Vittorio Orlando; the aged and cynical Georges Clemenceau of France, determined to avenge Germany's humiliating defeat of France in 1871; and David Lloyd George of Great Britain, of whom Wilson said, "He is slippery as an eel, and I never know when to count on him."

These European leaders represented bitter, vindictive nations that had suffered horrendously in the war. Their objectives bore little relationship to Wilson's vision of a liberal peace. As Clemenceau remarked, "God gave us the Ten Commandments and we broke them. Mr. Wilson has given us the Fourteen Points. We shall see." The squabbling among the Allies became intense.

Mirroring this poisonous political climate, the peace treaty signed by a sullen German delegation on June 28, 1919, was harshly punitive. Germany was disarmed, stripped of its colonies, forced to admit sole blame for the war, and saddled with unspecified but potentially enormous reparation payments. In all, Germany lost one-tenth of its population and one-eighth of its territory.

Wilson's idealism influenced some of the treaty's provisions. Germany's former colonies, as well as those of Turkey in the Middle East, went to various Allies under a trusteeship system by which they eventually, in theory, would become independent. The treaty recognized the independence of Poland; the Baltic states of Estonia, Latvia, and Lithuania, which Germany had seized from bolshevik Russia; and two new nations, Czechoslovakia and Yugoslavia, carved from the former Austro-Hungarian and Ottoman empires.

On balance, the Versailles treaty was a disaster. Its provisions fed festering resentment in Germany. Its framers, moreover, failed to come to terms with revolutionary Russia. Even as the treaty makers devised territorial settlements in eastern Europe that were designed to keep Russia as weak as possible, the Allies found themselves embroiled in the Russian civil war.

Indeed, in August 1918 a fourteen-nation Allied force had landed in Russian ports in Europe and Asia. The troops soon began assisting the counterrevolutionaries (including both democrats and tsarists) fighting to overthrow Lenin. Wilson approved of American participation. He had welcomed the liberal revolution of March 1917 but viewed Lenin's seizure of power in November 1917 as a betrayal of the Allied cause and of his hopes for a liberal Russian future.

Before leaving Versailles, the Allied leaders agreed to support a Russian military leader, Admiral Aleksandr Kolchak, who was waging an ultimately unsuccessful campaign against the bolsheviks. Wilson refused to recognize Lenin's communist government; not until 1933 would the United States open formal diplomatic relations with the Soviet Union.

The Fight over the League of Nations

In the summer of 1919, drained by months of bargaining and dismayed by the treaty's vindictive features, Wilson increasingly focused on his one shining achievement at Versailles: the League of Nations. The League, whose charter, or "covenant," was written into the treaty itself, represented the highest embodiment of Wilson's vision of a liberal, harmonious, and rational world order. As he wrote an adviser, "That instrument will work wonders, bring the blessing of peace, and then when the war psychosis has abated, it will not be difficult to settle all the disputes that baffle us now."

But within a few months, Wilson's dream lay shattered. Warning signs appeared as early as February 1919, when several leading Republicans, including Senate Majority Leader Henry Cabot Lodge, expressed serious doubts about the League. Wilson told them defiantly, "You cannot dissect the Covenant from the treaty without destroying the whole vital structure."

When Wilson returned to the United States in June 1919 and submitted the Versailles treaty to the Senate for ratification, Lodge bottled it up for weeks in the Foreign Relations Committee. Convinced that he could rally popular opinion, Wilson began a speaking tour in early September. He covered more than 9,000 miles and gave thirty-seven speeches in twenty-two days. Large, friendly crowds cheered Wilson's ideal of a world free of war.

But the grueling trip took a terrible toll. On September 25, outside Pueblo, Colorado, Wilson collapsed. Rushed back to Washington, he suffered a major stroke on October 2. Despite a partial recovery, he spent most of the rest of his term in bed or in a wheelchair, a reclusive invalid, his mind clouded, his fragile emotions betraying him into vengeful actions and petulant outbursts. Wilson's strong-willed second wife, Edith Galt, played a highly manipulative role during these difficult months. Fiercely guarding her husband, she and his doctor concealed his condition, controlled his access to information, and decided who could see him and who could not.

The final act of the League drama played itself out. Senators split into three camps: Democrats who supported the Covenant without changes, Republican "Irreconcilables" who opposed the League completely, and Republican "Reservationists," led by Lodge, who demanded significant modifications before they would accept the Covenant. Article 10 of the Covenant, pledging each member nation to preserve the political independence and territorial integrity of all members, concerned the Reservationists. They felt that it infringed on America's freedom of action in foreign affairs and on Congress's right to declare war.

Had Wilson compromised, the Senate would have ratified the treaty and the United States would have joined the League. But the president dug in his heels as his physical and emotional condition aggravated his tendency toward rigidity. He lashed out against the reservations demanded by the Republicans as "a knife thrust at the heart of the treaty." The American people, moreover, did not rise up in support of the League. The wartime reactionary mood persisted and political idealism waned. In November 1919 and again in March 1920, Irreconcilables and Democrats obeying Wilson's orders voted against the treaty that included Lodge's reservations. A president elected amid high popular enthusiasm in 1912, applauded when he called for war in 1917, and adulated when he arrived in Europe in 1918, lay isolated and sick, his political leadership repudiated. What should have been Wilson's supreme triumph turned to ashes in his grasp.

Racism and Red Scare

The wartime spirit of "100 percent Americanism" left an acrid aftertaste as 1919–1920 saw racial violence and fresh antiradical hysteria. Lynch mobs murdered seventy-six African-Americans in 1919, including ten military veterans, several still in uniform. The bloodiest disorder occurred in 1919 in Chicago, where an influx of southern African-Americans had intensified tensions. On a hot July afternoon, whites at a Lake Michigan beach threw stones at a black youth swimming offshore. He sank and drowned. A thirteen-day reign of terror followed as white and black marauders roamed the streets, randomly attacked innocent victims, and torched buildings. The violence left 15 whites and 23 blacks dead and more than 500 injured.

Wartime antiradical panic, reinforced by the fear and hatred of bolshevism, crested in the Red Scare of 1919–1920. Such emotions deepened as a rash of strikes broke out, representing an accumulation of grievances. When Seattle's labor unions organized an orderly general work stoppage early in 1919, the mayor accused the strikers of trying to "duplicate the anarchy of Russia" and called for federal troops. In April mail bombs were sent to various public officials. One blew off the hands of a senator's maid, and another damaged the U.S. attorney general's home.

The Election of 1920

Candidates	*Parties*	*Electoral Vote*	*Popular Vote*	*Percentage of Popular Vote*
WARREN G. HARDING	Republican	404	16,143,407	60.4
James M. Cox	Democratic	127	9,130,328	34.2
Eugene V. Debs	Socialist		919,799	3.4
P. P. Christensen	Farmer-Labor		265,411	1.0

The mounting frenzy over supposed radicals took political form. In November 1919 the House of Representatives refused to seat Milwaukee socialist Victor Berger. The New York legislature expelled several socialist members. The Justice Department established a countersubversive division under young J. Edgar Hoover, the future head of the Federal Bureau of Investigation, who arrested hundreds of suspected communists and aliens. In December 1919, 249 Russian-born aliens were deported.

On January 20, 1920, the Justice Department coordinated federal marshals and local police in raids on the homes of suspected radicals and the headquarters of radical organizations. Without bothering about search or arrest warrants, authorities arrested more than 4,000 people and ransacked homes and offices. These lightning raids grossly violated civil rights and simple decency. Marshals barged into one woman's bedroom to arrest her. In Lynn, Massachusetts, police arrested thirty-nine men and women meeting to discuss forming a cooperative bakery. The rabidly antiradical and politically ambitious attorney general, A. Mitchell Palmer, coordinated these "Red raids." Palmer had succumbed to the anticommunist hysteria of the early postwar period. He ominously predicted a "blaze of revolution . . . sweeping over every American institution of law and order . . . crawling into the sacred corners of American homes . . . burning up the foundations of society." The more outrageous manifestations of the Red Scare subsided as Palmer's irrational predictions failed to materialize. When a bomb exploded in New York City's financial district in September 1920, killing thirty-eight people, most Americans concluded that it was the work of an isolated fanatic rather than evidence of an approaching revolution.

The Election of 1920

In this disturbing climate, the nation prepared for the election of 1920. The Democrats, meeting in San Francisco, half-heartedly endorsed Wilson's League position and nominated James M. Cox, the progressive governor of Ohio. They chose as Cox's running mate the young assistant secretary of the navy, Franklin D. Roosevelt, who possessed a potent political name. The confident Republicans turned to Senator Warren G. Harding of Ohio, an amiable politician with few discernable qualifications beyond a lack of enemies. One Republican politician observed, "There ain't any first raters this year. . . . We got a lot of second raters, and Harding is the best of the second raters." For vice president they chose Governor Calvin Coolidge of Massachusetts.

Wilson declared the election a "solemn referendum" on the League, but the nation was spiritually spent, both by the war and by the emotional roller-coaster ride from lofty idealism to cynical disillusionment on which Wilson had taken it. Sensing the popular longing for calm, Harding promised a return to "normalcy." There would be no more idealistic crusades, no more cavalcades of reforms.

Harding and Coolidge piled up a landslide, winning 16 million votes to the Democrats' 9 million. Nearly a million voters defiantly cast their ballots for Socialist Eugene V. Debs, serving time in an Atlanta penitentiary.

The election dashed all hope for American entry into the League of Nations. Harding announced that the question of U.S. membership in the League was "dead." Two decades of reform at home and idealism abroad thus came to an abrupt, embittered end. The sense of national destiny and high purpose that Woodrow Wilson had evoked so eloquently in 1917 survived only as an ironic memory. Americans impatiently turned to a new president, a new decade, and a new era.

CONCLUSION

By conservative estimate, the First World War cost 10 million dead and 20 million wounded worldwide. Included in this staggering toll were 112,000 Americans—49,000 killed in combat, the rest dead of influenza and other diseases.

The war's social, political, economic, and technological impact extended far beyond the battlefield. Many of the technologies of slaughter that would dominate in the rest of the century emerged: torpedoes, bombs, toxic gases, and deadly efficient machine guns. The war furthered the goals of some reformers, bringing to fruition the women-suffrage and prohibition movements, for example. Government regulation of corporations expanded in the name of economic mobilization, and laws were passed to promote war workers' well-being and efficiency. Ultimately, however, the war undermined the progressive movement's commitment to social justice and its humanitarian concern for the underdog. When Americans repudiated Wilsonian idealism after the war, they also rejected reform. Internationally, the conflict propelled the United States to the center of world politics and left the nation's businesses and financial institutions poised for global expansion.

Some of these changes endured; others were fleeting. Their cumulative effect was profound. The United States that celebrated the armistice in November 1918 was a very different society from the one that Wilson had summoned to war only nineteen months earlier.

CHRONOLOGY

1905 President Theodore Roosevelt mediates the end of the Russo-Japanese War.

1906 San Francisco ends segregation of Asian schoolchildren.

1907 Roosevelt sends the "Great White Fleet" around the world.

1912 U.S. Marines occupy Nicaragua.

1914 U.S. troops occupy Vera Cruz, Mexico.
Archduke Franz Ferdinand of Austria assassinated.
World War I begins.
Wilson protests British interception of U.S. merchant ships.

1915 U.S. Marines occupy Haiti and the Dominican Republic.
Woman's Peace party organized.
British liner *Lusitania* sunk by German U-boat.
U.S. "preparedness" movement begins.
Germany restricts U-boat campaign.
Wilson permits U.S. bank loans to Allies.

1916 U.S. punitive expedition invades Mexico, seeking Pancho Villa.
After *Sussex* sinking, Germany pledges not to attack merchant ships without warning.
Wilson reelected as president.

1917 U.S. troops withdraw from Mexico.
Germany resumes unrestricted U-boat warfare; United States breaks diplomatic relations.
United States enters the war.
Selective Service Act sets up national draft.
War Industries Board, Committee on Public Information, and Food Administration created.
Espionage Act passed.
NAACP march in New York City.

Bolsheviks grab power in Russia; Russia leaves the war.
U.S. government seizes the nation's railroads.

1918 Wilson outlines Fourteen Points for peace.
Sedition Amendment to Espionage Act.
American Expeditionary Force (AEF) helps stop Germans at Château-Thierry and Belleau Wood, closes St. Mihiel salient, and plays key role in the Meuse-Argonne campaign.
Armistice signed (November 11).

1919 Eighteenth Amendment added to the Constitution.
Peace treaty, including League of Nations covenant, signed at Versailles.
Racial violence in Chicago.
Wilson suffers paralyzing stroke.
Versailles treaty, with League covenant, rejected by Senate.

1920 "Red raids" organized by Justice Department.
Nineteenth Amendment added to the Constitution.
Warren G. Harding elected president.

FOR FURTHER READING

Robert H. Ferrell, *Woodrow Wilson and World War I, 1917–1921* (1985). A vigorously written critical synthesis; especially good on the peace negotiations.

Frank Freidel, *Over There: The Story of America's First Great Overseas Crusade* (1964). Excellent, readable overview of the AEF experience based on soldiers' diaries and reminiscences.

Martin Gilbert, *The First World War: A Complete History* (1994). Weak on strategy, but vividly conveys the grim experience of ordinary soldiers.

David M. Kennedy, *Over Here: The First World War and American Society* (1980). Deeply researched interpretive study of the home front during the war.

Thomas J. Knock, *To End All Wars: World War I and the Quest for a New World Order* (1992). A compelling study of the origins of Wilson's internationalism and of the links between domestic reform and foreign policy.

Ronald Schaffer, *America in the Great War: The Rise of the War Welfare State* (1991). Explores the war's effect on corporate organization and business-government links as well as wartime initiatives to benefit industrial workers.

CHAPTER 24

The 1920s

To many observers, F. Scott and Zelda Fitzgerald symbolized the rich possibilities of the United States in the 1920s. They had it all: he was a talented and extravagantly handsome novelist; she, a breathtakingly beautiful and madcap companion. They danced their way through the decade on the front pages of the nation's newspapers, and the less daring gasped at the recklessness with which they consumed life. Fittingly, Scott Fitzgerald coined the term *Jazz Age* to describe the new America of flivvers and flappers, flagpole sitters, and get-rich-quick schemes. However, by the mid-1930s the Fitzgeralds' shocking decline made them seem a metaphor again, this time for American problems. Zelda had drifted far out of touch with reality and spent most of the last half of her life in asylums; Scott, in the grip of alcoholism, squandered his prodigious talent on Hollywood scripts that he despised. Their heady rise and sickening fall paralleled the 1920s in all too many ways.

(Right) 1920s Flapper Suzette Dewey, the daughter of a Treasury Department official, poses beside her roadster, December 1927

In the 1920s the nation's industrial machinery poured out a torrent of automobiles, electrical appliances, and other consumer goods. These new products brought prosperity to the national economy and far-reaching changes to daily life. The prosperity proved fragile; the changes did not. Economic transformations led to marked shifts in diet, dress, housekeeping, travel, entertainment, and thought.

Following several decades of immigration and urban growth, social tensions remained acute. As Republican presidents espoused conservative political and cultural values, conflicts ripped at the fabric of society. But this same ferment stimulated literature and the arts. When the decade ended, Americans summed up these turbulent and change-filled years in a phrase: the Roaring Twenties.

A New Economic Order

With consumer products aplenty, sophisticated advertising, and innovative forms of corporate organization, the economy raced forward in the 1920s, but not everyone benefited. Some key industries declined, workers lost jobs as factories automated, and farmers relapsed into chronic economic problems. Still, the overall picture seemed rosy, and most Americans celebrated the nation's thriving business culture.

A Decade of Prosperity

The war-induced boom continued until late 1920, when demobilization disrupted the economy. As the government canceled contracts and as veterans swamped labor markets, a recession struck. Business slowed, bankruptcies increased, and unemployment jumped. Recovery came in 1922, and, for the next few years, the economy grew spectacularly. Unemployment dropped as low as 3 percent, prices held steady, and gross national product climbed from $70 billion in 1922 to nearly $100 billion in 1929. By mid-decade the 1920–1922 recession seemed only a minor setback.

Electricity powered the general prosperity. Factories had started to electrify late in the nineteenth century, and by now the construction of hydroelectric generating plants had brought the age of electricity to urban households as well. By the mid-1920s, with more than 60 percent of the nation's homes wired for electricity, a wondrous array of electrical appliances—refrigerators, ranges, washing machines, vacuum cleaners, fans, razors, and mixers—stood gleaming in the stores. Their manufacture provided a potent economic stimulus.

The era's business boom also rested on the automobile. Passenger-car registrations bounded from 8 million in 1920 to more than 23 million in 1930. Ford's Model T led the market until mid-decade, when General Motors Corporation (GM) spurted ahead by touting a range of colors (the Model T came only in black) and improved passenger comfort. Particularly popular was GM's lowest-price car, named for automotive designer Louis Chevrolet. In response, in 1927 Ford introduced the stylish Model A in a spectrum of colors. By the end of the decade, the automobile industry accounted for 9 percent of all wages in manufacturing and had stimulated such related industries as rubber, gasoline and petroleum, advertising, and highway construction.

American capitalism remained vigorously expansionist. Ford, GM, General Electric, and other large corporations invested heavily in production facilities abroad. Other U.S. firms acquired foreign processing facilities or sources of raw materials. Swift and Armour built meatpacking plants in Argentina; Anaconda Copper acquired Chile's biggest copper mine; and the mammoth United Fruit Company established processing factories throughout Latin America. By 1930 U.S. private investment abroad totaled more than $15 billion.

New Modes of Producing, Managing, and Selling

In the 1920s assembly-line mass production boosted the per capita output of industrial workers by 40 percent. At the sprawling Ford plants near Detroit, workers stood in one place and performed simple, repetitive tasks as an endless chain conveyed the

Christmas in Consumerland

Giving a modern twist to an ancient symbol, this advertising catalog of the 1920s offered an enticing array of new electric products for the home.

partly assembled vehicles past them. The technique quickly spread, and *Fordism* became a worldwide synonym for American industrial prowess.

Corporate consolidation continued. By 1930 more than 1,000 companies a year were disappearing through merger. Corporate giants dominated major industries: Ford, GM, and Chrysler in automobiles; General Electric and Westinghouse in electricity; U.S. Steel in the steel industry. Consolidation reached epidemic proportions in public utilities. Samuel Insull of the Chicago Edison Company built an empire of local power companies that by 1929 had assets of $3.5 billion. At the decade's end, 100 corporations controlled nearly half the nation's business activity.

Merger mania was one expression of the search for a more integrated corporate order adapted for the new economic era. Where there were no mergers, companies that made the same product often cooperated on such matters as pricing, product specifications, and division of markets.

Streamlined operations resulted in a more bureaucratic management structure within individual businesses. Like the federal government, corporations nationalized their management in the twenties, establishing specialized divisions for product development, market research, economic forecasting, and employee relations. Professionals trained in management oversaw the day-to-day operations within this new corporate structure.

Wage policies also began to change. Some business leaders argued that employers should not necessarily pay the lowest wages possible; higher wages, they suggested, would generate higher productivity. Henry Ford led the way in 1914 by paying his workers an unprecedented five dollars a day, and other companies followed his lead in the 1920s.

In addition, new systems for distributing goods emerged. Automobiles now reached consumers through vast dealer networks; nearly 10,000 Ford dealerships had sprung up by 1926. A rapidly expanding network of chain stores accounted for about a quarter of all retail sales by 1930. Family-run roadside diners and tourist cabins prospered because of the spread of the automobile, but other small, locally owned businesses faded under relentless pressure from the chains. The A&P grocery chain expanded from 5,000 stores in 1922 to 17,500 in 1928. Installment buying represented another important mass-marketing innovation. By 1929, 75 percent of automobiles were bought on credit.

Above all, the 1920s business boom bobbed along on a sea of advertising. In 1919 corporations spent an estimated $1.8 billion promoting their wares. The advertising industry employed 600,000 people. Radio, the newest of the mass media, relied entirely on advertising for its income.

Advertisers used celebrity endorsements ("Nine

out of ten screen stars care for their skin with Lux toilet soap"), promises of social success, and threats of social embarrassment. Beneath a picture of a pretty but obviously unhappy young woman, a 1923 Listerine mouthwash ad proclaimed,

> *She was a beautiful girl and talented too. She had the advantages of education and better clothes than most girls of her set. She possessed that culture and poise that travel brings. Yet in the one pursuit that stands foremost in the mind of every girl and woman—marriage—she was a failure.*

The young woman's problem was *halitosis*, a hitherto little-known term for bad breath. The remedy, of course, was Listerine, and lots of it.

Beyond touting specific products, advertisers redefined popular aspirations by offering a seductive vision of a new era of consumption. Ads for automobiles, cigarettes, electrical conveniences, clothing, and home furnishings created a fantasy world of elegance, grace, and boundless pleasure.

Business influence saturated life in the 1920s. A 1921 article summed up the prevailing mood: "Among the nations of the earth today America stands for one idea: Business. . . . Thru business, properly conceived, managed, and conducted, the human race is finally to be redeemed." Americans venerated the magnates of business and the new world of material progress they had created. In *The Man Nobody Knows* (1925), ad man Bruce Barton, the son of a Protestant minister, described Jesus Christ as a managerial genius who "picked up twelve men from the bottom ranks of business and forged them into an organization that conquered the world." Observed sociologists Robert and Helen Lynd: "More and more of the activities of life are coming to be strained through the bars of the dollar sign."

Women in the New Economic Era

Automobiles, electrical appliances, and other technological wonders profoundly affected women's lives. In the decade's ubiquitous advertising, glamorous women smiled behind the steering wheel and happily operated electric appliances. Housework became an exciting technological challenge. As one ad said, "Men are judged successful according to their power to delegate work. Similarly the wise woman delegates to electricity all that electricity can do."

In the workplace the assembly line, offering less physically demanding work, should in theory have increased job opportunities for women. In fact, however, the assembly-line work force remained largely male. Although the number of women holding jobs increased by more than 2 million in the twenties, the *proportion* of women working outside the home remained unchanged, at 24 percent. The weakening of the union movement in the 1920s proved especially hard on women workers. By the end of the decade, a minuscule 3 percent of women workers belonged to unions.

Wage discrimination continued. In 1929 a male trimmer in the meatpacking industry earned fifty-two cents an hour; a female trimmer, thirty-seven cents an hour. Reflecting the widespread view that women worked only until marriage, employers relegated most female employees to low-paying piece-rate jobs.

Business bureaucratization increased female employment opportunities. By 1930, 2 million women were working as secretaries, typists, and filing clerks. Few became managers, however. In the professions, women worked in the limited spheres of nursing, librarianship, social work, and public-school teaching. As medical schools imposed a ceiling of 5 percent on female admissions, the number of women physicians declined.

The proportion of female high-school graduates attending college grew from 8 percent to 12 percent during the decade, and nearly 30,000 women received college degrees in 1930. More married women entered the work force, primarily in clerical jobs, in the lower ranks of business, or in traditional "women's professions" such as nursing, social work, and teaching. A handful followed Progressive Era trailblazers to become researchers and scholars in colleges and universities. As today, most found juggling marriage and a career difficult.

Workers in a Business Age

The labor movement faced tough sledding in the twenties. Several factors led to dwindling union membership, from 5 million in 1920 to 3.4 million in 1929. Overall wage rates crept upward in the 1920s. In the steel industry, for example, real hourly wages rose about 17 percent from 1923 to 1929. Despite continuing workplace inequities, employees' fatter pay envelopes helped to undermine the union movement. Changes in the industrial process also played a role. The trade unions' traditional strength lay in established industries such as printing, railroading, and construction. This craft-based pattern of union organization was ill suited to the new mass-production industries.

Management hostility further weakened organized labor. Sometimes this antagonism took physical form, as when Henry Ford hired thugs and spies to intimidate would-be organizers. Typically, however, the anti-union campaign was subtler. Manufacturers' associations renamed the nonunion shop the "open shop" and praised it as the "American Plan" of labor relations. Some companies sponsored their own "unions" and provided cafeterias, better rest rooms, and recreational facilities. Certain big corporations sold company stock to their workers at special prices.

Some corporate leaders heralded this new approach to labor relations as evidence of heightened ethical awareness in American business. General Electric's head insisted that workers' well-being stood second only to productivity in GE's hierarchy of values. Welfare capitalism, as this corporate paternalism was called, was intended to prevent the formation of independent unions.

Blacks' membership in unions remained low. Although the American Federation of Labor (AFL) officially prohibited racial discrimination, the independent unions composing the AFL discriminated against African-Americans in many ways. Some had constitutional clauses limiting membership to whites; others followed a de facto exclusionary policy. Corporations' hiring of African-Americans as strikebreakers further increased organized labor's hostility toward them.

African-Americans, women, Mexican-Americans, and recent immigrants clustered at the bottom of the wage scale. African-American workers entering the industrial labor force, last hired and first fired, typically performed the most menial jobs. Amid the general prosperity, wages for unskilled workers barely budged.

Agriculture: The Economy's Ailing Sector

The 1920s brought hard times for farmers. Dwindling military purchases and the revival of European agriculture sent prices plummeting 50 percent and more. In the period 1919–1921 total farm income fell from $10 billion to $4 billion. Increased production lowered prices even more. The real annual earnings of full-time agricultural workers fell from $528 in 1920 to $344 in 1921 and barely inched up for the rest of the decade. Farmers who had borrowed heavily to boost their harvests during the war found themselves unable to pay off loans and mortgages.

Farm groups turned to Washington for help. They asked for a price-support plan under which the government would purchase the surplus of six commodities—cotton, corn, rice, hogs, tobacco, and wheat—at a guaranteed high price and sell them on the world market. A tax, ultimately to be borne by consumers in the form of higher food costs, would make up the price differential. Congress passed the McNary-Haugen bill, embodying these ideas, in 1927 and again in 1928, but President Calvin Coolidge vetoed it both times. This failure to help financially strapped farmers reflected the conservative political climate of the decade.

Republicans in Power

Politics in the 1920s reflected the decade's business orientation. Republicans controlled Congress and supplied three presidents who mirrored the prevailing corporate outlook. In this atmosphere, former progressives and feminists faced difficult times.

Scandals and Silences: The Harding and Coolidge Years

In the 1920s the Republicans relied on a base of northern farmers, corporate leaders, small business-people, and skilled workers. The Democrats' base remained the white South and the urban political machines.

The conservatives who controlled the 1920 Republican convention selected Senator Warren G. Harding of Ohio as their nominee. A former newspaper editor and a genial backslapper, Harding enjoyed good liquor, good stories, poker with his cronies, and furtive encounters with his mistress. Yet this amiable second-rater won the presidency in a landslide (see Chapter 23). Harding's ordinariness appealed to war-weary voters longing for stability. Compared to Wilson's lofty sermons, Harding's vacuous oratory had a soothing appeal.

Realizing his lack of qualifications, Harding compensated by making some notable appointments: Henry A. Wallace, the respected editor of a farm periodical, became secretary of agriculture; Charles Evans Hughes, a former New York governor and presidential candidate, was named secretary of state; and Andrew Mellon, a Pittsburgh banker and financier, served as treasury secretary. Wartime food administrator Herbert Hoover dominated the cabinet as secretary of commerce. Unfortunately, Harding made some disastrous appointments as well, including Harry Daugherty, his political manager, as attorney general; Albert B. Fall, New Mexico senator, as secretary of the interior; and Charles Forbes, a wartime draft dodger, as director of the Veterans' Bureau. These men draped the Harding years in an aura of back-room sleaze reminiscent of the Grant administration.

By 1922 Washington rumor hinted at criminal activity in high places. Dismayed, Harding confessed, "I have no trouble with my enemies. . . . But . . . my goddamn friends . . . , they're the ones that keep me walking the floor nights." In 1923, returning from an Alaskan cruise, Harding suffered a heart attack and died in San Francisco.

In 1924 a Senate investigation exposed the full scope of the scandals. Charles Forbes, convicted of stealing Veterans' Bureau funds, evaded prison by fleeing abroad. The bureau's general counsel committed suicide, as did an associate of Attorney General Daugherty who had been accused of influence peddling. Daugherty himself, forced from office in 1924, escaped conviction in two criminal trials. The seamiest scandal involved Interior Secretary Fall, who went to jail for secretly leasing government oil reserves in Elk Hills, California, and Teapot Dome, Wyoming, to two oilmen while accepting "loans" from them totaling $400,000. "Teapot Dome" became shorthand, like "Watergate" in the 1970s, for an entire presidential legacy of scandal.

Vice President Calvin Coolidge learned of Harding's death while visiting his family in Vermont. His father, a local magistrate, administered the presidential oath by lantern light. Coolidge brought a distinctly different style to the White House. His determined silence contrasted with Harding's chattiness. Once as he left California, a radio reporter asked for a parting message to the people of the state. "Good-bye," Coolidge responded. Other than in style, however, Coolidge's advent meant little change. Tariff rates reached all-time highs, income taxes for the rich fell, and the Supreme Court overturned several progressive measures. Coolidge rejected a request for aid from Mississippi flood victims with the reminder that government had no duty to protect citizens "against the hazards of the elements."

In vetoing the McNary-Haugen farm bill, Coolidge warned against the "tyranny of bureaucratic regulation and control" and denounced the bill for benefiting farmers at the expense of "the general public welfare." Although his party had long championed high tariffs and other measures of benefit to business, Coolidge chafed when farmers pursued the same kind of special-interest politics.

Foreign Policy in an Isolationist Age

International relations produced President Harding's most notable achievement, the Washington Naval Arms Conference. To head off an expensive

The Election of 1924

Candidates	*Parties*	*Electoral Vote*	*Popular Vote*	*Percentage of Popular Vote*
CALVIN COOLIDGE	Republican	382	15,718,211	54.0
John W. Davis	Democratic	136	8,385,283	28.8
Robert M. La Follette	Progressive	13	4,831,289	16.6

international naval-arms race, Harding called for a conference. When the delegates of various nations met in October 1921, Secretary of State Hughes startled them by proposing the destruction of ships to achieve an agreed-upon ratio of craft among the world's naval powers. Consequently, in February 1924 five nations—Great Britain, the United States, Japan, France, and Italy—signed a treaty pledging to reduce battleship tonnage and to observe a ten-year moratorium on battleship construction. The United States and Japan also agreed to respect each other's territorial holdings in the Pacific. Although the treaty did not prevent war, it represented a pioneering arms-control effort.

America otherwise followed an isolationist foreign policy in the 1920s, joining neither the League of Nations nor the Court of International Justice (the World Court). Symbolic gestures replaced genuine engagement. For example, in 1928 the United States and France cosponsored the Kellogg-Briand Pact renouncing aggression and calling for the outlawing of war. Lacking enforcement mechanisms, the high-sounding document did nothing to prevent the militarism that would plunge the world into war a decade later.

U.S. insistence on the full repayment of wartime debts generated ill will among former allies. In 1922 a Senate commission calculated the total bill, including interest, at $22 billion. As the German economy collapsed under the weight of reparations payments, and as other European economies foundered, America scaled down its demands, but high U.S. tariffs prevented foreign powers from earning the dollars needed to pay their debts.

Progressive Stirrings, Democratic Divisions

In Congress the progressive spirit had survived. Senator George Norris of Nebraska blocked the Coolidge administration from selling a federal hydroelectric facility at Muscle Shoals, Alabama, to Henry Ford for a fraction of its value. Congress's creation of the Federal Radio Commission (1927) extended to the fledgling broadcasting industry the progressive principle of government regulation of business activity.

In 1922 labor and farm groups formed the Conference for Progressive Political Action (CPPA), and in 1924 the CPPA revived the Progressive party. It adopted a prolabor, profarmer platform calling for government ownership of railroads and water-power resources and nominated Senator Robert La Follette for president.

Split between urban and rural wings, the Democratic party held its 1924 convention in New York. The extent of the division became evident when a resolution condemning the Ku Klux Klan failed by one vote. Rural Democrats supported William Gibbs McAdoo, Wilson's treasury secretary; urban Democrats backed Governor Alfred E. Smith of New York, an Irish Roman Catholic. Ballot after ballot left both candidates short of the two-thirds majority necessary for nomination. Humorist Will Rogers observed, "This thing has got to end. New York invited you folks here as guests, not to live." After 102 ballots, exhausted delegates turned to a compromise candidate, John W. Davis. Despite the Democrats' support for some progressive reforms during the Wilson administration, the party's close identification with the interests of the poor and minorities still lay ahead.

On the Republican side, Coolidge easily won renomination. The GOP platform praised high tariffs, urged tax and spending cuts, and applauded the Washington Naval Arms Conference. With the economy humming and the opposition divided, Coolidge cruised to victory with about 16 million votes. Davis trailed with 8 million votes, and La Follette collected a little under 5 million.

Women and Politics in the 1920s: A Dream Deferred

Suffragists' belief that votes for women would transform politics died quickly after the war. Women did achieve notable gains: states passed laws permitting them to serve on juries and to hold public office, the League of Women Voters emerged, and the Sheppard-Towner Act of 1921 appropriated $1.2 million for rural prenatal and baby-care centers. Beyond these advances, however, the Nineteenth Amendment had little political impact. With the vote attained, women scattered to all points on the political spectrum, and many withdrew from politics completely.

As the women's movement splintered, it lost focus. Drawing mainly middle-class and professional women, the League of Women Voters abandoned reform activism for the study of civic issues. Some feminists worked for peace: Carrie Chapman Catt founded the National Conference on the Cause and Cure of War, and Jane Addams supported the Women's International League for Peace and Freedom. Meanwhile, Alice Paul and her National Woman's party campaigned for an equal-rights amendment to the Constitution, but many feminists condemned her position. Such an amendment might benefit professional women, they charged, but could harm female factory workers by abolishing protective legislation. The proposed amendment got nowhere.

Underlying the disarray in women's ranks were the conservative political atmosphere and materialistic mass culture of the 1920s. Right-wing groups accused Jane Addams and other women's rights leaders of communist sympathies. Young women, bombarded by advertising that defined liberation in terms of life-style and the purchase of goods, found civic idealism embarrassingly passé.

In this milieu, reforms achieved by organized women's groups often proved short-lived. The women's movement suffered serious setbacks when the Supreme Court struck down child-labor laws (1922) and women's protective laws (1923). A child-labor constitutional amendment squeezed through Congress in 1924 but won ratification in only a few states. The Sheppard-Towner program of rural prenatal and baby care ended in 1929.

Mass Society, Mass Culture

The automobiles, electrical appliances, and other manufactures that roared off the assembly lines in the 1920s heralded a new social and cultural era. These products utterly changed Americans' lives. The standardized mass production that spawned them, moreover, proved as adaptable to ideas as to roadsters and refrigerators.

A Nation of Cities, Consumer Goods, and Automobiles

The 1920 census showed that, for the first time, America's urban population outnumbered its rural dwellers. The tally recorded a dozen cities of more than 600,000. African-Americans constituted a major part of the movement to the cities. By 1930 more than 40 percent of the nation's 12 million African-Americans lived in cities, notably Chicago, Detroit, New York, and other northern and western metropolitan centers.

City growth reshaped American culture. The nation became increasingly urbanized "in the cast of its mind, in its ideals, and in its folkways," as one historian has written. The forces that molded culture—radio, the movies, corporations, advertising agencies, mass magazines—operated from cities.

Even when they nostalgically evoked rural values, they did so from big-city editorial offices and radio studios. The new consumer goods, particularly electrical appliances, had the most dramatic impact in the cities. (Most rural dwellers lacked electricity.)

These innovations reduced the hours and sheer physical effort of housework. In 1925, nearly 75 percent of working women surveyed said that they spent less time on housework than their mothers had. Vacuum cleaners supplanted brooms and carpet beaters, firing up wood stoves became a memory, and store-bought clothes replaced handmade apparel. Electricity altered the ritual of doing laundry and preparing food as well. Urban wives who had relied on commercial laundries began doing their own wash with the advent of the electric washing machine and iron. Cooking and eating patterns shifted. The rise of the supermarket made sharp inroads on the practice of canning. Commercially baked bread replaced home-baked bread. Refrigeration, supermarkets, and motor transport made fresh fruits and vegetables available year-round and led to significant improvement in the national diet.

The automobile, however, had the greatest social and cultural impact. Urban planners worriedly discussed traffic jams, parking problems, and the mounting accident rate (more than 26,000 Americans died in traffic accidents in 1924). Like electrical appliances, automobiles reached into the lives of ordinary Americans. Family vacations and long drives in the country became popular. The automobile diminished the isolation of rural life and gave farm dwellers easier access to the city for shopping and entertainment.

Family cohesion suffered from the new mobility. Young people welcomed the freedom from parental oversight that the car offered. On a whim, they could drive to a dance in a distant city. Complained one father, "It's getting so a fellow has to make a date with his family to see them."

The automobile's impact on individuality was similarly mixed. Car owners could travel where they wished, when they wished, freed from fixed routes and schedules. But the automobile also accelerated the standardization of American life. Millions chugged around in identical black vehicles. The one-room schoolhouse was abandoned as buses carried children to consolidated schools. Neighborhood shops and markets declined as people drove to chain stores. The automobile age brought the first suburban department stores, the first shopping center (in Kansas City), and the first fast-food chain (A&W Root Beer).

Yet even at $300 or $400, the automobile remained too expensive for the poor. The "automobile suburbs" that sprang up beyond the streetcar lines attracted the prosperous, but the urban poor, including the growing black population, remained behind.

At the same time, the automobile's farm cousin, the tractor, transformed agriculture. The horse and mule population declined in the 1920s, while the number of tractors grew to 920,000. As more and more farmers went into debt to buy mechanized equipment, the agricultural crisis worsened.

Soaring Energy Consumption and a Threatened Environment

The proliferation of electrical products and of passenger cars carried a high environmental price tag. Electrical use tripled in the 1920s, gobbling 42 million tons of coal, 10 million barrels of oil, and 112 million cubic feet of gas by 1929. And the 20 million automobiles clogging the nation's highways by 1929 guzzled fuel. As late as 1916, U.S. refineries had produced less than 50 million barrels of gasoline, but by 1929 gasoline production had catapulted to 435 million barrels—more than a billion barrels of crude oil pumped into thirsty fuel tanks.

The zooming demand for gasoline triggered feverish activity in the oilfields of Texas, Oklahoma, California, and elsewhere. Major oil companies such as Standard, Texaco, Gulf, and Atlantic solidified their dominance of the industry. Domestic oil production rose by 250 percent, and annual oil imports crept up to 76 million barrels.

Intense competition for oil bred massive waste. Natural gas, considered almost worthless, was burned off. The Bureau of Mines calculated that through the 1920s, more than a billion cubic feet of natural gas went up in smoke *every day* in America's oilfields. The heedless consumption of nonrenewable fossil fuels, which would reach massive proportions after World War II, had begun.

The environment suffered in less obvious ways, too. Power plants, steel mills, and automobile engines spewed tons of pollutants into the atmosphere. As ribbons of asphalt and cement snaked across the land, gas stations, billboards, restaurants, and tourist cabins followed. The wilderness that nineteenth-century Americans had so cherished came under heavy siege.

Isolated voices protested. The Sierra Club and the Audubon Society worked to preserve wilderness and wildlife. Aldo Leopold of the U.S. Forest Service warned that for too long "a stump was our symbol of progress." Americans accustomed to a seemingly boundless wilderness "are *unconscious* of what the disappearance of wild places would mean." Wilderness preservation demanded not just sentimental pronouncements, Leopold stressed, but careful planning and political savvy. But few listened. To most Americans of the day, energy resources appeared limitless. Pollution and a vanishing wilderness seemed small prices to pay for the benefits of the electric motor and the internal-combustion engine. Resources seemed boundless, and industry represented jobs, economic growth, and industrial development. The confident generation of the 1920s had little time for the environmental issues that would raise alarms two generations later.

Routinized Work, Mass-Produced Pleasure

Assembly-line techniques—repetitive, unvaried, and requiring little individual initiative—affected workers' views of themselves and their jobs. Factory managers even discouraged communication among workers: laughing or talking could divert them from their task. Ford employees learned to whisper without moving their lips and adopted a fixed, impassive mask. And as work became more routine, its psychic rewards diminished. The assembly line offered few skills to take pride in, no specialized knowledge, no prospect of advancement. Leisure-time activities grew more important as workers sought in their free hours the fulfillment that their jobs did not provide.

Amusement itself became standardized. The mass production of culture dated to the penny press and dime novel of the 1830s, but the process accelerated in the twenties. Mass-circulation magazines flourished. By 1922 ten American magazines boasted circulations of more than 2.5 million each. The *Saturday Evening Post,* with its bucolic Norman Rockwell covers and fiction featuring small-town life, specialized in prepackaged nostalgia. In 1921 DeWitt and Lila Wallace founded *Reader's Digest,* which condensed articles originally published elsewhere. The *Digest* served up traditionalist, probusiness views in simple prose. Pitched to the mass market, it represented the journalistic counterpart of the A&P. Bookselling also saw major changes as publishers began marketing their products through department stores and mail-order organizations such as the Book-of-the-Month Club (1924) and the Literary Guild (1926).

Radios and movies standardized culture even more dramatically. The radio era began on November 2, 1920, when station KDKA in Pittsburgh broadcast the news of Warren Harding's election. In 1922, 500 new stations went on the air, and by 1927 radio sales approached 7 million sets.

In 1926 three corporations—General Electric, Westinghouse, and the Radio Corporation of America—formed the first radio network, the National Broadcasting Company (NBC). The Columbia Broadcasting System (CBS) followed in 1927, and the networks soon ruled radio broadcasting. Elaborate research on audience preferences dictated programming. From Maine to California, Americans laughed at the same jokes, hummed the same tunes, and absorbed the same commercials. New York's WEAF broadcast the first commercially sponsored program in 1922, and the commercialization of radio proceeded rapidly. The first network comedy show, the popular (and racist) "Amos 'n' Andy" (1928), brought millions in sales to its sponsor, Pepsodent toothpaste.

The motion-picture business evolved similarly. Movies, having expanded from the immigrant slums into elegant uptown theaters with names such as

"Majestic," "Ritz," and "Palace," attracted audiences from all social levels. After Al Jolson's *The Jazz Singer* (1927) introduced sound, movies became even more popular and spawned a new generation of screen idols, including the western hero Gary Cooper and the aloof Scandinavian beauty Greta Garbo. Another enduring favorite, Mickey Mouse, debuted in 1928. By 1930 weekly movie attendance neared 80 million.

Movies transported their viewers to worlds far removed from reality. One movie ad succinctly promised "all the adventure, all the romance, all the excitement you lack in your daily life." The mass-produced fantasies shaped popular behavior and values, especially among the impressionable young. In the words of novelist John Dos Passos, Hollywood offered "a great bargain sale of five-and-ten-cent lusts and dreams."

Fads, Celebrities, and Heroes

In this era when news could reach every corner of the nation in seconds, fads and media-promoted events preoccupied Americans. In 1921 Atlantic City promoted itself with a new bathing-beauty competition, the Miss America Pageant. In 1922 millions played mah-jongg, a game of Chinese origin, and in 1924 a crossword-puzzle craze consumed the country.

Larger-than-life celebrities emerged in professional sports: Babe Ruth of the New York Yankees; Ty Cobb of the Detroit Tigers; Gertrude Ederle, the first woman to swim the English Channel; Jack Dempsey and Gene Tunney, whose two heavyweight title fights drew more than 200,000 spectators and millions of radio listeners. When Tunney won the 1927 bout thanks to a famous "long count" by a referee, five radio listeners dropped dead of heart attacks.

The idolization of celebrities illuminates the anxieties and hopes of ordinary Americans in these years. The young woman trying to define her role in a period of confusing social change could find an ideal in beauty pageants. For the man whose sense of mastery had been shaken by developments from feminism to Fordism, cheering himself hoarse for a towering hero like Dempsey or Ruth could momentarily restore a feeling of personal worth and self-confidence.

Charles A. Lindbergh (1902–1974) Begins His Epic Flight, May 20, 1927
Lindbergh's achievement helped reassure Americans that the lone individual could still make a mark in an age of mass production and mass culture.

Charles Lindbergh, "Lucky Lindy," the young pilot who made the first nonstop flight across the Atlantic, illustrates the hero worship of the times. Lindbergh had been a stunt flyer and airmail pilot before he competed for a $25,000 prize offered for the first nonstop New York–Paris flight. Lindbergh's daring flight on May 20–21, 1927, in his silver-winged *Spirit of St. Louis* captured the popular imagination. From the moment he touched down in

Paris, the glare of media attention enveloped him. Back home in America, radio, newspapers, magazines, and movie newsreels provided saturation coverage. The "Lone Eagle" handled his celebrity with dignity, proving an authentic hero in an age of scandals and scams. Many Americans saw his flight as evidence that the individual still counted in an era of standardization and mechanization. To conservatives, Lindbergh's solid virtues proved that the old verities survived in a time of moral disarray.

Clearly, the new mass media had mixed social effects. The technologies of mass communication promoted cultural standardization and a uniformity of thought that stifled local and regional diversity. But radio, the movies, and the mass magazines also helped to forge a national culture and introduced millions of Americans to fresh viewpoints and new behaviors. Mass media hammered home a powerful message: personal horizons need no longer be limited by one's immediate environment. The spread of mass culture in the 1920s opened up a large world for ordinary Americans. If that world was often vacuous and tawdry, it was also sometimes exciting and inspiring.

Cultural Ferment and Creativity

Ferment and creativity also characterized the culture of the 1920s. Writers, artists, musicians, and scientists compiled a record of remarkable achievement. African-Americans asserted their pride through the cultural flowering known as the Harlem Renaissance. Pulsing through the decade were the rhythms of jazz, the African-American musical idiom that was winning wild popularity.

The Jazz Age and the Postwar Crisis of Values

The war and its disillusioned aftermath brought to full boil the simmering cultural restlessness of the prewar years. The postwar crisis of values took many forms. The younger generation, especially college students, boisterously assailed older conventions of behavior. Taking advantage of prosperity and the mobility afforded by the automobile, they threw noisy parties, consumed bootleg liquor, flocked to jazz clubs, and danced the Charleston.

They also discussed sex freely and sometimes indulged openly in premarital sexual experimentation. Wrote novelist F. Scott Fitzgerald, "None of the Victorian mothers had any idea how casually their daughters were accustomed to be kissed." The ideas of Sigmund Freud, the Viennese physician whose studies of human sexuality first appeared in the 1890s, enjoyed a popular vogue in the 1920s, often in grossly oversimplified form.

But hard evidence for the "sexual revolution" of the 1920s remains skimpy. Premarital sexual activity may have increased, but it was still widely disapproved of by the young as well as their elders. Courtship patterns did change, however. In earlier periods "courting" implied a serious intention of marriage. In the 1920s the informal ritual of "dating" emerged, allowing young people to test compatibility and to gain confidence in dealing with the opposite sex without necessarily contemplating marriage.

The double standard, holding women to a stricter code of sexual conduct than men, remained in force. Young men could boast of their sexual activity, but "fast" women might be ostracized. The male's traditional role in initiating sexual activity also survived. Nonetheless, the 1920s did see some liberation for women. Female sexuality was acknowledged more openly. Skirts grew shorter, makeup (once the badge of the prostitute) appeared, and petticoats and constricting corsets disappeared. A trim, almost boyish figure replaced the Gibson girl as the ideal beauty. Thousands of young women began smoking cigarettes in defiance of convention.

Moral guardians protested these changes. A Methodist bishop denounced the new dances that brought "the bodies of men and women in unusual relation to each other." In 1925 when the president of the women's college Bryn Mawr permitted students to smoke, others were outraged.

The flapper—a sophisticated, fashionable, plea-

Doing the Charleston: A St. Louis Dance Contest in 1925
Media events like this helped shape the image of the 1920s as frivolous and pleasure mad. Originating among African-Americans of Charleston, South Carolina, the Charleston was popularized by the all-black Broadway musical review of 1923, Runnin' Wild.

sure-mad young woman—summed up the "flaming youth" of the twenties. The creation of magazine illustrator John Held, Jr., the flapper symbolized an elaborate complex of cultural values. Her bobbed hair, defiant cigarette, dangling beads, heavy make-up, and shockingly short skirt epitomized the rebelliousness that composed at least a part of the youth culture of the twenties.

Like the flapper, the Jazz Age itself—the "Roaring Twenties"—was partially a mass-media and novelistic creation. F. Scott Fitzgerald's romanticized interpretation of the affluent postwar young, *This Side of Paradise* (1920), spawned many imitators. Fitzgerald himself was only twenty-four when his novel of the "lost generation" appeared. With his sculpted good looks, wavy blond hair, and striking green eyes, he both wrote about and personified the Jazz Age. Flush with royalties, he and his wife, Zelda, partied away the early twenties in New York, Paris, and the French Mediterranean. A moralist at heart, Fitzgerald both admired and deplored his Jazz Age contemporaries. His finest novel, *The Great Gatsby* (1925), captured not only the gilded existence of the superrich and social climbers of the 1920s but also the cold-hearted selfishness and romantic illusions that ruled their lives.

As a description of the 1920s, the "Jazz Age" label must be used carefully. The upheaval in manners and morals was limited to a narrow social stratum. Old values did not vanish entirely in a haze of alcoholic parties, suggestive dances, and backseat sex. Millions of Americans adhered to traditional ways and traditional standards. Millions more—farmers, blacks, industrial workers, recent immigrants—found economic survival more important than the latest dance craze or the newest flapper fads and fashions.

Nonetheless, stereotypes such as the "flapper" and "Jazz Age" do capture the brassy, urban-based mass culture and hedonism that swamped the idealism and social commitment of earlier years. And during the Great Depression of the 1930s, Americans would look back nostalgically to the supposedly carefree Roaring Twenties.

Other American Writers of the Twenties

Like Fitzgerald, many other young writers found the cultural turbulence of the 1920s stimulating. They forged a remarkable body of work equally hostile to the moralistic pieties of the old order and the business pieties of the new.

Sinclair Lewis's novels skewered postwar America. In *Main Street* (1920) Lewis caustically depicted the cultural barrenness and smug self-satisfaction of a fictional midwestern farm town. In *Babbitt* (1922) he wielded his satirical scalpel to dissect George F. Babbitt, a middle-aged real-estate agent trapped in stifling middle-class conformity, one of the most memorable figures of American literature.

The scorn for middle-class America that dripped from Lewis's pen found a journalistic outlet in the work of H. L. Mencken, a Baltimore newspaperman who founded and became coeditor of *The American Mercury* (1924), the Bible of the decade's alienated intellectuals. A penetrating stylist, Mencken ridiculed small-town Americans, Protestant fundamentalists, the middle class (which he labeled the Booboisie), and mainstream America generally. His withering essays on Wilson, Harding, Coolidge, and Bryan are classics of American political satire.

Some young American writers spent the 1920s abroad, often in France. Even before the war, T. S. Eliot, Ezra Pound, and Gertrude Stein had become expatriates, and after the armistice others joined them. The most famous expatriate, Ernest Hemingway, had been a reporter before serving as a Red Cross volunteer in Italy during the war. Seriously wounded, he settled in Paris in 1921 and began to write. In *The Sun Also Rises* (1926), he evoked the experiences of a group of young Americans and British, shattered by the war, as they drifted around Spain. Even writers who stayed at home underwent a kind of spiritual expatriation, distancing themselves from the dominant business culture. The novels of Willa Cather, for example, implicitly repudiated modern mass society by evoking alternatives ranging from early New Mexico (*Death Comes for the Archbishop*, 1927) to seventeenth-century Quebec (*Shadows on the Rock*, 1931).

World War I represented a seminal experience for this generation of writers. The best war novel, Hemingway's *A Farewell to Arms* (1929), powerfully depicted the war's futility and leaders' inflated rhetoric and captured the disillusionment of the author's generation. Hemingway and his counterparts gagged at Wilsonian rhetoric, village narrowness, and chamber-of-commerce cant, yet they remained committed to American ideals. A desire to create an authentic national culture inspired their literary efforts, just as it had earlier inspired Hawthorne, Melville, and Whitman.

The social changes of these years energized African-American cultural life as well. The 1920s would spawn the cultural flowering known as the Harlem Renaissance, a surge of creativity that spanned musical reviews, poems, and novels exploring the African-American experience.

Achievements in Architecture, Painting, and Music

The creative energies of the 1920s found other outlets. A burst of architectural activity, for example, transformed the skylines of larger cities. Chaotically eclectic, this architecture displayed enormous vitality. By the end of the decade, the United States boasted 377 buildings more than seventy stories tall.

Artists turned to America itself for inspiration—whether the real nation around them or the country that they held in memory. Painter Thomas Hart Benton evoked a half-mythic land of cowboys, pioneers, and riverboat gamblers, while Edward Hopper starkly sketched a nation of faded small towns and lonely cities. Charles DeMuth painted boldly geometric grain elevators, factories, and urban scenes; Georgia O'Keeffe's early paintings evoked the congestion and excitement of Manhattan; and Charles Sheeler recorded a dramatic series of photographs of Ford's River Rouge plant near Detroit.

Musical performers and composers contributed to the creativity of this extraordinary decade, drawing on the cultural resources they knew best. Composer Aaron Copland tapped into folk-music traditions, and other composers evoked the new urban-industrial America. Frederick Converse's 1927 tone poem about the automobile, "Flivver Ten Million," featured "Dawn in Detroit," "May Night by the Roadside," and "The Collision."

Above all, American music in the 1920s meant jazz. The Original Dixieland Jazz Band—five white musicians imitating the black jazz bands of New Orleans—debuted in New York in January 1917, and a jazz vogue was soon under way. But the white bands that introduced jazz drained it of much of its energy. Paul Whiteman, the most popular white band leader of the decade, offered watered-down "jazz" versions of standard tunes and light classical works. Of the white composers who wrote in jazz idiom, George Gershwin, with *Rhapsody in Blue* (1924) and *An American in Paris* (1928), was the most original.

Meanwhile, African-American musicians were replenishing the creative springs of authentic jazz. Guitar picker Huddie Ledbetter (nicknamed Leadbelly) performed his field shouts and raw songs before appreciative African-American audiences in the South. Singers including Bessie Smith and Gertrude ("Ma") Rainey drew packed audiences on Chicago's South Side and sold thousands of records. Trumpeter Louis ("Satchmo") Armstrong and band leader Fletcher Henderson did some of their most creative work in the 1920s, and the enormously talented black pianist, composer, and band leader Duke Ellington performed to packed audiences at Harlem's Cotton Club.

The Harlem Renaissance

Much of the floodtide of southern black migration washed onto the shores of Manhattan Island. By 1929 New York City had become home to 327,000 African-Americans, the majority crowded into Harlem, formerly an elite suburb. Racism and lack of education condemned most of the new residents to low-paying, unskilled jobs or to unemployment, although black Harlem did boast a small middle class of entrepreneurs, ministers, and funeral directors.

Ironically, amid the social problems and disease spawned by poverty and overcrowding, a vibrant African-American culture emerged in Harlem in the 1920s. The Cotton Club and other Harlem cabarets featured jazz geniuses such as Duke Ellington, Fletcher Henderson, and Jelly Roll Morton. Musical comedy flourished, and muralist Aaron Douglas, concert tenor Roland Hayes, and singer-actor Paul Robeson contributed to the cultural ferment.

Above all, the Harlem Renaissance was a literary movement. Poet Langston Hughes transformed the oral traditions of transplanted southern blacks into *The Weary Blues* (1926), while in *Cane* (1923) Jean Toomer combined poems, drama, and short stories to portray the efforts of a young northern mulatto to penetrate the mysterious, sensual world of the black South. Alain Locke, a Rhodes scholar who taught at historically black Howard University, assembled essays, poems, and short stories in *The New Negro* (1925), a landmark work that hailed the Harlem Renaissance as black America's "spiritual coming of age."

White America quickly took notice. Book publishers courted African-American authors, white patrons funded them, and white writers discovered and sometimes distorted African-American life. Eugene O'Neill's play *The Emperor Jones* (1921) starred Charles Gilpin as a fear-crazed West Indian tyrant. The 1925 novel *Porgy*, by Dubose and Dorothy Heyward, offered a sentimentalized portrait of Charleston's African-American community; as a play, *Porgy* won the Pulitzer Prize in 1927; and as a George Gershwin musical, *Porgy and Bess*, first produced in 1935, it entered the cultural mainstream.

Whites turned to Harlem for the sensuality, eroticism, and escape from taboos of its speakeasies, prostitutes, and readily available drugs. Packing the late-night jazz clubs and the pulsating dance reviews, they praised black culture for its "spontaneous," "primitive," or "spiritual" qualities. Few were aware of, or cared much about, the more prosaic realities of Harlem life. Nor did it bother them that the popular Cotton Club, controlled by gangsters, featured black performers but barred most blacks from the audience.

At the same time, whites were quick to withdraw patronage from African-American artists who violated these stereotypes. In the 1930s when Langston Hughes shifted his focus to urban poverty, his white patron reacted angrily. Hughes later wrote, "She felt that [Negros] were America's great link with the primitive. . . . I was only an American Negro. I was not Africa. I was Chicago and Kansas City and Broadway and Harlem."

The Harlem Renaissance lacked either a political framework or ties to the larger African-American experience. The writers and artists of the 1920s ignored the racism, discrimination, and economic troubles most blacks faced and reacted with hostility to Marcus Garvey's attempt to mobilize the urban black masses. The stock market crash in 1929 and the ensuing Great Depression ended the Harlem Renaissance. In 1940 Langston Hughes tersely wrote its epitaph: "The ordinary Negros hadn't heard of the Negro Renaissance. And if they had, it hadn't raised their wages any."

Nonetheless, for all its naïveté, the Harlem Renaissance left an important legacy. The post-World War II literary flowering that began with Ralph Ellison's *Invisible Man* and continued with the works of James Baldwin, Toni Morrison, and Alice Walker, among others, owed a substantial debt to the Harlem Renaissance. A fragile flower withered by the cold winds of the Depression, it nevertheless remains a monument to African-American cultural creativity even under difficult circumstances.

Advances in Science and Medicine

The scientific developments of the 1920s would reverberate for decades. The first long-range television transmission, from New York to Washington, occurred in 1927. Arthur H. Compton won a Nobel Prize for his studies on X rays, and Ernest O. Lawrence laid the theoretical groundwork for the construction of the first cyclotron, a high-energy-particle accelerator vital in nuclear-physics research. Physicist Robert Goddard studied rocketry and in 1926 launched the first successful liquid-fuel rocket. His predictions of lunar landings and deep-space exploration, ridiculed at the time, proved prophetic.

The 1920s saw important gains in medical research as well. Harvey Cushing made dramatic advances in neurosurgery, and chemist Harry Steenbock discovered how to create Vitamin D in milk by bombarding it with ultraviolet rays. New discoveries in the treatment of diphtheria, whooping cough, measles, and influenza helped to significantly lengthen life expectancy.

A few observers sensed that a new era of scientific advance was dawning. In 1925 Harvard philosopher Alfred North Whitehead underscored science's growing power. "Individually powerless," White had concluded, scientists were "ultimately the rulers of the world." To many, the prospect of such power was simply part of the array of disorienting social changes that made the 1920s unusually stressful and conflict-ridden.

A Society in Conflict

Indeed, American society endured deep strains in the 1920s. Immigration, dizzying technological advances, urban growth, and Darwinian theory had shattered the cultural homogeneity of an earlier day. Rural Americans uneasily surveyed the mushrooming cities, native-born Protestants apprehensively eyed the swelling ranks of Catholics and Jews; and upholders of traditional standards viewed the revolution in manners and morals with dismay.

Immigration Restriction

Fed by wartime superpatriotism, the long-standing impulse to turn America into a nation of like-minded, culturally identical people culminated in the National Origins Act of 1924. This restrictive measure placed a ceiling of 164,000 on annual immigration and, more important, limited the number of people from any nation to 2 percent of the total number of that "national origin" living in the United States in 1890. Because the great influx of southern and eastern Europeans had occurred after 1890, the act virtually ended immigration from those areas. Calvin Coolidge observed when he signed the law: "America must be kept American." The law also excluded Asians entirely, deeply insulting the Chinese and Japanese.

In 1929 Congress made 1920 the base year for determining "national origins," but even this slightly liberalized formula kept the quota for Poland at 6,500; for Italy, 5,800; and for Russia, 2,700. This quota system, which survived into the 1960s, represented the most enduring counterattack of rural, native-born America against the immigrant cities.

Most proponents of restriction regarded Asia and southern and eastern Europe as sources of "undesirables," and the laws reflected this bias. No restrictions, however, were placed on immigration from the Western Hemisphere, and consequently immigration from French Canada and Latin America soared during the 1920s. By 1930 at least 2 million Mexican-born people lived in the United States. California's Mexican-American population quadrupled, from 90,000 to nearly 360,000, in the decade. Many of these newcomers became migratory workers in large-scale agribusiness.

The Sacco-Vanzetti Case

The nativist, antiradical sentiments that produced the 1919 Red Scare and the 1924 National Origins Act emerged starkly in a controversy over a Massachusetts murder case that quickly became a cause célèbre. On April 15, 1920, robbers shot and killed the paymaster and guard of a shoe factory in South Braintree, Massachusetts, and stole nearly $18,000. Three weeks later, two Italian immigrants, Nicola Sacco and Bartolomeo Vanzetti, were arrested and charged with the murders. They were found guilty in 1921.

Bare facts cannot convey the texture of the case or the emotions it aroused. Sacco and Vanzetti were avowed anarchists, and from the beginning the prosecution harped on their radicalism. The judge, a conservative Republican, was openly hostile to the defendants, whom he privately called "those anarchist bastards." The Sacco-Vanzetti case in fact mirrored the larger divisions in society. Nativists dwelled on the defendants' immigrant origins, conservatives insisted that the alien anarchists had to die, and prominent liberals rallied behind them.

In 1927 a commission appointed by the Massachusetts governor to review the case upheld the guilty verdict. Sacco and Vanzetti were executed in the electric chair. But whether they committed the murders remains uncertain. The original case against them was circumstantial and far from airtight. Recent findings, including ballistics tests on Sacco's gun, suggest that at least Sacco may have been guilty. But the poisonous political climate that tainted the trial remains indisputable, as does the case's importance in exposing divisions in American society.

The Ku Klux Klan

Nativism erupted viciously in the revived Ku Klux Klan. The original Klan had faded in the 1870s, but in November 1915 a group of hooded men met at Stone Mountain, Georgia, to revive it.

In 1920 two Atlanta public-relations specialists propelled the Klan into a national organization by stressing nativism and white supremacy. A recruitment campaign promised money to everyone within an elaborate sales web. The enterprising Atlantans held the exclusive rights to sell everything from Klan robes and masks to the genuine Chattahoochee River water used in initiation rites. This elaborate scam succeeded beyond anyone's wildest dreams. By the mid-1920s, estimates of membership in the Klan and its auxiliary, Women of the Klan, ranged from 2 million to 5 million. The revived Klan, its targets not only blacks but Catholics, Jews, and immigrants, thrived in the Midwest and Far West as well as the South. Most of its members came from blue-collar ranks.

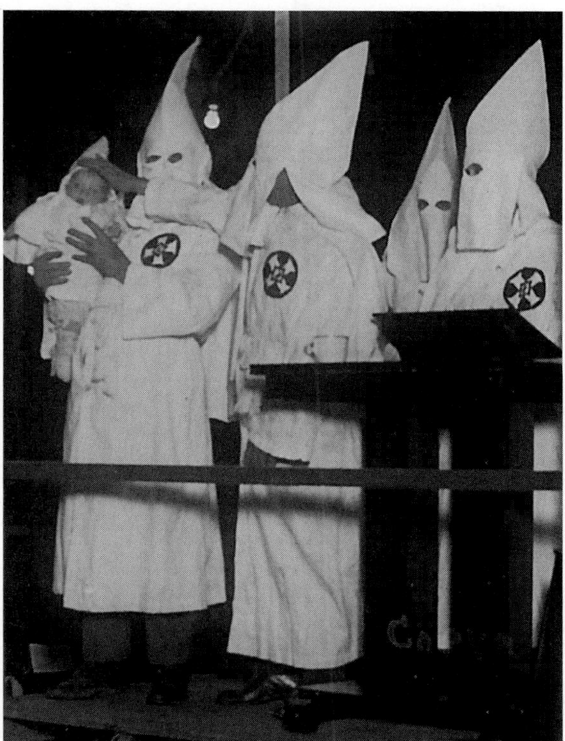

A Ku Klux Klan Ceremony on Long Island in the Early 1920s
The baby has been outfitted with its own white hood and robe. During a brief heyday after World War I, the revived Klan won many adherents all over the country to its message of white supremacy, moral purity, and 100 percent Americanism.

During its brief heyday, the Klan exercised real political power in many areas. In Oklahoma the Klan-controlled legislature impeached and removed an anti-Klan governor. The Klan elected a governor in Oregon and pushed through legislation (later overturned by the Supreme Court) requiring all the state's children to attend public schools.

Klan bigotry varied from region to region. In the South the antiblack theme loomed large, but Klaverns in the North and West more often targeted Catholics and Jews. In the Southwest the Klan focused on violators of prohibition and traditional morality, including adulterers and men who did not support their families.

The Klan filled important needs for its members. Although riddled with corruption at the top, the organization consisted primarily of ordinary people, not criminals or fanatics. The Klan's promise to restore the nation to an imagined purity—ethnic, moral, and religious—appealed powerfully to ill-educated, deeply religious, and economically marginal Americans disoriented by rapid social and moral change. Klan membership, moreover, bestowed a sense of importance and group cohesion on people who doubted their own worth. The Klan's rituals, ceremonials, and burning crosses lit up drab lives. One member wrote, "Who can look upon a multitude of white-robed Klansmen without thinking . . . of that throng of white-robed saints in the Glory Land?" But while the individual Klansman may seem more pitiful than sinister, the movement as a whole was violent. Klan members used intimidation, threats, beatings, and even murder in their quest for a "purified" America.

In March 1925 Indiana's politically influential Grand Dragon, David Stephenson, pressed bootleg liquor on a young secretary, forced her on a Pullman train, and raped her. When she later swallowed poison, Stephenson and his henchmen refused to call a physician. The woman died, and the Grand Dragon went to jail for first-degree manslaughter. From prison he revealed details of pervasive political corruption in Indiana. Its high moral pretensions shredded, the Klan faded rapidly but did not die. After World War II it would again surface as a malignant influence in American life.

The Garvey Movement

Among African-Americans, the decade's social strains ignited a different kind of mass movement. Blacks' widespread escape from southern rural poverty and racism led only to northern ghetto poverty similarly exacerbated by racism. Many poor urban African-Americans turned for relief to the spellbinding orator Marcus Garvey and his Universal Negro Improvement Association (UNIA). Garvey glorified all things black, urged black economic cooperation, and founded a chain of UNIA grocery stores and other businesses. He called on the world's blacks to return to "Motherland Africa" and establish a nation "strong enough to lend protection to the members of our race scattered all over the world." An estimated 80,000 blacks joined the UNIA, and thousands more felt the lure of Garvey's hypnotic oratory, the uplift of rousing UNIA parades, and the seduction of Garvey's dream of a mass return to Africa. White Americans were not the only people to find Garvey's mobilization of the black masses unsettling. Middle-class leaders of the African-American church and the NAACP, including W. E. B. Du Bois, were among Garvey's sharpest critics.

In 1923, however, a federal court convicted Garvey of fraud in connection with his Black Star Steamship Company. After two years' imprisonment, he was deported to Jamaica. Without this charismatic leader, the UNIA collapsed. But as the first mass movement in black America, it revealed the discontent seething in the ghettos and the potential for large-scale activism. "In a world where black is despised," wrote an African-American newspaper reporter upon Garvey's deportation, "he taught them that black is beautiful."

Fundamentalism and the Scopes Trial

In the half-century before 1920, American Protestantism had been severely tried. The prestige of science had increased steadily, challenging religion's cultural standing. Scholars had dissected the Bible's historical origins; psychologists had explained the religious impulse in terms of human emotional needs. Meanwhile, Catholic and Jewish immigrants had poured in.

Liberal Protestants responded by accepting the findings of science and emphasizing social service to the immigrants. But a powerful reaction, fundamentalism, was building. Named after *The Fundamentals*, a series of pamphlets published from 1909 to 1914, Protestant fundamentalism insisted on the divine inspiration of every word in the Bible, on the Genesis version of Creation, and on the virgin birth and resurrection of Jesus.

In the early 1920s fundamentalists took aim at the theory of evolution. Charles Darwin's ideas seemed to them a blatant rejection of biblical truth. In 1921–1922 fundamentalist legislators introduced bills to prohibit the teaching of evolution in twenty states' public schools, and several southern states enacted such legislation. Fundamentalism's best-known champion, aging politician William Jennings Bryan, vigorously endorsed the anti-evolution cause.

In 1925, when the Tennessee legislature outlawed the teaching of evolution in public schools, the American Civil Liberties Union (ACLU) volunteered to defend any teacher willing to challenge the law. A young high-school biology teacher in Dayton, Tennessee, John T. Scopes, accepted the offer. Scopes read a description of Darwin's theory to his class and was duly arrested.

Famed criminal lawyer Clarence Darrow headed the ACLU team of lawyers, and William Jennings Bryan enthusiastically assisted the prosecution. Journalists poured into Dayton, and radio stations broadcast the proceedings live. The Scopes "monkey trial" became an overnight sensation.

The trial's symbolic climax came when Darrow cross-examined Bryan on his religious beliefs and scientific knowledge. As Bryan insisted on the literal accuracy of the Bible, his ignorance of vast realms of human knowledge became painfully clear. Darrow succeeded in humiliating Bryan and ridiculing his ideas. The local jury found Scopes guilty, but the larger verdict, the one that really counted, differed. The Dayton trial marked a decisive setback for fundamentalism.

After the trial, fundamentalism diminished in mainstream Protestantism, but many local congregations and scores of radio preachers continued to embrace the traditional faith. Publicity, skilled musicians, and a flamboyant pulpit style enabled evangelist Billy Sunday to preach his fundamentalist message to 10,000 people at a time. Zealous new denominations and "full gospel" churches carried on the cause. Evangelist Aimee Semple McPherson regularly filled the 5,200 seats of her Angelus Temple in Los Angeles and reached thousands more by radio. Her followers embraced the beautiful, white-gowned McPherson's fundamentalist theology while reveling in her mastery of mass entertainment. In many ways she anticipated the television evangelists of a later day. When she died in 1944, her International Church of the Foursquare Gospel had more than 600 branches. Clearly, although fundamentalism had suffered a severe blow at Dayton, Tennessee, it was far from dead.

Prohibition

The fissure so evident in the Klan movement and in the Scopes trial also shaped the decade-long struggle to rid America of alcoholic beverages. Prohibition was simultaneously a way to deal with the serious social problems associated with alcohol abuse and a sign of native-born Americans' struggle to maintain cultural and political dominance over the immigrant cities. Both components of the anti-alcohol crusade loomed large in the 1920s.

The Election of 1928

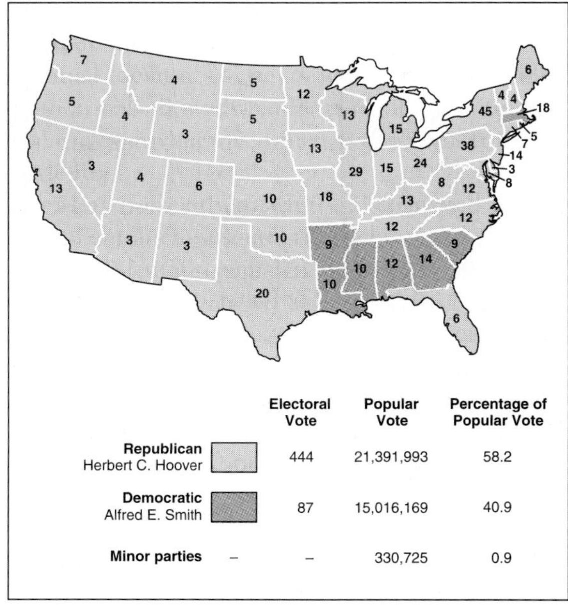

	Electoral Vote	Popular Vote	Percentage of Popular Vote
Republican Herbert C. Hoover	444	21,391,993	58.2
Democratic Alfred E. Smith	87	15,016,169	40.9
Minor parties –	–	330,725	0.9

When the Eighteenth Amendment took effect in January 1920, prohibitionists rejoiced. Their cause had triumphed. Saloons closed; liquor advertising stopped; arrests for drunkenness dwindled. But by the end of the decade, prohibition was discredited, and in 1933 it ended. What went wrong? Essentially, the prohibition debacle illustrates the virtual impossibility in a democracy of enforcing rules of behavior with which a significant portion of the population disagrees.

From the beginning, enforcement of the Volstead Act, the 1919 law that established the Prohibition Bureau within the Treasury Department, was underbudgeted and largely ineffective, especially in strongly antiprohibition states. New York, for example, repealed its prohibition-enforcement law in 1923. Further, the Volstead Act was riddled with loopholes. For example, alcohol could be purchased for religious or medicinal purposes and could be manufactured in private homes for personal consumption. Alcoholic beverages were not illegal; only their commercial manufacture, sale, or distribution was.

Would-be drinkers grew bold as enforcement faltered. For young people already rebelling against traditional standards, alcohol's illegality added to its appeal. Every city boasted speakeasies where customers could buy drinks, and rumrunners routinely smuggled in liquor. Many people even concocted their own home brew. By 1929 alcohol consumption had risen to 70 percent of the prewar level.

Organized crime entered the liquor business, facilitating drinkers' efforts to circumvent the law. In Chicago rival gangs engaged in bloody wars to control the liquor business; the 1920s saw 550 gangland killings. By 1929 Chicago mob king Al Capone controlled a network of speakeasies with annual profits of $60 million. Chicago's heavily publicized crime wave appeared dramatic proof of prohibition's failure. A reform designed to produce a more orderly, law-abiding America seemed to be having the opposite effect.

Prohibition became still another battleground in the decade's cultural wars. The "drys"—usually native-born Protestants—praised prohibition as a necessary and legitimate reform. The "wets"—liberals, alienated intellectuals, Jazz Age rebels, urban immigrants—condemned it as moralistic meddling. Prohibition figured prominently in the 1928 presidential campaign. Democratic candidate Al Smith made no secret of his support for repeal of the Eighteenth Amendment. Republican Herbert Hoover praised prohibition as "a great social and economic experiment, noble in motive and far-reaching in purpose." In 1931 a presidential commission acknowledged the breakdown of prohibition but urged its retention. Nevertheless, in 1933 prohibition ended with the Eighteenth Amendment's repeal. By then the nation had other worries.

Hoover at the Helm

Herbert Hoover, overwhelmingly elected president in 1928, seemed ideal to sustain the nation's booming prosperity. He brought a distinctive social and political philosophy that reflected his background in engineering.

The Election of 1928

The presidential candidates of 1928, Al Smith and Herbert Hoover, personified opposite ends of the political and social spectrum. Both self-made men, they were "as far apart as Pilsner and Coca-Cola," as H. L. Mencken cracked.

Four-term governor of New York, Smith easily sewed up the Democratic nomination. A Catholic and a "wet," his brown derby perpetually askew, Smith exuded the flavor of immigrant New York. Originally a machine politician, he represented progressivism's urban-immigrant component, championing social welfare and civil rights. Herbert Hoover won the Republican nomination with equal ease. Conservative party leaders, however, remained suspicious of this intelligent but aloof progressive who had never run for public office and had spent most of his pre-1920 adult life overseas. An Iowan, orphaned early in life, Hoover had put himself through Stanford University and made a fortune as a mining engineer in China and Australia. His service as wartime food administrator saved millions of lives in Europe and earned him a place in the Harding and Coolidge cabinets.

Eschewing the handshaking and baby kissing of the campaign trail, Hoover delivered laboriously composed radio speeches in a boring monotone so dull that people overlooked the originality of his ideas. Smith campaigned spiritedly throughout the country—a strategy that may have harmed him, for his big-city wisecracking and accent repelled many Americans west of the Hudson.

Smith's Catholicism figured importantly in the campaign as he faced a backlash of prejudice. Although Hoover urged tolerance, and Smith denied any conflict between his Catholic faith and the duties of the presidency, many Protestants, especially rural southerners and urban fundamentalists, found the issue of Smith's religion vital. But prosperity, not religion, was the decisive campaign issue. Republicans took credit for the booming economy and warned that Smith would create "soup kitchens instead of busy factories." Hoover predicted "the final triumph over poverty."

Hoover won in a landslide victory, making deep inroads in the Democratic "solid South." Smith carried a meager 87 electoral votes to Hoover's 444. But beneath Hoover's victory lay evidence of an emerging political realignment. Smith did well in the midwestern farm belt among financially strapped Republicans and in northern cities, where first- and second-generation Catholic and Jewish immigrants voted Democratic in record numbers. In 1924 the nation's twelve largest cities had all gone Republican; in 1928 Smith carried all twelve. If prosperity should end, these signs suggested, the Republican party would face trouble.

Herbert Hoover's Social Thought

Americans looked hopefully to their new president,

the Great Engineer. Hoover had a notable record of achievement and a well-developed social philosophy, expounded in his book *American Individualism* (1922). Although his own life followed the classic rags-to-riches formula, Hoover based his social outlook on his Quakerism, humanitarian activities, and engineering experience.

Like Theodore Roosevelt, Hoover believed that cutthroat competition was anachronistic. Rational economic development demanded corporate cooperation in marketing, wage policy, raw-material allocation, and product standardization. The economy should operate like a smoothly functioning machine. Capitalism, Hoover argued further, had social obligations. He welcomed the growth of welfare capitalism. But above all, Hoover believed in voluntarism. The cooperative, socially responsive economic order that he envisioned would arise through the voluntary action of capitalist leaders, not through government coercion or power struggles pitting labor against management.

As secretary of commerce, Hoover had reorganized the Commerce Department along rational lines, making it a model for private industry, and tried to accelerate the trend toward corporate consolidation and cooperation. He had convened more than 250 conferences at which business leaders discussed unemployment, pricing, labor-management relations, and the virtues of trade associations. He urged higher wages to increase consumer purchasing power and in 1923 persuaded the steel industry to adopt an eight-hour workday in the name of efficiency.

But Hoover's ideas had limits. He displayed more interest in cooperation among capitalists than among consumers or workers, and he greatly overestimated the role of altruism in business decision making. His unqualified opposition to direct government economic intervention would bring him to grief later in his administration when such intervention became urgently necessary.

Applying his ideology to specific issues, Hoover compiled an impressive record early in his administration. He created commissions to study public-policy issues, gathered data for policy makers' guidance, and established the Federal Farm Board to cope with farmers' problems. Indeed, as the summer of 1929 turned to autumn, the Hoover administration seemed off to a promising start. But ominous long-term economic trends were converging toward a crisis that would overwhelm and destroy the methodical Hoover's presidency.

CONCLUSION

Memorable events bracket the 1920s: World War I at the beginning, a catastrophic stock-market crash at the end. Americans of the era had to cope with massive technological and social change, adapting themselves to a mass-production, mass-consumption, mass-culture metropolitan world that had seemingly emerged overnight.

The most interesting responses to these broad changes unfolded outside politics. The stresses and disorientation that produced bitter social conflict also made the 1920s one of the most creative decades in American cultural and intellectual history. Champions of prohibition and fundamentalism, the Ku Klux Klan, rebellious youth, urban blacks who cheered Marcus Garvey, and the novelists and poets who revitalized American literature were all trying to make sense of an unfamiliar, often threatening social order. The twenties saw political failure and reactionary social movements, but the decade also generated positive and lasting achievements.

CHRONOLOGY

1915 Modern Ku Klux Klan founded.

1919 Volstead Act.

1920–1921 Sharp postwar recession; agricultural prices plummet.

1920 Warren G. Harding elected president.
Eighteenth Amendment takes effect.
F. Scott Fitzgerald, *This Side of Paradise*.
Sinclair Lewis, *Main Street*.

1921 Recovery from recession; economic boom begins; agriculture remains depressed.
Sheppard-Towner Act.
National Woman's party founded by Alice Paul.

1921–1922 Washington Naval Arms Conference.

1922 Supreme Court declares child-labor laws unconstitutional.
Herbert Hoover, *American Individualism*.
Sinclair Lewis, *Babbitt*.

1923 Harding dies; Calvin Coolidge becomes president.
Supreme Court strikes down minimum-wage laws for women.
Jean Toomer, *Cane*.

1924 Teapot Dome scandals investigated.
National Origins Act.
Calvin Coolidge elected president.
McNary-Haugen farm bill introduced.

1925 Scopes trial.
Ku Klux Klan scandal in Indiana.
Alain Locke, *The New Negro*.
F. Scott Fitzgerald, *The Great Gatsby*.

1926 Ernest Hemingway, *The Sun Also Rises*.
Langston Hughes, *The Weary Blues*.

1927 *The Jazz Singer*, first sound movie.
Coolidge vetoes the McNary-Haugen bill.
Willa Cather, *Death Comes for the Archbishop*.
Execution of Sacco and Vanzetti.
Charles A. Lindbergh's transatlantic flight.

1928 Kellogg-Briand Pact.
Herbert Hoover elected president.

1929 Sheppard-Towner program terminated.
Hallelujah, first all-black movie.
Ernest Hemingway, *A Farewell to Arms*.

FOR FURTHER READING

Charles C. Alexander, *Here the Country Lies: Nationalism and the Arts in Twentieth Century America* (1980). A useful revisionist study whose chapters on the 1920s stress the decade's positive achievements.

Loren Baritz, ed., *The Culture of the Twenties* (1970). A rich collection of primary documents with a helpful introductory essay.

Paul Carter, *The Twenties in America* (1968) and *Another Part of the Twenties* (1977). Two essays offering refreshingly personal interpretive judgments.

Lynn Dumenil, *The Modern Temper: America in the 1920s* (1995). A study offering a wealth of fresh insights, especially on often neglected groups and movements.

Ellis W. Hawley, *The Great War and the Search for a Modern Order* (1979). An economic study that traces the emergence (and collapse in 1929) of the first mass-consumption society.

William E. Leuchtenberg, *The Perils of Prosperity, 1914–1932* (1970). A cogent examination of the serious thinkers and mass culture of the twenties.

Nancy MacLean, *Behind the Mask of Chivalry: The Making of the Second Ku Klux Klan* (1994). An exploration of Klan members' anxieties about corporate growth, feminism, sexuality, and other issues of the 1920s.

Joan Shelley Rubin, *The Making of Middle-Brow Culture* (1992). An interpretive study of the Book-of-the-Month Club and other 1920s institutions by which high culture reached a larger public.

CHAPTER 25

Crash, Depression, and New Deal

In 1929 a stock-market collapse triggered the worst depression in American history. Crippled by his belief that voluntarism held the key to relieving individual suffering and that the economy would heal itself, President Herbert Hoover wrestled ineffectively with the crisis.

Franklin D. Roosevelt, who succeeded Hoover in 1933, dominated American politics until his death in 1945. As president, the forceful, ebullient Roosevelt not only directed American efforts to overcome the depression but also, as commander in chief during World War II, led the global struggle against Germany, Italy, and Japan.

This chapter focuses on the Great Depression and the New Deal, Roosevelt's economic and social programs to promote national recovery. A dizzying array of approaches, laws, and agencies characterized the New Deal, but certain patterns do emerge. From 1933 to 1935, the first phase of the New Deal emphasized relief

(Right) President Franklin D. Roosevelt with his dog Fala and a future voter

and recovery. While Roosevelt urged unity, his administration and a heavily Democratic Congress battled massive unemployment, business stagnation, and agricultural distress. Around 1935, responding to a political challenge on the Left and buoyed by a ringing endorsement in the 1934 midterm election, the New Deal shifted to a more reformist course. The so-called Second New Deal (1935–1938) stressed business regulation as well as social programs and tax policies benefiting working people, small farmers, and others at the low end of the economic scale. Arguments still roil about specific New Deal programs and even its general merits, but no one disputes that the New Deal marked a watershed in twentieth-century American history.

The laws and agencies that made up the New Deal represented a complex amalgam of approaches influenced by political crosscurrents and countless individuals. But in the public mind, the New Deal meant Roosevelt. Loved by some almost as a member of the family, and reviled by others as a demagogue and an opportunist, Roosevelt is recognized today as a consummate politician whose administration set the national political agenda for a generation.

Crash and Depression

Like a joyride that ends in screeching tires and crunching metal, the prosperity of the 1920s crashed in October 1929 with the stock-market collapse. The ensuing depression reached into every household in the land. President Hoover's commitment to private initiative and his horror of governmental coercion handcuffed him. In November 1932 a disillusioned nation gave an overwhelming electoral mandate to the Democratic party and Franklin D. Roosevelt.

The Crash

Stock prices had climbed throughout the 1920s as investors responded to growing prosperity and increasing productivity. Beginning in 1928, optimism turned into frenzy as speculators plunged into the market. Stock prices floated into what one contemporary called "the blue and cloudless empyrean." Stock speculation seemed the perfect form of gambling for an egalitarian society: everybody won.

In 1925 the market value of all stocks stood at $27 billion; by October 1929 it had hit $87 billion. Nine million Americans "played the market," often with borrowed funds. Optimistic pronouncements drew people in. "Everybody Ought to Be Rich," proclaimed a *Ladies' Home Journal* article. Stockbrokers loaned speculators up to 75 percent of a stock's purchase price, and credit buying became the rule. Brokers' loans reached $6 billion by the summer of 1929. Easy-credit policies on the part of the Federal Reserve Board, along with Treasury Secretary Andrew Mellon's pressure for tax cuts, increased the money available for speculation.

With corporations hungry for their share of speculators' money, new securities "were manufactured almost like cakes of soap," in one historian's words, simply because money could be made from their sale. Brokerage agents grew rich peddling American Can, Studebaker, Houston Oil, and Westinghouse. Totally unregulated "investment trusts," akin to today's mutual funds, offered novices the benefit of the supposedly superior wisdom of seasoned investors. This speculative frenzy rested on a precarious prosperity. Agriculture, mining, and textiles remained depressed, and automobile production slowed in the late 1920s. In 1928–1929 construction declined by 25 percent.

In July 1928 the Federal Reserve Board tried to dampen speculation by increasing interest rates, and early in 1929 it warned member banks not to lend money for stock-market speculation. But speculators paid up to 20 percent interest, and major banks and large corporations poured millions into the money market—somewhat like dumping gasoline onto a fire.

On October 24, 1929—"Black Thursday"—the collapse began. As prices plummeted, traders panicked. Some stocks found no buyers at all. Mounted police broke up crowds milling outside the New York Stock Exchange, while speculators huddled around ticker-tape machines "like friends around the bedside of a stricken friend," according to the *New York Times*. At midday a group of powerful bankers temporarily allayed the panic by issuing a reassuring statement and ostentatiously buying $30 million worth of major stocks. After a weak rally on Friday, prices continued to fall. The climax came on Tuesday, October 29, when a record 16 million stocks changed hands in frantic trading, most at inconceivably low prices. In the ensuing weeks, feeble upswings in stock prices alternated with further plunges.

On Black Thursday President Hoover issued the first of a series of optimistic pronouncements. "The fundamental business of the country . . . is on a sound and prosperous basis," he asserted. He was wrong. By mid-November stocks had lost $30 billion in value. The stock-market crash revealed the depth of other economic problems underlying the glittering prosperity of the 1920s.

Onset of the Depression

Despite confident predictions that business activity would quickly revive, the economy went into a prolonged tailspin that locked the country in a profound depression. Although it bottomed out in 1933, its effects lingered throughout the decade.

What caused the depression? Structural weaknesses in the American economy played a major role. Rises in productivity led not to higher wages but to high corporate profits. Between 1920 and 1929 the well-to-do increased their share of American income from 22 percent to 26 percent and spent much of that income on luxuries—discretionary spending that halted abruptly in 1929. The 40 percent of Americans at the lowest end of the economic scale received only 12 percent of the national income by 1929. At the same time, overproduction became a problem, in part because those at the lower end could not afford to buy goods, and consequently the summer of 1929 saw severe cutbacks in the output of durable commodities such as automobiles, tires, and homes. The decline in farm prices represented another weak spot. And some economists argue that major industries, such as railroads, steel, textiles, and mining, were lagging technologically and could not attract sufficient investment to stimulate the economy.

Other economists focus on the collapse of the banking system. The Federal Reserve System, they charge, failed to assure an adequate money supply to enable the economy to bounce back from the crash. In fact, the money supply did shrink by some 38 percent, but whether the Fed can be faulted is still hotly debated.

All analysts emphasize that the U.S. depression was part of a global economic crisis. Enfeebled by the devastation of World War I, massive debt payments, and a huge trade imbalance with the United States, European economies crashed in 1931. Austria's biggest bank failed in May; Germany imposed currency controls in July; Great Britain abandoned the gold standard in September. This larger crisis worsened an already bad American situation.

Statistics tell the bleak story of depression America. The gross national product slumped from $104 billion in 1929 to $59 billion in 1932. Farm prices, already low, fell nearly 60 percent from 1929 to 1932. Wheat prices plunged from $1.04 a bushel to $.51. Railroad corporations controlling one-third of the nation's track fell into bankruptcy. The banking system neared collapse as 5,500 banks closed their doors by early 1933. Unemployment soared from 3 percent in 1929 to 25 percent in 1933; 13 million Americans had no jobs, and many who worked faced cuts in wages and hours. These statistics translated into idled factories, bankrupted farms, closed banks, and hopelessness etched on the faces of the jobless as they waited in breadlines and trudged the streets looking for work.

The Depression's Human Toll

Most of the unemployed supported families, and so we must multiply the unemployment figures several times over to calculate the magnitude of human distress. The epidemic of bank closings deprived millions of their savings and even their pensions. African-Americans, Mexican-Americans, sharecroppers, and other groups endured particular hardships (see Chapter 26). Thousands of rural families lost their homes. In 1933 alone more than 5 percent of the nation's farms underwent mortgage foreclosures or forced sales because of tax delinquency. Reared on a work ethic that promised upward mobility in return for effort, many Americans found chronic unemployment a shattering psychic blow.

For the children of the depression, poor diet and inadequate medical and dental care laid the groundwork for long-term health problems. Malnutrition, rickets, pellagra, and other diet-related ailments increased alarmingly. By early 1933, as local school boards shortened the school year and even closed schools, more than 300,000 children were out of school.

Newspapers conveyed the human dimensions of the crisis by focusing on dramatic vignettes. The *New York Times* described "Hoover Valley"—a section of Central Park where jobless men built makeshift shelters of boxes and packing crates. In Washington State, reporters wrote of a rash of forest fires set by men hoping to earn a few dollars as fire fighters. Some gave up. The suicide rate climbed 30 percent from 1928 to 1932. In Youngstown, Ohio, a jobless father of ten jumped to his death as authorities prepared to evict his family from its home. Although extreme, such stories portrayed the terrible social costs of the nation's worst depression.

Hoover's Response

Historically, Americans had equated economic depressions with acts of nature—one simply had to ride out the storm. Although conservative cabinet members held this view, Hoover disagreed. Drawing on the legacy of progressive reform and his own experiences as food administrator during World War I, he responded to the crisis with energy and determination. But his course reflected his ideological commitment to localism and private initiative. He told an Iowa farm audience, "Every time we find solutions outside of government, we have not only strengthened character, but we have preserved our sense of real self-government."

Business leaders whom Hoover summoned to the White House pledged to maintain wages and employment. Seeing unemployment as a local issue, Hoover called on municipal and state governments to create public-works projects. In October 1930 he established the Emergency Committee for Employment to coordinate voluntary relief agencies, and in 1931 he persuaded the nation's largest bankers to establish the National Credit Corporation to lend smaller banks money for business loans. The crisis only intensified. As early as November 1930, voters rendered a harsh verdict on Hoover's policies: Republicans lost eight Senate seats and control of the House of Representatives as well.

Hoover's strategy failed dismally. Unemployment mounted, and in 1931 U.S. Steel, General Motors, and other large corporations broke their pledges and announced large wage cuts. Public charities and local welfare agencies faltered. In Philadelphia, joblessness rose to 300,000. The city cut relief payments to $4.23 per family per week and in June 1932 suspended them entirely.

By 1932, with an election looming and the voluntarist approach discredited, Hoover endorsed an unprecedented federal response. In January Congress provided $2 billion in funding to a new agency, the Reconstruction Finance Corporation (RFC), to make loans to major economic institutions such as banks, railroads, and insurance companies. In February Hoover signed the Glass-Steagall Act, allocating $750 million of the government's gold reserves for loans to private businesses. In July he signed legislation authorizing the RFC to give $2 billion to state and local governments for public-works programs. But Hoover gained little political benefit.

Hoover blamed the depression on global forces and argued that only international measures would help. He advocated a one-year moratorium on war-debt and reparations repayments, a sensible plan but one that seemed irrelevant to Americans. In 1931, dreading an unbalanced budget, Hoover called for a tax increase, thereby further alienating voters.

The man once portrayed as a masterful manager and humane philanthropist was now portrayed as bumbling and hard-hearted. Unable to concede error, Hoover told an aide, "No president must ever admit that he has been wrong." He even continued to support the increasingly unpopular, and unsuccessful, prohibition acts.

Mounting Discontent and Protest

A dark mood spread over the nation. Midwestern farmers organized the Farmers' Holiday Association to force prices up by withholding grain and livestock from the market, and dairy farmers dumped thousands of gallons of milk. World War I veterans mounted the most alarming protest. In 1924 Congress had voted a veterans' bonus to be paid twenty years later. In 1931 Congress received a proposal to pay the bonus immediately, and in June 1932, 10,000 veterans, many jobless, descended on Washington to lobby for its passage. When Congress rejected the proposal in mid-June, several thousand "bonus marchers" and their families stayed on. They organized protest parades and built a makeshift settlement of tents and packing crates—one of many ironically named "Hoovervilles"—on Anacostia Flats in southeastern Washington, D.C.

Hoover, afraid that the bonus marchers were the forerunners of revolution, ordered them confined to Anacostia Flats. Army Chief of Staff General Douglas MacArthur decided to break up the settlement. On July 28 1,000 armed soldiers, equipped with tear gas, tanks, and machine guns, drove the veterans from their encampment and burned it to the ground. For many Americans, the image of armed troops using force against peaceful veterans symbolized the Hoover administration's insensitivity to human suffering.

The Election of 1932

Herbert Hoover ran unopposed for the 1932 Republican nomination. Smelling defeat, delegates to the Republican convention gloomily adopted a platform praising Hoover's antidepression measures.

The Democrats, in contrast, scented victory. They drafted a platform to heal the divisions that had weakened the party in the 1920s and to appeal to urban immigrants, farmers, and fiscal conservatives. Delegates gave New York's governor, Franklin D. Roosevelt, the two-thirds majority he needed for nomination. Breaking precedent, FDR accepted the nomination in person, promising "a new deal for the American people."

Roosevelt's campaign provided no clear sense of the direction in which he would lead the country. He called for "bold, persistent experimentation" and promised more attention to "the forgotten man at the bottom of the economic pyramid" but also attacked Hoover's "reckless" spending.

If his campaign lacked specifics, Roosevelt himself exuded confidence. Above all, he was not Hoover! On November 8 FDR and his running mate, John Nance Garner of Texas, received nearly 23 million votes, almost half again as many as the Republicans. Both houses of Congress went heavily Democratic. After twelve years of Republican rule, the Democrats were back in charge.

The New Deal Takes Shape

The Roosevelt years began with feverish activity as FDR proposed a staggering array of emergency measures and as Congress passed most by wide margins. A strategy emerged from the welter of bills: *industrial recovery* through business-government cooperation and federal spending; *agricultural recovery* through subsidized crop reductions; and *short-term emergency relief for the jobless*, provided by the federal government if necessary. Presiding over this bustle was a smiling FDR, cigarette holder jauntily tilted upward, a symbol of confidence and renewed hope for millions.

New Beginnings

Shortly before FDR's inauguration, Congress passed the Twentieth Amendment, ending the nation's thirteen-year flirtation with prohibition. Supporters argued that repeal would stimulate economic recovery by producing a tax bonanza on the sale of alcoholic beverages. It would be a new beginning, they asserted.

Roosevelt's inaugural address also set an optimistic tone. The new president dedicated his administration to helping people weather the crisis. "The only thing we have to fear is fear itself," he reassured an anxious population. Americans responded with a surge of support. Within a few days, half a million approving letters deluged the White House.

In many ways, FDR seemed an unlikely figure to rally Americans in the depression. Like his distant cousin Theodore Roosevelt, FDR was a member of the social elite. His Dutch-immigrant ancestors had been merchants and landed aristocrats for three centuries, and his Groton-Harvard-Columbia background found little resonance with the average American. However, a battle against polio that left him unable to walk but strong in spirit had prepared FDR to struggle against adversity and feel empathy with other people. As governor of New York when the depression struck, he had proposed such innovative measures as unemployment insurance, emergency relief, and a public-works program.

The Election of 1932

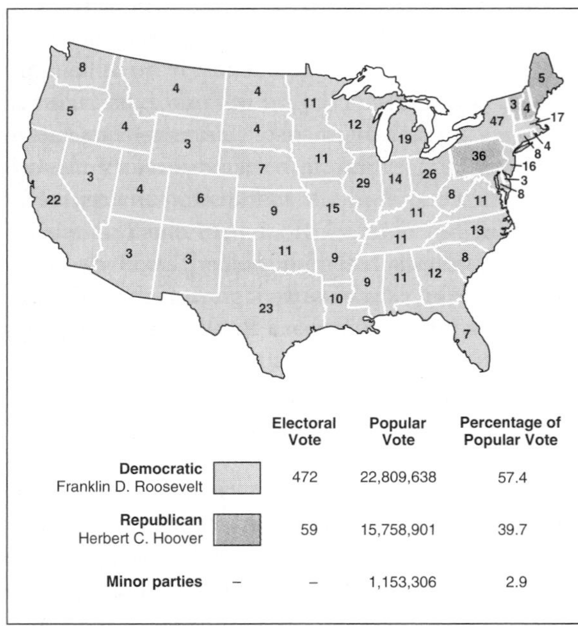

		Electoral Vote	Popular Vote	Percentage of Popular Vote
Democratic Franklin D. Roosevelt		472	22,809,638	57.4
Republican Herbert C. Hoover		59	15,758,901	39.7
Minor parties	–	–	1,153,306	2.9

Roosevelt entered the White House sensitive to the public mood and determined to restore the nation to economic health within the framework of capitalism and democracy. But he had no detailed agenda for achieving these goals. Not interested in theory, FDR encouraged competing proposals, compromised (or papered over) differences, and then threw his weight behind measures that he could sell to Congress and the people.

In New York Roosevelt had built up a circle of advisers, "the brain trust," many of them from universities. FDR sought a wide range of opinions, and his brain trust included both very conservative and very liberal viewpoints. Consequently, Roosevelt's New Deal reflected many ideological and political orientations.

Eleanor Roosevelt played a key White House role. Niece to Theodore Roosevelt, the president's wife had a keen social conscience and a background in Progressive Era settlement-house work. She influenced FDR's ideas by exposing him to reformers, social workers, and advocates of minority rights. She traveled ceaselessly and served as the eyes, ears, and sometimes the conscience for her wheelchair-bound husband. The Americans who poured out their troubles to her as they would to a personal friend had no idea of Eleanor Roosevelt's own emotional turmoil. She and Franklin had long been estranged and had found long-term intimacy outside their marriage, he with Lucy Mercer and she with Lorena Hickok. Details of their personal lives became public only years after their deaths.

Roosevelt's top political adviser, James Aloysius Farley, became postmaster general but spent more time on politics than on postage. He distributed patronage jobs, managed FDR's 1932 and 1936 campaigns, and smoothed White House relations with state and local Democrats. Bored by the substantive issues of the New Deal, Farley had a master sailor's sense of the treacherous currents of presidential politics.

Eleanor Roosevelt Visits a West Virginia Coal Mine, 1933
A New Yorker cartoon of 1933 portrayed one coal miner exclaiming to another, "Oh migosh, here comes Mrs. Roosevelt." But reality soon caught up with humor as the First Lady immersed herself in the plight of the poor and the exploited.

Roosevelt's cabinet reflected the diversity of the New Deal. Secretary of Labor Frances Perkins, the first woman cabinet member in U.S. history, had served as state industrial commissioner during FDR's years as governor of New York. Interior Secretary Harold Ickes was a prickly but able Republican progressive. Secretary of Agriculture Henry A. Wallace excelled as an agricultural economist and farm-policy theorist. Secretary of the Treasury Henry Morgenthau, a fiscal conservative, tolerated the unbalanced budgets if necessary to finance New Deal programs.

A host of other newcomers poured into Washington in 1933—former progressive reformers, settlement-house workers, political scientists, economics professors, bright young lawyers. They energized the capital, drafting bills, competing for the president's attention, and debating strategies of reform and recovery. From this pressure-cooker environment emerged a flood of laws, programs, and agencies encompassed within a single, catch-all label: the New Deal.

The Hundred Days

Between March 9 and June 16, 1933, the "Hundred Days," Congress enacted more than a dozen major bills. It was a period of remarkable legislative productivity. Rooted in the Progressive Era, these measures sharply expanded federal involvement in the national economy.

The banking crisis was FDR's most urgent challenge. On March 5 he ordered all banks to close for four days. At the end of this "bank holiday," the Emergency Banking Act, which had sailed through Congress, permitted healthy banks to reopen with a

Major Measures Enacted During the "Hundred Days" (March 9–June 16, 1933)

Month	Day	Measure
March	9	Emergency Banking Relief Act
	20	Economy Act
	31	Unemployment Relief Act (Civilian Conservation Corps)
May	12	Agricultural Adjustment Act
	12	Federal Emergency Relief Act
	18	Tennessee Valley Authority
	27	Federal Securities Act
June	13	Home Owners' Refinancing Act
	16	Farm Credit Act
	16	Banking Act of 1933 (Federal Deposit Insurance Corporation)
	16	National Industrial Recovery Act (National Recovery Administration; Public Works Administration)

Treasury Department license, provided for the orderly management of failed banks, and enlarged the government's regulatory power. In the first of a series of "fireside chats" broadcast by radio, FDR assured Americans that they could again entrust their money to banks. In June Congress created the Federal Deposit Insurance Corporation (FDIC) to insure all bank deposits up to $5,000.

To keep the budget-balancing pledges made in the Democratic platform, FDR proposed, and Congress passed, an economy measure cutting federal salaries, slashing veterans' pensions and benefits, and otherwise trimming spending. Other New Deal measures were more experimental. On March 31 Congress created the Civilian Conservation Corps (CCC) to employ jobless youths for reforestation, park maintenance, and erosion control. By 1935 half a million young men were earning $35 a month plus room and board in CCC camps from Maine to California. Even this small sum made a difference for families with no income at all. Two federal agencies addressed the heartbreak of foreclosure. The Home Owners Loan Corporation (HOLC) helped people to refinance home mortgages, and the Farm Credit Administration did the same for farmers.

The most comprehensive relief measure of the early New Deal, the Federal Emergency Relief Act of May 1933, provided $500 million to fill the empty relief coffers of states and cities. To run this program, Roosevelt appointed Harry Hopkins, a former social worker who emerged as one of the New Deal's most powerful figures. In his first two hours on the job, working from a makeshift desk in a hallway, Hopkins distributed $5 million.

The Tennessee Valley Authority (TVA), also created in May, sought to revitalize the entire Tennessee River valley, one of the nation's poorest regions. The TVA built a hydroelectric network that supplied cheap power to seven states while developing a flood-control system, recreational facilities, and a soil-conservation program. Widely praised in the early New Deal, the TVA later became controversial on several fronts. Conservatives disliked what they saw as "creeping socialism," and landowners objected to being displaced by dams and reservoirs. Environmentalists, energy conservationists, and critics of nuclear power also attacked the agency in subsequent years.

The two most important measures of the Hundred Days, the Agricultural Adjustment Act and the National Industrial Recovery Act, addressed economic revival. The Agricultural Adjustment Act sought to raise crop prices by reducing production. The objective was to blunt farmers' natural instinct to increase their production as prices fell, a process that drove prices still lower. In summer 1933, the government paid southern cotton planters to plow under much of their crop and midwestern farmers to slaughter 6 million piglets. The killing of pigs at a time when many people were going hungry became a public-relations debacle that the New Deal never fully lived down.

In May 1933 the Agricultural Adjustment Administration (AAA) began paying commodity producers to take acreage out of production. Food processors paid a tax that supported the program, and in turn they passed the cost on to consumers in the form of higher food prices. Parity—the restoration of farmers' purchasing power to its 1909–1914 level—was the AAA's goal.

Passed in June 1933, the National Industrial Recovery Act (NIRA) tried to kindle a spirit of cooperation and shared purpose. Along the lines of the trade associations that President Hoover had promoted, representatives of major industries, granted immunity from antitrust prosecution, drafted codes of "fair competition" for their industries. They set production limits, prescribed wages and working conditions, and forbade price cutting and unfair competitive practices. The National Recovery Administration (NRA) oversaw the codes.

The NRA aimed to foster recovery by breaking the cycle of wage cuts, falling prices, and layoffs. Social reformers, however, had further goals. Under pressure from Labor Secretary Perkins, the NRA's textile-industry code banned child labor. And Senator Robert Wagner of New York pushed through Section 7a of the NIRA, affirming workers' rights to organize and to bargain collectively.

Hugh Johnson, the NRA's head, organized a national campaign to persuade consumers to buy only from companies that subscribed to the NRA code. The campaign's ubiquitous symbol, the blue eagle, and its slogan, "We Do Our Part," adorned billboards, magazine advertisements, and storefronts.

The NIRA appropriated $3.3 billion for a public-works program to employ the jobless and to pump money into the economy. Headed by Secretary of the Interior Harold Ickes, the Public Works Administration (PWA) spent more than $4 billion on 34,000 projects, many involving the construction of dams, bridges, and public buildings.

The NRA philosophy echoed Hoover's theme of government-business cooperation. FDR included corporations as key players in the "all-American team" fighting the depression. Although the NRA codes, once signed by the president, had the force of law, Washington relied on voluntary compliance. Caught up in the spirit of national unity, most business leaders cooperated—initially.

Moreover, the probusiness Reconstruction Finance Corporation remained active. FDR appointed as RFC chairman Jesse H. Jones, a millionaire Houston banker. Under Jones, the RFC loaned billions of dollars to banks, insurance companies, and railroads. Jones also extended loans for new business ventures and thus made the RFC a potent financial instrument serving corporate America.

A few early New Deal measures anticipated a more adversarial approach to business. The 1929 crash had produced a bitter reaction against business executives. A Senate investigation of Wall Street in 1932–1934 discovered that not one of the twenty partners of the giant Morgan Bank had paid a penny of income tax in 1931 or 1932. People jeered when the president of the New York Stock Exchange told a Senate committee considering regulatory legislation, "You gentlemen are making a big mistake. The Exchange is a perfect institution."

Reflecting this public mood, Congress in May 1933 passed the Federal Securities Act, regulating the sale of stocks. It required corporate executives to give the Federal Trade Commission full information on all stock offerings and made them personally liable for any misrepresentation of securities issued by their companies. In 1934 Congress sharply curbed the purchase of stock on credit, which had contributed to the 1929 debacle, and created the powerful Securities and Exchange Commission (SEC) to oversee the stock market.

When Congress adjourned on June 16, 1933, the Hundred Days ended. For many Americans, this burst of legislative activity symbolized the dynamism, as well as the confusion, of the Roosevelt years. The Hundred Days spawned a galaxy of "alphabet soup" agencies whose initials few could keep straight.

The NRA Bogs Down

Although the economy improved for a short period in summer 1933, recovery proved elusive. Economic indicators remained bleak through 1934, and problems and controversy plagued the New Deal.

Hugh Johnson's hard-driving, hard-drinking ways created problems for the NRA, but its difficulties went deeper. As the crisis-induced national unity of early 1933 faded, corporate America grew unhappy with NRA regulation. Small business objected that the codes favored large business. Republicans and conservative jurists attacked the NRA as unconstitutional. The agency itself bogged down in drafting trivial codes. The trade associations that wrote and supervised the codes used them to restrict competition and maintain high prices, not to stimulate economic expansion.

Beset by problems and failing its essential aim, the NRA sank of its own weight. In May 1935 the Supreme Court unanimously declared the NRA unconstitutional. The Court ruled that the act gave the president regulatory powers that belonged to Congress and that the NRA tried to regulate *intrastate* commerce, violating the *interstate* commerce clause. As an economic-recovery measure, the NRA had failed.

Troubled Agriculture

The AAA also generated controversy. Drought as well as New Deal policies combined to reduce production and drive up prices. From 1933 to 1937, total farm income increased 50 percent. But the AAA often harmed, rather than helped, tenants and sharecroppers. Landowners banked crop-reduction checks, removed the acreage from production, and left the sharecroppers to shift for themselves.

Some victims of this process resisted. In 1934 the interracial Southern Tenant Farmers' Union, led by the Socialist party, emerged in Arkansas. An elderly black sharecropper told the organizing meeting, "The same chain that holds my people holds your people too. . . . The landlord is always betwixt us, beatin' us and starvin' us and makin' us fight each other. There ain't but one way. . . . That's for us to get together and stay together." Landowners struck back with a campaign of terror, chasing down union organizers as their ancestors had hunted runaway slaves.

In the mid-1930s nature itself conspired against farmers as drought turned the Great Plains into a dust bowl. In Oklahoma the temperatures rose above 100 degrees for thirty-six days in a row in summer 1934. Under a searing sun and rainless sky, dust storms rolled across the plains from the Dakotas to Texas. The choking, wind-driven clouds penetrated the tiniest cracks, covering furniture, clothing, and skin with fine dust. Drifting eastward, the clouds obscured the sky over Cleveland, dropped red snow in New England, and even sifted yellow dust into the White House.

Battered farmers of the South and Great Plains abandoned the land in droves. Some migrated to the cities; others packed their few belongings into old cars and headed west to become migrant workers in California and Arizona. The hardships they experienced symbolized the suffering and disruption of the 1930s.

In 1933–1935 debate raged within the New Deal between those who wanted to restore prosperity to agriculture as a whole and those who urged special attention to the nation's poorest farmers. Although FDR at first took the more conservative view, the advocates of a farm policy reflecting broader social objectives scored significant legislative victories in the later New Deal.

Controversy over Relief Strategy

Intense discussion focused on the issue of aid for the unemployed. Impatient with slow, inefficient state and local agencies, relief administrator Harry Hopkins had convinced FDR by November 1933 that only direct federal relief could prevent mass suffering that winter. FDR put Hopkins in charge of a temporary public-works agency, the Civil Works Administration (CWA), which expended nearly a billion dollars on short-term work projects for the unemployed.

When spring came, FDR abolished the CWA. No one would starve in warm weather, he believed. FDR shared with his conservative critics a horror of creating a permanent underclass dependent on welfare payments. But continuing mass unemployment, and local agencies' inability to cope with the challenge, made further federal relief inevitable.

Hopkins's growing influence sharpened the behind-the-scenes struggle between him and Harold Ickes to control federal relief policy. The supercautious Ickes went over every PWA proposal with a fine-toothed comb, leaving billions in relief dollars stalled in the pipeline. The impatient Hopkins sought above all to put people to work and to get money circulating. To him, even make-work projects such as raking leaves had merit if they provided jobs. In the unemployment crisis, Hopkins, not Ickes, became the chief architect of federal relief policy.

The New Deal in Midstream: Popularity and Problems

Despite the New Deal's brave beginnings, the depression continued as 1934 ended. Major problems gripped the NRA, conflict flared over farm policy, and the need for federal relief spending appeared to expand rather than taper off.

But the New Deal remained highly popular, reflecting both its achievements and FDR's political skills. Roosevelt commanded the public stage and marshaled support for his programs with seemingly perpetual buoyancy, self-assurance, and good humor. Although many staunchly Republican newspaper publishers remained hostile, FDR enjoyed excellent relations with the working press, and reporters painted an overwhelmingly favorable portrait of his administration.

FDR savored public appearances and took naturally to radio. He treated the radio audience not as an anonymous mass but as three or four listeners in a living room. In his fireside chats he patiently described his goals. To many, he seemed a family intimate. Roosevelt's easy mastery of radio provided a model for his successors in the television era.

The midterm election of November 1934 ratified the popular verdict on the New Deal as the Democrats increased their majorities in the House and Senate. Kansas journalist William Allen White observed of FDR that "he's been all but crowned by the people." Although some viewed the New Deal as complete, a different mood prevailed in Congress and the White House. As the 1934 election returns rolled in, Harry Hopkins turned to a group of New Deal friends and declared, "Boys, this is our hour!" A new surge of activism, rivaling the Hundred Days, lay ahead.

The New Deal Changes Course

As the initial mood of national unity waned, conservatives criticized the New Deal for going too far and radicals attacked it for not going far enough. FDR shelved the unity theme, veered leftward, and took up the cause of the underdog. Buoyed by the 1934 election and eying the 1936 presidential race, FDR in 1935 pushed through a bundle of reform measures known as the Second New Deal. In 1936 his landslide reelection victory cemented a new Democratic coalition that would long remain a potent political force.

Challenges from Right and Left

Although the early New Deal was hardly radical, some conservative business leaders saw it as a mortal threat to capitalism. In 1934 several top corporate leaders, joined by disgruntled Democrats, formed the American Liberty League, dedicated to the proposition that the New Deal restricted individual freedom and pointed the way to socialism. The U.S. Chamber of Commerce blasted the New Deal, and anti-Roosevelt jokes circulated among the rich, many of whom denounced FDR as a traitor to his class.

Stronger challenges came from spokespersons for those in the lower ranks who demanded radical social and economic changes. Father Charles Coughlin, a Detroit priest and radio spellbinder, won an audience of 40 million with his potent brew of economics, politics, and piety. An early New Deal supporter, Coughlin by 1935 was condemning FDR as a "great betrayer and liar," indulging in anti-Semitism, and peddling such panaceas as the nationalization of banks. Coughlin's radio followers, organized as the National Union of Social Justice and drawn mainly from the urban lower-middle class, threatened FDR's 1936 electoral hopes.

Millions of older Americans rallied to California physician Francis E. Townsend, who proposed that the government pay $200 monthly to retired citizens over sixty, stipulating that they spend the money within thirty days. This plan would thereby help elderly Americans and stimulate the economy, Townsend argued, and would open up jobs by encouraging early retirement. Although the scheme would have quickly bankrupted the nation, many older citizens embraced it.

Huey Long, a flamboyant political hell-raiser from Louisiana, became FDR's wiliest rival. A country lawyer who had won the state's governorship in 1928, Long ruled Louisiana as his personal fiefdom while building highways, schools, and public housing. He roared into Washington as a senator in 1932 and preached his "Share Our Wealth" program: a 100 percent tax on annual incomes exceeding $1 million and expropriation of fortunes over $5 million. Long proposed to give every American family a comfortable income, a house, a car, old-age benefits, and educational opportunities.

"Every man a king," proclaimed Long. His baiting of the rich appealed to Americans who resented gaping disparities of wealth. He fleetingly endorsed the New Deal, but his book *My First Days in the White House* (1935) showed clearly that the presidential bug had bitten him. By 1935 Long boasted 7.5 million supporters. When an assassin's bullet cut him down that September, Gerald L.K. Smith, even more demagogic, took over Share Our Wealth.

Adding to Roosevelt's worries, economic recovery remained elusive. By 1934 national income stood 25 percent above 1933 levels but still far below 1929 figures. Millions, jobless for three or four years, were deeply demoralized. In 1934 frustration erupted in nearly 2,000 strikes, from New York taxi drivers to San Francisco dock workers. Ultimately, however, Roosevelt regained the political high ground in 1935 with an impressive new series of legislative initiatives—the Second New Deal.

The Second New Deal: Expanding Federal Relief

In his January 1935 State of the Union address, FDR called for broad social reforms. His program contained six central elements: enlarged federal relief, assistance to the rural poor, support for organized labor, social-welfare benefits for older Americans and other disadvantaged groups, stricter business regulation, and heavier taxes on the well-to-do.

With unemployment still high, Congress in April 1935 passed the Emergency Relief Appropriation Act, granting FDR $5 billion to spend more or less as he wished. He swiftly established the Works Progress Administration (WPA) under Harry Hopkins. The WPA funneled relief directly to individuals. FDR's horror of "the dole," however, led him to insist that the WPA provide work, not handouts. In its eight-year life, the WPA put more than 8 million Americans to work, injected $11 billion into the economy, and completed a mind-boggling number of projects: 650,000 miles of roads built or improved; 124,000 bridges constructed or repaired; 125,000 schools, hospitals, and other public buildings erected.

The WPA also assisted writers, performers, and artists. The Federal Writers' Project employed out-of-work authors to produce state guides and histories of ethnic and immigrant groups. In Massachusetts, WPA workers transcribed hundreds of pages of handwritten legal documents from the witchcraft episode of 1692. In the South they collected the reminiscences of aged ex-slaves. The Federal Theatre Project (FTP) put unemployed actors to work across the nation. Touring FTP drama companies gave millions of small-town audiences their first taste of live theater. Artists working for the Federal Art Project designed posters, taught classes, and decorated post offices and courthouses with murals. These arts agencies helped thousands of creative people to survive the depression and enlivened a dismal decade.

Other New Deal agencies also distributed relief funds. The National Youth Administration provided part-time work for more than 2 million high-school and college youths. Harold Ickes's Public Works Administration picked up steam, employing thousands of workers on construction projects, including the Lincoln Tunnel in New York and the Grand Coulee Dam in Washington State.

Monumental relief spending generated monumental budget deficits, which soared as high as $4.4 billion in 1936 and dipped as low as $1.2 billion in 1938. The government borrowed heavily to cover the deficits. British economist John Maynard Keynes had advocated deficit spending during a depression in order to increase purchasing power and stimulate recovery. However, the New Deal was not Keynesian. The money that flowed into public-works programs was withdrawn from the economy by taxing or borrowing and thus exerted no stimulus effect. FDR saw deficit spending as a deplorable necessity, not a positive policy.

The Second New Deal: Turning Leftward

Roosevelt's legislative proposals of 1935 revealed a pronounced turn to the left. In 1933, heartened by a burst of national unity, FDR had played down class differences, stressed the common goal of recovery, and attempted an unprecedented degree of centralized economic planning. But by 1935 the political struggles inevitable in a democracy of conflicting social classes and diverse interests were reviving. The Second New Deal therefore abandoned the effort to devise programs with universal appeal. Roosevelt now offered a program openly geared to the needs of the poor, the disadvantaged, and the laboring masses.

Social-justice advocates, including Secretary of Labor Frances Perkins, helped to shape this program. So did hard-headed political calculation. Indeed, Roosevelt's advisers feared that Coughlin, Long, and Townsend could siphon off enough votes to deny Roosevelt reelection. This concern shone through in FDR's 1935 political agenda.

The New Deal's leftward turn became evident in agricultural policy as the plight of sharecroppers, tenants, migrants, and other poor farmers attracted fresh attention. The Resettlement Administration, created in May 1935, made loans to help small farmers buy their own farms and to enable sharecroppers and tenants to resettle on productive acreage. Although the agency achieved less than was hoped and lasted only two years, it kept the difficulties of tenants and sharecroppers alive as issues of government concern. In addition, the Rural Electrification Administration (REA), also established

Major Later New Deal Legislation (November 1933–1938)

1933 (Nov.)	Civil Works Administration
1934	Civil Works Emergency Relief Act
	Home Owners' Loan Act
	Securities Exchange Act (Securities and Exchange Commission)
	Communications Act (Federal Communications Commission)
	Federal Farm Bankruptcy Act
	National Housing Act (Federal Housing Administration)
1935	Emergency Relief Appropriations Act (Works Progress Administration)
	National Labor Relations Act (Wagner Act)
	Revenue Act of 1935
	Social Security Act
	Public Utilities Holding Company Act
	Banking Act of 1935
	Resettlement Administration
	Rural Electrification Act
1937	National Housing Act of 1937
	Bankhead-Jones Farm Tenancy Act
1938	Fair Labor Standards Act
	Agricultural Adjustment Act of 1938

in spring 1935, made low-interest loans to utility companies and farmers' cooperatives to extend electricity to the 90 percent of rural America that lacked it. By 1941, 40 percent of American farms enjoyed electricity.

In January 1936 the Supreme Court declared the Agricultural Adjustment Act unconstitutional. To replace the AAA, Congress passed the Soil Conservation and Domestic Allotment Act, which paid farmers to cut production of soil-depleting crops such as wheat and cotton (the major surplus commodities) and to plant soil-conserving grasses and legumes instead. When agricultural prices remained depressed, Congress passed another major farm law in 1938.

Organized labor won a key victory in the Second New Deal, thanks to the efforts of New York senator Robert Wagner. Although Roosevelt originally opposed a prolabor law as contrary to the early New Deal's national-unity theme, Wagner patiently built congressional support for his bill. In May 1935 when the Supreme Court ruled the NIRA unconstitutional, including Section 7a, which protected union members' rights, FDR announced his support for a labor law. The result, the National Labor Relations Act of July 1935, guaranteed collective-bargaining rights, permitted closed shops, and outlawed such management practices as spying on unions and blacklisting labor "agitators." The law created the National Labor Relations Board (NLRB) to supervise shop elections and to deal with labor-law violations. The legislation, called the Wagner Act after its chief supporter, stimulated a wave of unionization (see Chapter 26).

Of all the Second New Deal measures, the Social Security Act of 1935 had the most long-term significance. Drafted by a committee chaired by Frances Perkins, this measure combined ideas of Progressive Era reformers and the example of social-welfare programs in England and Germany. It established a mixed federal-state system of old-age pensions for workers, survivors' benefits for victims of industrial accidents, unemployment insurance, and aid for dependent mothers and children, the blind, and the crippled. Taxes, paid in part by employers and in part by wages withheld from workers' paychecks, funded pensions and survivors' benefits. In the short run, payroll withholding withdrew money from circulation and contributed to a steep recession in 1937. But it made sense politically because workers would fight the repeal of a social-security plan to which they had contributed. As FDR noted, "With those taxes in there, no damned politician can ever scrap my social security program."

The Social Security Act set benefit payments at low levels, contained no provision for health insurance, and excluded millions of farmers, domestic workers, and self-employed Americans. However, it established the principle of federal responsibility for social welfare and created the framework for a future welfare system.

The Second New Deal's more radical thrust resulted in two business regulatory measures in 1935. The Banking Act strengthened the Federal Reserve Board's control over the national banking system and money supply. The Public Utilities Holding Company Act regulated the interstate transmission of electricity and—targeting the sprawling public-utility empires of the 1920s—restricted gas and electric companies to one geographic region.

Finally, the Revenue Act of 1935 raised personal taxes at upper income levels, increased corporate taxes, and boosted levies on gifts and estates. Although this tax law had numerous loopholes and was not quite the "soak the rich" measure that some believed, it expressed the class-conscious mood of the Second New Deal.

By September 1935 the Second New Deal was complete. Laws had been enacted to promote the interests of the jobless, the elderly, the rural poor, and blue-collar workers; to regulate major business enterprises more closely than before; and to hike taxes on the wealthy. Without fully embracing the radical prescriptions of Coughlin, Townsend, or Long, FDR directed his program to the fears and inequities on which these critics had thrived. Nonetheless, FDR remained a firm supporter of the capitalist system. In his view, the New Deal had saved capitalism by reforming its excesses and addressing its less desirable social consequences.

The Election of 1936

Candidates	*Parties*	*Electoral Vote*	*Popular Vote*	*Percentage of Popular Vote*
FRANKLIN D. ROOSEVELT	Democratic	523	27,752,869	60.8
Alfred M. Landon	Republican	8	16,674,665	36.5
William Lemke	Union		882,479	1.9

The Election of 1936: The New Deal at High Tide

With the Second New Deal in place and unemployment declining, FDR faced the 1936 election confidently. "There's one issue in this campaign," he told an aide; "it's myself, and people must be either for me or against me."

A number of FDR's Republican foes lambasted Roosevelt's alleged dictatorial ambitions and charged that soon workers would have to wear metal dog tags engraved with their social-security numbers. The Republican party nominated progressive governor Alfred Landon of Kansas. A fiscal conservative who nevertheless believed that government must respond to social issues, Landon proved an inept campaigner.

FDR struck back against his challengers with typical zest. Only the forces of "selfishness and greed" opposed him, he told an election-eve rally in New York; "never before in history have these forces been so united against one candidate as they stand today. They are united in their hatred for me—and I welcome their hatred."

In the most crushing electoral victory since 1820, FDR carried every state but Maine and Vermont. FDR swamped Landon by a popular-vote margin of 11 million, and the Democrats increased their already-large majorities in the Senate and the House. The 1936 election underscored the message of 1932: Republican dominance was over. The Roosevelt landslide buried minor-party opponents as well. The Socialist candidate received fewer than 200,000 votes, and the Communist party candidate only 80,000. Congressman William Lemke, the candidate of the Coughlin, Townsend, and Share Our Wealth enthusiasts who had appeared so formidable in 1935, polled fewer than 900,000 votes.

The New Democratic Coalition

From 1860 to 1930, the Democrats had counted on three bases of support: the white South, parts of the West, and urban machines such as Tammany Hall. FDR retained these centers of strength but pushed far beyond them to forge a new Democratic majority. Five partially overlapping groups constituted the foundation of this new coalition: farmers, urban immigrants, unionized industrial workers, northern African-Americans, and women.

Midwestern farmers, longtime Republicans, found the New Deal's agricultural program congenial and widely switched to Roosevelt. For example, in 1936 FDR decisively carried Iowa, where Democratic candidates had been lucky to garner a mere 20 percent of the vote in the 1920s.

Urban voters, many of them immigrants or immigrants' children, followed the same pattern. In 1936 FDR carried the nation's twelve largest cities. New Deal relief programs aided the urban masses, and FDR wooed them persuasively. Further solidifying his urban base, FDR appointed many representatives of urban-immigrant groups, including unprecedented numbers of Catholics and Jews, to high New Deal positions.

Organized labor also joined the New Deal coalition. The unions pumped money into Roosevelt's reelection campaigns (although not nearly so much as big business gave to the Republicans), and rank-and-file union members voted overwhelmingly for FDR. Despite his early foot-dragging on the Wagner bill, FDR's reputation as a "friend of labor" proved unassailable. By 1936 administration ties to organized labor provoked a strong anti–New Deal mood in business circles. But FDR won some business support, particularly from officials of corporations that were aided by his programs—companies that provided equipment for TVA and PWA hydroelectric projects, for example—and from exporters profiting from the New Deal's aggressive free-trade policies.

Although most southern blacks remained disfranchised, the swelling black population of northern cities had become an influential force in electoral politics. As late as 1932, two-thirds of northern blacks had voted for the Republican Hoover. One African-American editor, annoyed by this enduring Republican allegiance, advised his readers to "turn Lincoln's picture to the wall. That debt has been paid in full." With the advent of the New Deal, a historic shift occurred. In 1934 Chicago's African-American voters had signaled the new order by electing a Democrat over a popular Republican congressman. In 1936 northern blacks voted in record numbers, and 76 percent cast their ballots for FDR.

Many factors played a part in blacks' turnaround. First, as employees last hired and first fired, African-Americans had higher jobless rates than the general work force, but unemployed blacks in the urban North benefited heavily from New Deal relief programs. Second, many African-Americans saw the New Deal as a force for racial justice, even though the record does not fully bear this perception out. Indeed, racially discriminatory clauses in some NRA codes led African-American activists to dismiss the agency as "Negroes Ruined Again," and other New Deal agencies tolerated racism. Roosevelt kept aloof from an NAACP campaign to make lynching a federal crime. In 1935 and 1938 he remained passive as antilynching bills were narrowly defeated in Congress.

Otherwise, however, the New Deal modestly advanced the black cause. Assuring an African-American student audience in Washington, D.C., that there would be "no . . . forgotten races" in his administration, FDR supported those seeking to eradicate racism from New Deal agencies. He appointed more than one hundred African-Americans to policy-level positions. The highest-ranking black appointee, educator Mary McLeod Bethune, the daughter of ex-slaves, became director of minority affairs in the National Youth Administration. The influential Bethune led the "black cabinet" that served as a link between the New Deal and African-American organizations. In addition, the "Roosevelt Supreme Court" that took shape after 1936 made important antidiscrimination rulings on voting rights, wage discrimination, jury selection, and real-estate transactions.

Thanks in large part to Eleanor Roosevelt, the New Deal also supported racial justice in symbolic ways. In 1939 when the Daughters of the American Revolution barred a performance by black contralto Marian Anderson in Washington's Constitution Hall, Mrs. Roosevelt resigned from the organization, and New Deal officials arranged for an Easter Sunday concert by Anderson on the Lincoln Memorial steps.

The Roosevelt administration also worked strenuously to attract women voters. Molly Dewson led the effort as head of the Democratic party's women's division. In 1936 she mobilized 15,000 women who went door-to-door distributing 80 million flyers describing New Deal programs.

Dewson, who believed that women had a special interest in issues relating to the home, stressed how social security, the National Youth Administration, federal school-lunch programs, and other New Deal initiatives strengthened the family. She did not push a specifically feminist agenda or women's rights legislation. New Deal programs of economic recovery and social welfare, in her view, offered the best promise of advancement for both men and women. Dewson did, however, advocate the appointment of women to federal policy-level positions and knew which strings to pull to place women in key New Deal posts. FDR appointed the first woman cabinet member, the first woman ambassador, and more female federal judges than any predecessor. The 1936 Democratic platform committee reflected a fifty-fifty gender balance.

Despite the visibility of a few African-Americans and women in New Deal circles, advancing the interests of these groups was not high on FDR's agenda. Racism and sexism had long pervaded American society, and Roosevelt's administration, preoccupied with the economic crisis, did little to change the situation.

The New Deal and the Environment

FDR's commitment to conservation ran deep. As early as 1910, he had chaired the Fish and Game Committee of the New York State Senate, trying to regulate tree cutting that threatened wildlife. Of all the New Deal agencies, moreover, the Civilian Conservation Corps lay closest to his heart. He valued its conservation role as much as its depression-fighting function. Under his prodding, the CCC thinned forests, built hiking trails and fire-lookout towers, and planted hundreds of thousands of trees.

Soil conservation became an urgent New Deal priority. The terrible Great Plains dust storms of 1933–1935 resulted not only from drought but also from overgrazing and unwise farming practices. Less dramatic than the dust bowl but no less damaging was soil erosion. By the 1930s erosion had destroyed 9 million acres of farmland, and 80 million acres more lay jeopardized.

Under director Hugh Bennett, the Soil Conservation Service of the Department of Agriculture established demonstration projects and research stations across the nation. Farmers learned the value of contour plowing, terracing, crop rotation, and cultivating grasses that strengthened the soil. The Taylor Grazing Act of 1934 restricted the grazing on public lands that had compounded the problem of erosion.

The Tennessee Valley Authority had an important environmental component: controlling the devastating floods that worsened soil erosion. TVA planners dreamed of harnessing the region's natural resources to serve its people—the goal of earlier conservationists, among them Gifford Pinchot. Although it fell short of this vision, the TVA became a model for similar multipurpose watershed projects in the United States and abroad.

During the 1930s, too, New Deal planners continued the national-park movement, creating Olympic National Park in Washington, Shenandoah National Park in Virginia, and Kings Canyon National Park in California. Wildlife preservation also gained ground. By 1940 the government had set aside 7.5 million acres for some 160 new wildlife refuges. In 1935 Robert Marshall of the U.S. Forest Service helped to form the Wilderness Society to lobby for the cause. Wilderness, said the society, was not "a luxury or plaything" but "a human need." Under pressure from wilderness advocates, Congress designated a large portion of Kings Canyon National Park a wilderness area.

The wilderness and wildlife movements brought together an unusual coalition: New Deal planners, men and women who cherished the wilderness on aesthetic and philosophical grounds, and corporations, particularly firearms companies, financially interested in preserving wildlife for hunters. The National Wildlife Federation (1935) was largely funded by the gun industry.

From a contemporary perspective, the New Deal's environmental record reveals gaps and blind spots. Matters of great concern today—atmospheric pollution, dwindling fossil fuels, pesticide hazards, and the pressures of an ever-growing population on limited global resources—received little attention. Vast hydroelectric projects such as TVA made sense at a time when rural America still lacked electric power, but they also reinforced an ideology of boundless energy consumption that in later years would seem heedless and wasteful. Nevertheless, the New Deal focused attention on conserving nature to a degree that had not been true for twenty years and would not again be true for a generation.

The New Deal Draws to a Close

After his enormous victory in the 1936 election,

Roosevelt launched an ill-conceived attack on the Supreme Court that weakened him politically. In the wake of this fight, he confronted a newly energized conservative opposition that helped to end the New Deal. But the legacy of the New Deal remained; in the span of a few years, it had rewritten the national political agenda.

FDR and the Supreme Court

Early in 1937, fresh from his second electoral triumph, FDR went after the one branch of government that had seemed immune to the New Deal, the Supreme Court. The Court comprised nine elderly men, one of whom had served since 1910; another, since 1914. Among these nine jurists, there were four archconservative justices who despised the New Deal. Joined by moderates, they had invalidated the NRA, the AAA, and progressive state laws and appeared determined to "tie Uncle Sam up in a hard knot," as liberal justice Harlan Stone observed. Roosevelt feared that key measures of the Second New Deal would meet a similar fate. Indeed, some lawyers were so sure that the Social Security Act would be found unconstitutional that they advised their clients to ignore it.

In February 1937 FDR unexpectedly proposed a sweeping court-reform bill that would have allowed the president to appoint an additional Supreme Court member for each justice over seventy, up to a total of six. Roosevelt insisted that this proposal reflected his concern for the heavy workload of aging justices, but his political motivation escaped no one.

FDR erroneously believed that his personal popularity would translate into support for his plan. Congress and the public, however, greeted it with skepticism that became disapproval. The size of the Supreme Court (unspecified in the Constitution) had been changed several times in the Republic's early years, but over the ensuing decades the membership of nine, set by Congress in 1869, had taken on an almost sacred quality. Conservatives blasted the president's "court-packing" scheme. Some feared a Rooseveltian grab for power in the wake of his electoral triumph; others resented the disingenuous way in which FDR presented the plan. Even some New Dealers abandoned the president on this issue. FDR pushed his court-reform bill for several months, but in July he gave up the fight. For one of the rare times in his presidency, he had suffered an embarrassing defeat.

But in fact the Supreme Court yielded to Roosevelt's pressure. One of the most conservative justices retired in May 1937, and others announced plans to step down. In April and May the Court upheld several key New Deal measures, including the Wagner Act and a state minimum-wage law. This shift away from anti–New Deal rulings may have been FDR's goal all along. From 1937 to 1939, FDR appointed four new members to the Court—Hugo Black, Stanley F. Reed, Felix Frankfurter, and William O. Douglas—laying the groundwork for a liberal majority that would endure long after the 1930s.

The Roosevelt Recession

As the Supreme Court fight ended, FDR confronted a far more serious problem: the economy plunged ominously in August 1937. Industrial production slumped to 1934 levels. Steel output sank from 80 percent to 19 percent of capacity. The jobless toll soared to 11 million in early 1938, encompassing more than 20 percent of the work force.

What caused this relapse? Federal policies that steeply reduced consumer income played a role. The new social-security program's payroll taxes withdrew some $2 billion from circulation. Concerned about mounting deficits, FDR had seized upon signs of recovery to terminate the PWA and to cut the WPA and other relief programs sharply. These economies reduced the federal deficit but contributed to the 1937–1938 downturn. So, too, did a drastic contraction of the money supply by the Federal Reserve Board to forestall inflation.

Echoing Hoover, FDR assured his cabinet, "Everything will work out all right if we just sit tight and keep quiet." However, Keynesian New Dealers recruited Harry Hopkins to warn the president of fierce political backlash should breadlines and soup kitchens return. Only a renewal of massive relief,

Capturing the Migrant Experience
This family of Texas tenant farmers in a California migrant-labor camp was photographed in 1935 by Dorothea Lange, one of the gifted photographers who compiled a memorable visual record for the Farm Security Administration of the Depression's human toll.

Hopkins insisted, would offer hope, and so in April 1938 FDR authorized heavy new spending. The WPA money machine clanked into action; the PWA received a new lease on life. By the end of 1938, unemployment had declined and industrial output had risen.

The End of the New Deal

Distracted by the Supreme Court fight, the 1937–1938 recession, and a menacing world situation (see Chapter 26), FDR offered relatively few reform initiatives in his second term. Congress, however, enacted several significant measures. The Bankhead-Jones Farm Tenancy Act of 1937 created the Farm Security Administration (FSA) to replace the short-lived Resettlement Administration. The FSA made low-interest loans that enabled tenant farmers and sharecroppers to buy their own family-size farms. Although the FSA did little to help the poorest tenants and sharecroppers, considered bad credit risks, it had loaned more than $1 billion by the end of 1941. Thousands of families became new farm owners.

The FSA also established camps offering clean, sanitary shelter and medical services to migrant farm workers, many of whom had lived under wretched, unhealthful conditions. In its most innovative program, the FSA commissioned talented photographers to preserve the lives of tenants, migrants, and dust bowl families on film. They collected a haunting album of stark images.

Other late New Deal measures set precedents. The National Housing Act (1937) appropriated $500 million for urban-slum clearance and public housing. The Fair Labor Standards Act of 1938 banned child labor and established a national minimum wage of forty cents an hour and a maximum workweek of forty hours. Humanitarianism mingled with northern legislators' desire to undermine the competitive edge of the South—its low wage scales—in securing passage of this law.

The Agricultural Adjustment Act of 1938 set up procedures for limiting the production of basic commodities such as cotton, wheat, corn, and tobacco. It also created a mechanism by which the government, in years of big harvests and low prices, would make loans to farmers and store their surplus crops in government warehouses. (These payments came directly from the federal treasury rather than a processors' tax, a feature that had caused the Agricultural Adjustment Act of 1933 to be declared unconstitutional.) In years of poor harvests and higher prices, farmers could repay their loans and market their commodities at a profit. These provisions helped to stabilize farm prices and established the framework of federal agricultural policy for decades to come.

The later 1930s also witnessed a leap in union membership (see Chapter 26). This labor activism, stimulated in part by Section 7a of the NIRA and by the Wagner Act, demonstrated the New Deal's continuing role in transforming the social contours of American life.

Despite such achievements, the New Deal clearly lost momentum after 1935, in part because of the growing strength of an anti–New Deal congressional coalition of Republicans and conservative southern Democrats. After the Supreme Court fight, the opposition became more outspoken. In 1937, with nerves rubbed raw by the Court fight, Congress rejected FDR's proposal to reorganize the executive branch by regrouping existing agencies, bureaus, and commissions into twelve superdepartments under the president's direct authority. Although the plan made administrative sense, FDR's critics claimed that it would create a virtual White House dictatorship. The conservative coalition also slashed relief appropriations, launched an investigation of the NLRB, cut corporate taxes, and killed the Federal Theatre Project. Suspecting that FDR used WPA staff members for political purposes, conservatives in 1939 passed the Hatch Act, forbidding federal workers from participating in electoral campaigns. The Fair Labor Standards Act of 1938 became law only after intense White House lobbying and watering down by conservatives. Harry Hopkins noted that as economic recovery proceeded, Congress and the public seemed "bored with the poor, the unemployed, the insecure."

Attempts by FDR to stem the anti–New Deal tide in 1938's midterm election notwithstanding, the Republicans gained heavily in the House and Senate and added thirteen governorships. Roosevelt had campaigned against several prominent anti–New Deal Democratic senators in 1938, but the major targets of his attempted purge all won handily.

Focusing mainly on unsettling foreign developments in his January 1939 State of the Union message, FDR proposed no new domestic measures and spoke of the need to "preserve our reforms." The New Deal was over.

CONCLUSION

The New Deal compiled a stunning record. Not all of its programs succeeded, nor did it achieve full economic recovery, but the New Deal nonetheless represents a watershed in U.S. history. The Roosevelt administration assumed that government was responsible for promoting economic prosperity and the well-being of all citizens. Social security, the Wagner Act, and the Fair Labor Standards Act defined the basic outline of the modern activist welfare state.

From the 1860s through the 1920s, the business class had dominated Washington. The New Deal eroded corporate sway over government: it acted as a broker for *all* organized interest groups—business, agriculture, labor, and other sectors. Although the unorganized, including sharecroppers and tenants, had little influence, government gradually grew more responsive to their interests.

New Dealers, unlike progressives, sought not to purify the nation but to solve practical problems of business stagnation, unemployment, and the maldistribution of economic resources. New Dealers' *style*, too, differed radically from that of progressives. As historian William E. Leuchtenberg has written, "If the archetypical progressive was Jane Addams singing 'Onward Christian Soldiers,' the representative New Dealer was Harry Hopkins betting on the horses at Laurel Race Track."

The New Deal vastly enlarged presidential power and prestige. Indeed, Roosevelt so commanded politics that Americans began to expect their president to formulate "programs" and to shape public debate. These developments forever altered the balance of power between the White House and Congress.

Any evaluation of the New Deal must come to grips with Franklin D. Roosevelt. Neither a saint nor a superman, he could be devious, as in the Supreme Court fight, and his administrative skills left much to be desired. But his strengths far outweighed his liabilities. He adopted an open, experimental approach in grappling with national problems. Above all, Roosevelt's infectious optimism renewed the confidence of a demoralized people. "We Americans of today . . . ," he said in 1939, "are characters in the living book of democracy. But we are also its author. It falls upon us now to say whether the chapters that are to come will tell a story of retreat or a story of continued advance."

CHRONOLOGY

1929 Stock-market crash; onset of depression.

1931 Farmers' Holiday Association.

1932 Reconstruction Finance Corporation.
Glass-Steagall Act.
Veterans' bonus march.
Franklin D. Roosevelt elected president.

1933 Repeal of Eighteenth Amendment (Prohibition).
Federal Deposit Insurance Corporation created.
Emergency Banking Act.
Civilian Conservation Corps (CCC).
Federal Emergency Relief Act (FERA).
Tennessee Valley Authority (TVA).
Agricultural Adjustment Administration (AAA).
National Recovery Administration (NRA).
Public Works Administration (PWA).
Civil Works Administration (CWA).

1934 Securities and Exchange Commission (SEC).
Civil Works Emergency Relief Act.

1935 Supreme Court declares NRA unconstitutional.
Emergency Relief Appropriation Act.
Works Progress Administration (WPA).
National Youth Administration.
Resettlement Administration.

Rural Electrification Administration (REA).
National Labor Relations Act (Wagner Act).
Social Security Act.
Banking Act.
NAACP campaign for federal antilynching law.
Huey Long assassinated.

1936 Supreme Court declares AAA unconstitutional.
Soil Conservation and Domestic Allotment Act.
Roosevelt wins landslide reelection victory.

1937 Roosevelt's "court-packing" plan defeated.
Farm Security Administration (FSA).

1937–1938 The "Roosevelt recession."

1938 Fair Labor Standards Act.
Agricultural Adjustment Act of 1938.

1939 Hatch Act.
Marian Anderson concert at Lincoln Memorial.

FOR FURTHER READING

Anthony J. Badger, *The New Deal: The Depression Years, 1933–1940* (1989). Good recent overview of the period and its politics.

Paul Conkin, *The New Deal*, 2d ed. (1975). A concise, balanced overview.

Steve Fraser and Gary Gerstle, eds., *The Rise and Fall of the New Deal Order, 1930–1980* (1989). Incisive critical essays on the New Deal's long-term legacy.

John A. Garraty, *The Great Depression* (1986). Especially valuable on the global aspects of the crisis.

William E. Leuchtenberg, *Franklin D. Roosevelt and the New Deal* (1983). A comprehensive, readable overview, rich in illuminating detail.

Albert U. Romasco, *The Politics of Recovery: Roosevelt's New Deal* (1983). A study particularly useful for the New Deal's policies toward business.

Harvard Sitkoff, *A New Deal for Blacks* (1978). An exploration of the Roosevelt administration's policies toward African-Americans.

Studs Terkel, *Hard Times* (1970). An oral history that poignantly convey the Depression's human toll.

Susan Ware, *Beyond Suffrage: Women and the New Deal* (1981). A study of the network of women who held high office in the New Deal.

CHAPTER 26

American Life in a Decade of Crisis at Home and Abroad

The Great Depression crashed down on America, bringing economic, social, and emotional havoc. To comprehend the depression, we must look beyond Wall Street and Washington to auto plants, harvest fields, artists' studios, and ordinary people's homes. We must look abroad as well, for in these cataclysmic years brutal dictators seized control of other powerful nations, raising the specter of war.

(Right) Striking Chevrolet workers in St. Louis holding an impromptu dance, 1937

The American People in the Depression Decade

For millions of industrial workers, the New Deal created a favorable climate for unionization. But union growth did not come easily, and workers often had to fight for the right to organize. Although some female and minority workers shared in the benefits of unionization, for others, the depression worsened a difficult situation. Indeed, the 1930s saw a backlash against working women and feminist goals, and the circumstances of African-Americans and Hispanic-Americans grew even more desperate.

Native Americans became the objects of well-meaning but sometimes misguided attention. And the depression profoundly affected the most basic social group of all, the family. But while many families experienced disruption and conflict, others drew together in the face of adversity.

The Plight of the People

The depression exacted an enormous toll in human suffering. Unemployment never fell below about 14 percent, and for much of the decade it ran considerably higher. (In the 1960s the government defined 5 percent unemployment as the maximum tolerable level.) As late as 1939, 9 million men and women remained jobless. Bankruptcies, foreclosures, and abandoned farms multiplied. A quarter of all farm families had to accept public or private assistance during the 1930s.

In some cities the jobless rate far exceeded the national average. In 1932, for example, Toledo's unemployment rate stood at an incredible 80 percent. The nation's jobless rolls included millions who had earned good wages before 1929. These newly impoverished individuals experienced intense stress over their sudden decline in income and status. Some went to great lengths to maintain appearances, even when they had barely enough to eat. Advertisements promoting products ranging from mouthwash and deodorant to encyclopedias and correspondence courses capitalized on widespread feelings of shame. The ads played on people's fears of being found out, of having their failings and pretenses exposed.

Among those fortunate enough to work, many took jobs below their level of training: college alumni pumped gas, and business-school graduates sold furniture. Others eked out a few dollars by peddling products to neighbors as poor as themselves. "I'll never forget watching my mother trying to sell Two-in-One Shoe Polish door-to-door," a child of the depression recalled.

Nutritional deficiencies and people's inability to pay for medical and dental care laid the groundwork for later problems. "You have to have money to be sick—or [you] did then," novelist John Dos Passos said; "any dentistry also was out of the question, with the result that my teeth went badly to pieces. Without dough you couldn't have a tooth filled." The savings of older Americans evaporated. By the mid-thirties, 1 million Americans over age 65 were on relief.

Industrial Workers Unionize

The economic crisis and widespread hardship energized and transformed organized labor. Although the number of unskilled or semiskilled factory workers had doubled between 1900 and 1930, they remained almost completely unorganized at the start of the depression. Managers of major industries—steel, automobiles, textiles—had blocked all attempts at unionization, viewing it as a threat to their right to run their businesses. The prosperity and probusiness mood of the 1920s had further sapped the labor movement's energies.

Then in the 1930s, hard times and a favorable government climate led to labor militancy and a surge of unionization. When the National Labor Relations Act of 1935 guaranteed labor's right to organize and to bargain collectively, militant labor leaders such as John L. Lewis of the United Mine Workers (UMW) and Sidney Hillman of the Amalgamated Clothing Workers chafed at the American Federation of Labor's slowness in organizing factory workers. In November 1935 Lewis and Hillman founded the Committee for Industrial Organization (CIO) within the AFL. CIO activists preached unionization to workers in Pittsburgh's steel mills, Detroit's auto plants, and Akron's rubber factories. Unlike the restrictive, craft-based AFL, the CIO unions welcomed all workers in a particular industry, regardless of their race, gender, or degree of skill.

In 1936 the CIO-sponsored Steel Workers Organizing Committee (SWOC) geared up for a major strike to win union recognition from U.S. Steel, which John L. Lewis described as "the crouching lion in the path of labor." The crouching lion proved a pussycat. Lewis had secretly negotiated a settlement with the head of U.S. Steel, Myron C. Taylor, who accepted unionization in the face of labor defiance and the strongly prolabor atmosphere in Washington. In March 1937 U.S. Steel recognized the union, granted a wage increase, and accepted a forty-hour workweek. Other steel companies followed, and by the year's end 400,000 steelworkers had signed their union cards.

Meanwhile, organizers for the United Auto Workers (UAW), led by the fiery Walter Reuther, mapped a campaign to organize General Motors, which was deeply hostile to unions. In December 1936 thousands of workers at GM's two body plants in Flint, Michigan, stopped work and occupied the factories, paralyzing GM's production by their "sit-down strike." Keeping their action peaceful, however, the strikers protected the equipment and the cars on the assembly lines.

Women played a key part in the Flint strike. They picketed and paraded, opened a kitchen to feed the strikers, organized a speakers' bureau to present the union's side, and even produced a drama, *The Strike Goes On*. Women also figured prominently in the confrontation on January 11, 1937, between strikers and Flint police that led to the officers' opening fire on the unarmed strikers. Only when women joined the picketers did the police cease shooting. Fourteen strikers were injured; astonishingly, none died.

This episode resulted in the formation of the Women's Emergency Brigade, whose 400 members, donning red berets and armbands, remained on twenty-four-hour alert for picket duty. Although the overall direction of the strike rested in male hands, the female participants discovered the exhilaration of working with others on a common cause. As one woman wrote in the UAW newspaper, "I only wish I'd gotten mad long ago, . . . but I didn't have time for anything outside of my own small circle. I'm living for the first time with a definite goal."

At first, GM fought unionization. Company officials called in the police to harass the strikers, sent spies to union meetings, and warned workers' families that strikers would be fired. The company also tried to persuade the Roosevelt administration to summon troops and to expel the strikers by force. Although FDR disapproved of the sit-down tactic, he refused to mobilize federal troops against the strikers. On February 11, seven weeks into the strike, GM signed a contract recognizing the UAW. Chrysler followed, and by the end of 1937 the UAW boasted more than 400,000 members.

In 1938 the Committee for Industrial Organization left the AFL to become the Congress of Industrial Organizations, a 2-million-member association of six major industrial unions. In response to the CIO challenge, the AFL became more vigorous and more flexible. Union membership shot up from under 3 million in 1933 to more than 8 million in 1941, with much of the increase after 1936.

These victories came hard as some big corporations battled unionization. Henry Ford, for example, hated unions, and his loyal lieutenant, a tough brawler named Harry Bennett, organized a squad of union-busting thugs to fight the UAW. In 1937 in a bloody encounter, Bennett's men beat Walter Reuther and other UAW officials outside Ford's River Rouge plant. Not until 1941 did Ford yield to union pressure. Another holdout was the Republic Steel Company, headed by union hater Tom Girdler. Even after U.S. Steel signed with the CIO in March 1937, Republic and other smaller companies known collectively as "Little Steel" adamantly refused.

In May 1937 workers in twenty-seven Little

Steel plants, including Republic's factory in South Chicago, walked off the job. Anticipating the strike, Girdler had assembled an arsenal of riot guns and tear gas. On May 30, Memorial Day, strikers approached the 264 police officers guarding the plant. Someone threw a large stick at the police, who opened fire, killing ten strikers and wounding more than eighty. A coroner's jury ruled the Memorial Day Massacre "justifiable homicide," but a Senate investigation concluded that it had been "clearly avoidable by the police." In 1941 Tom Girdler and the rest of Little Steel threw in the towel and finally signed union agreements with the CIO.

The union movement bypassed workers at the low end of the wage scale—domestics, farm workers, department-store clerks—who tended to be primarily female, black, or recent immigrants. More than three-quarters of all nonfarm workers remained unorganized as the decade ended. Nonetheless, the unionization of vast sectors of the industrial work force represents one of the decade's most memorable achievements.

Why did powerful corporations cave in to unions after years of resistance? Workers' militancy and the tactical skills of a new generation of labor leaders played a central role. So, too, did management's fears of violence and sabotage. But above all, labor's successes after 1936 reflected the changed political climate. Where government officials had once helped to break strikes by force and legal intimidation, Roosevelt and key state officials refused to intervene on the side of management. (The willingness of the South Chicago police to act as a kind of private army for Tom Girdler represents a rare exception.) The Fair Labor Standards Act of 1938 and the role of the National Labor Relations Board in assuring fair union votes made clear that Washington would not line up with management in labor disputes. Once the chiefs of the nation's major industries realized this fact, most came to terms with the union leaders.

Mixed Blessings for Women

Senator Robert Wagner called the working woman in the depression years "the first orphan in the storm." Indeed, for the 25 percent of women gainfully employed in 1930, the depression brought hard times. The female jobless rate hovered above 20 percent throughout much of the decade. Women who continued working often had to take lower-paying, lower-status jobs. Many young women entering the job market had to settle for temporary or part-time work.

In the face of heavy competition from displaced male workers, the number of women in white-collar professions such as librarianship, social work, and public-school teaching declined. Women who did cling to their jobs encountered wage discrimination. In 1939 the average woman schoolteacher earned 20 percent less than her male counterpart with comparable experience. A number of NRA codes actually endorsed lower pay for women workers. The minimum-wage clause of the Fair Labor Standards Act of 1938 helped thousands of women whose hourly wage fell below the new minimum but did not cover many categories of working women.

Married women workers encountered enormous resentment. Most took jobs out of economic necessity but were commonly accused of seeking to earn "pin money." People complained that married women had no right to hold jobs with so many men out of work. Many cities refused to employ married women as schoolteachers and fired women teachers who married.

The unionization drive of the later 1930s had mixed results for women workers. Some benefited from the campaign to organize the mass-production industries; for example, female workers helped to plan and to carry out a "slowdown" strategy that forced a large GM parts factory in Detroit to sign a union contract. However, unionization made little headway in heavily female sectors of the labor force, including the textile industry and the clerical, sales, and service occupations. For instance, by the 1930s office work had been almost completely feminized, and most women office workers earned far less than male factory workers. Many secretaries responded with enthusiasm when the CIO chartered an office workers' union in 1937, and several strikes occurred.

But the CIO drive to unionize clerical workers made little progress nationally.

The depression represented a low point for the women's movement. Battling the economic crisis, the nation had little patience for feminist issues or for the struggle to secure gender equality. Nonetheless, the proportion of women working for wages crept up slightly over the decade, from 25 percent to 26 percent. At the same time, the ratio of gainfully employed married women rose from 11.7 percent to 15.6 percent. Neither depression nor criticism could reverse the long-term movement of women into the workplace. Indeed, the depression may have accelerated that movement as married women worked to supplement the family income.

African-Americans, Hispanic-Americans, and Native Americans Cope with Hard Times

The depression markedly slowed the urbanization of African-Americans. Only 400,000 southern blacks moved to northern cities in the 1930s, far fewer than in the 1920s or the 1940s. In 1940, 77 percent of the nation's 12 million African-Americans still lived in the South.

Rural and urban blacks alike endured extreme hardships. New Deal agricultural policies often led to the eviction of African-American tenant farmers and sharecroppers. Among African-American industrial workers, persistent racism, discriminatory union policies, and fierce competition pushed the jobless rate far above that for whites.

Lynchings and miscarriages of justice continued for African-Americans as well, especially in the South. In the notorious "Scottsboro Boys" case, eight black youths were sentenced to death in 1931 by an all-white jury in Scottsboro, Alabama, on highly suspect charges of raping two white women. In 1935 the Supreme Court ordered a new trial because of the exclusion of African-Americans from the jury and the denial of legal counsel to the defendants. In 1936–1937 five of the defendants were again convicted, and they served lengthy prison terms.

African-Americans did not accept racism and discrimination passively. The National Association for the Advancement of Colored People battled in courts and legislatures against lynching, racial segregation, and the denial of black voting rights. Urban blacks particularly resented the fact that whites owned most businesses in African-American neighborhoods and employed only whites. Under the banner "DON'T SHOP WHERE YOU CAN'T WORK," protesters boycotted such businesses in several cities. In March 1935 hostility against white-owned businesses in Harlem, intensified by generalized anger about racism and chronic unemployment, erupted into a riot that caused $200 million in property damage and left three blacks dead.

To some extent, the depression diverted attention from racial issues and from the desperate economic condition of black Americans. But the rising tempo of activism gave warning that African-Americans would not forever ignore blatant racial discrimination and inequality.

The 1930s likewise brought trying times for Hispanic-Americans. Recent arrivals from Mexico, Puerto Rico, Cuba, and elsewhere in Latin America and South America made up most of the nation's 2 million Spanish-speaking residents. Most were manual laborers, many of them migratory agricultural workers. As the depression deepened, Mexican-born farm workers of the Southwest, welcomed for years as cheap labor, faced mounting hostility. The influx of "Okies" fleeing the dust bowl worsened the job crisis, and by 1937 more than half of the cotton workers in Arizona were out-of-staters who supplanted Mexican-American laborers.

With their access to migratory work disrupted, Mexican-Americans poured into southwestern cities and swelled the population of the Spanish-speaking neighborhoods (barrios). Discrimination pervaded the cities. Crude notices appeared trumpeting such warnings as "NO NIGGERS, MEXICANS, OR DOGS ALLOWED." Finding themselves expendable, half a million Mexicans returned to their native land in the 1930s. Some did so voluntarily, but in 1932 immigration officials and local authorities expelled more than 200,000 Mexican aliens.

Mexican-American agricultural workers faced appalling labor conditions and near-starvation wages. In the mid-1930s they rose up in waves of protests and strikes across California. In 1933 cotton workers and strawberry, pea, and grape pickers struck for higher wages. A labor organization called the Confederación de Uniones de Campesinos y Obreros Mexicanos (CUCOM, or Confederation of Unions of Mexican Workers and Farm Laborers) emerged. Under the impetus of CUCOM, more strikes erupted in 1935–1936, from the celery fields and citrus groves of the Los Angeles area to the lettuce fields of the Salinas Valley.

Well-financed agribusiness organizations such as the Associated Farmers of California and the California Fruit Growers Exchange (which marketed citrus under the Sunkist brand name) fought the unions, sometimes resorting to violence in the process. Against heavy odds, the labor movement among Mexican-American farm workers did achieve some successes. Striking cotton pickers, for example, increased the rate for a hundred pounds of cotton from $.60 to $.75. Their strikes also awakened some Americans to the inhumane working conditions and shamefully low wages of one of the nation's most exploited groups.

The 1930s also revived attention to the nation's 170,000 Native Americans, most of whom existed in a world of poverty, scant education, poor health care, and bleak prospects. The Dawes Act of 1887 had dissolved the tribes as legal entities and tried to promote the Indians' assimilation into the American mainstream by allocating some tribal lands to individuals and selling the rest. By the early 1930s, whites owned about two-thirds of the land that Native Americans had possessed in 1887, including much of the most valuable acreage. Meanwhile, officials of the Bureau of Indian Affairs, including several Quaker humanitarians appointed by Herbert Hoover, had become convinced that the Dawes Act approach should be reversed. A leading advocate of reform was John Collier, who in 1923 had founded the American Indian Defense Association to preserve the spiritual beauty and harmony of traditional Indian life.

Alabama Sharecropper
By paying landowners to take acreage out of production, New Deal agricultural policies often worsened the plight of share-croppers.

Appointed commissioner of Indian affairs in 1933, Collier translated his vision of renewed tribal life into policy. He secured funds from the Civilian Conservation Corps, the Public Works Administration, and the Works Progress Administration to build schools, hospitals, and irrigation systems on Indian reservations—and to provide jobs for Native American workers. But Collier had larger goals. In 1934 he presented Congress with a bill halting the sale of tribal land to individuals, restoring the remaining unallocated lands to tribal control, creating new reservations, and expanding existing ones. The bill also would have set up tribal councils with broad powers of home rule and required Indian schools to focus on Native American history and traditional arts and crafts.

This visionary bill drew angry opposition in western states. Some Indian leaders criticized it as a plan to transform the reservations into living museums and treat Native Americans as an exotic minority. In fact, Collier's bill was widely thought to reflect the sentimental idealism of a benevolent outsider who believed that he understood what was best for the Indians; from the perspective of many observers, it did not express the actual views of the Native American population.

The law that finally emerged during the New Deal, the Indian Reorganization Act of 1934, represented a compromise between Collier and his critics. It ended the sale of tribal lands and enabled tribes to regain title to unallocated lands, but it also scaled back tribal self-government and dropped Collier's call for the renewal of traditional tribal culture.

Like the New Deal itself, Indian reform ebbed in the late 1930s. Collier resigned in 1945, his dream of revitalized tribal life unfulfilled. The tribes' special standing with the federal government had been largely terminated, and Native Americans were once more encouraged to abandon reservations and to give up traditional ways.

Family Life and Population Trends

For many parents in the 1930s, daily life was a constant uphill climb to make ends meet and to keep families together. They patched clothes, stretched food resources, and, when all else failed, turned to public assistance. Very poor families developed survival skills that more affluent families lacked.

Hard times disrupted marital patterns. Marriage rates tumbled in the early 1930s as people confronted harsh economic realities. The birthrate, too, dropped precipitously in the early depression years. Couples postponed families or limited their children to one or two. Family planning became easier with the spread and growing acceptance of birth-control devices such as the condom and diaphragm.

The declining birthrate and restrictions on immigration held population growth in the 1930s to a scant 7 percent, in contrast to an average of 20 percent in the three preceding decades. The economic crisis temporarily slowed urban growth, and many jobless young people returned home from the cities to their parents' farms. However, another long-term demographic trend, the westward movement, continued. Thousands of American families responded to hard times by seeking opportunities in the West, especially California. The proportion of the population living in the Pacific region rose steeply, and Los Angeles advanced from tenth to fifth among U.S. cities.

The depression inflicted deep psychological wounds on many families. In households with a tradition of male authority, the husband's loss of a job and erosion of self-confidence often had devastating consequences. One man expressed the depression's threat to his masculinity in extreme form when he admitted, "I would rather turn on the gas and put an end to the whole family than let my wife support me." Desertions increased, and the divorce rate reached a then all-time high by 1940.

Parents ruefully canceled vacation plans. Children did without birthday presents and endured a home atmosphere tense with anxious discussions of family finances. Not all was bleak, however. People rediscovered skills such as painting their own houses and repairing their own cars. Home baking and canning thrived. Many later would look back at the depression as a time when adversity strengthened networks of sociability and support. One man recalled, "The feeling among people was beautiful. Supposing some guy was a hunter. He'd go out and get a hold of some ducks or some game, [and] they'd have their friends over and share it." But although sharing and making do could soften the depression's impact on family life, they could not eliminate the pain entirely, and the trials of the depression would long remain etched in the memories of those who lived through it.

The American Cultural Scene in the Thirties

The depression's cultural impact matched its broad social effects. Radio and movies provided diversion, and writers, artists, and social thinkers offered personal and probing views of American life. The mood shifted from critical pessimism to positive affirmation of the United States' history and traditions. This new tone reflected the renewed hope stimulated by the New Deal as well as the rallying of intellectuals against the rise of dictatorships abroad—regimes that made American democracy seem fragile and more valuable than some intellectuals had once appeared to think.

The Golden Age of Radio

Radio provided an antidote to hard times. Each evening millions of Americans gathered around their Silvertone or Atwater Kent consoles to listen to their favorite news commentators, musical programs, and—above all—comedy shows. Radio humor reached its zenith in the 1930s, when the real world was hardly laughable. Comedians Jack Benny, Fred Allen, and George Burns and Gracie Allen won fiercely loyal audiences.

So, too, did the fifteen-minute afternoon dramas known as soap operas (because soap companies usually sponsored them), the favorites of housewives across the land. Listeners became so deeply involved with these daily dollops of idealized romance and melodrama that the line between fantasy and reality blurred. They even wrote earnest letters to soap-opera characters advising them how to handle their problems. Identifying with the ordeals and traumas of the radio heroines, listeners gained temporary escape from their own difficulties.

The standardization of mass culture continued. As successful radio shows spawned eager imitators, programming took on a monotonous, formulaic quality.

The Silver Screen

In 1931 and 1932 the major movie studios tottered toward bankruptcy, but in true Hollywood fashion they staged a dramatic recovery in 1933 and prospered for the rest of the decade. Most people could still afford the quarter that it cost to see a movie, and the introduction of double features (1931) and drive-in theaters (1933) also boosted attendance. In 1939, 65 percent of the population saw at least one movie a week.

A few movies dealt realistically with contemporary issues such as labor unrest in the coal industry (*Black Fury*, 1935) and sharecroppers (*Cabin in the Cotton*, 1932). Two documentaries made in 1936, *The River* and *The Plow That Broke the Plains*, evoked the human and emotional toll of a century of westward expansion. Casting off the bleak pessimism of the early thirties, Warner Brothers studio made a series of movies in 1934–1936 that portrayed the New Deal in glowing terms. And in *Mr. Deeds Goes to Town* (1936) and *Mr. Smith Goes to Washington* (1939), director Frank Capra, the son of Italian immigrants, offered a patriotic, idealistic message: that "the people" would always triumph over entrenched interests.

Gangster movies served up a stark style of film realism. Taking advantage of the advent of sound, such movies as *Little Caesar* (1930) and *The Public Enemy* (1931) grittily portrayed an urban America of giant skyscrapers, raw and rain-swept streets, lonely bus depots and all-night diners, and the rat-tat-tat of machine guns as rival gangs battled it out. When civic groups protested that gangster movies glorified crime, Hollywood reversed the formula, making police and "G-men" (FBI agents) the heroes while maintaining the same level of violence. The lead characters, especially as played by actors Edward G. Robinson and James Cagney, struck a responsive chord with depression-era moviegoers, for whom the odds seemed equally discouraging and the social environment equally threatening.

Above all, movies offered the chance to forget the depression for a couple of hours. Indeed, cinema's narcotic function in the thirties is clear. Lush musicals featured catchy tunes and cheerful plots involving the triumph of luck and pluck. Walt Disney's *Snow White and the Seven Dwarfs* (1937) brought animation to a new level of sophistication. *The Wizard of Oz* (1939) became a classic, beloved by generations of children and adults alike. Comedies, too, provided cinematic escape and some of the decade's best movies. In films such as *Animal Crackers* (1930), *Duck Soup* (1933), and *A Night at the Opera* (1935), the Marx brothers, vaudeville troupers, created an anarchic world that satirized

Light Moments in a Dark Decade
The Marx Brothers clown around in Animal Crackers *(1930).*

authority, fractured the English language, and demolished all rules of logic.

Filmmakers continued to stereotype blacks and women. African-American actor Paul Robeson recreated his stage role in the movie *The Emperor Jones* (1933), but most African-American performers were confined to such parts as the weepy, scatterbrained maid played by Butterfly McQueen in *Gone with the Wind* (1939) or the indulgent house servant played by tap dancer Bill Robinson in the Shirley Temple feature *The Little Colonel* (1935). And Hollywood preached that women could find fulfillment only in marriage and domesticity, although a few films chipped away at the stereotype. In the comedy *Wedding Present* (1936), Joan Bennet played a strong-willed professional, and the tough, brassy, sexual, and fiercely independent Mae West, in *I'm No Angel* (1933) and other hits, cut her suitors down to size with a razor-sharp wit and made clear that she took orders from no one.

The Literature of the Early Thirties

American fiction of the early depression era exuded disillusionment, cynicism, and despair, challenging the fundamental premises of American ideology. James T. Farrell's *Studs Lonigan* trilogy (1932–1935) bleakly traced the hero's empty existence. The product of a chaotic working-class Irish-immigrant neighborhood, the young Lonigan stumbles through life, trying to piece together a coherent world view from the bits of mass culture that drift his way. Finally, not yet thirty, jobless, and alone, Lonigan dies of tuberculosis. John Dos Passos, in the innovative trilogy *U.S.A.* (1930–1936), sketched a dark portrait of American history from 1900 through the early 1930s, painting a bloated, money-mad, exploitive society utterly lacking social or spiritual coherence. The gloomiest view of the early thirties belonged to Nathaniel West. Drawing on his experiences as a night clerk in a seedy Manhattan hotel,

West in *Miss Lonelyhearts* (1933) wove a nightmarish story of a newspaper advice columnist so oppressed by the stream of human misery flowing across his desk that he retreats first into apathy and then into insanity. In West's *A Cool Million* (1934), a parody of Horatio Alger, brave and virtuous young Lemuel Pitkin comes to New York seeking his fortune, only to be cheated, betrayed, beaten, imprisoned, and murdered.

Some radical novelists of the 1930s, encouraged by Communist party clubs, wrote explicitly of the decadence of capitalism, the exploitation of workers, and the approaching revolution. Jack Conroy's *The Disinherited* (1933), about exploitation and labor violence in the Missouri coal fields, gained force from the fact that Conroy's father and brother had died in a mine disaster. And radical playwrights brought the class struggle to the stage, including Clifford Odets, whose *Waiting for Lefty* (1933) offered cartoonlike stereotypes of noble workers and evil bosses and ended with the audience chanting "Strike! Strike! Strike!"

The Later Thirties: The Popular Front and Cultural Nationalism

In 1933–1934 the American Communist party vehemently attacked FDR and the New Deal. But in 1935 Soviet dictator Joseph Stalin, fearful of an attack on the Soviet Union by Nazi Germany under Adolf Hitler, called for a worldwide "Popular Front" comprising opponents of fascism* and Nazism; American communist leaders then praised Roosevelt and recruited noncommunist intellectuals to the antifascist cause. For those who rallied to the Popular Front, few events aroused more passionate emotions than the Spanish Civil War (1936–1939). In July 1936 army units under fascist general Francisco Franco rebelled against Spain's legally elected government, a left-wing coalition. Spanish conservatives and monarchists, as well as landowners, industrialists, and the Roman Catholic hierarchy, supported Franco. His fellow fascists, Benito Mussolini of Italy and Adolf Hitler of Germany, provided military aid.

The anti-Franco loyalists, supporters of the elected government, won enthusiastic backing from many writers, artists, and intellectuals who sympathized with the Popular Front. Poet Archibald MacLeish pleaded eloquently for the loyalist cause. Ernest Hemingway, too, championed the loyalists' aims. His novel *For Whom the Bell Tolls* (1940) tells the story of a young American who joins a loyalist guerrilla band and eventually dies for the cause. Reflecting on his newfound capacity for political engagement, Hemingway wrote, "The Spanish Civil War offered something which you could believe in wholly and completely, and in which you felt an absolute brotherhood with the others who were engaged in it." (Franco's fascists gained control of Spain in 1939, and he ruled as a dictator, with American support, until his death in 1975.)

The Popular Front collapsed on August 24, 1939, when the Soviet Union and Nazi Germany signed a pact agreeing not to make war on each other and dividing Poland between them. Stalin's cynical exercise in power politics shocked idealistic Americans allied with the Popular Front. Enthusiasm for cooperating with the communists under the banner of "antifascism" evaporated, and membership in the American Communist party dwindled. Although short-lived, the Popular Front significantly influenced U.S. politics and culture in the later 1930s and alerted Americans to the danger of fascism.

The emergence of fascism and the renewal of political engagement inspired by the Popular Front combined with the achievements of the New Deal to stimulate a broad shift in America's cultural climate in the mid-1930s. The cynicism of the early depression yielded to more hopeful views. Writers abandoned the satirical tone of the twenties and voiced admiration for the courage and solid virtue of ordinary Americans.

---

*Fascism: a form of government involving one-party dictatorship, state control of production, extreme nationalism, and the forcible suppression of opposition.

This mood found many expressions. In John Steinbeck's *The Grapes of Wrath* (1939), an uprooted dust-bowl family, the Joads, experiences many setbacks as they make their way from Oklahoma to California. But they never give up and always help others. As Ma Joad says, "They ain't gonna wipe us out. Why, we're the people—we go on."

Another eloquent example of the new cultural experience dates from 1936, when writer James Agee and photographer Walker Evans spent weeks living with Alabama sharecroppers to research an article on rural poverty. It finally appeared in 1941 as *Let Us Now Praise Famous Men*. Enhanced by Evans's haunting photographs, Agee's beautifully written masterpiece evoked not only the precariousness of life at the bottom but also the strength and decency of Americans living at that level.

This positive assessment of American life reached the stage as well. Thornton Wilder's drama *Our Town* (1938) warmly portrayed a turn-of-the-century New England town where the deceptively ordinary routines of everyday life become, in memory, infinitely precious. William Saroyan's *The Time of Your Life* (1939) celebrated the foibles and virtues of a colorful collection of American "types" assembled in a San Francisco waterfront bar.

American music also reflected this swell of cultural nationalism. In *Billy the Kid* (1938) and other compositions, Aaron Copland drew upon American legends and folk memories. George Gershwin turned to a popular 1920s play about black life for his opera *Porgy and Bess* (1935). And jazz flourished in the later thirties, thanks to the big bands of Benny Goodman, Count Basie, Glenn Miller, and others who developed a smoother, flowing style known as swing. For the next decade, swing dominated popular music.

Cultural nationalism also heightened interest in regional literature and art. In such fictional works as *Absalom, Absalom!* (1936) and *The Hamlet* (1940), William Faulkner of Mississippi continued the complex and often tragic saga of his mythic Yoknapatawpha County. Artists Thomas Hart Benton of Missouri, John Steuart Curry of Kansas, and Grant Wood of Iowa contributed a strongly regional note to painting.

Americans also began to recognize their rich folk-art heritage. Galleries mounted shows of Amish quilts, New Hampshire weathervanes, itinerant portraiture from the colonial era, and lovingly crafted children's toys. Eighty-year-old Anna "Grandma" Moses was only the best known of many folk artists "discovered" during this decade.

The patriotic absorption with all things American generated a fascination with the nation's past. Americans flocked to historical re-creations such as Henry Ford's Greenfield Village in Michigan and Colonial Williamsburg in Virginia. In 1936–1939 Texans restored the Alamo in San Antonio, the "Cradle of Texas Liberty." Americans made Margaret Mitchell's romantic epic of the Old South, *Gone with the Wind* (1936), a best-selling novel. Poet Carl Sandburg won a Pulitzer Prize for a four-volume biography that elevated Abraham Lincoln to near-mythic status.

As the 1930s ended, Americans viewed their society, their history, and their political system with a newly appreciative eye. The nation had survived the economic crisis. Its social fabric remained whole; revolution had not erupted. Other societies had collapsed into dictatorship, but American democracy thrived. Intellectuals and writers now led the way in celebrating America and its people.

The Age of Streamlining

This restored confidence was captured in a bold style of industrial design called streamlining: which by the mid-1930s had become a national vogue. Inspired by the romance of flight, industrial designers preached the gospel of streamlining: smoothly flowing surfaces. Graceful curves replaced clunky, square shapes. The goal was to reduce products to their "utmost simplification in terms of function and form." Behind these aesthetic principles lay a social vision: that harmonious and functional consumer goods would produce a harmonious and functional society.

Streamlining appealed to American business. It also made products more attractive to consumers, a vital need during the economic stagnation. When Sears, Roebuck streamlined its Coldspot refrigerators, sales surged. Products ranging from stoves to toasters, alarm clocks, and cigarette lighters emerged in sleek new forms. Streamlining also helped business to rebuild its tattered reputation. By the mid-thirties, corporations were stressing the material benefits that business brought to society. Du Pont's "Better Things for Better Living Through Chemistry" summed up the new theme. Futuristic product designs fit perfectly with corporate America's effort to present itself as the benevolent shaper of the future.

The New York World's Fair of 1939 represented the high point of both the streamlining vogue and corporate America's public-relations counteroffensive. The hit of the fair was General Motors' Futurama, which gave visitors a vision of the United States in the distant year 1960—a nation of complex interstate highways complete with multiple lanes and stacked interchanges. For GM, Futurama represented a good public-relations investment that promoted GM vehicles and built public support for the costly highway system that the increasing number of cars and trucks would soon make essential.

Along with a first glimpse of such wonders as television and automatic dishwashers, the World's Fair offered its millions of visitors a memorable vision of "The World of Tomorrow"—a smoothly functioning technological utopia made possible by the nation's corporations. In one seductive, streamlined package, the fair epitomized capitalism's version of the cultural nationalism and reviving optimism that characterized the American mood as the thirties ended.

Undercurrents of Apprehension

Muted uneasiness and fear lay beneath the surface appearance of reviving confidence. Although the economic crisis had eased, danger was brewing overseas. The anxieties triggered by the menacing world situation flared at unexpected times and in unexpected ways. One such moment came on October 31, 1938, Halloween, when CBS radio aired a dramatic adaptation of H. G. Wells's *War of the Worlds*, directed by Orson Welles.

In realistic detail, the broadcast reported the landing of a spaceship near Princeton, New Jersey; the emergence of aliens with deadly ray guns; and their advance toward New York. The vivid dramatization sparked a national panic as more than a million horrified listeners believed that aliens had landed, that New York lay in ruins, and that the end of the world was at hand. When word of the alarm reached the CBS studio, Welles inserted several announcements that the program was fictional. By then many people had already fled their homes, and not for several hours did the nation's heartbeat return to normal.

Beneath the panic about "Martians" lay a far more rational fear, that of an approaching war. For while the depression had preoccupied Americans, the international situation had deteriorated, and by October 1938 a global conflict seemed near. Radio news bulletins had warned for weeks of an impending war between Germany and England. Some listeners to *War of the Worlds* blurred the broadcast's details and concluded that a foreign nation had launched a surprise attack against the United States. The reaction was understandable, for by this time the real world looked very scary indeed.

The United States in a Menacing World

Apart from efforts to improve Latin American relations, the early Roosevelt administration remained largely aloof from the rest of the world. As Italy, Germany, and Japan pursued aggressive and militaristic courses, American observers were torn between an impulse to resist fascism and an even stronger desire for peace. Determined not to stumble into war again, millions of Americans supported neutrality and peace. Others insisted that the United States help embattled democracies abroad. All the while, the world edged steadily closer to the precipice.

FDR's Nationalism and the Good Neighbor Policy

President Roosevelt at first put American economic interests above all else. Despite Secretary of State Cordell Hull's urging, FDR showed little interest in free trade or international economic cooperation.

Roosevelt did, however, commit himself to an internationalist approach in Latin America, where bitterness over decades of "Yankee imperialism" ran high. In his 1933 inaugural, he had announced a "Good Neighbor" policy toward Latin America, and at a conference in Uruguay in 1933 the United States endorsed a statement of principles that declared, "No state has the right to intervene in the internal or external affairs of another." Under this policy Roosevelt withdrew the last U.S. troops from Haiti and the Dominican Republic, persuaded American bankers to loosen their grip on Haiti's central banking system, and reduced the U.S. role in Panamanian affairs. However, the United States remained closely identified with the repressive regimes of Raphael Trujillo in the Dominican Republic and Anastasio Somoza in Nicaragua.

Cuba and Mexico provided major tests of the Good Neighbor policy. In Cuba economic problems triggered by the highly protectionist Smoot-Hawley Tariff of 1930 brought to power a radical leftist, Grau San Martín, in 1933. American opposition to the San Martín administration found expression in indirect action. Early in 1934, a conservative coalition enjoying U.S. support overthrew the San Martín regime. Strongman Fulgencio Batista gained power, aided by American manipulation of sugar quotas. He would retain power off and on until being overthrown by Fidel Castro in 1959.

In 1936 a reform government came to power in Mexico and nationalized several oil companies owned by U.S. and British corporations. The United States did not oppose nationalization but insisted on fair compensation. Economic pressure from Washington led to a compensation agreement that both the Mexican government and the oil companies accepted.

The Good Neighbor policy, in sum, did not terminate American interference in Latin America, but it did end heavy-handed intervention and military occupation.

The Rise of Fascism in Europe and Asia

Meanwhile, powerful forces raged across much of the world—forces that would once again pull the United States into war. As early as 1922, Italy's economic problems and social unrest had opened the way for Benito Mussolini and his Fascist party to seize power in Rome. The regime had swiftly suppressed dissent and imposed one-party rule.

More menacing events had unfolded in Germany with the rise of Adolf Hitler. An embittered war veteran, Hitler capitalized on the German people's resentment of the Versailles treaty and on the democratic government's inability to control runaway inflation. Briefly jailed after a 1923 grab for power failed, he had dictated his manifesto, *Mein Kampf* (My Struggle), filled with fanatic nationalism and anti-Semitism.

In 1929 an economic depression had struck Germany after a decade of runaway inflation and chronic recession. Hitler's National Socialist (Nazi) party had gained broad support as the economy deteriorated, and Hitler had become Germany's chancellor in January 1933. He promptly crushed rivals within the Nazi party and fastened a brutal dictatorship on Germany. Young Nazis staged towering bonfires to burn the work of authors—many of them Jewish—whom they accused of "un-German" ideas. A racist who believed that he had to purify Germany of "inferior" taint, Hitler began driving out German Jews, whom he blamed for Germany's defeat in World War I.

In the mid-1930s Hitler pursued a militaristic, expansionist foreign policy that violated the Versailles treaty by rearming Germany and reoccupying the Rhineland, the strip between the Rhine River and the French border specifically demilitarized at Versailles. Early in 1938 he proclaimed an *Anschluss* (union) between Austria and Germany. Meanwhile, Mussolini, intent on building an empire in Africa, had invaded Ethiopia in 1935. In London, Paris, Washington, and Geneva, the headquarters of the League of Nations, hand wringing but little firm action greeted these aggressive moves.

After Austria, Hitler turned to the Sudetenland, an area of Czechoslovakia containing 3 million ethnic Germans and 700,000 Czechs. Insisting that the Sudetenland was "racially" part of Germany, Hitler made clear his determination to take the area, by force if necessary. At a conference in

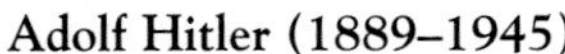

Adolf Hitler (1889–1945)
In this German magazine illustration from 1934, a belligerent Hitler is portrayed as his nation's savior.

European Aggression Before World War II
Less than twenty years after the end of World War I, war again loomed in Europe as Hitler launched Germany on a course of military and territorial expansion.

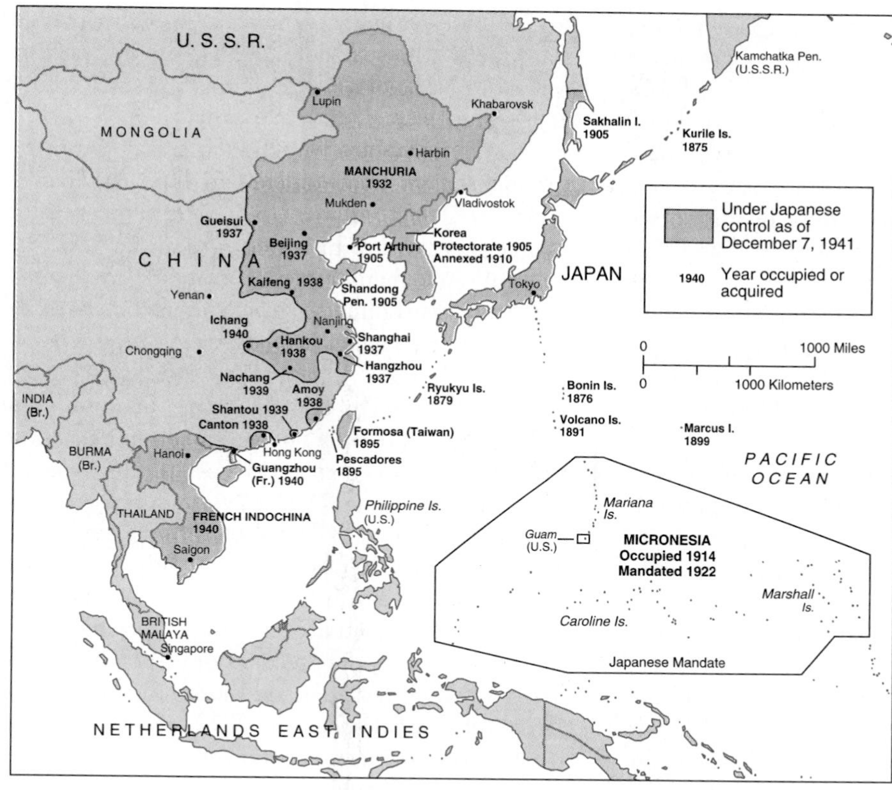

Japanese Expansion Before World War II *Dominated by militarists, Japan pursued an expansionist policy in Asia in the 1930s, extending its sphere of economic and political influence. In July 1937, having already occupied the Chinese province of Manchuria, Japan attacked China proper.*

Munich on September 29–30, 1938—which excluded the Czechs—British prime minister Neville Chamberlain and his French counterpart, Edouard Daladier, agreed to turn the Sudetenland over to Germany. Stripped of a third of its population and territory, Czechoslovakia now faced Germany's massed tanks and troops. Viewing this appeasement of Germany as a diplomatic victory, Chamberlain proclaimed "peace in our time." World War II was less than a year away.

In Tokyo, meanwhile, nationalistic militarists had gained control of Japan's government and begun a fateful course of expansion. In 1931–1933 Japanese troops had invaded the Chinese province of Manchuria, installed a puppet government, and forced China, with no outside support, to sign a treaty recognizing Japanese control of the province. In July 1937 Japan launched a full-scale war against China itself.

In 1936 and 1940 Germany, Italy, and Japan signed treaties of political alliance and mutual defense. This alignment, called the Axis, would soon join forces in war.

The American Mood: No More War

The American response to these developments reflected a revulsion against war. By the mid-1930s millions of Americans believed that the United States' decision to enter World War I in April 1917 had been a ghastly mistake. In mid-decade a series of books reinforced this conclusion, arguing that banking and corporate interests had dragged the United States into World War I to protect their loans and weapons sales to England and France.

Public concern over the "merchants of death" issue led to the creation of a special congressional investigating committee under Senator Gerald Nye, a North Dakota Republican. In hearings from 1934 to 1936, the Nye committee compiled mountainous evidence of the heavy involvement of U.S. banks and corporations in financing World War I and supplying arms to the Allies. It documented these groups' lobbying and public-relations activities in support of U.S. intervention. In these hearings, Progressive Era suspicions of "Wall Street" and "big business" resurfaced powerfully. And in the midst of the depression, it was not hard to convince Americans that bankers were evil. A January 1937 poll showed that an astonishing 70 percent of the people believed that the United States should have stayed out of World War I.

Mistakenly equating Hitler with Kaiser Wilhelm, and the rise of fascism with the militaristic posturing of the pre-1914 European empires, many Americans concluded that the United States, protected by two oceans, could safely remain aloof from the upheavals convulsing other parts of the world. Reflecting this outlook, a peace movement spread across the nation's college and university campuses in 1935–1938. A peace strike in spring 1936 saw half a million students boycott classes to attend antiwar events.

In 1935–1937 a series of Neutrality Acts echoed the longing for peace. To prevent a repetition of the circumstances that had brought the United States into war in 1917, these measures outlawed arms sales and loans to nations at war and forbade Americans from traveling on the ships of belligerent powers. But the high point of peace legislation came early in 1938 when Indiana congressman Louis Ludlow proposed a constitutional amendment requiring a national referendum on any U.S. declaration of war except in cases of actual attack. Only after a direct appeal from FDR, and then by a narrow margin, did Congress reject the Ludlow Amendment.

Hesitant Response to the Fascist Challenge

The American people took alarm slowly at the fascist and militaristic regimes in Germany, Italy, and Japan. Indeed, many Americans initially praised Mussolini for imposing order and discipline, making trains run on time, and energizing Italy with a flurry of government activity, and even Hitler had American admirers. Some—including Joseph P. Kennedy, the ambassador to Great Britain (and father of a future president)—found the German chancellor tolerable because of his fanatic opposition to communism. And many Americans at first considered Hitler and Mussolini more ridiculous than menacing. From the beginning, however, others viewed fascism with grave apprehension. As early as 1933, Harvard literature professor Howard Mumford Jones warned that Nazi book burnings and suppression of free speech put freedom at risk everywhere.

FDR reacted ambivalently to the fascist onslaught. Fascinated by global politics, he advocated adequate national defense, and as early as 1933 he proposed naval expansion. At the same time, personalizing international affairs as he did domestic issues, Roosevelt communicated directly with world leaders, including Hitler and Mussolini, seeking avenues of accommodation. FDR recognized the strength of American antiwar sentiment and never pushed ahead of public opinion. After the Munich Pact, the president sent a terse telegram of praise ("Good Man") to Prime Minister Chamberlain and wrote that he was "not a bit upset" at the agreement to hand the Sudetenland over to Germany.

Several factors shaped America's hesitant response to Europe's turmoil. The desire to avoid entanglement in European affairs reached back to the 1790s. The widespread conviction that American intervention in World War I was wrong fed this isolationist impulse, as did the focus on domestic issues during the depression.

The administration responded more uneasily to Japanese aggression against China throughout the 1930s than to Hitler and Mussolini. Americans regarded China with special sympathy and interest. Christian missionaries saw the vast Eastern nation as a field ripe for harvest, and top government policy makers clung to the old dream of a boundless China market. The Open Door policy of the late nineteenth century reflected the American outlook on Asian nations, "the great potential markets of the world" as Secretary of State Hull termed them.

Japanese expansion into Manchuria in 1931, and then into China itself in 1937, threatened the Open Door. On an immediate level, the closing of China to U.S. trade meant the loss of $100 million in annual cotton sales. But long-term concern that Japanese goods, especially textiles, might someday flood the world market heightened Washington's uneasiness. As early as 1934, General William "Billy" Mitchell, an advocate of air power, declared, "Japan is our most dangerous enemy, and our planes should be designed to attack her." In cabinet meetings, FDR openly speculated about eventual war with Japan.

Publicly, Washington reacted to Japan's moves with symbolic gestures, refusing to recognize the Japanese puppet government in Manchuria, extending modest loans to China, and urging Americans to boycott Japanese silk. In October 1938 the U.S. ambassador to Japan protested Japan's violation of the Open Door principle. The Japanese responded that the Open Door was "inapplicable." Apart from these cautious steps, the United States did little as the Japanese tightened their grip on China.

1938–1939: The Gathering Storm

The interlude of reduced tension that followed the Munich Pact proved tragically brief. "Peace in our time" lasted a mere 5½ months. At 6:00 A.M. on March 15, 1939, Nazi troops thundered across the border into Czechoslovakia. By evening the Nazi flag flew over Prague. Five months later, the signing of the Nazi-Soviet Pact gave Hitler a green light to invade Poland.

In the United States the debate over the American role intensified. Some almost desperately urged the nation to keep free of the approaching conflict. Opponents of intervention warned that American involvement in a war could shatter New Deal reforms and spawn repression and reaction, as it had a generation earlier. But opinion was shifting rapidly. Pacifism and neutralism weakened, and the voices urging activism strengthened. In 1938, warning of the "malignant character and cancerous spread" of fascism, cultural critic Lewis Mumford issued "A Call to Arms" in the *New Republic*. Archibald MacLeish, having earlier championed the cause of Spain, exhorted his fellow citizens to mobilize against Hitler.

After the fall of Czechoslovakia and Albania early in 1939, FDR publicly called on Hitler and Mussolini not to invade thirty-one specific nations. A jeering Hitler read FDR's message before the German Reichstag (legislative assembly), and Nazis roared with laughter as he proclaimed, "Mr. President, I fully understand that the vastness of your nation and the immense wealth of your country allow you to feel responsible for the history of the whole world and for the history of all nations. I, sir, am placed in a much more modest and smaller sphere."

In October 1938 Roosevelt asked Congress for a $300 million military appropriation; in November he instructed the Army Air Corps to plan for an annual production of 20,000 planes; in January 1939, calling for actions against "aggressor nations . . . more effective than mere words," he submitted a $1.3 billion defense budget. Hitler and Mussolini, he said, were "two madmen" who "respect force and force alone."

America and the Jewish Refugees

Hitler and the Nazis had translated their hatred of Jews into official policy. The Nuremberg Laws of 1935 had denied German Jews citizenship and many legal rights. Then in 1938 the anti-Jewish campaign grew more brutal as the Nazis barred Jews from attending concerts and plays, expelled Jewish students from schools and universities, and required Jews to register their property. When a distraught Jewish youth assassinated a German official in Paris, Hitler levied a "fine" of $400 million on the entire Jewish population of Germany.

This remorseless campaign reached a crescendo of violence on November 9–10, 1938: *Kristallnacht*, the "Night of Broken Glass." Throughout Germany and Austria, Nazis vandalized Jewish homes, burned synagogues, and wrecked and looted thousands of Jewish-owned businesses. Not even Jewish hospitals, old people's homes, or children's boarding schools escaped the terror.

No longer could anyone mistake Hitler's malignant intent. This brutish repression foreshadowed the policy of outright extermination that would emerge during World War II, Hitler's "final solution" to the "Jewish problem." Jews, who had been leaving Germany since 1933, streamed out by the tens of thousands, seeking haven. Between 1933 and 1938, 60,000 had fled to the United States.

Among the victims of fascism who found refuge in America were several hundred distinguished scholars, writers, musicians, artists, and scientists. This remarkable company included pianist Rudolph Serkin, composer Béla Bartók, architect Walter Gropius, political theorist Hannah Arendt, and future secretary of state Henry Kissinger. Also among the refugees were three gifted physicists, Leo Szilard, James Franck, and Enrico Fermi, who would play key roles in building the atomic bomb. American cultural and intellectual life in the second half of the twentieth century would have been immeasurably diminished without these refugees.

While it welcomed famous and distinguished Jewish refugees, the United States proved far more reluctant to grant sanctuary to the mass of Hitler's Jewish victims. Congress consistently rejected all efforts to liberalize the immigration law, with its discriminatory quotas. FDR bears some responsibility. While deploring Hitler's persecution of the Jews and helping to establish the Inter-Governmental Committee on Refugees in 1938, he did little else to translate his generalized sympathy for the Jews into political efforts to relax restrictions on immigration.

Most Americans, according to public-opinion polls, condemned the Jews' persecution, but only a minority favored admitting more refugees. In early 1938 when pollsters asked whether the immigration act should be amended to admit "a larger number of Jewish refugees from Germany," 75 percent responded no. Isolationism, anti-immigrant sentiment, and anti-Semitism sharply limited the American response to the tragedy of European Jewry.

The consequences of such attitudes were graphically illustrated in June 1939 when the *St. Louis*, a German passenger ship jammed with 900 Jewish refugees, asked permission to put its passengers ashore at Fort Lauderdale, Florida. Not only did immigration officials refuse this request, but also, according to the *New York Times*, a Coast Guard cutter stood by "to prevent possible attempts by refugees to jump off and swim ashore." The *St. Louis* turned slowly away from the lights of America and sailed back to Germany, where more than 700 of its passengers would die under Nazi brutality.

CONCLUSION

The ordeal of the *St. Louis* provides an appropriately somber conclusion to a decade that began with the stock-market plunge and ended with the nation teetering on the brink of war. Between these dismal developments, the 1930s brought bright moments of political creativity, social advance, and cultural achievement. American families showed sturdy resiliency, workers found solidarity in unions, and bold designs revolutionized consumer goods. Radio and movies provided standardized entertainment even as writers and others rediscovered the vitality of America's regional cultures. But by 1939 the world looked dark from the thunderheads of war gathering over Europe and Japan; it would soon look darker still.

CHRONOLOGY

1930 *Little Caesar*, gangster movie starring Edward G. Robinson.
Animal Crackers, classic Marx Brothers comedy.

1930–1936 John Dos Passos, *U.S.A.* trilogy.

1931–1932 Japan invades Manchuria and creates puppet government

1932–1935 James T. Farrell, *Studs Lonigan* trilogy.

1933 Nathanael West, *Miss Lonelyhearts*.
She Done Him Wrong and *I'm No Angel*, Mae West movie hits.
Adolf Hitler becomes chancellor of Germany and assumes dictatorial powers.

1934 Indian Reorganization Act.
Nathanael West, *A Cool Million*.
United States plays role in rise of Cuban strongman Fulgencio Batista.

1934–1936 Nye committee investigations.
Strikes by Mexican-American agricultural workers in the West.

1935 Supreme Court reverses conviction of the "Scottsboro Boys."
Clifford Odets, *Waiting for Lefty*.

1935–1937 Neutrality Acts.

1935–1938 Peace movement sweeps U.S. campuses.

1935–1939 Era of the Popular Front.

1936 William Faulkner, *Absalom, Absalom!*
Mr. Deeds Goes to Town, Frank Capra movie.

1936–1937 Autoworkers' sit-down strike against General Motors (December 1936–February 1937).

1936–1939 Spanish Civil War.

1937 U.S. Steel, General Motors, and Chrysler sign union contracts.
"Memorial Day Massacre" at Republic Steel Company in South Chicago.
Japan invades China.

1938 Formation of Congress of Industrial Organizations (CIO).
Thornton Wilder, *Our Town*.
War of the Worlds broadcast on CBS radio.
Nazis occupy Austria.
Munich Pact gives Sudetenland to Hitler.
Kristallnacht, night of Nazi terror against German and Austrian Jews.
United States protests Japanese violation of Open Door principle in China.

1939 John Steinbeck, *The Grapes of Wrath*.
New York World's Fair.
Nazis invade Czechoslovakia.
Nazi-Soviet Pact.
St. Louis, carrying Jewish refugees from Nazism, refused landing permission in Florida.

1940 Richard Wright, *Native Son*.
Ernest Hemingway, *For Whom the Bell Tolls*.

1941 James Agee and Walker Evans, *Let Us Now Praise Famous Men*.

FOR FURTHER READING

Caroline Bird, *The Invisible Scar* (1966). Moving look at the depression's human and psychological toll.

Lizabeth Cohen, *Making a New Deal: Industrial Workers in Chicago, 1919–1939* (1990). A well-researched interpretive study of working-class culture and the union movement.

Robert Dallek, *Franklin D. Roosevelt and American Foreign Policy, 1932–1945* (1979). A fine study stressing FDR's responsiveness to domestic political currents.

Anthony Heilbut, *Exiled in Paradise: German Refugee Artists and Intellectuals in America from the 1930s to the Present* (1983). Good account of a refugee movement that profoundly influenced American culture.

Jacqueline Jones, *The Dispossessed: America's Underclass from the Civil War to the Present* (1992). A broad-ranging work placing the plight of the depression-era poor in a larger historical context.

Jeffrey Meikle, *Twentieth Century Limited: Industrial Design in America, 1925–1939* (1979). Fascinating study of the streamlining movement, with a good chapter on the New York World's Fair.

Arnold A. Offner, *American Appeasement: United States*

Foreign Policy and Germany, 1933–1938 (1969). A comprehensive and well-written study.

Susan Ware, *Holding Their Own: American Women in the 1930s* (1982). A good overview incorporating recent scholarly research.

CHAPTER 27

Waging Global War, 1939–1945

To most Americans, World War II was "the good war." U.S. losses—some 300,000 dead—paled beside the tens of millions dead in Europe and Asia, and American soil was unscathed. In fact, the war made America once again a land of opportunity and hope as it ended the Depression and transformed the United States into a largely middle-class society. Many who had been left out of prewar society, women and African-Americans in particular, found liberation in the war. Simultaneously, "total war" fostered an increasingly active and powerful federal government, disrupted families, and laid bare social problems. And war's end found the United States a global leader in a world transformed.

(Right) Wartime security poster featuring a WAC, a member of the Women's Army Corps

Into the Storm, 1939–1941

Twenty years after World War I ended, Germany, Italy, and Japan unleashed campaigns of expansion and invasion that drew the United States into a second global conflict. After German victories in western Europe in spring 1940, President Franklin D. Roosevelt gave economic aid to nations resisting aggression by the so-called Rome-Berlin-Tokyo Axis. As the fascist menace grew, FDR accelerated rearmament and extended greater assistance to the Allies, principally Great Britain and France. Although reluctant to ask a divided Congress for a declaration of war, FDR understood that his uncompromising conduct toward Germany and Japan could cause the United States to be "pushed," as he said, into a worldwide war. Japan's attack in December 1941 on the U.S. fleet at Pearl Harbor would provide the push.

Hitler's Blitzkrieg
A Belgian mother and her children walk through rubble left by a German air attack.

Storm in Europe

Adolf Hitler had precipitated the war by demanding that Poland return to Germany the city of Danzig (Gdansk), lost after World War I. When Poland refused, Nazi armies poured into Poland at dawn on September 1, 1939, and the Luftwaffe (German air force) devastated Polish cities. Two days later, Britain and France, honoring commitments to Poland, declared war on Germany. Although FDR invoked the Neutrality Acts (see Chapter 26), he refused to ask Americans to be impartial. Even a neutral, Roosevelt declared, "cannot be asked to close his mind or his conscience."

Determined to avoid an Allied defeat that would leave the United States alone to confront Germany, the president in September 1939 asked Congress to amend the Neutrality Acts to allow the Allies to purchase weapons on a "cash-and-carry" basis. But there would be no loans to the Allies, and they would transport the weapons on their own ships. The cash-and-carry policy reflected a public mood that favored both aiding the Allies and staying out of war.

In spring 1940 Hitler unleashed his armies against western Europe; the Nazi *Wehrmacht* (war machine) swept all the way to the English Channel in a scant two months. In early June the British, rallied by the fighting spirit of their new prime minister, Winston Churchill, evacuated most of their army, but none of its equipment, from France. And on June 22 France surrendered.

Hitler then turned his fury against Great Britain, pounding the island from the air in preparation for a cross-channel invasion. When the Royal Air Force won the "Battle of Britain," the frustrated Nazi dictator turned to terror-bombing British cities in hopes of forcing a surrender. With Coventry destroyed and much of London in smoking ruins, the indomitable Churchill pleaded for all possible American aid. Most Americans favored additional support for Britain, but a large minority opposed it as wasteful or as a ruse to involve Americans in a war not vital to U.S. interests.

The Election of 1940

As the war escalated, Americans wondered whether Roosevelt would run for an unprecedented third term. On the eve of the Democrats' July convention, the president revealed that, given the world crisis, he would consent to a "draft" from his party. The Nazi menace forced conservative anti–New Deal Democrats to accept both the third term and the nomination of ultra liberal Henry Wallace as vice president.

German victories in Europe had an even greater impact on the Republican nomination. Dark-horse candidate Wendell Willkie, a former Democrat and a millionaire utility magnate, championed internationalism and aid to Britain; his conservative opponents criticized Roosevelt's handling of foreign affairs. As his supporters deafened the delegates with a "We Want Willkie!" chant, Willkie won the GOP nomination on the sixth ballot. A formidable contender, he supported internationalism but denounced FDR's third-term bid.

To counter Willkie's vigorous campaigning, Roosevelt adroitly played the role of a national leader too busy with defense and diplomacy to engage in partisan politics. To undercut GOP criticisms, he appointed Republicans to key cabinet positions: Henry L. Stimson as secretary of war and Frank Knox as secretary of the navy. With bipartisan support in Congress, Roosevelt approved a peacetime draft and a dramatic increase in defense funding. In September he engineered a "destroyers-for-bases" swap with England, sending fifty vintage American ships to Britain in exchange for leases on British air and naval bases in the Western Hemisphere. FDR claimed that the exchange was a way of averting American entry into the war—and it let him evade a congressional vote in the midst of his reelection campaign.

Anti-interventionist critics condemned Roosevelt's "dictatorial" methods and accused him of scheming to entangle the United States in the European conflict. Isolationists organized the Committee to Defend America First to protest the drift toward war. Financed in large part by Henry Ford, the America First Committee featured Charles Lindbergh as its most popular speaker and proclaimed that "Fortress America" could stand alone. Although America First drew backers from every region, ideology, and ethnic group, most Americans supported Roosevelt's attempt to aid Britain while avoiding war. Heartened by FDR's pledge—"I will never send an American boy to fight in a foreign war"—55 percent of Americans voted him into an unprecedented third term.

From Isolation to Intervention

His presidency secure, Roosevelt moved to support Britain, calling on the United States to become "the arsenal of democracy." He proposed a "lend-lease" program to supply war materiel to the cash-strapped British. Despite bitter opposition by the isolationists, Congress approved lend-lease in March 1941, and supplies began to flow across the Atlantic. When Hitler's armies invaded the U.S.S.R. in June

The Election of 1940

Candidates	*Parties*	*Electoral Vote*	*Popular Vote*	*Percentage of Popular Vote*
FRANKLIN D. ROOSEVELT	Democratic	449	27,307,819	54.8
Wendell L. Willkie	Republican	82	22,321,018	44.8

1941, FDR dispatched supplies to the Soviets despite American hostility toward communism. To defeat Hitler, FDR said, "I would hold hands with the Devil."

To counter the menace of German submarines that threatened to choke the transatlantic supply line, Roosevelt authorized the U.S. Navy to help the British track U-boats. By summer 1941 the U.S. Navy had begun convoying British ships, with orders to destroy enemy ships if necessary. U.S. forces also occupied Greenland and Iceland to keep them out of Nazi hands.

In mid-August Roosevelt met with Churchill aboard a warship off Newfoundland to discuss joint military objectives. They issued a document called the Atlantic Charter that contained their vision of a postwar world. Recalling Woodrow Wilson's Fourteen Points, the charter condemned aggression, affirmed national self-determination, and endorsed the principles of collective security and disarmament. After a German submarine fired at an American destroyer in September, Roosevelt authorized naval patrols to shoot on sight all Axis vessels operating in the western Atlantic. On October 31, 1941, a U-boat torpedoed and sank the destroyer *Reuben James*, killing 115 American sailors.

Now on a collision course with Germany, Roosevelt in November persuaded Congress to permit the arming of merchant ships and to allow the transport of lend-lease supplies to belligerent ports in war zones. Virtually nothing remained of the Neutrality Acts. Unprepared for a major war, America was nevertheless fighting a limited one, and a full-scale war seemed imminent.

Toward Pearl Harbor

Hitler's triumphs in western Europe encouraged Japan to expand its aggression from China to the resource-rich British, Dutch, and French colonial possessions in Southeast Asia. The United States opposed Japanese expansion virtually alone. But seeing Germany as America's primary threat, the Roosevelt administration tried to apply enough pressure to deter the Japanese without provoking Tokyo to war before the United States had built the "two-ocean navy" authorized by Congress in 1940. "It is terribly important for the control of the Atlantic for us to keep peace in the Pacific," Roosevelt told Harold Ickes, secretary of the interior, in mid-1941. "I simply have not got enough navy to go around—and every episode in the Pacific means fewer ships in the Atlantic." American military leaders agreed.

The Japanese, too, hoped to avoid war, but they would not compromise their goals. Japan's desire to create the Greater East Asia Co-Prosperity Sphere (an empire embracing much of China, Southeast Asia, and the western Pacific) matched America's insistence on the Open Door in China and the status quo in the rest of Asia. Japan saw America's stand as an attempt to block its rise to power, and Americans viewed Japan's talk of legitimate national aspirations as a smoke screen to cloak its brutal expansionism. Decades of "yellow-peril" propaganda had hardened U.S. attitudes toward Japan, and even those who were isolationist toward Europe tended to be interventionist toward Asia.

Initially Roosevelt employed economic pressure to halt Japanese expansion, ending a long-standing trade treaty and banning the sale of aviation fuel and scrap metal. When Japan responded in September 1940 by signing the Tripartite Pact with Germany and Italy, a pledge by each of the Axis nations to help the others in case of attack by a new enemy, Roosevelt also stopped the sale of steel and other metals. And when Japan occupied northern Indochina, a French colony, the list of embargoed goods lengthened.

In July 1941 the Japanese overran the rest of Indochina. Roosevelt then froze all Japanese assets in the United States and clamped a total embargo on trade with Japan. Tokyo had two choices: submit to the United States to gain a resumption of trade, or conquer new lands to obtain vital resources. In October expansionist war minister Hideki Tojo became Japan's prime minister. Tojo, who opposed compromise with the United States, set the first week in December as the deadline for Japanese forces to take the offensive if the United States did not yield. Watching fuel gauges drop toward empty, the Japanese believed that they had no option.

By late November U.S. intelligence's deciphering of Japan's top diplomatic code alerted the Roosevelt administration that war was imminent. The United States made no concessions during eleventh-hour negotiations under way in Washington, and Secretary of State Hull told Secretary of War Stimson, "I have washed my hands of it, and it is now in the hands of you and Knox—the Army and the Navy." War warnings went out to all U.S. commanders in the Pacific, advising that negotiations were deadlocked and that a Japanese attack was imminent. U.S. officials believed that the Japanese would strike British or Dutch possessions or even the Philippines—but the Japanese decided to gamble on a knockout punch. They hoped that a surprise Japanese raid on the American naval base at Pearl Harbor would destroy the U.S. Pacific Fleet and compel Roosevelt, preoccupied with Germany, to seek accommodation with Japan.

Waves of Japanese dive-bombers and torpedo planes thundered across the Hawaiian island of Oahu on the morning of December 7, 1941, bombing ships at anchor in Pearl Harbor and strafing planes parked wingtip to wingtip at nearby air bases. American forces suffered their most devastating loss in history. In less than three hours, eight battleships, three light cruisers, and two destroyers had been sunk or crippled, and 360 aircraft destroyed or damaged. The attack killed more than 2,000 Americans and opened the way for Japan's advance to the threshold of Australia in April 1942. It also ensured an aroused and united America to avenge what President Roosevelt called a "date which will live in infamy."

On December 8, when Roosevelt asked Congress to declare war on Japan, only one dissenting vote was cast (by Montana's Jeannette Rankin, who had also voted against entry into World War I). But FDR still hesitated to request a declaration of war against Germany. Hitler resolved the president's dilemma. Although Hitler's advisers begged him not to add the United States to the long list of anti-Nazi belligerents, he went before a cheering Reichstag on December 11 to declare war on the "half Judaized and the other half Negrified" Americans. Mussolini chimed in with his declaration of war, and Congress reciprocated that same afternoon. America faced a global war that it was not yet ready to fight.

On the Defensive

After Pearl Harbor, U-boats wreaked havoc in the North Atlantic and prowled the Caribbean and the East Coast of the United States. Every twenty-four hours, five more Allied vessels went to the bottom. By the end of 1942, Hitler's submarines had destroyed more than 1,000 Allied ships, offsetting the pace of American ship production. The United States was losing the Battle of the Atlantic.

The war news from Europe and Africa was, as Roosevelt admitted, "all bad." Hitler's rule covered an enormous swath of territory, from the outskirts of Moscow, deep in Russia, to the Pyrenees on the French-Spanish border, and from northern Norway to the Libyan desert. In spring 1942 Nazi armies inflicted more than 250,000 casualties on the Soviet army in Crimea, and Hitler launched a powerful offensive to seize the Caucasian oil fields. German forces moved relentlessly eastward in North Africa, threatening the Suez Canal, Britain's oil lifeline.

Apparently as invincible as the Nazis, the Japanese inflicted defeat after defeat on Allied Pacific forces. Tojo followed Pearl Harbor with a rampage across the Pacific that put Guam, Wake Island, Hong Kong, Singapore, Burma, and the Netherlands East Indies under Japan's control by the end of April 1942. American forces in the Philippines, besieged for months on the island of Corregidor, surrendered in May. Japan's Rising Sun blazed over hundreds of islands in the central and western Pacific and over the entire eastern rim of the Asian mainland from the border of Siberia to the border of India.

America Mobilizes for War

The United States had begun to prepare actively

for war after the fall of France in mid-1940. But many businesses, fearing a short-lived demand for war equipment, had hesitated. Constant bickering among the military, industry, and labor, combined with FDR's initial reluctance to speed mobilization, also hindered preparedness. In December 1941 American armed forces numbered only 1.6 million, and war production accounted for just 15 percent of U.S. industrial output. Moreover, Washington had not yet organized an efficient structure to direct mobilization.

Pearl Harbor changed everything. Within a week of the attack, Congress passed the War Powers Act, granting the president unprecedented authority. Hundreds of wartime agencies soon regulated American life. Volunteers and draftees swelled the army and navy. By the war's end 15 million men and nearly 350,000 women had served. To direct this military engine, Roosevelt formed the Joint Chiefs of Staff, made up of representatives of the army, navy, and army air force. The air force grew from a minor "corps" within the army to an autonomous, and vital, part of the military. The changing nature of modern warfare led to the creation of the Office of Strategic Services (OSS) to conduct espionage and to gather the information required for strategic planning. The far-reaching domestic changes under way would outlast the war and significantly alter the nation's attitudes, behavior, and institutions.

Organizing for Victory

After Pearl Harbor, Roosevelt called on Americans to produce an unprecedented quantity of supplies for the Allied fighting forces. He established the War Production Board (WPB) to allocate materials, to limit the production of civilian goods, and to distribute contracts. The newly created War Manpower Commission (WMC) supervised the mobilization of men and women for the military, war industry, and agriculture; the National War Labor Board (NWLB) mediated disputes between management and labor; and the Office of Price Administration (OPA) imposed strict price controls to check inflation.

In October 1942 FDR persuaded James F. Byrnes to leave the Supreme Court and take charge of America's domestic war effort. Byrnes was to increase coordination and cooperation among government agencies, industry, and the military. In May 1943 FDR appointed him to head the new Office of War Mobilization (OWM), which exercised control over the economy.

"The Americans can't build planes," a Nazi commander had jeered, "only electric iceboxes and razor blades." But in 1942 the United States achieved a miracle of war production. "It was not so much industrial conversion," one business leader remarked, "as industrial revolution, with months and years condensed into days." Car makers retooled to produce planes and tanks; a pinball-machine maker converted to armor-piercing shells. By late 1942, 33 percent of the economy was committed to war production. Whole new industries appeared virtually overnight. Ninety-seven percent of the nation's crude-rubber supply now lay in Japanese-controlled territory, but by 1944, 80 percent of the rubber consumed in the United States came from synthetic-rubber factories that had not existed two years earlier.

America also became the world's greatest weapons manufacturer, producing more war materiel by 1945 than its Axis enemies combined—300,000 military aircraft, 86,000 tanks, 2.6 million machine guns, and 6 million tons of bombs. The United States also built 5,000 cargo ships and 86,000 warships. Henry J. Kaiser, who had supervised the construction of Boulder Dam, introduced prefabrication to cut the time needed to build ships. In 1941 the construction of a Liberty-class merchant ship took six months; in 1943, less than two weeks; by 1945, Kaiser and other shipbuilders were completing a cargo ship every day.

Such breakneck production had costs. The size and powers of the government expanded as defense spending zoomed from 9 percent of gross national product (GNP) in 1940 to 46 percent in 1945; the federal budget soared from $9 billion to $98 billion. Federal civilian employees mushroomed from 1.1 million to 3.8 million. An alliance formed between the defense industry and the military. Because the government sought the maximum production in the shortest time, it encouraged corporate profits. "If you are going to try to go to war in a capitalist country," Secretary of War Stimson said, "you have to let business make money out of the process or business won't work."

To encourage business to convert to war production and expand its capacity, the government guaranteed profits, provided generous tax write-offs, and suspended antitrust prosecutions. Giant corporations benefited most from these actions. Two-thirds of all war-production dollars went to the hundred largest firms, and trends toward economic concentration accelerated.

A War Economy

The United States spent $250 million a day to defeat the Axis, ten times the cost of World War I. Wartime spending and the draft not only vanquished unemployment but also stimulated an industrial boom that made most Americans prosper. War expenditures doubled U.S. industrial output and nearly doubled the per capita GNP (to $1,074). By 1945 farm income had doubled from the 1940 level, net corporate profits had leaped 70 percent, and real wages, or purchasing power, had risen 50 percent.

Full employment, longer workweeks, larger paychecks, and the increased hiring of minorities, women, and the elderly brought a middle-class standard of living to millions of families. The war years produced the only significant shift in the distribution of income in the twentieth century. The fraction of total income going to the richest 5 percent shrank from 26 percent to 20 percent, whereas the share of the least affluent 40 percent climbed from 13 percent to 16 percent of all income. The middle class doubled in size.

The war reversed hard times for American farmers. With more than a million more new tractors in use in 1945 than in 1940, and with improved fertilizers and cultivation techniques, farmers harvested 477 million more bushels of corn, 324 million more bushels of wheat, and 500 million more pounds of rice. Higher prices, increased productivity, and a decline in the number of farmers raised the value of farm property by $20 billion. Radio comedians changed the words of a familiar nursery rhyme to "The farmer's in the dough." Mechanization and consolidation proceeded, farming became "agribusiness," and organized agriculture wielded power equal to organized labor, big government, and big business.

Organized labor expanded and grew wealthier. From 1940 to 1945 union membership rose from 9 million to 14.8 million workers, in part because of the expansion of the labor force. Although the National War Labor Board attempted to limit wage increases to restrain inflation, unions negotiated unprecedented fringe benefits for workers, including paid vacation time and health and pension plans. As most workers honored the "no-strike" pledge that they had given immediately after Pearl Harbor, less than one-tenth of 1 percent of wartime working time was lost to wildcat strikes. However, in 1943 United Mine Workers head John L. Lewis led more than half a million coal-field workers out of the pits and tunnels three times in two months. These strikes cost the union movement dearly as Congress passed the Smith-Connally War Labor Disputes Act in 1943, which limited workers' power to strike at a facility essential to the war effort.

Far more than strikes, inflation threatened the wartime economy. The OPA constantly battled inflation, which was fueled by greater spending power combined with a scarcity of goods. Throughout 1942 prices climbed at a 2 percent a month clip, but at the year's end Congress gave the president authority to freeze wages, prices, and rents. As the OPA clamped down, inflation slowed dramatically: consumer prices went up only 8 percent in the war's last two years.

The OPA also instituted rationing to combat inflation and to conserve scarce materials. Under the slogan "Use it up, wear it out, make it do or do without," the OPA rationed such products as gasoline, coffee, sugar, butter, cheese, and meat. Accepting rationing as a contribution to the security of loved ones fighting the war, most Americans cheerfully endured "meatless Tuesdays" and cuffless trousers, formed car pools, planted victory gardens, and recycled paper, fats, rubber, and scrap metal.

The sale of war bonds, like rationing, helped to limit inflation by draining consumer purchasing power. Bond buying gave civilians a sense of involvement in the war. Small investors bought $40 billion in "E" bonds, and wealthy individuals and corporations invested nearly twice that amount. Bond sales raised almost half the money needed to finance the war. FDR wanted to increase taxes to pay for the war, but Congress only grudgingly raised taxes. However, by the war's end the top income-tax rate had risen from 60 percent to 90 percent, and middle- and lower-income Americans were paying income taxes for the first time. The introduction of payroll deductions to withhold income taxes from wages facilitated tax collection.

Science and the War

Recognizing wartime scientific and technological developments, Winston Churchill dubbed World War II "a wizard war." In 1941 FDR created the Office of Scientific Research and Development (OSRD) for the development of new ordnance and medicines. The OSRD spent more than $1 billion to produce improved radar and sonar, rocket weapons, and proximity fuses for mines and artillery shells. It also funded the development of jet aircraft, pressurized cabins, and high-altitude bombsights. Other OSRD research hastened the widespread use of insecticides, contributed to improved blood transfusions, and produced "miracle drugs" such as penicillin. The agency's medical advances saved thousands of lives during the war and would increase life expectancy in peacetime. At the same, however, the environment often became a war casualty. For example, grapefruit groves shriveled under vapors from the Kaiser steel plant in Fontana, California, while radioactive waste from the plutonium-processing facility at Hanford, Washington, was haphazardly stored or dumped.

The atomic bomb project began in August 1939 when Albert Einstein, a Jewish refugee and Nobel prize–winning physicist, warned Roosevelt that Nazi scientists were seeking to use atomic physics to construct an extraordinarily destructive weapon. In 1941 FDR launched a massive Anglo-American secret program—the Soviets were excluded—to construct an atomic bomb. The next year the participating physicists, both Americans and Europeans, achieved a controlled chain reaction and acquired the basic knowledge necessary to develop the bomb. In 1943–1944 the Manhattan Engineering District—the code name for the atomic project—stockpiled fissionable materials. By July 1945 the Manhattan Project had employed more than 120,000 people and spent nearly $2 billion.

Just before dawn on July 16, 1945, a blinding fireball with "the brightness of several suns at midday" rose over the desert at Alamogordo, New Mexico, followed by a billowing mushroom cloud. Equivalent to 20,000 tons of TNT, the blast from this first atomic explosion was felt 100 miles away. The awesome spectacle reminded J. Robert Oppenheimer, the scientific director of the Manhattan Project, of a line from Hindu scripture: "Now I am become death, the destroyer of worlds." The atomic age had begun.

Propaganda and Politics

People as well as science and machinery had to be mobilized. To sustain a spirit of unity, the Roosevelt administration carefully managed public opinion. The Office of Censorship, established in December 1941, examined all letters going overseas and worked with publishers and broadcasters to suppress information that might damage the war effort, such as details of troop movements. Much was concealed. A year passed, for example, before the casualty and damage figures from Pearl Harbor were disclosed.

To shape public opinion, FDR created the Office of War Information (OWI) in June 1942. The OWI employed more than 4,000 writers, artists, and advertising specialists to explain the war and to counter enemy propaganda. Instead of stressing the

U.S. commitment to the preservation of democratic values, the OWI focused on the Axis nations' barbarism and the need to crush them. Anti-Japanese propaganda contained a strong dose of racism.

While the Roosevelt administration concentrated on the war, Republican critics seized the initiative in domestic politics. Full employment and high wages undermined the Democrats' class appeal, and many of the urban and working-class voters essential to the Roosevelt coalition were serving in the armed forces and did not vote in the 1942 elections. As Republicans gained nine seats in the Senate and forty-six in the House, congressional politics shifted to the right. Conservative Republicans and southern Democrats held the power to make or break legislation. Resentful of the wartime expansion of executive authority, and determined to curb labor unions and welfare spending, the conservatives abolished the CCC and the WPA and turned back attempts to extend the New Deal.

Despite the strength of the conservative coalition, the war enormously expanded governmental and executive power as the federal government's budget, size, and powers ballooned. As never before, Washington managed the economy, molded public opinion, funded scientific research, and influenced people's daily lives.

With more than $300 billion expended on the war, economic despondency yielded to buoyant prosperity. Unemployment ended, organized labor and agriculture thrived, and millions entered the middle class. Big business also prospered and grew bigger, more highly concentrated, and increasingly intertwined with the military. The wartime "miracle of production" strengthened confidence in business leaders and in the government's fiscal role in maintaining a robust economy. The United States stood second to none in economic and military power. Its citizens' expectations of what the federal government could and should be were turned upside down.

War and American Society

Fifteen million American men and 350,000 U.S. women went to war, grousing that they were as "GI"—government-issue—as their uniforms and equipment. Cartoonist Bill Mauldin's scruffy GI Joe and Willy, more interested in dry socks than in ideology, exemplified the reluctant warriors who filled out America's armed forces. They wanted to defeat Hitler, avenge Pearl Harbor, and return to a secure, familiar United States.

But the war dragged on for almost four years, transforming its participants. Millions who had never been far from home traveled to unfamiliar cities and remote nations. Sharing tents and foxholes with fellow Americans of different religions, nationalities, and social backgrounds helped to erase deep-seated prejudices. To many of the thousands of gay men and lesbian women in the armed forces, wartime liberated them from traditional expectations—and the scrutiny of family and neighbors. However, some suspected of homosexuality faced discharge as undesirables, psychiatric hospitals, or even imprisonment in "queer stockades." Wartime service sowed the seeds of a more homogenized national culture. The wartime experience also enlarged many GIs' sense of future possibilities and gave them skills in jobs and professions that they had barely known existed. And under the Servicemen's Readjustment Act, the "GI Bill of Rights," several million veterans would be studying for a high-school diploma or enrolling in college in 1946. Countless second-generation immigrant veterans would acquire an education under the GI Bill, and it would provide the springboard for their entry into the expanding middle class.

Returning GIs would find that America had changed as much as they had. Sweeping wartime alterations in society challenged established values, redefined traditional relationships, and created new problems. Adjusting to this new world could be difficult and painful, and the transition sometimes proved impossible.

The New Mobility

Nothing transformed the social topography more than the vast internal migration of an already mobile people. Americans swarmed to the centers of war production, especially the Pacific coast states, which manufactured one-half of the nation's wartime ships and airplanes. Six million people left farms to work in cities, and several million southern whites and blacks migrated northward and westward. This mass uprooting made Americans both more cosmopolitan and tolerant of differences and more lonely, alienated, and frustrated.

Life-styles became freewheeling as Americans moved far from their hometowns and traditional values. Housing shortages left millions living in converted garages, tent cities, trailer camps, or even their own cars. Overcrowding as well as wartime separations strained family and community life. High rates of divorce, family violence, and juvenile delinquency reflected the disruptions. Urban blight and conflicts between newcomers and old-timers accelerated.

Education and Entertainment

The war production boom that created both overcrowded communities and ghost towns played havoc with the nation's school systems. More than 350,000 teachers joined the armed services or took on better-paying war work, leaving schools woefully understaffed. Students abandoned school in record numbers. High-school enrollments sank as full-time teenage employment rose from 900,000 in 1940 to 3 million in 1944.

The loss of students to the armed services and war production forced colleges to admit large numbers of women and to contract themselves out to the military. Military training programs sent nearly a million servicemen and -women to college campuses to acquire skills in engineering, foreign languages, economics, and the sciences. Higher education became more dependent on the federal government, and universities competed for federal contracts and subsidies.

The war profoundly affected American culture. The media emphasized mass production and targeted mass audiences. Between 1941 and 1945 spending on books and theater entertainment more than doubled. Sixty million people attended movies weekly. Hollywood turned out a spate of war films that reinforced the image of Nazis and Japanese as fiends, portrayed GIs as freedom-loving heroes, and intensified Americans' appetites for unconditional victory. *Mission to Moscow* (1943), *Song of Russia* (1943), and other films glorified Soviet heroism. But as the war dragged on, people tired of propaganda, and Hollywood reemphasized romance and adventure.

Early in the war popular music featured patriotic themes. "Goodbye, Mama, I'm Off to Yokohama" was the first hit of 1942. As the war continued, themes of lost love and loneliness dominated songs. By 1945 bitterness pervaded the lyrics of best-selling records, and such hits as "Saturday Night Is the Loneliest Night of the Week" revealed an impatience for the war's end.

In bookstores, nonfiction crowed the shelves. Few war novels appeared, but Marion Hargrove's *See Here, Private Hargrove*, a comic account of army life, and John Hersey's *A Bell for Adano* (1946), about the occupation of Sicily, became instant classics. Magazines such as *Life*, *Look*, *The Saturday Evening Post*, and *Time* filled American hunger for reports of battle actions and of the prospects for peace. Wendell Willkie's *One World* (1943) became the fastest-selling title in publishing history to that time, with 2 million copies snapped up in two years. A vision of a world without military alliances and spheres of influence, this brief volume expressed hope that an international organization would extend peace and democracy through the postwar world. The Government Printing Office published Armed Services Editions, paperback reprints of classics and new releases, and nearly 350 million copies were distributed free to soldiers.

Americans also stayed glued to their radios during the war. The quest for up-to-date information kept radio audiences at record levels. The voices of Edward R. Murrow and Eric Sevareid reporting from the battlefields became as familiar as those of Jack Benny and Eddie Cantor on their comedy shows.

Women and the Family

Millions of American women donned pants, put their hair in bandannas, and went to work in defense plants. Reversing a decade of efforts to exclude women from the labor force, the federal government in 1942 urged women into war production. Songs such as "We're the Janes Who Make the Planes" appealed to women to take up war work, and propaganda called on them to "help save lives" and to "release able-bodied men for fighting." More than 6 million women entered the labor force during the war, bringing the number of employed women to 19 million. Less than a quarter of the labor force in 1940, women constituted well over a third of all workers in 1945.

The characteristics of female wage earners changed. Before the war women workers were predominantly young and single, but 75 percent of the new female workers were married, 60 percent were over thirty-five, and more than 33 percent had children under age fourteen. Women tended blast furnaces, operated cranes, drove taxis, welded hulls, and worked in shipyards. "Rosie the Riveter," her muscular arms cradling a pneumatic gun, symbolized the woman war worker; she was, as a popular song put it, "making history working for victory."

Women war workers implicitly challenged ideas of sexual inequality, but wartime strengthened traditional convictions. Men, not women, fought. This mindset allowed gender discrimination to flourish throughout the war, with women earning only 65 percent of what men did for the same work. Government propaganda portrayed women's war work as a temporary response to an emergency, and few women challenged traditional views of gender

Working for Victory *The federal government encouraged women to take on wartime defense work and pressured employers to hire them.*

roles. "A woman is a substitute," asserted a War Department brochure, "like plastic instead of metal." Work was pictured as an extension of women's traditional roles as wives and mothers. A newspaperwoman wrote of the "deep satisfaction which a woman of today knows who has made a rubber boat which may save the life of her aviator husband, or helped fashion a bullet which may avenge her son!" Given the concern about jobs for veterans after the war, attitudes toward women's employment changed little; in 1945 only 18 percent of respondents in a poll approved of married women's working.

Traditional convictions about a woman's place also shaped government resistance to establishing child-care centers for women employed in defense. "A mother's primary duty is to her home and children," the Labor Department's Children's Bureau stated. New York Mayor Fiorello La Guardia proclaimed that the worst mother was better than the best nursery. Funds for federal child-care centers covered few defense workers' children, and the young suffered. New terms such as *eight-hour orphans* and *latchkey children* described children forced to fend for themselves. Feeding the fears of those who believed that women's working outside the home would cause the family to disintegrate, juvenile delinquency increased fivefold, and the divorce rate nearly doubled.

The impact of war on women and children was multifaceted and even contradictory. Divorce rates soared, but so did marriage rates and birthrates. Although some women remained content to roll bandages for the Red Cross, 350,000 women joined the armed forces and for the first time served in positions there other than nurse. Female workers gained unprecedented employment opportunities and public recognition. Although many eagerly gave up their jobs at the end of the war, just as many did not relish losing their income and newfound independence. Overall, the war gave women a new sense of their potential. It allowed them to prove their capability and to participate in society outside the home. Most women still hoped to be wives and mothers, but the war had widened women's worlds and challenged sexist notions as nothing before ever had.

African-Americans and the War

The war also opened doors of opportunity for many African-Americans. The global conflict not only heightened blacks' aspirations but widened cracks in the wall of white racist attitudes and policies.

Realizing that the government needed the loyalty and work of a united people in order to win the war, African-American leaders saw new pathways to securing equal rights. In 1942 civil-rights spokesmen insisted that African-American support of the war hinged on the United States' commitment to racial justice. The battle against the Axis had to destroy racism at home as well as Nazi racism, and victory had to mean victory over racial discrimination as well as triumph on the battlefield, they said. African-Americans responded with passionate commitment.

Membership in the National Association for the Advancement of Colored People multiplied nearly ten times, reaching 500,000 in 1945. The association pressed for anti–poll tax and antilynching legislation, decried discrimination in defense industries and the armed services, and sought to end African-American disfranchisement. The campaign for black voting rights gained momentum when the Supreme Court, in *Smith* v. *Allwright* (1944), ruled Texas's all-white primary unconstitutional. This decision eliminated a barrier that had existed in eight states, although these states promptly resorted to other devices to minimize African-American voting.

A new civil-rights organization, the Congress of Racial Equality (CORE), founded in 1942, advanced the strategy of nonviolent resistance to challenge Jim Crow. In 1942 CORE staged a sit-in in a Chicago restaurant that had refused to serve blacks, and its success inspired interracial groups in other cities to experiment with nonviolent direct action. Also in 1942, A. Philip Randolph, the president of the Brotherhood of Sleeping Car Porters, worked to build his March-on-Washington Committee into an all-black protest movement that would engage in civil disobedience.

In 1941 Randolph had called for a "thundering march" of 100,000 blacks on Washington "to wake up and shock white America." He had warned Roosevelt that if the president did not abolish discrimination in the armed services and the defense industry, African-Americans would besiege the nation's capital. FDR had agreed to compromise, in June 1941 issuing Executive Order 8802, the first presidential directive on race since Reconstruction. It prohibited discriminatory employment practices by federal agencies and all unions and companies engaged in war-related work and established the Fair Employment Practices Commission (FEPC) to enforce this policy. Although the FEPC did not apply to the armed forces and lacked effective enforcement powers, roaring war production and a shrinking labor pool resulted in the employment of 2 million African-Americans in industry and 200,000 in the federal civil service. Between 1942 and 1945 the proportion of blacks in war production shot up from 3 percent to 9 percent. African-American membership in labor unions doubled, and the number of skilled and semiskilled African-American workers tripled. Average earnings for blacks increased from $457 to $1,976 a year, compared to $2,600 for whites.

About 1 million African-Americans served in the armed forces. Wartime needs forced the military to end policies of excluding blacks from combat units. The all-black 761st Tank Battalion gained distinction fighting in Germany, and the 99th Pursuit Squadron won eighty Distinguished Flying Crosses in combat against the Luftwaffe. Although the army and navy began experiments with integration in 1944, most blacks served in segregated units under white officers. Ironically, the Red Cross maintained separate black and white blood banks, even though a black physician, Dr. Charles Drew, had invented the process of storing blood plasma. The failure of military authorities to protect African-American servicemen off the post and the use of white military police to keep African-Americans "in their place" sparked conflict on many army bases. At least fifty African-American soldiers died in wartime racial encounters in the United States.

Violence within the military mirrored growing racial tensions at home. As African-Americans militantly protested against discrimination and rejected pleas to "go slow" in their campaign for first-class citizenship, many whites stiffened their resistance to raising blacks from their inferior economic and social positions. Numerous clashes occurred. In mid-1943 scores of cities reported pitched battles between whites and African-Americans. The bloodiest race riot exploded in Detroit that June. By its end, twenty-five blacks and nine whites lay dead, more than seven hundred had been injured, and more than $2 million in property had been destroyed. Fear of more violence led white liberals to emphasize racial tolerance and African-American leaders to reduce their militancy. Realizing that a war against racism at home could be interpreted as a hindrance to the war abroad, African-Americans organized programs to lessen aggressive behavior.

These wartime developments would lead to eventual success in the drive for black civil rights. As more than 700,000 blacks migrated from the South, blacks' status in society became a national concern. African-Americans were experiencing a new attitude of independence, and their greater educational and employment opportunities engendered hopefulness. With growing numbers of blacks voting in northern industrial cities, African-Americans held the balance of power in close elections. Consequently, politicians extended greater recognition to African-Americans and paid more attention to civil rights.

Blacks' optimism also flowed from the new prominence of the United States as a major power in a nonwhite world. As Japanese propaganda directed at Asians and Latin Americans emphasized lynchings of blacks and race riots in the United States, Americans confronted the peril that white racism posed to their national security. In addition, the horrors of Nazi racism made Americans sensitive to the harm caused by their own white-supremacist attitudes and practices. A former Alabama governor lamented that Nazism had "wrecked the theories of the master race with which we were so contented so long."

In a massive study of race problems entitled *An American Dilemma* (1944), Swedish economist Gunnar Myrdal concluded that "not since Reconstruction had there been more reason to anticipate fundamental changes in American race relations." Returning black veterans and African-Americans who had served the nation on the home front alike faced the postwar era resolved to gain all the rights enjoyed by whites.

Native Americans, Mexican-Americans, and Jews in Wartime

Wartime winds of change brought new opportunities, and problems, to other American minorities. Twenty-five thousand Native Americans served in the armed forces, many of them Navajo "code-talkers" who confounded the Japanese by relaying secret messages in an unbreakable code based on their native tongue. Another 75,000 Indians left reservations to work in defense. For most, it was the first experience of living in a non-Indian world, and after the war many would remain in the cities. Continued discrimination, however, would force a majority back to their reservations, which suffered severely from budget cuts during the war and the immediate postwar years. Prodded by those who coveted Indian lands, lawmakers demanded that Indians be taken off the backs of taxpayers and "freed from the reservations" to make their own way like other Americans. To mobilize against the campaign to end all reservations and trust protections, Native Americans in 1944 organized the National Congress of American Indians. Nonetheless, Native Americans who returned to reservations after the war found themselves ineligible for most of the benefits enjoyed by other veterans.

Unable to complain about prejudice and the way they were treated without risking deportation, hundreds of thousands of Mexicans became illegal aliens, exploited by Anglo planters and ranchers. At the same time, large numbers of Mexicans and Mexican-Americans moved to Los Angeles, Chicago, Detroit, and other large cities, where they found jobs in defense plants, garment factories, shipyards, and steel mills. Even as their occupational status and material conditions improved, most Mexican-Americans remained in communities segregated from the larger society.

In the military itself, Spanish-speaking Americans, like blacks, suffered discrimination. Nevertheless, nearly 350,000 Chicanos served in the armed forces, earning a disproportionate number of citations for distinguished service and Congressional Medals of Honor. And much like black and Indian veterans, Mexican-American veterans organized new groups to press for equal rights.

Despite the lip service paid to tolerance, American Jews also discovered that even a war against Nazism did not extinguish traditional prejudices. Anti-Semitism persisted in restrictive covenants to prevent the sale of homes to Jews, in employment ads stating that only Catholics or Protestants need apply, in rigid quota systems to limit the number of Jews in universities, and in "gentlemen's agreements" to exclude Jews from certain professions. Throughout the war, public-opinion polls revealed that a significant minority of Americans blamed either Wall Street Jews or Jewish communists for the war and thought Hitler justified in his treatment of Jews.

When reports of the Holocaust—the name later given to the Nazi effort to exterminate all European Jews—became known in the United States early in 1942, most Americans viewed it as a Jewish problem, of small concern to them. Most discounted the reports of Nazi massacres. Not until late November, with some 2.5 million Jews already dead, did the State Department admit knowledge of Hitler's genocide. Fourteen more months passed before Roosevelt established the War Refugee Board (WRB) to assist in the rescue and relocation of those condemned to the death camps. This tardy response condemned them to extermination or slave-labor concentration camps. Most American officials doubted that during war large numbers of Jews could be freed and transported to safety. Despite detailed photographs, the Allies refused to divert aircraft on bombing raids over Poland to destroy the gas chambers at Auschwitz, although the raids plastered nearby factories. Any diversion of airpower, the

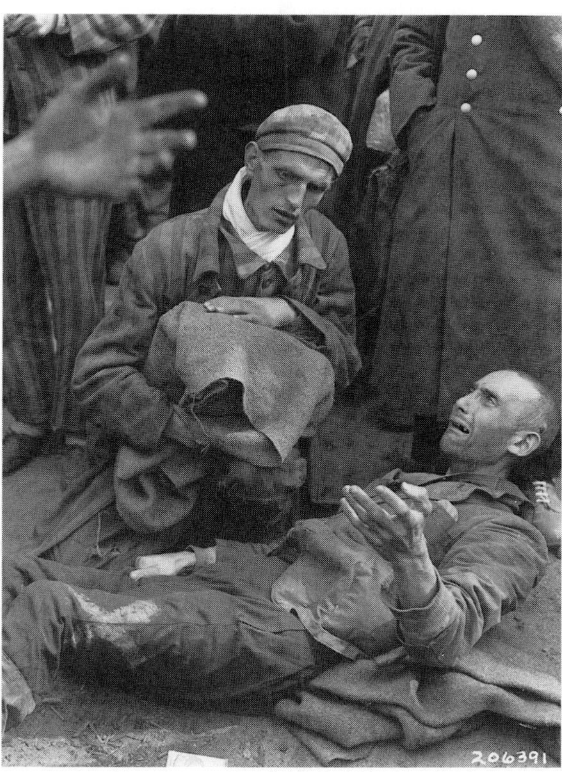

The Holocaust
Entering Germany in 1945, American and Russian soldiers discovered the horrors that the Nazis had perpetrated on European Jews and others. One anonymous American GI wrote of the ghastly concentration-camp scenes, "I've seen what wasn't ever meant for human eyes to see."

Allies alleged, would detract from the war effort and prolong the war.

Probably little could have been done to save most of Hitler's victims. However, the feeble U.S. response to the Nazis' "final solution" reflected not only America's single-minded determination to win the war with few American casualties but also a frightening indifference. America's inaction also grew from Britain's desire to placate its Arab allies by keeping Jewish settlers out of Palestine, congressional and public fears of an influx of destitute Jews into the United States, and the hesitancy of many American Jewish leaders to press the matter and risk increasing anti-Semitism at home. Because of State Department obstruction of rescue efforts, the WRB saved the lives of only 200,000 Jews and 20,000 non-Jews. Six million other Jews (about 75 percent of Europe's Jewish population) in addition to several million gypsies, Poles, communists, and gay men died in the camps.

The Internment of Japanese-Americans

A relative handful of Americans refused to support the war effort. Some 37,000 conscientious objectors accepted noncombat service, but 5,500 others, primarily Jehovah's Witnesses, refused to serve in any way and were imprisoned. A far greater abuse of civil liberties, however, was the internment of 112,000 Japanese-Americans, two-thirds of them native-born U.S. citizens, in relocation centers guarded by military police. The policy reflected forty years of anti-Japanese sentiment on the West Coast, rooted in racial prejudice and economic rivalry, as well as fears of Japanese saboteurs after Pearl Harbor. Self-serving politicians and farmers who wanted Japanese-American land had long decried the "yellow peril," and after the attack on Pearl Harbor they whipped up the rage and fears of many white Californians. In February 1942 Roosevelt gave in to the pressure and authorized the evacuation of all Japanese-Americans from the West Coast, despite the fact that not a single Japanese-American had been apprehended for espionage or sedition and neither the Federal Bureau of Investigation nor military intelligence had uncovered any disloyal behavior by Japanese-Americans.

Interestingly, only Japanese-Americans on the mainland fell victim to the internment policy. The Hawaiian islands were home to approximately 160,000 people of Japanese ancestry, one-third of the entire population. Nonetheless, despite the potential damage that saboteurs could have inflicted, Hawaiian officials maintained their tradition of interracial harmony. "This is America and we must do things the American way," announced Hawaii's military governor. Hawaii's Japanese committed no acts of sabotage; indeed, many became "superpatriots" in order to honor their obligations to the United States.

But on the mainland Japanese-Americans, forced to sell their lands and homes at whatever prices they could obtain, were herded into barbed-wire-encircled detention camps in desolate areas of the West. The Supreme Court, in *Korematsu* v. *U.S.* (1944), upheld the constitutionality of the evacuation, stating that it would not question government claims of military necessity during the war. By then, however, the hysteria had subsided, and the government had begun a program of gradual release. In 1982 a special government commission would formally blame the Roosevelt administration's action on "race prejudice, war hysteria, and a failure of political leadership" and would apologize to Japanese-Americans for "a grave injustice." In 1988 Congress voted to pay $20,000 as compensation to each of the nearly 60,000 Japanese-American internees still alive.

The Battlefront, 1942–1944

"No matter how long it may take us to overcome this premeditated invasion," President Roosevelt vowed in his war message on December 8, 1941, "the American people in their righteous might will win through to absolute victory." At the beginning of the new year, Britain, the Soviet Union, the United States, and twenty-three other countries signed the Declaration of the United Nations, creating a "Grand Alliance" pledged to devoting its full resources to victory. But in early 1942 the Allied outlook remained bleak. Nazi forces held much of Europe and threatened the Suez Canal; Japan controlled the western Pacific and a large part of Asia.

America's military might turned the tides of war. Diplomacy followed the fortunes of war, with Allied unity gradually diminishing as Germany and Japan weakened and as the United States, Britain, and the Soviet Union each sought wartime strategies and postwar arrangements best suited to its own national interest.

The Allied Drive in Europe

After Pearl Harbor, British and American officials agreed to concentrate first on defeating Germany and then on smashing Japan. But they differed on where to mount an attack. General George C. Marshall, army chief of staff, proposed an invasion of France to force Hitler to transfer troops west and thus to relieve pressure on the Russians, who faced the full fury of the Nazi armies. Prime Minister Churchill insisted on clearing the Mediterranean before invading France. He feared that a premature landing in France could mean slaughter, and he wanted American aid in North Africa to protect the Suez Canal, vital to the British. Over Soviet protests, Churchill persuaded Roosevelt to postpone the "second front" in western Europe and to invade North Africa instead. In November 1942 in Operation Torch, American and British troops under General Dwight D. Eisenhower landed in Morocco and Algeria. Pushing eastward, they trapped the German and Italian armies being driven westward by the British, and in May 1943 some 260,000 German-Italian troops surrendered.

Left alone to face two-thirds of the Nazi force, the Soviet Union hung on and, in the turning point of the European war, defeated Germany in the protracted Battle of Stalingrad (August 1942–January 1943). After destroying an entire German army—more than 600,000 men—at Stalingrad, the Red Army went on the offensive along a thousand-mile front. Stalingrad cost the Soviet Union more battle deaths in four months than the United States suffered in the entire war.

Although Stalin renewed his plea for a second front, Churchill again objected, and Roosevelt again agreed to a British plan: the invasion of Sicily. In summer 1943 Anglo-American forces gained control of Sicily in less than a month. Italian military leaders deposed Mussolini and surrendered to the Allies on September 8. As Allied forces moved up the Italian peninsula, German troops poured into Italy. Facing elite Nazi divisions in splendid defensive positions, the Allies spent eight months inching their way 150 miles to Rome and were still

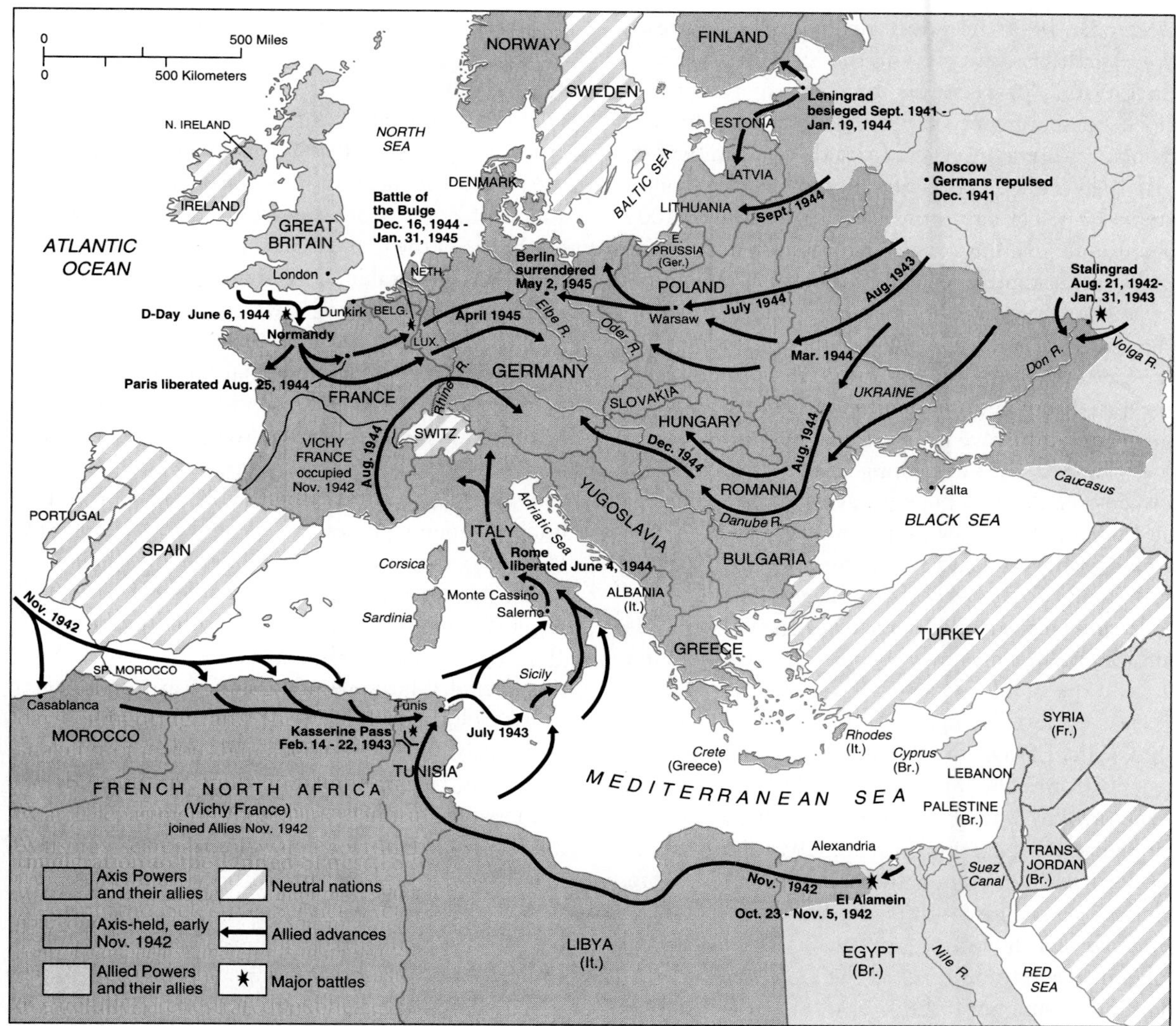

World War II in Europe and Africa

The momentous German defeats at Stalingrad and in Tunisia early in 1943 marked the turning point in the war against the Axis. By 1945 the Allied conquest of Hitler's "thousand year" Reich was imminent.

battling through the mud and snow of northern Italy when the war in Europe ended.

In 1943 and 1944 the United States and Britain turned the tide in the Atlantic and sent thousands of bombers over Germany. To the east, Soviet troops kept the Nazis in retreat.

American science and industry, as much as the American navy, won the Battle of the Atlantic. Advanced radar systems, high-frequency detection finders, and improved depth charges and torpedoes moved from laboratories to the oceans, while planes and ships poured from American factories. By

December 1943 the Allies had won the Battle of the Atlantic. Moreover, at the start of that year British and American air forces began round-the-clock bombardment, raining thousands of tons of bombs on German cities. In raids on Hamburg in July 1943, Allied planes dropping incendiary bombs created terrible firestorms, killing at least 60,000 people and leveling the city, much as they had done earlier at Cologne.

Meanwhile, in 1943 as the Soviet offensive reclaimed Russian cities and towns from the Nazis, the German armies fell into perpetual retreat across the vast north European plain. Advancing swiftly, the Red Army drove the Germans out of Soviet territory by mid-1944 and plunged into Poland, where the Soviets set up a puppet government. Late summer and early fall saw Soviet troops seize Romania and Bulgaria and aid communist guerrillas under Josip Broz Tito in liberating Yugoslavia. But the U.S.S.R. paid a terrible price for its victories: 24 million Soviet citizens, military and civilian, lay dead in the rubble of the western Soviet Union.

As eastern Europe fell under Soviet domination, Allied forces finally opened the long-delayed second front. On June 6, 1944—D-Day—150,000 Allied troops landed in Normandy in northwestern France, gaining a toehold on French soil. Within six weeks 1 million Allied troops had waded ashore. Under General Eisenhower, a man of superb administrative and diplomatic skills, the Allies liberated Paris in August and reached the German border by the end of summer. However, in the face of supply problems and stiffened German resistance, the Allied offensive ground to a halt.

In mid-December as the Allies prepared for a full-scale assault on the German heartland, Hitler in a desperate gamble threw his last reserves against American positions. The Battle of the Bulge—named for the "bulge" eighty miles long and fifty miles wide that Hitler's troops drove into the Allies' line—raged for nearly a month, and when it ended American troops stood on the banks of the Rhine. Fifty-five thousand had been killed or wounded and 18,000 taken prisoner. But the way to Germany lay open, and the end of the European war was in sight.

The War in the Pacific

The day after the Philippines fell to Japan in mid-May 1942, U.S. and Japanese fleets confronted each other in the Coral Sea off northeastern Australia, the first naval battle in history fought entirely from aircraft carriers. Both sides took heavy losses, but the Battle of the Coral Sea stopped the Japanese advance on Australia. Less than a month later, a Japanese armada turned toward Midway Island, the crucial American outpost between Hawaii and Japan. Because the U.S. Signal Corps had broken the Japanese naval code, the plans and locations of Japan's ships were known. American carriers and their planes consequently won a decisive victory, sinking four Japanese carriers and destroying several hundred enemy planes. After the Battle of Midway, Japanese expansion turned into a defensive effort to hold what the Imperial Navy had already won.

Eight months after Pearl Harbor, on August 7, 1942, the United States assumed the offensive in the Pacific. Marines waded ashore at Guadalcanal in the Solomon Islands. Tropical diseases—malaria, fungus, dysentery—afflicted both sides, but in six months of bloody fighting the United States drove the Japanese out of the Solomons. Japan left behind 25,000 dead, a gruesome preview of island battles to come.

In fall 1943 American forces began a two-pronged advance toward Japan. Under General Douglas MacArthur, who had commanded the heroic but futile defense of the Philippines, the army advanced north from Australia, "leapfrogging" from one strategic island to another. A second force under Admiral Chester Nimitz "island-hopped" across the central Pacific, isolating Japanese troops behind American lines and seizing key islands to serve as bases for American bombers sent against Japan itself.

Pacific operations remained secondary to the defeat of Germany, but the size of the conflict steadily increased. By late 1944 the United States had deployed 1.5 million marines and soldiers, along with the navy's fastest and largest aircraft carriers, in the Pacific. By the time MacArthur's troops

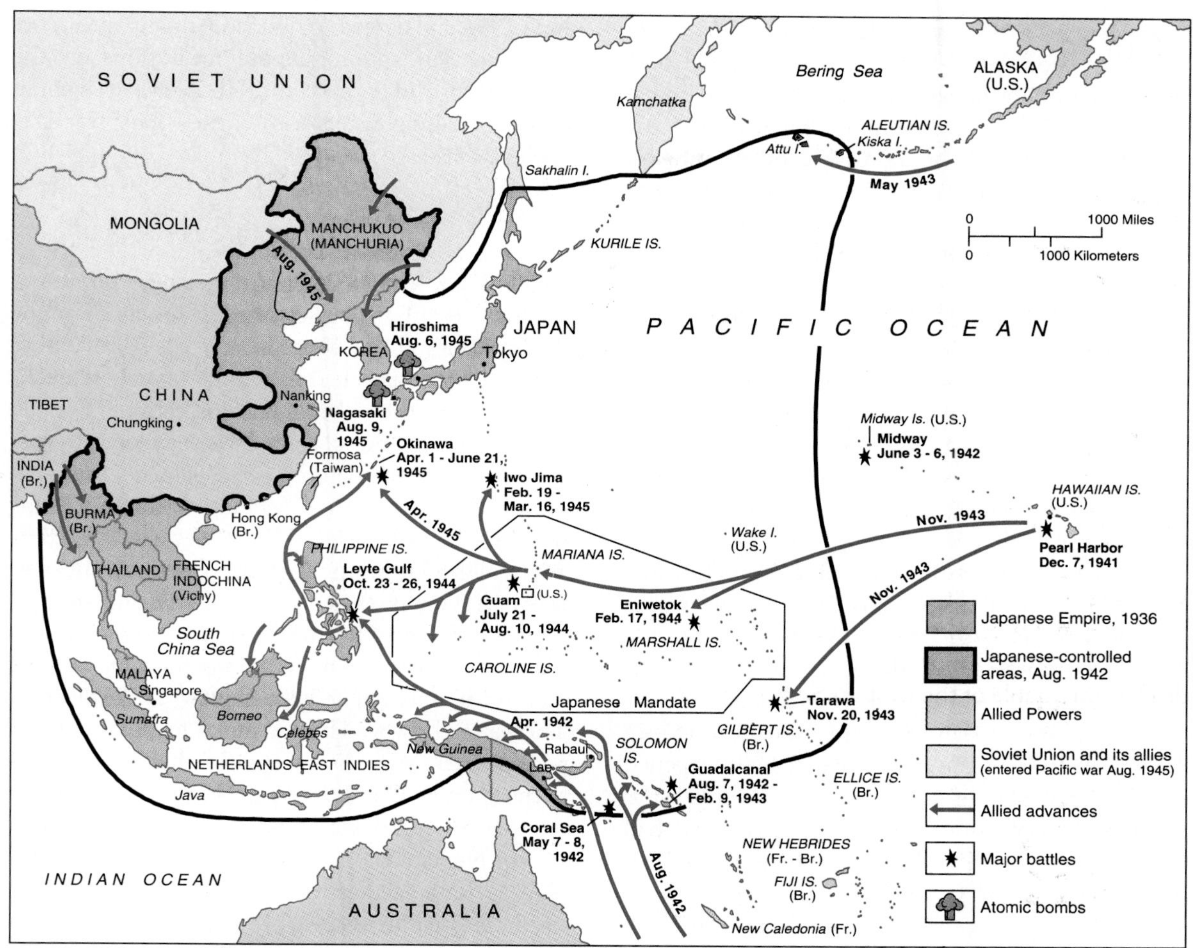

World War II in the Pacific

American ships and planes stemmed the Japanese offensive at the Battles of the Coral Sea and Midway Island. Thereafter, the Japanese were on the defensive against American amphibious assaults and air strikes.

liberated Manila in early 1945, they had lost 28,000 dead, fewer than the number killed in some individual battles in Europe. Under Nimitz, marines and naval forces seized strategic bases in the Gilbert Islands in November 1943 and the Marshall Islands in February 1944. Capture of the Marianas in summer 1944 put Tokyo within range of the new B-29 bombers, which by late 1944 were incinerating Japanese cities. In fall 1944 the American navy annihilated what remained of the imperial fleet at the battles of the Philippine Sea and Leyte Gulf. Japan's sea and air power were now totally shattered. Still, Japanese military leaders stymied attempts by civilians in the government to negotiate peace.

The Grand Alliance

Two primary goals underlay Roosevelt's wartime strategies: the total defeat of the Axis at the least possible cost in American lives and the establishment of a world order strong enough to preserve peace, to open trade, and to ensure national self-determination in the postwar era. Aware that only a common enemy fused the Grand Alliance together, FDR tried to promote harmony by concentrating on military victory and postponing divisive postwar matters.

But Churchill and Stalin had other goals. Britain sought to retain its imperial possessions and a balance of power against the U.S.S.R. in Europe. The Soviet Union wanted a permanently weakened Germany and a sphere of influence in eastern Europe in order to protect itself against future attacks from the West. To hold together this uneasy alliance, FDR used personal diplomacy and met frequently with foreign leaders to plan strategy and to mediate conflicts.

In January 1943 Roosevelt and Churchill had met at Casablanca, Morocco's main port, where they had resolved to attack Italy before invading France, and proclaimed that the war would continue until the Axis accepted "unconditional surrender." In this proclamation they sought to reduce Soviet mistrust of the West, which had deepened because of the postponement of the second front. Then in November 1943, at Cairo, Roosevelt had met with Churchill and Jiang Jieshi (Chiang Kai-shek), head of the Chinese government. To keep China in the war, FDR promised the return of Manchuria and Taiwan to China and guaranteed a free and independent Korea.

FDR and Churchill had continued on from Cairo to Tehran, Iran's capital, to confer with Stalin. Here they had set the invasion of France for June 1944 and agreed to divide Germany into zones of occupation and to impose reparations on the Reich. Most important to Roosevelt, at Tehran Stalin had also pledged to enter the Pacific war after Hitler's defeat.

The Election of 1944

As 1944 unfolded, Roosevelt turned his attention to domestic politics. Conservative gains in both the Republican and the Democratic parties drove FDR toward the center. He dumped the liberal Henry A. Wallace from the ticket and chose Harry S Truman as his vice-presidential candidate. A moderate senator from Missouri, Truman had gained a national profile by chairing a subcommittee investigating waste in the defense effort. Not strongly opposed by any major Democratic faction, Truman, "the new Missouri Compromise," restored a semblance of unity to the party for the 1944 campaign. The Republicans, hoping that unity would carry *them* to victory, nominated moderate New York governor Thomas E. Dewey. The campaign focused more on personalities than issues, with the Republicans harping on FDR's failing health and FDR touting American military victories.

In November the American electorate handed FDR an unprecedented fourth term, but with his narrowest margin ever—only 53 percent of the popular vote. Roosevelt owed his triumph largely to the urban vote and the support of organized labor. The president now directed his waning energies toward defeating the Axis and constructing a new international order.

The Election of 1944

Candidates	*Parties*	*Electoral Vote*	*Popular Vote*	*Percentage of Popular Vote*
FRANKLIN D. ROOSEVELT	Democratic	432	25,606,585	53.5
Thomas E. Dewey	Republican	99	22,014,745	46.0

Yalta Conference, 1945
The palaces where Roosevelt, Churchill, Stalin, and their advisers gathered were still standing, but the rest of Yalta had been reduced to ruin during the German occupation.

Triumph and Tragedy, 1945

Spring and summer 1945 brought stunning changes. In Europe the Yalta conference and the collapse of the Nazi Third Reich saw a new balance of power emerge. In Asia continued Japanese resistance and reluctance to surrender led to the use of a terrible new weapon, the atomic bomb. And in the United States, a new president, Harry Truman, presided over the end of war with Germany and Japan and the beginning of a new, "cold" war.

The Yalta Conference

By the time Roosevelt, Churchill, and Stalin met at the Soviet city of Yalta in February 1945, the military situation favored the Soviet Union, for the Soviet offensive was nearly complete. The Red Army had overrun eastern Europe; driven the Nazis out of Yugoslavia; begun to organize Poland, Romania, and Bulgaria as communist states; penetrated Austria, Hungary, and Czechoslovakia; and now massed only fifty miles from Berlin. American forces, in contrast, were still recovering from the Battle of the Bulge and faced fanatical resistance on the route to Japan. The Joint Chiefs of Staff, predicting that an invasion of Japan would cost 1 million American casualties, insisted that obtaining Stalin's help in Asia was worth almost any price. For his part, Stalin was in a position to make demands. Roosevelt and Churchill could do little about Stalin's domination of eastern Europe but considered Soviet aid essential in Asia. The United States anticipated a long, bloody battle against Japan. Stalin, however, had the luxury of deciding whether or not to enter the Pacific war.

The Yalta agreements mirrored the new balance of power. Stalin again promised to declare war on Japan "two or three months" after Germany's surrender, and in return Roosevelt and Churchill reneged on their arrangement with Jiang Jieshi (made earlier at Cairo) and promised the Soviet Union concessions in Manchuria and the territories that it had lost in the Russo-Japanese War forty years before. Stalin then recognized Jiang as the ruler of China and promised to press Mao Zedong's (Mao Tse-tung's) Chinese communists to cooperate with Jiang. Stalin also accepted the temporary partitioning of Germany and the postponement of discussions about reparations. On the matter dearest to FDR's heart, Stalin approved plans for a United Nations conference to establish a permanent international organization for collective security.

Stalin, however, proved adamant about Soviet domination in eastern Europe, particularly Poland. Twice in the twentieth century, German troops had used Poland as a pathway for invading Russia. Stalin would not expose his land again, and after the Red Army had captured Warsaw in January 1945, he encouraged the Polish communists to brutally subdue a noncommunist majority. Roosevelt and Churchill refused to recognize the communist Lublin regime, but they accepted Stalin's pledge to include noncommunist Poles in the new government and to allow free elections. They could do little else. Short of going to war against the Soviet Union while battling Germany and Japan, FDR could only hope that Stalin would keep his promises.

The Defeat of Germany

Meanwhile, Allied armies closed the vise on Germany. In early March 1945 American troops captured Cologne and encircled Germany's industrial heartland. To counter the threat of Soviet power in postwar Europe, Churchill proposed a rapid thrust to Berlin, but Eisenhower, with Roosevelt's backing, overruled the British. Instead, to minimize their casualties and to reassure Stalin, the Americans advanced methodically on a broad front until they met the Russians at the Elbe River at the end of April. By then the Red Army had overrun Vienna and reached the suburbs of Berlin. On April 30 Hitler committed suicide in a bunker under the ruins of Berlin; the city fell to the Soviets on May 2. A hastily assembled German government surrendered unconditionally on May 8.

Jubilant Americans celebrated Victory in Europe (V-E) Day with ticker-tape parades and dancing in the streets. The rejoicing subsided as attention turned to the Pacific. Moreover, in the last weeks of the German war, Allied troops had liberated those still alive in the concentration camps, and Americans had viewed newsreels of the gas chambers at Auschwitz, the ovens at Dachau, and the corpses stacked like cordwood at Belsen. They learned with horror of the systematic murder of 6 million Jews and several million others in the Nazi camps. And they mourned a death closer to home, the death of FDR. On April 12 the exhausted president, sitting for a portrait at his second home, in Warm Springs, Georgia, died of a cerebral hemorrhage. His unprepared successor inherited leadership of the most powerful nation in history—as well as troubles with the Soviet Union that seemed more intractable every day.

A New President

"I don't know whether you fellows ever had a load of hay or a bull fall on you," Harry S Truman told reporters on his first day in office, "but last night the moon, the stars, and all the planets fell on me." Unpretentious, awed by his new responsibilities, Truman had little familiarity with world affairs. He distrusted the Soviets and counted on American military power to maintain the peace. In office less than two weeks, he lashed out at Soviet ambassador V. M. Molotov that the United States was tired of waiting for Moscow to allow free elections in Poland, and he threatened to cut off lend-lease aid if the Soviet Union did not cooperate. The Truman administration reduced U.S. economic assistance to the Soviets and stalled on their request for a $1 billion reconstruction loan. Stalin consequently broke his Yalta promises and strengthened his control of eastern Europe. The bluster of Stalin and Truman accelerated the dissolution of the Grand Alliance.

The United States would neither concede the Soviet sphere of influence in eastern Europe nor take decisive steps to terminate it. Truman still sought Stalin's cooperation in establishing the United Nations and in defeating Japan, but Soviet-American relations rapidly deteriorated. By June 1945 when the Allied countries framed the United Nations Charter in San Francisco, hopes for a peaceful new international order had dimmed, and the United Nations emerged as a diplomatic battleground. Truman, Churchill, and Stalin met at Potsdam, Germany, from July 16 to August 2, to complete the postwar arrangements begun at Yalta. Each trying to preserve and enlarge his nation's sphere of influence, the allies could barely agree even to demilitarize Germany and to punish Nazi war criminals. All the major divisive issues were postponed. Given the diplomatic impasse, military power would determine the contours of the postwar world.

The Atomic Bombs

The war with Japan ground on. Early in 1945 marines landed on the tiny island of Iwo Jima, 700 miles from Japan. Because Japanese soldiers had hidden in tunnels and behind concrete bunkers and pillboxes, securing the island cost 25,000 marine casualties. A month later Americans landed on Okinawa, a key staging area for the planned invasion of the Japanese home islands, only 350 miles distant. In nearly three months of ferocious combat, U.S. forces sustained 40,000 casualties, while more than 110,000 Japanese military died and Japanese civilians took 80,000 casualties.

If the capture of these small islands had entailed such bloodshed, military planners asked, what would the invasion of Japan itself be like? Although a naval blockade had strangled Japan's commerce and its lands lay defenseless to U.S. bombers, the imperial government showed little disposition to surrender. Truman scheduled an invasion of Kyushu, the first of the home islands, for late 1945.

But the successful test of an atomic weapon at Alamogordo in mid-July presented an alternative. While at Potsdam, Truman, on July 25, secretly ordered that an atomic bomb be used if Japan did not surrender before August 3. He and Churchill publicly warned Japan to surrender unconditionally or face "prompt and utter destruction." When Japan rejected this Potsdam Declaration, Truman gave the military the go-ahead. On August 6 a B-29 named *Enola Gay* dropped a uranium bomb on Hiroshima, creating "a hell of unspeakable torments." A searing flash of heat, a fireball estimated at 300,000 degrees centigrade, incinerated buildings and vaporized people. Seventy thousand died of these "traditional" injuries, but an additional 70,000 would die of radiation poisoning. On August 8, as promised, Stalin declared war on Japan. The next day much of Nagasaki disappeared under the mushroom cloud of a plutonium bomb. Finally, on August 14 Japan surrendered, leaving the emperor on the throne but powerless. On September 2 General MacArthur, aboard the battleship *Missouri* in Tokyo Bay, formally accepted the Japanese surrender.

Many have questioned whether the war had to end with the atomic bombings. Some believe that racist American attitudes toward Japan motivated the decision to use the bombs. Yet from the beginning of the Manhattan Project, Germany had been the target; and considering the indiscriminate ferocity of the Allied bombings of Hamburg and Dresden, which killed tens of thousands of civilians, there is little reason to assume that the Allies would not have used atomic bombs against Germany had they been available. Others contend that demonstrating the bomb's destructiveness on an uninhabited island would have motivated the Japanese surrender. But American policy makers considered a demonstration too risky. Still others argue that Japan was ready to surrender and that an invasion of the home islands was unnecessary. We cannot know for sure. But we do know that as late as July 28, 1945, Japan rejected a demand for surrender and that not until after the Hiroshima bombing did the Japanese government discuss acceptance of the Potsdam Declaration.

Rapidly worsening relations between the United States and the U.S.S.R. convinced some that Truman dropped the atomic bomb primarily to intimidate Stalin. The failure of the Americans and Soviets to resolve their differences had led Truman to seek an end to the Pacific war before Stalin could enter. Truman recognized that such an awesome weapon might give the United States leverage to oust the communists from eastern Europe. Just before the Alamogordo test, Truman had said, "If it explodes, as I think it will, I'll certainly have a hammer on [Stalin]." Truman's new secretary of state, James Byrnes, thought that the bomb would "put us in a position to dictate our own terms at the end of the war."

Although the president and his advisers believed that the atomic bomb would strengthen their hand against the Soviets, that was not the main reason that the bombs were dropped. Throughout the war Americans had relied on production and technology to win the war with a minimum loss of American life. Every new weapon was used. "Total war" included the terror bombing of masses of civilians, and within this context the atomic bomb seemed simply one more weapon in an arsenal that had already wreaked enormous destruction on the enemy. No responsible official suggested that the United States accept the deaths of thousands of Americans while not using a weapon developed with 2 billion taxpayer dollars. Indeed, to the vast majority of Americans, the atomic bomb was, in Churchill's words, "a miracle of deliverance" that shortened the war and saved lives.

CONCLUSION

The dropping of the atomic bombs ended the deadliest war in history. More than 14 million combatants, including 300,000 Americans, had died. Twenty-five million civilians had perished. Much of Europe and Asia was rubble.

Although physically unscathed, the United States had changed profoundly. Mobilization had altered the structure of the economy; accelerated trends toward bigness in business, agriculture, and labor; and enlarged the role of the military. World War II had also transformed the scope and authority of the federal government, especially the presidency, and catalyzed vital changes in racial and social relations. Winning the greatest war in history infused an entire generation with a "can-do" spirit.

Isolationism had all but vanished as the United States, the strongest nation in the world in 1945, assumed a role in global affairs inconceivable five years earlier. Many hoped that the United Nations would ensure future peace. But instead, the war spawned a new conflict, the Cold War, whose influence would be at least as great as that of World War II itself.

CHRONOLOGY

1939 Germany invades Poland; World War II begins.
Soviet Union invades Poland.

1940 Germany conquers the Netherlands, Belgium, France, Denmark, Norway, and Luxembourg.
Germany, Italy, and Japan sign the Tripartite Pact.
Selective Service Act.
Franklin Roosevelt elected to a third term.

1941 Lend-Lease Act.
Roosevelt establishes the Fair Employment Practices Commission (FEPC).
Germany invades the Soviet Union.
Japan attacks Pearl Harbor; the United States enters World War II.
War Powers Act.

1942 Battle of Midway halts Japanese offensive.
Internment of Japanese-Americans.
Revenue Act expands graduated income-tax system.
Allies invade North Africa (Operation Torch).
First successful atomic chain reaction.
Congress of Racial Equality (CORE) founded.

1943 Soviet victory in Battle of Stalingrad.
Coal miners strike; Smith-Connally War Labor Disputes Act.
Detroit race riot.
Allied invasion of Italy.
Big Three meet in Tehran.

1944 Allied invasion of France (Operation Overlord).
GI Bill of Rights.
Roosevelt wins fourth term.
Battle of the Bulge.

1945 Big Three meet in Yalta.
Battles of Iwo Jima and Okinawa.
Roosevelt dies; Harry S Truman becomes president.
Germany surrenders.
Truman, Churchill, and Stalin meet in Potsdam.
United States drops atomic bombs on Hiroshima and Nagasaki; Japan surrenders.

FOR FURTHER READING

Beth Bailey and David Farber, *The First Strange Place: The Alchemy of Race and Sex in World War II Hawaii* (1992). A wide-ranging survey of the war's impact on Hawaiian society.

John Dower, *War Without Mercy* (1986). An insightful look at racism among the Americans and the Japanese.

Patrick Heardon, *Roosevelt Confronts Hitler: American Entry into World War II* (1987). An economic interpretation of U.S. foreign policy.

Warren Kimball, *The Juggler: Franklin Roosevelt as Wartime Statesman* (1991). A study of the president's war aims and postwar vision.

Gordon W. Prange, *At Dawn We Slept: The Untold Story of Pearl Harbor* (1981). A thoroughly researched, balanced examination of the controversies surrounding the Japanese attack.

Holly Cowan Shulman, *The Voice of America* (1991). An in-depth account of America's wartime propaganda policies and programs.

David Wyman, *The Abandonment of the Jews* (1985). A critical assessment of the United States' role in the Holocaust.

CHAPTER 28

Cold War America, 1945–1952

Optimistic that there would not soon be another war, and confident that the nation could solve any problems, ordinary Americans of the postwar years rushed to grab a share of the good life. They married, had babies, made Dr. Benjamin Spock's child-care manual the hottest book since best-seller lists had begun, bought cars with automatic transmissions, and moved to new split-level houses in suburbs. However, the peace of mind that they yearned for eluded them, for World War II had wrought decisive and disturbing changes in society and in the global balance of power.

Disagreement over Eastern Europe's postwar fate sparked a confrontation in which the Soviet Union and the United States each sought to reshape the world to serve its own interests. An uncompromising Harry S Truman squared off against an obsessive Joseph Stalin, each intensifying the insecurities of the other. A new form

(Right) Slicing an "atomic cake" at the Pentagon, 1946

The Postwar Political Setting

Anticommunism and Containment

The Truman Administration at Home

The Politics of Anticommunism

of international conflict—the Cold War—emerged, in which the two superpowers avoided direct military clashes while using all their resources to thwart the other's objectives.

The Cold War changed America. Abandoning its historical aloofness from events outside the Western Hemisphere, the United States now plunged into a global struggle to contain the Soviet Union and to stop communism. The nation that only a few years before had no military alliances, a small defense budget, and no troops on foreign soil built a giant military establishment, signed mutual-defense pacts with forty countries, directly intervened in the affairs of allies and enemies alike, built military bases on every continent, and embarked on a seemingly limitless nuclear-arms race. To oppose communist aggression in Asia, the United States dispatched thousands of Americans to fight in Korea.

The Cold War's political and social effects proved equally decisive. Preoccupation with the Soviet threat discredited the political Left and sapped liberalism's vitality. Conservatives remained convinced that the federal government's power should be strictly limited, but at the same time they applauded the growth of federal power when military expansion, sniffing out domestic disloyalty, and leading the world fight against communism were at issue. Socially, the free expression of ideas suffered during the Cold War, as popular fears of communist aggression and domestic subversion led to witch hunts against suspected communists that undermined civil liberties. In 1952 an anxious electorate turned hopefully to Dwight D. Eisenhower to deliver the stability for which they longed.

The Postwar Political Setting

In background and bearing, Harry S Truman could not have been more unlike FDR. The son of a Missouri horse and mule trader, Truman worked on his grandfather's farm until serving as an artillery captain in World War I. After returning from France, he operated a men's clothing store in Kansas City and dabbled in local politics until his business failed. Elected to the Senate in 1934, Truman was a diligent but colorless Democratic partisan, a supporter of FDR but not a committed New Dealer. Neither experienced in foreign policy nor supported by any major group within the Democratic party, Truman won the vice-presidential nomination in 1944 because he was a safe alternative to the liberal Henry A. Wallace and the conservative James F. Byrnes.

After FDR's death, liberals voiced dismay at this "usurper" in the White House. Truman made it clear that he would rule in his own way, replacing cabinet New Dealers with moderates and appointing political cronies to key posts. Conservatives were unhappy when Truman urged Congress to adopt a major economic reform program and emphasized his role as the champion of the common people against special interests.

Deeply concerned for the public welfare, Truman displayed on his desk a framed motto of Mark Twain: "Always do right. This will gratify some people and astonish the rest." He wanted the government to do more to help people, but without altering the existing social and economic systems. "I don't want any experiments," he told an aide; "the American people have been through a lot of experiments and they want a rest." They would not get much of that. Instead, aggressive Republican partisanship, a deeply divided Democratic party, and intense legislative suspicion of executive leadership would characterize the Truman years.

Demobilization and Reconversion

When the war ended, GIs and civilians alike wanted all those who had served overseas "home alive in '45." Troops demanding transport ships barraged Congress with threats of "no boats, no votes." On a single day in December 1945, 60,000 postcards arrived at the White House with the message "Bring the Boys Home by Christmas." Truman bowed to popular demand, and by 1948 American military strength had dropped from 12 million at war's end to just 1.5 million.

Returning veterans faced readjustment problems intensified by a soaring divorce rate and a drastic housing shortage. As war plants closed, moreover, veterans and civilians feared the return of mass unemployment and economic depression. Defense spending plummeted from $76 billion in 1945 to under $20 billion in 1946, and more than a million defense jobs vanished. However, an economic boom began in 1946 as U.S. economic output leaped from $200 billion to $318 billion by 1950.

The Serviceman's Readjustment Act of 1944, the "GI Bill of Rights," stimulated this economic growth. Under the GI Bill, 2.3 million veterans flocked to college, half of the total college enrollment between 1945 and 1950. The more than $15 billion that veterans received sent them to school, helped them buy homes, and financed their new businesses. A 1945 tax cut of $6 billion, coupled with huge wartime profits, enabled businesses to invest vigorously in new factories.

The Bretton Woods agreement (1944) among the Allies had set the stage for the United States to become economic leader of the noncommunist world. In addition to valuing ("pegging") other currencies in relation to the dollar, Bretton Woods created several institutions to oversee international trade and finance: the International Monetary Fund (IMF), the General Agreement on Tariffs and Trade (GATT), and the World Bank.

The United States' favorable position in international trade and finance bolstered the idea that "the American century" of world peace and prosperity was at hand. Fears of depression were replaced by visions of limitless growth. With many nations in ruins, American firms could import cheap raw materials; with little competition from other industrial nations, they could increase their export sales to record levels. Wartime advances in science and technology, especially electronics and synthetic materials, led to the development of new industries and drove up productivity in others.

Wartime savings and a pent-up demand for consumer goods also kindled postwar growth and prosperity. The men and women who had endured the Great Depression and the Second World War craved the "good life," and by the end of 1945, they possessed $140 billion in bank accounts and government bonds. The rage to consume, and the ability to do so, more than compensated for the decline in defense spending. Advertisements promising "a Ford in your future" and an "all-electric kitchen-of-the-future" became reality as sales of homes, furniture, cars, appliances, and clothing skyrocketed. Scores of new products—televisions, filter cigarettes, electric clothes dryers, freezers, automatic transmissions, air conditioners, hi-fis—emerged as hallmarks of the middle-class life-style.

Truman's Troubles

Americans' hunger for the fruits of affluence left them little appetite for extension of the New Deal. Truman's only major legislative accomplishment in the Seventy-ninth Congress, the Employment Act of 1946, committed the federal government to assuring economic growth and established the president's Council of Economic Advisers. Congress, however, had gutted from the proposed bill the goal of providing *full* employment, as well as the broad executive authority necessary to achieve that goal. Congress also blocked Truman's requests for public housing, a higher minimum wage, social-security expansion, a permanent Fair Employment Practices Commission, an anti–poll tax bill, federal aid to education, and government medical insurance.

Congressional eagerness to dismantle wartime controls, and inconsistent presidential leadership, hobbled the administration's ability to handle the major postwar economic problem: inflation. Consumer demand outran the supply of goods, putting intense pressure on prices. The Office of Price Administration (OPA) continued to set price controls after the war, but food producers, manufacturers, and retailers opposed controls strenuously. Many consumers favored preserving the OPA, but others saw the agency as a symbol of irksome wartime regulation. In June 1946, when Congress passed a bill that extended the OPA's life but removed its powers, Truman vetoed the bill. Within a week food costs rose 16 percent and the price of beef doubled.

Congress passed, and Truman signed, a second bill extending price controls in weakened form. Protesting any price controls, however, farmers and meat producers threatened to withhold food from the market. Observing that "meatless voters are opposition voters," Truman lifted controls on food prices just before the November 1946 midterm elections. Democratic candidates fared badly at the polls anyhow. By the time Truman lifted all price controls, shortly after the election, the consumer price index had already jumped nearly 25 percent and food prices had risen at an even faster rate.

Sharp price rises and shrinking paychecks goaded organized labor to demand higher wages. When employers resisted, worker dissatisfaction boiled over in a surge of strikes. In 1946 alone, more than 4.5 million men and women went on strike. After a United Mine Workers walkout paralyzed the economy for forty days, President Truman ordered government seizure of the mines. A week later the miners returned to work, after Truman had pressured owners to grant most of the demands. Six months later the drama repeated itself.

In spring 1946 railway engineers and trainmen struck, shutting down the railway system. Truman exploded. "If you think I'm going to sit here and let you tie up this whole country," the president shouted at the heads of the two unions, "you're crazy as hell." In May Truman asked Congress for authority to draft workers who struck in vital industries. Only when the rail workers gave in did the Senate reject Truman's proposals. His threat alienated labor leaders, and his encouragement of inflationary wage-price agreements between powerful unions and industries forced consumers to pay the bill in the form of higher prices.

By fall 1946 Truman had angered most major interest groups; polls showed that less than one-third of Americans approved of his performance. Summing up public discontent, Republicans asked, "Had enough?" In the 1946 elections they captured twenty-five governorships and, for the first time since 1928, won control of Congress.

President Triman with Union Supporters
Following his veto of the Taft-Hartley bill and 1948 election victory, won, in large part, by the strong backing of organized labor, a smiling Truman dons a hard hat with copper miners in Butte, Montana.

Anticommunism and Containment

By the end of 1946, smoldering antagonisms between Moscow and Washington had flared up. With the Nazis defeated, the "shotgun wedding" between the United States and the Soviet Union dissolved into a struggle to fill the power vacuum left by the defeat of Germany and Japan, the exhaustion and bankruptcy of Western Europe, and the crumbling of colonial empires in Asia and Africa. Misperception and misunderstanding proliferated as the two nations sought security, each feeding the other's fears. Fundamental ideological differences widened the chasm between the two powers.

Confrontation and Polarization

The destiny of Eastern Europe, especially Poland, remained at the heart of U.S.–Soviet contention. The Soviet Union wanted to end its vulnerability to invasions sweeping eastward across the plains of Poland. Stalin insisted on a demilitarized Germany and a buffer of nations friendly to the Soviet Union along its western flank. He considered a Soviet sphere of influence in Eastern Europe essential to national security, a just reward for the U.S.S.R.'s bearing the brunt of the war against Germany, and no different from the American spheres of influence in Western Europe, Japan, and Latin America. Stalin also believed that at Yalta, Roosevelt and Churchill had implicitly accepted a Soviet zone in Eastern Europe.

With the Red Army occupying half of Europe at the war's end, Stalin installed pro-Soviet governments in Bulgaria, Hungary, and Romania, while communist governments independent of Moscow came to power in Albania and Yugoslavia. Ignoring the Yalta Declaration of Liberated Europe, the Soviet Union barred free elections in Poland and brutally suppressed Polish democratic parties.

Stalin's refusal to abandon dominance in Eastern Europe collided with Truman's unwillingness to concede Soviet supremacy beyond Russia's borders. What Stalin saw as critical to Russian security, the Truman administration viewed as a violation of the right of national self-determination, a betrayal of democratic principles, and a cover for communism's spread. Furthermore, Truman and his advisers believed that history taught that the appeasement of dictators only fed their appetites for expansion. The new administration thus determined to be tough with Moscow, because any "generous and considerate attitude" by the United States would be interpreted as weakness by Stalin and would lead to a "barbarian invasion of Europe." Moreover, many in Truman's inner circle believed that traditional European balance-of-power politics and spheres of influence had precipitated both world wars. Only a new world order based on the self-determination of all nations working in good faith within the United Nations could guarantee peace.

Truman also thought that accepting the "enforced sovietization" of Eastern Europe would betray American war aims and condemn nations rescued from Hitler's tyranny to another totalitarian dictatorship. Too, Truman worried, a Soviet stranglehold in Eastern Europe would imperil the health of an American economy dependent on exports and on access to raw materials in the countries that Stalin appeared resolute to control solely for Soviet economic betterment.

Domestic political considerations also shaped Truman's response to Stalin. The Democratic party contained 6 million Polish-Americans as well as millions of other Americans of Eastern European origin, all of whom remained keenly interested in the fates of their homelands. The president realized that the Democratic party courted disaster by reneging on the Yalta agreements. He also recognized the strength of anticommunism in American politics and was determined not to appear "soft on communism."

Combativeness fit the temperament of the feisty Truman. Eager to demonstrate that he was in command, the president matched Stalin's intransigence on Polish elections with his own demands for a reorganization of Poland's government along democratic lines. Emboldened by America's monopoly of atomic bombs and its undisputed position as the world's economic superpower, the president hoped that the United States could control the terms of postwar settlement.

The Cold War Begins

But Truman's assertiveness inflamed Stalin's mistrust of the West and deepened the Soviets' obsession with their own security. Stalin stepped up his confiscation of materials and factories from occupied territories and forced his satellite nations to close their doors to Anglo-American trade and influence. In February 1946 he warned that there could be no lasting peace with capitalism and vowed to make the Soviet Union secure against the Western challenge—and to overcome the American edge in weapons.

Two weeks later a sixteen-page telegram from George F. Kennan, the American chargé d'affaires in Moscow, reached Washington. A leading student of Soviet politics, Kennan warned that the Soviet

Union was "committed fanatically to the belief" that there could be no permanent peace with the United States. The only way to deal with Soviet intransigence was "a long-term, patient but firm and vigilant containment of Russian expansive tendencies." Truman, who had already insisted that it was time "to get tough with Russia," accepted the idea of containment, as did many others in Washington who wanted "no compromise" with the communists. Containment soon became gospel. Republican leaders demanded that the United States "draw the line" with Moscow, and the Truman administration agreed.

In early March 1946 Truman accompanied Winston Churchill to Westminster College in Missouri, where the former British prime minister, in a famous speech, warned of a new threat to democracy, this time from Moscow. Stalin, he said, had drawn an iron curtain across the eastern half of Europe. Churchill called for an alliance of the English-speaking peoples against the Soviet Union and the maintenance of an Anglo-American monopoly on atomic weapons.

Convinced that American firmness could check Soviet expansionism, Truman in spring 1946 shifted his foreign policy in the direction prescribed by Kennan and Churchill. To force Stalin to keep an earlier promise to withdraw Soviet soldiers from the north of oil-rich Iran, Truman dispatched part of the Sixth Fleet to the Black Sea and threatened to send in American combat troops. In June Truman submitted to the United Nations an atomic-energy control plan requiring the Soviet Union to stop all work on nuclear weapons and to submit to a system of U.N. control and inspection before the United States would destroy its own atomic arsenal. As expected, the Soviets rejected the American proposal and offered an alternative plan equally unacceptable to the United States. As mutual hostility escalated, the Soviets and Americans rushed to develop doomsday weapons. In 1946 Congress established the Atomic Energy Commission (AEC) to regulate nuclear development. Although Congress specified that fissionable materials should be used for civilian purposes "so far as practicable," at least 90 percent of the AEC's effort focused on weapons.

Thus, less than a year after American and Soviet soldiers had jubilantly met at the Elbe River to celebrate nazism's defeat, the Cold War had begun. Economic pressure, nuclear intimidation, propaganda, and subversion, rather than military confrontation, characterized this conflict. Nonetheless, it would affect American life as decisively as any military engagement that the nation had fought.

European Crisis, American Commitment

In early 1947 America formally stated its commitment to combat Soviet power. On February 21 the British informed the United States that they could no longer afford to assist the governments of Greece and Turkey in their struggles against communist-supplied guerrilla insurgencies and against Soviet pressure for access to the Mediterranean. Britain asked the United States to assume the costs of thwarting communism in the eastern Mediterranean. The harsh European winter, the most severe in memory, heightened the sense of urgency in Washington. The economies of Western Europe had ground to a halt, famine and tuberculosis plagued the Continent, and colonies in Africa and Asia had risen in rebellion. Communist parties in France and Italy appeared ready to topple democratic coalition governments. Truman resolved to meet the Soviet challenge.

He first had to mobilize support for a radical departure from the American tradition of avoiding entangling alliances. In a tense White House meeting on February 27, the new secretary of state, former army chief of staff George C. Marshall, presented the case for massive aid to Greece and Turkey. Congressional leaders balked, more concerned about U.S. inflation than civil war in Greece. But Dean Acheson, the newly appointed undersecretary of state, seized the moment. The issue, he said, was not one of assisting the repressive Greek oligarchy and Turkey's military dictatorship—it was, rather, a universal struggle of freedom versus tyranny. "Like apples in a barrel infected by the corruption of one rotten one," he warned, the fall of Greece or Turkey would open Asia, Western Europe, and the oil fields of the Middle East to the Red menace. Shaken, the congressional leaders agreed to support the administration's request—if Truman could "scare hell out of the country."

Truman could and did. On March 12, 1947, addressing a joint session of Congress he painted global politics as a stark confrontation between liberty and oppression and asked for military aid for Greece and Turkey. Outlining what became known as the Truman Doctrine, the president declared that the United States must support any free people "resisting attempted subjugation by armed minorities or by outside pressures." This unilateral declaration effectively transformed the United States into a global policeman facing an almost limitless confrontation with the Soviet Union and its allies. Endorsed by the Republican Congress, the Truman Doctrine laid the foundation for American Cold War policy that would endure for much of the next four decades.

A month later the administration proposed massive U.S. assistance for European recovery. First proposed by the secretary of state and thus called the Marshall Plan, such aid would become another weapon in the arsenal against the spread of communism. Truman wanted to end the economic devastation in Europe that he believed could readily be exploited by communist revolutionaries. Although the Marshall Plan ostensibly would help the hungry and homeless of *all* European countries, Truman calculated, correctly, that the U.S.S.R. and its communist allies would reject it because of the conditions and controls that were linked to the aid. The administration also accurately foresaw that Western European economic recovery would lead to an expansion in the sales of American goods abroad and thus promote domestic prosperity.

The Marshall Plan fulfilled its sponsors' hopes. Over a five-year period Congress appropriated $17 billion for economic recovery in sixteen nations, and by 1952 the economic and social chaos that could have proved a fertile seedbed for communism had died down. Western Europe revived, prospered, and achieved an unprecedented unity. U.S. business, not coincidentally, boomed.

Confrontation

The Soviet Union initially reacted to the Truman Doctrine and the Marshall Plan by tightening its grip on Poland, Bulgaria, Albania, and Romania. Then in 1947–1948 communist coups added Hungary and Czechoslovakia to the Soviet bloc. Stalin next turned his attention to central Europe, determined to derail the prospect of a reunited Germany.

The Potsdam Agreement had divided Germany into four separate zones (administered by France, Great Britain, the Soviet Union, and the United States) and created a joint four-power administration for Germany's capital, Berlin, which lay 110 miles inside the Soviet-occupied eastern zone. As the Cold War intensified, however, the Western nations began to see a revived Germany as a buffer against Soviet expansion and gradually united their zones. An alarmed Stalin, still mindful of Russian casualties in World War II, in April 1948 impeded the flow of goods and people into Berlin and then in June blocked all rail and highway routes through the Soviet zone into Berlin. Stalin calculated that the Western powers, unable to feed the 2 million pro-Western Berliners under their control, would either have to abandon plans to create an independent West Germany or accept a communist Berlin.

Truman resolved neither to abandon Berlin nor to shoot his way into the city—and possibly trigger World War III. Instead, he ordered a daring airlift to provide Berliners with the food and fuel necessary for survival. American cargo planes landed at West Berlin's Templehof Airport virtually every three minutes, around the clock, carrying a mountain of supplies. Then in July 1948 Truman hinted that he would use "the bomb" if necessary and sent a fleet of B-29s, the only planes capable of delivering atomic bombs, to English bases. As tensions rose, Truman confided to his diary that "we are very close to war." The Berlin airlift continued for nearly a year.

In May 1949 the Soviets ended the block-

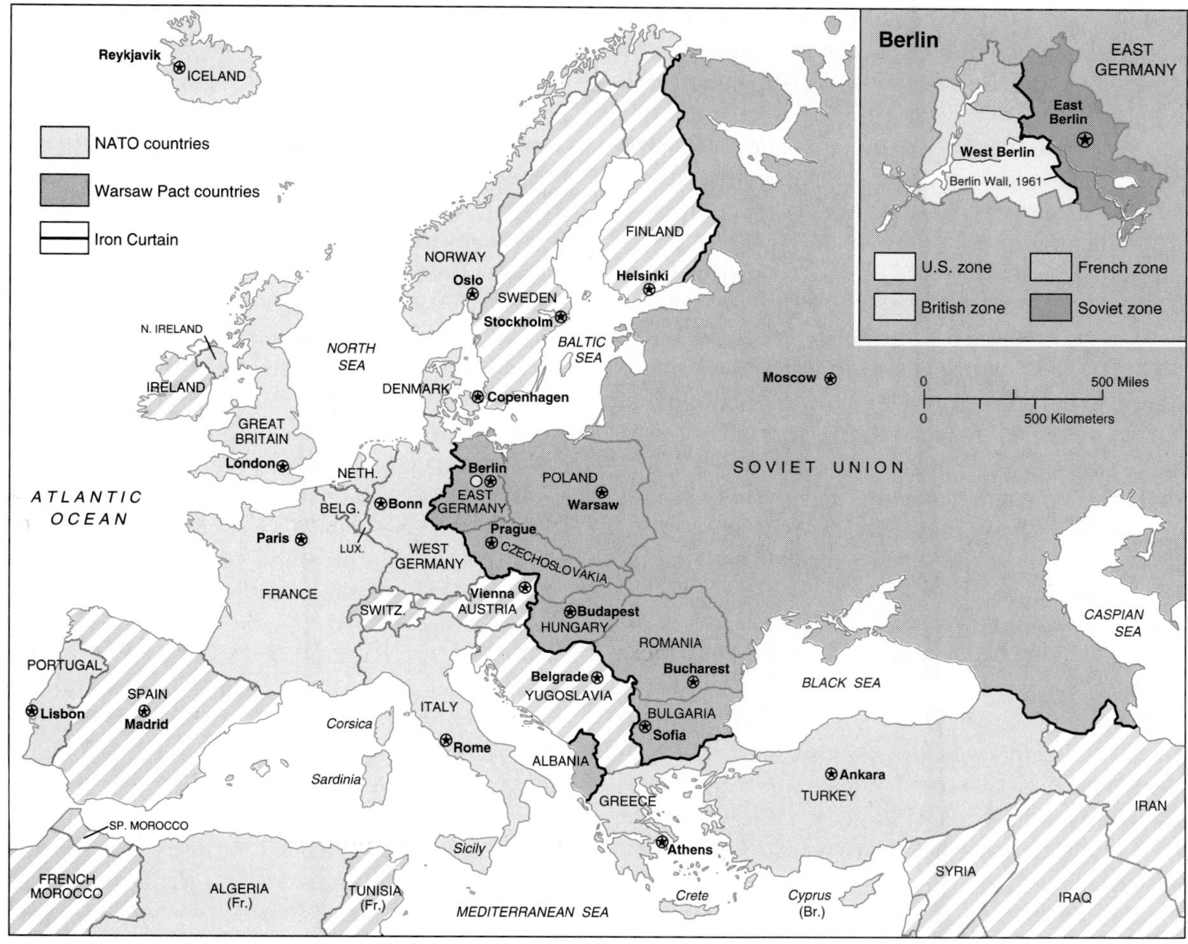

The Postwar Division of Europe
The wartime dispute between the Soviet Union and the Western Allies over Poland's future hardened after World War II into a cold war that split Europe into competing American and Russian spheres of influence. Across an "iron curtain," NATO countries faced the Warsaw Pact nations.

ade. Stalin's gamble had failed. The airlift highlighted American determination and technological prowess, revealed Stalin's willingness to use innocent citizens as pawns, and dramatically heightened anti-Soviet feeling in the West. In late 1948 U.S. public-opinion polls revealed an overwhelming demand for "firmness and increased 'toughness' in relations with Russia."

Continuing fears of a Soviet attack on Western Europe fostered support for a revitalized West German state and for an Atlantic collective-security alliance. Thus in May 1949 the United States, Britain, and France ended their occupation of Germany and approved the creation of the Federal Republic of Germany (West Germany). A month earlier ten nations of Western Europe had adopted the North Atlantic Treaty, establishing a military alliance with the United States and Canada and declaring that an attack on any member would be considered an attack against all. For the first time in its history, the United States entered into a peacetime military alliance. After overwhelming Senate approval, the United States officially joined the North Atlantic Treaty Organization (NATO).

Two days after Senate ratification, Truman asked Congress to authorize $1.3 billion for military assistance to NATO countries. To underscore his determination to contain communism, Truman persuaded General Dwight D. Eisenhower to become supreme commander of the new mutual-defense force and authorized the stationing of four U.S. army divisions in Europe as the nucleus of the NATO armed force. The Soviet Union responded by creating the German Democratic Republic (East Germany) in 1949, by exploding its own atomic bomb that same year, and by forming an Eastern bloc military alliance, the Warsaw Pact, in 1955. The United States and Soviet Union had divided Europe into two armed camps.

The Cold War in Asia

Moscow-Washington hostility also carved Asia into contending military and economic camps. The Russians created a sphere of influence in Manchuria, the United States denied Moscow a role in postwar Japan, and the two superpowers partitioned a helpless Korea.

As the head of the U.S. occupation forces in Japan, General Douglas MacArthur oversaw the country's transformation from an empire in ruins into a prosperous democracy. In 1952 the occupation ended, but a military security treaty allowed the U.S. to retain its Japanese bases on the Soviet-Asian perimeter and brought Japan under the American "nuclear umbrella." Both benefited: Japan could devote most of its resources to economic development, and the United States gained a staunch anti-communist ally. The containment policy in Asia also led the U.S. to help crush a procommunist guerrilla movement in the Philippines and to aid French efforts to reestablish colonial rule in Indochina (Vietnam, Laos, and Cambodia), despite American declarations in favor of national self-determination and against imperialism.

In China, however, U.S. efforts to block communism failed. The Truman administration initially tried to mediate the civil war raging between Jiang Jieshi's Nationalist government and Mao Zedong's communist forces. Between 1945 and 1949 the United States sent nearly $3 billion to the Nationalists. But American dollars could not force Jiang's corrupt government to reform itself and to win the support of the Chinese people, whom it had widely alienated. As Mao's well-disciplined and motivated forces marched south, Jiang's soldiers mutinied and surrendered without a fight. Unable to stem revolutionary sentiment or to build loyalty among the peasants, Jiang's regime collapsed, and he fled to exile on the island of Taiwan (Formosa).

Mao's establishment of the communist People's Republic of China shocked Americans. The most populous nation in the world, seen as a counterforce to Asian communism and a market for American trade, had become "Red China." Although the Truman administration insisted that it could have done little to alter the outcome and placed responsibility for Jiang's defeat on his failure to reform China, most Americans were unconvinced. China's fall to communism particularly embittered those conservatives who believed that America's future lay in Asia, not Europe. They launched an angry campaign to discover "Who lost China?" and assumed that the answer lay in the United States.

As the China debate raged, the president announced in September 1949 that the Soviet Union had exploded an atomic bomb. The loss of the nuclear monopoly shattered illusions of American invincibility. Combined with Mao's victory, this development would spawn an anticommunist hysteria and lead to irrational searches for scapegoats and subversives to explain American setbacks in world affairs.

A reeling Truman administration reassessed its strategy. In January 1950, stung by charges that he was soft on communism, the president ordered the development of a fusion-based hydrogen bomb (H-bomb), hundreds of times more powerful than an atomic bomb. Leading scientists, including J. Robert Oppenheimer, argued that hydrogen bombs were too complex to construct and too immorally destructive to use. But in the fearful atmosphere pervading Washington in early 1950, Truman accepted the report of his secretaries of defense and state recommending a crash thermonuclear program. In November 1952 the United States exploded its first H-bomb in the Marshall Islands, projecting a radioactive cloud twenty-five miles into the atmosphere and blasting a canyon a mile long and 175 feet deep in the ocean floor. Nine months later the Soviets detonated their own hydrogen bomb.

In April 1950 a presidentially appointed committee issued a top-secret review of defense policy. The report, NSC-68, emphasized the Soviet Union's aggressive intentions and military strength. To counter the U.S.S.R.'s "design for world domination"—the mortal challenge posed by the Soviet Union "not only to this Republic but to civilization itself"—NSC-68 called for a vast American military buildup, a large standing army, and a quadrupling of the defense budget to wage a global struggle against communism.

Truman hesitated to swallow his advisers' expensive medicine. An aide to Secretary of State Acheson recalled, "We were sweating over it, and then, with regard to NSC-68, thank God Korea came along." Indeed, on June 24, 1950, as Truman pondered NSC-68's implications, North Korean troops swept across the thirty-eighth parallel and invaded the Republic of Korea (South Korea). By the end of 1950, Truman would order the implementation of NSC-68 and triple the defense budget.

The Korean War

After Japan's defeat in World War II, the Soviet Union and United States had temporarily divided Korea at the thirty-eighth parallel for purposes of military occupation. The dividing line had solidified into a political frontier between the Soviet-backed People's Democratic Republic in North Korea and the American-supported Republic of Korea. Each government hoped to unify Korea under its exclusive control.

Chaos in Korea
In this photograph taken in 1950, South Korean women and children flee from the communist invaders as U.S. infantrymen move in to keep the North Koreans from making further advances.

Truman saw North Korea's invasion of South Korea not as an internal Korean matter but as Soviet-directed aggression. Despite ambiguous and often conflicting evidence, he never doubted that Stalin was testing American will. The president maintained, "If we are tough enough now, if we stand up to [the Soviets] . . . they won't take any next steps." Mindful of the failure of appeasement at Munich in 1938, Truman said that "if aggression is successful in Korea, we can expect it to spread through Asia and Europe to [the western] hemisphere." Failure to act would lead to a bloody "third world war, just as similar incidents had brought on the second world war." Truman also had to prove to Republican critics that the Democrats would not allow another country to "fall" to the communists.

The president decided to intervene in Korea. Without consulting Congress or asking for a formal declaration of war, Truman secured the United

Nations' sanction for a "police action" against the aggressor. Boycotting the Security Council in a dispute over recognition of the People's Republic of China, the Soviet Union could not veto this policy. On June 27 Truman ordered American air and sea forces to South Korea's aid and appointed General MacArthur to command the U.N. effort in Korea. Within three days American soldiers were fighting in Korea. U.S. forces provided most of the air and navy support and almost 50 percent of the troops fighting under the U.N. flag; South Korea supplied 43 percent of the forces, and fourteen other nations contributed less than 10 percent.

North Korea rapidly pushed the U.N. forces to the southeastern tip of the Korean peninsula. Then in mid-September a brilliant amphibious movement designed by MacArthur landed U.N. troops at Inchon, north of Seoul, and forced a North Korean retreat. Heartened, Truman permitted MacArthur to order U.N. armies across the thirty-eighth parallel toward the Yalu River, the boundary between Korea and China. The police action to restore the original border between the two Koreas was being transformed into a war of liberation to create "a unified, independent, and democratic" nation of Korea.

As U.N. troops approached the Yalu River, the Chinese warned that they would not "stand idly by" if their border was threatened. Ignoring this assertion, an overconfident MacArthur deployed his forces in a thin line below the river. On November 25 thirty-three Chinese divisions (about 300,000 men) counterattacked, driving stunned U.N. forces back below the thirty-eighth parallel. By March 1951 the fighting was stabilized at roughly the original dividing line between the two Koreas.

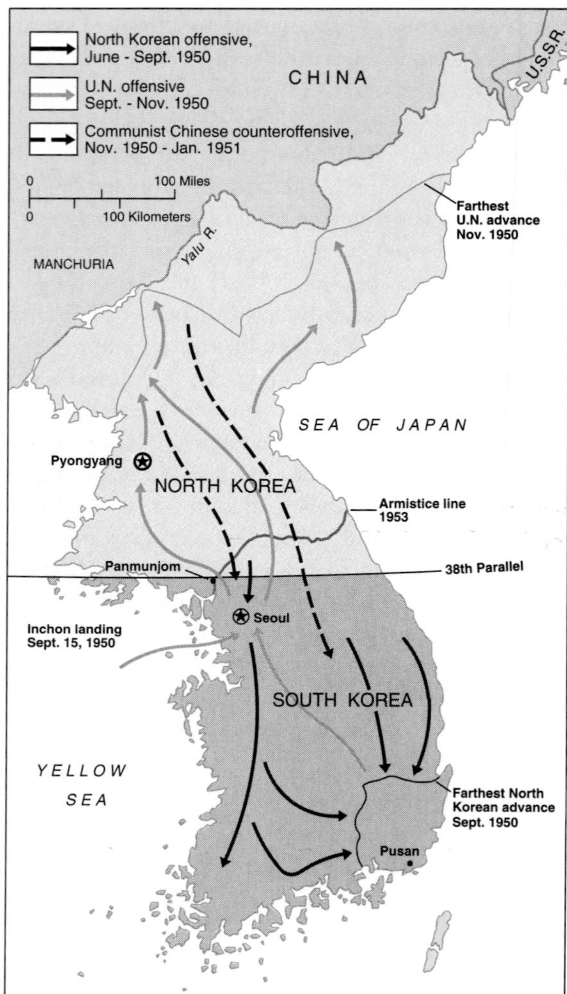

The Korean War, 1950–1953

The experience of fighting an undeclared and limited war for the limited objective of containing communism confused the generation of Americans who had just fought an all-out war for the total defeat of the Axis.

In spring 1951 Truman again reversed course and sought a negotiated peace based on the objective of restoring the integrity of South Korea. MacArthur rocked the boat, however, urging that he be allowed to bomb and blockade China, "unleash" Jiang Jieshi's troops against Mao's regime, and seek a total victory even at the risk of an all-out war with China. Truman rejected these ideas: "We are trying to prevent a world war—not to start one." Worried that the Soviet Union might take advantage of American involvement in Asia to pursue an aggressive course in Europe, he sought a limited war for a limited objective: to hold the line in Korea. But MacArthur would not accept a stalemate. "In war," he said, "there is no substitute for victory."

When MacArthur refused to stop criticizing administration policy, Truman relieved him of command, on April 10, 1951. To the president, the issue was civilian control of the military, a control that seemed threatened by MacArthur's public insubordination. Public opinion, however, backed the general. The very idea of limited war baffled many Americans, and a mounting casualty list added anger to the mix. Radical Republican criticisms, such as Indiana senator William Jenner's charge that "this country today is in the hands of a secret coterie which is directed by agents of the Soviet Union," won support in some quarters.

In July 1951 truce talks began, but they dragged on for two years as both sides continued their restricted but deadly war. By the time that wrangling over prisoner repatriation and the cease-fire line ended on July 26, 1953, the "limited war" had cost the United States almost 55,000 American lives, another 103,284 wounded or missing, and $54 billion. The conflict also accelerated implementation of NSC-68 and the expansion of containment into a global policy. From 1950 to 1953 defense spending zoomed from one-third to two-thirds of the entire federal budget. The United States acquired new bases around the world, committed itself to rearm West Germany, and joined a mutual-defense pact with Australia and New Zealand. Increased military aid flowed to Jiang Jieshi's troops on Taiwan, and American dollars were extended to the French army fighting the communist Ho Chi Minh in Indochina. By 1954 the United States was paying about three-quarters of French war costs in Vietnam.

Truman's intervention in Korea preserved a precarious balance of power in Asia by preventing the South Korean regime from falling to its communist rival in the north. It also underscored the administration's commitment to the anticommunist struggle, as well as the shift of that struggle's focus from Europe to Asia. Containment, originally designed to justify U.S. aid to Greece and Turkey, became in the early 1950s the ideological foundation for a major war in Korea and, ominously, for a deepening U.S. involvement with France's colonial war in Vietnam. By committing U.S. troops to battle with neither a declaration of war nor congressional approval, Truman set precedents for future undeclared wars, expanded presidential powers, and helped institutionalize the "warfare" state. Combined with the shock of China's "fall," the inconclusive Korean conflict created deep frustration among Americans and intensified their hatred of communism. This chain of unsettling events would have broad cultural as well as political consequences in the future.

The Truman Administration at Home

When World War II ended, Americans wanted to bring the troops home and enjoy peace. Since 1929 the nation had known little but the sufferings and shortages of depression and war, and now it was time to enjoy life! Widespread postwar affluence let dreams become reality as Americans flocked to the suburbs, launched a "baby boom" of howling proportions, and rushed to buy stoves, refrigerators, televisions, and cars.

Not all Americans shared the good times. Poverty remained a stark fact of life for millions in the cities and on farms. African-Americans experienced the grim reality of racism. Many refused to yield, however, and from the early postwar period there emerged a civil-rights movement that in a few years would sweep the nation.

Family and career, not social issues, preoccupied most Americans, however, and New Deal reform energies subsided into a mood of complacency. Although Truman sought to extend reform, the times were against him. Congressional conservatives wanted to reduce, not expand, federal power. Anticommunism intensified the American tendency to identify social radicalism with disloyalty, and undercut efforts to alter the status quo.

After 1949 the Truman administration increasingly reflected the popular mood. Federal expenditures were devoted to rearmament, not social welfare, and anticommunism replaced reform at the top of the American agenda.

The Eightieth Congress

Many Republicans in the Eightieth Congress, which convened in January 1947, interpreted the 1946 elections as a mandate to reverse the New Deal. Republican-controlled, Congress passed tax measures favoring the wealthy, and defeated proposals to raise the minimum wage and provide federal funds for education and housing.

Truman and the conservatives waged their major battle over the pro-union Wagner Act of 1935 (see Chapter 25). Postwar strikes had whipped up a national consensus for curbing union power. In 1947 Congress passed the Taft-Hartley Act (the Labor-Management Relations Act), which barred the closed shop and permitted the president to call a sixty-day cooling-off period to delay any strike that might endanger national safety or health. Unions termed the law a "slave labor bill" and demanded a presidential veto.

Truman did veto the measure, and he scolded Congress for "a shocking piece of legislation" biased against labor. Congress easily overrode the veto. But Truman had taken a major step toward regaining organized labor's support. This move reflected his recognition that his only hope for election in 1948 lay in reforging the New Deal coalition. To this end, he played the role of staunch New Dealer to the hilt, proposing a series of liberal reform bills—federal aid to education, housing, and health insurance; repeal of Taft-Hartley; and high farm-price supports.

Truman courted voters of Eastern European ancestry by emphasizing his opposition to the Iron Curtain. He overrode the objections of the State Department, which feared alienating the oil-rich Arab world, to extend diplomatic recognition to the new state of Israel immediately after it proclaimed independence. This move reflected both his deep sympathy toward Holocaust survivors who had immigrated to Israel and the strategic importance of Jewish-American voters.

The Politics of Civil Rights

Truman's desire for support from white southern Democrats initially tempered his support of the growing civil-rights movement. But the movement, and the violence it provoked, demanded a White House response.

Many African-Americans, especially veterans, demanded the right to vote after the war. Aggressive voter-registration drives raised the number of blacks registered to vote in the South from 2 percent in 1940 to 12 percent in 1947. Southern blacks risked intimidation, repression, and even murder in pursuing their right to vote, for white-supremacist politicians urged their followers to use any means to keep African-Americans from exercising that right.

Fearful of black assertiveness in seeking the vote and of other signs of a bold new spirit among African-Americans, some southern whites reacted brutally. In 1946 in rural Georgia, whites killed several black veterans who had voted that year, and in South Carolina whites blinded a black soldier for failing to sit in the rear of a bus. In Columbia, Tennessee, in 1946, whites rioted against blacks who insisted on their rights. Police arrested seventy blacks and looked the other way as a white mob broke into the jail to murder two African-American prisoners. Civil-rights leaders called for federal action.

In September 1946 Truman met with a delegation from some newly formed biracial groups to discuss racial terrorism in the South. Horrified by their accounts, he vowed to act. Truman believed that every American should enjoy the full rights of citizenship. He also understood the importance of the growing African-American vote, particularly in northern cities. The president realized, too, that white racism damaged U.S. relations with much of the world. The Soviet Union highlighted the mistreatment of American blacks, both to undercut U.S. appeals to racially diverse peoples in Africa, Asia, and Latin America and to counter U.S. condemnation of repression behind the Iron Curtain. After the 1946 elections, Truman established the President's Committee on Civil Rights to investigate race relations.

The committee's report, *To Secure These Rights*, called for the eradication of racial discrimination and segregation and proposed antilynching and anti–poll tax legislation. Boldly, Truman in February 1948 sent a special message to Congress urging lawmakers to enact most of the committee's proposals.

Southern segregationists denounced Truman's "stab in the back." Many influential southern politicians warned of a boycott of the national Democratic ticket. Truman backtracked, flinching at the prospect of major southern defections. He dropped his plans, for example, to submit specific civil-rights bills to Congress and endorsed a weak civil-rights plank for the Democratic platform.

At the Democratic convention in July 1948, liberals and urban politicians who needed African-American votes rejected the feeble civil-rights plank and committed the party to action on Truman's original proposals. Thirty-five delegates from Mississippi and Alabama responded by stalking out of the convention. They joined other southern segregationists to form the States' Rights Democratic party and nominated Governor Strom Thurmond of South Carolina for the presidency. The "Dixiecrats" hoped to win a hundred southern electoral votes, to restore their dominance in the Democratic party, and to preserve "the southern way of life" against an oppressive central government. They placed their electors on the ballot as the regular Democratic ticket in several states, erecting a major roadblock to Truman's chances of victory.

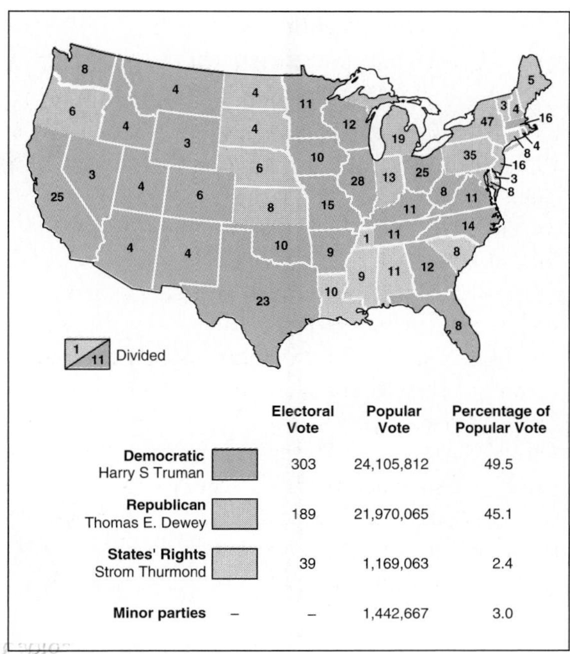

	Electoral Vote	Popular Vote	Percentage of Popular Vote
Democratic Harry S Truman	303	24,105,812	49.5
Republican Thomas E. Dewey	189	21,970,065	45.1
States' Rights Strom Thurmond	39	1,169,063	2.4
Minor parties –	–	1,442,667	3.0

The Election of 1948

The Election of 1948

Truman's electoral hopes faded when a band of left-wing Democrats joined with communists to launch a new Progressive party and nominated Henry A. Wallace for president. Truman had fired Wallace, his secretary of commerce and FDR's third-term vice president, for publicly questioning the administration's "get tough" stance toward the Soviet Union. The Wallace candidacy threatened Truman's chances in northern states, where many urban Democrats saw Wallace as the heir of New Deal liberalism.

To capitalize on Democratic divisions, Republicans tried to play it safe. Their platform vaguely endorsed much of the New Deal and the Truman administration's Cold War policy. They nominated the moderate governor of New York, Thomas E. Dewey, and ran a complacent campaign designed to offend the fewest people.

Truman, in contrast, campaigned tirelessly, blasting the "no-good, do-nothing" Republican-controlled Eightieth Congress. To shouts of "Give 'em hell, Harry," the president hammered away at the GOP as the party of "privilege, pride, and plunder." Pollsters applauded Truman's spunk but predicted a sure Dewey victory.

A surprised nation awoke the day after the election to learn that the president had won in the biggest upset in U.S. history, 24.1 million votes to Dewey's 22 million. Ironically, the Progressives and Dixiecrats had helped Truman. Their radicalism had kept both moderate liberals and moderate conservatives safely in the Democratic fold. The attorney general of Virginia explained, "The only sane and constructive course to follow is to remain in the house of our fathers—even though the roof leaks, and there be bats in the belfry, rats in the pantry, cockroaches in the kitchen, and skunks in the parlor." Moreover, Dixiecrat defections had freed Truman to campaign as a proponent of civil rights.

Harlem Residents Greet President Truman
Although stymied by Congress, Truman put forth unprecedented, sweeping civil-rights proposals that brought thousands of African-Americans out to see the president campaign in Harlem on October 29, 1948.

In July 1948 Truman had issued executive orders barring discrimination in federal employment and creating a committee to ensure "equality of treatment and opportunity for all persons in the armed services without regard to race, color, religion or national origin." Truman had also benefited from two Supreme Court decisions. In 1946 the Court had declared segregation in interstate bus transportation unconstitutional, and in 1948 it had outlawed restrictive housing covenants that forbade the sale or rental of property to minorities. In 1947 Jackie Robinson of the Brooklyn Dodgers shattered major-league baseball's color barrier. African-Americans had taken heart from these changes and had voted accordingly. Truman won a higher percentage of African-American votes than FDR ever had.

Truman had succeeded in 1948 by re-creating the New Deal coalition. With the crisis in Berlin helping to rally Americans behind their president, he had seized every opportunity to remind farmers and laborers that the Republican "gluttons of privilege" planned to "turn the clock back" and strip away New Deal benefits.

The Fair Deal

Despite his narrow victory margin, Truman saw his election as a mandate for liberalism. In his 1949 State of the Union message, he proposed an ambitious social and economic program, the Fair Deal. He asked Congress to enlarge New Deal programs in economic security, conservation, and housing and to go beyond the New Deal in other areas.

The Eighty-first Congress complied with the extension of existing programs but rejected new measures. Lawmakers raised the minimum wage; increased social-security coverage and benefits; expanded appropriations for public power, conservation, and slum clearance; and authorized the construction of nearly a million low-income housing units. But they rejected federal aid to education, national health insurance, civil-rights legislation, larger farm subsidies, and the repeal of Taft-Hartley.

Congress's rejection of most Fair Deal proposals stemmed from Truman's own lessening commitment to domestic reform in favor of foreign policy, as well as from the strengthening of the congressional conservative coalition. And widespread prosperity sapped public enthusiasm for more reform. The postwar congresses mirrored the sense of well-being that most Americans enjoyed and reflected the popular apprehensions over communism that doomed liberal hopes for social change.

The Politics of Anticommunism

As the Cold War evolved, some Americans concluded that the roots of the nation's foreign difficulties lay in domestic treason and subversion. How else could the communists have taken China and the Soviets have developed an atomic bomb? Millions of fearful Americans would eventually enlist in a crusade that would find scapegoats for the nation's problems and would equate dissent with disloyalty.

Since 1938 the House Committee on Un-American Activities (later called the House Un-American Activities Committee, or HUAC) had served as a platform for conservatives' denunciation of the New Deal as a communist plot. At first only the extreme Right had embraced this viewpoint seriously, but after World War II mounting numbers of Democrats and Republicans climbed aboard the anti-Red bandwagon.

This so-called second Red Scare influenced both governmental and personal actions. Millions of Americans were subjected to loyalty oaths and security investigations after the war. The anticommunist hysteria would destroy the Left, discredit liberalism, and undermine labor militancy. The purge of controversial government officials, furthermore, would ensure foreign-policy rigidity and the postponement of domestic social change.

Loyalty and Security

The Cold War raised legitimate concerns about American security. The Communist party had claimed 80,000 members during World War II, and no one knew how many occupied sensitive government positions. In mid-1945 a raid of the offices of a procommunist magazine revealed that classified documents had been given to the periodical by two State Department employees and a naval intelligence officer. Ten months later the Canadian government exposed a major spy network that had passed American military information and atomic secrets to the Soviets during the war.

Truman in late 1946 named a commission to study the loyalty problem and in March 1947 issued Executive Order 9835 establishing the Federal Employee Loyalty Program to provide a loyalty check on all government workers. The drive for absolute security soon overran concerns about rights, however, as civil servants suspected of disloyalty were allowed neither to face their accusers nor to require investigators to reveal sources. Instead of focusing on potential subversives in high-risk areas, the probe extended to the associations and beliefs of *every* government worker.

Mere criticism of American foreign policy could result in an accusation of disloyalty. People could lose their jobs if they liked foreign films, associated with radical friends or family members, or were past members of organizations now declared disloyal. Between 1947 and 1951 loyalty boards forced nearly 3,000 government employees to resign and fired 300 on charges of disloyalty. The probe uncovered no evidence of subversion or espionage, but it did spread fear among government employees. "If communists like apple pie and I do," said one federal worker, "I see no reason why I should stop eating it. But I would."

The Anticommunist Crusade

The very existence of a federal loyalty inquest fed mounting anticommunist hysteria. Federal investigators promoted fears of communist infiltration and legitimized other efforts to expose subversives. Universities banned controversial speakers, and popular magazines ran articles like "Reds Are After Your Child." Even comic books joined the fray: "Beware, commies, spies, traitors, and foreign agents! Captain America, with all loyal, free men behind him, is looking for you." By the end of Truman's term, thirty-nine states had created loyalty programs, most with virtually no procedural safeguards. Schoolteachers, college professors, and state and city employees throughout the nation signed loyalty oaths or lost their jobs.

In 1947 the House Un-American Activities Committee began hearings to expose communist influence in American life. HUAC's probes blurred distinctions between dissent and disloyalty, between radicalism and subversion. People who refused to answer HUAC questions often lost their livelihoods. HUAC also frightened labor unions into expelling communist members and avoiding progressive causes. Fearful that championing leftist causes would make them appear procommunist, unions concentrated on securing better pay and benefits and became bureaucratic special-interest pressure groups.

HUAC also left its mark on the entertainment industry. When certain prominent film directors and screenwriters refused to cooperate in 1947, HUAC had them cited for contempt and sent to federal prison. Blacklists in Hollywood and in radio broadcasting barred the employment of anyone with a slightly questionable past, thereby silencing many talented people.

The 1948 presidential campaign fed national anxieties. Truman lambasted Henry Wallace as a Stalinist dupe and accused the Republicans of being "unwittingly the ally of the communists in this country." In turn, the GOP dubbed the Democrats "the party of treason." A rising Republican star, Richard M. Nixon of California, charged that Democrats bore responsibility for "the unimpeded growth of the communist conspiracy in the United States."

To blunt the force of such accusations, the Justice Department prosecuted eleven top leaders of the American Communist party under the Smith Act of 1940, which outlawed any conspiracy advocating the overthrow of the government. In some cases, U.S. citizens consequently were convicted and jailed, not for anything they had done but only for what they had said. In 1951 the Supreme Court upheld the Smith Act's constitutionality, declaring that Congress could curtail freedom of speech if national security demanded such restrictions.

Ironically, the Communist party was fading into obscurity at the very time that politicians were magnifying the threat it posed. By 1950 its membership had shrunk to less than 30,000. Yet Truman's attorney general warned that American Reds "are everywhere—in factories, offices, butcher stores, on street corners, in private businesses—and each carries in himself the germ of death for society."

Hiss and the Rosenbergs

Nothing set off more alarms about the diabolic Red conspiracy in the federal government than the case of Alger Hiss. Amid the 1948 presidential campaign, HUAC conducted a sensational hearing in which Whittaker Chambers, a senior editor at *Time* and a former Soviet agent who had broken with the communists in 1938, identified Hiss as an underground party member in the 1930s.

In the hearing, Chambers appeared a tortured soul crusading to save the West from the Red peril. The elegant and cultured Hiss, in contrast, seemed the very symbol of the liberal establishment; a Harvard Law School graduate, he had clerked for Justice Oliver Wendell Holmes, served as a presidential adviser on foreign affairs (including the Yalta conference), and headed the Carnegie Endowment for International Peace.

Hiss denied any communist affiliation and claimed not to know Chambers. Most liberals believed Hiss. They thought him the victim of conservatives bent on tarnishing New Deal liberalism. Rushing to Hiss's defense, Truman denounced Chambers's allegations as a "red herring" to deflect attention from the failures of the Eightieth Congress.

To those suspicious of the Rooseveltian liberal tradition, Chambers's persistence and Hiss's fumbling retreat intensified fears that the Democratic administration was teeming with communists. Under rigorous questioning by Richard Nixon, Hiss admitted that he had known Chambers but denied having been a communist. Chambers broadened his accusation, claiming that Hiss had committed espionage in the 1930s by giving him secret State Department documents to be sent to the Soviet Union. Hiss protested his innocence, but a grand jury indicted him for perjury, or lying under oath. In January 1950 Hiss was convicted and received a five-year prison sentence. Emboldened congressional conservatives stalked other Hisses.

Just as the Hiss affair ended, another case shocked Americans. In early February 1950 the

Ethel and Julius Rosenberg
The couple is shown in 1951 leaving the New York City federal court after arraignment on spy charges.

British arrested Klaus Fuchs, a German-born scientist involved in the Manhattan Project, for passing atomic secrets to the Soviets. Fuchs's confession led to the arrest of two Americans, Ethel and Julius Rosenberg, as coconspirators. The Rosenbergs insisted that they were victims of anti-Semitism and were being prosecuted for their leftist beliefs. But in March 1951 a jury found them guilty of conspiring to commit espionage, and on June 19, 1953, the husband and wife were executed, although they maintained their innocence to the end.

At this point, some Americans could not separate fact from fantasy. For them, only conspiracy could explain U.S. weakness and Soviet might. Frustrated by unexpected failure in 1948, Republicans eagerly seized the theory. Doomed to four more years of exile from the White House, the GOP in 1949 hurled a series of reckless accusations at the administration, such as one senator's charge that it consisted of a "crazy assortment of collectivist cutthroat crackpots and Communist fellow-traveling appeasers."

McCarthyism

No individual would inflict so many wounds on the Democrats as Republican senator Joseph R. McCarthy of Wisconsin. Desperate for an issue to run on in 1952, McCarthy had noted the success of fellow Republicans who had labeled the Democrats "soft on communism." In February 1950 McCarthy boldly told a West Virginia audience that communists in the State Department had betrayed America. "I have here in my hand a list of 205," McCarthy reported as he waved a laundry list, "a list of names known to the Secretary of State as being members of the Communist party and who nevertheless are still working and shaping policy." Although he could produce no evidence to support his accusations, his senatorial stature and brazen style gave him a national forum. McCarthy soon repeated his charges, though lowering his numbers and reducing his indictment from "card-carrying communists" to "subversives" to "bad risks." A Senate committee found McCarthy's accusations "a fraud and a hoax," but he persisted. *McCarthyism* became synonymous with public charges of disloyalty without sufficient regard for evidence.

As the Korean War dragged on, McCarthy's efforts to "root out the skunks" escalated. He ridiculed Secretary of State Dean Acheson as the "Red Dean" and called Truman's dismissal of MacArthur "the greatest victory the communists have ever won." Buoyed by the partisan usefulness of McCarthy's onslaught, many Republicans encouraged him. McCarthyism especially appealed to midwestern party members indignant about the welfare state, restrictions on business, and the Europe-first emphasis of Truman's foreign policy. For them, anticommunism was a weapon of revenge against liberals and internationalists and a means to regain the controlling position that conservatism had once held. McCarthy also won a devoted following among blue-collar workers. His flag-waving patriotism appealed to traditionally Catholic ethnics, who wanted to gain acceptance as "100 percent Americans" through a show of anticommunist zeal. Countless Americans also shared McCarthy's scorn for privilege and gentility, for the "bright young men who are born with silver spoons in their mouths." And his conspiracy theory offered a simple answer to the perplexing questions of the Cold War.

McCarthy's political power had two bases: the Republican establishment and Democrats fearful of antagonizing him. The GOP support that McCarthy enjoyed made Democrats' condemnation look like mere partisan criticism. In the 1950 elections when he helped Republicans to defeat Democrats who had denounced him, McCarthy appeared invincible. "Joe will go that extra mile to destroy you," warned the new Senate majority leader, Lyndon B. Johnson of Texas.

Over Truman's veto, Congress in 1950 adopted the McCarran Internal Security Act, which required organizations deemed communist by the attorney general to register with the Department of Justice and to provide membership lists and financial statements. It also barred communists from employment in defense plants, authorized the government to deny passports to communists, and authorized the arrest and detention during a national emergency of "any person as to whom there is reason to believe might engage in acts of espionage or sabotage." The McCarran-Walter Immigration and Nationality Act of 1952, also passed over a presidential veto, maintained the discriminatory quotas based on national origins that gave immigrants from northern and Western Europe 85 percent of available slots, although it did end Asian exclusion. The new law also strengthened the attorney general's authority to exclude or deport aliens suspected of supporting communism.

The Election of 1952

By 1952 public apprehension about the loyalty of government employees combined with frustration over the Korean stalemate to sink Democratic presidential hopes to their lowest level since the 1920s. Both business and labor also resented Truman's freeze on wages and prices during the Korean conflict. In addition, revelations of bribery and influence peddling by some of Truman's old political associates gave Republicans ammunition for charging the Democrats with "plunder at home, and blunder abroad."

When Truman decided not to seek reelection, dispirited Democrats drafted Governor Adlai E. Stevenson of Illinois. But Stevenson could not separate himself from Truman, and his lofty speeches did not stir the average voter. Above all, Stevenson could not overcome the sentiment that twenty years of Democratic rule was enough.

The GOP once again bypassed conservative senator Robert A. Taft of Ohio, this time for the hugely popular war hero Dwight D. Eisenhower. Essentially apolitical, Eisenhower had once insisted that "lifelong professional soldiers should abstain

The Election of 1952

Candidates	*Parties*	*Electoral Vote*	*Popular Vote*	*Percentage of Popular Vote*
DWIGHT D. EISENHOWER	Republican	442	33,936,234	55.1
Adlai E. Stevenson	Democratic	89	27,314,992	44.4

from seeking higher political office," but he answered the call of the moderate wing of the Republican party and accepted the nomination. "Ike" chose as his running mate Richard M. Nixon, the former HUAC Red hunter.

Eisenhower and Nixon proved unbeatable. With a captivating grin and an unimpeachable record of public service, Eisenhower projected both personal warmth and the vigorous authority associated with military command. His smile, wrote one commentator, "was a smile of infinite reassurance." Indeed, Eisenhower symbolized the stability for which Americans yearned. At the same time, Nixon kept public apprehensions at the boiling point. Accusing the Democrats of treason, he charged that a Democratic victory would bring "more Alger Hisses, more atomic spies."

The GOP ticket stumbled when newspapers revealed the existence of a "slush fund" that California business leaders had created to keep Nixon in "financial comfort." But Nixon saved himself with a heart-tugging television defense. He explained the gifts, which included a cocker spaniel named Checkers given to his daughters, as intended to benefit his family. His appeal worked. The Republican ticket won 55 percent of the popular vote, cracked the solid South to carry thirty-nine states, and amassed 442 electoral votes. Enough Republicans rode Ike's coattails to give the GOP control of both houses of Congress by small margins.

CONCLUSION

The 1952 election closed the early postwar period. In many ways the years immediately following the war had confounded experts. The era had brought prosperity instead of renewed depression. America's costly triumph against fascism had led not to peace but to a new kind of dreadful conflict, the Cold War. Domestically, the era that was to have ushered in tranquillity instead saw bitter partisanship and an ugly mood of suspicion and repression.

This period laid the groundwork for trends that would mold the next half century of American history. Cold War rhetoric would shape a generation's perception of the world. The anticommunist offensive would strengthen presidential power and fundamentally reorient the federal government. The first stirrings of civil-rights activism and of entanglement in Vietnam foreshadowed issues that would dominate the 1960s.

Among ordinary Americans, although some vaguely realized that the bright promise of August 1945 had slipped away, many looked with hope to their new president and to better times ahead.

CHRONOLOGY

1945 Truman proposes economic reforms.

1946 Winston Churchill delivers his "iron curtain" speech.
Coal miners' strike.
More than a million GIs enroll in college.
Inflation soars to more than 18 percent.
Republicans win control of Congress.

1947 Truman Doctrine.
Federal Employee Loyalty Program.
Taft-Hartley Act.
Marshall Plan proposed to aid Europe.
President's Committee on Civil Rights issues *To Secure These Rights*.

1948 Communist coup in Czechoslovakia.

State of Israel founded.
Soviet Union blockades Berlin; United States begins airlift.
Congress approves Marshall Plan.
Truman orders an end to segregation in the armed forces.
Communist leaders put on trial under the Smith Act.
Truman elected president.

1949 North Atlantic Treaty Organization (NATO) established.
East and West Germany founded as separate nations.
Communist victory in China.
Soviet Union detonates an atomic bomb.

1950 Truman authorizes building a hydrogen bomb.
Soviet spy ring at Los Alamos uncovered.
Alger Hiss convicted of perjury.
Joseph McCarthy launches anticommunist crusade.
Korean War begins.
Julius and Ethel Rosenberg arrested as atomic spies.
McCarran Internal Security Act.
Truman accepts NSC-68.
China enters the Korean War.

1951 Douglas MacArthur dismissed from his Korean command.
Supreme Court upholds Smith Act.
Rosenbergs convicted of espionage.

1952 First hydrogen bomb exploded.
Dwight D. Eisenhower elected president.

FOR FURTHER READING

John Diggins, *The Proud Decades, 1941–1960* (1989). A wide-ranging survey of U.S. culture and politics.

Richard M. Fried, *Nightmare in Red: The McCarthy Era in Perspective* (1990). A cogent account of McCarthyism's rise and fall.

John L. Gaddis, *The United States and the Cold War* (1992). A probing reexamination of the major issues.

Robert Griffith and Athan Theoharis, eds., *The Specter: Original Essays on the Cold War and the Origins of McCarthyism* (1974). A collection of revisionist interpretations.

Alonzo L. Hamby, *Beyond the New Deal: Harry S. Truman and American Liberalism* (1973). A positive assessment of Truman's efforts to preserve and extend the New Deal.

Melvyn Leffler, *A Proponderance of Power: National Security, the Truman Administration, and the Cold War* (1992). The most comprehensive and incisive history of the Cold War's early stages.

Athan Theoharis and John Stuart Cox, *The Boss: J. Edgar Hoover and the Great American Inquisition* (1988). A biographical analysis highlighting the role of the Federal Bureau of Investigation in the Red Scare of the 1950s.

CHAPTER 29

America at Midcentury

Nostalgia has painted the 1950s as a decade of tranquillity, abundance, easy living, new homes in the suburbs, family togetherness, big cars, and cheap gasoline. In movies and television, the fifties are a sunny time when everybody liked Ike and loved Lucy. Teenagers wore poodle skirts, pedal pushers, and white bucks; danced to "Sh-boom" and "Rock Around the Clock"; and idolized Elvis Presley.

Behind these stereotypes lies a reality far more complex, and often far darker. Many Americans did enjoy the fruits of the decade's consumer culture. Having survived a depression and global war, they reveled in prosperity presided over by a popular president. They trusted Dwight D. Eisenhower and welcomed the thaw in the Cold War that came after the Korean War.

At the same time, the fifties saw the birth of the space age and of hydrogen bombs and intercontinental ballistic missiles. Senator Joseph McCarthy, the Warren Court, and Martin Luther King, Jr. kindled intense political passions. The

(Right) ***Family Photograph*** *by John Falter shows an idealized American family of the 1950s.*

The Eisenhower Presidency

The Cold War Continues

The Affluent Society

Consensus and Conservatism

The Other America

Seeds of Disquiet

arrival of an automated and computerized postindustrial society and television's growing power transformed life, as did the "baby boom," mass suburbanization, and a remarkable internal migration. Midcentury America encompassed peace and a widening Cold War, prosperity and persistent poverty, civil-rights triumphs and rampant racism.

The Eisenhower Presidency

Rarely in U.S. history has a president better fit the national mood than Dwight David Eisenhower. Exhausted by a quarter century of upheaval—the stock-market crash, the Great Depression, World War II, the Cold War—Americans craved stability and peace. And Eisenhower delivered. Eisenhower gave people weary of partisanship a sense of unity, and he inspired confidence. Most Americans overwhelmingly approved of his moderate policies.

Eisenhower epitomized the virtues and hopes of many Americans. The most distinguished general of World War II, he projected the image of a plain but good man. He expressed complicated issues in simple terms while governing a complex, urban, technological society and comforting an anxious people.

The General as Chief Executive

Dwight Eisenhower, born on October 14, 1890, in Denison, Texas, grew up in Abilene, Kansas, in a poor, strongly religious family. More athletic than studious, he graduated from the U.S. Military Academy at West Point in 1915. In directing the Allied invasion of North Africa in 1942, he revealed himself to be a brilliant war planner and organizer, and in 1944 he became Supreme Commander of Allied Forces on the Western Front. Respected for his managerial ability and talent for conciliation, Ike became a national hero.

Eisenhower's approach to the presidency reflected his wartime leadership style. He concentrated on major matters and worked to reconcile contending factions. His restrained view of presidential authority stemmed from his respect for the constitutional balance of power as well as his sense of the dignity of the Oval Office. Eisenhower rarely intervened publicly in the legislative process, shunned using his office as a "bully pulpit," and assured his cabinet members that he would "stay out of [their] hair." After establishing a chain of command, he delegated power to subordinates and conferred primarily with his top aides. This low-key style, combined with frequent fishing and golfing vacations, led Democrats to scoff at Eisenhower as a leader who "reigned but did not rule." In truth, Ike battled behind the scenes, his image of passivity masking an active and occasionally ruthless politician.

"Dynamic Conservatism"

Determined to govern the nation on business principles, Eisenhower staffed his administration with corporate executives. "Eight millionaires and a plumber," jested one journalist describing the new cabinet. In his first year Eisenhower worked with Congress to reduce farm-price subsidies, to cut the number of government employees, and to slash the federal budget. He also promoted the private development of hydroelectric and nuclear power and won congressional approval of a bill turning over to coastal states oil-rich "tidelands" that the Supreme Court had awarded to the federal government.

The Eisenhower administration followed a centrist course. More pragmatic than ideological, the president wished to reduce government spending and taxes, to contain inflation, and to govern efficiently. Instead of overturning the New Deal, he accommodated large-scale labor organizations and social-welfare policies. Milton Eisenhower, the president's brother and adviser, summed up Ike's views: "We should keep what we have, catch our breath for a while, and improve administration; it does not mean moving backward."

Eager to avoid a depression, Eisenhower relied heavily on the Council of Economic Advisers (CEA), despite conservative calls for its abolition. Arthur Burns, the head of the CEA, advocated a strong government effort to "fine-tune" the economy. The president promised to use "any and all weapons in the federal arsenal, including

The Election of 1956

Candidates	Parties	Electoral Vote	Popular Vote	Percentage of Popular Vote
DWIGHT D. EISENHOWER	Republican	457	35,590,472	57.6
Adlai E. Stevenson	Democratic	73	26,022,752	42.1

changes in monetary and credit policy, modifications of the tax structure, and a speed-up in the construction of public works" to stimulate economic growth. When recessions struck in 1953 and 1957, Eisenhower abandoned a balanced budget and increased spending to restore prosperity.

Eisenhower labeled his ideas "dynamic conservatism" and "modern Republicanism." Whatever the slogan, he supported extending social-security benefits, raising the minimum wage to a dollar an hour, adding 4 million workers to those eligible for unemployment benefits, and providing federally financed public housing for low-income families. He also approved construction of the St. Lawrence Seaway, linking the Great Lakes and the Atlantic Ocean, and creation of the Department of Health, Education, and Welfare. In 1956 Eisenhower backed the largest and most expensive public-works program in American history: the Interstate Highway Act, authorizing construction of a 41,000-mile system of expressways. Freeways would soon snake across America, accelerating suburban growth, heightening dependence on cars and trucks, contributing to urban decay and air pollution, and drastically increasing gasoline consumption.

Republicans renominated Ike by acclamation in 1956, and voters gave him a landslide victory over Democrat Adlai Stevenson. With the GOP crowing, "Everything's booming but the guns," the president won 36 million popular votes to Stevenson's 26 million and amassed 457 electoral votes.

The Downfall of Joseph McCarthy

Although he despised Joseph McCarthy, Eisenhower feared confronting the senator. Instead, he allowed McCarthy to grab plenty of rope in hopes that the demagogue would hang himself. He did. In 1954 McCarthy accused the army of harboring communist spies, and the army charged McCarthy

Caught in His Web

After four years of cowing opponents with accusations and intimidation, Joseph McCarthy's attacks on officers of the U.S.Army led in 1954 to a congressional investigation of the senator; six weeks of televised hearings in which McCarthy revealed his crude, bullying behavior to the American people; and, in December, to a Senate vote to censure him.

with using his influence to gain preferential treatment for a staff member who had been drafted.

Congress voted to investigate both charges, and on April 22, 1954, televised Army-McCarthy hearings began. A national audience witnessed McCarthy's boorish behavior. His dark scowl, raspy voice, endless interruptions, and disregard for the rights of others repelled many viewers. In June, when McCarthy smeared the reputation of a young lawyer assisting Joseph Welch, the army counsel, the mild-mannered Welch turned his wrath on McCarthy. "Until this moment, Senator, I think I really never gauged your cruelty or your recklessness. . . . Have you no sense of decency?" The gallery burst into applause.

The spell of the inquisitor broken, the Senate in December 1954 censured the Wisconsin senator for contemptuous behavior. This powerful rebuke demolished McCarthy as a political force.

McCarthy died in 1957, but the fears that he had exploited lingered. Congress continued to fund the House Un-American Activities Committee, and state and local governments continued to require loyalty oaths from teachers. Conservative groups, among them the John Birch Society, and self-proclaimed "new conservatives" such as William F. Buckley warned that domestic communists posed a major subversive threat. Stressing victory over communism instead of containment, they bemoaned the "creeping socialism" of Eisenhower and Truman, advocated a return to older moral standards, and attacked the Supreme Court.

The Warren Court

Liberalized by the presence of a new chief justice, Earl Warren (1953), the Supreme Court drew conservatives' wrath for defending the rights of those accused of subversive beliefs. In a 1957 decision, the Court held that the accused had the right to inspect government files used by the prosecution, and that same year the justices overturned convictions of Communist party officials under the Smith Act (see Chapter 28). Right-wing opponents plastered "Impeach Earl Warren" posters on highway billboards.

These condemnations paled beside those of segregationists after the *Brown* v. *Board of Education of Topeka* (May 1954) ruling. Unanimously reversing *Plessy* v. *Ferguson* (see Chapter 21), the Court held that separating schoolchildren "solely because of their race generates a feeling of inferiority as to their status in the community that may affect their hearts and minds in a way unlikely ever to be undone." Such segregation thus violated the equal-protection clause of the Fourteenth Amendment. The justices concluded that "separate educational facilities are inherently unequal." A year later the Court ordered the states to desegregate their schools "with all deliberate speed."

The border states complied, but when white southerners rejected the court's ruling, Eisenhower refused to force them. "I don't believe you can change the hearts of men with laws or decisions," he observed. Although not a racist, he never publicly endorsed the *Brown* decision, and privately he called his appointment of Earl Warren "the biggest damn fool mistake I ever made."

Encouraged by presidential inaction, southern white opposition stiffened. White Citizens Councils sprang up, and the Ku Klux Klan revived. Declaring the *Brown* decision "null, void, and of no effect," southern legislatures adopted "massive resistance" to thwart compliance with the law. They denied state aid to school systems that desegregated and then closed them down.

In 1955, 100 members of Congress signed the Southern Manifesto, denouncing *Brown* as "a clear abuse of judicial power." White southern politicians competed to "outnigger" each other in opposing integration. An Alabama candidate promised to go to jail to defend segregation, and his opponent promptly vowed to die for it. Segregationists also used violence and economic reprisals against blacks to maintain all-white schools. At the end of 1956, not a single African-American attended school with whites in the Deep South, and only a few did so in the Upper South.

The Laws of the Land

Southern resistance reached a climax in September 1957 when Arkansas governor Orval Faubus mobilized the state's National Guard to bar nine African-American students from entering Little Rock's Central High School under a federal court order. After another court order forced Faubus to withdraw the guardsmen, jeering whites blocked the black students' entry.

On national television Eisenhower decried this "disgraceful occurrence" and ordered those obstructing federal law "to disperse forthwith." When the mob defied him, the president federalized the Arkansas National Guard and dispatched federal troops to protect the blacks' rights. To ensure the blacks' safety, troops patrolled the high school for the rest of the year. Rather than accept integration, Faubus shut down Little Rock's public high schools for two years. When a federal court ruling reopened them, only three African-Americans attended Central High School. As the fifties ended, fewer than 1 percent of African-American students in the Deep South attended integrated schools.

Nonetheless, *Brown* and Little Rock galvanized the federal government's power to mandate changes in the South. And TV broadcasts of events at Little Rock foreshadowed television's vital role in the eventual demise of Jim Crow. A 1957 public-opinion poll showed that 90 percent of whites outside the South approved the use of federal troops in Little Rock.

Most nonsouthern whites also favored legislation to enfranchise southern blacks, and during the 1956 presidential campaign Eisenhower proposed a voting-rights bill. The Civil Rights Act of 1957, the first civil-rights law since Reconstruction, established a permanent commission on civil rights with broad investigatory powers but did little to guarantee the ballot to African-Americans. The Civil Rights Act of 1960 only slightly strengthened the first measure's enforcement powers. Like the *Brown* decision, however, these laws implied a changing attitude about race on the part of the federal government and encouraged African-Americans to fight on for their due.

The Cold War Continues

On the international front, the Eisenhower administration maintained Truman's containment policy. Joseph Stalin's death in 1953 and Eisenhower's resolve to reduce the risk of nuclear war did lead to a thaw in the Cold War, but ideological conflict still gripped the United States and the U.S.S.R. The Cold War did not end, nor did American determination to check communism waver.

Truce in Korea

Honoring his campaign pledge, Eisenhower visited Korea in December 1952, but he did not bring home a settlement. The fate of thousands of prisoners of war who did not want to return to communist rule remained the chief sticking point in negotiations. But the uncertainty in the communist world after Stalin's death, and Eisenhower's veiled threat to use nuclear weapons, broke the stalemate. The armistice signed on July 23, 1953, set the boundary between North and South Korea close to the thirty-eighth parallel (the prewar demarcation line) and established a panel of neutral nations to oversee the return of prisoners of war. The end of the fighting relieved many Americans but left Korea divided and its political problems unresolved.

Ike and Dulles

Eager to ease Cold War hostilities, Eisenhower first had to placate the Republican Old Guard, which rejected containment and clamored for forceful efforts to roll back the Red tide. He enlisted the aid of his secretary of state, John Foster Dulles, a stiff, self-righteous anticommunist.

Dulles advocated a holy war against "atheistic communism." He called for "liberation" of the captive peoples of Eastern Europe and the unleashing of

Jiang Jieshi against Communist China. Condemning neutralism on the part of other nations as "immoral," he threatened "an agonizing reappraisal" of American commitments if allies did not follow the U.S. lead. Believing that the Soviet Union understood only force, Dulles insisted on the necessity of "brinksmanship," the art of never backing down in a crisis, even if doing so meant risking war.

Such saber rattling pleased the Right, but Eisenhower preferred conciliation. Partly because he feared a nuclear war—the Soviet Union had tested its own hydrogen bomb in 1953—Eisenhower refused to translate Dulles's rhetoric into action. Too, the president understood the limits of American power. When the U.S.S.R. crushed insurrections in East Germany (1953) and Hungary (1956), the United States did not prevent the Soviet intervention. And despite talk of "unleashing" Jiang, a 1954 mutual-defense treaty with Taiwan specifically prohibited the Nationalists from any aggressive ventures without prior consultation with the United States.

Waging Peace

As multimegaton thermonuclear weapons replaced atomic bombs in American and Soviet arsenals, Eisenhower worked to reduce the probability of mutual annihilation. He proposed an "atoms for peace" plan whereby both superpowers would contribute fissionable materials to a new U.N. agency for use in industrial projects. Mounting fears about radioactive fallout from atomic tests, especially 1954 U.S. tests that spread strontium-90 over a wide area, heightened world concern about the nuclear-arms race.

In 1955 Eisenhower and Soviet leaders met in Geneva for the first East-West conference since World War II. Discussions produced no concrete results, but mutual talk of "peaceful coexistence" led reporters to hail the "spirit of Geneva." In March 1958 Moscow suspended atmospheric tests of nuclear weapons, and the United States followed suit.

But the Cold War continued. Dulles negotiated mutual-defense pacts with any nation that opposed communism. His "pactomania" committed the United States to the defense of forty-three nations. However, the United States relied primarily on nuclear weapons to deter the Soviets. A "New Look" defense program guaranteed "more bang for the buck" by emphasizing nuclear weapons while cutting back the army and navy. This New Look stressed "massive retaliation" rather than the deployment of U.S. troops to fight "brushfire" wars in remote places—and it spurred the Soviets to seek "more rubble for the ruble" by enlarging their nuclear stockpile.

Meanwhile, the focus of the Cold War shifted from Europe to the Third World, comprising largely nonwhite, developing nations. There the two superpowers waged war by proxy, using local guerrillas and military juntas to battle in isolated deserts and steamy jungles. There, too, the Central Intelligence Agency (CIA) fought covert wars against those thought to imperil American interests.

The Clandestine CIA

To command the CIA, Eisenhower appointed Allen Dulles, a veteran of wartime OSS operations and the brother of the secretary of state. Established in 1947 to conduct espionage and to analyze information on foreign nations, the CIA soon ranged far beyond its original purpose and carried out undercover operations to topple foreign regimes believed hostile to the United States. In 1953 the agency plotted with Iranian army officers to overthrow a popularly elected government that had taken possession of rich oil resources long exploited by Britain. Fearing a precedent that might jeopardize Western oil interests in the Middle East, the CIA returned the deposed shah of Iran to power and restored the oil wells to British firms. In return, the United States gained a loyal ally on the Soviet border, and American oil companies prospered from Iranian oil concessions. But the seeds of Iranian hatred of America had been sown—an enmity that would haunt the United States a quarter century later.

In 1953 the CIA intervened in Philippine elections to ensure a pro-American government. In 1954 in Guatemala it equipped and trained a Guatemalan force to destroy the incumbent regime, which had seized 225,000 acres from the American-owned United Fruit Company. The CIA's Guatemalan agents instituted a military dictatorship subservient to the United States, restored United Fruit's properties, and trampled political opposition, all with the approval of a handful of Washington officials.

In his second term Eisenhower allowed the CIA even greater leeway. By 1957 the agency was devoting 50 percent of its personnel and 80 percent of its budget to "covert action," subverting governments, bribing foreign politicians, and subsidizing foreign newspapers and labor unions that hewed to a pro-American line. Unwilling to be drawn into long, costly military conflicts, Eisenhower relied on the CIA to help the United States' allies and to weaken its opponents.

Conflict in Vietnam

The most extensive CIA secret operations during the 1950s took place in Indochina. As a result of the Korean War and Mao Zedong's victory in China, the United States viewed Indochina as a Cold War battleground. The Truman administration had provided the French, who were trying to reconquer their former colony of Vietnam, large-scale military assistance to fight the Vietminh, a broad-based Vietnamese nationalist coalition led by the communist Ho Chi Minh. By 1954 American aid accounted for 75 percent of French expenditures, but the French were losing. In early 1954 the Vietminh trapped and besieged 12,000 French troops in the valley of Dien Bien Phu.

France appealed for U.S. intervention, but the president demurred. Unwilling to commit American troops to a jungle war against a popular liberation front, people fighting to free their nation from colonialism, he voiced bitter opposition to American involvement: "I cannot conceive of a greater tragedy for America." On May 7, 1954, the French surrendered at Dien Bien Phu. In July an international peace conference in Geneva arranged a cease-fire and divided Vietnam at the seventeenth parallel, pending elections in 1956 to choose the government of a unified nation. The United States neither participated in the Geneva negotiations nor signed the final Geneva Accords.

Though opposed to committing the United States to an Asian land war, Eisenhower feared the consequences of a communist victory in Vietnam and refused to sign the Geneva Accords. If Vietnam fell, he warned, Thailand, Burma, Malaya, Indonesia, and ultimately all of America's Asian allies would follow. Because of his belief in this "domino theory," Eisenhower ignored the Geneva settlement.

In June 1954 the CIA Mission in Vietnam was established to help to install Ngo Dinh Diem, a fiercely anticommunist Catholic, as premier of France's puppet state. In 1955 Diem became president of an independent South Vietnam. CIA agents worked closely with him to train his armed forces and secret police, to eliminate political opposition, and to block the election to reunify Vietnam specified by the Geneva agreements. As Eisenhower later admitted, the United States opposed the election because "possibly 80 percent of the population would have voted for the communist Ho Chi Minh as their leader." Washington pinned its hopes on Diem to maintain a noncommunist South Vietnam.

But the autocratic Diem never rallied public support. His Catholicism alienated the predominantly Buddhist population, and his refusal to institute land reform and to end corruption raised widespread opposition. In 1957 former Vietminh guerrillas began sporadic antigovernment attacks, and in December 1960 opposition to Diem coalesced in the National Liberation Front (NLF). Organized by the Vietminh and backed by North Vietnam, the insurgency attracted broad support. Diem increasingly relied on the billions of dollars and growing corps of advisers that the Eisenhower administration supplied. Although he refused to make reforms that might have undercut the NLF's appeal, the United States remained committed to "sink or swim with Ngo Dinh Diem."

Antiwesternism in the Middle East

As troubles simmered in Vietnam, Eisenhower faced his greatest crisis in the Middle East. In 1954 Gamal Abdel Nasser came to power in Egypt. An Arab nationalist, he was determined to modernize Egypt and to buy arms from the Soviet bloc. To woo him, the United States offered financing for a dam at Aswan to harness the Nile River. But when Nasser declared neutrality in the Cold War and purchased arms from Czechoslovakia, John Foster Dulles canceled the loan. In retaliation, on July 26, 1956, Nasser nationalized the foreign-owned Suez Canal, intending to use Suez revenues to finance the dam.

U.S. allies reacted strongly to Nasser's provocation. The British, viewing the canal as the lifeline of the British Empire, were outraged. The French, fearful of Arab nationalism in their Algerian colony, expressed alarm. And the Israelis were threatened by that same Arab nationalism. Tensions between Egypt and Israel peaked when Nasser in 1955 blockaded the Gulf of Aqaba, Israel's only Red Sea outlet. Israel, France, and Britian invaded Egypt in October 1956. America's closest allies had not consulted the United States, and Moscow threatened intervention, possibly even nuclear confrontation. Furious, Eisenhower condemned the invasion and simultaneously put the Strategic Air Command on alert against the U.S.S.R. "If those fellows start something, we may have to hit 'em—and if necessary, with everything in the bucket," he warned. On November 6 Britain, France, and Israel promised to leave Egypt, and by March 1957 the last troops were gone.

The Suez crisis had two major consequences. It swelled Third World antiwestern sentiment, and the United States replaced Britain and France as the protector of western interests in the Middle East. Anxious to guarantee the flow of oil to the West, the president issued, and Congress approved, the Eisenhower Doctrine, a proclamation that the United States would send military aid and, if necessary, troops to any Middle Eastern nation that asked for help against "international communism."

In July 1958 Eisenhower implemented the doctrine. A nationalist coup in Iraq brought to power an antiwestern regime, and the neighboring prowestern Lebanese government requested U.S. support. Eisenhower ordered 14,000 marines into Lebanon. The marines soon left, but the United States continued to interpret Third World nationalism as communist inspired.

Frustration Abroad

Such interventions intensified the anti-American feelings of neutralists and nationalists in many small nations. In 1958 angry crowds in Peru and Venezuela spat at Vice President Nixon and stoned his car. In 1959 Fidel Castro overturned a dictatorial regime in Cuba and denounced "Yanqui imperialism." Anti-American riots in Japan in 1960 forced Eisenhower to cancel a trip to the United States' strongest Asian ally.

A tougher blow struck Eisenhower on May 1, 1960, two weeks before a scheduled summit conference with Soviet premier Nikita Khrushchev, when the Soviets shot down a U.S. spy plane 1,200 miles inside their border. Initially, Eisenhower announced that the downed plane was merely a weather reconnaissance aircraft that had strayed off course. An angry Khrushchev responded by displaying the captured CIA pilot, the U-2's spy cameras, and photos taken of Soviet missile sites. Although Eisenhower then admitted the spy mission, he refused to apologize, and the summit collapsed.

The Eisenhower Legacy

Three days before leaving office, Eisenhower offered Americans a farewell and a warning. The demands of national security, he stated, had produced the "conjunction of an immense military establishment and a large arms industry." Swollen Cold War defense budgets had tied American economic health to military expenditures, and military contracts had become a way of life for research scholars, for politicians, and for America's largest corporations. This intertwined combination of interests, Eisenhower believed, exerted enormous leverage and threatened the traditional subordination of the military in American life. He warned, "We must guard against the acquisition of unwarranted influence . . . by the military-industrial complex. The potential for the disastrous rise of misplaced power exists and will persist."

The president concluded by assessing his foreign policy. He admitted that he could not affirm that prolonged peace was in sight. Most scholars agreed. Eisenhower had ended the Korean War, maintained peace for more than seven years, avoided direct intervention in Vietnam, begun relaxing tensions with the Soviet Union, and suspended atmospheric nuclear testing. Yet he had also presided over an accelerating nuclear-arms race and a widening Cold War—and had given the CIA a green light to intervene in local conflicts around the globe. Domestically, the moderate Eisenhower pleased neither Left nor Right. His acceptance of New Deal social-welfare legislation angered the Republican Right, while liberals faulted him for passivity in the face of McCarthyism and racism. Nonetheless, Ike had given the majority of Americans what they most wanted—reassurance and a breathing spell in which to relish the comforts of life.

The Affluent Society

In 1958 economist John Kenneth Galbraith published *The Affluent Society*, a study of postwar America. The title reflected the broad-based prosperity that made the 1950s seem the fulfillment of the American dream. By the end of the decade, 60 percent of American families owned homes; 75 percent, cars; and 87 percent, at least one TV. Government spending, a large uptick in productivity, and steadily increasing consumer demand pushed the total gross national product (GNP) from $318 billion to $488 billion during the decade.

Three brief recessions and a rising national debt, almost $290 billion by 1961, evoked concern but did little to halt economic growth. Indeed, the United States achieved the highest living standard ever during the 1950s. By 1960 the average worker's income, adjusted for inflation, was 35 percent higher than in 1945 and 200 percent higher than in the 1920s. With just 6 percent of the world's population, the United States produced and consumed nearly 50 percent of everything made and sold on earth.

The New Industrial Society

Federal spending constituted a major source of economic growth, nearly doubling in the 1950s to $180 billion. The outlays of state and local governments more than kept pace. Federal expenditures, just 1 percent of the GNP in 1929, reached 17 percent by the mid-1950s. These funds built roads and airports, financed home mortgages, supported farm prices, and provided stipends for education. But more than *half* the federal budget—10 percent of the GNP—went to defense spending. Continued superpower rivalry in atomic weapons, missile-delivery systems, and the space race kept the federal government the nation's chief sponsor of both scientific and technological research and development (R&D).

Scientific breakthroughs brought both progress and problems. The nation's first nuclear power plant came on line in 1957, with no discussion of the dangers of accidental radiation releases or the dilemma of storing spent fuel rods. The chemical industry, building on massive research, surged from fiftieth to fourth place in the industrial economy. Americans enjoyed their Dacron suits, Orlon shirts, and Teflon-coated pots and pans and marveled at the array of produce that crowded store shelves—but chemical fertilizers and pesticides contaminated groundwater, and nearly indestructible plastics reduced landfill space. Electronics became the fifth-largest American industry, providing industrial equipment and consumer appliances. Electricity consumption tripled in the 1950s as industry automated and consumers learned to "live better electrically," as commercials urged. Cheap petroleum fueled expansion in both the chemical and the elec-

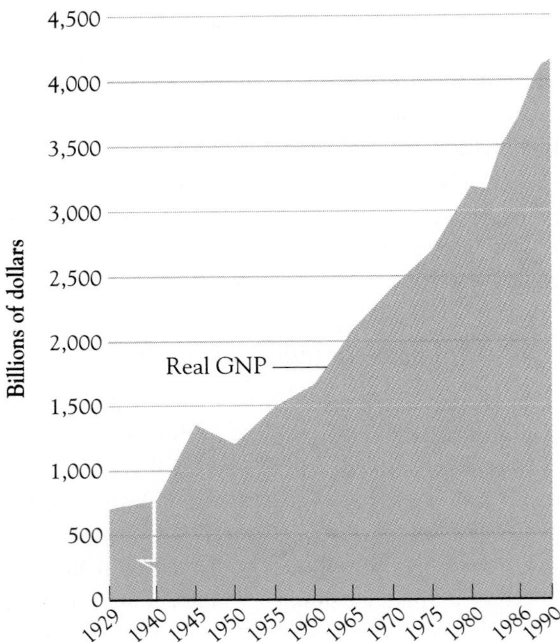

Gross National Product, 1929–1990

Following World War II, the United States achieved the highest living standard in world history. Between 1950 and 1970, the real GNP, which factors out inflation and reveals the actual amount of goods and services produced, steadily increased. However, in 1972, 1974–1975, 1980, and 1982 the real GNP declined.

NOTE: Data shown in 1982 dollars.
SOURCE: *Economic Report of the President*, 1991.

tronics industries. Domestic oil production and the importation of foreign oil rose steeply; by 1960 oil had replaced coal as the nation's main energy source. Hardly anyone paid attention to a warning in 1953 that escalating energy consumption was adding 6 billion tons of carbon dioxide to the earth's atmosphere every year and warming the planet.

Plentiful cheap gasoline fed the growth of the automobile and aircraft industries. Aircraft manufacture, the nation's third-largest industry in the 1950s, depended on massive defense spending, on commercial aviation's switch to jet propulsion, and on space research. The automobile industry, still the nation's largest, spent nearly one-fifth of its budget on R&D, using technology to fire up productivity. Just as machines had earlier replaced human workers in the automotive industry, automation now controlled the machines. Between 1945 and 1960 the number of hours and workers needed to produce a car both fell by 50 percent. Other industries followed, investing $10 billion a year throughout the fifties on labor-saving machinery.

The Age of Computers

The computer was a major key to technological revolution. In 1944 International Business Machines (IBM), cooperating with Harvard scientists, had produced the Mark I calculator, a slow, cumbersome maze of 500 miles of wiring and 3,000 electromechanical relays. Two years later, to calculate artillery trajectory, the U.S. Army had developed ENIAC, the first electronic computer. Although still unwieldy, with tens of thousands of vacuum tubes and resistors, ENIAC could multiply two ten-place numbers in less than 3/1,000 of a second, compared to Mark I's 3 seconds. Then had come the development of operating instructions, or programs; the replacement of wires by printed circuits; and, in 1948, Bell Lab's invention of tiny, solid-state transistors that ended reliance on radio tubes.

Computers fundamentally changed the American economy and society. The federal government became a major client, and computers became a billion-dollar business. Computers were as indispensable to Pentagon strategists playing war games as to the Internal Revenue Service, as integral to Weather Bureau meteorologists as to aerospace scientists. By the mid-1960s more than 30,000 mainframe computers would be used by banks, insurance companies, stock brokerages, hospitals, and universities. Computers enabled fewer workers to produce more goods in less time than ever before.

Concentration and Consolidation in Industry and Agriculture

Rapid technological advances accelerated the growth and power of big business. In 1950 only twenty-two firms had assets of more than $1 billion;

by 1960, fifty did. By then, one-half of 1 percent of corporations earned more than half the total corporate income in the United States. Wealthy firms, able to afford huge R&D outlays, swallowed weak competitors and became oligopolies. Three radio and television networks monopolized the nation's airwaves, and three automobile companies produced 90 percent of America's cars; large corporations controlled the lion's share of assets and sales in steel, petroleum, chemicals, and electrical machinery. Corporations formed conglomerates by merging companies in unrelated industries, and they acquired overseas facilities to become "multinational" enterprises.

Growth and consolidation meant greater bureaucratization. "Executives" continued to replace "capitalists"—by the mid-1950s American industry employed more than a quarter-million vice presidents. Divorced from the ownership of the corporations that they ran, professional managers oversaw R&D, production, advertising, sales, accounting, investments, and labor relations. Strong pressures for conformity emerged, rewarding those who gave in to social pressure rather than adhering to personal values. Sociologist David Riesman contrasted managers' "other-directed" behavior—an obsession to fit in and to gain acceptance by following the dictates of a group or organization—with the "inner-directed" orientation of small businesspeople and professionals of earlier years.

Changes in agriculture paralleled those in industry. Farming grew increasingly scientific and mechanized. Between 1945 and 1960, technology cut the work-hours necessary to grow crops by half. Many farm families migrated to cities. In 1956 alone, one-eleventh of the farm population left the land. Meanwhile, heavily capitalized farm businesses prospered by using new machines and by saturating their acreage with chemical fertilizers, herbicides, and pesticides.

Few Americans understood the extent to which synthetic chemicals poisoned the environment until the publication of Rachel Carson's *Silent Spring* in 1962. A former researcher for the Fish and Wildlife Services, Carson demonstrated the problems created by the indiscriminate use of the insecticide DDT and its spread through the food chain. (The "silent spring" of her title referred to the death of robins from DDT toxicity.) States would gradually ban DDT use, and in 1972 the federal government followed suit.

Meanwhile, agribusinesses grew rich from the intensive use of chemicals and from $5 billion in federal farm subsidies. A 1956 soil-conservation program, paying farmers to take cropland out of production, benefited large farm businesses that could afford to allow tens of thousands of acres to lie fallow.

Blue-Collar Blues

Consolidation also transformed the labor movement. In 1955 the American Federation of Labor and Congress of Industrial Organizations merged, bringing 85 percent of union members into a single unit. Although leaders promised aggressive unionism, the movement's old militancy was gone.

Organized labor had fallen victim to its own success. Benefits hard earned at the bargaining table, where management preferred higher costs (which it passed on in the form of higher prices) to strikes, bred complacency. Higher wages, a workweek under forty hours, paid vacations, health-care coverage, and automatic wage hikes tied to the cost of living led most workers to view themselves as middle class, not an aggrieved proletariat. Labor turbulence subsided.

A decrease in the number of blue-collar workers also sapped labor's momentum. As automation replaced more and more workers in steel, coal, and automobiles, membership in these industries' once-mighty unions dropped by more than 50 percent. New jobs in the 1950s were concentrated in the white-collar and service sectors of the economy and in public employment. Organized labor saw its portion of the labor force drop from 36 percent in 1953 to 31 percent in 1960.

Prosperity, Suburbanization, and Mobility

As real income (adjusted for inflation) rose, Americans spent less of their income on necessities. They enthusiastically bought powered lawn mowers, air conditioners, and striped toothpaste and heaped their shopping carts with frozen, dehydrated, and fortified foods. When they lacked cash, they borrowed. In 1950 Diners' Club issued the first credit card, and American Express soon followed. Installment buying, home mortgages, and auto loans raised Americans' private indebtedness in the 1950s from $73 billion to $196 billion. Consumer culture dominated American life, and advertising expenditures nearly tripled.

Americans purchased 58 million new cars during the 1950s. Manufacturers enticed people to trade in and up by offering bigger and flashier models, more chrome, two-tone color schemes, tail fins, and more powerful engines, such as Pontiac's 1955 "Sensational Strato-Streak V-8" that could go more than twice as fast as any existing speed limit. Hand in hand with these trends came rises in highway deaths, air pollution, oil consumption, and "autosclerosis"—clogged urban arteries.

Government policy as well as the proliferation of cars spurred white Americans' exodus to the suburbs. Federal spending on highways skyrocketed from $79 million in 1946 to $2.6 billion in 1960. Once-remote areas came within "commuting distance" for urban workers and became desirable places to live. The tax code further induced suburban home buying by allowing deductions for home-mortgage interest payments and for property taxes. The Federal Housing Administration (FHA) and the Veterans Administration (VA) offered low-interest loans.

Eighty-five percent of the 13 million new homes built in the 1950s were in the suburbs. Affordable single-family housing drew many Americans there. Others fled the central cities' crime, grime, and newly urbanized minorities, who were still targets of racial prejudice. Young couples headed for suburbia in quest of communities oriented toward children and education.

Social critics complained about the suburbs' rows of cookie-cutter houses inhabited by bored housewives and harried husbands, but most suburbanites enjoyed their new life-style, tranquil surroundings, and like-minded neighbors. To a nation of immigrants, most from countries where only the elite owned property, taking title to a home of one's own was at the core of the American dream.

1957 Chevrolet Bel Air
Advertisements alliteratively described this classic car's automatic transmission as the Triple-Turbine Turbo-Glide.

Whereas the urban population rose by 10 percent during the 1950s, the number of suburban dwellers nearly *doubled* as 18 million people moved to the suburbs. For the first time in the twentieth century, more Americans owned homes than lived in rented quarters. By 1960 the suburban population equaled that of the central cities, and by 1970 the suburbs contained two-thirds of the metropolitan-area population, and the cities, only one-third.

Americans moved not only from city to suburb but also from North to South and from East to West. California's climate and industry lured millions—it would surpass New York as the most populous state in 1963. The Gulf Coast and the Pacific Northwest also attracted millions of Americans. The shift of masses of people from the frosty North and East to the balmy South and West had a major political and economic impact. Drawn to the Sun Belt by low taxes, low energy costs, and right-to-work laws, industrialists transferred not only their plants and corporate headquarters but also their conservative outlooks. By 1980 the population of the Sun Belt, which stretched from the Old Confederacy across Texas to southern California, would exceed that of the North and East. The political power of the Republican party would rise correspondingly.

Twenty years after the Great Depression, America had been transformed. Affluence had replaced financial worry for countless Americans, the suburbs had blossomed, and automation, computers, and new management techniques were modernizing industry at a breakneck pace.

Consensus and Conservatism

Not everyone embraced the fifties' materialism or sank unquestioningly into a deep cushion of contentedness. Disaffected intellectuals found American life shallow and despaired of the United States as a "packaged society" and its people as "all items in a national supermarket—categorized, processed, labeled, priced, and readied for merchandising." Such attacks oversimplified reality. Ignored were the increasing diversity of American society, the materialism and conformity of earlier generations, and the currents of dissent swirling just beneath an apparently placid surface. Nonetheless, critics correctly spotlighted the elevation of comfort over challenge, safety over risk, and private pleasures over public affairs. Anxious for a respite from the trials of preceding decades and hungry for security, Americans plunged into the good life.

Togetherness and the "Baby Boom"

In 1954 *McCall's* magazine coined the term *togetherness* to celebrate the ideal couple: the man and woman who married young, had a large family, and centered their lives on home and children. Economic prosperity and Cold War saber-rattling led Americans in the 1950s to marry young, to have babies quickly, and to have lots of them. The fertility rate (the number of births per 1,000 women) peaked at 123 in 1957, when an American baby was born every seven seconds.

At the same time, medical science banished childhood diseases. Antibiotics virtually wiped out diphtheria and typhoid fever, while the Salk and Sabin vaccines eliminated polio. The plunge in childhood mortality helped to raise American life expectancy from 65.9 years in 1945 to 70.9 years in 1970. Coupled with the baby boom, this decline led to a 19 percent population spurt. During the 1950s, a time of negligible immigration, the U.S. population jumped from 151 million to 180 million. By 1960 children under fourteen constituted one-third of the population.

The sheer size of the baby-boom generation ensured its impact. Throughout the 1950s it helped to fuel the economic boom and to expand the nation's educational system. It made child rearing a foremost concern and reinforced the idea that women's place was in the home. With Americans convinced of the psychological potency of early childhood experiences, motherhood became an increasingly vital, demanding calling.

No one did more to emphasize the presumed link between full-time mothers and healthy children than Dr. Benjamin Spock; only the Bible outsold his *Baby and Child Care* (1946) in the fifties. Spock urged mothers to create an atmosphere of warmth and intimacy for their children. Crying babies were to be comforted; breast-feeding came back into vogue. At best, Spock's advice meant less spanking and more "democratic" family discussions; at worst, it produced a "filiarchy" in which children's needs predominated. Spock even suggested that the government pay mothers so that they would not have to work outside the home.

Domesticity

Popular culture throughout the fifties glorified marriage and parenthood, painting a woman's devotion to life in the home with her children as the most cherished goal. Television almost always pictured mother at home. Hollywood perpetuated the stereotype of career women as neurotic and of mothers and wives as happy. As Debbie Reynolds declared in

The Tender Trap (1955), "A woman isn't a woman until she's been married and had children."

The educational system reinforced these ideas. Alongside academic subjects, girls studied typing, etiquette, and cooking. Guidance counselors cautioned young women not to miss out on marriage by pursuing higher education. "Men are not interested in college degrees, but in the warmth and humanness of the girls they marry," stressed a textbook on family living. In the 1950s women constituted a smaller percentage of college students than in the 1920s or 1930s. Only one-third of college women completed their degrees, and except at the most prestigious colleges these degrees were concentrated in such fields as home economics and primary education.

However, profound changes were under way. Despite the wave of layoffs of women workers when World War II ended, women had quickly returned to the work force. By 1960 nearly 40 percent of American women held full- or part-time jobs; 40 percent of working women had school-age children.

Most women worked to augment family income, not to challenge stereotypes, and took low-paying, low-prestige jobs. Organized feminism ebbed to its lowest point of the century during the fifties. Most women responded to prosperity and atomic jitters by concentrating on private satisfactions and by trying to make the home a haven in an uncertain world.

Religion and Education

"Today in the U.S.," *Time* claimed in 1954, "the Christian faith is back in the center of things." Religious popularizers—fiery evangelist Billy Graham, riveting Roman Catholic bishop Fulton J. Sheen, and "positive-thinking" Protestant minister Norman Vincent Peale—had syndicated newspaper columns, best-selling books, and radio and television programs. Hollywood religious extravaganzas such as *The Robe* (1953) and *The Ten Commandments* (1956) became box-office hits, and TV commercials pronounced that "the family that prays together stays together."

Dial-a-Prayer offered telephone solutions for spiritual problems. Congress added "under God" to the Pledge of Allegiance and made "IN GOD WE TRUST" mandatory on all U.S. currency. Church attendance swelled from 64.5 million (48 percent of the population) in 1940 to 110 million (63 percent) in 1958.

Although millions embraced evangelical fundamentalism and became "born-again" Christians—a trend that would escalate—most Americans turned to religion mainly for reassurance in an anxious age. President Eisenhower declared, "Everybody should have a religious faith, and I don't care what it is." Despite the aura of religiosity in the fifties, the *intensity* of faith diminished for many people as mainstream churches downplayed sin and evil and preached Americanism and fellowship.

Similarly, education flourished in the 1950s, but seemed intellectually shallower than in prior decades. The baby boom inflated primary-school enrollment by 10 million. California opened a new school about every seven days throughout the decade and still faced a classroom shortage. The proportion of college-age Americans climbed from 15 percent in 1940 to more than 40 percent by the early 1960s. At every level, disciples of John Dewey promoted sociability and self-expression over science, math, and history. As community needs superseded intellectual rigor, the "well-rounded" student became more prized than the highly skilled or knowledgeable pupil.

Surveys of college students found them conservative, conformist, and careerist, a "silent generation" primarily seeking security and comfort. Business majors swamped majors in all other fields. Students' attitudes closely mirrored those of their elders in this decade.

Affirmation and Anxiety: The Culture of the Fifties

American culture reflected the expansive spirit of a prosperous era and an undercurrent of discontent. Enjoying more leisure time and bigger paychecks, Americans spent one-seventh of the GNP in 1950 on entertainment. Spectator sports boomed, new symphony halls opened, and book sales doubled.

New York replaced Paris as the capital of the art world. Like the immense abstract expressionist canvases of Jackson Pollock and Mark Rothko and the cool jazz trumpet of Miles Davis, the major novels of the fifties were characterized by introspection and improvisation. Sloan Wilson's *The Man in the Gray Flannel Suit* and John Updike's *Rabbit Run* (1960) presented characters vaguely dissatisfied with jobs and home, longing for a more vital and authentic existence but incapable of decisive action. J. D. Salinger's popular *The Catcher in the Rye* (1951) offered an adolescent version of the alienated, ineffectual protagonist. Young Holden Caulfield, expelled from prep school, is repelled by the "phoniness" of the adult world and considers a break for freedom. But he returns home, suffers a nervous collapse, and retreats into imagined heroism.

Southern, African-American, and Jewish-American writers turned out the decade's most vital fiction. William Faulkner continued his dense saga of a family in Yoknapatawpha County, Mississippi, in *The Town* (1957) and *The Mansion* (1960), while Eudora Welty evoked small-town Mississippi life in *The Ponder Heart* (1954). The black experience found memorable expression in James Baldwin's *Go Tell It on the Mountain* (1953) and Ralph Ellison's *Invisible Man* (1951). Bernard Malamud's *The Assistant* (1957) depicted the Jewish immigrant world of New York's Lower East Side; Philip Roth's *Goodbye Columbus* (1959) dissected the world of upwardly mobile Jews.

Hollywood reflected the diminished concern with social issues, churning out westerns, musicals, and costume spectacles. Movies about the 1950s portrayed Americans as one big, happy, white, middle-class family, exalting material success and romantic love. Career women were largely replaced by "dumb blondes," cute helpmates, and child-women. But as TV viewing soared, movie attendance plummeted by 50 percent, and 20 percent of the nation's theaters became bowling alleys and supermarkets.

The Message of the Medium

No cultural medium ever grew so huge so quickly, or so thoroughly reinforced the public mood, as American television in the 1950s. In 1946 several thousand households had TV sets; by 1950, 5 million did. By the early 1960s, 90 percent of all households owned at least one TV.

Business capitalized on the phenomenon. *TV Guide* soon outsold all other periodicals; by 1960 fifty-three separate editions went out to 7 million subscribers. First marketed in 1954, the TV dinner changed the nation's eating habits. By the mid-fifties the three major networks *each* had larger advertising revenues than any other communications medium in the world.

Early television showcased talent and creativity. High-quality shows appeared in prime time, including opera, documentaries such as Edward R. Murrow's "See It Now," and critically acclaimed original dramas on "Playhouse 90" and "Studio One." However, networks' drive for profits and McCarthy-era anxieties soon stunted innovation and transformed television into a cautious celebrator of conformity and consumerism. Corporations spent fortunes hawking their products—by 1960 they spent $2 billion on TV advertising—and networks competed for large audiences by appealing to the lowest common denominator of taste. Radio comedian Fred Allen observed, "They call television a medium because it's rare when it is well done."

Critics reviled television as an "idiot box" rotting viewers' minds. TV portrayed women as either zany madcaps ("I Love Lucy," "My Friend Irma") or saccharine-sweet housewives ("The Donna Reed Show," "Ozzie and Harriet"). "Father Knows Best," "Make Room for Daddy," and other popular programs celebrated the family's paternal protector and ignored the complexities of modern family life. An ongoing pageant of police dramas and westerns affirmed the value of violence in overcoming evil. Millions of children watched Howdy Doody, the Mouseketeers, and children's programs featuring mayhem and gunplay with equal enthusiasm.

Television reinforced consumerism and conformity, spawning fads: hula hoops, whiffle balls, Barbie dolls, and silly putty. It strengthened gender and racial stereotypes and encouraged passivity. And it transformed politics, elevating image above reality. Richard Nixon's televised "Checkers" speech in 1952 saved his political career. In 1960 John F. Kennedy's "telegenic" image would help him to win the presidency. And at another political level, TV's portrayal of contented citizens both reinforced complacency and obscured the existence of "the other America."

The Other America

"I am an invisible man," declared the African-American narrator of Ralph Ellison's *Invisible Man;* "I am invisible . . . because people refuse to see me." Indeed, few white middle-class Americans of the fifties perceived the extent of social inequality in the United States. "White flight" from cities to suburbs physically separated races and classes, while expressways walled off middle-class motorists from decaying urban ghettos and pockets of rural poverty. Popular culture focused on affluent Americans enjoying the "good life" and depicted minorities as servants, criminals, or buffoons. In this America, fundamental social change was unnecessary—material abundance, and just a bit of economic fine-tuning, were all that was needed. In 1956 both Adlai Stevenson and *Time* magazine announced that the elimination of poverty was in sight.

Poverty and Urban Blight

Economic realities belied such optimistic conclusions. In 1960 some 35 million Americans, one-fifth of the nation, lived below the poverty line, victims of malnutrition, disease, and squalor. Millions of senior citizens had neither medical nor hospital insurance, and nearly 8 million elderly had yearly incomes of less than a thousand dollars.

One-third of the poor lived in depressed rural areas, and 2 million migrant-farm workers lived in the most abject poverty. Observing a Texas migratory-labor camp in 1955, a journalist reported that 96 percent of the children had had no milk in the previous six months, eight out of ten adults had eaten no meat, and most slept "on the ground, in a cave, under a tree, or in a chicken house." In California's Imperial Valley, the infant death rate among migrant workers was more than seven times the statewide average.

The bulk of the poor huddled in decaying inner-city slums. Displaced Deep South blacks and Appalachian whites, Native Americans forced off reservations, Puerto Ricans, and Mexican migrants strained cities' already inadequate schools and housing. Nearly 200,000 Mexican-Americans herded into San Antonio's Westside barrio; a local newspaper described them as living like cattle in a stockyard, "with roofed-over corrals for homes and chutes for streets." Trapped in a cycle of want and poverty, children of the poor started school at a disadvantage and rapidly fell behind; many dropped out. Living with neither hope nor skills, they bequeathed a similar legacy to their children.

Urban problems intensified. Affluent residents and business moved to the suburbs as the poor flooded in. City governments, their tax bases shrinking, watched helplessly as antiquated schools and mass-transit facilities deteriorated.

The pressing need for low-cost housing went unanswered. Slum-clearance and urban-renewal projects shunted the poor from one ghetto to another to make room for parking garages and cultural centers. Bulldozers razed the Los Angeles barrio of Chavez Ravine to make way for Dodger Stadium. Landlords, realtors, and bankers deliberately excluded nonwhites from decent housing. One-half of the housing in New York's heavily black Harlem predated 1900. There, a dozen people might share a tiny apartment with broken windows, faulty plumbing, and gaping holes in the walls. Harlem's rates of illegitimacy, infant deaths, narcotics use, and crime towered above city and national averages. "Where flies and maggots breed . . . where rats bite helpless children," an African-American social psychologist observed, "the conditions of life are brutal and inhumane."

The Other America
The quality of life for citizens like these poor white children and the African-American North Carolina grandmother substantiated Michael Harrington's claim that too much had been made of American affluence in the 1950s.

African-Americans' Struggle for Justice

The collision between the hopes raised by the 1954 *Brown* decision and the indignities of persistent discrimination and segregation sparked a new phase in the civil-rights movement. To sweep away the separate but rarely equal facilities of Jim Crow, African-Americans developed new tactics, founded new organizations, and followed new leaders. They also devised direct-action confrontations with local power structures, both to engage large numbers of African-Americans in their own freedom fight and to arouse white America's conscience.

Racism touched even the smallest details of daily life. In Montgomery, Alabama, black bus riders had to surrender their seats so that no white rider would stand. Although the city's African-Americans represented more than three-fourths of all passengers, they had to pay their fare at the front of the bus, leave and reenter through the back door, and sit only in the rear. In December 1955, when Rosa Parks, a strong-willed black woman, refused to get up so that a white man could sit, she was arrested. Montgomery's black leaders organized a massive boycott. "There comes a time when people get tired, tired of being segregated and humiliated, tired of being kicked about by the brutal feet of oppression," declared Martin Luther King, Jr., an eloquent twenty-seven-year-old minister who articulated the anger of Montgomery blacks. The time had come, he continued, to stop being patient "with anything less than freedom and justice." With this speech began what would be a year-long bus boycott by 50,000 African-American Montgomerians.

African-Americans walked to work or organized car pools. Whites tried to crush the boycott by intimidation, but blacks stayed off the buses—and gained self-respect. "My soul has been tired for a long time," an old woman said; "now my feet are tired, and my soul is resting."

When city leaders would not budge, African-Americans filed suit, challenging bus segregation. In November 1956 the Supreme Court affirmed a lower-court decision outlawing such segregation.

The bus boycott demonstrated black strength and determination. It shattered the myth that African-Americans liked segregation and that only outside agitators fought Jim Crow. It affirmed for blacks everywhere the possibility of social change. And it gave the nation a persuasive African-American leader, Dr. King, whose oratory simultaneously inspired black political activism and touched white consciences.

King's philosophy of civil disobedience fused the spirit of evangelical Christianity with the strategy of nonviolent resistance. His emphasis on direct action gave every African-American an opportunity for activism; and his insistence on nonviolence diminished the threat of bloodshed. Preaching that they must lay their bodies on the line to provoke crises that would force whites to confront their racism, he urged his followers to love their enemies. In this way, he believed, blacks would convert their oppressors and build a community of true brotherhood. In 1957 King and a network of black ministers formed the Southern Christian Leadership Conference (SCLC) to direct this new campaign against Jim Crow.

The Hispanic-American and Native American Predicament

Meanwhile, Mexican-Americans and Native Americans made little headway in ending discrimination against them. The newest minority group, Puerto Ricans (who are U.S. citizens), reached nearly a million by 1960. Crowded mainly into New York's East Harlem, they suffered from inadequate schools, sanitation services, and police protection and were denied access to middle-class jobs. Like countless earlier immigrants, they gained personal freedom in the United States while losing the security of a strong cultural tradition.

Family frictions flared in the transition from Puerto Rican to American ways. Parents felt upstaged by children who learned English and who obtained jobs that were closed to their parents. As Puerto Rican women found readier access to employment than men did, relations between husbands and wives changed, often becoming strained. Many Puerto Ricans who tried to embrace American ways encountered prejudice because of their skin color and Spanish language.

Mexican-Americans suffered the same indignities. Most of them were also underpaid, cheated and discriminated against, forced to attend segregated schools, and excluded from mainstream American life. The presence of countless "undocumented aliens" compounded their difficulties.

After World War II the advent of new irrigation systems had added 7.5 million acres to the agricultural lands of the Southwest and stimulated demand for cheap Mexican labor. To stem the tide of illegal Mexican immigrants, in 1951 Congress established a temporary worker, or *bracero,* program that brought in tens of thousands of seasonal laborers. Many stayed, joining a growing number of illegal Hispanic immigrants. Between 1953 and 1955 the Eisenhower administration deported more than 3 million allegedly undocumented workers. Periodic roundups, however, proved no substitution for a sound labor policy or an effective enforcement strategy, and millions of Mexicans continued to cross the poorly guarded border. Employers meanwhile persisted in exploiting Mexican-American citizens. Often arrested and detained while walking the streets, Mexican-Americans had to prove their legal right to be in the United States. Such civil-rights violations reinforced Mexican-Americans' mistrust of the government and intensified their alienation from Anglo society.

Although the GI Bill had helped some Mexican-Americans to make it into the middle class, and despite antidiscrimination laws in several Southwestern cities, the one-third of Mexican-Americans below the poverty line saw their lives worsen. The influx of illegal workers as well as the *braceros* severely depressed wages. Whereas the newest arrivals worked in the fields, most Chicanos moved to urban *colonias* during the 1950s. By 1960 more than half a million Mexican-Americans resided in the Los Angeles metropolitan area. Denver, El Paso, Phoenix, and San Antonio also had large *colonias*.

Native Americans remained the poorest, most-ignored minority. Between 1900 and 1930 they had lost more than half their land. In 1953, pressured by agricultural, timber, and mining interests that coveted Indian lands, Congress adopted House Concurrent Resolution 108, which ended the Indians' status as wards of the United States, granted them citizenship, and called for the liquidation of the reservation system and the termination of special federal services to tribes. For the Menominees of Wisconsin and the Klamaths of Oregon, who owned valuable timberlands, the policy was disastrous. Further impoverishing the tribes, it transferred more than 500,000 acres of Native American lands to non-Indians. The federal Voluntary Relocation Program, designed to lure Indians off the reservations, provided Native Americans with moving costs, assistance in finding housing and jobs, and living expenses until they obtained work.

By 1960 more than 60,000 Indians had left their reservations. Some became middle class, some ended up in run-down urban shantytowns, and nearly a third eventually returned to their tribes. Their protests against termination and relocation ignored, Native Americans remained the most invisible of America's "invisible" men and women.

Seeds of Disquiet

Late in the 1950s breezes of self-scrutiny and apprehension ruffled the placid surface of American life. Questions about the nation's goals and values, periodic business recessions, rising unemployment, and the ballooning national debt contributed to the uneasiness. Third World anticolonialism, especially Fidel Castro's takeover of Cuba, diminished Americans' sense of national pride and power. And adding to the disquiet were the growing alienation of American youth and a technological breakthrough by the Soviet Union.

Sputnik

On October 4, 1957, the Soviet Union launched the first artificial earth satellite, *Sputnik* ("Fellow Traveler"). Weighing 184 pounds and only twenty-two inches in diameter, it circled the earth at 18,000 miles per hour. When *Sputnik II* went into a more distant orbit on November 3, critics indignantly said that Eisenhower had allowed a "technological Pearl Harbor." Democrats warned of a "missile gap" between the United States and the U.S.S.R.

Initially, the Eisenhower administration disparaged the Soviet achievement, but behind the scenes Eisenhower pushed to have the American Vanguard missile readied to launch a satellite. On December 6, with millions watching by TV, Vanguard rose a few feet into the air and exploded. Newspapers mockingly wrote of America's "Flopnik."

Eisenhower didn't laugh. Instead he doubled the funds for missile development to $4.3 billion in 1958 and then raised the level to $5.3 billion in 1959. He also established the Science Advisory Committee, whose recommendations led to creation of the National Aeronautics and Space Administration (NASA) in July 1958. By decade's end, the United States had launched several space probes and successfully tested the Atlas intercontinental ballistic missile.

Sputnik also set off a feverish effort to reshape American education. Critics pointed out that the Soviet Union produced twice as many scientists and engineers as the United States and complained that Americans honored football stars more than outstanding students. Progressive education fell into disrepute. Americans embarked on a crash program to raise educational standards. Federal funding built new classrooms and laboratories, raised teachers' salaries, and installed instructional television systems in schools. In 1958 Congress passed the National Defense Education Act, which provided loans to college students and funds for teacher training and for the development of new instructional materials in science, mathematics, and foreign languages.

America now banked on higher education to ensure national security. The number of college students skyrocketed from 1.5 million in 1940 to 3.6 million by 1960. That year, the government funneled $1.5 billion to universities, a hundredfold increase over 1940.

Linked directly to the Cold War, this hike in educational spending raised unsettling questions. By 1960 nearly a third of scientists and engineers on university faculties worked full-time on government research, primarily defense projects. Some observers feared that a military-industrial-*educational* complex was emerging.

A Rebellion of Youth

The fifties also bred cultural restiveness and a search for self-definition among adolescents. Few adults considered the implications of widespread affluence or the consequences of having a generation of teenagers who could stay in school instead of working. Few thought about the effects of growing up in an age when traditional values such as thrift and self-denial seemed of declining relevance. And despite talk of togetherness, fathers were often too busy to give their children much attention, and mothers sometimes seemed to spend more time chauffeuring adolescents than listening to them. Much of what adults knew about teen mores they learned from Hollywood and the mass media, which focused on the sensational and the superficial.

Accounts of juvenile delinquency abounded. News stories painted high schools as war zones, streets as jungles ruled by gangs, and teenagers as gun-carrying hoodlums. In truth, the delinquency rate remained steady. Nonetheless, teenagers who sported black-leather motorcycle jackets and slicked their hair into "ducktails" aroused adult alarm and disapproval.

Equally dismaying to parents, young Americans embraced rock-and-roll. In 1952 Alan Freed, the former host of a classical-music program on a Cleveland radio station, started a new program, "Moondog's Rock and Roll Party," after observing teenagers dancing to and enthusiastically buying rhythm-and-blues records, traditionally recorded by and for African-Americans. The show caught on, and in 1954 Freed moved it to New York and made rock-and-roll a national craze.

White performers transformed black rhythm-and-blues, with its heavy beat and suggestive lyrics, into "Top Ten" rock-and-roll. In 1954 Bill Haley and the Comets dropped some of the sexual allusions from Joe Turner's version of "Shake, Rattle, and Roll," added country-and-western guitar riffs, and produced the first major rock-and-roll hit. In the mid-fifties, too, Mississippi-born Elvis Presley swaggered onto the rock music scene. From January 1956, with the release of "Heartbreak Hotel," to March 1958, when he was drafted, Elvis produced fourteen consecutive million-selling records. Girls screamed at his voice and swooned at his pouty-surly expression; boys wore their hair long and greasy in imitation of their idol.

Melding the pentecostal music of his boyhood with the hillbilly boogie that he heard on "Grand Ole Opry" radio shows, Presley possessed a raw energy and strutting sexuality that shocked middle-class white adults. But the more adults condemned Presley and other rock-and-roll stars, the more teenagers loved them. Record sales tripled from 1954 to 1960, and Dick Clark's "American Bandstand" became the decade's biggest TV hit.

Portents of Change

Nonconformist writers known as the Beats expressed a more fundamental revolt against middle-class society. In Allen Ginsberg's *Howl* (1956) and Jack Kerouac's *On the Road* (1957), the Beats scorned materialism and "square" America. Kerouac scoffed at the "rows of well-to-do houses with lawns and television sets in each living room with everybody looking at the same thing and thinking the same thing at the same time." Romanticizing society's outcasts, the Beats glorified uninhibited sexuality, spontaneity, and spirituality.

The educated college-age youths who were among the Beats' greatest admirers rejected the era's complacency and caution. They protested the ongoing HUAC investigations, decried the nuclear-arms race, and, in 1958 and 1959, staged Youth Marches for Integrated Schools. Together with the Beats and rock-and-roll, this vocal minority of the "silent generation" heralded the youth movement that would explode in the 1960s.

CONCLUSION

The disquiet of the late fifties underlined the paradox of midcentury America. The United States, mightier than any nation in history, basked in prosperity. At the same time, Americans felt uneasiness as the arms race heated up and as booming times brought unsettling social change.

Most Americans applauded President Eisenhower's moderation while ignoring his warnings about the military-industrial complex. They also closed their eyes to the persistent poverty within society and to the concentration of power in the economy. White middle-class Americans looked forward to continued affluence and peace. Indeed, few who followed the presidential campaign of 1960, in which the two major-party candidates promised to outdo each other in expanding prosperity and containing communism, imagined that Americans would soon be waging a war against poverty and a land war in Asia. Even fewer anticipated that the rock-and-roll generation would help to topple white supremacy, to challenge their elders' most-cherished values, and to usher in an era of confrontation.

CHRONOLOGY

1944 Mark I calculator begins operation.

1946 Dr. Benjamin Spock, *Baby and Child Care*.
ENIAC, the first electronic computer, begins operation.

1947 Levittown, New York, development started.

1948 Bell Labs develops the transistor.

1950 Asociación Nacional México-Americana established.

1952 Dwight D. Eisenhower elected president.

1953 Korean War truce signed.
CIA-supported coup in Iran.
Earl Warren appointed U.S. chief justice.

1954 Army-McCarthy hearings.
Brown v. *Board of Education of Topeka*.
Fall of Dien Bien Phu; Geneva Conference.
CIA intervention in Guatemala.

1955 Salk polio vaccine developed.
AFL-CIO merger.
First postwar U.S.–Soviet summit meeting.
Montgomery bus boycott begins.

1956 Interstate Highway Act.
Suez crisis.
Soviet intervention in Poland and Hungary.
Allen Ginsberg, *Howl*.
Eisenhower reelected.

1957 Eisenhower Doctrine announced.
Civil Rights Act (first since Reconstruction).
Jack Kerouac, *On the Road*.
Little Rock school-desegregation crisis.
Soviet Union launches *Sputnik*.
Peak of "baby boom" (4.3 million births).

1958 U.S. troops sent to Lebanon.
National Defense Education Act.

1958 United States and Soviet Union halt atomic tests.
National Aeronautics and Space Administration (NASA) founded.

1959 Fidel Castro comes to power in Cuba.
Khrushchev and Eisenhower meet at Camp David.

1960 National Liberation Front of South Vietnam (NLF) established.
U-2 incident.
Second Civil Rights Act.

1962 Rachel Carson, *Silent Spring*.

FOR FURTHER READING

William H. Chafe, *The American Woman: Her Changing Social, Economic, and Political Roles, 1920–1970*, rev. ed. (1988). An incisive examination of discrimination against women and their efforts to overcome it.

Kenneth Jackson, *Crabgrass Frontier: The Suburbanization of the United States* (1985). An indispensable social history of suburban growth.

Jacqueline Jones, *The Dispossessed: America's Underclasses from the Civil War to the Present* (1992). A thorough analysis of the roots of modern poverty.

Elaine Tyler May, *Homeward Bound: American Families in the Cold War Era* (1988). A social history of how the Cold War influenced gender roles, marriage, parenting, and family life.

Larry May, ed., *Recasting America: Culture and Politics in the Age of the Cold War* (1989). A stimulating collection of essays.

Walter A. McDougall, . . . *The Heavens and the Earth: A Political History of the Space Age* (1985). A probing investigation of the diplomatic and political factors affecting the space program.

John Modell, *Into One's Own: From Youth to Adulthood in the United States, 1920–1975* (1989). An important, insightful survey of the coming of age of American youth.

Chester Pach, Jr., and Elmo Richardson, *The Presidency of Dwight D. Eisenhower* (1991). A fair, balanced, and thoughtful overview.

CHAPTER 30

The Turbulent Sixties

The complacency that characterized the 1950s was waning as the 1960s began. On February 1, 1960, four African-American students at North Carolina Agricultural and Technical College sat down at the lunch counter at the local Woolworth's and asked for coffee and doughnuts. When the waitress announced, "We don't serve colored here," the students remained seated, staying until the store closed. By the end of the week, hundreds of students had joined the sit-in. By April 1960 sit-ins had spread to seventy-eight southern communities, and by September 1961 some 70,000 African-American students had targeted segregated restaurants, churches, beaches, libraries, and movie theaters.

The Greensboro "coffee party" was only one part of a sweeping series of changes stirring. Even as African-Americans throughout the nation were greeting the students' activism with hope and pride, other voices of protest were puncturing the apathy and self-satisfaction of the fifties. Socialist Michael Harrington was investigating the plight of the poor,

(Right) The Selma to Montgomery March, 1965

Harvard Law School graduate Ralph Nader was sounding the alarm that many American automobiles were "unsafe at any speed," and mother and writer Betty Friedan was working on what would be a pathbreaking critique of sexism, *The Feminine Mystique* (1963).

These endeavors symbolized a spirit of new beginnings. Impatience and idealism, especially among the young, would lead many young Americans to embrace John F. Kennedy's New Frontier and to rally behind Lyndon Johnson's Great Society. Both administrations' rhetorical emphasis on social change would generate fervent hopes and lofty expectations. But assassinations of cherished leaders, ongoing racial strife, and a deepening quagmire in Vietnam would dampen optimism, and a reaction by the majority who opposed radical change would curtail reform. A decade that began with bright promise would end in discord and disillusionment.

The New Frontier, 1960–1963

Projecting an image of vigor and boldly proposing new approaches to old problems, John F. Kennedy personified the energy and self-confidence of American youth. His wealthy father, Joseph P. Kennedy, had held a series of appointive posts under Franklin D. Roosevelt. Joe Kennedy seethed with ambition, which he passed on to his sons, driving them to excel. Despite a severe back injury, John Kennedy had served in the navy during World War II. The elder Kennedy had arranged for a journalist to rework the Harvard-educated John's senior thesis into a book, *Why England Slept*, and persuaded a popular novelist to write articles lauding his heroism in rescuing his crew after their PT boat had been sunk in the South Pacific.

Esteemed as war hero and scholar, John Kennedy used his charm and his father's connections to win election in 1946 to the House of Representatives from a Boston district where he had never lived. Although Kennedy earned little distinction in Congress, Massachusetts voters sent him to the Senate in 1952 and overwhelmingly reelected him in 1958. By then he had a beautiful wife, Jacqueline, and a Pulitzer Prize for *Profiles in Courage* (1956), written largely by a staff member.

Despite the obstacle of his Roman Catholic faith, the popular Kennedy won a first-ballot victory at the 1960 Democratic convention, where, just forty-two years old, he sounded the theme of a "New Frontier" for reform at home and victory abroad, for "more sacrifice instead of more security."

The Election of 1960

Recalled a University of Nebraska student, "All at once you had something exciting. . . . Kennedy was talking about pumping new life into the nation and steering it in new directions." But most voters, middle-aged and middle class, seemed to be looking for the stability, security, and continuation of Eisenhower's "middle way" that the Republican candidate, Vice President Richard M. Nixon, promised. Although scorned by liberals for his McCarthyism, Nixon was better known and more experienced than Kennedy. A Protestant, he also was closely identified with the still popular Ike.

Nixon fumbled his opportunity. Conceding that he and Kennedy disagreed more about means than goals, he spent much of his time defending the Eisenhower record. His greatest mistake, however, was agreeing to meet Kennedy in televised debates.

More than 70 million people tuned in to the nation's first televised debate between presidential candidates—a broadcast that secured the dominance of television in American politics. The tanned and dynamic Kennedy contrasted strikingly with his pale, haggard opponent. The telegenic Democrat radiated confidence; Nixon, sweating under his pasty facial makeup, appeared insecure. Radio listeners called the debates a draw, but television viewers declared Kennedy the clear victor. Kennedy shot up in the polls, and Nixon never regained the lead.

Kennedy also benefited from the embarrassing U-2 incident and an economic recession, as well as from his choice of a southerner, Senate majority

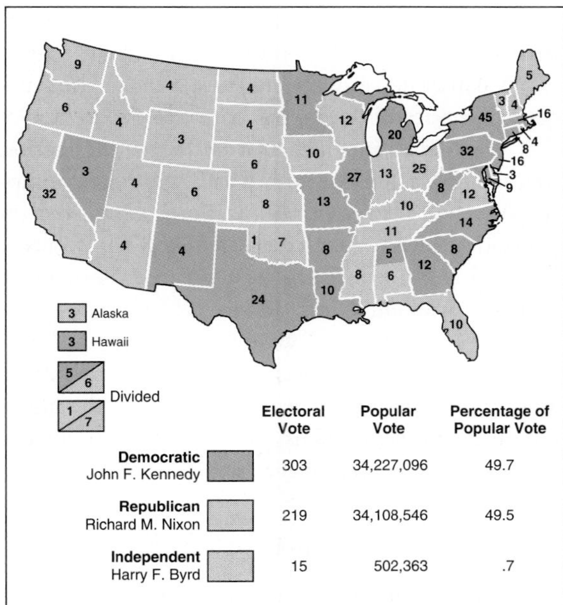

The Election of 1960

leader Lyndon B. Johnson, as his running mate. Still, the 1960 election was the closest since 1888. Kennedy's tiny margin of victory reflected both lingering fears about a Catholic president and a widespread reluctance to change. In the end, Kennedy's religion cut both ways: it cost him millions of votes in the South, but Catholic voters in closely contested midwestern and northeastern states delivered crucial margins. Although Nixon carried more states than Kennedy, the Democrat's popularity with urban minorities helped to give Kennedy a slender triumph.

Kennedy's inauguration set the tone of a new era: "Let the word go forth from this time and place, to friend and foe alike, that the torch has been passed to a new generation of Americans." In sharp contrast to the Eisenhower administration's "eight millionaires and a plumber," Kennedy surrounded himself with young intellectuals. For attorney general he selected his brother Robert Kennedy; "I see nothing wrong with giving Robert some legal expertise before he goes out to practice law," JFK joked.

Kennedy's dynamic style played well on TV and underscored the president's charisma and determination "to get America moving again." Aided by his wife, he adorned his presidency with the trappings of culture and excellence, filling government posts with Rhodes scholars and studding his speeches with references to Emerson and Aristotle. Awed by his taste and grace, reporters extolled the first family's glamour and vitality and ignored JFK's fragile health and extramarital affairs.

Kennedy's Domestic Record

The media focus on Kennedy's charisma and forceful rhetoric obscured his lackluster domestic record. Indeed, the conservative coalition of Republicans and southern Democrats that had stifled Truman's Fair Deal doomed the New Frontier as well. Lacking the votes in Congress to overcome these barriers, Kennedy rarely pressed Congress for reform, maintaining that "there is no sense in raising hell and then not being successful."

Instead, JFK made economic growth his domestic priority. To stimulate the economy, he combined higher defense and space expenditures with investment incentives for private enterprise. In 1961 Kennedy persuaded Congress to boost the defense budget by 20 percent, vastly increasing America's nuclear stockpile of intercontinental ballistic missiles, medium-range missiles, and Polaris submarines. Abandoning the "bigger bang for the buck" strategy, moreover, he sought stronger conventional forces and enhanced U.S. capability in countering Third World insurgencies. JFK also persuaded Congress to finance a "race to the moon," an effort that would cost more than $25 billion to land astronauts Neil Armstrong and Buzz Aldrin on the lunar surface in 1969.

In addition, JFK proposed lower business taxes through investment credits and generous depreciation allowances. But the business community and the Democratic president remained mutually suspicious. Business groups blamed the White House whenever stock prices tumbled. For his part, Kennedy reacted angrily when U.S. Steel raised

John Fitzgerald Kennedy (1917–1963)
The youthful, popular president throws out the first ball of the 1962 baseball season.

prices immediately after the president, to curb inflation, had pressured the steelworkers' union to accept a noninflationary contract with minimal raises. JFK threatened the company with antitrust suits and mobilized the Federal Bureau of Investigation (FBI) and the Federal Trade Commission to investigate price agreements among steel producers. Although U.S. Steel backed down this time, JFK then ignored the corporation's subsequent price hikes. And in January 1963 when he announced his major initiative to catalyze economic growth, the president rejected proposals for increased social spending and advocated personal and corporate tax reduction to encourage private investment and consumption.

When the Kennedy presidency ended tragically in November 1963, the proposed tax cut was bottled up in Congress, but JFK's economic program had doubled the rate of economic growth, decreased unemployment, and held inflation at 1.3 percent a year. He had stimulated the longest uninterrupted era of economic expansion in American history. But liberals complained that the Kennedy administration was promoting military spending at the expense of social welfare and the public sector.

Meanwhile, environmental pollution had become a matter of deepening concern. Awareness of the ecosystem's fragility grew with the publication in 1962 of Rachel Carson's *Silent Spring* (see Chapter 29). JFK appointed an advisory committee on pesticides, and tough federal regulations followed. In 1963 the Clean Air Act regulated automotive and industrial emissions, and in 1966 Congress outlawed the dumping of wastes and pollutants into lakes and rivers. After decades of heedless pollution, Washington hesitantly began to deal with the major environmental problems of a modern industrial order and consumer society.

Kennedy and Civil Rights

JFK neither anticipated nor welcomed the crusade for civil rights that engulfed the South. Fearful that a struggle over civil rights would divide the nation, split the Democratic party, and entangle Congress in lengthy filibusters, he straddled the issue for two years.

To JFK, racial problems were a thorny thicket to tiptoe around, not a dominant issue requiring decisive leadership. He appointed an unprecedented number of African-Americans to high offices while naming some white racists to federal judgeships. Kennedy remained aloof from attempts by congressional liberals to enact civil-rights legislation and stalled for two years before issuing a weak executive order banning discrimination in federally financed housing.

But the civil-rights movement kept pressure on the president. In the spring of 1961, the Congress of Racial Equality (CORE) organized a "freedom ride" through the Deep South to dramatize widespread violation of a 1960 Supreme Court decision banning segregation in interstate transportation. In Anniston, Alabama, Ku Klux Klansmen savagely beat the freedom riders and burned their bus, while in Birmingham a white mob mauled a CORE group. When whites in Montgomery viciously assaulted the freedom riders, Kennedy finally dispatched federal marshals to end the violence. Scores more freedom rides and the arrest of hundreds of young protesters forced the president to press the Interstate Commerce Commission to enforce the Supreme Court's ruling.

In fall 1962 Kennedy again applied federal force to quell white racist violence. When a federal court ordered the University of Mississippi to enroll James Meredith, an African-American air-force veteran, angry whites rioted. Rallying behind Confederate flags, students and troublemakers attacked federal marshals escorting Meredith to "Ole Miss." The clash left two dead, hundreds injured, and the campus shrouded in tear gas. Federal troops finally restored order and upheld the right of a black American to attend the university of his home state.

Birmingham, 1963
President Kennedy said this photograph of an African-American being attacked by a police dog during the protest demonstrations in Birmingham made him "sick." It helped galvanize the nation's conscience, leading Kennedy to submit a comprehensive civil-rights bill to Congress.

The African-American Revolution

In Birmingham on Good Friday, 1963, Martin Luther King, Jr., determined to expose the violent extremism of southern white racism and to force the president's hand, organized a series of marches, sit-ins, and pray-ins. With each protest bringing more arrests, police commissioner Eugene "Bull" Connor scoffed that King would soon "run out of niggers." Resorting to force, Connor unleashed his men, armed with electric cattle prods, high-pressure water hoses, and snarling attack dogs, on the nonviolent demonstrators. The ferocity of the attack, chronicled on television news programs, filled the world with revulsion.

"The civil-rights movement should thank God for Bull Connor," JFK remarked. "He's helped it as much as Abraham Lincoln." Indeed, the combination of African-American activism and growing white support for equal rights had stimulated Kennedy to arrange a behind-the-scenes compromise ending the Birmingham demonstrations in return for desegregating stores and upgrading the status of African-American workers. By mid-1963 the rallying cry "Freedom Now!" reverberated across the nation as the number and magnitude of similar protests grew. Increasingly concerned about America's image abroad and the "fires of frustration and discord" at home, Kennedy feared that if the federal government did not lead the way toward "peaceful and constructive" changes in race relations, blacks would turn to militancy. Accordingly, when Alabama governor George Wallace in June 1963 refused to allow two African-American students to enter the University of Alabama, Kennedy forced Wallace—who had pledged "Segregation now! Segregation tomorrow! Segregation forever!"—to capitulate to a court desegregation order.

On June 11 JFK went on television to define civil rights as "a moral issue" and to assert that "race has no place in American life or law." Describing

Martin Luther King, Jr. (1929–1968)
King warned of the "whirlwind of revolt" that would consume the nation if African-Americans' civil rights continued to be denied.

the plight of blacks in Jim Crow America, he asked, "Who among us would be content to have the color of his skin changed and stand in his place? Who among us would then be content with the counsels of patience and delay?" The president concluded, "It is time to act in the Congress, in your state and local legislative body, and, above all, in our daily lives." A week later, Kennedy proposed a comprehensive civil-rights measure—which most members of Congress ignored.

To compel Congress to act, nearly 250,000 Americans converged on the Capitol on August 28, 1963. There they heard the ringing words of Martin Luther King, Jr., proclaiming that he had a dream, a dream of brotherhood, of freedom and justice, a dream that "all of God's children, black men and white men, Jews and Gentiles, Protestants and Catholics, will be able to join hands and sing in the words of the old Negro spiritual, 'Free at last! Free at last! Thank God Almighty, we are free at last!' "

King's powerful oratory did not speed the civil-rights bill through Congress nor end racism, poverty, and despair. It prevented neither the ghetto riots that lay ahead nor the white backlash that smothered the civil-rights movement and destroyed King himself. But King had turned a political rally into a historic event. In one of the great speeches of history, he recalled America to the ideals of justice and equality.

Neither Kennedy's nor King's eloquence could quell the anger of white racists. On the night of the president's address, Medgar Evers, the head of the Mississippi branch of the National Association for the Advancement of Colored People, was murdered by a sniper in Jackson. In September the bombing of a black church in Birmingham killed four girls. And still, southern obstructionism kept the civil-rights bill stymied in Congress, with little hope of passage.

New Frontiers Abroad, 1960–1963

Having proclaimed in his inaugural address that "we shall pay any price, bear any burden, oppose any foe to assure the survival and success of liberty,"

Kennedy adopted a military strategy of "flexible response" to allow him "a wider choice than humiliation or all-out nuclear action." He tripled U.S. nuclear capabilities, increased conventional forces, and established counterinsurgency special units such as the Green Berets to fight Third World guerrilla revolutionaries.

At the same time, Kennedy gained congressional backing for new programs of economic assistance to Third World countries. The Agency for International Development coordinated foreign aid, the Food for Peace program distributed surplus agricultural products, and the Alliance for Progress worked for economic development and social reform in Latin America. The Peace Corps, created in 1961, exemplified the New Frontier blend of idealism and activism. By 1963, 5,000 Peace Corps volunteers were serving as teachers, crop specialists, and health workers in more than forty Third World nations. But despite these peaceful initiatives, containment and toughness remained central to American foreign policy.

Cold War Activism

Spring 1961 brought Kennedy's first foreign-policy crisis. Concerned about the presence of a communist outpost on the United States' doorstep, the president approved a CIA plan, drawn up under Eisenhower, to invade Cuba. In mid-April 1961, 1,500 anti-Castro exiles landed at Cuba's Bay of Pigs, assuming that their arrival would trigger a general uprising to overthrow Fidel Castro. The invasion was a fiasco.

Deprived of air cover by Kennedy's desire to conceal U.S. involvement, the invaders had no chance against Castro's superior forces. The Cuban people did not rise up, and in three days the island militia either killed or captured the entire brigade. Although Kennedy accepted blame for the failure, he neither apologized for nor ended attempts to overthrow Castro. Kennedy, determined to prove his strength, violated American treaty agreements and aroused the resentment of Latin Americans by supporting further raids on Cuba by exiles and even assassination plots against Castro.

In July 1961 on the heels of the Bay of Pigs failure, Kennedy met in Vienna with Soviet premier Nikita Khrushchev to try to resolve a number of issues involving a peace treaty with Germany. Comparing American troops in the divided city of Berlin to "a bone stuck in the throat," Khrushchev threatened war unless the West retreated. Believing the young president easily intimidated, Khrushchev then announced that he would sign a separate German peace agreement with East Germany. A shaken Kennedy returned to the United States and declared the defense of West Berlin essential to the Free World. He mobilized 150,000 reservists and National Guardsmen, sought higher defense spending, and, to prepare for a possible nuclear war, announced a crash program to build nuclear-fallout shelters. The threat of thermonuclear war with the U.S.S.R. escalated until mid-August when the Soviets settled for a stalemate. Leaving the American role in West Germany and Berlin unchanged, Moscow constructed a wall of concrete and barbed wire to seal off East Berlin, the Soviet-held sector, and later signed a peace treaty with East Germany. Designed to stop the flow of Germans from the communist zone—about 1,000 refugees a day by June 1961—the Berlin Wall and the mining of East Germany's western border ended the exodus of talent that had threatened East Germany's economic survival. "The Wall" became an enduring symbol of communism's denial of personal freedom until it fell in 1989.

To the Brink of Nuclear War

In mid-October 1962 aerial photographs revealed that the Soviet Union had begun constructing missile bases and had placed intermediate-range nuclear missiles, capable of striking most U.S. soil, in Cuba. Smarting from the Bay of Pigs disaster, fearing unchecked Soviet interference in the Western Hemisphere, and believing that his credibility was at stake, Kennedy responded forcefully. On October 22 the president went on television to denounce "this clandestine, reckless, and provocative threat to world peace" and to issue an ultimatum that the missiles be removed. The United States, he announced, would "quarantine" Cuba—impose a naval blockade—to prevent delivery of more missiles and would dismantle by force the missiles already in Cuba if the Soviet Union did not do so.

The world held its breath. The two superpowers appeared to be on a collision course toward nuclear war. Soviet technicians worked feverishly to complete the missile launch pads, and Soviet missile-carrying ships steamed toward the blockade. Nearly 200 U.S. Navy ships in the Caribbean, meanwhile, prepared to confront the Soviet freighters; B-52s armed with atomic bombs took to the air; and nearly 250,000 troops assembled in Florida to invade Cuba. On October 24 Secretary of State Dean Rusk reported, "We're eyeball to eyeball."

"I think the other fellow just blinked," a relieved Rusk announced on October 25. Kennedy received a conciliatory message from Khrushchev guaranteeing to remove the missiles if the United States promised never to invade Cuba. As Kennedy prepared to respond positively, a second, far more belligerent message arrived from the Soviet leader. Hours later an American U-2 reconnaissance plane was shot down over Cuba. It was "the blackest hour of the crisis," according to a Kennedy aide. As the military urged an invasion, Robert Kennedy persuaded his brother to accept the first letter and simply to ignore the second one. In the early morning hours of October 27, Khrushchev pledged to remove the missiles in return for Kennedy's noninvasion promise.

Only recently have the full dimensions of the crisis been revealed. In January 1992 the Russian military disclosed that Soviet forces in Cuba had possessed thirty-six nuclear warheads and nine tactical nuclear weapons for battlefield use. Soviet field commanders had independent authority to use these weapons. Worst of all, no Washington decision maker knew that the Soviets already had the ability to launch a nuclear strike from Cuba. Former secretary of defense Robert S. McNamara, speaking in 1992, recalled the pressure for an invasion in late October 1962. "We can predict the results with certainty. . . . U.S. troops could [not] have been attacked by tactical nuclear warheads without the U.S.'s responding with nuclear warheads. . . . Where would it have ended? In utter disaster."

Chastened by having stared over the brink of nuclear war, Kennedy and Khrushchev installed a telephone "hot line" so that the two sides could communicate instantly in future crises. In June 1963 JFK advocated a gradual relaxation of superpower tensions, and two months later the two nations agreed to the Limited Test Ban Treaty, which prohibited atmospheric and undersea nuclear testing.

These efforts signaled the beginning of a new phase of the Cold War, a phase later called détente, as the superpowers began to move from confrontation to negotiation. Ironically, the Cuban missile crisis escalated the arms race as both the United States and the Soviet Union increased their arsenals of intercontinental ballistic missiles and nuclear-missile submarines. The struggle for power in the Third World intensified as both superpowers sought to avoid direct confrontation by deploying surrogates.

Kennedy and Indochina

In early 1961 a crisis flared in Laos, a tiny, landlocked nation created by the Geneva agreement in 1954 (see Chapter 29). There a civil war between American-supported forces and procommunist rebels appeared headed for a communist triumph. Considering Laos strategically insignificant, Kennedy in July 1962 signed an accord restoring a neutralist government but leaving communist forces in the countryside. The Laotian settlement stiffened Kennedy's resolve not to allow further communist gains in Indochina, but it also confirmed North Vietnam's impression of American weakness.

Determined not to give further ground in Southeast Asia, Kennedy ordered large shipments of weapons to South Vietnam and increased the number of American "advisers" stationed there from about 700 in early 1961 to more than 16,000 by late 1963. He accepted Eisenhower's "domino theory" and viewed international communism as a monolithic force, a single global entity controlled by Moscow and Beijing. He was resolved to prove that the United States was not the "paper tiger" mocked by Mao Zedong.

To counter communist gains in South Vietnam, the United States uprooted Vietnamese peasants and moved them into fortified villages. Diem rejected American pressure to gain popular support through reform measures, instead choosing to crush demonstrations by students and Buddhists. By mid-1963 Buddhist monks were setting themselves on fire to protest Diem's repression and Diem's own military leaders were plotting a coup.

Frustrated American policy makers concluded that only a new government could stave off a Vietcong victory and secretly backed the coup efforts. On November 1, 1963, military leaders staged their coup, captured Diem and his brother, and shot them. Although the United States promptly recognized the new government, it made little headway against the Vietcong. JFK now faced two unpalatable alternatives: to use American combat forces or to withdraw and seek a negotiated settlement.

What Kennedy would have done remains unknown. Less than a month after Diem's death, John F. Kennedy himself fell to an assassin's bullet. His admirers contend that by late 1963 he was privately advocating the withdrawal of American forces after the 1964 election. JFK publicly proclaimed in fall 1963 that "it is their war. . . . In the final analysis it is their people and their government who have to win or lose the struggle." But skeptics note that the president followed this comment with a ringing restatement of the domino theory and a promise that the United States would not withdraw from the conflict.

The Thousand-Day Presidency

On November 22, 1963, during a trip to Texas to unite warring factions of the state Democratic party, a smiling JFK and Jackie rode in an open car along Dallas streets lined with cheering crowds. Suddenly gunshots rang out and the president slumped, his skull and throat shattered. While the driver sped the mortally wounded Kennedy to a nearby hospital, Secret Service agents rushed Lyndon B. Johnson to Air Force One to be sworn in as president.

Grief and disbelief gripped the nation as most Americans spent the next four days in front of their television sets. The images flickered in real time and then over and over in replay: the murder of the accused assassin, Lee Harvey Oswald; the somber state funeral, with the small boy saluting his father's casket; the grieving family lighting an eternal flame at Arlington National Cemetery. These images burned into the national memory. Television had made John F. Kennedy a celebrity in life; now, in death, it made him a hero, the fallen king of Camelot. The Kennedy magic has never died.

A balanced judgment on Kennedy remains elusive; historians are still too close in time for genuine perspective, and the Kennedy family has denied researchers access to many important documents. Kennedy loyalists have always stressed JFK's potential, his intelligence and grace, his ability to change and grow. His detractors—whose ranks have grown in recent years—point out the contrast between his public image as family man and his recklessly amoral private behavior. Liberal historians deplore his aggressive Cold War tactics, while conservatives fault him for stirring unrealistic expectations and setting in motion an enormous expansion of federal power that would reach fruition in the Great Society.

Nonetheless, some conclusions about the Kennedy presidency seem clear. Domestically, JFK's legacy was mixed. A conservative-dominated Congress blocked much of his agenda—only about one-third of his proposals became law. Kennedy also gave free rein to J. Edgar Hoover's FBI (in part because he himself was vulnerable to blackmail) and allowed the Central Intelligence Agency to connive with the Mafia to assassinate Fidel Castro. (Scholars are still sorting out the tangle of plots and policies that enmeshed the Kennedy brothers, Hoover, organized crime, and the national-security agencies.) The long economic expansion under Kennedy resulted from spending on missiles and the space race, not on social welfare and human needs, while environmental concerns languished. Internationally, Kennedy's record was equally mixed. He signed the world's first nuclear test ban treaty, but began a massive arms build-up. He compromised on Laos, but deepened U.S. involvement in Vietnam. And he remained a Cold Warrior whose rhetoric dangerously heated superpower confrontation.

By conveying a sense of concern for the underprivileged and by shaking the nation out of complacency, he gave reformers new hope, aroused the poor and powerless (especially African-Americans), and challenged the young, stimulating a flowering of social criticism and political activism rare in American history. Lyndon B. Johnson, sworn in as president on the plane that carried the murdered president's body back to Washington, inherited a dangerous combination of soaring expectations at home and deteriorating entanglement in Vietnam. Although Kennedy died with his luster untarnished, during LBJ's presidency events would shatter illusion after illusion. The American people would lose confidence in their nation and its leaders, with consequences that still reverberate.

The Great Society

Distrusted by liberals as "a Machiavelli in a Stetson," regarded as a usurper by Kennedy loyalists, the new president, Lyndon Baines Johnson, had achieved his highest ambition—but only through the assassination of a popular president in Johnson's home state, Texas. Though just nine years older than Kennedy, he seemed a relic of the past, a back-room wheeler-dealer. When many Americans compared the crude and domineering LBJ to the martyred Kennedy, JFK in death appeared even more eloquent and gifted than he had in life.

Yet Johnson had substantial political assets. He had served in Washington almost continuously since 1932, accruing enormous experience. He excelled at wooing allies, neutralizing enemies, forging compromise, and achieving legislative results. And he was a Protestant, a southerner, a moderate, and a close associate of Capitol Hill power brokers—all factors that would improve the chances for passage of the blocked Kennedy bills.

His first two years in office were extraordinarily successful. He deftly handled the transition of power, won a landslide electoral victory in 1964, and guided through Congress the greatest array of social-reform legislation in U.S. history. However, LBJ's swollen but fragile ego could not abide the sniping of the Kennedy loyalists, and he frequently complained that the media were not giving him "a fair shake." Wondering aloud, "Why don't people like me?" Johnson pressed on—to do more, to do it bigger and better, to vanquish all foes at home and abroad. Ironically, in seeking consensus and affection, Johnson would profoundly divide the nation.

Toward the Great Society

Calling for early passage of the tax-cut and civil-rights bills as a memorial to Kennedy, Johnson used his legislative skills to good effect. In February 1964 Congress passed a $10 billion tax-reduction bill that spurred economic growth and would shrink the budget deficit to $4 billion by 1966. In July lawmakers passed the Civil Rights Act of 1964, outlawing segregation in public accommodations, granting the federal government new powers to fight school segregation and black disfranchisement, and creating the Equal Employment Opportunity Commission (EEOC) to stop job discrimination because of race, religion, national origin, or gender.

In his boldest domestic initiative, LBJ also declared "unconditional war on poverty in America." Michael Harrington's *The Other America* (1962) had documented the persistence of widespread poverty in the larger affluent society. Some 40 million "invisible" people lived in substandard housing and subsisted on inadequate diets. Unaided by social welfare, they lived with little hope, mired in a culture of poverty, deprived of the education, medical care, and employment opportunities that most people took for granted.

LBJ championed a campaign to bring these "internal exiles" into the mainstream. Enacted in August 1964, the resulting Economic Opportunity Act established the Office of Economic Opportunity to fund and coordinate a job corps to train young people in marketable skills; VISTA (Volunteers in Service to America), a domestic peace corps; Project Head Start, to provide compensatory education for preschoolers from disadvantaged families; and an assortment of public-works and training programs.

Summing up his goals in 1964, Johnson offered a cheering crowd in Ann Arbor, Michigan, his vision of the "Great Society." First must come "an end to poverty and racial injustice," LBJ said. But that would be just the beginning. The Great Society would also be a place where all children could enrich their minds and enlarge their talents, where humans could renew their contact with nature, and where people would be deeply concerned with the quality of their goals. A cornucopia of liberal programs targeting health, education, conservation, the environment, and racial equality appeared ready to flow from Washington if Johnson won election in November.

The Election of 1964

Johnson's Great Society unsettled conservatives, whose movement had remained strong. Leaders of the Right particularly scorned Kennedy-Johnson welfarism. Conservatives supported active government and high federal spending to defeat communism but objected to similar activism and spending when the enemies were poverty, injustice, and lack of opportunity at home. To them, the lofty rhetoric of the Great Society only masked ever-greater government infringement on basic freedoms.

The Great Society's racial liberalism also frightened southern segregationists and a growing number of white laborers in northern cities who feared that the price of racial justice would be the integration of *their* neighborhoods, schools, and workplaces. Their support of Alabama's segregationist governor George Wallace in early 1964 presidential primaries heralded a "white backlash" against the civil-rights movement.

At the July 1964 Republican convention, these dissatisfied groups gained control of the GOP. They nominated right-wing Arizona senator Barry Goldwater for the presidency, named conservative William Miller of New York as his running mate, and wrote a platform repudiating liberal Republicanism. Determined to offer the nation "a choice, not an echo," Goldwater extolled his Senate votes against the civil-rights act and against the censure of Joseph McCarthy; suggested abolishing the graduated income tax; advocated eliminating "compulsory" social security; and hinted that he might use nuclear weapons against Cuba and North Vietnam if they did not give in to U.S. demands. Goldwater's stance appealed to Americans disturbed by the Cold War stalemate and the federal government's growing decision-making power.

Goldwater's conservative crusade let LBJ have the best of two worlds: he could run as a liberal reformer but still be the more moderate candidate. LBJ and his running mate, Senator Hubert Humphrey of Minnesota, painted Goldwater as an extremist not to be trusted with the nuclear trigger. When Goldwater charged that the Democrats had not pursued total victory in Vietnam, Johnson appeared the apostle of restraint: "We are not going to send American boys nine or ten thousand miles

The Election of 1964

Candidates	*Parties*	*Electoral Vote*	*Popular Vote*	*Percentage of Popular Vote*
LYNDON B. JOHNSON	Democratic	486	43,126,506	61.1
Barry M. Goldwater	Republican	52	27,176,799	38.5

from home to do what Asian boys ought to be doing for themselves."

To no one's surprise, LBJ won a landslide victory, 43 million votes to Goldwater's 27 million. The GOP, moreover, lost 500 of the state legislative seats that it had held. Commentators proclaimed the death of conservatism. But Goldwater's coalition of white southerners and blue-collar workers presaged conservatism's future triumph. In fact, nearly 40 percent of the electorate had voted for Goldwater, an uncompromising conservative who had demanded total victory over communism and an end to the welfare state. In the short run, the Democrats secured huge majorities in both houses of Congress, nullifying the conservative coalition's power to block the presidential proposals. For the first time in a quarter century, the liberals had a working majority.

Liberalism Triumphant

"Hurry, boys, hurry," LBJ urged his aides. "Get that legislation up to the hill and out. Eighteen months from now ol' Landslide Lyndon will be Lame-Duck Lyndon." Johnson flooded Congress with Great Society proposals, sixty-three in 1965 alone. And he got most of what he requested.

The Eighty-ninth Congress enlarged the War on Poverty and passed another milestone civil-rights act. Social security was expanded to include Medicare, health insurance for the aged, and Medicaid, medical care for the indigent. The expansion of the "guarantor state" begun under the New Deal continued with federal funds for education and housing, creation of the National Endowments for the Arts and Humanities, and establishment of new cabinet-level departments for transportation and housing and urban development. In 1965 a new immigration act abolished the quota system; most newcomers to the United States would thereafter emigrate from Asia and the Western Hemisphere.

The Great Society also sought to reduce pollution and to protect and preserve nature. Secretary of the Interior Stewart Udall played a major role in establishing Redwood National Park and in defeating efforts to dam the Colorado River and flood the lower Grand Canyon. Congress strengthened the Clean Water and Clean Air acts, protected endangered species and wildlands, and preserved scenic rivers and millions of acres of wilderness.

Summing up the Great Society, a presidential aide asserted, "There was no child we could not feed, no adult we could not put to work, no disease we could not cure, no toy, food or appliance we could not make safer, no air or water we could not clean." But programs so hopefully begun would largely wither—some because they were flawed, some because the liberal consensus supporting them vanished, and many because the administration ultimately opted for guns rather than butter. As Martin Luther King, Jr., observed, the hopes and expectations of the Great Society were "shot down on the battlefields of Vietnam."

From 1965 to 1968 the Office of Economic Opportunity spent an average of $1.7 billion a year. Military appropriations in the same period averaged $64 billion. LBJ's shift from welfare to warfare shattered his consensus and enraged those still mired in poverty. Resultant rising black militancy and urban riots would alienate "middle America." And growing bitterness about the Vietnam War would focus the wrath of liberals, particularly the young, on LBJ. The Democrats' loss of forty-seven House seats in 1966 would seal the Great Society's fate.

The Warren Court in the Sixties

By the mid-sixties the Supreme Court, headed by Chief Justice Earl Warren, was under siege. Its decisions from *Brown* v. *Board of Education* (1954) onward had incensed the Far Right. In 1962 John F. Kennedy had appointed two liberals to the Court, replacing moderates, and LBJ appointed the even more liberal Abe Fortas and Thurgood Marshall, the Court's first African-American justice. During the 1960s the Warren court handed down a series of decisions that changed the tenor of American life.

In a series of landmark cases, the Court prohibited Bible reading and prayer in public schools, limited communities' power to censor books and films, and overturned state bans on contraceptives. In *Baker* v. *Carr* (1962) and related decisions, the Warren court ruled that "one man, one vote" must prevail in both state and national elections and that representation in all legislative bodies must be allocated on the basis of "people, not land or trees, or pastures." Especially unsettling to many was the Court's commitment to due process of law for everyone caught up in the criminal-justice system. Rulings that a poor defendant charged with a felony must be provided an attorney, and that the accused has the right to counsel during interrogation, appeared to handcuff law enforcement even as crime proliferated.

In 1966 criticism of the Warren court reached a crescendo when it ruled in *Miranda* v. *Arizona* that police must warn all suspects that anything they say can be used against them in court and that they can choose to remain silent. In 1968 both Richard Nixon and George Wallace would promise to appoint judges who would emphasize "law and order" over individual rights and liberties.

The Changing Struggle for Equality, 1964–1968

The drive for black equality crested and receded in the two years following the 1963 March on Washington. The movement had brought the end of both legal discrimination and African-American disfranchisement and had gained improved educational and employment opportunities for African-Americans. But major problems remained: crime, drug addiction, family disorganization, and blacks' deep feelings of inadequacy. Persistent white racism, moreover, discouraged blacks, who increasingly questioned whether they would ever be seen as equals. For some, the movement had generated hopes that it could not fulfill and kindled a racial pride that rejected integration as a desirable goal. "The paths of Negro-white unity that had been converging," wrote Martin Luther King, Jr., "crossed at Selma and like a giant X began to diverge."

The Voting Rights Act of 1965

In 1964 CORE and SNCC (Student Nonviolent Coordinating Committee) activists, believing that the ballot box held the key to real power for southern blacks, mounted a major campaign to register African-American voters. Focusing on the state most hostile to equal rights, field workers organized the Mississippi Freedom Summer Project of 1964. One thousand college-student volunteers assisted blacks in registering to vote and in organizing "Freedom Schools" that taught black history and emphasized African-American self-worth. Harassed by Mississippi law-enforcement officials and Ku Klux Klansmen, the volunteers endured the firebombing of black churches and civil-rights headquarters, arrests, beatings, kidnappings, and even murders.

Although they registered only 1,200 African-Americans to vote, the workers enrolled nearly 60,000 disfranchised blacks in the Mississippi Freedom Democratic party (MFDP) and took their case to the national Democratic convention in August 1964. The MFDP insisted that the convention seat MFDP delegates instead of the all-white delegation chosen by the Mississippi Democratic party. LBJ, trying to head off white southern walkouts, forged a compromise that granted two at-large seats to the MFDP and barred from all future conventions any delegations from states that discriminated against African-Americans. The compromise alienated militants in the civil-rights movement.

Martin Luther King, Jr., and the Southern Christian Leadership Conference (SCLC), resolved to gain a voting-rights act, organized mass protests in Selma, Alabama, in March 1965. African-Americans constituted one-half the voting-age population in Dallas County, where Selma was located, but only 1 percent were registered to vote. Selma's county sheriff Jim Clark was every bit as ill tempered and violence prone as Birmingham's Bull Connor, and Clark's men attacked black protesters and bystanders indiscriminately and brutally. Showcased on television news, the vicious attacks provoked national outrage and fostered support for a voting-rights bill.

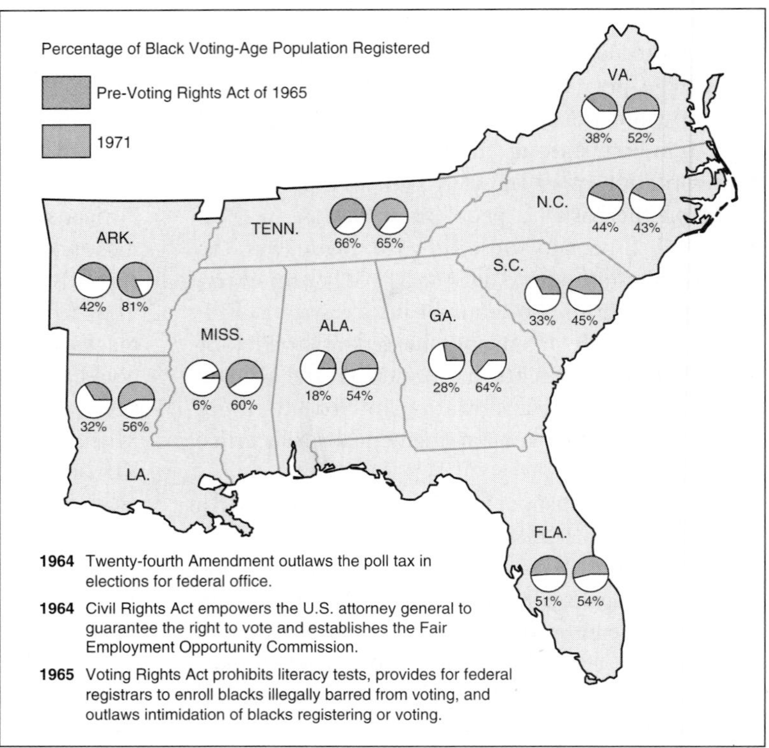

Voter Registration of African-Americans in the South, 1964–1971

As African-Americans overwhelmingly registered to vote as Democrats, some former segregationist politicians, among them George Wallace, started to court the African-American vote, and many southern whites began to cast their ballots for Republicans, inaugurating an era of real two-party competition in the South.

Signed by the president in August 1965, the resulting Voting Rights Act expanded black suffrage—and transformed southern politics. It authorized federal examiners to register voters and to suspend literacy tests in areas where fewer than one-half the minority residents of voting age were registered. Together with the Twenty-third Amendment, ratified in 1964, which outlawed the poll tax in federal elections, and a 1966 Supreme Court decision striking down the poll tax in *all* elections, the Voting Rights Act by 1968 had boosted the number of registered African-American voters in the South from 1 million to 3.1 million. For the first time since Reconstruction, African-Americans were a force to be reckoned with in southern politics.

The civil-rights movement altered, rather than revolutionized, race relations in the United States. Black voting power defeated some white supremacists while stirring other once ardent segregationists prudently to seek black support. Equal access to public accommodations gave African-Americans a new sense of dignity. "Now if we do want to go to McDonald's we can go to McDonald's," mused a black woman in Atlanta. "It's just knowing! It's a good feeling." But with discrimination lingering in many spheres and African-American unemployment still disproportionately high, the anger bubbling below the surface of the urban ghetto boiled over.

The Long, Hot Summers

On August 11, 1965, five days after the Voting Rights Act had been signed, a confrontation between white police and young blacks in Watts, Los Angeles's largest black district, ignited the most destructive race riot in two decades. For six days nearly 50,000 African-Americans looted shops, firebombed white-owned businesses, and sniped at police officers, fire fighters, and National Guard troops. When the riot ended, 34 people had been killed, 900 injured, and 4,000 arrested, and $30 million worth of property had been devastated. In rapid succession African-Americans in Chicago and in Springfield, Massachusetts, took to the streets, looting, burning, and battling police.

In summer 1966 rioting erupted in more than a score of northern ghettos, forcing whites to heed the squalor of the slums, the savage behavior of police in the ghetto, and urban poverty—issues that the civil-rights movement had ignored. The following summer brought nearly 150 racial outbreaks and 40 riots, the most intense and destructive period of racial violence that the United States had ever witnessed. In 1968 riots again would flare in the ghettos of more than one hundred cities after the assassination of Martin Luther King, Jr. (see Chapter 31). The 1964–1968 riot toll would include 200 dead, 7,000 injured, 40,000 arrested, and $200 million worth of property wrecked.

A frightened, bewildered nation asked why such widespread rioting was occurring just as African-Americans were beginning to achieve their goals. Explanations abounded. Militant blacks saw the uprisings as revolutionary violence directed at a racist, reactionary society. Conservatives described them as senseless outbursts by troublemakers. The National Advisory Commission on Civil Disorders (the Kerner Commission) indicted white racism for fostering "an explosive mixture" of poverty, slum housing, poor education, and police brutality. Warning that "our nation is moving toward two societies, one black, one white—separate and unequal," the commission recommended the creation of 2 million new jobs, the construction of 6 million units of public housing, an end to de facto school segregation in the North, and funding for a "national system of income supplementation." Aware of a swelling white backlash, LBJ ignored the commission's advice, and most whites approved of his inaction. Alarmed by demands for "Black Power" that had risen in recent riots, they preferred that their taxes be spent on strengthening local police forces instead of on improving ghetto conditions.

"Black Power"

Demands for Black Power in 1966 flowed from the same source as the riots: disappointment at the slow pace of racial change and black outrage toward a white society that blocked even minimal advances by African-Americans. Less an ideology than a cry of fury and frustration, Black Power rhetoric evolved from the teachings of Malcolm X. A former pimp, drug addict, and street hustler, Malcolm X had converted to the Nation of Islam, or Black Muslim faith, while in prison. Founded in Detroit in 1931 by Elijah Poole (who took the Islamic name Elijah Muhammed), the Nation of Islam insisted that blacks practice self-discipline and self-respect, and it rejected integration. Malcolm X accordingly urged African-Americans to separate themselves from the "white devil" and to take pride in their African roots and their blackness. Blacks, he claimed, had to rely on armed self-defense and had to seize their freedom "by any means necessary." Malcom X's assassination in February 1965 by members of the Nation of Islam, after he had broken with Elijah Muhammed, did not still his voice. *The Autobiography of Malcolm X* (1965) became the main text for the rising Black Power movement.

In summer 1966 Stokely Carmichael led SNCC away from its commitment to nonviolence and integration. "The only way we gonna stop them white men from whippin' us is to take over. We been saying freedom for six years and we ain't got nothin'. What we gonna start saying now is Black Power!" Carmichael's successor as SNCC head, H. Rap Brown, encouraged African-Americans "to get you some guns. . . . Don't be trying to love that honky [white man] to death. Shoot him to death." In 1966 two college students in Oakland, California, Huey Newton and Bobby Seale, organized the Black Panthers, who gained national publicity from a series of violent confrontations with the police and from Newton's repeated claim, quoting from

Chairman Mao, that "political power comes through the barrel of a gun."

African-American leaders of every persuasion adopted the "Black Power" slogan. Revolutionaries used it to preach guerrilla warfare; liberals, to demand reform; conservatives, to emphasize self-help. A generation of African-Americans was soon affirming that "black is beautiful." Young blacks donned dashikis, wore Afro hairstyles, enjoyed soul music and soul food, and established black-studies programs at colleges. Young SCLC leader Jesse Jackson asked students to repeat after him, "I may have lost hope, but I am . . . somebody. . . . I am . . . black . . . beautiful . . . proud. . . . I must be respected." Similar themes would reverberate through other social movements in the sixties.

Native American and Chicano Power

Activist Native Americans, whose peoples numbered nearly 800,000, also organized demonstrations to publicize their plight and to awaken self-respect and cultural pride. In 1961 representatives of sixty-seven tribes gathered in Chicago to draw up a Declaration of Purposes, and in 1964 hundreds of Indians assembled in Washington to lobby for recognition in the War on Poverty. Native Americans, they pointed out, suffered the worst poverty, the highest disease and death rates, and the poorest education and housing of any American group. President Johnson established the National Council on Indian Opportunity in 1965 and in 1968 sent Congress a special message seeking greater federal aid for the Indians.

By 1968 young activists were demanding "Red Power" and insisting on the name Native Americans. They agitated for preferential hiring, Native American studies programs, and reimbursement for lands taken from them in violation of federal laws and treaties. In 1968 Indians in Washington State tried to assert old treaty rights to fish in the Columbia River and Puget Sound, while Chippewa Indians in Minnesota inaugurated the American Indian Movement (AIM). Emphasizing Indians' rights to control their own affairs, AIM, like the Black Panthers, established armed patrols to protect Indians from police harassment.

Cesar Chávez

To dramatize the plight of migrant workers, Chávez drew on the tactics of the civil-rights movement. In 1965 he led striking grape pickers with the slogan "God is Beside You on the Picket Line."

Mexican-Americans also challenged whites' dominance. Their ethnic pride and solidarity were kindled by Cesar Chávez, founder of the National Farm Workers' Association, who sought improved working conditions for farm laborers and used nonviolent resistance to fight for social change. Portraying the farm workers' struggle as part of the larger national movement for civil rights, Chávez in 1965 organized a California grape pickers' strike and a nationwide consumer boycott of grapes (and later, lettuce).

By 1970, 85 percent of all Mexican-Americans lived in urban areas, and neighborhoods such as North Hollywood in Los Angeles became centers of

Mexican-American businesses. However, young activists rejected assimilation; they demanded to be called *Chicanos* and *Chicanas* and battled for bilingual and bicultural education. Organizations such as the Alianza in New Mexico, the Crusade for Justice in Colorado, and La Raza in Texas exemplified this new militancy. Young California Chicanos organized the Brown Berets and began to speak of "Chicano power." They demanded control over the institutions that most affected Mexican-Americans, particularly the Immigration and Naturalization Service, and called for an end to the *bracero* program.

The Black Power, Red Power, and Brown Power movements could not sustain the fervent activism and media attention that they attracted in the late sixties. But by elevating the consciousness and nurturing the confidence of the younger generation, each contributed to the cultural pride of its respective group.

A Second Feminist Wave

Following the victory of the woman-suffrage campaign in 1920, the American feminist movement had lost virtually all momentum. In the 1950s feminist consciousness had hit a low point. But in the 1960s, a new spirit of self-awareness and dissatisfaction stirred middle-class women. A revived feminist movement emerged, profoundly altering women's view of themselves and their role in American life.

Several events fanned the embers of discontent into a flame. In 1961 John F. Kennedy had established the Presidential Commission on the Status of Women. Its 1963 report documented occupational inequities suffered by women that were comparable to those endured by minorities. Women received less pay than men for comparable or identical work and had far less chance than their male counterparts of moving into professional or managerial careers. Women composed 51 percent of the population but made up only 7 percent of the nation's doctors and less than 4 percent of its lawyers. The women who served on the presidential commission successfully urged that the Civil Rights Act of 1964 prohibit gender-based as well as racial discrimination in employment.

Dismayed, however, by the Equal Employment Opportunity Commission's handling of gender-based discrimination complaints, these women formed the National Organization for Women (NOW) in 1966. Defined as a civil-rights group for women, NOW lobbied for equal opportunity, filed lawsuits against gender discrimination, and mobilized public opinion.

NOW's popularity owed much to the publication in 1963 of Betty Friedan's *The Feminine Mystique*. Calling it "the problem that has no name," Friedan deplored the narrow view that women should seek fulfillment only as wives and mothers. Suburban domesticity—the "velvet ghetto"—left many women with feelings of emptiness, with no sense of accomplishment, and afraid to ask "the silent question—'Is this all?'" Friedan asserted that women must pursue careers and establish "goals that will permit them to find their own identity." *The Feminine Mystique* revealed to disillusioned women that they were not alone. Friedan's demand for "something more than my husband, my children, and my home" rang true to many educated middle-class women who found the creativity of homemaking and the joys of motherhood exaggerated.

Still another catalyst for feminism came from the involvement of young women in the civil-rights and anti–Vietnam War movements. Women activists in these causes gained confidence in their own potential, an ideology to describe oppression and to justify resolve, and experience in the strategy and tactics of protest.

In 1968 militant feminists adopted "consciousness-raising" as a recruitment device and a means of transforming women's perceptions of themselves and society. Tens of thousands of women across the United States assembled in small groups to share their experiences and to air grievances. From such meetings came an understanding that their shared problems were not psychological issues but political problems amenable to political solutions, and from this new consciousness grew a sense of "sisterhood" and a commitment to end women's subordination.

Radical feminists set up "freedom trash cans" into which women could discard high-heeled shoes, bras, curlers, and other items that they considered demeaning. They staged sit-ins at all-male clubs and professional meetings to dramatize discrimination against women, established health collectives and day-care centers, and fought negative portrayals of women in the media, in advertising, and in language. Terms such as *sexism* and *male chauvinist pig* entered the American vocabulary.

In August 1970 various feminist factions put aside their differences to join the largest women's rights demonstration ever. Commemorating the fiftieth anniversary of woman suffrage, the Women's Strike for Equality brought out tens of thousands of women across the nation to parade for the right to equal employment and to safe, legal abortions. By then the women's movement had already pressured many financial institutions to issue credit to single women and to married women in their own name, ended newspapers' practice of listing employment opportunities under "Male" and "Female" headings, and secured guidelines that required corporations receiving federal funds to adopt nondiscriminatory hiring practices and equal pay scales. By 1970, moreover, more than 40 percent of all women held full-time jobs outside the home.

The changed consciousness of the feminist movement opened a larger world of choices and opportunities for American women. Domesticity remained an option, but it was no longer the *only* option. As never before, women were taking control of their own lives and defining their own goals.

The Lost Crusade in Vietnam, 1964–1968

Although the militancy of women, African-Americans, Indians, and Chicanos chipped away at the consensus that LBJ so desired, it was America's deepening involvement in Vietnam that most unraveled his hope for a united society. Despite the president's desire to concentrate on domestic affairs, developments in South Vietnam sidetracked and ensnared his administration. Diem's successors had proved incompetent, and in 1964 Vietcong attacks on noncommunist South Vietnam had become more damaging.

Johnson had to choose between intervening decisively or extricating the United States from Southeast Asia. While privately describing Vietnam as "a raggedy-ass fourth-rate country," LBJ feared that an all-out American military effort might lead to World War III. And he foresaw that a full-scale U.S. engagement in "that bitch of a war" would destroy "the woman I really loved—the Great Society." Yet Johnson did not want the United States to appear weak. Only American strength and resolve, he thought, would prevent a wider war. The president also worried that a pullout would leave him vulnerable to conservative attack. "I am not going to lose Vietnam," he insisted. "I am not going to be the president who saw Southeast Asia go the way China went."

Trapped between unacceptable alternatives, Johnson expanded the war, hoping that U.S. firepower would force Ho Chi Minh to the bargaining table. But the National Liberation Front and the North Vietnamese calculated that they could gain more by outlasting the United States than by negotiating. So the war ground on, devastating Southeast Asia and dividing the United States as nothing had since the Civil War.

The Gulf of Tonkin Resolution

In 1964 LBJ took bold steps to impress the North Vietnamese with American resolve and to block his vigorously anticommunist opponent, Barry Goldwater, from capitalizing on Vietnam in the presidential campaign. In February Johnson ordered the Pentagon to prepare for air strikes against North Vietnam. In May his advisers drafted a congressional resolution authorizing an escalation of American military action, and in July LBJ appointed General Maxwell Taylor, an advocate of a greater American role in Vietnam, as ambassador to Saigon. In early August, North Vietnamese patrol

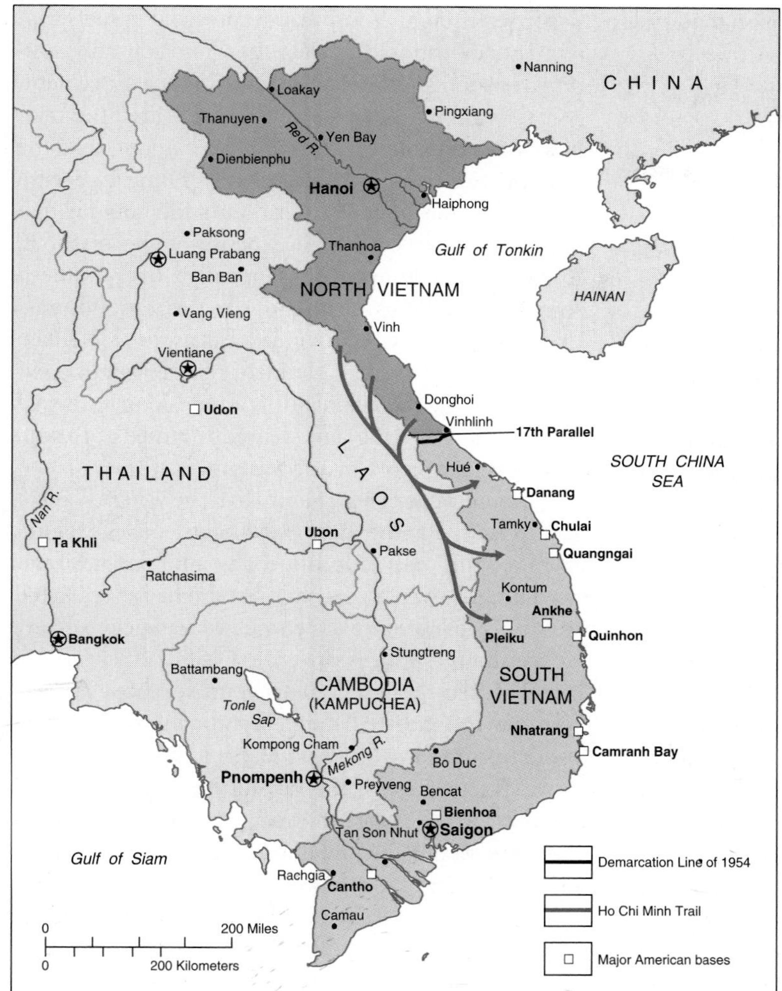

The Vietnam War, to 1968

Wishing to guarantee an independent, noncommunist government in South Vietnam, Lyndon Johnson remarked in 1965, "We fight because we must fight if we are to live in a world where every country can shape its own destiny. To withdraw from one battlefield means only to prepare for the next."

boats reportedly clashed with two U.S. destroyers patrolling the Gulf of Tonkin (see map). Despite virtually no evidence of an attack, Johnson announced that Americans had been victims of "open aggression on the high seas." Withholding the information that the U.S. destroyers had been aiding the South Vietnamese in clandestine raids against North Vietnam, the president condemned the alleged North Vietnamese attacks as unprovoked.

Johnson called on Congress to pass a resolution giving him the authority to "take all necessary measures to repel any armed attack against the forces of the United States and to prevent further aggression." Assured that this power would lead to no "extension of the present conflict," the Senate passed the Gulf of Tonkin Resolution by a vote of 88–2 and the House, by 416–0. Johnson called the resolution "grandma's nightshirt—it covered everything." The president, moreover, considered the resolution a mandate to commit U.S. forces to Vietnam as he saw fit. But the resolution would soon create a credibility problem for Johnson, allowing opponents of the war to charge that he had misled Congress and lied to the American people.

Americanization of the War

Interpreting the Gulf of Tonkin Resolution as a blank check to widen the war, Johnson early in 1965 ordered the sustained bombing of North Vietnam. Intended to inflict just enough damage to make Hanoi negotiate, to boost the morale of the Saigon government, and to stop the flow of soldiers and supplies southward from North Vietnam, the bombing accomplished none of these purposes. Further, for all of LBJ's concern about restraint, the United States dropped 800 tons of bombs daily on North Vietnam from 1965 to 1968, three times the tonnage used by all combatants in World War II.

Unable to turn the tide by bombing, Johnson escalated U.S. involvement by sending combat troops to Vietnam. Adopting a "meat-grinder" strategy of victory through attrition, Johnson intended to inflict heavy casualties on the communists in order to bring them to the peace table. Hanoi, however, was prepared to fight until American resolve waned, and the North became more and more involved in the conflict. Determined to prevent a North Vietnamese victory, Johnson had sent 485,000 troops to Vietnam by the end of 1967, more men than the United States had deployed in Korea at the peak of the earlier Asian war. North Vietnam had matched American escalation step for step, and there was no end in sight.

Opposition to the War

At first on college campuses and then in the wider society, a growing number of Americans doubted the wisdom of the Vietnam War and vocally opposed it. A week after marines splashed ashore at Danang, South Vietnam, in March 1965, students and faculty at the University of Michigan staged the first teach-in to raise questions about U.S. involvement. Later that spring, 25,000 people, mainly students, rallied in Washington to applaud two senators for their votes against the Gulf of Tonkin Resolution. As new draft calls went out in 1966, large-scale campus antiwar protests erupted. Students demonstrated against the Pentagon and military research and began a draft-resistance movement.

Liberal intellectuals and clergy joined the chorus of opposition to the war. Some argued that the United States had no business meddling in a civil quarrel; others doubted that the nation could win at any reasonable cost. The expense of the war, $20 billion annually and rising, appalled many Americans, especially as Great Society programs shrank. In 1967 critics who included Senators J. William Fulbright and Robert Kennedy, foreign-policy experts George Kennan and Walter Lippmann, and Martin Luther King, Jr., spurred hundreds of thousands to participate in antiwar protests.

Some opponents noted that the war fell especially hard on the poor. Owing to college deferments, the use of influence, and a military-assignment system that shunted the better educated to desk jobs, lower-class youths were twice as likely to be drafted and, if drafted, twice as likely to see combat duty as middle-class youths. About 80 percent of the enlisted men who fought in Vietnam were from poor or working-class families.

TV coverage of the war further eroded popular support. Scenes of shocking cruelty, of fleeing refugees, of children maimed by U.S. bombs, and of dying Americans replayed in living rooms night after night, undercutting the official optimism of government press agents. Americans shuddered in horror as they watched napalm (a burning glue that clings to skin and clothing) and defoliants lay waste Vietnam's countryside and leave thousands of civilians dead or mutilated. They saw American troops, who supposedly were winning the hearts and minds of the Vietnamese, uproot peasants, burn their villages, and desecrate their burial grounds.

Yet even at the height of the antiwar movement, most Americans either supported the war or remained undecided. As the war's costs rose and casualties surpassed those in the Korean War, however, the war's unpopularity deepened. The desire "to get out, but not give up" became a common sentiment. In mid-1967 Secretary of Defense McNamara admitted that "the picture of the world's greatest superpower killing or seriously injuring a

LBJ and Vietnam
The Vietnam War spelled President Lyndon Johnson's undoing. Here, young peace demonstrators express their feelings about the president's role in the war during a massive antiwar protest at the Pentagon in October 1967.

thousand noncombatants a week, while trying to pound a tiny backward country into submission on an issue whose merits are hotly disputed, is not a pretty one."

Equally disturbing was how polarized the nation had grown. "Hawks" would accept little short of quick and total victory, whereas "doves" insisted on negotiating, not fighting. The vast middle group of Americans, not opposed to the war on principle, was reaching the conclusion that the conflict was unwinnable. As Johnson lashed out at his critics and refused to de-escalate the conflict, demonstrators paraded past the White House and chanted, "Hey, hey, LBJ, how many kids did you kill today?" By 1968 the president had become a prisoner in the White House, unable to speak in public without drawing hecklers, and his Great Society lay in ruins.

CONCLUSION

Despite LBJ's woes in 1968, he had accomplished much. Under his predecessor, John F. Kennedy, idealistic young Americans had come to believe that it was time to rid the nation of racism and poverty. The civil-rights movement in the Kennedy years had vanquished legally enforced segregation, disfranchisement, and racial discrimination and nurtured blacks' self-respect. Other oppressed groups—women, Chicanos, Indians—had followed African-Americans' lead.

The reform impulse peaked during the first two years of the Johnson administration. Millions benefited from the Great Society as it made the United States a more caring and just nation. But the Great Society promised more than it could ultimately deliver. Despite LBJ's boast that the United States could fund a major war and still spend on social programs, the tremendous costs of the Vietnam War reduced the War on Poverty to a skirmish. By early 1966 the government was pouring $2 billion a month into Vietnam, more than it spent in an entire year to combat poverty. As U.S. involvement in Vietnam escalated, angry African-Americans and college-age youths turned to violence to hasten social change. Floundering in a futile war, Johnson and the Democratic party, like the American people as a whole, faced the election year 1968 in confusion and disarray.

CHRONOLOGY

1960 Sit-ins to protest segregation begin.
John F. Kennedy elected president.

1961 Peace Corps and Alliance for Progress created.
Bay of Pigs invasion.
Freedom rides.
Berlin Wall erected.

1962 Michael Harrington, *The Other America*.
Cuban missile crisis.

1963 Civil-rights demonstrations in Birmingham.
March on Washington.
Test-Ban Treaty between the Soviet Union and the United States.
Kennedy assassinated; Lyndon B. Johnson becomes president.
Betty Friedan, *The Feminine Mystique*.

1964 "Freedom Summer" in Mississippi.
Civil Rights Act.
Gulf of Tonkin incident and resolution.
Economic Opportunity Act initiates War on Poverty.
Johnson elected president.

1965 Bombing of North Vietnam and Americanization of the war begin.
Assassination of Malcolm X.
Civil-rights march from Selma to Montgomery.
Voting Rights Act.
Watts riot in Los Angeles.

1966 Stokely Carmichael calls for Black Power.
Black Panthers formed.
National Organization for Women (NOW) founded.

1967 Massive antiwar demonstrations.
Race riots in Newark, Detroit, and other cities.

FOR FURTHER READING

Irving Bernstein, *Promises Kept: John F. Kennedy's New Frontier* (1991), and Thomas Reeves, *A Question of Character: A Life of John F. Kennedy* (1991). Two conflicting interpretations of the man and his presidency.

William Chafe, *The Unfinished Journey: America Since World War II*, rev. ed. (1991). An interpretive history of social change emphasizing issues of class, gender, and race.

John Dittmer, *Local People: The Struggle for Civil Rights in Mississippi* (1994). An important study of the African-American freedom movement.

Sara Evans, *Personal Politics* (1979). An analysis of the roots of modern feminism in the civil-rights movement and in the New Left.

Samuel Hays, *Beauty, Health, and Permanence: Environmental Politics in the United States, 1955–1985* (1987). A pathbreaking account of modern environmentalism.

George Herring, *America's Longest War*, rev. ed. (1985). A comprehensive account of the reasons for America's involvement and ultimate failure in Vietnam.

Harvard Sitkoff, *The Struggle for Black Equality, 1954–1992* (1993). A dramatic account of the terror-laced struggle against white racism.

CHAPTER

31

A Troubled Journey: From Port Huron to Watergate

The Rise and Fall of the Youth Movement

1968: The Politics of Strife

Nixon and World Politics

Domestic Problems and Divisions

The Crisis of the Presidency

The Free Speech Movement . . . Students for a Democratic Society . . . "Make Love, Not War." . . . The baby boomers who deluged college campuses in the 1960s espousing these and other outlooks and causes spawned a student movement that gave the decade its distinctive cultural and political aura. In the short term, this movement, by assaulting traditional policies and values, produced vital changes. Ironically, in the longer run it contributed to a conservative resurgence.

Both agent in and beneficiary of the era's realignment, Republican Richard M. Nixon won the presidency in 1968 and gained a stunning reelection victory in 1972. Winning high marks for his management of world affairs, Nixon ended U.S. involvement in Vietnam and inaugurated a period of reduced tensions with China and the Soviet Union. In 1974, however, having flouted the very law and order that he had pledged to uphold on the domestic front, Nixon resigned in disgrace to avoid impeachment. He left as his legacy a public disrespect for the political system unparalleled in U.S. history.

(Right) American GI in Vietnam, 1972

The Rise and Fall of the Youth Movement

In the 1950s the number of American students pursuing higher education rose from 1 million to 4 million, and in the 1960s the number doubled again, to 8 million. By then more than half the U.S. population was under age thirty. Their sheer numbers and their concentration in higher education gave the baby boomers a collective identity and guaranteed that their actions would have impact.

Most baby boomers followed conventional paths in the 1960s. If they went to college—and fewer than half did—they typically took business and other career-oriented degrees. Whether they attended college or entered the work force directly after high school, the vast majority had their eyes fixed on a good job, a new car, a family, and a pleasant home. They had little incentive to turn radical. In fact, many young Americans disdained the long-haired protesters and displayed the same bumper stickers as their elders: "My Country—Right or Wrong" or "America—Love It or Leave It."

Although younger and more-educated Americans supported the war in higher percentages than did those older and less educated, far more college students protested the war than any other group. An insurgent minority of liberal-arts majors and graduate students at prestigious universities attracted considerable notice. They tended to be idealistic and to identify emotionally with the underprivileged; economically secure, they rejected the work ethic that had made their parents prosper; raised in indulgent, child-centered homes, they expected instant gratification and resented restrictions.

Toward a New Left

This liberal-minded student minority welcomed the idealism of the civil-rights movement, the rousing call of John F. Kennedy for service to the nation, and the campaign against nuclear testing that had led to the 1963 test ban treaty. Determined not to be a "silent generation," they admired the mavericks and outsiders of the 1950s: iconoclastic comedian Mort Sahl, Beat poet Allen Ginsberg, and pop-culture rebels like Elvis Presley and James Dean. Disillusionment and skepticism, however, mingled with idealism. Kennedy's assassination had cut down an idolized leader. And Lyndon Johnson's coarse personal style, political wheeling and dealing, and, above all, escalation of the war in Vietnam had alienated many of them.

The most alienated were the "red-diaper" babies, the offspring of parents with roots in 1930s radicalism. They provided the initial impetus for the campus awakening and for the rise of the radical movement that became known as the New Left in the 1960s. Indeed, Students for a Democratic Society (SDS), the embodiment of New Left campus radicalism, evolved from an old-time socialist organization.

In June 1962 an era of apathy ended when sixty students adopted the Port Huron (Michigan) Manifesto, a broad critique of American society and a call for more genuine human relationships. Written primarily by Tom Hayden, a twenty-two-year-old former editor of the University of Michigan student newspaper, the manifesto expressed SDS ideals: "We would replace power rooted in possession, privilege, or circumstances, with power rooted in love, reflectiveness, reason and creativity." Citing the success of civil-rights activists' sit-ins and freedom rides, SDS envisioned a nonviolent youth movement transforming the United States into a "participatory democracy" in which individuals would directly control the decisions that affected their lives and could end materialism, militarism, careerism, and racism.

SDS's early core consisted largely of red-diaper babies, altruistic youths typically raised in strongly religious homes that encouraged high ethics and political engagement. But many idealistic students never joined SDS and instead associated themselves with what they vaguely called the Movement. No matter what the label, a generation of activists found its agenda in the Port Huron Manifesto.

Thousands of students became radicalized in the sixties by what they saw as the impersonality and rigidity of campus administrators, the insensitivity of the nation's bureaucratic processes, and mainstream liberalism's inability to achieve deep, swift change. Only a radical rejection of compromise and consensus, they concluded, could restructure society along humane and democratic lines.

From Protest to Resistance

The first wave of student protest washed across the campus of the University of California, Berkeley. In fall 1964 civil-rights activists who were veterans of the Mississippi Freedom Summer Project tried to solicit funds and to recruit volunteers near the campus gate, a spot traditionally open to political activities. Prodded by local conservatives, however, the university suddenly banned such enterprises from the area. Organizing as the Berkeley Free Speech Movement, a coalition of student groups insisted on the right to campus political activity. The arrest of one student led to the occupation of the university administration building, more arrests, and a strike by nearly 70 percent of the student body. Mario Savio, a philosophy major, tried to place the Free Speech Movement in a broader context by claiming that the university not only greedily served the interests of corporate America but also treated students as interchangeable robots. Likening the university to a giant machine, Savio insisted, "There is a time when the operation of the machine becomes so odious, makes you so sick to heart, that . . . you've got to make it stop."

As unrest spread to other campuses, the protests took many forms. Students sat in to halt compulsory ROTC (Reserve Officers' Training Corps) programs, rallied to protest dress codes, marched to demand fewer required courses, and threatened to close down universities unless they admitted more minority students and stopped research for the military-industrial complex. The escalation of the Vietnam War in 1965 gave the New Left an opportunity to kindle a mass social movement. When the Johnson administration abolished automatic student deferments for the draft in January 1966, more than 200 new campus chapters of SDS appeared.

In 1966 SDS disrupted ROTC classes, organized draft-card burnings, and harassed campus recruiters for the military and for Dow Chemical Company, the chief producer of napalm and Agent Orange, chemicals used in Vietnam to burn villages and to defoliate forests. By 1967 SDS leaders were encouraging more provocative acts of defiance, orchestrating civil disobedience at selective-service centers, and counseling students to flee to Canada or Sweden rather than be drafted. At the Spring Mobilization to End the War in Vietnam, which attracted nearly a half-million protesters to New York's Central Park, SDS members led chants of "Burn cards, not people" and "Hell, no, we won't go!"

Spring 1968 saw at least 40,000 students on 100 campuses demonstrate against war and racism. Although the student movement was overwhelmingly peaceful, occasionally the confrontations turned violent. In April 1968, denouncing the university's proposed expansion into Harlem to construct a gymnasium, militant Columbia University students, shouting, "Gym Crow must go" took over the administration building and held a dean captive. The protest expanded into a demonstration against the war and university military research. A thousand students occupied other campus buildings and made them "revolutionary communes." Galvanized by the brutality of the police who retook the buildings, the moderate majority of Columbia students joined a general boycott of classes that shut down the university. A pitched battle between police and antiwar demonstrators at the Democratic National Convention in Chicago that summer illustrated how the antiwar movement was pushing the nation into increasingly emotional confrontation.

August 1969 saw a high point of the movement with the New Mobilization, a series of huge antiwar demonstrations culminating in mid-November with the March Against Death in Washington, D.C. The 300,000 protesters who descended on the nation's capital formed a march that began at Arlington National Cemetery, snaked past the White House, and ended at the Capitol, where twelve wooden coffins were set up. For forty hours the marchers proceeded single-file through a cold drizzle, carrying candles and signs with the names of soldiers killed or villages destroyed in Vietnam.

The Waning of Student Radicalism

A crescendo of violence in spring 1970 marked the effective end of the student movement as a political force. On April 30, 1970, President Richard M. Nixon, Lyndon Johnson's successor, jolted a war-weary nation by announcing that he had ordered U.S. troops to invade Cambodia, a neutral Indochinese nation that the president claimed was a staging area for North Vietnamese forces. Nixon had decided to extricate the United States from Vietnam by "Vietnamizing" the ground conflict and intensifying bombing. The many students who had been lulled by periodic announcements of troop withdrawals from Vietnam now felt infuriated, frightened, and betrayed. They exploded in hatred for Nixon and the war.

At Kent State University in Ohio, as elsewhere, these frustrations unleashed new turmoil. A few radicals broke windows, pelted police cars with rocks, and tried to firebomb the ROTC building. Nixon lashed out at them as "bums." Ohio governor James Rhodes slapped martial law on the university and ordered 3,000 National Guardsmen to Kent. Donning full battle gear, the troops rolled onto the Kent State campus in armored personnel carriers.

On May 4, the day after the Guard's arrival, 600 Kent State students peacefully demonstrated against the Cambodian invasion. Suddenly a campus policeman boomed through a bullhorn, "This assembly is unlawful! This is an order—disperse immediately!" Students shouted back, "Pigs off campus!" Some threw stones. With bayonets fixed, the guardsmen moved toward the rally and laid down a blanket of tear gas. Hundreds of demonstrators and onlookers, choking and weeping, ran from the advancing troops. Guardsmen in Troop G, apparently panicking, raised their rifles and fired a volley into the retreating crowd. When the shooting stopped, eleven students lay wounded; four were dead. None was a campus radical; two had simply been passing by on their way to lunch.

National Guardsmen at Kent State University, 1970
President Nixon's Commission on Campus Unrest concluded that "the [National Guard's] timing and manner of dispersal was disastrous. . . . The rally was peaceful and there was no impending violence."

The Guardsmen later alleged that they had fired to protect themselves from "a charging mob," but the Federal Bureau of Investigation (FBI) branded this claim a fabrication. A presidential commission investigating the Kent State incident denounced the shootings as "indiscriminate firing" and "unnecessary, unwarranted, and inexcusable."

Across the nation, students and others reacted with stunned disbelief followed by angry protest. Then on May 15 highway patrolmen looking into a campus demonstration fired into a women's dormitory at Jackson State College in Mississippi, killing two students and wounding eleven. Protests against such senseless violence, the war, and President Nixon thundered across campuses, and more than 400 colleges and universities shut down as students boycotted classes.

Popular reaction to these events demonstrated how polarized the nation had become. Although most college students blamed Nixon for widening the war and applauded the demonstrators' goals, far more Americans blamed the *victims* for the deaths at Kent State and criticized campus protesters for undermining U.S. foreign policy. Underlying these attitudes were a deep resentment of college students and impatience for an end to the social chaos. Symptomatically, Kent State students expressed profound alienation after the shootings, while a local merchant said that the National Guard "made only one mistake—they should have fired sooner and longer."

But the campus protests after Kent State and Jackson State represented the final spasm of a fragmenting, expiring movement. When a bomb planted by three antiwar radicals destroyed a science building at the University of Wisconsin in summer 1970, killing a graduate student, most students deplored the tactic. With the resumption of classes in the fall, the campus mood had changed dramatically. Frustrated by the failure to end the war, much less to revolutionize American society, antiwar activists at Wisconsin and elsewhere turned to other causes or to communes, careers, or parenthood. SDS fell prey to hard-line disciples of Chinese communist Mao Zedong or Argentina-born revolutionary Che Guevara. A handful of frustrated radicals went underground, planning and sometimes carrying out terrorist acts that justified the government's repression of the remnants of the antiwar movement. The New Left had fallen victim to government harassment, to its own internal contradictions, and to Nixon's success in winding down the Vietnam War.

The aftereffects of 1960s campus activism outlived the New Left. Student radicalism had catalyzed the resentments of millions of people into a rejection of liberalism. Fundamentalist Protestants upset by changing moral standards, white southerners angered by school desegregation, and blue-collar workers fed up with welfare spending united in a new conservatism that looked to the restoration of stability, patriotism, and traditional values.

Early stirrings of this backlash propelled Ronald Reagan to prominence. In 1966 he won California's governorship, in part because of his opposition to demonstrators at the University of California's Berkeley campus. The actor-turned-politician won a resounding reelection victory by railing against radicals: "If it takes a bloodbath," he said, "let's get it over with. No more appeasement." Other conservatives gained office nationwide. And memories of student radicalism would weaken liberalism's appeal during the 1970s and 1980s.

At the same time, the New Left had incubated the growth of public opposition to the Vietnam War. The movement had elevated the campuses into a force that the government could not ignore, and it had made continued U.S. involvement in Indochina difficult. The New Left had also aided in liberalizing many facets of campus life and making university governance less authoritarian. Dress codes and curfews virtually disappeared; ROTC became an elective, not a requirement; schools now recruited minorities; and students sat on the committees that shaped their education.

Some New Left veterans would remain active in post-1970 causes, including environmentalism, consumer advocacy, and the antinuclear movement. Female students who had learned organizing skills while enduring blatant male chauvinism in the sixties' antiwar movement would form the backbone of a resurgent women's movement in the seventies.

These outcomes fell far short of the original New Left vision of remaking the social and political order. Masses of students could be mobilized in the short run against the Vietnam War, but only a few had made long-term commitments to radical politics.

The Youth Culture

The alienation and desire for change that drew some youth to politics led others to seek new lifestyles and altered states of consciousness. In communes and tribes, they denounced individualism and private property, and in urban areas such as Chicago's Old Town or Atlanta's Fourteenth Street, "places where you could take a trip without a ticket," they experimented with drugs. Historian Theodore Roszak called them "a 'counter culture' . . . a culture so radically disaffiliated from the mainstream assumptions of our society that it scarcely looks to many as a culture at all, but takes on the alarming appearance of a barbarian intrusion."

The counterculture owed a debt to the Beats of the 1950s but went far beyond. Substituting the pleasure ethic for the work ethic, the "hippies" of the sixties scandalized the middle class with their sexual promiscuity and indulgence in drugs. Surveys estimated that least half the college students in the late sixties had tried marijuana and that a minority used mind-altering drugs, especially LSD and mescaline. Drug use came easy to a generation whose parents used nicotine, alcohol, amphetamines, and tranquilizers. Many youths, distancing themselves from middle-class respectability, flaunted outrageous personal styles. They showed their disdain for consumerism by wearing surplus military clothing, torn jeans, and tie-dyed T-shirts. Especially galling to adults, young men sported shaggy beards and long hair, which became the badge of the counterculture.

Popular music both echoed and influenced the youth culture. In the early sixties, college students listened to folk music. Songs protesting racism and injustice mirrored the idealistic, nonviolent commitment of the civil-rights movement. Bob Dylan sang hopefully of changes "blowin' in the wind" that would transform society. Then in 1964 Beatlemania swept the United States. Moving beyond their early romantic songs, the Beatles gloried in the youth culture's drugs ("I'd love to turn you on"), sex ("Why don't we do it in the road?"), and radicalism ("You say you want a revolution"). The Grateful Dead, Jefferson Airplane, and other bands launched "acid rock," which blended a heavy beat with lyrics extolling "sex, drugs, and rock-and-roll."

In August 1969, 400,000 young people gathered for the Woodstock festival in New York's Catskill Mountains to celebrate their vision of freedom and harmony. For three days and nights they reveled in the music of dozens of rock stars and openly shared drugs, sexual partners, and their contempt for the Establishment. The counterculture heralded Woodstock as the dawning of an era of love and peace, the Age of Aquarius.

In fact, the counterculture was disintegrating. Pilgrimages of "flower children" to San Francisco's Haight-Ashbury district and to New York's East Village in the mid-sixties had brought in their wake a train of muggers, rapists, and dope peddlers pushing hard drugs. With the decade's end came the shattering of the countercultural dream. In December 1969 the deranged Charles Manson and his "family" of runaways ritually murdered a pregnant movie actress and four of her friends. The tragedy revealed that something had gone profoundly wrong. Then a Rolling Stones concert at the Altamont Raceway near San Francisco deteriorated into a violent melee in which four concertgoers died. In July 1970 the Beatles disbanded. John Lennon sang, "The dream is over. What can I say?"

The Sexual Revolution

The counterculture's "do your own thing" idea of sex fit into an overall atmosphere of greater permissiveness. Indeed, many Americans became more open than before in pursuing sexual activity. These shifts in attitude and behavior unleashed a sexual revolution that would flourish until the mid-1980s, when the AIDS epidemic and the "graying" of the youth movement chilled the ardor of open sexuality.

Most commentators linked the sexual revolution to waning fears of unwanted pregnancy. In 1960 oral contraceptives reached the market, and by 1970, 12 million women were taking "the Pill." Even more women used the intrauterine device (later banned as unsafe) or the diaphragm for birth control. And states gradually legalized abortion. In 1970 in New York State, one fetus was legally aborted for every two babies born. The Supreme Court's *Roe* v. *Wade* decision (1973) struck down all remaining state laws infringing on a woman's right to abortion during the first three months of pregnancy.

The Court also threw out most laws restricting "sexually explicit" materials, and mass culture quickly exploited the new permissiveness. *Playboy* magazine featured ever-more-explicit erotica, and women's periodicals encouraged their readers to enjoy recreational sex. Barriers to public expression of sexuality fell as the Supreme Court extended First Amendment protection to books and films once banned as obscene and as Hollywood filled movie screens with scenes of explicit sex. Broadway presented plays featuring frontal nudity, mimed sex acts, and mock orgies, and even television presented frank discussions of once forbidden subjects.

The casual acceptance of sexuality influenced Americans' behavior. Many couples lived together without being married. Surveys showed that by the mid-1970s three-quarters of all college students had engaged in sexual intercourse before their senior year. The use of contraceptives (and to some extent, abortion) spread to women of all religious backgrounds—including Roman Catholics, despite the Catholic church's impassioned stand against "artificial" birth control.

In 1969 gay liberation emerged publicly from the semiunderground gay communities that had sprouted in major cities. By 1973 eight hundred openly gay groups were fighting for equal rights for homosexuals, the incorporation of lesbianism into the women's movement, and the removal of the stigmas of immorality and depravity attached to being gay. That year the American Psychiatric Association officially ended its classification of homosexuality as a mental disorder.

What some hailed as sexual liberation, others bemoaned as moral decay. Offended by "topless" bars, X-rated theaters, and "adult" bookstores, many Americans applauded politicians who promised a war on smut. The sexual revolution accentuated the "generation gap" that polarized the attitudes and behavior of many middle-class youths and their parents. Pubescent promiscuity, sex education in the schools, rising abortion rates, and homosexuals' "coming out of the closet" merged in many people's minds with pictures of student demonstrations and ghetto riots. In defense of embattled traditional morality, normally Democratic voters would swell the tide of conservatism as the sixties ended.

1968: The Politics of Strife

The social and cultural turmoil of the 1960s unfolded against a backdrop of frustration with the Vietnam War and an intensifying domestic political crisis. The stormy year 1968 brought these elements together explosively. The psychologically devastating Tet offensive was followed on the domestic scene by political assassinations, nominating conventions marred by violence, and new ghetto riots. Converging in the presidential campaign of 1968, the swirling currents of strife precipitated the first major realignment of American politics since the New Deal.

The Tet Offensive in Vietnam

In January 1968 liberal Democratic senator Eugene McCarthy of Minnesota, a Vietnam War critic, announced that he would challenge Lyndon B. Johnson for the presidential nomination. Pundits scoffed that McCarthy had no chance of unseating Johnson, who had won the presidency in 1964 by the largest margin in U.S. history. But McCarthy persisted, determined that at least one Democrat enter the primaries on an antiwar platform.

Shortly, America's hopes for victory in Vietnam sank, and with them LBJ's political fortunes. On January 31, the first day of Tet, the Vietnamese New Year, National Liberation Front (NLF) and North Vietnamese forces mounted a huge offensive, attacking more than one hundred towns in South Vietnam and even the U.S. Embassy in Saigon. U.S. troops repulsed the offensive after a month of ferocious fighting, inflicting a major military defeat on the communists.

The media, however, emphasized the staggering number of American casualties and the scope of the offensive. Americans at home reacted sharply to the realization that no area of South Vietnam was secure from the enemy and that a foe that the president had claimed was beaten could initiate such daring attacks. Many stopped believing reports of battlefield successes streaming from the White House and doubted that the United States could win the war at an acceptable cost.

After Tet, McCarthy's criticism of the war won new sympathizers. *Time, Newsweek,* and the *Wall Street Journal* published editorials urging a negotiated settlement. The nation's most respected newscaster, Walter Cronkite of CBS, observed that "it seems now more certain than ever that the bloody experience of Vietnam is to end in a stalemate." "If I've lost Walter," LBJ sighed, "then it's over. I've lost Mr. Average Citizen." Indeed, the president's approval rating dropped to a shocking 35 percent after Tet. The number of Americans who described themselves as prowar "hawks" slipped from 62 percent in January to 41 percent in March, while the antiwar "doves" jumped from 22 percent to 42 percent.

A Shaken President

Beleaguered, Johnson pondered a change in American policy. When the Joint Chiefs of Staff sought an additional 206,000 men for Vietnam, he consulted with advisers. Dean Acheson, the former secretary of state and a venerable Cold Warrior, told LBJ that "the Joint Chiefs of Staff don't know what they're talking about." Clark Clifford, the new secretary of defense, became convinced that the American course was hopeless.

Meanwhile, nearly 5,000 college students had swarmed to New Hampshire to stuff envelopes and ring doorbells for Eugene McCarthy. To be "Clean for Gene," they cut their long hair and dressed conservatively. McCarthy astonished the experts by winning nearly half the popular vote and twenty of twenty-four nominating-convention delegates in the primary contest of a state usually regarded as conservative.

After this upset, twice as many students converged on Wisconsin to canvass its more liberal Democratic voters, anticipating a resounding McCarthy triumph in the nation's second primary. Hurriedly, on March 16 Senator Robert Kennedy entered the Democratic contest, also promising to end the war. Projecting the familiar Kennedy glamour and magnetism, Kennedy was the one candidate whom Johnson feared could deny him renomination. Indeed, millions viewed Kennedy as the rightful heir to the White House. Appealing to minorities, the poor, and working-class ethnic whites, Kennedy became, according to one columnist, "our first politician for the pariahs, our great national outsider."

On March 31 LBJ informed a television audience that he was halting the bombing of North Vietnam. Saying that he wanted to devote all his efforts to the search for peace, Johnson then startlingly announced, "I shall not seek, and I will not accept, the nomination of my party for another term as your president." Embittered by the personal abuse that he had endured, and reluctant to polarize the nation further, the president called it quits. "The only difference between the Kennedy assassination and mine," he lamented, "is that I am alive and it has been more tortuous." Two days later, McCarthy trounced the president in the Wisconsin primary.

Assassinations and Turmoil

On April 4, three days after the Wisconsin primary, Martin Luther King, Jr. was killed in Memphis,

Tennessee, where he had gone to support striking sanitation workers. The assassin was James Earl Ray, a white escaped convict. As the news spread, African-American ghettos burst into violence in 125 cities. Twenty blocks of Chicago's West Side went up in flames, and Mayor Richard Daley ordered police to shoot to kill arsonists. In Washington, D.C., under night skies illuminated by 700 fires, army units in combat gear set up machine-gun emplacements outside the Capitol and White House. The rioting left 46 dead and 3,000 injured.

The Democratic contest for the presidential nomination became a three-cornered scramble as LBJ's vice president, Hubert Humphrey, entered the race as the standard-bearer of the New Deal coalition. McCarthy remained the candidate of the "new politics"—a moral crusade against war and injustice directed to affluent and educated liberals. And Kennedy campaigned as the tribune of the less privileged, the only candidate who appealed to white ethnics and the minority poor. But on June 5, 1968, as he celebrated victory in the California primary at a Los Angeles hotel, the brother of the murdered president was himself assassinated by a Palestinian refugee, Sirhan Sirhan, who loathed Kennedy's pro-Israel views.

The assassination crushed the dream of peace and racial justice, replacing it with despair. "I won't vote," one youth said. "Every good man we get they kill." Kennedy's death also dispirited the McCarthy forces and cleared the way for Humphrey, although some Democrats fumed that the party was about to nominate a prowar candidate who had not campaigned in a single primary.

Other Democrats turned to third-party candidate George Wallace or to Republican nominee Richard M. Nixon. Projecting a new image of maturity and inner tranquillity, Nixon allowed his vice-presidential running mate, Spiro Agnew, to play the shrill partisan. Nixon promised to end the war in Vietnam with honor, to restore "law and order," and to heed "the voice of the great majority of Americans, the forgotten Americans, the non-shouters, the non-demonstrators, those who do not break the law, people who pay their taxes and go to work, who send their children to school, who go to their churches, . . . who love this country." George Wallace tapped into the same wellspring of angry reaction as Nixon. Complaining that there was not "a dime's worth of difference" between the Democrats and the Republicans, Wallace pitched his message to blue-collar workers and southern whites fed up with antiwar protesters, black militants, hippies, and liberal intellectuals.

In August 1968 violence outside the Democratic National Convention in Chicago reinforced the appeal of both Wallace and Nixon. Thousands descended on the city to protest the Vietnam War, hoping to pressure the convention to repudiate the administration's policy. Radicals among the protesters wanted to provoke a confrontation to discredit the Democrats, and a handful ridiculed the system by creating their own "Youth International Party." These "Yippies'" guerrilla-theater stunts fascinated the media, which repeated with a straight face Yippie threats to dump LSD into Chicago's water system or to release greased pigs in the city's crowded Loop area.

Determined to avoid the rioting that had wracked Chicago after Martin Luther King, Jr.'s assassination, Mayor Richard Daley gave police a green light to attack "the hippies, the Yippies, and the flippies." The result was a police riot, televised live to a huge national audience. As protesters chanted, "The whole world is watching," Chicago police clubbed demonstrators and bystanders alike, beating them bloody or shoving them through plate-glass windows. The brutality on the streets overshadowed Humphrey's nomination and tore the Democrats further apart, fixing Americans' image of them as the party of dissent and disorder.

Conservative Resurgence

Nixon capitalized on the tumult. His TV campaign commercials flashed images of campus and ghetto uprisings. He portrayed himself as the representative of the Silent Majority, castigated the Supreme Court for safeguarding criminals at the expense of law-abiding citizens, and told white southerners that "our schools are for education—not integration."

George Wallace, also appealing to the broad revulsion against radicalism, burned across the political landscape. He stoked the fury of the working class against school integrationists, welfare mothers, and radical professors alike. Promising to keep peace even if it took "30,000 troops armed with three-foot bayonets," he vowed that "if any demonstrator ever lays down in front of my car, it'll be the last car he'll ever lie down in front of."

By September Wallace had climbed to 21 percent in voter-preference polls. Although many liked Wallace's views, few believed that he had any chance of winning and either did not vote or grudgingly supported one of his opponents. Still, nearly 14 percent of the electorate voted for Wallace in November.

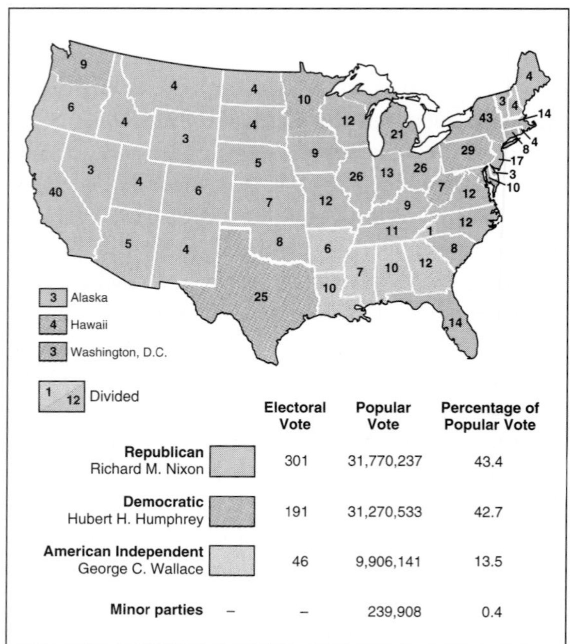

	Electoral Vote	Popular Vote	Percentage of Popular Vote
Republican Richard M. Nixon	301	31,770,237	43.4
Democratic Hubert H. Humphrey	191	31,270,533	42.7
American Independent George C. Wallace	46	9,906,141	13.5
Minor parties –	–	239,908	0.4

The Election of 1968

Despite a last-minute surge that brought Humphrey almost even with Nixon, the Republican candidate squeaked to victory with 43.4 percent of the popular vote. He garnered only 301 electoral votes, the narrowest victory since Woodrow Wilson's slender triumph in 1916. A conservative majority had supplanted the New Deal coalition—Humphrey received just 38 percent of the white vote.

The 57 percent of the electorate who chose Nixon or Wallace would dominate American presidential politics into the 1990s. While the national Democratic party fractured into a welter of contending groups, the Republicans attracted a new majority who lived in the suburbs and the Sun Belt, regarded the federal government as wasteful, disdained student radicalism and the forced busing of schoolchildren, and objected to special efforts to assist minorities and those on welfare. Yearning for restraint abroad and stability at home, a new majority looked hopefully to the new president to end the Vietnam War and to "bring us together again," as a campaign sign held by a young girl urged.

Nixon and World Politics

The new president, Richard M. Nixon, focused mainly on foreign affairs. Considering himself a master of realpolitik—a pragmatic approach stressing the advancement of the national interest rather than theoretical or ethical goals—he promoted a grand design to check Soviet expansionism and to promote global stability, to limit the nuclear-arms race, and to enhance the United States' economic well-being. Nixon recognized that the Vietnam War had eroded American support for similar armed interventions and that the Chinese-Soviet split had made the idea of monolithic communism obsolete. He planned to move the United States out of Vietnam and into an era of détente—an easing of tensions—with the communist world.

To manage diplomacy, Nixon chose Henry Kissinger, a refugee from Hitler's Germany and a Harvard professor of international relations who shared Nixon's desire to concentrate decision-making power in the White House. Both believed that effective diplomacy required secrecy, and they indulged their mutual passion for intrigue by keeping many of their actions hidden.

Vietnamization

The Nixon-Kissinger grand design meant ending the Vietnam War. The war was sapping American military strength, worsening inflation, and thwarting détente. In August 1969 the president unveiled what became known as the Nixon Doctrine, in which he redefined the United States' role in the Third World as that of a helpful partner rather than a military protector. In the future, Asian nations facing communist subversion could count on American financial and moral support, but they would have to defend themselves.

The Nixon Doctrine reflected the president's understanding of the war weariness of both the electorate and the U.S. troops in Vietnam. Johnson's decision to negotiate, rather than to escalate, had left American troops with the sense that nothing mattered except survival. Morale had plummeted and discipline had collapsed. Army desertions rocketed from 27,000 in 1967 to 76,000 in 1970, and the desertion rate in the marines rose even faster. Racial conflict among American soldiers became commonplace and drug use soared. The army reported more than 800 cases of "fragging"—enlisted men killing officers—and suspected as many as 1,400 more instances.

As fears and frustrations in U.S. forces mounted, so, too, did atrocities against the Vietnamese. Especially after 1967, growing cases of Americans dismembering enemy bodies, torturing captives, wantonly torching villages, and murdering civilians had come to light. In March 1968 an army unit led by an inexperienced lieutenant, William Calley, massacred several hundred defenseless civilians. Soldiers gang-raped girls, blew children apart with hand grenades, lined up women and old men in ditches and shot them, and then burned the village, My Lai. Revelations of such incidents, and the rising number of returned soldiers who joined Vietnam Veterans Against the War, had undercut the already diminished support for the war.

Despite pressure to end the war, Nixon was determined to salvage America's prestige. Seeking "peace with honor," Nixon pursued three simultaneous courses. First, he implemented "Vietnamization," replacing American troops with South Vietnamese. By 1972 U.S. forces in Vietnam would shrink from 500,000 to 30,000. Second, Nixon bypassed South Vietnamese leaders by sending Kissinger to negotiate secretly with North Vietnam's foreign minister, Le Duc Tho. Third, to force the communists to compromise despite U.S. withdrawal, the president radically escalated American bombing. To maximize the harm done to the enemy, Nixon in March 1969 secretly ordered the bombing of North Vietnamese supply routes in Cambodia and Laos and the intensification of bombing raids on North Vietnam. He told an aide, "We'll just slip the word to them that 'you know Nixon is obsessed about communism. We can't restrain him when he's angry—and he has his hand on the nuclear button'—and Ho Chi Minh . . . will be . . . begging for peace."

LBJ's War Becomes Nixon's War

But the secret B-52 raids against Cambodia neither made Hanoi beg for peace nor disrupted communist supply bases. They did, however, help to undermine the precarious stability of that tiny republic. In early 1970 North Vietnam increased its infiltration of troops into Cambodia, both to aid the Cambodian communists (the Khmer Rouge) and to facilitate the use of Cambodia as a staging area for attacks in South Vietnam. In turn, Nixon ordered a joint U.S.–South Vietnamese incursion into Cambodia at the end of April 1970. It was successful; the invaders seized large caches of arms and bought time for Vietnamization. But the costs were high. The invasion ended Cambodia's neutrality, widened the war throughout Indochina, and provoked massive American protests against the war, culminating in the student deaths at Kent State and Jackson State universities.

In 1971 Nixon continued to combine American withdrawal with renewed blows against the enemy. In February, at the administration's initiative, the South Vietnamese army invaded Laos to destroy communist bases there and to interfere with the flow of supplies southward from North Vietnam. The South Vietnamese, however, were routed. Em-

"The Blind Leading the Blind," 1971
Cartoonist David Levine depicted four presidents as being blind with regard to American involvement in Vietnam: Eisenhower, who first made an equivocal U.S. commitment in the faraway Asian nation; Kennedy, who deepened that commitment; Johnson, under whose administration the war escalated into a major conflict; and finally Nixon, who expanded American bombing targets to neutral Cambodia.
Reprinted with permission from *The New York Review of Books*, Copyright © 1971 NYREV, Inc.

boldened, in 1972 the North Vietnamese mounted the so-called Easter Offensive, their largest campaign since 1968. Nixon retaliated by mining North Vietnam's harbors and unleashing B-52s against its major cities.

America's Longest War Ends

On October 26, just days before the 1972 presidential election, Kissinger announced that "peace is at hand." The cease-fire agreement that he had secretly negotiated required the withdrawal of all American troops, provided for the return of U.S. prisoners of war, and allowed North Vietnamese troops to remain in South Vietnam.

Kissinger's negotiations had sealed Nixon's reelection, but Thieu refused to sign a cease-fire agreement permitting North Vietnamese troops to remain in the South. Angered by Thieu's rebuff, Le Duc Tho pressed for additional concessions. President Nixon again resorted to B-52 raids. The 1972 Christmas bombings of Hanoi and Haiphong, the most destructive of the war, roused fierce opposition domestically and globally but helped force the North Vietnamese to relent. Nixon's secret reassurance to Thieu that the United States would "respond with full force should the settlement be violated by North Vietnam" ended Saigon's recalcitrance.

The Paris Accords, signed in late January 1973, essentially reiterated the terms of the October truce. The agreement ended hostilities between the United States and North Vietnam but left unresolved the differences between North and South Vietnam, guaranteeing that Vietnam's future would yet be settled on the battlefield.

Thus ended America's longest war, a war that involved no vital U.S. interests, whose costs far outweighed potential benefits, and that intensified domestic problems and social divisions. It had cost 58,000 American deaths, 300,000 wounded, and at least $150 billion. Twenty percent of those who had served, nearly 500,000, received less-than-honorable discharges, a measure of the desertion rate, drug usage, strength of antiwar sentiment in the military, and immaturity of the troops (the average U.S. soldier in Vietnam was just nineteen years old, seven years younger than the average GI in World War II).

Virtually all who survived, wrote one marine, returned "as immigrants to a new world. For the culture we had known dissolved while we were in Vietnam, and the culture of combat we lived in . . . made us aliens when we returned." Beyond occasional media attention to the psychological difficulties that they faced in adjusting to civilian life, the nation paid little heed to its Vietnam veterans.

Instead, relieved that the long nightmare had ended, most Americans tried to forget the war. The bitterness of many veterans moderated with time. Few Americans gave much thought to how the war had devastated Vietnam, inflicting 2 million casualties. Laos, too, had suffered, but Cambodia had paid the highest price. After the war engulfed this previously peaceful land, the fanatical Khmer Rouge emerged victorious in 1975. Three million Cambodians—40 percent of the nation's population—died in the killings and "relocations" that followed.

Détente

Disengagement from Vietnam helped Nixon to achieve a turnabout in Chinese-American relations and détente with the communist superpowers. These developments, the most significant shift in U.S. foreign policy since the start of the Cold War, created a new relationship among the United States, China, and the Soviet Union.

The United States had refused to recognize the People's Republic of China in 1949. The United States had vetoed the admission of "Red China" to the United Nations and pressured American allies to restrict trade with the communist giant. But by 1969 a widening Chinese-Soviet split made the prospect of improved relations attractive to both Nixon and Mao Zedong. China wanted to end its isolation, the United States wanted to play one communist power against the other, and both wanted to thwart Soviet expansionism in Asia.

In fall 1970, Nixon opened what Kissinger called "the three-dimensional game" by calling China the People's Republic rather than Red China. In June 1971 Kissinger made a secret trip to China, and a month later Nixon announced that he would travel to the People's Republic "to seek the normalization of relations." In February 1972 the president's plane landed in China, beginning the first trip ever by a sitting American president to the largest nation in the world. Nixon toured the Great Wall and exchanged ceremonious toasts with Mao and Premier Zhou Enlai (Chou En-lai). Although differences between the two powers delayed official diplomatic relations until 1979, Nixon's visit signaled the end of more than twenty years of Chinese-American hostility.

Equally significantly, Nixon went to Moscow in May 1972. "There must be room in this world for two great nations with different systems to live together and work together," the president proclaimed. To that end, he concluded agreements with the Soviets on trade and technological cooperation (including the sale of $750 million in American grain) and, after the first Strategic Arms Limitation Talks (SALT I), signed two major arms-control pacts with Soviet leader Leonid Brezhnev. SALT I limited each nation to two antiballistic missile systems, froze each side's offensive nuclear missiles for five years, and committed both superpowers to strategic equality rather than nuclear superiority. Although it did not end the arms race, SALT I fundamentally altered U.S.–Soviet relations and moved both countries toward "peaceful coexistence." And in an election year it enhanced President Nixon's stature as a proponent of peace.

A Multipolar World

Not even rapproachement with China and détente with the Soviet Union could ensure global stability. In 1967 Israel, fearing that a massive Arab attack was imminent, launched a preemptive strike on its Arab neighbors, routing them in six days. In the war's aftermath, Israel occupied the Egyptian-

Nixon in China, 1972
American TV networks covered Nixon's dramatic visits to legendary landmarks such as the Great Wall, as well as his impromptu conversations with the Chinese people. One reporter remarked that "the White House was playing [the visit] as a pageant, not as a news story."

controlled Sinai and Gaza Strip, the Jordanian-ruled West Bank and East Jerusalem, and Syria's Golan Heights. The Middle East was more volatile than ever.

Israel promised to give up most of the occupied lands in exchange for direct negotiations and peace, but the Arab states refused to negotiate with Israel or to recognize its right to exist. The Palestinian population turned to the Palestine Liberation Organization (PLO), which had been founded in 1964, to defend its interests. The PLO sought international recognition of Palestinian rights and called for Israel's destruction. Competing PLO factions hijacked Western airliners, raided Israel, and murdered Israeli athletes at the 1972 Olympic games. To retaliate, Israel assassinated PLO agents abroad and bombed PLO bases and installations in refugee camps, especially in Lebanon.

War exploded again in 1973 when Egypt and Syria launched surprise attacks against Israel on the Jewish high holy day of Yom Kippur. Israel reeled under the attacks but, with military equipment airlifted by the United States, held firm and then counterattacked. In retaliation, the oil-producing Arab states, through the Organization of Petroleum Exporting Countries (OPEC), embargoed shipments of crude oil to the United States and its allies from October 1973 to March 1974. Acute oil shortages and soaring costs—the price of a barrel of crude oil soared from $3 to more than $12—fed inflation and spurred the use of nuclear power.

The Nixon administration, which had generally sided with Israel, now sought better relations with moderate Arab regimes in order to isolate Arab hard-liners. The dual shocks of the energy crisis at home and renewed Soviet influence among Arab hard-liners spurred Nixon and Kissinger to win Egypt for the prowestern camp, to conciliate the oil-rich Arab rulers of the Persian Gulf, and to force Arab-Israeli peace talks. Beginning in October 1973, Kissinger pursued "shuttle diplomacy," flying from capital to capital to engineer disengagement accords between Israel and Egypt, and Israel and Syria. He also persuaded OPEC to end its oil embargo. Kissinger's diplomacy, designed to establish the United States as the sole Middle Eastern peace-

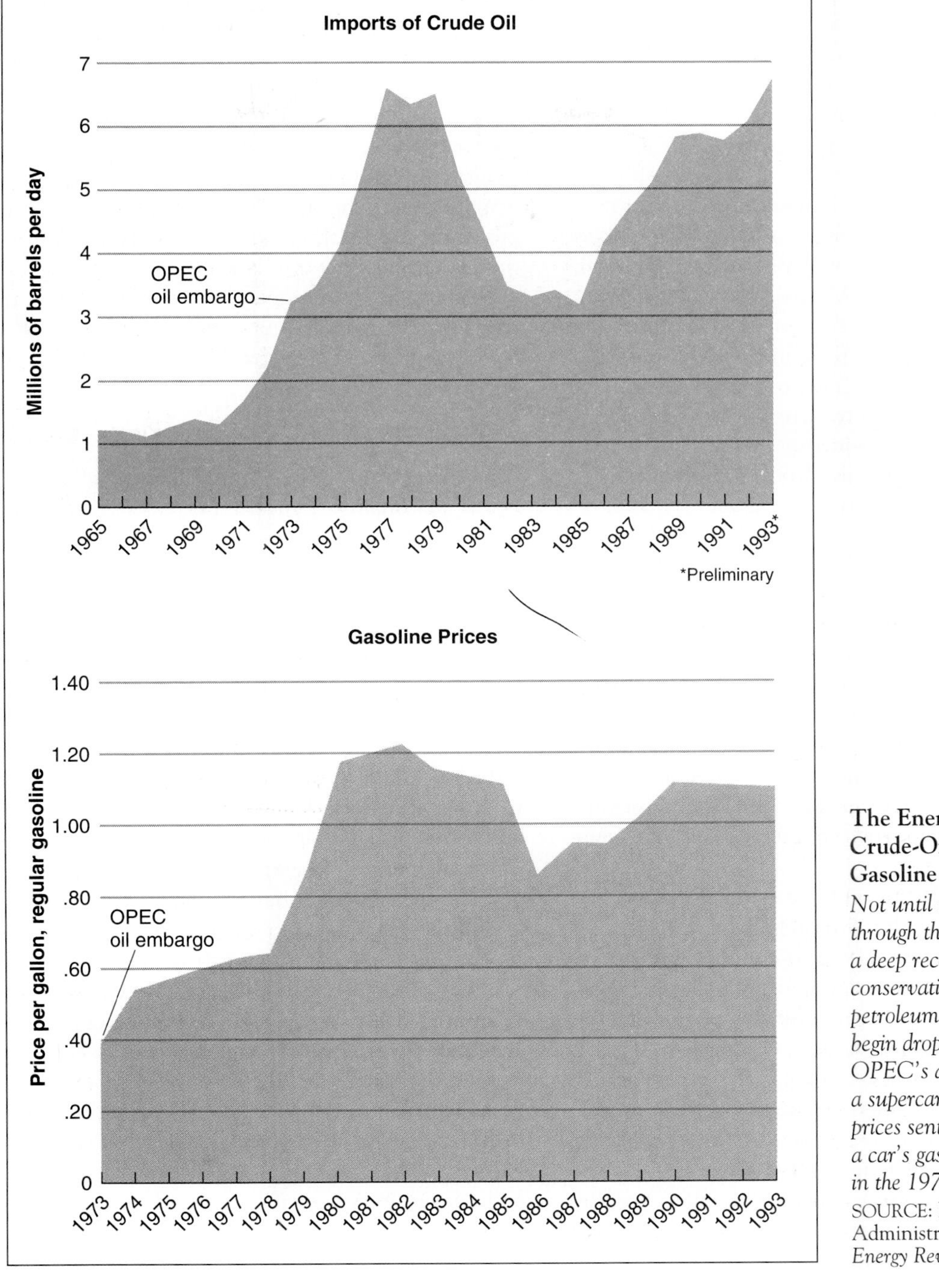

The Energy Crisis: Crude-Oil Imports and Gasoline Prices

Not until the 1980s, through the combination of a deep recession and fuel conservation, did U.S. petroleum imports finally begin dropping off (top). OPEC's ability to act as a supercartel in setting oil prices sent the cost of filling a car's gas tank skyrocketing in the 1970s (bottom).

SOURCE: Energy Information Administration, *Annual Energy Review*, 1993.

maker, had limited but notable success. Splits among the Arabs widened, Egypt moved closer to Washington, and Syria broke with Egypt. The PLO itself split between moderate and hard-line factions, and some Palestinian insurgents struck all the harder against Israel and against U.S. citizens abroad.

To counter Soviet influence and to protect American interests, the Nixon administration liberally supplied arms to the shah of Iran, Reza Pahlavi; to President Ferdinand Marcos in the Philippines; and to the white-supremacist regime of South Africa. Nixon-Kissinger realpolitik based American aid on a nation's willingness to oppose the Soviet Union, not on the nature of its government. Thus, the administration provided aid to antidemocratic regimes in Brazil and South Korea as well as to Portuguese colonial authorities in Angola.

When Chileans elected a Marxist, Salvador Allende, president in 1970, Nixon secretly funneled $10 million to the Central Intelligence Agency (CIA) to fund opponents of Allende's leftist regime. The United States also cut off economic aid to Chile, blocked private banks from granting loans, and successfully pressed the World Bank to drop Chile's credit rating. In September 1973 a military junta overthrew the Chilean government and killed Allende. Nixon quickly recognized the dictatorship, and economic aid and private investment again flowed to Chile.

The administration's active opposition to Allende reflected the extent to which American policy remained committed to containing communist influence. At the same time, Nixon understood the limits of U.S. power and the changed realities of world affairs. Discarding the vision of a bipolar world that had shaped American foreign policy since 1945, Nixon took advantage of the Chinese-Soviet split to improve American relations with both nations. The administration also ended American involvement in Vietnam and improved the U.S. position in the Middle East. Most significantly, the politician who had built his reputation as a staunch Cold Warrior initiated a new era of détente with the communist powers.

Domestic Problems and Divisions

Although Richard M. Nixon yearned to be remembered as an international statesman, domestic affairs kept intruding. In some ways, Nixon displayed domestic creativity, reforming welfare and abandoning traditional Republican hands-off conservatism to grapple with inflation and other complex economic problems. But another side of the Nixon administration appealed to the darker recesses of national character and intensified the fears and divisions among Americans. This underside was rooted in the complex character of Richard M. Nixon himself.

Richard Nixon: Man and Politician

Close observers of Nixon noted the multiple levels of his personality. Beneath the calculated public persona of the politician lurked a shadowy man who rarely revealed himself. Nixon the politician was highly intelligent, with phenomenal endurance and a capacity for total concentration. But the public Nixon also displayed the rigid self-control of a man monitoring his own every move. When the private Nixon did emerge, he was suspicious, insecure, and filled with anger. Nixon's conviction that enemies lurked on all sides, waiting to destroy him, verged on paranoia. He saw his life as a series of crises to be met and surmounted. A driven man, he sought to annihilate his partisan enemies, especially the "eastern liberal establishment" that had long opposed him.

Probing the source of his insecurities, some observers have viewed Nixon as the classic outsider: reared in pinched surroundings, physically awkward, unable to relate easily to others. Suspicious that others more cultivated and privileged were laughing at him, he sneered at "the so-called best circles in America." Many Americans shared his biases. As historian Garry Wills observed, Nixon's strengths and deficiencies uncannily matched what was "best and weakest in America."

In the early Nixon years, the president's strengths were most apparent. Nixon spoke of national reconciliation, took bold initiatives internationally, and dealt with domestic problems responsibly. But the darker side would ultimately prevail and drive him from office in disgrace.

The Nixon Presidency

Nixon began his presidency with a moderation reminiscent of Eisenhower. His calm rhetoric and selection of a well-qualified cabinet of flexible conservatives promised the respite from unrest that most Americans desired. Symbolic of this positive start, the nation joined the new president in celebrating the first successful manned mission to the moon on July 20, 1969, as astronaut Neil Armstrong descended from the lunar lander *Eagle* to the surface of the Sea of Tranquillity, announcing to enthralled television audiences back on Earth, "That's one small step for man, one giant leap for mankind."

The first newly elected president since 1849 whose party controlled neither house of Congress, Nixon initially approved a moderate extension of Great Society programs. He signed bills to increase social-security benefits, to build subsidized housing, to expand the Job Corps, and to grant the vote to eighteen-year-olds. Although Nixon sided with corporate leaders who claimed that the cost of meeting stringent environmental standards would make U.S. industry uncompetitive with foreign enterprises, the Democrat-controlled Congress enacted legislation targeting the adverse effects of material growth. Laws passed during the Nixon presidency limited pesticide use, protected endangered species, regulated consumer-product safety, and established maximum levels for the emission of pollutants into the air. The National Environmental Policy Act (1969) required environmental-impact analysis statements for proposed federal projects and established the Environmental Protection Agency in 1970. Congress also created the Occupational Safety and Health Administration to ensure workers' safety and well-being.

Growing environmental awareness culminated in the celebration of the first Earth Day in April 1970. Earth Day spotlighted such problems as thermal pollution, dying lakes, oil spills, and dwindling resources. The occasion also introduced Americans to the idea of "living lightly on the earth." Organic gardening, vegetarianism, solar power, recycling, and preventive health care became popular. Also in 1970, Nixon's Commission on Population Growth and the American Future promoted zero population growth, the idea that the birthrate should not exceed the death rate.

Conservatives grumbled as government grew larger and more intrusive and as race-conscious employment policies, including quotas, were mandated for all federal contractors. And conservatives grew nearly apoplectic when Nixon unveiled the Family Assistance Plan (FAP) in 1969. A bold effort to overhaul the welfare system, FAP proposed a guaranteed annual income for all Americans. Caught between liberals who considered it inadequate and conservatives who opposed it on principle, FAP made it through the House but died in the Senate.

Another Nixon innovation, revenue sharing, fared better. Nixon hailed what he termed "the New Federalism" as a way to reverse the flow of power, and funds, from the states to Washington, but the accompanying slashes in federal spending for social services left some financially pressed cities worse off than before.

A Troubled Economy

Nixon inherited the dire fiscal consequences of Lyndon B. Johnson's effort to wage the Vietnam War and finance the Great Society, to have both "guns and butter," by deficit financing. Nixon faced what was then considered a whopping budget deficit, $25 billion, and an inflation rate of 5 percent. A $2.5 billion tax cut in 1972 worsened the problem, so Nixon encouraged the Federal Reserve Board to raise interest rates and contract the money supply. Inflation continued to rise, but economic growth declined and unemployment soared, a combination of inflation and stagnation soon christened "stagflation."

Throughout 1971 Nixon lurched from policy to policy. Declaring, "I am now a Keynesian," he increased deficit spending to stimulate the private sector; gross national product spurted, as did the budget deficit, but economic decline continued. To the consternation of America's allies and trading partners, he devalued the dollar, allowing it to "float" in international monetary exchanges in a desperate attempt to correct the balance-of-payment deficit. Finally, Nixon froze wages, prices, and rents for ninety days, a bandaid that worked until after the 1972 election. Then he again reversed course, replacing controls with voluntary—and ineffective—guidelines. Nonetheless, inflation and sluggish growth would dog the U.S. economy throughout the decade.

Law and Order

Despite his public appeals for order, Nixon actually intensified social tensions when he tried to outflank George Wallace and appeal to southern whites, northern ethnics, blue-collar workers, and suburbanites—voters that political strategist Kevin Phillips vividly described as "in motion between a Democratic past and a Republican future." This strategy included a tough stand against crime, drug use, and domestic radicalism.

To combat the militants he despised, Nixon used full federal-government resources. The Internal Revenue Service (IRS) audited the tax returns of antiwar and civil-rights activists; the Small Business Administration denied them loans; and the FBI illegally wiretapped them. The FBI also infiltrated SDS and black radical groups with agents who, to discredit them, provoked violence within the movements. The Justice Department and the FBI worked with local officials to arrest Black Panthers on dubious charges. And the CIA illegally investigated and compiled dossiers on thousands of American dissidents. To focus the nation's fears on the radical threat, Nixon authorized the Department of Justice to prosecute antiwar activists and militant blacks in highly publicized trials.

Nixon also took steps to crush his opponents. Using unspent 1968 campaign funds, he created a secret task force in 1969 to spy on liberal columnists and congressional critics. Seeing political adversaries as personal enemies, Nixon compiled an "enemies list" of prominent Americans to be harassed by the government. "Anyone who opposes us, we'll destroy," warned a top White House official. "As a matter of fact, anyone who doesn't support us, we'll destroy."

In 1970 Nixon widened his offensive against the antiwar movement by approving the Huston Plan, which would use the CIA and FBI in various illegal missions. The plan called for extensive wiretapping and electronic surveillance, break-ins to find or plant evidence of illegal activity, and a new agency to centralize domestic covert operations under White House supervision. But FBI chief J. Edgar Hoover opposed the Huston Plan as a threat to the FBI's independence. Blocked, Nixon secretly

Inflation, 1946–1993

Inflation, which had been moderate during the two decades following the Second World War, began to soar with the escalation of the war in Vietnam in the mid-1960s. In 1979 and 1980 the nation experienced double-digit inflation in two consecutive years for the first time since World War I.

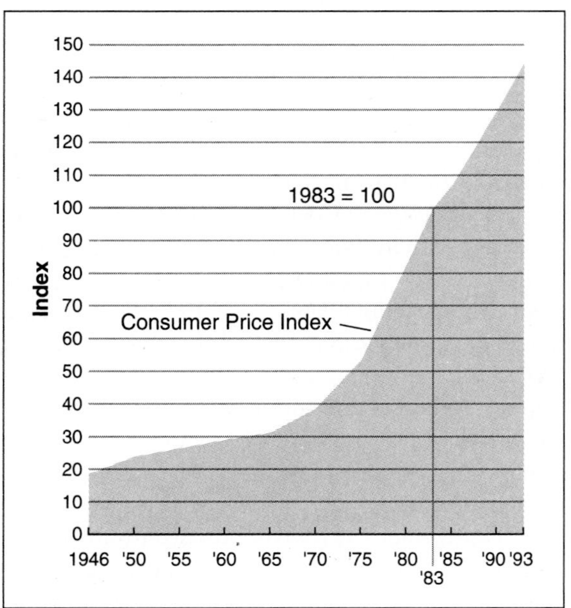

created his own White House unit to discredit his opposition and to ensure executive security. Nicknamed the plumbers because of their assignment to plug government leaks, the team was headed by ex-FBI agent G. Gordon Liddy and former CIA operative E. Howard Hunt.

The plumbers first targeted Daniel Ellsberg, a former Defense Department analyst who had turned over to the press the secret Pentagon Papers, a documentary history of U.S. involvement in Vietnam. On June 13 the *New York Times* began publishing the Pentagon Papers, which revealed a long history of government lies to foreign leaders, Congress, and the American people. Although the papers contained nothing damaging about his administration, Nixon feared that they would undermine public trust in government and establish a precedent for publishing classified material. The Supreme Court ultimately ruled that the documents' publication was protected under the First Amendment. Livid, Nixon directed the Justice Department to indict Ellsberg for theft and ordered the plumbers to discredit him. In August 1971 Liddy and Hunt broke into the office of Ellsberg's psychiatrist in search of information against the man who had become an instant hero to the antiwar movement.

The Southern Strategy

While attacking radicalism, Nixon courted whites upset by the drive for racial equality, especially southerners fearful of school desegregation. The administration testified before Congress against expanding the Voting Rights Act of 1965 and for modifications to the Fair Housing Act of 1968 that would have crippled its enforcement. Moreover, the administration pleaded for the postponement of desegregation in Mississippi schools and filed suits to prohibit the busing of children to desegregate schools. In 1971 when the Supreme Court upheld busing as a constitutional and necessary tactic, Nixon condemned the ruling and asked Congress to enact a moratorium on busing.

The strategy of wooing white southerners dictated Nixon's Supreme Court nominations. To reverse the Warren court's liberalism, he named strict constructionists, judges who would not "meddle" in social issues or be "soft" on criminals. In 1969 he appointed conservative judge Warren Burger as chief justice. Nixon then tried to appoint a Deep South conservative, but the Senate rejected both of his nominees. However, by 1972 Nixon had succeeded in appointing to the Supreme Court three justices with reputations as strict constructionists: Harry Blackmun of Minnesota, Lewis Powell of Virginia, and William Rehnquist of Arizona. The Nixon appointees would steer the court in a moderate direction. Although ruling liberally in cases involving abortion, desegregation, and the death penalty, the Burger court would shift to the right in rulings on civil liberties, community censorship, and police power.

The Silent Majority Speaks

To build a Republican majority, Nixon denounced the Democrats as the party of New Left "hooligans, hippies, and radical liberals," blaming them for fostering drug use, supporting abortion, and cultivating social disorder. As the 1970 elections neared, Nixon encouraged his vice president, Spiro T. Agnew, to step up attacks on the liberal opposition. Crisscrossing the nation, Agnew assailed students as "parasites of passions," Democrats as "sniveling handwringers," intellectuals as "an effete corps of intellectual snobs," and the news media as "nattering nabobs of negativism." Although liberals deplored Agnew's alarming alliterative allegations, a number of Democratic candidates joined their Republican opponents in appealing for a restoration of law and order, patriotism, and family values. The 1970 elections were a draw, with the Democrats gaining nine House seats and the Republicans two Senate seats.

The Election of 1972

Nixon's reelection in 1972 appeared certain. He counted on his diplomatic successes and his winding

The Election of 1972

Candidates	*Parties*	*Electoral Vote*	*Popular Vote*	*Percentage of Popular Vote*
RICHARD M. NIXON	Republican	520	47,169,911	60.7
George S. McGovern	Democratic	17	29,170,383	37.5

down of the Vietnam War to win over moderate voters. He expected his southern strategy and law-and-order posture to attract Wallace voters. Continuing Democratic divisions boosted Nixon's optimism.

Nixon's only major worry, another third-party candidacy by George Wallace, vanished on May 15, 1972. During a campaign stop, Wallace was shot and paralyzed from the waist down. He withdrew from the race, leaving Nixon a monopoly on the white-backlash, law-and-order vote.

The Senate's most outspoken dove, George McGovern of South Dakota, capitalized on the support of antiwar activists to blitz the Democratic primaries. New party rules requiring state delegations to include minority, female, and youthful delegates in approximate proportion to their numbers aided the liberal McGovern. A disapproving labor leader complained about "too much hair and not enough cigars at this convention," but McGovern won the nomination on the first ballot.

Perceptions of McGovern as inept and radical drove away all but the most committed supporters. After pledging to stand behind his vice-presidential running mate, Thomas Eagleton, "1,000 percent" when it became known that Eagleton had received electric-shock therapy for depression, McGovern dumped Eagleton and suffered the embarrassment of having several prominent Democrats decline to run with him. McGovern's endorsement of income redistribution, decriminalization of marijuana, immediate withdrawal from Vietnam, a $30 billion defense-budget cut, and pardons for those who had fled the United States to avoid the draft exposed him to GOP ridicule as the candidate of the radical fringe.

Meanwhile, Nixon, remembering his narrow loss to Kennedy in 1960 as well as his narrow victory over Humphrey in 1968, left no stone unturned. He created the Committee to Re-Elect the President (CREEP) to do everything necessary to ensure his reelection, and he appointed Attorney General John Mitchell as its head. The millions in contributions collected by CREEP financed a series of "dirty tricks" that spread dissension among Democrats and paid for a special internal espionage unit to spy on the opposition. Led by Liddy and Hunt of the White House plumbers, the Republican undercover team received Mitchell's approval to wiretap telephones at the Democratic National Committee headquarters in the Watergate apartment-office complex in Washington. Early one morning in June 1972, a security guard foiled the break-in to install the bugs. Arrested were James McCord, the security coordinator of CREEP, and several other Liddy and Hunt associates.

A White House cover-up began immediately. Nixon said "categorically" that "no one in the White House staff, no one in this administration, presently employed, was involved in this bizarre incident." Nixon ordered staff members to expunge Hunt's name from the White House telephone directory, to buy the silence of those arrested with $400,000 in hush money and hints of a presidential pardon, and to direct the CIA to halt the FBI's investigation of the Watergate break-in on the pretext that the probe would damage national security.

With the McGovern campaign a shambles and the Watergate incident seemingly contained, Nixon won the election overwhelmingly, amassing nearly 61 percent of the popular vote and 520 electoral votes. Strongly supported only by African-Americans, Mexican-Americans, and low-income voters, McGovern carried just Massachusetts and the District of Columbia. The election solidified the 1968 realignment.

However, the GOP gained only twelve seats in the House, and the Democrats increased their Senate majority by two. The outcome demonstrated the growing difficulty of unseating incumbents, the prevalence of ticket splitting among voters, and the decline of party loyalty. Only 55.7 percent of eligible voters went to the polls, down from 63.8 percent in 1960. Whether indifferent to politics or disenchanted with the choices offered, a growing number of citizens no longer bothered to participate in the electoral process.

The Crisis of the Presidency

In his second inaugural, Nixon pledged to make the next four years "the best four years in American history." Ironically, they would rank among its sorriest. His vice president would resign in disgrace, his closest confidants would go to jail, and he would serve barely a year and a half of his second term before resigning to avoid impeachment.

The Watergate Cover-up

The scheme to conceal links between the White House and the accused Watergate burglars had succeeded during the 1972 campaign. But after the election, federal judge John Sirica refused to accept the defendants' claim that they had acted on their own. Threatening severe prison sentences, Sirica coerced James McCord of CREEP into confessing that highly placed White House aides knew in advance of the break-in and that the defendants had committed perjury during the trial. McCord also stated that the White House had pressured him and his codefendants "to plead guilty and remain silent." Two *Washington Post* reporters, Carl Bernstein and Bob Woodward, following clues furnished by "Deep Throat," an unnamed informant, wrote a succession of front-page stories tying the break-in to illegal contributions and "dirty tricks" by CREEP.

In February 1973 the Senate established the Special Committee on Presidential Campaign Activities to investigate. As the trail of revelations led closer to the Oval Office, Nixon fired his special counsel, John Dean, who refused to be a scapegoat. On April 30 the president announced the resignations of his principal aides, H. R. Haldeman and John Ehrlichman, and pledged to get to the bottom of the scandal. He appointed Secretary of Defense Elliott Richardson, a Boston patrician of unassailable integrity, as his new attorney general and, bowing to Senate demands, instructed Richardson to appoint a special Watergate prosecutor with broad powers of investigation and subpoena. Richardson selected Archibald Cox, a Harvard law professor and Democrat.

In May the special Senate committee began a televised investigation. Chaired by Sam Ervin of North Carolina, an expert on constitutional law, the hearings revealed the existence of the "enemies list," the president's use of governmental agencies to harass his opponents, and administration favors in return for illegal campaign donations. Most damaging to Nixon, the hearings exposed the White House's active involvement in the Watergate cover-up. But the Senate still lacked concrete evidence of the president's criminality, the "smoking gun" that would prove Nixon's guilt. Because it was simply his word against that of John Dean, who testified that Nixon personally directed the cover-up, the president expected to survive the crisis.

Then another presidential aide revealed that Nixon had installed a secret taping system that recorded all conversations in the Oval Office. The Ervin committee and Cox insisted on access to the tapes, but Nixon refused, claiming executive privilege. In October when Cox sought a court order to obtain the tapes, Nixon ordered Attorney General Richardson to fire him. Richardson resigned in protest, as did the deputy attorney general. The third-ranking official in the Department of Justice, Solicitor General Robert Bork, dumped Cox. The furor raised by the "Saturday Night Massacre" sent Nixon's public-approval rating plunging downward. As Nixon named a new special prosecutor, Leon Jaworski, the House Judiciary Committee began impeachment proceedings.

A President Disgraced

Adding to Nixon's woes that October, Vice President Agnew, charged with income-tax evasion and acceptance of bribes, pleaded no contest—"the full equivalent of a plea of guilty," according to the trial judge. Agnew left office with a three-year suspended sentence and a $10,000 fine. Popular House minority leader Gerald R. Ford of Michigan replaced Agnew. Meanwhile, the unrelenting legal and political processes unfolding against Nixon made his continued presidency highly uncertain.

In March 1974 Jaworski and the House Judiciary Committee subpoenaed the president for the tape recordings of Oval Office conversations after the Watergate break-in. In April Nixon released edited transcripts of the tapes, filled with gaps and the phrase "expletive deleted." Despite the excisions, the president emerged as petty and vindictive. Although there was no smoking gun directly implicating the president, Nixon's standing was destroyed.

Nixon's sanitized version of the tapes satisfied neither Jaworski nor the House Judiciary Committee. Both pressed for unedited tapes. In late July the Supreme Court rebuffed the president's claim of executive privilege. Chief Justice Burger cited the president's obligation to provide evidence necessary for the due process of law and ordered Nixon to release the unexpurgated tapes.

On July 27 the House Judiciary Committee adopted the first article of impeachment, obstruction of justice for impeding the Watergate investigation. On July 29 the majority, including Republicans as well as Democrats, voted to condemn the president's abuse of power, especially his partisan use of the FBI and IRS. On July 30 the committee added as a third article of impeachment the president's contempt of Congress in refusing to obey a congressional subpoena for the tapes.

Nixon was checkmated. On August 5, 1974, he conceded in a televised address that he had withheld relevant evidence. He then surrendered the tapes, which contained the smoking gun proving that the president had ordered the cover-up, obstructed justice, subverted one government agency to prevent another from investigating a crime, and lied about his role for more than two years. Shocked Nixon loyalists on the Judiciary Committee switched their votes to favor impeachment. Nixon wavered, refusing to surrender, until Republican leaders informed him of the certainty of his impeachment and conviction. On August 9, 1974, Richard M. Nixon became the first American president to resign. Gerald Ford took office as the nation's first chief executive who had not been elected either president or vice president.

CONCLUSION

The conclusion of the Watergate scandal ended a period of extraordinary rancor. It capped a turbulent time in which one president elected by a record majority had feared to run for reelection, and his successor had won the next greatest percentage of the popular vote, only to resign in disgrace. Coming on the heels of the U.S. withdrawal from Vietnam, the energy crisis, and a deteriorating economy, Watergate intensified Americans' loss of confidence in their government.

American optimism is closely linked to the belief that Washington can govern effectively. In the 1940s and 1950s, people had faith in their government, which had decisively won World War II, ushered in unprecedented prosperity, provided social security, and built an impressive highway system. In the 1960s Presidents Kennedy and Johnson had raised expectations about goals that they could not fulfill: better schooling, good health care at reasonable cost, reduced crime, and harmonious race relations. By the middle of the decade, the percentage of Americans who trusted Washington to do the right thing had dropped precipitously.

Capitalizing on anti-Washington, antiliberal sentiment, Richard M. Nixon fashioned a new majority coalition to replace FDR's New Deal coalition. Although Nixon masterfully reduced international tensions, he fell victim to the gulf between popular expectations and continued domestic problems. Promising to unite a divided people, he polarized them further. Stressing law and order, he employed illegal means to secure his goals and then tried to conceal the facts. Nearly fifty Nixon administration officials were indicted for fraud, extortion, perjury, obstruction of justice, and other crimes, and more than a score, including the attorney general, went to prison.

Nixon's successor, Gerald R. Ford, proclaimed, "Our long national nightmare is over." But as Americans in 1976 contemplated the bicentennial of the Declaration of Independence, the malaise spread. Disillusioned with the mendacity of the nation's leaders, panicked by the end of the postwar economic boom, and helpless before foreign terrorists, oil sheiks, and street criminals, a pessimistic nation limited its ability to deal with such problems by deep distrust of its own political system.

CHRONOLOGY

1960 Birth-control pill marketed.

1964 Berkeley Free Speech Movement.

1967 March on the Pentagon.
Israeli-Arab Six-Day War.

1968 Tet Offensive.
President Lyndon Johnson announces that he will not seek reelection.
Martin Luther King, Jr. assassinated; race riots sweep nation.
Student strike at Columbia University.
Robert F. Kennedy assassinated.
Violence mars Democratic convention in Chicago.
Vietnam peace talks open in Paris.
Richard Nixon elected president.

1969 *Apollo 11* lands first Americans on the moon.
Nixon begins withdrawal of U.S. troops from Vietnam.
Woodstock festival.
March Against Death in Washington, D.C.
My Lai massacre.

1970 United States invades Cambodia.
Students killed at Kent State University and Jackson State College.
Nixon proposes Huston Plan.
Environmental Protection Agency established.
Earth Day first celebrated.

1971 United States invades Laos.
New York Times publishes Pentagon Papers.
Nixon institutes wage-and-price freeze.
South Vietnam invades Laos.

1972 Nixon visits China and the Soviet Union.
Strategic Arms Limitation Talks (SALT I) agreement approved.
Watergate break-in.
Nixon reelected in landslide victory.
Christmas bombing of North Vietnam.

1973 Vietnam cease-fire agreement signed.
Trial of Watergate burglars.
Senate establishes Special Committee on Presidential Campaign Activities to investigate Watergate.
President Salvador Allende murdered in Chile.
Vice President Spiro Agnew resigns; Gerald Ford appointed vice president.
Roe v. *Wade*.
Yom Kippur War; Organization of Petroleum Exporting Countries (OPEC) begins embargo of oil to the West.

1974 Supreme Court orders Nixon to release Watergate tapes.
House Judiciary Committee votes to impeach Nixon.
Nixon resigns; Ford becomes president.

FOR FURTHER READING

William Berman, *America's Right Turn: From Nixon to Bush* (1994). A valuable overview of the politics of conservatism.

William Chafe, *Never Stop Running: Allard Lowenstein and the Struggle to Save American Liberalism* (1993). The strife of the 1960s through the prism of a key liberal activist.

Kim McQuaid, *The Anxious Years* (1989). A chronicle of national passions and struggles from 1968 to Nixon's resignation.

Herbert Parmet, *Richard Nixon and His America* (1990). A solid survey of the presidency and the era.

W. J. Rorabaugh, *Berkeley at War* (1989). A lively analysis of the events that rocked Berkeley in the 1960s.

Robert Schulzinger, *Henry Kissinger: Doctor of Diplomacy* (1989). A balanced examination of Kissinger-Nixon foreign policies.

CHAPTER 32

Turning Inward: Society and Politics from Ford to Reagan

In the fifteen years after Watergate, personal preoccupations overshadowed public issues for many people, despite urgent national problems. Spiraling inflation gave rise to gnawing economic worries. The 1980 presidential election installed an administration committed to the free-enterprise system.

But however much Americans yearned to concentrate on private concerns, the world intruded. The later 1970s brought new crises in the Middle East and Central America even as American-Soviet relations deteriorated. This return to the bleakness of the early Cold War continued in the early 1980s. President Ronald Reagan, a long-time Cold Warrior as well as a free-market champion, pushed for big military spending increases and indulged in anti-Soviet rhetoric, galvanizing a vigorous antinuclear movement in this otherwise passive political era.

(Right) Hanging Jimmy Carter in effigy in Tehran, Iran

After the Sixties: Changing Social and Cultural Contours

Both the afterglow of the 1960s activism and reaction against that turbulent decade shaped American social and cultural trends in the 1970s and beyond. Environmentalism and feminism gained ground, but the violence that scarred the years from 1968 to 1970 turned many young adults toward personal goals, materialism, and self-indulgence. Yet millions of Americans remained mired in poverty. For example, although many African-Americans moved into the middle class, others became even more deeply alienated and cut off from the traditional avenues of upward mobility.

Radicals in the 1960s had celebrated sexual freedom and feminists had demanded reproductive choice, but the post-1970 years brought sexual caution as acquired immune deficiency syndrome (AIDS) took a fearsome toll and abortion rights became the center of fierce debate. As in the 1920s, individuals unsettled by rapid change sought moral certitude and spiritual solace, and organized religion prospered. And all these shifts were inextricably intertwined with political and economic developments.

America Turns Inward

The focus of social activism shifted after 1968, and demands for reform were as likely to come from the Right as the Left. The women's movement gained ground in the seventies. And in the aftermath of Rachel Carson's *Silent Spring* (1962) and Great Society programs, environmental consciousness remained high; Americans expressed concern about air and water pollution and endangered wildlife such as whales and certain species of owls and moths. In the late 1970s, concerns about nuclear power intensified, especially when a nearly catastrophic accident crippled the Three-Mile Island nuclear-power plant near Harrisburg, Pennsylvania.

For millions of young people, a sour political climate and a constricted economy acted against civic idealism. On the Left, the wreckage of the Kennedy-Johnson liberal consensus and the fragmentation of the New Left produced a vacuum of political leadership; on the Right, the Watergate debacle temporarily had the same effect. With politics in disarray, personal concerns beckoned, and President Ronald Reagan's message of individualism easily translated into self-centered materialism. Apart from calls for more military spending, Reagan offered no national agenda. The "campus radical" of the sixties became the "yuppie" (young urban professional), preoccupied with physical fitness, psychic harmony, and material consumption. But self-absorption too frequently became selfishness; writer Tom Wolfe christened yuppies the "Me Generation."

Mass media and an expanding entertainment industry drew Americans of all ages into the pursuit of private goals and pleasures. Average daily TV viewing crept upward from six hours in 1970 to seven hours by 1990. Prime-time soap operas such as "Dallas" and "Falcon Crest" engrossed millions. Super Bowl extravaganzas also drew huge audiences. Cable television featured specialized programming for everything from the stock market to rock music, and first-run movies on HBO and other "premium" channels offered even more choices. The major networks meanwhile watched their market share shrink. Disneyworld, opened in Florida in 1982, thrived, while blockbuster movies such as *Jaws*, *Close Encounters of the Third Kind*, *E.T.*, and *Star Wars* offered escapist fare for millions. Professional sports drew huge television audiences, and superstar sports celebrities earned multimillion-dollar salaries and signed multimillion-dollar product endorsements. Videocassette recorders (VCRs) allowed Americans to "time-shift" by taping TV shows for later viewing and to rent movies on cassette. By the early 1990s, 70 percent of U.S. households had VCRs. Entertainment became privatized as families could "go to the movies" at home. Using laser beams to digitize sound waves, compact discs (CDs) offered remarkably high-quality sound. Americans cast aside their stereos and bought millions of CD players.

And the personal computer arrived. In the late 1970s two young Californians, Steven Jobs and Stephen Wozniak, reduced computers from room size to desk-top size and marketed the phenomenally successful Apple computer. As Apple sales shot up, computer manufacturers multiplied, especially in California's "Silicon Valley," named after the silicon computer chip. In 1981 IBM launched its PC (personal computer) and quickly grabbed 40 percent of the market, but computer entrepreneurs continued to proliferate. By 1991, 60 million personal computers were in use in American offices, schools, and homes.

The Women's Movement: Gains and Uncertainties

Of all the legacies of the 1960s, perhaps the most far-reaching were a revitalized women's movement and basic changes in the status of women. Betty Friedan's *The Feminine Mystique* (1963) had heralded a new feminist activism. Millions of young, middle-class women had begun to reexamine their subordinate status in society. This rejuvenated feminism represented a rare source of social involvement in the generally quiescent 1970s. The 50,000 members of NOW (National Organization for Women), feminist support groups, and *Ms.* and other magazines spread the message.

Activism meant political clout—exemplified by the National Women's Political Caucus (1971), which promoted a feminist agenda. By 1972 many states had liberalized their abortion laws and outlawed gender discrimination in hiring. That same year, Congress passed the Equal Rights Amendment (ERA) to the Constitution, asserting that "equality of rights under the law shall not be denied or abridged by the United States or any State on the basis of sex." Twenty-eight states quickly ratified it, and adoption seemed sure. In 1973 the Supreme Court, in *Roe* v. *Wade*, proclaimed women's constitutional right to abortion; the decision relied heavily on the right to privacy, grounded in the due-process clause of the Fourteenth Amendment.

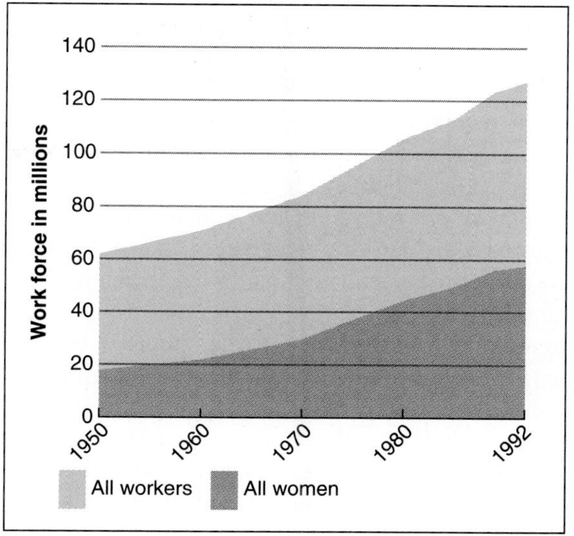

Women in the Work Force, 1950–1992

Since 1960 the proportion of American women who are gainfully employed has surged upward. As a result, young women coming of age in the 1990s have far different expectations about their lives than did their grandmothers or even their mothers.

SOURCES: *Statistical Abstract of the United States, 1988* (Washington, D.C.: GPO, 1987), 373; *World Almanac and Book of Facts, 1989* (New York: Pharos Books, 1988), 152; *Statistical Abstract of the United States, 1993* (Washington, D.C.: GPO, 1993), 400, 401.

By the early 1980s, however, the women's movement had splintered into moderate and radical camps. Although both espoused gender equality, moderates deplored the radicals' sometimes strident rhetoric. Betty Friedan's *The Second Stage* (1981) urged those feminists who had (controversially) downgraded family values to incorporate family issues into their campaign rather than leave this potent agenda to their opponents.

As the women's movement gained visibility, its opposition hardened. In 1972 President Nixon had vetoed a bill to establish a national network of day-care centers on the basis that it would weaken the family. Ratification of the ERA bogged down. Although polls showed that three-fourths of Americans supported the ERA, fiery opposition surfaced, and the amendment died in 1982, three states short of the required three-fourths.

Abortion became the most controversial issue relating to women. After the *Roe* v. *Wade* ruling, conservative Protestants and Roman Catholics organized a "right-to-life" movement and pressed for a constitutional amendment outlawing abortion. They charged that abortion undermined respect for human life and amounted to the murder of the unborn. Although the constitutional amendment failed, Congress in 1976 halted Medicaid funding for most abortions, thus putting abortion out of the reach of the poor. Most feminists, however, took a "pro-choice" stance and argued that individual women and their doctors, not laws, should dictate the decision. Polls showed that a majority of Americans agreed. Between 1973 and 1980 the number of women seeking abortions doubled, reaching 1.5 million, but then leveled off.

The baby boom yielded to the baby bust as birthrates reached a low in 1976. Couples were marrying later and having fewer children. By 1980 the statistically average American family had 1.6 children. The number of unmarried couples living together rose steadily, reaching 2.8 million by 1990, and the divorce rate catapulted to 480 per 1,000 marriages, up from 258 per 1,000 in 1960.

By 1992, 58 percent of women worked outside the home, up from 35 percent in 1960, as a through-the-roof cost of living sent women into the work force to supplement family income. Many women workers remained at the low end of the wage scale. Increasing numbers, however, entered corporate management and professions such as law and medicine. Working women juggled careers and family life—and coped with new kinds of stress. "Superwomen" pushed themselves to be successful professionals, attentive mothers, superb cooks, efficient housekeepers, and seductive wives. Conservatives increasingly voiced fears about the breakdown of the family.

Older feminists worried that young women had lost sight of the movement's original goals. They questioned whether women could function as equals in the male world without absorbing its competitiveness and careerism. But they recognized, too, that a long road lay ahead in overcoming ingrained gender discrimination. Working women's wages still lagged behind those of men. Gender segregation of the workplace largely persisted. Nursing and secretarial work remained overwhelmingly female, and, despite inroads by women, men still dominated high-prestige professions, especially at the upper ranks.

The eighties were not a favorable decade for confronting these inequities. The Reagan administration, suspicious of government activism on social issues, opposed many feminists' and other minorities' goals. Reagan appointees to the Civil Rights Commission hesitated to act. Reagan budgets cut social-welfare programs that benefited women and children. As women heading single-parent families swelled the welfare rolls, observers spoke of the "feminization of poverty." By 1990 feminist leaders and women would recognize that major challenges still loomed and complex problems remained unresolved.

The Two Worlds of Black America

The conservative trends that affected the women's movement in the 1970s and 1980s had repercussions for African-Americans as well. The Reagan administration's general contempt for government fueled a reluctance to use government powers to remedy racial injustice. This governmental foot-dragging came at a time of worsening crisis for the African-American community.

The story of African-Americans in the seventies and eighties was really two very different stories. Millions of blacks moved upward as the civil-rights movement opened long-closed doors. In 1965 African-American students had accounted for only 5 percent of college enrollment; by 1990, however, the figure reached 12 percent. And by 1990 some 46 percent of African-American workers held white-collar jobs.

But outside this circle lay a second, much grimmer realm of inner-city slums where blacks who had missed the "up" escalator were trapped. A third of all African-Americans inhabited this world, in which half the young people never finished high school and the jobless rate hovered around 60 percent.

Economic trends as well as racism contributed to their desperate situation. Structural changes in the American economy had eliminated many unskilled jobs once held by the urban poor. Recessions in the 1970s and early 1980s, moreover, battered the already struggling African-American underclass, and job cuts in steel, automaking, and other basic industries hit skilled African-American workers. Demands for a well-educated work force further shut out the poor and uneducated, and welfare payments lagged behind the rising cost of living.

Cocaine, especially the potent "crack," flooded urban ghettos in the 1980s. In some cases, eight- and nine-year-old black children earned up to $100 a day as lookouts for drug dealers; dealers in their early teens earned in two days as much as they would in a year at McDonald's. The cocaine plague stretched across the American landscape to include "yuppies," athletes, and entertainment figures.

Drugs and poverty in turn escalated urban violence. In the 1980s a young black male was six times as likely to be murdered as a young white male. In 1987 sixty black children under age seventeen were slain in Detroit. That same year, two major youth gangs, the Bloods and the Crips, accounted for more than 400 killings in Los Angeles. One observer summed up the situation in 1988: "Young black males in America's inner cities are an endangered species. . . . They are [the] rejects of our affluent society."

Meanwhile, among young, unmarried African-American women in the slums, the pregnancy rate soared. Single women, most of them young, poor, and uneducated, accounted for 63 percent of all black births in 1988. Millions of them, scarcely

Wounded Knee, South Dakota, 1973

In a gesture of symbolic protest, activists of the American Indian Movement occupied Wounded Knee, scene of the 1890 massacre of 300 Sioux by the U.S. Army.

more than children, depended on welfare payments for survival. Caught in a deep rut of dependence, they raised the specter of a permanent American underclass.

Unemployment, drug use, illegitimacy, and welfare dependency affected all racial and ethnic groups, but they emerged most starkly among inner-city African-American and Hispanic populations. Buffeted by complex economic and social forces, the predominantly nonwhite inner cities posed major social challenges.

New Patterns of Immigration

America's recent population growth—from 204 million in 1970 to more than 260 million in 1995—reflects a steady influx of both legal and illegal immigrants. Whereas most former immigrants came from Europe, 45 percent of the new immigrants hailed from the Western Hemisphere and 30 percent from Asia.

Immigration and a high birthrate made Hispanics the nation's fastest-growing ethnic group. In 1995 the Hispanic population stood at more than 26 million, up from 9 million in 1970. Mexican-Americans concentrated in the Southwest, while Cubans, Puerto Ricans, and other West Indians lived mainly in New York, Florida, Illinois, and New Jersey.

Desperate economic conditions had driven these newcomers to America. The collapse of world oil prices intensified unemployment and chronic poverty in Mexico during the 1980s, spurring many to seek opportunity in the north. These recent immigrants often faced hardship and poverty in their adopted land. In 1990 nearly 20 percent of Mexican-Americans and 30 percent of Puerto Ricans lived below the poverty line.

Proud of their language and traditions, these Hispanic newcomers strongly influenced U.S. culture. In some areas of Los Angeles, home to nearly 1 million Mexican-Americans, one could drive for miles in the 1980s and see only Spanish business signs and movie marquees. Large parts of Miami seemed wholly Hispanic.

By 1990 estimates of the number of illegal immigrants in the United States ranged as high as 12 million. Working long hours under harsh conditions with few legal protections, these impoverished immigrants, primarily Mexican and Haitian, performed hard manual labor, sweated in the garment trades, cleaned homes and cared for children, and bent their backs in agricultural fields. The Immigration Reform Control Act of 1986 outlawed the hiring of illegal immigrants and strengthened immigration controls at the border. The law also offered legal status to those immigrants who could prove that they had lived in the United States since January 1, 1982.

At the same time, immigration from Asia rose. Newcomers from Korea, Vietnam, and the Philippines joined well-established Chinese and Japanese communities in California, and many migrated eastward. These newest Americans worked hard, sought higher education, and moved up rapidly. All these trends made contemporary America a far more diverse and vibrant place than it had been a generation earlier.

Brightening Prospects for Native Americans

The status of American Indians had sunk to a new low in the 1950s as the federal government had promoted Indians' relocation to cities, where, it was tacitly hoped, they would disappear as a distinct ethnic group. Aroused by this destructive and ill-conceived policy, and influenced by the social-protest climate of the sixties, members of the militant American Indian Movement (AIM) had dramatized their cause by occupying Alcatraz Island in San Francisco Bay in 1969, the Bureau of Indian Affairs in Washington in 1972, and a trading post at Wounded Knee, South Dakota (the site of the 1890 massacre) in 1973.

Indians' militancy worked. In 1970 President Nixon rejected the "termination" approach and the federal government's traditional paternalism toward Indians and called for greater autonomy for Native Americans. The Indian Self-Determination Act of

1974 granted tribes control of federal-aid programs on reservations and oversight of their schools.

Indian peoples also felt heightened pride in their heritage. By 1990 more than 1.7 million persons identified themselves as Native Americans, up from 800,000 in 1970. Natural increase—in which the number of births surpasses the number of deaths—could not account for this growth, and census analysts concluded simply that more people than before chose to identify themselves as Indians. This upsurge reflected not only ethnic pride but also advantages associated with tribal membership, including the sharing of tribal revenues from casinos and other enterprises and employment opportunities under affirmative-action guidelines.

Ethnic pride inspired economic development on Indian reservations. Tribal ventures ranged from resorts to mining and logging enterprises. Food-processors, electronics firms, and other businesses built factories that created much-needed jobs on tribal lands. Certain tribes took advantage of their exemption from state gambling laws to open casinos, despite opposition from antigambling groups and from Native Americans who saw the casinos as a threat to Indian culture.

Indian tribes also reasserted long-ignored treaty rights. In 1971 native peoples in Alaska won 40 million acres of land and $1 billion in settlement of long-standing claims. In 1980 the Sioux received $107 million for South Dakota land taken from them illegally a century earlier, and the Penobscots of Maine won claims based on a 1790 law. In 1988 the tiny Puyallup tribe of Washington State was given $162 million to settle claims that the city of Tacoma occupied land granted them by treaty in the 1850s. The Puyallups announced plans to restore the salmon runs of the Puyallup River and to construct a deep-water port on Puget Sound.

It is true that high rates of unemployment, alcoholism, and disease persisted for Native Americans. But the renewal of tribal life, the new direction of federal policy, and the larger society's willingness to honor ancient treaties represented an advance. Movies such as *Little Big Man* (1970) and *Dances with Wolves* (1990) and TV series such as "Northern Exposure" reflected changing attitudes; although they tended to sentimentalize Indian culture, they were a vast improvement over the hostile stereotypes of earlier cowboys-and-Indians films.

Sexuality in the Era of AIDS

The sexual revolution of the 1960s had a particular impact on the homosexual community. Beginning in the early 1970s, many gay men and women "came out of the closest" to acknowledge their sexual orientation openly. They rallied, paraded, and organized to fight job discrimination and other forms of harassment. As one leader observed, "We are 20 million strong in this nation. We are moving from gay pride to gay politics."

Religious conservatives deplored this trend as evidence of society's moral disintegration. Evangelist Jerry Falwell proclaimed, "Homosexuality is . . . so abominable in the sight of God that he destroyed the cities of Sodom and Gomorrah because of this terrible sin."

The loosening of traditional sexual mores received a jolting setback in the 1980s with the proliferation of sexually transmitted diseases, including AIDS, first diagnosed in the United States in 1981. By 1994 more than 220,000 Americans had died of AIDS, and perhaps a million carried HIV (human immunodeficiency virus), the causative virus. Public-health officials warned that a vaccine lay far in the future. Although confined largely to sexually active homosexuals and bisexuals, intravenous drug users, and those having intercourse with these high-risk groups, AIDS appeared in the general population, too, and medical authorities warned of the need for caution and the use of condoms. This somber message was driven home in 1991 when basketball superstar Earvin "Magic" Johnson announced that he had tested positive for HIV. Young AIDS victims such as Ryan White and Kimberly Bergalis also heightened popular awareness of the disease.

The AIDS scare provided some Americans with an excuse to express their hatred of homosexuality. Others responded more sympathetically. Research on the mysterious disease received massive funding. Hospices opened to provide care and support for patients; a quilt bearing the names of AIDS victims toured the nation and grew steadily larger; candlelight marches memorialized the dead.

Fearful of exposure to AIDS, herpes, and other sexually transmitted diseases, Americans grew more cautious in their sexual behavior. The exuberant 1960s slogan "Make Love, Not War" gave way to "Safer Sex."

The Evangelical Renaissance

Religion became highly visible in the post-1970 United States as many Americans sought beliefs that gave meaning to life and resolved ethical dilemmas. Religious faith played a larger role after 1970 than it had for years.

This intensified religious interest took varied forms. Cults such as the Reverend Sun Myung Moon's Unification Church and the International Society for Krishna Consciousness prospered. A most significant development was the rapid growth of evangelical Protestant denominations, including the 2-million-member Assemblies of God and the 14-million-strong Southern Baptist Convention. All these groups believed in the Bible's literal truth, in "born-again" religious experience, and in an earthly life governed by personal piety and strict morality.

Evangelical Christians had pursued social reform before the Civil War, and many twentieth-century evangelicals also turned to political activism. In 1980 and 1984 Jerry Falwell's pro-Reagan Moral Majority registered nearly 2 million new voters. While targeting specific issues—abortion, pornography, and public-school prayer—evangelicals embraced a strongly conservative, anticommunist world view. Falwell disbanded his organization after 1984, but the Reverend Pat Robertson's well-organized Christian Coalition took its place, with the long-range goal of expanding conservative Christian influence at the state and national levels.

Fueling this rejuvenation was a network of religious bookstores, radio stations featuring religious programming, and, above all, television evangelists. Jerry Falwell, Pat Robertson, Jim and Tammy Bakker, Oral Roberts, and Jimmy Swaggart, among others, accounted for countless hours of broadcasting. Robertson's Christian Broadcasting Network became the nation's fourth-largest cable network. Televangelists repelled many Americans with their endless pleas for money, but millions of others found their spiritual message reassuring.

The "electronic church" suffered severe jolts after 1987. Jim Bakker resigned after acknowledging a sexual encounter with a church secretary and payoffs to buy her silence. The fiercely moralistic Jimmy Swaggart fell from grace when his repeated trysts with prostitutes were revealed. But the TV preachers' tribulations could not obscure the growing influence of evangelical religion. Confronting change on all sides, evangelicals found comfort in their faith and profoundly influenced American life in the late twentieth century.

"The Summer of '73"
Cartoonist Paul Szep used the stark image of a thirsty gasoline tanker to convey the gravity of the economic crisis spawned by the Arab oil embargo.

The Election of 1976

Candidates	Parties	Electoral Vote	Popular Vote	Percentage of Popular Vote
JIMMY CARTER	Democratic	297	40,827,394	49.9
Gerald R. Ford	Republican	240	39,145,977	47.9

Years of Malaise: Post-Watergate Politics and Diplomacy

Social change and public discontent shaped the politics of the 1970s and 1980s. With Richard Nixon's graceless exit from the presidency, the nation lost spirit and direction. His successors, Republican Gerald R. Ford and Democrat Jimmy Carter, grappled with a tangle of domestic and foreign problems—inflation, unemployment, and recession—and a foreboding sense of limits gripped many Americans.

Globally the years from 1974 to 1980 brought humiliations and setbacks from the withdrawal from Vietnam to the seizures of American hostages in Iran. The stark simplicities of the bipolar world blurred as complex problems arose in the Third World (Asia, the Middle East, Africa, and Latin America).

Americans felt adrift in an increasingly hostile world, no longer the masters of their fate and leaders of the Free World that they had been in the confident days of the 1950s and early 1960s. Post-Watergate America wallowed in a collective funk. Long convinced that it was exceptional, immune to the historical forces that hedged in other societies, the United States seemed diminished, ennervated, and buffeted by forces beyond its control. By 1980 accumulating frustration and anger were generating a powerful political revolt.

The Caretaker Presidency of Gerald Ford

Gerald Ford became president on August 9, 1974, after Richard M. Nixon's resignation. A former Michigan congressman who had served as Republican minority leader before becoming vice president, Ford displayed human decency, if little evidence of brilliance. While comedians poked fun at his verbal gaffes ("If Lincoln were alive today, he'd roll over in his grave"), most Americans found him a welcome relief after Nixon. Only a month into his term, however, Ford strained his popularity by pardoning Nixon for "any and all crimes" committed while in office, thus shielding the ex-president from prosecution for his Watergate role. Ford insisted that the pardon would help to heal the body politic, but many Americans were outraged.

More conservative than Nixon on domestic issues, Ford vetoed environmental, social-welfare, and public-interest measures, but the heavily Democratic Congress overrode most of the vetoes. Economic problems especially bedeviled Ford. Oil prices had shot up in 1973 as a result of the Arab oil embargo and OPEC (Organization of Petroleum Exporting Countries) price hikes. These blows fell hard on the United States, which imported one-third of its oil. The soaring cost of gasoline, home heating oil, and other petroleum-based products worsened already serious inflation. Consumer prices rose 12 percent in 1974 and 11 percent in 1975.

In October 1974 Ford initiated a program of voluntary restraint called Whip Inflation Now (WIN). Although the president gamely wore his big "WIN" button, prices continued to rise. Ford also cut federal spending and endorsed the Federal Reserve's attempt to cool the economy by raising the discount rate. However, a severe recession resulted in 1974–1975. Unemployment climbed to nearly 11 percent in 1975, tax receipts dropped as business stagnated, and the federal deficit spurted to record levels. Although Ford proposed a tax cut and measures to coax consumer spending, economic headaches persisted.

The oil crisis battered the U.S. auto industry. Americans stopped buying gas-guzzlers and turned to smaller, more fuel-efficient imports. General Motors, Ford, and Chrysler laid off 225,000 workers in 1974, and imports doubled their share of the U.S. market, reaching 33 percent by 1980.

President Ford retained Henry Kissinger as secretary of state and supported détente with China and the U.S.S.R. In 1974 the president and Soviet leader Leonid Brezhnev moved toward a new arms-control agreement, Strategic Arms Limitation Treaty (SALT) I, limiting each side to 2,400 nuclear missiles. The following year, Ford and Brezhnev joined thirty-one European nations in adopting the Helsinki Accords, formalizing Europe's post-1945 boundaries and vowing respect for human rights.The Helsinki Accords boosted the forces of change in the Soviet bloc and may well represent Ford's most important accomplishment.

In April 1975 battered American morale suffered a further blow when the South Vietnamese government fell. The triumphant northerners swiftly changed the name of Saigon to Ho Chi Minh City. TV chronicled desperate helicopter evacuations from the roof of the U. S. Embassy. A few weeks later, the new communist government in Cambodia seized an American merchant ship, the *Mayagüez*. Ford ordered a military rescue that freed the thirty-nine *Mayagüez* crewmen but cost the lives of forty-one U.S. servicemen.

Americans found little to cheer as the nation entered 1976, an election year and the bicentennial of the Declaration of Independence.

Outsider as Insider: President Jimmy Carter

President Ford won the Republican nomination in 1976. The Democratic nomination went to a little-known Georgia politician and peanut farmer, Jimmy Carter, who carried out a brilliant primary campaign. The folksy, toothy-grinned Carter made a virtue of his status as an outsider to Washington, pledged never to lie to the American people, and freely avowed his "born-again" Christianity. Carter and his running mate, Senator Walter Mondale of Minnesota, drew support by attacking the Ford administration's high inflation and unemployment rates.

The Democrats won by a narrow margin—49.9 percent of the popular vote to Ford's 47.9 and 297 electoral votes to the Republican's 240. The vote broke sharply along class lines: the well-to-do voted heavily for Ford; the disadvantaged, overwhelmingly for Carter. The Georgian swept the South and received 90 percent of the African-American vote.

As president, Carter rejected the trappings of what some in Nixon's day had called the imperial presidency. On inauguration day, he walked from the Capitol to the White House. In an attempt to echo FDR's radio chats, he later delivered some televised speeches from an easy chair by a fireplace.

But such symbolism could not ensure a successful presidency. Because Carter had entered the White House without a clear political philosophy, liberals and conservatives alike claimed him. Moreover, the intensely private Carter relied on a tight circle of young staff members from Georgia and avoided socializing with politicians. "Carter couldn't get the Pledge of Allegiance through Congress," groused one legislator. Disciplined and intelligent, Carter focused well on specific problems but lacked a larger political vision.

In his first year Carter used a tax cut and public-works programs to fight the recession. The unemployment rate dropped to 5 percent by late 1978. However, Carter showed little sympathy for social-welfare measures involving federal spending. Carter also introduced administrative reforms in civil service and the executive branch early in his presidency. But poor relations with Congress frustrated his attempts to promote national health insurance, to overhaul the welfare system, and to reform loophole-ridden income-tax laws. Responding to major social movements, he did appoint a substantial number of women and members of minority groups to federal judgeships.

Carter's foreign-affairs achievements outshone his domestic record, but even here the negatives outweighed the positives. Carter and his secretary of state, Cyrus Vance, worked vigorously to inject human rights into foreign policy and to combat abuses in Chile, Argentina, Ethiopia, South Africa, and other nations. Human-rights violations by American allies such as South Korea and the Philippines received far more gingerly treatment. Trying to adapt U.S. policy to a multipolar world, Carter also sought better relations with the new black nations of Africa. A State Department official summed up the administration's view: "It is not a sign of weakness to recognize that we alone cannot dictate events elsewhere. It is rather a sign of maturity in a complex world."

Carter, like Ford, also pursued initiatives launched by his predecessors. Earlier administrations had begun negotiating a more equitable treaty relationship with Panama. The Carter administration completed negotiations on two treaties transferring the Panama Canal and the Canal Zone to the Panamanians by 1999. Although the agreements protected U.S. interests, conservatives attacked them as proof of the United States' post-Vietnam loss of nerve. Why should the nation give up the canal? asked Ronald Reagan; "we stole it fair and square." In 1977 the Senate ratified both treaties.

The strengthening of ties with China accelerated after Mao Zedong's death in 1976. Carter initiated full diplomatic relations with the People's Republic of China on January 1, 1979, opening the door to scientific, cultural, academic, and commercial exchanges. And toward the world's other communist superpower, the Soviet Union, Carter showed both toughness and conciliation. In 1979 Carter and Brezhnev signed SALT II. Critics, however, charged that the agreement favored the Soviets, and after the U.S.S.R. invaded neighboring Afghanistan in January 1980, Carter withdrew the treaty from the Senate. He also took a series of hard-line measures against the Soviet Union, including a boycott of the 1980 Moscow Olympics. This get-tough policy reflected the views of Carter's national-security adviser, Zbigniew Brzezinski, a Polish-born political scientist who harbored hostility toward the Soviet Union and viewed détente with suspicion.

A Sea of Troubles as Carter's Term Ends

Inflation reached horrendous levels as Carter's term wore on. Prices vaulted by more than 13 percent in both 1979 and 1980, driven by staggering energy costs. In 1979 a second oil crisis hit as a revolution in Iran led to a diminished world oil reserve and as oil-guzzling nations, including the United States, waged a bidding war for the reduced supply. In response, OPEC boosted oil prices to above $30 a barrel. Americans who were used to paying $.30 for a gallon of gasoline saw prices edge toward $1 a gallon. As oil stopped flowing freely into the pipeline for international commerce, shortages arose and lines formed at gas stations. In 1979 alone, Americans paid $16.4 billion in added costs related to oil-price increases. Carter relied on voluntarism to curb the inflationary spiral; his Council on Wage and Price Stability urged workers and manufacturers to hold the line. But repeated hikes in oil prices thwarted his efforts.

As the Federal Reserve Board pushed the discount rate higher and higher, bank interest rates reached an unheard-of 20 percent by 1980. Mortgages and business loans consequently dried up, and economic activity remained in the doldrums. Government borrowing to compensate for slumping tax revenues drove up interest rates still more.

Carter had drawn a larger lesson from the oil crisis: that the nation's wasteful consumption of dwindling fossil fuels must yield to conservation. He recognized that two key factors underlying a generation of economic growth—cheap, unlimited energy and the lack of foreign competition—were about to disappear. Americans must learn to survive in a "zero-sum" society that could no longer anticipate endless expansion, the president believed. In 1975 Congress had set fuel-efficiency standards for cars and mandated a national speed limit of fifty-five miles per hour. Convinced that more had to be

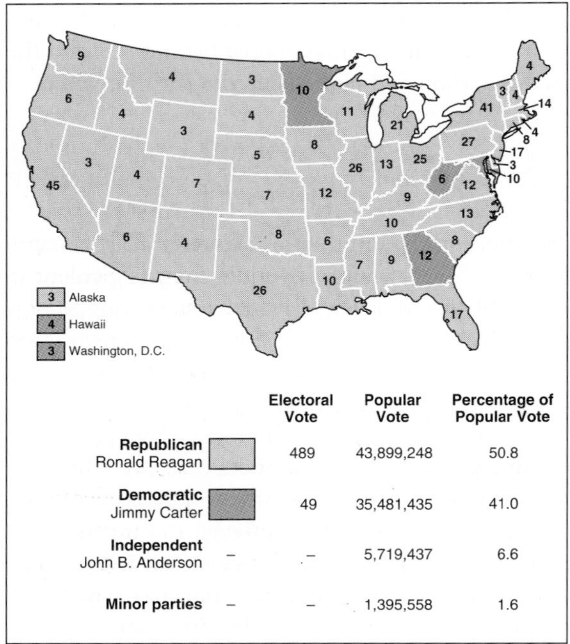

	Electoral Vote	Popular Vote	Percentage of Popular Vote
Republican Ronald Reagan	489	43,899,248	50.8
Democratic Jimmy Carter	49	35,481,435	41.0
Independent John B. Anderson	–	5,719,437	6.6
Minor parties	–	1,395,558	1.6

The Election of 1980

done, Carter in 1977 had created the Department of Energy and proposed taxes on oil and gasoline consumption, tax credits for conservation measures, and research on alternative energy resources. In 1978 Congress had passed a watered-down energy bill.

But with the oil crises and attendant economic jitters, Americans turned against the remote figure in the White House. Carter's approval rating plummeted to 26 percent in summer 1979. The president delivered a televised address discussing "national malaise" and "loss of confidence," but the speech only deepened the spreading suspicion that Carter himself was a large part of the problem. Frustration over the Iranian hostage crisis deepened Carter's problems, and by mid-1980 his approval rating had sunk to 23 percent.

The Democrats glumly renominated Jimmy Carter in 1980. But with double-digit inflation, 20 percent interest rates, an 8 percent unemployment rate, and the hostage crisis, he had no real chance of victory.

Carter remains a fascinating but controversial political figure. His sudden emergence vividly illustrates the power of television, which permitted an unknown candidate to bypass the laborious process of amassing support among power brokers and interest groups. Pursuing the presidency at a moment when Americans longed to see integrity and competency restored to that office, Carter seemed to fill the bill precisely. He identified issues that would dominate the national agenda in the future: energy policy; tax, welfare, and health-care reform; and the need to redefine America's world role. But he lacked the political skills to work well with Congress and to inspire the nation to confront its problems. By the end of his term, a victim of his own flaws and of forces largely beyond his control, Carter was lonely and discredited. A notable post-presidential career devoted to humanitarian service and the resolution of international conflicts would somewhat restore Carter's reputation, but few were sorry to see him leave in January 1981.

The Reagan Revolution

In 1980 voters turned to a presidential candidate who promised to break with the recent past—Ronald Reagan. His unabashed patriotism appealed to a nation still traumatized by Vietnam, and his denunciation of "tax-and-spend" policies seemed to strike at the root of "stagflation," that dismal combination of business stagnation and inflation. His attacks on liberal ideology resonated with millions of Americans.

As president, Reagan revived national pride and confidence. His economic policies lowered inflation and triggered a consumer buying spree and a surge of speculative investment. They also laid the groundwork, however, for serious economic difficulties after his departure.

Détente faltered in the early 1980s as President Reagan revived the belligerent rhetoric of the early Cold War, raised the stakes in the arms race with the Soviets, and supplied money and weapons to anticommunist forces in Latin America. But Reagan soon found himself enmeshed in foreign problems that did not easily fit into his highly ideological, bipolar world view.

Background of the Revolution

Several economic, ideological, and social trends contributed to Reagan's appeal. First, stagflation frightened and angered voters, and Carter's orthodox economic policies offered little hope for relief. Reagan promoted a simple idea: a dramatic tax cut would stimulate the economy, boost federal tax revenues, and achieve a balanced budget. Although George Bush, his chief rival for the Republican nomination, ridiculed these ideas as "voodoo economics," many voters thought them worth trying. Moreover, a belief in self-help and private enterprise had remained entrenched despite the New Deal–Great Society ideology of government activism. Simultaneously, decades of Cold War rhetoric had imprinted deeply on the American consciousness a determination to remain ahead of the Soviets militarily and to play a forceful world role. To many, Carter had seemed vacillating and unwilling to stand up for U.S. interests. Reagan's uncomplicated patriotism and eloquent assertions of the United States' continued greatness soothed a wounded national psyche.

Reagan also embraced the ideology of the New Right: a cultural conservatism stressing social and moral issues. Upset by social turmoil, the sexual revolution, the women's movement, and rising rates of divorce and abortion, millions of Americans called for a restoration of morality and "traditional values." TV evangelist Jerry Falwell's Moral Majority was one of many groups eager to translate public concerns into political action.

Population shifts in the 1970s also played a role in Reagan's success. New York, Chicago, and the other cities of the Northeast and upper Midwest had lost population as Texas, Florida, California, and the Sun Belt had grown rapidly. These areas were historically conservative and suspicious of Washington. Westerners had organized the "Sagebrush Revolution" to demand less government control and the return of federal lands to state control.

A skillful actor with a likeable manner and a ready smile, Ronald Reagan combined these themes into a potent message. Belying his sixty-nine years, he exuded youthful zest and jauntiness and offered a jittery nation the confident leadership for which it longed. Time would reveal a considerable gap between substance and image in Reagan's program, but in 1980 a majority of voters found his appeal irresistible.

The Man Behind the Movement

Reagan grew up in Dixon, Illinois, the son of an alcoholic father and a pious mother. After graduating from Eureka College, he worked as a sports announcer before striking out for Hollywood in 1937. His fifty-four films enjoyed only moderate success, but after 1954 he made a name for himself as a spokesperson for General Electric. A former New Dealer, Reagan moved to the right in the 1950s and won prominence through a TV speech for Barry Goldwater in 1964, praising individualism and free enterprise.

Recognizing Reagan's flair for politics, a group of California millionaires engineered his election as governor in 1966. In Sacramento he popularized conservative ideas while demonstrating an ability to compromise. After nearly winning the Republican presidential nomination in 1976, Reagan in 1980 had little trouble disposing of his principal opponent, George Bush, whom he then made his running mate.

Reagan promised Americans a new deal. Unlike FDR's New Deal, however, Reagan's version offered diminished government activity, reduced taxes and spending, and the unleashing of the free-enterprise system. Internationally, Reagan called for the restoration of American leadership and pride.

Asking, "Are you better off now than you were four years ago?" Reagan captured 51 percent of the popular vote to Carter's 41 percent. (An independent candidate, liberal Republican congressman John Anderson, collected most of the balance.)

Reaping the benefits of Nixon's southern strategy, Reagan carried every southern state except Carter's own Georgia and every state west of the Mississippi. More than half the nation's blue-collar workers voted Republican. Only African-American voters remained firmly Democratic. Republicans also gained eleven Senate seats and, for the first time since 1955, a majority. These Senate victories reflected the power of conservative political-action committees using computerized mass mailings to focus on such "hot-button" issues as abortion and gun control.

Reagan's term began auspiciously as the Iranian hostages boarded planes heading home. With this trauma past, the nation sized up its new leader. Few had a clear notion of his program beyond his rhetorical commitment to patriotism, military strength, the free market, and traditional values, but Reagan soon gave concrete substance to these generalities.

Ronald Reagan, Outdoorsman
Though President Reagan was often photographed in natural settings, his administration gave little support to the cause of environmental protection.

Reaganomics

"Reaganomics," the new president's economic program, boiled down to the belief that American capitalism, freed of heavy taxes and government regulation, would surge to great heights of productivity. Reagan's first budget message proposed a five-year, $750 billion tax cut built around a 30 percent reduction in federal income taxes over three years. Trimming the proposal slightly, Congress in May 1981 voted a 25 percent income-tax cut over three years.

To compensate for the lost revenues, Reagan proposed severe spending reductions for school lunches, student loans, job training, and urban mass transit. In all, Congress slashed more than $40 billion from domestic spending in 1981 (less than Reagan had requested). Conservative Democrats supported the reductions. Although mainstream economists warned that the tax cut would produce catastrophic federal deficits, Reagan remained convinced that lower tax rates would stimulate economic growth and raise total tax revenues. He was wrong.

Appointees to key agencies implemented another component of Reaganomics, radical cutbacks in the federal regulation of business. Reagan insisted that "government is not the solution to our problems; government *is* the problem." Deregulation, begun under Carter, was extended to banking, the savings-and-loan industry, transportation, and communications. The head of the Federal Communications Commission gutted federal rules governing the broadcast industry, and the secretary of transportation trimmed regulations reducing air pollution and increasing efficiency and safety in cars and trucks. Secretary of the Interior James

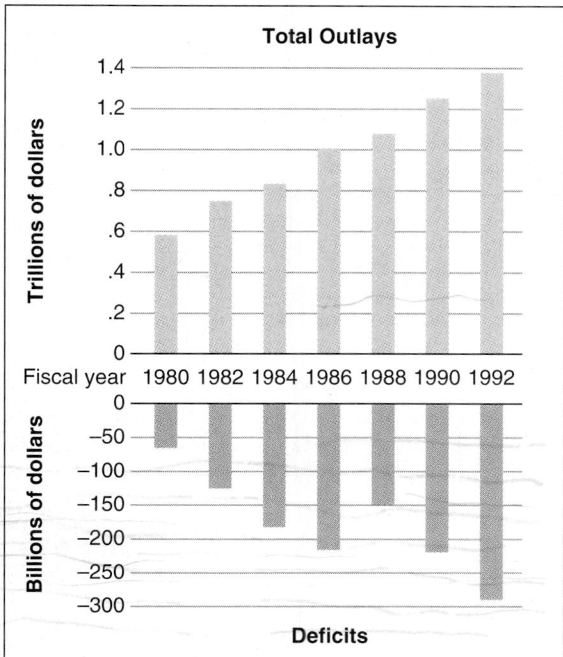

Federal Budget Expenditures and Deficits, Fiscal Years 1980–1992

After soaring to more than $200 billion in 1986, the runaway federal deficit declined somewhat, then surged again in 1990. Driven by mushrooming health-care costs, it could surpass $400 billion by 2002.

SOURCES: U.S. Department of the Treasury; Office of Management and Budget; *New York Times,* 1 March 1992, p. 1; *Statistical Abstract of the United States, 1993* (Washington, D.C.: GPO, 1993), p. 328.

Watt, a leader in the Sagebrush Rebellion, opened public lands in the West to commercial developers. But despite the administration's success in deregulation, Reagan's attack on "big government" had little effect on checking the steady growth of the federal budget and of the federal bureaucracy.

While implementing Reaganomics, the White House also had to cope with the immediate problem of inflation. The Federal Reserve Board led the charge against inflation, pushing the discount rate ever higher. This harsh medicine, coupled with a sharp downturn in world oil prices, worked. Inflation dropped to 4 percent in 1983 and held steady thereafter. But the high interest rates necessary to curb inflation spawned another severe recession, one that exceeded those of the Ford and Carter years. By late 1982 unemployment stood at 10 percent.

Falling exports added to the Reagan recession. As high U.S. interest rates lured foreign investors, the dollar rose in value vis-à-vis foreign currencies, making American goods more expensive abroad. The decline in U.S. exports—accompanied by enormous increases in imported TVs, stereos, and cars—propelled the U.S. trade deficit (the gap between exports and imports) from $31 billion in 1981 to $111 billion in 1984. The trade gap with Japan alone widened to a towering $33 billion in 1984.

Meanwhile, the United States' industrial heartland reeled under the triple blow of slumping exports, stiff foreign competition, and technological obsolescence. The aging steel mills, machinery plants, automobile companies, and other smokestack industries of the Midwest and Great Lakes laid off hordes of workers. Some plants closed. From 1979 through 1983, 11.5 million Americans lost jobs as a result of plant shutdowns or slack work. The drop in exports hurt farmers as well. From 1980 to 1985 wheat exports fell 38 percent and corn exports, 49 percent. Some lost farms that their families had run for generations.

Spiraling federal deficits compounded the economic muddle. Reagan's tax cuts reduced federal revenues without immediately stimulating business, and increases in military spending more than offset domestic spending cuts. With the economy in crisis, the government awash in red ink, and critics denouncing him as callous, Reagan offered assurances that his program would soon take effect. At the same time, he accepted a reduced rate of military spending, slower funding cuts in social programs, emergency job programs, and tax increases euphemistically described as "revenue-enhancement measures."

As recession's grip remained tight through 1982, the Democrats gained twenty-six House seats in the fall elections. The Reagan presidency appeared headed toward failure until early 1983 when the economy rebounded. Encouraged by tax cuts, declining interest rates, and evidence that inflation had been tamed, consumers went on a buying binge. The stock market surged, unemployment dropped, and the gross national product shot up by almost 10 percent.

The Great Bull Market

Revived consumer spending unleashed a wave of stock-market speculation reminiscent of the 1920s. The great bull market began on August 12, 1982, and lasted five years. Entrepreneurs such as Manhattan real-estate tycoon Donald Trump and stock analyst Ivan Boesky became celebrities. The 1984 autobiography of Lee Iacocca, who had rescued Chrysler from near bankruptcy, was a best-seller. Corporate mergers burgeoned. Chevron bought Gulf for $13 billion; GE acquired RCA for $6.3 billion. Meanwhile, the stock market steadily roared on. Banks and savings-and-loan companies, newly deregulated, loaned billions to developers for the construction of shopping malls, luxury apartments, retirement villages, and office buildings.

In the mid-1980s the dark side of this feeding frenzy emerged. The E. F. Hutton brokerage firm pleaded guilty to manipulating funds and defrauding hundreds of banks. Ivan Boesky went to prison after his 1986 conviction for insider trading. On October 19, 1987, "Black Monday," the Dow Jones plunged 508 points as one-fifth of the paper value of the nation's stocks evaporated. The downslide was eerily similar to the 1929 crash that precipitated the Great Depression, but prompt government action prevented another collapse.

Even at the height of the bull market, serious economic problems remained. The trade gap persisted, the deficit surpassed $200 billion in 1986, and farmers, the poor, and former industrial workers did not share in the renewed prosperity. The United States had been transformed from the world's largest creditor to the world's largest debtor. But—just in time to brighten Reagan's reelection prospects—the overall economic picture looked more hopeful than it had in years.

Reagan Confronts the "Evil Empire"

With the fading of détente in the late seventies, anti-Soviet rhetoric escalated when Ronald Reagan took office. The president blasted the Soviet Union as an "evil empire" and "the focus of evil in the modern world." Anti-Soviet sentiment crested in September 1983 when the Soviets shot down a Korean passenger aircraft that had strayed into their airspace, killing 269. Moscow claimed that the plane had been spying, but most Americans rejected this explanation.

Obsession with the Soviets also influenced Reagan policy in El Salvador and Nicaragua, two poor Central American nations caught up in revolutionary turmoil. In El Salvador the administration supported the ruling military junta in its ruthless suppression of a leftist insurgency backed by Cuba and Nicaragua. Even after the more moderate José Napoleon Duarte won the 1984 presidential election with U.S. support, death squads continued to operate. In Nicaragua, where Carter had at first aided the Sandinista revolutionaries who overthrew dictator Anastasio Somoza in 1979, Reagan accused the Sandinistas of creating another Cuba and a staging area for Soviet expansion. Under director William Casey, the Central Intelligence Agency in 1982 organized and financed a 10,000-man guerrilla army, the contras, based in Honduras and Costa Rica. The contras, many of them linked to the Somoza regime, conducted raids, planted mines, and carried out sabotage inside Nicaragua.

Fearing another Vietnam, Americans grew alarmed as details of this "covert" war leaked out. Congress imposed a series of bans on military aid to the contras, but Reagan's enthusiasm for the contras, whom he labeled "the moral equivalent of our Founding Fathers," held steady. Secret contra aid, organized within the White House by a National Security Council aide, Lieutenant Colonel Oliver North, and others, continued despite congressional prohibitions. In 1988 Reagan, still hoping for a contra victory, grudgingly supported a truce between the Sandinistas and the contras.

Reagan's militarization of American policy fell heavily on the West Indian island of Grenada, ruled by a radical leftist regime. In October 1983, 2,000 U.S. Marines invaded Grenada, overthrew the government, and installed one friendly to the United States. The Reagan administration maintained that American strategic interests had justified the action. Most Grenadians expressed their approval.

Tragedy and Frustration in the Middle East

At first the Reagan White House paid little attention to the Middle East. Hoping to stem Islamic fundamentalism, the United States tilted toward Saddam Hussein's Iraq in its long war with Iran. Attempts to court "moderates" in Iran culminated in a morass of arms-for-hostages deals, which would be exposed in 1985 as the Iran-contra scandal unfolded (see Chapter 33). Cold War policies dictated other U.S. actions in the Middle East.

In August 1981 Israel and the Palestine Liberation Organization (PLO) concluded a cease-fire, but the PLO continued building up its forces and carved out a sanctuary in southern Lebanon from which it could threaten Israel and defend itself against Syrian and Lebanese government hostility. In June 1982 when PLO extremists critically wounded the Israeli ambassador to Great Britain, Prime Minister Menachem Begin ordered Israeli troops to invade Lebanon and destroy the PLO. The incursion defeated the PLO militarily and forced its leaders to leave Lebanon. It also intensified civil war among Lebanese Christian and Islamic factions. A Christian militia took the opportunity to massacre Palestinians in a refugee camp near Beirut, Lebanon's capital.

Initially sympathetic to the Israeli invasion, the Reagan administration deployed 2,000 U.S. Marines to Beirut as part of a multinational peacekeeping force. The Muslim militias saw the Americans as pro-Israel and pro-Christian and began firing on the marines. The U.S. Navy shelled the Lebanese coast in retaliation. Then in October 1983 a Shiite Muslim crashed a truck laden with explosives into poorly guarded barracks, killing 239 marines. Because Reagan had never defined American interests in Lebanon, the disaster underscored the failure of his Lebanese policy. By early 1984 the marines had withdrawn, leaving Lebanon to its warring factions and to the Syrians.

Disappointment also dogged Reagan's attempt to promote a wider Middle East settlement. In September 1982 the president announced the "Reagan Plan" to restart Arab-Israeli peace talks along the lines envisioned by the Camp David Accords. Over the next four years, the administration tried to bring PLO leader Yasir Arafat and Jordan's King Hussein together for a "Jordanian solution" to the Palestinian question in the West Bank. But Reagan's efforts were scuttled by Syria's opposition, stemming from that nation's exclusion from the process; by PLO reluctance; and by Israel's fears for its security.

Military Buildup and Antinuclear Protest

Convinced that the United States had grown dangerously weak militarily, Reagan launched the most massive military expansion in American peacetime history. From 1981 to 1985, the Pentagon's budget swelled from $171 billion to more than $300 billion. Nuclear weapons were a key element of the U.S. buildup. In 1983 the administration deployed 572 cruise and Pershing II missiles in Western Europe, counterbalancing Soviet missiles in Eastern Europe. Reagan's supporters would later claim that the U.S.S.R.'s collapse in the late 1980s came from its efforts to match this American stockpiling. Others, however, would see the collapse as the result of internal events largely unaffected by American policy. There are no definitive answers yet.

On the domestic front, the Federal Emergency Management Agency responded to the nuclear

The Election of 1984

Candidates	*Parties*	*Electoral Vote*	*Popular Vote*	*Percentage of Popular Vote*
RONALD REAGAN	Republican	525	54,451,521	58.8
Walter Mondale	Democratic	13	37,565,334	40.5

buildup by designing an elaborate civil-defense plan whereby city residents would flee to remote "host communities" if nuclear war threatened. A Defense Department official averred that backyard shelters would save millions of people in a nuclear holocaust. "If there are enough shovels to go around," he asserted, "everybody's going to make it." Such talk, coupled with the military buildup and the faltering of arms control, sparked a grass-roots reaction as millions of Americans felt a growing threat of nuclear war. Concerned citizens campaigned for a freeze on the manufacture and deployment of nuclear weapons. In June 1982, 800,000 antinuclear protesters, the largest political demonstration in U.S. history, rallied in New York's Central Park. Nine states passed freeze resolutions in the following fall elections.

Responding to the "No nukes!" clamor, the administration in June 1982 proposed the total removal of medium-range nuclear missiles from Europe and commenced talks with the Soviets on strategic-arms reductions. In March 1983 Reagan proposed the Strategic Defense Initiative (SDI), a vast space-based defense system against nuclear missiles. Nicknamed Star Wars after the popular 1977 movie, SDI reflected America's deep faith in technology. But even as the Pentagon launched an SDI research program, critics pointed out not only the project's prohibitive cost and technological implausibility but also the likelihood that it would further escalate the arms race.

Reagan Reelected

As the 1984 election neared, liberal Democrats and independents found much to criticize in the Reagan presidency: runaway military spending, worsening Cold War tensions, yawning budget deficits, a cavernous foreign-trade gap, sharp cuts in social programs, and the assault on regulatory functions. To critics, Reaganism meant jingoism abroad and selfishness at home.

But many Americans applauded Reagan's attacks on government waste and inefficiency, as well as his get-tough policy toward the Soviets. Rhetoric aside, the administration *had* ended inflation and created a booming economy. Reagan's popularity remained high; some dubbed him the Teflon president because nothing bad seemed to stick to him. By 1984 many Americans believed that Reagan had revitalized the free-enterprise system, rebuilt U.S. military might, and made the nation "stand tall" in the world. Buoyed by evidence of broad support, Reagan confidently prepared to campaign for a second term. The 1984 Republican convention, scripted for TV, accentuated patriotism, prosperity, and the personality of Ronald Reagan.

Democratic hopefuls included Jesse Jackson, an African-American Chicago minister and one-time associate of Martin Luther King, Jr. Jackson attempted to build a broad "rainbow coalition" of African-Americans, Hispanic-Americans, displaced workers, and other outsiders in Reagan's America. Former vice president Walter Mondale, however, won the Democratic nomination. He ignited little enthusiasm, despite his choice of a woman, New York representative Geraldine Ferraro, as his running mate.

Reagan and Bush collected 59 percent of the popular vote and carried every state but Minnesota and the District of Columbia. Reagan's popular ideology and mastery of television teamed with a booming economy to secure his solid victory. Democrats remained in control of Congress, but Republican dominance of presidential politics, broken only by Carter's single term, held firm.

CONCLUSION

The United States of the 1970s and 1980s seemed to comprise two separate societies that barely recognized each other's existence. Yuppies abandoned social activism to enjoy the Me Decade and celebrated the successes of Donald Trump and Ivan Boesky, whose materialistic obsessions represented a grotesque intensification of widely shared values. The other America, the world of the poor, centered primarily in the inner cities, was a realm of crime, drugs, decaying housing projects, and a failing educational system, and it augured dire consequences. The middle and elite classes showed little concern for problems outside their own charmed circles.

Presidents Gerald Ford and Jimmy Carter tackled complex foreign and domestic problems with little success. In 1980 voters sent to the White House a man who had pledged radical changes in the government's role. The "Reagan Revolution," however, promised far more than it delivered, and its most enduring legacy may well be the crushing public debt that the nation is struggling with today.

Internationally, Reagan's first-term bellicosity heightened Cold War tensions and convinced many Americans that a full-scale nuclear war was no longer unthinkable. But in Reagan's second term, seismic shifts would rock the Soviet Union, transforming the Cold War and altering the world balance of power in ways that few could have dreamed of in 1984.

CHRONOLOGY

1963 Betty Friedan, *The Feminine Mystique*.

1966 Founding of National Organization for Women (NOW).

1972 Equal Rights Amendment passed by Congress.

1973 Major rise in Organization of Petroleum Exporting Countries (OPEC) prices; Arab oil boycott.
Roe v. *Wade*.

1974 Richard Nixon resigns presidency; Gerald Ford sworn in.
Whip Inflation Now (WIN) program.
Indian Self-Determination Act.
Ford-Brezhnev meeting.

1975 South Vietnamese government falls.
Mayagüez incident.

1976 Jimmy Carter elected president.

1977 Panama Canal treaties ratified.

1978–1980 Double-digit inflation and soaring interest rates.

1979 Menachem Begin and Anwar el-Sadat sign peace treaty at White House.
Second round of OPEC price increases.
Accident at Three-Mile Island nuclear plant.
Carter and Leonid Brezhnev sign Strategic Arms Limitation Treaty (SALT) II.
Carter restores full diplomatic relations with the People's Republic of China.

1980 Carter withdraws SALT II agreement from Senate after Soviet invasion of Afghanistan.
Iran hostage crisis preoccupies nation.
Ronald Reagan elected president.

1981 Major cuts in taxes and domestic spending, coupled with large increases in military budget.

1981–1983 Severe recession (late 1981–early 1983).

1982 Equal Rights Amendment dies.
Central Intelligence Agency organizes contra war against Nicaragua's Sandinista government.
Nuclear-freeze rally in Central Park.
Stock-market boom begins.

1983 239 U.S. Marines die in Beirut terrorist attack.
U.S. invasion of Grenada.
Reagan proposes Strategic Defense Initiative (SDI).

1984 Reagan defeats Walter Mondale in landslide.

1986 Immigration Reform and Control Act.
Federal deficit rises to $221 billion.

FOR FURTHER READING

James L. Baughman, *The Republic of Mass Culture: Journalism, Filmmaking, and Broadcasting in America Since 1941* (1992). Thorough, readable survey of the mass media's expanding role in contemporary America.

Paul Boyer, ed., *Reagan as President* (1990). Contemporary speeches, articles, and editorials commenting on Reagan and his program, with an introduction by the editor.

Peter Carroll, *It Seemed Like Nothing Happened* (1983). A perceptive, readable overview history of the 1970s.

Thomas Byrne Edsall with Mary D. Edsall, *Chain Reaction: The Impact of Race, Rights, and Taxes on American Politics* (1992). Insightful analysis of the social and economic sources of the rise of a conservative voting majority.

Haynes Johnson, *Sleepwalking Through History: America in the Reagan Years* (1991). A highly readable account of American politics and culture in the 1980s by a seasoned *Washington Post* reporter.

Carl H. Nightingale, *On the Edge: A History of Poor Black Children and Their American Dreams* (1993). Moving presentation of the effect of inner-city poverty on its most vulnerable victims.

Gaddis Smith, *Morality, Reason, and Power* (1986). Evaluation of Jimmy Carter's foreign policy by an able diplomatic historian.

Garry Wills, *Reagan's America: Innocents at Home* (1987). A stimulating, wide-ranging work by a distinguished political writer.

Daniel Yankelovich, *New Rules: Search for Self-Fulfillment in a World Turned Upside Down* (1981). An assessment of the American mood on the basis of public-opinion interviews and surveys.

CHAPTER

33

Beyond the Cold War

Optimism about foreign affairs dominated Ronald Reagan's second administration as new Soviet leadership under Mikhail Gorbachev edged away from the totalitarian repression of the old Stalinist system and toward a new openness, *glasnost*. At the same time, rocketing budget deficits and revelations of wrongdoing by Reagan administration officials soured domestic politics. Reagan's successor, George Bush, closed out the Cold War and reasserted American leadership in the Persian Gulf War, but he ignored thorny domestic problems, particularly a seemingly endless recession. Freed of Cold War concerns, Americans voted Bush out of office in 1992 in favor of Governor Bill Clinton of Arkansas, who pledged to focus on jobs and deficit reduction.

(Right) The destruction of the Berlin Wall in November 1989 marked the beginning of the end of the Cold War. Note the impassive East German border guards watching but not intervening.

Clinton took office riding a wave of hope, but image problems, policy disputes, and global complexities soon threatened to swamp his new administration. Despite economic recovery and victory in the Cold War, the national mood remained sour and edgy. Battered by political setbacks and misjudgments, Clinton saw his popularity erode as the Republicans carried both houses of Congress in 1994 and legislative gridlock—even to the point of shutting down the federal government—ensued. Ironically, the new administration would accomplish more in foreign policy than in domestic policy, despite the "policy wonk" backgrounds of both the president and vice president.

Problems and Opportunities in Reagan's Second Term

In his first term, Ronald Reagan had set a political agenda of tax cuts, deregulation, and expanded military spending. In his second term, a growing budget deficit and trade gap, and the Iran-contra scandal, overtook him. Foreign affairs temporarily eclipsed domestic issues, however, as a new era of Soviet-American cooperation and friendship replaced the "evil empire" confrontation of Reagan's first term. Despite chronic economic problems and misconduct at the highest levels of government, Reagan left office in 1989 with very favorable approval ratings, the first president since Dwight Eisenhower to complete two terms.

Tax Reform, Budget Deficits, and Trade Gaps

Reagan achieved significant legislative victories in his second term, including a new immigration law and tax reform. To make the system fairer, the tax-reform law eliminated many deductions, established uniform rates for people at comparable income levels, and removed 6 million low-income Americans from the tax rolls.

But sky-high federal deficits, the legacy of Reaganomics, persisted. In 1985 and 1986, the budget deficit reached $200 billion before settling at $150 billion in 1987 and 1988. Enormous federal debts and an escalating trade gap, which hit $154 billion in 1987, represented long-term economic problems bequeathed by Reagan to his successor.

Middle East Encore: Talks and Terrorism

The situation in the Middle East remained volatile. In December 1987 the Intifada, a Palestinian uprising against Israeli occupation, began in Gaza and spread to the West Bank. Reagan's secretary of state, George Shultz, attempted in 1988 to bring Jordan and the Palestinians into negotiations with Israel over an accelerated Palestinian autonomy plan. But the Israeli government rejected the "land for peace" formula and refused to negotiate until the Intifada ended; and the Palestinians rejected Shultz's proposals for not going far enough toward establishing a Palestinian state. Israel meanwhile continued to build Jewish settlements on the West Bank.

In the late 1980s the Middle East conflict generated a deadly by-product: kidnappings, airplane hijackings, airport attacks, and other terrorist acts. In April 1986 after terrorists bombed a Berlin nightclub popular with American GIs, President Reagan ordered a retaliatory air attack on Libya, which had been implicated in the bombing. In the worst of the terrorist incidents, a bomb exploded aboard a Pan Am jet over Scotland in December 1988, killing all 259 aboard, many of them Americans. In 1991 the U.S. and British governments formally charged Libya with complicity in the bombing. Colonel Muammar el-Qaddafi, Libya's ruler, denied the charges and refused to extradite the accused officials.

The Middle East was also the spawning ground for a crisis that would rock the Reagan presidency to its core.

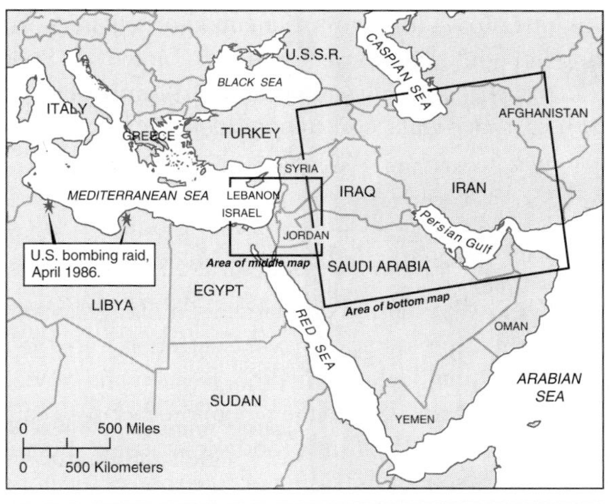

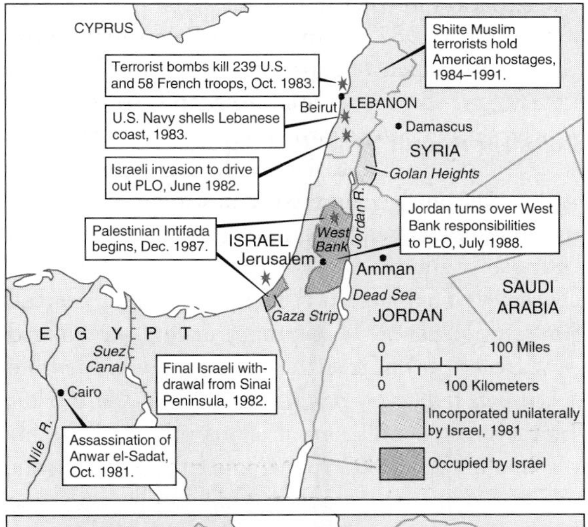

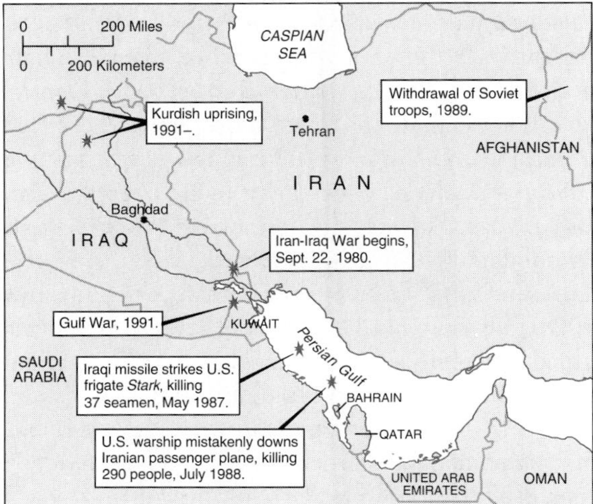

The Mideast Crises, 1980–Present

The Bush administration, like its predecessors, had trouble formulating a coherent and effective policy toward the Middle East, a region torn by ethnic, religious, and national conflicts.

The Iran-Contra Scandal

On November 3, 1986, a Beirut newspaper reported that in 1985 the United States had shipped 508 antitank missiles to the violently anti-American Iranian government. Thus began the worst scandal of the Reagan administration. Acknowledging the sale, Reagan declared that his goal had been to encourage "moderate elements" in Iran and to secure the release of American hostages held in Lebanon by pro-Iranian radicals. In February 1987 a presidential investigative panel placed heavy blame on the administration, prompting the resignation of Chief of Staff Donald Regan.

Soon more details surfaced. It was learned that national-security adviser Robert McFarlane had accompanied the second arms shipment to Iran and had carried a chocolate cake and a Bible autographed by President Reagan for Ayatollah Khomeini. The most explosive revelation was that Lieutenant Colonel Oliver North had diverted millions in profits from the arms sales to the Nicaraguan contras (see Chapter 32) at a time when Congress had made such aid illegal. In November 1986 North and his secretary had altered or deleted computer files and had held a "shredding party" to destroy incriminating documents.

In summer 1987 a joint House-Senate investigative committee on the Iran-contra affair heard 250 hours of testimony from twenty-eight witnesses. A fascinated nation watched "Ollie" North, resplendent in his military uniform, portray himself as a true patriot. Former national-security adviser John Poindexter testified that he had deliberately concealed the diversion of funds from Reagan.

The committee found no evidence that President Reagan personally knew of illegalities, but it severely criticized the casual management style and disregard for the law that had fed the scandal. In early 1988 a court-appointed special prosecutor, Lawrence Walsh, won criminal indictments against Poindexter, North, and others. In 1989 a federal jury convicted North of obstructing a congressional inquiry, destroying and falsifying National Security Council documents, and accepting an illegal gratuity, but the conviction was later reversed on the technical grounds that certain incriminating testimony had been given under a promise of immunity. Proclaiming himself vindicated, North began a public-speaking career and published memoirs claiming that Reagan had been fully aware of his activities. In 1994 North narrowly lost a bid for a senatorial seat from Virginia. The Iran-contra scandal dogged the Reagan administration's final years as a shocking abuse of executive power.

More Scandals and Embarrassments

Other disturbing revelations, some of them involving the president's closest associates, plagued Reagan's second term. His old friend Attorney General Edward Meese was accused of influence peddling and resigned in July 1988. That same year, former chief of staff Donald Regan's *For the Record* painted Reagan as little more than an automaton: "Every moment of every public appearance, every word was scripted, every place where Reagan was expected to stand was chalked with toe marks." Regan also revealed that first lady Nancy Reagan regularly consulted an astrologer about the president's schedule and pending decisions. News broke of bribery and conspiracy involving some of the Pentagon's largest suppliers. In 1989 still other revelations came, this time about former interior secretary James Watt's and other prominent Republicans' acceptance of hundreds of thousands of dollars for interceding with the Department of Housing and Urban Development on behalf of developers seeking federal subsidies.

But the dirty linen did not sully Reagan's own popularity. His admirers did not look to him for administrative brilliance or conventional political skills. The sources of his popularity lay far deeper, in his uncanny ability to articulate the beliefs, fears, and hopes of millions of Americans. Moreover, Reagan benefited from an unanticipated turn of events abroad that would end his presidency on a note of triumph.

Reagan's Mission to Moscow

The Cold War thawed dramatically in Reagan's second term. Meeting at Geneva, Switzerland, in 1985 and Reykjavík, Iceland, in 1986, Reagan and Soviet leader Mikhail Gorbachev explored large-scale weapons cuts. Beset by economic crisis at home, Gorbachev sought an easing of superpower tensions to gain a breathing space for reform and crafted a

President Reagan Visits Red Square
As the Cold War crumbled, President Reagan flew to Moscow in 1988 to sign a nuclear-arms reduction treaty with Soviet premier Mikhail Gorbachev.

policy of *glasnost*, or openness, to begin *perestroika*, the restructuring of Soviet society.

In December 1987 Gorbachev came to Washington to sign the Intermediate Nuclear Forces (INF) Treaty. Providing for the removal of 2,500 American and Soviet missiles from Europe, this treaty revived the arms-control process and for the first time eliminated an entire class of nuclear weapons. INF also provided on-site inspections to verify compliance.

This agreement led to Reagan's historic visit to Moscow in May 1988. The two leaders not only signed the INF Treaty but also established a cordial personal relationship. Asked about the evil empire, Reagan replied that he had been talking about an earlier era. Gorbachev announced Soviet withdrawal from Afghanistan, resolving another major sticking point.

Détente, derailed in the 1970s, was back on track and barreling ahead. Even critics of Reagan's domestic policies applauded the turnabout. The ardent Cold Warrior, denouncer of earlier arms-control treaties and champion of mammoth military spending, seemed destined to be remembered for bettering superpower relations, signing an important arms-limitation agreement, and reducing the risk of global war.

The Election of 1988

Vice President George Bush nailed down the Republican nomination for the presidency. A seven-way battle among Democrats narrowed into a contest between Jesse Jackson and Massachusetts governor Michael Dukakis. Preaching concern for the poor and urging a full-scale war on drugs, Jackson drew impressive numbers of white as well as black votes. However, Dukakis victories in major primary states, including New York and California, proved decisive. He chose Texas senator Lloyd Bentsen as his running mate.

On the Republican side, Bush surprised everyone by choosing a little-known conservative senator from Indiana, J. Danforth ("Dan") Quayle III, as his vice-presidential selection. The press soon learned that in 1969 Quayle had pulled strings to avoid service in Vietnam, but the issue faded.

Bush called for a "kinder, gentler America" and promised no new taxes. He emphasized peace and prosperity, pointing to better superpower relations, low inflation, and the 14 million new jobs created during the eighties. While Bush personally took the high road, some of his commercials took the low road. One campaign ad, playing on latent racist stereotypes, featured a black man who had committed rape and murder after his release under a Massachusetts prisoner-furlough program. Bush assailed Dukakis's veto of a bill requiring Massachusetts schoolchildren to recite the Pledge of Allegiance, although the Supreme Court had already declared such a law unconstitutional. For his part, Dukakis declined to attack Bush and stressed that "this election is not about ideology, it's about competence." Boasting his accomplishments as governor, he hammered at the failures of the "Swiss-cheese" Reagan economy. But Dukakis seemed edgy and defensive, and his dismissal of ideology made it difficult for him to define his vision of America.

Both candidates avoided serious issues in favor of TV-oriented "photo opportunities" and "sound bites." Bush visited flag factories and military plants; Dukakis looked spectacularly out of place posing in a tank. Editorial writers grumbled about the "junk-food" campaign, but images, catchy phrases, and twenty-second spots on the evening news became the essence of presidential politics. On November 8 Bush gained 54 percent of the vote, won forty states, and emerged with a lopsided 426–112 electoral margin. The Democrats retained control of both houses of Congress.

The departing president could look back on foreign policy triumphs, having had the good fortune to serve as the Cold War and the Soviet menace had ended. Reagan had also restored national pride; but his domestic record was mixed. Luxuriating in apparent prosperity, the administration—and the American people—had ignored serious social issues and structural weaknesses in the economy. Some Reagan policies, in fact, laid the groundwork for later problems. And despite his popularity, Reagan's

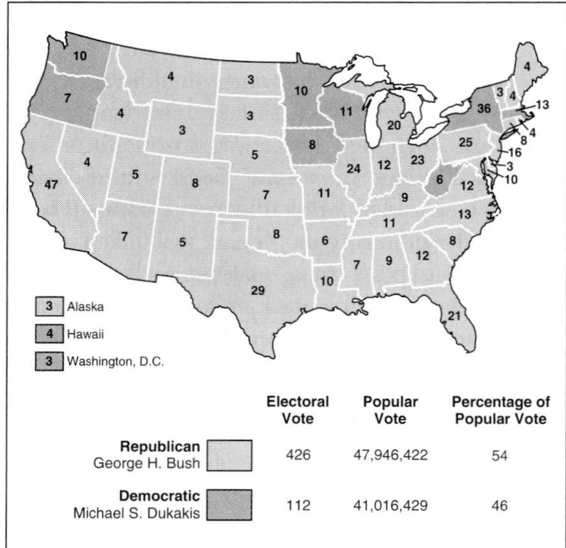

The Election of 1988

image dimmed quickly. From the perspective of the early 1990s, his presidency seemed more an interlude of nostalgia and drift than one of positive achievement and a time when individual gain took precedence over the public good.

The Bush Years: Resolve Abroad, Drift at Home

The son of a powerful Connecticut senator, George Bush had fought in World War II and attended Yale before entering the Texas oil business. He had served in Congress, lost a Senate race, directed the Central Intelligence Agency (CIA), and fought for the 1980 Republican nomination before being tapped as Ronald Reagan's running mate in 1980.

As president, Bush compiled a curiously uneven record. Despite a series of international triumphs, especially orchestration of the Gulf War, in the domestic theater Bush often appeared asleep at the switch, substituting platitudes for policy. In retrospect, the Bush interlude seems primarily a postscript to the Reagan era.

The Cold War Ends

Amid the changing of the guard in Washington, Soviet power collapsed with breathtaking speed. When Gorbachev refused to use Soviet troops to prop up Eastern Europe's unpopular communist regimes, they swiftly fell. New democratic governments sprang up behind what had been the iron curtain. In November 1989 exuberant Germans tore down the Berlin Wall, and within a year Germany was reunited for the first time since 1945. The Baltic republics—Latvia, Lithuania, and Estonia—forcibly annexed by the Soviet Union on the eve of World War II, declared their independence. Other Soviet republics followed.

The Cold War was suddenly over; the arms race, the Cold War's evil twin, seemed to wind down as well. In August 1991 President Bush and Gorbachev signed a treaty reducing their strategic arsenals by 25 percent. Secretary of Defense Dick Cheney proposed a 25 percent reduction in U.S. military forces over five years. With the Warsaw Pact gone, the North Atlantic Treaty Organization (NATO) planned a 50 percent troop reduction.

In August 1991 as the Soviet Union inched toward a market economy, increasing economic chaos led hard-line Communist party leaders to stage a coup against Gorbachev. Rallied by Boris Yeltsin, the president of the Russian Republic, the Russian people protectively surrounded the Russian parliament to defy the plotters and their tanks. Gorbachev returned to power, but Yeltsin assumed a dominant role.

The failed coup accelerated the death of the Soviet Communist party and of the Soviet Union itself. Exultant crowds toppled statues of Lenin and other communist leaders across the nation, and Leningrad reverted to its tsarist name, St. Petersburg. As the Soviet republics rushed to independence, Gorbachev was overwhelmed by the forces that he had released. Seeking to reform the Soviet economic and political system, he had also tried to preserve a unified Soviet Union, to retain a role for the Communist party, and to remain in charge of the reform process. In these latter goals he failed. The August 1991 coup stripped the last shred of legitimacy from the Soviet Communist party. Later

The End of the Cold War

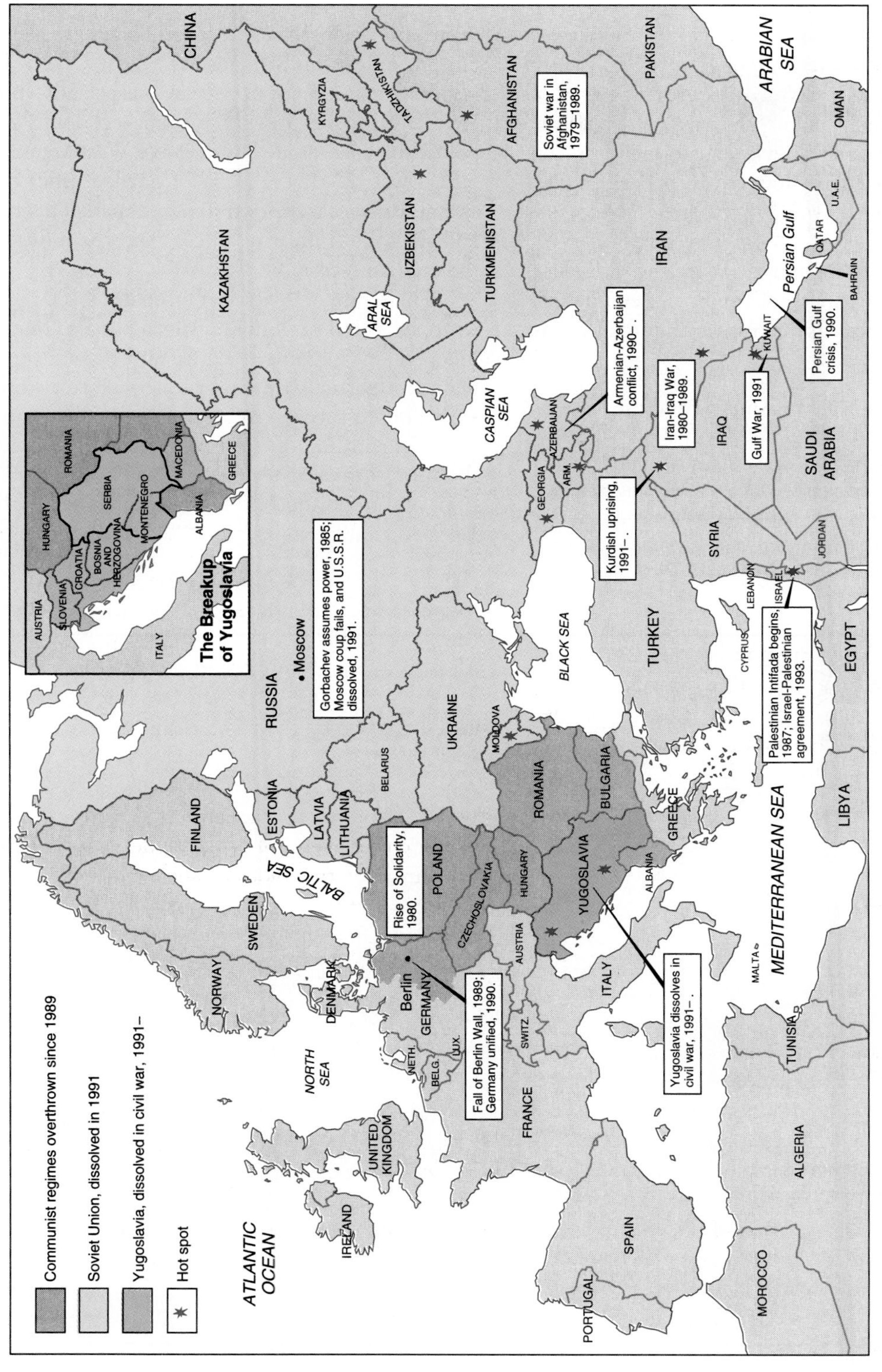

that year, led by Yeltsin, most of the Soviet republics proclaimed the end of the U.S.S.R. and formed the vaguely defined Commonwealth of Independent States. On Christmas Day 1991, enthralled American TV viewers watched as the hammer and sickle were lowered over the Kremlin for the last time. Bowing to the inevitable, Gorbachev resigned.

Secretary of State James Baker and President Bush proceeded cautiously as the Soviet empire disintegrated. American influence was limited, in any event, as nationalism and ethnic issues exploded in Eastern Europe and the former Soviet Union. Economic chaos and social upheaval especially threatened the Russian Republic. Some economists and political leaders argued for massive Western aid, but others warned that a flood of outside relief could swamp Russia's transition to a free-market economy and slow the shift of resources from the military to the civilian sector.

The future of the Soviet arsenal, 27,000 nuclear weapons, based not only in Russia but also in newly independent Ukraine, Belarus, and Kazakhstan, remained a particularly vital concern. Baker worked, with limited success, to assure the security and orderly dismantling of these weapons and to prevent the flow of nuclear technology to Third World nations and to nonnuclear European nations. Early in 1992, as strategic talks progressed, Bush announced

The United States in Latin America and the Caribbean

Plagued by poverty, population pressures, repressive regimes, and drug trafficking, Latin America saw turmoil and conflict—but also some hopeful developments—in the 1980s and 1990s. In the long tradition of Yanqui *intervention, U.S. forces invaded Grenada in 1983 and Panama in 1989.*

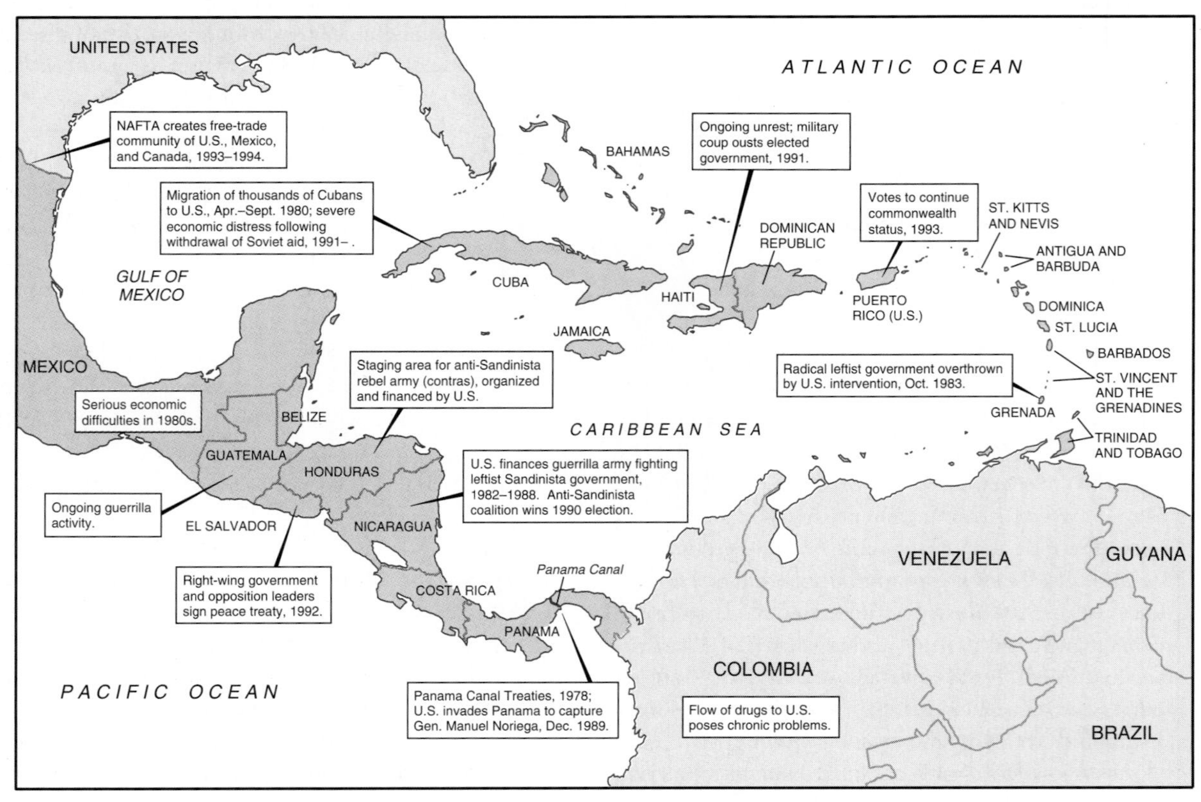

major reductions in the American nuclear arsenal.

The Cold War's end offered opportunities for the resolution of regional conflicts elsewhere in the world. For decades, the superpowers had aided allies, client states, and rebel forces throughout the Third World. But with the Cold War over and only one superpower left, the prospects for resolving local disputes brightened.

In Latin America, the bloody civil wars of the Cold War era wound down. The Bush administration abandoned its predecessors' financing of the Nicaraguan contras and worked at reintegrating them into Nicaragua's life and politics. In 1989 the Sandinistas and contras agreed to elections the next year, greater press freedom, and an end to their war. Victory in the elections went to newspaper publisher Violetta Chamorro, the leader of an anti-Sandinista coalition. In tiny El Salvador, where the United States had spent more than $1 billion to keep leftist guerrillas from power, the right-wing government and the guerrillas signed a treaty in 1992, ending a twelve-year civil war that had left 75,000 dead.

As the Cold War waned, the underlying causes of Latin America's social turbulence came into sharper focus. Enormous problems linked to poverty, ignorance, and economic exploitation still plagued Latin America. Open guerrilla warfare continued in Peru. Cocaine and heroin flowed from South and Central America to U.S. cities. In December 1989 concern over the drug traffic led to a U.S. invasion of Panama to capture the nation's strongman ruler, General Manuel Noriega. Formerly on the CIA payroll, Noriega was a corrupt thug who, in return for lucrative bribes, permitted Panama to serve as a conduit for the northward movement of drugs. Convicted in a U.S. court, Noriega received a life prison term for drug trafficking.

America's relations with the Philippines, a former colony and longtime ally, shifted as well. Resistance to the corrupt government of President Ferdinand Marcos intensified after the 1983 assassination of Benigno Aquino, a popular opposition leader. After a fraud-ridden election in 1986, Aquino's widow, Corazon, proclaimed herself victor, and the United States recognized her government. Marcos accepted exile in Hawaii. But the Philippines remained turbulent. In 1991 the Philippines legislature ended long-term American leases on two military bases. In the post–Cold War climate of eased world tensions, the Bush administration accepted this decision and withdrew from the bases.

South Africa became a focus of debate in Reagan's second term. Anglican bishop Desmond Tutu, a leader of South Africa's blacks, appealed for U.S. support against apartheid, the white government's policy of racial segregation. In 1986 Congress, over Reagan's veto, imposed stiff sanctions, banning South African products and prohibiting U.S. investments there. Worldwide sanctions helped to bring extraordinary changes to South Africa. In 1990 President F. W. de Klerk released black leader Nelson Mandela after twenty-seven years in prison and opened negotiations with his African National Congress. The South African parliament scrapped most apartheid laws in 1991, and Bush lifted some U.S. sanctions. In 1992 a strong majority of the nation's whites voted to continue dismantling apartheid and to extend political rights to South Africa's black majority.

China proved a major exception to the world trend toward democracy. In 1989 U.S. relations with China suffered a serious setback when the Chinese army brutally crushed a prodemocracy demonstration by thousands of unarmed students in Beijing's Tiananmen Square. As many as 1,000 students died, and repression, arrests, and public executions followed. The Bush administration protested but neither broke diplomatic relations nor canceled trade agreements with China, leaving these and a host of other foreign-policy headaches for his successor.

As Cold War worries waned, international trade issues took on growing significance. The towering U.S. trade deficit with Japan, which ranged from $40 billion to $55 billion in the late 1980s, aroused particular concern. In early 1992 President Bush led a high-level trade mission to Japan, accompanied by the heads of the "big three" U.S. auto companies. But efforts to open Japanese markets proved futile. When Bush collapsed from the flu during a state dinner in Tokyo, the mishap seemed unhappily symbolic

As the Bush administration grappled with a tangle of global issues, one regional provocation elicited a dramatic response.

Operation Desert Storm

On August 2, 1990, the Middle Eastern nation of Iraq invaded its oil-rich neighbor, Kuwait. Iraq's dictator, Saddam Hussein, had dismissed Kuwait's nation-state status as a creation of western imperialists and asserted Iraq's claim to the area.

Under Saddam, Iraq had for years threatened not only its Arab neighbors but also Israel. Iraq's military buildup, including chemical- and nuclear-weapons programs, had worried many governments in the 1980s. However, during the Iraq-Iran war (1980–1988), the United States had tilted toward Iraq because of Iran's rabid anti-Americanism. But lessened Iranian hostility after Ayatollah Khomeini's death in 1989 had removed the United States' incentive to placate Iraq. Thus, when Iraq invaded Kuwait, Washington denounced the aggression.

Determined to avoid the mistakes of the Vietnam era, Bush carefully built a consensus for anti-Iraqi action in Congress, in the United Nations, and among the American people. He also articulated a clear military objective—Iraqi withdrawal from Kuwait—and provided the necessary military force. More than 400,000 troops were shuttled to Saudi Arabia.

The United Nations imposed economic sanctions on Iraq and insisted that Saddam withdraw from Kuwait by January 15, 1991. On January 12, after somber debate, both houses of Congress endorsed military action against Iraq. Most Democrats, however, voted against war, favoring continued economic sanctions.

On January 16 a massive air assault opened the war. For nearly six weeks both American and allied land- and carrier-based planes pounded troops, supply depots, and command and communications targets in Iraq's capital, Baghdad. They flew up to 3,000 sorties daily. Iraq offered little direct resistance to the air attacks. But Saddam ordered Soviet-made Scud missiles fired against Israeli and Saudi Arabian cities. Americans watched transfixed as the Cable News Network carried live coverage of U.S. Patriot missiles streaking off to intercept incoming Scuds. Carefully edited for mass television viewers, the war often seemed a glorified video game. The reality of an estimated 100,000 Iraqi deaths, both military and civilian, hardly impinged on Americans' consciousness.

On February 23, 200,000 U.N. forces, comprising U.S. troops and their allies under General H. Norman Schwarzkopf, advanced across the desert toward Kuwait. Within three days Iraqi soldiers were in full flight or surrendering en masse. U.N. forces destroyed 3,700 Iraqi tanks while losing only three. One hundred hours after the ground war had begun, with Iraqi resistance crushed and Kuwait City liberated, President Bush declared a cease-fire. American casualties numbered 148 dead, including 35 killed by "friendly fire," and 467 wounded.

As victory celebrations back in the United States receded, the war's political aftermath came into focus. Kuwait created a refugee nightmare by expelling thousands of Palestinian workers who had supported Iraq. Within Iraq, amid widespread civilian hardship and malnutrition, Saddam clung to power. His army brutally suppressed rebellions by Shiite Muslims in the south and by a large Kurdish ethnic minority in the north. U.N. inspectors found convincing evidence of an advanced nuclear-weapons project under way in Iraq, and its discontinuance brought general relief.

Capitalizing on the favorable diplomatic climate created by the outcome of the Gulf War, Bush called for a renewed Middle Eastern peace effort. Secretary of State James Baker orchestrated the diplomacy, which culminated in the opening of talks involving Israel, the Palestinians, and various Arab states in November 1991. Polls showed that 80 percent of Israelis favored a settlement, but whether the longtime enemies could reach agreement remained unclear. Frustrating though it was, the peace process continued and would bear fruit under Bush's successor.

Domestic Discontents

The tax cuts, Pentagon spending, and deregulatory fever of the "Reagan revolution" had unleashed entrepreneurial energies, powered a stock-market surge and a wave of corporate takeovers, and set off an economic boom that gave the 1980s a patina of prosperity. But in the 1990s the longer-term effects of Reaganism began to be felt. As the economy slowed, the go-go eighties seemed remote. Under George Bush, Americans, especially the middle class, bristled with economic discontent.

Economic Strains

As president, Bush confronted—or evaded—a morass of economic problems directly related to Reagan policies. First came the collapse of the savings-and-loan (S&L) industry, long a source of home loans to borrowers and of a secure return to depositors. In the late seventies, S&Ls had paid high interest rates to attract depositors, even though their assets were tied up in fixed-rate mortgages. In the early eighties, capital freed up by the Reagan tax cuts had flowed to S&Ls just as they were deregulated. Caught up in the high-flying economic mood of the eighties, S&Ls across the nation had made risky loans on speculative real-estate ventures. As the economy cooled, many such investments went bad. In the period 1988–1990, nearly 600 S&Ls failed, wiping out thousands of depositors' savings.

Because the federal government insures S&L deposits, the Bush administration in 1989 set up a program to repay depositors and to sell millions of dollars' worth of foreclosed office towers and apartment buildings in a depressed real-estate market. Estimates of the cost of the bailout topped $400 billion.

Meanwhile, the federal deficit, already worsened by the Reagan tax cuts and runaway military spending, mounted. In fall 1990 Congress and Bush agreed on a five-year deficit-reduction package that clipped government spending and increased taxes. Controversially, Bush had abandoned his 1988 campaign pledge "Read my lips: no new taxes." But the red ink flowed on; the deficit reached $269 billion in 1991 and $290 billion in 1992. The Gulf War, the S&L bailout, and soaring welfare and Medicare-Medicaid payments shattered the budget-balancing effort.

Making matters worse, a recession struck in summer 1990. Retail sales slumped, housing starts declined, and unemployment rose. Troubled times continued into 1992, with a jobless rate of more than 7 percent. Hard-pressed states gutted social-welfare funding—Michigan cut AFDC (Aid to Families with Dependent Children) payments by 17 percent. As the number of Americans below the poverty line rose by 2.1 million, the plight of the poor roused more resentment than sympathy. Ohio's governor declared, "Most Ohioans have had enough welfare, enough poverty, enough drugs, enough crime." The middle class, political strategists discovered, were suffering from "compassion fatigue." Battered by Japanese imports, the U.S. auto industry fared disastrously in 1991. A week before Christmas, GM unveiled plans to close twenty-one plants and cut its work force by more than 70,000.

Economic jitters made many Americans look back on Reagan's policies skeptically. If 1984 was "morning in America," wrote a columnist, quoting a Reagan campaign slogan, 1989–1990 was the "morning after." For most middle-class Americans, the situation produced more anxiety than desperation, but the gloomy economic picture clouded much of Bush's presidency.

Hard times worsened already bleak inner-city conditions. In April 1992 violence erupted in a poor black section of Los Angeles and quickly spread. The immediate trigger was the Rodney King case. Videotapes showed white California police officers beating an African-American motorist, Rodney King, who seemed to be trying to escape. When an all-white jury acquitted the four officers, the predominantly black south-central section of Los Angeles exploded into riots that took a terrible toll in both life and property.

Among African-Americans, the gulf between the middle class and the inner-city poor widened. By 1990 one-third of black high school graduates went on to college, up from one-quarter in 1985. More than 7,300 blacks held public office in America in 1990, up from 1,300 in 1970. Most visible were New York City's first African-American mayor, David Dinkins, and the nation's first African-American governor, Virginia's Douglas Wilder. Bush appointed African-Americans Colin Powell chairman of the Joint Chiefs of Staff, Louis Sullivan secretary of health and human services, and Clarence Thomas Supreme Court justice. But the record of black achievement could not obscure the harsh realities for the one-third of African-Americans below the poverty level.

Similar patterns emerged in the Hispanic-American population. By 1991 more than 4,000 Hispanics held public office in California alone. At the same time, more than a quarter of all Hispanics remained poor, eking out a living in urban barrios or on the exhausting migrant-labor circuit.

Reflecting middle-class white and business priorities, the Bush administration did little to address these issues. In 1990 Bush vetoed a bill broadening federal protection against job discrimination, claiming that it would encourage "racial quotas." In 1991 he signed a similar bill. When Bush showed up in Atlanta in 1992 to sing "We Shall Overcome" on the birthday of Martin Luther King, Jr., King's daughter, the Reverend Bernice King, asked bitterly, "How dare we celebrate in the midst of a recession, when nobody is sure whether their jobs are secure?"

An inrushing stream of immigrants from many nations raised concerns about whether the country could absorb so many newcomers, the vast majority of them from Latin America and Asia. Debate focused on the issue of whether the United States should become a "salad bowl" of multiple cultures, a society not only tolerating but even encouraging diverse ethnic groups and languages. In the academic world, similar concerns led to attacks upon, and fervent defense of, the "canon" of traditional Western literature. Critics argued that this canon drew almost exclusively from "dead white males" and demanded the inclusion of non-European literature and philosophy.

In the realm of public education, the recession stung school budgets at a moment of much hand-wringing over shortcomings in the American educational system. Remedies proved elusive. Bush ballyhooed himself as the "education president" but addressed the issue only fitfully. Bush called for standardized national testing of schoolchildren, supported a voucher system by which parents could withdraw their children from public schools and enroll them in private or church schools, and urged corporate America to support a fund for experimental schools. These proposals hardly matched the magnitude of the problem.

The environmental issue was spotlighted in March 1989 when a 987-foot oil tanker, the *Exxon Valdez*, ran aground in Alaska's beautiful Prince William Sound and spilled more than 10 million gallons of crude oil. The accident fouled 600 acres of coastal and marine habitats, killed thousands of sea otters and shore birds, and jeopardized vital salmon and herring industries. Then in summer 1989 the Environmental Protection Agency (EPA) reported that air pollution exceeded federal standards in more than one hundred cities. In Louisiana alone, industry pumped 2 million pounds of pollutants into the air daily. In 1991 the EPA reported that pollutants were depleting the ozone shield—the layer that protects humans from cancer-causing solar radiation—over the United States at twice the rate that scientists had predicted.

Caught between public pressure for change and corporate calls for a go-slow policy, the Bush administration compiled a mixed environmental record. Bush called the *Exxon Valdez* spill a "major tragedy" but supported offshore oil exploration and drilling. In a rare bipartisan effort, the White House and the Democratic Congress passed a tough Federal Clean Air Act in 1990. The government also began the

Cleaning Up After the *Exxon Valdez* Disaster
Volunteers on Green Island in Alaska's Prince William Sound collect and bag sea otters killed in the Exxon Valdez *oil spill of March 1989, a catastrophe that focused attention on the mounting ecological toll of industrialization.*

multibillion-dollar task of disposing of radioactive waste and cleaning up nuclear-weapons facilities and nuclear-power plants that had been contaminating soil and ground water for years.

But the Bush administration, like the Reagan government, generally dismissed environmental concerns. Vice President Dan Quayle ridiculed environmentalists; the administration scuttled international treaties on global warming and mining in Antarctica, recommended oil exploration in the Alaskan wilderness, and proposed opening vast tracts of protected wetlands to development. In 1992 Bush addressed the Earth Summit, a United Nations–sponsored environmental conference in Brazil, but his defensive, self-serving speech further alienated environmental activists.

The Supreme Court Moves Right

Like all presidents, Reagan and Bush sought to perpetuate their political ideology through Supreme Court appointments. In addition to nominating Sandra Day O'Connor, Reagan in 1986 elevated William Rehnquist to chief justice and chose judicial conservative Antonin Scalia to fill the vacant seat. Then in 1987 Reagan named Robert Bork, a judge and legal scholar whose intellectual rigidity, doctrinaire opposition to judicial activism, and scant regard for the Supreme Court's role in protecting individual liberties led the Senate to reject him. Reagan's next nominee withdrew after admitting that he had smoked marijuana, but Reagan's third choice, Anthony Kennedy, also very conservative, won speedy confirmation.

President Bush made two nominations, in 1990 and 1991: David Souter and Clarence Thomas. Souter, a New Hampshire judge, gained easy confirmation, but the Thomas nomination proved controversial. Bush nominated him to fill the seat vacated by Thurgood Marshall, a black who had fought segregation as a lawyer for the National Association for the Advancement of Colored People. Thomas, also an African-American, espoused a conservative political ideology, praised Oliver North as a maligned hero, and opposed affirmative-action programs. The head of the Equal Employment Opportunity Commission (EEOC) under Reagan, Thomas saw individual effort, not government programs, as the avenue for black progress. Noting Thomas's right-wing ideology and his thin record as a federal judge, critics charged Bush with cynically playing racial politics.

The nomination drew even more challenges when a former Thomas associate at EEOC, law professor Anita Hill, charged him with sexual harassment years before. For several days, the Senate Judiciary Committee's hearings on Hill's accusations filled the nation's TV screens. Thomas narrowly won confirmation, 52–48.

These Reagan-Bush appointments seemed to ensure that a conservative majority would rule the Court into the twenty-first century. The liberal social activism that had characterized the Court from the New Deal through the Earl Warren years was blunted. Hints of the Court's new conservatism came early. In a series of 5–4 rulings in 1989, the Court upheld a Missouri law limiting women's right to abortion and imposed confining new definitions on widely used civil-rights laws aimed at protecting the employment rights of women and minorities and at remedying past inequities. In the 1990–1991 term, the Court narrowed the rights of an arrested person and upheld regulations barring physicians in federally funded family-planning clinics from discussing abortion with their patients. Then in a 5–4 decision in June 1992, the Supreme Court upheld a Pennsylvania law placing various restrictions on abortion. At the same time, however, the majority affirmed *Roe* v. *Wade* (1973), the decision that had upheld women's constitutional right to abortion.

The Politics of Frustration

Bush's shifting political fortunes were a barometer of the public mood. In the afterglow of Operation Desert Storm, his approval ratings shot up to 88 percent, only to plummet below 50 percent as the recession eroded national confidence. In a 1991 election to fill a Senate vacancy in Pennsylvania, Bush's weakened influence showed when his attorney general, Richard Thornburgh, lost to a political novice who articulated middle-class concerns about high taxes and ever-escalating health-care costs.

Heeding such warning signals, Bush proclaimed economic recovery his "Number 1 priority." Yet in late 1991, a damning *New York Times* editorial commented, "Nearly three years into his term, George Bush remains mystifyingly incomplete: shrewd and energetic in foreign policy and . . . clumsy and irresolute—at home. . . . The domestic Bush flops like a fish, leaving the impression that he doesn't know what he thinks or doesn't much care, apart from the political gains to be extracted from an issue."

Bush's 1992 State of the Union message contained a recession-fighting package, including middle-class tax relief, tax breaks for first-time home buyers, and tax credits to help Americans buy health insurance. Refurbishing traditional Republican formulas, Bush also asked for lower taxes on capital gains, tax incentives for business investment, and an end to the luxury tax on yachts and private planes. Democrats dismissed Bush's belated attention to domestic issues as politically motivated and inadequate.

In the 1992 race for the White House, the Bush-Quayle ticket coasted to renomination. But the Republican right dominated the convention and platform, while moderates deplored this rightward turn. Undaunted by Bush's apparent invulnerability after Desert Storm, Governor William ("Bill") Clinton of Arkansas withstood doubts about his character and accusations of marital infidelities to defeat his opponents in the primaries and sew up the Democratic presidential nomination in early summer 1992. Choosing Senator Albert Gore of Tennessee, an advocate for the environment, as his running mate, Clinton pledged an activist government and oriented the Democratic party toward middle-class concerns.

Folksy billionaire H. Ross Perot presented a political challenge to politics-as-usual. His insistence that the nation's economic problems were simple, and that only party politics stood in the way of their solution, carried Perot to a nearly 40 percent peak in the polls. However, the Texan's autocratic ways and thin-skinned response to criticism turned off many supporters. In July 1992 he left the race for poorly explained reasons, but he returned in October 1992, spent millions of his own dollars on television advertising, and participated in televised presidential debates.

Bush ran a negative campaign, attacking Clinton's character and charging that the Arkansas governor had been a draft dodger during the Vietnam War. Toward the campaign's end, Bush ridiculed Clinton and Gore as "crazies" and "bozos." Clinton called for an industrial policy that would give Washington an active role in promoting economic

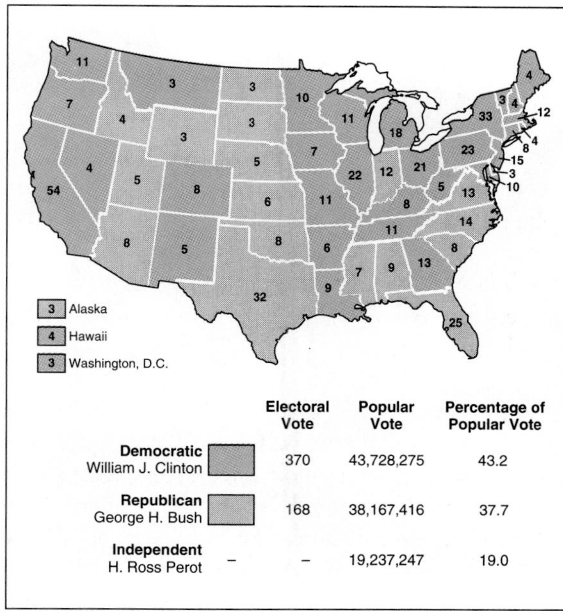

	Electoral Vote	Popular Vote	Percentage of Popular Vote
Democratic William J. Clinton	370	43,728,275	43.2
Republican George H. Bush	168	38,167,416	37.7
Independent H. Ross Perot	–	19,237,247	19.0

The Election of 1992

recovery and innovative technologies, and he put health-care reform high on his agenda.

The voters spoke on November 3 when 43 percent chose Clinton. Bush trailed with 38 percent, and Perot amassed 19 percent—the largest share for a third party since Teddy Roosevelt's 1912 Bull Moose party. In the electoral tally, Clinton carried 370 votes to Bush's 168.

Clinton's electoral success rested largely on his ability to resurrect the Democratic coalition, luring blue-collar and "Reagan Democrat" voters as well as reclaiming parts of the South. With the presidency and both houses of Congress in Democratic hands, Americans hoped for the end of legislative gridlock. The new Congress itself was more representative of U.S. society as a whole as thirty-eight African-American and seventeen Hispanic-Americans won election to the 1993–1994 session, up from twenty-five and ten, respectively. And the new Congress included fifty-three women: six in the Senate and forty-seven in the House. This outcome, combined with the advent of Hillary Rodham Clinton, the first presidential spouse to have a career in her own right, buoyed those who had declared 1992 the "Year of the Woman."

The Clinton Years: Politics Moves Right

William Jefferson Clinton—Bill Clinton, as he preferred—was the first baby-boomer president: born after World War II, shaped by JFK, the Beatles, and Vietnam. Born in Arkansas in 1946, he attended Georgetown University and then, after a stint at Oxford as a Rhodes Scholar, Yale Law School. Fascinated by politics, he returned to Arkansas, married his law-school classmate Hillary Rodham, and won the governorship in 1979, at thirty-two.

Clinton entered the White House in January 1993 exuding confidence and energy, but he quickly encountered rough seas—some of his own making and some rooted in the complexity of the issues the nation faced. In the 1994 midterm election, disgruntled voters gave the Republicans a stunning victory. As Clinton moved right, however, his standing improved.

Clinton's difficulties stemmed in part from the "character issue" rooted in his desire to please and his consequent tendency to shift positions. Political cartoonist Garry Trudeau routinely portrayed him as a waffle. The Clintons' Arkansas financial dealings, especially their real-estate venture with the Whitewater Development Company, presented critics with ammunition and led to Senate hearings and the appointment of a special counsel. By 1996 Whitewater had resulted in several criminal convictions, including Clinton's successor as Arkansas's governor, but had not directly implicated the Clintons. Other issues dogged the White House as well, including Hillary Clinton's $100,000 profit on a $1,000 commodities investment; the suicide of White House aide Vincent Foster, a close Clinton friend and former law partner of Hillary Clinton; controversy over the firing of the White House Travel Office staff; White House mishandling of

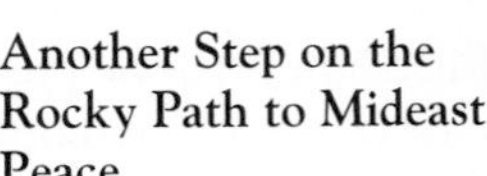

Another Step on the Rocky Path to Mideast Peace
President Clinton presides as Israeli prime minister Yitzhak Rabin and PLO chairman Yasir Arafat shake hands after signing a peace accord at the White House, September 13, 1993.

confidential Federal Bureau of Investigation files; and a sexual harassment lawsuit filed against the president by a former Arkansas state employee.

The Quest for a Coherent Foreign Policy

The new administration faced difficult foreign-policy challenges, including responding to turmoil in the former Soviet empire, defining America's role as the sole remaining superpower, and shaping a "New World Order" in which a nation's trade balance loomed as large as its military might. Complicating the situation was the emergence of Japan and Germany as economic powerhouses and of the European Union (EU) as a formidable trading bloc. Bill Clinton, like George Bush, failed to craft a coherent foreign policy comparable to the containment doctrine of the Cold War years. Ironically, however, his first term brought more success in the diplomatic arena than in the domestic realm.

The collapse of Soviet hegemony in Eastern Europe unleashed ancient ethnic hatreds. While the Czechs and Slovaks peacefully divided Czechoslovakia into two separate nations, attempts at ethnic separation in Yugoslavia proved catastrophic. In pursuit of a "Greater Serbia," Orthodox Christian Serbs seized territory from Roman Catholic Croats and Muslim Bosnians (with the Croats occasionally joining the Serbs in attacking the Bosnians) and carried out a brutal "ethnic cleansing" all too reminiscent of Nazi genocide. The bloody conflict dragged on until 1995 when the Clinton administration brought leaders of the warring groups to Dayton, Ohio, to sign a peace treaty and arrange a partition of Serbian, Croatian and Bosnian lands. At the end of 1995, Clinton dispatched some 20,000 U. S. troops to Bosnia-Herzegovina as part of a NATO peacekeeping contingent, despite serious misgivings by many Americans.

In Russia itself, political and economic upheaval spawned widespread unrest, especially among older and rural Russians who saw themselves as victims more than beneficiaries of the new order. The economy reeled, criminal gangs flourished in major cities, ultranationalists scored disturbing electoral gains, and many Russians recalled the communist era with nostalgia born of desperation. The

Clinton administration supported President Boris Yeltsin despite his lurches from reform to repression. Yeltsin eked out a victory in the 1996 presidential election, but Russia's future remained deeply clouded.

Lingering Vietnam-era fears of overseas commitment narrowed Clinton's foreign-policy options. He withdrew from Somalia the troops that Bush had dispatched on a humanitarian mission that had turned bloody. In Haiti, Clinton employed very tentative threats of force to dislodge a dictatorship and restore the elected leader, Bertrand Aristide. When tribal rivalries flared in the Central African nation of Rwanda, leaving perhaps 1 million dead and another 1 million refugees, Clinton pledged equipment to a U.N. aid mission but did little else.

Elsewhere, however, the diplomatic scene looked somewhat brighter. In Northern Ireland, the Clinton administration promoted peace talks between hostile Protestant and Roman Catholic factions. In South Africa, where a move to multiracial democracy had been hastened by economic sanctions imposed by the United States and other nations, Nelson Mandela moved from prison to the presidency in the nation's first multiracial election.

In the Middle East, the administration helped forge an agreement between the Palestine Liberation Organization (PLO) and the Israeli government granting the Palestinians limited self-rule in the Gaza Strip and the West Bank city of Jericho. PLO leader Yasir Arafat and Israeli prime minister Yitzhak Rabin signed the accord at the White House as a smiling Bill Clinton looked on. But hopes for a broader Middle East peace agreement faded with the assassination of Rabin in fall 1995 and the election of Benjamin Netanyahu, a hardliner hostile to Rabin's peace policy, as Israel's prime minister in 1996.

Increasingly, however, trade issues dominated Clinton's foreign-policy agenda, symbolized by the globe-trotting of Secretary of Commerce Ron Brown in search of investment opportunities for U.S. firms, until his 1996 death in a plane crash. "Trade as much as troops," Clinton proclaimed, "will . . . define the ties that bind nations in the twenty-first century"—and many foreign-policy experts agreed.

A mushrooming U.S. trade deficit, which shot to $150 billion in 1994, lent urgency to the trade issue. So did the coalescence of fifteen European nations, including most of America's NATO partners, into the European Union, the world's largest trading bloc. Partially in response, the Clinton administration successfully urged ratification of the North American Free Trade Agreement (NAFTA), negotiated during the Bush administration. Under NAFTA, the United States, Canada, and Mexico formed a single free-trade zone, a Western Hemisphere bloc to compete with the EU. The administration also agreed to participate in the Asian Pacific Economic Community (APEC), a Pacific Rim trading bloc, but full implementation of the APEC agreement lay far in the future.

The Clinton administration took a major step toward global economic cooperation in 1994 by securing the ratification of a restructured General Agreement on Tariffs and Trade (GATT), the first major reordering of the world trade system since the 1944 Bretton Woods conference. The revised GATT provided for gradual elimination of trade barriers worldwide and established the World Trade Organization (WTO) to settle disputes. Despite critics' misgivings that WTO membership undermined U.S. sovereignty, economists hailed the new system as a key step toward a truly integrated world economy.

The shift of focus from military to economic competition brought its own problems, however. Trade disputes with Japan continued to plague Clinton as they had Bush. Trade issues, coupled with human-rights abuses, also dogged U.S. relations with China, an emerging economic superpower in Asia.

Although no grand theme or unifying strategic vision arose during Clinton's first term, his administration compiled a creditable record on the diplomatic and world-trade fronts. And even the president's critics conceded the difficulty of crafting a foreign policy in a post–Cold War world where one big challenge—containing communism—had given way to an ever-shifting kaleidoscope of smaller challenges.

Struggling to Shape a Domestic Agenda

At home no less than abroad, the Clinton administration confronted both immediate problems and long-term challenges. Profound structural changes associated with the rise of a post-industrial, service-oriented, information-based economy demanded attention, as did the related emergence of a growing underclass, mostly African-American and Hispanic, cut off from economic opportunity in decaying inner-city slums.

Both Clinton and Vice President Al Gore belonged to the New Democratic Coalition, a group of fiscal moderates who stood for economic growth, attention to the economic concerns of the middle class, and reduced federal spending on social programs. Clinton's campaign, designed to lure blue-collar and middle-class voters back to the Democratic fold, stressed economic growth, middle-class tax relief, health-care reform, and welfare programs based on work rather than the dole. The campaign also echoed themes of the sixties and seventies such as feminism, abortion rights, and environmental concerns.

The transition from campaigning to governing proved rocky for Clinton. His effort to implement a campaign pledge to end the exclusion of homosexuals from military service stirred a hornet's nest of controversy. He soon retreated to a compromise position summed up in the phrase "Don't ask, don't tell."

A slogan on the wall of Clinton's campaign headquarters had proclaimed "It's the Economy, Stupid," and as president Clinton offered an economic program to cut the deficit and stimulate long-term growth. After six months of debate, Congress narrowly passed a five-year economic plan that cut military spending, increased taxes on upper-income families, and trimmed the projected budget deficit—but omitted a $169 billion package intended to stimulate job creation and economic expansion.

Clinton touted health-care reform as his central domestic goal. Although Americans in general enjoyed the world's best health care, the system had serious problems, including the fact that some 37 million citizens lacked health insurance and the spiraling cost of Medicare and Medicaid. If unchecked, analysts calculated, health costs would eat up nearly 20 percent of the gross domestic product by 2000, twice the rate of other industrialized nations.

Clinton appointed his wife to head a task force on reforming health care. Working behind closed doors, the task force devised a sweeping plan that the president presented to Congress in September 1993. As insurance-industry lobbyists and the health-care professions criticized aspects of the plan, polls made clear that the public favored incremental, rather than radical, reform. The key role of Hillary Clinton, who held no elective office or official government position, in shaping the proposal also rankled many voters. Ultimately the health-care bill died.

Clinton scored a major success on another front, however, with enactment of the administration's anticrime bill, which provided $30 billion for drug treatment, more prisons and more police officers, and boot camps for first-time offenders. It also included a controversial ban on assault weapons.

The 1994 Elections: A Sharp Right Turn

As the midterm elections neared, frustration with Clinton, and with politics in general, intensified. Newt Gingrich, a Republican congressman from Georgia, capitalized on the sour mood by drafting a conservative "Contract with America" and bringing some 300 GOP candidates to Washington to sign it. This strategy turned the midterm elections, normally dominated by local issues, into a national referendum. In a landslide that galvanized conservatives and stunned liberals, voters gave Republicans control of both houses of Congress for the first time since 1954.

Speaker of the House Newt Gingrich
A key architect of the Republican electoral victory in 1994, Gingrich led a right-wing assault on sixty years of welfare-state liberalism.

In the House, a jubilant horde of Republicans, including seventy-three freshmen, chose Gingrich as Speaker of the House and rapidly enacted most of the provisions of the Contract with America. These measures—including a balanced-budget amendment, repeal of the assault-weapon ban, and major tax cuts—soon bogged down in the Senate, however.

Gingrich's own popularity underwent a meteoric rise and fall. Initially, the new Speaker seemed to be everywhere, appearing on talk shows, giving interviews, calling press conferences. However, his loquacious "shoot-from-the-lip" style and his glib rhetoric, a blend of computer-age technobabble and harsh, sink-or-swim individualism, alienated many. An ethically dubious $4.5 million book advance (which he eventually repudiated) further tarnished Gingrich's reputation.

When Clinton and Congress failed to agree on a budget in 1995, much of the federal government shut down twice, once for almost two weeks. Americans blamed Gingrich when they could not obtain passports, visit national parks, or tour the Smithsonian Institution. By 1996 Gingrich's revolution had lost steam and Clinton's poll ratings had rebounded.

But the 1994 elections had driven Clinton to the right, as his position on welfare reform soon made clear. Candidate Clinton had pledged to "end welfare as we know it," but he and a reluctant Democratic Congress had made little headway on welfare reform in 1993–94. The Republican revolutionaries of 1995, by contrast, outdid Clinton in their zest for junking the welfare system. It cost too much, they charged, undermined the work ethic, sustained a bloated federal bureaucracy, and trapped the poor in a cycle of dependence.

Advocates for the poor warned that abandonment of the welfare system, however flawed, could have catastrophic results. Only a large-scale (and expensive) program to provide jobs, job training, better schools, and other services in the inner cities, they insisted, offered hope of ending welfare dependence.

But the warning went unheeded in the rush to "end welfare as we know it." In August 1996, having

The Election of 1996

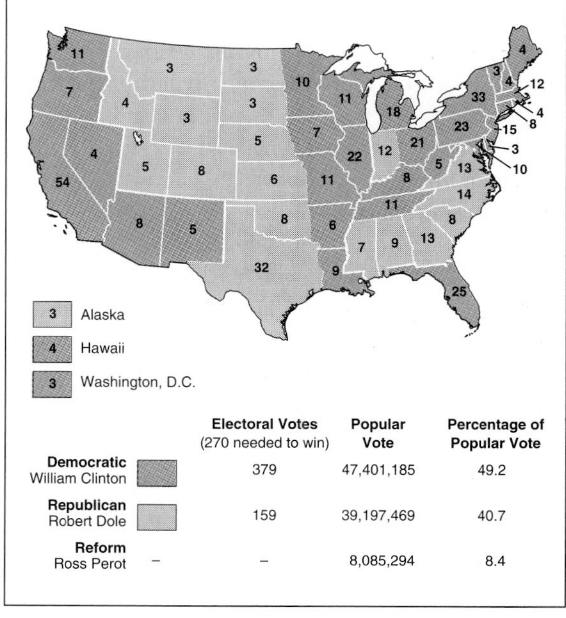

	Electoral Votes (270 needed to win)	Popular Vote	Percentage of Popular Vote
Democratic William Clinton	379	47,401,185	49.2
Republican Robert Dole	159	39,197,469	40.7
Reform Ross Perot –	–	8,085,294	8.4

vetoed two earlier bills, Clinton agreed to sign a Republican welfare-reform bill—thereby depriving the GOP of a potent campaign issue. Ending a sixty-year commitment of unconditional support to those in need, this bill turned responsibility for welfare back to the states, which would receive lump-sum grants to devise their own programs. Along with sharp cuts in overall welfare spending, the bill set a five-year lifetime limit on benefits, required all able-bodied adults to work after two years on the dole, cut the federal food stamp program, and denied all but emergency aid to legal immigrants. Serious questions about job training, work programs, and the fate of those destined to be cut off from public assistance—including millions of children—remained unanswered.

As the 1996 presidential election neared, seventy-three-year-old Bob Dole, a long-time Kansas senator, won the Republican nomination, naming former congressman Jack Kemp as his running mate. Recycling Ronald Reagan's supply-side economics, Dole pledged to cut taxes by 15 percent while balancing the budget—a feat that would require massive cuts in domestic spending. GOP conservatives, led by the Christian Coalition of televangelist Pat Robertson, wrote the party platform, calling for an absolute ban on abortions, among other goals. But the Republican convention presented a cheerful "feel-good" image geared for prime-time TV. General Colin Powell, the popular ex-chairman of the Joint Chiefs of Staff, and Dole's personable wife, Elizabeth, stressed the party's "inclusiveness" and Dole's heroic World War II service, which had left him partially disabled.

The 1996 campaign made clear that party conventions, once raucous free-for-alls, had increasingly become slick, made-for-TV productions, with the real decisions hammered out behind the scenes. When the staged nature of these events became clear, public interest in them diminished.

As the Dole-Kemp ticket tried to reclaim the political center, it found that ground occupied by President Clinton, who had increasingly adopted Republican positions after the 1994 election debacle. Adding to the confusion, the eccentric Texas billionaire Ross Perot, founder and financier of the budget-balancing Reform Party, again threw his hat in the ring.

In November 1996 voters returned Clinton to the White House; at the same time, they increased the Republican majority in the Senate and kept the Republican majority in the House. The rightward drift of American politics, and the dominant role of television in the process, seemed likely to continue.

CONCLUSION

U.S. society has evolved with dizzying speed in the closing years of the twentieth century. Many Americans are thriving in the service-based high-technology economy, but many other citizens lag behind, raising the danger of a permanent "underclass" and a nation permanently divided between an educated professional elite and a huge lower caste mired in poverty and despair. The pace of social and demographic change has fed uneasiness, cultural tensions, and explosions of reactionary venom. As familiar international power alignments have vanished, Americans have watched anxiously to discern the shape of the new world order and their place in it.

Politicians, the media, and citizens in general are only beginning to come to terms with the scope of these changes. Is an increasingly media-driven political system equal to this challenge, they ask, or will it implode into demagoguery and reaction? Can a multicultural society of diverse ethnic groups, culture values, and religious beliefs sustain a sense of common national identity? As the United States moves further into its third century as a nation, no one can be certain of the answers to these questions.

CHRONOLOGY

1984–1986 Congress bars military aid to contras.

1985 Palestinian airline hijackings and other terrorism.

1986 Congress passes South African sanctions.
U.S. air raid on Libya.

1987 Congressional hearings on Iran-contra scandal.
Stock-market crash.
Trade deficit reaches $170 billion.

1988 U.S. warship *Vincennes,* in Persian Gulf, shoots down Iranian passenger plane, killing 290.
Oliver North, John Poindexter, and other Iran-contra figures indicted.
Reagan signs Intermediate Nuclear Forces Treaty (INF) in Moscow.
George Bush elected president.

1989 Oliver North convicted for Iran-contra role.
Massive Alaskan oil spill by *Exxon Valdez.*
Supreme Court limits access to abortion.
Supreme Court restricts civil-rights laws.
U.S. invasion of Panama; Manuel Noriega overthrown.
China's rulers crush prodemocracy movement.
Berlin Wall is opened.

1990 Federal Clean Air Act passed.
President Bush and Congress agree on five-year budget-deficit reduction package.
Iraq invades Kuwait.
Recession begins.
Germany reunified; Soviet troops start withdrawal from East Germany and rest of Eastern Europe.

1991 Gulf War (Operation Desert Storm).
United States and U.S.S.R. sign treaty reducing strategic nuclear arms by 25 percent.
Political and economic upheavals in Soviet Union after Gorbachev survives coup attempt.
Clarence Thomas seated on Supreme Court amid controversy.
Soviet Union collapses.

1992 Supreme Court upholds *Roe* v. *Wade.*
Arkansas governor Bill Clinton elected president.
American troops deployed in Somalia.

1993 North American Free Trade Agreement (NAFTA) approved.
General Agreement on Tariffs and Trade (GATT) renegotiated.
Israel, Palestinians reach peace agreement.
Clinton health plan developed, revealed.
Congress enacts modified version of Clinton economic plan.
Congress approves North American Free Trade Agreement (NAFTA).
Recession ends.

1993 Congress debates health-care reform (1993–1994).
Ruth Bader Ginsberg joins Supreme Court.
World Trade Center bombed.

1994 Christian Coalition gains control of Republican party in several states.
Somalia intervention ends.
United States seeks ouster of military junta in Haiti.
Nelson Mandela elected president of South Africa.
Israeli–Palestine Liberation Organization (PLO) accord on limited Palestinian self-rule in Gaza and Jericho.
Stephen G. Breyer joins Supreme Court.
Republican victory in 1994 elections.

1995 Bombing of Murrah Federal Building in Oklahoma City.
U.S. brokers peace treaty in Bosnia.
Israeli Prime Minister Itzhak Rabin assassinated.
Budget impasse shuts down federal government twice.
U.S. troops deployed to Bosnia on peacekeeping mission.

1996 Yeltsin reelected Russian president.
Gingrich popularity plummets.
Sweeping changes in welfare system enacted.
Clinton reelected.
Apparent breakthrough in AIDS treatment.

FOR FURTHER READING

Mary Jo Bane and David T. Ellwood, *Welfare Realities: From Rhetoric to Reform* (1994). Exploration by Ellwood, assistant secretary of health and human services in the Clinton administration, and his co-author of the complexities of welfare reform.

Robert Bellah et al., *The Good Society* (1991). Thoughtful reflections on the sources of community in the American historical experience.

Al Gore, *Earth in the Balance: Ecology and the Human Spirit* (1992). Assessment by a soon-to-be vice president of the environmental challenges facing humankind.

Philip K. Howard, *The Death of Common Sense: How the Law Is Suffocating America* (1995). A look by a lawyer at how well-intentioned but overly detailed government regulations can get out of hand.

James Davis Hunter, *Culture Wars: The Struggle to Define America* (1991). A sociologist's analysis of the sources of moral and cultural conflict in contemporary U.S. society.

Haynes Johnson, *Divided We Fall: Gambling with History in the Nineties* (1994). A journalist's disturbing report, based on grassroots interviews, on a divided and apprehensive populace.

David Maraniss, *First in His Class: A Biography of Bill Clinton* (1995). Exploration of the sources of Clinton's political drive and his almost desperate need to be liked.

Mark Robert Rank, *Living on the Edge: The Realities of Welfare in America* (1994). A compelling look at the human face of some of society's most marginal members.

Statistical Abstract of the United States, 1993: The National Data Book (1993). A treasure trove of information on economic and social trends, from the budget deficit to college enrollments.

U.S. News and World Report, *Triumph Without Victory: The Unreported History of the Persian Gulf War* (1992). The most complete early history of Operation Desert Storm, by the editors of a leading news magazine.

Lawrence E. Walsh, *Iran-Contra: The Final Report* (1994). Independent counsel Walsh's full record of the crimes and cover-ups associated with the Iran-Contra affair.

Appendix

Declaration of Independence

IN CONGRESS, JULY 4, 1776

The Unanimous Declaration of the Thirteen United States of America

When, in the course of human events, it becomes necessary for one people to dissolve the political bands which have connected them with another, and to assume, among the powers of the earth, the separate and equal station to which the laws of nature and of nature's God entitle them, a decent respect to the opinions of mankind requires that they should declare the causes which impel them to the separation.

We hold these truths to be self-evident: That all men are created equal; that they are endowed by their Creator with certain unalienable rights; that among these are life, liberty, and the pursuit of happiness; that, to secure these rights, governments are instituted among men, deriving their just powers from the consent of the governed; that whenever any form of government becomes destructive of these ends, it is the right of the people to alter or to abolish it, and to institute new government, laying its foundation on such principles, and organizing its powers in such form, as to them shall seem most likely to effect their safety and happiness. Prudence, indeed, will dictate that governments long established should not be changed for light and transient causes; and accordingly all experience hath shown that mankind are more disposed to suffer, while evils are sufferable, than to right themselves by abolishing the forms to which they are accustomed. But when a long train of abuses and usurpations, pursuing invariably the same object, evinces a design to reduce them under absolute despotism, it is their right, it is their duty, to throw off such government, and to provide new guards for their future security. Such has been the patient sufferance of these colonies; and such is now the necessity which constrains them to alter their former systems of government. The history of the present King of Great Britain is a history of repeated injuries and usurpations, all having in direct object the establishment of an absolute tyranny over these states. To prove this, let facts be submitted to a candid world.

He has refused his assent to laws, the most wholesome and necessary for the public good.

He has forbidden his governors to pass laws of immediate and pressing importance, unless suspended in their operation till his assent should be obtained; and, when so suspended, he has utterly neglected to attend to them.

He has refused to pass other laws for the accommodation of large districts of people, unless those people would relinquish the right of representation in the legislature, a right inestimable to them, and formidable to tyrants only.

He has called together legislative bodies at places unusual, uncomfortable, and distant from the depository of their public records, for the sole purpose of fatiguing them into compliance with his measures.

He has dissolved representative houses repeatedly, for opposing, with manly firmness, his invasions on the rights of the people.

He has refused for a long time, after such dissolutions, to cause others to be elected; whereby the legislative powers, incapable of annihilation, have returned to the people at large for their exercise; the state remaining, in the mean time, exposed to all the dangers of invasions from without and convulsions within.

He has endeavored to prevent the population of these states; for that purpose obstructing the laws of naturalization of foreigners; refusing to pass others to encourage their migration hither, and raising the conditions of new appropriation of lands.

He has obstructed the administration of justice, by refusing his assent to laws for establishing judiciary powers.

He has made judges dependent on his will alone, for the tenure of their offices, and the amount and payment of their salaries.

He has erected a multitude of new offices, and sent hither swarms of officers to harass our people and eat out their substance.

He has kept among us, in times of peace, standing armies, without the consent of our legislatures.

He has affected to render the military independent of, and superior to, the civil power.

He has combined with others to subject us to a jurisdiction foreign to our constitution, and unacknowledged by our laws, giving his assent to their acts of pretended legislation:

For quartering large bodies of armed troops among us;

For protecting them, by a mock trial, from punishment for any murders which they should commit on the inhabitants of these states;

For cutting off our trade with all parts of the world;

For imposing taxes on us without our consent;

For depriving us, in many cases, of the benefits of trial by jury;

For transporting us beyond seas, to be tried for pretended offenses;

For abolishing the free system of English laws in a neighboring province, establishing therein an arbitrary government, and enlarging its boundaries, so as to render it at once an example and fit instrument for introducing the same absolute rule into these colonies;

For taking away our charters, abolishing our most valuable laws, and altering fundamentally the forms of our governments;

For suspending our own legislatures, and declaring themselves invested with power to legislate for us in all cases whatsoever.

He has abdicated government here, by declaring us out of his protection and waging war against us.

He has plundered our seas, ravaged our coasts, burned our towns, and destroyed the lives of our people.

He is at this time transporting large armies of foreign mercenaries to complete the works of death, desolation, and tyranny already begun with circumstances of cruelty and perfidy scarcely paralleled in the most barbarous ages, and totally unworthy of the head of a civilized nation.

He has constrained our fellow-citizens, taken captive on the high seas, to bear arms against their country, to become the executioners of their friends and brethren, or to fall themselves by their hands.

He has excited domestic insurrection among us, and has endeavored to bring on the inhabitants of our frontiers the merciless Indian savages, whose known rule of warfare is an undistinguished destruction of all ages, sexes, and conditions.

In every stage of these oppressions we have petitioned for redress in the most humble terms; our repeated petitions have been answered only by repeated injury. A prince, whose character is thus marked by every act which may define a tyrant, is unfit to be the ruler of a free people.

Nor have we been wanting in our attentions to our British brethren. We have warned them, from time to time, of attempts by their legislature to extend an unwarrantable jurisdiction over us. We have reminded them of the circumstances of our emigration and settlement here. We have appealed to their native justice and magnanimity; and we have conjured them by the ties of our common kindred, to disavow these usurpations, which would inevitably interrupt our connections and correspondence. They, too, have been deaf to the voice of justice and of consanguinity. We must, therefore, acquiesce in the necessity which denounces our separation, and hold them, as we hold the rest of mankind, enemies in war, in peace friends.

We, therefore, the representatives of the United States of America, in General Congress assembled, appealing to the Supreme Judge of the world for the rectitude of our intentions, do, in the name and by the authority of the good people of these colonies, solemnly publish and declare, that these United Colonies are, and of right ought to be, FREE AND INDEPENDENT STATES; that they are absolved from all allegiance to the British crown, and that all political connection between them and the state of Great Britain is, and ought to be, totally dissolved; and that, as free and independent states, they have full power to levy war, conclude peace, contract alliances, establish commerce, and do all other acts and things which independent states may of right do. And for the support of this declaration, with a firm reliance on the protection of Divine Providence, we mutually pledge to each other our lives, our fortunes, and our sacred honor.

JOHN HANCOCK [*President*]
[*and fifty-five others*]

Constitution of the United States of America

PREAMBLE

We the people of the United States, in order to form a more perfect union, establish justice, insure domestic tranquility, provide for the common defense, promote the general welfare, and secure the blessings of liberty to ourselves and our posterity, do ordain and establish this CONSTITUTION for the United States of America.

ARTICLE I

Section 1. All legislative powers herein granted shall be vested in a Congress of the United States, which shall consist of a Senate and a House of Representatives.

Section 2. The House of Representatives shall be composed of members chosen every second year by the people of the several States, and the electors in each State shall have the qualifications requisite for electors of the most numerous branch of the State Legislature.

No person shall be a Representative who shall not have attained to the age of twenty-five years, and been seven years a citizen of the United States, and who shall not, when elected, be an inhabitant of that State in which he shall be chosen.

Representatives and direct taxes shall be apportioned among the several States which may be included within this Union, according to their respective numbers, *which shall be determined by adding to the whole number of free persons, including those bound to service for a term of years and excluding Indians not taxed, three-fifths of all other persons*. The actual enumeration shall be made within three years after the first meeting of the Congress of the United States, and within every subsequent term of ten years, in such manner as they shall by law direct. The number of Representatives shall not exceed one for every thirty thousand, but each State shall have at least one Representative; *and until such enumeration shall be made, the State of New Hampshire shall be entitled to choose three, Massachusetts eight, Rhode Island and Providence Plantations one, Connecticut five, New York six, New Jersey four, Pennsylvania eight, Delaware one, Maryland six, Virginia ten, North Carolina five, South Carolina five, and Georgia three*.

When vacancies happen in the representation from any State, the Executive authority thereof shall issue writs of election to fill such vacancies.

The House of Representatives shall choose their Speaker and other officers; and shall have the sole power of impeachment.

Section 3. The Senate of the United States shall be composed of two Senators from each State, *chosen by the legislature thereof*, for six years; and each Senator shall have one vote.

Immediately after they shall be assembled in consequence of the first election, they shall be divided as equally as may be into three classes. The seats of the Senators of the first class shall be vacated at the expiration of the second year, of the second class at the expiration of the fourth year, and of the third class at the expiration of the sixth year, so that one-third may be chosen every second year; *and if vacancies happen by resignation or otherwise, during the recess of the legislature of any State, the Executive thereof may make*

NOTE: Passages no longer in effect are printed in italic type.

temporary appointments until the next meeting of the legislature, which shall then fill such vacancies.

No person shall be a Senator who shall not have attained to the age of thirty years, and been nine years a citizen of the United States, and who shall not, when elected, be an inhabitant of that State for which he shall be chosen.

The Vice President of the United States shall be President of the Senate, but shall have no vote, unless they be equally divided.

The Senate shall choose their other officers, and also a President *pro tempore,* in the absence of the Vice President, or when he shall exercise the office of the President of the United States.

The Senate shall have the sole power to try all impeachments. When sitting for that purpose, they shall be on oath or affirmation. When the President of the United States is tried, the Chief Justice shall preside: and no person shall be convicted without the concurrence of two-thirds of the members present.

Judgment in cases of impeachment shall not extend further than to removal from the office, and disqualification to hold and enjoy any office of honor, trust or profit under the United States; but the party convicted shall nevertheless be liable and subject to indictment, trial, judgment and punishment, according to law.

Section 4. The times, places and manner of holding elections for Senators and Representatives shall be prescribed in each State by the legislature thereof; but the Congress may at any time by law make or alter such regulations, except as to the places of choosing Senators.

The Congress shall assemble at least once in every year, and such meeting *shall be on the first Monday in December, unless they shall by law appoint a different day.*

Section 5. Each house shall be the judge of the elections, returns and qualifications of its own members, and a majority of each shall constitute a quorum to do business; but a smaller number may adjourn from day to day, and may be authorized to compel the attendance of absent members, in such manner, and under such penalties, as each house may provide.

Each house may determine the rules of its proceedings, punish its members for disorderly behavior, and with the concurrence of two-thirds, expel a member.

Each house shall keep a journal of its proceedings, and from time to time publish the same, excepting such parts as may in their judgment require secrecy; and the yeas and nays of the members of either house on any question shall, at the desire of one-fifth of those present, be entered on the journal.

Neither house, during the session of Congress, shall, without the consent of the other, adjourn for more than three days, nor to any other place than that in which the two houses shall be sitting.

Section 6. The Senators and Representatives shall receive a compensation for their services, to be ascertained by law and paid out of the treasury of the United States. They shall in all cases except treason, felony and breach of the peace, be privileged from arrest during their attendance at the session of their respective houses, and in going to and returning from the same; and for any speech or debate in either house, they shall not be questioned in any other place.

No Senator or Representative shall, during the time for which he was elected, be appointed to any civil office under the authority of the United States, which shall have been created, or the emoluments whereof shall have been increased, during such time; and no person holding any office under the United States shall be a member of either house during his continuance in office.

Section 7. All bills for raising revenue shall originate in the House of Representatives; but the Senate may propose or concur with amendments as on other bills.

Every bill which shall have passed the House of Representatives and the Senate, shall, before it become a law, be presented to the President of the United States; if he approve he shall sign it, but if not he shall return it with objections to that house in which it originated, who shall enter the objections at large on their journal, and proceed to reconsider it. If after such reconsideration two-thirds of that house shall agree to pass the bill, it shall be sent, together with the objections, to the other house, by which it shall likewise be reconsidered, and, if approved by two-thirds of that house, it shall become a law. But in all such cases the votes of both houses shall be determined by yeas and nays, and the names of the persons voting for and against the bill shall be entered on the journal of each house respectively. If any bill shall not be returned by the President within ten days (Sundays excepted) after it shall have been presented to him, the same shall be a law, in like manner as if he had signed it, unless the Congress by their adjournment prevent its return, in which case it shall not be a law.

Every order, resolution, or vote to which the concurrence of the Senate and House of Representatives may be necessary (except on a question of adjournment) shall be presented to the President of the United States; and before the same shall take effect, shall be approved by him, or being disapproved by him, shall be repassed by two-thirds of the Senate and House of Representatives, according to the rules and limitations prescribed in the case of a bill.

Section 8. The Congress shall have power

To lay and collect taxes, duties, imposts, and excises, to pay the debts and provide for the common defense and general welfare of the United States; but all duties, imposts and excises shall be uniform throughout the United States;

To borrow money on the credit of the United States;

To regulate commerce with foreign nations, and among the several States, and with the Indian tribes;

To establish an uniform rule of naturalization, and uniform laws on the subject of bankruptcies throughout the United States;

To coin money, regulate the value thereof, and of foreign coin, and fix the standard of weights and measures;

To provide for the punishment of counterfeiting the securities and current coin of the United States;

To establish post offices and post roads;

To promote the progress of science and useful arts by securing for limited times to authors and inventors the exclusive right to their respective writings and discoveries;

To constitute tribunals inferior to the Supreme Court;

To define and punish piracies and felonies committed on the high seas and offenses against the law of nations;

To declare war, grant letters of marque and reprisal, and make rules concerning captures on land and water;

To raise and support armies, but no appropriation of money to that use shall be for a longer term than two years;

To provide and maintain a navy;

To make rules for the government and regulation of the land and naval forces;

To provide for calling forth the militia to execute the laws of the Union, suppress insurrections, and repel invasions;

To provide for organizing, arming, and disciplining the militia, and for governing such part of them as may be employed in the service of the United States, reserving to the States respectively the appointment of the officers, and the authority of training the militia according to the discipline prescribed by Congress;

To exercise exclusive legislation in all cases whatsoever, over such district (not exceeding ten miles square) as may, by cession of particular States, and the acceptance of Congress, become the seat of government of the United States, and to exercise like authority over all places purchased by the consent of the legislature of the State, in which the same shall be, for erection of forts, magazines, arsenals, dock-yards, and other needful buildings;—and

To make all laws which shall be necessary and proper for carrying into execution the foregoing powers, and all other powers vested by this Constitution in the government of the United States, or in any department or officer thereof.

Section 9. *The migration or importation of such persons as any of the States now existing shall think proper to admit shall not be prohibited by the Congress prior to the year 1808; but a tax or duty may be imposed on such importation, not exceeding $10 for each person.*

The privilege of the writ of habeas corpus shall not be suspended, unless when in cases of rebellion or invasion the public safety may require it.

No bill of attainder or ex post facto law shall be passed.

No capitation, or other direct, tax shall be laid, unless in proportion to the census or enumeration herein before directed to be taken.

No tax or duty shall be laid on articles exported from any State.

No preference shall be given by any regulation of commerce or revenue to the ports of one State over those of another; nor shall vessels bound to, or from, one State, be obliged to enter, clear, or pay duties in another.

No money shall be drawn from the treasury, but in consequence of appropriations made by law; and a regular statement and account of the receipts and expenditures of all public money shall be published from time to time.

No title of nobility shall be granted by the United States: and no person holding any office of profit or trust under them, shall, without the consent of the Congress, accept of any present, emolument, office, or title, of any kind whatever, from any king, prince, or foreign state.

Section 10. No State shall enter into any treaty, alliance, or confederation; grant letters of marque and reprisal; coin money; emit bills of credit; make anything but gold and silver coin a tender in payment of debts; pass any bill of attainder, ex post facto law, or law impairing the obligation of contracts, or grant any title of nobility.

No State shall, without the consent of Congress, lay any imposts or duties on imports or exports, except what may be absolutely necessary for executing its inspection laws: and the net produce of all duties and imposts, laid by any State on imports or exports, shall be for the use of the treasury of the United States; and all such laws shall be subject to the revision and control of the Congress.

No State shall, without the consent of Congress, lay any duty of tonnage, keep troops or ships of war in time of peace, enter into any agreement or compact with another State, or with a foreign power, or engage in war, unless actually invaded, or in such imminent danger as will not admit of delay.

ARTICLE II

Section 1. The executive power shall be vested in a President of the United States of America. He shall hold his office during the term of four years, and, together with the Vice President, chosen for the same term, be elected as follows:

Each state shall appoint, in such manner as the legislature thereof may direct, a number of electors, equal to the whole number of Senators and Representatives to which the State may be entitled in the Congress; but no Senator or Representative, or person holding an office of trust or profit under the United States, shall be appointed an elector.

The electors shall meet in their respective States, and vote by ballot for two persons, of whom one at least shall not be an inhabitant of the same State with themselves. And they shall make a list of all the persons voted for, and of the number of votes for each; which list they shall sign and certify, and transmit sealed to the seat of government of the United States, directed to the President of the Senate. The President of the Senate shall, in the presence of the Senate and the House of Representatives, open all the certificates, and the votes shall then be counted. The person having the greatest number of votes shall be the President, if such number be a majority of the whole number of electors appointed; and if there be more than one who have such majority, and have an equal number of votes, then the House of Representatives shall immediately choose by ballot one of them for President; and if no person have a majority, then from the five highest on the list said house shall in like manner choose the President. But in choosing the President the votes shall be taken by States, the representation from each State having one vote; a quorum for this purpose shall consist of a member or members from two-thirds of the States, and a majority of all the States shall be necessary to a choice. In every case, after the choice of the President, the person having the greatest number of votes of the electors shall be the Vice President. But if there should remain two or more who have equal votes, the Senate shall choose from them by ballot the Vice President.

The Congress may determine the time of choosing the electors and the day on which they shall give their votes; which day shall be the same throughout the United States.

No person except a natural-born citizen, *or a citizen of the United States at the time of the adoption of this Constitution,* shall be eligible to the office of President; neither shall any person be eligible to that office who shall not have attained to the age of thirty-five years, and been fourteen years a resident within the United States.

In case of the removal of the President from office or of his death, resignation, or inability to discharge the powers and duties of the said office, the same shall devolve on the Vice President, and the Congress may by law provide for the case of removal, death, resignation, or inability, both of the President and Vice President, declaring what officer shall then act as President, and such officer shall act accordingly, until the disability be removed, or a President shall be elected.

The President shall, at stated times, receive for his services a compensation, which shall neither be increased nor diminished during the period for which he shall have been elected, and he shall not receive within that period any other emolument from the United States, or any of them.

Before he enter on the execution of his office, he shall take the following oath or affirmation:—"I do solemnly swear (or affirm) that I will faithfully execute the office of the President of the United States, and will to the best of my ability preserve, protect and defend the Constitution of the United States."

Section 2. The President shall be commander in chief of the army and navy of the United States, and of the militia of the several States, when called into the actual service of the United States; he may require the opinion, in writing, of the principal officer in each of the executive departments, upon any subject relating to the duties of their respective offices, and he shall have power to grant reprieves and pardons for offenses against the United States, except in cases of impeachment.

He shall have power, by and with the advice and consent of the Senate, to make treaties, provided two-thirds of the Senators present concur; and he shall nominate, and by and with the advice and consent of the Senate, shall appoint ambassadors, other public ministers and consuls, judges of the Supreme Court, and all other officers of the United States, whose appointments are not herein otherwise provided for, and which shall be established by law: but Congress may by law vest the appointment of such inferior officers, as they think proper, in the President alone, in the courts of law, or in the heads of departments.

The President shall have power to fill up all vacancies that may happen during the recess of the Senate, by granting commissions which shall expire at the end of their next session.

Section 3. He shall from time to time give to the Congress information of the state of the Union, and recommend to their consideration such measures as he shall judge necessary and expedient; he may, on extraordinary occasions, convene both houses, or either of them, and in case of disagreement between them, with respect to the time of adjournment, he may adjourn them to such time as he shall think proper; he shall receive ambassadors and other public ministers; he shall take care that the laws be faithfully executed, and shall commission all the officers of the United States.

Section 4. The President, Vice President and all civil officers of the United States shall be removed from office on impeachment for, and on conviction of, treason, bribery, or other high crimes and misdemeanors.

ARTICLE III

Section 1. The judicial power of the United States shall be vested in one Supreme Court, and in such inferior courts as the Congress may from time to time ordain and establish. The judges, both of the Supreme and inferior courts, shall hold their offices during good behavior, and shall, at stated times, receive for their services a compensation which shall not be diminished during their continuance in office.

Section 2. The judicial power shall extend to all cases, in law and equity, arising under this Constitution, the laws of the United States, and treaties made, or which shall be made, under their authority;—to all cases affecting ambassadors, other public ministers and consuls;—to all cases of admiralty and maritime jurisdiction;—to controversies to which the United States shall be a party;—to controversies between two or more States;—*between a State and citizens of another State*;—between citizens of different States;—between citizens of the same State claiming lands under grants of different States, and between a State, or the citizens thereof, and foreign states, citizens or subjects.

In all cases affecting ambassadors, other public ministers and consuls, and those in which a State shall be party, the Supreme Court shall have original jurisdiction. In all the other cases before mentioned, the Supreme Court shall have appellate jurisdiction, both as to law and fact, with such exceptions, and under such regulations, as the Congress shall make.

The trial of all crimes, except in cases of impeachment, shall be by jury; and such trial shall be held in the State where said crimes shall have been committed; but when not committed within any State, the trial shall be at such place or places as the Congress may by law have directed.

Section 3. Treason against the United States shall consist only in levying war against them, or in adhering to their enemies, giving them aid and comfort. No person shall be convicted of treason unless on the testimony of two witnesses to the same overt act, or on confession in open court.

The Congress shall have power to declare the punishment of treason, but no attainder of treason shall work corruption of blood, or forfeiture except during the life of the person attainted.

ARTICLE IV

Section 1. Full faith and credit shall be given in each State to the public acts, records, and judicial proceedings of every other State. And the Congress may by general laws prescribe the manner in which such acts, records, and proceedings shall be proved, and the effect thereof.

Section 2. The citizens of each State shall be entitled to all privileges and immunities of citizens in the several States.

A person charged in any State with treason, felony, or other crime, who shall flee from justice, and be found in another State, shall on demand of the executive authority of the State from which he fled, be delivered up, to be removed to the State having jurisdiction of the crime.

No person held to service or labor in one State, under the laws thereof, escaping into another, shall, in consequence of any law or regulation therein, be discharged from such service or labor, but shall be delivered up on claim of the party to whom such service or labor may be due.

Section 3. New States may be admitted by the Congress into this Union; but no new State shall be formed or erected within the jurisdiction of any other State; nor any State be formed by the junction of two or more States, or parts of States, without the consent of the legislatures of the States concerned as well as of the Congress.

The Congress shall have power to dispose of and make all needful rules and regulations respecting the territory or other property belonging to the United States; and nothing in this Constitution shall be so construed as to prejudice any claims of the United States, or of any particular State.

Section 4. The United States shall guarantee to every State in this Union a republican form of government, and shall protect each of them against invasion; and on application of the legislature, or of the executive (when the legislature cannot be convened), against domestic violence.

ARTICLE V

The Congress, whenever two-thirds of both houses shall deem it necessary, shall propose amendments to this Constitution, or, on the application of the legislatures of two-thirds of the several States, shall call a convention for proposing amendments, which, in either case, shall be valid to all intents and purposes, as part of this Constitution, when ratified by the legislatures of three-fourths of the several States, or by conventions in three-fourths thereof, as the one or the other mode of ratification may be proposed by the Congress; provided *that no amendments which may be made prior to the year one thousand eight hundred and eight shall in any manner affect the first and fourth clauses in the ninth section of the first article;* and that no State, without its consent, shall be deprived of its equal suffrage in the Senate.

ARTICLE VI

All debts contracted and engagements entered into, before the adoption of this Constitution, shall be as valid against the United States under this Constitution, as under the Confederation.

This Constitution, and the laws of the United States which shall be made in pursuance thereof; and all treaties made, or which shall be made, under the authority of the United States, shall be the supreme law of the land; and the judges in every State shall be bound thereby, anything in the Constitution or laws of any State to the contrary notwithstanding.

The Senators and Representatives before mentioned, and the members of the several State legislatures, and all executive and judicial officers, both of the United States and of the several States, shall be bound by oath or affirmation to support this Constitution; but no religious test shall ever be required as a qualification to any office or public trust under the United States.

ARTICLE VII

The ratification of the conventions of nine States shall be sufficient for the establishment of this Constitution between the States so ratifying the same.

Done in Convention by the unanimous consent of the States present, the seventeenth day of September in the year of our Lord one thousand seven hundred and eighty-seven and of the Independence of the United States of America the twelfth. In witness whereof we have hereunto subscribed our names.

[Signed by]
G° WASHINGTON
Presidt and Deputy from Virginia
[*and thirty-eight others*]

Amendments to the Constitution

ARTICLE I*

Congress shall make no law respecting an establishment of religion, or prohibiting the free exercise thereof; or abridging the freedom of speech, or of the press; or the right of the people peaceably to assemble, and to petition the government for a redress of grievances.

ARTICLE II

A well-regulated militia being necessary to the security of a free State, the right of the people to keep and bear arms shall not be infringed.

ARTICLE III

No soldier shall, in time of peace, be quartered in any house without the consent of the owner, nor in time of war, but in a manner to be prescribed by law.

ARTICLE IV

The right of the people to be secure in their persons, houses, papers, and effects, against unreasonable searches and seizures, shall not be violated, and no warrants shall issue but upon probable cause, supported by oath or affirmation, and particularly describing the place to be searched, and the persons or things to be seized.

ARTICLE V

No person shall be held to answer for a capital, or otherwise infamous crime, unless on a presentment or indictment of a grand jury, except in cases arising in the land or naval forces, or in the militia, when in actual service in time of war or public danger; nor shall any person be subject for the same offense to be twice put in jeopardy of life or limb; nor shall be compelled in any criminal case to be a witness against himself, nor be deprived of life, liberty, or property, without due process of law; nor shall private property be taken for public use without just compensation.

*The first ten Amendments (Bill of Rights) were adopted in 1791.

ARTICLE VI

In all criminal prosecutions, the accused shall enjoy the right to a speedy and public trial, by an impartial jury of the State and district wherein the crime shall have been committed, which district shall have been previously ascertained by law, and to be informed of the nature and cause of the accusation; to be confronted with the witnesses against him; to have compulsory process for obtaining witnesses in his favor, and to have the assistance of counsel for his defense.

ARTICLE VII

In suits at common law, where the value in controversy shall exceed twenty dollars, the right of trial by jury shall be preserved, and no fact tried by a jury shall be otherwise reexamined in any court of the United States, than according to the rules of the common law.

ARTICLE VIII

Excessive bail shall not be required, nor excessive fines imposed, nor cruel and unusual punishments inflicted.

ARTICLE IX

The enumeration in the Constitution, of certain rights, shall not be construed to deny or disparage others retained by the people.

ARTICLE X

The powers not delegated to the United States by the Constitution, not prohibited by it to the States, are reserved to the States respectively, or to the people.

ARTICLE XI [*Adopted 1798*]

The judicial power of the United States shall not be construed to extend to any suit in law or equity, commenced or prosecuted against one of the United States by citizens of another State, or by citizens or subjects of any foreign state.

ARTICLE XII [*Adopted 1804*]

The electors shall meet in their respective States, and vote by ballot for President and Vice President, one of whom, at least, shall not be an inhabitant of the same State with themselves; they shall name in their ballots the person voted for as President, and in distinct ballots the person voted for as Vice President, and they shall make distinct lists of all persons voted for as President, and of all persons voted for as Vice President, and of the number of votes for each, which lists they shall sign and certify, and transmit sealed to the seat of government of the United States, directed to the President of the Senate;—the President of the Senate shall, in the presence of the Senate and House of Representatives, open all the certificates and the votes shall then be counted;—the person having the greatest number of votes for President shall be the President, if such number be a majority of the whole number of electors appointed; and if no person have such majority, then from the persons having the highest numbers not exceeding three on the list of those voted for as President, the House of Representatives shall choose immediately, by ballot, the President. But in choosing the President, the votes shall be taken by States, the representation from each State having one vote; a quorum for this purpose shall consist of a member or members from two-thirds of the States, and a majority of all the States shall be necessary to a choice. And if the House of Representatives shall not choose a President whenever the right of choice shall devolve upon them, before *the fourth day of March* next following, then the Vice President shall act as President, as in the case of the death or other constitutional disability of the President.

The person having the greatest number of votes as Vice President shall be the Vice President, if such a number be a majority of the whole number of electors appointed; and if no person have a majority, then from the two highest numbers on the list the Senate shall choose the Vice President; a quorum for the purpose shall consist of two-thirds of the whole number of Senators, and a majority of the whole number shall be necessary to a choice. But no person constitutionally ineligible to the office of President shall be eligible to that of Vice President of the United States.

ARTICLE XIII [*Adopted 1865*]

Section 1. Neither slavery nor involuntary servitude, except as a punishment for crime whereof the party shall have been duly convicted, shall exist within the United States, or any place subject to their jurisdiction.

Section 2. Congress shall have power to enforce this article by appropriate legislation.

ARTICLE XIV [*Adopted 1868*]

Section 1. All persons born or naturalized in the United States, and subject to the jurisdiction thereof, are citizens of the United States and of the State wherein they reside. No State shall make or enforce any law which shall abridge the privileges or immunities of citizens of the United States; nor shall any State deprive any person of life, liberty, or property, without due process of law; nor deny to any person within its jurisdiction the equal protection of the laws.

Section 2. Representatives shall be apportioned among the several States according to their respective numbers, counting the whole number of persons in each State, excluding Indians not taxed. But when the right to vote at any election for the choice of Electors for President and Vice President of the United States, Representatives in Congress, the executive and judicial officers of a State, or the members of the legislature thereof, is denied to any of the male inhabitants of such State, being twenty-one years of age and citizens of the United States, or in any way abridged, except for participation in rebellion, or other crime, the basis of representation therein shall be reduced in the proportion which the number of such male citizens shall bear to the whole number of male citizens twenty-one years of age in such State.

Section 3. No person shall be a Senator or Representative in Congress or Elector of President and Vice President, or hold any office, civil or military, under the United States, or under any State, who, having previously taken an oath, as a member of Congress, or as an officer of the United States, or as a member of any State legislature, or as an executive or judicial officer of any State, to support the Constitution of the United States, shall have engaged in insurrection or rebellion against the same, or given aid and comfort to the enemies thereof. Congress may, by a vote of two-thirds of each house, remove such disability.

Section 4. The validity of the public debt of the United States, authorized by law, including debts incurred for payment of pensions and bounties for services in suppressing insurrection or rebellion, shall not be questioned. But neither the United States nor any State shall assume or pay any debt or obligation incurred in aid of insurrection or rebellion against the United States, or any claim for the loss or emancipation of any slave; but all such debts, obligations, and claims shall be held illegal and void.

Section 5. The Congress shall have the power to enforce, by appropriate legislation, the provisions of this article.

ARTICLE XV [*Adopted 1870*]

Section 1. The right of citizens of the United States to vote shall not be denied or abridged by the United States or by any State on account of race, color, or previous condition of servitude.

Section 2. The Congress shall have power to enforce this article by appropriate legislation.

ARTICLE XVI [*Adopted 1913*]

The Congress shall have power to lay and collect taxes on incomes, from whatever source derived, without apportionment among the several States, and without regard to any census or enumeration.

ARTICLE XVII [*Adopted 1913*]

Section 1. The Senate of the United States shall be composed of two Senators from each State, elected by the people thereof, for six years; and each Senator shall have one vote. The electors in each State shall have the qualifications requisite for electors of [voters for] the most numerous branch of the State legislatures.

Section 2. When vacancies happen in the representation of any State in the Senate, the executive authority of such State shall issue writs of election to fill such vacancies: Provided, that the Legislature of any State may empower the executive thereof to make temporary appointments until the people fill the vacancies by election as the Legislature may direct.

Section 3. This amendment shall not be so construed as to affect the election or term of any Senator chosen before it becomes valid as part of the Constitution.

ARTICLE XVIII [*Adopted 1919; repealed 1933*]

Section 1. *After one year from the ratification of this article the manufacture, sale, or transportation of intoxicating liquors within, the importation thereof into,* *or the exportation thereof from the United States and all territory subject to the jurisdiction thereof, for beverage purposes, is hereby prohibited.*

Section 2. *The Congress and the several States shall have concurrent power to enforce this article by appropriate legislation.*

Section 3. *This article shall be inoperative unless it shall have been ratified as an amendment to the Constitution by the legislatures of the several States, as provided by the Constitution, within seven years from the date of the submission thereof to the States by the Congress.*

ARTICLE XIX [*Adopted 1920*]

Section 1. The right of citizens of the United States to vote shall not be denied or abridged by the United States or by any State on account of sex.

Section 2. The Congress shall have the power to enforce this article by appropriate legislation.

ARTICLE XX [*Adopted 1933*]

Section 1. The terms of the President and Vice President shall end at noon on the 20th day of January, and the terms of Senators and Representatives at noon on the 3d day of January, of the years in which such terms would have ended if this article had not been ratified; and the terms of their successors shall then begin.

Section 2. The Congress shall assemble at least once in every year, and such meeting shall begin at noon on the 3d day of January, unless they shall by law appoint a different day.

Section 3. If, at the time fixed for the beginning of the term of the President, the President-elect shall have died, the Vice President-elect shall become President. If a President shall not have been chosen before the time fixed for the beginning of his term, or if the President-elect shall have failed to qualify, then the Vice President-elect shall act as President until a President shall have qualified; and the Congress may by law provide for the case wherein neither a President-elect nor a Vice President-elect shall have qualified, declaring who shall then act as President, or the manner in which one who is to act shall be selected, and such persons shall act accordingly until a President or Vice President shall have qualified.

Section 4. The Congress may by law provide for the case of the death of any of the persons from whom the House of Representatives may choose a President whenever the right of choice shall have devolved upon them, and for the case of the death of any of the persons from whom the Senate may choose a Vice President whenever the right of choice shall have devolved upon them.

Section 5. Sections 1 and 2 shall take effect on the 15th day of October following the ratification of this article.

Section 6. This article shall be inoperative unless it shall have been ratified as an amendment to the Constitution by the Legislatures of three-fourths of the several States within seven years from the date of its submission.

ARTICLE XXI [*Adopted 1933*]

Section 1. The eighteenth article of amendment to the Constitution of the United States is hereby repealed.

Section 2. The transportation or importation into any State, Territory, or Possession of the United States for delivery or use therein of intoxicating liquors, in violation of the laws thereof, is hereby prohibited.

Section 3. This article shall be inoperative unless it shall have been ratified as an amendment to the Constitution by conventions in the several States, as provided in the Constitution, within seven years from the date of submission thereof to the States by the Congress.

ARTICLE XXII [*Adopted 1951*]

Section 1. No person shall be elected to the office of President more than twice, and no person who has held the office of President, or acted as President, for more than two years of a term to which some other person was elected President shall be elected to the office of President more than once. But this article shall not apply to any person holding the office of President when this article was proposed by the Congress, and shall not prevent any person who may be holding the office of President, or acting as President, during the term within which this article becomes operative from holding the office of President or acting as President during the remainder of such term.

Section 2. This article shall be inoperative unless it shall have been ratified as an amendment to the Constitution by the legislatures of three-fourths of the several States within seven years from the date of its submission to the States by the Congress.

ARTICLE XXIII [*Adopted 1961*]

Section 1. The District constituting the seat of Government of the United States shall appoint in such manner as the Congress may direct:

A number of electors of President and Vice President equal to the whole number of Senators and Representatives in Congress to which the District would be entitled if it were a State, but in no event more than the least populous State; they shall be in addition to those appointed by the States, but they shall be considered for the purposes of the election of President and Vice President, to be electors appointed by a State; and they shall meet in the District and perform such duties as provided by the twelfth article of amendment.

Section 2. The Congress shall have the power to enforce this article by appropriate legislation.

ARTICLE XXIV [*Adopted 1964*]

Section 1. The right of citizens of the United States to vote in any primary or other election for President or Vice President, for electors for President or Vice President, or for Senator or Representative in Congress, shall not be denied or abridged by the United States or any State by reason of failure to pay any poll tax or other tax.

Section 2. The Congress shall have the power to enforce this article by appropriate legislation.

ARTICLE XXV [*Adopted 1967*]

Section 1. In case of the removal of the President from office or of his death or resignation, the Vice President shall become President.

Section 2. Whenever there is a vacancy in the office of the Vice President, the President shall nominate a Vice President who shall take office upon confirmation by a majority vote of both Houses of Congress.

Section 3. Whenever the President transmits to the President pro tempore of the Senate and the Speaker of the House of Representatives his written declaration that he is unable to discharge the powers and duties of his office, and until he transmits to them a written declaration to the contrary, such powers and duties shall be discharged by the Vice President as Acting President.

Section 4. Whenever the Vice President and a majority of either the principal officers of the executive departments or of such other body as Congress may by law provide, transmit to the President pro tempore of the Senate and the Speaker of the House of Representatives their written declaration that the President is unable to discharge the powers and duties of his office, the Vice President shall immediately assume the powers and duties of the office as Acting President.

Thereafter, when the President transmits to the President pro tempore of the Senate and the

Speaker of the House of Representatives his written declaration that no inability exists, he shall resume the powers and duties of his office unless the Vice President and a majority of either the principal officers of the executive department[s] or of such other body as Congress may by law provide, transmit within four days to the President pro tempore of the Senate and the Speaker of the House of Representatives their written declaration that the President is unable to discharge the powers and duties of his office. Thereupon Congress shall decide the issue, assembling within forty-eight hours for that purpose if not in session. If the Congress, within twenty-one days after receipt of the latter written declaration, or, if Congress is not in session, within twenty-one days after Congress is required to assemble, determines by two-thirds vote of both Houses that the President is unable to discharge the powers and duties of his office, the Vice President shall continue to discharge the same as Acting President; otherwise, the President shall resume the powers and duties of his office.

ARTICLE XXVI [*Adopted 1971*]

Section 1. The right of citizens of the United States, who are eighteen years of age or older, to vote shall not be denied or abridged by the United States or by any State on account of age.

Section 2. The Congress shall have power to enforce this article by appropriate legislation.

ARTICLE XXVII* [*Adopted 1992*]

No law, varying the compensation for services of the Senators and Representatives, shall take effect, until an election of Representatives shall have intervened.

---

*Originally proposed in 1789 by James Madison, this amendment failed to win ratification along with the other parts of what became the Bill of Rights. However, the proposed amendment contained no deadline for ratification, and over the years other state legislatures voted to add it to the Constitution; many such ratifications occurred during the 1980s and early 1990s as public frustration with Congress's performance mounted. In May 1992 the Archivist of the United States certified that, with the Michigan legislature's ratification, the article had been approved by three-fourths of the states and thus automatically became part of the Constitution. But congressional leaders and constitutional specialists questioned whether an amendment that took 202 years to win ratification was valid, and the issue had not been resolved by the time this book went to press.

Presidential Elections, 1789–1996

Year	*States in the Union*	*Candidates*	*Parties*	*Electoral Vote*	*Popular Vote*	*Percentage of Popular Vote*
1789	11	GEORGE WASHINGTON	No party designations	69		
		John Adams		34		
		Minor candidates		35		
1792	15	GEORGE WASHINGTON	No party designations	132		
		John Adams		77		
		George Clinton		50		
		Minor candidates		5		
1796	16	JOHN ADAMS	Federalist	71		
		Thomas Jefferson	Democratic-Republican	68		
		Thomas Pinckney	Federalist	59		
		Aaron Burr	Democratic-Republican	30		
		Minor candidates		48		
1800	16	THOMAS JEFFERSON	Democratic-Republican	73		
		Aaron Burr	Democratic-Republican	73		
		John Adams	Federalist	65		
		Charles C. Pinckney	Federalist	64		
		John Jay	Federalist	1		
1804	17	THOMAS JEFFERSON	Democratic-Republican	162		
		Charles C. Pinckney	Federalist	14		
1808	17	JAMES MADISON	Democratic-Republican	122		
		Charles C. Pinckney	Federalist	47		
		George Clinton	Democratic-Republican	6		
1812	18	JAMES MADISON	Democratic-Republican	128		
		DeWitt Clinton	Federalist	89		
1816	19	JAMES MONROE	Democratic-Republican	183		
		Rufus King	Federalist	34		
1820	24	JAMES MONROE	Democratic-Republican	231		
		John Quincy Adams	Independent Republican	1		
1824	24	JOHN QUINCY ADAMS	Democratic-Republican	84	108,740	30.5
		Andrew Jackson	Democratic-Republican	99	153,544	43.1
		William H. Crawford	Democratic-Republican	41	46,618	13.1
		Henry Clay	Democratic-Republican	37	47,136	13.2
1828	24	ANDREW JACKSON	Democratic	178	642,553	56.0
		John Quincy Adams	National Republican	83	500,897	44.0
1832	24	ANDREW JACKSON	Democratic	219	687,502	55.0
		Henry Clay	National Republican	49	530,189	42.4
		William Wirt	Anti-Masonic	7	33,108	2.6
		John Floyd	National Republican	11		

Because candidates receiving less than 1 percent of the popular vote are omitted, the percentage of popular vote may not total 100 percent.

Before the Twelfth Amendment was passed in 1804, the electoral college voted for two presidential candidates; the runner-up became vice president.

Year	States in the Union	Candidates	Parties	Electoral Vote	Popular Vote	Percentage of Popular Vote
1836	26	MARTIN VAN BUREN	Democratic	170	765,483	50.9
		William H. Harrison	Whig	73	739,795	49.1
		Hugh L. White	Whig	26		
		Daniel Webster	Whig	14		
		W. P. Mangum	Whig	11		
1840	26	WILLIAM H. HARRISON	Whig	234	1,274,624	53.1
		Martin Van Buren	Democratic	60	1,127,781	46.9
1844	26	JAMES K. POLK	Democratic	170	1,338,464	49.6
		Henry Clay	Whig	105	1,300,097	48.1
		James G. Birney	Liberty		62,300	2.3
1848	30	ZACHARY TAYLOR	Whig	163	1,360,967	47.4
		Lewis Cass	Democratic	127	1,222,342	42.5
		Martin Van Buren	Free Soil		291,263	10.1
1852	31	FRANKLIN PIERCE	Democratic	254	1,601,117	50.9
		Winfield Scott	Whig	42	1,385,453	44.1
		John P. Hale	Free Soil		155,825	5.0
1856	31	JAMES BUCHANAN	Democratic	174	1,832,955	45.3
		John C. Frémont	Republican	114	1,339,932	33.1
		Millard Fillmore	American	8	871,731	21.6
1860	33	ABRAHAM LINCOLN	Republican	180	1,865,593	39.8
		Stephen A. Douglas	Democratic	12	1,382,713	29.5
		John C. Breckinridge	Democratic	72	848,356	18.1
		John Bell	Constitutional Union	39	592,906	12.6
1864	36	ABRAHAM LINCOLN	Republican	212	2,206,938	55.0
		George B. McClellan	Democratic	21	1,803,787	45.0
1868	37	ULYSSES S. GRANT	Republican	214	3,013,421	52.7
		Horatio Seymour	Democratic	80	2,706,829	47.3
1872	37	ULYSSES S. GRANT	Republican	286	3,596,745	55.6
		Horace Greeley	Democratic	*	2,843,446	43.9
1876	38	RUTHERFORD B. HAYES	Republican	185	4,034,311	48.0
		Samuel J. Tilden	Democratic	184	4,288,546	51.0
		Peter Cooper	Greenback		75,973	1.0
1880	38	JAMES A. GARFIELD	Republican	214	4,453,295	48.5
		Winfield S. Hancock	Democratic	155	4,414,082	48.1
		James B. Weaver	Greenback-Labor		308,578	3.4
1884	38	GROVER CLEVELAND	Democratic	219	4,879,507	48.5
		James G. Blaine	Republican	182	4,850,293	48.2
		Benjamin F. Butler	Greenback-Labor		175,370	1.8
		John P. St. John	Prohibition		150,369	1.5

*When Greeley died shortly after the election, his supporters divided their votes among the minor candidates.
Because candidates receiving less than 1 percent of the popular vote are omitted, the percentage of popular vote may not total 100 percent.

Year	States in the Union	Candidates	Parties	Electoral Vote	Popular Vote	Percentage of Popular Vote
1888	38	BENJAMIN HARRISON	Republican	233	5,477,129	47.9
		Grover Cleveland	Democratic	168	5,537,857	48.6
		Clinton B. Fisk	Prohibition		249,506	2.2
		Anson J. Streeter	Union Labor		146,935	1.3
1892	44	GROVER CLEVELAND	Democratic	277	5,555,426	46.1
		Benjamin Harrison	Republican	145	5,182,690	43.0
		James B. Weaver	People's	22	1,029,846	8.5
		John Bidwell	Prohibition		264,133	2.2
1896	45	WILLIAM McKINLEY	Republican	271	7,102,246	51.1
		William J. Bryan	Democratic	176	6,492,559	47.7
1900	45	WILLIAM McKINLEY	Republican	292	7,218,491	51.7
		William J. Bryan	Democratic; Populist	155	6,356,734	45.5
		John C. Wooley	Prohibition		208,914	1.5
1904	45	THEODORE ROOSEVELT	Republican	336	7,628,461	57.4
		Alton B. Parker	Democratic	140	5,084,223	37.6
		Eugene V. Debs	Socialist		402,283	3.0
		Silas C. Swallow	Prohibition		258,536	1.9
1908	46	WILLIAM H. TAFT	Republican	321	7,675,320	51.6
		William J. Bryan	Democratic	162	6,412,294	43.1
		Eugene V. Debs	Socialist		420,793	2.8
		Eugene W. Chafin	Prohibition		253,840	1.7
1912	48	WOODROW WILSON	Democratic	435	6,296,547	41.9
		Theodore Roosevelt	Progressive	88	4,118,571	27.4
		William H. Taft	Republican	8	3,486,720	23.2
		Eugene V. Debs	Socialist		900,672	6.0
		Eugene W. Chafin	Prohibition		206,275	1.4
1916	48	WOODROW WILSON	Democratic	277	9,127,695	49.4
		Charles E. Hughes	Republican	254	8,533,507	46.2
		A. L. Benson	Socialist		585,113	3.2
		J. Frank Hanly	Prohibition		220,506	1.2
1920	48	WARREN G. HARDING	Republican	404	16,143,407	60.4
		James N. Cox	Democratic	127	9,130,328	34.2
		Eugene V. Debs	Socialist		919,799	3.4
		P. P. Christensen	Farmer-Labor		265,411	1.0
1924	48	CALVIN COOLIDGE	Republican	382	15,718,211	54.0
		John W. Davis	Democratic	136	8,385,283	28.8
		Robert M. La Follette	Progressive	13	4,831,289	16.6
1928	48	HERBERT C. HOOVER	Republican	444	21,391,993	58.2
		Alfred E. Smith	Democratic	87	15,016,169	40.9

Because candidates receiving less than 1 percent of the popular vote are omitted, the percentage of popular vote may not total 100 percent.

Year	*States in the Union*	*Candidates*	*Parties*	*Electoral Vote*	*Popular Vote*	*Percentage of Popular Vote*
1932	48	FRANKLIN D. ROOSEVELT	Democratic	472	22,809,638	57.4
		Herbert C. Hoover	Republican	59	15,758,901	39.7
		Norman Thomas	Socialist		881,951	2.2
1936	48	FRANKLIN D. ROOSEVELT	Democratic	523	27,752,869	60.8
		Alfred M. Landon	Republican	8	16,674,665	36.5
		William Lemke	Union		882,479	1.9
1940	48	FRANKLIN D. ROOSEVELT	Democratic	449	27,307,819	54.8
		Wendell L. Willkie	Republican	82	22,321,018	44.8
1944	48	FRANKLIN D. ROOSEVELT	Democratic	432	25,606,585	53.5
		Thomas E. Dewey	Republican	99	22,014,745	46.0
1948	48	HARRY S TRUMAN	Democratic	303	24,105,812	49.5
		Thomas E. Dewey	Republican	189	21,970,065	45.1
		Strom Thurmond	States' Rights	39	1,169,063	2.4
		Henry A. Wallace	Progressive		1,157,172	2.4
1952	48	DWIGHT D. EISENHOWER	Republican	442	33,936,234	55.1
		Adlai E. Stevenson	Democratic	89	27,314,992	44.4
1956	48	DWIGHT D. EISENHOWER	Republican	457	35,590,472	57.6
		Adlai E. Stevenson	Democratic	73	26,022,752	42.1
1960	50	JOHN F. KENNEDY	Democratic	303	34,227,096	49.7
		Richard M. Nixon	Republican	219	34,108,546	49.5
		Harry F. Byrd	Independent	15	502,363	.7
1964	50	LYNDON B. JOHNSON	Democratic	486	43,126,506	61.1
		Barry M. Goldwater	Republican	52	27,176,799	38.5
1968	50	RICHARD M. NIXON	Republican	301	31,770,237	43.4
		Hubert H. Humphrey	Democratic	191	31,270,533	42.7
		George C. Wallace	American Independent	46	9,906,141	13.5
1972	50	RICHARD M. NIXON	Republican	520	47,169,911	60.7
		George S. McGovern	Democratic	17	29,170,383	37.5
1976	50	JIMMY CARTER	Democratic	297	40,827,394	49.9
		Gerald R. Ford	Republican	240	39,145,977	47.9
1980	50	RONALD W. REAGAN	Republican	489	43,899,248	50.8
		Jimmy Carter	Democratic	49	35,481,435	41.0
		John B. Anderson	Independent		5,719,437	6.6
		Ed Clark	Libertarian		920,859	1.0
1984	50	RONALD W. REAGAN	Republican	525	54,451,521	58.8
		Walter F. Mondale	Democratic	13	37,565,334	40.5
1988	50	GEORGE H. W. BUSH	Republican	426	47,946,422	54.0
		Michael S. Dukakis	Democratic	112	41,016,429	46.0
1992	50	WILLIAM J. CLINTON	Democratic	370	43,728,275	43.2
		George H. W. Bush	Republican	168	38,167,416	37.7
		H. Ross Perot	Independent		19,237,247	19.0
1996	50	WILLIAM J. CLINTON	Democratic	379	47,401,185	49.2
		Robert Dole	Republican	159	39,197,469	40.7
		H. Ross Perot	Reform		8,085,294	8.4

Because candidates receiving less than 1 percent of the popular vote are omitted, the percentage of popular vote may not total 100 percent.

Supreme Court Justices

Name	*Terms of Service*	*Appointed By*
JOHN JAY	1789–1795	Washington
James Wilson	1789–1798	Washington
John Rutledge	1790–1791	Washington
William Cushing	1790–1810	Washington
John Blair	1790–1796	Washington
James Iredell	1790–1799	Washington
Thomas Johnson	1792–1793	Washington
William Paterson	1793–1806	Washington
JOHN RUTLEDGE*	1795	Washington
Samuel Chase	1796–1811	Washington
OLIVER ELLSWORTH	1796–1800	Washington
Bushrod Washington	1799–1829	J. Adams
Alfred Moore	1800–1804	J. Adams
JOHN MARSHALL	1801–1835	J. Adams
William Johnson	1804–1834	Jefferson
Brockholst Livingston	1807–1823	Jefferson
Thomas Todd	1807–1826	Jefferson
Gabriel Duvall	1811–1835	Madison
Joseph Story	1812–1845	Madison
Smith Thompson	1823–1843	Monroe
Robert Trimble	1826–1828	J. Q. Adams
John McLean	1830–1861	Jackson
Henry Baldwin	1830–1844	Jackson
James M. Wayne	1835–1867	Jackson
ROGER B. TANEY	1836–1864	Jackson
Philip P. Barbour	1836–1841	Jackson
John Cartron	1837–1865	Van Buren
John McKinley	1838–1852	Van Buren
Peter V. Daniel	1842–1860	Van Buren
Samuel Nelson	1845–1872	Tyler
Levi Woodbury	1845–1851	Polk
Robert C. Grier	1846–1870	Polk
Benjamin R. Curtis	1851–1857	Fillmore
John A. Campbell	1853–1861	Pierce
Nathan Clifford	1858–1881	Buchanan
Noah H. Swayne	1862–1881	Lincoln
Samuel F. Miller	1862–1890	Lincoln
David Davis	1862–1877	Lincoln
Stephen J. Field	1863–1897	Lincoln
SALMON P. CHASE	1864–1873	Lincoln

NOTE: The names of chief justices are printed in capital letters.

*Although Rutledge acted as chief justice, the Senate refused to confirm his appointment.

Name	*Terms of Service*	*Appointed By*
William Strong	1870–1880	Grant
Joseph P. Bradley	1870–1892	Grant
Ward Hunt	1873–1882	Grant
MORRISON R. WAITE	1874–1888	Grant
John M. Harlan	1877–1911	Hayes
William B. Woods	1881–1887	Hayes
Stanley Matthews	1881–1889	Garfield
Horace Gray	1882–1902	Arthur
Samuel Blatchford	1882–1893	Arthur
Lucious Q. C. Lamar	1888–1893	Cleveland
MELVILLE W. FULLER	1888–1910	Cleveland
David J. Brewer	1890–1910	B. Harrison
Henry B. Brown	1891–1906	B. Harrison
George Shiras, Jr.	1892–1903	B. Harrison
Howell E. Jackson	1893–1895	B. Harrison
Edward D. White	1894–1910	Cleveland
Rufus W. Peckham	1896–1909	Cleveland
Joseph McKenna	1898–1925	McKinley
Oliver W. Holmes	1902–1932	T. Roosevelt
William R. Day	1903–1922	T. Roosevelt
William H. Moody	1906–1910	T. Roosevelt
Horace H. Lurton	1910–1914	Taft
Charles E. Hughes	1910–1916	Taft
EDWARD D. WHITE	1910–1921	Taft
Willis Van Devanter	1911–1937	Taft
Joseph R. Lamar	1911–1916	Taft
Mahlon Pitney	1912–1922	Taft
James C. McReynolds	1914–1941	Wilson
Louis D. Brandeis	1916–1939	Wilson
John H. Clarke	1916–1922	Wilson
WILLIAM H. TAFT	1921–1930	Harding
George Sutherland	1922–1938	Harding
Pierce Butler	1923–1939	Harding
Edward T. Sanford	1923–1930	Harding
Harlan F. Stone	1925–1941	Coolidge
CHARLES E. HUGHES	1930–1941	Hoover
Owen J. Roberts	1930–1945	Hoover
Benjamin N. Cardozo	1932–1938	Hoover
Hugo L. Black	1937–1971	F. Roosevelt
Stanley F. Reed	1938–1957	F. Roosevelt
Felix Frankfurter	1939–1962	F. Roosevelt
William O. Douglas	1939–1975	F. Roosevelt
Frank Murphy	1940–1949	F. Roosevelt
HARLAN F. STONE	1941–1946	F. Roosevelt

Name	*Terms of Service*	*Appointed By*
James F. Byrnes	1941–1942	F. Roosevelt
Robert H. Jackson	1941–1954	F. Roosevelt
Wiley B. Rutledge	1943–1949	F. Roosevelt
Harold H. Burton	1945–1958	Truman
FREDERICK M. VINSON	1946–1953	Truman
Tom C. Clark	1949–1967	Truman
Sherman Minton	1949–1956	Truman
EARL WARREN	1953–1969	Eisenhower
John Marshall Harlan	1955–1971	Eisenhower
William J. Brennan, Jr.	1956–1990	Eisenhower
Charles E. Whittaker	1957–1962	Eisenhower
Potter Stewart	1958–1981	Eisenhower
Byron R. White	1962–1993	Kennedy
Arthur J. Goldberg	1962–1965	Kennedy
Abe Fortas	1965–1970	L. Johnson
Thurgood Marshall	1967–1991	L. Johnson
WARREN E. BURGER	1969–1986	Nixon
Harry A. Blackmun	1970–1994	Nixon
Lewis F. Powell, Jr.	1971–1987	Nixon
William H. Rehnquist	1971–1986	Nixon
John Paul Stevens	1975–	Ford
Sandra Day O'Connor	1981–	Reagan
WILLIAM H. REHNQUIST	1986–	Reagan
Antonin Scalia	1986–	Reagan
Anthony Kennedy	1988–	Reagan
David Souter	1990–	Bush
Clarence Thomas	1991–	Bush
Ruth Bader Ginsburg	1993–	Clinton
Stephen Breyer	1994–	Clinton

Growth of U.S. Population and Area

Census	Population of United States	Increase over the Preceding Census: Number	Increase over the Preceding Census: Percentage	Land Area (Sq. Mi.)	Pop. Per. Sq. Mi.	Percentage of Pop. in Urban and Rural Territory: Urban	Percentage of Pop. in Urban and Rural Territory: Rural
1790	3,929,214			867,980	4.5	5.1	94.9
1800	5,308,483	1,379,269	35.1	867,980	6.1	6.1	93.9
1810	7,239,881	1,931,398	36.4	1,685,865	4.3	7.2	92.8
1820	9,638,453	2,398,572	33.1	1,753,588	5.5	7.2	92.8
1830	12,866,020	3,227,567	33.5	1,753,588	7.3	8.8	91.2
1840	17,069,453	4,203,433	32.7	1,753,588	9.7	10.8	89.2
1850	23,191,876	6,122,423	35.9	2,944,337	7.9	15.3	84.7
1860	31,433,321	8,251,445	35.6	2,973,965	10.6	19.8	80.2
1870	39,818,449	8,375,128	26.6	2,973,965	13.4	24.9	75.1
1880	50,155,783	10,337,334	26.0	2,973,965	16.9	28.2	71.8
1890	62,947,714	12,791,931	25.5	2,973,965	21.2	35.1	64.9
1900	75,994,575	13,046,861	20.7	2,974,159	25.6	39.7	60.3
1910	91,972,266	15,997,691	21.0	2,973,890	30.9	45.7	54.3
1920	105,710,620	13,738,354	14.9	2,973,776	35.5	51.2	48.8
1930	122,775,046	17,064,426	16.1	2,977,128	41.2	56.2	43.8
1940	131,669,275	8,894,229	7.2	2,977,128	44.2	56.5	43.5
1950	150,697,361	19,028,086	14.5	2,974,726*	50.7	64.0	36.0
1960†	179,323,175	28,625,814	19.0	3,540,911	50.6	69.9	30.1
1970	203,235,298	23,912,123	13.3	3,536,855	57.5	73.5	26.5
1980	226,504,825	23,269,527	11.4	3,536,855	64.0	73.7	26.3
1990	249,975,000	22,164,068	9.8	3,536,855	70.3	N.A.	N.A.

*As measured in 1940; shrinkage offset by increase in water area.

†First year for which figures include Alaska and Hawaii.

SOURCES: Census Bureau, *Historical Statistics of the United States*, updated by relevant *Statistical Abstract of the United States*.

Admission of States into the Union

State	*Date of Admission*	*State*	*Date of Admission*
1. Delaware	December 7, 1787	26. Michigan	January 26, 1837
2. Pennsylvania	December 12, 1787	27. Florida	March 3, 1845
3. New Jersey	December 18, 1787	28. Texas	December 29, 1845
4. Georgia	January 2, 1788	29. Iowa	December 28, 1846
5. Connecticut	January 9, 1788	30. Wisconsin	May 29, 1848
6. Massachusetts	February 6, 1788	31. California	September 9, 1850
7. Maryland	April 28, 1788	32. Minnesota	May 11, 1858
8. South Carolina	May 23, 1788	33. Oregon	February 14, 1859
9. New Hampshire	June 21, 1788	34. Kansas	January 29, 1861
10. Virginia	June 25, 1788	35. West Virginia	June 20, 1863
11. New York	July 26, 1788	36. Nevada	October 31, 1864
12. North Carolina	November 21, 1789	37. Nebraska	March 1, 1867
13. Rhode Island	May 29, 1790	38. Colorado	August 1, 1876
14. Vermont	March 4, 1791	39. North Dakota	November 2, 1889
15. Kentucky	June 1, 1792	40. South Dakota	November 2, 1889
16. Tennessee	June 1, 1796	41. Montana	November 8, 1889
17. Ohio	March 1, 1803	42. Washington	November 11, 1889
18. Louisiana	April 30, 1812	43. Idaho	July 3, 1890
19. Indiana	December 11, 1816	44. Wyoming	July 10, 1890
20. Mississippi	December 10, 1817	45. Utah	January 4, 1896
21. Illinois	December 3, 1818	46. Oklahoma	November 16, 1907
22. Alabama	December 14, 1819	47. New Mexico	January 6, 1912
23. Maine	March 15, 1820	48. Arizona	February 14, 1912
24. Missouri	August 10, 1821	49. Alaska	January 3, 1959
25. Arkansas	June 15, 1836	50. Hawaii	August 21, 1959

Profile of the U.S. Population

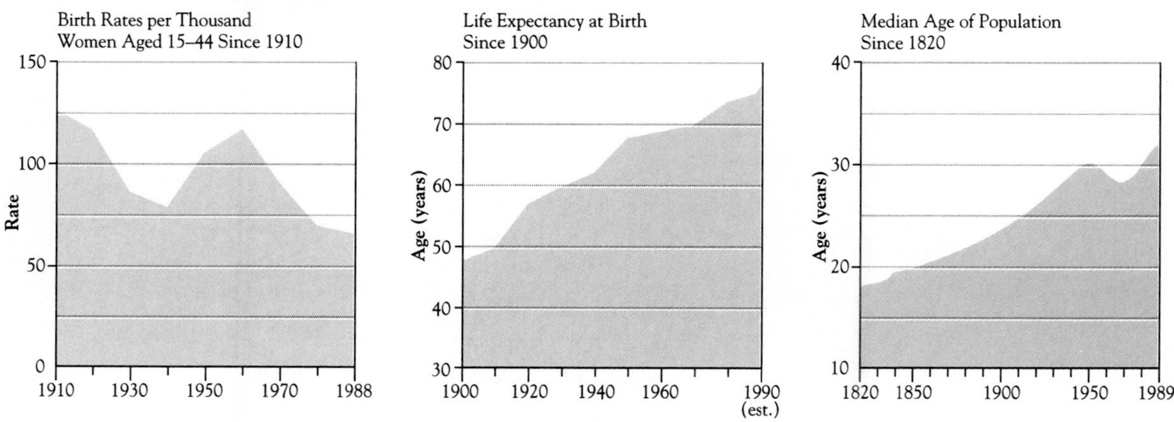

SOURCES: *Historical Statistics of the United States* and *Statistical Abstract of the United States*, relevant years.

Political and Physical Map of the United States

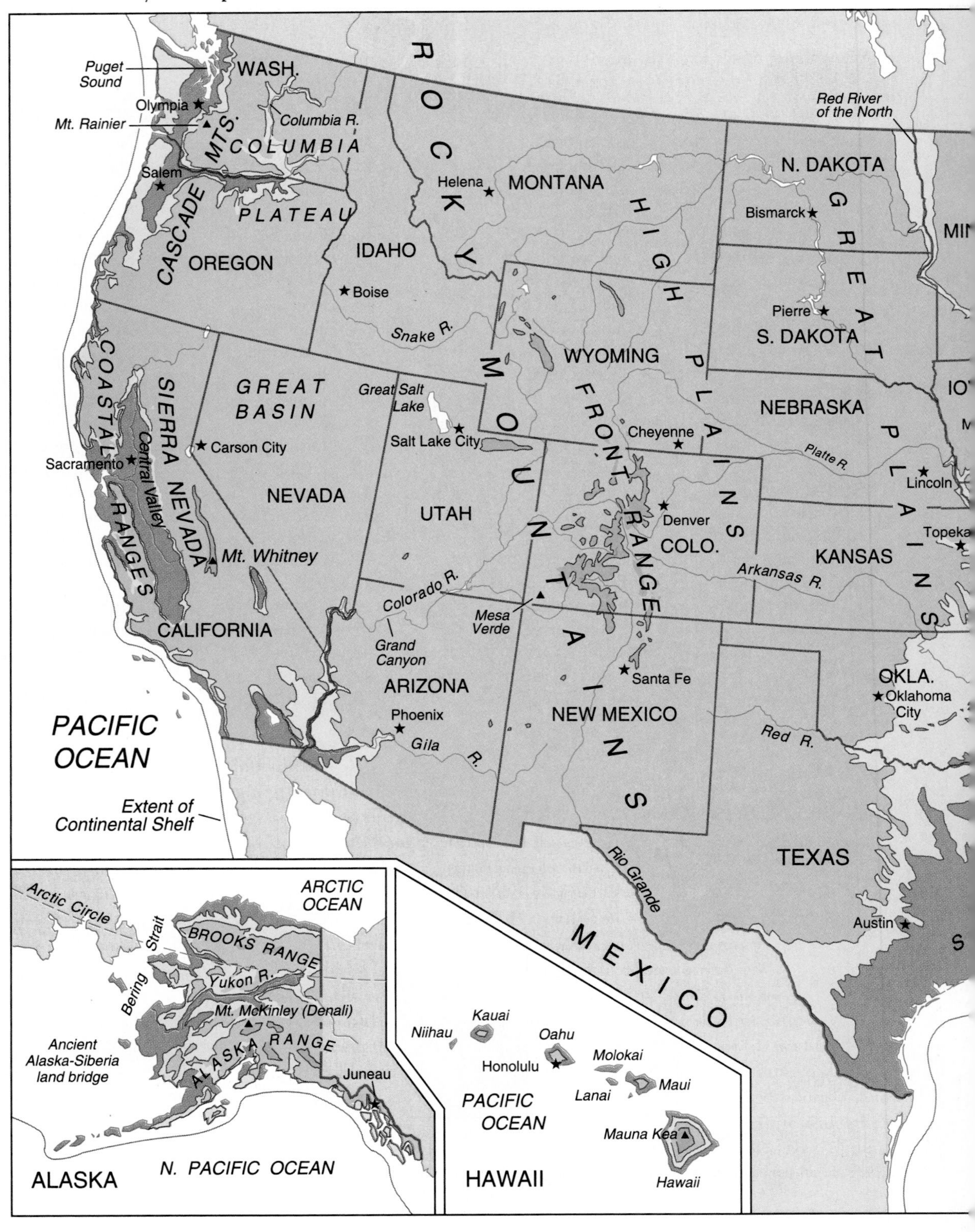

CANADA
L. Superior
L. Michigan
L. Huron
L. Ontario
L. Erie
St. Lawrence R.
Grand Banks
ME.
Augusta
VT.
Montpelier
Concord
N.H.
Adirondack Mts.
N.Y.
Albany
Hudson R.
MASS.
Boston
Cape Cod
Hartford
R.I.
Providence
CONN.
Long I.
Niagara Falls
WIS.
Madison
MICH.
Lansing
PA.
Trenton
N.J.
Susquehanna R.
Harrisburg
Delaware R.
Dover
Delaware Bay
MD.
Annapolis
DEL.
Chesapeake Bay
OHIO
Columbus
Springfield
ILL.
Wabash R.
Indianapolis
IND.
W.VA.
Charleston
VA.
Potomac R.
Richmond
Ohio R.
Frankfort
KY.
N.C.
Raleigh
Cape Hatteras
Nashville
TENN.
Tennessee R.
S.C.
Columbia
Savannah R.
Atlanta
GA.
Mississippi R.
Little Rock
MISS.
Jackson
ALA.
Montgomery
Tallahassee
FLA.
Everglades
APPALACHIAN MTS.
PIEDMONT
TIDEWATER
COASTAL PLAIN
ATLANTIC OCEAN
GULF STREAM
Extent of Continental Shelf
0
500 Miles
0
500 Kilometers
ATLANTIC OCEAN
San Juan
PUERTO RICO
Gulf of Mexico
San Salvador (Watling I.)
Over 10,000 feet
1,000 – 10,000 feet
500 – 1,000 feet
Sea level – 500 feet

Photograph Credits

Chapter 1 p. 1: Ohio Historical Society; p. 8: Field Museum of Natural History, Chicago/Art Resource, New York; p. 9: Courtesy of Cahokia Mounds Historic Site, painting by Lloyd K. Townsend.

Chapter 2 p. 15: John Carter Brown Library; p. 18: Entwistle Gallery, London/Werner Forman Archive/Art Resource, New York; p. 25: Pierpont Morgan Library, New York. MS 3900, Folio 100; p. 28: Arizona State Museum, University of Arizona. Helen Teiwes, photographer; p. 32: By permission of The British Library.

Chapter 3 p. 39: Library Company of Philadelphia; p. 41: Courtesy, American Antiquarian Society; p. 53: The British Museum, London; p. 56: Arents Tobacco Collection, New York Public Library. Miriam and Ira D. Wallach Division of Art, Prints & Photographs. Astor, Lenox, and Tilden Foundation; p. 61 (both): Historical Society of Pennsylvania; p. 64: Photograph by John K. Hillers. Courtesy, Museum of New Mexico, Neg. No. 16096.

Chapter 4 p. 67: Newport Historical Society; p. 73: Peabody Essex Museum, Salem, Massachusetts; p. 75: Courtesy, Wethersfield Historical Society; p. 86: Yale University. Bequest of Eugene Phelps Edwards, 1938.

Chapter 5 p. 90: Courtesy, Winterthur Museum. Bequest of Henry Francis du Pont; p. 98: Courtesy, American Antiquarian Society; p. 104: Deposited by the City of Boston. Courtesy, Museum of Fine Arts, Boston; p. 108: Library of Congress.

Chapter 6 p. 117: New York Historical Society; p. 121: Metropolitan Museum of Art. Bequest of Charles Allen Munn, 1924; p. 136 (detail): Boston Athenaeum; p. 138: Colonial Williamsburg Foundation.

Chapter 7 p. 144: New York State Historical Association, Cooperstown; p. 150: Yale University Art Gallery; p. 155: Smithsonian Institution. Photo #BAE1169-L-3.

Chapter 8 p. 168: White House Historical Association; p. 170 (left): Monticello/Thomas Jefferson Memorial Foundation, Inc.; p. 170 (right): Collection of Mr. and Mrs. Jack W. Warner, Tuscaloosa, Alabama; p. 179: Granger Collection.

Chapter 9 p. 190: Walters Art Gallery, Baltimore; p. 192: Metropolitan Museum of Art, Rogers Fund, 1942. #42.95.12; p. 193: William L. Clements Library/University of Michigan, Ann Arbor; p. 199: University of Massachusetts, Lowell, Center for Lowell History, Lyndon Library; p. 202: Witt Library/Courtauld Institute of Art.

Chapter 10 p. 208: Massachusetts Historical Society; p. 213 (left): Andrew W. Mellon Collection © 1996 Board of Trustees, National Gallery of Art; p. 213 (right): Redwood Library and Athenaeum, Newport, Rhode Island; p. 224: Boston Athenaeum; p. 226 (left): Chicago Historical Society; p. 226 (right): Library of Congress.

Chapter 11 p. 230: Courtesy George Eastman House; p. 231: AP/Wide World Photos; p. 241: Corbis-Bettmann; p. 244: Photograph courtesy of the Louisa May Alcott Memorial Association.

Chapter 12 p. 249: Gibbes Museum of Art/Carolina Art Association; p. 255: Collection of Dr. Richard G. Saloom; p. 262: New York Historical Society; p. 268: Hampton University Museum, Hampton, Virginia.

Chapter 13 p. 271: Amon Carter Museum, Fort Worth, Texas; p. 275: Boston Athenaeum; p. 280: Courtesy George Eastman House; p. 285: Chicago Historical Society; p. 291: Courtesy, Bancroft Library.

Chapter 14 p. 293: Metropolitan Museum of Art, Arthur Hoppock Hearn Fund #50.94.1; p. 295: Library of Congress; p. 297: Metropolitan Museum of Art, Gift of I.N. Phelps Stokes, Edward S. Hawes, Alice Mary Hawes, Marion Augusta Hawes, 1937 #37.14.40; p. 306 (left): National Portrait Gallery, Washington, DC/Art Resource, NY; p. 306 (right): Corbis-Bettmann.

Chapter 15 p. 315: Cook Collection, Valentine Museum, Richmond, Virginia; p. 318: Corbis-Bettmann; p. 322: Library of Congress; p. 327: Chicago Historical Society; p. 329: National Archives.

Chapter 16 p. 341: Library of Congress; p. 344: Harper's Weekly, 1866; p. 351: Tennessee State Museum Collection. Copy photograph by June Dorman; p. 352: The William Gladstone Collection.

Chapter 17 p. 365: D.C. Heath Photo Files; p. 367: DeGolyer Library, Southern Methodist University, Dallas, Texas. Photograph by Robert Benecke. #Ag82.86.60; p. 373: Huntington Library, San Marino, California; p. 380: Santa Barbara Historical Society; p. 381: Library of Congress.

Chapter 18 p. 389: Detail of photograph of Lewis Hine. Library of Congress; p. 390: Corbis-Bettmann; p. 397: Corbis-Bettmann; p. 399: Library of Congress; p. 405: Library of Congress.

Chapter 19 p. 411: Detail of photograph by Jacob Riis. Library of Congress; p. 415: By courtesy of the Ellis Island Immigration Museum; p. 421: *Harper's Weekly*, 1871; p. 424: Jane Addams Memorial Collection/Special Collections/University Library/University of Illinois at Chicago.

Chapter 20 p. 430: State Historical Society of Wisconsin. Photo by Charles Van Schaick WHi(V2)600; p. 433: AT&T Archives; p. 437: Corbis-Bettmann; p. 443: North Wind Picture Agency; p. 445: Granger Collection.

Chapter 21 p. 450: Harold B. Lee Library/Brigham Young University, Provo, Utah; p. 452: Watertown Historical Society; p. 465: Division of Political History, Smithsonian Institution; p. 470: California Museum of Photography, University of California, Riverside.

Chapter 22 p. 475: Museum of American Textile History; p. 476: Denver Public Library, Western History Department; p. 485: Corbis-Bettmann; p. 490: Special Collections Division, University of Washington Libraries, A. Curtis #19943; p. 493: Library of Congress.

Chapter 23 p. 502: National Archives; p. 504: Granger Collection; p. 507: D.C. Heath Photo Files; p. 511: National Archives.

Chapter 24 p. 524: Library of Congress; p. 526: Courtesy, Strong Museum, Rochester, NY; p. 534: Corbis-Bettmann; p. 536: Missouri Historical Society; p. 541: Corbis-Bettmann.

Chapter 25 p. 547: Franklin D. Roosevelt Library. Photo by Margaret Suckley; p. 553: Corbis-Bettmann Newsphotos; p. 565: Photograph by Dorothea Lange. Library of Congress.

Chapter 26 p. 569: AP/Wide World Photos; p. 574: Photograph by Arthur Rothstein. Library of Congress; p. 577: Corbis-Bettmann; p. 582: The Granger Collection.

Chapter 27 p. 589: National Archives; p. 590: Corbis-Bettmann/UPI Newsphoto; p. 599: FPG International; p. 603: U.S. Army Photo; p. 609: Imperial War Museum, London.

Chapter 28 p. 614: Historical Pictures Collection/Stock, Montage, Inc.; p. 617: Corbis-UPI/Bettmann Newsphotos; p. 623: Corbis-UPI/Bettmann Newsphotos; p. 628: Corbis-UPI/Bettmann Newsphotos; p. 631: Corbis-UPI/Bettmann Newsphotos.

Chapter 29 p. 635: Family Photo by John Falter, *Saturday Evening Post* cover, July 5, 1952 © The Curtis Publishing Company; p. 637: "Caught in His Web" from *Herblock's Here and Now*. Simon and Schuster, 1955; p. 646: Bruce Wrighton © Laurence Miller Gallery; p. 651 (both): Magnum Photos.

Chapter 30 p. 657: Dan Budnik/Woodfin Camp & Associates; p. 660: Fred Ward/Black Star; p. 661: AP/Wide World Photos; p. 662: Magnum Photos; p. 672: Bob Fitch/Black Star; p. 677: Corbis-UPI/Bettmann Newsphotos.

Chapter 31 p. 679: Larry Burrows/Life Picture Service; p. 682: AP/Wide World Photos; p. 690: Reprinted with permission from *The New York Review of Books*, Copyright © 1971 NYREV, Inc.; p. 692: Sygma.

Chapter 32 p. 703: Henri Bureau/Sygma; p. 707: Corbis-UPI/Bettmann Newsphotos; p. 710: Paul Szep/Boston Globe; p. 716: Ronald Reagan Presidential Library.

Chapter 33 p. 723: Corbis-Reuters/Bettmann; p. 726: AP/Wide World Photos; p. 735: Corbis-UPI/Bettmann Newsphotos; p. 738: Corbis-Reuters/Bettmann; p. 741: Dennis Brack/Black Star

Index